r	Interest rate (usually real rate) or rate of return (profitability rate)
R	Nominal interest rate
$E(R)$	Expected (required) rate of return on new investment (in CAPM)
R^o	Estimated rate of return
R_M	Return on the market portfolio
R_F	Risk-free rate of interest
R_j	Returns to individual firm or security
ρ_{jk} (rho)	Correlation coefficient
s	Subscript referring to alternative states-of-the-world
S	Market value of a firm's common equity; also sales when indicated
σ (sigma)	Standard deviation
σ^2	Variance; also VAR( )
t	Time period or time index
T	Time to maturity in OPM
T_c	Marginal corporate income tax rate; also T
T_{ps}	Capital gains tax rate
T_{pb}	Ordinary personal income tax rate
u	Upward movement in asset price in BOP
V	Market value of a firm; also total variable costs
v	Variable costs per unit
v_{ps}	Value of preferred stock per share
w	Weights in capital structure or portfolio proportions
X	Net operating income of a firm; also equals EBIT = NOI; also exercise price of option

Managerial Finance

Eighth Edition

Managerial Finance

Eighth Edition

J. Fred Weston
Graduate School of Management
University of California, Los Angeles

Thomas E. Copeland
Graduate School of Management
University of California, Los Angeles

The Dryden Press

Chicago New York Philadelphia San Francisco Montreal Toronto
London Sydney Tokyo Mexico City Rio de Janeiro Madrid

Acquisitions Editor: Elizabeth Widdicombe
Developmental Editor: Penny Gaffney
Project Editor: Cate Rzasa
Managing Editor: Jane Perkins
Design Director: Alan Wendt
Design Supervisor: Jeanne Calabrese
Production Manager: Mary Jarvis

Copy Editor: Lorraine Wolf
Compositor: York Graphic Services
Text Type: Palatino

Library of Congress Cataloging-in-Publication Data

Weston, J. Fred (John Fred), 1916–
    Managerial finance.

    Includes bibliographies and index.
    1. Corporations—Finance.   I. Copeland, Thomas E., 1946–   .   II. Title.
HG4026.W45   1986   658.1'5   85-12974
ISBN 0-03-064041-5

Printed in the United States of America
678-039-98765432

Address orders:
383 Madison Avenue
New York, NY 10017

Address editorial correspondence:
One Salt Creek Lane
Hinsdale, IL 60521

CBS COLLEGE PUBLISHING
The Dryden Press
Holt, Rinehart and Winston
Saunders College Publishing

About the Authors

J. Fred Weston earned his A.B. in Political Science, his MBA in Business Economics, and his Ph.D. in Finance, all from the University of Chicago. Dr. Weston began his teaching career at the University of Chicago and in 1949 joined the staff of the University of California, Los Angeles, where he has been professor of managerial economics and finance in the Graduate School of Management since 1955 and has served as Chairman of Finance and Chairman of Business Economics. In 1979, Professor Weston was selected one of the five outstanding teachers on the UCLA campus. He is currently the Cordner Professor of Money and Financial Markets.

Dr. Weston was Associate Editor of *The Journal of Finance* from 1948 to 1955, and a member of the journal's editorial board. He has served as President of the American Finance Association, President of the Western Economic Association, and President of the Financial Management Association. He was also a member of the American Economic Association Census Advisory Committee.

Dr. Weston has published extensively in the financial literature. In addition to *Managerial Finance*, he is the author of several other books, including *The Role of Mergers in the Growth of Large Firms*, *Public Policy toward Mergers* (with Sam Peltzman), and *Financial Theory and Corporate Policy* (with Thomas E. Copeland).

Dr. Weston has served extensively as a consultant to business firms on financial and economic policies.

Thomas E. Copeland received his B.A. in Economics from Johns Hopkins University, his MBA in Finance from the Wharton School, and his Ph.D. from the University of Pennsylvania. Since that time he has been a member of the faculty at UCLA's Graduate School of Management where he has served as Chairman of the Finance Curriculum Area. He has twice received an award for best teacher in the MBA program, is active in executive education, and has directed UCLA's program for the Young President's Organization.

Also with J. Fred Weston, Dr. Copeland has authored *Financial Theory and Corporate Policy*, the most widely used advanced level corporation finance text. His academic publications include articles about stock splits, theory of market trading activity, receivables policy, leasing, bid–ask spreads, nonprofit organizations, and portfolio performance measurement. His current research focuses on the value of listing on the NYSE, empirical evidence on block and new issue liquidity premia, spinoffs, and issues in experimental economics. Dr. Copeland is a member of the editorial board of *The Midland Corporate Financial Journal* and the *Financial Review*.

Dr. Copeland is a member of the board of directors of Kalama Chemical, Seattle, Washington, and is experienced in the valuation of privately held corporations.

The Dryden Press Series in Finance

Preface

In the eighth edition of *Managerial Finance,* we have tried to rethink the material in a fundamental way to reflect the important developments that continue to take place in the field of finance. In reworking the materials, we have sought to achieve a smoother, more cohesive and integrated treatment of managerial finance. Topic coverage is more complete, and the modern finance literature has been fully utilized to provide guidance to practicing financial managers. Our aim is to present the state of the art of received theory as a guide to making practical financial decisions.

The central unifying theme in the eighth edition is the *valuation orientation.* Valuation is the basis for decisions in all major areas of finance: time value of money, capital budgeting, capital structure, cost of capital, dividend policy, financing decisions, mergers, and financial reorganizations.

Impacts of New Developments

Managerial Finance continues to reflect important new developments in the financial environment. The changing value of the U.S. dollar, for example, dramatizes the increased importance of international finance. The relative value of the dollar has created serious problems for some industries and new challenges and opportunities for others. In making the necessary adjustments to economic changes in both domestic and international markets, finance plays a significant role along with the other disciplines important in managing organizations.

New financial instruments and new financial institutions also continuously change the environment in which business firms must operate. Academic researchers have made significant advances, especially in the areas of capital budgeting, asset pricing, cost of capital, and applications of option pricing theory. At the same time, business firms are making increased use of financial theory, and feedback from the world of financial practitioners is affecting financial theory. These developments have guided the revisions made in the eighth edition of *Managerial Finance.*

Changes in the Eighth Edition

Although there are many changes in the eighth edition, this edition continues the basic philosophy of previous editions: to provide users with coverage of all important areas of financial management while providing flexibility in the use of materials. We have continued to reflect important new advances in the applications of valuation analysis, asset pricing models, option pricing models, and the state-preference framework.

Specific changes in the eighth edition of *Managerial Finance* include the following:

1. End-of-chapter problems have been updated and revised where appropriate. We have also added new problems to round out the coverage of concepts and to provide appropriate emphasis on areas of central importance. Interest rate levels used in the problems seek to strike a middle range between the extreme highs of the early summer of 1982 and the lows reached in early 1983 and mid-1985.
2. Time value of money and capital budgeting have been introduced early (Chapters 5 and 6) so they can be used as tools of analysis in all subsequent decision areas.

3. A new chapter (Chapter 7) has been added to describe how the market determines discount rates.

4. The materials on financial forecasting (Chapter 10) have been revised to introduce some statistical concepts used in subsequent topics, particularly decision making under uncertainty and its applications.

5. Decision models for credit management and policy (Chapter 14) reflect the new capital budgeting approach taken in recent literature.

6. The treatment of decision making under uncertainty and its applications (Chapters 16 and 17) has been streamlined and clarified.

7. Option pricing (Chapter 18) begins with the simplified binomial option pricing model, which is then generalized to the Black-Scholes model.

8. The literature on market efficiency has been summarized (Chapter 19) because the concepts are basic to correct thinking about financial decision making.

9. The theory and measurement of the cost of capital discussions (Chapter 21) have been reorganized and clarified.

10. Dividend policy (Chapter 22) has been rewritten to reflect the theoretical literature as well as practical applications of dividend policy, including consideration of clientele effects.

11. Valuation measurement (Chapter 23) has been reworked and clarified.

12. The analysis of refunding decisions (Appendix A to Chapter 26) has been reformulated and streamlined.

13. The discussion of warrants and convertibles (Chapter 28) has been rewritten to integrate the material with the recent literature, which reflects the application of option pricing models.

14. Pension fund management (Chapter 29) has been added to reflect the increasing responsibility of financial managers in this area and to illustrate the impact of ERISA on the corporate debt implications of pension liabilities.

15. Merger analysis (Chapter 30) has been refocused to a fundamental valuation approach and extended to incorporate broader issues of corporate restructuring and control.

16. The reorganization and bankruptcy materials (Chapter 31) have been rewritten to integrate more fully the impact of the Bankruptcy Reform Act of 1978.

We hope that as a result of these substantial revisions, the reader will have a gratifying intellectual experience with the new *Managerial Finance*. The increased rigor of the eighth edition will pay off in increased insights and ease of moving from concept to concept as well facilitating practical applications in decision making.

Flexibility in the Use of the Materials

Much of the book's specific content is the result of our classroom teaching experience over a number of years, including executive development programs. This experience, in addition to our consulting with business firms on financial problems and policies, has helped us to identify the most significant responsibilities of financial managers, the most fundamental problems facing firms, and the most feasible approaches to practical decision making. Some topics are conceptually difficult, but so are the issues faced by financial managers. Business managers must be prepared to handle complex problems, and finding solutions to these problems necessarily involves the use of advanced tools and techniques.

We have not avoided the many unresolved areas of business financial theory and practice. Although we could have simplified the text in many places by side-stepping the difficult issues, we preferred to provide a basic framework based on the "received doctrine" and then go on to present materials (sometimes in chapter appendixes) on a number of important but controversial issues. We hope that our presentation, along with the additional references provided at the end of each chapter, will stimulate the reader to further inquiry.

We acknowledge that the level and difficulty of the material are uneven. Certain sections are simply descriptions of the institutional features of the financial environment and, as such, can be comprehended easily and rapidly. Other parts—notably the materials on capital budgeting, uncertainty, option pricing, and the cost of capital—are difficult. We hope that by alternating easy and tough material, we will provide a refreshing change of pace for the reader.

Managerial Finance has traditionally been a highly flexible text, and this flexibility has been increased in the eighth edition. This book can be used in a one-quarter or one-semester introductory course. However, when so used, it will not be possible to cover all of the chapters. Some instructors concentrate on the basic theory chapters for a one-quarter or one-semester course, which would include Chapters 1, 5–7, 16–18, and 20–23, representing 11 of the 32 chapters. For a one-semester course of 15 to 18 weeks, one or more additional major parts of the book can be added. Other instructors simply take the chapters in sequence, covering Chapters 1–19 or Chapters 1–23 as time permits. Still others cover the entire book in a sequence of two quarters or two semesters. We have also found that business executives can work through the book on their own with the assistance of the book's *Study Guide* described below.

Several reviewers suggested that it might be desirable to reduce the total length of the book. Although the idea was appealing, we did not follow the suggestion for several reasons. We want the book to cover the entire field of business finance and to deal with all of the financial management functions. Eliminating institutional material and concentrating only on theory and technique would give the student an unrealistic, sterile view of finance. Some of the more advanced theories and techniques could have been eliminated because they are difficult, but they are essential for sound decision making. These considerations, plus the flexibility in the use of materials, which makes it unnecessary to cover the entire book in one course, caused us to refrain from eliminating these sections. Furthermore, the book has a tradition of functioning as a text or reference work for use in subsequent courses and for the practicing financial executive as well.

Ancillary Materials

Several items are available to supplement *Managerial Finance*. For the professor, there is a comprehensive *Instructor's Manual*, which contains alternative subject sequences and teaching methods, course outlines, answers to all text questions, solutions to all text problems, and an extensive array of test questions and problems. Also available to the instructor is a comprehensive set of *Transparency Masters*, which feature solutions to selected end-of-chapter problems. As a supplement to problems in the text, an additional set of *Supplemental Problems* and solutions is available to adopters. These were developed with the assistance of Roger Bey, Keith Johnson, and Ramon Johnson, among others.

For the student, the *Study Guide* highlights key points in the text and presents a comprehensive set of problems similar to those at the end of each chapter. Each problem is solved in detail, so a student who has difficulty working the end-of-chapter problems can be aided by use of the *Study Guide*.

A casebook and a book of readings can also be used to supplement *Managerial Finance*. *Cases in Managerial Finance*, sixth edition, by Roy L. Crum and Eugene F. Brigham and *Issues in Managerial Finance*, second edition, by Eugene F. Brigham and Ramon E. Johnson, are available.

Acknowledgments

In its several revisions, this book has been worked on and critically reviewed by numerous individuals, and we have received many detailed comments and suggestions from instructors and students using the book in our own schools and elsewhere. All this help has improved the quality of the book, and we are deeply indebted to the following individuals, and others, for their help: M. Adler, E. Altman, J. Andrews, R. Aubey, P. Bacon, W. Beranek, V. Brewer, W. Brueggeman, R. Carleson, S. Choudhur, P. Cooley, C. Cox, D. Fischer, G. Granger, R. Gray, J. Griggs, R. Haugen, S. Hawk, R. Hehre, J. Henry, A. Herrmann, G. Hettenhouse, R. Himes, C. C. Hsia, C. Johnson, R. Jones, D. Kaplan, M. Kaufman, D. Knight, H. Krogh, R. LeClair, W. Lee, D. Longmore, J. Longstreet, H. Magee, P. Malone, R. Masulis, R. Moore, T. Morton, T. Nantell, R. Nelson, R. Norgaard, J. Pappas, R. Pettit, R. Pettway, J. Pinkerton, G. Pogue, W. Regan, F. Reilly, R. Rentz, R. Richards, C. Rini, R. Roenfeldt, W. Sharpe, K. Smith, P. Smith, R. Smith, D. Sorenson, B. Trueman, M. Tysseland, P. Vanderheiden, D. Woods, J. Yeakel, and D. Ziegenhein.

For providing us with detailed reviews of the manuscript for this edition, we owe special thanks to Michael L. Baker, Severin C. Carlson, Dosoung Choi, Peter K. Ewald, Keith Wm. Fairchild, Roger P. Hill, Herb Johnson, Morris Lamberson, Glenn H. Petry, John G. Preston, John M. Wachowicz, Jr., Dennis Zocco, and, particularly, Mary Jean Scheuer.

The Graduate School of Management at UCLA and our colleagues provided us with intellectual support in bringing this edition to completion. We owe special thanks to Susan Hoag for her good judgment and assistance in all phases of writing the book and to Marilyn McElroy for her dedication and creative abilities in putting the manuscript through many revisions and on to the computer. For assistance in developing and refining problems and solutions, we thank Sally Hamilton, Mark Ewing, and Jeffrey Shepard. For help in the typing and preparation process, we thank Karen Withem and Solomon Jones.

We are also indebted to The Dryden Press staff—principally, Liz Widdicombe, Cate Rzasa, Penny Gaffney, Alan Wendt, Jeanne Calabrese, Judy Sarwark, Debby Ruck, and Bill Schoof— for their creative efforts in seeing the manuscript through development and production to the bound book.

The field of finance will continue to experience significant changes. It is stimulating to participate in these exciting developments, and we hope that *Managerial Finance* will contribute to continued advances in the theory and practice of finance. We welcome comments and suggestions of any kind from our readers.

J. Fred Weston
Thomas E. Copeland

Graduate School of Management
UCLA
Los Angeles, California 90024

September 1985

Contents

and Other Aspects of Corporate Control 912   Terms of Mergers 914   Holding
Companies 920   Leveraged Buy-Outs 923   Managerial Policies in a Valuation
Framework 927

Part One   Fundamental Concepts of Managerial Finance

Part One provides basic background material. The scope and nature of managerial finance are described in Chapter 1. Chapter 2 discusses the financial statements of the firm and the complex financial reporting environment in which the firm operates. Chapter 3 presents an overview of the total financial network of the modern economy, viewing the functions of financial managers within the perspective of the money and capital markets. In Chapter 4, the key elements of the U.S. tax system are summarized. The discussion emphasizes that since a high percentage of business income is paid to the government, taxes have an important influence on many kinds of business decisions, and particularly on the form of business organization chosen (proprietorship, partnership, or corporation).

Chapter 1   The Finance Function

What is managerial finance? What is the finance function in the firm? What specific tasks are assigned to financial managers? What tools and techniques are available to them, and how can their performance be measured? On a broader scale, what is the role of finance in the U.S. economy, and how can managerial finance be used to further national goals? Providing at least tentative answers to these questions is the principal purpose of this book.

The Finance Function

Managerial finance is defined by the functions and responsibilities of financial managers. While the specifics vary among organizations, *the key finance functions are the investment, financing, and dividend decisions of an organization.*[1] Funds are raised from external financial sources and allocated for different uses. The flow of funds in the operations of an enterprise is monitored. Benefits to the financing sources take the form of returns, repayments, products, and services. These finance functions must be performed in all organizations — from business firms to government units or agencies, aid groups such as the Red Cross or the Salvation Army, and other nonprofit organizations such as art museums and theater groups. Thus, *the financial manager's main functions are to plan for, obtain, and use funds to maximize the value of a firm.* Several important activities are involved. First, in planning and forecasting, the financial manager must interact with the executives who are responsible for the general planning activities of the firm.

Second, the financial manager is concerned with investment and financing decisions and their interactions. A successful firm usually achieves a high rate of growth in sales, which requires the support of increased investments by the firm. Financial managers must determine a sound rate of sales growth and must rank alternative investment opportunities. They help decide the specific investments to be made and the alternative sources and forms of funds for financing these investments. Decisions must be made about the use of internal versus external funds, of debt versus owners' funds, and of long-term versus short-term financing.

Third, the financial manager interacts with other managers in the business to help the firm operate as efficiently as possible. All business decisions have financial implications, and all managers — financial and otherwise — need to take this into account. For example, marketing decisions, which affect sales growth and, consequently, change investment requirements, must allow for their effect on (and how they are affected by) the availability of funds, inventory policies, plant capacity utilization, and so on.

---

[1]"Dividend decisions" determine how the firm pays a return to all different types of investors for the use of their funds.

The fourth aspect involves the use of the money and capital markets. As we shall explain in a subsequent chapter, the financial manager links his firm to the financial markets in which funds are raised and in which the firm's securities are traded.

In sum, the central responsibilities of financial managers relate to decisions on investments and how they are financed. In the performance of these functions, the financial manager's responsibilities have a direct bearing on the key decisions affecting the value of the firm.

Finance in the Organizational Structure of the Firm

The chief financial officer is high in the organization hierarchy of the firm because of the central role of finance in top-level decision making. Figure 1.1 depicts the typical organization structure for large firms in the United States. The board of directors represents the shareholders and is the source of ultimate authority in the firm. The president is the chief executive officer to whom the senior vice presidents report. One of these key executives is the *vice president of finance*, the chief financial officer (CFO), who is responsible for the formulation of major financial policies in the firm. He also interacts with other senior officers to present the financial implications of major decisions in other areas, defines the

Figure 1.1   Finance in the Organization Structure

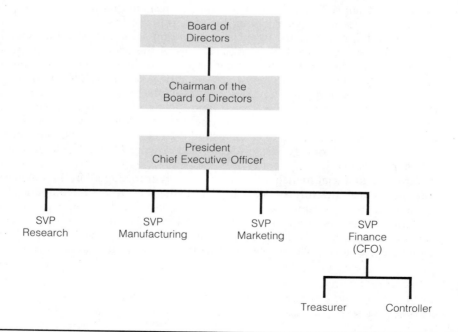

duties of other financial officers who report to him, and is held accountable for the analytical aspects of the treasurer's and controller's activities.

Specific finance functions are typically divided between two top financial officers — the treasurer and the controller. The *treasurer* handles the acquisition and custody of funds. The areas of responsibility for the *controller* are accounting, reporting, and control. In addition to these core responsibilities, the two positions often include related activities. For example, the treasurer is typically responsible for the acquisition of cash and, therefore, the relationships with commercial banks and investment bankers. The treasurer is likely to provide reports on the daily cash position of the firm and its working capital position; he is also responsible for the formulation of cash budgets. Although the controller has the main reporting responsibilities, the treasurer generally reports on cash flows and cash conservation. The treasurer is also usually responsible for credit management, insurance, and pensions management.

The controller's central function includes the recording and reporting of financial information. This typically involves the preparation of budgets and financial statements, two instruments for carrying out control responsibility. Other duties of the controller include payroll, taxes, and internal auditing.

In smaller organizations, the owner of the firm may carry out (or supervise the execution of) the treasurer and controller functions, or one financial officer may perform both functions under the title of treasurer, controller, or vice president of finance.

Some large firms include a fourth corporate officer whose activities are sometimes considered to be financial in nature — the *corporate secretary*. The corporate secretary is responsible for communications relating to the company's financial instruments. These encompass legal affairs and recording minutes in connection with top-level committee meetings. The corporate secretary's duties include record keeping in connection with the instruments of ownership, and financial records related to the borrowing activities of the company.

Company history and the abilities of individual officers greatly influence the areas of responsibility of these four financial offices. A very able and active financial officer will be involved in all top management policies and decisions, often providing a training ground for the movement of the chief financial officer into the top management positions of the company — the president or chief executive officer.

In addition to individual financial officers, larger enterprises use *finance committees*. Ideally, a committee assembles persons of different backgrounds and abilities to formulate policies and decisions. Financing decisions require a wide scope of knowledge and balanced judgments. For example, obtaining outside funds represents a major decision. The difference of a quarter- or half-percent in interest rates may represent a large amount of money in absolute terms. When such firms as IBM, General Motors, and Kellogg borrow $600 million, a difference of one-half of one percent amounts to $3 million per year. Therefore, the judgments of senior managers with financial backgrounds are valuable in arriving at decisions with bankers on the timing and terms of a loan. Also, the finance committee, working closely with the board of directors, characteristically has major responsibility for administering the capital and the operating budgets.

Finance committees are classified further into subgroups in larger firms. In addition to the general finance committee, there may be a *capital appropriations committee*, responsible primarily for capital budgets and expenditures; a *budget committee*, dealing with the operating budgets of the forthcoming year; and a *pension committee*, because the amounts of funds involved are so large.

The *salary and profit-sharing committee* is responsible for salary administration as well as for setting classifications and compensation for top-level officers. Usually tied to the general planning and control processes of the firm, this committee seeks to provide the rewards and penalties necessary to make the planning and control system work effectively.

The finance function is typically close to the top in the organizational structure of the firm because financial decisions are crucial to the survival and success of the firm. All important episodes in the life of a corporation have major financial implications. Such decisions include adding a new product line or reducing participation in an old one; expanding or adding a plant or changing locations; selling additional new securities; entering into leasing arrangements; and paying dividends and making share repurchases. These decisions have a lasting effect upon the long-run profitability of the firm and, therefore, require top management consideration. Hence, finance is typically involved in high-level decisions of the firm.

The Nature of the Firm and Its Goals

A new theory of the nature of the firm, the "contractual theory," has now become widely held.[2] It views the firm as a network of contracts, actual and implicit, which specify the roles of the various participants in the organization (workers, managers, owners, lenders) and define their rights, obligations, and payoffs under various conditions. Most participants bargain for limited risk and fixed payoffs, whereas the firm's owners are liable for any residual risk and thus hold a residual claim on any assets and earnings of the firm which remain after covering costs. Yet although contracts reduce conflicts of interest in a firm, they cannot eliminate entirely the potential conflict which arises in any organization characterized by separation of ownership and control.

In the modern corporation, ownership is commonly widely diffused. The day-to-day operations of the firm are conducted by its managers, who usually do not have the predominant stock ownership. Technically, the managers are the agents of the owners but, in fact, exercise control over the firm. Thus, there is a potential conflict of interest between the owners, who expect the managers to act on their behalf, and the managers, who have their own interests as well. This gives rise to what has been called "the agency problem," that is, the divergence of interests that arises between a principal and his agent.

Jensen and Meckling [1976] have developed the most analytical treatment of the relationship between managers and owners. In their formulation, the agency problem arises when a manager owns less than the total common stock of the firm. This fractional ownership can lead the managers to work less strenuously and to acquire more perquisites (luxurious offices, furniture and rugs, company cars) than if they had to bear all of the costs.

To deal with such agency problems, additional expenditures would be required. These other forms of agency costs include (1) auditing systems to limit this kind of management behavior, (2) various kinds of bonding assurances by the managers that such abuses will not be practiced, and (3) changes in organization systems to limit the ability of managers to engage in the undesirable practices.

There is some disagreement as to the magnitude of the agency problem. A number of people argue that because managers know more about the firm than its shareholders do, they may come to dominate the board of directors, which in theory is supposed to repre-

---

[2]A good summary statement with reference to the origins and development of the theory is found in Alchian [1982]. See also Fama and Jensen [1983a, 1983b].

sent the shareholders. In addition, they contend that managers are interested in the firm's growth or size because managers' salaries and other benefits are related to sales or total assets.

While there is some basis for this view of managerial control, others point to compensation plans for managers with bonuses tied to profits and to stock options which give managers incentive to increase the value of the firm's common stock. In addition, they note that shareholders do, in fact, exercise their ultimate power to replace management. This carrot and stick approach, they contend, is sufficient to keep the agency problem under control.

For large, publicly traded corporations, the stock market serves as a performance monitor. While stock prices may react to the general economy (for example, changes in interest rates) or industry-wide factors (for example, the impact on the automobile industry of a change in steel prices), the basic component of the stock price is the market's perception of the particular firm's current and expected future performance. Empirical studies have demonstrated that stock prices respond quickly and accurately to publicly available information. Thus, if managers are not performing effectively relative to the potential of the assets under their control, it will not be long before this is reflected in a lower stock price.

Two additional mechanisms are said to keep managerialism in check. (The term *managerialism* refers to self-serving behavior by managers at the expense of shareholders.) One control is the managerial labor market which prices out the human capital of managers. The market is continuously reassessing the value of managerial human capital on the basis of potential or contracted performance versus actual performance.[3] If the assessment is unfavorable, the competition among managers assures that a replacement will be made. But some argue that the wide dispersion of ownership of common stock of most large corporations may make it difficult for shareholders to exercise their control through the board of directors. The individual shareholder does not have a large enough investment to justify his spending money and time to closely monitor the managers and board of directors. If so, the second control mechanism comes into action. This is the market for corporate takeovers. Poor management will cause the price of the firm's stock to decline, making the firm a bargain for a corporate acquirer and a tender offer will be made.[4]

Goals of the Firm

Within the above framework, *the goal of financial management is to maximize the value of the firm.* However, there are potential conflicts between a firm's owners and its creditors. For example, consider a firm financed half from the owners' funds and half from debt funds borrowed at a fixed interest rate, such as 10 percent. No matter how high the firm's earnings, the bondholders still receive only their 10 percent return. Yet if the firm is highly successful, the market value of the ownership funds (the common stock of the company) is likely to rise greatly.

If the company does very well, the value of its common stock will increase, while the value of the firm's debt is not likely to be greatly affected. On the other hand, if the firm does poorly, the claims of the debtholders will have to be honored first and the value of the common stock will decline greatly. Thus, the value of the ownership shares provides a

---

[3]For a discussion of the role of the managerial labor market, see Fama [1980].

[4]For a more complete discussion of the role of mergers and tender offers, see Chapter 30.

good index for measuring the degree of a company's effectiveness in performance. It is for this reason that the goal of financial management is generally expressed in terms of maximizing the value of the ownership shares of the firm — in short, maximizing share price.

By formulating clear objectives in terms of stock price values, the discipline of the financial markets is implemented. Thus, firms that perform better than others have higher stock prices and can raise additional funds under more favorable terms. When funds go to firms with favorable stock price trends, the economy's resources are directed to their most efficient uses. For this reason, the finance literature has generally adopted the basic objective of maximizing the price of the firm's common stock. Financial theories have been developed from this postulate and receive considerable support from empirical studies. Shareholder wealth maximization also provides a basis for rational decision making with respect to a wide range of financial issues faced by the firm.

The goal of maximizing share price does not imply that managers should seek to increase the value of common stock at the expense of bondholders. For example, managers should not substantially alter the riskiness of the firm's product-market investment activities. Riskier investments, if they are successful, will benefit the shareholders greatly. On the other hand, risky investments that fail will reduce the security to bondholders and decrease bond values. As a practical matter, if a firm does not give strong assurances to bondholders that investment policies will not be changed to their disadvantage, it must pay interest rates high enough to compensate bondholders against the possibility of such adverse policy changes.

Social Responsibility

Another important aspect of the goals of the firm and the goals of financial management is consideration of social responsibility. There are a number of dimensions to be taken into account. First, if financial management seeks to maximize share price, this requires efficient, well-managed operations related to consumer demand patterns. Successful firms are at the forefront of efficiency and innovation, so that value maximization leads to new products, new technologies, and greater employment; hence, the more successful the firm in value maximization, the better the quality and quantity of the total "pie" to be distributed.

But in recent years, "externalities" (such as pollution, product safety, and job safety) have increased in importance. As economic agents whose actions have considerable impact, business firms must take into account the effects of their policies and actions on society as a whole. It has long been recognized that the external economic environment is highly important to a firm's decision making. Fluctuations in the overall level of business activity and related changes in the conditions of financial markets are important aspects of the external environment. In a like manner, the expectations of workers, consumers, and various interest groups create other dimensions of the external environment that firms must respond to in order to achieve long-run wealth maximization. Indeed, responsiveness to these new and powerful constituencies may be required for the survival of the private enterprise system. This point of view argues that business firms must recognize a wider range of influences from the external environment.

It is critical that industry and government cooperate in establishing rules for corporate behavior and that firms follow the spirit as well as the letter of the law in their actions. Thus, firms should strive to maximize shareholder wealth within external constraints. Throughout this book, we shall assume that managements operate in this manner.

Value Maximization as a Goal

We have discussed some broad aspects of value maximization as a goal. Now we turn to a consideration of technical distinctions and implementation aspects of the role of financial management in value maximization.

It is important to recognize that value maximization is broader than "profit maximization." This is true for several reasons. First, maximizing value takes the time value of money into account. Funds that are received this year have more value than funds that may be received ten years from now. Second, value maximization considers the riskiness of the income stream. For example, the rate of return required on riskless government securities would be lower than the rate of return required on an investment in starting a new business.

Third, the "quality" of the expected future fund flows may vary. Profit figures can vary widely depending upon the accounting rules and conventions used. Value maximization avoids some of these problems by emphasizing cash or fund flows rather than being dependent on the way that profit or net income is measured. There is considerable evidence that the financial markets see through differences in accounting procedures and get closer to true, underlying values.

Thus, value maximization is broader and more general than profit maximization and, as such, provides a solid basis for decision making. Value maximization is the unifying conceptual idea used throughout the book.

Performance Measurement by the Financial Markets

The basic finance functions must be performed in all types of organizations. What is unique about business organizations is that they are directly and measurably subject to the discipline of the financial markets. These markets are continuously determining the valuations of business firms' securities, thereby providing measures of the firms' performance.[5] A consequence of this continuous assessment of a firm by the capital markets is the change in its valuation level (stock market price).

The presence of the capital markets' continuous assessment therefore stimulates efficiency and provides incentive to business managers to improve their performance.

The Risk-Return Tradeoff

Financial decisions affect the level of a firm's stock prices by influencing the size of the cash flow stream and the riskiness of the firm. These relationships are diagrammed in Figure 1.2. Policy decisions, which are subject to government constraints, affect both profitability and risk; these two factors jointly determine the value of the firm.

The primary policy decision is made in choosing the industry in which the firm is operating. Profitability and risk are further influenced by decisions relating to the size of the firm, its growth rate, the types and amounts of equipment used, the extent to which debt is employed, the firm's liquidity position, and so on. An increase in the cash position, for instance, reduces risk; however, since cash is not an earning asset, converting other assets

---

[5]The financial markets discussed in Chapter 3 provide valuation of firms whose shares are traded. The relationships between return and risk provide the basis for the valuation of companies whose ownership shares are not actively traded.

Figure 1.2   Valuation as the Central Focus of the Finance Function

---

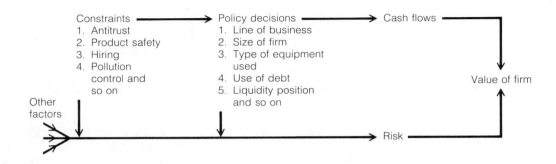

to cash also reduces profitability. Similarly, the use of additional debt raises the rate of return, or the profitability, on the stockholders' net worth; at the same time, more debt means more risk. The financial manager seeks to strike the particular balance between risk and profitability that will maximize the wealth of the firm's stockholders, that is, the *risk-return tradeoff*. Most financial decisions involve such tradeoffs.

The Changing Role of Financial Management

When finance first emerged as a separate field of study in the early 1900s, the emphasis was on legalistic matters relating to mergers, consolidations, the formation of new firms, and the various types of securities issued by corporations. Industrialization was sweeping the country, and the critical problem faced by firms was obtaining capital for expansion. The capital markets were relatively primitive, and transfers of funds from individual savers to businesses were quite difficult. Accounting statements of earnings and asset values were unreliable, and stock trading by insiders and manipulators caused prices to fluctuate wildly; consequently, investors were reluctant to purchase stocks and bonds. In this environment, it is easy to see why finance concentrated so heavily on legal issues relating to the issuance of securities.

The emphasis remained on securities through the 1920s; however, radical changes occurred during the depression of the 1930s. Business failures during that period caused finance to focus on bankruptcy and reorganization, corporate liquidity, and government regulation of securities markets. Finance was still a descriptive, legalistic subject, but the emphasis shifted to survival rather than expansion.

During the 1940s and early 1950s, finance continued to be taught as a descriptive, institutional subject, viewed from the outside rather than from within the firm's management. However, some effort was devoted to budgeting and other internal control procedures, and stimulated by the work of Dean, capital budgeting began to receive attention.

The evolutionary pace quickened during the late 1950s. While the right-hand side of the balance sheet (liabilities and capital) had received more attention in the earlier era, increasing emphasis was placed on asset analysis during the last half of that decade. Mathematical models were developed and applied to inventories, cash, accounts receivable, and fixed assets. Increasingly, the focus of finance shifted from the outsider's to the insider's point of view, as financial decisions within the firm were recognized to be the critical issues in corporate finance. Descriptive, institutional materials on capital markets and financing instruments were still studied, but within the context of corporate financial decisions.

The emphasis on decision making has continued in recent years. First, there has been increasing belief that sound investment decisions require accurate measurements of the cost of capital. Accordingly, ways of quantifying the cost of capital now play a key role in finance. Second, capital has been in short supply, rekindling the interest in methods of raising funds. Third, there has been continued merger activity, leading to renewed interest in takeovers. Fourth, accelerated progress in transportation and communications has stimulated interest in international finance. Fifth, an increasing awareness of social problems, such as air and water pollution, work safety, urban blight, and unemployment among minorities, has demanded a greater proportion of the time of financial managers in their efforts to determine the firm's appropriate role in relation to these problems. Finally, another important change in the economic environment is the persistent high rate of inflation.

The Impact of Inflation on Financial Management

Inflation has become such a pervasive part of the economic environment that it must be viewed as an important new influence on business financial decisions. During the 1950s and 1960s, prices rose at an average rate of about 1 to 2 percent per year, but in the 1970s, the rate of inflation in some years rose to more than 10 percent. In 1982-84, although the inflation rate in the United States was reduced, the prospect of continuing large government deficits raised the specter of the return of inflation. Thus, the fear of inflation continues to exert a strong influence on financial policies. Some major effects of inflation are briefly sketched here.

Interest Rates. The rate of interest that any security would yield if there were zero inflation is called the "real rate of interest." The interest rates that are actually observed in the financial markets are called "nominal rates of interest," which represent the real rate plus an "inflation premium." The inflation premium reflects the expected long-run rate of inflation.[6] Accordingly, an increase in the expected rate of inflation is translated into higher interest rates. So higher rates of inflation mean that the costs of obtaining funds by governments, business, and individuals will be increased. Thus, inflation makes obtaining funds more expensive for everybody.

Planning Difficulties. Businesses operate on the basis of long-run plans. For example, a firm builds a plant only after making a thorough analysis of expected costs and revenues over the life of the plant. Reaching such estimates is not easy under the best of conditions. During rapid inflation, when labor and materials costs are changing unevenly, accurate forecasts are especially important yet exceedingly difficult to make.

---

[6]From 1982 to the present (April 1985), when the current rate of inflation of 4 to 6 percent was deducted from prevailing nominal rates of interest, the "real rate of interest" appeared to be very high, 7 to 9 percent. One explanation is that high uncertainty about future rates of inflation causes this premium.

Demand for Capital. Inflation increases the amount of capital required to conduct a given volume of business. When inventories are sold, they must be replaced with more expensive goods. The costs of expanding or replacing plants are also greater, and workers demand higher wages. While financial managers are pressured to raise additional capital, the monetary authorities may restrict the supply of loanable funds in an effort to hold down the rate of inflation. The ensuing scramble for limited funds drives interest rates still higher.

Bond Price Declines. Long-term bond prices fall as interest rates rise. In the effort to protect themselves against such capital losses, lenders are beginning (1) to put more funds into short-term rather than long-term debt and (2) to insist upon bonds whose interest rates vary with "the general level of interest rates" as measured by an index of interest rates. Brazil and other inflation-plagued South American countries have used such indexed bonds for years.

Accounting Problems. With high rates of inflation, reported profits are distorted. The sale of low-cost inventories results in higher reported profits, but cash flows are held down as firms restock with higher-cost inventories. Similarly, depreciation charges are inaccurate, since they do not reflect the new costs of replacing plant and equipment. Higher reported profits caused by inadequate inventory valuation and depreciation charges result in higher income taxes and reduced cash flows. If a firm plans dividends and capital expenditures based on these "paper" profits, it may develop serious financial problems.

Inflation is a disturbing and challenging new experience for financial managers in the United States. If it returns, financial policies and practices will undergo still further modifications.

Organization of This Book

The aim of this book is to explain the procedures, practices, and policies by which financial management can contribute to the successful performance of organizations. We begin with an emphasis on the tradeoffs between risk and return in seeking to make decisions that will maximize the value of the firm. Each subsequent topic is treated within this basic framework.

The eight major parts of the book are as follows:

Part One: Fundamental Concepts of Managerial Finance
Part Two: The Time Dimension in Financial Decisions
Part Three: Financial Analysis, Planning, and Control
Part Four: Working Capital Management
Part Five: Decision Making under Uncertainty
Part Six: Cost of Capital and Valuation
Part Seven: The Treasurer's Point of View: Policy Decisions
Part Eight: Integrated Topics in Managerial Finance

Part One includes basic background material on financial statements, financial markets, and the tax environment. In Part Two, the time value of money and capital budgeting decisions are discussed. Part Three covers financial analysis, financial models of the firm, and planning and control systems. The foregoing parts provide a framework for Part Four, which covers all aspects of working capital management.

Part Five discusses the impact of decision making under uncertainty and develops a foundation for determining the risk adjustment component of discount rates. This leads to Part Six, which deals with the cost of capital concepts required both for the capital budgeting analysis previously treated and for the valuation chapter which concludes Part Six.

With the analytic framework established, the long-term financing decisions of the firm are treated in Part Seven from the treasurer's point of view. This section builds on the financial structure issues discussed in the cost of capital chapter but in a setting related to individual financial decisions. The increasingly important uses of newer forms of financing are also presented. Part Seven concludes with a discussion of pension fund management, for which the corporate treasurer usually has considerable responsibility.

Finally, in Part Eight, the general concepts and principles of managerial finance are used in integrative applications. Three areas of major importance are covered — mergers, financial readjustments, and international business finance.

Summary

Managerial finance involves the investment, financing, and dividend decisions of the firm. The main functions of financial managers are to plan for, acquire, and use funds to make the maximum contribution to the efficient operation of an organization. This requires that financial managers be familiar with the financial markets from which funds are drawn as well as know how to make sound investment decisions and how to stimulate efficient operations in the organization. All financial decisions involve alternative choices, which include the use of internal versus external funds, long-term versus short-term projects, long-term versus short-term fund sources, and a higher rate of growth versus a lower rate of growth.

We have set forth the view of the firm as a network of contracts among the various participants in the organization. The generally accepted goal of the firm is value maximization, which leads to the efficient use of resources. We discussed potential conflicts between owners and managers as well as between owners and creditors and how they might be resolved. For practical implementation in making financial decisions, stock price maximization is used as a proxy for value maximization. Decisions relating to value maximization typically involve a tradeoff between prospective risks and prospective returns. With this background, we turn to the remaining chapters of the book, which seek to implement the objectives we have set forth.

Questions

1.1 What are the main functions of financial managers?

1.2 Why is shareholder wealth maximization a better operating goal than profit maximization?

1.3 What is the difference between firm value maximization and shareholder wealth maximization?

1.4 What are the issues in the conflict of interest between stockholders and managers, and how can they be resolved?

1.5 What are the potential conflicts of interest between shareholders and bondholders? How can they be resolved?

1.6 What role does social responsibility have in formulating business and financial goals?

1.7   What have been the major developmental periods in the field of finance? What circumstances led to the evolution of the emphasis in each period?

1.8   What is the nature of the risk-return tradeoff faced in financial decision making?

Selected References

Alchian, A. A., "Property Rights, Specialization and the Firm," J. Fred Weston and Michael E. Granfield, Eds., *Corporate Enterprise in a New Environment*, New York: KCG Productions, Inc., 1982, pp. 11-36.

Branch, Ben, "Corporate Objectives and Market Performance," *Financial Management*, 2 (Summer 1973), pp. 24-29.

Ciscel, David H., and Carroll, Thomas M., "The Determinants of Executive Salaries: An Econometric Survey," *Review of Economics and Statistics*, 62 (February 1980), pp. 7-13.

Cooley, Phillip L., "Managerial Pay and Financial Performances of Small Business," *Journal of Business*, 7 (September 1979), pp. 267-276.

Diamond, Douglas W., and Verrecchia, Robert E., "Optimal Managerial Contracts and Equilibrium Security Prices," *Journal of Finance*, 37 (May 1982), pp. 275-287.

Eaton, Jonathan, and Rosen, Harvey S., "Agency, Delayed Compensation, and the Structure of Executive Remuneration," *Journal of Finance*, 38 (December 1983), pp. 1489-1505.

Elliott, J. W., "Control, Size, Growth, and Financial Performance in the Firm," *Journal of Financial and Quantitative Analysis*, 7 (January 1972), pp. 1309-1320.

Fama, Eugene F., "Agency Problems and the Theory of the Firm," *Journal of Political Economy*, 88 (April 1980), pp. 288-307.

——, and Jensen, Michael C., "Separation of Ownership and Control," *The Journal of Law and Economics*, 26 (June 1983a), pp. 301-325.

——, "Agency Problems and Residual Claims," *The Journal of Law and Economics*, 26 (June 1983b), pp. 327-349.

Findlay, Chapman M., and Whitmore, G. A., "Beyond Shareholder Wealth Maximization," *Financial Management*, 3 (Winter 1974), pp. 25-35.

Grossman, S. J., and Stiglitz, J. E., "On Value Maximization and Alternative Objectives of the Firm," *Journal of Finance*, 32 (May 1977), pp. 389-415.

Hakansson, Nils H., "The Fantastic World of Finance: Progress and the Free Lunch," *Journal of Financial and Quantitative Analysis*, 14 (November 1979), pp. 717-734.

Jensen, M. C., and Meckling, W. H., "Theory of the Firm: Managerial Behavior, Agency Costs and Ownership Structure," *Journal of Financial Economics*, 3 (October 1976), pp. 350-360.

Lewellen, Wilbur G., "Management and Ownership in the Large Firm," *Journal of Finance*, 24 (May 1969), pp. 299-322.

Seitz, Neil, "Shareholder Goals, Firm Goals and Firm Financing Decisions," *Financial Management*, 11 (Autumn 1982), pp. 20-26.

Treynor, Jack L., "The Financial Objective in the Widely Held Corporation," *Financial Analysts Journal*, 37 (March/April 1981), pp. 68-71.

Wacht, Richard F., "A Financial Management Theory of the Nonprofit Organization," *Journal of Financial Research*, 7 (Spring 1984), pp. 37-45.

Weston, J. Fred, "Developments in Finance Theory," *Financial Management*, 10 (June 1981), pp. 5-22.

——, "New Themes in Finance," *Journal of Finance*, 24 (March 1974), pp. 237-243.

——, *The Scope and Methodology of Finance*, Englewood Cliffs, N. J.: Prentice-Hall, 1966.

——, "Toward Theories of Financial Policy," *Journal of Finance*, 10 (May 1955), pp. 130-143.

Chapter 2 Financial Statements

Financial statements report the historical performance of a firm and provide clues to its future. The annual report is a document which informs shareholders and is audited in accordance with generally accepted accounting principles. The 10K and 8K are documents provided, under very specific guidelines, to the Securities and Exchange Commission. Tax statements are supplied by the firm to the Internal Revenue Service, to state and local tax authorities (for income and property tax purposes), and to foreign governments (when the firm is multinational).

Sample Income Statement

Table 2.1 shows a highly stylized version of a firm's income statement, which measures the *flows* of revenues and expenses during an interval of time, usually one year. The other major financial statement is the firm's balance sheet, which measures *stocks* of assets and liabilities at a point in time. A complete description of a firm's activities during a year consists of three financial statements: (1) a beginning-of-year balance sheet, which gives a snapshot of the firm at the start of its fiscal year; (2) an income statement, which shows the flows of revenues and expenses during the year; and (3) an end-of-year balance sheet, which provides a snapshot of the ending assets and liabilities. Both a beginning and an end-of-year balance sheet are necessary in order to measure any changes in stock balances, for example, changes in inventory held.

A discussion of our illustrative income statement and balance sheet serves three purposes. First, it familiarizes the reader with the accounting terminology used throughout the remainder of this text. Second, it may be used as an introduction to many of the corporate finance topics which are covered in later chapters. And third, it illustrates the sources and uses of funds statement, an important financial planning tool, which is presented later on in this chapter.

Table 2.1, the sample income statement, begins with the revenues of the firm, $\tilde{R}$, which are not known with certainty (at least for planning purposes). The symbol tilde ($\sim$) is used to distinguish between those flow items which are random variables and those (such as fixed cash costs, depreciation, and interest expenses) which typically are not random. The very nature of a firm's product has much to do with the riskiness of its revenue stream. For example, consumer products such as food, tobacco, and electricity have relatively low variability, and annual sales are easy to predict. By comparison, the variation in demand for steel or housing is relatively uncertain. Some of the risk can be eliminated by choosing to diversify across product lines (for example, conglomerate merger), but it is impossible to diversify away all risk. The general subject of risk and return tradeoffs is discussed in Chapters 16 and 17. Conglomerate mergers are discussed in Chapter 30.

The production technology of the firm is reflected in the costs which are reported in the sample income statement. There are many different ways to produce a given product. For

Table 2.1   Sample Income Statement

Income for the Year 19XX

$\tilde{R}$	=	revenues
$-\tilde{VC}$	=	variable costs
$-FCC$	=	fixed cash costs
$-dep$	=	noncash fixed costs (for example, depreciation)
$\widetilde{EBIT}$	=	earnings before interest and taxes
$-rD$	=	fixed rate interest payments
$\widetilde{EBT}$	=	earnings before taxes
$-\widetilde{tax}$	=	taxes = $T(\widetilde{EBT})$
$\widetilde{NI}$	=	net income
$-\widetilde{Div}$	=	dividends paid out to shareholders
$\widetilde{Rtd.E.}$	=	retained earnings (added to retained earnings on the sample balance sheet)

example, a hydroelectric dam could be built by using 100,000 men with picks, shovels, and buckets or by using 100 men with bulldozers, cranes, and cement mixers. Economic theory tells us that the choice of technology will be determined by the relative costs of the major inputs, namely, capital and labor. The income statement reflects the choice of production technology by the ratio of fixed costs (FCC and dep) to variable costs of production. Variable costs are the salaries, wages, materials, and services used in production. Total variable costs in a given year depend on how much output is sold.[1] If there are no sales, then variable costs are zero. On the other hand, fixed costs are constant and must be written off regardless of the firm's sales. Fixed costs have two components, fixed cash costs (FCC), such as property taxes and certain administrative salaries and wages, and noncash fixed costs (dep), whose major component is usually depreciation. We distinguish between cash costs and noncash costs because the market value of the firm is determined by cash flows. Depreciation is not a cash flow. Rather, it is an estimate of the decline in the value of physical capital employed in production (obsolesence or wear and tear).

The choice of production technology affects the riskiness of the earnings from operations, or $\widetilde{EBIT}$, earnings before interest and taxes. If revenue, $\tilde{R}$, is uncertain, then so is EBIT. The amount of fixed costs determines the extent to which $\widetilde{EBIT}$ is more variable than revenues.[2] This concept is called *operating leverage*, and it is discussed in detail in Chapter 9. To illustrate the idea, consider a simple example. Suppose a firm has no fixed operating costs at all. If it has no sales or production, its revenue is zero, its variable costs are zero,

---

[1]Accrual accounting requires that manufacturing expenses (the cost of goods sold) be entered onto the income statement when an item is sold. Before then, the item is carried (at cost) in inventory. Hence, the variable cost of manufacturing does not appear on the income statement when the item is produced. It appears as an expense only when the item is recorded as sold.

[2]Hereafter, EBIT will be understood to be a random variable; hence, we will omit the tilde ($\sim$).

and hence its EBIT also is zero. But if the same firm has $1 million of fixed costs and no sales or production, then it loses $1 million. Intuitively, it is clear that the greater the ratio of fixed costs to total costs, the greater is the firm's operating leverage and the higher is the riskiness of its EBIT stream.

The combination of revenue risk and operating leverage, that is, the variability of the EBIT stream, is called the firm's *business risk*. Managers can modify a firm's business risk through their choice of product lines (revenue risk) and production technology (operating leverage). Next, we move down the income statement and consider *financial risk*.

To keep things simple, assume that all debt financing is in the form of contracts with fixed interest payments.[3] These interest payments are represented in Table 2.1 by rD, where r is the fixed coupon rate on a bond (say 10 percent per year) and D is the face value of the bond issue (say $1 million); hence, rD is the annual fixed interest charge ($100,000). Fixed interest payments have the effect of increasing the riskiness of the net income stream to shareholders. As the use of debt financing increases, the firm has greater *financial leverage*.[4] The explanation of why financial leverage affects the riskiness of net income is similar to that used for operating leverage. With no interest expenses, a firm with zero EBIT would also have zero net income, but with zero EBIT and positive interest charges, net income would be negative (a loss). Hence, as interest charges increase, so does the riskiness of the net income stream. Financial leverage is the responsibility of the firm's chief financial officer, and is a major issue in corporation finance. The concept of financial leverage as a measure of risk is presented in Chapter 8, and its effects on risk and return are discussed in Chapter 20. The effect of financial leverage on the value of the firm is the subject of Chapter 21. The interesting issue in Chapter 21 is whether or not the form of financing makes a difference.

After subtracting interest expenses from EBIT, we are left with taxable income. Actual taxes paid, "tax," are the product of the firm's tax rate, T, and the amount of earnings before taxes, EBT. The firm's tax environment is discussed in detail in Chapter 4.

Net income, NI, is the residual stream of earnings owned by shareholders. We have seen that its riskiness is affected by both the business risk and the financial risk chosen by the managers of the firm. The board of directors must decide, on behalf of shareholders, what portion of net income should be paid out to shareholders in the form of dividends, Div, and what part to reinvest in the firm. The portion reinvested is called retained earnings, Rtd.E., and it represents a form of corporate savings (as opposed to consumption). Historically, about 60 percent of all savings in the United States has come from corporate retained earnings. The dividend decision is discussed in Chapter 22, where the central issue is whether the market value of shares is affected by the firm's dividend policy. Note that financial leverage and dividend policy are closely related. If the firm decides to pay out a relatively large fraction of its earnings in the form of dividends, then it has less retained earnings to reinvest, raising the probability that it will have to borrow funds for investment. Hence, the decision not to pay dividends is related to a choice of lower financial leverage.

Table 2.2 summarizes the topics of interest which have been discussed in connection with the sample income statement. Next, we turn our attention to the sample balance sheet.

---

[3]The alternative is variable interest debt, which might stipulate that interest payments change with general inflation in the economy (indexed bonds) or with the operating income (EBIT) of the company (income bonds).

[4]Outside of the United States, financial leverage is usually called "gearing."

Table 2.2   Finance Topics and the Sample Income Statement

Income for the Year 19XX

$\tilde{R}$	revenue risk
$-\widetilde{VC}$	
$-FCC$	operating leverage
$-\widetilde{dep}$	
$\widetilde{EBIT}$	business risk
$-rD$	financial leverage
$\widetilde{EBT}$	
$-\widetilde{tax}$	tax strategy
$\widetilde{NI}$	shareholder's risk and return
$-Div$	dividend policy
$\widetilde{Rtd.E.}$	

Sample Balance Sheet

It should be emphasized that in order to have complete information about a firm during a given year, we need an income statement and *two* balance sheets, one at the beginning and another at the end of the year. Each provides a snapshot of the firm's assets and liabilities, and the change between snapshots is a moving picture.

Table 2.3 is a sample balance sheet. We can use it to introduce some additional topics and terminology.

Table 2.3   Sample Balance Sheet

Assets and Liabilities as of Fiscal Year End 19XX

Assets	Liabilities
Short-term	Short-term
Cash	Accounts payable
Marketable securities	Short-term debt (notes payable)
Accounts receivable	Accruals (taxes due, salaries, and wages)
Inventory	Long-term
Long-term	Debt
Gross property, plant, and equipment	Preferred stock
Less accumulated depreciation	Equity
Net property, plant	Common at par
and equipment	Common in excess of par
	Retained earnings
	Less Treasury stock
Total assets	Total liabilities

First, let's take an overall point of view. By construction, the book value of total assets must equal the book value of total liabilities. Two major components, equity and various forms of debt (including accounts payable, notes payable, accruals, and long-term debt), make up total liabilities. Equity is considered to be a liability because the firm is a legal entity which "owes" its net worth (its equity) to its owners, the shareholders.

The difference between short-term assets and short-term liabilities is called the *net working capital* of the firm. As long as there are more short-term assets than liabilities, the firm is said to be in a liquid position because it can pay off all of its short-term obligations without having to liquidate any long-term assets. Part Four of this text discusses the major issues of working capital management. For example, what ratio of short-term assets to short-term liabilities is optimal? What constitutes the optimal management of cash balances, marketable securities, and inventories? And what is the best way to manage accounts receivable and accounts payable?

For most manufacturing firms, the most profitable and least liquid assets are the tangible assets composed of property, plant, and equipment. Although almost any corporate decision may be thought of as maximizing the net present value of shareholders' wealth, the project selection decision is the usual focus of value maximization. This all-important topic is discussed in detail in Chapter 6, where it is called the *capital budgeting decision*. It is also the focus of Chapter 16, where the firm is viewed as a portfolio of risky assets.

Note that the long-term assets account (in Table 2.3) is divided into three components. Gross property, plant, and equipment represent the original purchase price of long-term assets. Each year, an estimate of the depreciation of each asset is made and then added to all prior depreciation. The result, accumulated depreciation, is then deducted from gross property, plant, and equipment to arrive at net property, plant, and equipment. Annual depreciation appears as an expense on the income statement (see Table 2.1). Net property, plant, and equipment represents the current depreciated book value of tangible assets. If an asset is sold, its original book value is removed from gross property, plant, and equipment, and its accumulated depreciation is subtracted from that account. Finally, if its market value is above (below) its net book value, then a capital gain (loss) is recorded on the income statement.

Turning to the liabilities side of the balance sheet, we can focus briefly on short-term liabilities. Accounts payable are IOUs for unpaid bills. Frequently referred to as trade credit, they represent short-term borrowing from suppliers of goods and services. The management of trade credit is discussed in Chapter 14. Notes payable represent short-term debt, usually borrowed as a line of credit from a commercial bank. Accruals are unpaid obligations — for example, salary and wages or taxes due. As was mentioned earlier, the management of short-term liabilities is discussed in Part Four on working capital management.

The choice among sources of financing is the most important financial decision of the firm. The ratio of debt to equity establishes the firm's *capital structure*, and as mentioned earlier, it determines the amount of financial leverage. The firm's cost of financing is called the *weighted average cost of capital* and is a weighted average of the marginal after-tax costs of its sources of capital — its debt and equity. Capital structure and the cost of capital are discussed in Chapters 20 and 21. From an investor's point of view, debt is less risky than equity because interest payments are a contractual obligation and because, in the event of bankruptcy, debtholders have prior claim to the firm's assets. Equity payments, that is, the dividend stream, are residual claims on the firm's cash flows. Hence, they are riskier than debt. One can conclude, therefore, that debt capital will require a lower nominal rate of return than equity because it is less risky.

The choice of capital structure is important because there may be a mixture of debt and equity which (for a given set of cash flows from operations) minimizes the weighted average cost of capital and, consequently, maximizes the market value of the firm. As we shall see in Chapter 21, the firm's optimal capital structure depends on its tax situation, on potential bankruptcy costs, on its ability to unambiguously signal its future prospects to investors, and on agency costs between managers and suppliers of various sources of capital. The determination of optimal capital structure is a difficult problem which is not yet completely resolved in the academic literature.

Preferred stock is a hybrid security having some of the characteristics of both debt and equity. Payments to owners of preferred stock are called preferred dividends. Being of fixed size, they are contractual just like interest payments on debt. However, if cash flow is insufficient to cover preferred dividends, the firm cannot be forced into bankruptcy or reorganization. Instead, the preferred dividends are deferred. Cumulative preferred dividends must be paid before any dividends can be declared to shareholders. Thus, we see that preferred stock is riskier than debt but less risky than equity.

The equity portion of Table 2.3 is subdivided into four parts. When new shares are sold, the value per share received by the firm is broken down into common at par and common in excess of par. For example, if the firm receives $20 per share for $1 par value, then $19 per share issued is added to common in excess of par and the remainder is added to common at par. Par value is an anachronistic concept. Many firms have stock with no par value. It used to be that if an investor purchased a share for less than its par value, then in the event of bankruptcy, the investor could be made personally liable for the difference between the purchase price and the par value of the share. The details of issuing new equity are discussed in Chapter 25. The third item in the equity section is retained earnings, which represents the chronological sum of the retained earnings taken each year from the income statement. For a firm founded in 1920, for example, the retained earnings figure will be the accumulation of all earnings retained since 1920. Recall that the firm's net income is the sum of dividends, which are paid out to shareholders, and retained earnings, which is added to the balance sheet:

$$\text{NI} = \text{Dividends} + \text{Retained earnings.} \qquad \textbf{(2.1)}$$

Hence, retained earnings is the link between the flows of cash on the income statement and the stocks of assets and liabilities on the balance sheet.

The final equity item is Treasury stock. It is subtracted from the other equity items because it represents the cost of repurchasing common stock (either via tender offer or open market purchases). The purchase of Treasury stock has the effect of reducing the number of shares outstanding without changing the firm's expected earnings stream. Consequently, earnings per share (and the price per share of the remaining shares) go up following a repurchase of Treasury stock. Share repurchase is intimately related to dividend policy, as shown by the following example. Suppose your firm has $3,000,000 in earnings and that $1,000,000 will be spent either to repurchase shares or paid out as a cash dividend. If dividends are paid, $2,000,000 in retained earnings will be added to the liabilities side of the balance sheet. Shareholders will receive $1,000,000 before taxes but must pay income taxes on the dividends received. Alternately, if we assume that there is a pro rata (that is, an equal percentage) repurchase of shares from each shareholder, then $3,000,000 is added to retained earnings and $1,000,000 to Treasury stock, which is subtracted from the equity portion of the balance sheet. The net effect on the liabilities is the addition of $2,000,000. Thus, cash dividends and share repurchase have the same effect on the book value of liabilities, but not on shareholders' wealth. Dividends are taxed at the ordinary income tax rate, but share repurchases result in capital gains (because the stock price goes up), which do not have to be taxed until the shares are actually sold, and then at

Table 2.4   Finance Topics and the Sample Balance Sheet

Assets		Liabilities	
	Short-term	Short-term	
Cash management ⟵	Cash	A/P ⟶ Trade credit	Working
Security analysis ⟵	Marketable securities	STD ⟶ Bank credit	capital
Receivables policy ⟵	Accounts receivable	Accruals	policy
Inventory policy ⟵	Inventory		
	Long-term	Long-term	
Capital	Gross PP&E	Long-term debt	Capital structure
budgeting	−Accumulated depreciation	Preferred stock	and the cost
	Net PP&E	Equity	of capital
		Common at par	
		Common in excess of par	
		Retained earnings	Dividend
		Less Treasury stock	policy
	Total assets	Total liabilities	

the capital gains rate, which is lower than the ordinary income tax rate. Hence, it would appear that share repurchase would be preferred to dividends by shareholders who pay a higher tax rate on dividends than on capital gains. This issue is discussed in detail in Chapter 22.

Table 2.4 summarizes the finance topics which are highlighted on the balance sheet.

Sources and Uses of Funds

One of the most important responsibilities of the corporate treasurer is the management of sources and uses of funds. Not only must the treasurer be sure that cash is available to meet short-term needs, such as payrolls and invoice payments, but also he or she must plan for strategic funds management to facilitate long-term growth via capital expansion or acquisition. The tool for this analysis is the *sources and uses of funds statement*. It is computed from an income statement and two balance sheets, one at the beginning of the period and one at the end. Although a sources and uses statement may be estimated for any interval of time (for example, a week, a month, or a quarter), we shall focus on an annual statement. The change in the firm's cash position will be defined as the difference between sources and uses of funds.[5]

$$\Delta\text{Cash} = \text{Sources of funds} - \text{Uses of funds}. \qquad (2.2)$$

Table 2.5 summarizes the sources and uses of funds.

[5]Alternately, one could define increases in cash balances as a use of funds and decreases as a source. If so, then total sources would have to equal total uses. Sources and uses statements in annual reports usually adopt this procedure.

Table 2.5   Sources and Uses of Funds

Sources	Uses
1. From operations = NI + dep	1. Dividends
2. Decreases in short-term assets (excluding cash)	2. Increases in short-term assets (excluding cash)
3. Increases in short-term liabilities	3. Decreases in short-term liabilities
4. Decreases in gross property, plant, and equipment	4. Increases in gross property, plant, and equipment
5. Increases in long-term debt	5. Decreases in long-term debt
6. Sale of preferred or common stock	6. Repurchase of preferred or common stock (Treasury stock)

The explanation for each category of sources and uses is straightforward. First, note that NI + dep (net income plus depreciation) is a way of summarizing the sources (or uses) of funds from operations. The equation below is the definition of net income, taken from the Sample Income Statement (Table 2.1).

$$NI = R - VC - FCC - dep - rD - T(R - VC - FCC - dep - rD). \qquad (2.3)$$

Revenue, R, is the major source of funds. All negative terms are uses of funds except for depreciation, which is a noncash charge. Consequently, we must add depreciation to net income in order to obtain a summary number for sources of funds from operations.

$$NI + dep = \text{Sources of funds from operations.} \qquad (2.4)$$

Of course, depreciation is not literally a source of funds because no cash flow is associated with depreciation expenses.

Depreciation is an annual charge against income that reflects the cost of the equipment used in the production process. For example, suppose a machine with an expected useful life of ten years and no expected salvage value was purchased in 1978 for $100,000. This cost must be charged against production during the machine's ten-year life; otherwise, profits will be overstated. If the machine is depreciated by the straight line method, the annual charge is $10,000. To determine income, this amount is deducted from sales revenues, along with such other costs as labor and raw materials. However, depreciation is not a cash cost. Funds were expended in 1978, so the depreciation charged against income each year is not a cash outlay. In this way, it differs from labor or raw materials payments, which are cash costs.

To illustrate the significance of depreciation in cash flow analysis, consider the Dallas Fertilizer and Chemical Company, which has the following income statement for 19X1:

Sales revenues	$300,000,000
Costs excluding depreciation	$270,000,000
Depreciation	10,000,000
Net income before taxes	$ 20,000,000
Taxes @ 40%	8,000,000
Net income after taxes	$ 12,000,000

Assuming that sales are for cash and that all costs except depreciation are paid by cash during 19X1, how much cash is available from operations to pay dividends, retire debt, or make investments in fixed or current assets (or both)? The answer is $22 million, the sum of after-tax profit plus depreciation. The sales are all for cash, so the firm took in $300 million in cash. Its costs other than depreciation were $270 million, paid in cash, leaving $30 million. *Depreciation is not a cash charge*—the firm does not pay out the $10 million of depreciation expenses—so $30 million of funds remains after depreciation. Taxes, on the other hand, are paid in cash, so $8 million for taxes must be deducted from the $30 million gross operating cash flow, leaving a net cash flow from operations of $22 million. Since $300,000,000 flows in and $278,000,000 flows out, $22,000,000 *must* remain. This $22 million is, of course, exactly equal to net income after taxes plus depreciation: $12 million plus $10 million equals $22 million. Depreciation is a noncash charge which is added to net income to arrive at funds generated by operations.

In the uses column, opposite sources from operations (NI + dep), are dividends, which are definitely a cash outflow and are usually a major use of funds. From Equation 2.1, we recall that net income minus dividends is equal to retained earnings. Hence, the first row in the table of sources and uses of funds (Table 2.5) summarizes all information on cash flows from the income statement. All other rows are changes in balance sheet accounts.

Decreases (increases) in short-term assets, excepting cash, are sources (uses) of funds. For example, a decrease in inventories is a source of funds because some product has been sold. On the other hand, increases (decreases) in short-term liabilities are sources (uses) of funds. If accounts payable increase, the firm has, in effect, borrowed from suppliers of trade credit. This is an increase of funds available, a source. We focus on gross property, plant, and equipment because it is easier to use. An increase in gross PP&E means a use of funds and vice versa for a decrease. Unfortunately, sometimes a firm may report only its net property, plant, and equipment and accumulated depreciation. If so, we can show that the change in gross property, plant, and equipment (ΔGPP&E) is equal to the net property, plant, and equipment on the end-of-year balance sheet, NPP&E(end), plus depreciation during the period, dep, minus net property, plant, and equipment at the beginning of the period, NPP&E(begin).

$$\Delta\text{GPP\&E} = \text{NPP\&E(end)} + \text{dep} - \text{NPP\&E(begin)}. \qquad (2.5)$$

To see that this is true, construct beginning and ending PP&E accounts for a simple example as shown below.

	Beginning	Ending
Gross PP&E	1000	1100
Less accumulated depreciation	500	550
Net PP&E	500	550

The change in gross PP&E is 100. Depreciation during the period is 50, that is, the change in accumulated depreciation. Finally, the change in net PP&E is 50. Hence, we have

$$\Delta\text{GPP\&E} = 100 = \text{NPP\&E(end)} + \text{dep} - \text{NPP\&E(begin)}$$
$$= 550 + 50 - 500 = 100.$$

Thus, either of two calculations can be used to compute the effect of changes in long-term assets on sources and uses of funds.

The remaining items in Table 2.5 are straightforward. An increase (decrease) in long-term debt is a source (use) of funds because it represents borrowing (repayment of a loan). Sale (repurchase) of equity is also a source (use) of funds.

Table 2.6 gives Dallas Fertilizer's comparative balance sheets for 19X0 and 19X1, along with net changes in each item (except for cash), classified as a source or a use.

The next step in constructing a sources and uses statement involves (1) making adjustments to reflect net income and dividends and (2) isolating changes in working capital (current assets and current liabilities). These changes are reflected in the statement shown in Table 2.7. Net income in 19X1 amounted to $12 million, a source, and dividends of $2 million, a use, were paid. The $10 million in retained earnings shown in Table 2.6 is deleted from Table 2.7 to avoid double counting. This statement of sources and uses of funds tells the financial manager that plant size was expanded, that fixed assets amounting to $25 million were acquired, that inventories and net receivables increased as sales increased, and that the firm needed funds to meet working capital and fixed assets demands.

Previously, Dallas had been financing its growth through bank credit (notes payable). In the present period of growth, management decided to obtain some financing from permanent sources, namely, long-term debt, to finance some of the asset growth and also pay back some of its bank credit, thereby reducing notes payable. It also obtained funds from earnings and from depreciation charges. Moreover, the firm had been accumulating mar-

Table 2.6	Dallas Fertilizer and Chemical Company Comparative Balance Sheets and Sources and Uses of Funds (Millions of Dollars)				
		Dec. 31, 19X0	**Dec. 31, 19X1**	**Source**	**Use**
Assets					
Cash		$ 10	$ 5		
Marketable securities		25	15	$10	
Net receivables		15	20		$ 5
Inventories		25	35		10
Gross fixed assets		$150	$175		25
(Less accumulated depreciation)[a]		−40	−50		
Net fixed assets		110	125		
Total assets		$185	$200		
Liabilities					
Accounts payable		$ 10	$ 6		$4
Notes payable		15	10		5
Other current liabilities		10	14	4	
Long-term debt		60	70	10	
Preferred stock		10	10	—	—
Common stock		50	50	—	—
Retained earnings		30	40	10	
Total claims on assets		$185	$200		

[a] The accumulated depreciation is actually a liability account (a contra-asset) that appears on the left side of the balance sheet. Note that it is deducted, not added, when totaling the column.

Table 2.7   Dallas Fertilizer and Chemical Company
Statement of Changes in Financial Position, 19X1
(Millions of Dollars)

	Amount		Percent	
Sources of funds (excluding cash)				
Net income		$12	26.1	
Depreciation		10	21.7	
Decreases in working capital				47.8
Sale of marketable securities	$10		21.7	
Increase in other liabilities	4		8.7	
Total decrease in working capital		14		30.4
Increase in long-term debt		10		21.7
Total sources of funds		$46		100.0
Uses of funds				
Increases in working capital				
Inventory investment	$10		19.6	
Increase in receivables	5		9.8	
Reduction in notes payable	5		9.8	
Reduction in accounts payable	4		7.9	
Total increase in working capital		$24		47.1
Gross fixed assets expansion		25	49.0	
Dividends to stockholders		2	3.9	52.9
Total uses of funds		$51		100.0

Total sources − Total uses = ΔCash = $−5.

ketable securities in anticipation of this expansion program, and some were sold to pay for new buildings and equipment. Finally, note that total uses exceed total sources by $5 million. Therefore, the firm's cash position was worked down. This fact is confirmed by looking at the balance sheets in Table 2.6. The cash account decreases from $10 million to $5 million.

In summary, the example illustrates how the sources and uses of funds statement can provide both a fairly complete picture of recent operations and a good perspective on the flow of funds within the company. Given the projected balance sheet and supplementary projected data on earnings, dividends, and depreciation, the financial manager can construct a pro forma, or projected, sources and uses of funds statement to show how a firm plans to acquire and employ funds during some future period. Such a statement is obviously of much interest to lenders as well as to the firm's own management.

Reporting Requirements

One of the important responsibilities of the chief financial officer is to manage all financial reporting requirements both inside and outside of the firm. Figure 2.1 illustrates the scope of the many types of financial statements which may be necessary.

While carrying out his or her reporting duties, the chief financial officer (CFO) must interact with many different users of financial information. For example, let's look at inter-

Figure 2.1   Financial Reporting Requirements of the Firm

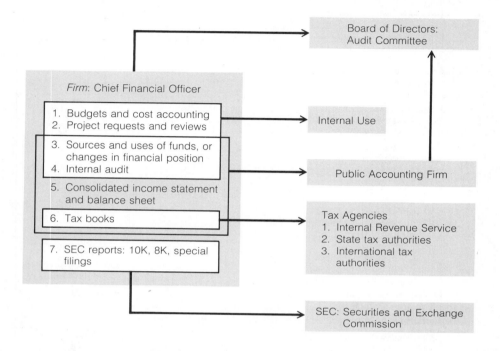

nal users. The firm's managers must be given budgets, which are governed by cost accounting conventions. In turn, managers supply the CFO with requests for new project funding. Also, ongoing projects are constantly reviewed, sources and uses of funds are monitored, and internal audits are performed to check on the accuracy and validity of data being reported to corporate headquarters.

In addition to these numerous internal reporting requirements, the CFO must supply financial data to shareholders, the board of directors, public accounting firms, the Securities and Exchange Commission (SEC), and various tax agencies, such as the Internal Revenue Service (IRS), state and local tax authorities, and even to international tax authorities. These external users of accounting information each have separate data requirements, and even worse, their demands are not necessarily consistent. For example, the accounting treatment of the annual report can cause earnings per share to increase while cash flows may decrease because taxes have increased on the IRS forms.

First, let's turn our attention to the reporting requirements of shareholders on the annual report. Why require an annual report at all? And why have the annual report audited (at some expense) by an independent public accounting firm? One reasonable answer to these questions is suggested by Watts and Zimmerman [1978]. As a corporation grows in size, it often needs to raise external equity capital. Consequently, there arises a separation between ownership and control. Specialized managers actually operate the firm while external equity capital is supplied by numerous shareholders whose ownership is quite diffuse. In the absence of some kind of monitoring agreement, shareholders would supply new capital only at a high cost because managers could either shirk their duties or consume excess perquisites at shareholder expense. It is in the best interest of both managers and shareholders to agree in advance on some form of independent monitoring if the cost of the monitoring arrangement is less than the costs in the absence of monitoring.

The usual procedure is for shareholders to elect a board of directors, who, in turn, select (1) an audit committee to oversee the external audit of the firm's accounts and to direct the preparation of an annual report to shareholders and (2) a public accounting firm to perform the audit and to approve (or disapprove) the annual report. The audit committee often contains a majority of outside or nonmanagement directors as well as the CFO.

Congress has accepted the ultimate responsibility for the determination of accounting principles. However, in the Securities Act of 1933, the authority was delegated to the Securities and Exchange Commission (SEC). Choosing not to become directly involved in the regulation of accounting principles, the SEC has elected to oversee self-regulation by the accounting profession. Public accounting firms are guided by a set of generally accepted accounting principles, which are governed by opinions, issued between 1959 and 1973, of the Accounting Principles Board (APB) and by the Financial Accounting Standards Board (FASB), which has been the principal agency outside of the federal government since 1973.

The SEC requires that nearly all publicly held corporations submit a standardized annual report called the 10K, which usually contains more information than the annual report. Firms are required to send the 10K to all shareholders who request it. In addition, there is a quarterly filing called the 10Q. The SEC further requires that whenever a corporation wishes to issue securities to the public, it must file a registration statement which discloses current financial data as well as such items as the purpose for issuing the securities.

Last in order of our discussion, but never least important, are the ubiquitous tax statements which must be filed with the Internal Revenue Service of the federal government, with state tax collection agencies, and with foreign governments. It is not unusual to discover that accounting rules for tax reporting are different from those in the generally accepted accounting principles used in preparation of the annual report. For example, most corporations use some form of accelerated depreciation in order to maximize the present value of the depreciation tax shield on their tax statements. Simultaneously, they use straight line depreciation on the annual report to their shareholders.

Summary

This chapter has provided an overview of the financial statements of the firm: the income statement, the balance sheet, and the sources and uses of funds statement. At the same time, we have introduced some of the important issues and definitions which will be discussed later on in the book. We also discussed the complex financial reporting environment in which a U.S. firm operates. The chief financial officer must be familiar with the regulations of the Securities and Exchange Commission, the Financial Accounting Standards Board, the Internal Revenue Service, state tax codes, and international tax codes.

Questions

2.1 What are the three financial statements necessary to have a complete picture of the firm during an interval of time, say one year?

2.2 What happens to the operating leverage of a firm if it decides to undertake a project which increases fixed costs but decreases variable costs in such a way that total costs do not change?

2.3 How does one summarize the sources of funds from operations?

2.4 If a firm buys Treasury stock, what happens to the number of shares outstanding?

2.5 Is an increase in accounts payable a source or a use of funds? Why?

2.6 Who are the primary external users of the firm's financial statements?

2.7 Why is it in the best interest of managers to have the financial statements of the firm audited by an independent public accounting firm?

Problems

2.1 Given below are the Tiptop Corporation's income statement and balance sheets ending in the year 19X4. Compute the sources and uses of funds.

Income Statement for the Year 19X4

Revenue	$300,000
Cost of goods sold	−270,000
Selling and administrative expenses	−10,000
Earnings before interest and taxes	20,000
Interest expense	−10,000
Earnings before taxes	10,000
Taxes @ 40%	−4,000
Net income	6,000

Balance Sheets

	Dec. 31, 19X3		Dec. 31, 19X4	
Assets				
Cash		$ 10,000		$ 5,000
Accounts receivable		15,000		20,000
Marketable securities		25,000		15,000
Inventories		25,000		35,000
Gross PP&E	150,000		175,000	
Less accumulated depreciation	−40,000		−50,000	
Net PP&E		110,000		125,000
Total assets		185,000		200,000
Liabilities				
Accounts payable		$ 10,000		$ 6,000
Notes due		25,000		24,000
Long-term debt		60,000		70,000
Equity				
Common		50,000		70,000
Retained earnings		50,000		45,000
Less Treasury stock		−10,000		−15,000
Total liabilities		185,000		200,000

2.2 Given the following information, calculate the sources and uses of funds for the XYZ Company:

Income Statement for the Year 19X4

Revenue	$1000
Cost of goods sold	−600
Selling and administrative expenses	−500
Net operating income	−100
Interest charges	−50
Earnings before taxes	−150
Taxes @ 40%	+60
Net income	−90

Balance Sheets	Dec. 31, 19X3		Dec. 31, 19X4	
Assets				
Cash		60		40
Accounts receivable		40		50
Marketable securities		100		0
Inventories		50		100
Gross PP&E	385		405	
Less accumulated depreciation	−85		−95	
Net PP&E		300		310
Total assets		550		500
Liabilities				
Accounts payable		40		60
Notes due		60		100
Long-term debt		100		90
Equity				
Common		200		200
Retained earnings		150		50
Total liabilities		550		500

Selected References

Davidson, S.; Stickney, C. P.; and Weil, R. L., *Financial Accounting,* Hinsdale, Illinois: Dryden Press, 1985.

Watts, R., and Zimmerman, J., "Towards a Positive Theory of the Determination of Accounting Standards," *Accounting Review,* (January 1978), pp. 112-134.

Chapter 3 The Financial Environment

An important part of the environment within which financial managers function is the financial sector of the economy, which consists of financial markets, financial institutions, and financial instruments. This chapter will discuss each of these three aspects of the financial environment.

Financial Markets

The financial manager functions in a complex financial network because the savings and investment functions in a modern economy are performed by different economic agents. Savings surplus units (a "unit" could be a business firm or an individual), whose savings exceed their investment in real assets, own financial assets. On the other hand, savings deficit units, whose current savings are less than their investment in real assets, incur financial liabilities. A wide variety of financial claims, including promissory notes, bonds, and common stocks, are issued by savings deficit units.

The transfer of funds from a savings surplus unit or the acquisition of funds by a savings deficit unit creates a financial asset and a financial liability. For example, funds deposited in a savings account in a bank or a savings and loan association represent a financial asset on the account holder's personal balance sheet but a liability account to the financial institution. Conversely, a loan from a financial institution, for, say, the purchase of a home, represents a financial asset on its balance sheet but a financial liability to the borrower.

A *financial transaction* results in the simultaneous creation of a financial asset and a financial liability. The creation and transfer of such assets and liabilities constitute *financial markets*. The nature of financial markets can be explained by an analogy to the market for actual goods. The automobile market, for example, is defined by all transactions in automobiles, whether they occur at auto dealers' showrooms, at wholesale auctions of used cars, or at individuals' homes, because they make up the total demand and supply for autos.

Similarly, financial markets are comprised of all trades that result in the creation of financial assets and financial liabilities. Trades are made through organized institutions, such as the New York Stock Exchange or the regional stock exchanges, or through the thousands of brokers and dealers who buy and sell securities off the exchange, comprising the *over-the-counter market*. Individual transactions with department stores, savings banks, or other financial institutions also create financial assets and financial liabilities. Thus, financial markets are not specific physical structures remote to the average individual. Rather, everyone participates in the trading process to some degree.

Different segments of the financial markets are characterized by somewhat different demand and supply influences. When the financial claims and obligations bought and sold have maturities of less than one year, the transactions constitute *money markets*. If the maturities are more than one year, the markets are referred to as *capital markets*. Although real capital in an economy is represented by things — for example, plants, machinery, and equipment — long-term financial instruments are regarded as ultimately representing claims on the real resources in an economy; for that reason, the markets in which these instruments are traded are referred to as capital markets.

Financing Sources and Financial Intermediation

Financial intermediation brings together, through transactions in the financial markets, the savings surplus units and the savings deficit units so that savings can be redistributed into their most productive uses. The specialized business firms whose activities include the creation of financial assets and liabilities are called *financial intermediaries*. Without these intermediaries and the processes of financial intermediation, the allocation of savings into real investment would be limited by whatever the distribution of savings happened to be. With financial intermediation, savings are transferred to economic units that have opportunities for profitable investment. In the process, real resources are allocated more effectively, and real output for the economy as a whole is increased.

The major types of financial intermediaries are briefly described. Commercial banks are defined by their ability to accept demand deposits subject to transfer by depositors' checks. Such checks represent a widely accepted medium of exchange, accounting for over 90 percent of the transactions that take place. Savings and loan associations receive funds from passbook savings and invest them primarily in real estate mortgages that represent long-term borrowing, mostly by individuals.[1] Finance companies are business firms whose main activity is making loans to other business firms and to individuals. Life insurance companies sell protection against the loss of income from premature death or disability, and the insurance policies they sell typically have a savings element in them. Pension funds collect contributions from employees and/or employers to make periodic payments upon employees' retirement. Investment funds, also called mutual funds, sell shares to investors and use the proceeds to purchase existing equity securities.

Investment bankers are financial firms that buy new issues of securities from business firms at a guaranteed, agreed-upon price and seek immediately to resell the securities to other investors. Related financial firms that function simply as agents linking buyers and sellers are called investment brokers. Investment dealers are those who purchase for their own account from sellers and ultimately resell to other buyers. While investment bankers (discussed in Chapter 24) operate in the new issues market, brokers and dealers engage in transactions of securities that have already been issued. Other sources of funds are other business firms, households, and governments. At any point in time, some of these will be net borrowers and others net lenders.

The Role of the Financial Manager

In Figure 3.1, the financial manager is shown linking the financing of an organization to its financing sources via the financial markets.

In the aggregate, business firms are savings deficit units that obtain funds to make investments to produce more goods and services. As part of the process by which funds

---

[1]New laws have broadened the scope of S&L operations so that they may increasingly become department stores of finance, as are the other financial intermediaries.

Figure 3.1   Financial Markets, the Financial Manager, and the Firm

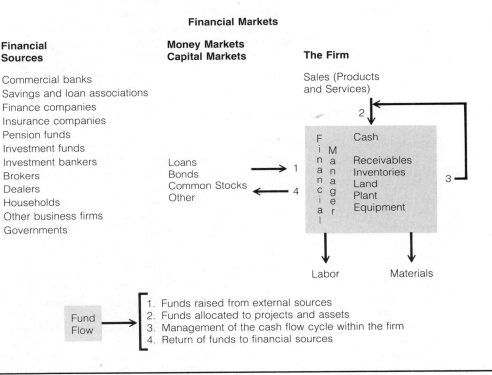

It is the financial manager's responsibility to implement these choices in the various financial markets to meet the firm's capital requirements.

are allocated to their most productive uses, financial managers have two important areas of responsibility:

To obtain external funds through the financial markets.
— What financing forms and sources are available?
— How can the funds be acquired efficiently?
— What is the most economical mix of financing?
— What will be the timing and form of returns and repayments to financing sources?

To see that the funds obtained are used effectively.
— To what projects and products should funds be allocated?
— What assets and resources must be acquired in order to produce the product or service?
— How should the use of funds be monitored so that they are most effectively distributed among the various operating activities?

It is the financial manager's responsibility to implement these choices in the various financial markets to meet the firm's capital requirements.

Types of Financial Instruments

Financial institutions make use of three major types of financial instruments: money, stock, and debt. *Money* is issued by the U.S. Treasury as coins and paper currency. The central bank, the Federal Reserve System, interacts with the commercial banking system in creating the demand deposits (the familiar checking accounts) by which about 90 percent of commercial transactions are conducted. *Stock* generally means common stock, which represents ownership of a firm. *Debt* is a promise to pay to the creditor a specified amount plus interest at a future date.

The Federal Reserve System

Fundamental to an understanding of the behavior of the money and capital markets is an analysis of the role of the Federal Reserve System. The Fed, as it is called, has a set of instruments with which to influence the operations of commercial banks, whose loan and investment activities, in turn, have an important influence on the cost and availability of money. The most powerful of the Fed's instruments, and hence the one used most sparingly, is the right to change reserve requirements (the percentage of deposits that must be kept in reserve with the Fed). Most often, the Fed will exercise its option to alter the pattern of open-market operations (the Fed's buying and selling of securities), increasing and decreasing the amount of funds in the public's hands.

Changes may also be made in the interest rate the Fed charges its borrowers, mainly the commercial banks. This interest charge is called its discount rate for the following reason. A commercial bank makes loans to its customers, resulting in the creation of debt instruments, such as promissory notes. The bank may, in turn, sell these promissory notes to the Fed. When a commercial bank sells debt instruments to the Fed, they are discounted from face value. To illustrate, suppose a bank sells a promissory note in the amount of $1,210, which the borrower has promised to pay the bank at the end of one year. If the Fed's discount rate at that time is 10 percent, it will pay the bank $1,210 divided by 1.10, or $1,100, the discounted value of the promissory note.

Changes in the discount rate change the interest rates paid by banks and, consequently, the rates they charge their customers. In addition, changes in the Fed's discount rate may have "announcement effects." These changes represent an implicit announcement by Federal Reserve authorities that a change in economic conditions has occurred and that the new conditions call for a tightening or easing of monetary conditions. The data demonstrate that increases in the Federal Reserve Bank discount rate have been followed by rising interest rate levels and decreases by lowered levels. When the Federal Reserve System purchases or sells securities in the open market, makes changes in the discount rate, or varies reserve requirements, the supply and price of funds are influenced and the interest rates on most securities change as a result.

Fiscal Policy

The fiscal policy of the federal government may also cause fluctuating interest rates. A cash budget deficit represents a stimulating influence by the federal government, and a cash surplus exerts a restraining influence. However, this generalization must be modified to reflect the way a deficit is financed and the way a surplus is used. To have the most stimulating effect, a deficit should be financed by a sale of securities through the banking system, particularly the central bank, thus providing a maximum amount of bank reserves and permitting a multiple expansion in the money supply. To have the most restrictive effect, the surplus should be used to retire bonds held by the banking system, particularly the central bank, thereby reducing bank reserves and causing a multiple contraction in the supply of money.

The impact of Treasury financing programs varies. Ordinarily, when the Treasury needs to draw funds from the money market, it competes with other potential users of funds, possibly resulting in a rise in interest rate levels. However, the desire to hold down interest rates also influences Treasury and Federal Reserve policy. To ensure the success of a large new offering, Federal Reserve authorities may temporarily ease money conditions, which may soften interest rates. If the Treasury encounters resistance in selling securities in the nonbanking sector, it may sell them in large volume to the commercial banking system, a move that expands its reserves and thereby increases the monetary base. This change, in turn, may lower the level of interest rates. The opposite effects may also occur. If the money supply expands faster than new goods and new investments, there may be too much money chasing too few goods, with inflation as the result. Lenders may then require an inflation component in the nominal interest rates charged, resulting in a rise in interest rates. This more sophisticated reaction to monetary policy has been called a "rational expectations" model in that it takes into account the longer term effects of changes in government policy.

Securities Markets

Within the framework of the broad functions of financial intermediation and the monetary and fiscal policies briefly summarized in the preceding sections is another important set of institutions in the operation of the financial system — the securities markets. One basis for classifying securities markets is the distinction between *primary markets*, in which stocks and bonds are initially sold, and *secondary markets*, in which they are subsequently traded. Initial sales of securities are made by investment banking firms, which purchase them from the issuing firm and sell them through an underwriting syndicate or group. Subsequent transactions take place on organized securities exchanges or in less formal markets. The operations of securities markets provide a framework within which the nature of investment banking and the new issues market (discussed in Chapter 24) can be understood. Accordingly, the organized security exchanges, the over-the-counter markets (the third market), and the fourth market will be discussed in this section.

The major exchange is the New York Stock Exchange (NYSE), with about 1,500 common stocks listed. In 1982, the NYSE alone accounted for 85 percent of the dollar volume and over 80 percent of the share volume of annual exchange trading. This represented trading of over $488 billion on a volume of over 16 billion shares.[2] Second largest is the American Stock Exchange (AMEX), with about 900 listed issues accounting for about 3 percent of the dollar volume. The remaining 12 percent of dollar volume exchange trading is divided among 11 registered regional exchanges.

The organized security exchanges are tangible physical entities. Each of the larger ones occupies its own building and has specifically designated members and an elected governing body, its board of governors. Members may buy seats, which represent the right to trade on the exchange. In 1968, seats on the NYSE sold at a record high of $515,000; in 1974, about $85,000. During 1981, they ranged between $220,000 and $285,000; seats on

---

[2]National Association of Securities Dealers, *NASDAQ Fact Book 1982*, Washington, D.C., 1982, p. 8.

the AMEX ranged from $200,000 to $275,000. Most of the larger stock-brokerage firms own seats on the exchanges and designate one or more of their officers as members of the exchange.

Over-the-Counter (OTC) Security Markets

Over-the-counter security markets is the term used for all the buying and selling activity in securities that does not take place on a stock exchange. The OTC market, which includes stocks of all types and for all sizes of U.S. corporations, as well as some foreign issues, handles transactions in (1) almost all bonds of U.S. corporations; (2) almost all bonds of federal, state, and local governments; (3) open-end investment company shares of mutual funds; (4) new issues of securities; (5) most secondary distributions of large blocks of stock, regardless of whether they are listed on an exchange; and (6) stocks of most of the country's banks and insurance companies.[3]

The exchanges operate as auction markets; the trading process is achieved through agents making transactions at one geographically centralized exchange location. On an exchange, firms known as "specialists" are responsible for matching buy and sell orders and for maintaining an orderly market in a particular security. In contrast, the OTC market is a dealer market; that is, business is conducted across the country by broker/dealers known as *market makers*, who stand ready to buy and sell securities in a manner similar to wholesale suppliers of goods or merchandise. The exchanges are used to match buy and sell orders that come in more or less simultaneously. But if a stock is traded less frequently (perhaps because it is a new or a small firm), matching buy and sell orders might require an extended period of time. To avoid this problem, some broker/dealer firms maintain an inventory of stocks. They buy when individual investors want to sell and sell when investors want to buy. At one time, these securities were kept in a safe; when they were bought and sold, they were literally passed over the counter.

The National Association of Securities Dealers, Inc., is the self-regulatory organization of the OTC markets. The brokers and dealers in the OTC markets communicate primarily through a computerized quotation system called NASDAQ, which presently enables current price quotations for over 3,600 actively traded OTC securities to be displayed on terminals in subscribers' offices. Daily newspaper information is available on over 1,900 NASDAQ securities.

The *third market* refers to these transactions from dealer accounts in the OTC market. Unlisted stocks will be handled only in the OTC market, but listed stocks may also be involved in these transactions. They can also include trades of large blocks of listed stocks off the floor of the exchange, with a brokerage house acting as intermediary between two institutional investors.

The *fourth market* refers to direct transfers of blocks of stock among institutional investors without an intermediary broker. A well-known example is the arrangement between

---

[3]Banks earlier had a tradition against listing stocks. The historic reason was fear that a falling market price for their stocks could lead depositors to think a particular bank was in danger, causing a run on the bank. Some basis for such fears may have existed before the creation of the Federal Deposit Insurance Corporation in 1935, but that fear is no longer justified. The other reason for banks not listing had to do with the disclosure of financial information which banks had been reluctant to provide. In the late 1960s, SEC rules were changed to require less disclosure from listed companies; and, increasingly, bank regulatory agencies were requiring additional disclosure. As this disclosure gap narrowed, banks and other financial institutions increasingly sought exchange listing. A notable first was the Chase Manhattan Bank, which was listed on the New York Stock Exchange in 1965. During the period 1971 to 1977, over 50 percent of the new listings per year were financial institutions.

the Ford Foundation and the Rockefeller Foundation to exchange the common stocks of the Ford Motor Company and Standard Oil of New Jersey. Such transactions have led to the development of Instinet, a computerized quotation system with display terminals to provide communications among major institutional investors.

The development of the third and fourth markets reflects the increased importance of institutional investors (for example, insurance companies and bank pension departments) in stock trading. Between 1972 and 1979, the number of block trades (transactions over 10,000 shares) on the NYSE more than tripled to almost 100,000 block trades per year. The NYSE equity holdings of pension funds more than doubled between 1975 to 1980. In the same period, the estimated institutional holdings of NYSE-listed stocks rose from $241.8 billion to $440.2 billion, representing over one-third of the total market value of all NYSE stocks and approximately 70 percent of the dollar volume of public trading.

The National Market System

The securities markets are in a state of flux. After four years of research and investigation, Congress enacted the Securities Acts Amendments of 1975,[4] which departed from the concept of self-regulation that had previously been followed in the relationships between the government and the securities industry, representing the most far-reaching piece of securities legislation since the 1930s. The purpose of the legislation is to encourage nationwide competition in securities trading through the development of a national market system, in which securities markets across the country are linked electronically. The Securities and Exchange Commission, in conjunction with the securities industry, is mandated to work out the operational details of the system. While the national market system is far from being fully implemented, the progress that has been made has impacted the securities industry in a number of ways. Investors have already benefited from generally lower transaction costs due to the prohibition of minimum fixed commission rates. In 1981 alone, security commission income dropped 6 percent. This has led to the "unbundling" of such peripheral services as research reports from the buying and selling functions performed by brokerage firms and the rise of the so-called "discount" brokers, whose sole function is to execute the buy and sell orders of clients who make their own investment decisions. The increasing computerization of investment operations, on the other hand, is bringing about greater economic concentration in the securities industry, with fewer but larger brokerage concerns.

Progress toward a national market system has been somewhat slow. Developments to date include the Intermarket Trading System (ITS), which electronically links the NYSE, the AMEX, and five major regional exchanges. By early 1983, over 1,000 listed issues were eligible for ITS trading. In 1979, the SEC authorized a pilot project for nationwide reporting of both on- and off-floor trading for a small sample of 30 recently listed stocks. This experiment, linking the exchanges with off-board market makers (the National Association of Securities Dealers), is continuing within the Intermarket Trading System. Within the NASDAQ system, the SEC has proposed that OTC securities meeting specified trading volume and other financial criteria should be included in the national market system, subject to the same kind of real-time transaction reporting as is available on exchange-listed securities.

---

[4]The original Securities Acts of 1933 and 1934, which established the Securities and Exchange Commission (SEC) for federal regulation of the financial markets, are discussed in Chapter 24.

Decision to List Stock

In order to list their stock, firms must meet exchange requirements relating to such factors as size of company, number of years in business, earnings record, and number of shares outstanding and their market value. In general, requirements become more stringent if viewed on a spectrum ranging from the regional exchanges toward the NYSE.

The firm itself makes the decision on whether to seek to list its securities on an exchange. Typically, the stock of a new and small company is traded over the counter; there is simply not enough activity to justify the use of an auction market for such stocks. As the company grows and establishes an earnings record, expands its number of shares outstanding, and increases its list of stockholders, it may decide to apply for listing on one of the regional exchanges. For example, a Chicago company may list on the Midwest Stock Exchange and a West Coast company on the Pacific Stock Exchange. As the company grows still more, and its stock becomes distributed throughout the country, it may seek a listing on the American Stock Exchange, the smaller of the two national exchanges. Finally, if it becomes one of the nation's leading firms, it may, if it qualifies, switch to the Big Board, the New York Stock Exchange.

Many people believe that listing is beneficial to both the company and its stockholders. Listed companies receive a certain amount of free advertising and publicity, and the status of being listed enhances their prestige and reputations. The exchanges maintain that listing is advantageous in terms of lowering the required rate of return on a firm's common stock. Investors, of course, respond favorably to increased information, increased liquidity, and increased prestige. By providing investors with these benefits by listing their companies' stocks, financial managers presumably lower their firms' costs of capital.

With increased computerization, electronic communication, and preliminary steps toward a national market system, the information gap between listed and unlisted stocks appears to be narrowing. Between 1981 and 1982, there was a 44 percent decline in the number of firms leaving the NASD system for the AMEX or the NYSE (110 in 1981 versus 62 in 1982). It is not clear whether this is a trend or only the cyclical effects of the economic recession in 1982. Some studies have concluded that listing status does not affect the cost of capital for otherwise comparable companies [Baker and Spitzfaden (1981); Phillips and Zecher (1982)]. Information availability, at least in terms of newspaper coverage, appears to be related more to firm size and trading volume than to listing status. Other empirical studies appear to indicate that there is some value to listing [Cary and Copeland (1984); Dhaliwal (1983)]. However, there has been little research on the causes of this value increase.

Benefits Provided by Security Exchanges

Organized security exchanges are said to provide at least four economic functions.

1. Security exchanges facilitate the investment process by providing a marketplace in which to conduct efficient and relatively inexpensive transactions. Investors are thus assured that they will have a place in which to sell their securities if they decide to do so. The increased liquidity provided by the exchanges makes investors willing to accept a lower rate of return on securities than they would otherwise require. If so, exchanges may lower the cost of capital to businesses.
2. They are capable of handling continuous transactions, testing the values of securities. The purchases and sales of securities record judgments on the values and pros-

pects of companies. Those whose prospects are judged favorably by the investment community have higher values, which facilitate new financing and growth.

3. Security prices are relatively more stable because of the operation of the security exchanges. Organized markets improve liquidity by providing continuous markets that make for more frequent but smaller price changes. In the absence of organized markets, price changes are less frequent but more violent.
4. The securities markets aid in the digestion of new security issues and facilitate their successful flotation.

Increasingly, firms that cannot utilize the exchanges can get many of these same benefits by having their securities traded in the over-the-counter market.

Stock Market Reporting

We cannot delve deeply into the matter of financial reporting (which is more properly the field of investment analysis), but we will attempt to explain the most widely used service — the New York Stock Exchange reporting system.

Figure 3.2 is a section of the stock market page taken from *The Wall Street Journal* reporting of NYSE composite transactions, which include trades on five regional exchanges and those reported by the National Association of Securities Dealers and Instinet. Stocks are listed alphabetically, with those whose names consist of capital letters listed first. The items are explained by reference to information on the Gannett Company, a newspaper chain.

The two columns on the left show the highest and lowest prices at which the stock has sold during the previous 365 days; Gannett has traded in the range of \$31 1/8 (\$31.125) to \$72. The figure just to the right of the company's abbreviated name is the dividend rate based on the most recent quarterly payment. In 1983, Gannett was expected to pay \$1.80 per share, representing a dividend yield of 2.6 percent based on the closing price of \$69. Next comes the price-earnings (P-E) ratio of 20, which is the current price divided by the last year's earnings per share.

Figure 3.2 Stock Market Transactions

52 Weeks High	Low	Stock	Div.	Yld %	P-E Ratio	Sales 100s	High	low	Close	Net Chg.
		– G–G–G –								
19¾	9	GAF	.05i	..	17	1486	18¾	17¼	18⅜	– ¼
25¼	12⅜	GAF pf	1.20	4.9	..	26	24¾	24½	24½	– ¼
31½	20½	GATX	2.40	7.8	17	71	31	30⅝	30⅝	– ⅜
40¾	11⅛	GCA		..	33	570	36	34¾	35⅞	– ⅜
59⅜	21	GEICO	.72	1.2	15	118	59⅛	58¼	58¼	– ⅝
18⅛	7½	GEO	.24	2.5	..	137	9⅝	9½	9½	.....
7⅞	3⅞	GF Eqp		..	..	7	7¼	7⅛	7¼	+ ⅛
46⅜	26⅜	GTE	2.92	6.5	9	4691	45½	44⅜	44⅝	– ¾
23⅜	16⅜	GTE pf	2.48	11.	..	17	23¼	23	23¼	+ ⅛
31¾	10⅛	GalHou	.20	1.7	..	120	11¾	11⅜	11½	+ ⅛
72	31⅛	Gannett	1.80	2.6	20	716	69½	68½	69	+ ½

Source: *The Wall Street Journal*, May 12, 1983, p. 50 (reporting transactions of May 11, 1983). Reprinted by permission of *The Wall Street Journal*.

After the P-E ratio comes the volume of trading for the day; 71,600 shares of Gannett stock were traded on May 11, 1983. Following the volume are the high and low prices for the day and the closing price. On May 11, 1983, Gannett traded as high as $69.50 and as low as $68.50, while the last trade was at $69. The last column gives the change from the closing price on the previous day; Gannett was up $1/2, so the previous close must have been $68.50. A set of footnotes giving additional information about specific issues always accompanies the stock market quotes.

Other useful information not directly given in the stock transaction data is easily inferred. For example, the P-E ratio implies that last year's earnings were $3.45 per share, and this, in turn, implies that the dividend payout ratio is approximately 50 percent of earnings.

Margin Trading and Short Selling

Margin trading and short selling are two practices said to contribute to the securities markets' efficiency. *Margin trading* involves the buying of securities on credit. For example, when margin requirements are 60 percent, 100 shares of a stock selling for $100 a share can be bought by putting up, in cash, only $6,000, or 60 percent of the purchase price, and borrowing the remaining $4,000. The stockbroker lends the margin purchaser the funds, retaining custody of the stock as collateral. Margin requirements are determined by the Federal Reserve Board. When the Fed judges that stock market activity and prices are unduly stimulated by easy credit, it raises margin requirements and thus reduces the amount of credit available for the purchase of stocks. On the other hand, if the Fed wants to stimulate the market as part of its overall monetary policy, it reduces margin requirements.

Margin trading is a form of leverage that magnifies the percentage gain (or the loss) from a given swing in security prices. An oversimplified example (disregarding dividends or transaction costs) will suffice to demonstrate the impact of margin trading.

Walter Smith buys 100 shares of Provo Company's stock at $20 per share. He holds the stock for one year and sells when the price is $25 per share. His initial cash outlay is $2,000, and his cash inflow one year later is $2,500. We can thus calculate Smith's return on investment:

$$\text{Return on investment} = \text{Net cash inflow/Initial cash outflow}$$

$$= (\$2,500 - \$2,000)/\$2,000$$

$$= \$500/\$2,000$$

$$= 25\%.$$

Now suppose that instead of investing the entire $2,000, Smith bought the Provo Company stock on the margin when the margin requirement was 60 percent. Smith's initial investment is reduced to $1,200 (that is, 60 percent of $2,000), and he borrows the remaining $800 from his broker (assume that the broker charges 10 percent annual interest on the loan). As before, Smith sells his stock after one year at $25 per share, for a cash inflow of $2,500. To calculate Smith's return on investment in this case, we must reduce his gross cash inflow by the initial $1,200 investment, by the repayment of the $800 loan, and by the $80 interest due on the loan.

$$\text{Net cash inflow} = \$2,500 - \$1,200 - \$800 - \$80 = \$420$$

$$\text{Return on investment} = \$420/\$1,200$$

$$= 35\%.$$

Although the dollar amount of net cash inflow is less, the investment required to initiate the transaction is also less, and the percentage return on investment rises from 25 to 35 percent.

On the other hand, if the price of Provo Company stock fell to $15 by the end of the year, Smith would experience a loss by selling. The cash inflow at year end would be only $1,500, for a $500 loss, and the percentage return on investment for the nonmargin case would be $-\$500/\$2,000 = -25\%$.

For the 60 percent margin example, net cash inflows would be $1,500 - $1,200 - $800 - $80 = -$580, and the percentage return on investment would be $-\$580/\$1,200 = -48\%$. Thus, we have illustrated how both gains and losses are magnified by margin trading. The use of debt makes investment returns riskier, since the range of probable returns is extended in both the positive and negative directions. This applies not only to individual transactions but to investments by business firms as well. Leverage decisions by business firms will be one of the central issues of financing to be discussed in subsequent chapters.

Short selling means selling a security that is not owned by the seller. Suppose you own 100 shares of ZN, which is currently selling for $80 a share. If you become convinced that ZN is overpriced and that it is going to fall to $40 within the next year, you will probably sell your stock. Now suppose you do not own any ZN, but you still think the price will fall from $80 to $40. You can, through a lending arrangement with a broker, *go short* in ZN, or *sell ZN short*.

Instead of borrowing cash from the broker as in margin trading, the investor borrows shares of street-name stock (that is, shares registered in the broker's name although they may in fact belong to another investor, who, for example, purchased them on the margin and thus are being held by the broker as collateral). The borrowed shares are then sold at the current market price. The short seller anticipates that by the time he must return the borrowed shares, the price will have fallen; he will then purchase the shares on the open market to repay the broker. Thus, his upside gain will be the difference between the (higher) price at which he sells the borrowed shares and the (lower) price at which he later buys shares to substitute for those borrowed. Of course, if the investor is wrong, and the stock price rises rather than falls, he will suffer a loss. Brokerage houses recognize this possibility by establishing *maintenance requirements*. For example, they may stipulate a 50 percent margin on the proceeds of the short sale, with additional cash deposits for each 2.5 point rise in the price of the stock sold short. These requirements vary from firm to firm.

Short selling involves such other problems as the need for double coverage of any dividends paid — one for the individual whose stock was borrowed to make the short sale and one for the purchaser of the stock. One dividend will be paid by the company, and the other will have to be paid by the short seller, reducing his gain.

Margin trading and short selling contribute to the making of a continuous market. They broaden ownership of securities by increasing the ability of people to buy them and provide for a more active market, effecting narrower price fluctuations. However, when a strong speculative psychology grips the market, margin trading can be a fuel that feeds the speculative fervor. Short selling, on the other hand, can aggravate pessimism on the downside. The downside effects of short selling are somewhat restricted, however, since the SEC has ruled that a short sale cannot be made at a price lower than that of the last previously recorded sale. If a stock is in a continuous decline, short selling cannot occur; hence, it cannot be used to push the stock down. In the 1920s, before this rule was put into effect, market manipulators could and did use short sales to drive prices down.

Financial Instruments

Within the framework of the financial markets and financial institutions we have described, financial managers have a wide range of financial instruments in which they can invest and forms of financing by which they can raise funds. We have already noted that common stock represents the ownership claims in corporations. In addition, a wide range of debt financing is used. This includes short-term debt, such as notes payable to banks and accounts payable to the suppliers of goods. Long-term debt can be secured by the physical assets of the firm, such as mortgage debt. Unsecured long-term debt instruments are called debentures. Preferred stock is a hybrid form of financing which has elements of debt, in that the dividend payments are usually of a fixed dollar amount, and of equity, in that if the firm does not earn enough to pay the dividends, they can be omitted or postponed without the firm being in legal default of its obligations.

International financial markets extend the range of alternatives available to financial managers. Surplus funds can be invested at advantageous rates in the many different types of international financial instruments. Financing can be obtained in the Eurocurrency market for short-term borrowing or in the Eurobond market for longer-term debt financing.

Summary

The financial sector of the economy, an important part of the financial manager's environment, is comprised of financial markets, financial institutions, and financial instruments.

Financial markets involve the creation and transfer of financial assets and liabilities. The financial manager uses these markets to obtain needed funds for the operation and growth of the business and to employ funds temporarily not needed by the business. Funds are provided by savings surplus units to be used by savings deficit units. This transfer of funds creates a financial asset for the surplus unit and a financial liability for the deficit unit. Transfers can be made directly between a surplus and a deficit unit or can involve a financial intermediary, such as a bank. Intermediaries take on financial liabilities in order to create financial assets, typically profiting from their expertise in packaging these assets and liabilities. The operations of intermediaries, and financial markets in general, bring about a more efficient allocation of real resources.

The money markets involve financial assets and liabilities with maturities of less than one year, and the capital markets involve transfers for longer periods. Since most businesses are savings deficit units, the financial manager is concerned with the choice of financial markets, intermediaries, and instruments best suited to the financing needs of the firm and with the decision of how best to employ excess funds for short periods.

The initial sale of stocks and bonds is known as the primary market. Subsequent trading takes place in the secondary market, the organized exchanges. The over-the-counter market, the third market, is a dealer market, where broker/dealers throughout the country act as market makers. Sometimes large blocks of stock are traded directly among institutional investors, constituting the fourth market.

In addition to the cash purchase or sale of stocks or bonds, margin trading involves borrowing. Margin requirements, set by the Fed, change from time to time. Short selling is the practice of selling securities that are not presently owned, anticipating an opportunity to repurchase them later at a lower price. (That is, the short seller benefits if the price falls.) Short selling and margin trading make markets more active and may contribute to the ability to buy or sell securities with smaller price swings than otherwise would occur.

Two major forms of financing are used by business firms: equity financing through common stock and various forms of debt financing. Numerous alternative types of debt instruments exist; they differ in maturity, in terms, and in the degree of risk that the borrower (the issuer of the debt) will become unable to meet the obligation. Sources of financing have become increasingly international in scope.

Questions

3.1 What activities of financial managers are depicted by Figure 3.1?

3.2 What are financial intermediaries, and what economic functions do they perform?

3.3 How could each tool of the Fed be used to slow down expansion?

3.4 Evaluate each of the arguments in favor of organized securities exchanges relative to OTC markets 100 years ago versus today.

3.5 One day, the New York Stock Exchange composite transactions reported in *The Wall Street Journal* showed XYZ Corporation as follows:

49   27   XYZ   1.20   3.8   8   60   33   30   32   +1

    a) Is XYZ trading near its high or its low for the year?

    b) What was yesterday's closing price?

    c) In terms of the closing price, what is the expected dividend yield on XYZ stock?

    d) Based on the information given in the report, what would you estimate XYZ's annual earnings per share to be?

3.6 Why might an investor want to sell short?

3.7 As the financial manager of a business, what factors would you want to consider in deciding how to invest some temporary surplus funds?

3.8 If your firm needs more long-term capital, can you think of a situation where you might want to use a short-term source of funds?

Problems

3.1 Select a recent issue of the *Federal Reserve Bulletin* and locate the table giving information on margin requirements for margin stocks, convertible bonds, and short sales.

    a) Do *margin requirements* refer to the percentage of borrowing to market value of the collateral or to the percentage of funds provided by the investor?

    b) Are the requirements always the same for the three types of securities?

    c) What has been the trend in margin requirements since March 11, 1968?

    d) What are current margin requirements?

3.2 Using a recent issue of *The Wall Street Journal*, answer the following questions with respect to General Electric Company common stock:

    a) On what exchange is it listed?

    b) What is the annual dollar amount of dividends based on the last quarterly or semiannual distribution?

c) What percentage yield is represented by this dollar amount of dividends based on the closing price of the stock?

d) How does this compare with the rate of interest the same funds could earn in a savings account?

e) What is the indicated price-earnings ratio of the stock based on the closing price and the most recent 12 months' earnings?

f) By what percentage is the closing price below the high price for the previous 52 weeks?

g) By what percentage is the closing price above the low price for the previous 52 weeks?

h) Would you say that the common stock of General Electric has experienced high, low, or moderate volatility during the previous 52 weeks?

3.3 Using a recent issue of *The Wall Street Journal*, answer the following questions about the 8 1/2 percent bonds of the Dow Chemical Company maturing 2006. (You may have to check more than one issue to find a trade for this particular bond.)

a) On what exchange are they listed?

b) What is their current yield?

c) What was their closing price?

d) Was their closing price below or above their par value of 100?

Selected References

Baker, H. Kent, and Spitzfaden, J., "The Impact of Exchange Listing on the Cost of Equity Capital," Washington, D.C.: American University, Kogod College of Business Administration, 1981.

Cary, David, and Copeland, Thomas E., "Listing on the New York Stock Exchange, Prediction and Changes in Value: An Empirical Study," working paper, University of California, Los Angeles, 1984.

Dhaliwal, Dan S., "Exchange-Lister Effects on a Firm's Cost of Equity Capital," *Journal of Business Research*, 11 (1983), pp. 139-151.

Fabozzi, Frank J., "Does Listing on the AMEX Increase the Value of Equity?" *Financial Management*, 10 (Spring 1981), pp. 43-50.

Johnson, Ramon E., "Term Structures of Corporate Bond Yields as a Function of Risk of Default," *Journal of Finance*, 22 (May 1967), pp. 313-345.

Kaufman, George G., *The U.S. Financial System: Money, Markets, and Institutions*, 2d ed., Englewood Cliffs, N. J.: Prentice-Hall, 1983.

Klemkosky, Robert C., and Wright, David J., "The Changing Structure of the Stock Market: The National Market System," *Business Horizons*, 24 (July-August 1981), pp. 10-20.

Malkiel, Burton G., *The Term Structure of Interest Rates*, Princeton, N. J.: Princeton University Press, 1966.

Phillips, Susan M., and Zecher, J. Richard, "Exchange Listing and the Cost of Equity Capital," U.S. Securities and Exchange Commission, Directorate of Economic and Policy Analysis, Capital Market Working Paper No. 8 (1982).

Pyle, David H., "On the Theory of Financial Intermediation," *Journal of Finance*, 26 (June 1971), pp. 737-747.

Torell, John R., III, "U.S. Financial Deregulation: Upheaval and Promise," *Journal of Banking and Finance*, 7 (December 1983), pp. 561-565.

Van Horne, James C., *Financial Market Rates and Flows*, Englewood Cliffs, N. J.: Prentice-Hall, 1978.

Chapter 4 The Tax Environment

The federal government is often called the most important stockholder in the U.S. economy. While this is not literally true, since the government does not own corporate shares in the strict sense of the word, the government is by far the largest recipient of business profits. Income of unincorporated businesses is subject to tax rates ranging up to 50 percent, while corporate income in excess of $100,000 is taxed at a 46 percent rate. Furthermore, dividends received by stockholders are subject to personal income taxes at the stockholders' individual tax rates. State, and sometimes city or county, taxes must be added to these federal taxes.

With such a large percentage of business income going to the government, it is not surprising that taxes play an important role in financial decisions. To lease or to buy, to issue common stock or debt, to make or not to make a particular investment, to merge or not to merge — all these decisions are influenced by tax factors.

Tax laws are constantly changing in response to different political and public policy goals, and thus the specific rules of taxation cannot be treated in a book of this type. Nevertheless, this chapter summarizes certain basic elements of the tax structure relating to financial decisions.

Introduction

Three major revisions in the tax laws have been enacted in recent years. First, there was the Economic Recovery Tax Act of 1981 (ERTA). Next came TEFRA, the Tax Equity and Fiscal Responsibility Act of 1982. Still another major piece of tax legislation, entitled the Deficit Reduction Act of 1984, also referred to as the Tax Reform Act of 1984, was signed into law in mid-year. These laws made an almost unbelievable number of changes in the Internal Revenue Code. Yet, some basic patterns of relations important for financial decisions remained basically unchanged. It is these basic relations that are the emphasis of this brief summary of the key aspects of the tax laws and regulations. It is not intended to substitute for the need to use tax accountants and tax lawyers on real-life matters of complexity.

Corporate Income Tax

The Economic Recovery Tax Act of 1981 (ERTA) adopted the following rates, effective 1983, for the corporate income tax:

Rate Structure

First $25,000	15%
Second $25,000	18%
Third $25,000	30%

$$
\begin{array}{ll}
\text{Fourth } \$25,000 & 40\% \\
\text{Over } \$100,000 & 46\%
\end{array}
$$

For example, if in 1983 a corporation has a taxable net income of $110,000, its tax will be computed as follows:

$$
\begin{array}{ll}
0.15(\$25,000) = & \$\ 3,750 \\
0.18(\$25,000) = & 4,500 \\
0.30(\$25,000) = & 7,500 \\
0.40(\$25,000) = & 10,000 \\
0.46(\$10,000) = & \underline{4,600} \\
\text{Total tax} \quad = & \$30,350
\end{array}
$$

Thus, the corporation's average tax rate will be $30,350 ÷ $110,000 = 27.6 percent. However, on any amount over $100,000, the *marginal* tax rate on incremental income will be 46 percent. Table 4.1 shows that the *average* corporate income tax is moderately progressive up to $11 million, after which it becomes virtually a flat 46 percent.

This relatively simple tax structure has wide implications for business planning. Because the tax rate increases sharply when corporate income rises above $100,000, it clearly seems advantageous to break moderate-sized companies into two or more separate corporations in order to make the lower corporate income tax rates applicable. This was, in fact, done for many years by a number of firms, with some groups (such as retail chains and small loan companies) having literally thousands of separate corporations. However, from a tax standpoint, the Tax Reform Act of 1969 substantially eliminated the advantages of multiple corporations.

Depreciation

Depreciation expenses are deductible in computing federal income taxes; the larger the depreciation charge, the lower the actual tax liability. The tax laws specify the methods for calculating depreciation for purposes of computing federal income taxes. When tax laws

Table 4.1   Marginal and Average Corporate Tax Rates, 1983

Taxable Corporate Income (in Dollars) (1)	Marginal Tax Rate (Percent) (2)	Incremental Taxes Paid (3)	Total Taxes Paid (4)	Average Tax Rate (Percent) (5)
0 - 25,000	15	3,750	3,750	15.00
25,001 - 50,000	18	4,500	8,250	16.50
50,001 - 75,000	30	7,500	15,750	21.00
75,001 - 100,000	40	10,000	25,750	25.75
100,001 - 200,000	46	46,000	71,750	35.88
200,001 - 1,000,000	46	368,000	439,750	43.98
1,000,001 - 11,000,000	46	4,600,000	5,039,750	45.82
11,000,001 - 111,000,000	46	46,000,000	51,039,750	45.98

Columns (4) and (5) are based on upper limit of income range.

are changed to permit more rapid, or accelerated, depreciation, this reduces tax payments and stimulates business investments.[1]

A number of different depreciation methods are authorized for tax purposes: (1) straight line, (2) units of production, (3) sum-of-years'-digits, and (4) declining balance. These methods are explained in Appendix A to this chapter. The last two methods listed are generally referred to as accelerated depreciation methods; from a tax standpoint, they are ordinarily more favorable than straight line depreciation.

The fiscal policy implications of depreciation methods stem from two factors: (1) accelerated depreciation reduces taxes in the early years of an asset's life, thus increasing corporate cash flows and making more funds available for investment; and (2) faster cash flows increase the profitability, or rate of return, on an investment. The second point is discussed in the context of capital budgeting in Chapter 6.

Depreciation methods, like tax rates, are regulated by Congress and are occasionally altered to influence the level of investment and thereby to stimulate or retard the economy. Sweeping changes, which were made in 1981 and 1984, allow companies to rapidly recoup capital expenditures on assets purchased after 1980 under a system called the Accelerated Cost Recovery System (ACRS). Under this system, it is no longer necessary to select a depreciation method or to determine an asset's useful life or salvage value. ACRS provides statutory recovery periods of 3, 5, 10, 15, or 18 years for various classes of assets, and the allowable depreciation reflects approximately the 150 percent declining balance method. (See Appendix A.) This method results in higher depreciation deductions in early years and lower deductions in the later years of an asset's life. (The 1982 tax act, the Tax Equity and Fiscal Responsibility Act, or TEFRA, repealed the 1981 act's provisions for even further liberalization.) The specific rules are quite technical and beyond the scope of this book.

Investment Tax Credit

The concept of an investment tax credit was first incorporated into the federal income tax laws in 1962. Under the investment tax credit program, business firms can deduct, as a credit against their income tax, a specified percentage of the dollar amount of new investment in each of certain categories of assets. The 1981 tax law specified a 6 percent investment tax credit for qualifying property with a life of three years or less and a 10 percent credit for all qualifying property with a life of more than three years. Thus, if a firm that otherwise will have a $100,000 tax bill purchases an asset costing $200,000 and having a 20-year life, it will receive a tax credit of $20,000 (10 percent of $200,000), and its adjusted tax bill will be $80,000.

Additional credit may be allowed for qualified energy investments and rehabilitation of historic structures. There are rules that impose a recapture tax on investment credit property not held for a specified minimum period of time.

The investment tax credit, like tax rates and depreciation methods, is subject to congressional changes reflecting public policy considerations. During the economic boom in the early part of 1966, the investment credit was suspended in an effort to reduce investment; it was reinstated later that year, removed again in 1969, and reinstated again in 1971. The

---

[1]Federal tax statutes also consider the time over which assets must be depreciated. A reduction in that period has the same stimulating effect on the economy as does a change in permitted depreciation methods that speeds up depreciation expenses for tax purposes.

1982 tax act modified the 1981 legislation by requiring firms to reduce the tax basis of the property by one-half of the investment tax credit taken for purposes of calculating depreciation and determining gain or loss on disposal.

Corporate Capital Gains and Losses

Corporate taxable income consists of two kinds: profits from the sale of capital assets and all other income (defined as *ordinary income*). *Capital assets* (for example, buildings or security investments) are defined as assets not bought and sold in the ordinary course of a firm's business. Gains and losses on the sale of capital assets are defined as capital gains and losses, and under certain circumstances, they receive special tax treatment.[2] Real and depreciable property used in the business is not defined as a capital asset, although the Internal Revenue Code specifies that such property is treated as a capital asset in the event of a net gain. (However, the recapture of depreciation provisions may eliminate much of this benefit.) If there is a net loss, the full amount can be deducted from ordinary income without any of the limitations described below for capital loss treatment.[3]

Until 1977, the distinction between short-term and long-term capital gains was based on a 6-month holding period. Assets held 6 months or less gave rise to short-term capital gains or losses on their sale. If held more than 6 months, the gain or loss was considered long-term. The Tax Reform Act of 1976 increased the period over which assets must be held for purposes of determining long-term capital gain or loss from 6 months to 9 months in 1977 and to 12 months thereafter. The Deficit Reduction Act of 1984 provides for 6 months for property acquired after June 22, 1984, and for 12 months for property acquired after 1987.

Short-term capital gains less short-term capital losses equal net short-term gains, which are added to the firm's ordinary income and taxed at regular corporate income tax rates. For net long-term capital gains (long-term gains less long-term losses), the tax is limited to 20 percent plus a minimum tax factor on part of a corporation's gains, making the maximum rate on corporate capital gains slightly higher. Of course, if income is below $50,000, regular tax rates of 15 or 18 percent apply.

Depreciable Assets

If a building is subject to depreciation, its tax basis is defined as the original purchase price less allowable accumulated depreciation. To illustrate, suppose a building cost $100,000, and $40,000 of (allowable) depreciation has been taken on it. Its tax basis is $100,000 − $40,000 = $60,000.

A building cannot be depreciated by an accelerated method to transfer ordinary income to capital gains. Thus, a problem may arise when it is bought, depreciated by an accelerated method, and subsequently sold. If the sale is at a price above book value, the differ-

---

[2]Corporate capital gains and losses (as well as most other tax matters) are subject to many technical provisions. This section and the others dealing with tax matters include only the most general provisions. For special cases, see *Federal Tax Course* (Englewood Cliffs, N.J.: Prentice-Hall, 1985).

[3]The special treatment of depreciable properties should be kept in mind in connection with the material in Chapter 6 on capital budgeting. The difference between the book value of an asset and its salvage or abandonment value (if lower than book value) can be deducted from ordinary income; thus, the full amount of this difference is a deductible expense.

ence between straight line and accelerated depreciation is not allowable for determining the capital gain or loss. To illustrate: In the above example, if straight line depreciation had been $25,000, then $15,000 of the $40,000 depreciation would be recaptured. Thus, the tax cost of figuring a capital gain would be $75,000 ($100,000 − $25,000). If the asset were sold for $85,000, a long-term capital gain of $10,000 ($85,000 − $75,000) would result. The $15,000 difference between allowable depreciation and depreciation claimed would be taxed as ordinary income. This rule is intended to prevent firms from converting regular income to capital gains by accelerated depreciation in order to reduce income tax obligations.

In the case of personal property, such as machinery, the entire gain is recaptured as ordinary income up to the amount of the depreciation taken, regardless of the method employed. In the case of depreciation of buildings, the recapture provisions apply only to the excess of depreciation deducted over straight line depreciation.

Deductibility of Capital Losses

A corporation's net capital loss is not deductible from ordinary income. It can only be offset against capital gains. For example, if in 1983 a corporation had ordinary income of $100,000 and a net capital loss of $25,000 (that is, capital losses for the year exceeded capital gains for the year by $25,000), it still paid a tax of $25,750 on the $100,000 ordinary income. The net capital loss, however, can be carried back three years and forward five years and can be used to offset capital gains during that period.

Dividend Income

Another important rule is that 85 percent of the dividends received by one corporation from another are exempt from taxation.[4] For example, if Corporation H owns stock in Corporation J and receives $100,000 in dividends from that corporation, it pays taxes on only $15,000 of the $100,000. Assuming H is in the 46 percent tax bracket, the tax is $6,900, or 6.9 percent of the dividends received. The reason for this reduced tax is that subjecting inter-corporate dividends to the full corporate tax rate would eventually lead to triple taxation. First, Corporation J would pay its regular taxes. Then, Corporation H would pay a second tax. Finally, H's own stockholders would be subject to taxes on their dividends. The 85 percent dividend deduction thus reduces the multiple taxation of corporate income.

Deductibility of Interest and Dividends

Interest payments made by a corporation are a deductible expense to the firm, but dividends paid on its common stock are not. Thus, if a firm raises (through debt) $100,000 and contracts to pay the suppliers of this money 10 percent, or $10,000 a year, the $10,000 is deductible if the $100,000 is debt. It is not deductible if the $100,000 is raised as stock and

---

[4]If the corporation owns 80 percent or more of the stock of another firm, it can file a consolidated tax return. In this situation, there are no dividends as far as the Internal Revenue Service is concerned, so there is obviously no tax on fund transfers between the two entities.

the $10,000 is paid as dividends.[5] This differential treatment of dividends and interest payments has an important effect on the manner in which firms raise capital, as later chapters will show.

Payment of Tax in Installments

Firms must estimate their taxable income for the current year and, if reporting on a calendar year basis, pay one-fourth of the estimated tax on April 15, June 15, September 15, and December 15 of that year. The estimated taxes paid must be identical to those of the previous year or at least 90 percent of actual tax liability for the current year, or the firm will be subject to penalties. Any differences between estimated and actual taxes are payable by March 15 of the following year. For example, if a firm expected to earn $100,000 in 1983 and to owe a tax of $25,750 on this income, then it had to file an estimated income statement and pay $6,438 on the 15th of April, June, September, and December of 1983. By March 15, 1984, it must have filed a final income statement and paid any shortfall (or received a refund for overages) between estimated and actual taxes.

Net Operating Losses Carryover

For most businesses, net operating losses incurred in taxable years ending after 1975 can now be carried forward for 15 years. The allowable carryback period for net operating losses is 3 years, thereby giving firms an 18-year period in which to absorb losses against future profits or to recoup taxes paid on past profits. The purpose of permitting this loss averaging is to avoid penalizing firms whose incomes fluctuate widely. To illustrate: Suppose the Ritz Hotel made $100,000 before taxes in all years except 1983, when it suffered a $600,000 operating loss. The Ritz could utilize the carryback feature to recompute its taxes for 1980, using $100,000 of the operating losses to reduce the 1980 profit to zero and recovering the amount of taxes paid in that year. Since $500,000 of unrecovered losses would still be available, it could do the same thing for 1981 and 1982. Then, in 1984, 1985, and 1986, it could apply the carryover loss to reduce its profits to zero in each of these years. Alternately, the Ritz could have chosen to start this procedure in 1984.

The Tax Reform Act of 1976 limits the use of a company's net operating losses in periods following a change in its ownership. The carryover is disallowed if the following conditions exist: (1) 50 percent or more of the corporation's stock changes hands during a two-year period as a result of purchase or redemption of stock, and (2) the corporation changes its trade or business. (There are other important restrictions on the acquisition of a loss company, but they are too complex to be covered in this brief summary.)

Improper Accumulation

A special surtax on improperly accumulated income is provided for by Section 531 of the Internal Revenue Code, which states that earnings accumulated by a corporation are subject to penalty rates *if the purpose of the accumulation is to enable the stockholders to avoid the personal income tax*. The penalty rate is 27.5 percent on the first $100,000 of improperly

---

[5]Limits have been placed on the deductibility of interest payments on some forms of securities issued in connection with mergers.

accumulated taxable income for the current year and 38.5 percent on all amounts over $100,000. Of income not paid out in dividends, a cumulative total of $250,000 (the balance sheet item of retained earnings) is prima facie retainable for the reasonable needs of the business; this benefits small corporations. Of course, most companies have legitimate reasons for retaining earnings over $250,000, and they are not subject to the penalty.

Earnings retention can be justified if the firm is paying off debt, financing growth, or increasing marketable securities to seek to provide the corporation with a cushion against possible cash drains caused by losses. How much a firm should properly accumulate for uncertain contingencies is a matter of judgment. Fear of the penalty taxes that can be imposed under Section 531 may cause a firm to pay out a higher rate of dividends than it otherwise would.[6]

Sometimes Section 531 stimulates mergers. A clear illustration is provided by the purchase of the Toni Company (home permanents) by the Gillette Safety Razor Company.[7] The sale was made at a time when Toni's sales volume had begun to level off. Since earnings retention might have been difficult to justify, Toni's owners, the Harris brothers, were faced with the alternatives of paying penalty rates for improper accumulation of earnings or of paying out the income as dividends. Toni's income after corporate taxes was $4 million a year; with the Harris brothers' average personal income tax of 75 percent, only $1 million a year would have been left after they had paid personal taxes on dividends. By selling Toni for $13 million, they realized a $12 million capital gain because their book value was $1 million. After paying the 25 percent capital gains tax on the $12 million, or $3 million, the Harrises realized $10 million after taxes ($13 million sale price minus $3 million tax). Thus, Gillette paid the equivalent of three and one-quarter years' after-corporate-tax earnings for Toni, while the Harris brothers received ten years' after-personal-tax net income for it. The tax factor made the transaction advantageous to both parties.

The broad aspects of the federal corporate income tax have now been covered. Because the federal income tax on individuals is equally important for many business decisions, the individual tax structure will now be examined and compared with the corporate tax structure. This will provide a basis for making an intelligent choice as to which form of organization a firm should elect for tax purposes.

Personal Income Tax

Of some 5 million business firms in the United States, about 4 million are organized as sole proprietorships or partnerships. The income of these firms is taxed as personal income to the owners or the partners. The net income of a proprietorship or partnership provides a basis for determining the individual's income tax liability. Thus, as a business tax, the individual income tax can be as important as the corporate income tax.

The personal income tax is conceptually straightforward, although many taxpayers find it confusing. Virtually all the income a person or family receives goes into determining the tax liability. For tax purposes, income is classified as earned (wages or salary) and nonearned (primarily capital gains, rents, interest, and dividends). Under existing tax laws, different kinds of income may be taxed in different ways or at different rates.

[6]See materials in Hall [1952], especially Appendix 3.

[7]See Butters, Lintner, and Cary [1951]. The lucid presentation by these authors has been drawn on for the general background, but the data have been approximated to simplify the illustration. The principle involved is not affected by the modifications of the facts.

Total income from all sources is called gross income. All taxpayers are permitted to make deductions from their gross income before computing any tax. These deductions are of two types: deductions and personal exemptions.

Deductions.   State and local taxes, medical expenses, interest payments, and charitable contributions, along with miscellaneous casualty losses, are tax deductible expenses. The standard deduction can be claimed in lieu of these actual expenses. Since 1979, the standard deduction has been $3,400 for joint returns of married couples and $2,300 for single taxpayers. Taxpayers with actual expenses in excess of the standard deduction reduce the amount of taxable income by itemizing their deductible expenses.

Personal Exemptions.   A $1,000 deduction is allowed for the taxpayer and each of that person's dependents. An additional exemption of $1,000 is permitted for any taxpayer who is over 65 years old or blind. In 1983, a family of four—husband, wife, and two dependent children, none blind or over 65—had personal exemptions totaling $4,000. The apparent intent of the personal exemption is to exempt the first part of income from taxation, thereby enabling the family to obtain the basic necessities of life, such as food and shelter. The same intent appears in the form of the graduated income tax, where the highest tax rates are levied against "discretionary" income.

The following classifications are used in connection with calculating an individual's income tax liability:

Income

Wages, salaries, tips, and so on

Interest income less exclusion

Dividends less exclusion

Business income

Applicable capital gains or losses

Pensions, annuities, rents, royalties, partnerships, and so on

Alimony received

Other categories

Gross income (the sum of the above)

Adjustments to income

Moving expenses

Employee business expenses

Payments to an individual retirement account

Alimony paid

Other categories

Total adjustments (the sum of the above)

Adjusted gross income =

Total income less adjustments to income

Less: Number of personal exemptions times $1,000

Less: Itemized deductions in excess of the applicable standard deduction

Equals taxable income

Table 4.2   Marginal and Average Personal Income Tax Rates, 1984–

Taxable Income		Tax Liability			Total Tax	Average Tax
				Percent of Excess over Column 1	(Based on Upper Limit of Bracket)	
Over	Not Over	(3)	+	(4)	(5)	(6)
(1)	(2)					
$ 3,400	$ 5,500	$ 0		11%	$ 231	4.20%
5,500	7,600	231		12	483	6.36
7,600	11,900	483		14	1,085	9.12
11,900	16,000	1,085		16	1,741	10.88
16,000	20,200	1,741		18	2,497	12.36
20,200	24,600	2,497		22	3,465	14.09
24,600	29,900	3,465		25	4,790	16.02
29,900	35,200	4,790		28	6,274	17.82
35,200	45,800	6,274		33	9,772	21.34
45,800	60,000	9,772		38	15,168	25.28
60,000	85,600	15,168		42	25,920	30.28
85,600	109,400	25,920		45	36,630	33.48
109,400	162,400	36,630		49	62,600	38.55
162,400	and over	62,600		50	a	a

The table shows a joint return for a married couple or surviving spouse.
[a]Not calculable.

Among the itemized deductions that enable adjusted gross income to be reduced is interest paid on borrowings. Thus, for both corporations and individuals, interest expenses paid are deductible for tax purposes.

Tax Rates for the Personal Income Tax. Tax rates for taxable years beginning after 1983 are indicated in Table 4.2. The tax rates presented are for the joint return of a married couple or surviving spouse. The taxable income is adjusted gross income less personal exemptions less the excess of itemized deductions over the applicable standard deduction. The average and marginal tax rates rise slowly; the marginal rate goes up to a maximum of 50 percent on income over $162,400. (Table 4.2 will be used in an upcoming comparison of the tax differences between sole proprietorships and corporations.)

Individual Capital Gains and Losses

As with corporations, the distinction between short-term and long-term gains and losses is the 6- or 12-month holding period. Net short-term gains are taxed at regular rates. The tax on net long-term capital gains is computed by deducting 60 percent of the amount, with the remaining 40 percent subject to tax at the marginal tax rate on ordinary income.

Dividend and Interest Income

The tax law in effect in 1983 provides a $100 dividend exclusion, plus an interest exclusion of up to 15 percent of net interest income by 1985 (to a maximum of $450). The law includes further incentives to saving in the form of a $1,000 interest exclusion on qualifying savings certificates. (All of these exclusions may be doubled on a joint return whether the interest and dividends are received by either one or both spouses.)

To illustrate, if a family's gross income in 1985 consists of $12,000 in salary, $500 in stock dividends, and $1,000 in net ordinary interest income, the gross income is $13,500, but gross taxable income (before deductions) is only $13,000 (that is, $13,500 − (2 × $100) − (2 × .15 × $1,000) = $13,000).

Choices among Alternative Forms of Business Organization

Taxes are an important influence in choosing among alternative forms of business organization. In the following sections, the nature of the various alternatives and their advantages and disadvantages will be described. Then the tax aspects will be considered.

From a technical and legal standpoint, there are three major forms of business organization: the sole proprietorship, the partnership, and the corporation.[8] In terms of numbers, 70 percent of business firms are operated as sole proprietorships, 8 percent are partnerships, and 14 percent are corporations. By dollar value of sales, however, about 80 percent of business is conducted by corporations, about 13 percent by sole proprietorships, and about 7 percent by partnerships. The remainder of this section describes and compares the characteristics of these alternative forms of business organization.

Sole Proprietorship

A sole proprietorship is a business owned by one individual. Going into business as a sole proprietor is very simple; a person merely begins business operations. However, cities or counties may require even the smallest establishments to be licensed or registered. State licenses may also be required.

The proprietorship has key advantages for small operations. It is easily and inexpensively formed, requires no formal charter for operations, and is subject to few government regulations. Further, it pays no corporate income taxes, although all earnings of the firm are subject to personal income taxes, regardless of whether or not the owner withdraws the funds for personal use.

The proprietorship also has important limitations. Most significant is its inability to obtain large sums of capital. Further, the proprietor has unlimited personal liability for business debts; creditors can look to both business assets and personal assets to satisfy their claims. Finally, the proprietorship is limited to the life of the individual who creates it. For all these reasons, the sole proprietorship is limited primarily to small business operations. However, businesses frequently are started as proprietorships and then converted to corporations when their growth causes the disadvantages of the proprietorship form to outweigh its advantages.

---

[8]Other less common forms of organization include business trusts, joint stock companies, and cooperatives.

Partnership

When two or more persons associate to conduct a business enterprise, a partnership is said to exist. Partnerships can operate under different degrees of formality, ranging from an informal oral understanding to a written partnership agreement to a formal agreement filed with the state government. Like the proprietorship, the partnership has the advantages of ease and economy of formation as well as freedom from special government regulations. Partnership profits are taxed as personal income in proportion to the partners' claims, whether or not they are distributed to them.

One of the advantages of the partnership over the proprietorship is that it makes possible a pooling of various types of resources. Some partners contribute particular skills or contacts, while others contribute funds. However, there are practical limits to the number of co-owners who can join in an enterprise without destructive conflict, so most partnership agreements provide that the individual partners cannot sell their share of the business unless all the partners agree to accept the new partner (or partners).

If a new partner comes into the business, the old partnership ceases to exist and a new one is created. The withdrawal or death of any of the partners also dissolves the partnership. To prevent disputes under such circumstances, the articles of the partnership agreement should include terms and conditions under which assets are to be distributed upon dissolution. Of course, dissolution of the partnership does not necessarily mean the end of the business; the remaining partners may simply buy out the one who left the firm. To avoid financial pressures caused by the death of one of the partners, it is a common practice for each partner to carry life insurance naming the remaining partners as beneficiaries. The proceeds of such policies can be used to buy out the investment of the deceased partner.

A number of drawbacks stemming from the characteristics of the partnership limit its use. They include impermanence, difficulty of transferring ownership, and unlimited liability (except for limited partners). Partners risk their personal assets as well as their investments in the business. Further, under partnership law, the partners are jointly and separately liable for business debts. This means that if any partner is unable to meet the claims resulting from the liquidation of the partnership, the remaining partners must take over the unsatisfied claims, drawing on their personal assets if necessary.[9]

Corporation

A corporation is a legal entity created by a governmental unit — mostly states in the United States.[10] It is a separate entity, distinct from its owners and managers. This separateness gives the corporation four major advantages: (1) It has an unlimited life — changes of owners and managers do not affect its continuity; (2) it permits limited liability — stockholders are not personally liable for the debts of the firm;[11] (3) the residual risk

---

[9]However, it is possible to limit the liabilities of some partners by establishing a limited partnership, wherein certain partners are designated general partners and others limited partners. Limited partnerships are quite common in the area of real estate investment.

[10]Certain types of firms (for example, banks) are also chartered by the federal government.

[11]In the case of small corporations, the limited liability feature is often a fiction, since bankers and credit managers frequently require personal guarantees from the stockholders of small, weak businesses.

of the owners is divided into many units so that the risk exposure in any one firm can be small and diversification by investors across many firms is facilitated; and (4) it permits easy transferability of ownership interest in the firm — the divided ownership interests can be transferred far more easily than partnership interests.

While a proprietorship or a partnership can commence operations without much paperwork, the chartering of a corporation involves more legal formalities. First, a certificate of incorporation is drawn up; in most states, it includes the following information: (1) name of proposed corporation, (2) purposes, (3) amount of capital stock, (4) number of directors, (5) names and addresses of directors, and (6) duration (if limited). The certificate is notarized and sent to the secretary of the state in which the business seeks incorporation. If approved, the corporation officially comes into being.

The actual operations of the firm are governed by two documents, the charter and the bylaws. The corporate charter technically consists of a certificate of incorporation and, by reference, the general corporation laws of the state. Thus, the corporation is bound by the general corporation laws of the state as well as by the unique provisions of its certificate of incorporation. The bylaws are a set of rules drawn up by the founders of the corporation to aid in governing the internal management of the company. Included are such points as (1) how directors are to be elected (all elected each year or, say, one-third each year, and whether cumulative voting will be used); (2) whether the preemptive first right of purchase is granted to existing stockholders in the event new securities are sold; and (3) provisions for management committees, such as an executive committee or a finance committee, and their duties. Also included is the procedure for changing the bylaws themselves if necessary.

Tax Aspects of the Forms of Organization

To a small, growing firm, there may be advantages in the corporate form of organization. There is "double taxation" of dividends, but salaries paid to principals in the corporation are a tax-deductible expense and so are not subject to double taxation. The income of a proprietorship or partnership is subject to personal tax rates up to 50 percent. While this rate is only 4 percentage points higher than the maximum corporate tax rate (the maximum personal tax rate had been as high as 90 percent in earlier decades), the tax aspects of organizational form are still important. By splitting organizational earnings between the corporation and the individual, both may be put into a much lower tax bracket. Also of importance is that all the earnings of partnerships and proprietorships are taxable at the personal tax rate whether they are reinvested in the business or withdrawn from it.

A specific example will illustrate the application of several factors influencing the amount of taxes under alternative forms of business organization. Craig Vernon, a married man with two children, is planning to start a new business, CV Manufacturing. He is trying to decide between a corporation or a sole proprietorship as the form of organization. Under either form, he will initially own 100 percent of the firm. Tax considerations are very important to him because he plans to finance the expected growth of the firm by drawing a salary sufficient for living expenses for his family (about $50,000) and plowing the remainder back into the enterprise.

Vernon will have no outside income, since he is liquidating all his investments in order to initially finance CV Manufacturing. He estimates that his itemized deductions will be $5,800 in excess of the standard deduction. He expects the following income before deducting his salary:

1984 $ 70,000
1985 100,000
1986 120,000

To determine whether Vernon should form the new business as a corporation or a proprietorship, we will first calculate the total taxes to be paid if it is organized as a corporation (see Table 4.3). Then we will calculate total taxes on the basis of a proprietorship (see Table 4.4).

By comparing Tables 4.3 and 4.4, we see that the taxes are lower for a corporation in each of the years. The reason is that the corporate form of ownership enables Vernon to split his income so that it is taxed at low marginal rates (most of it at less than 30 percent). But under the single proprietorship, much of the income is subject to higher rates.

We can compare the results and see that the corporate form of organization will yield Vernon the greatest bottom-line profits.

	1984	1985	1986
Taxes paid as proprietorship	$15,252	$27,990	$37,022
Taxes paid as corporation	10,924	16,174	22,174
Advantage as corporation	$ 4,328	$11,816	$14,848

However, the advantage of the corporate form of organization is somewhat illusory. The figures shown for the corporation deal with dollars that have not yet come into the hands of the shareholders. If the earnings are distributed as a dividend, there will be further taxes to be borne by the shareholders individually. If a shareholder sells his or her stock

Table 4.3 Total Taxes for CV as a Corporation

	1984	1985	1986
Income before salary and tax	$70,000	$100,000	$120,000
Less salary	50,000	50,000	50,000
Taxable income, corporate	$20,000	$ 50,000	$ 70,000
Corporate taxes:			
$25,000 at 15%	3,000	3,750	3,750
$25,000 at 18%	0	4,500	4,500
$25,000 at 30%	0	0	6,000
Total corporate tax	3,000	8,250	14,250
Salary	50,000	50,000	50,000
Less exemptions	4,000	4,000	4,000
Total	46,000	46,000	46,000
Less excess deductions	5,800	5,800	5,800
Taxable income, personal	40,200	40,200	40,200
Total personal tax	7,924	7,924	7,924
Combined total tax	10,924	16,174	22,174

Table 4.4   Total Taxes for CV as a Proprietorship

Total income	$70,000	$100,000	$120,000
Less exemptions	4,000	4,000	4,000
Total	66,000	96,000	116,000
Less excess deductions	5,800	5,800	5,800
Taxable income, personal	60,200	90,200	110,200
Tax liability	15,252	27,990	37,022

and gets the benefit of corporate earnings in the form of a capital gain, the person will have to pay a capital gains tax. The extent of the ultimate additional tax is currently unknown, but the shareholder does benefit from having at least temporary use of the tax dollars saved. Of course, for a large enterprise with income of several hundred million dollars, the "tax splitting" effect does not have as great an influence. However, in that case, the corporation's effectiveness in raising large sums of capital from a large number of sources becomes the major consideration in selecting the corporate form of organization.

While broad generalizations are not possible, these are factors that should at least be taken into account in making the decision about the form of organization for any business enterprise.

Special Provisions for Small Businesses

A number of provisions of the Internal Revenue Code favor small business firms. Two in particular are of practical importance.

Subchapter S Corporations

Subchapter S of the Internal Revenue Code provides that some small, incorporated businesses may still elect to be taxed as proprietorships or partnerships if some technical requirements are met, for example, a maximum of 25 shareholders. Thus, the firm may enjoy the protection of the limited liability provided by incorporation but still retain some tax advantages.

These benefits are particularly important to a small new firm, which may incur losses while it seeks to become established in its beginning years. Its operating losses may be used on a pro rata basis by its stockholders as deductions against their ordinary income. This would stimulate persons in high marginal personal income tax brackets to invest in small, new, risky enterprises. Similarly, investment tax credits (deductions against tax liabilities and therefore very valuable) can be taken by the stockholders. New firms making large capital investments may not have income sufficient to fully utilize such tax credits. But the deductions would be very valuable to individuals with high incomes. In circumstances in which an analysis favored the use of a sole proprietorship, the owners can still gain the benefits of limited liability but pay taxes as a sole proprietorship. This would avoid the double taxation involved in the payment of a corporate income tax.

Section 1244 Provisions

Section 1244 of the Revenue Act of 1978 provides that individuals who invest in the stock of certain small domestic corporations, and suffer a loss on that stock, may, for tax purposes, treat such a loss up to $50,000 a year ($100,000 on a joint return) as an ordinary loss rather than as a capital loss. A small business corporation is defined for this purpose if its designated Section 1244 common stock and paid-in surplus does not exceed $1 million. This provision also encourages the formation of, and investment in, small corporations.

Although the foregoing special provisions make it difficult to generalize on whether the corporate or the noncorporate form is more advantageous from a tax standpoint, the essential variables for making an analysis are provided. In general, the advantage now seems to be on the side of the corporation, particularly since a small firm may obtain the many benefits of its corporate status and yet elect to be taxed as a proprietorship or a partnership.

Summary

This chapter provides some basic background on the tax environment within which business firms operate. The corporate tax rate structure is relatively simple. The tax rate is 15 percent on income up to $25,000; 18, 30, and 40 percent respectively on the next three increments of $25,000; and 46 percent on all income over $100,000. Estimated taxes are paid in quarterly installments during the year in which the income is earned; when the returns are filed, the actual tax liability results either in additional payments or in a refund due. Any operating loss incurred by the corporation can be carried back 3 years and forward 15 years against income in those years. The firm can elect not to employ the carryback provision.

Assets that are not bought and sold in the ordinary course of business are subject to capital gains tax on disposition. If an asset is held more than the specified period, any gain on the sale is classified as long-term and taxed at a maximum rate of 20 percent. Gains on assets held for a shorter period are subject to taxation at the company's regular rate. Capital losses can be offset against capital gains to arrive at net long-term gains and net short-term gains. These losses can be carried back against gains for three years and carried forward for five years but cannot be offset against ordinary income.

Of the dividends received by a corporation owning stock in another firm, 85 percent are excluded from the receiving firm's taxable income, but the firm must pay full taxes on the remaining 15 percent. Dividends paid are not treated as a tax-deductible expense. Regardless of the size of its earnings, a corporation does not have to pay dividends if it needs funds for expansion. If, however, the funds are not needed for business purposes — if earnings are retained merely to enable stockholders to avoid paying personal income taxes on dividends received — the firm is subject to an improper accumulations tax. Interest received is taxable as ordinary income; interest paid is a deductible expense.

Unincorporated business income is taxed at the personal tax rates of the owners. Personal income tax rates for both individuals and married persons filing jointly are progressive — the higher the income, the higher the tax rate. The rates start at 11 percent of taxable income and rise to 50 percent.

The holding period for long-term capital gains and losses is the same as for corporations. Short-term gains are taxed as ordinary income, and 40 percent of long-term gains are taxed at the regular tax rate.

The information presented here on the tax system is not designed to make a tax expert of the reader. It merely provides a few essentials for recognizing the tax aspects of business financial problems and for developing an awareness of the kinds of situations that should be dealt with by tax specialists. These basics are, however, referred to frequently throughout the text, because income taxes are often an important factor in business financial decisions.

Sole proprietorships and partnerships are easily formed. All earnings are taxed as regular income at the rate of the owner or partner. Owners and partners are also personally liable for the debts of the business.

The corporation has the advantage of limiting the liability of the participants, but it is generally more expensive to organize. Once organized, a corporation provides an easy means to transfer ownership to others. Corporate earnings paid as dividends are subject to double taxation. The other tax differences between corporations and proprietorships or partnerships depend on the facts of individual cases.

Questions

4.1 Compare the marginal and the average tax rates of corporations for taxable incomes of $5,000, $50,000, $500,000, and $50,000,000. Can you make such a comparison for sole proprietorships or for partnerships?

4.2 Which is the more relevant tax rate — the marginal or the average — in determining the form of organization for a new firm? Discuss aspects of the tax laws that make the form of organization less important.

4.3 For tax purposes, how does the treatment of interest expense compare with the treatment of common stock dividends from each of the following standpoints: a firm paying the interest or dividends, an individual recipient, and a corporate recipient?

4.4 What is the purpose of the Internal Revenue Code provision dealing with improper accumulation of corporate surplus revenue?

4.5 Why is personal income tax information important for a study of business finance?

4.6 How do the tax rates for capital gains and losses affect an individual's investment policies and opportunities for financing a small business?

4.7 What are the advantages and disadvantages of the use of a sole proprietorship versus a partnership for conducting the operations of a small business firm?

4.8 Under what circumstances does it become advantageous for the small business to incorporate?

4.9 In what sense is the corporation a person?

4.10 Would it be practical for General Motors to be organized as a partnership?

Problems

4.1 A corporation had net taxable income of $60,000 in 1984.
   a)   How much income tax must the corporation pay?
   b)   What is the marginal tax rate?
   c)   What is the average tax rate?

4.2 The Dolmite Corporation had net income from operations of $40,000. It also had $20,000 of interest expense and $35,000 of interest revenue during 1984.
   a)   How much income tax must the corporation pay?

    b)   What is the marginal tax rate?

    c)   What is the average tax rate?

4.3   The Triangle Corporation had net income from operations of $130,000 in 1984, including $30,000 in dividend income on stocks of various major publicly held corporations.

    a)   How much tax must the corporation pay?

    b)   What is the average tax rate on net income?

    c)   What is its marginal tax rate?

4.4   Determine the effective marginal and average income tax rates for a corporation earning (a) $10,000, (b) $100,000, (c) $1,000,000, and (d) $100,000,000.

4.5   The taxable income of the Pennock Corporation, formed in 1980, is indicated below. (Losses are shown as minuses.)

Year	Taxable Income
1980	−$ 80,000
1981	60,000
1982	50,000
1983	70,000
1984	−120,000

What is the corporate tax liability for each year? (Use 1984 tax rates.)

4.6   Victor Stone has operated his small machine shop as a sole proprietorship for several years, but recent changes in the corporate tax structure have led him to consider incorporating. Stone is married and has two children. His only income, an annual salary of $40,000, is from operating the business. He reinvests any additional earnings in the business. In addition to the applicable personal exemptions, he has $6,100 of itemized deductions in excess of the standard deductions already incorporated in the tax tables (for example, in Table 4.2). Stone estimates that his proprietorship earnings before salary and taxes for the period of 1984 to 1986 will be:

Year	Income before Salary and Taxes
1984	$50,000
1985	70,000
1986	90,000

    a)   What will his total taxes be under:

        1.   A proprietorship?

        2.   A corporate form of organization?

    b)   Should Stone incorporate? Discuss.

Selected References

Barro, Robert J., and Sahasakul, Chaipat, "Measuring the Average Marginal Tax Rate from the Individual Income Tax," *Journal of Business*, 56 (October 1983), pp. 419-452.

Butters, J. K.; Lintner, J.; and Cary, W. L., *Effects of Taxation on Corporate Mergers*, Boston: Harvard Business School, 1951, pp. 96-111.

Caks, John, "Sense and Nonsense About Depreciation," *Financial Management*, 10 (Autumn 1981), pp. 80-86.

Comiskey, Eugene E., and Hasselback, James R., "Analyzing the Profit-Tax Relationship," *Financial Management*, 2 (Winter 1973), pp. 57-62.

Dyl, Edward A., "Capital Gains Taxation and Year-End Stock Market Behavior," *Journal of Finance*, 32 (March 1977), pp. 165-175.

Federal Tax Course, Englewood Cliffs, N. J.: Prentice-Hall, 1985.

Hall, J. K., *The Taxation of Corporate Surplus Accumulations*, Washington, D. C.: The Government Printing Office, 1952.

McCarty, Daniel E., and McDaniel, William R., "A Note on Expensing Versus Depreciating Under the Accelerated Cost Recovery System: Comment," *Financial Management*, 12 (Summer 1983), pp. 37-39.

Appendix A to Chapter 4
Depreciation Methods

The four principal methods of depreciation — straight line, sum-of-years'-digits, declining balance, and units of production — and their effects on a firm's taxes are illustrated in this appendix. We will begin by assuming that a machine is purchased for $1,100 and has an estimated useful life of ten years or 10,000 hours. It will have a scrap value of $100 after ten years or 10,000 hours of use, whichever comes first. Table 4A.1 illustrates each of the four depreciation methods and compares the depreciation charges of each method over the ten-year period.

Straight Line

With the straight line method, a uniform annual depreciation charge of $100 a year is provided. This figure is arrived at by simply dividing the economic life into the total cost of the machine minus the estimated salvage value:

Table 4A.1 Comparison of Depreciation Methods for a 10-Year, $1,100 Asset with a $100 Salvage Value

Year	Straight Line	Sum-of-Years'-Digits	Units of Production[a]	Declining Balance (150%)
1	$ 100	$ 182	200	$ 165
2	100	164	180	140
3	100	145	150	119
4	100	127	130	101
5	100	109	100	86
6	100	91	80	78
7	100	73	60	78
8	100	55	50	78
9	100	36	30	78
10	100	18	20	78
Total	$1,000	$1,000	$1,000	$1,000

Columns may not add to the total because of rounding.
[a]The assumption is made that the machine is used the following number of hours: first year, 2,000; second year, 1,800; third year, 1,500; fourth year, 1,300; fifth year, 1,000; sixth year, 800; seventh year, 600; eighth year, 500; ninth year, 300; tenth year, 200.

$$\frac{(\$1,100 \text{ cost} - \$100 \text{ salvage value})}{10 \text{ years}} = \$100 \text{ a year depreciation charge.}$$

If the estimated salvage value is not in excess of 10 percent of the original cost, it can be ignored, but we are leaving it in for illustrative purposes.

Sum-of-Years'-Digits

Under the sum-of-years'-digits method, the yearly depreciation allowance is determined as follows:

1.   Calculate the sum of the years' digits; in our example, there is a total of 55 digits:

$$1 + 2 + 3 + 4 + 5 + 6 + 7 + 8 + 9 + 10 = 55.$$

This figure can also be arrived at by means of the sum of an algebraic progression equation, where n is the life of the asset:

$$\text{Sum} = n\left(\frac{n+1}{2}\right) = 10\left(\frac{10+1}{2}\right) = 55. \qquad \textbf{(4A.1)}$$

2.   Divide the number of remaining years by the sum-of-years'-digits and multiply this fraction by the depreciable cost (total cost minus salvage value) of the asset:

$$\text{Year 1: } \frac{10}{55}(\$1,000) = \$182 \text{ depreciation.}$$

$$\text{Year 2: } \frac{9}{55}(\$1,000) = \$164 \text{ depreciation.}$$

$$\text{Year 10: } \frac{1}{55}(\$1,000) = \$18 \text{ depreciation.}$$

It will be noted that in the above expressions, the numerator of each fraction can be written as $(n + 1 - t)$, where t is the number of years in use; the denominator, of course, is the sum of the digits expression which we set forth in Equation 4A.1. This fraction is multiplied times the original depreciable amount, which we will call I. Hence, the formula for the annual amount of the sum-of-years'-digits can be written as:

$$\text{Dep}_t = \frac{2(n + 1 - t)I}{n(n + 1)}. \qquad \textbf{(4A.2)}$$

Units of Production

Under the units of production method, the expected useful life of 10,000 hours is divided into the depreciable cost (purchase price minus salvage value) to arrive at an hourly depreciation rate of ten cents. Since, in our example, the machine is run for 2,000 hours in the first year, the depreciation in that year is $200; in the second year, $180; and so on. With this method, depreciation charges cannot be estimated precisely ahead of time; the firm must wait until the end of the year to determine what usage has been made of the machine and hence its depreciation.

Declining Balance Methods

In the declining balance methods of accelerated depreciation, the annual depreciation charge is calculated by multiplying a fixed rate times the undepreciated balance, or net book value (that is, the cost less accumulated depreciation). Since the undepreciated balance becomes smaller in each successive period, the amount of depreciation declines during each successive period; the rate applied to the undepreciated balance is fixed. The method permitted for income tax purposes under the Accelerated Cost Recovery System (ACRS) of the 1981 and 1982 tax acts is the 150 percent declining balance — that is, 1.5 times the straight line rate. (The 1981 act had scheduled accelerations to 175 percent declining balance in 1985 and to 200 percent, known as double declining balance, in 1986, but these were repealed by the 1982 act.) For example, on an asset with a ten-year life, straight line depreciation would be at a uniform rate of 10 percent per year; for the 150 percent declining balance method, the fixed rate would be $150\% \times 10\% = 15\%$ per year (applied to the undepreciated balance); for the 175 percent declining balance method, the rate would be 17.5 percent; and for double declining balance, 20 percent.

In the declining balance methods, under IRS rules, the estimated salvage value need not be subtracted from the cost of the asset in making the depreciation calculation as is done in other depreciation methods. The 150 percent method is illustrated for the data of our example in Table 4A.2.

Column (2) is the net book value subject to depreciation. It is the purchase price of the asset less the depreciation taken. For the second year, the depreciation rate is applied to

---

Table 4A.2   150% Declining Balance Method

Year (1)	Net Book Value (1,100 − Col. 4 of Previous Year) (2)	150% DB Deprec. (0.15 × Col. 2) (3)	Total Depreciation (Sum of Col. 3) (4)	Test of Straight Line Method (5)	Adjusted Total Depreciation (6)
1	$1,100	$165	$165		
2	935	140	305		
3	795	119	424		
4	676	101	525		
5	575	86	611	79[a]	
6	489	73	684	78[b]	689
7	416	62	746	78	767
8	354	53	799	78	845
9	301	45	844	78	923
10	256	38	882	78	1,001

[a]$1,100 - 100 - 525 = 475 \div 6 = 79.$
[b]$1,100 - 100 - 611 = 389 \div 5 = 78.$

$1,100 less $165, or $935. Then, 15 percent of $935 is $140, the amount of depreciation for Year 2; and this procedure continues for each successive year.

The company makes a switch from the declining balance method to straight line whenever straight line depreciation on the remaining net book value of the asset exceeds the depreciation amount under the declining balance method. In switching from double-declining balance to straight line depreciation, however, we must remember to deduct the salvage value to obtain the depreciable amount of the asset. In Table 4A.2, we test for this in the fifth year, but declining balance depreciation is still somewhat higher. In the sixth year, the depreciable amount of $1,000 less accumulated depreciation of $611 equals $389, which is $78 per year for the remaining five years. The switch is made at this point so that the adjusted accumulated depreciation as shown in Column (6) is the full $1,000 net depreciable value of the asset. Thus, although salvage value is not initially taken into account in applying the declining balance method, it is brought in at the point where the switch to straight line depreciation is made. A compact formula can be written for calculating the annual amount of depreciation under the 150 percent declining balance method. Using the symbols we have employed before, the formula can be written as:

$$\text{Dep}_t = \frac{1.5[1 - (1.5/n)]^{t-1}I}{n}. \qquad (4A.3)$$

The logic of this formula is: The expression in the brackets in the numerator, when multiplied times I, gives us the undepreciated balance. We multiply this by 1.5 and divide by n to obtain the depreciation for the year.

Similarly, the formula for the annual amount of depreciation under the double declining balance method is the following:

$$\text{Dep}_t = \frac{2[1 - (2/n)]^{t-1}I}{n}. \qquad (4A.4)$$

The logic of the formula is, of course, exactly the same as for the 150 percent declining balance except that the 2 is substituted for the 1.5.

Effect of Depreciation on Taxes Paid

The effect of the accelerated methods on a firm's income tax payment is easily demonstrated. If a firm chooses in the first year to use the straight line method, it can deduct only $100 from its earnings to arrive at earnings before taxes (the amount of earnings to which the tax rate applies). However, using any one of the other three methods, the firm would have a much greater deduction and, therefore, a lower tax liability. Eventually, there is less depreciation in later years, but there is a benefit from the time value of money.

Changing the Depreciable Life of an Asset

While Congress sets broad rules, the U.S. Department of the Treasury establishes various guidelines that set legal limits on the minimum life of classes of assets; by lowering these limits, the government can accomplish ends similar to permitting accelerated depreciation methods. Halving the minimum depreciable life of an asset, for example, would effectively double the annual rate of depreciation.

Problems

4A.1 The Altmont Corporation has purchased an asset for $5,200. It has an estimated salvage value of $200 at the end of its five-year life. Calculate the annual depreciation expense under each of the following methods:
a)   Straight line method
b)   Declining balance method (use 150%)
c)   Sum-of-years'-digits method

4A.2 The Rudd Corporation has purchased for $8,500 a machine with an expected useful life of eight years or 6,000 hours. It has an expected salvage value of $500. The annual usage of the machine is estimated as follows:

Year	Hours of Usage
1	1,500
2	1,200
3	1,000
4	800
5	500
6	400
7	300
8	300
	6,000

a)   Calculate the annual depreciation expense under each of the following methods:
1.   Straight line method
2.   Sum-of-years'-digits method
3.   Units of production method
4.   Declining balance method (use 150%)
b)   Add the depreciation expenses for the first two years and rank each method in descending order of the amount of tax deductible depreciation expenses.

4A.3 Assume the same facts as in the above problem except for a four-year life and hours of usage per year of:

Year	Hours of Usage
1	6,000
2	1,800
3	1,200
4	1,000
	10,000

Answer the same questions asked in Problem 4A.2, parts a and b.

Part Two The Time Dimension in Financial Decisions

Compound interest relationships are used in virtually every financial decision. Hence, in this section, we seek to establish some fundamental concepts that will be used throughout the remainder of the book. Chapter 5 sets forth the central concepts of compound interest and present value relationships.

In Chapter 6, we show how these central concepts are applied in the important area of investment decisions by the firm. The capital budgeting decisions described in Chapter 6 involve the use of discount rates and assume a world with certainty. Later on, in Chapters 16 and 17, where we discuss decision making in a world with uncertainty, the capital budgeting decision is revisited. Chapter 7 explains how the market determines discount rates that are used in making investment decisions.

Chapter 5   The Time Value of Money

A clear view of the time value of money is essential to an understanding of many topics throughout this book. Financial structure decisions, lease versus purchase decisions, bond refunding operations, security valuation techniques, and the whole question of the cost of capital are subjects that cannot be understood without a knowledge of compound interest. Many people are afraid of the subject and avoid it. However, a fear of compound interest relationships is quite unfounded; the subject matter is not inherently difficult. Almost all problems involving compound interest can be handled with only a few basic formulas.

Future Value

A person invests $1,000 in a security that pays 10 percent interest compounded annually. How much will this person have at the end of one year? To treat the matter systematically, let us define the following terms:

$P_0 =$ principal, or beginning amount, at time 0 (that is, $1,000)
$r =$ interest rate (that is, 10%)
$P_0r =$ total dollar amount of interest earned at r%
$FV_{r,n} =$ value at the end of n periods at r%.

When n equals 1, $FV_{r,n}$ can be calculated as follows:

$$FV_{r,1} = P_0 + P_0r \qquad (5.1)$$
$$= P_0(1 + r).$$

Equation 5.1 shows that the ending amount ($FV_{r,1}$) is equal to the beginning amount (P_0) times the factor $(1 + r)$. In the example, where P_0 is $1,000, r is 10 percent, and n is one year, $FV_{r,n}$ is determined as follows:

$$FV_{10\%,1 \text{ yr.}} = \$1,000(1.0 + 0.10) = \$1,000(1.10) = \$1,100.$$

Multiple Periods

If the person leaves the $1,000 on deposit for five years, to what amount will it have grown at the end of that period? Equation 5.1 can be used to construct Table 5.1, which indicates the answer. Note that $FV_{r,2}$, the balance at the end of the second year, is found as follows:

$$FV_{r,2} = FV_{r,1} (1 + r) = P_0(1 + r)(1 + r) = P_0(1 + r)^2$$
$$= \$1,000(1.10)^2 = \$1,210.00.$$

Table 5.1   Compound Interest Calculations

Period	Beginning Amount	×	$(1 + r)$	=	Ending Amount $(FV_{r,n})$
1	$1,000.00		1.10		$1,100.00
2	1,100.00		1.10		1,210.00
3	1,210.00		1.10		1,331.00
4	1,331.00		1.10		1,464.10
5	1,464.10		1.10		1,610.51

Similarly, $FV_{r,3}$, the balance after three years, is found as

$$FV_{r,3} = FV_{r,2}(1 + r) = P_0(1 + r)^3$$

$$= \$1,000(1.1)^3 = \$1,331.00.$$

In general, $FV_{r,n}$, the compound amount at the end of any future year n, is found as

$$FV_{r,n} = P_0(1 + r)^n. \tag{5.2}$$

Equation 5.2 is the fundamental equation of compound interest. Equation 5.1 is simply a special case of Equation 5.2, where $n = 1$.

While an understanding of the derivation of Equation 5.2 will help in understanding much of the remaining material in this chapter (and in subsequent chapters), the concept can be applied quite readily in a mechanical sense. Tables have been constructed for values of $(1 + r)^n$ for wide ranges of r and n. (See Table A.1 in Appendix A at the end of the book.)

Letting the *future value interest factor* (FVIF) equal $(1 + r)^n$, we can write Equation 5.2 as $FV_{r,n} = P_0[\text{FVIF}(r,n)]$. It is necessary only to go to an appropriate interest table to find the proper interest factor. For example, the correct interest factor for the illustration given in Table 5.1 can be found in Table A.1. Look down the period column to 5, then across this row to the appropriate number in the 10 percent column to find the interest factor, 1.6105. Then, using this interest factor, the future value of the $1,000 after five years is

$$FV_{10\%,5 \text{ yrs.}} = P_0\text{FVIF}(10\%, 5 \text{ yrs.}) = \$1,000(1.6105) = \$1,610.50.$$

This is the same figure that was obtained by the long method in Table 5.1.

Graphic View of the Compounding Process: Growth

Figure 5.1 shows how the interest factors for compounding grow as the compounding period increases. Curves can be drawn for any interest rate, including fractional rates; we have plotted curves for 0 percent, 5 percent, and 10 percent from data in Table A.1.

Figure 5.1 also shows how $1 (or any other sum) grows over time at various rates of interest — the higher the rate of interest, the faster the rate of growth. The interest rate is, in fact, the compound growth rate; if a deposited sum earns 5 percent, then the funds on deposit grow at the rate of 5 percent per year.

Figure 5.1   Relationships among Compound Value Interest Factors, Interest Rates, and Time

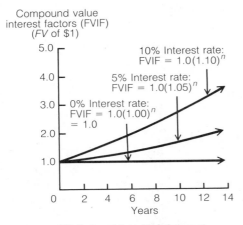

(a) Amount to which interest factor (or $1) grows after *n* years at various interest (or growth) rates

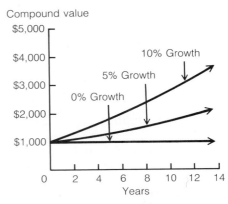

(b) Amount to which $1,000 grows after *n* years at various interest (or growth) rates

Present Value

Suppose you are offered the alternative of either $1,610.51 at the end of five years or X dollars today. There is no question that the $1,610.51 will be paid in full (perhaps the payer is the U.S. government). Having no current need for the money, you could deposit the X dollars in a savings association paying 10 percent interest; the 10 percent is your *opportunity cost*. How small must X be to induce you to accept the promise of $1,610.51 five years hence?

Table 5.1 shows that the initial amount of $1,000 growing at 10 percent a year yields $1,610.51 at the end of five years. Thus, you should be indifferent about the choice between $1,000 today and $1,610.51 at the end of five years. The $1,000 is the present value of $1,610.51 due in five years when the applicable interest rate is 10 percent. The subscript zero in the term P_0 indicates the present. Hence, present value quantities can be identified by either P_0 or $PV_{r,n}$.

Finding present values (*discounting*, as it is commonly called) is simply the reverse of compounding, and Equation 5.2 can readily be transformed into a present value formula by dividing both sides by the discount factor $(1 + r)^n$.

$$FV_{r,n} = P_0(1 + r)^n. \tag{5.2}$$

$$\text{Present value} = P_0 = \frac{FV_{r,n}}{(1 + r)^n} = FV_{r,n}\left[\frac{1}{(1 + r)^n}\right] \tag{5.3}$$

$$= FV_{r,n}[(1 + r)^{-n}] = FV_{r,n}\text{PVIF}(r,n).$$

Tables have been constructed for the interest rate factors — $(1 + r)^{-n}$ — for various rates, r, and time intervals, n. (See Table A.2 in Appendix A at the end of the book.) For the case being considered, look down the 10 percent column in Table A.2 to the fifth row. The figure shown there, 0.6209, is the present value interest factor (PVIF) used to determine the present value of $1,610.51 payable in five years, discounted at 10 percent.

$$P_0 = FV_{10\%,5\ \text{yrs.}}[\text{PVIF}(10\%,5\ \text{yrs.})]$$

$$= \$1,610.51(0.6209)$$

$$= \$1,000.$$

Graphic View of the Discounting Process

Figure 5.2 shows how the interest factors for discounting decrease as the discounting period increases. The curves in the figure, plotted from data in Table A.2, show that the present value of a sum to be received at some future date decreases (1) as the payment date is extended further into the future and (2) as the discount rate increases. If relatively high discount rates apply, funds due in the future are worth very little today; even at relatively low discount rates, funds due in the distant future are not worth much today. For example, $1,000 due in ten years is worth $247 today if the discount rate is 15 percent,

Figure 5.2   Relationships among Present Value Interest Factors, Interest Rates, and Time

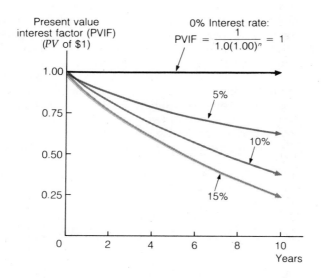

but it is worth $614 today at a 5 percent discount rate. Similarly, $1,000 due in ten years at 10 percent is worth $386 today, but the same amount at the same discount rate due in five years is worth $621 today.[1]

Future Value versus Present Value

Because a thorough understanding of future value concepts is vital to understanding the remainder of this book and because the subject gives many students trouble, it will be useful to examine in more detail the relationship between compounding and discounting.

Notice that Equation 5.2, the basic equation for compounding, is developed from the logical sequence set forth in Table 5.1; the equation merely presents in mathematical form the steps outlined in the table. The present value interest factor [PVIF(r,n)] in Equation 5.3 (the basic equation for discounting or finding present values) is the reciprocal of the future value interest factor [FVIF(r,n)] for the same (r,n) combination:

$$\text{PVIF}(r,n) = \frac{1}{\text{FVIF}(r,n)}.$$

For example, the *future value interest factor* for 10 percent over five years is seen in Table A.1 to be 1.6105. The *present value interest factor* for 10 percent over five years, therefore, must be the reciprocal of 1.6105:

$$\text{PVIF}(10\%,5 \text{ yrs.}) = \frac{1}{1.6105} = 0.6209.$$

The PVIF found in this manner must, of course, correspond with the PVIF shown in Table A.2 at the end of this book.

The reciprocal nature of the relationship between present value and future value permits us to find present values in two ways — by multiplying or by dividing. Thus, the present value of $1,000 due in five years and discounted at 10 percent can be found as

$$P_0 = PV_{r,n} = FV_{r,n}[\text{PVIF}(r,n)] = FV_{r,n}\frac{1}{(1+r)^n}$$

$$= \$1,000(0.6209) = \$620.90,$$

or

$$P_0 = PV_{r,n} = \frac{FV_{r,n}}{\text{FVIF}(r,n)} = \frac{FV_{r,n}}{(1+r)^n} = \frac{\$1,000}{1.6105} = \$620.90.$$

[1]Note that Figure 5.2 is not a mirror image of Figure 5.1. The curves in Figure 5.1 approach ∞ as n increases; in Figure 5.2, the curves approach zero, not $-\infty$, as n increases.

In the second form, it is easy to see why the present value of a given future amount ($FV_{r,n}$) declines as the discount rate increases.

To conclude this comparison of present and future values, compare Figures 5.1 and 5.2. Notice that the vertical intercept is at 1.0 in each case, but future value interest factors rise while present value interest factors decline. The reason for this divergence is, of course, that present value factors are reciprocals of future value factors.

Future Value of an Annuity

An *annuity* is defined as a series of payments of a fixed amount for a specified number of years. Each payment occurs at the end of the year.[2] For example, a promise to pay $1,000 a year for three years is a three-year annuity. If you were to receive such an annuity and were to invest each annual payment in a security paying 10 percent interest, how much would you have at the end of three years? The answer is shown graphically in Figure 5.3. The first payment is made at the end of Year 1, the second at the end of Year 2, and the third at the end of Year 3. The last payment is not compounded at all; the next to the last is compounded for one year; the first is compounded for two years, that is, for $(n - 1)$ years. When the future values of each of the payments are added, their total is the sum of the annuity. In the example, this total is $3,310.

Expressed algebraically, with $FVA_{r,t}$ defined as the future value, a as the periodic receipt, t as the length of the annuity, and FVIFA as the future value interest factor for an annuity, the formula for $FVA_{r,t}$ is

$$FVA_{r,t} = a(1 + r)^{n-1} + a(1 + r)^{n-2} + \ldots + a(1 + r)^1 + a(1 + r)^0$$
$$= a[(1 + r)^{n-1} + (1 + r)^{n-2} + \ldots + (1 + r)^1 + (1 + r)^0].$$

This expression is called a geometric series. It appears many times in different applications throughout the text. Consequently, it's worth the effort to show how a series with n terms

---

Figure 5.3   Graphic Illustration of an Annuity: Compound Sum

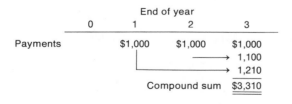

	End of year			
	0	1	2	3
Payments		$1,000	$1,000	$1,000
				1,100
				1,210
		Compound sum		$3,310

---

[2]For payments made at the beginning of the period, each receipt is shifted back one year. The annuity is then called an *annuity due*; the one in the present discussion, where payments are made at the end of each period, is called a *regular annuity*, or, sometimes, a *deferred annuity*.

(possibly an infinite number of terms) can be reduced to a simple equation. In order to do so, let $(1 + r) = u$. Then, we can rewrite the above series as

$$FVA_{r,t} = a(u^{n-1} + u^{n-2} + \ldots + u + 1), \text{ since } u^0 = 1.$$

Multiplying both sides of the equation by u, we have

$$uFVA_{r,t} = a(u^n + u^{n-1} + \ldots + u^2 + u).$$

Now subtract $uFVA_{r,t}$ from $FVA_{r,t}$ in order to reduce the series,

$$FVA_{r,t} - uFVA_{r,t} = a(-u^n + 1),$$

and simplify as follows:

$$FVA_{r,t}(1 - u) = a(1 - u^n)$$

$$FVA_{r,t} = a(1 - u^n)/(1 - u).$$

Substituting back the value of u, we have

$$FVA_{r,t} = a[1 - (1 + r)^n]/(1 - 1 - r)$$

$$= a[(1 + r)^n - 1]/r \qquad\qquad \textbf{(5.4a)}$$

$$= a\text{FVIFA}(r,t). \qquad\qquad \textbf{(5.4b)}$$

FVIFA has been given values for various combinations of r and t. To find these, see Table A.3 in Appendix A. To find the answer to the three-year, $1,000 annuity problem, simply refer to Table A.3, look down the 10 percent column to the row for the third year, and multiply the factor 3.3100 by $1,000. The answer using (5.4b) is the same as the one derived by the long method illustrated in Figure 5.3:

$$FVA_{r,t} = a \times \text{FVIFA}(r,t)$$

$$FVA_{10\%, 3 \text{ yrs.}} = \$1,000 \times 3.3100 = \$3,310.$$

Notice that the FVIFA for the sum of an annuity is always larger than the number of years the annuity runs. The reader should verify that the same result can be obtained with a hand calculator, using the formula in (5.4a).

It is useful to recognize some relationships between the formulas for a simple future value and for the future value of an annuity by looking at them together.

$$\text{Future sum: } FV_{r,n} = P_0\text{FVIF}(r,n).$$

$$\text{Future value of an annuity: } FVA_{r,t} = a\text{FVIFA}(r,t).$$

Both formulas involve an interest rate, r. But time is indexed as n in the future sum and as t in the future value of an annuity. An example will illustrate the reason. You place $1,000 in a savings account and want to know what its value will be at the end of three years at a compound interest rate of 10 percent. The compound interest factor at 10 percent for three years is 1.3310 as shown by Table A.1. So the future value at the end of three years is $1,331.

The sum of an annuity formula is based on making a deposit of $1,000 at the end of the first year and also at the end of the second and third years. So we have to use t to indicate that the annuity deposits are made at the end of each of the years 1, 2, and 3. The third year in this example is the nth, or the terminal (final), year. This is the reason n is used in the future and present value formulas, but t is used in the formulas involving annuities. In Table A.3, we find that the sum of an annuity factor at 10 percent for three years is 3.3100, giving an annuity future value of $3,310. This is much larger than the result for the simple future value because three deposits (rather than one) were made. Even at a zero interest rate, the annuity factor for the three deposits (three annuity payments) would be 3, which is much larger than the simple future value factor of 1.3310 with a 10 percent interest rate.

Present Value of an Annuity

Suppose you were offered the following alternatives: a three-year annuity of $1,000 a year or a lump-sum payment today. You have no need for the money during the next three years, so if you accept the annuity, you will simply invest the funds in a security paying 10 percent interest. What must be the lump-sum payment received today to make it equivalent to the annuity? Figure 5.4 helps explain the problem.

The present value of the first receipt is $a[1/(1 + r)]$, that of the second is $a[1/(1 + r)^2]$, or $a[1/(1 + r)]^2$, and so on. Defining the present value of an annuity of t years as $PVA_{r,t}$ and the present value interest factor for an annuity as PVIFA, we can write the following equation:

$$PVA_{r,t} = a\left[\frac{1}{1 + r}\right] + a\left[\frac{1}{1 + r}\right]^2 + \ldots + a\left[\frac{1}{1 + r}\right]^n$$

$$= a\left[\frac{1}{(1 + r)} + \frac{1}{(1 + r)^2} + \ldots + \frac{1}{(1 + r)^n}\right].$$

Figure 5.4   Graphic Illustration of an Annuity: Present Value

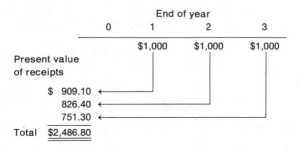

A procedure similar to that used to derive (5.4a) and (5.4b) can be used to show that the above geometric series reduces to

$$PVA_{r,t} = a[1 - (1 + r)^{-n}]/r \qquad \text{(5.5a)}$$

$$= a[\text{PVIFA}(r,t)]. \qquad \text{(5.5b)}$$

Again, tables have been worked out for the PVIFA, the expression after a in Equation 5.5b. (See Table A.4 in Appendix A.) From Table A.4, the PVIFA for a three-year, 10 percent annuity is found to be 2.4869. Multiplying this factor by the $1,000 annual receipt gives $2,486.90, the present value of the annuity:

$$PVA_{r,t} = a\text{PVIFA}(r,t)$$

$$PVA_{10\%,3 \text{ yrs.}} = \$1,000 \times 2.4869 = \$2,486.90.$$

Notice that the PVIFA for the present value of an annuity is always less than the number of years the annuity runs, whereas the FVIFA for the sum of an annuity is larger than the number of years. Again, the reader should verify that the same result is obtained with a hand calculator, using Equation 5.5a.

Annual Payments for Accumulation of a Future Sum

Thus far in the chapter, all the equations have been based on Equation 5.2. The present value equation merely involves a transposition of Equation 5.2, and the annuity equations simply take the sum of the basic compound interest equation for different values of t. We now examine some additional modifications of the equations.

Suppose we want to know the amount of money that must be deposited at the end of each of five years at 10 percent in order to have $10,000 available to pay off a debt at the end of the fifth year. Dividing both sides of Equation 5.4b by the FVIFA, in order to isolate a, the annual payment, we obtain

$$a\text{FVIFA}(r,t) = FVA_{r,t}. \qquad \text{(5.4b)}$$

$$a = \frac{FVA_{r,t}}{\text{FVIFA}(r,t)}. \qquad \text{(5.6)}$$

Looking up the sum of an annuity interest factor for five years at 10 percent in Table A.3 at the end of the book and dividing that figure into $10,000, the future value of the annuity, $FVA_{r,t}$, we find

$$a = \frac{\$10,000}{6.1051} = \$1,638.$$

Thus, if $1,638 is deposited each year in an account paying a 10 percent return, at the end of five years, the account will have accumulated $10,000. The procedure is called setting up a sinking fund; such funds are used, for example, to provide for bond retirements.

Annual Annuity Payments

Suppose that you receive a second mortgage loan for $20,000 at an interest rate of 10 percent. You are required to pay it off in three annual installments to begin at the end of the first year. The solution requires application of the present value of an annuity formula, Equation 5.5b. Here, however, we know that the present value of the annuity is $20,000, and the problem is to find the three equal annual payments when the interest rate is 10 percent. This calls for dividing both sides of Equation 5.5b by the PVIFA to obtain Equation 5.7.

$$PVA_{r,t} = a\text{PVIFA}(r,t). \tag{5.5b}$$

$$a = \frac{PVA_{r,t}}{\text{PVIFA}(r,t)}. \tag{5.7}$$

The interest factor (PVIFA) is found in Appendix A, Table A.4, to be 2.4869. Substituting this value in Equation 5.7, we find the three equal annual amounts to be $8,042.14:

$$a = \frac{\$20,000}{2.4869} = \$8,042.141.$$

This kind of calculation is also used in setting up insurance and pension plan benefit schedules. For example, if you have accumulated $200,000 and if it were to be paid to you in three annual installments beginning at the end of each year, your annual benefit would be $80,421.41 (ten times the amount in the previous example).

Determining Interest Rates

In many instances, the present values and cash flows associated with a payment stream are known, but the interest rate is not known. Suppose a bank offers to lend you $1,000 today if you sign a note agreeing to pay the bank $1,762.30 at the end of five years. What rate of interest would you be paying on the loan? To answer the question, we use Equation 5.2:

$$FV_{r,n} = P_0(1 + r)^n = P_0\text{FVIF}(r,n). \tag{5.2}$$

We simply solve for the FVIF and then look up this value in Table A.1 along the row for the fifth year:

$$\text{FVIF}(r,n) = \frac{FV_{r,5 \text{ yrs.}}}{P_0} = \frac{\$1,762.30}{\$1,000} = 1.7623.$$

Looking across the row for the fifth year, we find the value 1.7623 in the 12 percent column; therefore, the interest rate on the loan is 12 percent.

Precisely the same approach is taken to determine the interest rate implicit in an annuity. For example, suppose a bank will lend you $2,401.80 if you sign a note in which you agree to pay the bank $1,000 at the end of each of the next three years. What interest rate is the bank charging you? To answer the question, we solve Equation 5.5b for PVIFA and then look up the PVIFA in Table A.4:

$$PV_{r,t} = a\text{PVIFA}(r,t) \tag{5.5b}$$

$$\text{PVIFA}(r,t) = \frac{PV_{r,3 \text{ yrs.}}}{a} = \frac{\$2,401.8}{\$1,000} = 2.4018.$$

Looking across the third-year row, we find the factor 2.4018 under the 12 percent column; therefore, the bank is lending you money at a 12 percent interest rate.

Present Value of an Unequal Series of Receipts

In illustrating annuities to this point, we assumed that the payments or receipts were the same fixed amount — sometimes called constant or level annuities. Although some financial problems do involve constant annuities, many others (as will be illustrated in the following chapter on capital budgeting) are concerned with unequal flows of cash. Consequently, it is necessary to expand our analysis to handle payments or receipts that may be of different size in different years. Most of these applications involve present value calculations. This section will be restricted to illustrating the present value of an unequal series of payments, since other applications are made throughout the remainder of the book and the principles are the same.

To do the calculating procedure, suppose someone offers to sell you a series of payments consisting of $300 after one year, $100 after two years, and $200 after three years. How much will you be willing to pay for the series, assuming the appropriate discount rate (interest rate) is 10 percent? To determine the purchase price, we simply compute the present value of each payment. The calculations are worked out in Table 5.2. The receipts for each year are shown in the second column; the discount factors are given in the third column; and the product of these two columns, the present value of each individual receipt, is given in the last column. When the individual present values in the last column are added together, the sum is the present value of the investment — $505.63. Under the assumptions of the example, you should be willing to pay this amount for the investment.

Table 5.2   Calculating the Present Value of an Unequal Series of Payments

Period	Receipt	×	Interest Factor (PVIF)	=	Present Value (PV or P_0)
1	$300		0.9091		$272.73
2	100		0.8264		82.64
3	200		0.7513		150.26
			PV of investment		$505.63

Noninteger Values of Interest Rates

In the interest tables at the end of the book we have given interest factor values for integer values such as 8 or 9 percent. Sometimes practical problems involve fractional interest rates, such as $8\frac{1}{4}$ percent. Or the interest rate calculation problem you encounter may involve time periods outside the range of the years provided in the tables. (Compounding for periods other than the annual basis given in the tables will be discussed in the following section.) For fractional interest rates, the use of the formulas and a hand calculator will enable us to determine the interest factors required. Recall that in the interest rate formulas presented, there was a component (FVIF, PVIF, FVIFA, or PVIFA) for the interest factor. Assuming that our problem involved alternatively using each of the four types of interest factors for an interest rate of $8\frac{1}{4}$ percent and a ten-year period, the formulas and the resulting values are shown below:

$$FVIF = (1 + r)^n = 1.0825^{10} = 2.2094.$$

$$PVIF = 1/(1 + r)^n = 1/1.0825^{10} = 0.4526.$$

$$FVIFA = [(1 + r)^n - 1]/r = (1.0825^{10} - 1)/0.0825$$

$$= 14.6597.$$

$$PVIFA = [1 - (1 + r)^{-n}]/r = (1 - 1.0825^{-10})/0.0825 = 6.6351.$$

Notice that in performing the calculations, we take $(1.0825)^{10}$ and then simply use this result in a slightly different way for each of the four interest factors that we calculate. However, many hand-held calculators are preprogrammed to carry out these kinds of calculations. All of these internal programs are based on the logic involved in using each of the four basic compound interest formulas.

Sometimes the problem involves obtaining interest rates when only the interest factors are provided. For example, suppose we make an investment of $663,510, which will yield $100,000 a year for ten years. We want to know the rate of return on that investment. We use Equation 5.5b to find the PVIFA:

$$PVIFA = \$663,510 \div \$100,000 = 6.6351.$$

From our calculations above, we recognize that this result is the PVIFA in which the interest rate is $8\frac{1}{4}$ percent. If we are using a preprogrammed hand calculator, we can solve for the required interest rate. With a less sophisticated hand calculator, we would have to obtain the result by trial and error. But with hand calculators of any degree of sophistication, if we keep in mind the expressions for the four basic compound interest relations, we can obtain what we need to solve any real-world problem that might come up. This is even true when compounding is other than on an annual basis, as we shall demonstrate in the following section.

Semiannual and Other Compounding Periods

In all the examples used thus far, it has been assumed that returns were received annually. For example, in the section dealing with future values, it was assumed that the funds earned 10 percent a year. However, suppose the earnings rate had been 10 percent com-

---

Table 5.3   Compound Interest Calculations with Semiannual Compounding

Period	Beginning Amount (P_0)	×	$(1 + r)$	=	Ending Amount $(FV_{r,n})$
1	$1,000.00		1.05		$1,050.00
2	1,050.00		1.05		1,102.50

---

pounded semiannually (that is, every six months). What would this have meant? Consider the following example.

You invest $1,000 in a security to receive a return of 10 percent compounded semiannually. How much will you have at the end of one year? Since semiannual compounding means that interest is actually paid each six months, this fact is taken into account in the tabular calculations in Table 5.3. Here, the annual interest rate is divided by 2, but twice as many compounding periods are used because interest is paid twice a year. Comparing the amount on hand at the end of the second six-month period, $1,102.50, with what would have been on hand under annual compounding, $1,100.00, shows that semiannual compounding is better for the investor. This result occurs, of course, because the saver earns interest on interest more frequently.

We can extend this simple example for more frequent compounding within the year. We shall calculate the future sum for one year for multiple compounding within the year for an interest rate of 12 percent and an initial principal of $1 as shown in Table 5.4. We see that daily compounding increases the interest rate by 0.75 percent.

Equation 5.8 is a generalization of the procedure for within-the-year compounding:

$$q \text{ frequency, } n \text{ years } FV_{r,n} = P_0\left(1 + \frac{r}{q}\right)^{nq}. \tag{5.8}$$

The interest tables can be used when compounding occurs more than once a year. Simply divide the nominal, or stated, interest rate by the number of times compounding occurs and multiply the years by the number of compounding periods per year. For example, to find the amount to which $1,000 will grow after five years if semiannual compound-

---

Table 5.4   Multiple Compounding within One Year

Annual	$FV_{r,1} = P_0(1 + r)$		$= 1.1200.\ (q = 1)$
Semiannual	$= P_0\left(1 + \dfrac{r}{2}\right)^2$		$= 1.1236.\ (q = 2)$
Quarterly	$= P_0\left(1 + \dfrac{r}{4}\right)^4$		$= 1.1255.\ (q = 4)$
Monthly	$= P_0\left(1 + \dfrac{r}{12}\right)^{12}$		$= 1.1268.\ (q = 12)$
Daily	$= P_0\left(1 + \dfrac{r}{365}\right)^{365}$		$= 1.1275.\ (q = 365)$

ing is applied to a stated 10 percent interest rate, divide 10 percent by 2 and multiply the five years by 2. Then look in Table A.1 at the end of the book under the 5 percent column and in the row for the tenth period, where you will find an interest factor of 1.6289. Multiplying this by the initial $1,000 gives a value of $1,628.90, the amount to which $1,000 will grow in five years at 10 percent compounded semiannually. This compares with $1,610.50 for annual compounding.

The same procedure is applied in all the cases covered — compounding, discounting, single payments, and annuities. To illustrate semiannual compounding in calculating the present value of an annuity, for example, consider the case described in the section on the present value of an annuity — $1,000 a year for three years, discounted at 10 percent. With annual discounting or compounding, the interest factor is 2.4869 and the present value of the annuity is $2,486.90. For semiannual compounding, look under the 5 percent column and in the Year 6 row of Table A.4 to find an interest factor of 5.0757. Then multiply by half of $1,000, or the $500 received each six months, to get the present value of the annuity, $2,537.85. The payments come a little more rapidly (the first $500 is paid after only six months), so the annuity is a little more valuable if payments are received semiannually rather than annually.

By letting q approach infinity, Equation 5.8 can be modified to the special case of *continuous compounding*.[3] Continuous compounding is extremely useful in theoretical finance as well as in practical applications.

The Annual Percentage Rate (APR)

Different types of financial contracts use different compounding periods. Most bonds pay interest semiannually. Some savings accounts pay interest quarterly, but the new money market accounts at most financial institutions pay interest daily. Department stores, oil companies, and credit cards also specify a daily rate of interest. In addition, to obtain a home mortgage loan, the lender charges points, up front. To compare the costs of different credit sources, it is necessary to calculate the effective rate of interest, or the annual percentage rate (APR), as it is generally called.

To calculate the APR, we should recognize that we are simply making another application of Equation 5.8, where $n = 1$. Equation 5.8 then becomes Equation 5.8a:

$$PV_{r,1} = P_0\left(1 + \frac{r}{q}\right)^q. \tag{5.8a}$$

The annual effective rate of interest (APR), r_e, can be determined as follows:

$$\frac{PV_{r,1}}{P_0} = \left(1 + \frac{r}{q}\right)^q = 1 + r_e.$$

Solving for r_e, we have

$$r_e = APR = \left(1 + \frac{r}{q}\right)^q - 1. \tag{5.9}$$

[3]Discussed in Appendix A to this chapter.

Since we have already calculated $(1 + r_e)$ in Table 5.4, the effective rate of interest in each of the examples is obtained by subtracting 1. For example, the effective rate of interest rises from 12.36 percent for semiannual compounding to 12.68 percent for monthly compounding.

We can generalize further. At an interest rate of 12 percent, we want to know the future sum of $100 with quarterly compounding for five years. First we use Equation 5.8:

$$FV_{r,n} = P_0\left(1 + \frac{r}{q}\right)^{nq} = \$100\left(1 + \frac{.12}{4}\right)^{5(4)} = \$100(1.03)^{20} = \$180.611.$$

Alternating, we can use the effective interest rate, or APR, in Table 5.4 for quarterly compounding. This is 12.55 percent, which we can use in Equation 5.2:

$$FV_{r,n} = P_0(1 + r_e)^n = \$100(1.1255)^5 = 180.604.$$

Since the results are the same (except for rounding), we can use either method in making calculations. In many transactions, government regulations require that the lender provide the borrower with a written statement of the APR in the transaction. We have described how it can be calculated.

Amortized Loans

Corporate bonds are typically payable in full at maturity, with only the interest paid semiannually. Thus a 30-year corporate bond with a face amount of $100,000 and a coupon rate of 12 percent would pay $6,000 in interest each six months for a yearly total of $12,000. The principal of $100,000 would be paid at the end of 30 years. However, business term loans, automobile loans, and home mortgage loans typically provide for repayment of principal as each periodic payment is made. These are called *amortized loans*.

An example will illustrate the ideas involved in amortized loans. A firm borrows $100,000, which will be paid off by three equal payments made at the end of each of the subsequent three years. The applicable annual interest rate is 12 percent. The equal annual payments will combine both interest and repayment of principal so that the loan is completely repaid by the end of the third year. The key concept involved is to determine the amount of the equal annual payments.[4]

We use Equation 5.7 derived previously to determine the annual payment or annuity.

$$a = \frac{PVA_{r,t}}{PVIFA(r,t)}$$

$$= \frac{\$100,000}{PVIFA(12\%,3\ \text{yrs.})}$$

We can determine from the table for the present value of an annuity that the interest factor is 2.4018; divided into the initial $100,000 gives us the amount of the equal annual payment of $41,635.44 that has to be made. (If we use a hand calculator and carry the

---

[4]Unequal payments could accomplish the same result, but the arithmetic would be somewhat more complicated.

Table 5.5   Loan Amortization Schedule ($100,000 @12%) 3 Years, Annually

Year	(1) Payment	(2) Interest [.12 × Col. (4)]	(3) Repayment of Principal [Col. (1) − Col. (2)]	(4) End-of-Year Balance
0	—	—	—	$100,000.00
1	$ 41,634.90	$12,000.00	$ 29,634.90	70,365.10
2	41,634.90	8,443.81	33,191.09	37,174.01
3	41,634.90	4,460.88	37,174.02	≈0
	$124,904.70	$24,904.69	$100,000.01	

interest factor out to nine places, the equal annual payment is $41,634.90. This is the amount used in the subsequent analysis.)

Remember that the equal annual payment consists of an interest component and a repayment of principal component. The amount of each component varies each year, as illustrated in Table 5.5, which represents an amortization schedule.

Column (1) represents the equal annual payments. Column (2) represents the interest component. The amount for Year 1 is 12 percent of the original amount borrowed. This is subtracted from the annual payment to obtain the repayment of principal shown in Column (3). The repayment of principal deducted from the original $100,000 gives the end-of-year balance shown in Column (4) for Year 1. In the subsequent years, interest is calculated on the previous end-of-year balance in Column (4). This new amount of interest is deducted from the equal payment in Column (1) to determine the repayment of principal in Column (3). Column (4) continues to be the balance at the end of the previous year less the repayment of principal during the current year.

The total of the three equal payments made is $124,904.70. This is the total in Column (1). This also represents the sum of the interest payments shown in Column (2) plus the repayment of the $100,000, which is the total of Column (3). In subsequent discussions that involve tax factors, the interest payments for each year in Column (2) represent a deductible cost for the borrower and an addition to taxable income for the lender.

Automobile loans and home mortgage loans typically involve amortization of the principal in equal monthly installments. We will illustrate a home mortgage with the same dollar amount and the same quoted interest rate as in the previous illustration but will change the amortization period to 30 years with equal monthly payments. The expression for the interest factor for the present value of an annuity was given by Equation 5.5a:

$$\frac{1 - (1 + r)^{-n}}{r}.$$

We insert (.12/12 = .01) for the monthly interest rate, r, and 360 for the number of months, n. The resulting interest factor is 97.21833. This is divided into $100,000 to obtain the equal monthly mortgage loan payment of $1,028.61. The monthly pattern is illustrated in Table 5.6. The logic of the relation between the columns is exactly the same as for Table 5.5. In the early years, most of the payment represents interest with relatively little left

| Table 5.6 | Illustration of Amortization for a Home Mortgage ($100,000 @12%) 30 Years, Monthly |

Month	(1) Payment	(2) Interest [.01 × Col. (4)]	(3) Repayment of Principal [Col. (1) − Col. (2)]	(4) End-of- Month Balance
0	—	—	—	$100,000.00
1	$ 1,028.61	$ 1,000.00	$ 28.61	99,971.39
2	1,028.61	999.71	28.90	99,942.49
3	1,028.61	999.42	29.19	99,913.30
—	—	—	—	—
—	—	—	—	—
—	—	—	—	—
359	1,028.61	—	—	1,018.43
360	1,028.61	10.18	1,018.43	0
	$370,299.60	$270,299.60	$100,000.00	

over for repayment of principal. However, as shown, for the final month, most of the payment is repayment of principal with a relatively small amount of interest expense.

The sum of the monthly payments over the entire 30-year period is $370,299.60. Thus, the total of payments made over the 360 periods is almost four times the amount of the original principal of $100,000 borrowed under the home mortgage. However, the lender is simply earning a quoted rate of 12 percent compounded monthly (which is an APR of 12.683 percent).[5] The dollar amount of interest is so large because the payments are made over the extended 360-month period.

Appropriate Interest Rates

Throughout this chapter, the rates we have used for compounding or discounting have simply been assumed for illustrative purposes. A natural question is how do we know what the appropriate interest rate for a particular financial decision might be.[6] We will give an overview in Chapter 7, "How the Market Determines Discount Rates," but a complete development is not achieved until we have finished Part Six dealing with cost of capital and valuation. The background essential for handling the material in Part Six is covered in Parts Two through Five. At this point, it is sufficient to note that the major influences are the general patterns of interest rates in the economy as a whole, differences in risks among different investments and securities, and, finally, the opportunity costs of making one investment as compared to another. The later materials will explain these concepts.

---

[5] $r_e = \text{APR} = \left(1 + \dfrac{.12}{12}\right)^{12} - 1 = 12.683\%.$

[6]For convenience, in this chapter, we speak of *interest rates*, which implies that only debt is involved. In later chapters, the concept is broadened considerably, and the term *rate of return* or *discount factor* is used in place of *interest rate*.

Summary

A knowledge of compound interest and present value techniques is essential to an understanding of several important aspects of finance: capital budgeting, financial structure, security valuation, and many other topics.

The four basic equations with the notation that will be used throughout the book are

1. $FV_{r,n} = P_0 FVIF(r,n)$.
2. $PV_{r,n} = FV_{r,n} PVIF(r,n)$.
3. $FVA_{r,t} = aFVIFA(r,t)$.
4. $PVA_{r,t} = aPVIFA(r,t)$.

The future value ($FV_{r,n}$), or the future amount, is defined as the sum to which a beginning amount of principal (P_0) will grow over n years when interest is earned at the rate of r percent a year. The equation for finding the future value is

$$FV_{r,n} = P_0(1 + r)^n.$$

Tables giving the future value of $1 for a large number of different years and interest rates have been prepared. The future value of $1 is called the future value interest factor (FVIF), given in Table A.1 in Appendix A.

The present value of a future payment ($PV_{r,n}$) is the amount that, if we had it now and if we invested it at the specified interest rate (r), would equal the future payment ($FV_{r,n}$) on the date the future payment is due. For example, if a person were to receive $1,610 after five years and then decided 10 percent were the appropriate interest rate (called the *discount rate* when computing present values), then that person could find the present value of the $1,610 by applying the following equation:

$$PV_{r,n} = FV_{r,n}\left[\frac{1}{(1 + r)^n}\right] = \$1,610(0.6209) = \$1,000.$$

The term in brackets is called the present value interest factor (PVIF), and values for it have been worked out in Table A.2 of Appendix A.

An *annuity* is defined as a series of payments of a fixed amount (a) for a specified number of years. The future value of an annuity is the total amount one will have at the end of the annuity period if each payment is invested at a certain interest rate and is held to the end of the annuity period. For example, suppose we have a three-year, $1,000 annuity invested at 10 percent. Using the formulas for annuities, tables have been constructed for various interest rates. The FVIFA for the future value of a three-year annuity at 10 percent is 3.3100, and it can be used to find the future value:

$$FVA_{r,t} = \text{Future value of annuity} = FVIFA(r,t) \times \text{Annual cash flow}$$

$$= 3.3100 \times \$1,000 = \$3,310.$$

Thus, $3,310 is the future value of the annuity.

The present value of an annuity is the lump sum we would need to have on hand today in order to be able to withdraw equal amounts (a) each year and end up with a balance exactly equal to zero at the end of the annuity period. For example, if we wish to withdraw $1,000 a year for three years, we could deposit $2,486.90 today in a bank account paying 10 percent interest, withdraw the $1,000 in each of the next three years, and end up with a zero balance. Thus, $2,486.90 is the present value of an annuity of $1,000 a year for three years when the appropriate discount rate is 10 percent. Again, tables are available for finding the present value of annuities. To use them, we simply look up the interest factor (PVIFA) for the appropriate number of years and interest rate and then multiply the PVIFA by the annual receipt:

$$PVA_{r,t} = \text{Present value of annuity} = \text{PVIFA}(r,t) \times \text{Annual cash flow}$$

$$= 2.4869 \times \$1,000 = \$2,486.90.$$

The four basic interest formulas can be used in combination to find such things as the present value of an uneven series of receipts. The formulas can also be transformed to find (1) the annual payments necessary to accumulate a future sum, (2) the annual receipts from a specified annuity, (3) the periodic payments necessary to amortize a loan, and (4) the interest rate implicit in a loan contract.

Questions

5.1 When do financial decisions require explicit consideration of the interest factor?
5.2 Explain the relationship of discount rate levels to both present value and future value. Do the same for time to maturity.
5.3 Why do lending firms prefer 360 days per year as a basis for interest calculations, while borrowing firms prefer 365 days?
5.4 Compound interest relationships are important for decisions other than financial ones. Why are they important to marketing managers?
5.5 Would you rather have a savings account that pays 5 percent interest compounded semiannually or one that pays 5 percent interest compounded daily? Why?
5.6 For a given interest rate and a given number of years, is the interest factor for the sum of an annuity greater or smaller than the interest factor for the present value of the annuity?
5.7 Suppose you are examining two investments, A and B. Both have the same maturity, but A pays a 6 percent return and B yields 5 percent. Which investment is probably riskier? How do you know?

Problems

5.1 Which amount is worth more at 9 percent: $1,000 today or $2,000 after eight years?
5.2 The current production target for the five-year plan of the Logo Company is to increase output by 8 percent a year. If the 1985 production is 3.81 million tons, what is the target production for 1990?
5.3 At a growth rate of 9 percent, how long does it take a sum to double?
5.4 Assuming you had extra cash, how much would you be willing to loan somebody who agreed to pay you $50,000 in five years, if interest rates are 8 percent?
5.5 If, at age 25, you open an IRA account paying 10 percent annual interest, and you put $2,000 in at the end of each year, what will be your balance at age 65?
5.6 You are offered two alternatives: a $2,000 annuity for seven years or a lump sum today. If current interest rates are 9 percent, how large will the lump sum have to be to make you indifferent between the alternatives?

5.7 The Lowell Company's sales last year were $1 million.
- **a)** Assuming that sales grow 18 percent a year, calculate sales for each of the next six years.
- **b)** Plot the sales projections.
- **c)** If your graph is correct, your projected sales curve is nonlinear. If it had been linear, would this have indicated a constant, increasing, or decreasing percentage growth rate? Explain.

5.8 The Hull Company has established a sinking fund to retire a $900,000 mortgage that matures on December 31, 1992. The company plans to put a fixed amount into the fund each year for ten years. The first payment was made on December 31, 1983; the last will be made on December 31, 1992. The company anticipates that the fund will earn 10 percent a year. What annual contributions must be made to accumulate the $900,000 as of December 31, 1992?

5.9 You need $135,500 at the end of 14 years. You know that the best you can do is to make equal payments into a bank account on which you can earn 6 percent interest compounded annually. Your first payment is to be made at the end of the first year.
- **a)** What amount must you plan to pay annually to achieve your objective?
- **b)** Instead of making annual payments, you decide to make one lump-sum payment today. To achieve your objective of $135,500 at the end of the 14-year period, what should this sum be? (You can still earn 6 percent interest compounded annually on your account.)

5.10 You have just purchased a newly issued $1,000 five-year Malley Company bond at par. The bond (Bond A) pays $60 in interest semiannually ($120 a year). You are also negotiating the purchase of a $1,000 six-year Malley Company bond (Bond B) that returns $30 in semiannual interest payments and has six years remaining before it matures.
- **a)** What is the going rate of return on bonds of the risk and maturity of Malley Company's Bond A?
- **b)** What should you be willing to pay for Bond B?
- **c)** How will your answer to Part b change if Bond A pays $40 in semiannual interest instead of $60 but still sells for $1,000? (Bond B still pays $30 semiannually and $1,000 at the end of six years.)

5.11 If you buy a note for $11,300, you will receive ten annual payments of $2,000, the first payment to be made one year from today. What rate of return, or yield, does the note offer?

5.12 You can buy a bond for $1,000 that will pay no interest during its seven-year life but will have a value of $2,502 when it matures. What rate of interest will you earn if you buy the bond and hold it to maturity?

5.13 A bank agrees to lend you $1,000 today in return for your promise to pay back $1,838.50 nine years from today. What rate of interest is the bank charging you?

5.14 If earnings in 1984 are $1.99 a share, while eight years earlier (in 1976) they were $1, what has been the annual rate of growth in earnings?

5.15 You are considering two investment opportunities, A and B. A is expected to pay $300 a year for the first 10 years, $700 a year for the next 15 years, and nothing thereafter. B is expected to pay $1,000 a year for 10 years and nothing thereafter. You find that other investments of similar risk to A and B yield 8 percent and 14 percent, respectively.
- **a)** Find the present value of each investment. Show your calculations.
- **b)** Which is the riskier investment? Why?
- **c)** Assume that your rich uncle will give you a choice of A or B without cost to you and that you (1) must hold the investment for its entire life (cannot sell it) or (2)

are free to sell it at its going market price. Which investment would you prefer under each of the two conditions?

5.16 On December 31, Helen Ventor buys a building for $175,000, paying 20 percent down and agreeing to pay the balance in 20 equal annual installments that are to include principal plus 15 percent compound interest on the declining balance. What are the equal installments?

5.17 You wish to borrow $50,000 from your savings and loan for a home mortgage. The quoted interest rate is 11 percent compounded monthly for a 25-year mortgage.
a)   What annual percentage rate is equal to 11 percent compounded monthly?
b)   What will your monthly mortgage payments be (assuming that they are paid at the end of each month)?

5.18 Suppose you open a savings account with $1,800 earned in a summer job. The account's stated interest rate is 11 percent. Calculate your account's balance after one year if interest is paid (a) annually, (b) semiannually, (c) quarterly, (d) monthly, and (e) daily.

5.19 a)   What amount will be paid for a $1,000 ten-year bond that pays $40 interest semiannually ($80 a year) and that yields 10 percent, compounded semiannually?
b)   What will be paid if the bond is sold to yield 8 percent?
c)   What will be paid if semiannual interest payments are $50 and the bond yields 6 percent?

5.20 Bank A offers to make you a school loan at an effective annual rate of 10 percent. Bank B offers the money at 9.6 percent compounded monthly. Which one should you accept?

5.21 The Hardy Company's common stock paid a dividend of $1 last year. Dividends are expected to grow at a rate of 18 percent for each of the next six years.
a)   Calculate the expected dividend for each of the next six years.
b)   Assuming that the first of these six dividends will be paid one year from now, what is the present value of the six dividends? (Given the riskiness of the dividend stream, 18 percent is the appropriate discount rate.)
c)   Assume that the price of the stock will be $27 six years from now. What is the present value of this "terminal value"? Use an 18 percent discount rate.
d)   Assume that you will buy the stock, receive the six dividends, and then sell the stock. How much should you be willing to pay for it?
e)   What would happen to the price of this stock if the discount rate declined because the riskiness of the stock declined? If the growth rate of the dividend stream increased?

Selected References

Cissell, R.; Cissell, H.; and Flaspohler, D. C., *Mathematics of Finance*, 5th ed., Boston: Houghton Mifflin, 1978.

Scott, David L., and Moore, W. Kent, *Fundamentals of the Time Value of Money* (New York: Praeger, 1984).

U.S. Department of Commerce, *Handbook of Mathematical Functions*. Edited by M. Abramowitz and I. A. Stegum. Washington, D.C.: Government Printing Office, December 1972.

Vichas, Robert P., *Handbook of Financial Mathematics, Formulas and Tables*. Englewood Cliffs, N.J.: Prentice-Hall, 1979.

Appendix A to Chapter 5

Continuous Compounding and Discounting

Continuous Compounding

In Chapter 5, we assumed that growth occurs at discrete intervals—annually, semiannually, and so forth. For some purposes, it is better to assume instantaneous, or *continuous*, growth. Continuous compounding is used extensively in theoretical work. Also, as demonstrated in later chapters, some computations are simplified when continuously compounded interest rates are used. The relationship between discrete and continuous compounding is illustrated in Figure 5A.1, for $P_0 = \$100$ and $r = 20\%$. Figure 5A.1(a) shows the annual compounding case, where interest is added once a year; in Figure 5A.1(b), compounding occurs twice a year; and in Figure 5A.1(c), interest is earned continuously.

We developed Equation 5.8 in Chapter 5 to allow for any number of compounding periods per year:

Figure 5A.1   Annual, Semiannual, and Continuous Compounding

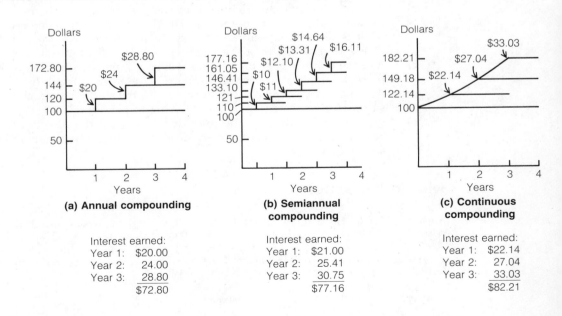

(a) Annual compounding

Interest earned:
Year 1: $20.00
Year 2:   24.00
Year 3:   28.80
          $72.80

(b) Semiannual compounding

Interest earned:
Year 1: $21.00
Year 2:   25.41
Year 3:   30.75
          $77.16

(c) Continuous compounding

Interest earned:
Year 1: $22.14
Year 2:   27.04
Year 3:   33.03
          $82.21

$$FV_{r,n} = P_0\left(1 + \frac{r}{q}\right)^{nq}.$$ (5.8)

Equation 5.8, in turn, can be modified to allow for continuous compounding. The steps in this modification are developed below. In the literature of finance, where continuous compounding is employed, V_t is used in place of $FV_{r,n}$ and t is used for years (time). We will also shift from r to k, since r is a market interest rate and k is the firm's cost of capital to which this material will be applied.

Step 1. Returning to Equation 5.8, the general case of compound growth, but using the new notation, can be expressed as follows:

$$V_t = P_0\left(1 + \frac{k}{q}\right)^{qt}.$$ (5.8)

Noting that since we can multiply qt by k/k, we can set $qt = (q/k)(kt)$ and rewrite Equation 5.8 as

$$V_t = P_0\left[\left(1 + \frac{k}{q}\right)^{(q/k)}\right]^{(kt)}.$$ (5A.1)

Step 2. Defining $m = q/k$ and noting that $k/q = 1/(q/k) = 1/m$, we can rewrite Equation 5A.1 as

$$V_t = P_0\left[\left(1 + \frac{1}{m}\right)^{m}\right]^{kt}.$$ (5A.2)

Step 3. As the number of compounding periods (q) increases, m also increases; this causes the term in brackets in Equation 5A.2 to increase. At the limit, when q and m approach infinity (and compounding is instantaneous, or continuous), the term in brackets approaches the value 2.718 . . . . The value e is defined as this limiting case:

$$e = \lim_{m \to \infty} \left(1 + \frac{1}{m}\right)^{m} = 2.718 \ldots .$$ (5A.3)

Thus, we may substitute e for the bracketed term, rewriting Equation 5A.2 as

$$V_t = P_0 e^{kt}$$ (5A.4)

for the case of continuous compounding (or continuous growth).

Step 4. Interest factors (IF) can be developed for continuous compounding; developing the factors requires the use of natural, or Naperian, logarithms.[1] First, letting $P_0 = 1$, we can rewrite Equation 5A.4 as

$$V_t = e^{kt}.$$ (5A.5)

---

[1]Recall that the logarithm of a number is the power, or exponent, to which a specified base must be raised to equal the number; that is, the log (base 10) of 100 is 2 because $(10)^2 = 100$. In the system of natural logs, the base is $e \approx 2.718$.

Setting Equation 5A.5 in log form and noting that ln denotes the log to the base e, we obtain

$$\ln V_t = kt \ln e. \tag{5A.6}$$

Since e is defined as the base of the system of natural logarithms, $\ln e$ must equal 1.0 (that is, $e^1 = e$, so $\ln e = 1.0$). Therefore,

$$\ln V_t = kt. \tag{5A.7}$$

One simply looks up the product kt in a table of natural logarithms and obtains the value V_t as the antilog. For example, if $t = $ five years and $k = 10$ percent, the product is 0.50. Looking up this value in Appendix B at the end of the book, we find in this table of natural logs that 0.5 lies between 0.49470 and 0.50078, whose antilogs are 1.64 and 1.65 respectively. Interpolating, we find the antilog of 0.5 to be 1.649. Thus, 1.649 is the interest factor for a 10 percent growth rate compounded continuously for five years. One dollar growing continuously at this compound rate would equal $1.649 after five years.

   Even simpler is the use of a hand calculator. If it has an e^x key, punch in the .5 and push the e^x key; the result is 1.648721. If the hand calculator does not have an e^x key, punch in the .5 and then first punch INV followed by the lnx key to obtain the same result.

Continuous Discounting

Equation 5A.4 can be transformed into Equation 5A.8 and used to determine present values under continuous compounding. Using k as the discount rate (again, this is the standard notation: k is used as the discount rate and g as the growth rate for compounding), we obtain

$$PV = \frac{V_t}{e^{kt}} = V_t e^{-kt}. \tag{5A.8}$$

Thus, if $1,649 is due in five years and if the appropriate *continuous* discount rate k is 10 percent, the present value of this future payment is

$$PV = \frac{\$1,649}{1.649} = \$1,000.$$

Continuous Compounding and Discounting for Annuities

For continuously compounding and discounting *streams* of payments ("annuities"), elementary integral calculus must be employed. The procedures involved are outlined below.

Step 1.   An amount a is received at the end of each year. The amount received grows at the rate g; thus, the accumulated sum of the receipts at the end of any year n is S_t, calculated as

$$S_t = a(1 + g)^0 + a(1 + g)^1 + a(1 + g)^2 + \cdots + a(1 + g)^{t-1}$$
$$= a + a(1 + g)^1 + a(1 + g)^2 + \cdots + a(1 + g)^{t-1}$$
$$= \sum_{t=1}^{n} a(1 + g)^{t-1}. \tag{5A.9}$$

S_t is the accumulated sum of the receipts, and it is equal to the sum of the rectangles in Figure 5A.2a; this is the area under the discontinuous curve formed by the tops of the rectangles.

Step 2.   Exactly the same principle is involved in finding the accumulated sum of the continuous equivalent of an annuity, or a stream of receipts received continuously. The accumulated sum is again represented by the area under a curve, but now the curve is continuous as in Figure 5A.2b. In the discrete case, the area under the curve was obtained by adding the rectangles; in the continuous case, the area must be found by the process of integration.

The stream of receipts (or the value of a_t) uses the initial receipt a_0. It grows at the continuous rate g for t periods.

$$a_t = a_0 e^{gt} \tag{5A.10}$$

Equation 5A.10 defines the curve, and the area under the curve (S_t) is represented by the integral:

$$S_t = \int_{t=0}^{n} a_0 e^{gt}\, dt = a_0 \int_{t=0}^{n} e^{gt}\, dt. \tag{5A.11}$$

Figure 5A.2   Sum of an "Annuity" under Discrete and Continuous Compounding

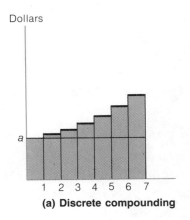

(a) Discrete compounding

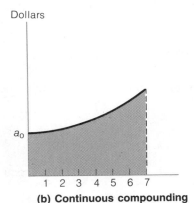

(b) Continuous compounding

Step 3. Given a discrete series of receipts such as those shown in Figure 5A.2a and a discount rate, k, we find their PV as

$$PV = \sum_{t=1}^{n} a_t(1 + k)^{-t}.$$

If the receipts accrue continuously, as do those in Figure 5A.2b, we must find the present value of the stream of payments by calculus. First, note that by Equation 5A.8, we find the PV of the instantaneous receipt for period t as

$$PV = a_t e^{-kt}. \tag{5A.8}$$

The present value of the entire stream of receipts is given as the integral:

$$PV = \int_{t=0}^{n} a_t e^{-kt}\, dt. \tag{5A.12}$$

Step 4. Although the primary Equations 5A.11 and 5A.12 developed thus far in this section are seldom used individually, the basic dividend valuation model is developed by combining them.

First, note from Equation 5A.10 that $a_t = a_0 e^{gt}$. Substitute this value into Equation 5A.12, obtaining

$$PV = \int_{t=0}^{n} a_0 e^{gt} e^{-kt}\, dt. \tag{5A.13}$$

Now remove the constant term a_0 from within the integral and combine the exponents of the e term, obtaining

$$PV = a_0 \int_{t=0}^{n} e^{gt-kt}\, dt$$

$$= a_0 \int_{t=0}^{n} e^{-(k-g)t}\, dt. \tag{5A.14}$$

Therefore, the integration of Equation 5A.14 yields an indefinite integral of the form

$$PV = \frac{a_0 e^{-(k-g)t}}{k - g},$$

which, when evaluated at $t = \infty$, is equal to 0, and when evaluated at $t = 0$, is equal to

$$-\frac{a_0}{k - g}.$$

Subtracting the lower bound from the upper yields

$$PV = 0 - \left[-\frac{a_0}{k - g} \right]$$

$$= \frac{a_0}{k - g}. \tag{5A.15}$$

Equation 5A.15 is thus the present value of a continuous stream of receipts growing at rate g and discounted at rate k. This is similar to the constant growth dividend valuation model, discussed in Chapter 23.[2]

The Relationship between Discrete and Continuous Interest Rates

Discrete growth or compounding can always be transformed into an equivalent continuous version. Let d represent a discrete rate of compounding, while c is a continuous compounding rate. Suppose we have the following pattern of discrete compounding of interest:

$$I, \ I(1 + d), \ I(1 + d)^2, \ I(1 + d)^3, \ \dots$$

The exponent of the expression $(1 + d)$ represents the number of periods covered in the compounding. Let b represent $(1 + d)$ so that we can write

$$I(1 + d)^t = Ib^t = Ie^{ct}.$$

Thus, even though a discrete case $I(1 + d)^t$ is being considered, there is an equivalent continuous natural exponential function Ie^{ct}. Now, we can demonstrate the relationship between d and c. Start with the first and last term of the above expression. Having cancelled I, we have

$$(1 + d)^t = e^{ct}.$$

We take natural logs of both sides to obtain

$$t \ln(1 + d) = ct.$$

Since the relationship is not dependent on the number of time periods involved we can cancel the t's. We thus have

$$\ln(1 + d) = c. \tag{5A.16}$$

---

[2]With a continuous stream, the first payments start at the beginning of period zero. With discrete time periods, the first payment occurs at the end of period zero. This latter is the constant growth dividend model which is

$$PV = \frac{a_0(1 + g)}{k - g}.$$

This is a general expression. We can see that the continuous rate will, in general, be lower than the discrete rate. For example, if the discrete rate of interest is 12 percent, the continuous rate would be ln(1.12) = 11.33 percent. This is quite logical, since the interest is working harder when it is compounding every second than when it is compounding only once a year, for example.

Conversely, if a given interest rate is being compounded continuously, the equivalent discrete rate is larger. Thus, if we are using a nominal 12 percent rate but applying it continuously, the equivalent discrete rate will be higher. The appropriate formula to apply requires solving Equation 5A.16 for d. The result we get is Equation 5A.17.

$$d = e^c - 1. \tag{5A.17}$$

Compounding the 12 percent nominal rate continuously, the equivalent discrete rate is 12.7497. The result we had earlier obtained for daily compounding carried to the same number of decimal places was 12.7475. This illustrates that the equivalent discrete rate for continuous compounding is somewhat higher (but not by much) than for daily compounding. Note that Equation 5A.17 is the continuous compounding equivalent of Equation 5.9, which was the expression for calculating the annual percentage rate under discrete compounding. Thus, we see that the equivalent discrete rate when a nominal interest rate is compounded continuously really represents the annual percentage rate (APR).

To accomplish the same result as a given discrete rate, the continuous rate is smaller (because it works harder). On the other hand, when a given nominal annual rate is compounded monthly or daily or (in the limit) continuously, the APR is higher. The initial point of reference in the statement of the problem must be kept clearly in mind.

Problems

5A.1 What annual rate of interest would make you indifferent between it and 10 percent compounded continuously?

5A.2 The First Security Bank pays 9 percent interest compounded annually on time deposits. The Second Security Bank pays 8 percent interest compounded continuously.
   a)   In which bank would you prefer to deposit your money?
   b)   Would your choice of banks be influenced by the fact that you might want to withdraw your funds during the year as opposed to the end of the year? (Assume that funds must be left on deposit during the entire compounding period in order to receive any interest.)

5A.3 If you have an account that compounds interest continuously and has an effective annual yield of 6.18 percent, what is the stated annual interest rate?

5A.4 What rate of interest compounded monthly is equivalent to 18 percent compounded continuously?

5A.5 For a 20-year deposit, what annual rate, payable quarterly, will produce the same effective rate as 6 percent, compounded continuously?

5A.6 You have $32,604 in a 15-year-old account, which has been paying a 12.5 percent nominal rate of interest, compounded continuously. How much was your initial deposit?

Chapter 6 Capital Budgeting Techniques

Capital budgeting involves the entire process of planning expenditures whose returns are expected to extend beyond one year. The choice of one year is arbitrary, of course, but it is a convenient cutoff point for distinguishing between kinds of expenditures. Obvious examples of capital outlays are expenditures for land, buildings, and equipment, and for permanent additions to working capital associated with plant expansion. An advertising or promotion campaign or a research and development program is also likely to have an impact beyond one year, so they too can be classified as capital budgeting expenditures.

To facilitate an exposition of the investment decision process, we have broken the topic down into its major components. In this chapter, we consider the capital budgeting process and the techniques generally employed by reasonably sophisticated business firms. The compound interest concepts covered in the preceding chapter are used extensively. Uncertainty is explicitly and formally considered in Chapters 16 and 17, and the cost of capital concept is developed and related to capital budgeting in Chapter 21.

Significance of Capital Budgeting

A number of factors combine to make capital budgeting perhaps the most important decision with which financial management is involved. Further, all departments of a firm — production, marketing, and so on — are vitally affected by the capital budgeting decisions; so all executives, no matter what their primary responsibility, must be aware of how capital budgeting decisions are made.

Long-Term Effects

First and foremost, capital budgeting requires a commitment into the future, often in the face of considerable uncertainty. For example, the purchase of an asset with an economic life of ten years requires a long period of waiting before the final results of the action can be known.

An erroneous forecast of asset requirements can result in serious consequences. If the firm has invested too much in fixed assets, it will incur unnecessarily heavy expenses. If it has not spent enough, it will have inadequate capacity and may lose a portion of its share of the market to rival firms. To regain lost customers typically requires heavy selling expenses, price reduction, product improvements, and so forth.

A related problem is how to properly phase the availability of capital assets in order to have them come "on stream" at the correct time. For example, the executive vice president of a decorative tile company gave the authors an illustration of the importance of capital budgeting. His firm tried to operate near capacity most of the time. For about four years, there had been intermittent spurts in the demand for its product; when these spurts occurred, the firm had to turn away orders. After a sharp increase in demand, the firm would add capacity by renting an additional building and then purchasing and installing the appropriate equipment. It would take six to eight months to have the additional capacity ready. At this point, the company frequently found that there was no demand for its increased output — other firms had already expanded their operations and had taken an increased share of the market, with the result that demand for this firm had leveled off. If the firm had properly forecast demand and had planned its increase in capacity six months or one year in advance, it would have been able to maintain its market — indeed, to obtain a larger share of the market.

Good capital budgeting will improve the timing of asset acquisitions and the quality of assets purchased. This result follows from the nature of capital goods and their producers. Capital goods are not ordered by firms until they see that sales are beginning to press on capacity. Such occasions occur simultaneously for many firms. When the heavy orders come in, the producers of capital goods go from a situation of idle capacity to one where they cannot meet all the orders that have been placed. Consequently, large backlogs accumulate. Since the production of capital goods involves a relatively long work-in-process period, a year or more of waiting may be involved before the additional modern capital goods are available. Furthermore, the quality of the capital goods, produced on rush order, may deteriorate. These factors have obvious implications for purchasing agents and plant managers.

Raising Funds

Another reason for the importance of capital budgeting is that asset expansion typically involves substantial expenditures. Before a firm spends a large amount of money, it must make the proper plans — large amounts of funds are not available automatically. A firm contemplating a major capital expenditure program may need to plan its financing several years in advance to be sure of having the funds required for the expansion.

An Overview of Capital Budgeting

Capital budgeting is, in essence, an application of a classic proposition from the economic theory of the firm: Namely, a firm should operate at the point where its marginal revenue is just equal to its marginal cost. When this role is applied to the capital budgeting decision, marginal revenue is taken to be the percentage rate of return on investments, while marginal cost is the firm's marginal cost of capital. Proper implementation of this rule will result in capital budgeting decisions which maximize shareholders' wealth.

In order to keep the analysis simple, we shall initially assume that all potential projects have exactly the same risk as the firm as a whole. This implies that the same marginal cost of capital is relevant for all projects. Later on, in Chapter 17, we shall investigate capital budgeting procedures when projects have different risk.

A simplified version of the capital budgeting problem is depicted in Figure 6.1(a). The horizontal axis measures the dollars of investment during a year, while the vertical axis shows both the percentage cost of capital and the rate of return on projects. The projects are denoted by boxes — Project A, for example, calls for an outlay of $3 million and promises a 17 percent rate of return; Project B requires $1 million and yields about 16 percent; and so on. The last investment, Project G, requires $5 million and is expected to return

---

Figure 6.1   Illustrative Capital Budgeting Decision Process

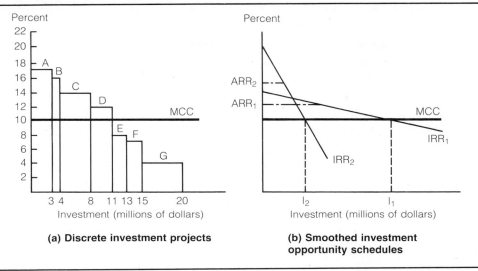

(a) **Discrete investment projects**   (b) **Smoothed investment opportunity schedules**

---

only 4 percent. In Figure 6.1(b), the concept is generalized to show smoothed investment opportunity schedules (IRR), and two alternative schedules are presented.[1]

The curve MCC designates the marginal cost of capital, or the cost of each additional dollar acquired for purposes of making capital expenditures. As it is drawn in Figure 6.1(a), the marginal cost of capital is constant at 10 percent, a rate which is assumed to be appropriate given the firm's riskiness.[2] To maximize profits, the firm should accept Projects A through D, obtaining and investing $11 million, and reject E, F, and G.

Notice that two alternative investment opportunity schedules are shown in Figure 6.1(b). Both are stylized versions of the investment schedule in Figure 6.1(a). IRR_1 designates relatively many desirable investment opportunities, while IRR_2 designates relatively few desirable projects. The curves could be interpreted as applying either to different firms or to one firm at two different times. Note also that both firms optimally apply the same decision rule for accepting projects. *Take all projects which earn a rate of return greater than the marginal cost of capital.* Thus, Firm 1 undertakes an amount of investment, I_1, while Firm 2 invests only I_2. The marginal rate of return on the last project undertaken is the same for both firms, even though the average rate of return for Firm 2, ARR_2, is greater than for Firm 1, ARR_1.[3] For both firms, the marginal rate of return is equal to the marginal cost of capital, MCC.

---

[1]The investment opportunity schedules measure the rate of return on each project. The rate of return on a project is generally called the *internal rate of return (IRR)*. This is why we label the investment opportunity schedules IRR. The process of calculating the IRR is explained later in this chapter. Briefly, it is defined as the discount rate which equates the present value of cash inflows with the present value of cash outlays.

[2]The reasons for assuming a perfectly horizontal marginal cost of capital curve are discussed in Chapter 21.

[3]For straight lines, the ARR is the midpoint of the line segment above the marginal cost of capital, MCC. The ARR is the average return on all projects accepted.

At the applied level, the capital budgeting process is much more complex than the preceding example suggests. Projects do not just appear; a continuing stream of good investment opportunities results from hard thinking, careful planning, and, often, large outlays for research and development. Moreover, some very difficult measurement problems are involved: The sales and costs associated with particular projects must be estimated, frequently for many years into the future, in the face of great uncertainty. Finally, some difficult conceptual and empirical problems arise over the methods of calculating rates of return and the cost of capital.

Investment Proposals

Aside from the actual generation of ideas, the first step in the capital budgeting process is to assemble a list of the proposed new investments, together with the data necessary to appraise them. Although practices vary from firm to firm, proposals dealing with asset acquisitions are frequently grouped according to the following four categories:

1.   Replacements.
2.   Expansion: additional capacity in existing product lines.
3.   Growth: new product lines.
4.   Other (for example, pollution control equipment).

These groupings are somewhat arbitrary, and it is frequently difficult to decide the appropriate category for a particular investment. In spite of such problems, the scheme is used quite widely and, as we shall see, with good reason.

Ordinarily, replacement decisions are the simplest to make. Assets wear out or become obsolete, and they must be replaced if production efficiency is to be maintained. The firm has a very good idea of the cost savings to be obtained by replacing an old asset, and it knows the consequences of nonreplacement. All in all, the outcomes of most replacement decisions can be predicted with a high degree of confidence.

Examples of the second investment classification are proposals for adding more machines of the type already in use or the opening of new branches in a city-wide chain of food stores. Expansion investments are frequently incorporated in replacement decisions. To illustrate, an old, inefficient machine may be replaced by a larger and more efficient one. A degree of uncertainty — sometimes extremely high — is clearly involved in expansion, but the firm at least has the advantage of examining past production and sales experience with similar machines or stores.

When it considers an investment of the third kind, growth into new product lines, little, if any, experience is available on which to base decisions. To illustrate, when Union Carbide decided to develop the laser for commercial application, it had very little idea of either the development costs or the specific applications to which lasers could be put. Under such circumstances, any estimates must at best be treated as very crude approximations.

The "other" category is a catchall and includes intangibles; an example is a proposal to boost employee morale and productivity by installing a music system. Mandatory pollution control devices, which must be undertaken even though they produce no revenues, are another example of the "other" category. Major strategic decisions, such as plans for overseas expansion or mergers, might also be included here, but more frequently, they are treated separately from the regular capital budget.

Administrative Aspects

Other important aspects of capital budgeting involve administrative matters. Approvals are typically required at higher levels within the organization as we move away from replacement decisions and as the sums involved increase. One of the most important functions of the board of directors is to approve the major outlays in a capital budgeting program as well as the total capital budget for each planning period. Such decisions are crucial for the future well-being of the firm.

The planning horizon for capital budgeting programs varies with the nature of the industry. When sales can be forecast with a high degree of reliability for 10 to 20 years, the planning period is likely to be correspondingly long; electric utilities are an example of such an industry. Also, when the product-technology developments in the industry require an 8-to-10-year cycle to develop a new major product, as in certain segments of the aerospace industry, a correspondingly long planning period is necessary.

After a capital budget has been adopted, funding must be scheduled. Characteristically, the finance department is responsible for scheduling and acquiring funds to meet scheduled requirements. The finance department is also primarily responsible for cooperating with the operating divisions to compile systematic records on the uses of funds and the installation of equipment purchased. Effective capital budgeting programs require such information as the basis for periodic review and evaluation of capital expenditure decisions — the feedback and control phase of capital budgeting, often called the *post-audit review*.

The foregoing represents a brief overview of the administrative aspects of capital budgeting; the analytical problems involved are considered next.

Choosing among Alternative Proposals

In most firms, there are more proposals for projects than the firm is able or willing to finance. Some proposals are good, others are poor, and methods must be developed for distinguishing between the good and the poor. Essentially, the end product is a ranking of the proposals and a cutoff point for determining how far down the ranked list to go.

In part, proposals are eliminated because some are *mutually exclusive*. Mutually exclusive proposals are alternative methods of doing the same job. If one piece of equipment is chosen, others will not be required. Thus, if there is a need to improve the materials handling system in a chemical plant, the job may be done either by conveyer belts or by forklift trucks. The selection of one method makes it unnecessary to use the others: They are mutually exclusive items.

Independent projects are those that are being considered for different kinds of tasks that need to be accomplished. For example, in addition to the materials handling system, the chemical firm may need equipment to package the end product. The work would require a packaging machine, and the purchase of equipment for this purpose would be independent of the equipment purchased for materials handling. The firm may undertake any or all independent projects.

Finally, projects may be *contingent*. For example, there may be only one way to build a football stadium but two ways of housing it (in a metal structure or a geodesic dome). Because the stadium and its housing are contingent, the analysis requires that we consider them together. Hence, we would want to compare the stadium within a metal structure with the alternative of the stadium within a geodesic dome.

To distinguish among the many items that compete for the allocation of the firm's capital funds, a ranking procedure must be developed. This procedure requires calculating the estimated cash flows from the use of equipment and then translating them into a measure of their effect on shareholders' wealth. First, we turn our attention to the problem of estimating cash flows for capital budgeting purposes.

Measures of Cash Flows for Capital Budgeting

Cash flows for capital budgeting purposes are defined as the after-tax cash flows for an all-equity financed firm.[4] Algebraically, this definition is equivalent to earnings before interest and taxes, EBIT, less the taxes the firm would pay if it had no debt, T(EBIT), plus noncash depreciation charges, Δdep,

$$\Delta\text{Cash flow} = \Delta\text{EBIT} - T(\Delta\text{EBIT}) + \Delta\text{dep}.$$

Notice that this definition of cash flows is unaffected by the firm's financing decision, for example the amount of debt which it uses. Consequently, the investment decision and the financing decision are kept separate when we use this definition of cash flows for capital budgeting purposes.

We focus on how the firm's cash flows will be changed. Table 6.1 provides an example of a pro-forma income statement which can be used to illustrate a cash flow calculation.

To arrive at the change in after-tax cash flows created by the project, we start with increased revenues, ΔR, then subtract out all items which are expensable for tax purposes (ΔVC + ΔFCC + Δdep). The result is taxable income, assuming the firm has no debt. Next, we subtract the change in taxes and add back the change in depreciation because depreciation is not a cash outflow. The appropriate algebraic expression is:

$$\Delta\text{Cash flow} = (\Delta R - \Delta VC - \Delta FCC - \Delta\text{dep}) - T(\Delta R - \Delta VC - \Delta FCC - \Delta\text{dep}) + \Delta\text{dep}.$$

Table 6.1   Pro-forma Income Statement

Description	Symbol	Amount
Change in sales revenue	ΔR	$145,000
Change in variable operating costs	ΔVC	−90,000
Change in fixed cash costs	ΔFCC	−10,000
Change in depreciation	Δdep	−15,000
Change in earnings before interest and taxes	ΔEBIT	30,000
Change in interest expense	ΔrD	−5,000
Change in earnings before tax	ΔEBT	25,000
Change in taxes (@T = 40%)	ΔTax	−10,000
Change in net income	ΔNI	15,000

---

[4]This definition is still correct when the firm does use some leverage in the form of debt financing, as will be shown in the example which follows.

This equation can be simplified as follows:

$$\Delta \text{Cash flow} = (1 - T)(\Delta R - \Delta VC - \Delta FCC - \Delta dep) + \Delta dep.$$

Note that the term in brackets is the same as the change in earnings before interest and taxes, $\Delta EBIT$; hence, the equation becomes:[5]

$$\Delta \text{Cash flow} = (1 - T)\Delta EBIT + \Delta dep. \tag{6.1}$$

Substituting in the numbers from Table 6.1, we have:

$$\Delta \text{Cash flow} = (1 - .4)(\$145,000 - \$90,000 - \$10,000 - \$15,000) + \$15,000$$

$$= .6(\$30,000) + \$15,000$$

$$= \$33,000.$$

The procedure described above starts with revenues at the top of the income statement and then works down to obtain the definition of cash flows for capital budgeting purposes. Alternately, one can start at the bottom of the income statement, with changes in net income (ΔNI) and build upward to arrive at the same definition. Sometimes this approach is easier to use. The algebraic expression for the change in cash flows is

$$\Delta \text{Cash flow} = \Delta NI + \Delta dep + (1 - T)\Delta rD. \tag{6.2}$$

In order to prove that it is equivalent to Equation 6.1, start by writing out the full expression for the change in net income,

$$\Delta NI = (1 - T)(\Delta R - \Delta VC - \Delta FCC - \Delta dep - \Delta rD),$$

and substitute it into Equation 6.2,

$$\Delta \text{Cash flow} = (1 - T)(\Delta R - \Delta VC - \Delta FCC - \Delta dep - \Delta rD) + \Delta dep + (1 - T)\Delta rD.$$

Separating out the ΔrD terms, we have

$$\Delta \text{Cash flow} = (1 - T)(\Delta R - \Delta VC - \Delta FCC - \Delta dep) - (1 - T)\Delta rD + \Delta dep + (1 - T)\Delta rD$$

$$= (1 - T)(\Delta R - \Delta VC - \Delta FCC - \Delta dep) + \Delta dep$$

$$= (1 - T)\Delta EBIT + \Delta dep.$$

---

[5]Sometimes we see the cash flow equation expressed somewhat differently. For example, start with

$$\Delta \text{Cash flow} = (1 - T)(\Delta R - \Delta VC - \Delta FCC - \Delta dep) + \Delta dep.$$

Then separate out the depreciation term as follows:

$$\Delta \text{Cash flow} = (1 - T)(\Delta R - \Delta VC - \Delta FCC) - \Delta dep + T\Delta dep + \Delta dep.$$

The result is a definition of cash flows equivalent to Equation 6.1:

$$\Delta \text{Cash flow} = (1 - T)(\Delta R - \Delta VC - \Delta FCC) + T\Delta dep.$$

Thus, we have shown that the definitions of cash flows for capital budgeting purposes are equivalent in Equations 6.1 and 6.2.

Importance of Good Data

Most discussions of cash flows associated with capital projects are relatively brief, but it is important to emphasize this: *In the entire capital budgeting procedure, probably nothing is of greater importance than a reliable estimate of the cost savings or revenue increases that will be achieved from the prospective outlay of capital funds.* The increased output and sales revenue resulting from expansion programs are obvious benefits. Cost reduction benefits include changes in quality and quantity of direct labor; in amount and cost of scrap and rework time; in fuel costs; and in maintenance expenses, down time, safety, flexibility, and so on. Each capital equipment expenditure must be examined in detail for possible additional costs and savings.

All the procedures for ranking projects (described in the next section) are no better than the data input — the old saying, "garbage in, garbage out," is certainly applicable to capital budgeting analysis. Thus, the data assembly process is not a routine clerical task to be performed on a mechanical basis. It requires continuous monitoring and evaluation of estimates by those competent to make such evaluations — engineers, accountants, economists, cost analysts, and other qualified persons.

After costs and benefits have been estimated, they are utilized for ranking alternative investment proposals. How this ranking is accomplished is our next topic.

Ranking Investment Proposals

The point of capital budgeting — indeed, the point of all financial analysis — is to make decisions that will maximize the value of the firm. The capital budgeting process is designed to answer two questions: (1) Which of several mutually exclusive investments should be selected? (2) How many projects, in total, should be accepted?

Among the many methods used for ranking investment proposals, four are discussed here.

1. *Payback method (or payback period):* Number of years required to return the original investment.
2. *Return on assets (ROA) or return on investment (ROI):* An average rate of return on assets employed.
3. *Net present value (NPV) method:* Present value of expected future cash flows discounted at the appropriate cost of capital, minus the cost of the investment.
4. *Internal rate of return (IRR) method:* Interest rate which equates the present value of future cash flows to the investment outlay.

In the next sections of this chapter, the nature and characteristics of the four methods are illustrated and explained. To make the explanations more meaningful, the same data set is used to illustrate each procedure.

General Principles

When comparing various capital budgeting criteria, it is useful to establish some guidelines. What are the properties of an ideal criterion? The optimal decision rule will have four characteristics:

1. It will select from a group of mutually exclusive projects the one which maximizes shareholders' wealth.
2. It will appropriately consider all cash flows.
3. It will discount the cash flows at the appropriate market-determined opportunity cost of capital.
4. It will allow managers to consider each project independently from all others. This has come to be known as the *value additivity principle*.

The value additivity principle implies that if we know the value of separate projects accepted by management, then simply adding their values, V_j, will give us the value of the firm. If there are N projects, then the value of the firm will be:[6]

$$V = \sum_{j=1}^{N} V_j, \ j = 1, \ \ldots \ N.$$

This is a particularly important point because it means that projects can be considered on their own merit without the necessity of looking at them in an infinite variety of combinations with other projects.

Table 6.2 gives the cash flows for four mutually exclusive projects. They all have the same life, five years, and they all require the same investment outlay, $1,500. Once accepted, no project can be abandoned without incurring the outflows indicated. For example, Project A has negative cash flows during its fourth and fifth years. Once the project is accepted these expected cash outflows must be incurred. An example of a project of this type is a nuclear power plant. Decommissioning costs at the end of the economic life of the facility can be as large as the initial construction costs and they must be taken into account.

Table 6.2 Cash Flows of Four Mutually Exclusive Projects

	Cash Flows				
Year	A	B	C	D	PVIF @10%
0	−1,500	−1,500	−1,500	−1,500	1.000
1	150	0	150	300	.909
2	1,350	0	300	450	.826
3	150	450	450	750	.751
4	−150	1,050	600	750	.683
5	−600	1,950	1,875	900	.621

[6]The summation sign, Σ, simply means that we add up the present values of the projects. For example, if there are three projects, then $N = 3$ and

$$\sum_{j=1}^{N} V_j = \sum_{j=1}^{3} V_j = V_1 + V_2 + V_3.$$

The last column of Table 6.2 shows the appropriate discount factor for the present value of cash flows, assuming that the appropriate opportunity cost of capital is 10 percent.[7] Since all four projects are assumed to have the same risk, they can be discounted at the same interest rate.

Now we turn our attention to the actual implementation of the four above-mentioned capital budgeting techniques (1) the payback method, (2) the return on assets, (3) the net present value, and (4) the internal rate of return. We shall see that only one technique — the net present value method — satisfies all four of the desirable properties for capital budgeting criteria.

Payback Method

The payback period is the number of years required to recover the initial capital outlay on a project. The payback periods for the four projects in Table 6.2 are given below.

Project A, 2-year payback

Project B, 4-year payback

Project C, 4-year payback

Project D, 3-year payback

If management were adhering strictly to the payback method, then Project A would be chosen as the best among the four mutually exclusive alternatives. Even a casual look at the numbers indicates that this would be a bad decision. The difficulty with the payback method is that it does not consider all cash flows and it fails to discount them. Failure to consider all cash flows results in ignoring the large negative cash flows which occur in the last two years of Project A. Failure to discount them means that management would be indifferent between the following two cash flow patterns:

	Cash Flows	
Year	G	G*
0	−1,000	−1,000
1	100	900
2	900	100

because they have the same payback period. Yet no one with a positive opportunity cost of funds would choose Project G because Project G* returns cash much faster.

The payback method also violates the value additivity principle. Consider the following example. Projects 1 and 2 are mutually exclusive but Project 3 is independent. Hence, it is possible to undertake Projects 1 and 3 in combination, 2 and 3 in combination, or any of the projects in isolation. The table on page 109 shows the alternatives and their cash flows.

[7]A discussion of how the cost of capital is calculated is presented in Chapter 21. For now, the cost of capital should be considered as the firm's opportunity cost of making a particular investment. That is, if the firm does not make a particular investment, it saves the cost of this investment; and if it can invest these funds in another project of equivalent risk that provides a return of 10 percent, then its opportunity cost of making the first investment is 10 percent.

Year	1	2	Cash Flows 3	1 and 3	2 and 3
0	−1	−1	−1	−2	−2
1	0	1	0	0	1
2	2	0	0	2	0
3	−1	1	3	2	4
Payback in years	2	1	3	2	3

If projects are considered separately, then Project 2 looks best, with a one-year payback. But if combinations of projects are considered, now 1 and 3 looks better than 2 and 3. This is a clear violation of the value additivity principle because the decision we reach by studying mutually exclusive alternatives (for example, Project 2 is best) is different from the decision reached when projects are considered as combinations (for example, 1 and 3 is best). Shortly, we shall show that the internal rate of return method also violates the value additivity principle, but the net present value method does not.

The only argument in favor of using the payback method is that it is easy to use, but with the advent of pocket calculators and computers, we feel that other more correct capital budgeting techniques are just as easy to use.

Return on Assets (ROA)

The return on assets (ROA) which is also sometimes called the return on investment (ROI) is an average rate of return technique. It is computed by averaging the expected cash flows over the life of a project and then dividing the average annual cash flow by the initial investment outlay.[8] For example, the ROA for Project B in Table 6.2 is computed from the following definition:

$$\text{ROA} = \left(\sum_{t=0}^{n} \text{Cash flow}_t / n \right) \div I_0$$

where

$$I_0 = \text{Initial cash outlay} = \$1,500$$

$$n = \text{Life of the project} = 5 \text{ years.}$$

Substituting in the correct numbers from Table 6.2, we have

$$\text{ROA} = \left[\frac{-\$1,500 + \$0 + \$0 + \$450 + \$1,050 + \$1,950}{5} \right] \div \$1,500$$

$$= \frac{\$1,950}{5} \div \$1,500$$

$$= \frac{\$390}{\$1,500} = 26\%.$$

---

[8]Sometimes the definition of cash flows for the ROA technique is different from Equations 6.1 or 6.2. Alternate definitions invalidate the technique even beyond the criticisms which we mention. This particular illustration is based on the practice of a large food products company described in a published finance case.

The ROA's for the four projects are

Project A, -8%

Project B, 26%

Project C, 25%

Project D, 22%

The ROA criterion chooses Project B as best. The major problem with ROA is that it does not take the time value of money into account. We would have obtained exactly the same ROA for Project B, even if the order of cash flows had been reversed with $1,950 received now, $1,050 at the end of Year 1, $450 at the end of Year 2, and $-$1,500 at the end of Year 5. But no one with a positive opportunity cost of capital would be indifferent between the alternatives. The opposite ordering of cash flows would always be preferred.

Net Present Value Method

As the flaws in the payback and ROA methods were recognized, people began to search for methods of evaluating projects that would recognize that a dollar received immediately is preferable to a dollar received at some future date. This recognition led to the development of *discounted cash flow (DCF) techniques* to take account of the time value of money. One such discounted cash flow technique is called the net present value method. *To implement this approach, find the present value of the expected net cash flows of an investment, discounted at the cost of capital, and subtract from it the initial cost outlay of the project.*[9] If the net present value is positive, the project should be accepted; if negative, it should be rejected. If two projects are mutually exclusive, the one with the higher net present value should be chosen.

The equation for the net present value (NPV) is[10]

$$\text{NPV} = \left[\frac{\text{CF}_1}{(1 + k)^1} + \frac{\text{CF}_2}{(1 + k)^2} + \ldots + \frac{\text{CF}_n}{(1 + k)^n} \right] - I_0.$$

$$= \sum_{t=1}^{n} \frac{\text{CF}_t}{(1 + k)^t} - I_0. \qquad (6.3)$$

Here CF_1, CF_2, and so forth represent the net cash flows; k is the firm's cost of capital; I_0 is the initial cost of the project; and n is the project's expected life.

The net present value of Project C in Table 6.2 is calculated below by multiplying each cash flow by the appropriate discount factor (PVIF), assuming that the cost of capital, k, is 10 percent.

---

[9]If costs are spread over several years, the present value of capital outlays must be taken into account. Suppose, for example, that a firm bought land in 1978, erected a building in 1979, installed equipment in 1980, and started production in 1981. One could treat 1978 as the base year, comparing the present value of the costs as of 1978 to the present value of the benefit stream as of that date.

[10]The second equation is simply a shorthand expression in which sigma (Σ) signifies "sum up" or add the present values of n cash flow terms. If $t = 1$, then $\text{CF}_t = \text{CF}_1$ and $1/(1 + k)^t = 1/(1 + k)^1$; if $t = 2$, then $\text{CF}_t = \text{CF}_2$ and $1/(1 + k)^t = 1/(1 + k)^2$; and so on, until $t = n$, the last year the project provides any cash flows. The symbol $\sum\limits_{t=1}^{n}$ simply says, "Go through the following process: Let $t = 1$ and find the PV of CF_1; then let $t = 2$ and find the PV of CF_2. Continue until the PV of each individual cash flow has been found and then add the PV's of these individual cash flows to find the PV of the asset."

Year	Cash Flow	×	PVIF	=	PV
0	−1,500		1.000		−1,500.00
1	150		.909		136.35
2	300		.826		247.80
3	450		.751		337.95
4	600		.683		409.80
5	1,875		.621		1,164.38
				NPV =	796.28

The net present values of all four projects in Table 6.2 are:

Project A   NPV = $−610.95.

Project B   NPV = $ 766.05.

Project C   NPV = $ 796.28.

Project D   NPV = $ 778.80.

If these projects were independent instead of mutually exclusive, we would reject A and accept B, C, and D. Why? Since they are mutually exclusive, we select the project with the greatest NPV, Project C. The NPV of the project is exactly the same as the increase in shareholders' wealth. This fact makes it the correct decision rule for capital budgeting purposes. The NPV rule also meets the other three general principles required for an optimal capital budgeting criterion. It takes all cash flows into account. All cash flows are discounted at the appropriate market-determined opportunity cost of capital in order to determine their present values. Also, the NPV rule obeys the value additivity principle.

   The net present value of a project is exactly the same as the increase in shareholders' wealth. To see why, start by assuming a project has zero net present value. In this case, the project returns enough cash flow to do three things:

1.   To pay off all interest payments to creditors who have lent money to finance the project,
2.   To pay all expected returns (dividends and capital gains) to shareholders who have put up equity for the project, and
3.   To pay off the original principal, I_0, which was invested in the project.

Thus, a zero net present value project is one which earns a fair return to compensate both debt holders and equity holders, each according to the returns which they expect for the risk they take. A positive NPV project earns more than the required rate of return, and equity holders receive all excess cash flows because debt holders have a fixed claim on the firm. Consequently, equity holders' wealth increases by exactly the NPV of the project. It is this direct link between shareholders' wealth and the NPV definition which makes the net present value criterion so important in decision making.

Internal Rate of Return Method

The internal rate of return (IRR) is defined as the *interest rate that equates the present value of the expected future cash flows, or receipts, to the initial cost outlay.* The equation for calculating the internal rate of return is

$$\frac{CF_1}{(1 + IRR)^1} + \frac{CF_2}{(1 + IRR)^2} + \ldots + \frac{CF_n}{(1 + IRR)^n} - I_0 = 0 \qquad \text{(6.4)}$$

$$\sum_{t=1}^{n} \frac{CF_t}{(1 + IRR)^t} - I_0 = 0.$$

Here we know the value of I_0 and also the values of CF_1, CF_2, . . . , CF_n, but we do not know the value of IRR. Thus, we have an equation with one unknown, and we can solve for the value of IRR. Some value of IRR will cause the sum of the discounted receipts to equal the initial cost of the project, making the equation equal to zero, and that value of IRR is defined as the internal rate of return.

Notice that the internal rate of return formula, Equation 6.4, is simply the NPV formula, Equation 6.3, solved for that particular value of k that causes the NPV to equal zero. In other words, the same basic equation is used for both methods, but in the NPV method, the discount rate (k) is specified as the market-determined opportunity cost of capital, while in the IRR method, the NPV is set equal to zero and the value of IRR that forces the NPV to equal zero is found.

The internal rate of return may be found by trial and error. First, compute the present value of the cash flows from an investment, using an arbitrarily selected interest rate — for example, 10 percent. Then compare the present value so obtained with the investment's cost. If the present value is higher than the cost figure, try a higher interest rate and go through the procedure again. Conversely, if the present value is lower than the cost, lower the interest rate and repeat the process. Continue until the present value of the flows from the investment is approximately equal to its cost. *The interest rate that brings about this equality is defined as the internal rate of return.*[11]

Table 6.3 shows computations for the IRR of Project D in Table 6.2, and Figure 6.2 graphs the relationship between the discount rate and the NPV of the project.

Table 6.3 IRR for Project D

Year	Cash Flow	PV @10%		PV @20%		PV @25%		PV @25.4%	
0	−1,500	1.000	−1,500.00	1.000	−1,500.00	1.000	−1,500.00	1.000	−1,500.00
1	300	.909	272.70	.833	249.90	.800	240.00	.797	239.10
2	450	.826	371.70	.694	312.30	.640	288.00	.636	286.20
3	750	.751	563.25	.579	434.25	.512	384.00	.507	380.25
4	750	.683	512.25	.482	361.50	.410	307.50	.404	303.00
5	900	.621	558.90	.402	361.80	.328	295.20	.322	289.80
	1,650		778.80		219.75		14.70		−1.65

---

[11]In order to reduce the number of trials required to find the internal rate of return, it is important to minimize the error at each iteration. One reasonable approach is to make as good a first approximation as possible and then to "straddle" the internal rate of return by making fairly large changes in the interest rate early in the iterative process. In practice, if many projects are to be evaluated or if many years are involved, relatively inexpensive hand calculators can be used to solve for the internal rate of return.

Figure 6.2 NPV of Project D at Different Discount Rates

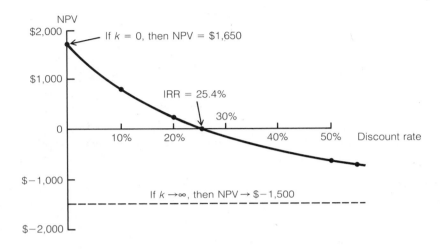

In Figure 6.2, the NPV of Project D's cash flows decreases as the discount rate is increased. If the discount rate is zero, there is no time value of money and the NPV of a project is simply the sum of its cash flows. For Project D, the NPV equals $1,650 when the discount rate is zero. At the opposite extreme, if the discount rate is infinite, then the future cash flows are valueless and the NPV of Project D is its current cash flow, −$1,500. Somewhere between these two extremes is a discount rate which makes the NPV equal to zero. In Figure 6.2, we see that the IRR for Project D is 25.4 percent. The IRR's for each of the four projects in Table 6.2 are given below.

Project A   IRR = −200%.
Project B   IRR =   20.9%.
Project C   IRR =   22.8%.
Project D   IRR =   25.4%.

If we use the IRR criterion and the projects are independent, we accept any project which has an IRR greater than the opportunity cost of capital, which is 10 percent. Therefore, we would accept Projects B, C, and D. However, since these projects are mutually exclusive, the IRR rule leads us to accept Project D as best.

Comparison of the NPV and IRR Methods

The numerical example given in Table 6.2 illustrates that each of the four capital budgeting criteria favors a different project. The results are summarized in Table 6.4 where the "best" project for each criterion is shown in a box.

We have already rejected the payback and ROA techniques because they fail to discount cash flows, but what about the NPV and IRR criteria? They both are discounted cash flow

Criterion	Project A	Project B	Project C	Project D
Payback	2 years	4 years	4 years	3 years
ROA	−8%	26%	25%	22%
NPV	$−610.95	$766.05	$796.28	$778.80
IRR	−200%	20.9%	22.8%	25.4%

Table 6.4   Mutually Exclusive Projects Selected by Different Capital Budgeting Criteria

techniques, yet they select different mutually exclusive projects as optimal. Which technique is best? After all, only one criterion can select the mutually exclusive project which maximizes shareholders' wealth. We shall see that *the NPV criterion is the only capital budgeting method which is always consistent with shareholder wealth maximization*. The material in this section shows why.

As noted above, the NPV method (1) accepts all independent projects whose NPV's are greater than zero and (2) ranks mutually exclusive projects by their NPV's, selecting the project with the higher NPV according to Equation 6.5:

$$\text{NPV} = \sum_{t=1}^{n} \frac{\text{CF}_t}{(1 + k)^t} - I_0. \tag{6.5}$$

The IRR method, on the other hand, finds the value of IRR that forces Equation 6.6 to equal zero:

$$\text{NPV} = \sum_{t=1}^{n} \frac{\text{CF}_t}{(1 + \text{IRR})^t} - I_0 = 0. \tag{6.6}$$

The IRR method calls for accepting independent projects where IRR, the internal rate of return, is greater than k, the cost of capital, and for selecting among mutually exclusive projects depending on which has the highest IRR.

It is apparent that the only structural difference between the NPV and IRR methods lies in the discount rates used in the two equations — all the values in the equations are identical except for IRR and k. Further, we can see that if IRR > k, then NPV > 0.[12] Accordingly, it would appear that the two methods give the same accept/reject decisions for specific projects — if a project is acceptable under the NPV criterion, it is also acceptable if the IRR method is used. However, the following example illustrates that this statement is incorrect. Consider the following pattern of cash flows:

---

[12]This can be seen by noting that NPV = 0 only when IRR = k:

$$\text{NPV} = \sum_{t=1}^{n} \frac{\text{CF}_t}{(1 + k)^t} - I_0 = \sum_{t=1}^{n} \frac{\text{CF}_t}{(1 + \text{IRR})^t} - I_0 = 0,$$

if and only if IRR = k. If IRR > k, then NPV > 0, and if IRR < k, then NPV < 0.

Year	Cash Flow	PV @10%
1	400	363.60
2	400	330.40
3	−1,000	−751.00
		− 57.00

Figure 6.3 illustrates the NPV for different discount rates. The internal rate of return is 15.8 percent. If the appropriate opportunity cost of capital is $k = 10\%$, then strict adherence to the IRR rule would lead us to accept the project since IRR $> k$. However, when we discount the cash flows at 10 percent, we discover that the NPV is $\$-57.00$. According to the NPV rule, the project should be rejected. Once again, the NPV and IRR rules give different answers.

Upon careful examination, we shall see that there are (at least) three reasons why the IRR rule is an inferior capital budgeting criterion: It (1) makes a bad reinvestment rate assumption, (2) violates the value additivity principle, and (3) can result in multiple IRR's for the same project. We shall examine each of these problems in turn.

1.   The *reinvestment rate assumption* is actually an inaccurate use of terminology for what should be called the *opportunity cost assumption*.[13] All investment projects of equal risk will have the same opportunity cost from the point of view of all investors. We have assumed throughout the chapter that all four projects in Table 6.2 are equally risky and that all investors require at least a 10 percent rate of return in order to invest in the projects. The rate of 10 percent is the appropriate opportunity cost of capital for the assumed level of risk. That is why we discount the cash flows at a 10

Figure 6.3   The IRR versus the NPV

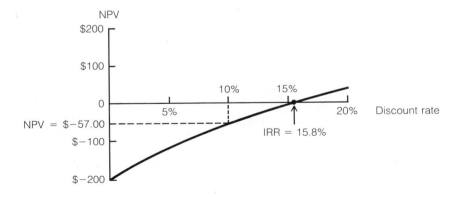

---

[13]The phrase "reinvestment rate" is misleading because it causes people to become involved in a debate about whether or not cash flows from the project can be reinvested at the IRR of the project. The real issue is, given the risk of the project, then at what rate can funds be invested (or reinvested) somewhere else for the same level of risk. Thus the appropriate "reinvestment rate" is the opportunity cost of capital.

percent rate. It would not be appropriate to discount the cash flows at a higher rate unless they had higher risk. But this is exactly what the IRR method does. The cash flows for Project C are discounted at a 22.8 percent rate (the IRR for Project C), and for Project D, they are discounted at 25.4 percent (the IRR for Project D). Although the projects have the same risk, they are discounted at different rates, neither of which is the correct opportunity cost of capital given the risk of the projects. The major difficulty with the IRR method is that it makes an inappropriate opportunity cost assumption. Projects of equal risk do not have different opportunity costs of capital.

The NPV rule, on the other hand, makes the correct assumption that the cash flows for all projects of equal risk must be discounted at the same rate. Figure 6.4 illustrates this point by graphing the relationship between the NPV and various discount rates for the two projects whose cash flows are given below. Notice that the IRR is the rate which causes the NPV to be equal to zero. As illustrated, the IRR for Project A (that is, 23 percent) is greater than for Project B (17 percent). Yet, given that these two projects have equivalent risk, every investor would discount their cash flows at, let's say, a 10 percent opportunity cost of capital.[14] And at a 10 percent

Figure 6.4   Comparison of Two Mutually Exclusive Projects

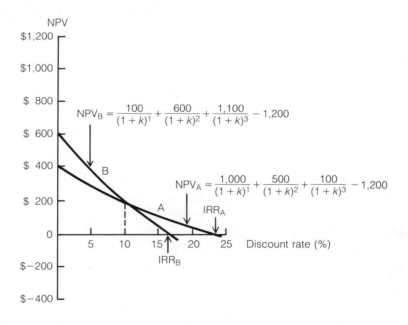

$$NPV_B = \frac{100}{(1+k)^1} + \frac{600}{(1+k)^2} + \frac{1,100}{(1+k)^3} - 1,200$$

$$NPV_A = \frac{1,000}{(1+k)^1} + \frac{500}{(1+k)^2} + \frac{100}{(1+k)^3} - 1,200$$

[14]We have to wait until Chapters 16 and 17 to learn how to actually estimate the riskiness of different projects and how to modify our capital budgeting procedures to evaluate projects of different risk.

discount rate, Project B has the higher NPV (NPV for A = $197 and NPV for B = $213). If the opportunity cost of capital is higher than approximately 11 percent, then Project A has the higher NPV.

	Cash Flow from Project		Interest Factor	Present Values	
Year	A	B	PVIF @10%	A	B
0	$-1,200	$-1,200	1.000	$-1,200.00	$-1,200.00
1	1,000	100	.909	909.00	90.90
2	500	600	.826	413.00	495.60
3	100	1,100	.751	75.10	826.10
				$ 197.10	$ 212.60

2. *NPV, the IRR, and Terminal Value.* As mentioned earlier, the correct interpretation of the reinvestment rate is that it is the opportunity cost of capital. The reinvestment rate refers to investing funds elsewhere, in projects of equivalent risk. It does not refer to the rate at which funds can be put back into a given project. Consider the two projects whose cash flows are provided below.

Project	Year 0	Year 1	Year 2	Year 3	Cost of Capital	NPV	IRR
X	$-10,000	$5,000	$5,000	$ 5,000	10%	$2,430	23.4%
Y	$-10,000	$ 0	$ 0	$17,280	10%	$2,977	20.0%

The NPV rule is unambiguous. Project Y should be chosen, if they are mutually exclusive, because it has the greater NPV at a discount rate of 10 percent.

There is the temptation, however, to argue that Project X is superior because its cash flows can be reinvested each year at its IRR, which is 23.4 percent. Project Y, on the other hand, has no intermediate cash flows to be reinvested. In fact, the cash inflows from X will have a terminal value of $18,783 if reinvested at 23.4 percent. Project Y's terminal value remains at $17,280. On this basis, Project X seems better because it has a higher terminal value. The fallacy with this line of reasoning is that the cash inflows from Project X cannot be reinvested back into Project X. It required only a $10,000 initial outlay. Additional investments of $5,000 in years 2 and 3 are impossible. The only reasonable assumption is that the cash flows from either project can be reinvested somewhere else at the fair rate of return for projects of equivalent risk. This rate is the opportunity cost of capital, 10 percent, which is used to determine the project NPV's in the first place.

Terminal values, when correctly calculated, always provide the same capital budgeting decision as net present values. The correct reinvestment rate is the project's cost of capital, not its IRR.

3. The *value additivity principle* demands that managers be able to consider one project independently of all others. In order to demonstrate that the IRR criterion can violate the value additivity principle, consider the three projects whose cash flows are given in Table 6.5.[15]

---

[15]This example is taken from Copeland and Weston [1983, p. 32].

Table 6.5   The IRR Rule Violates Value Additivity

Year	Project 1	Project 2	Project 3	PV Factor @10%	1 + 3	2 + 3
0	−100	−100	−100	1.000	−200	−200
1	0	225	450	.909	450	675
2	550	0	0	.826	550	0

Project	NPV @10%	IRR
1	$354.30	134.5%
2	104.53	125.0%
3	309.05	350.0%
1 + 3	663.35	212.8%
2 + 3	413.58	237.5%

Projects 1 and 2 are mutually exclusive, and Project 3 is independent of them. If the value additivity principle holds, we should be able to choose the better of the two mutually exclusive projects without having to consider the independent project. The NPV's of the three projects as well as their IRR's are also given in Table 6.5. If we use the IRR rule to choose between Projects 1 and 2, we would select Project 1. But if we consider combinations of projects, then the IRR rule would prefer Projects 2 and 3 to Projects 1 and 3. The IRR rule prefers Project 1 in isolation but Project 2 in combination with the independent project. In this example, the IRR rule does not obey the value additivity principle. The implication for management is that it would have to consider all possible combinations of projects and choose the combination which has the greatest internal rate of return. If, for example, a firm had only five projects, it would need to consider 32 different combinations.

The NPV rule always obeys the value additivity principle. Given that the opportunity cost of capital is 10 percent, we would choose Project 1 as being the best either by itself or in combination with Project 3. Note that the combinations of 1 and 3 or 2 and 3 are simply the sums of the NPV's of the projects considered separately. Consequently, if we adopt the NPV rule, the value of the firm is the sum of the values of the separate projects. Later (in Chapter 17) we shall see that this result holds even in a world with uncertainty where the firm may be viewed as a portfolio of risky projects.

4.   *Multiple rates of return* are another difficulty with the IRR rule. A classic example of this situation has come to be known as the oil-well pump problem. An oil company is trying to decide whether or not to install a high-speed pump on a well which is already in operation. The estimated incremental cash flows are given in Table 6.6. The pump will cost $1,600 to install. During its first year of operation, it will produce $10,000 more oil than the pump which is currently in place. But during the second year, the high-speed pump produces $10,000 less oil because the well has been depleted. The question is whether or not to accept the rapid pumping technique, which speeds up cash flows in the near term at the expense of cash flows in the long term. Figure 6.5 shows the NPV of the project for different discount rates. If the

---

Table 6.6   Oil-Well Pump Incremental Cash Flows

Year	Estimated Cash Flow
0	− 1,600
1	10,000
2	−10,000

---

opportunity cost of capital is 10 percent, the NPV rule would reject the project because it has negative NPV at that rate. If we are using the IRR rule, the project has two IRR's, 25 percent and 400 percent. Since both exceed the opportunity cost of capital, the project would probably be accepted.

Mathematically, the multiple IRR's are a result of Descartes' rule of signs, which implies that every time the cash flows change signs, there may be a new (positive, real) root to the problem. For the above example, the signs of cash flows change twice. There are two roots, that is, two IRR's, and neither of them has any economic meaning.

5.   *Summarizing the comparison between the NPV and IRR criteria*, we see that the IRR has many difficulties which invalidate it as a generally acceptable capital budgeting rule. First, the IRR method assumes that funds invested in projects have opportunity

---

Figure 6.5   Multiple Internal Rates of Return

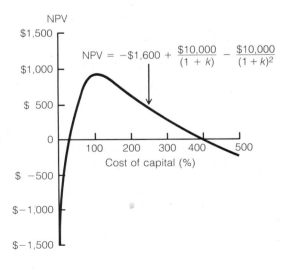

$$NPV = -\$1,600 + \frac{\$10,000}{(1 + k)} - \frac{\$10,000}{(1 + k)^2}$$

costs equal to the IRR for the project. This implicit reinvestment rate assumption violates the requirement that cash flows be discounted at the market-determined opportunity cost of capital which is appropriate for their risk. Second, the IRR does not obey the value additivity principle, and, consequently, managers who use the IRR cannot consider projects independently of each other. Finally, the IRR rule can lead to multiple rates of return whenever the sign of cash flows changes more than once. The NPV rule avoids all the problems to which the IRR is heir. It discounts cash flows at the opportunity cost of funds; it obeys the value additivity principle; and most important, it is precisely the same thing as maximizing shareholders' wealth.

Capital Budgeting: An Example

From this point forward, we shall use the net present value method for all capital budgeting decisions. The following replacement decision is an example of a typical problem. It illustrates the use of cash flows for capital budgeting decisions. It emphasizes that all project cash flows must be represented as *changes* in the firm's cash flows. And it demonstrates the NPV method of discounted cash flows.

The Widget Division of the Culver Company, a profitable, diversified manufacturing firm, purchased a machine 5 years ago at a cost of $7,500. The machine had an expected life of 15 years at time of purchase and a zero estimated salvage value at the end of the 15 years. It is being depreciated on a straight line basis and has a book value of $5,000 at present. The division manager reports that, for $12,000 (including installation), a new machine can be bought which, over its 10-year life, will expand sales from $10,000 to $11,000 a year. Further, it will reduce labor and raw materials usage sufficiently to cut operating costs from $7,000 to $5,000. The new machine has an estimated salvage value of $2,000 at the end of 10 years. The old machine's current market value is $1,000. Taxes are at a 40 percent rate and are paid quarterly, and the firm's cost of capital is 10 percent. Should Culver buy the new machine?

The decision calls for five steps: (1) estimating the actual cash outlay attributable to the new investment, (2) determining the incremental cash flows, (3) finding the present value of the incremental cash flows, (4) adding the present value of the expected salvage value to the present value of the total cash flows, and (5) seeing whether the NPV is positive. These steps are explained further in the following sections.

Estimated Cash Outlay.   The net initial cash outlay consists of these items: (1) payment to the manufacturer, (2) tax effects, and (3) proceeds from the sale of the old machine. Culver must make a $12,000 payment to the manufacturer of the machine, but its next quarterly tax bill will be reduced because of the loss it will incur when it sells the old machine: Tax saving = (Loss)(Tax rate) = ($4,000)(0.4) = $1,600. The tax reduction will occur because the old machine, which is carried at $5,000, will be written down by $4,000 ($5,000 less $1,000 salvage value) immediately upon the purchase of the new one.

To illustrate, suppose the Culver Company's taxable income in the quarter in which the new machine is to be purchased would have been $100,000 without the purchase of the new machine and the consequent write-off of the old machine. With a 40 percent tax rate, Culver would have had to write a check for $40,000 to pay its tax bill. However, if it bought the new machine and sold the old one, it would take an operating loss of $4,000 — the $5,000 book value on the old machine less the salvage value of $1,000. (The loss is an operating loss, not a capital loss, because it is simply recognizing that depreciation charges, an operating cost, were too low during the old machine's five-year life.)[16] With this $4,000 additional operating cost, the next quarter's taxable income would be reduced from $100,000 to $96,000, and the tax bill from $40,000 to $38,400. This means, of course, that the firm's cash outflow for taxes would be $1,600 less *because* of the purchase of the new machine.

In addition, there would be a cash inflow of $1,000 from the sale of the old machine. The net result is that the purchase of the new machine would involve an immediate net cash outlay of $9,400, the cost used for capital budgeting purposes:

Invoice price of new machine	$12,000
Less: Tax savings	−1,600
Salvage of old machine	−1,000
Net cash outflow (cost)	$ 9,400

If additional working capital is required as a result of a capital budgeting decision, as would generally be true for expansion investments (as opposed to cost-reducing replacement investments), this factor must be taken into account. The amount of *net* working capital (additional current assets required as a result of the expansion minus any spontaneous funds generated by the expansion) is estimated and added to the initial cost outlay. We assume that Culver will not need any additional working capital, so this factor is ignored in the example.

Annual Benefits. Column 1 in Table 6.7 shows the Widget Division's estimated income statement as it would be without the new machine; Column 2 shows the statement as it would look if the new investment were made. (It is assumed that these figures are

---

Table 6.7   Comparative Accounting Income Statement Framework for Considering Cash Flows

	Without New Investment (1)		With New Investment (2)		Difference: (2) − (1) (3)	
Sales		$10,000		$11,000		$1,000
Operating costs	$7,000		$5,000		($2,000)	
Depreciation	500		1,000		500	
Interest charges	500		1,000		500	
Income before taxes		$ 2,000		$ 4,000		$2,000
Taxes (T = 0.4)		800		1,600		800
Income after taxes		$ 1,200		$ 2,400		$1,200
Dividends paid		600		1,200		600
Additions to retained earnings		$ 600		$ 1,200		$ 600

---

[16]If Culver traded in the old machine as partial payment for the new one, the loss would be added to the depreciable cost of the new machine, and there would be no immediate tax saving.

Table 6.8   Net Operating Cash Flow Statement

	Without New Investment (1)	With New Investment (2)	Difference or Incremental Flows: (2) − (1) (3)
Sales	$10,000	$11,000	$1,000
Operating cash costs (O)[a]	7,000	5,000	(2,000)
Net operating cash income (NOI)[a]	$ 3,000	$ 6,000	$3,000
Taxes (T = 0.4)	1,200	2,400	1,200
After-tax operating income: NOI (1 − T)	$ 1,800	$ 3,600	$1,800
Depreciation tax benefit (T × Dep)	200	400	200
Net cash flows (CF)	$ 2,000	$ 4,000	$2,000

[a]Does not include depreciation as a cash cost, since this is a cash flow statement and depreciation is not a cash cost.

applicable for each of the next ten years; if this is not the case, then cash flow estimates must be made for each year.) Column 3 shows the differences between the first two columns.

For capital budgeting analysis, the cash flows that are discounted are the net after-tax operating cash flows. The data in Table 6.7 represent accounting income and must be adjusted in order to be on a cash rather than accrual basis and also to exclude all payments to the sources of financing. In Table 6.7, depreciation is a noncash charge; interest charges and dividends paid are cash flows to the financing sources.

While depreciation is a noncash charge, it is deductible for computing income tax, and income tax payments are cash flows. The cash flows must include the depreciation tax benefits.

Table 6.8 shows the operating cash flows without the new investment, with the new investment, and the difference, or incremental flows.

Finding the _PV_ of the Benefits. We have explained in detail how to measure the annual benefits. The next step is to determine the present value of the benefit stream. The interest factor for a ten-year, 10 percent annuity is found to be 6.1446 from Table A.4. This factor, when multiplied by the $2,000 incremental cash flow, results in a present value of $12,289.

Salvage Value. The new machine has an estimated salvage value of $2,000; that is, Culver expects to be able to sell the machine for $2,000 after ten years of use. The present value of an inflow of $2,000 due in ten years is $771, found as $2,000 × 0.3855. If additional working capital had been required and included in the initial cash outlay, this amount would be added to the salvage value of the machine because the working capital would be recovered if and when the project is abandoned.

Notice that the salvage value is a return of capital, not taxable income, so it is _not_ subject to income taxes. Of course, when the new machine is actually retired ten years hence, it might be sold for more or less than the expected $2,000, so either taxable income or a deductible operating loss could arise, but $2,000 is the best present estimate of the new machine's salvage value.

Determining the Net Present Value.   The project's net present value is found as the sum of the present values of the inflows, or benefits, less the outflows, or costs:

Inflows: *PV* of annual benefits	$12,289
 *PV* of salvage value, new machine	771
Less: Net cash outflow, or cost	(9,400)
Net present value (NPV)	$ 3,660

Since the NPV is positive, the project should be accepted.

Capital Budgeting Worksheet

Table 6.9 presents a worksheet for evaluating capital projects. The top section shows net cash flows at the time of investment; since all these flows occur immediately, no discounting is required and the interest factor is 1.0. The lower section of the table shows future cash flows — benefits from increased sales and/or reduced costs, depreciation, and salvage value. These flows occur over time, so it is necessary to convert them to present values. The NPV as determined in the alternative format, $3,660, agrees with the figure calculated earlier.

Table 6.9   Alternative Worksheet for Capital Budgeting Project Evaluation

	Amount before Tax	Amount after Tax[a]	Year Event Occurs	PV Factor @10%	PV
Outflows at time investment is made					
$\quad$ Investment in new equipment	$12,000	$12,000	0	1.0000	$12,000
$\quad$ Salvage value of old	(1,000)	(1,000)	0	1.0000	(1,000)
$\quad$ Tax effect of the sale[b]	(4,000)	(1,600)	0	1.0000	(1,600)
$\quad$ Increased working capital (if necessary)	c	—	0	1.0000	—
$\quad\quad$ Total initial outflows (*PV* of costs)					$ 9,400
Inflows, or annual returns					
$\quad$ Benefits[d] (NOI)	$ 3,000	$ 1,800	1-10	6.1446	$11,060
$\quad$ Depreciation on new (annual)[b]	1,000	400	1-10	6.1446	2,458
$\quad$ Depreciation on old (annual)[b]	(500)	(200)	1-10	6.1446	(1,229)
$\quad$ Salvage value on new	2,000	2,000	10	0.3855	771
$\quad$ Return of working capital (if necessary)	c	—	10	0.3855	—
$\quad\quad$ Total periodic inflows (*PV* of benefits)					$13,060

NPV = *PV* of benefits less *PV* of cost = $13,060 − $9,400 = $3,660.

[a]Amount after tax equals amount before tax times T or (1 − T), where T = Tax rate.
[b]Deductions (tax loss and depreciation) are multiplied by T.
[c]Not applicable.
[d]Benefits are multiplied by (1 − T).

Accelerated Depreciation

Thus far in our illustrations of capital budgeting, it has been assumed that straight line depreciation was used, thus enabling us to derive uniform cash flows over the life of the investment. Realistically, however, firms usually employ *accelerated depreciation* methods; when such is the case, it is necessary to modify the procedures outlined thus far. With accelerated depreciation, the deduction for depreciation expense is no longer a constant amount. It is, rather, larger in the earlier years and then declining. But for the entire period of a capital budgeting analysis, the present value of all of the accelerated depreciation tax deductions can be calculated.

Appendix C (at the end of the book) contains present value factors for accelerated depreciation. The factors in the table are developed as shown in the example in Table 6.10. In this example, we are interested in the factor for depreciation by the sum-of-years'-digits method over a five-year period with a 10 percent cost of capital. We first find the fraction of $1 that is received in each year and then discount that amount at 10 percent. The sum of the present values of the amounts received during the five years, shown in the product column, equals the accelerated depreciation factor (0.806 in this example).

To find the present value of the depreciation tax savings when an investment is depreciated by an accelerated method, we multiply the tax rate by the accelerated depreciation factor by the amount of the investment. For a $20,000 investment:

$$PV = T(\text{accelerated depreciation } PV \text{ factor})I$$

$$= 0.4(0.806)(\$20,000) = \$6,448.$$

Appendix C gives factors for both the sum-of-years'-digits and double declining balance depreciation methods, for various asset lives, and for different discount rates. The factor of 0.806 calculated in Table 6.10 can also be found in Appendix C—in the 10 percent column in the fifth period.

Table 6.10   Calculation of the Accelerated Depreciation Factor

Year	Depreciation Fraction Applied to Asset Cost	Amount of Depreciation	10% Discount Factor	Product
1	5/15	0.33333	0.9091	0.3030
2	4/15	0.26667	0.8264	0.2204
3	3/15	0.20000	0.7513	0.1503
4	2/15	0.13333	0.6830	0.0911
5	1/15	0.06667	0.6209	0.0414
	Totals 1.00	1.00000		Factor = 0.8062

Projects with Different Lives

All of the previous numerical examples in this chapter have compared mutually exclusive projects with the same economic life and the same initial capital outlay, that is, the same scale. We now turn our attention to capital budgeting techniques which handle the more realistic problem of projects with different lives and different scale.

Projects A and B in Table 6.11 are mutually exclusive and have different lives. If the opportunity cost of capital is 10 percent, the (simple) NPV's of the projects are

$$NPV(A) = \$723.14.$$
$$NPV(B) = \$894.44.$$

However, if these projects can be replicated at constant scale, then Project A should be superior to Project B because it recovers cash flow faster. As long as a project is not unique, we can reasonably assume that it can be repeated.

One way to put the two projects onto an equal footing is to string them together until the series of Project A repetitions lasts just as long as the series for Project B. An example which repeats Project A three times and Project B twice is illustrated in Figure 6.6. If Project A is repeated three times, it is equivalent to receiving an NPV of \$723.14 now, at the end of Year 2, and at the end of Year 4. This is really an annuity (paid in advance) with payments every two years. Its net present value is

$$NPV(2,3) = \$723.14 + \frac{\$723.14}{(1.1)^2} + \frac{\$723.14}{(1.1)^4} = \$1,814.69.$$

The notation NPV(2,3) means that we are finding the NPV of a two-year project which is replicated three times. A similar calculation for Project B shows that NPV(3,2) = \$1,566.45. Consequently, if the projects are repeated so that they both have a six-year cycle, we see that Project A is really superior.

The procedure which we have just described is very cumbersome. What would we do, for example, if we were comparing five projects whose expected lives were 3, 5, 7, 11, and 13 years? Each project would have to be replicated for $3 \times 5 \times 7 \times 11 \times 13 = 1,155$ years, a tedious task. The easiest thing to do (believe it or not) is to assume that each project is replicated at constant scale forever. Not only does every project have the same (infinite) life with this procedure, but also it is equivalent to maximizing shareholders' wealth. The

---

Table 6.11   Mutually Exclusive Projects with Different Lives

Year	Project A	Project B
0	$-17,500	$-17,500
1	10,500	7,000
2	10,500	7,000
3		8,313

Figure 6.6   An Ad Hoc Procedure for Comparing Projects with Different Lives

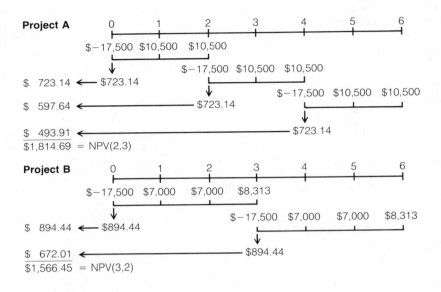

NPV of an infinite stream of projects which are replicated every n years is really the same thing as the present value of a long-run strategy of investing in the n-year project.

In order to compute NPV(n,∞), the net present value of an n-year project which is replicated at constant scale forever, we can write out the discounted present value of each net present value as follows:

$$\text{NPV}(n,\infty) = \text{NPV}(n) + \frac{\text{NPV}(n)}{(1 + k)^n} + \frac{\text{NPV}(n)}{(1 + k)^{2n}} + \cdots . \qquad (6.7)$$

Notice that the second term is the net present value received n years hence, which is then discounted at the opportunity cost of capital, k, for n years. The third term discounts NPV(n) for $2n$ years, and so forth. In order to simplify this expression, we employ exactly the same "trick" that was used in Chapter 5, for Equation 5.4a. First, let

$$\frac{1}{(1 + k)^n} = U.$$

Substituting this back into Equation 6.7, we have

$$\text{NPV}(n,\infty) = \text{NPV}(n) + U\,\text{NPV}(n) + U^2\,\text{NPV}(n) + \cdots + U^N\text{NPV}(n), \qquad (6.7a)$$

$$\text{NPV}(n,\infty) = \text{NPV}(n)[1 + U + U^2 + \cdots + U^N].$$

Next multiply both sides by U.

$$U[\text{NPV}(n,\infty)] = \text{NPV}(n)[U + U^2 + \cdots + U^N + U^{N+1}]. \tag{6.8}$$

Then, we subtract Equation 6.8 from Equation 6.7a in order to eliminate the infinite number of intermediate terms. The result leaves only the first term and the last as shown below:

$$\text{NPV}(n,\infty) - U\,\text{NPV}(n,\infty) = \text{NPV}(n)[1 - U^{N+1}].$$

Solving for $\text{NPV}(n,\infty)$, we have

$$\text{NPV}(n,\infty) = \text{NPV}(n)\,\frac{[1 - U^{N+1}]}{1 - U}.$$

Of course, the second term in the numerator on the right-hand side of the equation diminishes to zero if the number of terms is infinite.

$$\lim_{N\to\infty} U^{N+1} = \lim_{N\to\infty}\left[\frac{1}{1+k}\right]^{N+1} \to 0 \text{ since } \frac{1}{1+k} < 1.$$

The resulting, simplified equation is

$$\text{NPV}(n,\infty) = \text{NPV}(n)\,\frac{1}{1 - U}.$$

Substituting back the value of U, we have

$$\text{NPV}(n,\infty) = \text{NPV}(n)\left[\frac{1}{1 - (1/(1+k)^n)}\right].$$

Multiplying numerator and denominator by $(1+k)^n$, we have

$$\text{NPV}(n,\infty) = \text{NPV}(n)\left[\frac{(1+k)^n}{(1+k)^n - 1}\right]. \tag{6.9}$$

Equation 6.9 is the NPV of an n-year project replicated at constant scale an infinite number of times. We can use it to compare replicable projects with different lives because when their cash flow streams are replicated forever, it is as if they had the same (infinite) life.[17]

---

[17]It is often suggested that an equally good ranking criterion is the annual equivalent value which is obtained by multiplying $\text{NPV}(n,\infty)$ by the cost of capital, k.

$$\text{Annual equivalent value} = k[\text{NPV}(n,\infty)].$$

However, if projects have different risk, the annual equivalent value should not be used, because if two projects have exactly the same $\text{NPV}(n,\infty)$, then the one with the higher cost of capital (that is, the riskier project) will appear (incorrectly) to have the greater annual equivalent value.

If we apply Equation 6.9 to the projects in Table 6.11, we see that for the two-year project,

$$\text{NPV}(2,\infty) = \text{NPV}(2)\left[\frac{(1 + .1)^2}{(1 + .1)^2 - 1}\right]$$

$$= \$723.14\left[\frac{1.21}{1.21 - 1}\right]$$

$$= \$723.14(5.76) = \$4,165.29,$$

and for the three-year project,

$$\text{NPV}(3,\infty) = \$894.44\left[\frac{(1.1)^3}{(1.1)^3 - 1}\right]$$

$$= \$894.44(4.02) = \$3,595.65.$$

If you had the opportunity to purchase the right to own Project A and repeat it forever, you would pay up to \$4,165.29 for it. Thus, $\text{NPV}(n,\infty)$ is exactly the same thing as the increase in shareholders' wealth if Project A is replicable (not unique).

A good example of choosing among mutually exclusive projects with different lives is the decision of when to harvest an area of growing trees or when to bottle aging whiskey. For example, we could harvest trees after four years, five years, or nine years. Example cash flows are given in Table 6.12.[18] Each harvesting date is a mutually exclusive alternative. In fact, there are an infinite number of mutually exclusive harvesting decisions, and only the optimal harvest time will maximize shareholders' wealth.

One of the important aspects of the tree-harvesting problem is that the project can be repeated indefinitely. If we decide to harvest after five years, we will replicate the project by replanting the same acreage and then waiting five years before we harvest again. Consequently, the decision to harvest after five years is really a long-run strategy which goes on indefinitely. We can think of an infinite series of five-year projects which are replicated at constant scale, and $\text{NPV}(5,\infty)$ is the current value of the strategy.

If we were to employ the simple net present value technique (without replicating the project), and if the opportunity cost of capital is $k = 5\%$, we would discover that a strategy

Table 6.12   Cash Flows for Three Different Tree-Harvesting Strategies, $k = 5\%$

Strategy	I_0 = Initial outlay	CF = Revenue at harvest	NPV(n)	IRR	NPV(n, ∞)
Harvest every 4 years	\$−15,000	\$22,361	\$3,396	10.50%	\$19,154
Harvest every 5 years	\$−15,000	\$24,494	\$4,192	10.31%	\$19,365
Harvest every 9 years	\$−15,000	\$31,664	\$5,411	8.64%	\$15,225

[18]This example is taken from Copeland and Weston [1983, p. 54].

of harvesting every nine years yields the highest NPV(n). The results for all three mutually exclusive alternatives are shown in Table 6.12. The calculation for the nine-year strategy is

$$NPV(9) = \frac{CF_9}{(1 + k)^9} - I_0$$

$$= \frac{\$31,664}{(1.05)^9} - \$15,000$$

$$= \$31,664(.6446) - \$15,000 = \$5,411.$$

Unfortunately, the nine-year harvesting strategy does not maximize shareholders' wealth. Because the projects can be replicated, shareholders' wealth is the NPV of a harvesting strategy repeated forever; that is, it is NPV(n,∞). The calculation for the five-year strategy uses Equation 6.9:

$$NPV(5,\infty) = NPV(5)\left[\frac{(1 + .05)^5}{(1.05)^5 - 1}\right]$$

$$= \$4,192\left[\frac{1.27628}{1.27628 - 1}\right]$$

$$= \$4,192(4.6195) = \$19,365.$$

Since NPV(n,∞) is largest for the five-year strategy, it is the best choice among the mutually exclusive alternatives given in Table 6.12. It is the strategy which maximizes shareholders' wealth.[19]

Generally speaking, most projects are replicable in an approximate way. Even though technology may change, it is usually reasonable to assume that projects are replicable. Consequently, we recommend using the NPV(n,∞) procedure for comparing projects of different lives.

Projects with Different Scale

Next, let's turn our attention to projects with different scale, that is, different initial investment outlays. Table 6.13 provides data for five independent projects. All projects are assumed to have the same economic life of five years; hence, using the simple NPV criterion will give the same accept/reject decision as using NPV(n,∞). If there are no capital constraints, then the first four projects should be accepted because they all have a positive NPV. The total outlay would be $1,300,000.

Suppose that there is a capital rationing situation where our budget is restricted to $600,000. How shall we choose projects? First, note that under conditions of true capital rationing, the firm's value is not being maximized. If management were maximizing shareholders' wealth, it would accept all positive NPV projects and make an outlay of the full $1,300,000. If a financial manager does face strict capital rationing and cannot get the

---

[19]Note that the IRR for each project is also given in Table 6.12. Once again, the IRR gives the incorrect answer. It chooses a four-year harvest cycle, when five years is the best.

Table 6.13   Four Projects with Different Scale (5-year lives, k = 10%)

Project	Outlay = I_0	Annual CF	PV of CF	NPV	IRR	PI
A	$400,000	$121,347	$460,000	$60,000	15.7%	1.15
B	250,000	74,523	282,500	32,500	14.9	1.13
C	350,000	102,485	388,500	38,500	14.2	1.11
D	300,000	85,470	324,000	24,000	13.1	1.08
E	100,000	23,742	90,000	−10,000	6.0	.90

---

constraint lifted, the objective should be to maximize value subject to the constraint that the capital budget is not exceeded. This amounts to a linear (or integer) programming problem. If we designate V_j as the net present value of each project, w_j as the fraction of each project accepted, and I_j as the initial cash outlay, then the linear programming problem may be written[20]

$$\text{MAX} \sum_j w_j V_j \tag{6.10}$$

subject to:

$$\sum_j w_j I_j \leq \text{Budget},$$

$$w_j \leq 1.0.$$

The *profitability index* is an equivalent procedure for solving a one-period capital constraint problem. It has also often been proposed for dealing with the issue of projects of different scale. As we shall see, when correctly implemented, it is exactly the same as the NPV technique. We discuss it here because it is often misused. The profitability index (PI), or the benefit/cost ratio, as it is sometimes called, is defined as

$$PI = \frac{PV \text{ Benefits}}{Cost} = \left[\sum_{t=1}^{n} \frac{CF_t}{(1+k)^t} \right] \div I_0. \tag{6.11}$$

The PI shows the *relative* profitability of any project, or the *PV* of benefits per dollar cost.[21]

Looking at the last column of Table 6.13, it is tempting to meet our assumed $600,000 budget by accepting only Project A, which costs $400,000 and has the highest profitability index (PI = 1.15). However, this would be incorrect because there is $200,000 left over which must be invested in cash or marketable securities which have a profitability index of

---

[20]For further readings on this topic, the reader is referred to articles by Lorie and Savage [1955], Weingartner [1963], Baumol and Quandt [1965], Carleton [1969], Bernhard [1969], and Myers [1972].

[21]If costs are incurred in more than one year, they should be netted against cash inflows in the corresponding years; if costs exceed cash inflows in some years, the denominator must be the *PV* of the costs.

1.0. At best, the unused budget can earn only the opportunity cost of capital; therefore, the PV of the inflows will just equal the $200,000, leaving us with a PI of 1.0 for the excess funds.

Correct use of the PI requires that we find the combination of projects and excess funds which maximizes a weighted average profitability index. For example, if Projects B and C are selected, the weighted average PI is

$$PI = \frac{250,000}{600,000}(1.13) + \frac{350,000}{600,000}(1.11) = 1.1183.$$

It is computed by multiplying the PI of each project by the percentage of the total budget allocated to it. If Project A is selected, two-thirds of the total budget will be invested in the project, but the remaining one-third will be invested in cash and marketable securities which have a profitability index of only 1.0; hence, the weighted average profitability index will be

$$PI = \frac{400,000}{600,000}(1.15) + \frac{200,000}{600,000}(1.00) = 1.1000.$$

This example shows that, given a $600,000 budget, and the characteristics of the projects available, it is better to choose Projects B and C rather than Project A and excess cash. Note that this decision is exactly the same as maximizing the NPV of the firm subject to a budget constraint. The NPV of Projects B and C is $71,000 while Project A is worth only $60,000. Our advice to the reader is to stick with the NPV maximization principle and ignore the PI because, at best, it provides exactly the same results.

Summary

Capital budgeting, which involves commitments for large outlays whose benefits (or drawbacks) extend well into the future, is of the greatest significance to a firm. Decisions in these areas, therefore, will have a major impact on the future well-being of the firm. This chapter focused on how capital budgeting decisions can be made more effective in contributing to the health and growth of a firm. The discussion stressed the development of systematic procedures and rules for preparing a list of investment proposals, for evaluating them, and for selecting a cutoff point.

The chapter emphasized that one of the most crucial phases in the process of evaluating capital budget proposals is obtaining a dependable estimate of the benefits that will be obtained from undertaking the project. It cannot be overemphasized that the firm must allocate to competent and experienced personnel the making of these judgments.

Determining Cash Flows. The cash inflows from an investment are the incremental change in after-tax net operating cash income plus the incremental depreciation tax benefit; the cash outflow is the cost of the investment less the salvage value received on an old machine plus any tax loss (or less any tax savings) when the machine is sold.

Ranking Investment Proposals. Four commonly used procedures for ranking investment proposals were discussed in the chapter: payback, return on assets, net present value, and internal rate of return.

Payback is defined as the number of years required to return the original investment. Although the payback method is used frequently, it has serious conceptual weaknesses, because it ignores the facts that (1) some receipts come in beyond the payback period and (2) a dollar received today is more valuable than a dollar received in the future.

Return on assets is the average annual cash inflow divided by the original capital outlay. Like the payback method, its major conceptual problem is that it does not discount cash flows.

Net present value is defined as the present value of future returns, discounted at the cost of capital, minus the cost of the investment. The NPV method overcomes the conceptual flaws noted in the use of the payback method and ROA.

Internal rate of return is defined as the interest rate that equates the present value of future returns to the investment outlay. The internal rate of return method, like the NPV method, discounts cash flows.

In most cases, the two discounted cash flow methods give identical answers to these questions: Which of two mutually exclusive projects should be selected? How large should the total capital budget be? However, under certain circumstances, conflicts may arise. Such conflicts are caused primarily by the fact that the NPV and IRR methods make different assumptions about the rate at which cash flows may be reinvested, or the opportunity cost of cash flows. The assumption of the NPV method (that the opportunity cost is the cost of capital) is the correct one. Accordingly, our preference is for using the NPV method to make capital budgeting decisions.

Questions

6.1 A firm has $100 million available for capital expenditures. Suppose Project A involves purchasing $100 million of grain, shipping it overseas, and selling it within a year at a profit of $20 million. The project has an IRR of 20 percent and an NPV of $20 million, and it will cause earnings per share (EPS) to rise within one year. Project B calls for the use of the $100 million to develop a new process, acquire land, build a plant, and begin processing. Project B, which, if chosen, cannot be postponed, has an NPV of $50 million and an IRR of 30 percent. But the fact that some of the plant costs will be written off immediately, combined with the fact that no revenues will be generated for several years, means that accepting Project B will reduce short-run earnings per share (EPS).

    a) Should the short-run effects on EPS influence the choice between the two projects?

    b) How might situations such as the one described here influence a firm's decision to use payback as a screening criterion?

6.2 Are there conditions under which a firm might be better off if it chose a machine with a rapid payback rather than one with the largest rate of return?

6.3 Company X uses the payback method in evaluating investment proposals and is considering new equipment whose additional net after-tax earnings will be $150 a year. The equipment costs $500, and its expected life is ten years (straight line depreciation). The company uses a three-year payback as its criterion. Should the equipment be purchased under the above assumptions?

6.4 What are the most critical problems that arise in calculating a rate of return for a prospective investment?

6.5 What other factors in addition to rate of return analysis should be considered in determining capital expenditures?

6.6   Would it be beneficial for a firm to review its past capital expenditures and capital budgeting procedures? Explain.

6.7   Fiscal and monetary policies are tools used by the government to stimulate the economy. Using the analytical devices developed in this chapter, explain how each of the following might be expected to stimulate the economy by encouraging investment.
   a)   A speedup of tax-allowable depreciation
   b)   An easing of interest rates
   c)   Passage of a new federal program giving more aid to the poor
   d)   An investment tax credit

Problems

6.1   A firm has an opportunity to invest in a machine at a cost of $656,670. The net cash flows after taxes from the machine would be $210,000 per year and would continue for five years. The applicable cost of capital for this project is 12 percent.
   a)   Calculate the net present value for the investment.
   b)   What is the internal rate of return for the investment?
   c)   Should the investment be made?

6.2   The following facts are presented on an opportunity to invest in Machine A: Cost of equipment is $120,000. The life is ten years. The estimated after-tax salvage value at the end of ten years would be $20,000. The additional investment in working capital required would be $30,000. The applicable tax rate is 40 percent. The cost savings per year are estimated to be cash flows of $40,000 per year for ten years. The applicable cost of capital is 12 percent. The pro-forma income statement for this activity would be

Sales	$140,000
Operating costs	100,000
Earnings before depreciation, interest, and taxes	40,000
Depreciation	10,000
Earnings before interest and taxes = (EBIT) = (NOI)	30,000
Taxes @40 percent	12,000
Net income = NI	$ 18,000

   a)   Use the worksheet method to calculate the NPV from the project.
   b)   Present two formulations of the tax-adjusted net cash flows.
   c)   Should the investment be made?

6.3   After using Machine A in Problem 6.2 for five years, the firm has an opportunity to invest in Machine B, which would replace Machine A. Machine B would have a five-year life, cost $80,000, have an after-tax salvage value of $20,000, generate sales of $150,000 per year, and reduce operating expenses by $10,000 per year. If the replacement were made by investing in Machine B, the amount realized on the sale of Machine A would be $30,000.
   a)   Present the comparative income statements and cash flows for machines A and B and for the change created by adding Machine B.
   b)   Calculate the NPV for the investment in Machine B.
   c)   Compare your results for the NPV of Machine B to the NPV for Machine A previously calculated. Should the investment in Machine B be made?

6.4 The Farlow Company is considering the replacement of a riveting machine with a new one that will increase the earnings before depreciation from $20,000 per year to $51,000 per year. The new machine will cost $100,000 and have an estimated life of eight years with no salvage value. The applicable corporate tax rate is 40 percent, and the firm's cost of capital is 12 percent. The old machine has been fully depreciated and has no salvage value.

    a) Evaluate the replacement decision, using straight line depreciation.

    b) Evaluate the replacement decision, using sum-of-years'-digits accelerated depreciation.

6.5 Assume that the Farlow Company in Problem 6.4 will be able to realize an investment tax credit of 10 percent on the purchase of the new machine for $100,000 with savings of $31,000 per year; the machine will have a life of eight years and a salvage value of $12,000. Assume further that the old machine has a book value of $40,000 and a remaining life of eight years. If replaced, the old machine can be sold now for $15,000. Use straight line depreciation. Evaluate the investment decision.

6.6 Natural Beverages is contemplating the replacement of one of its bottling machines with a newer and more efficient one. The old machine has a book value of $500,000 and a remaining useful life of five years. The firm does not expect to realize any return from scrapping the old machine in five years, but it can sell the machine now to another firm in the industry for $300,000.

    The new machine has a purchase price of $1.1 million, an estimated useful life of five years, and an estimated salvage value of $200,000. It is expected to economize on electric power usage, labor, and repair costs and to reduce the number of defective bottles. In total, an annual saving of $250,000 will be realized if the new machine is installed. The company is in the 40 percent tax bracket, has a 10 percent cost of capital, and uses straight line depreciation. (Note: To calculate depreciation, assume that the salvage value is deducted from initial cost to get the depreciable cost.)

    a) What is the initial cash outlay required for the new machine?

    b) What are the cash flows in years 1 to 5?

    c) What is the cash flow from the salvage value in Year 5?

    d) Should Natural Beverages purchase the new machine? Support your answer.

6.7 The FM Company has cash inflows of $275,000 and cash outflows of $210,000 per year on Project A. The investment outlay is $144,000; its life is eight years; the tax rate is 40 percent. The applicable cost of capital is 14 percent.

    a) Calculate the net cash flows and the net present value for Project A, using straight line depreciation for tax purposes.

    b) If the earnings before depreciation, interest, and taxes are $40,000 per year, what is the net present value for Project A, using straight line depreciation?

    c) Recalculate your answer under Part (b), using sum-of-years'-digits depreciation.

6.8 The Starbuck Company is considering the purchase of a new machine tool to replace an obsolete one. The machine being used for the operation has both a tax book value and a market value of zero; it is in good working order and will last, physically, for at least an additional 15 years. The proposed machine will perform the operation so much more efficiently that Starbuck engineers estimate that labor, material, and other direct costs of the operation will be reduced $4,500 a year if it is installed. The proposed machine costs $24,000 delivered and installed, and its economic life is estimated to be 15 years, with zero salvage value. The company expects to earn 12 percent on its investment after taxes (12 percent is the firm's cost of capital). The tax rate is 40 percent, and the firm uses straight line depreciation.

    a) Should Starbuck buy the new machine?

b) Assume that the tax book value of the old machine is $6,000, that the annual depreciation charge is $400, and that the machine has no market value. How do these assumptions affect your answer?

c) Answer Part (b), assuming that the old machine has a market value of $4,000.

d) Answer Part (b), assuming that the annual saving will be $6,000.

e) Answer Part (a), assuming that the relevant cost of capital is now 6 percent. What is the significance of this change? What can be said about parts (b), (c), and (d) under this assumption?

6.9 Each of two mutually exclusive projects involves an investment of $120,000. Cash flows (after-tax profits plus depreciation) for the two projects have a different time pattern, although the totals are approximately the same. Project M will yield high returns early and lower returns in later years. (It is a mining type of investment, and the expense of removing the ore is lower at the entrance to the mine, where there is easier access.) Project O yields low returns in the early years and higher returns in the later years. (It is an orchard type of investment, and it takes a number of years for trees to mature and be fully bearing.) The cash flows from the two investments are as follows:

Year	Project M	Project O
1	$70,000	$10,000
2	40,000	20,000
3	30,000	30,000
4	10,000	50,000
5	10,000	80,000

a) Compute the present value of each project when the firm's cost of capital is 0 percent, 6 percent, 10 percent, and 20 percent.

b) Compute the internal rate of return (IRR) for each project.

c) Graph the present value of the two projects, putting net present value (NPV) on the Y-axis and the cost of capital on the X-axis.

d) Can you determine the IRR of the projects from your graph? Explain.

e) Which project would you select, assuming no capital rationing and a constant cost of capital of 8 percent? of 10 percent? of 12 percent? Explain.

6.10 Because of increasing energy prices, David Bradshaw, the chief financial officer of General Tools Company, is quite concerned about the gas bill of his firm.

Also, Bradshaw is interested in the new tax benefits from installing energy conservation equipment. To encourage energy conservation and to promote industrial and agricultural conversions from oil and gas to alternative forms of energy, the Energy Tax Act of 1978 provided a 10 percent credit in addition to the regular investment credit for "alternative energy property," such as equipment that uses fuel other than oil or natural gas, and for "specially defined energy property" intended to reduce energy waste in existing facilities. The credit is not refundable, but it can be used to offset 100 percent of tax liability.

Bradshaw is considering the installation of new energy-saving solar equipment to replace the conventional boiler, which uses gas as the only energy source and which can be used for another 15 years. The new solar system is estimated to have a lifetime of 15 years and requires a capital investment of $24,000. The net book value of the old boiler is $10,000. There is no salvage value for either equipment. However, the new system is expected to have an energy saving of 1 billion BTU's per year. The firm will have a combined 20 percent tax credit on the investment in the new solar system.

The current price is $2.04 for 1,000 cubic feet of natural gas, which contains 1 million BTU's. The required rate of return on investment is 15 percent after tax; the annual operating and maintenance expenses for the new solar system are estimated to be $400 less than for the conventional boiler; and the old boiler has a current market value of $8,000. The corporate tax rate is 40 percent, and the firm uses straight line depreciation.

a)   As a financial analyst, what is your recommendation to Bradshaw?

b)   Suppose the annual growth rate of gas prices is expected to be 15 percent. How will this affect your evaluation?

6.11 The Grant Corporation is considering a project which has a five-year life and costs $2,500. It would save $410 per year in operating costs and increase revenue by $300 per year. It would be financed with a five-year loan with the following payment schedule (the annual rate of interest is 8 percent). No salvage value for the new purchased equipment is assumed at the end of the project.

Payment	Interest	Repayment of Principal	Balance
$626.14	$200.00	$426.14	$2,073.86
626.14	165.91	460.23	1,613.63
626.14	129.09	497.05	1,116.58
626.14	89.33	536.81	579.77
626.14	46.37	579.77	0
	$630.70	$2,500.00	

If the company has a 12 percent after-tax cost of capital and a 40 percent tax rate, what is the net present value of the project if the company uses

a)   straight line depreciation?

b)   double declining balance depreciation (DDB) for the first four years of the project and then straight line depreciation in the fifth year?

6.12 You are considering the economic value of an MBA. Assuming that you can and do enroll in a business school immediately, expenses are $8,000 per year and foregone income is $12,000 per year for the required 2 years. Your expected yearly income for the following 18 years is increased by $12,919.

a)   What is the return on investment earned? (Hint: It is more than 10 percent.)

b)   What are some of the major complicating factors ignored in the information presented?

6.13 A firm is comparing the purchase of two mutually exclusive machine investments. Machine F involves an investment of $40,000 and would produce annual net cash flows after taxes of $12,000 for five years. Machine H would require an investment of $100,000 and would produce annual cash flows after taxes of $30,000 for seven years. Machine H is somewhat more risky and requires a cost of capital of 12 percent, compared to 10 percent for Machine F. Which machine should be selected?

6.14 The Longdon Company has two alternative investment projects, E and F. As a result of a capital rationing policy, the management is contemplating which project they should accept. The following table provides the management with all the related financial information:

	Project E	Project F
Cost	$15,000	$15,000
Cash flow per year (CF_t)	$ 5,500	$ 3,200
Life	4 years	8 years
Cost of capital	12%	12%

Calculate the NPV and IRR for each project and make your recommendation.

6.15 If the opportunity cost of capital is 15 percent, which of the following three projects has the highest PI? Which will increase shareholders' wealth the most?

Year	Project A	Project B	Project C
0	$-300	$-1,000	$-600
1	320	750	1,100
2	320	750	—
3	—	750	—

6.16 A coal mining firm is considering opening a strip mine, the cost of which is $4.4 million. Cash flows will be $27.7 million, all coming at the end of one year. The land must be returned to its natural state at a cost of $25 million, payable after two years. The IRR is found to be either 9.2 percent or 420 percent. Should the project be accepted (a) if $k = 8$ percent or (b) if $k = 14$ percent? Explain your reasoning.

Selected References

Baumol, William J., and Quandt, Richard E., "Investment and Discount Rates under Capital Rationing—A Programming Approach," *Economic Journal*, 75 (June 1965), pp. 317-329.

Bernhard, Richard H., "Mathematical Programming Models for Capital Budgeting—A Survey, Generalization, and Critique," *Journal of Financial and Quantitative Analysis*, 4 (June 1969), pp. 111-158.

Bierman, Harold, Jr., and Smidt, Seymour, *The Capital Budgeting Decision*, 4th ed. New York: Macmillan, 1975.

Booth, Laurence D., "Correct Procedures for the Evaluation of Risky Cash Outflows," *Journal of Financial and Quantitative Analysis*, 17 (June 1982), pp. 287-300.

Carleton, W., "Linear Programming and Capital Budgeting Models: A New Interpretation," *Journal of Finance*, (December 1969), pp. 825-833.

Cooley, Philip L.; Roenfeldt, Rodney L.; and Chew, It-Keong, "Capital Budgeting Procedures under Inflation," *Financial Management*, 4 (Winter 1975), pp. 18-27.

Copeland, Thomas E., and Weston, J. Fred, *Financial Theory and Corporate Policy*, 2nd ed., Reading, Mass.: Addison-Wesley, 1983.

Emery, Gary W., "Some Guidelines for Evaluating Capital Investment Alternatives with Unequal Lives," *Financial Management*, 11 (Spring 1982), pp. 14-19.

Findlay, M. Chapman, and Williams, Edward E., "The Problem of 'Unequal Lives' Reconsidered," *Journal of Business Finance & Accounting*, 8 (Summer 1981), pp. 161-164.

Lorie, J. H., and Savage, L. J., "Three Problems in Capital Rationing," *Journal of Business*, (October 1955), pp. 229-239.

Meyer, Richard L., "A Note on Capital Budgeting Techniques and the Reinvestment Rate," *Journal of Finance*, 34 (December 1979), pp. 1251-1254.

Myers, S. C., "A Note on Linear Programming and Capital Budgeting," *Journal of Finance*, (March 1972), pp. 89-92.

Rappaport, Alfred, and Taggart, Robert A., Jr., "Evaluation of Capital Expenditure Proposals Under Inflation," *Financial Management*, 11 (Spring 1982), pp. 5-13.

Sarnat, Marshall, and Levy, Haim, "The Relationship of Rules of Thumb to the Internal Rate of Return: A Restatement and Generalization," *Journal of Finance*, 24 (June 1969), pp. 479-489.

Schall, Lawrence D.; Sundem, Gary L.; and Geijsbeek, William R., "Survey and Analysis of Capital Budgeting Methods," *Journal of Finance*, 33 (March 1978), pp. 281-292.

Schwab, Bernhard, and Lusztig, Peter, "A Note on Abandonment Value and Capital Budgeting," *Journal of Financial and Quantitative Analysis*, 5 (September 1970), pp. 377-380.

Smidt, Seymour, "A Bayesian Analysis of Project Selection and of Post Audit Evaluations," *Journal of Finance*, 34 (June 1979), pp. 675-688.

Taggart, Robert A., Jr., "Capital Budgeting and the Financing Decision: An Exposition," *Financial Management*, 6 (Summer 1977), pp. 59-64.

Weingartner, H. Martin, *Mathematical Programming and the Analysis of Capital Budgeting Problems*, Englewood Cliffs, N. J.: Prentice-Hall, 1963.

Chapter 7   How the Market Determines Discount Rates

In the previous chapter, we discussed capital budgeting — the firm's investment decision. We emphasized that the net present value criterion was consistent with the goal of shareholder wealth maximization because it discounted cash flows for capital budgeting purposes at the appropriate market-determined cost of capital. This chapter shows how the marketplace determines discount rates. Where do they come from? Why do they differ from security to security? How are they affected by productivity, expected inflation, liquidity, and risk? We shall also see how to apply a more sophisticated understanding of discount rates to capital budgeting in an inflationary environment.

Productivity, Inflation, Liquidity, and Risk

There are a wide variety of assets and securities in which one might invest, and they all appear to have different rates of return. For example, Ibbotson and Sinquefield [1982] compiled data on various types of securities over the time period 1926 to 1981 and found the following long-run pretax rates of return (compounded annually):

Common stocks	9.1%
Stocks of smaller companies	12.1%
Long-term corporate bonds	3.6%
Long-term U.S. government bonds	3.0%
Short-term U.S. Treasury bills	3.0%
Inflation	3.0%

As we shall see, the pretax nominal rate of return on any asset can be explained by four components: the expected real rate of return, expected inflation over the life of the asset, the liquidity of the asset, and the riskiness of the asset. For example, most of the difference between the rate of return on common stocks, 9.1 percent, and on long-term government bonds, 3.0 percent, can be explained by the extra risk of common stock. Equation 7.1 shows that interest rates are a function of four components:

$$\text{Nominal rate of return} = f[E(\text{real rate}), E(\text{inflation}), \qquad (7.1)$$
$$E(\text{liquidity premium}), E(\text{risk premium})].$$

Note that each term on the right-hand side is preceded by an expectations operator, E. For example, $E(\text{inflation})$ is the market's estimate of expected future inflation. Investors try to estimate what inflation will be, and, consequently, the market rates of return on securities with different lives will reflect the market's expectation of inflation over the life of the asset.

The remainder of this chapter will proceed by starting with the simplest possible type of market instrument, one which lasts only one time period in a world without any inflation and with no risk. Then, we will complicate things step by step. First, we will add in the effect of expected inflation and liquidity in an effort to explain how rates of return on default-free U.S. government bonds depend on their maturity. Second, we will look at the effect of default risk in order to show why corporate bonds, which are subject to bankruptcy, have higher expected rates of return than U.S. government bonds of equal maturity. Finally, we will introduce return risk (later the subject of Chapters 16 to 18) in order to explain why common stocks have higher expected rates of return than long-term U.S. government bonds.

The Real Rate of Interest

We can best develop our understanding of how interest rates are determined by starting with market equilibrium in a simple one-period setting where there is no inflation and no risk. The market equilibrium interest rate is a price of money across time. It is the rate of return which equates borrowing and lending in the economy, and, as we shall see, it is the opportunity cost of capital which determines the optimal amount of investment for every individual. In order to illustrate these facts, Figure 7.1 shows the investment opportunity schedules for two individuals (similar to Figure 6.1). Initially, they are unable to exchange funds via borrowing and lending. Individual A, who is relatively impatient, requires a subjective rate of return of $r_A = 10\%$, while individual B requires only $r_B = 5\%$. The difference in their subjective required rates of return simply reflects the fact that different people have different preferences for the time value of money. It has nothing to do with differ-

Figure 7.1   Investment Opportunity Schedules for Two Individuals

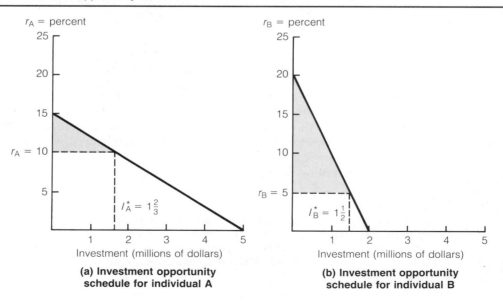

(a) Investment opportunity
schedule for individual A

(b) Investment opportunity
schedule for individual B

ences in the riskiness of their investments because we have assumed that all investments are risk free.

Equations 7.1a and 7.1b are algebraic representations of the investment schedules in Figure 7.1.

$$r_A = \$15 - 3I_A \text{ or } I_A = \$5 - (1/3)r_A. \tag{7.1a}$$

$$r_B = \$20 - 10I_B \text{ or } I_B = \$2 - (1/10)r_B. \tag{7.1b}$$

Given a subjective rate of 10 percent, individual A will invest $I_A^* = \$1\frac{2}{3}$ million while individual B, with a rate of 5 percent, will invest $I_B^* = \$1\frac{1}{2}$ million. Individual A's subjectively measured wealth increases by the shaded area in Figure 7.1(a), because every project in this area earns more than a 10 percent return. Since the shaded area is a triangle, its area is $A = 1/2 \ bh$ or $A = .5(\$1\frac{2}{3} \text{ million})(5\%) = \$41,667$. Similarly, the subjectively determined wealth of individual B is \$112,500.

If we allow the exchange of funds via borrowing and lending, then (1) there will be an equilibrium rate of interest which equates the amount of borrowing with the amount of lending, (2) individuals will disregard their own subjective interest rates and will use the market equilibrium rate of return for making optimal investment decisions, and (3) all individuals will be better off than they would have been in a world without borrowing and lending opportunities. These results have come to be known as the *Fisher separation principle* (after Irving Fisher [1930] who first described them). The idea is that all individuals will maximize their wealth if they base their consumption/investment decisions on the market-determined interest rate rather than on their own subjective rates of return. Hence, optimal investment decisions are separate from individuals' subjective tastes and preferences. To see why the Fisher separation principle works, let's return to our example.

Previously, individuals A and B had made their investment decisions without the opportunity to borrow and lend.[1] How will their behavior change if borrowing and lending are permitted? Individual A, who has a subjective rate of 10 percent, will be willing to borrow if the market interest rate is less than 10 percent, or lend if it is higher. Individual B also borrows or lends depending on the relationship between her subjective rate and the market rate. Figure 7.2 shows the total amount of borrowed funds which will be supplied and demanded at different market rates of interest.

The total amount of borrowed funds demanded (or supplied) is determined by substituting a market rate of interest into Equations 7.1a and 7.1b and then comparing the new amount of desired investment with original amount, I^*. Table 7.1 gives the resulting supply and demand schedules. In our example, the equilibrium rate of return which equates supply and demand is 8.85 percent. It can be determined algebraically by noting that individual A's demand for borrowed funds, B_A, is the difference between his investment in a world without capital markets, $I_A^* = \$1\frac{2}{3}$ million, and his desired investment given the opportunity to borrow and lend.

$$B_A = I_A - I_A^*$$

$$= [5 - (1/3)r] - 1 \ 2/3$$

$$B_A = 3 \ 1/3 - (1/3)r.$$

---

[1]For convenience, we assume that I_A^* and I_B^* are the desired savings of the individuals; hence, desired savings (that is, funds available for investment) equals desired investment, and there is no residual cash to borrow or lend without actually changing the investment decision. For a more advanced presentation, which includes initial endowments, indifference curves for future and current consumption, and the production opportunity set, see Hirshleifer [1970] or Copeland and Weston [1983].

Figure 7.2   The Supply and Demand for Borrowed Funds

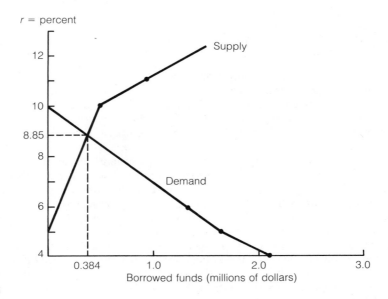

Similarly, for individual B, we have

$$B_B = I_B - I_B^*$$

$$= [2 - (1/10)r] - 1\ 1/2$$

$$B = 1/2 - (1/10)r.$$

In equilibrium, the aggregate amount of borrowing must equal the amount of lending; hence,

$$B_A + B_B = 0.$$

$$3\ 1/3 - (1/3)r + 1/2 - (1/10)r = 0$$

$$\frac{100}{30} - \frac{10r}{30} + \frac{15}{30} - \frac{3r}{30} = 0$$

$$13r = 115$$

$$r = 8.84615\%.$$

At the equilibrium rate of 8.85 percent, individual A will borrow $.384 million from individual B. Both are better off than before. Individual A is able to borrow at 8.85 percent, which is below his subjective rate of 10 percent, while B lends at 8.85 percent, which is

Table 7.1   Demand and Supply Schedules for Borrowed Funds

Market Rate	A's Borrowing		B's Borrowing		Excess Demand	D	S
	Demand	Supply	Demand	Supply			
0.00%	$3 1/3	$0	$1/2	$0	$3 5/6	3.83	
3.00%	2 1/3	0	2/10	0	2 16/30	2.53	0
6.00%	1 1/3	0	0	1/10	1 7/30	1.23	.10
8.85%	.384	0	0	.384	0	.38	.38
12.00%	0	2/3	0	7/10	−(41/30)		1.37
15.00%	0	1 2/3	0	1	−(2 2/3)		2.67

higher than her 5 percent subjective rate. Before borrowing and lending were allowed, individual A invested $1.67 million and his wealth was $41,667. Now, he borrows in order to invest $2.05 million, and his wealth increases by the average rate of return on new investment, that is, 10% − 8.85%, times the amount of new investment, $.384 million. His new wealth is $41,667 + $4,416 = $46,083, and he is better off than before. Individual B is also better off. Even though she invests less than before in real investments ($1.116 million instead of $1.5 million), she receives a higher rate on each dollar lent. Her wealth increases by the average return on lending, that is, 8.85% − 5%, times the amount lent, $.384 million. Her new wealth is $14,784 higher than before.

Both investors make their borrowing/lending decision by comparing their subjective rate with the market rate; hence, the market rate is used as a signal to determine their optimal investment decisions. *Regardless of their subjective rates of time preference, all individuals maximize their wealth by undertaking projects until the marginal rate of return on the last project just equals the market equilibrium rate.* It is hard to overemphasize the importance of Fisher separation because it is the basis for capital budgeting. The NPV rule, discussed in Chapter 6, is merely an application of the Fisher separation principle because all cash flows are discounted at the market equilibrium opportunity cost of funds. All individuals, regardless of their personal preferences, will unanimously agree that the market rate is the correct discount rate.

The simple example given above serves to demonstrate that market interest rates are determined by the supply and demand for funds. Supply and demand depend on people's subjective rates of time preference, their endowments, and the schedule of invest-ment opportunities which is available. If more profitable investments become available, then there will be greater competition for funds, interest rates will rise, and some projects at the margin will be dropped. The average rate of return on investments will increase. Thus, when the economy is more productive, the real rate of interest rises to reflect the increased productivity. Referring to Equation 7.1, we see that changes in the real rate of interest are related directly to the real rates of return on investment in the economy. However, this relationship is complicated somewhat by the fact that the government may invest in unprofitable projects. If the government competes for funds, due to deficit spending, interest rates will go up and investment in the private sector of the economy will fall. This effect is known as "crowding out." If the government projects which are undertaken provide no net benefit to the economy, then we are made worse off. The relationship between the real rate of return and the availability of productive investment opportunities is weakened.

The Term Structure of Interest Rates

We now extend our understanding of equilibrium interest rates to incorporate expected inflation and liquidity while holding default risk and return risk constant. For example, all U.S. government debt, regardless of its maturity, may be assumed to have zero default risk. Yet, as shown in Figure 7.3, the yield changes with the term to maturity of the debt. The *term structure of interest rates* describes the relationship between interest rates and loan maturity.

The yield to maturity on a long-term bond is computed in exactly the same way one would solve for the internal rate of return on a security. For example, suppose a bond promises to pay a 14 percent coupon at the end of each year for three years and then pay a face value of $1,000. The current market price of the bond, B_0, is $1,099.47. The yield to maturity on the bond, which we shall designate as $_0R_T$, may be computed by solving the following expression:

$$B_0 = \sum_{t=1}^{T} \frac{coupon_t}{(1 + {_0R_T})^t} + \frac{face\ value}{(1 + {_0R_T})^T} \tag{7.2}$$

Figure 7.3   Term Structure of Rates on U.S. Government Securities, 1976, 1980, and 1984

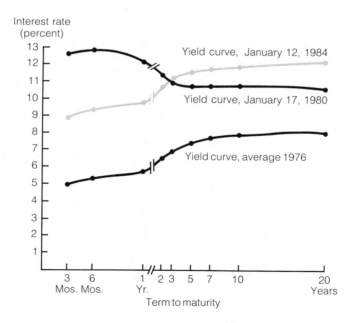

Sources: Curve for January 17, 1980, is from Salomon Brothers, *Bond Market Roundup*, week ending January 18, 1980; curve for 1976 is from *Federal Reserve Bulletin*, February 1978, p. A27; and curve for January 12, 1984, is from *The Wall Street Journal*, January 13, 1984.

$$\$1,099.47 = \sum_{t=1}^{3} \frac{\$140}{(1 + {_0}R_3)^t} + \frac{\$1,000}{(1 + {_0}R_3)^3}.$$

Solving iteratively, we find that the yield to maturity, ${_0}R_3$, is 10 percent.

One problem with this procedure is that it implicitly assumes that the annual interest rate is the same for each year of the bond's life. As we shall see, this is usually not true. For example, an average return of 10 percent for three years can be earned by receiving 8 percent in the first year, 10.5 percent in the second, and 11.53 percent in the third year.[2] Later on, we will show how it is possible to use the observed term structure in order to estimate the market's prediction of future one-period interest rates.

Figure 7.3 shows the term structure of rates in three years, 1976, 1980, and 1984. In the lowest curve, for 1976, we see a pattern of rising yields. The shorter term maturities carry lower rates of interest than the longer term maturities. This rising yield structure has been characteristic of most years since 1930. The yield curve for 1984 had a similar pattern but was shifted up from the 1976 curve. The curve for 1980 shows a pattern which starts high and then declines until the fifth year, becoming relatively flat thereafter. By May 1980, the yield curve had dropped and its slope became positive, rising from 10 percent on short-term issues to about 11 percent on 30-year maturities.

In addition to illustrating the changing term structure of interest rates, Figure 7.3 also reveals a shift in the *level of rates*. Between 1976 and 1980, the interest rate on all govern-ment securities — long-term and short-term — increased. Such movements represent changes in the general level of interest rates.[3] The historical pattern of the relation-ship between long- and short-term interest rates is shown for the period 1910 through 1984 in Figure 7.4. The long-term rate is represented by the Aaa bond rate — the rate on high-grade, long-term (25 years or more) corporate bonds. The short-term rate is represented by the rate on prime commercial paper — the four-to-six-month debt of top-quality firms.

Three points should be made about the graph: (1) both long-term and short-term rates generally rose over the period; (2) short-term rates were more volatile than long-term rates; and (3) long-term rates were generally above short-term rates.

Except for a few months in the mid-1950s, the long-term rate was consistently above the short-term rate in all years from 1929 to 1966. However, in recent years, short-term rates have more often been above long-term rates. This change occurred during 1966 and dur-ing parts of 1969, 1970, 1973, and again in late 1978, continuing persistently through mid-1981.

Both short-term and long-term rates experienced unprecedented volatility from 1979 to 1984. Rates rose to historic highs several times, and in 1980 alone, the prime bank loan rate ranged from 19.8 percent in April to 11.1 percent in August and back up to over 20 percent by year-end.[4]

---

[2]In other words,

$$(1.10)^3 = (1.08)(1.105)(1.1153).$$

[3]In addition to the level and term structure of rates on a given class of securities (in this case, government securities) there is also the pattern of relationships among different classes of securities — for example, mortgages, government bonds, corporates, and bank business loans. In general, movements in the term structure and level of rates are similar for most classes of securities.

[4]Federal Reserve Bank of St. Louis, *U.S. Financial Data*, weekly issues, 1979-1982.

Figure 7.4   Long- and Short-Term Interest Rates

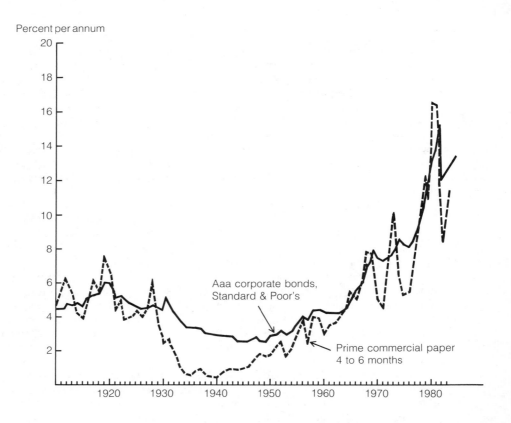

Source: *Economic Indicators*, July 1984, U.S. Government Printing Office, Washington, D.C., p. 30.

Theoretical Explanations for the Term Structure of Interest Rates

Three theories have been advanced to explain the term structure — the relationship between short-term and long-term interest rates: the expectations theory, the liquidity preference theory, and the market segmentation theory. We will consider each in turn.

Expectations Theory

The unbiased *expectations theory* asserts that *expected future interest rates* are equal to *forward rates* computed from observed bond prices. The *n*-period forward rate is the yield to maturity which is fixed today on a *T*-year bond from Year *T* - *n* to Year *T*. In order to keep things simple, we will stick to one-period forward rates. For example, in 1989 we can calculate the one-year forward rate for 1992 — a rate predicted by the current market prices of forward contracts. To illustrate, let us consider an investor whose planning horizon is two years. Let $_0R_T$ be the yield to maturity for a T-year bond; let $_tf_{t+1}$ be the observed one-period forward rate from Year t to Year $(t + 1)$, which is computed from the market prices of bonds; and let $E(_tr_{t+1})$ be the expected one-period future rate of interest. Suppose our investor is considering two alternative investment strategies: (1) purchasing a two-year bond with a yield of 9 percent per year or (2) purchasing a one-year bond that yields 8 percent, and then reinvesting the $108 he will have at the end of the year in another one-year bond. If he chooses Strategy 1, at the end of two years, he will have

$$\text{Ending value} = \$100(1.09)(1.09) = \$118.81.$$

If he follows Strategy 2, his expected value at the end of two years will depend upon his expected future rate on the one-year bond during the second year $[E(_1r_2)]$:

$$\text{Ending value} = \$100(1.08)[1 + E(_1r_2)] = \$108[1 + E(_1r_2)].$$

Under the expectations theory, the expected value of $E(_1r_2)$ will be 10.01 percent, found as follows:

$$\$118.81 = \$108[1 + E(_1r_2)]$$
$$1 + E(_1r_2) = 1.1001$$
$$E(_1r_2) = 0.1001 = 10.01\%.$$

Now, suppose that actual market prices showed the observed one-period forward rate in the second year $(_1f_2)$ to be greater than 10.01 percent, say 10.5 percent. In that case, if our investor is maximizing his expected payoff, he (and others) would be better off investing short term, because he would end up with $119.34, which is greater than $118.81.[5] Just the reverse would hold if $_1f_2 < 10.01$ percent. Thus, according to the expectations theory, capital market competition forces forward rates to be equal to expected future rates over the holding period.

$$E(_tr_{t+1}) = {}_tf_{t+1}. \qquad (7.3)$$

Observed forward rates of interest are easy to measure because we can use observed yields to maturity. The T-year yield to maturity on a bond must be equal to the geometric average of the forward rates over its life. In general,

$$(1 + {}_0R_T)^T = (1 + {}_0r_1)(1 + {}_1f_2) \ldots (1 + {}_{T-1}f_T). \qquad (7.4)$$

---

[5]If he starts with $100 and invests it at 8 percent in the first year and 10.5 percent the second year, investing in this series of one-year bonds, he obtains

$$\$100(1.08)(1.105) = \$119.34.$$

This result is better than investing in a two-year bond. As more investors adopt the strategy of buying two one-year bonds, the prices of the bonds go up and their yield falls — back into equilibrium.

Figure 7.5   A Simple Term Structure Example

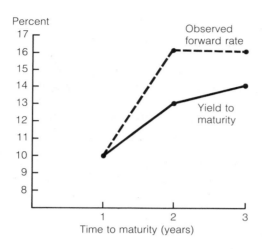

Note that in the first time period (that is, for the shortest bond), the future rate ($_0r_1$) is equal to the forward rate, by definition.

To illustrate the computation of forward rates, suppose that we have three default-free bonds, each paying $140 (at the end of each year) and having a face value of $1,000 at maturity. They mature one, two, and three years hence and are observed to have current market prices of $1,036.36, $1,016.68, and $1,000.00 respectively. Using Equation 7.2, their computed yields to maturity are 10 percent, 13 percent, and 14 percent. The term structure for this example is shown in Figure 7.5. Suppose we want to know the forward rate implied for the third time period. It can be computed by taking the ratio of the (geometric product of the) yields to maturity on the three- and two-period bonds as shown below:

$$1 + {_2f_3} = \frac{(1 + {_0R_3})^3}{(1 + {_0R_2})^2}$$

$$= \frac{(1 + {_0r_1})(1 + {_1f_2})(1 + {_2f_3})}{(1 + {_0r_1})(1 + {_1f_2})}$$

$$= \frac{(1.14)^3}{(1.13)^2} = \frac{1.481544}{1.2769} = 1.1603$$

$${_2f_3} = 16.03\%.$$

Similarly, one can compute the second-period forward rate as 16.08 percent, and, of course, the one-period rate is observed directly to be 10 percent.

By itself, the forward rate is merely an algebraic computation from observed bond data. The unbiased expectations theory attempts to explain observed forward rates by saying (as in Equation 7.3) that expected future rates $E(_t r_{t+1})$ will, on average, be equal to the forward rates. There are, however, reasons why this may not be true. First, the transactions costs of rolling over a one-year bond n times may be such that a series of one-year bonds is not a perfect substitute for an n-year bond. Second, there is uncertainty about future one-year rates of interest which is not immediately resolved. These issues lead to the possibility of a liquidity premium in the term structure.

Liquidity Preference Theory

The future is inherently uncertain, and when uncertainty is considered, the pure expectations theory must be modified. To illustrate, let us consider a situation where future short-term rates are expected to remain unchanged on average, but they may be higher or lower depending on changes in the money supply. In this case, the pure expectations theory predicts that short- and long-term bonds sell at equal yields. The *liquidity preference theory*, on the other hand, holds that long-term bonds must yield more than short-term bonds for two reasons. First, in a world of uncertainty, investors will, in general, prefer to hold short-term securities because they are more liquid; they can be converted to cash without danger of loss of principal. Investors will, therefore, accept lower yields on short-term securities. Second, borrowers react in exactly the opposite way from investors — business borrowers generally prefer long-term debt because short-term debt subjects a firm to greater dangers of having to refund debt under adverse conditions. Accordingly, firms are willing to pay a higher rate, other things held constant, for long-term than for short-term funds.

We see, then, that pressures on both the supply and demand sides — caused by liquidity preferences of both lenders and borrowers — will tend to make the yield curve slope upward. Figure 7.6 illustrates this effect for constant, rising, and falling term structures.

Figure 7.6   Term Structure with and without a Liquidity Premium

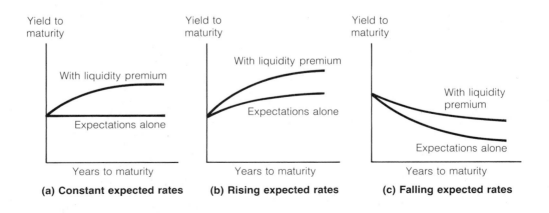

(a) **Constant expected rates**   (b) **Rising expected rates**   (c) **Falling expected rates**

Market Segmentation Hypothesis

The expectations theory assumes that, in the aggregate, lenders and borrowers are indifferent between long- and short-term bonds except for any expected yield differentials based on maturity. The liquidity preference theory states that an upward bias exists — the yield curve slopes upward to a greater extent than is justified by expectations about future rates because investors prefer to lend short while borrowers prefer to borrow long.

The *market segmentation, institutional, or hedging-pressure theory* admits the liquidity preference argument as a good description of the behavior of investors with short horizons, such as commercial banks, which regard certainty of principal as more important than certainty of income because of the nature of their deposit liabilities. However, certain other investors with long-term liabilities, such as insurance companies, might prefer to buy long-term bonds because, given the nature of their liabilities, they find certainty of income highly desirable. On the other hand, borrowers relate the maturity of their debt to the maturity of their assets. Thus, the market segmentation theory characterizes market participants as having strong maturity preferences, then argues that interest rates are determined by supply and demand in each segmented market, with each maturity constituting a segment. In the strictest version of this theory, expectations play no role — bonds with different maturities are not substitutes for one another because of different demand preferences or the preferred habitat of both lenders and borrowers.

Empirical Evidence

Empirical studies suggest that there is some validity to each of these theories. Specifically, the recent work indicates that if lenders and borrowers have no reason for expecting a change in the general level of interest rates, the yield curve will be upward sloping because of liquidity preferences. (Under the expectations theory, the term structure of interest rates would be flat if there were no expectations of a change in the level of short-term rates.) However, it is a fact that during periods of extremely high interest rates, the yield curve is downward sloping; this proves that the expectations theory also operates. At still other times, when supply and demand conditions in particular maturity sectors change, the term structure seems to be modified, thus confirming the market segmentation theory. In summary, each theory has an element of truth, and each must be taken into account in seeking to understand the changing patterns observed in the term structure of interest rates.

Inflation and the Term Structure

Anyone who has lived through an inflationary economy is well aware of the fact that there is an important difference between nominal and constant dollar prices and between nominal and real interest rates. What really counts is what you can consume, not the unit of exchange in which it is denominated. Suppose that you are indifferent between a loaf of bread today and 1.2 loaves at the end of one year. This implies a 20 percent real rate of interest. But suppose that a loaf costs $1.00 today and you expect that it will cost $1.80 at the year's end. This implies an inflation rate of 80 percent. What nominal rate of interest must you charge in order to maintain a real rate of 20 percent? The answer is that if you lend one loaf today, you must require that the borrower repay enough tomorrow so that you consume 1.2 loaves of bread, each costing $1.80. Your computation would be

$$\text{Loan repayment amount} = (1.2 \text{ loaves})(\$1.80/\text{loaf})$$

$$= \$2.16.$$

Thus, your nominal rate of interest is 116 percent. To generalize this example, we see that the nominal rate of interest, R, is the product of the real rate of interest, r, and expected inflation $E(i)$ as shown below:

$$1 + R = (1 + r)[1 + E(i)] \qquad\qquad (7.5)$$

$$1 + R = 1 + r + E(i) + rE(i).$$

Usually the cross product term $[rE(i)]$ is small and is ignored. This is why the nominal rate (assuming no liquidity premium and no default or rate of return risk) is often expressed as the sum of the real rate and the expected inflation rate, that is,

$$\text{Nominal rate} = E(\text{real rate}) + E(\text{inflation}).$$

If the real rate of return is relatively constant, then we can turn this equation around to say that expected inflation is the observed nominal rate minus the real rate, a constant.

$$E(\text{inflation}) = \text{Nominal rate} - \text{Real rate}.$$

If the marketplace makes unbiased forecasts of inflation, then actual inflation should be equal to expected inflation plus a random error term.

$$\text{Actual inflation} = E(\text{inflation}) + \text{Error term} \qquad\qquad (7.6)$$

$$= \text{Nominal rate} - \text{Real rate} + \text{Error term}.$$

This relationship has been studied by Fama [1975], by Nelson and Schwert [1977], and by Hess and Bicksler [1975] via regression equations similar to the following:

$$\text{Actual inflation} = a + b(\text{nominal rate}) + \text{Error term}. \qquad\qquad (7.7)$$

If the real rate is constant, the intercept (a) in Equation 7.7 will be equal to minus the real rate, and the slope term (b) should be close to 1.0. Fama [1975] fit this equation to data on U.S. Treasury bills between 1953 and 1971 and found that b was .98. This suggests that changes in current nominal rates are fairly good forecasts of inflation. Nelson and Schwert [1977] and Hess and Bicksler [1975] have pointed out that although the real rate appears to have been relatively constant during 1953-1971, in general it does vary across time and was much more variable after 1971.

These empirical results are useful because they imply that the term structure of interest rates contains useful information about expected inflation. If the term structure is downward sloping, as in Figure 7.6(c), the market is telling us that it expects near-term inflation to be higher than in the long run. An upward-sloping term structure, as in Figure 7.6(b), implies higher long-run inflation.

Table 7.2　　　The Term Structure and Capital Budgeting

Year	Yield to Maturity	Forward Rate	Cash Flows for A	Cash Flows for B	Discount Factor
0	—	—	$-110	$-110	1.0000
1	10%	10.00%	28	48	.9091
2	13	16.08	59	51	.7832
3	14	16.03	63	46	.6750

If one could estimate the expected real rate and the expected liquidity premium for a given maturity of riskless debt, then observed forward rates on U.S. government bonds could be used to forecast inflation as follows:

$$E(\text{inflation}) = \text{Nominal rate} - E(\text{real rate}) - E(\text{liquidity premium}).$$

Capital Budgeting and the Term Structure

Regardless of which theory of the term structure is correct, the fact that forward rates are not constant is relevant for the capital budgeting decision. The cash flows estimated for each year should be discounted to the present using the information revealed in the term structure of interest rates. Table 7.2 gives the yields to maturity, the implied forward rates, and cash flows for two mutually exclusive projects.

It is not uncommon for corporate treasurers to compute the NPV of these projects by discounting at the cost of capital for "three-year money," namely 14 percent. After all, both projects have a three-year life. When the cash flows are discounted at 14 percent, Project A has a NPV of $2.48 while B has a lower NPV of $2.40. Project A appears to be superior. Unfortunately, this procedure does not account for the fact that the real opportunity cost of funds is 10 percent for cash flows received in the first year, 16.08 percent for second-year cash flows, and 16.03 percent for third-year cash flows. The correct discount rate for cash flows in each year is the forward rate for that year. Note that this is also equal to the product of the implied forward rates from Year 1 up to the year of the cash flows. For example, in order to discount Project A's third year cash flow back to the present, it should be divided by 1.1603 to get it back to the second year, by 1.1608 to get it back to the first year, and by 1.1 to return it to a present value. This is equivalent to dividing by the yield to maturity on a three-year bond, that is, $(1.14)^3$. Thus, the third-year discount factor is

$$(1.14)^{-3} = [(1.10)(1.1608)(1.1603)]^{-1} = .6750.$$

The correct discount factors are given in the last column of Table 7.2. When the cash flows are appropriately discounted, the NPV's of Projects A and B are $4.19 and $4.63 respectively. Now Project B is preferred over A.

When the term structure is upward sloping, as in our simple example, a firm which uses the long-term rate (the three-year rate) to discount all cash flows will tend to overestimate the NPV's of projects. Of course, when the term structure is downward sloping, the opposite bias exists. In addition, as the example has shown, it is possible for the wrong project to be selected if the information given in the term structure is ignored.

Capital Budgeting and Inflation

It has been suggested that the term structure provides the best estimate of expected inflation. If so, a downward-sloping term structure implies that investors expect near-term inflation to be higher than long-term. An upward-sloping term structure (removing the liquidity premium) implies the opposite. If the firm's capital budgeting procedure discounts nominal cash flows (cum inflation) at market rates, then the cash flow estimates should reflect inflationary estimates on a year-by-year basis.

An additional problem created by inflation is that expected inflation may vary across different sectors of the economy. It may not be enough to know expected inflation for the entire economy. For capital budgeting purposes, we need to know how inflation will affect the revenues and costs for our line of business.[6] In order to keep things simple, we assume that the term structure is flat, that is, that expected inflation is constant across time.

Table 7.3 gives data for the expected cash flows for a project without inflation effects. A capital outlay of $75,000 is required for the five-year project. The corporate tax rate is 50 percent and the real rate of return, r, required for projects of equivalent risk is 9 percent. We will calculate the NPV of the project without inflation, and then we will see how inflation can change the results.

The expected cash flows in Table 7.3 are calculated using Equation 6.1:

$$\Delta CF = \Delta EBIT(1 - T) + \Delta dep \qquad (6.1)$$

$$= 10,000(1 - .5) + 15,000$$

$$= 20,000.$$

Table 7.3 Expected Net Cash Flows without Inflation Effects

	1	2	3	4	5
Expected revenue (ΔR)	$40,000	$50,000	$60,000	$70,000	$80,000
− Expected cash costs (ΔVC)	15,000	25,000	35,000	45,000	55,000
− Depreciation (Δdep)	15,000	15,000	15,000	15,000	15,000
= $\Delta EBIT$	10,000	10,000	10,000	10,000	10,000
− Taxes at 50% (T)	5,000	5,000	5,000	5,000	5,000
+ Depreciation (Δdep)	15,000	15,000	15,000	15,000	15,000
= Expected cash flows (ΔCF)	20,000	20,000	20,000	20,000	20,000

[6]For articles on inflation and capital budgeting, see Van Horne [1971] and Cooley, Roenfeldt, and Chew [1975]. Also see Cooley, Roenfeldt, and Chew's exchange with Findlay and Frankle [1976].

Table 7.4   Expected Net Cash Flows with Inflation Effects

	1	2	3	4	5
Expected revenue [$E(i) = 7\%$]	$42,800	$57,245	$73,503	$91,755	$112,204
− Expected cash costs [$E(i) = 8\%$]	16,200	29,160	44,090	61,222	80,813
− Depreciation	15,000	15,000	15,000	15,000	15,000
= $\Delta EBIT$	11,600	13,085	14,413	15,534	16,391
− Taxes at 50%	5,800	6,542	7,206	7,767	8,195
+ Depreciation	15,000	15,000	15,000	15,000	15,000
= Expected cash flows	20,800	21,542	22,206	22,767	23,195

The NPV of the project is

$$\text{NPV} = \sum_{t=1}^{5} \frac{\Delta CF_t}{(1 + r)^t} - I_0$$

$$= \$20,000 \text{ PVIFA } (9\%, 5 \text{ yrs.}) - \$75,000$$

$$= \$20,000(3.8897) - \$75,000$$

$$= \$77,794 - \$75,000 = \$2,794.$$

Table 7.4 shows the expected cash flows for the same project except that now revenues are subject to a 7 percent inflation rate while cash costs are subject to an 8 percent inflation rate. We also assume that general inflation in the economy is 6 percent, so the inflation-adjusted discount rate becomes approximately

$$\text{Nominal rate} = \text{Real rate} + E(\text{inflation}) = r + E(i)$$

$$= 9\% + 6\% = 15\%.$$

The calculation of the NPV of the project with inflation is shown in Table 7.5. Taking all the inflation influences into account, the NPV is $−1,473 and the project would be rejected. The fact that cash costs accelerated faster than revenues did not help. Also, the depreciation tax shield remained fixed in constant dollars. Consequently, it became less and less valuable and the firm's real tax rate increased with time. Some have suggested that this influence has been sufficiently widespread to account for the sluggish rate of capital investment in the United States since the early 1970s.

In the situation we illustrated initially, failure to take inflation into account in the expected cash flows resulted in an erroneous capital budgeting analysis. A project was accepted that, measured correctly, produced a return below the required rate of return. There would be an unsound allocation of capital if the inflation-caused bias in the analysis had not been taken into account. When inflationary effects were accounted for, cash outflows grew at a higher rate than the cash inflows. As a consequence, the expected net present value of the project was negative. Making the inflation adjustment does not always necessarily result in a negative net present value for the project — it simply results in a more accurate estimate of the net benefits from the project, positive or negative.

Table 7.5   Calculation of NPV with Inflationary Effects

Year	Cash Flow (1)	Discount Factor (15%) (2)	Present Value (1) × (2)
1	$20,800	0.8696	$18,088
2	21,542	0.7561	16,288
3	22,206	0.6575	14,600
4	22,767	0.5718	13,018
5	23,195	0.4972	11,533
			NPV = $73,527
			−75,000
			$−1,473

Note that the recommended procedure was to multiply constant dollar estimates of revenues and cash costs by the appropriate inflation factor and then discount the nominal dollar cash flows by the inflation-adjusted discount rate. In the special case that cash flows are expected to be inflated at the same rate as the economy, an alternate, equivalent procedure is to discount constant dollar costs at the real interest rate. To show this result, take the constant dollar numbers in Table 7.3. The NPV computation was

$$NPV = \sum_{t=1}^{5} \frac{\$20,000}{(1.09)^t} - \$75,000.$$

Now, suppose that all cash flows increase at 6 percent per year and the discount rate increases a like amount. The NPV equation now becomes

$$NPV = \sum_{t=1}^{5} \frac{\$20,000(1.06)^t}{(1.09)^t(1.06)^t} - \$75,000.$$

Since inflation factors are now in both the numerator and the denominator and are the same, they can be cancelled. Consequently, it makes no difference whether we discount constant dollar cash flow estimates at the real rate or nominal cash flow estimates at the nominal market discount rate. In this special case, we get the same NPV either way.

Risk and the Market Discount Rate

So far, we have discussed three of the four components of a security's rate of return: the real rate, expected inflation over the life of the security, and the liquidity premium. The remaining element is risk and it can be broken down into two categories: default risk and covariance risk. *Default risk* is most relevant for corporate long-term debt where there is a chance of bankruptcy. We will discuss it first, and then move on to *covariance risk*, which has to do with the sensitivity of security prices to changes in general economic conditions.

The usual method for determining the default risk of corporate long-term debt is to refer to the *bond ratings* supplied by various agencies. Major bond rating agencies are Moody's

Table 7.6   Sample of New Issues by Moody's Rating of Issue

Rating	Industrials	% of Total	Utilities	% of Total
Aaa	29	26.1	14	20.6
Aa	18	16.2	14	20.6
A	38	34.3	18	26.5
Baa	20	18.0	20	29.4
Ba	1	0.9	2	2.9
B	5	4.5	0	0
	111	100.0	68	100.0

Source: Adapted from Mark Weinstein, "The Effect of a Rating Change Announcement on Bond Price," *Journal of Financial Economics*, December 1977.

Investors Service Inc., Standard & Poor's Corp., and Fitch Investor Service. Moody's bond rating has seven classifications ranging from Aaa, which is the highest quality bond, down to Caa, the lowest quality. Weinstein [1977] collected data on 179 new bond issues between 1962 and 1964. Table 7.6 shows the distribution by risk class. About 40 percent of the new bonds qualified for the two highest quality ratings. Figure 7.7 shows the yields on bonds of different risk. Just as expected, the high-quality, low-risk bonds have lower yields than do the low-quality, high-risk bonds. Of the roughly 2,000 major corporations that are evaluated by the agencies, approximately 500 are rerated quarterly because they issue commercial paper, another 500 are rerated annually (most of the utilities), and the remaining 1,000 have no established review date but are usually reviewed annually.

From an investor's point of view, one might ask the following question: Do the agencies determine the prices and interest rates paid for bonds or do investors in the capital markets? The evidence collected by Wakeman [1978] and Weinstein [1978] shows that changes in bond ratings are not treated as new information by capital markets. In fact, changes in ratings usually occur several months after the capital markets have already reacted to the fundamental change in the bond's quality. Changes in agency ratings do not cause changes in required yields to maturity. It is the other way around. However, this does not imply that bond ratings are without value. On average, the ratings provide unbiased estimates of bond risk and are therefore a useful source of information.

The yields to maturity plotted in Figure 7.7 are only *promised* yields. They are calculated by assuming that a bond, regardless of its rating, will pay off all cash flows as promised. For example, consider a 10 percent coupon bond with only one year to maturity which promises to pay a $1,000 face value and a coupon of $100 at maturity. If it was riskless and if the market risk-free rate was 10 percent, then the current price of the bond, B_0, would be

$$B_0 = \$1,000 = \frac{\$1,000 + \$100}{1.1}.$$

But, suppose it has a high probability of default, so that the market prices it at $700. Then, the yield to maturity would be calculated as follows:

$$B_0 = \$700 = \frac{\$1,000 + \$100}{1 + R}$$

Figure 7.7   Comparison of Bond Yields for Bonds of Different Risks

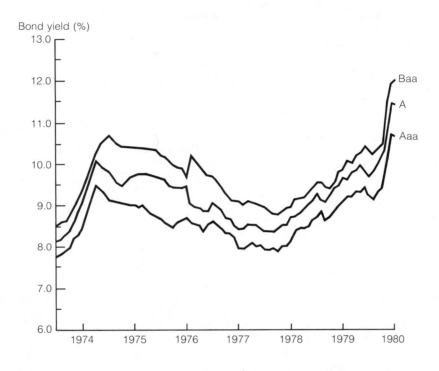

Source: *Federal Reserve Bulletin*, Board of Governors of the Federal Reserve System, various issues.

$$R = \frac{\$1,100}{\$700} - 1 = 57.14\%.$$

Thus, 57.14 percent is the yield which would be plotted in Figure 7.7. But, 57.14 percent is actually only a *promised* yield. Suppose there is a 30 percent chance of default (with no payment at all). Then, the expected end-of-year payout is really a 30 percent chance of receiving nothing and a 70 percent chance of receiving $1,100. If you receive nothing, your rate of return is −100 percent:

$$\text{Return} = \frac{\$0 - \$700}{\$700} = -100\%,$$

and if you receive $1,100, your return is 57.14 percent.

In order to compute the *expected rate of return* on the risky bond, it is necessary to use the expected cash flows in the numerator. Therefore, we must rewrite the bond valuation equation as follows:

$$B_0 = \frac{E(\text{coupon} + \text{face value})}{1 + E(\text{rate of return})}.$$

The expected, or average, cash flows are the promised cash flows, each multiplied by its respective probability. In our example, they are

$$E(\text{coupon} + \text{face value}) = .3(\text{no payment}) + .7(\$1,100)$$

$$= \$770.$$

The expected cash flow is what you would receive if you held a large well-diversified portfolio of bonds of similar default risk (but no market covariance risk). If the market value (B_0) of our bond is $700, then the expected return is

$$\$700 = \frac{\$770}{1 + E(\text{rate of return})}$$

$$E(\text{rate of return}) = 10\%.$$

This is the same return as expected on a completely default-free bond. The purpose of this example is to show that the difference in yields on bonds of different risk, as illustrated in Figure 7.7, is really a difference in promised yields and is therefore a measure of the market's estimate of the default risk of various grades of bonds.[7] If yields to maturity were calculated by using expected cash flows instead of promised cash flows, most of the yield differences in Figure 7.7 would disappear.

To the extent that default risk is independent of whatever else is happening in the economy, it can be diversified away at relatively low cost by simply holding a large portfolio of risky debt. This is how commercial banks form their loan portfolios. However, when risk cannot be diversified away because returns covary with the economy, then investors will require higher *expected* rates of return to compensate them for the covariance risk they undertake. A complete explanation of covariance risk and how it is priced in equilibrium will fill all of Chapters 16 and 17. Figure 7.8, however, gives a rough idea of how differences in covariance risk affect the expected rates of return on different types of securities. Treasury bills are virtually risk-free. Long-term corporate bonds are riskier because their probability of default depends in part on whether the economy is in a recession or recovery. Common stock is much more sensitive to the state of the economy and, consequently, has greater undiversifiable risk and a higher expected return. Finally, options are very risky and require among the highest expected rates of return.

Summary

The observed nominal pretax rate of return on any asset can be explained by four factors: the real rate of return, expected inflation, liquidity, and risk.

Nominal rate $= f\,[E(\text{real rate}), E(\text{inflation}), E(\text{liquidity premium}), E(\text{risk premium})]$.

---

[7]We used a one-period bond to illustrate the expected yield. If multi-period bonds are used, one merely uses the *expected* coupons and face value and then solves for the expected yield to maturity which equates the present value of the bond's expected cash flows with its current market price. Problem 7.11 illustrates the procedure.

Figure 7.8   The Risk-Return Tradeoff

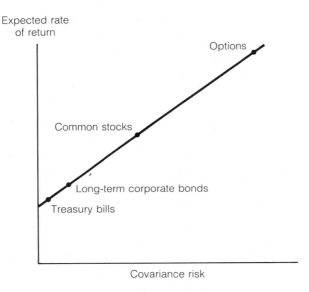

Assets can be grouped according to how they fit these characteristics. For example, one can collect all Aaa rated corporate bonds with ten years to maturity. Within this group, all four factors are held constant. Consequently, all securities within the group are close economic substitutes and will have the same nominal rate of return. Other characteristics, such as the name of the company issuing the bond, its date of issue, or the name of the investor currently holding it are completely irrelevant.

Understanding the economic determinants of nominal rates of return helps to sort out the confusion about why rates of return differ from security to security. Common stocks have averaged 9.1 percent per year between 1926 and 1981 primarily because they are riskier than long-term corporate bonds which have yielded 3.6 percent. On any given day, long-term bonds of a given default risk will have higher (or lower) promised yields than short-term bonds with the same default risk either because the long-term bonds are less liquid (or because expected inflation is higher in the long run).

We have also seen that sophisticated capital budgeting requires that the term structure of interest rates and expected inflation be taken into account. This has become particularly important in recent years, when double-digit inflation has been common worldwide.

Questions

7.1   What happens to the real rate of interest when the demand for capital increases because technological innovations have caused the aggregate investment opportunity set to increase?

7.2   What happens to the real rate of interest and to the amount of investment in the private sector if the government decides to borrow in the capital markets in order to fund a large unexpected deficit?

7.3   Why is the long-run rate of return on long-term corporate bonds (3.6 percent) higher than the long-run rate of return on long-term U.S. government debt (3.0 percent)?

7.4   If the rate of return on long-term U.S. government bonds has been 3.0 percent, if long-run inflation (1926–1982) has been 3 percent and the rate of return on U.S. Treasury bills (that is, short-term U.S. government bonds) has also been 3.0 percent, what does this suggest about the liquidity premium on long-term bonds?

7.5   Given that the liquidity premium is positive, how can you explain a downward-sloping term structure?

7.6   What is the major implication of Fisher separation?

7.7   There have been times when the term structure of interest rates has been such that short-term rates were higher than long-term rates. Does this necessarily imply that the best financial policy for a firm is to use all long-term debt and no short-term debt? Explain.

7.8   How would you use the term structure to predict inflation?

7.9   What is the difference between the promised return and the expected return on risky long-term bonds?

7.10 Why is the historical rate of return on common stock (9.1 percent) higher than the rate on long-term corporate bonds (3.6 percent)?

Problems

7.1   Given below are the investment opportunity schedules and subjective rates of return for two investors:

$$\text{Mr. A} \qquad r_A = 20 - 5I_A, \text{ subjective rate} = r_A = 10\%.$$

$$\text{Ms. B} \qquad r_B = 15 - I_B, \text{ subjective rate} = r_B = 5\%.$$

   a)   How much will each investor seek to invest if they cannot borrow or lend?
   b)   If they can borrow and lend, (1) what will the market equilibrium interest rate be? and (2) how much will each borrow or lend?
   c)   How will your answers to Part (b) change if Mr. A's subjective rate increases to 15 percent?

7.2   From the pair of yield curves presented in Figure P7.2, what generalizations can be made on the behavior of financial markets between 1981 and 1984?

7.3   From a recent issue of the *Federal Reserve Bulletin* or from another convenient source:
   a)   Construct a yield curve for the most recent monthly 1979 data for U.S. government securities, using market yields for maturities of one year or less and the capital market rates for constant maturities for the maturities from 2 to 20 years.
   b)   Why does the yield curve show only U.S. government security yields instead of including yields on commercial paper and corporate bonds?

Figure P7.2　　Term Structures in 1981 and 1984

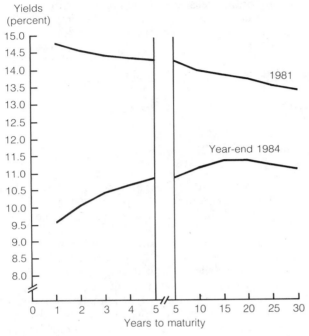

Source: *Federal Reserve Bulletin*, February 1985, Table 1.35, p. A26.

7.4　Suppose that expected future short-term interest rates have the following alternative patterns:

Year	A	B	C	D
1	4%	8%	4%	8%
2	5	7	6	7
3	6	6	15	5
4	7	5	6	7
5	8	4	4	8

a)　Using a simple arithmetic average, what is the current rate on a five-year note for each of the four patterns?

b)　Using a geometric average, answer the same question as for Part (a). (Hint: Add 1 to each percentage (for example, 1.04), then multiply the five numbers, and then take their fifth root. Subtract 1 from the result. On a hand calculator, use the y^x or x^x button with 0.2, which equals 1/5. For example, for interest rate A, the product is 1.3376, and the fifth root minus 1 is 5.991 percent.)

c) Optional:
  1. Calculate the current two-, three-, and four-year note yields using both the arithmetic and geometric averages and then graph the resulting yield curves in four graphs of two curves each.
  2. Is the height of the yield curve based on the arithmetic averages higher or lower than that based on the geometric averages?

7.5 Given below are the yields to maturity on a five-year bond:

Years to Maturity	Yield to Maturity
1	8.0
2	9.0
3	10.0
4	10.5
5	10.8

a) What is the implied forward rate of interest for the third year?
b) What (geometric) average annual rate of interest would you receive if you bought a bond at the beginning of the third year and sold it at the beginning of the fifth year?

7.6 The Comex Company is considering investing in a machine that produces Frisbees. The cost of the machine is $40,000. Production by year during the four-year life of the machine is expected to be as follows: 12,000 units, 16,000 units, 20,000 units, and 18,000 units. The market for Frisbees is increasing; hence, management believes that the price of Frisbees will increase at about 10 percent annually, compared to the general rate of inflation of 9 percent. The price of Frisbees in the first year will be $2, but plastic used to produce Frisbees is rapidly becoming more expensive. Because of this, production cash outflows are expected to grow at 15 percent per year. First-year production cost will be $1 per unit.

The company will use sum-of-years'-digits depreciation on the new machine. There will be no salvage value at the end of the fourth year. The company's tax rate is 40 percent, and its cost of capital is 18 percent, based on the existing rate of inflation. Should the project be undertaken?

7.7 Your firm is considering an investment in a machine that produces bowling balls. The cost of the machine is $100,000 with zero expected salvage value. Annual production in units during the five-year life of the machine is expected to be 5,000, 8,000, 12,000, 10,000, and 6,000.

The price of bowling balls is expected to rise from $20 during Year 1 at a rate of 2 percent per year for the following four years. Production cash outflows are expected to grow at 10 percent per year from the first-year production costs of $10 per unit.

Depreciation of the machine will be on a straight line basis. The applicable tax rate is 40 percent, and the applicable cost of capital is 15 percent. Should the investment in the machine be made?

7.8 You are given the following information about an investment of $40,000: It is expected to yield benefits over a five-year period. It is also expected that there will be annual cash inflows of $90,000 and annual cash outflows of $75,000, excluding taxes and the depreciation tax shelter. There will be no salvage value; straight line depreciation is used. The tax rate is 40 percent, and the cost of capital is 8 percent.
a) Compute the net present value of the investment.

b)   On investigation, you discover that no adjustments have been made for inflation or price level changes. Year 1 data are correct, but after that, inflows are expected to increase at 4 percent per year and outflows at 6 percent per year. The general rate of inflation is expected to be about 6 percent, causing the cost of capital to rise to 14 percent. Reevaluate the net present value of the project in light of this information.

7.9   The table below gives the yields to maturity and implied forward rates on bonds which are expected to have about the same risk as two projects which your firm is considering (Projects A and B). Cash flows are also given in the table.

Year	Yield to Maturity	Forward Rate	Cash Flow for A	Cash Flow for B
0	—	—	$-100	$-100
1	21%	21.00%	62	48
2	18	15.07	50	52
3	16	12.10	28	44

You have been asked to answer the following questions.

a)   Common practice is to use the yield to maturity on three-year bonds as the appropriate discount rate for the project's cash flows. What is the NPV of the two projects if you use this rate?

b)   An alternative is to use the annual forward rates to discount the cash flows. What is the NPV of each project if you use this procedure?

c)   Which procedure is correct? Why?

7.10   The table below gives the yields to maturity for bonds with approximately the same risk as Project X and Project Y, for which cash flows are also given.

Year	Yield to Maturity	Cash Flows	
		X	Y
0	—	-1,000	-1,000
1	14.00%	300	600
2	15.00%	400	500
3	15.99%	600	200

a)   Find the NPV of each project using the three-year yield to maturity.

b)   Find the NPV of each project using the annual forward rates to discount cash flows.

7.11   You have priced two pure discount bonds, each with five years to maturity and with a face value of $1,000. They pay no coupons. The first bond sells for $780.58 and the second sells for $667.43.

a)   What are their yields to maturity?

b)   Why does the second bond sell for less than the first?

c)   If their default risk is uncorrelated with the rest of the economy, then their expected cash flows can be discounted at the riskless rate, which is 5 percent. If they have the same expected yield, what is the probability of default for the second bond? (Assume that if the bond defaults, you receive nothing, but if it does not default, you receive the full face value.)

Selected References

Bierman, H., Jr., and Smidt, S., *The Capital Budgeting Decision*, 4th ed., New York: Macmillan, 1975.

Cooley, P. L.; Roenfeldt, R. L.; and Chew, I. K., "Capital Budgeting Procedures Under Inflation," *Financial Management*, (Winter 1975), pp. 18-27.

Copeland, Thomas E., and Weston, J. Fred, *Financial Theory and Corporate Policy*, 2nd edition, Reading, Massachusetts: Addison Wesley, 1983.

Cornell, Bradford, "Money Supply Announcements and Interest Rates: Another View," *Journal of Business*, 56 (January 1983), pp. 1-23.

Cox, John C.; Ingersoll, Jonathan E., Jr.; and Ross, Stephen A., "The Relation Between Forward Prices and Future Prices," *Journal of Financial Economics*, 9 (December 1981), pp. 321-346.

————, "A Re-examination of Traditional Hypotheses about the Term Structure of Interest Rates," *Journal of Finance*, 36 (September 1981), pp. 769-799.

————, "A Theory of the Term Structure of Interest Rates," unpublished working paper, Stanford University, 1980.

Culbertson, J. M., "The Term Structure of Interest Rates," *Quarterly Journal of Economics*, (November 1957), pp. 489-504.

Dobson, Steven W.; Sutch, Richard C.; and Vanderford, David F., "An Evaluation of Alternative Empirical Models of the Term Structure of Interest Rates," *Journal of Finance*, 31 (September 1976), pp. 1035-1065.

Fama, Eugene F., "Term Premiums in Bond Returns," working paper, University of Chicago, (August 1983).

————, "The Information in the Term Structure," working paper, University of Chicago, (March 1983).

————, "Stock Returns, Real Activity, Inflation and Money," *American Economic Review*, (September 1981), pp. 545-565.

————, "Interest Rates and Inflation: The Message in the Entrails," *American Economic Review*, (June 1977), pp. 487-496.

————, "Short-term Interest Rates as Predictors of Inflation," *American Economic Review*, (June 1975), pp. 269-282.

Fama, Eugene F., and Schwert, G. William, "Inflation, Interest, and Relative Prices," *Journal of Business*, 52 (April 1979), pp. 183-209.

————, "Asset Returns and Inflation," *Journal of Financial Economics*, (November 1977), pp. 113-146.

Findlay, M. C., and Frankle, A. W., "Capital Budgeting Procedures under Inflation: Cooley, Roenfeldt and Chew vs. Findlay and Frankle," *Financial Management*, (Autumn 1976), pp. 83-90.

Fisher, I., *The Theory of Interest*, New York: Macmillan, 1930.

————, "Appreciation and Interest," *Publications of the American Economic Association*, (August 1896), pp. 23-29, 91-92.

Gultekin, N. Bulent, "Stock Market Returns and Inflation: Evidence from Other Countries," *Journal of Finance*, (March 1983), pp. 49-65.

Hess, P., and Bicksler, J., "Capital Asset Prices versus Time Series Models as Predictors of Inflation," *Journal of Financial Economics*, (December 1975), pp. 341-360.

Hicks, J. R., *Value and Capital*, 2nd edition, London: Oxford University Press, 1946.

Hirshleifer, J., "Liquidity, Uncertainty, and the Accumulation of Information," in Carter and Ford, eds., *Essays in Honor of G. L. S. Shackle*, Oxford: Basil Blackwell, 1972.

————, *Investment, Interest and Capital*, Englewood Cliffs, New Jersey: Prentice-Hall, 1970.

Ibbotson, Roger G., and Sinquefield, Rex A., *Stocks, Bonds, Bills, and Inflation: The Past and the Future*, Charlottesville, Virginia: The Financial Analysts Research Foundation, Monograph #15, 1982.

Long, J. B., "Stock Prices, Inflation and the Term Structure of Interest Rates," *Journal of Financial Economics*, 1 (July 1974), pp. 131-170.

Lutz, F. A., "The Structure of Interest Rates," *Quarterly Journal of Economics*, (November 1940), pp. 36-63.

Malkiel, B. G., "Expectations, Bond Prices, and the Term Structure of Interest Rates," *Quarterly Journal of Economics*, (May 1962), pp. 197-218.

McCulloch, J. H., "An Estimate of the Liquidity Premium," *Journal of Political Economy*, (January-February 1975), pp. 95-119.

Meiselman, D., *The Term Structure of Interest Rates*, Princeton, New Jersey: Princeton University Press, 1966.

Modigliani, F., and Sutch, R., "Debt Management and the Term Structure of Interest Rates: An Empirical Analysis," *Journal of Political Economy*, 75 (August 1967), pp. 569-589.

Nelson, C., and Schwert, G. William, "Short-term Interest Rates as Predictors of Inflation: On Testing the Hypothesis that the Real Rate is Constant," *American Economic Review*, (June 1977), pp. 478-486.

Roley, V. Vance, "The Determinants of the Treasury Security Yield Curve," *Journal of Finance*, 36 (December 1981), pp. 1103-1126.

Roll, R., *The Behavior of Interest Rates: An Application of the Efficient Market Model to U.S. Treasury Bills*, New York: Basic Books, 1970.

Sargent, T., "Rational Expectations and the Term Structure of Interest Rates," *Journal of Money, Credit and Banking*, (February 1972), pp. 74-97.

Solnik, B., "The Relation Between Stock Prices and Inflationary Expectations: The International Evidence," *Journal of Finance*, (March 1983), pp. 35-48.

Van Horne, J. C., *Financial Markets and Flows*, Englewood Cliffs, N. J.: Prentice Hall, 1978.

———, "A Note on Biases on Capital Budgeting Introduced by Inflation," *Journal of Financial and Quantitative Analysis*, (January 1971), pp. 653-658.

Wakeman, Lee, "Bond Rating Agencies and Capital Markets," working paper, Graduate School of Management, University of Rochester, Rochester, New York, 1978.

Weinstein, Mark, "The Seasoning Process of New Corporate Bond Issues," *Journal of Finance*, (December 1978), pp. 1343-1354.

———, "The Effect of a Rating Change Announcement on Bond Price," *Journal of Financial Economics*, (December 1977), pp. 329-350.

Wood, J. H., "Expectations, Error and the Term Structure of Interest Rates," *Journal of Political Economy*, (April 1963), pp. 160-171.

Woodward, Susan, "The Liquidity Premium and the Solidity Premium," *The American Economic Review*, (June 1983), pp. 348-361.

Appendix A to Chapter 7
Interest Rate Futures and Riding the Yield Curve

Forward Rates and Futures Rates

Equation 7.4 showed how forward rates could be computed by taking the ratio of yields to maturity for bonds of adjacent maturity. Mathematically, this was

$$1 + {}_tf_{t+1} = \frac{(1 + {}_0R_{t+1})^{t+1}}{(1 + {}_0R_t)^t}.$$ (7A.1)

Forward rates are of importance because of their economic nature. The forward rate is the marginal return gained from an investment by holding or committing the investment for one additional time period. Thus, the forward rate represents a return that will be realized over a future time period if the expectations implied by the current term structure of interest rates are realized.

Another form of return from an investment held over a future time period is measured by the *futures rate*. Interest rate futures are contracts that call for transactions in specified financial instruments to take place on stated future dates. The yields on futures contracts for a series of years into the future would, in the absence of frictions or other types of market imperfections, be the same as the implied forward rates. The only difference between forward and futures contracts is that the daily gain or loss from holding a futures contract is transferred between traders at the end of each day, while the profits and losses from holding a forward contract accumulate until the contract matures. Whether or not this distinction makes any difference is, in actuality, a matter of empirical testing. Strong divergences between the two sets of rates may offer possible profit-making opportunities. The relationship between futures and forward rates has become significant in recent years with the development of a market in interest rate futures.

The Establishment of an Interest Rate Futures Market

Interest rate futures are a relatively new development. In the fall of 1975, the Chicago Board of Trade established a contract for GNMA's (Government National Mortgage Association Securities). In early 1976, the International Monetary Market (IMM) of the Chicago Mercantile Exchange introduced a contract for 90-day Treasury bills. In 1977, the Chicago Board of Trade (CBT) extended trading to Treasury bond futures contracts. On August 7, 1980, the New York Stock Exchange, through its wholly owned subsidiary, the New York Futures Exchange, began trading in futures contracts for five major currencies plus 20-year Treasury bonds. At the opening, it was estimated that during 1979 the trading volume averaged about 50,000 contracts a day on the Chicago Board of Trade and on the IMM and that the New York Futures Exchange would reach between 15 percent and 20 percent of that volume in its first year.

The volume in these interest rate futures has grown substantially. For example, on an average day in 1979, futures contracts representing about $7 1/2 billion in three-month Treasury bills were traded on the International Monetary Market of the Chicago Mercantile Exchange. On an average day in 1979 at the Chicago Board of Trade, futures contracts representing almost $1 billion of long-term Treasury bonds were traded. Also, futures contracts representing over $1/2 billion of GNMA's changed hands on an average day in 1979.

The financial futures markets operate as do other futures markets. One of the most active futures markets is for three-month Treasury bills at the IMM. Through this exchange, a customer might buy a contract to take delivery of and pay for $1 million of three-month Treasury bills on March 20, 1986. There are eight contract delivery months extending at quarterly intervals for about two years into the future.

The contract price is quoted as the difference between $100 and the discount rate on the bill in question. Thus, a contract fixing a bill rate at 8.5 percent would be quoted at $91.50. A clearinghouse places itself between the buyer and the seller, so that the buyer's contract is not with the seller but with the clearinghouse. Also, the seller's contract is with the clearinghouse and not with the original buyer. For the financial liability of the clearinghouse, the clearing member firms must place margins on their contracts. For each purchase or sale of a three-month Treasury bill contract of $1 million on the IMM, the clearing member firm must post a margin of $1,200, which can be in the form of cash or a bank letter of credit. The clearing member firm, in turn, imposes an initial margin of at least $1,500 on the individual trader.

While the position is outstanding, the contract will be "marked-to-market" by the clearinghouse at the end of each business day. Either profits or losses are recorded, based on the position and price movements. Profits in the margin account may be withdrawn. If losses reduce the firm's margin below $1,200, the firm must make up the difference to the clearinghouse in cash before the clearinghouse opens the next day. The customer's margin account may fall below the initial $1,500; but if it falls below the $1,200 maintenance margin, the account must be brought back up to $1,500. There are also daily limits on the degree of price fluctuations. At the IMM, for example, no futures trades in Treasury bills can involve prices more than 50 basis points above or below the final settlement price of the previous day, though these margins may be temporarily increased if the daily limit restricts trading for a few days. (One hundred basis points equal 1 percent. The number of basis points is a convenient way to describe interest rate changes of fractions of a percent.)

The Relationship between the Forward and Futures Rates

In theory, in the absence of frictions and other market imperfections, a divergence between forward and futures rates could not persist. We shall illustrate how arbitrage operations under idealized conditions would prevent the persistence of a divergence. The basic data to be used in the analysis are set forth in Figure 7A.1.

Arbitrage operations simply imply that transactions can be made to obtain a sure profit without any risk. This will be illustrated by the pattern of data assumed in Figure 7A.1. In that figure, rates are presented for four categories of Treasury bills. Treasury bill A is a 182-day bill yielding 10.6 percent. T-bill B is a 91-day bill starting immediately and carrying a yield of 10 percent. T-bill C is a 91-day bill starting 91 days later and bearing a yield of 11.2 percent. Continuous compounding is assumed, so the yield on the 182-day bill is a

Figure 7A.1   Pattern of Rates to Illustrate Arbitrage Operations

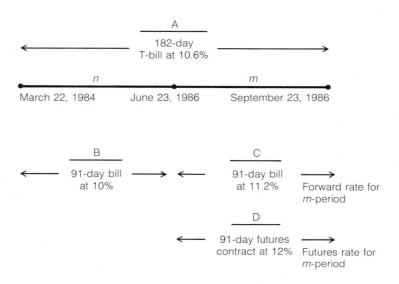

simple average of the yields on the successive 91-day bills spanned by bill A. Finally, Item D is a 91-day futures contract covering the second 91-day period and carrying a yield of 12 percent. The 12 percent yield for the T-bill futures contract is chosen arbitrarily above bill C to illustrate the arbitrage transactions that would be stimulated.

The patterns imply a positive term structure with the rate on the futures contract assumed to be above the rate on the forward contract. In the example, the implied forward rate is the 11.2 percent on T-bill C. Under the relationships assumed, the following actions would be taken.

1.   Buying the 91-day T-bill futures contract to run for the *m* period after the elapse of the *n* period.
2.   Taking a long position in the 91-day T-bill B for the *n* period.
3.   Selling short the 182-day T-bill A for the (*n* + *m*) period.

The second and third transactions are equivalent to shorting a 91-day T-bill for the *m* period.

Thus, one earns 12 percent on the futures contract while paying only 11.2 percent in the short position in the 91-day T-bill for the *m* period. The results could also be expressed in terms of the lower price paid for the futures contract in which the buyer is taking a long position and the higher price on the forward contract that is sold short.

In expressing the results in the prices of the Treasury bills, we will follow the pattern laid out by Capozza and Cornell [1979]. Although the T-bill futures contracts are denominated in units of $1 million, for ease of encompassing the numbers, we will assume units of $1,000. The results are shown in Table 7A.1.

Table 7A.1   Gain from Arbitraging When the Futures Rate Exceeds the Forward Rate

---

At time t:
Inflow from shorting 182-day bill $(n + m)$ $\quad = \exp[-0.106(0.5)](\$1,000)^a \quad = \$ \ 948.38$
Outflow for investment in n-day bills
(91 days) $\qquad\qquad\qquad\qquad\qquad\qquad\qquad\qquad\qquad\qquad\qquad\qquad\quad \$ \ 948.38$

Net $\qquad\qquad\qquad\qquad\qquad\qquad\qquad\qquad\qquad\qquad\qquad\qquad\qquad\quad = \$ \quad 0$

At time $t + n$ (end of 91 days):
Inflow from maturation of n-day bills $\qquad = (948.38/975.31)(\$1,000)^b \quad = \$ \ 972.39$
Outflow from taking delivery of bills on
the futures contracts $\qquad\qquad\qquad\qquad = \exp[-0.12(0.25)](\$1,000) \quad = \$ \ 970.45$

Net gain $\qquad\qquad\qquad\qquad\qquad\qquad\qquad\qquad\qquad\qquad\qquad\qquad\quad = \$ \qquad 1.94 \text{ per bond}$

At time $t + n + m$:
Inflow from maturation of the m-day bill
bought through the futures market $\qquad\qquad\qquad\qquad\qquad\qquad\qquad\qquad =\$1,000.00$
Outflow from maturation of the shorted
$(n + m)$-day bill $\qquad\qquad\qquad\qquad\qquad\qquad\qquad\qquad\qquad\qquad = \$1,000.00$

Net $\qquad\qquad\qquad\qquad\qquad\qquad\qquad\qquad\qquad\qquad\qquad\qquad\qquad = \$ \quad 0$

---

[a]Since continuous compounding of a discount bond is assumed, to have an annual yield of 10.6 percent requires that its price with six months to run is $e^{-0.106(0.5)}$ times the maturity value of the bond (here assumed to be $1,000). The "exp" is a generally used method of indicating the power to which e is raised.
[b]$975.31 represents the price of the n-day bill at t, so the fraction represents the portion of the $1,000 maturity value purchased from the proceeds of shorting the $(n + m)$-day bill at time t.

The net gain is thus $1.94 per $1,000 of bonds or $1,940 on the standard $1 million T-bill futures contract. In the illustration, the transactor is completely hedged, that is, he takes no risk, and no net investment is required to achieve the sure gain. The transactions would be expected to eliminate this arbitrage opportunity. Selling short the 182-day bill would tend to decrease its price, driving up its yield. Purchase of the futures contracts would tend to drive up their price and reduce their yield until profitable arbitrage opportunities no longer existed. Before reviewing the empirical studies on the relationship between forward and futures rates, we have laid the necessary foundation of discussing the concept of riding the yield curve.

Riding the Yield Curve

As interest rates have risen in recent years, cash managers have tried to avoid holding idle cash. Rather, they have sought to obtain a return by investing cash balances. A substantial amount of such funds has been placed in highly liquid, interest-earning marketable securities. U.S. Treasury bills have been used substantially as investment instruments. The Treasury bills futures market has enabled investments in Treasury bills to be made in a number of ways.

Suppose a cash manager has $1 million and will need it in 91 days to meet a commitment. During this time period, however, the cash manager wishes to earn interest on the $1 million and so invests in Treasury bills. There are at least three ways the cash manager can invest in the T-bills:

1. Invest for a maturity of less than 91 days, planning to roll over the investment into other, successive bills maturing at the end of 91 days.
2. Buy a Treasury bill maturing in exactly 91 days.
3. Buy a Treasury bill of maturity longer than 91 days with a plan to sell the bill at the end of the 91 days.

The strategy of purchasing bills of maturities longer than the planned holding period and selling them prior to maturity is referred to as *riding the yield curve.*

If the term structure of interest rates is positive, the longer maturity the cash manager can get into, the higher will be the yield. But the term structure itself reflects expectations of future supply and demand relationships, and these are subject to change. Risks can come from a number of sources. Changes may take place in the term structure of interest rates. The relation between the spot, forward, and futures markets may change. Hence, among the alternatives that the cash manager may take to invest available funds are different kinds and degrees of risk in relation to potential movements and changes in the money and capital markets.

One alternative is to *match maturities*. This would represent simply buying, under our example, a 91-day Treasury bill. The funds earn whatever Treasury bills earn during that 91-day period of time. Another alternative would be to ride the yield curve on an unhedged basis. An illustration would be to buy 182-day Treasury bills with the intention of selling them at the end of 91 days.

A third alternative would be to ride the yield curve in a hedged position. To illustrate this concretely, we will use the data in Figure 7A.1, except that the rate on the futures contract for Period m will be assumed to be equal to the forward rate for the same time period (at 11.2 percent). With the positively sloped yield curve reflected in the data of Figure 7A.1, the transactions to ride the yield curve in a hedged position would be the following:

1. On March 22, 1984, buy the 182-day T-bill on a 10.6 percent basis at \$948.38.
2. Sell a 91-day futures contract on an 11.2 percent basis at \$972.39.
3. On June 23, 1984, deliver the T-bill with 91 days remaining to meet the futures contract requirement.

The cash manager has locked in the 10.6 percent yield on the 182-day bill as compared with the lower 10 percent yield on the 91-day bill available on March 22, 1984.

The differential gain from riding the yield curve in a hedged position results from the positive slope of the term structure curve and the relationship between short-term and long-term rates, which reflects the unbiased expectations theory. But compared with simply taking a position in the 91-day T-bill, riding the yield curve in a hedged position requires two transactions and commissions instead of one. So the results also depend on the commission levels in relation to the extent to which the yield curve is positively sloped. Also, of course, the higher demand for the 182-day bill as compared with the 91-day bill will tend to drive up the price (lower the yield) of the longer-term bill (as compared with the shorter-term bill). The sale of the T-bill futures will tend to drive down their prices (raise the required yields). Thus, the actions taken to benefit from the positively sloped term structure will tend to flatten the slope of the curve.

In the light of transactions of the types described above, it is not likely that opportunities for abnormal returns would persist. But the matter is best settled by empirical studies in the area.

Empirical Studies of Yields on Futures Contracts and the Behavior of Forward Rates

Empirical studies of opportunities for arbitrage profits in the relationship between forward and futures market rates have yielded different results through time. Both Puglisi [1978] and Branch [1978] found gains derived from hedged riding of the yield curve. Ederington [1979] found the results to be less consistent. Capozza and Cornell [1979] observed a substantial differential of futures rates above implied forward rates for contracts whose maturities extended beyond 17 to 18 weeks. A study of a later time period by Arak and McCurdy [1979] observed forward rates higher than futures rates on the June 1979 Treasury bills contracts over the period from November 1978 through April 1979. Arak and McCurdy also observed a substantial spread, with higher forward rates than futures rates in the September 1979 Treasury bill futures contracts traded on the International Monetary Market, particularly in June and July of 1979.

Most studies have found that the futures rates are below the forward rates near the maturity date of the futures contracts. The explanation generally given is the lower transactions costs in the futures contracts as compared with the spot or forward markets, in which transactions costs are generally greater.

For longer maturities, the persistently higher futures rates over forward rates that Capozza and Cornell observed are explained by the higher risk in futures contracts. Transactions in the Treasury bill cash and forward markets involve the creditworthiness of the instrument itself, and the T-bill presumably has no credit risk. The futures contracts, by contrast, involve the creditworthiness of the customers, of the trading firms, and of the clearinghouses. Therefore, futures contracts may involve some greater risks than do spot and forward contracts.

Conclusions on Opportunities in the Interest Rate Futures Markets

Like other futures markets, the interest rate futures markets perform socially useful economic functions. The futures markets rates themselves record expectations of future interest rate levels. And, as with other futures markets, the futures markets in interest rates can be used to reduce the risk of taking or holding a position in financial instruments.

Opportunities for arbitrage gains depend on the relationships among the spot, forward, and futures markets. The positive or negative yield curve structure also determines the kind of strategies that may be profitable, and so, of course, the yield curve acts both as a stimulus and as a restraint. The cost of hedging will depend on the relative costs of using the forward and futures markets. In addition, transactions costs are important in determining the potential benefits of using the interest rate futures markets. If transactions costs are high, arbitrage opportunities are more limited. If transactions costs are low, periods can occur when arbitrage opportunities may exist.

Interest rate futures markets have been used in part to avoid taxes, the trader in this instance converts ordinary income into capital gains. However, Treasury rulings have greatly restricted the use of the interest rate futures markets in this way. One would expect different results from empirical studies done before and after these key rulings. One would also expect that competition would cause some of the tax avoidance benefits to be passed on to traders on the other side of the transactions.

It is also not surprising that speculators use the interest rate futures markets. To the extent that they do, the increased activity should be helpful to traders who have a need for hedging. This will be true only if the speculative activity does not introduce abnormal fluctuations and shifts in the underlying patterns of relationships.

In the long run, we would expect the interest rate futures markets to provide another alternative in the range of potential risk-return positions that a cash or a financial manager might employ. The interest rate futures markets can be viewed from two standpoints. First, the patterns between forward rates and interest rate futures provide opportunities for reducing risk by hedging and for bearing risk by taking speculative positions.

A second way to view the interest rate futures markets is in terms of the basic relations between spot and futures markets. If a commodity is storable, it can be bought today, stored, and sold at a future date. If the futures price were to exceed the spot price by more than the costs involved in storing, arbitrageurs would buy the commodity in the spot market — raising the price — and would sell it in the futures market, lowering the futures price. These activities would reduce the disparity between the futures price and the current price. Thus, a second benefit a futures market provides is to develop appropriate relationships between spot prices and futures prices.

Selected References

Arak, Marcelle, and McCurdy, Christopher J., "Interest Rate Futures," *Quarterly Review, Federal Reserve Bank of New York*, 4 (Winter 1979-1980), pp. 33-46.

Baesel, Jerome, and Grant, Dwight, "Optimal Sequential Futures Trading," *Journal of Financial and Quantitative Analysis*, 17 (December 1982), pp. 683-695.

Black, Fisher, "The Pricing of Commodity Contracts," *Journal of Financial Economics*, 3 (March 1976), pp. 167-179.

Branch, Ben, "Testing the Unbiased Expectations Theory of Interest Rates," *Financial Review*, (Fall 1978), pp. 51-66.

Capozza, Dennis R., and Cornell, Bradford, "Treasury Bill Pricing in the Spot and Futures Markets," *Review of Economics and Statistics*, 61 (November 1979), pp. 513-520.

Cornell, Bradford, and Reinganum, Mark, "Forward and Futures Prices: Evidence from the Foreign Exchange Markets," *Journal of Finance*, 36 (December 1981), pp. 1035-1045.

Cox, John; Ingersoll, Jon; and Ross, Steve, "The Relation Between Forward Prices and Futures Prices," *Journal of Financial Economics*, (December 1981), pp. 321-346.

Ederington, Louis H., "The Hedging Performance of the New Futures Market," *Journal of Finance*, 34 (March 1979), pp. 157-170.

Fama, Eugene F., "Forward Rates as Predictors of Future Spot Rates," *Journal of Financial Economics*, 3 (October 1976), pp. 361-378.

French, Kenneth R., "A Comparison of Futures and Forward Prices," *Journal of Financial Economics*, 12 (November 1983), pp. 311-342.

Hansen, L., and Hodrick, R., "Forward Exchange Rates as Optimal Predictors of Future Spot Prices: An Econometric Analysis," *Journal of Political Economy*, (October 1980), pp. 829-853.

Jarrow, R., and Oldfield, George, "Forward Contracts and Futures Contracts," *Journal of Financial Economics*, (December 1981), pp. 373-382.

Kolb, Robert W., *Interest Rate Futures: A Comprehensive Introduction*, Richmond, Virginia: Robert F. Dame, Inc., 1982.

Osteryoung, Jerome S.; Roberts, Gordon S.; and McCarty, Daniel E., "Ride the Yield Curve When Investing Idle Funds in Treasury Bills?" *Financial Executive*, 47 (April 1979), pp. 10-15.

Puglisi, Donald J., "Is the Futures Market for Treasury Bills Efficient?" *Journal of Portfolio Management*, 4 (Winter 1978), pp. 64-67.

Rendleman, Richard J., Jr., and Carabini, Christopher E., "The Efficiency of the Treasury Bill Futures Market," *Journal of Finance*, 34 (September 1979), pp. 895-914.

Richard, Scott F., and Sundareson, M., "A Continuous Time Model of Forward Prices and Futures Prices in a Multigood Economy," *Journal of Financial Economics*, (December 1981), pp. 347-372.

Part Three Financial Analysis, Planning, and Control

The chapters of Part Three discuss financial planning and control systems in firms. They provide the framework for planning the firm's growth and the development of financial controls for efficiency. Although these areas of finance do not have the sophistication of the formal models developed in other parts of the book, they are vital to the firm's healthy profitability. Chapter 8 examines the construction and use of the basic ratios of financial analysis; through this ratio analysis, we can pinpoint the firm's strengths and weaknesses.

Chapter 9 begins with the broad planning framework of the relations among revenues, volume, and profits in a breakeven analysis. The chapter then continues with a more detailed consideration of budget systems and controls for decentralized operations.

Chapter 10 takes up financial forecasting: Given a projected increase in sales, how much money must the financial manager raise to support this level of sales?

Finance deals, largely, with very specific questions. Should we lease or buy the new machine? Should we expand capacity at the Hartford plant? Should we raise capital this year by long-term or short-term debt or by selling stock? Should we go along with the marketing department, which wants to expand inventories, or with the production department, which wants to reduce them? Such specific questions, typical of those facing the financial manager, are considered in the remainder of the book. But Part Three takes an overview of the firm. Because all particular decisions are made within the context of the firm's overall position, this overview is critical to an understanding of any individual proposal.

Chapter 8 Financial Ratio Analysis

Planning is the key to the financial manager's success. Financial plans may take many forms, but any good plan must be related to the firm's existing strengths and weaknesses. The strengths must be understood if they are to be used to proper advantage, and the weaknesses must be recognized if corrective action is to be taken. For example, are inventories adequate to support the projected level of sales? Does the firm have too heavy an investment in accounts receivable, and does this condition reflect a lax collection policy? The financial manager can plan future financial requirements in accordance with the forecasting and budgeting procedures we will present in succeeding chapters, but the plan must begin with the type of financial analysis developed in this chapter.

Basic Financial Statements

Because ratio analysis employs financial data taken from the firm's balance sheet and income statement, it is useful to begin with a review of these accounting reports. For illustrative purposes, we shall use data taken from the Walker-Wilson Manufacturing Company, a manufacturer of specialized machinery used in the automobile repair business. Formed in 1961, when Charles Walker and Ben Wilson set up a small plant to produce certain tools they had developed while in the army, Walker-Wilson grew steadily and earned the reputation of being one of the best small firms in its line of business. In December 1983, both Walker and Wilson were killed in a crash of their private plane, and for the next two years, the firm was managed by Walker-Wilson's accountant.

In 1986, the widows, who are the principal stockholders in Walker-Wilson (WW) acting on the advice of the firm's bankers and attorneys, engaged David Thompson as president and general manager. Although Thompson is experienced in the machinery business, especially in production and sales, he does not have a detailed knowledge of his new company. So he has decided to conduct a careful appraisal of the firm's position and, on the basis of this position, to draw up a plan for future operations.

The main financial statements, the income statement and the balance sheet, were described in Chapter 2. Here three types of financial statements for WW are presented to illustrate the use of financial ratio analysis.

Balance Sheet

Walker-Wilson's balance sheet, given in Table 8.1, shows the value of the firm's assets, and of the claims on these assets, at two particular points in time, December 31, 1984, and December 31, 1985. The assets are arranged from top to bottom in order of decreasing

Table 8.1   Walker-Wilson Company Illustrative Balance Sheet (Thousands of Dollars)

Assets		Dec. 31, 1984		Dec. 31, 1985
Cash		$ 52		$ 50
Marketable securities		175		150
Receivables		250		200
Inventories		355		300
Total current assets		$ 832		$ 700
Gross plant and equipment	$1,610		1,800	
Less depreciation	400		500	
Net plant and equipment		1,210		1,300
Total assets		$2,042		$2,000

Claims on Assets		Dec. 31, 1984		Dec. 31, 1985
Accounts payable		$ 87		$ 60
Notes payable (@ 10%)		110		100
Accruals		10		10
Provision for federal income taxes		135		130
Total current liabilities		$ 342		$ 300
First mortgage bonds (@ 8%)[a]		520		500
Debentures (@ 10%)		200		200
Common stock (200,000 shares)	$ 600		$ 600	
Retained earnings	380		400	
Total net worth		980		1,000
Total claims on assets		$2,042		$2,000

[a]The sinking fund requirement for the mortgage bonds is $20,000 a year.

liquidity; that is, assets toward the top of the column will be converted to cash sooner than those toward the bottom of the column. The top group of assets — cash, marketable securities, accounts receivable, and inventories, which are expected to be converted into cash within one year — is defined as *current assets*. Assets in the lower part of the statement — plant and equipment, which are not expected to be converted to cash within one year — are defined as *fixed assets*.

The right side of the balance sheet is arranged similarly. Those items toward the top of the claims column will mature and have to be paid off relatively soon; those further down the column will be due in the more distant future. Current liabilities must be paid within one year; because the firm never has to "pay off" common stockholders, common stock and retained earnings represent "permanent" capital.

Income Statement

Walker-Wilson's income statement is shown in Table 8.2. Sales are at the top of the statement; various costs, including taxes, are deducted to arrive at the net income available to common stockholders.[1] The figure on the last line represents earnings per share (EPS), calculated as net income divided by number of shares outstanding.

Statement of Retained Earnings

Earnings can be paid out to stockholders as dividends or retained and reinvested in the business. Stockholders like to receive dividends, of course; but if earnings are plowed back into the business, the value of the stockholders' position in the company increases. Later in the book, we shall consider the pros and cons of retaining earnings versus paying them out in dividends, but for now, we are simply interested in the effects of dividends and retained earnings on the balance sheet. For this purpose, accountants use the statement of retained earnings, illustrated for Walker-Wilson in Table 8.3. Walker-Wilson earned $120,000 during the year, paid $100,000 in dividends to stockholders, and plowed

Table 8.2   Walker-Wilson Company Illustrative Income Statement
for Year Ended December 31, 1985

Net sales		$3,000,000
Cost of goods sold		2,555,000
Gross profit		$ 445,000
Less operating expenses		
Selling	$22,000	
General and administrative	40,000	
Lease payment on office building	28,000	90,000
Gross operating revenue		$ 355,000
Depreciation		100,000
Net operating income		$ 255,000
Other income and expense except interest		15,000
Earnings before interest and taxes		$ 270,000
Less interest expense		
Interest on notes payable	$10,000	
Interest on first mortgage	40,000	
Interest on debentures	20,000	70,000
Net income before income tax		$ 200,000
Federal income tax (@ 40%)		80,000
Net income, after income tax, available to common stockholders		$ 120,000
Earnings per share (EPS)		$ .60

[1]Note that net operating income (NOI) is adjusted for other nonoperating income and expense to obtain earnings before interest and taxes (EBIT). If other income and expense are small, NOI and EBIT are approximately the same, as we shall usually assume in subsequent chapters.

Table 8.3	Walker-Wilson Company Statement of Retained Earnings for Year Ended December 31, 1985

Balance of retained earnings, December 31, 1984	$380,000
Plus net income, 1985	120,000
	$500,000
Less dividends to stockholders	100,000
Balance of retained earnings, December 31, 1985	$400,000

$20,000 back into the business. Thus, the retained earnings at the end of 1985, as shown both on the balance sheet and on the statement of retained earnings, is $400,000, which is $20,000 larger than the year-end 1984 figure.

Relationships among the Three Statements

It is important to recognize that the balance sheet is a statement of the firm's financial position *at a point in time*, whereas the income statement shows the results of operations *during an interval of time*. Thus, the balance sheet represents a snapshot of the firm's position on a given date, while the income statement is based on a flow concept, showing what occurred between two points in time.

The statement of retained earnings indicates how the retained earnings account on the balance sheet is adjusted between balance sheet dates. Since its inception, Walker-Wilson had retained a total of $380,000 by December 31, 1984. In 1985, it earned $120,000 and retained $20,000 of this amount. Thus, the retained earnings shown on the balance sheet for December 31, 1985, is $400,000.

A firm that retains earnings generally does so to expand the business — that is, to finance the purchase of assets such as plant, equipment, and inventories. As a result of operations in 1985, Walker-Wilson has $20,000 available for that purpose. Sometimes, retained earnings are used to build up the cash account, but, as shown on the balance sheet, they are *not* cash. Through the years, they have been invested in bricks and mortar and other assets, so they are not "available" for anything. The earnings *for the current year* may be available for investment, but the *past retained earnings* have already been employed.

Stated another way, the balance sheet item "retained earnings" simply shows how much of the earnings the stockholders, through the years, have elected to retain in the business. Thus, the retained earnings account shows the additional investment the stockholders as a group have made in the business over and above their initial investment at the inception of the company and through any subsequent issues of stock.

Basic Types of Financial Ratios

Each type of analysis has a purpose or use that determines the different relationships emphasized. The analyst may, for example, be a banker considering whether to grant a short-term loan to a firm. Bankers are primarily interested in the firm's near-term, or liquidity, position, so they stress ratios that measure liquidity. In contrast, long-term creditors place far more emphasis on earning power and operating efficiency. They know that unprofitable operations erode asset values and that a strong current position is no guarantee that funds will be available to repay a 20-year bond issue. Equity investors are similarly interested in long-term profitability and efficiency. Management is, of course, concerned with all these aspects of financial analysis; it must be able to repay its debts to long- and short-term creditors as well as earn profits for stockholders.

It is useful to classify ratios into six fundamental types:

1. *Liquidity ratios*, which measure the firm's ability to meet its maturing short-term obligations.
2. *Leverage ratios*, which measure the extent to which the firm has been financed by debt.
3. *Activity ratios*, which measure how effectively the firm is using its resources.
4. *Profitability ratios*, which measure management's effectiveness as shown by the returns generated on sales and investment.
5. *Growth ratios*, which measure the firm's ability to maintain its economic position in the growth of the economy and industry.
6. *Valuation ratios*, which measure the ability of management to create market values in excess of investment cost outlays. Valuation ratios are the most complete measure of performance in that they reflect the risk ratios (the first two) and the returns ratios (the following three). Valuation ratios are of great importance, since they relate directly to the goal of maximizing the value of the firm and shareholder wealth.

Financial Ratio Standards

Suppose we calculate a financial ratio as the number 5, for example. Is this good, bad, or indifferent? To make use of financial ratios, we need to have some standards for comparison. The general practice is to compare the ratios for the firm with the patterns for the industry or lines of business in which the firm operates.

If the financial ratios of individual firms in an industry bunched closely together, this would suggest that there were some underlying economic and business forces that compelled all firms in an industry to behave similarly. There is some disagreement on the actual pattern of the statistical distribution of financial ratios by industries.[2] From a practical standpoint, it is likely that well-managed firms will have some ratios better than the industry average. Other firms may have ratios not as good as the industry average. The industry average is not a magic number that all firms must match. However, if a firm's ratios are greatly different from the industry average, the analyst should find out the reasons. This emphasizes the main purpose of financial ratio analysis: It is a part of the detective work performed to try to evaluate how a firm is performing and how it is positioned for the future. Financial ratio analysis should not be done mechanically but rather with judgment as a part of a broader evaluation process.

Use of Financial Ratios

Specific examples of each ratio are given in the following sections, where the Walker-Wilson case history illustrates its calculation and use.

---

[2]This issue has been explored in the following articles and the references therein cited: Barnes [1982], Horrigan [1983], and Barnes [1983].

Liquidity Ratios

Generally, the first concern of the financial analyst is liquidity: Is the firm able to meet its maturing obligations? Walker-Wilson has debts totaling $300,000 that must be paid within the coming year. Can these obligations be satisfied? Although a full liquidity analysis requires the use of cash budgets (described in Chapter 9), ratio analysis, by relating the amount of cash and other current assets to the current obligations, provides a quick and easy-to-use measure of liquidity. Two commonly used liquidity ratios are presented here.

Current Ratio. The current ratio is computed by dividing current assets by current liabilities. Current assets normally include cash, marketable securities, accounts receivable, and inventories; current liabilities consist of accounts payable, short-term notes payable, current maturities of long-term debt, accrued income taxes, and other accrued expenses (principally wages). The current ratio is the most commonly used measure of short-term solvency, since it indicates the extent to which the claims of short-term creditors are covered by assets that are expected to be converted to cash in a period roughly corresponding to the maturity of the claims.

The calculation of the current ratio for Walker-Wilson at year-end 1985 is shown below.

$$\text{Current ratio} = \frac{\text{Current assets}}{\text{Current liabilities}} = \frac{\$700,000}{\$300,000} = 2.3 \text{ times.}$$

$$\text{Industry average} = 2.5 \text{ times.}$$

The current ratio is slightly below the average for the industry, 2.5, but not low enough to cause concern. It appears that Walker-Wilson is about in line with most other firms in this particular line of business. Since current assets are near maturity, it is highly probable that they could be liquidated at close to book value. With a current ratio of 2.3, Walker-Wilson could liquidate current assets at only 43 percent of book value and still pay off current creditors in full.[3]

Quick Ratio or Acid Test. The quick ratio is calculated by deducting inventories from current assets and dividing the remainder by current liabilities. Inventories are typically the least liquid of a firm's current assets and the assets on which losses are most likely to occur in the event of liquidation. Therefore, this measure of the firm's ability to pay off short-term obligations without relying on the sale of inventories is important.

$$\text{Quick ratio or acid test} = \frac{\text{Current assets} - \text{Inventory}}{\text{Current liabilities}} = \frac{\$400,000}{\$300,000}$$

$$= 1.3 \text{ times.}$$

$$\text{Industry average} = 1.0 \text{ times.}$$

The industry average quick ratio is 1, so Walker-Wilson's 1.3 ratio compares favorably with other firms in the industry. Thompson knows that if the marketable securities can be sold at par and if he can collect the accounts receivable, he can pay off his current liabilities without selling any inventory.

---

[3](1/2.3) = .43, or 43 percent. Note that (.43)($700,000) ≈ $300,000, the amount of current liabilities.

Leverage Ratios

Leverage ratios, which measure the funds supplied by owners as compared with the financing provided by the firm's creditors, have a number of implications. First, creditors look to the equity, or owner-supplied funds, to provide a margin of safety. If owners have provided only a small proportion of total financing, the risks of the enterprise are borne mainly by the creditors. Second, by raising funds through debt, the owners gain the benefits of maintaining control of the firm with a limited investment. Third, if the firm earns more on the borrowed funds than it pays in interest, the return to the owners is magnified. For example, if assets earn 10 percent and debt costs only 8 percent, there is a 2 percent differential accruing to the stockholders. Leverage cuts both ways, however; if the return on assets falls to 3 percent, the differential between that figure and the cost of debt must be made up from equity's share of total profits. In the first instance, where assets earn more than the cost of debt, leverage is favorable; in the second, it is unfavorable.

Firms with low leverage ratios have less risk of loss when the economy is in a downturn, but they also have lower expected returns when the economy booms. Conversely, firms with high leverage ratios run the risk of large losses but also have a chance of gaining high profits. The prospects of high returns are desirable, but investors are averse to risk. Decisions about the use of leverage, then, must balance higher expected returns against increased risk.[4]

In practice, leverage is approached in two ways. One approach examines balance sheet ratios and determines the extent to which borrowed funds have been used to finance the firm. The other approach measures the risks of debt by income statement ratios designed to determine the number of times fixed charges are covered by operating profits. These sets of ratios are complementary, and most analysts examine both.

Total Debt to Total Assets. The ratio of total debt to total assets, generally called the *debt ratio*, measures the percentage of total funds provided by creditors. Debt includes current liabilities and all bonds. Creditors prefer moderate debt ratios, since the lower the ratio, the greater the cushion against creditors' losses in the event of liquidation. In contrast to the creditors' preference for a low debt ratio, the owners may seek high leverage to magnify earnings or because raising new equity means giving up some degree of control. If the debt ratio is too high, there is a danger of encouraging irresponsibility on the part of the owners. The owners' stake can become so small that speculative activity, if it is successful, will yield them a substantial percentage return. If the venture is unsuccessful, however, they will incur only a moderate loss because their investment is small.

$$\text{Debt ratio} = \frac{\text{Total debt}}{\text{Total assets}} = \frac{\$1,000,000}{\$2,000,000} = 50\%.$$

$$\text{Industry average} = 33\%.$$

Walker-Wilson's debt ratio is 50 percent; this means that creditors have supplied half the firm's total financing. Since the average debt ratio for this industry is about 33 percent,

---

[4]The problem of determining optimum leverage for a firm with given risk characteristics is examined extensively in Chapters 20 and 21.

Walker-Wilson would find it difficult to borrow additional funds without first raising more equity capital. Creditors would be reluctant to lend the firm more money, and Thompson would probably be subjecting the stockholders to undue danger if he sought to increase the debt ratio even more by borrowing.[5]

Times Interest Earned. The times-interest-earned ratio (also called the "coverage ratio") is determined by dividing earnings before interest and taxes (EBIT) from Table 8.2 by the interest charges. The ratio measures the extent to which earnings can decline without resultant financial embarrassment to the firm because of inability to meet annual interest costs. Failure to meet this obligation can bring legal action by the creditors, possibly resulting in bankruptcy. Note that the before-tax income figure is used in the numerator. Because income taxes are computed after interest expense is deducted, the ability to pay current interest is not affected by income taxes. Walker-Wilson's interest charges consist of three payments totaling $70,000 (see Table 8.2). The firm's EBIT available for servicing these charges is $270,000, so the interest is covered 3.9 times. Since the industry average is 8 times, the company is covering its interest charges by a minimum margin of safety and deserves only a poor rating. This ratio reinforces the conclusion based on the debt ratio that the company is likely to face some difficulties if it attempts to borrow additional funds.

$$\text{Times interest earned} = \frac{\text{Earnings before interest and taxes (EBIT)}}{\text{Interest charges}}$$

$$= \frac{\text{Income before taxes} + \text{Interest charges}}{\text{Interest charges}}$$

$$= \frac{\$270,000}{\$70,000} = 3.9 \text{ times.}$$

$$\text{Industry average} = 8.0 \text{ times.}$$

Fixed Charge Coverage. The fixed charge coverage ratio is similar to the times-interest-earned ratio, but it is somewhat more inclusive in that it recognizes that many firms lease assets and incur long-term obligations under lease contracts.[6] As we show in Chapter 27, leasing has become widespread in recent years, making this ratio preferable to the times-interest-earned ratio for most financial analyses. Fixed charges are defined as interest plus annual long-term lease obligations, and the fixed charge coverage ratio is defined as follows:

[5]The ratio of debt to equity is also used in financial analysis. The debt to assets (B/A) and debt to equity (B/S) ratios are simply transformations of one another:

$$B/S = \frac{B/A}{1 - B/A} \quad \text{and} \quad B/A = \frac{B/S}{1 + B/S}.$$

Both ratios increase as a firm of a given size (total assets) uses a greater proportion of debt, but B/A rises linearly and approaches a limit of 100 percent while B/S rises exponentially and approaches infinity.

[6]Generally, a long-term lease is defined as one that is at least three years long. Thus, rent incurred under a one-year lease would not be included in the fixed charge coverage ratio, but rental payments under a three-year or longer lease would be defined as fixed charges.

$$\text{Fixed charge coverage} = \frac{\text{Income before taxes} + \text{Interest charges} + \text{Lease obligations}}{\text{Interest charges} + \text{Lease obligations}}$$

$$= \frac{\$200,000 + \$70,000 + \$28,000}{\$70,000 + \$28,000} = \frac{\$298,000}{\$98,000}$$

$$= 3.0 \text{ times.}$$

$$\text{Industry average} = 5.5 \text{ times.}$$

Walker-Wilson's fixed charges are covered 3.0 times, as opposed to an industry average of 5.5 times. Again, this indicates that the firm is somewhat weaker than creditors would prefer it to be, and it points up the difficulties Thompson would likely encounter if he attempted additional borrowing.

Cash Flow Coverage. Suppose Walker-Wilson issued preferred stock which required payment of dividends of $12,000 per year and had to make annual payments of principal on its various debt obligations of $42,000 per year. To the numerator of the previous ratio, we will add depreciation. To the denominator, we shall add the two additional items on a before-tax basis. We divide each by $(1 - T)$ because neither is a tax-deductible expense. Hence, the firm must have enough cash flow so that it can meet all cash flow obligations after taxes are paid.

$$\text{Cash flow coverage} = \frac{\text{Cash inflows}}{\text{Fixed charges} + \dfrac{\text{Preferred stock dividends}}{(1 - T)} + \dfrac{\text{Debt repayment}}{(1 - T)}}$$

$$= \frac{\$298,000 + \$100,000}{\$98,000 + \$12,000/.6 + \$42,000/.6} = \frac{\$398,000}{\$188,000}$$

$$= 2.1 \text{ times.}$$

While there are not generally published industry standards on this ratio, logic suggests that a cash coverage ratio of at least two times be achieved. This allows for a substantial decline in cash inflows before a cash solvency problem is encountered. Walker-Wilson meets this standard minimally.

Activity Ratios

Activity ratios measure how effectively the firm employs the resources at its command. These ratios all involve comparisons between the level of sales and the investment in various asset accounts. They presume that a "proper" balance should exist between sales and the various asset accounts — inventories, accounts receivable, fixed assets, and others. As we shall see in the following chapters, this is generally a good assumption.

Inventory Turnover. The inventory turnover, defined as sales divided by inventory, is shown as follows:

$$\text{Inventory turnover} = \frac{\text{Sales}}{\text{Inventory}} = \frac{\$3,000,000}{\$300,000} = 10 \text{ times.}$$

$$\text{Industry average} = 9 \text{ times.}$$

Walker-Wilson's turnover of 10 times compares favorably with an industry average of 9 times. This suggests that the company does not hold excessive stocks of inventory; excess stocks are, of course, unproductive and represent an investment with a low or zero rate of return. The company's high inventory turnover also reinforces Thompson's faith in the current ratio. If turnover were low — say three or four times — Thompson would wonder if the firm were holding damaged or obsolete materials not actually worth their stated value.

Two problems arise in calculating and analyzing the inventory turnover ratio. First, sales are at market prices; if inventories are carried at cost, as they generally are, it is more appropriate to use cost of goods sold in place of sales in the numerator of the formula. However, established compilers of financial ratio statistics, such as Dun & Bradstreet, use the ratio of sales to inventories carried at cost. Therefore, to develop a figure that can be compared with those developed by Dun & Bradstreet, it is necessary to measure inventory turnover with sales in the numerator, as we do here.

Second, sales occur over the entire year, whereas the inventory figure is for one point in time. This makes it better to use an average inventory, computed by adding beginning and ending inventories and dividing by 2. If it is determined that the firm's business is highly seasonal or if there has been a strong upward or downward sales trend during the year, it is essential to make some such adjustment. Neither of these conditions holds for Walker-Wilson, so Thompson used the year-end inventory figure.

Average Collection Period.   The average collection period, which is a measure of the accounts receivable turnover, is computed in two steps: (1) annual sales are divided by 360 to get the average daily sales[7] and (2) daily sales are divided into accounts receivable to find the number of days' sales tied up in receivables. This is defined as the *average collection period*, because it represents the average length of time the firm must wait after making a sale before receiving payment. The calculations for Walker-Wilson show an average collection period of 24 days, slightly above the 20-day industry average.

$$\text{Sales per day} = \frac{\$3,000,000}{360} = \$8,333.$$

$$\text{Average collection period} = \frac{\text{Receivables}}{\text{Sales per day}} = \frac{\$200,000}{\$8,333} = 24 \text{ days.}$$

$$\text{Industry average} = 20 \text{ days.}$$

This ratio can also be evaluated by comparison with the terms on which the firm sells its goods. For example, Walker-Wilson's sales terms call for payment within 20 days, so the

---

[7]Because information on credit sales is generally unavailable, total sales must be used. Since firms do not all have the same percentage of credit sales, there is a good chance that the average collection period will be somewhat in error. Also, note that in this illustration, we have simplified the computation by using 360 rather than 365 as the number of days in a year. Both figures are used in the financial community, and the difference in results would not affect the decision involved.

24-day collection period indicates that customers, on the average, are not paying their bills on time. If the collection period over the past few years had been lengthening while the credit policy had not changed, this would have been even stronger evidence that steps should be taken to expedite the collection of accounts receivable.

One additional financial tool should be mentioned in connection with accounts receivable analysis — the *aging schedule*, which breaks down accounts receivable according to how long they have been outstanding. The aging schedule for Walker-Wilson is given below.

Age of Account (Days)	% of Total Value of Accounts Receivable
0-20	50
21-30	20
31-45	15
46-60	3
Over 60	12
Total	100

The 24-day collection period looks bad by comparison with the 20-day sales term, and the aging schedule shows that the firm is having especially serious collection problems with some of its accounts: 50 percent are overdue, many for over a month; others pay quite promptly, bringing the average down to only 24 days. But the aging schedule shows this average to be somewhat misleading.

Fixed Assets Turnover.   The ratio of sales to fixed assets measures the turnover of plant and equipment.

$$\text{Fixed assets turnover} = \frac{\text{Sales}}{\text{Net fixed assets}} = \frac{\$3,000,000}{\$1,300,000} = 2.3 \text{ times.}$$

$$\text{Industry average} = 5.0 \text{ times.}$$

Walker-Wilson's turnover of 2.3 times compares poorly with the industry average of 5 times, indicating that the firm is not using its fixed assets to as high a percentage of capacity as are the other firms in the industry. Thompson should bear this in mind when his production people request funds for new capital investments.

Total Assets Turnover.   The final activity ratio, which measures the turnover of all the firm's assets, is calculated by dividing sales by total assets.

$$\text{Total assets turnover} = \frac{\text{Sales}}{\text{Total assets}} = \frac{\$3,000,000}{\$2,000,000} = 1.5 \text{ times.}$$

$$\text{Industry average} = 2.0 \text{ times.}$$

Walker-Wilson's turnover of total assets is well below the industry average. The company is simply not generating a sufficient volume of business for the size of its asset investment. Sales should be increased, or some assets should be disposed of, or both.

Profitability Ratios

Profitability is the net result of a large number of policies and decisions. The ratios examined thus far reveal some interesting things about the way the firm is operating, but the profitability ratios give final answers about how effectively the firm is being managed.

Profit Margin on Sales.   The profit margin on sales, computed by dividing net income after taxes by sales, gives the profit per dollar of sales.

$$\text{Profit margin} = \frac{\text{Net income}}{\text{Sales}} = \frac{\$120,000}{\$3,000,000} = 4\%.$$

$$\text{Industry average} = 5\%.$$

Walker-Wilson's profit margin is somewhat below the industry average of 5 percent, indicating that the firm's prices are relatively low or that its costs are relatively high, or both.

Return on Total Assets.   The return on total assets seeks to measure the effectiveness with which the firm has employed its total resources; it is sometimes called the return on investment, or ROI. On a before-tax basis, the ratio would be (EBIT/Total assets). We also need to know what is left after taxes, but this introduces a complication since interest, as we saw in Chapter 4, is tax deductible. Because of the tax shelter benefit of interest, we add the after-tax interest expenses to net income for the numerator of the ratio:

$$\text{Return on total assets} = \frac{\text{Net income} + \text{Interest}(1 - T)}{\text{Total assets}}$$

$$= \frac{\$120,000 + \$70,000(.6)}{\$2,000,000} = \frac{\$162,000}{\$2,000,000} = 8.1\%.$$

$$\text{Industry average} = 11.4\%.$$

Walker-Wilson's 8.1 percent return is well below the percent average for the industry. This low rate results from the low profit margin on sales (4 percent vs. industry average of 5 percent) and from the low turnover of total assets (1.5 vs. industry average of 2).

Return on Net Worth.   The ratio of net profit after taxes to net worth measures the rate of return on the stockholders' investment.

$$\text{Return on net worth} = \frac{\text{Net income}}{\text{Net worth}} = \frac{\$120,000}{\$1,000,000} = 12\%.$$

$$\text{Industry average} = 15\%.$$

Walker-Wilson's 12 percent return is below the 15 percent industry average, but not as far below as the return on total assets. In Chapter 9, where the du Pont method of analysis is introduced, we will see why this is so.

Growth Ratios

Growth ratios measure how well the firm is maintaining its economic position in the economy as a whole as well as in its own industry. During the recent period of inflation, the interpretation of growth ratios has become more difficult. Since the early 1970s nominal growth rates have increased greatly. The growth of the economy as well as of industries and firms has reflected the inflation factor as well as the underlying (real) growth. Before the onset of persistent inflation in the late 1960s real growth rates were about 3 to 3 1/2 percent per year with an inflation rate of 2 to 3 percent. This made for a total growth rate in the 5 to 7 percent area. However, since the early 1970s the inflation rate has been in the range of 7 to 10 percent, while real growth has declined to 1 or 2 percent. Thus, nominal growth has been from 8 to 12 percent while real growth has been much lower. Since reported figures are reflected in nominal terms, the growth rate reference standards we shall employ will include the inflation factor. However, as a part of the further internal analysis by business firms, a separation needs to be made between growth coming from the inflation influence alone, which just changes the measuring stick, and that coming from underlying real growth, which reflects the basic productivity of the economy.

The annual reports of business firms will generally include a section of historical data on selected financial items. These may be used to develop the growth and valuation ratios. The data for Walker-Wilson are presented in Table 8.4.

From the basic data in Table 8.4, we have calculated the five-year growth rates for six items for Walker-Wilson covering the years 1980 to 1985 in Table 8.5. We have calculated growth by dividing the last-period figure by the first-period figure, which gives a compound sum interest factor. Then, by referring to the compound interest tables, we can determine the growth rate represented by the ratio.[8] We observe that the growth rate in

---

Table 8.4   Some Historical Data for Walker-Wilson Company

	1980	1981	1982	1983	1984	1985
Firm (in thousands)						
Sales	$2,100	$2,200	$2,500	$3,400	$3,200	$3,000
Net income	100	120	150	180	160	120
Per share earnings	.50	.60	.75	.90	.80	.60
Dividends	.10	.12	.12	.12	.12	.12
Market price, common stock						
high	5.00	7.00	8.00	9.00	5.00	6.00
low	4.00	5.00	6.00	7.00	4.00	3.00
average	4.50	6.00	7.00	8.00	4.50	4.50
Book value of common stock, year end	4.10	4.30	4.40	4.70	4.90	5.00

---

[8]This is equivalent to

$$g = \left[\frac{X_n}{X_0} \right]^{1/n} - 1,$$

which represents taking the geometric average of the growth over the period.

Table 8.5   Growth Rate Data

| | Five-Year Growth Rates, 1980–1985 | |
	Walker-Wilson	Industry
Sales	7.4	7.2
Net income	3.7	7.8
Earnings per share	3.7	8.2
Dividends per share	3.7	6.4
Market price: average	0.0	2.0
Book value per share	4.0	7.0

sales for Walker-Wilson was about the same as for the industry. However, net income, which is the measure of the profitability performance of the firm, has grown at only about half the industry standard rate.

Next, we turn to per share growth analysis. First, we consider earnings per share, which reflect the methods by which the firm has financed its overall growth. Here again, the growth rate is less than half that of the industry. Dividends per share have grown at the same rate as earnings per share. However, Table 8.4 shows that all of the dividend growth came in the first year while the earnings growth has been declining during the two most recent years.

Market price represents the results of the valuation of the firm's earnings. Market price growth for the industry as a whole has been weak, only 2 percent. But the market price change for Walker-Wilson has been zero. While its average price increased from $4.50 to $8.00 in the early years, it declined again to $4.50 in the last two years.

Book value per share indicates the resources in the company per share of stockholder investment. This grew at a 7 percent rate for the industry but at only a 4 percent rate for Walker-Wilson. Again, the weakened performance of the last two years has pulled down the growth rate in the book value per share. Thus, the growth performance of Walker-Wilson has been relatively weak, which should have some implications for the valuation ratios as well.

Valuation Ratios

Valuation ratios are the most comprehensive measures of performance for the firm in that they reflect the combined influence of risk ratios and return ratios. We have calculated two valuation ratios and summarized their patterns in Table 8.6.

We first analyzed trends in the price to earnings ratios. At the beginning of the period, they were higher for the company than for the industry. However, by the end of the period, the ratios were higher for the industry than for the company, reflecting the company's poor performance in the last two years.

Price to earnings ratios must be interpreted with caution. Note that between 1984 and 1985, the price-earnings ratio for the company rose from 5.6 to 7.5. However, the average market price of the company stock stayed at $4.50. The price-earnings ratio rose while earnings dropped only because the average price remained the same.

The market to book ratio is also an important valuation ratio. In a way, it indicates the value that the financial markets attach to the management and the organization of the

Table 8.6 Valuation Ratios

	1980	1981	1982	1983	1984	1985
Price to earnings ratios						
Company	9.0	10.0	9.3	8.9	5.6	7.5
Industry	7.0	8.0	8.0	8.0	9.0	8.0
Market to book ratios						
Company	1.1	1.4	1.6	1.7	0.9	0.9
Industry	0.9	1.0	1.0	1.2	1.1	1.0

company as a going concern. In some sense, book value represents the historical costs of brick and mortar — the physical assets of the company. A well-run company with strong management and an organization that functions efficiently should have a market value greater than or at least equal to the book value of its physical assets.

As we see from Table 8.6, the market to book ratio of the company exceeded 1.0 in the early years. In fact, it had become 1.7 by 1983. The industry did not perform as well but in most years had a market to book ratio of at least 1.0. However, during the last two years, while the market to book ratio for the industry has remained at 1.0 or better, it has dipped below 1.0 for the company.

Summary of the Ratios

The individual ratios, which are summarized in Table 8.7, give Thompson a reasonably good idea of Walker-Wilson's main strengths and weaknesses. First, the company's liquidity position is reasonably good; its current and quick ratios appear to be satisfactory by comparison with the industry averages. Second, the leverage ratios suggest that the company is rather heavily indebted. With a debt ratio substantially higher than the industry average, and with coverage ratios well below the industry averages, it is doubtful that Walker-Wilson could do much additional debt financing except on relatively unfavorable terms. Even if Thompson could borrow more, to do so would be subjecting the company to the danger of default and bankruptcy in the event of a business downturn.

Turning to the activity ratios, the inventory turnover and average collection period both indicate that the company's current assets are pretty well in balance, but the low fixed asset turnover suggests that there has been too heavy an investment in fixed assets. This low turnover means, in effect, that the company probably could have operated with a smaller investment in fixed assets. Had the excessive fixed asset investment not been made, the company could have avoided some of its debt financing and would now have lower interest payments. This, in turn, would have led to improved leverage and coverage ratios.

The profit margin on sales is low, indicating that costs are too high or prices too low or both. In this particular case, the sales prices are in line with those of other firms; high costs are, in fact, the cause of the low margin. Further, the high costs can be traced to high depreciation charges and high interest expenses, both of which are, in turn, attributable to the excessive investment in fixed assets.

Returns on total investment and net worth are also below the industry averages. These relatively poor results are directly attributable to the low profit margin on sales, which

Table 8.7   Summary of Financial Ratio Analyses

Ratio	Formula for Calculation	Calculation		Industry Average	Evaluation
Liquidity					
Current	$\dfrac{\text{Current assets}}{\text{Current liabilities}}$	$\dfrac{\$700,000}{\$300,000}$	$= 2.3$ times.	2.5 times	Satisfactory
Quick ratio or acid test	$\dfrac{\text{Current assets} - \text{Inventory}}{\text{Current liabilities}}$	$\dfrac{\$400,000}{\$300,000}$	$= 1.3$ times.	1 time	Good
Leverage					
Debt to total assets	$\dfrac{\text{Total debt}}{\text{Total assets}}$	$\dfrac{\$1,000,000}{\$2,000,000}$	$= 50\%.$	33%	Poor
Times interest earned	$\dfrac{\text{Earnings before taxes and interest charges}}{\text{Interest charges}}$	$\dfrac{\$270,000}{\$70,000}$	$= 3.9$ times.	8 times	Poor
Fixed charge coverage	$\dfrac{\text{Income available for meeting fixed charges}}{\text{Fixed charges}}$	$\dfrac{\$298,000}{\$98,000}$	$= 3.0$ times.	5.5 times	Poor
Activity					
Inventory turnover	$\dfrac{\text{Sales}}{\text{Inventory}}$	$\dfrac{\$3,000,000}{\$300,000}$	$= 10$ times.	9 times	Satisfactory
Average collection period	$\dfrac{\text{Receivables}}{\text{Sales per day}}$	$\dfrac{\$200,000}{\$8,333}$	$= 24$ days.	20 days	Satisfactory
Fixed assets turnover	$\dfrac{\text{Sales}}{\text{Fixed assets}}$	$\dfrac{\$3,000,000}{\$1,300,000}$	$= 2.3$ times.	5 times	Poor
Total assets turnover	$\dfrac{\text{Sales}}{\text{Total assets}}$	$\dfrac{\$3,000,000}{\$2,000,000}$	$= 1.5$ times.	2 times	Poor

lowers the numerators of the ratios, and the excessive investment, which raises the denominators.

Sales growth of Walker-Wilson is satisfactory in relation to the industry standard. However, all of the profitability growth measures are weak. Valuation relationships are also unfavorable. Additional perspective on the growth performance of Walker-Wilson is provided by the trend analysis, which supplements the single measure provided by the growth percentage.

Trend Analysis

While the preceding ratio analysis gives a reasonably good picture of Walker-Wilson's operation, it is incomplete in one important respect — it ignores the time dimension. The ratios are snapshots of the position at one point in time, but there may be trends in motion that are in the process of rapidly eroding a relatively good present position. Conversely,

Table 8.7 Summary of Financial Ratio Analyses (*Continued*)

Ratio	Formula for Calculation	Calculation		Industry Average	Evaluation
Profitability					
Profit margin on sales	$\dfrac{\text{Net income}}{\text{Sales}}$	$\dfrac{\$120,000}{\$3,000,000}$	$= 4\%.$	5%	Fair
Return on total assets	$\dfrac{\text{Net income} + \text{Interest}\,(1-T)}{\text{Total assets}}$	$\dfrac{\$162,000}{\$2,000,000}$	$= 8.1\%.$	11.4%	Poor
Return on net worth	$\dfrac{\text{Net income}}{\text{Net worth}}$	$\dfrac{\$120,000}{\$1,000,000}$	$= 12\%.$	15%	Poor
Growth					
Sales	$\dfrac{\text{Ending values}}{\text{Beginning values}} = \text{FVIF}(r,5).$	$\dfrac{\$3,000}{\$2,100}$	$= 1.4286;\ r = 7.4\%.$	7.2%	Satisfactory
Net income	$\dfrac{\text{Ending values}}{\text{Beginning values}} = \text{FVIF}(r,5).$	$\dfrac{\$120}{\$100}$	$= 1.2;\ r = 3.7\%.$	7.8%	Poor
Earnings per share	$\dfrac{\text{Ending values}}{\text{Beginning values}} = \text{FVIF}(r,5).$	$\dfrac{\$0.60}{\$0.50}$	$= 1.2;\ r = 3.7\%.$	8.2%	Poor
Dividends per share	$\dfrac{\text{Ending values}}{\text{Beginning values}} = \text{FVIF}(r,5).$	$\dfrac{\$0.12}{\$0.10}$	$= 1.2;\ r = 3.7\%.$	6.4%	Poor
Valuation					
Price to earnings ratio	$\dfrac{\text{Price}}{\text{Earnings}}$	$\dfrac{\$4.50}{\$0.60}$	$= 7.5\text{ times.}$	8 times	Fair
Market to book ratio	$\dfrac{\text{Market value}}{\text{Book value}}$	$\dfrac{\$4.50}{\$5.00}$	$= 0.9\text{ times.}$	1.0 times	Poor

an analysis of the ratios over the past few years may suggest that a relatively weak position is improving at a rapid rate.

The method of trend analysis is illustrated in Figure 8.1, which shows graphs of Walker-Wilson's sales, current ratio, debt ratio, fixed assets turnover, and return on net worth. The figures are compared with industry averages. Industry sales have been rising steadily over the entire period, and the industry average ratios have been relatively stable throughout. Thus, any trends in the company's ratios are due to its own internal conditions, not to environmental influences on all firms. In addition, Walker-Wilson's deterioration since the death of the two principal officers is quite apparent. Prior to 1983, the company grew more rapidly than the average firm in the industry; during the following two years, however, sales actually declined.

Walker-Wilson's liquidity position as measured by its current ratio has also gone downhill in the past two years. Although the ratio is only slightly below the industry average at the present time, the trend suggests that a real liquidity crisis may develop during the next year or two unless corrective action is taken immediately.

Figure 8.1   Illustration of Trend Analysis

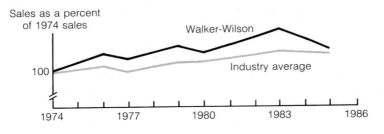

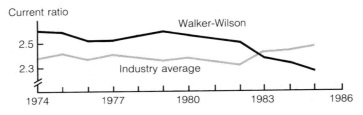

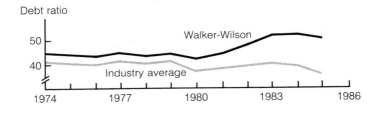

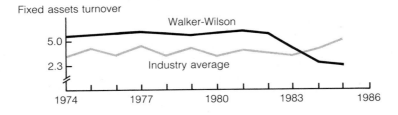

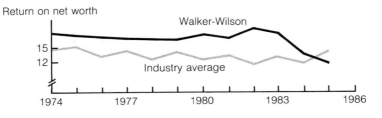

   The debt ratio trend line shows that Walker-Wilson followed industry practices closely until 1983, when the ratio jumped to a full 10 percentage points above the industry average. Similarly, the fixed assets turnover declined during 1983, even though sales were still rising. The records reveal that the company borrowed heavily during 1983 to finance a major expansion of plant and equipment. Walker and Wilson had intended to use this additional capacity to generate a still higher volume of sales and to retire the debt out of expected high profits. Their untimely death, however, led to a decrease rather than an increase in sales, and the expected high profits that were to be used to retire the debt did not materialize. The analysis suggests that the bankers were correct when they advised Mrs. Walker and Mrs. Wilson of the need for a change in management.

Sources of Comparative Ratios

In our analysis of the Walker-Wilson Company, we frequently used industry average ratios. Where are such averages obtained? Some important sources are listed below.

Dun & Bradstreet

Dun & Bradstreet (D&B) provides 14 ratios calculated for a large number of industries. The complete data give the 14 ratios, with the interquartile ranges, for 800 types of business activity based on their financial statements.[9] The compilations include 400,000 companies. The figures are also grouped by annual sales into three size categories.

Robert Morris Associates

Another group of useful ratios can be found in the annual *Statement Studies*, compiled and published by Robert Morris Associates, the national association of bank loan officers. These are representative averages based on 80,000 financial statements of commercial borrowers. Average balance sheet and income data and 17 ratios are calculated for 341 industries. Asset items are all expressed as a percent of total assets. Income statement data are expressed as a percent of net sales. Data are presented for four size categories as well as for all of the firms in the industry. Industry trend data are presented for a five-year period. The industry names are related to the Standard Industrial Classification (SIC) codes of the U.S. Bureau of the Census. Sixteen ratios are presented as well as the total dollar amount of net sales and total assets for each category covered.

---

[9]The median and quartile ratios can be illustrated by an example. The median ratio of current assets to current debt of manufacturers of airplane parts and accessories in a recent year was 2.30. To obtain this figure, the ratios of current assets to current debt for each of some 41 firms were arranged in a graduated series, with the largest ratio at the top and the smallest at the bottom. The median ratio of 2.30 is the ratio halfway between the top and the bottom. The ratio of 4.40, representing the upper quartile, is one-quarter of the way down from the top (or halfway between the top and the median). The ratio 1.50, representing the lower quartile, is one-quarter of the way up from the bottom (or halfway between the median and the bottom).

Quarterly Financial Report for Manufacturing Corporations

The Bureau of the Census in the U.S. Department of Commerce publishes quarterly financial data on manufacturing companies. Both balance sheet and income statement data are developed from a systematic sample of corporations. The reports are published about six months after the financial data have been made available by the companies. They include an analysis by industry groups and by asset size, and financial statements in ratio form (or common-size analysis) as well. The reports are a rich source of information and can be purchased directly from the U.S. Government Printing Office.

Trade Associations and Public Accountants

Financial ratios for many industries, compiled by trade associations and public accountants, constitute an important source to be checked by a financial manager seeking comparative data. These averages are usually the best obtainable. In addition to balance sheet data, they provide detailed information on operating expenses, which makes possible an informed analysis of the firms' efficiency. Credit departments of individual firms also compile financial ratios and averages on their customers in order to judge their ability to meet obligations and on their suppliers in order to evaluate their financial ability to fulfill contracts.

External Use of Financial Ratios

We have analyzed a rather long list of ratios, determining what each ratio is designed to measure. What one ratio may not indicate, another will. Also, a relationship vaguely suggested by one ratio may be corroborated by another. For these reasons, it is generally useful to calculate a number of different ratios.

In numerous situations, however, a few ratios tell the story. For example, a credit manager confronted with many invoices each day may limit the analysis to three ratios as evidence of whether the prospective buyer of goods will pay promptly. The analyst may use (1) the debt to total assets ratio to determine how much of the prospective buyer's own funds are invested in the business, (2) either the current or the quick ratio to determine how burdened the prospective buyer is with current liabilities, and (3) any of the profitability ratios to determine whether the firm has favorable prospects. There are relationships among the ratios. If the debt ratio is high, the owners have too little funds in the business and may need to use supplier financing which increases current liabilities and reduces the current ratio. High leverage will aggravate poor profitability and vice versa. If the profit margin is high enough, it may justify the risk of dealing with a slow-paying customer (profitable companies are likely to grow and thus become better customers in the future). However, if the profit margin is low in relation to other firms in the industry, if the current ratio is low, and if the debt ratio is high, a credit manager probably will not approve a sale involving an extension of credit.[10]

---

[10]Statistical techniques have been developed to improve the use of ratios in credit analysis. One such development is the discriminant analysis model reported by Altman [1968]. Altman's model is discussed in Appendix B to this chapter. See also Altman, Haldeman, and Narayanan [1977].

Of necessity, the credit manager is more than a calculator and reader of financial ratios. Qualitative factors may override quantitative analysis. For instance, in selling to truckers, oil companies often find that the financial ratios are adverse and that if they based their decisions solely on financial ratios, they would never make sales. Or, to take another example, profits may have been low for a period, but if the customer understands why and can remove the cause of the difficulty, a credit manager may be willing to approve a sale to that customer. This decision is also influenced by the profit margin of the selling firm. If it is making a large profit on sales, it is in a better position to take credit risks than if its own margin is low. Ultimately, the credit manager must judge each customer on character and management ability, and intelligent credit decisions must be based on careful consideration of conditions in the selling firm as well as in the buying firm.

Use of Financial Ratios in Security Analysis

We have emphasized the use of ratio analysis by the financial manager and by outside credit analysts. However, financial ratios are also useful in security analysis — the evaluation of the investment merits of stocks and bonds. When the emphasis is on security analysis, the principal focus is on judging the long-run profit potential of the firm. Profitability is dependent in large part on the efficiency with which the firm is run; because financial ratio analysis provides insights into this factor, it is useful to the security analyst.

Some Limitations of Ratio Analysis

Although ratios are exceptionally useful tools, they do have limitations and must be used with caution. Ratios are constructed from accounting data, and these data are subject to different interpretations and even to manipulation. For example, two firms may use different depreciation methods or inventory valuation methods; depending on the procedures followed, reported profits can be raised or lowered. Similar differences can be encountered in the treatment of research and development expenditures, pension plan costs, mergers, product warranties, and bad-debt reserves. Further, if firms use different fiscal years, and if seasonal factors are important, this can influence the comparative ratios. Thus, if the ratios of two firms are to be compared, it is important to analyze the basic accounting data upon which the ratios were based and to reconcile any major differences.

A financial manager must also be cautious in judging whether a particular ratio is "good" or "bad" and in forming a composite judgment about a firm on the basis of a set of ratios. For example, a high inventory turnover ratio could indicate efficient inventory management, but it could also indicate a serious shortage of inventories and suggest the likelihood of stock-outs. When financial ratio analysis indicates that the patterns of a firm depart from industry norms, this is a basis for questions and further investigation and analysis. Additional information and discussions may establish sound explanations for the difference between the pattern for the individual firm and industry composite ratios. Or the differences may reveal forms of mismanagement or supermanagement.

Conversely, conformance to industry composite ratios does not establish with certainty that the firm is performing normally and is managed well. In the short run, many tricks can be used to make a firm look good in relation to industry standards. The analyst must develop firsthand knowledge of the operations and management of the firm to provide a check on the financial ratios. In addition, the analyst must develop a sixth sense — a touch, a smell, a feel — for what is going on in the firm. Sometimes it is this kind of business judgment that uncovers weaknesses in the firm. The analyst should not be anesthetized by financial ratios that appear to conform with normality.

Ratios, then, are extremely useful tools. But as with other analytical methods, they must be used with judgment and caution, not in an unthinking, mechanical manner. Financial ratio analysis is a useful part of an investigation process. But financial ratios alone are not the complete answer to questions about the performance of a firm.

Summary

Ratio analysis, which relates balance sheet and income statement items to one another, permits the charting of a firm's history and the evaluation of its present position. It also allows the financial manager to anticipate reactions of investors and creditors and thus to gain insight into how attempts to acquire funds are likely to be received.

Ratios are classified into six basic types: liquidity, leverage, activity, profitability, growth, and valuation. Data from the Walker-Wilson Manufacturing Company were used to compute each type of ratio and to show how a financial analysis is made in practice. An almost unlimited number of ratios can be calculated, but, in practice, a limited number of each type is sufficient.

A ratio is not a meaningful number in and of itself; it must be compared with something before it becomes useful. The two basic kinds of comparative analysis are (1) trend analysis, which involves computing the ratios of a particular firm for several years and comparing the ratios over time to see if the firm is improving or deteriorating; and (2) comparisons with other firms in the same industry. These two comparisons are often combined in the graphic analysis illustrated in Figure 8.1.

Questions

8.1 "A uniform system of accounts, including identical forms for balance sheets and income statements, would be a most reasonable requirement for the SEC to impose on all publicly owned firms." Discuss this statement.

8.2 We have divided financial ratios into six groups: liquidity, leverage, activity, profitability, growth, and valuation. We could also consider financial analysis as being conducted by four groups of analysts: management, equity investors, long-term creditors, and short-term creditors.
    a)   Explain the nature of each type of ratio.
    b)   Explain the emphasis of each type of analyst in dealing with the ratios.

8.3 Why can norms with relatively well-defined limits be stated in advance for some financial ratios but not for others?

8.4 How does trend analysis supplement the basic financial ratio calculations and their interpretation?

8.5 Why should the inventory turnover figure be more important to a grocery store than to a shoe repair store?

8.6 How can a firm have a high current ratio and still be unable to pay its bills?

8.7 "The higher the rate of return on investment (ROI), the better the firm's management." Is this statement true for all firms? Explain. If you disagree with the statement, give examples of cases in which it might not be true.

8.8 What factors would you, as a financial manager, want to examine if a firm's rate of return (a) on assets or (b) on net worth was too low?

8.9   Profit margins and turnover rates vary from industry to industry. What industry characteristics account for these variations? Give some contrasting examples to illustrate your answer.

8.10 Which relation would you, as a financial manager, prefer: (a) a profit margin of 10 percent and a capital turnover of 2 or (b) a profit margin of 20 percent and a capital turnover of 1? Can you think of any firm with a relationship similar to (b)?

Problems

8.1   The Wagner Company has $2,400,000 in current assets and $950,000 in current liabilities. How much can its short-term debt (notes payable) increase without violating a current ratio of 2 to 1? (The funds from the additional notes payable will be used to increase inventory.)

8.2   Complete the balance sheet and sales information (fill in the blanks) for the Goodrich Company using the following financial data:

Debt/net worth: 1.5
Acid test ratio: 0.40
Total asset turnover: 1.5 times
Days' sales outstanding in accounts receivable: 20
Gross profit margin: 25%
Sales to inventory turnover: 5 times

Balance Sheet

Cash	_____	Accounts payable	_____
Accounts receivable	_____	Common stock	$10,000
Inventories	_____	Retained earnings	$20,000
Plant and equipment	_____	Total liabilities and capital	_____
Total assets	_____		
Sales	_____	Cost of goods sold	_____

8.3   The following data were taken from the financial statements of the Wisconsin Furniture Company for the calendar year 1985. The norms given below are composite industry averages for the wood and upholstered furniture industry based on various sources for industry composite data.

a)   Fill in the ratios for the Wisconsin Furniture Company.

b)   Indicate by comparison with industry norms the possible errors in management policies reflected in these financial statements.

Wisconsin Furniture Company
Balance Sheet as of December 31, 1985

Assets		Liabilities	
Cash	$ 19,000	Accounts payable	$ 77,500
Receivables	180,000	Notes payable (@ 9%)	36,000
Inventory	433,000	Other current liabilities	67,000
Total current assets	$632,000	Total current liabilities	$180,500
Net fixed assets	190,500	Long-term debt (@ 10%)	200,000
		Net worth	442,000
Total assets	$822,500	Total claims on assets	$822,500

Wisconsin Furniture Company
Income Statement for Year Ended December 31, 1985

Sales		$1,315,000
Cost of goods sold		
Material	$415,000	
Labor	360,000	
Heat, light, and power	45,000	
Indirect labor	52,000	
Depreciation	40,000	912,000
Gross profit		$ 403,000
Selling expense	$137,500	
General and administrative expense	195,000	332,500
Net operating profit (EBIT)		$ 70,500
Less interest expense		23,000
Net income before tax		$ 47,500
Less federal income tax (@ 40%)		19,000
Net income		$ 28,500

Wisconsin Furniture Company

Ratio	Ratio	Industry Norm
$\dfrac{\text{Current assets}}{\text{Current liabilities}}$	_____	3.1 times
$\dfrac{\text{Debt}}{\text{Total assets}}$	_____	45%
Times interest earned	_____	5.8 times
$\dfrac{\text{Cost of goods sold}}{\text{Inventory}}$	_____	6.2 times
Average collection period	_____	46 days
$\dfrac{\text{Sales}}{\text{Total assets}}$	_____	2.0 times
$\dfrac{\text{Net income}}{\text{Sales}}$	_____	2.8%
$\dfrac{\text{EBIT}(1-T)}{\text{Total assets}}$	_____	8.6%
$\dfrac{\text{Net income}}{\text{Net worth}}$	_____	10.2%

8.4 The following data were taken from the financial statements of Wheatland Pharmaceuticals Company, a wholesaler of drugs, drug proprietaries, and sundries, for the calendar year 1985. The norms given below are the industry averages for wholesale drugs, drug proprietaries, and sundries.

a) Fill in the ratios for Wheatland Pharmaceuticals Company.

b) Indicate by comparison with the industry norms the possible errors in management policies reflected in these financial statements.

Wheatland Pharmaceuticals Company Balance Sheet as of December 31, 1985 (Thousands of Dollars)

Assets		Liabilities	
Cash	$ 155	Accounts payable	$ 258
Receivables	672	Notes payable (@ 10%)	168
Inventory	483	Other current liabilities	234
Total current assets	$1,310	Total current liabilities	$ 660
Net fixed assets	585	Long-term debt (@ 12%)	513
		Net worth	722
Total assets	$1,895	Total claims on assets	$1,895

Wheatland Pharmaceuticals Company Income Statement for Year Ended December 31, 1985 (Thousands of Dollars)

Sales	$3,244
Cost of goods sold	2,845
Gross profit	$ 399
Operating expenses	230
EBIT	$ 169
Interest expense	78
Net income before tax	$ 91
Taxes (@ 40%)	36
Net income	$ 55

Wheatland Pharmaceuticals Company

Ratio	Ratio	Industry Norm
$\dfrac{\text{Current assets}}{\text{Current liabilities}}$	_____	2.0 times
$\dfrac{\text{Debt}}{\text{Total assets}}$	_____	60%
Times interest earned	_____	3.8 times
$\dfrac{\text{Cost of goods sold}}{\text{Inventory}}$	_____	6.7 times
Average collection period	_____	35 days
$\dfrac{\text{Sales}}{\text{Total assets}}$	_____	2.9 times
$\dfrac{\text{Net income}}{\text{Sales}}$	_____	1.2%
$\dfrac{\text{EBIT}(1-T)}{\text{Total assets}}$	_____	7.4%
$\dfrac{\text{Net income}}{\text{Net worth}}$	_____	8.3%

8.5 Richard Rutledge, a retired schoolteacher, holds a large number of shares of stock in the Bangor Corporation. The dividend payments from this stock make up a significant portion of Mr. Rutledge's income, so he was concerned when Bangor dropped its 1984 dividend to $1.25 per share from the $1.75 per share it had paid for the previous two years.

Mr. Rutledge gathered the information below for analysis to determine whether the financial condition of Bangor was indeed deteriorating.

Bangor Corporation Balance Sheets as of December 31

	1982	1983	1984
Cash	$ 76,250	$ 72,000	$ 40,000
Accounts receivable	401,600	439,000	672,000
Inventory	493,000	794,000	1,270,000
Total current assets	$ 970,850	$1,305,000	$1,982,000
Land and building	126,150	138,000	125,000
Machinery	169,000	182,000	153,000
Other fixed assets	74,600	91,000	82,000
Total assets	$1,340,600	$1,716,000	$2,342,000
Accounts and notes payable	$ 171,100	$ 368,800	$ 679,240
Accruals	78,500	170,000	335,000
Total current liabilities	$ 249,600	$ 538,800	$1,014,240
Long-term debt	304,250	304,290	408,600
Common stock	575,000	575,000	575,000
Retained earnings	211,750	297,910	344,160
Total liabilities and equity	$1,340,600	$1,716,000	$2,342,000

Bangor Corporation Yearly Income Statements for the Year Ending December 31

	1982	1983	1984
Sales	$4,135,000	$4,290,000	$4,450,000
Cost of goods sold	3,308,000	3,550,000	3,560,000
Gross operating profit	$ 827,000	$ 740,000	$ 890,000
Gen. admin. & selling expense	318,000	236,320	256,000
Other operating expenses	127,000	159,000	191,000
EBIT	$ 382,000	$ 344,680	$ 443,000
Interest expense	64,000	134,000	318,000
Net income before taxes	$ 318,000	$ 210,680	$ 125,000
Taxes (40%)	127,000	84,270	50,000
Net income	$ 191,000	$ 126,410	$ 75,000
Number of shares outstanding	23,000	23,000	23,000
Per share data			
EPS	$8.30	$5.50	$3.26
Cash dividend per share	$1.75	$1.75	$1.25
Market price (average)	48 7/8	25 1/2	13 1/4

	Industry Financial Ratios (1984)[a]
Quick ratio	1.0
Current ratio	2.7
Inventory turnover[b]	7 times
Average collection period	32 days
Fixed asset turnover[b]	13.0 times
Total asset turnover[b]	2.6 times
EBIT$(1 - T)$ to total assets	14%
Net income to net worth	18%
Equity ratio	50%
Profit margin on sales	3.5%
P/E ratio	6 times

[a]Industry average ratios have been roughly constant for the past four years.
[b]Based on year-end balance sheet figures.

a) Calculate the key financial ratios for Bangor Corporation, graph them, and analyze the trends in the firm's ratios in relation to the industry averages.

b) What strengths and weaknesses are revealed by the ratio analysis?

Selected References

Altman, Edward I., "Financial Ratios, Discriminant Analysis, and the Prediction of Corporate Bankruptcy," *Journal of Finance*, 23 (September 1968), pp. 589-609.

———; Haldeman, Robert G.; and Narayanan, P., "ZETA Analysis: A New Model to Identify Bankruptcy Risk of Corporations," *Journal of Banking and Finance*, 1 (June 1977), pp. 29-54.

Barnes, Paul, "Methodological Implications of Non-Normally Distributed Financial Ratios: A Reply," *Journal of Business Finance & Accounting*, 10 (Winter 1983), pp. 691-693.

———, "Methodological Implications of Non-Normally Distributed Financial Ratios," *Journal of Business Finance & Accounting*, 9 (Spring 1982), pp. 51-62.

Beaver, William H., "Financial Ratios as Predictors of Failure," in *Empirical Research in Accounting: Selected Studies* in *Journal of Accounting Research*, (1966), pp. 71-111.

Branch, Ben, "The Impact of Operating Decisions on ROI Dynamics," *Financial Management*, 7 (Winter 1978), pp. 54-60.

Chen, Kung H., and Shimerda, Thomas A., "An Empirical Analysis of Useful Financial Ratios," *Financial Management*, 10 (Spring 1981), pp. 51-60.

Gombola, Michael J., and Ketz, J. Edward, "Financial Ratio Patterns in Retail and Manufacturing Organizations," *Financial Management*, 12 (Summer 1983), pp. 45-56.

Horrigan, James O., "Methodological Implications of Non-Normally Distributed Financial Ratios: A Comment," *Journal of Business Finance & Accounting*, 10 (Winter 1983), pp. 683-689.

———, "A Short History of Financial Ratio Analysis," *Accounting Review*, 43 (April 1968), pp. 284-294.

Johnson, W. Bruce, "The Cross-sectional Stability of Financial Ratio Patterns," *Journal of Financial and Quantitative Analysis*, 14 (December 1979), pp. 1035-1048.

Appendix A to Chapter 8
Effects of Changing Price Levels

Immediately after World War II, with the removal of price controls that had held prices to arbitrary levels, there was a burst of inflation. Thereafter, prices increased at a rate of 2 to 3 percent per year until the escalation of hostilities in Southeast Asia in 1966, when inflation again erupted in the United States. In 1971, the United States departed from the convertibility of the dollar into gold, and the major nations adopted floating exchange rates in place of nominally fixed exchange rates. Double-digit inflation (as measured by the wholesale price index or consumer price index) has been a reality or a threat in the United States for more than a decade.

Inflation and the Measurement of Profitability

In an economy experiencing a high rate of price increases, the measurement of profitability becomes complicated. The times at which assets are purchased have a great impact on accounting profitability measures and on taxation. For example, Firm A purchased its assets in Year 1, when their cost was $20 million, while Firm B purchased virtually identical assets five years later at a cost of $40 million. Let us assume that the assets will have an average 20-year life, that both firms use straight line depreciation, that the income before taxes and depreciation for both firms is $5 million per year over the life of the assets, and that their tax rate is 50 percent. Let us compare the financial profiles of the two companies:

	Firm A	Firm B
Income before taxes and depreciation	$5,000,000	$5,000,000
Less depreciation expense	−1,000,000	−2,000,000
Income before taxes	$4,000,000	$3,000,000
Taxes (@ 50%)	2,000,000	1,500,000
Net income after taxes	$2,000,000	$1,500,000
Average return on investment	20%	7.5%

Since the cost of the assets will be depreciated down to zero over their 20-year lives, their average value is half the original cost. The net income after taxes is assumed to be constant for each year so that the average annual returns are 20 percent for Firm A and 7.5 percent for Firm B. But does Firm A really have a return almost three times greater than Firm B's? The replacement value of Firm A's assets is $40 million, on which the current depreciation expense would be $2 million per year, not $1 million. Is it correct for an investor to project Firm A's earning power into the future at 20 percent, or should the higher replacement cost of Firm A's assets that are being used up be taken into account? Should the tax-deductible depreciation expense for Firm A be $2 million per year rather than $1 million?

There are no easy answers to these questions, which arise because of the changing values of assets. Some people feel that Firm A is gaining windfall profits because it is using assets that it was able to purchase at lower than current costs. Others argue that Firm A is paying excessive taxes because the real depreciation expense should be doubled.

Inflation and Inventory Valuation Methods

The divergence between economic and accounting measures of profitability results from the valuation of both fixed assets and inventories. During periods of inflation, the method of inventory valuation for income statements and balance sheets has a major impact on profitability measurement.

By comparing FIFO (first-in-first-out) and LIFO (last-in-first-out) inventory costing and valuation methods, Table 8A.1 illustrates the difficulty of obtaining a meaningful economic measure of profitability during a period of unstable prices. During such a period, Firms C and D each have two batches of inventory. The first batch of 100 units was acquired at a cost of $1.00 per unit; the second was acquired later at $1.50 per unit. Firm C uses the FIFO method, and Firm D uses the LIFO method. The income statement for each firm shows that it sold 100 units at $5.00 apiece. Since Firm C uses the FIFO method, it has figured the cost of goods sold (inventories used) as $100 (the cost of Batch 1). Since Firm D uses the LIFO method, it has figured the cost of goods sold as $150 (the cost of Batch 2). As a consequence, Firm C reports a net income of $100 and Firm D a net income of only $50.

However, the effects are reversed on the balance sheet, where Firm C carries inventories at $150 and Firm D at $100. On this basis, Firm C reports total assets of $1,000 and Firm D $950. The return on assets is thus 10 percent for Firm C and 5.3 percent for Firm D.

During a period of rising price levels, the use of LIFO results in an expense item on the income statement that is closer to the current replacement cost of items used from inventories. However, using LIFO also means that the balance sheet amount of inventory investment is carried at historical costs rather than current costs. Thus, although LIFO comes closer to a correct measure of *expenses* for the income statement, it results in an understate-

---

Table 8A.1   Effects of FIFO and LIFO Inventory Costing and Valuation

Firm C (FIFO)			Firm D (LIFO)		
Income statement			**Income statement**		
Sales (100 at $5)		$ 500	Sales (100 at $5)		$500
Inventories used	$100		Inventories used	$150	
Other costs	300		Other costs	300	
Total costs		400	Total costs		450
Net income		$ 100	Net income		$ 50
Balance sheet			**Balance sheet**		
Inventories on hand		$ 150	Inventories on hand		$100
Other assets		850	Other assets		850
Total assets		$1,000	Total assets		$950
Return on assets		10%	Return on assets		5.3%

Note: Inventories for both companies: Batch 1 — 100 units at $1.00 per unit, for a total of $100; Batch 2 — 100 units at $1.50 per unit, for a total of $150.

ment of *investment* on the balance sheet. Conversely, if FIFO is used, the expense item on the income statement is understated and the balance sheet valuation of inventories is closer to current costs. The consequences are similar to those for depreciation based on historical acquisition costs versus current replacement costs.

Thus, in a period of inflation, distortions will result from the use of the historical cost postulate. Assets are recorded at cost, but revenue and other expense flows are in dollars of different purchasing power. The amortization of fixed costs does not reflect the current cost of these assets. Furthermore, net income during periods when assets are held does not reflect the effects of management's decision to hold the assets rather than sell them. Assets are not stated on the balance sheet at their current values, so the firm's financial position cannot be accurately evaluated. When assets are sold, gains or losses are reported during that period even though these results reflect decisions in prior periods to hold the assets.

Proposals for Accounting Policies to Adjust for Inflation

As a consequence of a continued high rate of inflation, proposals have been made to modify accounting procedures to recognize that the traditional postulate of a stable measuring unit is no longer valid. In December 1974, the Financial Accounting Standards Board issued a proposed statement entitled "Financial Reporting in Units of General Purchasing Power." On March 23, 1976, the Securities and Exchange Commission issued Accounting Series Release No. 190. SEC Release 190 requires disclosure of replacement costs for inventory items and depreciable plant from registrants with $100 million or more (at historical cost) of gross plant assets and inventories constituting 10 percent or more of total assets.

In September 1979, the Financial Accounting Standards Board (FASB) issued Statement No. 33, *Financial Reporting and Changing Prices*. A related publication, *Illustrations of Financial Reporting and Changing Prices*, was issued in December 1979. FASB 33 requires major companies to disclose the effects of both general inflation (purchasing power) and specific price changes (current costs) as supplementary information in their published annual reports. FASB No. 33 applies to public enterprises having either (1) inventories and property, plant, and equipment (before deducting accumulated depreciation) amounting to more than $125 million or (2) total assets amounting to more than $1 billion (after deducting accumulated depreciation). Statement No. 33 is effective for fiscal years ended on or after December 22, 1979.[1]

Financial statements and financial ratio analysis are used to understand the past performance of a business firm as well as to lay a foundation for future projections. Traditional accounting methods assumed that the general price level was relatively stable. In addition, traditional accounting assumed that no major structural changes were taking place that caused the relative values of individual assets to change greatly. These assumptions were severely violated in the 1970s. It is, therefore, particularly important that methods be developed to make the appropriate adjustments in accounting data if they are to be used effectively in financial decision making.

---

[1]In its Accounting Series Release No. 271, issued shortly after the publication of FASB No. 33, the Securities and Exchange Commission ruled that companies giving supplemental current-cost information in accordance with FASB No. 33 need not provide the SEC with replacement-cost information.

Selected References

Davidson, S., and Weil, R. L., "Replacement Cost Disclosure," *Financial Analysts Journal*, 32 (March-April 1976), pp. 57-66.

——, "Inflation Accounting and 1974 Earnings," *Financial Analysts Journal*, 31 (September-October 1975), pp. 42-54.

——, "Predicting Inflation-Adjusted Results," *Financial Analysts Journal*, 31 (January-February 1975), pp. 27-31.

Dhavale, Dileep G., and Wilson, Hoyt G., "Breakeven Analysis with Inflationary Cost and Prices," *Engineering Economist*, 25 (Winter 1980), pp. 107-122.

Financial Accounting Standards Board, *Illustrations of Financial Reporting and Changing Prices: Statement of Financial Accounting Standards No. 33*, Stamford, Conn.: Financial Accounting Standards Board, December 1979.

——, *Statement of Financial Accounting Standards No. 33: Financial Reporting and Changing Prices*, Stamford, Conn.: Financial Accounting Standards Board, September 1979.

——, *Summary Statement of Financial Accounting Standards No. 33: Financial Reporting and Changing Prices*, Stamford, Conn.: Financial Accounting Standards Board, September 1979.

Hong, Hai, "Inflationary Tax Effects on the Assets of Business Corporations," *Financial Management*, 6 (Fall 1977), pp. 51-59.

Weston, J. Fred, and Goudzwaard, Maurice B., "Financial Policies in an Inflationary Environment," in *The Treasurer's Handbook*, edited by J. Fred Weston and Maurice B. Goudzwaard, Homewood, Ill.: Dow Jones-Irwin, 1976, pp. 20-42.

Appendix B to Chapter 8
Financial Ratios in Discriminant Analysis

Financial ratios give an indication of the financial strength of a company. The limitations of ratio analysis arise from the fact that the methodology is basically *univariate*; that is, each ratio is examined in isolation. The combined effects of several ratios are based solely on the judgment of the financial analyst. Therefore, to overcome these shortcomings of ratio analysis, it is necessary to combine different ratios into a meaningful predictive model. Two statistical techniques, namely, regression analysis and discriminant analysis, have been used for this purpose. *Regression analysis* uses past data to predict future values of a dependent variable, while *discriminant analysis* results in an index that allows classification of an observation into one of several *a priori* groupings.

Classification of Observations by Discriminant Analysis

The general problem of classification arises when an analyst has certain characteristics of an observation and wishes to classify that observation into one of several predetermined categories on the basis of these characteristics. For example, a financial analyst has on hand various financial ratios of a business enterprise and wishes to use these ratios to classify it as either a bankrupt firm or a nonbankrupt firm. Discriminant analysis is one statistical technique that allows such classification.

Basically, discriminant analysis consists of three steps:

1. Establish mutually exclusive group classifications. Each group is distinguished by a probability distribution of the characteristics.
2. Collect data for observations in the groups.
3. Derive linear combinations of these characteristics which "best" discriminate between the groups. (By "best," we mean the ones that minimize the probability of misclassification.)

Altman's Applications of Discriminant Analysis

Altman [1968] used discriminant analysis to establish a model for predicting bankruptcy of firms. His sample was composed of 66 manufacturing firms, half of which went bankrupt. From their financial statements one period prior to bankruptcy, Altman obtained 22 financial ratios, of which 5 were found to contribute most to the prediction model. The discriminant function Z was found to be

$$Z = .012X_1 + .014X_2 + .033X_3 + .006X_4 + .999X_5, \tag{8B.1}$$

where

$X_1 =$ Working capital/Total assets (in %)
$X_2 =$ Retained earnings/Total assets (in %)
$X_3 =$ EBIT/Total assets (in %)
$X_4 =$ Market value of equity/Book value of debt (in %)
$X_5 =$ Sales/Total assets (times).

Applications to Groups of Firms

We can illustrate how this discriminant function can be used by applying it to the group means reported by Altman for his groups of bankrupt and nonbankrupt firms.

	Group Means[a]	
	Bankrupt	Nonbankrupt
X_1	−6.1%	41.4%
X_2	−62.6%	35.5%
X_3	−31.8%	15.4%
X_4	40.1%	247.7%
X_5	1.5X	1.9X

[a]E. I. Altman, *Corporate Bankruptcy in America* (Lexington, Mass.: Heath-Lexington Books, 1971), p. 65.

The resulting Z values are as follows:

$$\underline{X_1} \qquad \underline{X_2} \qquad \underline{X_3} \qquad \underline{X_4} \qquad \underline{X_5} \qquad \underline{Z}$$

$$Z_{br} = -.0732 - .8764 - 1.0494 + .2406 + 1.4985 = -0.2599.$$

$$Z_{nbr} = +.4968 + .4970 + .5082 + 1.4862 + 1.8981 = +4.8863.$$

We observe that the group means for bankrupt firms produced a Z value of −0.2599, while the group means for nonbankrupt firms produced a Z value of 4.8863. To establish a guideline for classifying firms, a cutoff value for Z is chosen to be 2.675, the midpoint of the range of values of Z that results in minimal misclassifications. Thus, a firm with a Z score of greater (less) than 2.675 is classified as a nonbankrupt (bankrupt) firm. The largest contributor to group separation of the discriminant function was found to be the profitability ratio X_3, followed by X_5, X_4, X_2, and X_1, in that order. The model correctly classifies 95 percent of the total sample, as indicated by the following matrix:

	Predicted Group Membership	
Actual Group Membership	Bankrupt	Nonbankrupt
Bankrupt	31	2
Nonbankrupt	1	32

By applying the above discriminant function to data obtained two to five years prior to bankruptcy, it was found that the model correctly classified 72 percent of the initial sample two years prior to failure. A trend analysis shows that all five observed ratios $X_1, \ldots ,X_5$ deteriorated as bankruptcy approached and that the most serious change in the majority of these ratios occurred between the third and second years prior to failure.

Application to an Individual Firm

The Altman model can also be applied to individual companies. For example, in Table 8B.1, the income statement and balance sheet for Chrysler Corporation are presented for the year ending December 31, 1979. These abbreviated financial statements provide the data needed to utilize the discriminant Z function presented in Equation 8B.1.

Using the data on Chrysler, we can make calculations of the five key financial ratios as presented in Table 8B.2. The data required for each ratio can be taken from the information in Table 8B.1. With the X values calculated in Table 8B.2, we can utilize Equation 8B.1 to calculate the Z value for Chrysler as of the end of 1979. This is done in Equation 8B.2.

$$Z = .012(-1.67) + .014(7.46) + .033(-13.33) + .006(11.74) + .999(1.8) \quad \textbf{(8B.2)}$$

$$= -.020 + .104 - .440 + .070 + 1.798$$

$$= 1.512.$$

Table 8B.1   Chrysler Corporation Financial Statements

A. Chrysler Corporation income statement for year ended December 31, 1979 (in millions)

Revenues	$12,004
Costs (except depreciation and interest)	12,710
Depreciation	181
Interest expense, net	215
Income taxes (credit)	5
Net income	($1,097)

B. Chrysler Corporation balance sheet as of December 31, 1979

Current assets	$3,121	Current liabilities	$3,232	
Other assets	3,532	Long-term debt	1,597	
		Total debt		$4,829
		Preferred stock		219
		Common stock[a]	417	
		(66.7 million shares)		
		Paid-in capital	692	
		Retained earnings	496	
		Shareholders' equity		$1,605
Total assets	$6,653	Total claims		$6,653

[a]Average price in 1979 was approximately $8.50.

Table 8B.2   Use of Chrysler Data in the Z Equation

$$X_1 = \frac{\text{Current assets less Current liabilities}}{\text{Total assets}} = \frac{3{,}121 - 3{,}232}{6{,}653} = -1.67\%.$$

$$X_2 = \frac{\text{Retained earnings}}{\text{Total assets}} = \frac{496}{6{,}653} = 7.46\%.$$

$$X_3 = \frac{\text{Earnings before interest and taxes}}{\text{Total assets}} = \frac{(887)}{6{,}653} = -13.33\%.$$

$$X_4 = \frac{\text{Market value of equity}}{\text{Book value of debt}} = \frac{66.7 \times 8.50}{4{,}829} = \frac{567}{4{,}829} = 11.74\%.$$

$$X_5 = \frac{\text{Sales}}{\text{Total assets}} = \frac{12{,}004}{6{,}653} = 1.8 \times$$

The resulting Z value is 1.512. Recall that the critical Z value that appeared to discriminate between bankrupt and nonbankrupt firms was 2.675. Chrysler's Z value of 1.512 is below the critical value and places it in the category of firms likely to go bankrupt. However, Chrysler's situation was not as bad as the group of bankrupt firms whose Z value was $-.26$. The intermediate result for Chrysler suggests that it was indeed in difficulty but that even on a purely mechanical basis the loan guarantee might rescue Chrysler. Obviously, fundamental analysis of Chrysler's place in the dynamically changing automobile industry was required for a final decision. However, it is interesting to note that the discriminant analysis of Chrysler's position was consistent with the judgment that Chrysler was having problems but had some possibility of rescue in one form or another.

Selected References

Altman, Edward I., "Examining Moyer's Re-examination of Forecasting Financial Failure," *Financial Management*, 7 (Winter 1978), pp. 76-79.

————, "Financial Ratios, Discriminant Analysis and the Prediction of Corporate Bankruptcy," *Journal of Finance*, 23 (September 1968), pp. 589-609.

————, and Eisenbeis, Robert A., "Financial Applications of Discriminant Analysis: A Clarification," *Journal of Financial and Quantitative Analysis*, 13 (March 1978), pp. 185-195.

Altman, Edward I.; Haldeman, Robert G.; and Narayanan, P., "ZETA Analysis: A New Model to Identify Bankruptcy Risk," *Journal of Banking and Finance*, 1 (June 1977), pp. 29-54.

Eisenbeis, Robert A., "Pitfalls in the Application of Discriminant Analysis in Business, Finance, and Economics," *Journal of Finance*, 32 (June 1977), pp. 875-900.

————, and Avery, Robert B., *Discriminant Analysis and Classification Procedures: Theory and Applications*, Lexington, Mass.: D. C. Heath, 1972.

Joy, O. Maurice, and Tollefson, John O., "On the Financial Applications of Discriminant Analysis," *Journal of Financial and Quantitative Analysis*, 10 (December 1975), pp. 723-739.

Moyer, R. Charles, "Reply to 'Examining Moyer's Re-examination of Forecasting Failure,'" *Financial Management*, 7 (Winter 1978), pp. 80-81.

————, "Forecasting Financial Failure: A Re-examination," *Financial Management*, 6 (Spring 1977), pp. 11-17.

Tollefson, John O., and Joy, O. Maurice, "Some Clarifying Comments on Discriminant Analysis," *Journal of Financial and Quantitative Analysis*, 13 (March 1978), pp. 197-200.

Chapter 9 Financial Planning and Control

In the present chapter, we emphasize the planning framework. The focus is on profitability analysis, both in a broad long-term framework and in connection with shorter-term forecasting, which is the focus of the budgeting process. In addition to long-range forecasts, the financial manager is concerned with short-term needs for funds. It is embarrassing for a corporate treasurer to "run out of money." Even though a bank loan can probably be negotiated on short notice, this plight may cause the banker to question the soundness of the firm's management and, accordingly, to reduce the company's line of credit or raise the interest rate. Therefore, attention must be given to short-term budgeting, with special emphasis on cash forecasting, or cash budgeting, as it is commonly called. Since modern business involves many large corporations with a number of individual divisions, the application of financial planning and control to divisions is also surveyed.

Five major areas are covered in this chapter:
1. *Breakeven analysis, or profit planning*
2. *Operating leverage — the sensitivity of operating income to changes in the volume of operations*
3. *Cash forecasting and budgeting*
4. *Divisional control in a decentralized firm*
5. *Overall planning models.*

These five topics are tied together by the framework of financial planning and control.

Financial Planning and Control Processes

Financial planning and control involve the use of projections based on standards and the development of a feedback and adjustment process to improve performance. This financial planning and control process involves forecasts and the use of several types of budgets. Budget systems are developed for every significant area of the firm's activities, as shown by Figure 9.1.

The production budget analyzes the use of materials, parts, labor, and facilities. Each of its major elements is likely to have its own budget as well: a materials budget, a personnel budget, and a facilities budget. To achieve sales of the products produced requires the use of a marketing budget. A budget is also developed to cover general office and executive requirements.

The results of projecting all these elements of cost are reflected in the budgeted (also called "pro forma" or "projected") income statement. Anticipated sales give rise to contemplation of the various types of investments needed to produce the products. These investments, plus the beginning balance sheet, provide the necessary data for developing the assets side of the balance sheet.

Assets must be financed, but first a cash flow analysis (the cash budget) is needed. The cash budget indicates the combined effects of the budgeted operations on the firm's cash

Figure 9.1   Overview of the Financial Planning and Control Process

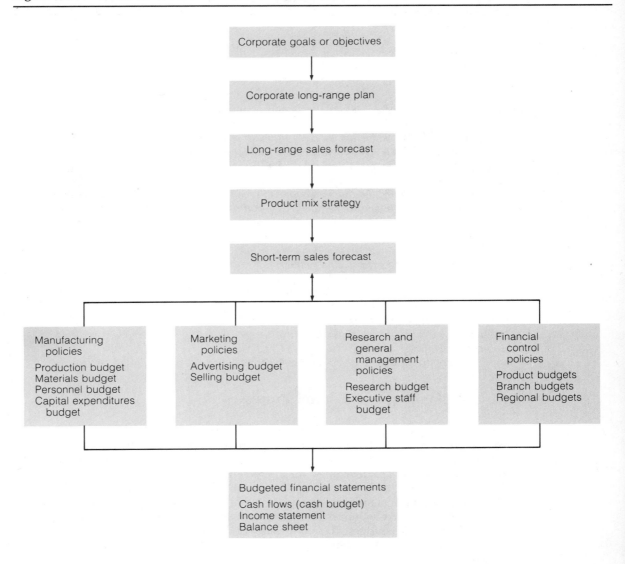

flows. A positive net cash flow indicates that the firm has sufficient financing. However, if an increase in the volume of operations leads to a negative cash flow, additional financing is required. The longer the lead time in arranging for the required financing, the greater is the opportunity for developing the required documentation and for working out arrangements with financing sources.

Financial planning and control seek to improve profitability, avoid cash squeezes, and improve the performance of individual divisions of a company. These areas represent the main sections covered in this chapter.

Breakeven Analysis

The relationships between the size of investment outlays and the required volume to achieve profitability are referred to as breakeven analysis or profit planning. Breakeven analysis is a device for determining the point at which sales will just cover costs. If all of a firm's costs were variable, the subject of breakeven volume would not come up. But since the level of total costs can be greatly influenced by the size of the fixed investments the firm makes, the resulting fixed costs will put the firm in a loss position unless a sufficient volume of sales is achieved.

If a firm is to avoid accounting losses, its sales must cover all costs — those that vary directly with production and those that do not change as production levels change. Costs that fall into each of these categories are outlined in Table 9.1.

The nature of breakeven analysis is depicted in Figure 9.2, the basic breakeven chart. The chart is presented on a unit basis, with units produced shown on the horizontal axis and income and costs measured on the vertical axis. Fixed costs of $40,000 are represented by a horizontal line; they are the same (fixed) regardless of the number of units produced. Variable costs are assumed to be $1.20 a unit. Units are assumed to be sold at $2.00 each, so the total revenue is pictured as a straight line, which increases with production. The slope (or rate of ascent) of the total revenue line is steeper than that of the total cost line. This must be true, because the firm is gaining $2.00 of revenue for every $1.20 paid out for labor and materials — the variable costs. Until the breakeven point (found at the intersection of the total income and total cost lines), the firm suffers losses. After that point, it begins to make profits. Figure 9.2 indicates a breakeven point at a sales and cost level of $100,000 and a production level of 50,000 units.

Calculations of the breakeven point can also be carried out algebraically. From the data given, the firm's total revenue or sales function, TR, is

$$TR = \$2Q,$$

where Q is the number of units of production per period.

Table 9.1 Fixed and Variable Costs

Fixed Costs[a]	Direct or Variable Costs
Depreciation on plant and equipment	Factory labor
Rentals	Materials
Salaries of research staff	Sales commissions
Salaries of executive staff	
General office expenses	

[a]Some of these costs (for example, salaries and office expenses) can be varied to some degree; however, firms are reluctant to reduce these expenditures in response to temporary fluctuations in sales. Such costs are often called *semivariable* costs.

Figure 9.2   Breakeven Chart

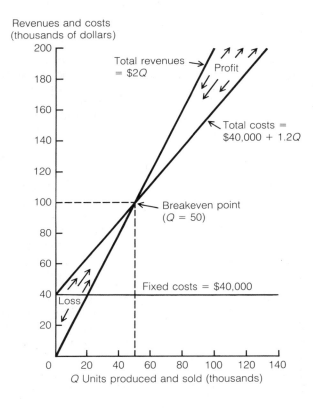

The total cost function is

$$TC = \$40{,}000 + \$1.20Q.$$

At the breakeven quantity, Q^*, total revenues and total costs are equal. So equating the sales and total cost functions,

$$\$2Q = \$40{,}000 + \$1.20Q$$

$$Q^* = 50{,}000.$$

The relationships are clarified further by use of a contribution income statement for various levels of units sold, as shown by Table 9.2. From Table 9.2, we can readily observe that the breakeven quantity is 50,000 units sold. The breakeven level of sales is $100,000. To develop these relationships algebraically, we define them as follows:

Table 9.2   Contribution Income Statement at Various Quantities of Units Sold

Units sold (Q)	20,000	40,000	50,000	80,000	100,000	200,000
Sales revenues (TR)	$40,000	$80,000	$100,000	$160,000	$200,000	$400,000
Total variable expenses (V)	24,000	48,000	60,000	96,000	120,000	240,000
Contribution margin (C)	16,000	32,000	40,000	64,000	80,000	160,000
Fixed operating expenses (F)	40,000	40,000	40,000	40,000	40,000	40,000
Net operating income (X)	($24,000)	($ 8,000)	—	$ 24,000	$ 40,000	$120,000

Note: $C = cQ$ and $X = cQ - F = C - F$

$$TR^* = \text{breakeven revenues} = PQ^*$$
$$Q^* = \text{the breakeven quantity of units sold}$$
$$P = \text{selling price per unit}$$
$$F = \text{fixed costs}$$
$$v = \text{variable cost per unit}$$
$$V = \text{total variable costs} = vQ$$
$$c = \text{contribution margin per unit} = (P - v)$$
$$C = \text{total contribution margin} = cQ = (P - v)Q$$
$$CR = \text{contribution ratio} = \left(1 - \frac{vQ}{PQ}\right) = \left(1 - \frac{v}{P}\right).$$

We can then readily develop the breakeven quantity and the breakeven dollar volume of sales by beginning with the relationship that total revenues or sales equal total costs at breakeven. We then have the following:

Breakeven quantity = Q^*.

$$P \cdot Q^* = vQ^* + F$$

$$P \cdot Q^* - vQ^* = F$$

$$Q^* = \frac{F}{P - v}$$

$$= \frac{F}{c}. \qquad \textbf{(9.1a)}$$

Breakeven revenues = TR^*.

$$TR^* = F + V$$

$$= F + \frac{V \cdot TR^*}{TR^*}$$

$$= PQ$$

$$TR^* - \frac{V}{PQ}TR^* = F$$

$$TR^* = \frac{F}{1 - \dfrac{V}{PQ}}$$

$$= \frac{F}{CR}. \qquad \textbf{(9.1b)}$$

We can illustrate the calculation of both Q^* and TR^* from the data of our numerical example.

$$Q^* = \frac{F}{c} \qquad\qquad\qquad TR^* = \frac{F}{CR}$$

$$= \frac{\$40,000}{\$.80} \qquad\qquad \frac{V}{PQ} = .6 \text{ at all quantities sold;}$$

$$= 50,000 \text{ units.} \qquad\qquad \text{therefore,}$$

$$CR = \left(1 - \frac{V}{PQ}\right) = .4.$$

Hence,

$$TR^* = \frac{\$40,000}{.4} = \$100,000.$$

Thus, the breakeven quantity or breakeven sales volume can readily be calculated by use of the total fixed costs and a contribution margin relationship.

Limitations of Breakeven Analysis

Breakeven analysis is useful in studying the relations among volume, prices, and costs; it is thus helpful in pricing, cost control, and decisions about expansion programs. It has limitations, however, as a guide to managerial actions.

Linear breakeven analysis is especially weak in what it implies about the sales possibilities for the firm. Any linear breakeven chart is based on a constant sales price. Therefore, in order to study profit possibilities under different prices, a whole series of charts is necessary — one for each price.

Breakeven analysis may also be deficient with regard to costs. If sales increase to levels at which the existing plant and equipment are worked to capacity, additional workers are hired and overtime pay increases. All this causes variable costs to rise sharply. If additional equipment and plant are required, fixed costs are also increased. Finally, the products sold by the firm may change in quality and quantity. Such changes in product mix influence the level and slope of the cost function. Breakeven analysis is useful as a first step in developing the basic data required for pricing and for financial decisions. But more detailed analysis is required before final judgments can be made.

Nonlinear Breakeven Analysis

Some of the deficiencies in traditional breakeven analysis are avoided by recognizing that the relationships are likely to be nonlinear. For example, it is reasonable to think that increased sales can be obtained only by successively reducing prices. Similarly, empirical studies suggest that average variable cost per unit falls over some range of output and then begins to rise. These assumptions are illustrated in Figure 9.3, which reflects the usual assumptions of economists about the shapes of the curves that depict total revenues and total costs.

Because of the role of fixed costs, there is an initial region where losses are incurred when sales are relatively low. This is followed by an area in which there is a positive profit. Subsequently, an upper breakeven point is reached beyond which losses are again incurred. Figure 9.3 illustrates that output in the profit region at which maximum profit is achieved. This is shown graphically as the point at which the slope of the total revenue

Figure 9.3　　　Nonlinear Breakeven Chart

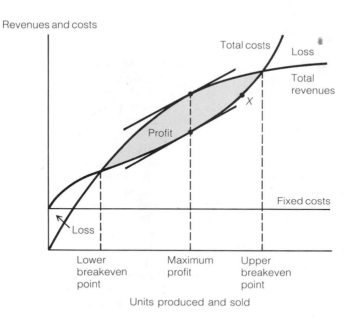

curve is equal to the slope of the total cost curve. In economic terms, the slopes of these two curves are respectively marginal revenue and marginal cost. Hence, maximum profit is achieved when, in economic terms, marginal revenue equals marginal cost. Figure 9.3 illustrates that at that output, the amount by which total revenue exceeds total cost is the largest. Thus, traditional economic principles represent a form of breakeven analysis. Alternatively, we may say that breakeven analysis can be made more useful by putting it in the framework of less restrictive assumptions about the shapes of the total revenue and total cost functions.

Applications of Breakeven Analysis

Used appropriately, breakeven analysis can shed light on a number of important business decisions. In general, breakeven analysis can be used by the firm in three separate but related ways. In new-product decisions, breakeven analysis helps determine how large sales of a new product must be for the firm to achieve profitability. Breakeven analysis can also be used as a broad framework for studying the effects of a general expansion in the level of operations. Finally, in analyzing programs to modernize and automate, where the firm would be operating in a more mechanized, automated manner and thus substituting fixed costs for variable costs, breakeven analysis helps analyze the consequences of shifting from variable costs to fixed costs. The key factor is the influence of volume changes on profitability when firms have different relationships between fixed and variable costs. Understanding these relationships involves understanding the idea of *operating leverage*, to which we now turn.

Operating Leverage

To a physicist, *leverage* implies the use of a lever to raise a heavy object with a small force. In business terminology, a high degree of operating leverage implies that a relatively small change in sales results in a large change in net operating income.

The significance of the degree of operating leverage is illustrated by Figure 9.4. Three firms — A, B, and C — with differing degrees of leverage are contrasted. Firm A has a relatively small amount of fixed charges; it does not have much automated equipment, so its depreciation cost is low. However, its variable cost line has a relatively steep slope, denoting that its variable costs per unit are higher than those of the other firms.

Firm B is considered to have a normal amount of fixed costs in its operations. It uses automated equipment (with which one operator can turn out a few or many units at the same labor cost) to about the same extent as the average firm in the industry. Firm B breaks even at a higher level of operations than does Firm A. At a production level of 40,000 units, B loses $8,000 but A breaks even.

Firm C has the highest fixed costs. It is highly automated, using expensive, high-speed machines that require very little labor per unit produced. With such an operation, its variable costs rise slowly. Because of the high overhead resulting from charges associated with the expensive machinery, Firm C's breakeven point is higher than that for either Firm A or Firm B. Once Firm C reaches its breakeven point, however, its profits rise faster than do those of the other firms.

Alternative operating leverage decisions can have a great impact on the unit cost position of each firm. When 200,000 units are sold, the average per unit cost of production for each firm, calculated by dividing total costs by the 200,000 units sold, is

	Average Cost per Unit at 200,000 Units
Firm A	$1.60
Firm B	$1.40
Firm C	$1.30

These results have important implications. At a high volume of operations of 200,000 units per period, Firm C has a substantial cost superiority over the other two firms and particularly over Firm A. Firm C could cut the price of its product to $1.50 per unit, which represents a level that would be unprofitable for Firm A, and still have more than a 13 percent ($.20/$1.50) return on sales. (The average pretax margin on sales for manufacturing firms is about 9 to 11 percent.) Another illustration of this idea is the difference in unit costs for Japanese versus U.S. steel companies. Most Japanese steel companies can produce 10 million tons or more per year, while only one or two U.S. steel companies can produce as much as 5 million tons per year. Operating at such a high capacity (in part due to the benefit of growth through export sales), the Japanese companies have been able to sell steel in the United States at prices below the costs of the U.S. steel companies. While the total story is complex, the firms' operating leverage factor is an important influence on their relative costs per unit.

Figure 9.4   Operating Leverage

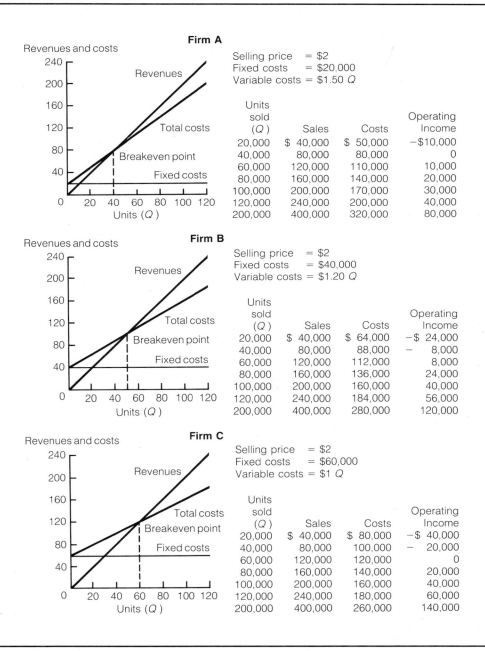

Firm A

Revenues and costs

Selling price   = $2
Fixed costs   = $20,000
Variable costs = $1.50 Q

Units sold (Q)	Sales	Costs	Operating Income
20,000	$ 40,000	$ 50,000	−$10,000
40,000	80,000	80,000	0
60,000	120,000	110,000	10,000
80,000	160,000	140,000	20,000
100,000	200,000	170,000	30,000
120,000	240,000	200,000	40,000
200,000	400,000	320,000	80,000

Firm B

Revenues and costs

Selling price   = $2
Fixed costs   = $40,000
Variable costs = $1.20 Q

Units sold (Q)	Sales	Costs	Operating Income
20,000	$ 40,000	$ 64,000	−$ 24,000
40,000	80,000	88,000	− 8,000
60,000	120,000	112,000	8,000
80,000	160,000	136,000	24,000
100,000	200,000	160,000	40,000
120,000	240,000	184,000	56,000
200,000	400,000	280,000	120,000

Firm C

Revenues and costs

Selling price   = $2
Fixed costs   = $60,000
Variable costs = $1 Q

Units sold (Q)	Sales	Costs	Operating Income
20,000	$ 40,000	$ 80,000	−$ 40,000
40,000	80,000	100,000	− 20,000
60,000	120,000	120,000	0
80,000	160,000	140,000	20,000
100,000	200,000	160,000	40,000
120,000	240,000	180,000	60,000
200,000	400,000	260,000	140,000

Degree of Operating Leverage

Operating leverage can be defined more precisely in terms of the way a given change in sales volume affects net operating income (NOI). To measure the effect on profitability of a change in volume, we calculate the *degree of operating leverage,* the ratio of the percentage change in operating income to the percentage change in units sold or in total revenues. Algebraically,

$$\frac{\text{Degree of}}{\text{operating leverage}} = \frac{\text{Percentage change in operating income}}{\text{Percentage change in units sold or in total revenues}}.$$

For Firm B in Figure 9.4, the degree of operating leverage (DOL_B) for a change in units of output from 100,000 to 120,000 is

$$DOL_B = \frac{\frac{\Delta \text{Income}}{\text{Income}}}{\frac{\Delta Q}{Q}} = \frac{\frac{\Delta X}{X}}{\frac{\Delta Q}{Q}}$$

$$= \frac{\frac{\$56,000 - \$40,000}{\$40,000}}{\frac{120,000 - 100,000}{100,000}} = \frac{\frac{\$16,000}{\$40,000}}{\frac{20,000}{100,000}}$$

$$= \frac{40\%}{20\%} = 2.0.$$

Here, ΔX is the increase in net operating income, Q is the quantity of output in units, and ΔQ is the increase in output.[1]

Using the same equation, the degree of operating leverage at 100,000 units is 1.67 for Firm A and 2.5 for Firm C. Thus, for a 10 percent change in volume, Firm C, the company with the most operating leverage, will experience a profit gain of 25 percent, while Firm A,

---

[1] Note that an alternative formulation for calculating DOL at any level of output Q can be derived:

$$DOL = \frac{\frac{\Delta X}{X}}{\frac{\Delta Q}{Q}}$$

$$= \frac{\frac{c\Delta Q}{cQ - F}}{\frac{\Delta Q}{Q}}$$

$$= \frac{Qc\Delta Q}{\Delta Q(cQ - F)}$$

$$= \frac{cQ}{X}$$

$$= \frac{C}{X}.$$

the one with the least leverage, will have only a 16.7 percent profit gain. The profits of Firm C are more sensitive to changes in sales volume than those of Firm A. Thus, the higher the degree of operating leverage, the more profits will fluctuate, both in an upward and downward direction, in response to changes in volume.

The degree of operating leverage of a firm has important implications for a number of areas of business and financial policy.[2] Firm C's high degree of operating leverage suggests gains from increasing volume. Suppose Firm C could increase its quantity sold from 100,000 units to 120,000 units by cutting the price per unit to $1.90. The equation for net operating income is

$$\text{Net operating income } (X) = PQ - vQ - F$$

$$= \$1.90(120{,}000) - (\$1)120{,}000 - \$60{,}000$$

$$= \$228{,}000 - \$120{,}000 - \$60{,}000$$

$$= \$48{,}000.$$

The equation shows that Firm C could increase its profits from $40,000 at a volume of 100,000 to $48,000 at a volume of 120,000. Thus, a high degree of operating leverage suggests that an aggressive price policy may increase profits, particularly if the market is responsive to small price cuts.

On the other hand, Firm C's high degree of operating leverage tells us that the company is subject to large swings in profits as its volume fluctuates. Thus, if Firm C's industry is one whose sales are greatly affected by changes in the overall level of economic activity (as are, for example, the durable goods industries, such as machine tools, steel, and autos), its profits are subject to large fluctuations. Hence, the degree of financial leverage appropriate for Firm C to take on is lower than that for a firm with a lower degree of operating leverage and for industries whose sales are less sensitive to fluctuations in the level of the economy. (Financial leverage is discussed in Chapters 20 and 21.)

Cash Breakeven Analysis

Some of the firm's fixed costs are noncash outlays, and, for a period, some of its revenues may be in receivables. The cash breakeven chart for Firm B, constructed on the assumption that $30,000 of the fixed costs from the previous illustration are depreciation charges and, therefore, a noncash outlay, is shown in Figure 9.5. Because fixed cash outlays are only $10,000, the cash breakeven point is at 12,500 units rather than 50,000 units, which is the profit breakeven point.

An equation for the cash breakeven point based on sales revenues can be derived from the equation for the profit breakeven point. The only change is to reduce fixed costs by the amount of noncash outlays:

[2]The degree of operating leverage is a form of *elasticity concept* and thus is akin to the familiar price elasticity developed in economics. Since operating leverage is an elasticity, it varies depending on the particular part of the breakeven graph that is being considered. For example, in terms of our illustrative firms, the degree of operating leverage is greatest close to the breakeven point, where a very small change in volume can produce a very large percentage increase in profits simply because the base profits are close to zero near the breakeven point.

Figure 9.5   Cash Breakeven Analysis for Firm B

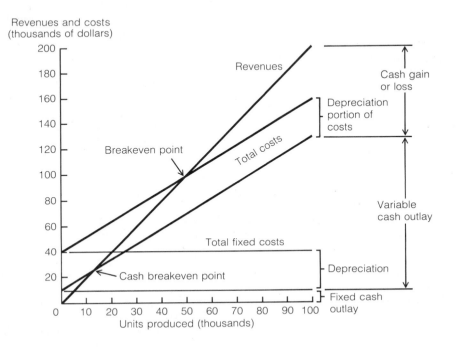

$$TR^* = \frac{F - \text{Noncash outlays}}{(CR)}.$$

If noncash outlays are very close to total fixed costs, the cash breakeven point approaches zero. The cash breakeven point based on units of output is comparable to the profit breakeven quantity, except that fixed costs must be adjusted for noncash outlays:

$$Q^* = \frac{F - \text{Noncash outlays}}{c}.$$

Here again, if noncash outlays are very large, the cash breakeven point may be low, despite a large amount of fixed charges.

Cash breakeven analysis does not fully represent cash flows; for this, a cash budget is required. But it is useful because it provides a picture of the flow of funds from operations. A firm may incur a level of fixed costs that will result in losses during business downswings but large profits during upswings. If cash outlays are small, the firm may be able to operate above the cash breakeven point even during periods of loss. Thus, the risk of insolvency (in the sense of being unable to meet cash obligations) is small. This allows a firm to reach out for higher profits through automation and operating leverage.

Cash Budgets

A natural extension of the ideas involved in cash breakeven analysis is a consideration of cash budgeting. The cash budget, a highly significant tool in the financial planning and control processes of business firms, is a projection of future cash receipts and cash disbursements over some time interval. This provides the financial manager with a framework for reviewing and controlling future cash receipts and future cash disbursements and an overview of the probable patterns of cash flows in the future. The financial manager may then review his collection and disbursement procedures to determine whether he is maximizing the firm's net cash flows. If despite his best efforts in controlling cash inflows and outflows, the cash budget indicates that additional financing will be required, the financial manager will have some lead time for taking the actions necessary to provide for future financing.

In this chapter, we shall describe the procedures for preparing the cash budget. In Chapter 12 on cash and marketable securities, we shall use the cash budget framework for analyzing how cash collections and cash disbursements can be efficiently managed and controlled to optimize the firm's net cash flows.

Procedures for Preparing a Cash Budget

The cash budget is forward-looking. It seeks to estimate future cash receipts and cash disbursements. Some forecasts are necessarily involved. As we shall see over and over, the key to financial forecasts and to the analysis of many financial decisions is the sales forecast. We shall comment briefly on the main elements involved in making a sales forecast, but the details would involve another separate book-length treatment.

Two fundamental approaches to the sales forecast are typically used. These are referred to as the "top-down" and "bottoms-up" approaches.

In the "top-down" approach, the analysis begins with forecasts of the economy. Then a relationship between the economy and industry sales is developed.[3] Implicit recognition of the role of the economy is often found in annual reports reflected in statements such as "the economy was weak, which impacted severely on our industry." With an industry forecast, an attempt is next made to estimate the firm's market share by individual products. This may also include the expected performance of new products that are going to be introduced. Market share times industry sales in each product-market area will provide a sales forecast by product and, when summed, for the firm as a whole.

The "bottoms-up" approach typically begins with sales estimates by individual sales representatives. Product sales managers will then consolidate these individual forecasts into sales estimates by product lines. Combining the sales forecast by product lines results in a sales forecast for the firm as a whole.

Both methods come to the same final figure — sales forecast by product lines and for the firm as a whole. The advantage of the "bottoms-up" approach is that it can take into account unusual developments, such as particularly large new orders or substantial cancellations from individual customers. The advantage of the "top-down" approach is that trends in the economy and in the industry may greatly alter customer behavior. Orders may be cancelled or increased depending upon general economic developments. But mak-

---

[3]Chapter 10, "Financial Forecasting," gives examples of several different ways of relating sales forecasts to economy-wide factors.

ing the sales forecasts for product lines and for the firm as a whole is a critical activity in every firm. It is the basis for other forecasts and budgets affecting not only finance but such factors as procurement, production, and employment policies. Since the sales forecasts are so important, all of the key executives of the firm are likely to be involved. Finance is only one of the users of the sales forecast, but it is especially critical to financial planning and control.

The financial manager, in conjunction with other executives, has in hand a sales forecast. We now describe how this sales forecast is used in developing a cash budget for the next six months. In Table 9.3, we set forth a schedule of sales and cash collections. The sales forecast is given for January through June of the forthcoming year. It is assumed that the sales level for the months prior to January are at the same $600,000 level and that the sales for the months following June are also at the same $600,000 level since lead-and-lag relationships require forecasts prior to and following the specific six-month period. The firm sells on a 30-days basis (that is, customers have 30 days to pay). Its experience establishes that, on average, 80 percent of the sales are collected in the month following the sales and 20 percent during the second month following the sales. Row 1 in Table 9.3 presents the sales forecast. Row 2 sets forth collections made during the following month. Since it has been assumed that sales for the months prior to January were also at the $600,000 level, the entry in Row 2 would be 80 percent of $600,000, or $480,000. In Row 3, the collections during the second month after sales would be 20 percent of $600,000, which is $120,000. Total cash receipts for January would, therefore, be $600,000. For February, the total cash receipts would be the same. In March, collections during one month following sales would be 80 percent of $800,000, or $640,000. The collections related to sales two months previously would be 20 percent of $600,000, or $120,000. Total cash receipts for March would, therefore, be $760,000. The total cash receipts for the subsequent months would be calculated following the same logic.

In Table 9.4, we consider the schedule of cash expenses based on the sales forecast in Table 9.3, which we refer to as "Sales Forecast One." Row 1 starts with the sales forecast. Purchases have to be made in anticipation of sales. Experience for this firm indicates that purchases on average represent about 50 percent of sales that are expected to be made in the following month. Hence, purchases would represent 50 percent of the sales forecast for the month following. It is assumed further that purchases are paid for on average in the month after they have been made. Hence, taking the Row 2 figures and shifting them forward one month gives us the cash outflows for payment of purchases shown in Row 3.

It is assumed that wages and other expenses in a given month represent the processing of goods which were purchased in the previous month. It is also assumed that wages and other expenses are paid during the month that they are incurred. Hence Row 4, which

---

Table 9.3　　　Schedule of Sales and Cash Collections—Sales Forecast One (Thousands of Dollars)

	Jan.	Feb.	Mar.	Apr.	May	June
1. Sales forecast one	$600	$800	$800	$1,000	$1,000	$ 600
2. Collections — 80% of sales ($t-1$)	480	480	640	640	800	800
3. Collections — 20% of sales ($t-2$)	120	120	120	160	160	200
4. Total cash receipts	$600	$600	$760	$ 800	$ 960	$1,000

Table 9.4   Schedule of Cash Expenses — Sales Forecast One (Thousands of Dollars)

	Dec.	Jan.	Feb.	Mar.	Apr.	May	June	July
1. Sales forecast one		$600	$800	$800	$1,000	$1,000	$600	
2. Purchases — 50% of sales ($t + 1$)	$300	400	400	500	500	300	300	$300
3. Payment — purchases ($t - 1$)		300	400	400	500	500	300	
4. Wages — 60% of purchases ($t - 1$)		180	240	240	300	300	180	
5. Other expenses — 30% of purchases ($t + 1$)		120	150	150	90	90	90	
6. Total cash expenses		$600	$790	$790	$ 890	$ 890	$570	

represents cash outlays for wages, is 60 percent of purchases made in the previous month. It is assumed that other expenses are incurred and paid in the month preceding the month in which purchases are made. Hence Row 5 would be 30 percent of purchases made in the following month. Total cash expenses in Row 6 represent the sum of payments set forth in Rows 3 through 5.

If these were the only receipts and expenses for the firm, the cash budget or schedule of net cash flows would be as depicted in Table 9.5. Rows 2 and 3 of Table 9.5 simply summarize the results of the previous two tables. The difference between total cash receipts and total cash expenses are the net cash flows shown in Row 4. These are accumulated to give us the cumulative cash flow in Row 5. Under the data assumed, the firm has a zero cash flow position at the end of January. Moreover, the cumulative position is negative for the following months through the end of May. It moves into a positive cumulative cash flow position in June. The pattern of cumulative cash flows provides information to the financial manager on the financing needs that will be required during the months that the cumulative cash flows are in a negative position. For the data presented in Table 9.5, the financial manager will have to finance on a temporary short-term seasonal basis the cumulative negative cash flow position during the months from February through May but will be able to repay this short-term loan during the month of June.

It is interesting to see the effect of continuing sales at the $1 million level in June instead of the sales level of $600,000 previously assumed. It is easy to see that total cash receipts would reflect the "steady state" level of sales at $1 million. Hence, total cash receipts in June would be $1 million as shown in Table 9.6. The projection of total cash expenses is somewhat more complicated and is detailed in Table 9.7. Following the same logic that

Table 9.5   Schedule of Net Cash Flows — Sales Forecast One (Thousands of Dollars)

	Jan.	Feb.	Mar.	Apr.	May	June
1. Sales	$600	$800	$800	$1,000	$1,000	$ 600
2. Total cash receipts	600	600	760	800	960	1,000
3. Total cash expenses	600	790	790	890	890	570
4. Net cash flow	0	(190)	(30)	(90)	70	430
5. Cumulative cash flow	0	(190)	(220)	(310)	(240)	190

Table 9.6   Schedule of Net Cash Flows — Sales Forecast Two (Thousands of Dollars)

	Jan.	Feb.	Mar.	Apr.	May	June
1. Sales	$600	$800	$800	$1,000	$1,000	$1,000
2. Total cash receipts	600	600	760	800	960	1,000
3. Total cash expenses	600	790	790	890	950	950
4. Net cash flow	0	(190)	(30)	(90)	10	50
5. Cumulative cash flow	0	(190)	(220)	(310)	(300)	(250)

was employed in Table 9.4, we obtain total cash expenses of $950,000 in Row 6 of Table 9.7. This is used as Row 3 in Table 9.6. We can then calculate the net cash flows in Row 4 of Table 9.6. Accumulating the results in Row 5, we observe that from the month of February on, the firm is in a cumulative negative cash flow position. In planning the financing, the financial manager must, therefore, forecast beyond the six months to determine the period for which financing of the negative cash flows shown in Table 9.6 will have to be planned.

Realistically, the firm will have other cash receipts and other cash disbursements in addition to those directly related to sales and purchases. We shall illustrate additional types of cash disbursements as shown in Table 9.8. We start with the total cash expenses that we had obtained in Table 9.4 based on Sales Forecast One. In Row 2 of Table 9.8, we assume capital outlays for machinery to take place in the months of March and June. In addition, we assume in Row 3 interest payments of $50,000 to be made in June. Income taxes are estimated for the months of January and April. Finally, we provide in Row 5 for quarterly dividend payments in the months of March and June. Total cash disbursements are, therefore, the figures shown in Row 6.

In Table 9.9, we present net cash flows and cash balances, taking the additional types of cash disbursements into account. The new net cash flows are shown in Row 3. They are accumulated in Row 4. Assuming an initial cash balance at the beginning of January (the end of December) of 100, we can, therefore, calculate in Row 6 the end-of-month cash balance without financing. Again, under the numbers postulated, the firm is in a cumulative negative cash flow position after January. This provides a forewarning to the financial manager of the financing that will be required during the forthcoming six-month period.

Table 9.7   Schedule of Cash Expenses — Sales Forecast Two (Thousands of Dollars)

	May	June	July
1. Sales	$1,000	$1,000	$1,000
2. Purchases — 50% of sales $(t + 1)$	500	500	500
3. Payment of purchases $(t - 1)$	500	500	
4. Wages — 60% of purchases $(t - 1)$	300	300	
5. Other expenses — 30% of purchases $(t + 1)$	150	150	
6. Total cash expenses	$ 950	$ 950	

Table 9.8   Schedule of Cash Disbursements—Sales Forecast One (Thousands of Dollars)

	Jan.	Feb.	Mar.	Apr.	May	June
1. Total cash expenses (Table 9.4)	$600	$790	$790	$890	$890	$570
2. Capital expenditures			100			200
3. Interest payments						50
4. Income taxes	40			40		
5. Dividends			10			10
6. Total cash disbursements	$640	$790	$900	$930	$890	$830

The basic methodology for developing the cash budget has been described. Some additional variations will now be indicated. Clearly for longer-term planning, the firm needs a cash budget beyond a six-month period. Typically, cash budgets will be prepared on a one-year basis for annual budgeting and then for periods up to five or ten years for longer-term financial planning. The end objective is the same—to get a picture of what the firm's cash balance position will be regarding the availability of funds or the financing that will be required.

In addition to requiring longer-term plans, the firm needs to take into account the variability that is likely to be experienced in the cash flows actually realized. We have seen that each segment of the cash budget is based on a sales forecast. Sales are obviously subject to variation. Provision must be made for altering the cash budget based on different possible levels of sales. In addition to variability in sales, other receipts and disbursements are subject to error as well. Collections may not actually follow the exact pattern that has been assumed. Expenses and other disbursements may differ because of the performance in controlling material, labor, and other costs.

Variability can be experienced in all elements of the cash budget. This has given rise to sophisticated computer techniques for analyzing the cash budget (as well as other elements of financial planning). No matter how complex the computerized approaches to cash planning and other aspects of financial planning employed, the underlying logic must follow the principles set forth in the previous discussion. If these are understood, they can readily be applied in any sophisticated type of computerized handling of the mechanics of the financial planning processes.

Table 9.9   Net Cash Flows and Cash Balances—Sales Forecast One (Thousands of Dollars)

	Dec.	Jan.	Feb.	Mar.	Apr.	May	June
1. Total cash receipts (Table 9.3)		$600	$600	$760	$800	$960	$1,000
2. Total cash disbursements (Table 9.8)		640	790	900	930	890	830
3. Net cash flow		(40)	(190)	(140)	(130)	70	170
4. Cumulative net cash flow		(40)	(230)	(370)	(500)	(430)	(260)
5. Initial cash balance (end of Dec.)	$100						
6. End-of-month cash balance without financing	100	60	(130)	(270)	(400)	(330)	(160)

We have indicated that cash budgets may have to be extended over a long number of years into the future to relate to other long-term plans. In addition, in some business firms in highly volatile types of business activities, cash budgets may be required for time intervals of less than one month. It is not uncommon for firms to engage in daily cash forecasting.[4]

It should be emphasized that the cash budget, like other elements of the firm's financial planning, does not represent an end in itself. It provides a tool for the more effective management of the firm. With modern computer techniques, it is possible to reflect the effects on future cash flows of a large number of alternative possibilities that may occur. The effects of an increase or decrease in sales, a change in the average collection period, a change in labor costs, and so forth, can all be analyzed, and their effects on the firm's future cash flow position can be estimated.

The purpose of such exercises is to provide the firm with an early lead time for adjusting to changes that may take place in its future. The emphasis should be on considering how the firm might best adjust to possible future changes. Also, the value of cash budgets and other financial planning tools is to enable the firm to determine which changes have major impacts and which have only minor impacts.

But the main emphasis is on how the firm might adjust to deal with future contingencies. If sales fall off, can expenses be quickly adjusted downward? If sales increase, can additional purchases be made and will additional labor be available? At what level of increase in sales will additional machinery and equipment be required? What will be the effect of a change in sales or changes in materials or labor costs on the firm's profitability and on cash flows? Does the firm have any maneuverability in adjusting to such changes? Again, we emphasize financial plans are not an end in themselves. They are tools to guide the firm in formulating sound policies and in making rapid adjustments to changes in the economic environment and to competitive changes that are always taking place.

Control in Multidivision Companies

For organizational reasons, large firms are generally set up on a decentralized basis. For example, General Electric establishes separate divisions for heavy appliances, light appliances, power transformers, fossil fuel generating equipment, nuclear generating equipment, and so on. Each division is defined as a *profit center*, and each has its own investments — fixed and current assets, together with a share of such general corporate assets as research labs and headquarters buildings — and is expected to earn an appropriate return on them.

The corporate headquarters, or central staff, typically controls the various divisions by a form of the du Pont system.

The du Pont System of Financial Analysis

The du Pont system of financial analysis has achieved wide recognition in American industry, and properly so. It brings together the activity ratios and profit margin on sales and shows how these ratios interact to determine the profitability of assets. The nature of the system, modified somewhat, is set forth in Figure 9.6.

---

[4]Illustrative of a methodology for relating cash forecasts to a firm's total information system is the article by Stone and Miller [1981].

Figure 9.6   du Pont Chart for Divisional Control

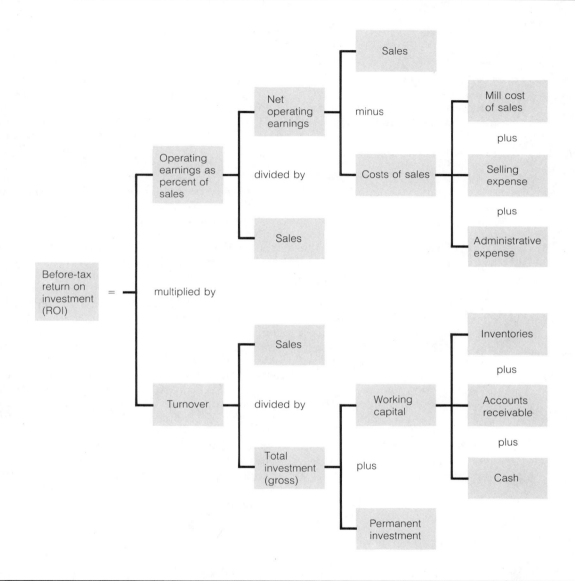

The bottom part of the figure develops the turnover ratio. It shows how current assets (cash, marketable securities, accounts receivable, and inventories) added to fixed assets give total investment. Total investment divided into sales gives the turnover of investment.

The upper part of the figure can develop the net operating income. The individual expense items are subtracted from sales to produce net operating income. This figure divided by sales gives the margin on sales. When the asset turnover ratio is multiplied by this margin on sales, the product is the before-tax return on total investment (ROI) in the firm. This can be seen from the following formula:

$$\frac{\text{NOI}}{\text{Sales}} \times \frac{\text{Sales}}{\text{Investment}} = \text{ROI}.$$

Would it be better to have a 10 percent margin on sales and a total asset turnover of two times or a 5 percent sales margin and a turnover of four times? It makes no difference; in either case, the firm has a 20 percent return on investment. Actually, most firms are not free to make the kind of choice posed in this question. Depending on the nature of its industry, the firm *must* operate with more or fewer assets, and its turnover will depend on the characteristics of its particular line of business. In the case of a dealer in fresh fruits and vegetables, fish, or other perishable items, the turnover should be high—every day or two is most desirable. In contrast, some lines of business require heavy fixed investment or long production periods. A hydroelectric utility company, with its heavy investment in dams and transmission lines, requires heavy fixed investment; a shipbuilder or an aircraft producer needs a long production period. Such companies necessarily have a low asset turnover rate but a correspondingly higher profit margin on sales.

When the du Pont system is used for divisional control, the process is often called return on investment (ROI) control. Return is measured by operating earnings—income before interest and taxes—as shown in Figure 9.6. Sometimes the earnings figure is calculated before depreciation, and total gross assets are measured before deduction of the depreciation reserve. Measurement on gross assets has the advantage of avoiding differences in ROI due to differences in the average age of the fixed assets. Older assets are more fully depreciated and have a higher depreciation reserve and lower net fixed asset amount. This causes the ROI on net total assets to be higher when fixed assets are older.

If a particular division's ROI falls below a target figure, then the centralized corporate staff helps the division's own financial staff trace back through the du Pont system to determine the cause of the substandard ROI. Each division manager is judged by the division's ROI and rewarded or penalized accordingly. Division managers are thus motivated to keep their ROI up to the target level. Their individual actions should in turn maintain the firm's ROI at an appropriate level.

In addition to its use in managerial control, ROI can be used to allocate funds to the various divisions. The firm as a whole has financial resources—retained earnings, cash flow from depreciation, and the ability to obtain additional debt and equity funds from capital markets. These funds can be allocated on the basis of the divisional ROI's, with divisions having high ROI's receiving more funds than those with low ones.

Pitfalls in the Use of ROI Control

Any system of divisional control runs the risk that executives will devise methods for "beating the system." Hence, a number of problems can arise if ROI control is used without proper safeguards.[5] Since the divisional managers are rewarded on the basis of their

---

[5]For a discussion of how to avoid the pitfalls of a static approach to ROI control and an emphasis on its use as a dynamic information feedback control process, see Weston [1972].

ROI performance, it is absolutely essential for their morale that they feel their divisional ROI does indeed provide an accurate measure of relative performance. But ROI is dependent on a number of factors in addition to managerial competence; some of these factors are listed below.

1. *Depreciation.* ROI is very sensitive to depreciation policy. If one division is writing off assets at a relatively rapid rate, its annual profits — and hence its ROI — will be reduced.

2. *Book value of assets.* If an older division is using assets that have been largely written off, both its current depreciation charges and its investment base will be low. This will make its ROI high in relation to newer divisions.

3. *Transfer pricing.* In most corporations, some divisions sell to other divisions. At General Motors, for example, the Fisher Body division sells to the Chevrolet division. In such cases, the price at which goods are transferred between divisions has a fundamental effect on divisional profits. If the transfer price of auto bodies is set relatively high, then Fisher Body will have a relatively high ROI and Chevrolet a relatively low one.

4. *Time periods.* Many projects have long gestation periods, during which expenditures must be made for research and development, plant construction, market development, and the like. Such expenditures add to the investment base without a commensurate increase in profits for several years. During this period, a division's ROI can be seriously reduced; and without proper constraints, its manager may be improperly penalized. Given the frequency of personnel transfers in larger corporations, it is easy to see how the timing problem can keep managers from making long-term investments that are in the best interests of the firm.

5. *Industry conditions.* If one division is operating in an industry where conditions are favorable and rates of return are high, while another is in an industry suffering from excessive competition, these differences may cause the favored division to look good and the unfavored one to look bad, quite apart from any differences in their managers. For example, Signal Companies' aerospace division could hardly have been expected to perform as well as their truck division did in 1973, when the entire aerospace industry suffered severe problems and truck sales soared. External conditions must be taken into account when appraising ROI performance.

Because of these factors, a division's ROI must be supplemented with other criteria for evaluating performance. For example, its growth rate in sales, profits, and market share (as well as its ROI) in comparison with other firms in its own industry has been used in such evaluations. Although ROI control has been used with great success in U.S. industry, the system cannot be used in a mechanical sense by inexperienced personnel. As with most other tools, it is helpful if used properly but destructive if misused.

Overall Planning Models

The logic of the du Pont system for control in multidivision companies has been extended into broader overall planning models. These models provide a broad framework for understanding fundamental financial planning and control relationships. Since they generally emphasize the point of view of the firm as a whole, the focus is on the return on equity after the influence of financial leverage and taxes are taken into account. To illustrate these fundamental planning and control relationships, the following factors will be employed with numerical values that correspond to the average for all manufacturing firms in the United States in recent years. The notation will follow the literature on the subject.[6]

Symbol		Relationship	Numerical Value
T	=	asset turnover	$2\times$
m	=	margin on sales	5%
L	=	financial leverage	$2\times$
b	=	retention rate	.6
BV	=	book value	
BVS	=	book value per share	
EPS	=	earnings per share	
DPS	=	dividends per share	
G	=	sustainable growth rate	

The return on equity (ROE) involves the three fundamental factors of turnover, margin, and leverage:

Asset turnover $\times$ Margin on sales $\times$ Financial leverage = Return on equity.

These three fundamental factors are also expressed in terms of ratios.

$$\frac{\text{Sales}}{\text{Total assets}} \times \frac{\text{Net income}}{\text{Sales}} \times \frac{\text{Total assets}}{\text{Equity}} = \frac{\text{Net income}}{\text{Equity}}.$$

In symbols, we have TmL = ROE. With the numerical values suggested above, ROE equals

$$2(.05)(2) = .20 = 20\%.$$

With the knowledge of return on equity, we can then calculate earnings per share (EPS).

Return on equity $\times$ Book value per share = Earnings per share (EPS).

$$\frac{\text{Net income}}{\text{Equity}} \times \frac{\text{Equity}}{\text{No. of shares}} = \frac{\text{Net income}}{\text{No. of shares}} = EPS.$$

The earnings per share figure is widely used but reflects such arbitrary elements as the number of shares outstanding. In order to provide a numerical illustration, we therefore need two additional items of information. One is the size of the firm. The other is the number of equity shares outstanding. It will be noted that the return on equity measure above could be calculated independent of these two additional pieces of information. Let us assume a firm with total assets of $100 million and 1 million shares of equity stock outstanding. The earnings per share would therefore be

$$\frac{\$10 \text{ million}}{\$50 \text{ million}} \times \frac{\$50 \text{ million}}{1 \text{ million}} = \$10 \text{ per share.}$$

[6]See Higgins [1981], Babcock [1970, 1980], and Zakon [1976].

Having earnings per share, it is a short step to obtain dividends per share. The additional item needed is the dividend payout. The dividend payout is 1 minus the retention rate or is equal to

$$(1 - b) = (1 - .6) = .4.$$

For dividends per share we therefore have

Earnings per share × Dividend payout = Dividends per share.

$$\frac{\text{Net income}}{\text{No. of shares}} \times \frac{\text{Dividends}}{\text{Net income}} = \frac{\text{Dividends}}{\text{No. of shares}}.$$

We already have all of the numerical values for making the calculation. It is simply

$$\$10(.4) = \$4.$$

Much has been written on the concept of *sustainable dividends*. This can be expressed as the dollar amount of total dividends or the dollar amount of dividends per share. The concept involves nothing more than bringing together all of the factors for each of the target measures discussed to this point. The full set of factors for calculating dividends per share is now exhibited.

$$\frac{\text{Sales}}{\text{Total assets}} \times \frac{\text{Net income}}{\text{Sales}} \times \frac{\text{Total assets}}{\text{Equity}} \times \frac{\text{Equity}}{\text{No. of shares}}$$

$$\times \frac{\text{Dividends paid}}{\text{Net income}} = \text{Dividends per share.}$$

In symbols and numbers, we have

$$T \times m \times L \times BVS \times (1 - b) = DPS$$

$$2 \times .05 \times 2 \times \$50 \times .4 = \$4 \text{ per share.}$$

To obtain the total amount of dividends, we would use total book value rather than book value per share. In symbols,

$$T \times m \times L \times BV \times (1 - b) = \text{Dividends.}$$

The $50 would now represent $50 million, and the total amount of dividends would be $4 million.

Related to the idea of sustainable dividends is the concept of sustainable growth rate. It again involves the use of factors we have already discussed arranged in a slightly different manner. (See Babcock [1970].) The sustainable growth rate is simply the return on equity times the retention rate. Hence, we have

$$T \times m \times L \times b = \text{Sustainable growth rate.}$$

For our example, we would have

$$2 \times .05 \times 2 \times .6 = 12\% = \text{Sustainable growth rate.}$$

While the relationship appears to be simple, there is much business and financial analysis involved in the concept of sustainable growth rate. Each of the factors in the equation represents an important aspect of business decision making. Turnover refers to the effectiveness with which the firm's assets or resources are utilized. The profit margin on sales is an important measure of how well the firm has managed its costs in relationship to the prices received for its products. Financial leverage is one of the key aspects of financial decision making. The retention rate reflects investment requirements in relation to an important component of the firm's free cash flows.

While the above relationships are relatively simple, they provide the basic framework for highly sophisticated computerized business and financial planning models. No matter how bulky the computer output analysis may appear, the underlying relationships involved are the patterns which have been discussed in this section. These relationships can be calculated for business firms or segments of an operation with the use of hand calculators. They provide important insights for financial planning and control. Additional refinements and details may then be explored with the use of more elaborate computerized models.

Summary

The general theme of this chapter is the financial planning and control process. A number of analytical approaches are set forth to help implement financial planning and control. The relationship between investment outlays and the volume required to achieve profitability is referred to as breakeven analysis. Breakeven analysis focuses on the pattern of relations between total revenues and total costs. It is a method of relating fixed costs, variable costs, and total revenues to show the level of sales that must be attained if the firm is to operate at a profit. The analysis can be based on the number of units produced or on total dollar sales. It can be used for the entire company or for a particular product or division. With minor modifications, it can be put on a cash basis instead of a profit basis.

Operating leverage is defined as the extent to which fixed costs are used in operations. The degree of operating leverage (DOL), then, is the ratio of the percentage change in operating income to the percentage change in units sold or in sales. A firm's DOL is a precise measure of how much operating leverage the firm is employing. Breakeven analysis emphasizes the volume of sales the firm needs to be profitable. The degree of operating leverage measures how sensitive the firm's profits are to changes in the volume of sales. Both concepts measure the effects of the relative proportion of fixed costs in the total cost function of the firm.

The budgeting process provides detailed analysis for the control of revenues and costs. Its overall purpose is to improve internal operations, thereby reducing costs and raising profitability. A budgeting system starts with a set of performance standards, or targets. The targets represent the firm's financial plan. The budgeted amounts are compared with the actual results. If there are differences, the reasons should be identified and appropriate adjustments in the firm's policies should be made. These changes include the correction of deficiencies and more aggressive pursuit of opportunities. This is the feedback and control part of the budget process. It is critical to achieving a high level of managerial performance.

Although the entire budget system is vital to corporate management, one aspect of the system is especially important to the financial manager—the cash budget. The cash budget is, in fact, the principal tool for making short-run financial forecasts. If used properly, it can pinpoint the funds that will be needed, when they will be needed, and when cash flows will be sufficient to retire the company's loans.

As a firm becomes larger, it is necessary for it to decentralize operations to some extent. But decentralized operations still require some centralized control. The principal tool used for such control is the return on investment (ROI) method. There are problems with ROI control; but if budgeting and ROI control are viewed as a communication system that aids the flow of information among managers of the firm, a dynamic interaction among managers can be developed. If the emphasis is on an informed interaction process, the results of operations as measured by ROI will be improved. Communication and motivation, the behavioral aspects of the budgeting process, cannot be overemphasized.

Questions

9.1 What benefits can be derived from breakeven analysis?

9.2 What is operating leverage? Explain how profits or losses can be magnified in a firm with high operating leverage as opposed to a firm without this characteristic.

9.3 What data are necessary to construct a breakeven chart?

9.4 What is the general effect of each of the following changes on a firm's breakeven point?
a) An increase in selling price with no change in units sold.
b) A change from the leasing of a machine for $5,000 a year to the purchase of the machine for $100,000. The useful life of this machine will be 20 years, with no salvage value. Assume straight line depreciation.
c) A reduction in variable labor costs.

9.5 In what sense can depreciation be considered a source of funds?

9.6 Why is a cash budget important even when there is plenty of cash in the bank?

9.7 Assume that a firm is making up its long-run financial budget. What period should this budget cover—one month, six months, one year, three years, five years, or some other period? Justify your answer.

9.8 Is a detailed budget more important to a large, multidivisional firm than to a small, single-product firm?

9.9 Assume that your uncle is a major stockholder in a multidivisional firm that uses a naive ROI criterion for evaluating divisional managers and that bases managers' salaries in large part on this evaluation. You can have the job of division manager in any division you choose. If you are a salary maximizer, what divisional characteristics will you seek? If, because of your good performance, you become president of the firm, what changes will you make?

Problems

9.1 The Bentley Corporation produces tea kettles, which it sells for $10. Fixed costs are $600,000 for up to 400,000 units of output. Variable costs are $7 per unit.
a) What is the firm's gain or loss at sales of 175,000 units? Of 300,000 units?
b) What is the breakeven point? Illustrate by means of a chart.
c) What is Bentley's degree of operating leverage at sales of 225,000 units? Of 300,000 units?

9.2 For Pratt Industries, the following relationships exist. Each unit of output is sold for $35; the fixed costs are $160,000; variable costs are $15 a unit.

  a) What is the firm's gain or loss at sales of 6,000 units? Of 9,000 units?

  b) What is the breakeven point? Illustrate by means of a chart.

  c) What is Pratt's degree of operating leverage at sales of 6,000 units? Of 9,000 units?

  d) What happens to the breakeven point if the selling price rises to $40? What is the significance of the change to financial management? Illustrate by means of a chart.

  e) What happens to the breakeven point if the selling price rises to $40 but variable costs rise to $20 a unit? Illustrate by means of a chart.

9.3 For Ardell Industries, the following relations exist. Each unit of output is sold for $100; the fixed costs are $312,500, of which $250,000 are annual depreciation charges; variable costs are $37.50 per unit.

  a) What is the firm's gain or loss at sales of 4,000 units? Of 7,000 units?

  b) What is the profit breakeven point? Illustrate by means of a chart.

  c) What is the cash breakeven point? Illustrate by means of a chart.

  d) Assume Ardell is operating at a level of 3,500 units. Are creditors likely to seek the liquidation of the company if it is slow in paying its bills?

9.4 The Ortho Company is planning to request a line of credit from its bank. The following sales forecasts have been made for parts of 19X1 and 19X2:

May 19X1	$150,000
June	150,000
July	300,000
August	450,000
September	600,000
October	300,000
November	300,000
December	75,000
January 19X2	150,000

Collection estimates obtained from the credit and collection department are as follows: collected within the month of sale, 5 percent; collected the month following the sale, 80 percent; collected the second month following the sale, 15 percent. Payments for labor and raw materials are typically made during the month following the month in which these costs are incurred. Total labor and raw materials costs are estimated for each month as follows:

May 19X1	$ 75,000
June	75,000
July	105,000
August	735,000
September	255,000
October	195,000
November	135,000
December	75,000

General and administrative salaries will amount to approximately $22,500 a month; lease payments under long-term lease contracts will be $7,500 a month; depreciation charges will be $30,000 a month; miscellaneous expenses will be $2,250 a month; income tax payments of $52,500 will be due in both September and December; and a progress payment of $150,000 on a new research laboratory must be paid in October.

Cash on hand on July 1 will amount to $110,000, and a minimum cash balance of $75,000 must be maintained throughout the cash budget period.

a)   Prepare a monthly cash budget for the last six months of 19X1.

b)   Prepare an estimate of required financing (or excess funds)—that is, the amount of money the Ortho Company will need to borrow (or will have available to invest)—for each month during the period.

c)   Assume that receipts from sales come in uniformly during the month (that is, cash receipts come in at the rate of 1/30 each day), but all outflows are paid on the fifth of the month. Will this have an effect on the cash budget (that is, will the cash budget you have prepared be valid under these assumptions)? If not, what can be done to make a valid estimate of financing requirements?

9.5   The board of directors of the San Jose Microprocessor Company has received numerous complaints from shareholders regarding the performance of the firm's management. In an effort to verify the validity of these complaints, the board has collected the information below.

a)   Calculate the relevant financial ratios for San Jose Microprocessor.

b)   Apply a du Pont chart analysis on San Jose and compare it to the du Pont chart analysis based on composite ratios for the industry as a whole.

c)   Evaluate management's performance and list specific areas where improvement is needed.

San Jose Microprocessor Company
Balance Sheet as of December 31, 19X0 (Thousands of Dollars)

Assets		Liabilities		
Cash	$ 90	Accounts payable	$450	
Marketable securities	40	Notes payable (@ 11%)	380	
Receivables	1,550	Other current liabilities	280	
Inventory	1,190	Total current liabilities		$1,110
Total current assets	$2,870	Long-term debt (@ 9%)		880
Net fixed assets	1,130	Total liabilities		$1,990
		Net worth		2,010
Total assets	$4,000	Total claims on assets		$4,000

San Jose Microprocessor Company
Income Statement for Year Ended December 31, 19X0 (Thousands of Dollars)

Sales		$6,200
Cost of goods sold		
Materials	$2,440	
Labor	1,540	
Heat, light, and power	230	
Indirect labor	370	
Depreciation	140	4,720
Gross profit		$1,480
Selling expenses	490	
General and administrative expenses	530	1,020
Net operating income (NOI)(EBIT)		$ 460
Less interest expense		121

Net income before taxes	$ 339
Less federal income taxes	152
Net income	$ 187

Industry du Pont Analysis

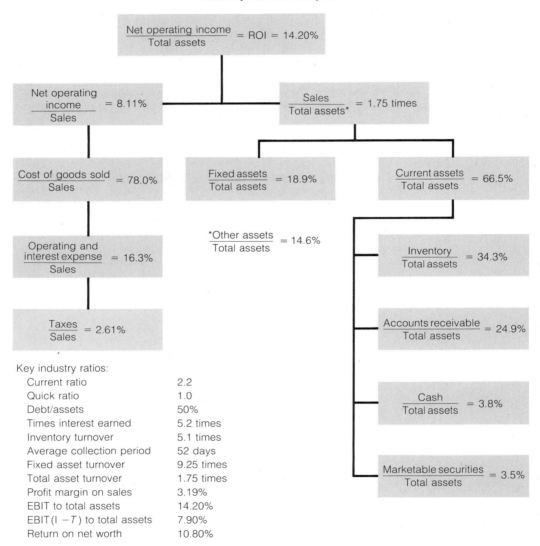

Key industry ratios:

Current ratio	2.2
Quick ratio	1.0
Debt/assets	50%
Times interest earned	5.2 times
Inventory turnover	5.1 times
Average collection period	52 days
Fixed asset turnover	9.25 times
Total asset turnover	1.75 times
Profit margin on sales	3.19%
EBIT to total assets	14.20%
EBIT$(I-T)$ to total assets	7.90%
Return on net worth	10.80%

9.6 Gulf and Eastern, Inc., is a diversified multinational corporation that produces a wide variety of goods and services, including chemicals, soaps, tobacco products, toys, plastics, pollution control equipment, canned food, sugar, motion pictures, and computer software. The corporation's major divisions were brought together in the early 1960s under a decentralized form of management; each division was evaluated in terms of its profitability, efficiency, and return on investments. This decentralized organization persisted through most of the decade, during which Gulf and Eastern experienced a high average growth rate in total assets, earnings, and stock prices.

Toward the end of 1975, however, those trends were reversed. The organization was faced with declining earnings, unstable stock prices, and a generally uncertain future. This situation persisted into 1976, but during that year, a new president, Lynn Thompson, was appointed by the board of directors. Thompson, who had served for a time on the financial staff of I. E. du Pont, used the du Pont system to evaluate the various divisions. All showed definite weaknesses.

Thompson reported to the board that a principal reason for the poor overall performance was a lack of control by central management over each division's activities. She was particularly disturbed by the consistently poor results of the corporation's budgeting procedures. Under that system, each division manager drew up a projected budget for the next quarter, along with estimated sales, revenue, and profit; funds were then allocated to the divisions, basically in proportion to their budget requests. However, actual budgets seldom matched the projections; wide discrepancies occurred; and this, of course, resulted in a highly inefficient use of capital.

In an attempt to correct the situation, Thompson asked the firm's chief financial officer to draw up a plan to improve the budgeting, planning, and control processes. When the plan was submitted, its basic provisions included the following:

1. To improve the quality of the divisional budgets, the division managers should be informed that the continuance of wide variation between their projected and actual budgets would result in dismissal.

2. A system should be instituted under which funds would be allocated to divisions on the basis of their average return on investment (ROI) during the last four quarters. Since funds were short, divisions with high ROI's would get most of the available money.

3. Only about half of each division manager's present compensation should be received as salary; the rest should be in the form of a bonus related to the division's average ROI for the quarter.

4. Each division should submit to the central office for approval all capital expenditure requests, production schedules, and price changes. Thus, the company would be recentralized.

a) 1. Is it reasonable to expect the new procedures to improve the accuracy of budget forecasts?

    2. Should all divisions be expected to maintain the same degree of accuracy?

    3. In what other ways might the budgets be made?

b) 1. What problems would be associated with the use of the ROI criterion in allocating funds among the divisions?

    2. What effect would the period used in computing ROI (that is, four quarters, one quarter, two years, and so on) have on the effectiveness of this method?

    3. What problems might occur in evaluating the ROI in the crude rubber and auto tires divisions? Between the sugar products and pollution control equipment divisions?

c) What problems would be associated with rewarding each manager on the basis of the division's ROI?

d) How well would the policy of recentralization work in this highly diversified corporation, particularly in light of the financial officer's three other proposals?

Selected References

Babcock, G. C., "The Roots of Risk and Return," *Financial Analysts Journal*, 36 (January-February 1980), pp. 56-63.

———, "The Concept of Sustainable Growth," *Financial Analysts Journal*, 26 (May-June 1970), pp. 108-114.

Dearden, John, "The Case Against ROI Control," *Harvard Business Review*, 47 (May-June 1969), pp. 124-135.

Dhavale, Dileep G., and Wilson, Hoyt G., "Breakeven Analysis with Inflationary Cost and Prices," *Engineering Economist*, 25 (Winter 1980), pp. 107-121.

Higgins, Robert C., "Sustainable Growth under Inflation," *Financial Management*, 10 (Autumn 1981), pp. 36-40.

Lee, Cheng F., and Junkus, Joan C., "Financing Analysis and Planning: An Overview," *Journal of Economics and Business*, 35 (August 1983), pp. 259-284.

Rappaport, Alfred, "Measuring Company Growth Capacity during Inflation," *Harvard Business Review*, 57 (January-February 1979), pp. 91-100.

———, "A Capital Budgeting Approach to Divisional Planning and Control," *Financial Executive*, 36 (October 1968), pp. 47-63.

Reinhardt, U. E., "Breakeven Analysis for Lockheed's Tri Star: An Application of Financial Theory," *Journal of Finance*, 28 (September 1973), pp. 821-838.

Searby, Frederick W., "Return to Return on Investment," *Harvard Business Review*, 53 (March-April 1975), pp. 113-119.

Soldofsky, R. M., "Accountant's versus Economist's Concepts of Breakeven Analysis," *N.A.A. Bulletin*, 41 (December 1959), pp. 5-18.

Stone, Bernell K., and Miller, T. W., "Daily Cash Forecasting: A Structuring Framework," *Journal of Cash Management*, 1 (October 1981), pp. 35-50.

Stone, Bernell K.; Downes, David H.; and Magee, Robert P., "Computer-Assisted Financial Planning: The Planner-Model Interface," *Journal of Business Research*, 5 (September 1977), pp. 215-233.

Weston, J. Fred, "ROI Planning and Control: A Dynamic Management System," *Business Horizons*, (August 1972), pp. 35–42.

Zakon, Alan J., "Capital Structure Organization," Chapter 30 in *The Treasurer's Handbook*, Eds., J. Fred Weston and Maurice B. Goudzwaard, Homewood, Ill.: Dow Jones-Irwin, 1976, pp. 641-668.

Chapter 10 Financial Forecasting

The planning process is an integral part of the financial manager's job. As we shall see in subsequent chapters, long-term debt and equity funds are raised infrequently and in large amounts, primarily because the cost per dollar raised by selling such securities decreases as the size of the issue increases. Because of these considerations, it is important that the firm have a working estimate of its total needs for funds for the next few years. It is therefore useful to examine methods of forecasting the firm's needs for funds, and this is the subject of the present chapter. We shall examine the percent of sales method for projecting cash needs and then move on to discuss more sophisticated linear regression techniques. Linear regression is a tool of analysis which is used throughout the remainder of the book.

Cash Flow Cycle

We must recognize that firms need assets to make sales; if sales are to be increased, assets must also be expanded. Growing firms require new investments — immediate investment in current assets and, as full capacity is reached, investment in fixed assets as well. New investments must be financed, and new financing carries with it commitments and obligations to service the capital obtained.[1] A growing, profitable firm is likely to require additional cash for investments in receivables, inventories, and fixed assets. Such a firm can, therefore, have a cash flow problem. The nature of this problem, as well as the cause and effect relationship between assets and sales, is illustrated in the following discussion, in which we trace the consequences of a series of transactions.

Effects on the Balance Sheet

1. Two partners invest a total of $50,000 to create the Glamour Galore Dress Company. The firm rents a plant; equipment and other fixed assets cost $30,000. The resulting financial situation is shown by Balance Sheet 1.

---

[1]*Servicing* capital refers to the payment of interest and principal on debt and dividends on common stocks.

Balance Sheet 1

Assets		Liabilities	
Current assets		Capital stock	$50,000
Cash	$20,000		
Fixed assets			
Plant and equipment	30,000		
Total assets	$50,000	Total liabilities and net worth	$50,000

2. Glamour Galore receives an order to manufacture 10,000 dresses. The receipt of an order in itself has no effect on the balance sheet, but the preparation for the manufacturing activity often does. Say that the firm buys $20,000 worth of cotton cloth on terms of net 30 days. Without additional investment by the owners, total assets increase by $20,000, financed by the trade accounts payable to the supplier of the cotton cloth.

   After the purchase, the firm spends $20,000 on labor for cutting the cloth to the required pattern. Of the $20,000 total labor cost, $10,000 is paid in cash and $10,000 is owed in the form of accrued wages. These two transactions are reflected in Balance Sheet 2, which shows that total assets increase to $80,000. Current assets are increased; net working capital — total current assets minus total current liabilities — remains constant. The current ratio at 1.67 is below the "bankers' rule of thumb" of 2, and the debt ratio rises to 38 percent. The financial position of the firm is weakening. If it should seek to borrow at this point, Glamour Galore could not use the work-in-process inventories as collateral, because a lender could find little use for partially manufactured dresses.

Balance Sheet 2

Assets		Liabilities	
Current assets		Accounts payable	$20,000
Cash	$10,000	Accrued wages payable	10,000
Inventories		Total current liabilities	$30,000
Work in process			
Materials	20,000	Capital stock	$50,000
Labor	20,000		
Total current assets	$50,000		
Fixed assets			
Plant and equipment	30,000		
Total assets	$80,000	Total liabilities and net worth	$80,000

3. In order to complete the dresses, the firm incurs additional labor costs of $20,000 and pays in cash. It is assumed that the firm desires to maintain a minimum cash balance of $5,000. Since the initial cash balance is $10,000, Glamour Galore must borrow an additional $15,000 from its bank to meet the wage bill. The borrowing is reflected in notes payable in Balance Sheet 3. Total assets rise to $95,000, with a finished goods inventory of $60,000. The current ratio drops to 1.4, and the debt ratio rises to 47 percent. These ratios show a further weakening of the financial position.

Balance Sheet 3

Assets			Liabilities	
Current assets			Accounts payable	$20,000
Cash		$ 5,000	Notes payable	15,000
Inventory			Accrued wages payable	10,000
Finished goods		60,000	Total current liabilities	$45,000
Total current assets		$65,000		
			Capital stock	50,000
Fixed assets				
Plant and equipment		30,000		
Total assets		$95,000	Total liabilities and net worth	$95,000

4. Glamour Galore ships the dresses on the basis of the original order, invoicing the purchaser for $100,000 within 30 days. Accrued wages and accounts payable have to be paid now, so Glamour Galore must borrow an additional $30,000 in order to maintain the $5,000 minimum cash balance. These transactions are shown in Balance Sheet 4. Note that in Balance Sheet 4, finished goods inventory is replaced by receivables, with the markup reflected as retained earnings. This causes the debt ratio to drop to 33 percent. Since the receivables are carried at the sales price, current assets increase to $105,000 and the current ratio rises to 2.3. Compared with the conditions reflected in Balance Sheet 3, most of the financial ratios show improvement. However, the absolute amount of debt is large.

    Whether the firm's financial position is really improved depends upon the creditworthiness of the purchaser of the dresses. If the purchaser is a good credit risk, Glamour Galore may be able to borrow further on the basis of the accounts receivable.

Balance Sheet 4

Assets			Liabilities	
Current assets			Notes payable	$ 45,000
Cash		$ 5,000	Total current liabilities	$ 45,000
Accounts receivable		100,000	Capital stock	50,000
Total current assets		$105,000	Retained earnings	40,000
			Total net worth	$ 90,000
Fixed assets				
Plant and equipment		30,000		
Total assets		$135,000	Total liabilities and net worth	$135,000

5. The firm receives payment for the accounts receivable, pays off the bank loan, and is in the highly liquid position shown by Balance Sheet 5. If a new order for 10,000 dresses is received, it will have no effect on the balance sheet, but a cycle similar to the one we have been describing will begin.

Balance Sheet 5

Assets		Liabilities	
Current assets		Capital stock	$50,000
Cash	$60,000	Retained earnings	40,000
Fixed assets			
Plant and equipment	30,000		
Total assets	$90,000	Total liabilities and net worth	$90,000

6.   The idea of the cash flow cycle can now be generalized. An order that requires the purchase of raw materials is placed with the firm. The purchase, in turn, generates an account payable. As labor is applied, work-in-process inventories build up. To the extent that wages are not fully paid at the time labor is used, accrued wages will appear on the liability side of the balance sheet. As goods are completed, they move into finished goods inventories. The cash needed to pay for the labor to complete the goods may make it necessary for the firm to borrow.

   Finished goods inventories are sold, usually on credit, which gives rise to accounts receivable. As the firm has not received cash, this point in the cycle represents the peak in financing requirements. If the firm did not borrow at the time finished goods inventories were at their maximum, it may do so as inventories are converted into receivables by credit sales. Income taxes, which were not considered in the example, can add to the problem. As accounts receivable become cash, short-term obligations can be paid off.

Financing Patterns

The influence of sales on current asset levels has just been illustrated. Over the course of several cycles, the fluctuations in sales will be accompanied in most industries by a rising long-term trend. Figure 10.1 shows the consequences of such a pattern. Total permanent assets increase steadily in the form of current and fixed assets. Assets should be financed by liabilities with similar maturity. Long-term increases in current assets such as inventories and accounts receivable are usually financed by "permanent" increases in current liabilities, such as accrued taxes and wages and accounts payable, which naturally accompany increasing sales. Temporary increases in assets can be covered by other forms of short-term liabilities. The distinction between temporary and permanent asset levels may be difficult to make in practice, but it is neither illusory nor unimportant. Short-term financing for the financing of long-term needs is dangerous. A profitable firm may become unable to meet its cash obligations if funds borrowed on a short-term basis have become tied up in permanent asset needs.

Percent of Sales Method

It is apparent from the preceding discussion that *the most important variable that influences a firm's financing requirements is its projected dollar volume of sales. A good sales forecast is an essential foundation for forecasting financial requirements.* In spite of its importance, we shall not go into sales forecasting until later in the chapter; rather, we simply assume that a

Figure 10.1   Fluctuating versus Permanent Assets

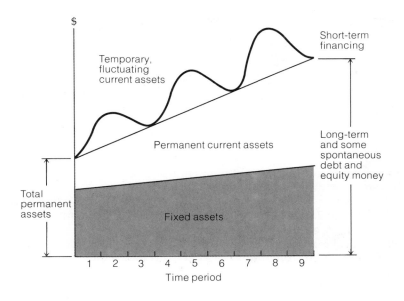

sales forecast has been made and then estimate financial requirements on the basis of this forecast.

The simplest approach to forecasting financial requirements expresses the firm's needs in terms of the percentage of annual sales invested in each individual balance sheet item. As an example, consider the Moore Company, whose balance sheet as of December 31, 19X1, is shown in Table 10.1. The company's sales are running at about $500,000 a year, which is its capacity limit; the profit margin after tax on sales is 4 percent. During 19X1, the company earned $20,000 after taxes and paid out $10,000 in dividends, and it plans to continue paying out half of net profits as dividends. How much additional financing will be needed if sales expand to $800,000 during 19X2? The calculating procedure, using the percent of sales method, is explained below.[2]

First, isolate those balance sheet items that can be expected to vary directly with sales. In the case of the Moore Company, this step applies to each category of assets — a higher level of sales necessitates more cash for transactions, more receivables, higher inventory levels, and additional fixed plant capacity. On the liability side, accounts payable as well as accruals may be expected to increase as sales do. Retained earnings will go up as long as the company is profitable and does not pay out 100 percent of earnings, but the percent-

---

[2]We recognize, of course, that as a practical matter, business firms plan their needs in terms of specific items of equipment, square feet of floor space, and other factors, and not as a percentage of sales. However, the outside analyst does not have access to this information. Also, even though the information on specific items is available, a manager needs to check forecasts in aggregate terms. The percent of sales method serves both these needs surprisingly well.

Table 10.1   The Moore Company Balance Sheet as of December 31, 19X1

Assets		Liabilities	
Cash	$ 10,000	Accounts payable	$ 50,000
Receivables	85,000	Accrued taxes and wages	25,000
Inventories	100,000	Mortgage bonds	70,000
Fixed assets (net)	150,000	Common stocks	100,000
		Retained earnings	100,000
Total assets	$345,000	Total liabilities and net worth	$345,000

age increase is not constant. In addition, neither common stock nor mortgage bonds will increase spontaneously with an increase in sales.

The items that can be expected to vary directly with sales are tabulated as a percentage of sales in Table 10.2. For every $1.00 increase in sales, assets must increase by $.69; this $.69 must be financed in some manner. Accounts payable will increase spontaneously with sales, as will accruals; these two items will supply $.15 of new funds for each $1.00 increase in sales. Subtracting the 15 percent for spontaneously generated funds from the 69 percent funds requirement leaves 54 percent. Thus, for each $1.00 increase in sales, the Moore Company must obtain $.54 of financing either from internally generated funds or from external sources.

In the case at hand, sales are scheduled to increase from $500,000 to $800,000, or by $300,000. Applying the 54 percent developed in the table to the expected increase in sales leads to the conclusion that $162,000 will be needed.

Some of that need will be met by retained earnings. Total revenues during 19X2 will be $800,000; if the company earns 4 percent after taxes on this volume, profits will amount to $32,000. Assuming that the 50 percent dividend payout ratio is maintained, dividends will be $16,000 and $16,000 will be retained. Subtracting the retained earnings from the

Table 10.2   The Moore Company Balance Sheet as of December 31, 19X1 (Percent of Sales)

Assets (%)		Liabilities (%)	
Cash	2.0	Accounts payable	10.0
Receivables	17.0	Accrued taxes and wages	5.0
Inventories	20.0	Mortgage bonds[a]	—
Fixed assets (net)	30.0	Common stock[a]	—
		Retained earnings[a]	—
Total assets	69.0	Total liabilities and net worth	15.0
Assets as percent of sales			69.0
Less: Spontaneous increase in liabilities			15.0
Percent of each additional dollar of sales that must be financed			54.0

[a]Not applicable.

$162,000 that was needed leaves a figure of $146,000 — the amount of funds that must be obtained through borrowing or by selling new common stock.

This process may be expressed in equation form:

$$\text{External funds needed} = \frac{A}{TR}(\Delta TR) - \frac{L}{TR}(\Delta TR) - bc(TR_2). \qquad \textbf{(10.1)}$$

Here:

$\dfrac{A}{TR} =$ assets that increase spontaneously with total revenues or sales as a percent of total revenues or sales $= .69$

$\dfrac{L}{TR} =$ those liabilities that increase spontaneously with total revenues or sales as a percent of total revenues or sales $= .15$

$\Delta TR =$ change in total revenues or sales $= \$300,000$

$c =$ profit margin on sales $= .04$

$TR_2 =$ total revenues projected for the year $= \$800,000$

$b =$ earnings retention ratio $= .5.$

For the Moore Company, then,

$$\text{External funds needed} = 0.69(\$300,000) - 0.15(\$300,000) - 0.5(0.04)(\$800,000)$$

$$= 0.54(\$300,000) - 0.02(\$800,000)$$

$$= \$146,000.$$

The $146,000 found by the formula method must, of course, equal the amount derived previously.

Notice what would have occurred if the Moore Company's sales forecast for 19X2 had been only $515,000, or a 3 percent increase. Applying the formula, we find the external funds requirements as follows:

$$\text{External funds needed} = 0.54(\$15,000) - 0.02(\$515,000)$$

$$= \$8,100 - \$10,300$$

$$= (\$2,200).$$

In this case, no external funds are required. In fact, the company will have $2,200 in excess of its requirements; it, therefore, could plan to increase dividends, retire debt, or seek additional investment opportunities. The example shows that while small percentage increases in sales can be financed through internally generated funds, larger percentage increases cause the firm to go into the market for outside capital. In other words, small rates of sales growth for profitable companies can be financed from internal sources, but higher rates of sales growth require external financing.[3]

---

[3]At this point, one might ask two questions: "Shouldn't depreciation be considered as a source of funds, and won't this reduce the amount of external funds needed?" The answer to both questions is no. In the percent of sales method, we are relating fixed assets, net of the reserve for depreciation, to sales. This process implicitly assumes that funds related to the depreciation policies are used to replace assets to which the depreciation is applicable and are, therefore, not available for asset expansion. The net fixed assets related to sales already have the reserve for depreciation (which is a cumulative sum of each year's depreciation expense charge) deducted from gross fixed assets.

Note that the sales level equals $(1 + g)TR_1$, where g equals the growth rate in sales. The increase in sales, therefore, can be written:

$$\Delta TR = (1 + g)TR_1 - TR_1 = TR_1(1 + g - 1) = gTR_1.$$

Let us next take the expression for external funds needed, Equation 10.1, and use it to derive the percentage of the increase in sales that will have to be financed externally (percentage of external funds required, or PEFR) as a function of the critical variables involved. In Equation 10.1, let $\left(\dfrac{A}{TR} - \dfrac{L}{TR}\right) = I$, substitute for ΔTR and TR_2, and divide both sides by $\Delta TR = gTR_1$.

$$\text{PEFR} = I - \frac{c}{g}(1 + g)b = I - cb\left(\frac{1 + g}{g}\right) \tag{10.2}$$

Using Equation 10.2, we can now investigate the influence of factors such as an increased rate of inflation on the percentage of sales growth that must be financed externally. Based on the relationships for all manufacturing industries, some representative values of the terms on the right-hand side of the equation are $I = 0.5$, $c = 0.05$, and $b = 0.60$.

During the period that preceded the onset of inflation in the United States after 1966, the economy was growing at about 6 to 7 percent per annum. If a firm was in an industry that grew at the same rate as the economy as a whole and if a firm maintained its market share position in its industry, the firm grew at 6 to 7 percent per annum as well. Let us see what the implications for external financing requirements would be. With a growth rate of 6 percent, the percentage of an increase in sales that would have to be financed externally would be as follows:

$$\text{PEFR} = 0.5 - \frac{0.05}{0.06}(1.06)(0.6)$$

$$= 0.50 - 0.53 = -0.03 = -3\%.$$

At 7 percent growth, the PEFR would be

$$\text{PEFR} = 0.5 - \frac{0.05}{0.07}(1.07)(0.6)$$

$$= 0.50 - 0.46 = 0.04 = 4\%.$$

Thus, at a growth rate of 6 percent, the percentage of external financing to sales growth would be a negative 3 percent. In other words, the firm would have excess funds which it could use to increase dividends or increase its investment in marketable securities. With a growth rate of 7 percent, the firm would have a requirement of external financing of 4 percent of the sales increase.

Following 1966, the inflation rate in some years was in the two-digit range; that is, 10 percent or more. Suppose we add sufficient percentage points per annum of an inflation rate to the previous 6 to 7 percent growth rate to obtain a growth rate of 15 or 20 percent for a firm. Then, the external financing requirements will be as follows:

$$\text{PEFR} = 0.5 - \frac{0.05}{0.15}(1.15)(0.6)$$

$$= 0.50 - 0.23 = 0.27 = 27\%.$$

$$\text{PEFR} = 0.5 - \frac{0.05}{0.20}(1.20)(0.6)$$

$$= 0.50 - 0.18 = 0.32 = 32\%.$$

With a growth rate in sales of 15 percent, external financing rises to 27 percent of the firm's sales growth. If inflation caused the growth rate of the firm to rise to 20 percent, then the external financing percentage would rise to 32 percent. The substantial increase in the growth rate of sales of firms measured in inflated dollars in recent years points up why external financing has become more important for firms.[4] It underscores also why the finance function in firms has taken on increased importance in recent years. There is just a much bigger job to be done, particularly in requirements for using external financing sources to maintain the sales growth of a firm. Even if the firm were not growing in real terms, an inflation rate of 10 percent, for example, would make it necessary for the firm to raise external financing of 17 percent of its growth in sales of inflated dollars — even though the real growth of the firm was zero.

The percent of sales method of forecasting financial requirements is neither simple nor mechanical, although an explanation of the ideas requires simple illustrations. Experience in applying the technique in practice suggests the importance of understanding (1) the basic technology of the firm and (2) the logic of the relation between sales and assets for the particular firm in question. A great deal of experience and judgment is required to apply the technique in actual practice.

Linear Regression: One Variable

Linear regression is a much better forecasting technique than the percent of sales method and is the most common quantitative forecasting methodology.[5] Financial managers often use linear regression as a forecasting tool. Furthermore, they need to be familiar with the advantages and disadvantages of regression analysis in order to successfully communicate with their economics staff.

Comparing Linear Regression with the Percent of Sales Method

Figure 10.2 illustrates the difference between the percent of sales method and linear regression for the data in Table 10.3, which shows the sales and inventory levels for a major integrated oil company in recent years. The percent of sales method uses the average of

---

[4]Note, however, that PEFR has an upper limit, even when the growth in sales becomes very high. From Equation 10.2, it can be seen that as g becomes very large, $\left(\frac{1+g}{g}\right)$ approaches 1 so that the upper limit for PEFR is $(I - cb)$.

[5]This section can be skipped by those readers who are already familiar with regression analysis.

Figure 10.2 Comparing the Percent of Sales Method with Simple Linear Regression

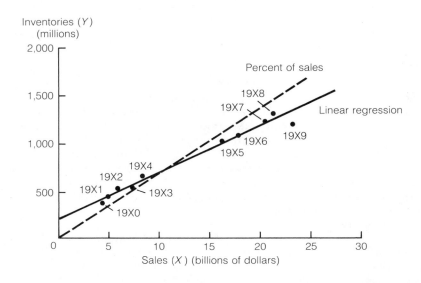

the inventory to sales ratios in order to predict inventories. For example, the ten-year average shows inventories to be 7.31 percent of sales. Using the percent of sales method, we would predict 19X9 inventory to be $1,762 million when it was actually $1,216 million, an error of $546 million. In Figure 10.2, the percent of sales method is illustrated by the dashed line. It is a ray from the origin with a slope of 7.31 percent. Its equation is

$$\text{Inventory} = .0731 \text{ Sales}$$

or

$$Y = bX,$$

where b is the slope of the line.

Linear regression is a better technique because it does not assume that the line which best fits the data automatically goes through the origin. Instead, it allows us to find the straight line which best fits the data. As shown in Figure 10.2, the solid linear regression line is an improvement over the percent of sales (dashed) line because it fits the data much better. The equation for the linear regression is

$$\text{Inventory} = \$.216 \text{ billion} + .04987 \text{ Sales} \tag{10.3}$$

or

$$Y = a + bX,$$

where a is the intercept where the regression line meets the Y-axis and b is the slope of the line. If we use the regression line to predict 19X9 inventory, given 19X9 sales, we have

Table 10.3   Inventory to Sales Relationships for a Major Integrated Oil Company
for a Ten-Year Period (Billions of Dollars)

	Inventory (Y)	Sales (X)	Inventory to Sales Ratio (Y/X)
19X0	$ .403	$ 4.560	0.088
19X1	.461	4.962	0.093
19X2	.506	5.728	0.088
19X3	.507	6.477	0.078
19X4	.665	8.480	0.078
19X5	1.087	17.924	0.061
19X6	1.165	17.524	0.066
19X7	1.278	20.181	0.063
19X8	1.438	21.752	0.066
19X9	1.216	24.106	0.050

$$\text{Inventory} = \$.216 \text{ billion} + .04987(\$24.106 \text{ billion})$$

$$= \$1.418 \text{ billion.}$$

Actual inventory was $1.216 billion; hence, the linear regression was off by $.202 billion, a much smaller error than the percent of sales method, which was off by $.546 billion.[6]

Exactly how is the "best" linear regression line calculated? What criterion is used to determine the "best" fit? These are a few of the questions which we will address in the remainder of the chapter. If we recognize that our forecasts are likely to have some error, then the linear regression line can be written as follows:

$$Y_t = a + bX_t + \epsilon_t. \tag{10.4}$$

The only difference between Equation 10.3 and Equation 10.4 is that we have added subscripts, t, to designate the time periods from which observations are taken and there is a random error term, ϵ_t. It represents the difference between the predicted value of the *dependent variable* on the left-hand side of the equation (in our example, it was inventory in Year t) and the actual value of the dependent variable. The variable on the left-hand side of the equation is called the dependent variable because it is the one we are trying to explain. The *independent variable* (sales in Year t) on the right-hand side is the explanatory variable.

The object of linear regression is to find the intercept, a, and the slope, b, which minimize the sum of the squared prediction errors, ϵ_t, in Equation 10.4. The line which has the lowest squared error terms will be the one with the best fit. But why minimize the sum of the *squared* error terms? And how can this be done mathematically?

---

[6]An even better forecast can be attained by regressing inventory against the square root of sales. See Chapter 13 for an explanation of why inventory is usually a function of the square root of sales.

Definition of Mean and Variance

We must begin by defining the mean and variance of a distribution of random variables. As we shall see, the variance is the same thing as the expectation of the sum of the squared error terms. When they are minimized, we are also minimizing the variance of prediction errors.

First, let's take a look at the *unconditional* mean and variance of inventory — unconditional because we will not use any information about sales to improve our estimates. The mean, or average, is defined as the expected value, $E(Y)$.

$$\overline{Y} = E(Y) \equiv \sum_{i=1}^{N} p_i Y_i = \frac{1}{N} \sum_{i=1}^{N} Y_i. \tag{10.5}$$

In Equation 10.5, N is defined as the number of observations ($N = 10$), p_i is the probability of each observation ($p_i = 1/N = 1/10$), and Y_i are the individual observations. The calculations in Column (2) of Table 10.4 show that the mean inventory is \$.873 billion over the last ten years.

Table 10.4   Statistics for Inventory and Sales (Billions of Dollars)

(1) Year	(2) Inventory (Y)	(3) Sales (X)	(4) $Y - \overline{Y}$	(5) $(Y - \overline{Y})^2$	(6) $X - \overline{X}$	(7) $(X - \overline{X})^2$	(8) $(Y - \overline{Y})(X - \overline{X})$	(9) $\epsilon = Y - \hat{Y}$	(10) ϵ^2
19X0	.403	4.560	−.469	.221	−8.61	74.122	4.043	−.0403	.00162
19X1	.461	4.962	−.411	.169	−8.21	67.361	3.378	−.0023	.00001
19X2	.506	5.728	−.366	.134	−7.44	55.374	2.728	.0045	.00002
19X3	.507	6.477	−.365	.134	−6.69	44.788	2.447	−.0319	.00101
19X4	.665	8.480	−.208	.043	−4.69	21.990	.974	.0263	.00069
19X5	1.087	17.924	.214	.046	4.76	22.606	1.019	−.0227	.00052
19X6	1.165	17.524	.292	.085	4.35	18.963	1.273	.0752	.00566
19X7	1.278	20.181	.405	.164	7.01	49.163	2.843	.0557	.00310
19X8	1.438	21.752	.565	.320	8.58	73.661	4.853	.1374	.01888
19X9	1.216	24.106	.343	.118	10.94	119.609	3.756	−.2020	.04081
Sum	8.726	131.694	0	1.435	0	574.638	27.313	−.0001	.07232

$\overline{Y} = E(Y) = \Sigma Y_i / N = 8.726/10 = .873.$ 　　　　　　$\overline{X} = E(X) = \Sigma X_i / N = 131.694/10 = 13.169.$

$\sigma_Y^2 = \Sigma(Y - \overline{Y})^2/(N - 1) = 1.435/9 = .159.$ 　　$\sigma_X^2 = \Sigma(X - \overline{X})^2/(N - 1) = 574.638/9 = 60.849.$

$\sigma_Y = \sqrt{\sigma_Y^2} = \sqrt{.159} = .399.$ 　　　　　　　　$\sigma_X = \sqrt{\sigma_X^2} = \sqrt{60.849} = 7.801.$

$\text{COV}(Y,X) = \Sigma(Y - \overline{Y})(X - \overline{X})/(N - 1) = 27.313/9 = 3.035.$ 　　$r^2 = (\sigma_Y^2 - \sigma_\epsilon^2)/\sigma_Y^2 = .9496.$

$\hat{b} = \text{COV}(Y,X)/\sigma_X^2 = 3.035/60.849 = .04987.$ 　　　　$r = \sqrt{r^2} = \text{COV}(Y,X)/\sigma_Y\sigma_X = .9745.$

$\hat{a} = \overline{Y} - \hat{b}\overline{X} = .873 - .04987(13.169) = .216.$ 　　　　$\sigma_\epsilon^2 = .07232/9 = .0080.$

Symbol definitions:	$\overline{Y}, \overline{X}$ = the means of inventory and sales, respectively.	$\hat{a}, \hat{b}$ = the intercept and slope estimates.
	N = the number of observations in the sample.	ϵ = the error term.
	σ_Y^2, σ_X^2 = the variances of inventory and sales, respectively.	r^2 = the coefficient of determination.
	$\text{COV}(Y,X)$ = the covariance between inventory and sales.	

The variance is defined as the expectation (or average) of the mean deviations squared.

$$\text{VAR}(Y) \equiv E\{[Y_i - E(Y)]^2\} \tag{10.6}$$

Because we are estimating the true variance from only a ten-year sample of statistics, we have to use an estimated mean, $E(Y)$, rather than the true mean. The implication is that, in order to compute an unbiased estimate of the true variance, we have to sum the mean deviations squared and divide by $N - 1$ instead of by N. We use $N - 1$ because one degree of freedom is lost when estimating the mean. The definition of variance for sampling statistics is

$$\sigma_Y^2 = \text{VAR}(Y) = \sum_{i=1}^{N} [Y_i - E(Y)]^2/(N - 1). \tag{10.7}$$

The variance is a good statistic for measuring the variability of a set of numbers. It places higher weights on observations which are far away from the mean because it squares the mean deviations. Look at Table 10.4, Columns (4) and (5). In 19X4, the difference between the actual inventory and the mean was only $.208 billion. When squared it contributes .0431 to the variance statistic. On the other hand, the 19X9 inventory is $.343 billion above the mean. Its departure from the mean is about 1.65 times larger than 19X4 inventory, but it contributes .1179 to the variance statistic—an amount which is 2.74 times larger than the amount contributed by 19X4 inventory. Thus, the variance statistic is sensitive to observations which depart widely from the mean.

Sometimes, rather than using the standard deviation as a measure of variability, we will use a scaled measure of variability, called the coefficient of variation. It is defined as

$$\text{Coefficient of variation} = CV(Y) = \frac{\sqrt{\text{VAR}(Y)}}{E(Y)}. \tag{10.7a}$$

This measure of variability is a relative measure because it converts the square root of variance (called the standard deviation) into a percentage by dividing through by the average value of Y, that is, $E(Y)$. Relative measures of variability, like the coefficient of variation, are useful for comparing numbers of vastly different size. For example, a large company with $\sqrt{\text{VAR(Sales)}} = \$100$ million and $E(\text{Sales})$ of $500 million has the same *relative* variability (that is, the same coefficient of variation) as a smaller company with $\sqrt{\text{VAR(Sales)}} = \$.2$ million and $E(\text{Sales})$ of only $1 million.

The Unconditional Distribution of Sales

Figure 10.3 pictures the *unconditional distribution* of inventory assuming that it is drawn from a bell-shaped or normal distribution.[7] The vertical axis measures the frequency of different inventory levels and the horizontal axis measures the level of inventory. The mean (or average) inventory is $.873 billion and its variance is $.159 billion squared. Be-

---

[7]The appendix to this chapter provides a more complete description of the normal distribution.

Figure 10.3   Unconditional Distribution of Sales Assuming a Normal Distribution (in Billions of Dollars)

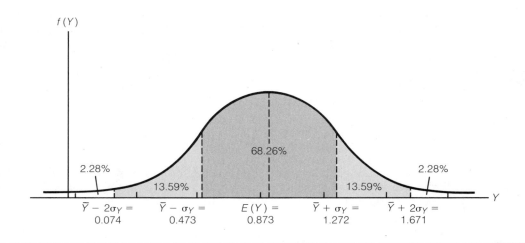

cause people don't usually think in terms of dollars squared, we usually employ the standard deviation, σ, which is the square root of the variance:

$$\sigma_Y = \sqrt{\text{VAR}(Y)} = \sqrt{\sigma_Y^2} = \sqrt{.159} = .399. \qquad (10.8)$$

If we knew nothing but the inventory figures, our forecast would probably be that expected inventory would be $.873 billion plus or minus one standard deviation of $.399 billion.

For a normal distribution, we know that 68.3 percent of the time, our observations will fall within plus or minus one standard deviation. This is shown by the cross-hatched area in Figure 10.3. And 95.4 percent of the time, inventory would fall within plus or minus two standard deviations.

Fortunately, we know much more than the unconditional distribution for inventory. We know that inventory is positively related to sales. The extra information provided by sales will allow us to come up with a *conditional distribution* of inventory *given* an estimate of sales. The conditional distribution will be much more accurate (that is, it will have a much lower standard deviation) than the unconditional distribution.

If we are trying to explain the conditional distribution of inventory given sales, we might choose a linear model such as Equation 10.4:

$$Y_t = a + bX_t + \epsilon_t, \qquad (10.4)$$

where

$Y_t =$ inventory in Year t
$X_t =$ sales in Year t
$\epsilon_t =$ a random error term (the difference between actual inventory and inventory predicted by the model).

Linear relationships have the virtue that they are simple and robust. Although many natural phenomena are not linearly related, in most cases linear approximations usually work well within a limited range.

Figure 10.4 shows a plot of inventory versus sales. The straight solid line is the linear regression line which minimizes the sum of the squared error terms. It is the best linear fit to the points. We saw, earlier, that the equation for the regression line is

$$\text{Inventory}_t = .216 + .04987 \text{ Sales}_t.$$

The slope of the linear regression, $b = .04987$, tells us how much inventory will change when sales does. For example, a \$1 billion increase (decrease) in sales will result in a

Figure 10.4 A Linear Regression of Inventory on Sales

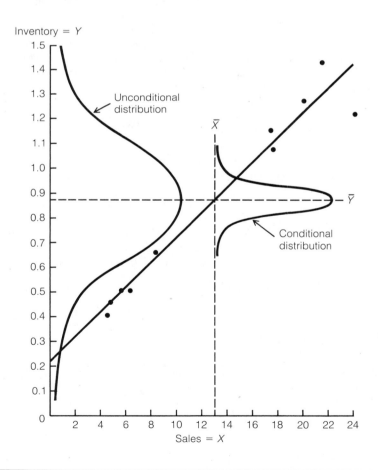

$49.87 million increase (decrease) in inventory. The sensitivity of inventory to sales depends on the *covariance* between the two variables. The formal definition of the slope, b, is

$$b = \frac{\text{COV}(Y,X)}{\text{VAR}(X)}. \qquad (10.9)$$

The slope is the covariance between inventory, Y_t, and sales, X_t, divided by the variance of sales. Later on, in Chapter 16, when we discuss decision making under uncertainty (portfolio theory), the covariance between random variables will become an extremely important concept. In fact, the covariance between the return on a risky asset and the return on a market portfolio such as the New York Stock Exchange Index will be the way we measure the risk of a marketable asset (for example, common stock). The formal definition of covariance for sampling statistics is

$$\text{COV}(Y,X) = \frac{1}{N-1}\sum_{i=1}^{N}[(Y_i - E(Y))(X_i - E(X))]. \qquad (10.10)$$

Intuitively, the covariance is a measure of how random variables Y and X depart from their means at the same time. A positive covariance will result if Y is above its mean when X is also above its mean. A negative covariance is the opposite. When Y is high, X is low, so that the two tend to be offsetting. Table 10.4 shows the calculations for the variance of sales in Column (7) and for the covariance between inventory and sales in Column (8). Thus, the slope estimate, $\hat{b}$, is[8]

$$\hat{b} = \frac{3.035}{60.849} = .04987.$$

Because the linear regression line must pass through the mean of Y and the mean of X, the definition of the intercept estimate, $\hat{a}$, is

$$\hat{a} = E(Y) - \hat{b}\ E(X). \qquad (10.11)$$

Substituting in the values of $E(Y)$, $\hat{b}$, and $E(X)$, we have

$$\hat{a} = .873 - .04987(13.169) = .216.$$

This intercept estimate implies that inventory would be $.216 billion even if sales were zero.

The Coefficient of Determination

The residual errors, shown in Column (9) of Table 10.4, are the difference between the actual inventory, Y, and the inventory predicted by the linear regression, $\hat{Y}$. The residual errors indicate the extent of movement in the dependent variable (Y) which is not ex-

---

[8]We put a "hat" over b to designate that this is only an estimate of the true relationship between inventory and sales. It is not the true relationship.

plained by the independent variable (X). If the residuals are small relative to the total variability of the dependent variable, then it follows that a major part of the unconditional distribution of the dependent variable has been explained. The unconditional variance of inventory was computed to be $\sigma_Y^2 = .159$. The conditional variance, given sales, is the variance of the residual terms. Since the average residual is equal to zero, the variance of the residuals is the sum of the squared error terms divided by $N - 1$.

$$\sigma_\epsilon^2 = \Sigma\epsilon_i^2/(N - 1) = .07232/9 = .0080.$$

Both the unconditional and conditional distributions are illustrated in Figure 10.4. From the graph, we can see that the extra information provided by sales has provided a dramatic increase in our ability to explain inventory. A statistic which measures the extent of the increased explanatory power is called the *coefficient of determination*, r^2.

$$r^2 = \frac{\text{Variation explained by the linear regression}}{\text{Unconditional variation of the dependent variable}} \qquad \textbf{(10.12)}$$

$$= \frac{\Sigma(Y - \overline{Y})^2 - \Sigma(\epsilon - \overline{\epsilon})^2}{\Sigma(Y - \overline{Y})^2}.$$

Equation 10.12 says that we can estimate the percentage of the unconditional variance of the dependent variable which is explained by the independent variable if we subtract the variance of the error terms from the unconditional variance and then divide the result by the unconditional variance. The numbers for our example are

$$r^2 = \frac{.159 - .008}{.159} = .9496.$$

This means that 94.96 percent of the unconditional variance of inventory is explained by sales. If all of the variance were explained, then the sum of the squared residuals would be zero and the coefficient of determination would be $r^2 = 1$. At the opposite extreme, the equation would not reduce the variance of the dependent variable at all, and we would have $r^2 = 0$.

Tests of Significance

In addition to finding the best linear relationship between inventory and sales, it is also important to know whether or not the intercept and slope are statistically significant. Can we be confident that the results are good explanations for the relationship between inventory and sales, or did they happen merely by chance? Can we reject the null hypothesis that the intercept and slope are equal to zero?

The significance of the intercept and slope is determined by t-tests. If the t-statistics are large enough, we can be confident that our results are significant. The t-statistics are defined as the estimates of the intercept, $\hat{a}$, and the slope, $\hat{b}$, divided by their respective standard errors of estimate:

$$t(\hat{a}) = \frac{\hat{a}}{se(\hat{a})}, \qquad t(\hat{b}) = \frac{\hat{b}}{se(\hat{b})}. \qquad \textbf{(10.13)}$$

While the definition of the standard errors of estimate and the derivation of the t-statistics is beyond the scope of this text, we should discuss how to interpret them because they are usually included in the output from computer software linear regression packages.

When inventory is regressed on sales, the results, with t-statistics in parentheses, are

$$\text{Inventory} = .216 + .04987 \quad \text{Sales} \qquad r^2 = .9496$$
$$\qquad\qquad (3.516) \quad (12.276) \qquad\qquad F = 150.7$$

For our example, at the 95 percent confidence level, the t-statistics are significant if they are greater than 2.262. Hence, both the slope and the intercept are significantly greater than zero.[9]

The computer regression package also gives an F-statistic which is used to determine whether or not the coefficient of determination is significantly above zero. For our example, the F-statistic must be greater than 5.12 at the 95 percent confidence level. Since it is, we can infer that sales explains a significant portion of the variance of inventory.

Summary

Financial forecasting is one of the most important tools for planning. The cash flow necessary for paying expenses, for working capital, and for long-term investment can be forecast from pro forma income statements and balance sheets. The most important variable that influences financing requirements for most firms is the projected dollar volume of sales. We have shown how inventory, for example, is related to sales.

We have reviewed two different procedures for financial forecasting. The percent of sales method is the simplest but also the most restrictive because it implicitly assumes a linear relationship which is forced to pass through the origin. Simple linear regression differs because it does not assume that the line passes through the origin. Linear regression finds the slope and intercept which minimize the sum of squared errors from the line. We showed how to compute the least squares estimates of the intercept and slope, and we discussed the meaning of t-tests and F-statistics. These forecasting techniques can be used to estimate the seasonal and cyclical fluctuations in the firm's financial statements. These forecasts are then used to plan to meet the financial needs of the company. Temporary fluctuations in working capital are usually financed via lines of credit with lending institutions. Permanent build-ups in working capital and long-term assets are usually financed with long-term capital sources such as bonds and stock.

Questions

10.1   What should be the approximate point of intersection between the sales-to-asset regression line and the vertical axis (Y-axis intercept) for the following: inventory, accounts receivable, fixed assets? State your answer in terms of positive, zero, or negative intercept. Can you think of any accounts that might have a negative intercept?

10.2   How does forecasting financial requirements in advance of needs help financial managers perform their responsibilities more effectively?

---

[9]For more on how to use t-statistics see Hoel [1954], pp. 274-283, or any other good statistics textbook.

10.3 What is the difference between the long-range financial forecasting concept (for example, the percent-of-sales method) and the budgeting concept? How might they be used together?

10.4 Explain how a downturn in the business cycle could either cause a cash shortage for a firm or generate excess cash.

10.5 Explain this statement: To a considerable extent, current assets represent permanent assets.

10.6 What advantages does a simple linear regression have over the percent of sales method for financial forecasting?

10.7 Define the mean and variance for a sampling distribution.

10.8 Define the slope of a linear regression. What equation do you use? What does the slope mean?

10.9 What are t-statistics? How are they used?

10.10 What is an F-statistic? How is it used?

10.11 Define the coefficient of determination. What does it mean?

Problems

10.1 The Blume Company's 19X0 balance sheet is given below. Sales in 19X0 totaled $2 million. The ratio of net profit to sales was 5 percent, with a dividend payout ratio of 40 percent of net income. Sales are expected to increase by 30 percent during 19X1. No long-term debt will be retired. Using the percentage of sales method, determine how much outside financing is required in 19X1.

Blume Company Balance Sheet as of December 31, 19X0

Assets		Liabilities	
Cash	$ 75,000	Accounts payable	$ 40,000
Accounts receivable	150,000	Accruals	25,000
Inventory	240,000	Notes payable	85,000
Current assets	$ 465,000	Total current liabilities	$ 150,000
Net fixed assets	735,000	Long-term debt	250,000
		Total debt	$ 400,000
		Capital stock	450,000
		Retained earnings	350,000
Total assets	$1,200,000	Total liabilities and net worth	$1,200,000

10.2 Given the following data on Hanes Corporation, predict next year's balance sheet:

This year's sales: $80,000,000

Next year's sales: $100,000,000

After-tax profits: 6% of sales

Dividend payout: 40%

Retained earnings at the end of this year: $21,500,000

Cash as percent of sales: 3%

Receivables as percent of sales: 12%

Inventory as percent of sales: 25%

Net fixed assets as percent of sales: 40%

Accounts payable as percent of sales: 8%

Accruals as percent of sales: 20%

Next year's common stock: $20,000,000.

Hanes Corporation Balance Sheet as of December 31, 19X0

Assets		Liabilities	
Cash	_____	Accounts payable	_____
Accounts receivable	_____	Notes payable	_____
Inventory	_____	Accruals	_____
Total current assets	_____	Total current liabilities	_____
Fixed assets	_____	Common stock	_____
		Retained earnings	_____
Total assets	══════	Total liabilities	══════

10.3 One useful method of evaluating a firm's financial structure in relation to its industry is to compare it with financial ratio composites for the industry. A new firm, or an established firm contemplating entry into a new industry, may use such composites as a guide to its likely approximate financial position after the initial settling-down period.

The following data represent ratios for the publishing and printing industry for 19X0.

Sales to net worth: 2.2 times

Current debt to net worth: 45%

Total debt to net worth: 80%

Current ratio: 2.4 times

Net sales to inventory: 5.1 times

Average collection period: 60 days

Net fixed assets to net worth: 72%.

a) Complete the pro forma balance sheet (round to nearest thousand) for Original Printers, whose 19X0 sales are $5 million.

b) What does the use of the financial ratio composites accomplish?

c) What other factors will influence the financial structure of the firm?

Original Printers, Inc. Pro Forma Balance Sheet as of December 31, 19X0

Assets		Liabilities	
Cash	_____	Current debt	_____
Accounts receivable	_____	Long-term debt	_____
Inventory	_____	Total debt	_____
Current assets	_____	Net worth	_____
Fixed assets	_____		
Total assets	══════	Total liabilities and net worth	══════

10.4 The Kamberg Supply Company is a wholesale steel distributor. It purchases steel in carload lots from more than 20 producing mills and sells to several thousand steel users. The items carried include sheets, plates, wire products, bolts, windows, pipe, and tubing.

The company owns two warehouses of 25,000 square feet each and is contemplating the erection of another warehouse of 30,000 square feet. The nature of a steel supply business requires that the company maintain large inventories to take care of customer requirements in the event of mill strikes or other delays.

In examining historical patterns, the company found consistent relationships among the following accounts as a percent of sales.

Current assets: 65%

Net fixed assets: 25%

Accounts payable: 10%

Other current liabilities, including accruals and provision for income taxes but not bank loans: 12%

Net profit after taxes: 5%.

The company's sales for 1985 were $10 million, and its balance sheet on December 31, 1985, is shown below. The company expects its sales to increase by $1 million each year. If this level is achieved, what will the company's financial requirements be at the end of the five-year period? Assume that accounts not tied directly to sales (for example, notes payable) remain constant and that the company pays no dividends.

a) Construct a pro forma balance sheet for the end of 1990, using "additional financing needed" as the balancing item.

b) What are the crucial assumptions you made in your projection method?

Kamberg Supply Company Balance Sheet as of December 31, 1985

Assets		Liabilities	
Current assets	$6,500,000	Accounts payable	$1,000,000
Fixed assets	2,500,000	Notes payable	1,200,000
		Other current liabilities	1,200,000
		Total current liabilities	$3,400,000
		Mortgage loan	1,000,000
		Common stock	2,000,000
		Retained earnings	2,600,000
Total assets	$9,000,000	Total liabilities and net worth	$9,000,000

10.5 The 19X1 sales of Ultrasonics, Inc., were $12 million. Common stock and notes payable are constant. The dividend payout ratio is 40 percent. Retained earnings shown on the December 31, 19X0, balance sheet were $80,000. The percent of sales in each balance sheet item that varies directly with sales is expected to be

	Percent
Cash	5
Receivables	15
Inventories	20
Net fixed assets	40
Accounts payable	10
Accruals	5
Profit rate (after taxes) on sales	4

a) Complete the balance sheet given below.

b) Suppose that in 19X2, sales will increase by 20 percent over 19X1 sales. How much additional (external) capital will be required?

c) Construct the year-end 19X2 balance sheet. Set up an account for "financing needed" or "funds available."

d) What would happen to capital requirements under each of the following conditions?

  1. The profit margin went from 4 percent to 6 percent; from 4 percent to 2 percent. Set up an equation to illustrate your answers.

  2. The dividend payout rate was raised from 40 percent to 80 percent; was lowered from 40 percent to 20 percent. Set up an equation to illustrate your answers.

  3. Slower collections caused receivables to rise to 72 days of sales.

Ultrasonics, Inc., Balance Sheet as of December 31, 19X1

Assets		Liabilities	
Cash	_____	Accounts payable	_____
Receivables	_____	Notes payable	$ 900,000
Inventory	_____	Accruals	_____
Total current assets	_____	Total current liabilities	_____
Fixed assets	_____	Common stock	$6,532,000
		Retained earnings	_____
Total assets	_____	Total liabilities and net worth	_____

10.6 A firm has the following relationships. The ratio of assets to sales is 55 percent. Liabilities that increase spontaneously with sales are 15 percent. The profit margin on sales after taxes is 6 percent. The firm's dividend payout ratio is 40 percent.

a) If the firm's growth rate on sales is 15 percent per annum, what percentage of the sales increase in any year must be financed externally?

b) If the firm's growth rate on sales increases to 25 percent per annum, what percentage of the sales increase in any year must be financed externally?

c) How will your answer to Part (a) change if the profit margin increases to 8 percent?

d) How will your answer to Part (b) change if the firm's dividend payout is reduced to 10 percent?

e) If the profit margin increases from 6 percent to 8 percent and the dividend payout ratio is 20 percent, at what growth rate in sales will the external financing requirement percentage be exactly zero?

10.7 You are starting a new business. You know only two things: (1) the business you are planning to enter and (2) an estimated volume of sales. With the use of industry financial composites, you can project the balance sheet and income statement you are likely to have. Departures from this projection will provide a basis for analyzing causes of the deviations.

To illustrate: You plan to enter the manufacturing of industrial electrical instruments. Sales in your first full year of operation are expected to be $14 million. Based on the following industry composites for 19X8, write the pro forma balance sheet and income statement for your company for 19X9.

Current ratio: 2.4 times

Net income to sales: 5%

Sales to net worth: 3.5 times

Average collection period: 50 days

Sales to inventory: 5.5 times

Fixed assets on net worth: 60%

Current debt to net worth: 50%

Total debt to net worth: 80%

Cost of sales to sales: 60%

Operating expenses to sales: 30%

Profit before taxes to sales: 10%.

10.8   Using the following data, calculate the sampling mean, variance, and standard deviation for sales.

Year	Sales	GNP
19X8	721.3	3998.9
19X7	525.1	3513.6
19X6	462.3	3172.5
19X5	315.7	2937.7
19X4	256.8	2633.1
19X3	111.5	2417.8
19X2	82.9	2163.9

10.9   Using the data given in Problem 10.8, estimate the intercept and slope of the regression line:

$$\text{Sales} = \hat{a} + \hat{b}\ \text{GNP}.$$

Next, estimate the coefficient of determination for the above regression.

10.10   The data in Table 10.3 can be used to explain inventory as a function of sales. The percent of sales method gave the following relationship:

$$\text{Inventory} = .0731\ \text{Sales}.$$

Linear regression gave

$$\text{Inventory} = .216 + .05\ \text{Sales}.$$

a) What is the r^2 for the linear regression of inventory as a function of sales?

b) Suppose we transform sales by taking its square root and then regress inventory on the square root of sales as follows:

$$\text{Inventory} = \hat{a} + \hat{b}\ \sqrt{\text{Sales}}.$$

Estimate the intercept and slope terms for this linear regression and compare the r^2 with the r^2 which you computed for Part (a) of this question.

Selected References

Chambers, John, C.; Mullick, Satinder K.; and Smith, Donald D., "How to Choose the Right Forecasting Technique," *Harvard Business Review*, 49 (July-August 1971), pp. 45-74.

Christ, C. G., *Econometric Models and Methods*, New York: Wiley, 1966.

Dhrymes, P. J., *Econometrics: Statistical Foundations and Applications*, New York: Harper and Row, 1970.

Francis, Jack Clark, and Rowell, Dexter R., "A Simultaneous Equation Model of the Firm for Financial Analysis and Planning," *Financial Management*, 7 (Spring 1978), pp. 29-44.

Gershefski, George W., "Building a Corporate Financial Model," *Harvard Business Review*, 47 (July-August 1969), pp. 61-72.

Goldberger, A. S., *Econometric Theory*, New York: Wiley, 1964.

Gup, Benton E., "The Financial Consequences of Corporate Growth," *Journal of Finance*, 35 (December 1980), pp. 1257-1265.

Higgins, Robert C., "Sustainable Growth Under Inflation," *Financial Management*, 10 (Autumn 1981), pp. 36-40.

Hoel, P. G., *Introduction to Mathematical Statistics*, 3rd ed., New York: Wiley, 1954.

Johnston, J., *Econometric Methods*, New York: McGraw-Hill, 1963.

Rao, P., and Miller, L., *Applied Econometrics*, Belmont, Calif.: Wadsworth, 1971.

Wonnacott, R. J., and Wonnacott, T. H., *Econometrics*, New York: Wiley, 1970.

Appendix A to Chapter 10
The Normal Distribution

One of the assumptions made in the development of linear regression is that the distribution of returns is approximately normal. The mean and variance (or standard deviation) can then be used to compare entire probability distributions. Because the normal distribution plays such an important role in financial economics, it is useful to know more about it.

Suppose that we have the continuous probability distribution shown in Figure 10A.1. This is a normal curve with a mean of 20 and a standard deviation of 5; X could be dollars, percentage rates of return, or any other units. If we want to know the probability that an outcome will fall between 15 and 30, we must calculate the area beneath the curve between these points, the shaded area in the diagram.

The area under the curve between 15 and 30 can be determined by integrating the curve over this interval, or, since the distribution is normal, by reference to statistical tables of the area under the normal curve, such as Appendix D.[1] To use these tables, it is necessary only to know the mean and standard deviation of the distribution.[2] The distribution to be investigated must first be standardized by using the following formula:

$$z = \frac{X - \mu}{\sigma},$$ (10A.1)

where z is the standardized variable, or the number of standard deviations from the mean;[3] X is the outcome of interest; and μ and σ are the mean and standard deviation of the distribution, respectively. For our example, where we are interested in the probability that an outcome will fall between 15 and 30, we first normalize these points of interest using Equation 10A.1:

$$z_1 = \frac{15 - 20}{5} = -1.0; \; z_2 = \frac{30 - 20}{5} = 2.0.$$

---

[1] The equation for the normal curve is tedious to integrate, thus making the use of tables much more convenient. The equation for the normal curve is:

$$f(X) = \frac{1}{\sqrt{2\pi\sigma^2}} e^{-(X-\mu)^2/2\sigma^2},$$

where $f(X)$ is the frequency of a given value of X, π is the ratio of the circumference to the diameter of a circle, and e is the base of natural logarithms; μ and σ denote the mean and standard deviation of the probability distribution, and X is any possible outcome.

[2] The definitions for means and standard deviations for sampling statistics are given in Equations 10.5 and 10.7.

[3] Note that if the point of interest is 1σ away from the mean, then $X - \mu = \sigma$, so $z = \sigma/\sigma = 1.0$. Thus, when $z = 1.0$, the point of interest is 1σ away from the mean; when $z = 2$, the value is 2σ, and so forth.

Figure 10A.1   Continuous Probability Distribution

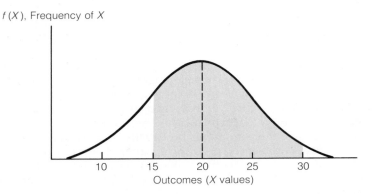

The areas associated with these z values are found in Table 10A.1 to be 0.3413 and 0.4773.[4] This means that the probability is 0.3413 that the actual outcome will fall between 15 and 20, and 0.4773 that it will fall between 20 and 30. Summing these probabilities shows that the probability of an outcome falling between 15 and 30 is 0.8186, or 81.86 percent.

Suppose we had been interested in determining the probability that the actual outcome would be greater than 15. Here, we would first note that the probability that the outcome will be between 15 and 20 is 0.3413. Then, we would observe that the probability of an

Table 10A.1   Area under the Normal Curve of Error

z	Area from the Mean to the Point of Interest	$f(z)$ Ordinate
0.0	0.0000	0.3989
0.5	0.1915	0.3521
1.0	0.3413	0.2420
1.5	0.4332	0.1295
2.0	0.4773	0.0540
2.5	0.4938	0.0175
3.0	0.4987	0.0044

z = number of standard deviations from the mean. Some area tables are set up to indicate the area to the left or right of the point of interest; in this book, we indicate the area between the mean and the point of interest.

[4]Note that the negative sign on z_1 is ignored, since the normal curve is symmetrical around the mean; the minus sign merely indicates that the point lies to the left of the mean.

Figure 10A.2   The Normal Curve

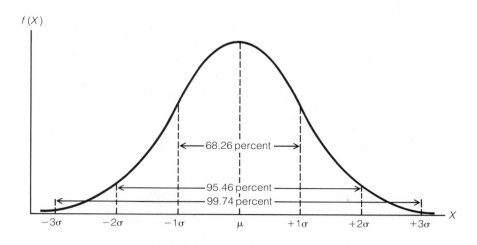

outcome greater than the mean, 20, is 0.5000. Thus, the probability is 0.3413 + 0.5000 = 0.8413, or 84.13 percent, that the outcome will exceed 15.

Some interesting properties of normal probability distributions can be seen by examining Table 10A.1 and Figure 10A.2, which is a graph of the normal curve. For any normal distribution, the probability of an outcome falling within plus or minus one standard deviation from the mean is 0.6826, or 68.26 percent; 34.13 percent × 2.0. If we take the range within two standard deviations of the mean, the probability of an occurrence within this range is 95.46 percent; and 99.74 percent of all outcomes will fall within three standard deviations of the mean. Although the distribution theoretically runs from minus infinity to plus infinity, the probability of occurrences beyond about three standard deviations is very near zero.

Illustrating the Use of Probability Concepts

The concepts discussed in the preceding section of this appendix can be clarified by a numerical example. Consider three states of the economy; boom, normal, and recession. Next, assume that we can attach a probability of occurrence to each state of the economy and, further, that we can estimate the dollar returns that will occur on each of two projects under each possible state. With this information, we construct Table 10A.2.

The expected values of Projects A and B are calculated by Equation 10A.2,

$$E(X) = \sum_{i=1}^{N} p_i X_i, \qquad \text{(10A.2)}$$

and the standard deviations of their respective returns are found by Equation 10A.3.

Table 10A.2   Means and Standard Deviations of Projects A and B

State of the Economy	Probability of Its Occurring p_i	Return X_i	p_iX_i
Project A			
Recession	0.2	$400	$ 80
Normal	0.6	500	300
Boom	0.2	600	120
	1.0		Expected value = $500

Standard deviation $= \sigma_A = \$63.25$.

Project B			
Recession	0.2	$300	$ 60
Normal	0.6	500	300
Boom	0.2	700	140
	1.0		Expected value = $500

Standard deviation $= \sigma_B = \$126.49$.

Figure 10A.3   Probability Distributions for Projects A and B

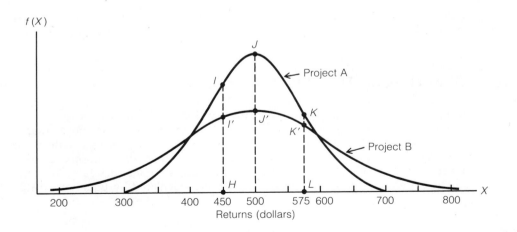

$$\sigma_i = \sqrt{\sum_{i=1}^{N} p_i[X_i - E(X)]^2} \qquad\qquad \textbf{(10A.3)}$$

Note that since the probabilities of events are subjectively estimated, and are not sampling statistics, we multiply each event by its probability, p_i, instead of dividing by the number of observations. On the assumption that the returns from Projects A and B are normally distributed, knowing the mean and the standard deviation as calculated in Table 10A.2 permits us to graph probability distributions for Projects A and B; these distributions are shown in Figure 10A.3.[5] The expected value of each project's cash flow is seen to be $500; however, the flatter graph of B indicates that this is the riskier project.

Suppose we want to determine the probabilities that the actual returns of Projects A and B will be in the interval $450 to $575. Using Equation 10A.1 and Figure 10A.3, we can calculate the respective probability distributions. The first step is to calculate the z values of the interval limits for the two projects:

Project A

$$\text{lower } z_1 = \frac{\$450 - \$500}{\$63.25} = -0.79.$$

$$\text{upper } z_2 = \frac{\$575 - \$500}{\$63.25} = 1.19.$$

[5]Normal probability distributions can be constructed once the mean and standard deviation are known, using a table of *ordinates* of the normal curve. (See Column 3 of Table 10A.1.) This table is similar to the table of areas used above, except that the ordinate table gives relative *heights* of probability curve $f(X)$ at various z values rather than areas beneath the curve. Figure 10A.3 was constructed by plotting points at various z values according to the following formula:

$$f(X) = \frac{1}{\sigma} \times (\text{Ordinate for } z \text{ value}),$$

where the ordinate value is read from a table of ordinates.

For example, the points corresponding to the mean and +1 and +2 standard deviations for Projects A and B were calculated as follows:

Project A (1)	z (2)	Ordinate at z (3)	1/σ (4)	f(X): (3) × (4) =(5)
Mean = 500.00	0	0.3989	1/63.25	0.0063
+1σ = 563.25	1	0.2420	1/63.25	0.0038
+2σ = 626.50	2	0.0540	1/63.25	0.0009
Project B				
Mean = 500.00	0	0.3989	1/126.49	0.0032
+1σ = 626.49	1	0.2420	1/126.49	0.0019
+2σ = 752.98	2	0.0540	1/126.49	0.0004

Column 5 above gives the relative heights of the two distributions: Thus, if we decide (for pictorial convenience) to let the curve for Project B be 3.2 inches high at the mean, then the curve should be 1.9 inches high at $\mu \pm 1\sigma$, and the curve for Project A should be 6.3 inches at the mean and 3.8 inches at $\pm 1\sigma$. Other points in Figure 10A.3 were determined in like manner.

Project B

$$\text{lower } z_1 = \frac{\$450 - \$500}{\$126.49} = -0.40.$$

$$\text{upper } z_2 = \frac{\$575 - \$500}{\$126.49} = 0.59.$$

In Appendix D, which is a more complete table of z values, we find the areas under a normal curve for each of these four z values:

Project A	*z* Value	Area
lower z:	−.79	0.2852
upper z:	1.19	0.3830
	Total area =	0.6682, or 66.82 percent.

Project B	*z* Value	Area
lower z:	−0.40	0.1554
upper z:	0.59	0.2224
	Total area =	0.3778, or 37.78 percent.

Thus, there is about a 67 percent chance that the actual cash flow from Project A will lie in the interval $450 to $575 and about a 38 percent probability that B's cash flow will fall in this interval.

Now look at Figure 10A.3 and observe the two areas that were just calculated. For Project A, the area bounded by *HIJKL* represents about 67 percent of the area under A's curve. For Project B, that area bounded by *HI'J'K'L* includes about 38 percent of the total area.

Cumulative Probability

Suppose we ask these questions: What is the probability that the cash flows from Project A will be at least $100? $150? $200? and so on. Obviously, there is a higher probability of their being at least $100 rather than $150, at least $150 rather than $200, and so on. In general, the most convenient way of expressing the answer to such "at least" questions is through the use of *cumulative probability distributions*; these distributions for Projects A and B are calculated in Table 10A.3 and are plotted in Figure 10A.4.

Suppose Projects A and B each cost $450; then, if each project returns at least $450, they will both break even. What is the probability of breaking even on each project? From Figure 10A.4, we see that the probability is 78 percent that Project A will break even, while the breakeven probability is only 65 percent for the riskier Project B. However, there is virtually no chance that A will yield more than $650, while B has a 5 percent chance of returning $700 or more.

Table 10A.3 Cumulative Probability Distributions for Projects A and B

Expected Return	z Value	Cumulative Probability
Project A		
300	−3.16	0.9992[a]
400	−1.58	0.9429[b]
450	−0.79	0.7852
500	0.00	0.5000[c]
575	1.19	0.1170[d]
600	1.58	0.0571
700	3.16	0.0008[a]
Project B		
200	−2.37	0.9911[b]
300	−1.58	0.9429
400	−0.79	0.7852
450	−0.40	0.6554
500	0.00	0.5000[c]
575	0.59	0.2776[d]
600	0.79	0.2148
700	1.58	0.0571
800	2.37	0.0089

[a]Not shown in Appendix D.
[b]0.5000 plus area under left tail of the normal curve; for example, for Project A, 0.5000 + 0.4429 = 0.9429 = 94.3 percent for $z = -1.58$.
[c]The mean has a cumulative probability of 0.5000 = 50 percent.
[d]0.5000 less area under right tail of the normal curve; for example, for Project A, 0.5000 − 0.3830 = 0.1170 = 11.7 percent for $z = 1.19$.

Figure 10A.4 Cumulative Probability Distributions for Projects A and B

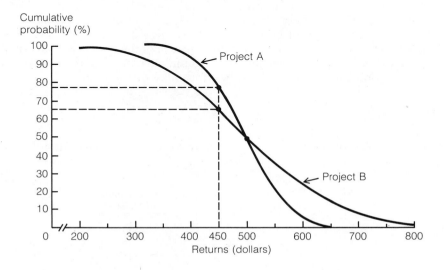

Figure 10A.5   Skewed Distributions

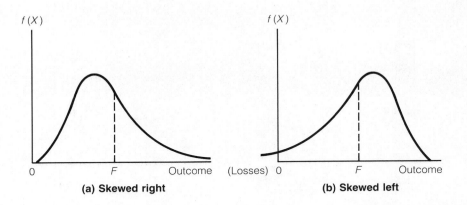

(a) Skewed right   (b) Skewed left

Other Distributions

Thus far, we have assumed that project returns fit a probability distribution that is approximately normal. Many distributions do fit this pattern, and normal distributions are relatively easy to work with. Therefore, much of the work done on risk measurement assumes a normal distribution. However, other distributions are certainly possible; Figure 10A.5 shows distributions skewed to the right and left, respectively. For two possible investments with equal expected returns, F, would an investor prefer a normal, a left-skewed, or a right-skewed distribution? A distribution skewed to the right, such as the one in Figure 10A.5(a), would probably be chosen because the odds on a very low return are small, while there is some chance of very high returns. For the left-skewed distributions, there is little likelihood of large gains but a large cumulative probability of losses. Skewness is in the direction of the "long tail" of the probability distribution.

Problems

10A.1 The sales of the Cleveland Company for next year have the following probability distribution:

Probability	Sales (Millions of Dollars)
0.1	$10
0.2	12
0.4	15
0.2	18
0.1	20

a) On graph paper, plot sales on the horizontal axis and probability of sales on the vertical axis, using the points given above. Draw a smooth curve connecting your plotted points. What can you say about this curve?

b) Compute the mean of the probability distribution.

c) Compute the standard deviation of the probability distribution.

d) Compute the coefficient of variation of the probability distribution.

e) What is the probability that sales will exceed $16 million?

f) What is the probability that sales will fall below $13 million?

g) What is the probability that sales will be between $13 and $16 million?

h) What is the probability that sales will exceed $17 million?

10A.2 Mutual of Poughkeepsie offers to sell your firm a $1 million, one-year term insurance policy on your corporate jet for a premium of $7,500. The probability that the plane will be lost or incur damages in that amount in any 12-month period is 0.001.

a) What is the insurance company's expected gain from sale of the policy?

b) What is the insurance company's expected gain or loss if the probability of a $1 million fire loss is 0.01? Would the insurance company still offer your firm the same policy for the same premium? Explain.

Part Four   **Working Capital Management**

Up to this point, we have analyzed the firm's operations from an overall aggregate standpoint. We now turn to an examination of the various aspects of financial management of the firm in more detail. In Part Four, we focus on the top half of the balance sheet, studying current assets, current liabilities, and the interrelationship between these two sets of accounts. This type of analysis is commonly called working capital management.

Chapter 11 examines some general principles of overall working capital management. In the next three chapters, we analyze the major current asset accounts. Chapter 12 covers several aspects of cash management, including cash disbursements, management of the firm's marketable securities portfolio, and cash management models. Chapter 13 provides an overview of inventory models, which has broad implications since all investments represent an inventory decision to some degree. In Chapter 14, we analyze credit management decisions calculating NPV's, utilizing the capital budgeting framework developed earlier. Chapter 15 describes the important sources of short-term financing.

In broad perspective, working capital management represents the efforts of the firm to make adjustments to short-run changes. These represent the developments to which the firm must make prompt and effective responses. We take up these aspects of financial decision making early, because they occupy the major portion of the financial manager's time and represent areas in which activity takes place on a continuing basis.

Chapter 11 Working Capital Policy

The term working capital is used in different ways by different writers. We take a practical approach by adopting the usage found in the annual reports of corporations where working capital is defined as current assets minus current liabilities. Thus, working capital represents the firm's investment in cash, marketable securities, accounts receivable, and inventories less the current liabilities used to finance the current assets. Some refer to this measure as net working capital, but if working capital is what is left after taking account of current liabilities, it is redundant to add the term net. Working capital management is defined broadly to encompass all aspects of the administration of both current assets and current liabilities.

In this chapter, we deal with two central aspects of working capital management. One is how much financial resources should be invested in current assets. The other is the proportions of short-term versus long-term debt to be used in financing current assets.

Importance of Working Capital Management

Working capital management includes a number of aspects that make it an important topic for study:

1. Surveys indicate that the largest portion of a financial manager's time is devoted to the day-by-day internal operations of the firm, which can appropriately be subsumed under the heading of working capital management.
2. Characteristically, current assets represent more than half the total assets of a business firm. Because they represent such a large investment and because this investment tends to be relatively volatile, current assets are worthy of the financial manager's careful attention.
3. Working capital management is particularly important for small firms. Although such firms can minimize their investment in fixed assets by renting or leasing plant and equipment, they cannot avoid investment in cash, receivables, and inventories. Therefore, current assets are particularly significant for the financial manager of a small firm. Further, because a small firm has relatively limited access to the long-term capital markets, it must necessarily rely heavily on trade credit and short-term bank loans, both of which affect working capital by increasing current liabilities.
4. The relationship between sales growth and the need to finance current assets is close and direct. For example, if the firm's average collection period is 40 days and its credit sales are $1,000 a day, it has an investment of $40,000 in accounts receivable. If sales rise to $2,000 a day, the investment in accounts receivable rises to $80,000. Sales increases produce similar immediate needs for additional inventories and, perhaps, for cash balances. All such needs must be financed; and since they are so closely related to sales volume, it is imperative that the financial manager keep aware of developments in the working capital segment of the firm. Of course, continued sales

increases require additional long-term assets, which must also be financed. However, fixed asset investments, while critically important to the firm in a strategic, long-run sense, generally have more lead time in financing than do current asset investments.

Risk-Return Tradeoff for Current Asset Investments

If it could forecast perfectly, a firm would hold exactly enough cash to make disbursements as required, exactly enough inventories to meet production and sales requirements, exactly the accounts receivable called for by an optimal credit policy, and no marketable securities unless the interest returns on such assets exceeded the cost of capital (an unlikely occurrence). The current asset holdings under the perfect foresight case would be the theoretical optimum for a profit-maximizing firm. The middle solid line in Figure 11.1 shows the theoretical optimum at different output levels. Any holdings larger than the optimum would increase the firm's assets without a proportionate increase in its returns, thus lowering its rate of return on investment. Any smaller holdings would mean the

Figure 11.1   Relationship between Current Assets and Output under Certainty and Uncertainty

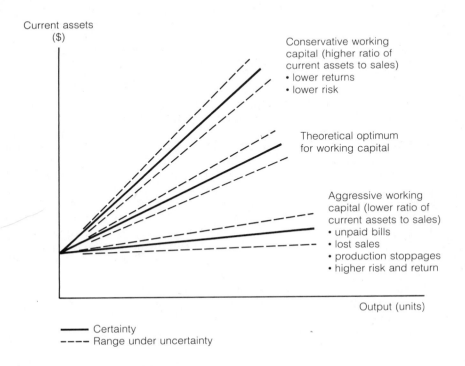

inability to pay bills on time, lost sales and production stoppages because of inventory shortages, and lost sales because of an overly restrictive credit policy.

When uncertainty is introduced into the picture, current asset management involves (1) determination of the minimum required balances of each type of asset and (2) addition of a safety stock to account for the fact that forecasts are imperfect. The broken lines in Figure 11.1 illustrate variations in alternative current asset policies. The lines with the steepest slopes represent conservative policies. Under conservative current asset policies, relatively large balances of cash and marketable securities are maintained, large amounts of inventories are kept on hand, and sales are stimulated by the use of a credit policy that provides liberal financing to customers and that results in a high level of accounts receivable. The lowest of the lines in Figure 11.1 have the smallest slopes, representing the most aggressive current asset policy in which holdings of cash, receivables, and inventories are sharply restricted. The intermediate lines represent a middle-ground approach.

Current asset holdings are the highest at any output level under the conservative policy and the lowest under the aggressive policy. For example, a firm which follows a conservative current asset policy holds relatively large safety stocks. If it follows an aggressive policy, its safety stocks are minimal. The aggressive policy requires the smallest investment, but the return on investment in current assets depends upon the degree to which the more restrictive asset management policies reduce sales levels below those that would be achieved under other policies. Numerical illustrations of some possibilities are presented in Table 11.1.

In Part A, it is assumed that the less aggressive current asset investment policies stimulate sales to a slight degree by having more variety in inventory, fewer stock-out problems, and so forth. But still, the indicated rate of return on assets is highest for the current asset policy of greatest aggressiveness.

In Part B of Table 11.1, an alternative set of assumptions is illustrated. It is assumed that the aggressive current asset investment policy results in a larger adverse sales effect and also lowers the earnings rate. As a consequence, the most aggressive policy now results in the lowest indicated return on assets. It is assumed that the middle-ground policy pro-

---

Table 11.1   Effects of Alternative Current Asset Policies on Rates of Return

	Conservative	Middle-Ground	Aggressive
Part A			
Sales	$110,000,000	$105,000,000	$100,000,000
EBIT @15%	16,500,000	15,750,000	15,000,000
Current assets	70,000,000	55,000,000	40,000,000
Fixed assets	50,000,000	50,000,000	50,000,000
Total assets	$120,000,000	$105,000,000	$ 90,000,000
Rate of return on assets (EBIT/assets)	13.75%	15%	16.7%
Part B			
Sales	$115,000,000	$105,000,000	$ 80,000,000
EBIT rate	15%	15%	12%
EBIT amount	17,250,000	15,750,000	9,600,000
Total assets	$120,000,000	$105,000,000	$ 90,000,000
Rate of return on assets (EBIT/assets)	14.4%	15%	10.7%

duces the same results as before. The results of the conservative policy are assumed to improve somewhat. Still the outcome for the middle-ground policy represents the highest return on assets for the relationships postulated.

Table 11.1 illustrates the general idea that the kind of current asset policy a firm follows may result in a stimulus to sales and profitability or in negative effects on both the volume of sales and profitability.

In the real world, things are considerably more complex than this simple example suggests. For one thing, different types of current assets affect both risk and returns differently. Increased holdings of cash do more to improve the firm's risk posture than a similar dollar increase in receivables or inventories; idle cash penalizes earnings more severely than does the same investment in marketable securities. Generalizations are difficult when we consider accounts receivable and inventories, because it is difficult to measure either the earnings penalty or the risk reduction that results from increasing the balances of these items beyond their theoretical optimum levels.

Financing Current Assets

In Chapter 6 on capital budgeting, we saw that capital budgeting decisions involve estimating the stream of benefits expected from a given project and then discounting the expected cash flows back to the present to find the present value of the project. Although current asset investment analysis is similar to fixed asset analysis in the sense that it also requires estimates of the effects of such investments on profits, it is different in two key respects:

1. The cash and marketable securities portion of current assets provides liquidity to the firm and reduces its vulnerability to adverse patterns of cash flows. This increased liquidity reduces the risk that the firm would not have cash assets to meet maturing obligations from the liability side of the balance sheet. In this respect, the riskiness of the firm is reduced. But to the extent that liquid assets earn less than other assets and to the extent that having large safety stocks of cash and marketable securities increases the current and total assets over what they might otherwise be, the overall return on assets is reduced.

2. Although both fixed and current asset holdings are functions of *expected* sales, only current assets can be adjusted to *actual* sales in the short run; hence, adjustments to short-run fluctuations in demand lie in the domain of working capital management.

An Idealized Model of Financing Current Assets

Up to now, we have been focusing on the asset side of the balance sheet, assuming that the liability structure was being held constant. Now we turn to the liability side of the balance sheet and assume that the asset pattern is being held constant.

The term *working capital* originated at a time when most industries were closely related to agriculture. Processors would buy crops in the fall, process them, sell the finished product, and end up just before the next harvest with relatively low inventories. Bank loans with maximum maturities of one year were used to finance both the purchase and the processing costs, and these loans were retired with the proceeds from the sale of the finished products.

This situation is depicted in Figure 11.2, where fixed assets are shown to be growing steadily over time, while current assets jump at harvest season and then decline during

Figure 11.2   Fixed and Current Asset Patterns in Agriculture

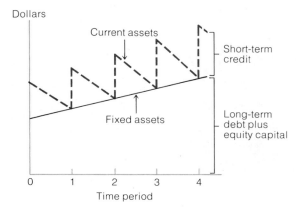

the year, ending at zero just before the next crop is harvested. Current assets are financed with short-term credit, and fixed assets are financed with long-term funds. Thus, the top segment of the graph deals with working capital.

The figure represents, of course, an idealized situation for agriculture. In manufacturing and distribution, current assets may build up gradually and decline in various patterns. Nevertheless, the example does illustrate the general nature of seasonal patterns in working capital. Working capital management consists of decisions relating to the top section of the graph — managing current assets and arranging the short-term credit used to finance them.

Financing the "Permanent" Portion of Current Assets

As the economy became less oriented toward agriculture, the production and financing cycles of typical businesses changed. Although seasonal patterns still exist and business cycles cause asset requirements to fluctuate, it is less likely that current assets will drop to zero. As sales increase, the investment in cash, receivables, and inventories must grow proportionately. A steadily rising level of sales over the years will result in permanent increases in current assets. Although individual receivables accounts are paid off and individual inventory items become embodied in completed products and are sold, the continuous operations of the firm will result in rising investments in receivables and inventories as sales increase. Temporary seasonal fluctuations in sales would be followed by similar fluctuations in current asset requirements.

Figures 11.3 through 11.5 illustrate three alternative patterns of financing current and fixed assets. In Figure 11.3, financing is matched to the permanence of assets; that is, the firm attempts to match the maturity structure of its assets and liabilities exactly. As total permanent assets increase, they are financed by equity, long-term debt, and by the "permanent" portion of spontaneous current liabilities. (Spontaneous current liabilities refers

Figure 11.3   Average Working Capital Financing

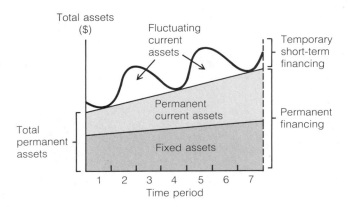

to accounts payable, accrued taxes, and accrued wages, which grow with sales and represent a form of financing.)

An alternative policy would be an aggressive working capital management policy (Figure 11.4) in which all fixed assets are financed with long-term capital, but part of the permanent current assets are financed with temporary short-term credit. The dashed line could even have been drawn *below* the line designating fixed assets, indicating that all the current assets and part of the fixed assets are financed with short-term credit; this would be a very aggressive policy.

Figure 11.4   Aggressive Working Capital Financing

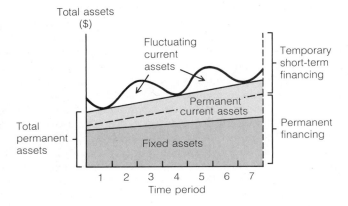

Figure 11.5   Conservative Working Capital Financing

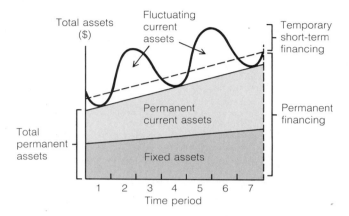

Alternatively, as in Figure 11.5, the dashed line could be drawn *above* the line designating permanent current assets, indicating that permanent capital is being used to meet seasonal demands. In this case, the firm uses a small amount of short-term credit to meet its peak seasonal requirements, but it also meets part of its seasonal needs by "storing liquidity" in the form of marketable securities during the off-season. The peaks above the dashed line represent short-term financing; the troughs below it represent short-term security holdings. This represents a conservative policy.

Another basic policy decision in working capital management is the choice between the use of short-term versus long-term financing. To analyze this decision, we shall first consider the relative advantages and disadvantages of these two financing methods.

The Costs and Risks of Alternative Debt Maturities

Interest rate volatility and uncertainty have greatly increased in recent years. Firms have been reluctant to borrow long term while interest rates have been high and have been concerned that they may go even higher. Like a policy of rolling over short-term debt, floating rate financing is used to reduce the risks to borrowers. Floating rate financing ties the interest rate on the borrowing to interest rate levels in general, measured by the levels of the bank prime lending rate or to the yield on ten-year U.S. Treasury bonds. So long as interest levels are correlated with the health of the economy, this has the advantage of reducing the swings in the profitability of the borrowing firm. We demonstrate this by using the numerical examples in Tables 11.2 and 11.3. Fixed rate versus flexible financing under favorable general economic conditions is illustrated in Table 11.2, while Table 11.3 makes a similar analysis under recessionary conditions.

Under favorable economic conditions, we postulate that both sales and interest rate levels will be higher. Flexible rate financing is shown at 15 percent, while fixed rate financ-

Table 11.2   Fixed Rate vs. Flexible Rate Financing, Prosperity

	Fixed Rate Financing	Flexible Rate Financing
Total assets	$ 800,000	$ 800,000
Flexible rate debt @15%		400,000
Fixed rate debt @12%	400,000	
Equity	400,000	400,000
Total claims	$ 800,000	$ 800,000
Sales	$1,200,000	$1,200,000
Net operating income @12%	144,000	144,000
Less interest	48,000	60,000
Taxable income	96,000	84,000
Less taxes @40%	38,400	33,600
Net income	57,600	50,400
Return on equity	14.4%	12.6%

ing locks in the cost to 12 percent. Fixed rate financing results in a return on equity of 14.4 percent as compared with the lower 12.6 percent for flexible rate financing.

In Table 11.3, the results are depicted for unfavorable conditions in the general economy when government policy and other factors cause interest rates to decline. The fixed rate financing stays at 12 percent, but flexible rate financing would be expected to be lower than the cost of fixed rate financing on average. The return on equity for fixed rate financing drops to 7.8 percent, but to only 10.2 percent for flexible rate financing. The decline in

Table 11.3   Fixed Rate vs. Flexible Rate Financing, Recession

	Fixed Rate Financing	Flexible Rate Financing
Total assets	$ 800,000	$ 800,000
Flexible rate debt @8%		400,000
Fixed rate debt @12%	400,000	
Equity	400,000	400,000
Total claims	$ 800,000	$ 800,000
Sales	$1,000,000	$1,000,000
Net operating income @10%	100,000	100,000
Less interest	48,000	32,000
Taxable income	52,000	68,000
Less taxes @40%	20,800	27,200
Net income	31,200	40,800
Return on equity	7.8%	10.2%

return on equity is 6.6 percentage points for fixed rate financing, but only 2.4 percentage points for flexible rate financing.

Thus, the firm's profitability, given flexible rate financing, is more stable and less influenced by overall economic conditions than under fixed rate financing. This example shows the relative degree to which the profitability of a firm covaries with general market conditions. As long as interest rates are positively correlated with the health of the firm and the economy, we will have the result that flexible rate financing (or the roll-over of short-term debt) is less risky than long-term financing. Thus, this material on working capital policy is linked to the central issues of such financing decisions as the firm's cost of capital, which will be developed in subsequent chapters.

Summary

Working capital is current assets minus current liabilities. *Working capital management* involves all aspects of the administration of current assets and current liabilities.

The first policy question deals with the determination of the level of total current assets to be held. Current assets vary with sales, but the ratio of current assets to sales is a policy matter. A firm that elects to operate aggressively will hold relatively small stocks of current assets, a policy that will reduce the required level of investment and increase the expected rate of return on investment. However, an aggressive policy also increases the likelihood of running out of inventories or losing sales because of an excessively tough credit policy.

The second policy question concerns the relationships among types of assets and the way these assets are financed. One policy calls for matching asset and liability maturities by financing current assets with short-term debt and fixed assets with long-term debt or equity. But this policy is unsound, because current assets include "permanent" investments that increase as sales grow. In our judgment, the financing of current assets should recognize that some portion bears a constant relationship to sales, so that this portion represents "permanent" investment. This would call for financing the permanent portion of current assets with the permanent portion of short-term debt (the spontaneous portion provided by accounts payable and accruals) and by long-term debt and equity financing to the extent required.

The final section of the chapter describes how flexible rate financing enables a firm to reduce the variability of its return to equity investors. This reduction of the firm's market covariance risk will enable the firm to reduce its costs of financing. Hence, working capital policy is related to the central issues of a firm's financial policies.

Questions

11.1 Give your reaction to this statement: Merely increasing the level of current asset holdings does not necessarily reduce the riskiness of the firm. Rather, the composition of the current assets, whether highly liquid or highly illiquid, is the important factor to consider.

11.2 How does the seasonal nature of a firm's sales influence the decision about the amount of short-term credit in the financial structure?

11.3 What is the advantage of matching the maturities of assets and liabilities? What are the disadvantages?

11.4   There have been times when the term structure of interest rates has been such that short-term rates were higher than long-term rates. Does this necessarily imply that the best financial policy for a firm is to use all long-term debt and no short-term debt? Explain.

11.5   Assuming a firm's volume of business remained constant, would you expect it to have higher cash balances (demand deposits) during a tight-money period or an easy-money period? Does this situation have any ramifications for federal monetary policy?

Problems

11.1   Indicate the effects of the transactions listed below on each of the following: total current assets, working capital, current ratio, and net profit. Use "+" to indicate an increase, "−" to indicate a decrease, and "0" to indicate no effect. State necessary assumptions and assume an initial current ratio of more than 1 to 1.

	Total Current Assets	Working Capital[a]	Current Ratio	Net Profit
1. Cash is acquired through issuance of additional common stock.	___	___	___	___
2. Merchandise is sold for cash.	___	___	___	___
3. Federal income tax due for the previous year is paid.	___	___	___	___
4. A fixed asset is sold for less than book value.	___	___	___	___
5. A fixed asset is sold for more than book value.	___	___	___	___
6. Merchandise is sold on credit.	___	___	___	___
7. Payment is made to trade creditors for previous purchases.	___	___	___	___
8. A cash dividend is declared and paid.	___	___	___	___
9. Cash is obtained through short-term bank loans.	___	___	___	___
10. Short-term notes receivable are sold at a discount.	___	___	___	___
11. A profitable firm increases its fixed assets depreciation allowance account.	___	___	___	___
12. Marketable securities are sold below cost.	___	___	___	___
13. Uncollectible accounts are written off against the allowance account.	___	___	___	___
14. Advances are made to employees.	___	___	___	___
15. Current operating expenses are paid.	___	___	___	___
16. Short-term promissory notes are issued to trade creditors for prior purchases.	___	___	___	___
17. Ten-year notes are issued to pay off accounts payable.	___	___	___	___
18. A wholly depreciated asset is retired.	___	___	___	___
19. Accounts receivable are collected.	___	___	___	___
20. A stock dividend is declared and paid.	___	___	___	___
21. Equipment is purchased with short-term notes.	___	___	___	___
22. The allowance for doubtful accounts is increased.	___	___	___	___
23. Merchandise is purchased on credit.	___	___	___	___
24. The estimated taxes payable are increased.	___	___	___	___

[a]Working capital is defined as current assets minus current liabilities.

11.2 The Warner Flooring Corporation is attempting to determine the optimal level of current assets for the coming year. Management expects sales to increase to approximately $1.2 million as a result of asset expansion presently being undertaken. Fixed assets total $500,000, and the firm wishes to maintain a 60 percent debt ratio. Warner's interest cost is currently 10 percent on both short-term debt and longer-term debt (which the firm uses in its permanent capital structure). Three alternatives regarding the projected current asset level are available to the firm: (1) an aggressive policy requiring current assets of only 45 percent of projected sales, (2) an average policy of 50 percent of sales in current assets, and (3) a conservative policy requiring current assets of 60 percent of sales. The firm expects to generate earnings before interest and taxes at a rate of 12 percent on total sales.

a) What is the expected return on equity under each current asset level? (Assume a 40 percent tax rate.)

b) In this problem, we have assumed that the earnings rate and the level of expected sales are independent of current asset policy. Is this a valid assumption?

c) How would the overall riskiness of the firm vary under each policy? Discuss specifically the effect of current asset management on demand, expenses, fixed charge coverage, risk of insolvency, and so on.

11.3 Three companies — Aggressive, Between, and Conservative — have different working capital management policies as implied by their names. For example, Aggressive employs only minimal current assets and finances entirely with current liabilities and equity. The "tight-ship" approach has a dual effect. It keeps total assets low, and this tends to increase return on assets. But for reasons such as stock-outs, total sales are reduced; and since inventory is ordered more frequently and in smaller quantities, variable costs are increased. Condensed balance sheets for the three companies are presented below.

Balance Sheets

	Aggressive	Between	Conservative
Current assets	$150,000	$200,000	$300,000
Fixed assets	200,000	200,000	200,000
Total assets	$350,000	$400,000	$500,000
Current liabilities (@12%)	$200,000	$100,000	$ 50,000
Long-term debt (@10%)	0	100,000	200,000
Total debt	$200,000	$200,000	$250,000
Equity	150,000	200,000	250,000
Total claims on assets	$350,000	$400,000	$500,000
Current ratio	0.75:1	2:1	6:1

The cost of goods sold functions for the three firms are as follows:

$$\text{Cost of goods sold} = \text{Fixed costs} + \text{Variable costs}$$

$$\text{Aggressive: Cost of goods sold} = \$200,000 + 0.70 \text{ (Sales)}$$

$$\text{Between: Cost of goods sold} = \$270,000 + 0.65 \text{ (Sales)}$$

$$\text{Conservative: Cost of goods sold} = \$385,000 + 0.60 \text{ (Sales)}$$

Because of the working capital differences, sales for the three firms under different economic conditions are expected to vary as indicated below:

	Aggressive	Between	Conservative
Strong economy	$1,200,000	$1,200,000	$1,200,000
Average economy	900,000	1,000,000	1,150,000
Weak economy	700,000	800,000	1,050,000

a) Make out income statements for each company for strong, average, and weak economies using the following pattern:
Sales
Less cost of goods sold
Earnings before interest and taxes (EBIT)
Less·interest expense
Taxable income
Less taxes (@40%)
Net income

b) Compare the rates of return (EBIT/Total Assets and Return on Equity). Which company is best in a strong economy? In an average economy? In a weak economy?

c) What considerations for management of working capital are indicated by this problem?

Selected References

Merville, L. J., and Tavis, L. A., "Optimal Working Capital Policies: A Chance-Constrained Programming Approach," *Journal of Financial and Quantitative Analysis*, 8 (January 1973), pp. 47-60.

Sartoris, William L., and Hill, Ned C., "A Generalized Cash Flow Approach to Short-Term Financial Decisions," *Journal of Finance*, 38 (May 1983), pp. 349-360.

Smith, Keith V., *Readings on the Management of Working Capital*, 2nd Ed., New York: West Publishing Company, 1980.

———, *Guide to Working Capital Management*, New York: McGraw-Hill, 1975.

Stancill, James M., *The Management of Working Capital*, Scranton, Pa.: Intext Educational Publishers, 1971.

Tinsley, P. A., "Capital Structure, Precautionary Balances, and Valuation of the Firm: The Problem of Financial Risk," *Journal of Financial and Quantitative Analysis*, 5 (March 1970), pp. 33-62.

Walker, Ernest W., "Towards a Theory of Working Capital," *Engineering Economist*, 9 (January-February 1964), pp. 21-35.

Yardini, Edward E., "A Portfolio-Balance Model of Corporate Working Capital," *Journal of Finance*, 33 (May 1978), pp. 535-552.

Chapter 12 Cash and Marketable Securities Management

Cash management has taken on increased importance in recent years as the relatively high level of interest rates on short-term investments has raised the opportunity cost of holding cash balances. Financial managers, therefore, have developed and refined techniques of cash collection and disbursement to try to optimize the availability of funds and to reduce the interest costs of outside financing.

Closely allied with the cash management function is the management of marketable securities, the portfolio of highly liquid, near-cash assets which serves as a backup to the cash account.

Computerization has increased the sophistication of the techniques employed. In addition to access to large-scale computer systems, many financial managers use desk-top personal computers (PC's) with the capabilities of continuously accessing information on financial markets as well as on internal developments of the firm. We shall seek to emphasize the concepts that guide the use of modern developments in information management.

Cash and Marketable Securities Management

Several issues are involved in the management of the firm's liquidity position. One is to develop efficient systems for the management of cash inflows and cash outflows. Efficient cash-gathering and disbursal has become a major area of managerial finance. So many high-level corporate executives are involved and so many conceptual issues are raised that important institutional developments in cash management have taken place. Because the developments in this field are so rapid and the literature has become so substantial, our treatment of the subject will be streamlined to focus on a more generalized framework for approaching the subject. The treatment of more specific techniques and procedures would rapidly become obsolete.

Why Hold Cash and Marketable Securities?

Cash and marketable securities are discussed together because marketable securities can be quickly converted into cash with only small transactions costs and hence can be regarded as a form of backup cash. When we refer to cash itself, we are using cash in the broad sense of demand deposits and money market accounts as well as currency holdings (of the "green stuff"). Business firms, like individuals, now hold their "cash" mostly in the form of some kind of an account that earns interest in a financial institution.

Since investments in cash and marketable securities represent assets with less risk than product or project investments, they may be expected to have returns less than the weighted average returns on all of the assets of a firm. We would expect investments in marketable securities to cover their proportionate cost of capital in relation to the liquidity function that they perform for the firm. In general, given the highly competitive and efficient nature of the financial markets, we would not expect that investments in marketable securities would be positive NPV investments. It is the investment in projects that hopefully will earn positive NPV's and thereby increase the value of the firm.

Businesses and individuals have four primary motives for holding cash and cash backup in the form of marketable securities: (1) the transactions motive, (2) the precautionary motive, (3) to meet future needs, and (4) compensating balance requirements.

Transactions Motive.   The principal motive for holding cash is to enable the firm to conduct its ordinary business — making purchases and sales. In lines of business where billings are predictable (such as the utilities), cash inflows can be scheduled and synchronized with the need for the cash outflows. We expect the cash-to-revenues ratio and cash-to-total-assets ratio for such firms to be relatively low. In retail trade, by contrast, sales are more random, and a number of transactions may actually be conducted with physical currency. A number of large transactions may occur unexpectedly, creating a surge in cash flows. As a consequence, retail trade requires a higher ratio of cash-to-sales and of cash-to-total assets.

The seasonality of a business may give rise to a need for cash to purchase inventories. For example, raw materials may be available only during a harvest season and may be perishable, as in the food-canning business. Or sales may be seasonal, as they are in department stores (with the peaks around the Christmas and Easter holidays), giving rise to an increase in cash needs during the busy periods.

Precautionary Motive.   The precautionary motive for holding safety stocks of cash relates primarily to the predictability of cash inflows and outflows. If the predictability is high, less cash need be held against an emergency or any other contingency. Another factor that strongly influences the precautionary motive is the ability to borrow additional cash on short notice. Borrowing flexibility is primarily a matter of the strength of the firm's relationships with banking institutions and other credit sources. The need for holding cash is satisfied in large part by having near-money assets, such as short-term government securities.

Future Needs.   The firm's cash and marketable securities accounts may rise to rather sizable levels on a temporary basis as funds are accumulated to meet specific future needs. For example, at the end of 1977, IBM held $252 million in cash and $5.2 billion in marketable securities. Combined, these items represented 38.9 percent of IBM's year-end total assets of $14.0 billion. Whenever IBM introduces a new computer development, the cash requirements are quite substantial, since the total investment and production costs will be recovered over several years in monthly rental receipts. By the end of 1982, IBM's total assets had risen to over $32 billion, representing 232 percent of its 1977 total assets. But cash plus marketable securities had fallen to $3.3 billion, representing only 10 percent of total assets.

Compensating Balance Requirements.   The commercial banking system performs many functions for business firms. Business firms pay for these services in part by direct fees and sometimes in part by maintaining compensating balances at the bank. Compensating balances represent the minimum levels that the firm agrees to maintain in its checking account with the bank. With this assurance, the bank can loan such funds on a longer basis, earning a return, which is an indirect fee to the bank. This represents an institutional reason why a firm holds cash.

A firm holds cash and marketable securities primarily for transactions purposes. Additional holdings for precautionary purposes and to meet future needs represent in concept a type of a safety stock. With respect to the precautionary motive, the safety stock holdings relate primarily to the fact that cash inflows and cash outflows cannot be predicted perfectly. Holding cash for future needs represents another type of safety stock motive, so that, temporarily less favorable conditions in the money and capital markets will not delay or increase the cost of an otherwise favorable positive NPV investment opportunity.

Thus, decisions with regard to holding cash and marketable securities require careful analysis in order to approach optimal holdings. To hold an inadequate amount of cash and marketable securities may interrupt the normal operations of a business. An inadequate safety stock may cause the embarrassment of having inadequate funds to meet emergencies or to seize favorable opportunities. But, the dangers of having inadequate cash are not solved by holding excess amounts of cash and marketable securities. Excess conservatism has disadvantages, although they may be different from those associated with excess aggressiveness. If the amount of cash and marketable securities held is either inadequate or excessive, this area of financial management is not being handled in an optimal fashion. Thus, a number of important functions are involved in cash and marketable securities management. One is effective design and management of cash inflows and outflows. Second, cash and marketable securities should be held in amounts that are close to an optimal level. Third, cash and marketable securities should be placed in the proper institutions and in the proper forms of securities.

Specific Advantages of Adequate Cash

In addition to these general motives, sound working capital management requires maintenance of an ample amount of cash for several other specific reasons.

1. It is essential that the firm have sufficient cash to take trade discounts. The payment schedule for purchases is referred to as the *term of the sale*. A commonly encountered billing procedure, or *term of trade*, is that of a 2 percent discount on a bill paid within 10 days, with full payment required in 30 days, if the discount is not taken. (This is usually stated as 2/10, net 30.) Since the net amount is due in 30 days, failure to take the discount means paying the extra 2 percent for using the money an additional 20 days. The following equation can be used for calculating the cost, on an annual basis, of not taking discounts:

$$\text{Cost} = \frac{\text{Discount } \%}{(100 - \text{Discount } \%)} \times \frac{365}{(\text{Final due date} - \text{Discount period})}.$$

The denominator in the first term (100 − Discount percent) equals the funds made available by not taking the discount. To illustrate, the cost of not taking a discount and paying on the 30th day when the terms are 2/10, net 30 is computed:

$$\text{Cost} = \frac{2}{98} \times \frac{365}{20} = 0.0204 \times 18.25 = 37.23\% = \text{Calculated cost.}$$

We then determine the APR or effective interest rate:

$$\text{APR} = r_e = \left(1 + \frac{.3723}{18.25}\right)^{18.25} - 1 = 44.56\%.$$

This represents an annual effective interest rate of about 45 percent. Most firms' cost of capital is substantially lower than 45 percent, so they should borrow funds, if necessary, to take the discount when the implicit interest rates in foregoing cash discounts are this high.

2. Since the current and acid test ratios are key items in credit analysis, it is essential that the firm, in order to maintain its credit standing, meet the standards of the line of business in which it is engaged. A strong credit standing enables the firm to purchase goods from trade suppliers on favorable terms and to maintain its line of credit with banks and other sources of credit.

3. Ample cash is useful for taking advantage of favorable business opportunities that may come along from time to time, such as special cash offers.

4. The firm should have sufficient liquidity to meet emergencies, such as strikes, fires, or marketing campaigns of competitors.

Financial managers may be able to improve the inflow-outflow pattern of cash. They can do so by better synchronization of flows and by reduction of float, explained in the following sections.

Sources of Float

Whenever a customer mails a check, some amount of time passes before the check is received by the seller. This is called *mail-time float*. After the firm receives the check, processing time is involved in crediting the customer's account and in getting the check into the banking system. This kind of time lag is called *processing float*. A third type of lag, related to the clearing time within the banking system, is called *transit float*. The seller's bank may use the Federal Reserve System or a local clearinghouse for clearing its checks. The banks and clearinghouse mechanisms involved may have an availability schedule for checks involving specified distances, and so forth. The time required by the system to communicate the information needed to clear the checks may be longer or shorter than the availability schedule. Thus, *availability time* may differ from *clear time*.

Considerable progress has been made by business firms and the banking system in an attempt to manage the clearing process efficiently. The development of an efficient cash mobilization system requires decisions with respect to (1) collection points, (2) bank-gathering systems, and (3) alternative methods of transferring funds.

If a firm makes sales to distant cities, mail float alone can be as much as three or four days. This can be reduced by setting up collection points and banking relationships in the areas where sales are made.

Since the firm is likely to have field sales offices in the major regions in which it sells, it can provide for direct collection by these units. As payments are received by the field office, they are recorded and deposited in a local bank (a field depository bank). Since the local offices are close to the customer, mail-time float is reduced.

A *lockbox system* can significantly reduce all types of float.[1] A firm will set up a lockbox arrangement in a city (or cities) corresponding to the geographic distribution of its customers. Customers are directed to mail payments to the lockbox (a post office box) administered by a local bank which collects checks from the box, sometimes several times a day, and deposits the checks to the firm's account. The bank begins the clearing process and

---

[1]The analytics of designing a lockbox system have become quite sophisticated. See, for example, the August 1981 issue of *Management Science*, which carries three articles on the subject by Nauss and Markland, by Stone, and by Fielitz and Fennell.

notifies the firm that a check has been received, reducing processing float. The bank charges the receiving firm for the services rendered. To determine whether a lockbox system is advantageous, the firm will compare the bank fees (including compensating balances) against the gains from reducing float. A rule of thumb in estimating potential lockbox savings is that for every $1 million in annual sales, accelerating the collection time by one-quarter of a day results in $1,000 in savings. Thus, the savings can be of significant magnitude.[2]

Cash-Gathering System

Several categories of banks are used when a firm gathers cash. The general relationships are illustrated in Figure 12.1 for local depository banks, regional concentration banks, and a central bank. *Local depository banks* are those into which field collections are channeled. They are not necessarily limited to cities in which the firm has sales offices. A *regional*

Figure 12.1   Cash-Gathering System of a National Company

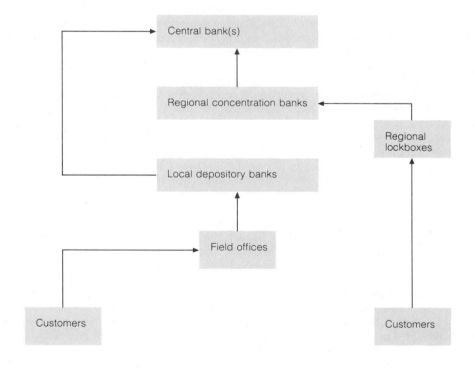

[2]See Ferguson [1983].

concentration bank is one to which a firm seeks to channel funds to have them available for disbursements. Firms usually maintain a major disbursing account at such a bank. As illustrated in Figure 12.1, the regional concentration banks are part of the *concentration banking system* of the firm. Figure 12.1 also indicates that the regional concentration banks usually also handle a lockbox arrangement. Since a lockbox system uses data processing, check handling, and other banking services with substantial fixed costs and other expenses, there will be fewer regional concentration banks than local depository banks.

The concentration banking system developed by the firm seeks to mobilize its funds as efficiently as possible. In addition to a cash-gathering system, the firm needs to work out some policies and decision rules for the rapid transfer of funds. These rules are considered next.

Transfer Mechanisms

A *transfer mechanism* is a system for moving funds between accounts at different banks. The three main transfer mechanisms are

1. Depository transfer checks (DTC)
2. Electronic depository transfer checks (EDTC)
3. Wire transfers

A *depository transfer check (DTC)* is a check restricted for deposit at a particular bank. Except for the deposit-only restriction, a DTC is an ordinary check. DTC's provide a means for moving funds from local depository banks into concentration banks. A DTC is payable only to the bank of deposit for credit to the firm's specific account. In a mail-based initiation procedure, the local office or a company's field unit prepares the DTC and mails it with the deposit slip to a regional concentration bank, which is often a "lockbox bank." (This bank will subsequently transfer the funds to the central bank along with other checks received at the lockbox.) The concentration bank credits the funds to the firm's account, placing the check into the clearing process. While this process is automatic in that no action is required by the firm's cash managers, funds availability is limited by postal and clearing times. DTC's may also be initiated by central company management in response to deposit reports from local offices and/or lockbox banks, or on a pre-arranged schedule.

An *electronic DTC (EDTC)* is a paperless electronic image transfer via the Automated Clearinghouse (ACH) network developed by the Federal Reserve System. The EDTC avoids the use of the mails and has a uniform one-business-day clearing time. EDTC's are generally initiated by central company management.

Wire transfer of funds between banks makes funds collected at one bank immediately available for use at another bank, even in a different city. It is the fastest way to move cash between banks, eliminating transit float. The bank wire method is a private wire service used and supported by about 300 banks in the United States. They use the bank wire system for transferring funds, exchanging credit information, and making securities transactions. The Federal Reserve wire system can be used by commercial banks that are members of the Federal Reserve System. However, commercial banks not on the bank wire or not members of the Federal Reserve System can obtain access to the wire transfer system through their correspondent banks.

Wire transfers are typically initiated on a standing order basis. Company headquarters will make a written authorization to a local depository bank to transfer funds to the firm's concentration bank when the amount exceeds some target level, such as $80,000. The use of standing instructions to transfer funds can be an effective way of managing complex cash-gathering systems, avoiding the need for daily communication with distant locations.

An efficient cash management system must consider the timing and amount of cash transfers which will minimize costs while conforming to bank balance requirements and company policy. The majority of companies (80 percent of the largest 1,200 industrial firms) simply make daily transfers of each day's reported deposits, leaving a minimum required balance in the account.[3] Other firms use simple rules of thumb, for example, the anticipation of deposits, so that the firm reduces float by initiating the transfer before being notified that deposits have been made; firms also take advantage of week-end timing and another form of float termed "dual balance." *Dual balance* refers to the balances resulting when the DTC clearing time is longer than the availability time specified. Dual balances involve only DTC's, since both wires and EDTC's have the same clear time and availability time. For example, availability time at the concentration bank may be one business day, while the actual DTC clearing time back to the depository bank upon which the DTC is written is *two* business days. Thus, a $15,000 DTC deposited in the concentration bank on Tuesday would result in a $15,000 available balance addition at the concentration bank on Wednesday, but with $15,000 still not charged at the depository bank until Thursday. Thus, the same $15,000 is an available balance in both the concentration bank and the depository bank on Wednesday — hence the term *dual balance*.

Comparing the Costs of Alternative Transfer Mechanisms

The use of a wire transfer is the quickest transfer mechanism but the most expensive. There is no delay on a wire transfer, but the typical cost range is $6 to $8. A mail depository transfer check (DTC) may cost only 40 to 50 cents but may involve delays from two to seven days. An evaluation of the alternatives has conventionally involved a comparison of the value of the extra interest from the faster transfer related to the extra cost involved. The conventional cost comparisons are giving way to newer, more sophisticated programming techniques.[4] The conventional formula for the breakeven transfer size is as follows:

$$S^* = \Delta COST/r\Delta T, \tag{12.1}$$

where

$\quad S^* =$ the breakeven size of transfer above which the faster, higher cost mechanism is preferred
$\Delta COST =$ the incremental cost of the faster mechanism
$\quad r =$ the applicable daily interest rate
$\quad \Delta T =$ the difference in transfer time in days

If the cost difference between a wire and a DTC is $6, with a time difference of two days and an interest value of funds at the concentration bank of 0.03 percent per day, the

---

[3]See Stone and Hill [1980].

[4]This discussion is based on Stone and Hill [1980].

breakeven transfer size would be

$$S^* = \frac{\$6.00}{.0003(2)} = \$10,000. \tag{12.2}$$

Thus, on amounts above $10,000, a wire transfer would be used. If the time saved is only one day, the breakeven size is $20,000.

Stone and Hill criticize the above conventional procedure on a number of grounds.[5] They argue that the conventional breakeven analysis assumes no value for funds in the depository bank. They observe that compensating balances are recognized by banks in assigning "service credits" to the firm in the bank's analysis of the profitability of the account and the need to make service charges to the company. Hence, it is argued that the opportunity costs of not having funds in the concentration bank is not the full interest rate but rather the *difference* between the interest rate and the earnings credit rate at the depository bank.

A number of other considerations must be taken into account in evaluating the cost/benefit tradeoffs of alternative transfer systems. The benefit of one system over another may be small relative to the cost of disrupting existing relationships. These different tradeoffs, plus the service credits earned by leaving some funds in the gathering system as compensating balances, result in the use of a variety of transfer mechanisms under different circumstances. Systematic decision models are under development, but the judgment of the financial manager still plays a key role.

Managing Disbursements

Just as expediting the collection process conserves cash, slowing disbursements accomplishes the same thing by keeping cash on hand for longer periods. An obvious way to do this is simply to delay payments, but this involves equally obvious difficulties. Firms have, in the past, devised rather ingenious methods for "legitimately" lengthening the collection period on their own checks, ranging from maintaining disbursement accounts in remote banks to using slow, awkward payment procedures. Since such practices are usually recognized for what they are, their use should be severely limited.

One procedure for delaying disbursements is the use of drafts. While a check is written by the payer and, once written, payable on demand, a draft is, in theory, drawn by the recipient. It is submitted to the payer who must approve it and deposit funds to cover it. Only then can it be collected.

AT&T has used drafts in the following way: In handling its payrolls, for instance, AT&T can pay an employee by draft on Friday. The employee cashes the draft at his local bank, which sends it on to AT&T's New York bank. It may be Wednesday or Thursday before the draft arrives. The bank then sends it to the company's accounting department, which has until 3 P.M. that day to inspect and approve it. Not until then does AT&T deposit funds in its bank to pay the draft.[6] Insurance companies also use drafts to pay claims.

---

[5]Stone and Hill [1980], pp. 46–57.

[6]"More Firms Substitute Drafts for Checks to Pay, Collect Bills," *Wall Street Journal*, August 29, 1971.

Using Float

Checks written by firms (or individuals) are not deducted from bank records until they are actually received by the bank, possibly a matter of several days. The lag between the time the check is written until the time the bank receives it is also known as *float*.

Some firms are able to exploit float to create what is effectively an interest-free loan. For example, a firm with only a moderate balance in its business checking account (which does not pay interest) and $100,000 in its savings account may write a check for $100,000, knowing that it will not clear for six or seven days. After six days, it can move the $100,000 from the savings account to the checking account so the check will be covered. In the meantime, six days of interest will have been earned on the savings account. This is the gain from float.

In reality, the problem is more complex. The check-writing firm in the illustration also receives checks, which it deposits in its savings account. Historically, banks have considered these deposits to be available to the company when they are deposited. If the firm is slow to deposit such checks, float is reduced.

Suppose a firm writes checks totaling about $5,000 each day. It takes about six or seven days for these checks to clear and to be deducted from the firm's bank account. Thus, the firm's own checking records show a balance $30,000 less than that shown by the bank's records. If the firm receives checks in the amount of $5,000 daily and loses only four days while these checks are being deposited, its own books show a balance that is $20,000 larger than the bank's balance. Thus, the firm's float — the difference between the $30,000 and the $20,000 — is $10,000.

Bank Charge Analysis

In the past, banks have compensated for funds lost through float by raising prices of other services, which are paid for by all customers. They have, for example, offset float costs by higher interest rates on loans or higher service charges. Thus, other customers of the bank bore part of the cost if a firm used float successfully. Clearly, this was not desirable for either the bank or the other customers, and efforts to reduce the gains from using float have intensified in recent years.

One method banks would like to employ to reduce these gains is the electronic funds transfer system. EFTS, as it is called, would create a nation-wide computer network that would substantially reduce float time. It presently takes several days to clear checks across the country. Under EFTS, the time could be reduced to hours or even minutes. As yet, no nation-wide system exists, but developments in that direction are moving rapidly.

In addition to reducing the actual time it takes to clear a check, banks are attempting to more accurately match costs and revenues on individual accounts. One effect of this matching is a further reduction in the gains from using float. Table 12.1 depicts a typical commercial checking account service charge analysis. In the earnings credit section, the customer is credited for the average collected balance at the interest rate of 5 percent. The collected balance is the daily balance adjusted for the typical time it takes for the bank to collect on checks deposited. Thus, the estimated days of float will be low for a business dealing mostly with local customers and high for a business that receives payments from out-of-state customers. In this way, the individual firm bears the cost of float directly. The expense part of the analysis is straightforward. In reality, there are many more expense

Table 12.1   State National Bank Commercial Service Charge Analysis
Mail Order Supply Company, September 1983

Earnings Credit

1. Days in month	31	
2. Less average days float	6	
3. Basis for earnings credit	25	
4. Average daily balance	$21,300.00	
5. Daily rate factor (@ 5%)	0.000139	
6. Earnings credit (3 × 4 × 5)		$74.02

Service Debits

7. 20 deposits (@ $.25 each)	$ 5.00	
8. 3,200 checks deposited (@ $.02 each)	64.00	
9. 200 checks written (@ $.08 each)	16.00	
10. Total service debits (7 + 8 + 9)		85.00
Service charge (10 − 6)		$10.98

classifications than the few itemized here—among them lockbox charges, computer service billings, and required compensating balances. In Table 12.1, the service charge to the firm is $10.98 after allowing for the earnings credit.

Cost of Cash Management

We have described a number of procedures that can be used to hold down cash balance requirements.[7] Implementing these procedures, however, is not a costless operation. How far should a firm go in making its cash operations more efficient? As a general rule, a firm should incur these expenses so long as its marginal returns exceed its marginal expenses.

For example, suppose that by establishing a lockbox system and increasing the accuracy of cash inflow and outflow forecasts, a firm can reduce its investment in cash by $1.2 million. Further suppose that the firm borrows at an effective rate of 10 percent.[8] The steps taken release $1.2 million, and the cost of capital required to carry this $1.2 million investment in cash is $120,000. If the costs of the procedures necessary to release the $1.2 million are less than $120,000, the move is a good one; if the costs exceed $120,000, the greater efficiency is not worth the cost. It is clear that larger firms, with larger cash balances, can better afford to hire the personnel necessary to maintain tight control over their cash positions. Cash management is one element of business operations in which economies of scale are clearly present. In sum, the value of careful cash management depends on the cost of funds invested in cash, which, in turn, depends on the current rate of interest. Since the 1970s, with interest rates rising to historic highs in 1982, firms began devoting more care than ever to cash management.

[7]We are abstracting from the security aspects of cash management — the prevention of fraud and embezzlement. These topics are better covered in accounting than in finance courses.

[8]The borrowing rate, 10 percent, is used rather than the firm's average cost of capital, because cash is a less risky investment than the firm's average assets. Notice also that before-tax figures are used here; the analysis can employ either before-tax or after-tax figures so long as consistency is maintained.

Marketable Securities

Firms sometimes report sizable amounts of short-term marketable securities such as Treasury bills or bank certificates of deposit among their current assets. Why are marketable securities held? The two primary reasons — the need for a substitute for cash and the need for a temporary investment — are considered in this section.

Substitute for Cash

Some firms hold portfolios of marketable securities in lieu of large cash balances, liquidating part of the portfolio to increase the cash account when cash outflows exceed inflows. Data are not available to indicate the extent of this practice, but our impression is that it is not common. Most firms prefer to let their banks maintain such liquid reserves, and they borrow to meet temporary cash shortages.

Temporary Investment

In addition to using marketable securities as a buffer against cash shortages, firms also hold them on a strictly temporary basis. Firms engaged in seasonal operations, for example, frequently have surplus cash flows during a part of the year and deficit cash flows the rest of the time. (Recall the cash budgeting illustration in Chapter 9.) Such firms may purchase marketable securities during their surplus periods and then liquidate them when cash deficits occur. Other firms, particularly those in capital goods industries, where fluctuations are violent, attempt to accumulate cash or near-cash securities during a downturn in volume in order to be ready to finance an upturn.

Firms also accumulate liquid assets to meet predictable financial requirements. For example, if a major modernization program is planned for the near future, or if a bond issue is about to mature, the marketable securities portfolio may be increased to provide the required funds. Marketable securities holdings are also frequently increased immediately before quarterly corporate tax payments are due.

Some firms accumulate resources as a protection against a number of contingencies. When they make uninsurable product warranties, for example, companies must be ready to meet any claims that may arise. Firms in highly competitive industries must have resources to carry them through substantial shifts in the market structure. And firms in an industry in which new markets are emerging — for example, foreign markets — need to have resources to meet developments. These funds may be on hand for fairly long periods.

Criteria for Selecting Securities

The applicable criteria for selection among the wide range of securities available include (1) financial risk, (2) interest rate risk, (3) purchasing power risk, (4) liquidity or marketability, (5) taxability, and (6) relative yields. Each will be considered in turn.

Financial Risk. The greater the degree to which the price and returns of a security fluctuate, the greater is the financial risk. Many factors may influence the size and frequency of a security's price changes, but the greater the fluctuations, the greater is the risk that a loss may be incurred. In the extreme, the most serious unfavorable event is that the issuer cannot meet interest payments or principal payments — the risk of default. U.S. government securities do not carry the risk of default and, therefore, are considered "safer" than other securities. Bonds issued by state and local governments, as well as corporate securities, are considered to be subject to some degree of default risk. Rating agencies such as Moody's Investors Service and the Standard & Poor's Corporation assign quality ratings to securities. Among the factors influencing a security's rating is the degree of likelihood that default may occur. These quality assessments can and do change with time. For many years, the securities of utility companies were regarded as of the highest quality with minimum risk of default. In recent years, however, utility securities have been downgraded to lower quality ratings.

Interest Rate Risk.   Changes in the general level of interest rates will cause the prices of securities to fluctuate. This is especially true of such securities as notes or bonds, which carry a fixed rate of interest. In general, the shorter the maturity of a debt instrument, the smaller is the size of fluctuations in its price. A partial exception to this generalization should be noted. For bonds selling at 20 to 30 percent below maturity value with maturities of less than 30 years, the degree of fluctuation in their prices reaches a maximum around a maturity of about 15 to 18 years and then declines with longer maturities.[9]

In general, long-term bonds are riskier than short-term securities for a firm's marketable securities portfolio. However, partly because of this risk differential, higher yields are more frequently available on long-term than on short-term securities.

Given the motives most firms have for holding marketable securities portfolios, it is generally not feasible for them to be exposed to a high degree of risk from interest rate fluctuations. Accordingly, firms usually confine their portfolios to securities with short maturities. Only if the securities are expected to be held for a long period and not be subject to forced liquidation on short notice will long-term securities be chosen. Additional protection from interest rate fluctuations is provided by the use of the interest rate futures markets described in the Appendix to Chapter 7.

Purchasing Power Risk.   Changes in general price levels will affect the purchasing power of both the principal and the income from investments in securities. The total return from a security is measured by the capital gain or loss plus the income yield. Varied relationships have developed for different types of assets during the prolonged inflation since the late 1960s in the United States. Bonds with fixed dollar amounts of income and a fixed dollar amount at maturity have declined in value as inflation has caused interest rate levels to rise. But common stocks whose dividends theoretically are not fixed in amount have also declined in value because the underlying earning power of corporations appears to have been impaired during the persistent inflation. Commodities such as gold and diamonds have risen in value even though they pay no interest or other forms of income. Real estate is a hybrid case in that rentals have not risen as fast as the general price level, but the values of homes and commercial properties have outpaced the rise in the general price level.

Liquidity or Marketability Risk.   The potential decline from a security's quoted market price when the security is sold is its liquidity or marketability risk. Liquidity risk is related to the breadth or thinness of the market for a security. U.S. Treasury bonds or AT&T securities will be more widely held and have greater liquidity than the securities of the Podunk Printing Company.

---

[9]For the mathematics and reasons for this result, see Hsia and Weston [1981].

Taxability.   The tax position of a firm's marketable securities portfolio is influenced by the overall tax position of a firm. A firm with prior years' losses to carry forward can ignore taxability. A firm that pays the full 46 percent marginal corporate tax rate must take taxability into account. The market yields on a security will reflect the total demand and supply of tax influences. Yet, the position of the individual firm may be different from the overall pattern. To the extent that a firm may have a need for tax protection different from the overall pattern of the market, it might find that taxability considerations are either favorable or unfavorable. A number of kinds of securities, such as the bonds of state and local governments, have varying degrees of tax exemption. In addition, securities that sell at a discount offer opportunities for taking returns in the form of capital gains rather than ordinary income.

Returns on Securities.   The higher the risk, the higher is the required return. Thus, in building a marketable securities portfolio, corporate treasurers must evaluate the risk-return tradeoffs. Since the motive for holding marketable securities is protection against uncertain and fluctuating inflows and outflows, the dominant policy is to choose relatively less risky alternatives at the sacrifice of some return. Accordingly, corporate treasurers will emphasize relatively short-term, highly liquid assets in constructing the marketable securities portfolio.

Investment Alternatives

The main kinds of investments meeting the objectives just set forth are listed in Table 12.2. These represent the highly liquid, short-term securities issued by the U.S. government and by the very strongest domestic and foreign banks and other business corporations.

   The financial manager decides on a suitable maturity pattern for the holdings on the basis of how long the funds are to be held. The numerous alternatives can be selected and balanced in such a way that maturities and risks appropriate to the financial situation of the firm are obtained. Commercial bankers, investment bankers, and brokers provide the financial manager with detailed information on each of the forms of investment listed. The yields on these marketable securities change with shifts in financial market conditions. The financial manager should keep up to date on these characteristics and follow the principle of making investment selections that offer maturities, yields, and risks appropriate to the firm.

The Price of Securities Quoted on a Discount Basis

Some securities are quoted on a discount basis. The relation between the discount and price can be illustrated using U.S. Treasury bills with maturities of less than one year. The computation is based on the actual number of days to maturity, using 360 days per year.[10] The following expressions are used to compute the discount basis and dollar price:

$$D = \frac{M}{360} B,$$

$$P = \$100 - D,$$

---

[10]The number of days in the year used in interest rate calculations varies in different applications. The number 360 had been widely used for many years. For some uses, 365 has begun to be assumed. But the established practice for calculations related to Treasury bills is still 360 days.

Table 12.2   Alternative Marketable Securities for Investment

---

Treasury bills (T-bills)	Obligations of the U.S. government. Exempt from state and local income taxes.
U.S. Treasury notes and bonds	Original maturities of more than one year, but maturing issues have high liquidity. Also exempt from state and local income taxes.
Federal agency issues	Notes issued by corporations and agencies created by the U.S. government.
Short-term tax exempts	Notes issued by states, municipalities, local housing agencies, and urban renewal agencies. Exempt from state and local taxes and from the federal income tax.
Commercial paper	Unsecured notes issued by finance companies, bank holding companies, and industrial firms.
Bonds of domestic and foreign corporations (highest grade)	Original maturities of more than one year, but issues near maturity behave similarly to short-term instruments.
Negotiable certificates of deposits (CD's)	Receipts for time deposits at commercial banks that can be sold before maturity.
Bankers' acceptances	Time drafts (or orders to pay) issued by a business firm (usually an importer) that have been accepted by a bank which guarantees payment.
Eurodollars	Dollar-denominated time deposits at overseas banks.
Repurchase agreements (repos)	Sale of government securities by a bank or securities dealer with a simultaneous agreement to repurchase.
Money market mutual funds	Investment companies whose portfolios are limited to short-term money-market instruments.

Note: The marketable securities listed on this table are illustrative of a much larger range of available alternatives. For a more complete listing, including prices and yields, see, for example, Salomon Brothers, "Bond Market Roundup" and "International Bond Market Roundup," each published weekly.

where

$D =$ full discount
$M =$ days to maturity
$B =$ discount basis in percent
$P =$ dollar price

For example, calculate the dollar price for a Treasury bill due in 275 days on an 8 percent discount basis.

$$D = \frac{275}{360} \times 8\%$$

$$= 6.111\%.$$

$$P = \$100 - D$$

$$= \$100 - \$6.111.$$

$$= \$93.889 \text{ (the dollar price on an 8\% discount basis).}$$

Note that the price is greater than simply deducting the 8 percent discount factor from $100. Income from Treasury bills is subject to all federal taxes. The difference between the purchase price and the sale price or maturity value is treated as ordinary income, not a capital gain or loss.

Effects of Inflation

Inflation devalues money, making the careful investment of cash essential to the health of the firm. An improved cash management system keeps track of idle cash; but once this cash has been found, it can act as a hedge against inflation only if it is invested appropriately. During periods of tight money, neither small nor large firms can be confident of receiving bank loans to meet cash shortages. Therefore, it is imperative for them to keep cash reserves for future contingencies.

To protect these cash reserves against inflation, companies have begun to invest the funds aggressively, seeking higher yields. Idle cash is no longer merely kept in the bank or invested exclusively in Treasury bills. Certificates of deposit, municipal securities, and commercial paper offer higher rates of return and, therefore, are gaining in popularity. Firms are even using foreign instruments. For example, NCR invests in commercial paper, the Euromarket, and both domestic and Japanese certificates of deposit to increase pretax earnings by about $1 million per year. Litton Industries invests part of its portfolio in Swiss franc- and German mark-denominated time deposits and in foreign certificates of deposit. AT&T trades Treasury bills, looking for the best yield, rather than holding them to maturity. Its other investments include commercial paper, bankers' acceptances, certificates of deposit, and overnight repurchase agreements. *Repurchase agreements*, or repos, have a very short maturity of one or a few days.[11] Therefore, they are especially appropriate for investing money for short periods of time while avoiding most types of risks.

An example of the marketable securities portfolio of IBM as of December 31, 1983, is presented in Table 12.3. The largest single investment is in U.S. Treasury securities. It is of interest to note also that $2.314 billion of the marketable security investments were in foreign accounts. These included $290 million in foreign investments denominated in dollars, probably representing mostly Eurodollar deposits.

Cash Management Models

Investment in cash and marketable securities is analogous to investment in inventory. (All asset investments represent an inventory decision to some degree.) First, a basic stock must be on hand to balance inflows and outflows of the items, the size of the stock depending on the patterns of flows, whether regular or irregular. Second, because the unexpected may always occur, it is necessary to have safety stocks on hand, representing the little extra to avoid the costs of not having enough to meet current needs. Third, additional amounts may be required to meet future growth needs; these are called *anticipation stocks*. Related to anticipation stocks is the recognition that there are optimum purchase sizes, defined as *economic ordering quantities*.

---

[11]The repurchase time and price are specified in advance. Thus, the return to the seller and the yield to the buyer are "locked in" with no interest rate fluctuation risk.

Table 12.3   Schedule I: International Business Machines Corporation & Subsidiary Companies
                   December 31, 1983 Marketable Securities (Millions of Dollars)

		Amount Included in Statement of Financial Position
U.S. Treasury securities		$1,745
Other investments — U.S. institutions		202
Government securities and other investments, non-U.S.		659
Non-U.S. time deposits and other bank obligations		
German marks	486	
U.S. dollars	290	
British pounds	267	
Italian lire	240	
Swiss francs	176	
Canadian dollars	165	
Swedish kroner	87	
Dutch guilders	82	
French francs	71	
Austrian schillings	67	
Norwegian kroner	53	
Danish kroner	52	
Belgian francs	48	
Japanese yen	45	
Other currencies	185	
Total non-U.S. bank obligations	2,314	
Total marketable securities		$4,920

Source: 1983 International Business Machines 10-K.

As we will demonstrate in Chapter 13, which develops the basic inventory decision model, there are both rising and falling costs associated with maintaining various levels of stocks or balances (whether of inventory or of any other asset); that is, there are costs associated with both too high and too low a level, and thus there exists some optimal level at which these costs are balanced. In cash management, the basic stock is the minimum cash balance, which may be determined, in part, by bank compensating balance requirements. This cash stock must be sufficient to cover at least the transactions needs of the firm. Inflows come principally from receipts, borrowing, and sales of securities; outflows are represented by cash disbursements. The marketable securities portfolio acts as a reserve, or safety stock, against anticipated (or unanticipated) future needs and opportunities.

The primary cost associated with too high a level of cash is the opportunity cost of having funds tied up in a nonpositive NPV asset. The costs of too low a level of cash include the costs of running short (including the inability to take cash discounts) and the more quantifiable transactions costs associated with borrowing funds or converting marketable securities to cash. Since the opportunity costs rise with holding more cash, and the transactions costs rise with less cash (and thus more frequent transfers from marketable securities to cash), there is some optimal level of cash and size of transfer which minimizes the total cost of cash management.

Several types of mathematical models have been developed to help determine optimal cash balances. An early model developed by Baumol essentially applies a basic inventory model to cash management.[12] In this model, it is assumed that the firm on average is growing and is a net user of cash. Marketable securities represent a buffer stock between episodes of external financing, which is drawn down as required periodically. Ordering costs are represented by the clerical and transactions costs of making transfers between the investment portfolio and the cash account. The holding cost is the interest foregone on cash balances held. Assuming that expenditures occur evenly over time and that cash replenishments come in lump sums at periodic intervals, the optimal size of the cash transfer is formulated as follows:

$$C^* = \sqrt{\frac{2bT}{i}},$$

where

$C^* =$ the optimal size of the cash transfer
$T =$ the total cash usage for the period of time involved
$b =$ the cost of the transaction in the purchase or sale of marketable securities
$i =$ the applicable interest rate on marketable securities

The formula can be illustrated in a specific numerical example. The total demand for cash (T) over the period of time involved (one year) is $1.8 million. The cost per transaction is $25. The applicable interest rate is 10 percent.

Using the data in the formula, we obtain

$$C^* = \sqrt{\frac{2bT}{i}} = \sqrt{\frac{2(\$25)(\$1,800,000)}{.10}} = \$30,000.$$

Having calculated C^*, the optimal amount of cash transfer, the average cash balance for the period will be

$$\frac{C^*}{2} = \frac{\$30,000}{2} = \$15,000.$$

The total number of transactions or transfers required per year can also be readily determined:

$$\frac{\$1,800,000}{\$30,000} = 60, \text{ or somewhat more than one transaction per week.}$$

Finally, the total cost per year of maintaining cash balances can be calculated:

$$TC = b\left(\frac{T}{C}\right) + i\left(\frac{C}{2}\right)$$

$$= \$25(60) + .10(\$15,000) = \$1,500 + \$1,500$$

$$= \$3,000.$$

---

[12]The interested reader is referred to the Appendix to this chapter for a more complete development of the Baumol and other cash management models.

On the basis of the data of the example, the total cost is \$3,000 per year. Under the assumptions of the analysis, this minimizes the costs of managing the inventory of cash.

Estimating the Firm's Daily Cash Balance

The cash management models of the type just described call for transfers from the marketable securities portfolio to the firm's demand deposit accounts (cash) when the firm's cash balances reach predetermined levels. This requires that the firm seek to anticipate the levels of its cash balances on a continuing basis. With the aid of computerization, some firms develop daily cash forecasts [Stone and Miller, 1981]. The procedures for doing this can be outlined. The monthly cash budgets (described in Chapter 9) provide the initial framework. The items in the cash budget can be broken into daily repetitive transactions that can be modeled into patterns of daily inflows and outflows. Weekly, monthly, and seasonal influences can be taken into account. In addition, major outflows and inflows are scheduled. The major scheduled outflows would be taxes, lease payments, debt service obligations, and so forth. The major scheduled inflows would be the maturing of investments, sales of assets, and so on. The timing of major scheduled inflows and outflows can be superimposed on the pattern of repetitive flows.

Taking both repetitive flows and scheduled flows into account permits the formulation of projections of expected daily cash balances. Computerization permits closely tracking the projected balances against the actual daily cash balances. Analysis of the divergences between the two should enable the financial manager to improve the estimating model, to improve cash gathering and cash disbursing practices, and to provide dependable lead times for adjustments of the actual cash balances by transfers into and from the marketable securities portfolio. Here, as in many other aspects of the responsibilities of financial managers, computerization permits a rapid flow of information and prompt adjustments to change. These adjustments call for improvements in policies and procedures and in the refinement of forecasting models.

Summary

Recent high levels of interest rates have increased the importance of cash management, while, at the same time, advances in technology have changed the nature of the cash management function. Financial managers have developed new techniques for optimizing cash balances and determining the appropriate relation between holding cash and holding investments in marketable securities.

The four primary reasons for holding cash are the transactions motive, the precautionary motive, to meet future needs, and to satisfy bank compensating balance requirements. The two major aspects of a cash flow system involve the gathering and disbursement of cash, with the firm's objective to speed collections and legitimately slow disbursements.

Float arises from lags in the payment process (mail, processing, and bank clearing delays). Float is an advantage to the firm as a buyer and a disadvantage to the firm as a seller. An efficient cash-gathering system will focus on reducing negative mail float with decentralized collections and a lockbox system. The use of the lockbox also reduces processing time by starting checks through the bank clearing process before they have been recorded in the firm's accounting system.

A concentration banking system seeks to speed the cash-gathering process by mobilizing funds efficiently through a hierarchy of local depository banks, regional concentration banks, and a central bank. The local depository banks are used to channel field office collections. The concentration banks, which usually handle the lockbox arrangement, channel funds to a major disbursement account. A key element in the selection of concentration banks is their location relative to a firm's customers and to Federal Reserve System check-clearing facilities and their access to the bank wire system to facilitate the transfer of funds to the firm's central bank, where greater control can be exercised over a single cash pool.

The financial manager has a range of mechanisms from which to choose for the rapid transfer of funds and must balance speed against cost. The conventional model for the cost comparison arrives at a breakeven size of transfer (above which a more rapid, more expensive method would be preferred) by comparing the value of the extra interest which would be earned in the central bank with the incremental cost of the faster mechanism. This method has been criticized for failing to consider any other value for the funds than the interest foregone by not transferring them to the central bank. For example, balances left in the concentration banks can earn service credits, reducing the cost to the firm of using the bank's services. Timing considerations further complicate the cost-benefit analysis of transfer mechanisms, and systematic models which reflect these considerations are under development.

With respect to disbursements, several methods can be used to lengthen the payment period. However, banks seek to offset the gains from float; they attempt to charge for their services in such a way that firms bear the cost of the float directly.

Companies' liquidity policies vary with individual circumstances and needs. In selecting the firm's portfolio of marketable securities, the financial manager must consider financial risk, interest rate risk, purchasing power risk, liquidity or marketability, taxability, and relative yields. The securities which have best suited the financial manager's objectives are short-term U.S. government issues, plus those of the very strongest domestic and foreign banks and corporations. The effects of inflation, however, with its rapid devaluation of the purchasing power of idle cash, have led firms to be somewhat more aggressive in their efforts to seek out the highest yielding opportunities for given levels of risk.

The performance of mathematical models designed to determine the optimal cash balance depends on how well the firm's patterns of cash flows conform to the assumptions of the model. The Baumol model applies the EOQ inventory model to cash management (with an assumption of continuous expenditures) to determine the economic quantity of cash to have on hand.

Questions

12.1 How can better methods of communication reduce the necessity for firms to hold large cash balances?

12.2 Discuss this statement: The highly developed financial system of the United States, with its many different near-cash assets, has greatly reduced cash balance requirements by reducing the need for transactions balances.

12.3 Would you expect a firm with a high growth rate to hold more or fewer precautionary and speculative cash balances than a firm with a low growth rate? Explain.

12.4 Many firms that find themselves with temporary surplus cash invest these funds in Treasury bills. Since Treasury bills frequently have the lowest yield of any investment security, why are they chosen as investments?

12.5 Discuss the differences between financial risk and interest rate risk. Which has the greater effect on the selection of marketable securities?

12.6 Explain the possible effects on a firm's cash balance of each of the following factors (other things held constant):

      a)   The level of interest rates rises.
      b)   The cost of trading in marketable securities rises.
      c)   The cost of trading in marketable securities falls.
      d)   Sales forecasts are improved through the use of a more accurate forecasting technique.

12.7 Discuss possible sources of resistance to a concentration banking system instituted in a decentralized firm.

Problems

12.1 Hayes Associates is short on cash and is attempting to determine whether it would be advantageous to forego the discount on this month's purchases or to borrow funds to take advantage of the discount. The discount terms are 2/10, net 45.

      a)   What is the maximum annual interest rate that Hayes Associates should pay on borrowed funds? Why?
      b)   What are some of the intangible disadvantages associated with foregoing the discount?

12.2 Scott, Inc., currently has a centralized billing system located in New York City. However, over the years, its customers gradually have become less concentrated on the East Coast and now cover the entire United States. On average, it requires five days from the time customers mail payments until Scott is able to receive, process, and deposit their payments. To shorten this time, Scott is considering the installation of a lockbox collection system. It estimates that the system will reduce the time lag from customer mailing to deposit by three and one-half days. Scott has a daily average collection of $700,000.

      a)   What reduction in cash balances can Scott achieve by initiating the lockbox system?
      b)   If Scott has an opportunity cost of 8 percent, how much is the lockbox system worth on an annual basis?
      c)   What is the maximum monthly charge Scott can pay for the lockbox system?

12.3 A firm issues checks in the amount of $1 million each day and deducts them from its own records at the close of business on the day they are written. On average, the bank receives and clears the checks (deducts them from the firm's bank balance) the evening of the fourth day after they are written; for example, a check written on Monday will be cleared on Friday afternoon. The firm's loan agreement with the bank requires it to maintain a $750,000 minimum average compensating balance; this is $250,000 greater than the cash safety stock the firm would otherwise have on deposit.

      a)   Assuming that the firm makes its deposit in the late afternoon (and the bank includes the deposit in the day's transactions), how much must the firm deposit each day to maintain a sufficient balance once it reaches a steady state?
      b)   How many days of float does the firm carry?
      c)   What ending daily balance should the firm try to maintain at the bank and on its own records?
      d)   Explain how float can help increase the value of the firm's common stock. Use a partial balance sheet and the du Pont system concept (Chapter 9) in your answer.

12.4   The New York field office of the Metallux Corporation has sold a quantity of silver ingots for $15,000. Metallux wants to transfer this amount to its concentration bank in San Francisco as economically as possible. Two means of transfer are being considered.

   1.   A mail depository transfer check (DTC) costs 50 cents and takes three days.
   2.   A wire transfer costs $7.50 and funds are immediately available in San Francisco.

Metallux earns 14.5 percent annual interest on funds in its concentration bank. Which transfer method should be used?

12.5   Warrior Industries projects that annual cash usage of $3.75 million will occur uniformly throughout the forthcoming year. Warrior plans to meet these demands for cash by periodically selling marketable securities from its portfolio. The firm's marketable securities are invested to earn 12 percent, and the cost per transaction of converting funds to cash is $40.

   a)   Use the Baumol model to determine the optimal transaction size for transfers from marketable securities to cash.
   b)   What will be Warrior's average cash balance?
   c)   How many transfers per year will be required?

Selected References

Batlin, Carl Alan, and Hinko, Susan, "A Game Theoretic Approach to Cash Management," *Journal of Business*, 55 (July 1982), pp. 367-382.

Ferguson, Daniel, "Optimize Your Firm's Lockbox Selection System," *Financial Executive*, (April 1983), p. 19.

Frost, Peter A., "Banking Services, Minimum Cash Balances and the Firm's Demand for Money," *Journal of Finance*, 25 (December 1970), pp. 1029-1039.

Gitman, Lawrence J., and Goodwin, Mark D., "An Assessment of Marketable Securities Management Practices," *Journal of Financial Research*, 2 (Fall 1979), pp. 161-169.

Gitman, Lawrence J.; Moses, Edward A.; and White, Thomas I., "An Assessment of Corporate Cash Management Practices," *Financial Management*, 8 (Spring 1979), pp. 32-42.

Hsia, Chi-Cheng, and Weston, J. Fred, "Price Behavior of Deep Discount Bonds," *Journal of Banking and Finance*, 5 (1981), pp. 357-361.

Journal of Cash Management, see every issue since October 1981.

Lewellen, Wilbur G., "Finance Subsidiaries and Corporate Borrowing Capacity," *Financial Management*, 1 (Spring 1972), pp. 21-32.

Maier, Steven F., and Vander Weide, James H., "What Lockbox and Disbursement Models Really Do," *Journal of Finance*, 38 (May 1983), pp. 361-371.

Punter, Alan, "Optimal Cash Management Under Conditions of Uncertainty," *Journal of Business Finance & Accounting*, 9 (Autumn 1982), pp. 329-340.

Sartoris, William L., and Hill, Ned C., "A Generalized Cash Flow Approach to Short-Term Financial Decisions," *Journal of Finance*, 38 (May 1983), pp. 349-360.

Scott, James H., Jr., "The Tax Effects of Investment in Marketable Securities on Firm Valuation," *Journal of Finance*, 34 (May 1979), pp. 307-324.

Searby, Frederick W., "Cash Management: Helping Meet the Capital Crisis," in *The Treasurer's Handbook*, edited by J. Fred Weston and Maurice Goudzwaard, Homewood Ill.: Dow Jones-Irwin, 1976, pp. 440-456.

Stone, Bernell K., "The Design of a Company's Banking System," *Journal of Finance*, 38 (May 1983), pp. 373-385.

Stone, Bernell K., and Hill, Ned C., "Cash Transfer Scheduling for Efficient Cash Concentration," *Financial Management*, (Autumn 1980), pp. 35-43.

——, "The Evaluation of Alternative Cash Transfer Mechanisms and Methods," *Proceedings of the Nineteenth Annual Meeting of the Southwestern Finance Association*, 1980, pp. 39-58.

Stone, Bernell K., and Miller, Tom W., "Daily Cash Forecasting: A Structuring Framework," *Journal of Cash Management*, 1 (October 1981), pp. 35, 38-50.

Appendix A to Chapter 12[1]
Cash Management Models

Inventory-like models have been constructed to aid the financial manager in determining the firm's optimum cash balances. Three such models—those developed by William J. Baumol, Merton H. Miller and Daniel Orr, and William Beranek—are presented in this appendix.

Baumol Model

The classic article on cash management by Baumol [1952] applies the EOQ model to the cash management problem. Although Baumol's article emphasized the macroeconomic implications for monetary theory, he recognized the implications for business finance and set the stage for further work in this area. In essence, Baumol recognized the fundamental similarities of inventories and cash from a financial viewpoint. In the case of inventories, ordering and stock-out costs make it expensive to keep inventories at a zero level by placing orders for immediate requirements only. But costs are also involved with *holding* inventories, and an optimal policy balances the opposing costs of ordering and holding inventory.

With cash and securities, the situation is very similar. Order costs come in the form of clerical work and brokerage fees in the making of transfers between the cash account and an investment portfolio. On the other side of the coin, there are holding costs, such as interest foregone, when large cash balances are held to avoid the costs of making transfers. Further, costs are associated with running out of cash, just as in the case of inventories. As with inventories, the optimal cash balance minimizes these costs.

In its most operational form, the Baumol model assumes that a firm's cash balances behave, over time, in a sawtooth pattern, as shown in Figure 12A.1. Receipts come in at periodic intervals, such as Time 0, 1, 2, 3, and so forth; expenditures occur continuously throughout the periods. Since the model assumes certainty, the firm can adopt an optimal policy that calls for investing I dollars in a short-term investment portfolio at the beginning of each period and then withdrawing C dollars from the portfolio and placing them in the cash account at regular intervals during the period. The model must, of course, take into account both the costs of investment transactions and the costs of holding cash balances.

The decision variables facing the financial manager for a single period are illustrated in Figure 12A.2. The manager has an amount of cash equal to T for the period's transactions. A portion of the initial cash, $R = T - I$, is retained in the form of cash, and the balance, I, is invested in a portfolio of short-term liquid assets that earns a rate of return, i. The retained cash, R, is sufficient to meet expenditures during the period from t_0 to t_1. An

[1]We would like to acknowledge the assistance of Richard A. Samuelson in the preparation of this appendix.

Figure 12A.1 Baumol's Pattern of Receipts and Expenditures

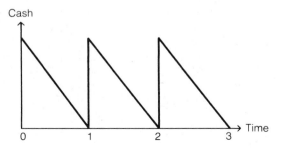

additional C dollars will be transferred from the investment portfolio to the cash account at time t_1 to cover expenditures for the period from t_1 to t_2; C dollars will again be withdrawn at time t_2 and t_3. Receipts of T dollars flow into the cash account again at t_4, and the same process is repeated during the following period.

If the disbursements are assumed to be continuous, then $R = T - I$ dollars withheld from the initial cash receipt will serve to meet payments during a fraction of the period between receipts equal to $(T - I)/T$ times the length of the period. Further, since the average cash holding for that time will be $(T - I)/2$, the interest cost (opportunity cost) of

Figure 12A.2 Baumol's Transfers from Securities to Cash

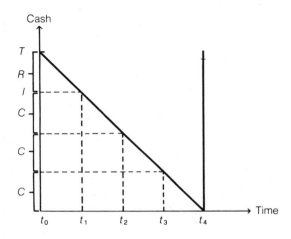

withholding that money will be

$$\left(\frac{T-I}{2}\right)i\left(\frac{T-I}{T}\right),$$

where i is the interest rate on invested funds. Brokerage fees required to invest I dollars will vary with the number of deposits (investments) and with the size of each deposit. The fee per deposit is equal to $b_d + k_dI$, where b_d is the base cost per deposit and k_dI is the component which varies with the size of the deposit. Similarly, b_w and k_wC represent the variable costs of making withdrawals.

The cost of obtaining cash for the remainder of the period is found, similarly, to be

$$\left(\frac{C}{2}\right)i\left(\frac{I}{T}\right) + (b_w + k_wC)\frac{I}{C}.$$

The first term is the interest (opportunity) cost of holding the average amount ($C/2$) of cash over the subperiod, and the second term is the brokerage cost of making withdrawals from the investment account.

Combining these component costs, the total cost function is given by

$$Z = \left(\frac{T-I}{2}\right)i\left(\frac{T-I}{T}\right) + b_d + k_dI + \left(\frac{C}{2}\right)i\left(\frac{I}{T}\right) + (b_w + k_wC)\frac{I}{C}. \qquad \textbf{(12A.1)}$$

The optimal value for C is found by differentiating Equation 12A.1 with respect to C and setting the derivative equal to zero. This gives

$$C = \sqrt{\frac{2b_wT}{i}}. \qquad \textbf{(12A.2)}$$

R, the optimum cash balance to withhold from the initial receipt, is found by differentiating Equation 12A.1 with respect to I, which gives

$$R = T - I = C + T\left(\frac{k_w + k_d}{i}\right). \qquad \textbf{(12A.3)}$$

In order to minimize costs, the financial manager will then withhold R dollars from the initial receipts to cover expenditures for the beginning of the period and will withdraw C dollars from the investment portfolio I/C times per period.

To illustrate the Baumol model, let $T = \$1,200,000$ per year, $b_d = \$10$, $k_d = 0$, $i = 10\%$, $b_w = \$26$, and $k_w = 0$. Using Equation 12A.2, solve for C:

$$C = \sqrt{\frac{2(\$26)(\$1,200,000)}{0.10}} \approx \$25,000.$$

With $T = \$1,200,000$ (or $\$100,000$ per month), and $C = \$25,000$, or an optimum of four cash withdrawals from investments per month. Using Equation 12A.3,

$$R = \$25,000 + \$100,000\left(\frac{0+0}{0.10}\right) = \$25,000.$$

These results illustrate the pattern depicted by Figure 12A.2. Then, using Equation 12A.1:

$$Z = \left(\frac{\$25,000}{2}\right)\left(\frac{0.10}{12}\right)\left(\frac{\$25,000}{\$100,000}\right) + \$10$$

$$+ \left(\frac{\$25,000}{2}\right)\left(\frac{0.10}{12}\right)\left(\frac{\$75,000}{\$100,000}\right) + \$26\left(\frac{\$75,000}{\$25,000}\right)$$

$$= (\$12,500)(0.00833)(0.25) + \$10 + (\$12,500)(0.00833)(0.75) + (\$26)(3)$$

$$= \$26.03 + \$10 + \$78.09 + \$78$$

$$= \$192.12.$$

The financial manager knows all of the items listed as input information but does not know C, R, I, or Z. Using Equation 12A.2, the manager obtains C. Using Equation 12A.3, the manager calculates R, from which I can also be obtained. The manager then has all the information required to calculate Equation 12A.1, which represents Z, the total cost function for cash management when the size of the cash withdrawals, C, from investments is optimal. (R and I will also be optimal.)

While the Baumol model captures the essential elements of the problem, its restrictive assumptions about the behavior of cash inflows and outflows are probably more applicable to an individual than to a business firm. For the firm, inflows are likely to be less lumpy and outflows are likely to be less smooth. Instead, the behavior of cash balances might resemble the pattern of Figure 12A.3. Daily changes in the cash balance may be up or down, following an irregular and somewhat unpredictable pattern. When the balance drifts upward for some length of time, a point is reached at which the financial officer orders a transfer of cash to the investment portfolio, and the cash balance is returned to some lower level. When disbursements exceed receipts for some period of time, investments are sold and a transfer is made to the cash account to restore the cash balance to a higher level. If this particular behavior is typical, then the certainty assumptions of the Baumol model are too restrictive to make it operational.

Figure 12A.3   Realistic Pattern of Receipts and Expenditures for a Firm

Miller-Orr Model

Miller and Orr [1966] expanded the Baumol model by incorporating a stochastic generating process for periodic changes in cash balances so that the cash pattern resembles that shown in Figure 12A.3. In contrast to the completely deterministic assumptions of the Baumol model, Miller and Orr assume that net cash flows behave as if they were generated by a "stationary random walk." This means that changes in the cash balance over a given period are random in both size and direction and that they form a normal distribution as the number of periods observed increases. The model allows for *a priori* knowledge, however, that changes at a certain time have a greater probability of being either positive or negative.[2]

The Miller-Orr model is designed to determine the time and size of transfers between an investment account and the cash account according to a decision process illustrated in Figure 12A.4. Changes in cash balances are allowed to go up until they reach some level h at time t_1; they are then reduced to level z, the *return point*, by investing $(h - z)$ dollars in the investment portfolio. Next, the cash balance wanders aimlessly until it reaches the minimum balance point, r, at t_2. At this time, enough earning assets are sold to return the cash balance to its return point, z. Miller and Orr define t so that $1/t$ is "some small fraction of a working day such as 1/8," or, equivalently, "the number of operating cash transactions per day." We suppose that during any such hour, the cash balance will either increase by m dollars with probability p or decrease by m dollars with probability $q = 1 - p$. Most of their analysis is based on the "special symmetric or zero-drift case in which $p = q = 1/2$." For this special case, the variance of daily changes in the cash balance is equal to $m^2 t$. The model is based on a cost function similar to Baumol's, and it includes elements for the cost of making transfers to and from cash and for the opportunity cost of holding

---

Figure 12A.4 Miller-Orr Cash Management Model

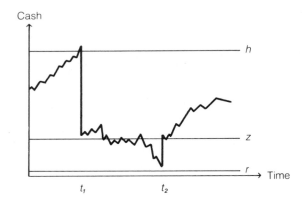

---

[2]See Miller and Orr [1966], pp. 418, 419, 422.

cash. The upper limit, h, which cash balances should not be allowed to surpass, and the return point, z, to which the balance is returned after every transfer either to or from the cash account, are computed so as to minimize the cost function. The lower limit is assumed to be given, and it could be the minimum balance required by the banks in which the cash is deposited.

The cost function for the Miller-Orr model can be stated as $E(c) = bE(N)/T + iE(m)$, where $E(N)$ = the expected number of transfers between cash and the investment portfolio during the planning period; b = the cost per transfer; T = the number of days in the planning period; $E(m)$ = the expected average daily cash balance; and i = the daily rate of interest earned on the investments. The objective is to minimize $E(c)$ by choice of the variables h and z, the upper control limit and the return point, respectively.

The solution as derived by Miller and Orr becomes

$$z^* = \left(\frac{3b\sigma^2}{4i} \right)^{1/3}. \tag{12A.4}$$

The variance of the daily changes in the cash balance is represented by σ^2. As would be expected, a higher transfer cost, b, or variance, σ^2, would imply a greater spread between the upper and lower control limits. For the special case where p (the probability that cash balances will increase) equals 0.5, and q (the probability that cash balances will decrease) equals 0.5 (and $r = 0$), the upper control limit will always be three times greater than the return point, z:

$$h^* = 3z^*. \tag{12A.4a}$$

To illustrate the Miller-Orr model, let $b = \$25$, $m = \$10$, $t = 8$, $i = 20\%$, $r = 0$, and $\sigma^2 = m^2t = 800$. Given Equation 12A.4:

$$z^* = \left[\frac{3(\$25)(800)}{4(0.20/365)} \right]^{1/3} = \left(\frac{\$60,000}{0.0021917808} \right)^{1/3}$$

$$= (\$27,375,000)^{1/3}$$

$$= \$301.38 \approx \$300.$$

$$h^* = 3(\$301.38) = \$904.14 \approx \$900.$$

For $r = 100$, h^* would be $1,000 and z would be $400.

Miller and Orr tested their model by applying it to nine months of data on the daily cash balances and purchases and sales of short-term securities of a large industrial company. When the decisions of the model were compared to those actually made by the treasurer of the company, the model was found to produce an average daily cash balance that was about 40 percent *lower* ($160,000 for the model and $275,000 for the treasurer). Looking at it from another side, the model would have been able to match the $275,000 average daily balance with only 80 transactions, as compared to the treasurer's 112 actual transactions.

As with most inventory control models, the Miller-Orr model's performance depends not only on how well the conditional predictions (in this case, the expected number of transfers and the expected average cash balance) conform to actuality but also on how well the parameters are estimated. In this model, b, the transfer cost, is sometimes difficult to estimate. In Miller and Orr's study, the order costs included such components as "(a) making two or more long-distance phone calls plus 15 minutes to a half-hour of the assistant treasurer's time, (b) typing up and carefully checking an authorization letter with four copies, (c) carrying the original of the letter to be signed by the treasurer, and (d) carrying the copies to the controller's office where special accounts are opened, the entries are posted and further checks of the arithmetic are made."[3] These clerical procedures were thought to be in the magnitude of $20 to $50 per order. In the application of their model, however, Miller and Orr did not rely on their estimate for order costs; instead, they tested the model through the use of a series of "assumed" order costs until the model used the same number of transactions as did the treasurer. They could then determine the order cost implied by the treasurer's own action. The results were then used to evaluate the treasurer's performance in managing the cash balances and so provided valuable information to the treasurer.

The treasurer found, for example, that his action in purchasing securities was often inconsistent. Too often, he made small-lot purchases well below the minimum of $(h - z)$ computed by the model, while, at other times, he allowed cash balances to drift to as much as double the upper control limit before making a purchase. If it did no more than give the treasurer some perspective about his buying and selling activities, the model was used successfully.[4]

Beranek Model

Beranek [1963] devoted a chapter in his text, *Analysis for Financial Decisions*, to the problem of determining the optimal allocation of available funds between the cash balance and marketable securities.[5] His approach differs from Baumol's in that he includes a probability distribution for expected cash flows and a cost function for the loss of cash discounts and deterioration of credit rating when the firm is caught short of cash. The decision variable in Beranek's model is the allocation of funds between cash and investments at the beginning of the period. Withdrawals from investment are assumed to be possible only at the end of each planning period.

According to Beranek, it is more helpful for the analysis of cash management problems to regard cash *disbursements* as being directly controllable by management and relatively lumpy and to regard *receipts* as being uncontrollable and continuous. In the certainty case, this pattern of cash balance behavior would be the reverse of the sawtooth pattern assumed by Baumol, and it would look like the pattern illustrated in Figure 12A.5. In explaining this approach, one can argue that institutional customs and arrangements might cause cash outflows to be concentrated at periodic intervals. Wages and salaries are ordinarily paid weekly or monthly; credit terms for merchandise purchases may allow payment on the tenth and final days of the month; and other significant outflows, such as tax and dividend payments, will be concentrated at regular intervals. Insofar as cash outflows are controllable and recur in a cyclical manner, the financial manager can predict cash needs over a planning period and can invest that portion of the funds that is not expected to be needed during the planning period.

In Beranek's model, the financial manager is regarded as having total resources of k dollars available at the beginning of a planning period. The manager expects the net cash drain (receipts less disbursements) at the end of the period to be y dollars (either positive

[3]Miller and Orr [1967].

[4]For a cash planning approach related to credit decisions by the use of a financial simulation model, see Stone [1973].

[5]Beranek [1963].

Figure 12A.5   Beranek's Pattern of Receipts and Expenditures

---

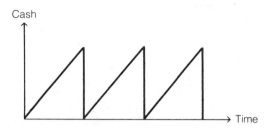

or negative), with a probability distribution $g(y)$. The financial manager's objective of maximizing returns by investment in securities is constrained by transactions costs and the risk of being short of cash when funds are needed for expenditures. Beranek considers that *short costs* consist of cash discounts foregone and the deterioration of the firm's credit rating when it is unable to meet payments in time. It might be more realistic, however, to think of short costs as the cost of borrowing on a line of credit, since the company would undoubtedly prefer short-term borrowing to foregoing cash discounts or allowing its credit rating to deteriorate.

Given the probability distribution of net cash flows, the costs of running short of cash, and the opportunity cost of holding cash balances, Beranek develops a cost function and differentiates it to find the optimal initial cash balance, which is the amount of cash that should be on hand at the start of the period. His solution calls for setting the cash balance at a level such that, once the critical level is set, the cumulative probability of running short of cash is equal to the ratio d/a, where d = net return on the investment portfolio, and a = incremental cost of being short \$1 of cash. This means that the financial manager should continue shifting resources from the opening cash balance to securities until the expectation that the ending cash balance will be below the critical minimum is equal to the ratio of the incremental net return per dollar of investment to the incremental short cost per dollar.

A Comparison of the Models

The models described in this appendix differ primarily in the emphasis given to various costs affecting their solutions. The Baumol and the Miller-Orr models give critical emphasis to the costs arising from transfers between the cash account and the investment portfolio. They ignore the alternative of borrowing and concentrate on the liquidation of investments to meet the needs for cash outflows. The Beranek model, on the other hand, gives critical emphasis to the costs arising from the shortage of cash (the cost of borrowing, from one viewpoint), while transactions costs are only indirectly considered. The latter model ignores the alternatives of liquidating investments to meet cash needs. A model that directly incorporates both the possibility of borrowing and the possibility of holding a portfolio of liquid assets would be desirable, since it is not clear that liquidation of investments would always be preferable to borrowing or vice versa.

Of all the models, the Miller-Orr version appears to be the easiest to implement, if for no other reason than the simplicity of its decision rules. Decision models are more likely to be used when management can easily understand their application. In addition, the Miller-Orr decision model's planning period covers a longer period of time, so it does not have to be revised as often as the Beranek model. The financial manager who uses the Beranek model must feed information into the model and derive a decision each time a transfer between cash and securities is being considered. While this must be counted as a disadvantage of this model, it could result in better decisions by making the model more responsive to conditions existing at the time decisions are made.

The Miller-Orr model has an element of flexibility, moreover, that should not be overlooked. Expectations that cash balances are more likely to either increase or decrease over a given period can be incorporated into the calculation of the optimal values for the decision variables. Thus, if a business is subject to seasonal trends, the optimal control limits can be adjusted for each season by using different values for p and q, the respective probabilities that cash will increase and decrease.

The Miller-Orr model is built on the assumption that cash balances behave as if they were generated by a random walk. To the extent that this assumption is erroneous, management will find the model of little use. If management can significantly control the timing of cash outflows (and perhaps even cash inflows), then a model of the Beranek type may be more suitable. In this case, management should not have too much difficulty forming the subjective probability distributions that are needed for this model. In reality, it would probably be true that cash flows are partly random and partly controllable, so the applicability of any of the models can be determined only by testing them with actual data.

It should be remembered that decision models of the type discussed in this appendix are not intended to be applied blindly. There are difficulties in estimating parameters and probabilities. But even more important, the financial manager often has available information that is not directly incorporated into the model. Thus a model, acting ignorantly and unaware of other relevant information, might provide completely erroneous advice. On the other hand, despite their restrictive assumptions and errors, decision models perform effectively if they capture the essential elements in a decision problem. Cash management models should be used as a guide to intelligent decision making, tempered by the manager's own good judgment.

Selected References

Baumol, William J., "The Transactions Demand for Cash: An Inventory Theoretic Approach," *Quarterly Journal of Economics*, 65 (November 1952), pp. 545-556.

Beranek, William, *Analysis for Financial Decisions*, Homewood, Illinois: Irwin, 1963, pp. 345-387.

Constantinides, George M., "Stochastic Cash Management with Fixed and Proportional Transaction Costs," *Management Science*, 22 (August 1976), pp. 1320-1331.

Daellenbach, Hans G., "Are Cash Management Optimization Models Worthwhile?" *Journal of Financial and Quantitative Analysis*, 9 (September 1974), pp. 607-626.

Eppen, Gary D., and Fama, Eugene F., "Cash Balance and Simple Dynamic Portfolio Problems with Proportional Costs," *International Economic Review*, 10 (June 1969), pp. 110-133.

Mao, James C. T., and Sarndal, Carl E., "Cash Management: Theory and Practice," *Journal of Business Finance & Accounting*, 5 (Autumn 1978), pp. 329-338.

Miller, Merton H., and Orr, Daniel, "The Demand for Money by Firms: Extension of Analytic Results," *Journal of Finance*, 23 (December 1968), pp. 735-759.

————, "An Application of Control-Limit Models to the Management of Corporate Cash Balances," in *Financial Research and Management Decisions*, Edited by A. A. Robichek, New York: Wiley, 1967, pp. 133-151.

————, "A Model of the Demand for Money by Firms," *Quarterly Journal of Economics*, 80 (August 1966), pp. 413-435.

Orgler, Yair E., *Cash Management*, Belmont, Calif.: Wadsworth, 1970.

Sethi, Suresh P., and Thompson, Gerald L., "Application of Mathematical Control Theory to Finance: Modeling Simple Dynamic Cash Balance Problems," *Journal of Financial and Quantitative Analysis*, 5 (December 1970), pp. 381-394.

Stone, Bernell K., "Cash Planning and Credit-Line Determination with a Financial Statement Simulator: A Cash Report on Short-Term Financial Planning," *Journal of Financial and Quantitative Analysis*, 8 (November 1973), pp. 711-730.

Chapter 13 Inventory Management

Inventory and accounts receivable are the two largest current asset accounts. Of approximately equal magnitude, together they comprised almost 80 percent of current assets and over 30 percent of total assets for all manufacturing industries in 1982.[1]

While the complexities of inventory decision modeling may be more appropriately the province of operations management, financial managers must also be concerned with inventory as part of the overall cycle of cash flows; the financial manager must understand the logic of the inventory control model, which is one of the most widely used mathematical models in business and which has more general applicability beyond inventory (for example, to cash management).[2]

Inventory

Manufacturing firms generally have three kinds of inventories: (1) raw materials, (2) work in process, and (3) finished goods. The level of *raw materials inventories* is influenced by anticipated production, seasonality of production, reliability of sources of supply, and the efficiency of scheduling purchases and production operations. *Work-in-process inventory* is strongly influenced by the length of the production period, which is the time between placing raw material in production and completing the finished product. Inventory turnover can be increased by decreasing the production period. One means of accomplishing this is to perfect engineering techniques, thereby speeding up the manufacturing process. Another means is to buy items rather than make them.

The level of *finished goods inventory* is a matter of coordinating production and sales. The financial manager can stimulate sales by changing credit terms or by granting credit to marginal risks. But whether the goods remain on the books as inventories or as receivables, the financial manager has to finance them. Many times, firms find it desirable to make the sale so that they are one step nearer to realizing cash. The potential profits can outweigh the additional collection risk.

Our primary focus in this section is control of investment in inventories. Inventory models, developed as an aid in this task, have proved extremely useful in minimizing inventory costs. As our examination of the du Pont system in Chapter 9 showed, any procedure that can reduce the investment required to generate a given sales volume may have a beneficial effect on the firm's rate of return and hence on the value of the firm.

---

[1]U.S. Bureau of the Census, *Quarterly Financial Report for Manufacturing, Mining, and Trade Corporations,* Fourth Quarter, 1982, Series QFR-82-4, U.S. Government Printing Office, Washington, D. C. 20402, 1983.

[2]In rewriting this chapter, we incorporated many suggestions from Professor C. C. Hsia of Washington State University.

Determinants of the Size of Inventories

Although wide variations occur, inventory to sales ratios are generally concentrated in the 12 to 20 percent range. The major determinants of investment in inventory are (1) level of sales, (2) length and technical nature of the production processes, and (3) durability versus perishability (the style factors) in the end product. Inventories in the tobacco industry, for example, are large because of the long curing process. Similarly, in the machinery manufacturing industries, inventories are large because of the long work-in-process period. However, inventories in oil and gas production are low, because raw materials and goods in process are small in relation to sales. In the canning industry, average inventories are large because of the seasonality of the raw materials.

With respect to durability and style factors, large inventories are found in the hardware and the precious metals industries because durability is great and the style factor is small. Inventories are small in baking because of the perishability of the final product and in printing because the items are manufactured to order.

Within limits set by the economics of a firm's industry, there exists a potential for improvement in inventory control from the use of computers and operations research. Although the techniques are far too diverse and complicated for a complete treatment in this text, the financial manager should be prepared to use the contributions of specialists who have developed effective procedures for minimizing the investment in inventory.

An illustration of the techniques at the practical level is Harris Electronics' inventory system, which works like this: Tabulator cards are inserted in each package of five electronic tubes leaving Harris's warehouse. They are identified by account number, type of merchandise, and price of the units ordered. As the merchandise is sold, the distributor collects the cards and files the replacement order with no paperwork, simply by sending in the cards.

Western Union Telegraph Company equipment accepts the punched cards and transmits information on them to the warehouse, where it is duplicated on other punched cards. A typical order of 5,000 tubes of varying types can be received in about 17 minutes, assembled in about 90 minutes, and delivered to Boston's Logan Airport in an additional 45 minutes. Orders from 3,000 miles away can be delivered within 24 hours, a savings of 13 days in some cases.

Information on the order also goes into a computer, which keeps track of stock-on-hand data for each item. When an order draws the stock down below the *order point*, this triggers action in the production department, where additional units of the item are then manufactured for stock. In the next section, we will examine both the optimal order point and the number of units that should be manufactured — called the *economic ordering quantity (EOQ)*.

Generality of Inventory Analysis

Managing assets of all kinds is basically an inventory problem; the same method of analysis applies to cash and fixed assets as to inventories themselves. In borrowing money, in buying raw materials for production, or in purchasing plant and equipment, it is cheaper to buy more than just enough to meet immediate needs.

With the foregoing as a basic foundation, we can develop the theoretical basis for determining the optimal size of the purchase order, which also implies the optimal investment in inventory and the choice of the time to reorder. The model involves a tradeoff between rising and declining costs. Costs such as those related to storage rise with larger inventories, which result from larger orders placed less frequently. But with larger orders placed less frequently, the costs of placing orders would be lower. The goal is to balance these two types of influences to minimize the costs of ordering and of inventory investment. Since entire books and courses are devoted to inventory management, we will not cover the total subject. The model we illustrate, however, is the most widely used and can be developed to encompass any desired extensions.

Classification of Costs

The first step in the process of building an inventory model is to specify those costs that rise and those that decline with the size and frequency of orders and the resulting levels of inventory. Table 13.1 lists some typical costs associated with ordering goods and with carrying inventories. Part A involves carrying costs. Obviously, the larger the inventory, the larger will be storage costs, insurance, and property taxes. Warehousing costs are likely to be more directly related to the size of the inventory item rather than to the value of the item purchased. However, all of the other carrying costs vary with the value of the item. For example, both insurance costs and property taxes are related to the value of inventories. In addition, more valuable items in inventory may require extra protection and extra safeguards. It is, therefore, general practice to express storage costs and carrying costs generally as a percentage of inventory value. Since carrying cost is usually measured as some percentage of inventory value, carrying costs are a type of variable cost. As in economics, when a cost is a fixed amount per quantity produced or sold, this is generally regarded as a "variable cost." To the extent that a firm has safety stocks (discussed later), the carrying costs related to a fixed amount of safety stocks may be regarded as a fixed cost.

The second category of costs set forth in Table 13.1 is ordering costs. Ordering costs are the costs of placing an order if the items are purchased from others or production setup costs if produced within the firm. Ordering costs include the costs of running a purchasing department, personnel and telephone or letter writing expenses associated with plac-

---

Table 13.1   Costs Associated with Inventories

A. Carrying Costs
1. Storage costs
2. Insurance
3. Property taxes
4. Cost of capital tied up
5. Depreciation and obsolescence

B. Ordering Costs
1. Cost of placing order or production setup costs
2. Shipping and handling costs
3. Quantity discounts taken or lost

C. Costs Related to Safety Stocks
1. Loss of sales
2. Loss of customer goodwill
3. Disruption of production schedules

ing orders, and the costs of preparing specifications. Ordering costs would also include the related costs of receiving and inspecting the material and the costs of paying invoices. Another type of "ordering cost" is represented by quantity discounts (negative cost) which may be available if the size of the purchase order is large enough.

In practice, it is difficult to draw the line between variable and fixed ordering costs. The basic costs of running an order department, including the salary of the purchasing agent and the cost of typewriters, desks, and telephones, may be regarded as fixed. Given this basic purchasing facility, the cost of increasing the number of orders over a moderate range may be relatively small. As the number of orders increases, it may be necessary at some point to increase the space allocated to the purchasing department, to acquire additional personnel, and so forth. In these situations, the ordering costs become variable.

The third category of costs presented in Table 13.1 is costs related to safety stocks. Safety stocks represent the inventories held by the firm in the effort to avoid running short of goods to meet sales opportunities. If safety stocks are inadequate, the firm will incur lost sales and the loss of customer goodwill. If we are considering an inventory production system, running short may require overtime and other disruptions of production schedules.

Having classified costs associated with inventories, we are now in a position to present the basic inventory model. We shall do this by a specific numerical example for purposes of clarity. We will assume that the Emerson Company expects to achieve a sales volume of 3,600 widgets during 19X0 and that Emerson is quite confident of hitting this target. Further, these sales are expected to be evenly distributed over the year, so inventories will decline smoothly and gradually. The widgets are purchased for $40 each.

The notation and illustrative numerical amounts that we shall use in the analysis are shown in Table 13.2.

Carrying Costs

Field studies indicate that carrying costs vary among companies but are likely to be in the range of 20 to 25 percent of inventory value.[3] Storage and insurance costs are likely to vary with the type of product as well as product value. Obsolescence, shrinkage, and spoilage will be especially influenced by the type of product. For standard, staple items, such costs may be relatively low. For perishables or products with a very important element of style (for example, clothing), obsolescence costs may be very substantial.

We will assume that this is a warehousing model in which the company is not producing the products it sells. Supplies appear all at once and are used uniformly over time. We will assume initially that there is no safety stock. Thus, carrying costs will rise in direct proportion to the average amount of inventory carried. For example, Emerson's cost of capital is 10 percent, and depreciation is estimated to amount to 5 percent per year. Lumping together these and Emerson's other costs of carrying inventory produces a total cost of 25 percent of the investment in inventory.

Defining the percentage cost as C, we can, in general, find the total carrying costs as the percentage carrying cost (C) times the price per unit (P) times the average number of units (A) (which is $Q/2$ since inventory falls evenly to zero during the inventory cycle).

[3]*Techniques in Inventory Management*, National Association of Accountants, NAA Research Report No. 40, New York, February 1, 1964, pp. 18–21.

Table 13.2   Notation and Data Inputs for EOQ Example

A = average inventory
C = carrying cost expressed as a percentage of inventory purchase price = 25% per year
CP = carrying cost expressed in dollars per unit of inventory = $10 per year
EOQ = economic order quantity
F = fixed ordering costs = $5,400 per year
N = number of orders placed per year = U/Q
P = purchase price per unit of inventory = $40
Q = order quantity
S = safety stock
T = total inventory costs
U = annual usage in units = 3,600
V = variable ordering costs per order = $125

$$\text{Total carrying costs} = (C)(P)(A).$$

If Emerson elects to order only once a year, average inventories will be 3,600/2 = 1,800 units, and the cost of carrying the inventory will be 0.25 × $40 × 1,800 = $18,000. If the company orders twice a year and hence has average inventories that are half as large, total carrying costs will decline to $9,000, and so on. For our example, total carrying costs will equal $10 × $Q/2$, or 5Q$.

Ordering Costs

The fixed costs of the order department in our example are estimated to be $5,400. There are in addition costs of placing an order — for example, preparing specifications, telephone calls, and delivery charges. Total variable ordering costs will be the cost of placing an order (V) times the number of orders placed (N). The company's cost of ordering, shipping, and receiving, which we define as V, is $125 per order.

$$\text{Total ordering costs} = F + (V)(N)$$

$$= \$5,400 + \$125(U/Q)$$

$$= \$5,400 + \$125(3,600)/Q.$$

The EOQ Model

The economic order quantity (EOQ) model can be developed algebraically and graphically. Although total inventory costs are affected by both fixed and variable ordering and carrying costs, the EOQ is determined solely by variable inventory costs. The intersection point of the (rising) variable carrying costs curve with the (declining) variable ordering costs curve lies directly below the minimum point of the total inventory costs curve, as illustrated in Figure 13.1, where T^* is the minimum level of total inventory costs, and Q^* is the optimal quantity of inventory for periodic reordering, that is, the EOQ.

We can also determine the optimal order quantity algebraically. This is the quantity, Q, that minimizes total costs, T. Total inventory costs (T) can be defined as the sum of variable carrying costs, variable ordering costs, and fixed ordering costs.

Figure 13.1   Inventory Costs and the EOQ with Only Variable Costs

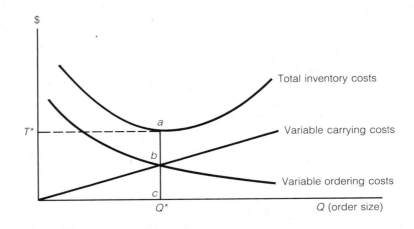

$$T = CPA + VN + F. \tag{13.1}$$

Recognizing that $A = Q/2$ and $N = U/Q$, Equation 13.1 can be written as an explicit function of Q:

$$T = CP\left(\frac{Q}{2}\right) + V\left(\frac{U}{Q}\right) + F \tag{13.2}$$

$$= CP\left(\frac{Q}{2}\right) + VUQ^{-1} + F.$$

We differentiate Equation 13.2 with respect to Q, set the result equal to zero, and solve for Q. We thereby minimize total costs and obtain the basic economic order quantity model:[4]

$$\frac{dT}{dQ} = \frac{CP}{2} - \frac{VU}{Q^2} = 0 \tag{13.3}$$

$$\frac{CP}{2} = \frac{VU}{Q^2}$$

$$Q^2 = \frac{2VU}{CP}$$

$$Q = \sqrt{\frac{2VU}{CP}} = Q^* = \text{EOQ}.$$

[4]When we differentiate, fixed costs do not vary with Q, so they drop out.

In the Emerson case, we find

$$EOQ = \sqrt{\frac{2(\$125)(3,600)}{(0.25)(\$40)}}$$

$$= \sqrt{\frac{\$900,000}{\$10}}$$

$$= \sqrt{90,000}$$

$$= 300 \text{ units per order.}$$

If the EOQ is ordered 12 times a year ($3,600/300 = 12$), or every 30 days, the total costs of ordering and carrying inventories will be minimized.

Relationship between Sales and Inventories

Intuitively, we would suppose that the higher the ordering or processing costs, the less frequently orders should be placed. However, the higher the carrying costs of inventory, the more frequently stocks should be ordered. These two features are incorporated in the EOQ formula. Notice also that if Emerson's sales had been estimated at 900 units, the EOQ would have been 150, while the average inventory would have been 75 units instead of the 150 called for with sales of 3,600 units. Thus, a quadrupling of sales leads to only a doubling of inventories. The general rule is that the EOQ increases with the *square root* of sales, so any increase in sales results in a less than proportionate increase in inventories. The financial manager should keep this in mind in establishing standards for inventory control.

We will now examine the effect of fixed ordering costs on the properties of the EOQ model. From the derivation of the EOQ model, we know that

$$Q^{*2} = 2VU/CP.$$

Rearranging terms yields

$$CP(Q^*/2) = V(U/Q^*). \tag{13.4}$$

Note that $(Q^*/2) = A^*$, the optimal average inventory, and that $(U/Q^*) = N^*$, the optimal number of orders placed. Thus, Equation 13.4 can be written as

$$CPA^* = VN^*. \tag{13.5}$$

Equation 13.5 indicates that, at the order quantity where the total inventory costs are minimized, the variable carrying costs equal the variable ordering costs. Figure 13.1 illustrates this case. It can be proved that point b, the intersection between the variable ordering costs curve and the variable carrying costs curve, lies midway between points a and c, and is directly below the minimum point on the total inventory costs curve.

Note that the fixed ordering costs are not a function of the order size Q. The existence of F merely raises the level of the total inventory costs as shown in Figure 13.2. It has nothing to do with the determination of EOQ, and, thus, the minimum point on the total cost curve can still be proved to lie directly above the intersection of the variable carrying and variable ordering costs curves.

Figure 13.2   Inventory Costs and the EOQ with Fixed Ordering Costs

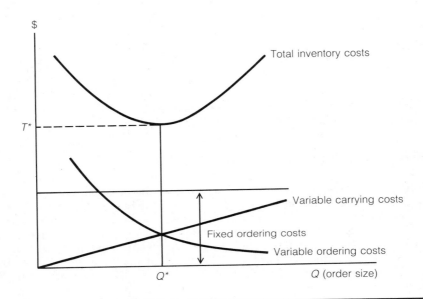

For the Emerson example with fixed ordering costs, the total costs of ordering and carrying inventories are shown in Equation 13.6.

$$T = CPA + VN + F \qquad (13.6)$$

$$= CP\left(\frac{Q}{2}\right) + V\left(\frac{U}{Q}\right) + F$$

$$= (.25)(40)\left(\frac{300}{2}\right) + \$125\left(\frac{3,600}{300}\right) + \$5,400$$

$$= \$1,500 + \$1,500 + \$5,400$$

$$= \$8,400.$$

This is Emerson's lowest possible cost of ordering and carrying inventories.

The EOQ model gives us the optimum, or cost minimizing, order quantity for given levels of usage (U) and inventory carrying cost (C). Knowing the EOQ and continuing our assumption that the pattern of inventory across time is a sawtooth as shown in Figure 13.3, we can find the optimal average inventory as

$$A = \frac{\text{EOQ}}{2} = \frac{300}{2} = 150 \text{ units.} \qquad (13.7)$$

Emerson will thus have an average inventory investment of 150 units at $40 each, or $6,000.

Extending the EOQ Model

The basic EOQ model assumes a predictable sales activity, a constant usage over the year, and an immediate replenishment of the inventory stocks. For the Emerson Company, with an annual demand of 3,600 units and an EOQ of 300 units, there is a need to order 12 times each year, once every 30 days. If the beginning and ending inventory balances are zero, the maximum inventory would be 300 units, with an average of 150 units. The slope of the daily usage line is 10 units. We now can extend the analysis to see what happens (1) if inventory stocks are not replenished instantaneously and (2) if inventory usage is uncertain instead of constant throughout the year.[5]

Inventory Policy with Lead Time

We can relax the assumption of instantaneous order and delivery. Let us assume Emerson requires eight days to place an order and receive the delivery. In order not to interrupt its sales activities, Emerson must keep an eight-day stock, or 80 units, on hand whenever it places an order (Daily usage × Lead time = 10 × 8 = 80). The stock that must be on hand at the time of ordering is defined as the order point; whenever inventory falls below this point, a new order will be placed. If Emerson's inventory control process is automated, the computer will generate an order when the stock on hand falls to 80 units.[6] These conditions are reflected in Figure 13.3.

Figure 13.3   Demand Forecast with Certainty

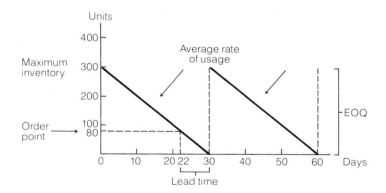

[5]This section may be omitted without loss of continuity.
[6]If a new order must be placed before a prior order is received — that is, if the normal delivery lead time is longer than the time between orders — then what is called a "goods in transit inventory" builds up. This complicates matters somewhat, but the simplest solution to the problem is to deduct goods in transit when calculating the order point. In other words, the order point would be calculated as (Order point = Lead time × Daily usage − Goods in transit).

EOQ for Production Runs

Until now, we have assumed that inventory is delivered all at once in a pattern like that shown in Figure 13.3. This is a typical warehouse example. However, in many cases, firms produce their own finished goods inventory during production runs of R units per day. If a firm is producing its own inventory, the sawtooth pattern changes from that shown in Figure 13.3 to the pattern illustrated in Figure 13.4. Instead of arriving all at once, inventory builds up slowly over a period of time (as shown by line XY) while the production rate (R) exceeds the usage rate (U). When the production run stops, the inventory is drawn down at the normal usage rate, U (as shown in line segment YZ).

In order to derive the economic order quantity when a firm produces its own finished goods, let's keep the same set of facts as before, but now interpret the variable ordering costs per order as production run setup costs ($V = \$125$ per production run) and assume that the Emerson Company can produce at the rate of $R = 4,800$ units per year. In order to determine the economic order quantity, we need to know the carrying costs and the ordering costs.

Emerson's maximum inventory will be the number of days in a production run times the rate of increase in inventory each day. The number of days per production run (that is, length of a production run) will be the number of units per run (that is, the order quantity) divided by the number of units produced per day. The equation is[7]

$$\text{Length of a production run} = \frac{Q \text{ units}}{R \text{ units per year}/360 \text{ days per year}}.$$

And the rate of increase in inventory during each day of the production run is

$$\text{Rate of increase in inventory} = \frac{R \text{ units per year} - U \text{ units per year}}{360 \text{ days per year}}.$$

Figure 13.4   Demand Forecast Assuming Production Runs of R Units Per Day for Q/R Days

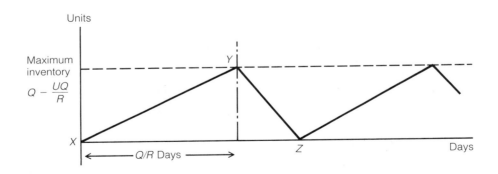

Putting these together, we see that the maximum inventory is

$$\text{Maximum inventory} = \frac{Q}{R}(R - U) = Q - \frac{UQ}{R}.$$

The average inventory (A) is half the maximum, since inventory rises and falls in linear fashion during and between production.

$$A = \frac{1}{2}\frac{Q}{R}(R - U) \tag{13.8}$$

$$= \frac{Q}{2}\left(1 - \frac{U}{R}\right).$$

Comparing the average inventory in the production case (Equation 13.8) with the warehouse case (Equation 13.7) shows that the producer needs to carry a smaller average inventory than that of a warehouser. We will demonstrate this numerically once we have determined the EOQ.

The last step in determining carrying costs is to multiply the average inventory times the dollar carrying cost per unit, CP.

$$\text{Total carrying costs} = (C)(P)\frac{Q}{2}\left(1 - \frac{U}{R}\right).$$

Emerson's total ordering costs may be expressed exactly as before because the rate of production has no effect on the cost per order (or the cost per setup). Hence, total ordering costs are

$$\text{Total ordering cost} = F + (V)(N)$$

$$= F + V\left(\frac{U}{Q}\right).$$

By adding carrying and ordering costs, we have the total inventory cost.

$$T = CP\frac{Q}{2}\left(1 - \frac{U}{R}\right) + F + V\left(\frac{U}{Q}\right). \tag{13.9}$$

When we differentiate Equation 13.9 with respect to Q, set it equal to zero, and solve for Q, we minimize total costs.

$$\frac{dT}{dQ} = \frac{CP}{2}\left(1 - \frac{U}{R}\right) - \frac{VU}{Q^2} = 0 \tag{13.10}$$

$$\frac{CP}{2} - \frac{CPU}{2R} - \frac{VU}{Q^2} = 0$$

$$\frac{CPR\ Q^2 - CPU\ Q^2 - 2URV}{2R\ Q^2} = 0$$

$$Q^2(CPR - CPU) = 2URV$$

$$Q^* = \text{EOQ} = \sqrt{\frac{2URV}{CP(R - U)}}.$$

Substituting in the numbers for Emerson Company, we find that the economic order quantity is

$$\text{EOQ} = \sqrt{\frac{2(4{,}800)(3{,}600)(\$125)}{.25(\$40)(4{,}800 - 3{,}600)}}$$

$$= \sqrt{360{,}000}$$

$$= 600 \text{ units per production run.}$$

Using this result, we see that the average inventory is

$$A = \frac{Q}{2}\left(1 - \frac{U}{R}\right)$$

$$= \frac{600}{2}\left(1 - \frac{3{,}600}{4{,}800}\right) = 75 \text{ units.}$$

The difference between Emerson Company as a distributor and the same company as a producer is that the economic order quantity rises from 300 to 600 units and the average inventory falls from 150 to 75 units. Also, if we compare total inventory costs, they were $8,400 in the warehousing case and in the production case are

$$T = CP\frac{Q}{2}\left(1 - \frac{U}{R}\right) + F + V\left(\frac{U}{Q}\right)$$

$$= .25(\$40)\frac{600}{2}\left(1 - \frac{3{,}600}{4{,}800}\right) + \$5{,}400 + \$125\left(\frac{3{,}600}{600}\right)$$

$$= \$750 + \$5{,}400 + \$750$$

$$= \$6{,}900.$$

The lower average inventory and lower inventory cost in the production case result from the fact that inventories are being replenished continuously instead of intermittently as in the warehousing example. By comparing the two situations, we have seen that the actual pattern of inventory is critical. For many realistic situations, the problem becomes so complex that it is necessary to solve it via computer simulation.

EOQ Model with Uncertainty: Safety Stocks

To this point, we have assumed that usage (demand) is known with certainty and is uniform throughout time and that the order lead time never varies. Either or both of these assumptions could be incorrect, so it is necessary to modify the EOQ model to allow for this possibility. This modification generally takes the form of adding a *safety stock* to average inventories.

An optimal policy will minimize the total cost of the safety stock. The increased carrying costs of the safety stock must be traded off against the costs of stockout. The increased carrying costs are the annual carrying costs per unit (CP) times the safety stock (S).[8] The annual stockout cost depends on four factors:

Expected annual stockout cost = Unit stockout cost × Units of stockout × Probability of stockout in a cycle × Number of inventory cycles per year.

If we return to our initial assumption that inventory is delivered, not produced, then the number of inventory cycles per year for the Emerson Company is $N = U/EOQ = 3,600/300 = 12$. Thus, Emerson Company would order every 30 days if there were no uncertainty about the rate of inventory usage. We assume, for the time being, that the order lead time is also 30 days. Suppose that the Emerson Company sales force has provided estimates of the usage rate during one inventory cycle as shown in Table 13.3. Note that the EOQ in a world without any uncertainty was 300 units. This is the unweighted average usage rate in Table 13.3, but actual usage could be as high as 450 units or as low as 150 units in a 30-day period.

If we are also told that the stockout cost is $5.21 per unit, it should be possible to determine the optimal safety stock. For example, suppose we decide to carry 150 units of safety stock. Then, as shown in Table 13.4, we start with 450 units at the beginning of the inventory cycle (that is, the sum of an EOQ of 300 units and the 150-unit safety stock). There is no chance of stockout, and hence the expected stockout cost is zero. However, the expected carrying cost is

$$E(\text{Carrying cost per 30-day cycle}) = \left(\frac{\$10 \text{ per year}}{12 \text{ cycles per year}} \right) \times \text{Safety stock}$$

$$= \left(\frac{\$10}{12} \right) 150 = \$125.$$

Table 13.3   The Distribution of Usage during One 30-Day Inventory Cycle

Usage/30-Day Period	Daily Usage	Probability
150 units	5.00 units	.04
200	6.67	.08
250	8.33	.20
300	10.00	.36
350	11.67	.20
400	13.33	.08
450	15.00	.04

---

[8]Note that we have multiplied CP by the *entire* safety stock, not by one-half of the safety stock. The reason is that the EOQ represents the expected (or average) usage rate. There is a 50-50 chance of using more or less (see Table 13.3). Hence, the entire safety stock is also the average safety stock.

Table 13.4   Safety Stock Computations (30-Day Inventory Cycle)

Safety Stock	Total Inventory	Stockout Quantity	Stockout Cost	Probability	Expected Stockout Cost	Expected Carrying Cost	Expected Total Cost
150	450	0	0	0	0	$125.00	$125.00
100	400	50	$260.50	.04	$ 10.42	83.33	93.75
50	350	50	260.50	.08	20.84		
		100	521.00	.04	20.84		
					$ 41.68	41.67	83.35
0	300	50	260.50	.20	52.10		
		100	521.00	.08	41.68		
		150	781.50	.04	31.26		
					$125.04	0	125.04

Thus, the total cost of a 150-unit safety stock is $125. Alternately, we could choose a 100-unit safety stock. As shown in Table 13.4, the expected stockout cost in this case is $10.42 because the company expects to stockout 4 percent of the time at a cost of $260.50. Carrying costs have decreased to $83.33, and hence the 100-unit safety stock is superior to the 150-unit policy because total costs have dropped from $125 to $93.75.

The optimal policy is the one where expected stockout costs equal expected carrying costs. In our example, this is a safety stock of 50 units. Emerson Company expects to stockout 12 percent of the time under this policy. Emerson's initial order would be 350 units instead of 300 units, and subsequent orders would be for 300 units each.

The lead time is important in this type of analysis. For example, suppose we reduce the assumed lead time from 30 days (equal to the inventory cycle) to only 5 days.[9] The maximum usage is 15 units per day, so if we set our order point at $5 \times 15 = 75$ units, we will never stockout. When the lead time is less than the inventory cycle, it is necessary to compute the optimal safety stock using the lead time instead of the inventory cycle.

Note that even with a safety stock, the EOQ remains at 300 units. The increase in total carrying costs resulting from an addition of a fixed amount for carrying the safety stocks of 50 units at $10 per unit does not affect the cost minimizing quantity. And, as we shall demonstrate, the minimum point of the total inventory cost curve still lies directly above the intersection of the variable ordering and variable carrying costs curves.

Given a safety stock (S), which has annual expected stockout costs of $$K$, total inventory costs are

$$T = CPA + VN + F + CPS + K.$$

Since the EOQ is not a function of the fixed ordering costs, nor a function of the costs for carrying the safety stock, the existence of expected stockout costs and the costs for carrying the safety stock merely raises further the level of the total inventory costs. Therefore, the same principle as shown for the simplest case with no fixed costs remains valid for this case, which is illustrated in Figure 13.5.

[9]The assumed lead time is known with certainty.

Figure 13.5   Inventory Costs and EOQ with Two Types of Fixed Costs

---

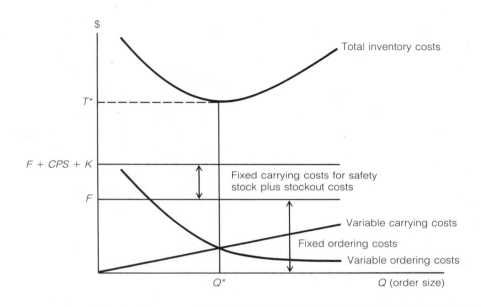

For our example, with a safety stock of 50 units, Emerson's total inventory costs will increase to

$$T = CPA + VN + F + CPS + K$$

$$= \$8{,}400 + \$10(50) + \$41.68$$

$$= \$9{,}400.00.$$

Effects of Inflation on EOQ

During inflation, formal models such as the EOQ must be adjusted. As freight costs rise, the cost of placing an order may increase rapidly. Purchase prices may also rise abruptly and repeatedly. Also, in recent years, the cost of capital has changed rapidly. Therefore, the values used in the EOQ equation may not remain constant for any appreciable length of time. If so, the optimal order quantity will not remain fixed. Some companies will need greater flexibility in the timing of their orders than that afforded by the automatic order point because they may be able to buy marginal production at reduced prices. Also, certain companies may stockpile inventories, taking advantage of the opportunity to purchase supplies before major price increases and gaining protection against shortages. Therefore, during periods of inflation and tight money, a firm may need more flexible inventory management as it attempts to take advantage of bargains and to provide for future contingencies. The basic logic of the inventory model remains intact: Some costs will rise with larger inventories, and others will fall. Although an optimum is still there to be found, it may change and require repeated reassessments.

Management of Accounts Receivable

Once inventories have been sold, there is some time lag until payment is received. This interim stage is represented by accounts receivable for the selling firm and by accounts payable for the buying firm. As we shall see in Chapter 15, accounts payable is an important source of short-term financing for the buying firm. Particularly in an inflationary period, when interest rates are high and financing requirements large, buyers may delay their payments beyond the normal credit period. This, in turn, causes the selling firm's investment in accounts receivable to rise, increasing the seller's financing requirements. Thus, one of the consequences of persistent inflation is to increase the importance of the role of credit and collection policies. The next chapter will discuss the principles of extending credit and the effects of various credit policies on the sales and profitability of the firm.

Summary

This chapter focused on the management of inventories, a major component of current assets.

Inventories — raw materials, work in process, and finished goods — are necessary in most businesses. Rather elaborate systems for controlling the level of inventories have been designed. These systems frequently use computers for keeping records of all the items in stock. An inventory control model that considers anticipated sales, ordering costs, and carrying costs can be used to determine EOQ's for each item.

The basic inventory model recognizes that certain costs (carrying costs) rise as average inventory holdings increase but that certain other costs (ordering costs and stockout costs) fall as these holdings increase. The two sets of costs make up the total cost of ordering and carrying inventories, and the EOQ model is designed to locate an optimal order size that will minimize total inventory costs.

Questions

13.1 Inventory decision models are designed to help minimize the cost of obtaining and carrying inventory. Describe the basic nature of the fundamental inventory control model, discussing specifically the nature of increasing costs, decreasing costs, and total costs.

13.2 What are the probable effects of the following on inventory holdings?
   a) Manufacture of a part formerly purchased from an outside supplier.
   b) Greater use of air freight.
   c) Increase, from 7 to 17, in the number of styles produced.
   d) Large price reductions to your firm from a manufacturer of bathing suits if the suits are purchased in December and January.

13.3 What factors are likely to reduce the holdings of inventory in relation to sales in the future? What factors will tend to increase the ratio? What, in your judgment, is the net effect?

13.4   Explain how a firm can reduce its investment in inventory by having its supplier hold raw materials inventories and its customers hold finished goods inventories. What are the limitations of such a policy?

Problems

13.1   You are given the following information:

> Annual demand: 2,800 units
> Cost per order placed: $5.25
> Carrying cost: 20%
> Price per unit: $30.

a)   Fill in the blanks in the table below.

Order size	35	56	70	140	200	2,800
Number of orders	___	___	___	___	___	___
Average inventory	___	___	___	___	___	___
Carrying cost	___	___	___	___	___	___
Order cost	___	___	___	___	___	___
Total cost	___	___	___	___	___	___

b)   What is the EOQ?

13.2   The following relationships for inventory purchase and storage costs have been established for the Norman Corporation.
  1. Orders must be placed in multiples of 100 units.
  2. Requirements for the year are 180,000 units (U). (Use 50 weeks in a year for calculations.)
  3. The purchase price per unit (P) is $2.
  4. The carrying cost (C) is 50 percent of the purchase price of goods.
  5. The cost per order placed (V) is $400.
  6. Desired safety stock (S) is 10,000 units (on hand initially).
  7. One week is required for delivery.

a)   What is the most economical order quantity?
b)   What is the optimal number of orders to be placed?
c)   At what inventory level should a reorder be made?

13.3   The following relationships for inventory purchase and storage costs have been established for the Lomer Fabricating Corporation.
  1. Orders must be placed in multiples of 100 units.
  2. Requirements for the year are 400,000 units (U). (Use 50 weeks in a year for calculations.)
  3. The purchase price per unit (P) is $2.
  4. The carrying cost (C) is 20 percent of the purchase price of goods.
  5. The cost per order placed (V) is $50.
  6. Desired safety stock (S) is 10,000 units (on hand initially).
  7. One week is required for delivery.

a)   What is the most economical order quantity?
b)   What is the optimal number of orders to be placed?
c)   At what inventory level should a reorder be made?

13.4   The following relationships for inventory purchases and storage costs have been established for the Milton Processing Corporation.

Basic facts:
1. Orders must be placed in multiples of 100 units.
2. Requirements for the year are 500,000 units (U). (Use 50 weeks in a year for calculations.)
3. The purchase price per unit is $5.
4. The carrying cost is 20 percent of the purchase price of goods.
5. The cost per order placed is $25.
6. Desired safety stock is 10,000 units (on hand initially).
7. One week is required for delivery.

a) What is the most economical order quantity?
b) What is the optimal number of orders to be placed?
c) At what inventory level should a reorder be made?
d) If annual unit sales double, what is the percent increase in the EOQ? What is the elasticity of EOQ with respect to sales (percent change in EOQ/percent change in sales)?
e) If the purchase price per unit doubles, what is the percent change in EOQ? What is the elasticity of EOQ with respect to purchase price per unit?

13.5 Professors Tiernan and Tanner have identified the variables which determine the degree of sensitivity of total inventory costs to order quantity.[10] Their model can be briefly summarized within our framework. Recall Equation 13.2 reproduced below:

$$T = CP(Q/2) + V(U/Q) + F. \qquad (13.2)$$

This can be slightly rearranged as shown in Equation 13.2.a:

$$T = F + VU/Q + \frac{CP}{2}(Q). \qquad (13.2a)$$

Their numerical example illustrates the factors that determine the sensitivity of inventory costs to order size. To illustrate, assume that fixed costs are $20 and that total usage (U) is 1,000 units. One set of curves is defined by Cases A and B, where ordering costs and carrying costs are as follows:

	V	CP
A	.10	.01
B	50.00	.01

a) What are the resulting equations in the format of Equation 13.2a for Cases A and B?
b) In contrast are Cases C and D, the data for which are presented below:

	V	CP
C	.10	20
D	.50	20

[10]Tiernan and Tanner [1983].

What are the resulting equations?

c)   Graph the four sets of equations identifying the EOQ.

d)   Comment on the sensitivity of total costs to order size for each case.

Selected References

Beranek, William, "Financial Implications of Lot-Size Inventory Models," *Management Science*, 13 (April 1967), pp. 401-408.

Buffa, Elwood S., *Modern Production/Operations Management*, 6th Ed., New York: John Wiley & Sons, 1980.

Magee, John F., and Meal, Harlan C., "Inventory Management and Standards," in *The Treasurer's*

Handbook, Edited by J. Fred Weston and Maurice B. Goudzwaard, Homewood, Ill.: Dow Jones-Irwin, 1976, pp. 496-542.

Snyder, Arthur, "Principles of Inventory Management," *Financial Executive*, 32 (April 1964), pp. 13-21.

Tiernan, Frank M., and Tanner, Dennis A., "How Economic Order Quantity Controls Inventory Expense," *Financial Executive*, 51 (July 1983), pp. 46-52.

Chapter 14 Credit Management and Policy

Credit management and policy are closely allied to inventory management. In this chapter, we discuss the basis for making decisions on extending credit. Such decisions involve credit standards, credit terms, and the determination of who shall receive credit. A framework for evaluating decisions on changing credit policies is also presented.

The level of accounts receivable is determined by the volume of credit sales and the average period between sales and collections. The average collection period is dependent partly on economic conditions (during a recession or a period of extremely tight money, for example, customers may be forced to delay payment) and partly on a set of controllable factors — *credit policy variables*. The major aspects include credit standards and credit terms. Credit terms (discussed in Chapter 15) cover matters such as the length of the credit period and the use of cash discounts. After discussing the policy variables, we will illustrate their interaction and how they influence the actual establishment of a firm's credit policy.

Credit Standards

If a firm makes credit sales to only the strongest of customers, it will experience only small amounts of bad debt losses. On the other hand, it will probably lose sales, and the profit it foregoes on these lost sales may be greater than the costs it avoids. To determine the optimal credit standard, the firm relates the marginal costs of credit to the marginal profits on the increased sales.

Marginal costs include production and selling costs; but abstracting from them at this point, we will consider only those costs associated with the quality of the marginal accounts, or *credit quality costs*. These costs include (1) default, or bad debt losses; (2) higher investigation and collection costs; and (3) higher amounts tied up in receivables, resulting in higher costs of capital, due to less creditworthy customers who delay payment.

Since credit costs and credit quality are correlated, it is important to be able to judge the quality of an account, and perhaps the best way to do this is in terms of the probability of default. Probability estimates are for the most part subjective; but credit rating is a well-established practice, and a good credit manager can make reasonably accurate judgments of the probability of default by different classes of customers.

Five C's of Credit.   To evaluate the credit risk, credit managers consider the five C's of credit: character, capacity, capital, collateral, and conditions.

Character has to do with the probability that a customer will try to honor obligations. This factor is of considerable importance, because every credit transaction implies a promise to pay. Will the creditor make an honest effort to pay the debts, or is this credit applicant likely to try to get away with something? Experienced credit managers frequently insist that character is the most important issue in a credit evaluation.

Capacity describes a subjective judgment of the customer's ability to pay. It is gauged by the customer's past business performance record, supplemented by physical observation of the plant or store and business methods.

Capital is measured by the general financial position of the firm as indicated by a financial ratio analysis, with special emphasis on the tangible net worth of the enterprise.

Collateral is represented by assets offered by the customer as a pledge for security of the credit extended.

The fifth C, *conditions*, has to do with the impact of general economic trends on the firm or special developments in certain areas of the economy that may affect the customer's ability to meet the obligation.

The five C's of credit represent the factors by which the credit risk is judged. Information on these items is obtained from a number of sources, including the firm's prior experience with the customer. If it is a new account, audited financial statements for the three previous years may be requested. (Applicants sometimes submit income tax returns in lieu of other statements.)

Two major sources of external information are available. First, by periodic meetings of local groups and by correspondence, information on experience with debtors is exchanged through the credit associations. More formally, Credit Interchange, a system developed by the National Association of Credit Management for assembling and distributing information on debtors' past performance, is provided. The interchange reports show the paying record of the debtor, the industries from which he or she is buying, and the trading areas in which the purchases are being made.

The second source of external information is the credit-reporting agencies, the best known of which is Dun & Bradstreet. Agencies that specialize in coverage of a limited number of industries also provide information. Representative of these are the National Credit Office and Lyon Furniture Mercantile Agency. These agencies provide data that can be used by the credit manager in the credit analysis; they also provide ratings similar to those available on corporate bonds.

Another source of credit information is the customer's commercial bank. While the bank cannot disclose account balances and loan balances without the applicant's consent, some general information can be provided. Typically, the bank will express the magnitude of the customer's account balance (for example, a "medium six-figure" balance). The extent to which the bank will disclose information will also depend in part on the creditor firm's past dealings with the bank and the personal relationships of the executives involved.

An individual firm can translate its credit information into risk classes, grouped according to the probability of loss associated with sales to a customer. The combination of rating and supplementary information might lead to the groupings of probable loss experience below.

Risk Class Number	Probable Loss Ratio (in Percentages)
1	None
2	0-1/2
3	Over 1/2-1
4	Over 1-2
5	Over 2-5
6	Over 5-10
7	Over 10-20
8	Over 20

If the selling firm has a 20 percent margin over the sum of direct operating costs and all delivery and selling costs, and if it is producing at less than full capacity, it may adopt the following credit policies: selling on customary credit terms to Groups 1 through 5; selling to Groups 6 and 7 under more stringent credit terms, such as cash on delivery; and requiring advance payment from Group 8. As long as the bad debt loss ratios are less than 20 percent, the additional sales are contributing something to overhead. However, the opportunity costs of the increased investment in receivables also must be taken into account in the analysis, as will be shown in the examples later in the chapter.

Statistical techniques, especially regression analysis and discriminant analysis, have been used with some success in judging creditworthiness.[1] These methods work best when individual credits are relatively small and a large number of borrowers are involved, as in retail credit, consumer loans, and mortgage lending. As the increase in credit card use and similar procedures builds up, as computers are used more frequently, and as credit records on individuals and small firms are developed, statistical techniques promise to become much more important than they are today.[2]

Analysis of Credit Information

The evaluation will start with a relatively standard financial ratio analysis, with emphasis on the liquidity, leverage, and profitability ratios. The ratios will be compared to composites for the lines of business in which the firm operates. In addition, the analysis may become even more quantitative by employing some procedures for credit scoring. This represents an extension of the multiple discriminant analysis described in Appendix B to Chapter 8.

In addition to a general financial analysis, some specific tests related to credit activity will be performed. Information on the payment practices of the prospective customer will be factored into the analysis. This is done by taking the accounts payable data from the financial statements and calculating an average age of accounts payable. This average payment period can then be used in two comparisons. The first one relates the actual payment period to the terms of credit. For example, if credit terms are net 30 days and the average payment period is 55 days, a slippage of 25 days is involved. The second comparison examines the customer's payment period against the average for its line of business. The average payment period might be 40 days. Continuing the assumption of credit terms of net 30 days, this represents a lag of 10 days as general practice and therefore "normal" in some sense. The additional 15 days beyond the 40 days represents a further "abnormal" lag by this particular customer.

Credit information may be used in a formal scoring and evaluation system, or quantitative analysis will be combined with qualitative information on the prospective customer. Based on both kinds of information and the experience of the credit manager in dealing with similar situations, a number of decisions can be reached. One decision may be the approval or disapproval of a particular sale on the firm's standard credit terms. Also, a line of credit may be determined for this customer. One rule of thumb for a line of credit is a

---

[1]Discriminant analysis, discussed in Appendix B to Chapter 8, partitions a sample into two or more components on the basis of a set of characteristics. The sample, for instance, might be loan applicants at a consumer loan company. The components into which they are classified might be those likely to make prompt repayment and those likely to default. The characteristics might be whether the applicant owns a home, how long the person has been with the current employer, level of income, and so on.

[2]It has been said that the biggest single deterrent to the increased automation of credit processes is George Orwell's classic book, *1984*, in which he described the social dangers of centralized files of information on individuals. Orwell's omnipresent watcher, Big Brother, is mentioned frequently in congressional sessions discussing mass storage of information relevant to credit analysis.

percentage of the customer's net worth (or "estimated financial strength") related to the number of its major suppliers. For example, if the credit-supplying firm has a general standard of trying to keep total trade credit below 60 percent of the customer's net worth and it is determined that there are four other major suppliers, then the credit limit may be established at no more than 12 percent of the customer's net worth (60% ÷ 5 total suppliers). Or, the figure may be set at 10 percent to provide a margin of safety and to allow for fluctuations in the volume of business among the customer's major suppliers.

Counseling

Credit executives have a substantial positive function in a firm. They are not simply "heavies," whose job it is to bully delinquent accounts. The basic objective of credit management is to add value to the firm by contributing to an optimal amount of profitable sales. It is especially in the evaluation of credit information and in the collections functions that credit managers can perform a valuable role for the firm. If the potential borrower does not meet credit standards, one simple approach is to turn down the order. This could probably be justified by comparing probable gain with probable loss on the order. But in analyzing the applicant's credit information, the credit manager may have identified causes of or factors in the firm's poor financial performance that could alter the credit decision.

Similarly, when payments are delinquent, the temptation is to follow standard collections patterns. These include sending letters of increasing insistence, making phone calls, seeking intervention by the firm's legal department, using outside collection agencies, and instigating lawsuits. Such methods may succeed in collecting all or part of the money. But the credit manager's larger objective is to build a broad and increasing base of profitable sales.

A good credit manager will strive to learn the business of his firm's customers as well as (or better than) the executives of those firms. He should seek to keep current on their sales trends, management performance, liquidity, leverage, and profitability. The creative credit manager keeps abreast of external factors affecting his customers' businesses and is in continuous communication with the large accounts. He should seek to serve as a valued sounding board for discussions of trends affecting his customers' industries as well as of important policy decisions in the individual firms. He should provide a source of counsel on important policy and decision areas affecting his customers' future well-being. To be sure, these recommendations reflect the ideal and must be compromised with practical considerations of time and cost. But to the degree that these potentials are realized, a credit manager can make an important contribution to his own firm. He can help his customers' businesses expand profitably and can increase sales volume for his own firm. Thus, the credit granting and collection functions can be part of an effective sales activity strategy.

Terms of Trade Credit

The terms of credit specify the period for which credit is extended and the discount, if any, for early payment. For example, if a firm's credit terms to all approved customers are stated as 2/10, net 30, then a 2 percent discount from the stated sales price is granted if payment is made within 10 days, and the entire amount is due 30 days from the invoice date if the discount is not taken. If the terms are stated "net 60," this indicates that no discount is offered and that the bill is due and payable 60 days after the invoice date.

If sales are seasonal, a firm may use seasonal dating. Jensen, Inc., a bathing suit manufacturer, sells on terms of 2/10, net 30, May 1 dating. This means that the effective invoice date is May 1, so the discount can be taken until May 10, or the full amount must be paid on May 30, regardless of when the sale was made. Jensen produces output throughout the year, but retail sales of bathing suits are concentrated in the spring and early summer. Because of its practice of offering seasonal datings, Jensen induces some customers to stock up early, saving Jensen storage costs and also nailing down sales.

Credit Period

Lengthening the credit period stimulates sales, but there is a cost to tying up funds in receivables. For example, if a firm changes its terms from net 30 to net 60, the average receivables for the year may rise from $100,000 to $300,000 — the increase caused partly by the longer credit terms and partly by the larger volume of sales. The optimal credit period is determined by the point where marginal profits on increased sales are exactly offset by the costs of carrying the higher amounts of accounts receivable.

Cash Discounts

The effect of granting cash discounts can be analyzed similarly to the credit period. For example, if a firm changes its terms from net 30 to 2/10, net 30, it may well attract new customers who want to take discounts, thereby increasing gross sales. Also, the average collection period will be shortened, as some existing customers pay more promptly to take advantage of the discount. Offsetting these benefits is the cost of the discounts taken. The optimal discount is established at the point where costs and benefits are exactly offsetting.

Accounts Receivable versus Accounts Payable

Whenever goods are sold on credit, two accounts are created. An asset item called an *accounts receivable* appears on the books of the selling firm, and a liability item called an *accounts payable* appears on the books of the purchaser. At this point, we are analyzing the transaction from the viewpoint of the seller, so we have concentrated on the type of variables under the seller's control. In Chapter 15, we will examine the transaction from the viewpoint of the purchaser, discussing accounts payable as a source of funds and considering the cost of these funds vis-à-vis funds obtained from other sources.

Evaluating Changes in Credit Policy

Thus far in our treatment of current asset management, we have dealt with each area individually, and in actual practice, similar compartmentalization is often reinforced by organizational structures in which cash managers manage cash, payables managers manage payables, credit managers manage receivables, and operations managers manage inventories. However, it is important to note that such fragmentation is illusory and may lead to erroneous decision criteria in any one area unless consideration is given to the decision's impact on other areas. For example, a decision to deny credit to slow-paying customers would likely reduce the collection period but would also reduce total sales and production volume, thus altering the level of cash flows in these areas, and perhaps their timing as well. An integrated model must consider the interrelationships between both the timing and the amount of all cash flows involved in current asset policy decisions.

A number of authors have attempted to formulate decision models which integrate several elements of working capital management, for example, the relationship between inventory control and payables and receivables management. By concentrating on cash flows over time (rather than accounting measures) in an NPV framework, the Sartoris-Hill [1981] credit policy decision model discussed below goes a long way towards integrating all of the elements of current asset management to the goal of maximizing the value of the firm. Sartoris and Hill (building on the earlier work of Kim and Atkins [1978], of Hill and Riener [1979], and of Dyl [1977]) formulate a net present value cash flow approach to the analysis of alternative credit policies. Their decision model is based on calculating the net gain or loss resulting from a change in credit policy. It is sufficiently flexible to account for differences of price, cost, trade discount, bad debt loss rate, timing of cash flows, inventory effects, and growth rate of sales, all simultaneously or in any combination.

Their cash flow timeline, in Figure 14.1, is a useful tool for illustrating that evaluation of a change in credit policy extends beyond its impact on the level of accounts receivable. The timeline shifts the focus to changes in the timing and amount of cash flows over the entire cycle, which encompasses inventory and payables management, credit management, and cash collections.

An example will illustrate how the Sartoris-Hill model incorporates the interrelation of current asset variables into the evaluation of a credit policy. The Halbard Company manufactures electric typewriters. Credit sales are constant throughout the year, averaging 200 units per day at $500 each; costs are $350 per unit. Based on a weighted average, cash collections are received 40 days from the date of sale. (Terms of sale are net 30; however, some customers delay payment.) The current bad debt loss rate is 2 percent, and Halbard estimates its daily interest rate to be 0.05 percent.[3] Halbard is considering extending its

Figure 14.1   The Cash Flow Timeline

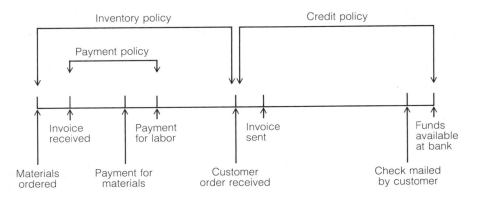

terms of sale to net 45 days. It is estimated that sales will rise to 250 units per day but that the bad debt loss rate will also rise, to 3 percent and that the average collection period will rise to 50 days.

Using the Sartoris-Hill notation, in which the subscripts "0" and "1" refer to the current and proposed credit policies respectively, we have

Factors	Current Policy	Proposed Policy
P = price per unit	$P_0 = \$500$	$P_1 = \$500$
C = cost per unit	$C_0 = \$350$	$C_1 = \$350$
Q = daily sales	$Q_0 = 200$ units	$Q_1 = 250$ units
b = bad debt loss rate	$b_0 = 2\%$	$b_1 = 3\%$
t = average collection period	$t_0 = 40$ days	$t_1 = 50$ days
k = daily interest rate	$k_0 = 0.05\%$	$k_1 = 0.05\%$

The net present value under the current policy consists of net revenues discounted for t_0 days, less costs (inventory is assumed to be purchased or produced and paid for on the date of sale).

$$\text{NPV}_0 = \left[\frac{P_0 Q_0(1 - b_0)}{(1 + k_0)^{t_0}} \right] - C_0 Q_0$$

$$= \frac{\$500(200)(1 - .02)}{(1.0005)^{40}} - \$350(200)$$

$$= \frac{\$98,000}{1.0202} - \$70,000$$

$$= \$96,060 - \$70,000$$

$$= \$26,060.$$

Likewise, the NPV of one day's operations under the proposed new policy will be

$$\text{NPV}_1 = \left[\frac{P_1 Q_1(1 - b_1)}{(1 + k_1)^{t_1}} \right] - C_1 Q_1$$

$$= \frac{\$500(250)(1 - .03)}{(1.0005)^{50}} - (\$350)(250)$$

$$= \frac{\$121,250}{1.0253} - \$87,500$$

$$= \$118,258 - \$87,500$$

$$= \$30,758.$$

The decision criterion for the change in credit policy should be to adopt the policy with the higher net present value; in this case, NPV_1 is greater than NPV_0 by \$4,698, and thus the proposed change in credit policy should be adopted.

For simplicity, we have excluded until now the impact on the NPV analysis of changes in working capital resulting from changes in credit terms. As the amount of sales increases so does the amount of working capital required to support that level of sales. Cash, inventories, and accounts receivables all increase. For our example, we will assume other working capital (receivables are already reflected in the model) to be a constant percentage, w, of sales. Assume $w = 25$ percent. In evaluating the proposed credit policy, we need to subtract an additional cost due to the additional working capital. Thus, NPV_0 becomes

$$NPV_0 = \left[\frac{P_0 Q_0 (1 - b_0)}{(1 + k_0)^{t_0}} \right] - C_0 Q_0 - w \left[P_0 Q_0 - \frac{P_0 Q_0}{(1 + k_0)^{t_0}} \right]$$

$$= \frac{\$500(200)(1 - .02)}{(1.0005)^{40}} - \$350(200) - .25 \left[\$500(200) - \frac{\$500(200)}{(1.0005)^{40}} \right]$$

$$= \$96,060 - \$70,000 - \$495 = \$25,565.$$

The term $w P_0 Q_0$ represents our outlay for the current level of working capital, and the term

$$\frac{w P_0 Q_0}{(1 + k_0)^{t_0}}$$

represents what we get back in 40 days collection time. We do the same for NPV_1, which becomes

$$NPV_1 = \left[\frac{P_1 Q_1 (1 - b_1)}{(1 + k_1)^{t_1}} \right] - C_1 Q_1 - w \left[P_1 Q_1 - \frac{P_1 Q_1}{(1 + k_1)^{t_1}} \right].$$

Again, the term $w P_1 Q_1$ represents the working capital outlay for the proposed level of receivables, and the term

$$\frac{w P_1 Q_1}{(1 + k_1)^{t_1}}$$

represents what we get back after the increase in collection time to 50 days.

$$NPV_1 = \frac{\$500(250)(1 - .03)}{(1.0005)^{50}} - \$350(250) - .25 \left[\$500(250) - \frac{\$500(250)}{(1.0005)^{50}} \right]$$

$$= \$118,258 - \$87,500 - \$771 = \$29,987.$$

The result for $NPV_1 - NPV_0$ is $4,422; hence, the new credit policy remains favorable.

Thus, additional working capital requirements such as additional inventories occur when credit policy changes result in increased sales and the NPV calculation of the credit change is affected.

This example demonstrates the interrelation of aspects of current asset management. Credit policy affects not only accounts receivable but also sales and working capital requirements. Other examples could show how production costs might change, or the optimum inventory level might change. Still others might incorporate changing prices or the timing of cash flows. The model is capable of including all effects of the credit policy by focusing on cash flow impacts and the resulting NPV of a given credit policy change.

As with any analytical tool, the results can only be as valid as the data inputs. Estimates of the effects of a policy change might be made on the basis of market research or by comparison with existing product line/credit policy combinations within the firm or in other firms. Alternatively, the model can be used in a sensitivity framework to calculate the change in sales or bad debt loss rate (for example) required to justify a change in credit policy, in conjunction with an analysis of the probabilities of various changes occurring.[4]

Use of Computers in Credit Management

By nature, credit management lends itself to the use of computer controls. Credit management requires the collection, compilation, storage, analysis, and retrieval of information. Since accurate information on fund flows is critical to good credit management, efficient information processing is important.

All of the accounts receivable materials can be organized into a computer record system giving the credit manager current information on the status of accounts. Records will include the date the account was opened, the amount currently owed, the customer's maximum credit line, and a record of the customer's past payments. The credit rating assigned to the customer by Dun & Bradstreet or other rating agencies can be noted. Periodically, the credit manager may draw off various types of analyses of the customer accounts. These may include the days' sales outstanding, the aging schedule, and a payments pattern analysis as described in Appendix A to this chapter.

In addition, particular controls can be set up to monitor account delinquency. The computer can periodically flag past-due accounts for the credit manager's attention. The computer may be programmed to provide information on how close the account balance is to the established maximum line of credit. Such information provides the credit manager with the opportunity to contact the customer on a timely basis.

Indeed, the computer can be programmed to perform selected credit decisions. Based on credit limits set in advance, credit standards can be expressed quantitatively, and the computer can approve or reject credit applications or flag them for further analysis. Aided by a computer, a relatively small staff can manage a greatly increased volume of credit activity.

In addition to information on individual accounts, the computer can provide the credit manager with information on groups of companies. Periodically, the credit manager may receive a summary of all receivable accounts with respect to each account individually and in total. Information can be provided on billings, payments, discounts taken, and amounts owed. In addition, the computer can prepare special reports to provide analytical information that may be useful in making credit decisions. For example, the payment history of companies in the same industry may be compared. Do companies in a particular industry tend to pay slowly during certain months of the year? If this appears to be a trend, the credit manager should analyze the economic factors that cause firms in a particular industry to respond in similar ways. On the other hand, if a customer performs differently from most firms in the industry, the credit manager can examine the circumstances behind that firm's behavior. The credit manager may also analyze, before the problems escalate, any management or operating problems that may be developing in a firm making the account a serious credit risk.

Using a computer increases both the amount and frequency of information available to the credit manager. This information facilitates interaction with the customer and enables the credit management department to communicate promptly and effectively with other divisions in its own company as well as with general management. Thus, the effectiveness

---

[4]Sartoris and Hill [1983]. Also, see Copeland and Khoury [1981].

of the credit department has been greatly enhanced by making feasible computer-generated information flows which otherwise would be too expensive and time consuming to develop.

Summary

In this chapter, we discussed the management of accounts receivable, including the major credit policy variables and the effects which alternate credit policies have on the value of the firm.

In establishing a credit policy, a firm formulates its credit standards and its credit terms. Credit standards that are too strict will lose sales; credit standards that are too easy will result in excessive bad debt losses. To determine optimal credit standards, the firm relates the marginal costs of credit to the marginal profits on the increased sales. Individual customers are evaluated on the five C's of credit: character, capacity, capital, collateral, and conditions, all of which indicate the likelihood that the buyer will pay its obligations. Credit analysis and the evaluation of prospective customers typically include analysis of financial ratios, the average age of accounts receivable, and record of past payments. It also incorporates the experience of the credit manager in similar situations.

The terms of credit specify the credit period and the use of cash discounts. Longer credit periods stimulate sales, but the optimal credit period balances the marginal profits on increased sales against the costs of carrying the higher amounts of accounts receivable. Similarly, an optimal cash discount policy balances the benefit of increased sales and the costs of discounts taken.

Our discussion of evaluating alternate credit policies recognized the interdependence of current asset variables. Credit policy changes can involve overall changes in the level and composition of all current assets. The Sartoris-Hill credit policy decision model uses a capital budgeting framework to determine the effects of alternative credit policies on the value of the firm.

Computerized accounts receivable can provide a valuable information tool to credit managers. Computer records include such information as the amount currently owed, the customer's maximum credit line, and record of past payments. The computer can flag past-due accounts, make note of accounts approaching their credit limit, and even perform some selected credit decisions. It can also provide summary information on all accounts or help analyze customers in a specific industry.

Questions

14.1   Assume that a firm sells on terms of net 30 and that its accounts are, on the average, 30 days overdue. What will its investment in receivables be if its annual credit sales are approximately $720,000?

14.2   Evaluate this statement: It is difficult to judge the performance of many of our employees but not that of the credit manager. If the credit manager is performing perfectly, credit losses are zero; the higher our losses (as a percent of sales), the worse is the performance.

14.3   Apco Corporation's 19X1 sales were $990,000. In April 19X1, the accounts receivable balance was $41,250; by July 19X1, accounts receivable had more than doubled to $96,250. Calculate the Days' Sales Outstanding for each period. Did the increase necessarily represent a problem for Apco?

14.4 How would a new business go about setting up credit standards? Would its credit policies be likely to vary from those of established firms in the same line of business?

14.5 Explain how the credit terms of a firm's suppliers can affect the terms offered to the firm's customers.

Problems

14.1 The Fulton Company has been reviewing its credit policies. The credit standards it has been applying have resulted in annual credit sales of $5 million. Its average collection period is 30 days, with a bad debt loss ratio of 1 percent. Because persistent inflation has caused deterioration in the financial position of many of its customers, Fulton is considering a reduction in its credit standards. As a result, it expects incremental credit sales of $400,000, on which the average collection period (ACP) would be 60 days and on which the bad debt loss (BDL) ratio would be 3 percent. The variable cost ratio (VCR) to sales for Fulton is 70 percent. The required return on investment in receivables is 15 percent.

Evaluate the relaxation in credit standards that Fulton is considering.

14.2 Instead of relaxing credit standards, Fulton is considering simply lengthening credit terms from net 20 to net 50, a procedure that would increase the average collection period from 30 days to 60 days. Under the new policy, Fulton expects incremental sales to be $500,000 and the new bad debt loss ratio to rise to 2 percent on *all* sales. Assume all other returns hold. Evaluate the lengthening in credit terms that Fulton is considering.

14.3 Gulf Distributors makes all sales on a credit basis; once each year, it routinely evaluates the creditworthiness of all its customers. The evaluation procedure ranks customers from 1 to 5, in order of increasing risk. Results of the ranking are given below.

Category	Percentage Bad Debts	Average Collection Period (Days)	Credit Decision	Annual Sales Lost through Credit Restrictions
1	None	10	Unlimited credit	None
2	1.0	12	Unlimited credit	None
3	3.0	20	Limited credit	$360,000
4	9.0	60	Limited credit	$180,000
5	30.0	90	No credit	$360,000

The variable cost ratio is 75 percent. The opportunity cost of investment in receivables is 15 percent.

What will be the effect on profitability of extending full credit to Category 3? to Category 4? to Category 5?

14.4 Milburn Auto Parts is considering changing its credit terms from 2/15, net 30 to 3/10, net 30 in order to speed collections. At present, 60 percent of Milburn's customers take the 2 percent discount. Under the new terms, this number is expected to rise to 70 percent, reducing the average collection period from 25 to 22 days. Bad-debt losses are expected to rise from 1 percent to the 2 percent level. However, the more generous cash discount terms are expected to increase credit sales from $800,000 to

$1 million per year. Milburn's variable cost ratio is 80 percent, and its cost of accounts receivable is 15 percent. Evaluate the change.

14.5   Charles Roberts, the new credit manager of the Baskin Corporation, was alarmed to find that Baskin sells on credit terms of net 90 days, when industry-wide credit terms are net 30 days. On annual credit sales of $2.5 million, Baskin currently averages 95 days' sales in accounts receivable. Roberts estimates that tightening the credit terms to 30 days will reduce annual sales to $2,375,000 but that accounts receivable will drop to 35 days of sales and the bad debt loss ratio drop from 3 percent of sales to 1 percent of sales.

Baskin's variable cost ratio is 85 percent. If Baskin's opportunity cost of funds is 18 percent, should the change be made?

Selected References

Atkins, Joseph C., and Kim, Yong H., "Comment and Correction: Opportunity Cost in the Evaluation of Investment in Accounts Receivable," *Financial Management*, 6 (Winter 1977), pp. 71-74.

Ben-Horim, Moshe, and Levy, Haim, "Management of Accounts Receivable Under Inflation," *Financial Management*, 12 (Spring 1983), pp. 42-48.

Copeland, Thomas E., and Khoury, Nabil, "A Theory of Credit Extensions with Default Risk and Systematic Risk," *The Engineering Economist*, (1981), pp. 35-51.

Dyl, Edward A., "Another Look at the Evaluation of Investments in Accounts Receivable," *Financial Management*, 6 (Winter 1977), pp. 67-70.

Greer, Carl C., "The Optimal Credit Acceptance Policy," *Journal of Financial and Quantitative Analysis*, 2 (December 1967), pp. 399-415.

Hawkins, Gregory D., "An Analysis of Revolving Credit Agreements," *Journal of Financial Economics*, 10 (March 1982), pp. 59-82.

Hill, Ned C., and Riener, Kenneth D., "Determining the Cash Discount in the Firm's Credit Policy," *Financial Management*, 8 (Spring 1979), pp. 68-73.

Kim, Yong H., and Atkins, Joseph C., "Evaluating Investments in Accounts Receivable: A Maximizing Framework," *Journal of Finance*, 33 (May 1978), pp. 403-412.

Lane, Sylvia, "Submarginal Credit Risk Classification," *Journal of Financial and Quantitative Analysis*, 7 (January 1972), pp. 1379-1385.

Lewellen, Wilbur G.; McConnell, John J.; and Scott, Jonathan A., "Capital Market Influences on Trade Credit Policies," *The Journal of Financial Research*, 3 (Summer 1980), pp. 105-114.

Lieber, Ziv, and Orgler, Yair E., "An Integrated Model for Accounts Receivable Management," *Management Science*, 22 (October 1975), pp. 212-219.

Long, Michael S., "Credit Screening System Selection," *Journal of Financial and Quantitative Analysis*, 11 (June 1976), pp. 313-328.

Mehta, Dileep, "Optimal Credit Policy Selection: A Dynamic Approach," *Journal of Financial and Quantitative Analysis*, 5 (December 1970), pp. 421-444.

———, "The Formulation of Credit Policy Models," *Management Science*, 15 (October 1968), pp. 30-50.

Oh, John S., "Opportunity Cost in the Evaluation of Investment in Accounts Receivable," *Financial Management*, 5 (Summer 1976), pp. 32-36.

Sartoris, William, and Hill, Ned C., "A Generalized Cash Flow Approach to Short-term Financial Decisions," *Journal of Finance*, 38 (May 1983), pp. 349-360.

———, "Evaluating Credit Policy Alternatives: A Present Value Framework," *The Journal of Financial Research*, 4 (Spring 1981), pp. 81-89.

Schiff, M., and Lieber, Z., "A Model for the Integration of Credit and Inventory Management," *Journal of Finance*, 29 (March 1974), pp. 133-141.

Schwartz, Robert A., "An Economic Model of Trade Credit," *Journal of Financial and Quantitative Analysis*, 9 (September 1974), pp. 643-657.

Walia, Tirlochan S., "Explicit and Implicit Cost of Changes in the Level of Accounts Receivable and the Credit Policy Decision of the Firm," *Financial Management*, 6 (Winter 1977), pp. 75-78.

Weston, J. Fred, and Tuan, Pham D., "Comment on Analysis of Credit Policy Changes," *Financial Management*, (Winter 1980), pp. 59-63.

Appendix A to Chapter 14

The Payments Pattern Approach

The management of accounts receivable is an important aspect of working capital management for a firm that sells on credit. The rate at which credit sales are converted into cash measures the efficiency of a firm's collection policy and the performance of its collection efforts. Two key issues facing the financial executive in accounts receivable management are the forecasting and the control of accounts receivable. We first examine two methods widely used by corporations, namely, the Days' Sales Outstanding (DSO) and the Aging Schedule (AS). We then focus our attention on the payments pattern approach, which offers a better means of monitoring accounts receivable.

Corporate Practice

According to a survey by Stone [1976], out of the companies which reported the use of some systematic procedures to project accounts receivable, a great majority used either a pro forma projection of DSO or some other ratio of receivables to a measure of sales. In the control of receivables, the AS is reportedly the popular method.

Days' Sales Outstanding

The average Days' Sales Outstanding (DSO) at a given time t is usually calculated as the ratio of receivables to a measure of daily sales:

$$DSO_t = \frac{\text{Total AR}_t}{\text{Daily sales}}.$$

The daily sales figure is obtained by averaging sales over a recent time period. The averaging period may be 30 days, 60 days, 90 days, or another relevant period. Clearly, DSO is affected by both the level of sales and the averaging period used.

The Aging Schedule

The Aging Schedule (AS) is the percentage of end-of-quarter accounts receivable in different age groups. Here, the phrase *age group* refers to the period of time that receivables have been outstanding from the time of sales. A strong AS shows only a small percentage of end-of-quarter receivables based on old sales, with the highest percentage based on the most recent month's sales.

Problems with These Approaches

Both the DSO and the AS are affected by the pattern of sales within a quarter. Table 14A.1 shows the end-of-quarter DSO for three different sales patterns. Total sales for the three quarters are identical at $180,000; only the monthly distributions differ from quarter to quarter. The payments pattern is assumed to be constant, with collections of 10 percent of sales during the month that sales are made and 30 percent, 40 percent, and 20 percent in the three months that follow. As a result, end-of-quarter receivables are 20 percent of the first month's sales, 60 percent of the second, and 90 percent of the third. If sales were level at $60,000 per month, the DSO would be constant at 51 days, as shown for the first quarter in Table 14A.1 (look in the 30 days column under End-of-Quarter DSO). With changing sales patterns, the DSO varies, changing to 41 for the second quarter and 81 for the third when the averaging period is for 30 days.

Table 14A.2 shows the aging schedule for the same sales and collections data. If sales were level at $60,000 monthly, the AS would be constant, with 53 percent in the 0 to 30 days group, 35 percent in the 31 to 60 days group, and 12 percent in the 61 to 90 days group (shown for the first quarter in the Percent of Total column). But with a changing sales pattern, the AS becomes erratic. If sales are rising, as in the second quarter, the uncollected receivables from the first two months make up a relatively small portion (34 percent) of end-of-quarter receivables. Consequently, the payments experience appears to be improving. When sales are falling, as in the third quarter, uncollected receivables based on heavy sales for the first two months make up 67 percent of end-of-quarter receivables, and the payments experience appears to be worsening. Thus, seasonal variations in sales can send false signals to the credit manager, even though the true collection experience is unchanged.

Other factors can also cause DSO and AS figures to shift. The DSO figures can be further distorted when alternative averaging periods are used to calculate daily sales. For the data in Table 14A.1, third quarter daily sales rise from $1,000 based on a 30-day average to $2,000 based on a 90-day average. The corresponding end-of-quarter DSO falls from

---

Table 14A.1   DSO with Varying Sales Pattern and Varying Averaging Periods (Dollars in Thousands)

Month	Sales	Receivables at End of Quarter	Daily Sales if Averaging Period Is the Most Recent:			End-of-Quarter DSO (in Days) If Averaging Period Is:		
			30 Days	60 Days	90 Days	30 Days	60 Days	90 Days
January	$60	$ 12						
February	60	36						
March	60	54						
		$102	$2	$2	$2	51	51	51
April	$30	$ 6						
May	60	36						
June	90	81						
		$123	$3	$2.50	$2	41	49	62.
July	$90	$ 18						
August	60	36						
September	30	27						
		$ 81	$1	$1.50	$2	81	54	41

Table 14A.2   Aging Schedules (Dollars in Thousands)

Month	Sales	Total Receivables at End of Quarter	Age Group (in Days)	Percent of Total
January	$60	$ 12	61-90	12%
February	60	36	31-60	35
March	60	54	0-30	53
		$102		100%
April	$30	$ 6	61-90	5%
May	60	36	31-60	29
June	90	81	0-30	66
		$123		100%
July	$90	$ 18	61-90	22%
August	60	36	31-60	45
September	30	27	0-30	33
		$ 81		100%

an alarming 81 days to a healthy 41 days. The way the credit manager perceives the collection experience as measured by the DSO will depend on which averaging period is chosen.

The AS figures can be further distorted if payments on the most recent month's sales are unusually high or low. A high proportion of payments on the most recent month's sales means that receivables for the previous two months will make up a higher percentage of end-of-quarter receivables, even though the old receivables may be normal in relation to the sales for those months. For instance, if receivables from September sales were $10,000 (instead of the $27,000 shown in Table 14A.2) because customers paid $20,000 during September instead of the normal $3,000, the proportion of receivables in the three age groups would have been:

Month	Receivables	Age Groups	Percent of Total
July	$18	61-90	28%
August	36	31-60	56
September	10	0-30	16
	$64		100%

In this example, the exceptionally high collections on September sales — a condition favorable to the firm — distort the percentages to create the impression that the aging schedule has deteriorated.

Payments Pattern Approach

We have seen that the DSO and AS procedures can be unreliable in the forecasting and control of accounts receivable. The major deficiency of both methods lies in their aggregation of sales and accounts receivable over a particular time period, a quarter in the above example. The payments pattern approach, suggested by Lewellen and Johnson [1972] and by Stone [1976], overcomes this difficulty to produce an analysis of payments behavior which is, of course, the real issue of interest to management.

The Payments Pattern

A (monthly) payments pattern is characterized by the proportions of credit sales in a given month that are paid in that month and a number of subsequent months. Table 14A.3 gives the monthly cash flows and accounts receivable arising from $60,000 of credit sales in January. The payments pattern is reflected in the last column: We see that 90 percent of payments for January sales remains outstanding at the end of that month, 60 percent at the end of February, and 20 percent at the end of March. A graphical representation of the payments pattern is given in Figure 14A.1; the rectangles represent the accounts receivable proportions and the accumulated paid proportions of January sales at different points in time.

Mathematically, a payments pattern can be expressed as a sequence of numbers $(P_0, P_1, P_2, \ldots, P_H)$, where P_i, called the payments proportion, denotes the proportion of credit sales paid i months after the month of sale, and $P_0 + P_1 + \ldots + P_H = 1$. H is the payments horizon, that is, the number of months required for a given month's credit sales to be completely collected. Once a payments pattern is known, we can easily derive the accounts receivable pattern to be the sequence of numbers

$$(F_0, F_1, \ldots, F_{H-1}),$$

where F_i, called the balance fraction, is the remaining accounts receivable i months after the month of sale, and $F_i = 1 - (P_0 + P_1 + \ldots + P_i)$. At the end of the payments horizon, the credit sales in any particular month are fully paid so that $F_H = 1 - (P_0 + P_1 + \ldots + P_H) = 0$. In the above numerical example, $H = 3$, $P_0 = 0.1$, $P_1 = 0.3$, $P_2 = 0.4$, $P_3 = 0.2$, and $F_0 = 1 - 0.1 = 0.9$, $F_1 = 1 - (0.1 + 0.3) = 0.6$, and $F_2 = 1 - (0.1 + 0.3 + 0.4) = 0.2$.

When the payments pattern remains the same, that is, the numbers $P_0, P_1, \ldots, P_H$ remain unchanged from month to month, it is said to be constant. For example, using the same data as in Table 14A.1, we observe a constant payments pattern (0.1, 0.3, 0.4, 0.2) and, consequently, a constant accounts receivable pattern (0.9, 0.6, 0.2) as exhibited in Table 14A.4.

Table 14A.3   Payments Pattern of $60,000 of Credit Sales in January

Month	Collections from January Sales during Month		Receivables from January Sales Outstanding at End of Month	
	Percent	in Thousands	in Thousands	Percent
January	10	$ 6	$54	90
February	30	18	36	60
March	40	24	12	20
April	20	12	0	0

Figure 14A.1   Graph of Payments Pattern of $60,000 of Credit Sales in January

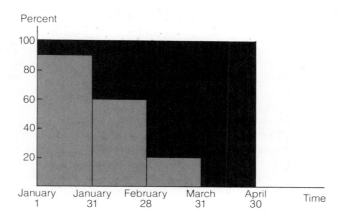

The major deficiency of the DSO and AS methods is due to the aggregation of sales and accounts receivable over a number of time periods. This aggregation makes it difficult to detect changes in the payments behavior. In the payments pattern approach, the problem is overcome by matching accounts receivable to sales in the month of origin. As a consequence, the payments pattern approach, in contrast to the DSO and AS, is not sales-level dependent. No matter what the sales pattern may be, the last column in Table 14A.4 remains unchanged, provided the payments pattern is constant. Conversely, any change

Table 14A.4   Accounts Receivable as Percentages of Original Sales

Month of Origin	Sales during That Month (in Thousands)	Receivables at End of Quarter (in Thousands)	Percentage Outstanding (Receivables/Sales in Month of Origin)
January	$60	$ 12	20%
February	60	36	60
March	60	54	90
		$102	
April	$30	$ 6	20%
May	60	36	60
June	90	81	90
		$123	
July	$90	$ 18	20%
August	60	36	60
September	30	27	90
		$81	

in payments behavior would be immediately reflected and recognized. Thus, the payments proportions (P_i) and the balance proportions (F_i) provide efficient means of control for the credit manager. For example, assume that a firm's historical accounts receivable pattern was (0.9, 0.6, 0.2). In early March, assume that the report on actual payments for January and February credit sales showed a current balance fraction for January sales of $F_1 = 0.70$ versus the pro forma value of 0.60, and a balance fraction for February sales of $F_0 = 0.95$ versus the pro forma value of 0.90. A problem, created by two consecutive adverse and large deviations from the normal pattern, is indicated.

The procedures proposed by Carpenter and Miller [1979] build on the payments pattern framework. For brevity, their study will be referred to by the initials CM. The emphasis of the sales pattern approach presented by Lewellen and Johnson and by Stone was to express receivables as a percent of sales in the month of origin. Control standards are developed from the percentages based on the payments pattern and corresponding receivables pattern. CM built upon the payments pattern concept to develop some additional evaluation relations. The key measure is the weighted DSO (WDSO). The changes in the WDSO, or changes in the average daily sales (ADS) in relation to the WDSO of the previous reference period, enable them to calculate efficiency and volume variances in receivables. The resulting data enable the credit executive to separate the changes in collection experience from changes in the sales patterns. The executive is thus better able to evaluate the current state of collections and receivables investment. Since it is now possible to distinguish between changes in credit experience and in sales volume, the credit executive can plan to work on changing collection performance or to alter the credit-related variables that influence the volume of sales.

Selected References

Carpenter, Michael D., and Miller, Jack E., "A Reliable Framework for Monitoring Accounts Receivable," *Financial Management*, 8 (Winter 1979), pp. 37-40.

Lewellen, W. G., and Edmister, R. O., "A General Model for Accounts Receivable Analysis and Control," *Journal of Financial and Quantitative Analysis*, 8 (March 1973), pp. 195-206.

Lewellen, W. G., and Johnson, R. W., "Better Way to Monitor Accounts Receivable," *Harvard Business Review*, 50 (May-June 1972), pp. 101-109.

Stone, B. K., "Payments-Pattern Approach to Forecasting and Control of Accounts Receivable," *Financial Management*, 5 (1976), pp. 65-82.

Chapter 15 Short-Term Financing

Our final topic in the discussion of working capital management is short-term financing. Short-term credit is defined as debt originally scheduled for repayment within one year. A variety of short-term credits are available to the firm, and the financial manager must know the advantages and disadvantages of each. In this chapter, we evaluate the three major sources of funds with short maturities. Ranked in descending order by volume of credit supplied, they are (1) trade credit among firms, (2) loans from commercial banks, and (3) commercial paper.

Short-term credits are often secured with some form of collateral. Hence, we will also discuss two common methods for securing loans: accounts receivable financing and inventory financing.

Trade Credit

In the ordinary course of events, a firm buys its supplies and materials on credit from other firms, recording the debt as an *account payable*. Accounts payable, or *trade credit*, is the largest single category of short-term credit, representing about one-third of the current liabilities of nonfinancial corporations.[1] This percentage is somewhat larger for small firms. Because these firms may not qualify for financing from other sources, they rely rather heavily on trade credit.

Trade credit is a spontaneous source of financing in that it arises from ordinary business transactions. For example, suppose a firm makes average purchases of $2,000 a day on terms of net 30. On the average, it will owe 30 times $2,000, or $60,000, to its suppliers. If its sales and, consequently, its purchases double, accounts payable will also double — to $120,000. The firm will have spontaneously generated an additional $60,000 of financing. Similarly, if the terms of credit are extended from 30 to 40 days, accounts payable will expand from $60,000 to $80,000; thus, lengthening the average payment period generates additional financing.

Credit Terms

The terms of sales, or *credit terms*, describe the payment obligation of the buyer. The following discussion outlines the four main factors that influence the length of credit terms: the economic nature of the product, the seller's circumstances, the buyer's circumstances, and cash discounts.[2]

---

[1]In Chapter 14, we discussed trade credit from the viewpoint of minimizing investment in current assets. In the present chapter, we look at the other side of the coin — trade credit as a source, rather than a use, of financing. In Chapter 14, the use of trade credit by customers resulted in an asset investment called *accounts receivable*. In the present chapter, the use of trade credit gives rise to short-term obligations, generally called *accounts payable*.

[2]For a discussion of the determinants of credit policy, see Hill, Wood, and Sorenson [1981].

Economic Nature of the Product. Commodities with high sales turnover are sold on relatively short credit terms; buyers resell the products rapidly, generating cash that enables them to pay the suppliers. Groceries have a high turnover, but perishability also plays a role. The credit extended for fresh fruits and vegetables might run from 5 to 10 days, whereas the credit extended on canned fruits and vegetables would more likely be 15 to 30 days. Terms for items that have a slow retail turnover, such as jewelry, may run six months or longer.

Seller Circumstances. Financially weak sellers must require cash or exceptionally short credit terms. For example, farmers sell livestock to meat-packing companies on a cash basis. In many industries, variations in credit terms can be used as a sales promotion device. Although the use of credit as a selling device could endanger sound credit management, the practice does occur, especially when the seller's industry has excess capacity. Also, large sellers can use their position to impose relatively short credit terms. However, the reverse appears more often in practice; that is, financially strong sellers are suppliers of funds to small firms.

Buyer Circumstances. In general, financially sound retailers who sell on credit may, in turn, receive slightly longer terms. Some classes of retailers regarded as selling in particularly risky areas (such as clothing) receive extended credit terms but are offered large discounts to encourage early payment.

Cash Discounts. A *cash discount* is a reduction in price based on payment within a specified period. The costs of not taking cash discounts often exceed the rate of interest at which the buyer can borrow, so it is important that a firm be cautious in its use of trade credit as a source of financing; it could be quite expensive. If the firm borrows and takes the cash discount, the period during which accounts payable remain on the books is reduced. The effective length of credit is thus influenced by the size of discounts offered. Credit terms typically express the amount of the cash discount and the date of its expiration, as well as the final due date. We noted earlier that one of the most frequently encountered terms is 2/10, net 30. (If payment is made within 10 days of the invoice date, a 2 percent cash discount is allowed. If the cash discount is not taken, payment is due 30 days after the date of invoicing.) The cost of not taking cash discounts can be substantial, as shown here.

Cost of Credit if the Cash Discount Is Not Taken

$$r_c = \frac{\%}{100 - \%} \times \frac{365}{\# \text{ days}}$$

Credit Terms	Computed Interest (r_c) (Percent)	Effective Interest with 36.5 times or 18.25 times Compounding per Year (Percent)
1/10, net 20	36.87	$r_e = \left(1 + \dfrac{.3687}{36.5}\right)^{36.5} - 1 = 44.32\%.$
1/10, net 30	18.43	$r_e = \left(1 + \dfrac{.1843}{18.25}\right)^{18.25} - 1 = 20.13\%.$
2/10, net 20	74.49	$r_e = \left(1 + \dfrac{.7449}{36.5}\right)^{36.5} - 1 = 109.05\%.$
2/10, net 30	37.24	$r_e = \left(1 + \dfrac{.3724}{18.25}\right)^{18.25} - 1 = 44.58\%.$

Concept of Net Credit

Trade credit has double-edged significance for the firm. It is a source of credit for financing purchases, and it is a use of funds to the extent that the firm finances credit sales to customers. For example, if, on the average, a firm sells $3,000 worth of goods a day and has an average collection period of 40 days, at any balance sheet date, it will have accounts receivable of approximately $120,000.

If the same firm buys $2,000 worth of materials a day and the balance is outstanding for 20 days, accounts payable will average $40,000. The firm is thus extending net credit of $80,000 — the difference between accounts receivable and accounts payable.

Large firms and well-financed firms of all sizes tend to be net suppliers of trade credit; small firms and undercapitalized firms of all sizes tend to be net users of trade credit. It is impossible to generalize about whether it is better to be a net supplier or a net user; the choice depends on the firm's circumstances and on the various costs and benefits of receiving and using trade credit.

Advantages of Trade Credit as a Source of Financing

Trade credit, a customary part of doing business in most industries, is convenient and informal. A firm that does not qualify for credit from a financial institution may receive trade credit because previous experience has familiarized the seller with the creditworthiness of the customer. The seller knows the merchandising practices of the industry and is usually in a good position to judge the capacity of the customer and the risk of selling on credit. The amount of trade credit fluctuates with the buyer's purchases, subject to any credit limits that may be operative.

Whether trade credit costs more or less than other forms of financing is a moot question. The buyer often has no alternative form of financing available, and the costs may be commensurate with the risks to the seller. But in some instances, trade credit is used simply because the buyer does not realize how expensive it is. In such circumstances, careful financial analysis may lead to the substitution of alternative forms of financing.

At the other extreme, trade credit may represent a virtual subsidy or sales promotion device offered by the seller. The authors know, for example, of cases where manufacturers quite literally supplied *all* the financing for new firms by selling on credit terms substantially longer than those of the new company. In one instance, a manufacturer, eager to obtain a dealership in a particular area, made a loan to the new company to cover operating expenses during the initial phases and geared the payment of accounts payable to cash receipts. Even in such instances, however, the buying firm must be careful that it is not really paying a hidden financing cost in the form of higher product prices than could be obtained elsewhere. Extending credit involves a cost to the selling firm, and this firm may well be raising its own prices to offset the apparently free credit it extends.

Importance of Good Supplier Relations during Inflation

During periods of inflation and tight money, firms raise their standards for extending trade credit to their customers. Since cleaning up accounts receivable is one way to obtain a more favorable liquidity position, suppliers become more selective when extending trade credit. This shows that it is important for a firm to earn the confidence of its suppliers. Showing good financial ratios and paying promptly are excellent ways to achieve this goal. But even if these indicators are unfavorable, a firm may still be able to obtain trade credit by offering realistic plans for improving its situation. Illustrative was the W. T. Grant Company experience in 1975. After announcing policy changes and a program for improvement, W. T. Grant's suppliers were willing to continue to extend trade credit for a period of time. The more recent experience of the Wickes Companies in 1982 is similar. Sanford Sigoloff, who had a record of success in rehabilitating bankrupt companies, was appointed to turn around the Wickes Companies. Mr. Sigoloff's appointment, and the subsequent program for rehabilitation that he announced, enabled the company to maintain relationships with an important number of its suppliers. The Wickes reorganization involved the largest amount of debt ($2 billion) for any industrial company in bankruptcy.

Short-Term Financing by Commercial Banks

Commercial bank lending, which appears on the balance sheet as *notes payable*, is second in importance to trade credit as a source of short-term financing. Banks occupy a pivotal position in the short-term and intermediate-term money markets. Their influence is greater than it appears to be from the dollar amounts they lend, because the banks provide nonspontaneous funds. As a firm's financing needs increase, it requests additional funds from banks. If the request is denied, often the alternative is to slow down the rate of growth or to cut back operations.

Characteristics of Loans from Commercial Banks

In the following sections, the main characteristics of lending patterns of commercial banks are briefly described.

Forms of Loans. A single loan obtained from a bank by a business firm is not different in principle from a loan obtained by an individual. In fact, it is often difficult to distinguish a bank loan to a small business from a personal loan. The loan is obtained by signing a conventional promissory note. Repayment is made in a lump sum at maturity (when the note is due) or in installments throughout the life of the loan.

A *line of credit* is a formal or informal understanding between the bank and the borrower concerning the maximum loan balance the bank will allow the borrower. For example, a bank loan officer may indicate to a financial manager that the bank regards the firm as "good" for up to $80,000 for the forthcoming year. Subsequently, the manager signs a promissory note for $15,000 for 90 days, thereby "taking down" $15,000 of the total line of $80,000 in credit. This amount is credited to the firm's checking account at the bank. At maturity, the checking account is charged for the amount of the loan. Interest may be deducted in advance or may be paid at maturity. Before repayment of the $15,000, the firm may borrow additional amounts up to the total of $80,000.

A more formal procedure may be followed. To illustrate, Chrysler Corporation arranged a line of credit for over $100 million with a group of banks. The banks were formally committed to lend Chrysler the funds if they were needed. Chrysler, in turn, paid a commitment fee of approximately one-quarter of 1 percent of the unused balance of the commitment to compensate the banks for making the funds available.

Size of Customers. Banks make loans to firms of all sizes. By dollar amount, the major proportion of loans from commercial banks is obtained by large firms. But by number of loans, small firms account for over one-half of bank loans.

Maturity. Commercial banks concentrate on the short-term lending market. Short-term loans make up about two-thirds of bank loans by dollar amount, whereas term loans (loans with maturities longer than one year) make up only one-third.

Security. If a potential borrower is a questionable credit risk, or if the firm's financing needs exceed the amount that the loan officer of the bank considers to be prudent on an unsecured basis, some form of security is required. More than half the dollar value of bank loans is secured. (The forms of security are described later in this chapter.) In terms of the number of bank loans, two-thirds are secured through the endorsement of a third party, who guarantees payment of the loan in the event the borrower defaults.

Compensating Balances. Banks typically require that a regular borrower maintain an average checking account balance equal to 15 or 20 percent of the outstanding loan. These balances, commonly called *compensating balances,* are a method of raising the effective interest rate. For example, if a firm needs $80,000 to pay off outstanding obligations but must maintain a 20 percent compensating balance, it must borrow $100,000 in order to obtain the required $80,000. If the stated interest rate is 5 percent, the effective cost is actually $6\frac{1}{4}$ percent ($5,000 divided by $80,000). These *loan* compensating balances are, of course, added to any *service* compensating balances (discussed in Chapter 12) that the firm's bank may require.

Repayment of Bank Loans. Because most bank deposits are subject to withdrawal on demand, commercial banks seek to prevent firms from using bank credit for permanent financing. A bank, therefore, may require its borrowers to "clean up" their short-term bank loans for at least one month each year. If a firm is unable to become free of bank debt at least part of each year, it is using bank financing for permanent needs and should develop additional sources of long-term or permanent financing.

Cost of Commercial Bank Loans. Most loans from commercial banks have recently cost from 10 to 20 percent, with the effective rate depending on the characteristics of the firm and the level of interest rates in the economy. If the firm can qualify as a prime risk because of its size and financial strength, the rate of interest will be one-half to three-quarters of a percent above the discount rate charged by federal reserve banks to commercial banks. This is called the *prime interest rate*. On the other hand, a small firm with below-average financial ratios may be required to provide collateral security and to pay an effective rate of interest of 2 to 3 points above the prime rate.

"Regular" Interest. Determination of the effective, or true, rate of interest on a loan depends on the stated rate of interest and the lender's method of charging interest. If the interest is paid at the maturity of the loan, the stated rate of interest is the effective rate of interest. For example, on a $20,000 loan for one year at 10 percent, the interest is $2,000.

$$\text{``Regular'' loan, interest paid at maturity} = \frac{\text{Interest}}{\text{Borrowed amount}}$$

$$= \frac{\$2,000}{\$20,000} = 10\%.$$

Discounted Interest. If the bank deducts the interest in advance (discounts the loan), the effective rate of interest is increased. On the $20,000 loan for one year at 10 percent, the discount is $2,000, and the borrower obtains the use of only $18,000. The effective rate of interest is 11.1 percent (versus 10 percent on a "regular" loan):

$$\text{Discounted loan} = \frac{\text{Interest}}{\text{Borrowed amount} - \text{Interest}} = \frac{\$2,000}{\$18,000} = 11.1\%.$$

Installment Loan.   The "regular" and discounted interest loans above are both characterized by repayment of the loan principal at maturity. Under the installment method, principal payments are made periodically (for example, monthly) over the term of the loan; on a one-year loan, the borrower has the full amount of the money only during the first month and by the last month has already paid back eleven-twelfths of the loan. Thus, the effective rate (that is, the annual percentage rate, or APR) of interest on an installment loan is significantly higher than the stated rate. Installment loans can be arranged in two ways. In an add-on installment loan, net loan proceeds are the same as the face amount of the loan, but interest is added to the loan principal to calculate the monthly installments. In a discounted installment loan, interest is subtracted from the principal to obtain the net loan proceeds while the installments are based on the full face value of the loan. The add-on installment loan results in higher monthly payments but a lower effective interest rate; the discounted installment loan results in lower monthly payments but a higher effective interest rate. Examples will illustrate the calculation of the effective interest rate under the two methods for a one-year installment loan of $20,000 at a 10 percent nominal interest rate.

1.   Add-on Installment Loan

Amount borrowed	$20,000.00
Stated interest rate	10%
Add-on interest	$2,000.00
Total	$22,000.00
Monthly installment ($22,000/12)	$1,833.33

The computed interest rate, r_c, implicit in these terms can be found as

$$\text{Borrowed amount} = \text{Periodic payment} \times \text{PVIFA}(r_c, n \text{ periods}).$$

Substituting the numerical values and using the formula for the PVIFA, we have

$$\$20,000 = \$1,833.33 \left[\frac{1 - \dfrac{1}{\left(1 + \dfrac{r}{q}\right)^q}}{r/q} \right].$$

Solving for (r/q) (on a programmed hand-calculator), we find that (r/q) is approximately equal to .015 on a monthly basis, implying a computed annual interest rate of 18 percent compounded monthly and an effective or annual percentage rate of 19.56 percent, computed from $(1 + .015)^{12} - 1$.

2.   Discounted Installment Loan

Amount borrowed	$20,000.00
Stated interest rate	10%
Subtract interest	$2,000.00
Amount received	$18,000.00
Monthly installment ($20,000/12)	$1,666.67

Again, the computed interest rate can be found as

$$\text{Amount received} = \text{Periodic payment} \times \text{PVIFA}(r/q,\ n \text{ periods}),$$

or

$$\$18,000 = \$1,666.67 \left[\frac{1 - \dfrac{1}{\left(1 + \dfrac{r}{q}\right)^q}}{r/q} \right].$$

Solving, we find $r/q = .01659$ for a computed annual rate of approximately 19.91 percent, compounded monthly, and an APR of 21.83 percent, computed from $(1.01659)^{12} - 1$.

In both cases, the interest is calculated on the original amount of the loan, not on the amount actually outstanding (the declining balance), and this causes the effective interest rate to be almost double the stated rate. Interest is calculated by the installment method on most consumer loans (for example, automobile loans), but the installment method is not often used for business loans larger than about $15,000.

Choice of Banks

Banks have direct relationships with their borrowers. There is much personal association over the years, and the business problems of the borrower are frequently discussed. Thus, banks often provide informal management counseling services. A potential borrower seeking such a relationship should recognize the important differences among banks considered in the following discussion.

1. Banks have different basic policies towards risk. Some are inclined to follow relatively conservative lending practices; others engage in what are properly termed creative banking practices. The policies reflect partly the personalities of the bank officers and partly the characteristics of the bank's deposit liabilities. Thus, a bank with fluctuating deposit liabilities in a static community tends to be a conservative lender. A bank whose deposits are growing with little interruption may follow liberal credit policies. A large bank with diversification over broad geographical regions or among several industries can obtain the benefit of combining and averaging risks. Thus, marginal credit risks that may be unacceptable to a small bank or to a specialized unit bank can be pooled by a branch banking system to reduce the overall risks of a group of marginal accounts.

2. Some bank loan officers are active in providing counsel and in stimulating development loans to firms in their early and formative years. Certain banks even have specialized departments to make loans to firms expected to become growth firms. Bankers in such departments can provide much counseling to customers.

3. Banks differ in the extent to which they support a borrower's activities in bad times. This characteristic is referred to as the bank's degree of loyalty. Some banks put great pressure on a business to liquidate its loans when the firm's outlook becomes clouded, whereas others stand by the firm and work diligently to help it attain a more favorable condition.

4. Another characteristic by which banks differ is the degree of deposit stability. Instability arises not only from fluctuations in the level of deposits but also from the composition of deposits. Deposits can take the form of *demand deposits* (checking accounts) or *time deposits* (savings accounts, certificates of deposit, Christmas clubs).

Total deposits tend to be more stable when time deposits are substantial. Differences in deposit stability go a long way toward explaining differences in the extent to which banks are willing or able to help borrowers work their way out of difficulties or even crises.

5. Banks differ greatly in the degree of loan specialization. Larger banks have separate departments specializing in different kinds of loans, such as real estate, installment, and commercial loans. Within these broad categories, they may specialize by line of business, such as steel, machinery, or textiles. Smaller banks are likely to reflect the nature of the business and economic environment in which they operate. They tend to become specialists in specific lines, such as oil, construction, or agriculture. The borrower can obtain more creative cooperation and more active support at the bank that has the greatest experience and familiarity with the borrower's particular type of business. The financial manager, therefore, should choose a bank with care. The bank that is excellent for one firm may be unsatisfactory for another.

6. The size of a bank can be an important characteristic. Since the maximum loan a bank can make to any customer is generally limited to 10 percent of the bank's capital accounts (capital stock plus retained earnings), it generally is not appropriate for large firms to develop borrowing relationships with small banks.

7. With the heightened competition among commercial banks and other financial institutions, the aggressiveness of banks has increased. Modern commercial banks now offer a wide range of financial and business services. Most large banks have business development departments that provide counseling to firms and serve as intermediaries on a wide variety of their requirements.

Commercial Paper

Commercial paper consists of unsecured promissory notes issued by firms to finance short-term credit needs. In recent years, the issuance of commercial paper has become an increasingly important source of short-term financing for many types of corporations, including utilities, finance companies, insurance companies, bank holding companies, and manufacturing companies. It is used not only to finance seasonal working capital needs but also as a means of interim financing of major projects such as bank buildings, ships, pipelines, nuclear fuel cores, and plant expansion. Between December 1979 and December 1984, the amount of commercial paper outstanding increased from $113 billion to $239 billion, an increase of over 100 percent. By comparison, the total of the commercial and industrial loans of all commercial banks in December 1984 was $468 billion. So commercial paper outstanding represented 51 percent of the total of bank business loans.[3]

Some commercial paper — especially the large volume of it issued by finance companies — is sold directly to investors, including business corporations, commercial banks, insurance companies, and state and local government units. As of December 1984, about 50 percent of the commercial paper outstanding had been directly placed with investors. The remainder represented that sold through commercial paper dealers, who function as intermediaries in the commercial paper market.

[3]*Federal Reserve Bulletin*, May 1985 pp. A16 and A23.

Maturity and Cost

Maturities of commercial paper generally vary from two months to one year, with an average of about five months. The rates on prime commercial paper vary, but they are generally about half a percent below those on prime business loans. And since compensating balances are not required for commercial paper, the *effective* cost differential is still wider.[4]

Use

The use of the open market for commercial paper is restricted to a comparatively small number of concerns that are exceptionally good credit risks. Dealers prefer to handle the paper of concerns whose net worth is $10 million or more and whose annual borrowing exceeds $1 million.

Advantages and Disadvantages

The commercial paper market has some significant advantages:

1.   It permits the broadest and the most advantageous distribution of paper.
2.   It provides more funds at lower rates than do other methods.
3.   The borrower avoids the inconvenience and expense of financing arrangements with a number of institutions, each of which requires a compensating balance.
4.   Publicity and prestige accrue to the borrower as its product and paper become more widely known.
5.   The commercial paper dealer frequently offers valuable advice to clients.

A basic limitation of the commercial paper market is that the size of the funds available is limited to the excess liquidity that corporations (the main suppliers of funds) have at any particular time. Another disadvantage is that a debtor who is in temporary financial difficulty receives little help because commercial paper dealings are impersonal. Banks are much more personal and much more likely to help a good customer weather a temporary storm.[5]

---

[4]However, this factor is offset to some extent by the fact that firms issuing commercial paper are sometimes required by commercial paper dealers to have unused bank lines of credit to back up their outstanding commercial paper, and fees must be paid on these lines.

[5]This point was emphasized dramatically in the aftermath of the Penn Central bankruptcy. Penn Central had a large amount of commercial paper that went into default, embarrassing corporate treasurers who had been holding the paper as part of their liquidity reserves. Immediately after the bankruptcy, the commercial paper market dried up to a large extent, and some companies that had relied heavily on this market found themselves under severe liquidity pressure as their commercial paper matured and could not be refunded. Chrysler, for example, had to seek bank loans of over $500 million because it could not sell commercial paper for a time. Without adequate bank lines, Chrysler might well have been forced into bankruptcy itself, even though it was then basically sound, because of the Penn Central panic. Incidentally, the Federal Reserve Board recognized that many other firms would be in the same position as Chrysler and so expanded bank reserves in order to enable the banking system to take up the slack caused by the withdrawal of funds from the commercial paper market.

Effects of Inflation

During periods of inflation and tight money, many commercial paper sellers are pushed out of the market because the sources of purchasing commercial paper do not have the ability to expand their assets as does a fractional reserve commercial banking system. Ryder System, a Florida trucking company, was forced to turn to bank loans for $10 million of financing during 1974 because they were able to find buyers for only $15 million of their commercial paper. Thus, during inflationary periods, firms may be forced to seek the more expensive bank loans since they can no longer sell the cheaper commercial paper.

Bankers' Acceptances

A *banker's acceptance* is a debt instrument created by the creditor and arises out of a self-liquidating business transaction, mainly from import and export activity. For example, a U.S. coffee processor may arrange with a U.S. commercial bank for the issuance of an irrevocable letter of credit in favor of a Brazilian exporter with whom the U.S. processor has negotiated a transaction. The letter of credit covers the details of the shipment and states that the Brazilian exporter can draw a draft for a specified amount on the U.S. bank.[6] On the basis of the letter of credit, the exporter draws a draft on the bank and negotiates the draft with a local Brazilian bank, receiving immediate payment. The Brazilian bank then forwards the draft to the United States for presentation to the bank that issued the letter of credit. When this bank stamps the draft "accepted," it accepts the obligation to pay the draft at maturity, thereby creating an acceptance. Typically, the acceptance is then sold to an acceptance dealer, and the proceeds are credited to the account of the Brazilian bank. The shipping documents are released to the U.S. importer against a trust receipt, enabling the U.S. company to process and sell the coffee.

The proceeds of the coffee sales are deposited by the importer at the accepting bank in time to meet the required payment on the draft at maturity. The holder of the acceptance at maturity presents it to the accepting bank for payment, completing the transaction. The cost of the acceptance reflects the discount in the acceptance dealer's bid plus the accepting bank's commission rate. The cost can be borne by either the seller or buyer of the goods in accordance with the agreement made with the accepting bank. It reflects the tradeoffs involved in the selling price of the goods (which is related to provisions for bearing the risks that may be involved in the transaction) and the payment of fees for various instruments created by the transaction (such as the acceptance itself).

Bankers' acceptances are an effective method of short-term financing since the drawer gains time before funds are due. The appeal of bankers' acceptances, which are traded in an active secondary market, results from two basic characteristics. First, they are safe. Since they usually finance the shipment and storage of goods, the inventory can be pledged as collateral. Return to investors is usually comparable to the return on a good certificate of deposit. During periods of inflation, when investors become increasingly selective, a banker's acceptance may look safer than commercial paper or even the certifi-

---

[6]A *draft* is similar to an ordinary check. A check is drawn up by those *making* the payment, but a draft is drawn up by those who are to *receive* payment. Also a draft can be a sight draft which, like a check, is to be paid when received by the bank on which it is drawn. But a time draft will specify payment at a future date. This is similar to a post-dated check, except that time drafts represent a customary procedure, unlike post-dated checks.

cates of deposit of some banks. Second, when an acceptance is backed by readily market-able goods and a warehouse receipt has been issued, the acceptance is eligible for redis-count with the Federal Reserve.

Secured Short-Term Financing

Given a choice, it is ordinarily better to borrow on an unsecured basis, since the bookkeep-ing costs of secured loans are often high. However, a potential borrower's credit rating may not be sufficiently strong to justify the loan. If the loan can be secured by some form of collateral to be claimed by the lender in the event of default, then the lender may extend credit to an otherwise unacceptable firm. Similarly, a firm that can borrow on an unse-cured basis may elect to use security if it finds that this will induce lenders to quote a lower interest rate.

Several different kinds of collateral can be employed — marketable stocks or bonds, land or buildings, equipment, inventory, and accounts receivable. Marketable securities make excellent collateral, but few firms hold portfolios of stocks and bonds. Similarly, real prop-erty (land and buildings) and equipment are good forms of collateral, but they are gener-ally used as security for long-term loans. The bulk of secured short-term business borrow-ing involves the pledge of short-term assets — accounts receivable or inventories.

In the past, state laws varied greatly with regard to the use of security in financing. By the late 1960s, however, most states had adopted the *Uniform Commercial Code (UCC)*, which standardized and simplified the procedure for establishing loan security.

The heart of the UCC is the *security agreement*, a standardized document, or form, on which are stated the specific pledged assets. The assets can be items of equipment, ac-counts receivable, or inventories. Procedures for financing under the UCC are described in the following sections.

Accounts Receivable Financing

Accounts receivable financing involves either the assigning of receivables or the selling of receivables (factoring). Assigning, or pledging, or discounting of accounts receivable is characterized by the fact that the lender not only has a lien on the receivables but also has recourse to the borrower (seller of the goods); if the person or firm that bought the goods does not pay, the selling firm must take the loss. In other words, the risk of default on the accounts receivable pledged remains with the borrower. Also, the buyer of the goods is not ordinarily notified about the pledging of the receivables. The financial institution that lends on the security of accounts receivable is generally either a commercial bank or one of the large industrial finance companies.

Factoring, or selling accounts receivable, involves the purchase of accounts receivable by the lender without recourse to the borrower (seller of the goods). The buyer of the goods is notified of the transfer and makes payment directly to the lender. Since the factoring firm assumes the risk of default on bad accounts, it must do the credit checking. Accordingly, factors provide not only money but also a credit department for the borrower.

Procedure for Pledging Accounts Receivable

The financing of accounts receivable is initiated by a legally binding agreement between the seller of the goods and the financing institution. The agreement sets forth in detail the procedure to be followed and the legal obligations of both parties. Once the working relationship has been established, the seller periodically takes a batch of invoices to the financing institution. The lender reviews the invoices and makes an appraisal of the buyers. Invoices of companies that do not meet the lender's credit standards are not accepted for pledging. The financial institution seeks to protect itself at every phase of the operation. Selection of good invoices is the essential first step. If the buyer of the goods does not pay the invoice, the lender still has recourse against the seller of the goods. However, if many buyers default, the seller may be unable to meet the obligation to the financial institution. Additional protection afforded the lender is that the loan is generally for less than 100 percent of the pledged receivables; for example, the lender may advance the selling firm 75 percent of the amount of the pledged receivables.

An example will illustrate how the effective cost of accounts receivable financing is a function of accounts receivable turnover and the nominal interest rate: The Commerce Electronics Company has annual credit sales of $1 million, and its average accounts receivable balance is $200,000. Thus, its receivables turn over five times per year. Commerce is considering the use of accounts receivable financing to provide needed funds. The proposed pledging agreement specifies that a 15 percent reserve be deducted from funds advanced to protect against returns on disputed items. The annual interest rate is 16 percent [a 2 percent premium over the (then current) prime rate], charged on the amount of receivables less the reserve requirement. Interest is deducted in advance.

The formula for calculating the computed interest rate, r_c, is

$$r_c = \frac{1}{\left(\dfrac{1}{r}\right) - \left(\dfrac{1}{n}\right)},$$

where

$r_c =$ the computed interest rate
$r =$ the nominal interest rate $= 16$ percent
$n =$ the annual accounts receivable turnover $= 5$ times.

Thus,

$$r_c = \frac{1}{\left(\dfrac{1}{.16}\right) - \left(\dfrac{1}{5}\right)}$$

$$= \frac{1}{6.25 - 0.2}$$

$$= \frac{1}{6.05}$$

$$= 16.53\%.$$

We can verify this computed rate using a worksheet methodology:

Average duration of advance	$360/5 = 72$ days
Periodic interest rate	$16\%/5 = 3.2\%$
Reserve	$(.15)\$200,000 = \$30,000$
Periodic interest charge	$.032(\$200,000 - \$30,000) = \$5,440$

Annual interest charge	(5)\$5,440 = \$27,200
Net amount received	\$200,000 − \$30,000 − \$5,440 = \$164,560
Computed interest rate	\$27,200/\$164,560 = 16.53%.

Thus, the computed annual interest rate is 16.53 percent, the same result achieved above based solely on the nominal interest rate and turnover. The reserve requirement does not impact the computed interest rate since interest is calculated after deducting the reserve. Nor does the level of sales affect the computed interest rate, so long as the accounts receivable turnover remains constant. However, given the nominal interest rate, a higher turnover will result in a lower computed interest rate, and conversely. For example, with an accounts receivable turnover of 3, the computed rate for Commerce would be

$$r_c = \cfrac{1}{\left(\cfrac{1}{.16}\right) - \left(\cfrac{1}{3}\right)}$$

$$= \frac{1}{6.25 - .33}$$

$$= 16.90\%.$$

And with a turnover of 7, the computed cost would be

$$r_c = \frac{1}{6.25 - .143}$$

$$= 16.37\%.$$

Procedure for Factoring Accounts Receivable

The procedure for factoring is somewhat different from that for simply using accounts receivable as collateral for a loan. Again, an agreement between the seller and the factor is made to specify legal obligations and procedural arrangements. When the seller receives an order from a buyer, a credit approval slip is written and immediately sent to the factoring company for a credit check. If the factor does not approve the sale, the seller generally refuses to fill the order. This procedure informs the seller, prior to the sale, about the buyer's creditworthiness and acceptability to the factor. If the sale is approved, shipment is made and the invoice is stamped to notify the buyer to make payment directly to the factoring company.

The factor performs three functions in carrying out the procedure outlined above: (1) credit checking, (2) lending, and (3) risk bearing. The seller can select various combinations of these functions by changing provisions in the factoring agreement. For example, a small- or medium-sized firm can avoid establishing a credit department. The factor's service may well be less costly than a department that has a capacity in excess of the firm's credit volume. Also, if the firm uses a part-time noncredit specialist to perform credit checking, the person's lack of education, training, and experience may result in excessive losses. In some situations, the seller may have the factor perform the credit-checking and risk-taking functions but not the lending function.

To illustrate the more typical situation in which the factor also performs a lending function by making payment in advance of collection, we return to the Commerce Electronics

Company example. Instead of pledging or using its accounts receivable as collateral, Commerce is now considering a factoring arrangement. The factor would approve Commerce's invoices and advance funds as soon as the goods are shipped. The factoring commission or fee for credit checking is $1\frac{1}{2}$ percent of the invoice amount, deducted in advance. As in pledging, the factor sets up a 15 percent reserve against returns on disputed items. Interest expense is computed at a 16 percent annual rate on the invoice amount less the reserve and is deducted in advance. Recall that Commerce has annual sales of $1 million, with an average accounts receivable balance of $200,000; thus, the receivables turnover is five times, implying an average collection period of 72 days. This is the length of time the factor's funds will be at risk. (This 72-day collection period is approximately double the average collection period for all manufacturing firms and may be the reason that Commerce is motivated to consider pledging or factoring receivables in the first place.) We can calculate the effective cost of the factoring arrangement using the worksheet method:

Factoring commission	$(.015)\$200,000 = \$ \ \ 3,000$
Reserve	$(.15)\$200,000 = \$ \ 30,000$
Interest expense	$(.16)\left(\dfrac{72}{360}\right)(\$200,000 - \$30,000) = \$ \ \ 5,440$
Funds advanced	$\$200,000 - \$3,000 - \$30,000 - \$5,440 = \$161,560$
Annual interest expense	$5 \times \$5,440 = \$ \ 27,200$
Annual factoring commission	$5 \times \$3,000 = \$ \ 15,000$
Total annual expense	$\$ \ 42,200$
Computed interest rate	$\$42,200/\$161,560 = 26.12\%.$

Note that this is much higher than the effective interest rate in the pledging scenario (16.53 percent); this is due solely to the addition of the factoring commission or credit-checking fee, since other variables were not altered.[7] But since the use of factoring may reduce the firm's costs of a credit department, it may still be cost-efficient.

Once a factoring arrangement is established, a continuous circular flow of goods and funds takes place among the seller, the buyers, and the factor. The seller of the goods receives orders and transmits the purchase orders to the factor for approval; on approval, the goods are shipped; the factor advances the money to the seller; the buyers pay the factor; and the factor periodically remits any excess reserve to the seller of goods. Thus, once the agreement is in force, funds from this source are "spontaneous."

Evaluation of Receivables Financing

Accounts receivable financing essentially occurs because the seller needs to borrow, but his credit position isn't strong enough to borrow on an unsecured basis. Pledging of accounts receivable involves this financing aspect alone, with the receivables treated as collateral for the loan. Pledging would be appropriate where a firm's buyers tend to be very high-quality companies. Factoring, on the other hand, involves both the financing aspect and the issue of credit evaluation and the assumption of credit risk by the factor. Thus, in a sense, it is misleading to include the factoring commission in calculating the effective cost of factoring as in the worksheet above. The key issue for this "insurance" element of the cost is whether the credit-checking and risk-bearing functions can be car-

---

[7]There can be considerable variation in the terms of accounts receivable financing contracts; for example, a factoring agreement may call for interest to be computed on the invoice price less both the reserve and the factoring commission. The worksheet methodology is flexible enough to handle these variations, while, for example, the compact formula used in the pledging analysis is not.

ried out more cheaply by the factor or by the firm itself. An efficient factor has the advantage that having done a credit evaluation of a buyer firm, it can "sell" its evaluation to, for example, ten different selling firms for as little as $\frac{1}{10}$ of the cost of the evaluation. In contrast, each individual seller would have to bear the entire cost of the evaluation alone, and the evaluation would have to be duplicated as many times as there are sellers. (It is not surprising that we find factoring companies specializing in particular seller industry groups.) This raises the question why a company would ever do credit evaluation on its own. The answer may be that, when done properly, credit evaluation involves continuing interaction between the sales and credit departments of the selling firm with the buyers, which can benefit follow-on sales. Also, the cost difference may not be large, so that the issue comes down to the relative efficiency of the selling company versus the factoring company. For example, where the number of buyers is large but the dollar amount of sales to each is relatively small, the efficiency factor may hinge on the sheer mechanics of handling the paperwork.

Accounts receivable financing also has disadvantages. First, when invoices are numerous and relatively small in dollar amount, the administrative costs involved may render this method of financing inconvenient and expensive. Second, the firm is using a highly liquid asset as security. For a long time, accounts receivable financing was frowned on by most trade creditors; it was regarded as confession of a firm's unsound financial position. It is no longer regarded in this light, however, and many sound firms engage in receivables pledging or factoring. Still, the traditional attitude causes some trade creditors to refuse to sell on credit to a firm that is factoring or pledging its receivables, on the ground that this practice removes one of the most liquid of the firm's assets and, accordingly, weakens the position of other creditors.

In the future, accounts receivable financing is likely to continue to increase in relative importance. Computer technology is rapidly advancing towards the point where credit records of individuals and firms can be kept in computer memory units. Systems already have been devised whereby a retailer can insert an individual's magnetic credit card into a box and receive a signal showing whether the person's credit is good and whether a bank is willing to buy the receivable created when the store completes the sale. The cost of handling invoices will be greatly reduced from present-day costs because the new systems will be so highly automated. This will make it possible to use accounts receivable financing for very small sales, and it will reduce the cost of all receivables financing. This suggests a continued expansion of accounts receivable financing.

Inventory Financing

If a firm is a relatively good credit risk, the mere existence of the inventory may be a sufficient basis for receiving an unsecured loan. If the firm is a relatively poor risk, the lending institution may insist on security, which often takes the form of a blanket lien against the inventory. Alternatively, trust receipts, field warehouse financing, or collateral certificates can be used to secure loans. These methods of using inventories as security are discussed below.

Blanket Inventory Lien

The *blanket inventory lien* gives the lending institution a lien against all inventories of the borrower. However, the borrower is free to sell the inventories; thus, the value of the collateral can be reduced. This fact often makes an inventory lien a less desirable arrangement to a bank.

Trust Receipts

Because of the weaknesses of the blanket lien for inventory financing, another kind of security is often used — the trust receipt. A *trust receipt* is an instrument acknowledging that the borrower holds the goods in trust for the lender. On receiving funds from the lender, the borrowing firm conveys a trust receipt for the goods. The goods can be stored in a public warehouse or held on the borrower's premises. The trust receipt provides that the goods are held in trust for the lender or are segregated on the borrower's premises on behalf of the lender and that proceeds from the sale of such goods are transmitted to the lender at the end of each day. Automobile dealer financing is the best example of trust receipt financing.

One defect of this form of financing is the requirement that a trust receipt must be issued for specific goods. For example, if the security is bags of coffee beans, the trust receipts must indicate the bags by number. In order to validate its trust receipts, the lending institution must send someone to the borrower's premises to see that the bag numbers are correctly listed. Furthermore, complex legal requirements for trust receipts require the attention of a bank officer. Problems are compounded if borrowers are widely separated geographically from the lender. To offset these inconveniences, warehousing is coming into wide use as a method of securing loans with inventory.

Field Warehouse Financing

Like trust receipts, field warehouse financing uses inventory as security. A public warehouse represents an independent third party engaged in the business of storing goods. Sometimes the warehouse is not practical because of the bulkiness of goods and the expense of transporting them to and from the borrower's premises. Field warehouse financing represents an economical method of inventory financing in which the "warehouse" is established on the borrower's premises. To provide inventory supervision, the lending institution employs a third party in the arrangement, the field warehousing company. This company acts as the control (or supervisory) agent for the lending institution.

Field warehousing is illustrated by a simple example. Suppose a potential borrower has stacked iron in an open yard on its premises. A field warehouse can be established if, say, a field warehousing concern places a temporary fence around the iron and erects a sign stating: "This is a field warehouse supervised and conducted by the Smith Field Warehousing Corporation."

The example illustrates the two elements in the establishment of a warehouse: (1) public notification of the field warehouse arrangement and (2) supervision of the warehouse by a custodian of the field warehouse concern. When the field warehousing operation is relatively small, the second condition is sometimes violated by hiring an employee of the borrower to supervise the inventory. This practice is viewed as undesirable by the lending institution because there is no control over the collateral by a person independent of the borrowing concern.[8]

---

[8]This absence of independent control was the main cause of the breakdown that resulted in the huge losses connected with loans to the Allied Crude Vegetable Oil Company headed by Anthony (Tino) DeAngelis. American Express Field Warehousing Company hired men from Allied's staff as custodians. Their dishonesty was not discovered because of another breakdown — the fact that the American Express touring inspector did not actually take a physical inventory of the warehouses. As a consequence, the swindle was not discovered until losses running into the hundreds of millions of dollars had been suffered. See Norman C. Miller, *The Great Salad Oil Swindle* (Baltimore, Md.: Penguin Books, 1965), pp. 72-77.

The field warehouse financing operation is described best by a specific illustration. Assume that a tomato canner is interested in financing operations by bank borrowing. The canner has funds sufficient to finance 15 to 20 percent of operations during the canning season. These funds are adequate to purchase and process an initial batch of tomatoes. As the cans are put into boxes and rolled into the storerooms, the canner needs additional funds for both raw materials and labor.

Because of the canner's poor credit rating, the bank decides that a field warehousing operation is necessary to secure its loans. The field warehouse is established, and the custodian notifies the lending institution of the description, by number, of the boxes of canned tomatoes in storage and under his control. Thereupon, the lending institution establishes for the canner a deposit on which it can draw. From this point on, the bank finances the operations. The canner needs only enough cash to initiate the cycle. The farmers bring more tomatoes; the canner processes them; the cans are boxed and the boxes put into the field warehouse; field warehouse receipts are drawn up and sent to the bank; the bank establishes further deposits for the canner on the basis of the receipts; and the canner can draw on the deposits to continue the cycle.

Of course, the canner's ultimate objective is to sell the canned tomatoes. As the canner receives purchase orders, it transmits them to the bank, and the bank directs the custodian to release the inventories. It is agreed that, as remittances are received by the canner, they will be turned over to the bank. These remittances pay off the loans made by the bank.

Typically, a seasonal pattern exists. At the beginning of the tomato harvesting and canning season, the canner's cash needs and loan requirements begin to rise, and they reach a maximum by the end of the canning season. It is hoped that, just before the new canning season begins, the canner has sold a sufficient volume to have paid off the loan completely. If for some reason the canner has had a bad year, the bank may carry the company over another year to enable it to sell off its inventory.

Acceptable Products. In addition to canned foods, which account for about 17 percent of all field warehouse loans, many other product inventories provide a basis for field warehouse financing. Some of these are miscellaneous groceries, which represent about 13 percent; lumber products, about 10 percent; and coal and coke, about 6 percent.

These products are relatively nonperishable and are sold in well developed, organized markets. Nonperishability protects the lender who has to take over the security. For this reason, a bank will not make a field warehousing loan on perishables such as fresh fish. However, frozen fish, which can be stored for a long time, can be field warehoused. An organized market also aids the lender in disposing of inventory that it takes over. Banks are not interested in going into the canning or the fish business. They want to be able to dispose of an inventory quickly and with the expenditure of a minimum amount of their own time.

Cost of Financing. The fixed costs of a field warehousing arrangement are relatively high; such financing, therefore, is not suitable for a very small firm. If a field warehouse company sets up the warehouse itself, it typically sets a minimum fixed charge, plus about 1 or 2 percent of the amount of credit extended to the borrower. Furthermore, the financing institution charges interest at a rate somewhat above the prevailing prime rate. The minimum size of an efficient warehousing operation requires an inventory of about $100,000.

Appraisal. The use of field warehouse financing as a source of funds for business firms has many advantages. First, the amount of funds available is flexible because the financing is tied to the growth of inventories, which, in turn, is related directly to financing needs.

Second, the arrangement increases the acceptability of inventories as loan collateral. Some inventories are not accepted by a bank as a security without a field warehousing arrangement. Third, the necessity for inventory control, safekeeping, and the use of specialists in warehousing has resulted in improved warehouse practices. The services of the field warehouse companies have often saved money for the firm, in spite of the financing costs mentioned above. The field warehouse company may suggest inventory practices that reduce both the number of people the firm has to employ and inventory damage and loss as well.

The major disadvantage of a field warehousing operation is the fixed cost element, which reduces the feasibility of this form of financing for small firms.

Collateral Certificates

A *collateral certificate* guarantees the existence of the amount of inventory pledged as loan collateral. It is a statement issued periodically to the lender by a third party, who certifies that the inventory exists and that it will be available if needed.

This method of bank financing is becoming increasingly popular, primarily because of its flexibility. First, there is no need for physical segregation or possession of inventories. Therefore, collateral certificates can even be used to cover work-in-process inventories, facilitating more freedom in the movement of goods. Second, the collateral certificate can provide for a receivables financing plan, allowing financing to continue smoothly as inventories are converted into receivables. Third, the certificate issuer usually provides a number of services to simplify loan administration for both the borrower and the lender.

Summary

Short-term credit is debt originally scheduled for repayment within one year. The three major sources of short-term credit are trade credit among firms, loans from commercial banks, and commercial paper.

Trade credit (represented by accounts payable) is the largest single category of short-term credit; it is especially important for smaller firms. Trade credit is a *spontaneous source of financing* in that it arises from ordinary business transactions; as sales increase so does the supply of financing from accounts payable.

Bank credit occupies a pivotal position in the short-term money market. Banks provide the marginal credit that allows firms to expand more rapidly than is possible through retained earnings and trade credit. A denial of bank credit often means that a firm must slow its rate of growth.

Bank interest rates are quoted in three ways — regular compound interest, discount interest, and installment interest. Regular interest needs no adjustment; it is correct as stated. Discount interest requires a small upward adjustment to make it comparable to regular compound interest rates. Installment interest rates require a large adjustment, and, frequently, the true interest rate is double the quoted rate for an installment loan.

Bank loans are personal in the sense that the financial manager meets with the banker, discusses the terms of the loan, and reaches an agreement that requires direct and personal negotiation. Commercial paper, however, although it is physically similar to a bank loan, is sold in a broad, impersonal market. A California firm might, for example, sell commercial paper to a manufacturer in the Midwest.

Only the very strongest firms are able to use the commercial paper markets. The nature of these markets is such that the firm selling the paper must have a reputation so good that buyers of the paper are willing to buy it without any sort of credit check. Interest rates in the commercial paper market are the lowest available to business borrowers.

The most common forms of collateral used for short-term credit are inventories and accounts receivable. Accounts receivable financing can be done either by pledging the receivables or by selling them outright (often called factoring). When the receivables are pledged, the borrower retains the risk that the person or firm owing the receivables will not pay; in factoring, this risk is typically passed on to the lender. Because factors take the risk of default, they investigate the purchaser's credit; therefore, factors can perform three functions: lending, risk bearing, and credit checking. When receivables are pledged, the lender typically performs only the first of these functions.

Loans secured by inventories are not satisfactory under many circumstances. For certain kinds of inventory, however, the technique known as field warehousing is used to provide adequate security to the lender. Under a field warehousing arrangement, the inventory is physically controlled by a warehouse company, which releases the inventory only on order from the lending institution. Canned goods, lumber, steel, coal, and other standardized products are goods usually covered in field warehouse arrangements. Blanket inventory liens, trust receipts, and collateral certificates are also used in securing loans with inventories.

Questions

15.1 It is inevitable that firms will obtain a certain amount of their financing in the form of trade credit, which is (to some extent) a free source of funds. What are some other reasons for firms to use trade credit?

15.2 Discuss the statement: Commercial paper interest rates are always lower than bank loan rates to a given borrower. Nevertheless, many firms perfectly capable of selling commercial paper employ higher-cost bank credit. Indicate (a) why commercial paper rates are lower than bank rates and (b) why firms might use bank credit in spite of its higher cost.

15.3 Discuss these statements: Trade credit has an explicit interest rate cost if discounts are available but not taken. There are also some intangible costs associated with the failure to take discounts.

15.4 A large manufacturing firm that had been selling its products on a 3/10, net 30 basis changed its credit terms to 1/20, net 90. What changes might be anticipated on the balance sheets of the manufacturer and of its customers?

15.5 The availability of bank credit is more important to small firms than to large ones. Why?

15.6 What factors should a firm consider in selecting its primary bank? Would it be feasible for a firm to have a primary deposit bank (the bank where most of its funds are deposited) and a different primary loan bank (the bank where it does most of its borrowing)?

15.7 Indicate whether each of the following changes will raise or lower the cost of a firm's accounts receivable financing and explain why this occurs:
a) The firm eases up on its credit standards in order to increase sales.
b) The firm institutes a policy of refusing to make credit sales if the amount of the purchase (invoice) is below $100. Previously, about 40 percent of all invoices were below $100.

c)   The firm agrees to give recourse to the finance company for all defaults.

d)   A firm that already has a recourse arrangement is merged into a larger, stronger company.

e)   A firm without a recourse arrangement changes its terms of trade from net 30 to net 90.

15.8   Would a firm that manufactures specialized machinery for a few large customers be more likely to use a form of inventory financing or a form of accounts receivable financing? Why?

15.9   Discuss the statement: A firm that factors its accounts receivable will have a stronger current ratio than one that discounts its receivables.

15.10   Why would it not be practical for a typical retailer to use field warehouse financing?

15.11   Describe an industry that might be expected to use each of the following forms of credit and explain your reasons for choosing each one:
a)   Field warehouse financing
b)   Factoring
c)   Accounts receivable discounting
d)   Trust receipts
e)   None of these

Problems

15.1   What is the equivalent annual interest rate (APR) that would be lost if a firm failed to take the cash discount under each of the following terms?
a)   1/15, net 30
b)   2/10, net 60
c)   3/10, net 60
d)   2/10, net 40
e)   1/10, net 40

15.2   Wilber Corp. is negotiating with the Citizen's Bank for a $500,000 one-year loan. Citizen has offered Wilber the following three alternatives:
1.   A 15 percent interest rate, no compensating balance, and interest due at the end of the year.
2.   A 13 percent interest rate, a 20 percent compensating balance, and interest due at the end of the year.
3.   An 11 percent interest rate, a 15 percent compensating balance, and the loan discounted.

If Wilber wishes to minimize the effective interest rate, which alternative will it choose?

15.3   Mark Industries is having difficulty paying its bills and is considering foregoing its trade discounts on $300,000 of accounts payable. As an alternative, Mark can obtain a 60-day note with a 14 percent annual interest rate. The note will be discounted, and the trade credit terms are 2/10, net 60.
a)   Which alternative has the lower effective cost?
b)   If Mark does not take its trade discounts, what conclusions may outsiders draw?

15.4   Best Catsup Company is considering the following two alternatives for financing next year's canning operations:
1.   Establishing a $1 million line of credit with a 1 percent interest rate on the used amount at the end of each month and a 1 percent per annum com-

mitment fee rate on the unused portion (.0833 percent on unused amount at the end of each month). A $150,000 compensating balance will be required at all times on the entire $1 million line.

2. Using field warehousing to finance the inventory. Financing charges will be a flat fee of $500, plus 2 percent of the maximum amount of credit extended, plus a 10 percent annual interest rate (.833 percent on amount outstanding at the end of each month) on all outstanding credit.

Best has $150,000 of funds available for inventory financing. All financing is done on the first of the month and is sufficient to cover the value of the expected inventory at the end of the month. Expected month-end inventory levels are given below.

Month	Amount	Month	Amount
July 19X0	$ 150,000	January 19X1	$600,000
August	400,000	February	450,000
September	600,000	March	350,000
October	800,000	April	225,000
November	1,000,000	May	100,000
December	750,000	June	0

Which financing plan has the lower cost? (Hints: Under the bank loan plan, borrowings in July are $150,000 and in December $750,000; under the field warehousing plan, July borrowings are zero and December borrowings are $600,000.)

15.5 Collins Manufacturing needs an additional $100,000. The financial manager is considering two methods of obtaining this money: a loan from a commercial bank or a factoring arrangement. The bank charges 12 percent per annum interest, discount basis. It also requires a 15 percent compensating balance. The factor is willing to purchase Collins's accounts receivable and to advance the invoice amount less a 3 percent factoring commission on the invoices purchased each month. (All sales are on 30-day terms.) A 10 percent annual interest rate will be charged on the total invoice price and deducted in advance. Also, under the factoring agreement, Collins can eliminate its credit department and reduce credit expenses by $2,000 per month. Bad debt losses of 10 percent on the factored amount can also be avoided.

a) How much should the bank loan be in order to net $100,000? How much accounts receivable should be factored to net $100,000?

b) What are the computed interest rates and the annual total dollar costs, including credit department expenses and bad debt losses, associated with each financing arrangement?

c) Discuss some considerations other than cost that may influence management's choice between factoring and a commercial bank loan.

15.6 Sunlight Sailboats estimates that due to the seasonal nature of its business, it will require an additional $200,000 of cash for the month of July. Sunlight has four options available to provide the needed funds. It can

1. Establish a one-year line of credit for $200,000 with a commercial bank. The commitment fee will be 0.5 percent, and the interest charge on the used funds will be 15 percent per annum. The minimum time the funds can be used is 30 days.

2. Forego the July trade discount of 2/10, net 40 on $200,000 of accounts payable.

3.　Issue $200,000 of 30-day commercial paper at a 13.8 percent per annum interest rate.

4.　Issue $200,000 of 60-day commercial paper at a 14 percent per annum interest rate. Since the funds are required for only 30 days, the excess funds ($200,000) can be invested in 13 percent per annum marketable securities for the month of August. The total transaction fee on purchasing and selling the marketable securities is 0.5 percent of the fair value.

a)　Which financing arrangement results in the lowest cost?

b)　Is the source with the lowest expected cost necessarily the source to select? Why or why not?

15.7　The balance sheet of the Pacific Finance Corporation is shown below.

Pacific Finance Corporation Balance Sheet
(Millions of Dollars)

Assets		Liabilities	
Cash	$ 75	Bank loans	$ 250
Net receivables	2,400	Commercial paper	825
Marketable securities	150	Others	375
Repossessions	5	Total due within a year	$1,450
Total current assets	$2,630	Long-term debt	1,000
Other assets	170	Total shareholders' equity	350
Total assets	$2,800	Total claims	$2,800

a)　Calculate commercial paper as a percentage of short-term financing, as a percentage of total-debt financing, and as a percentage of all financing.

b)　Why do finance companies such as Pacific Finance use commercial paper to such a great extent?

c)　Why do they use both bank loans and commercial paper?

15.8　Wilkins Manufacturing needs an additional $250,000, which it plans to obtain through a factoring arrangement. The factor would purchase Wilkins's accounts receivable and advance the invoice amount, less a 2 percent commission, on the invoices purchased each month. (Wilkins sells on terms of net 30 days.) In addition, the factor charges 16 percent annual interest on the total invoice amount, to be deducted in advance.

a)　What amount of accounts receivable must be factored to net $250,000?

b)　If Wilkins can reduce credit expenses by $1,500 per month and avoid bad-debt losses of 3 percent on the factored amount, what is the total dollar cost of the factoring arrangement?

15.9　The Shelby Saw Corporation has fallen behind in its accounts payable. Although its terms of purchase are net 30 days, the current accounts payable balance represents 60 days' purchases. Shelby is seeking to increase bank borrowings in order to become current in meeting its trade obligations (that is, to reduce accounts payable to 30 days' purchases). The company's balance sheet is shown below:

Balance Sheet
Shelby Saw Corporation

Assets		Liabilities	
Cash	$ 100,000	Accounts payable	$ 600,000
Accounts receivable	300,000	Bank loans	900,000
Inventory	1,400,000	Current liabilities	$1,500,000
Current assets	$1,800,000	Long-term debt	700,000
Fixed assets	1,200,000	Net worth	800,000
Total assets	$3,000,000	Total liabilities	$3,000,000

a)   How much financing is required to eliminate past due accounts payable?

b)   As a bank loan officer, would you make the loan? Explain.

15.10   The Shandow Insulation Company has been growing rapidly, but because of insufficient working capital, it has now become slow in paying bills. Of its total accounts payable, $96,000 is overdue. This threatens Shandow's relationship with its main supplier of powders used in the manufacture of various kinds of insulation materials for aircraft and missiles. Over 75 percent of its sales are to six large, financially strong defense contractors. The company's balance sheet, sales, and net profit for the past year are shown below.

Balance Sheet
Shandow Corporation

Cash	$ 28,800	Trade credit[a]	$240,000
Receivables	320,000	Bank loans	192,000
Inventories		Accruals[a]	48,000
Raw material	38,400	Total current debt	$480,000
Work in process	192,000	Mortgages on equipment	288,000
Finished goods	57,600	Capital stock	96,000
Total current assets	636,800	Retained earnings	96,000
Equipment	323,200		
Total assets	$ 960,000	Total liabilities/net worth	$960,000
Sales	$1,920,000		
Profit after taxes	96,000		

[a]Increases spontaneously with sales increases.

Shandow is considering two alternative methods to solve its payments problem: factoring and receivables financing. Additional information:

Receivables turn over six times a year. (Sales/receivables = 6.) All sales are made on credit. The factor requires a 15 percent reserve for returns on disputed items. The factor also requires a 1.5 percent commission on average receivables outstanding, payable at the time the receivable is purchased, to cover the costs of credit checking. There is an interest charge by the factor at the prime rate (12 percent) plus 3 percent based on receivables *less* any reserve requirements and commissions. This payment is made at the beginning of the period and is deducted from the advance. Receivables financing would involve the same costs as factoring except the factoring commission and a 20 percent reserve rather than 15 percent under factoring.

a)   When sales are $1,920,000, on average, what is the total amount of receivables outstanding?

b)   What is the average duration of advances, on the basis of 360 days a year?

c)   How much cash does the firm actually receive under factoring as compared with receivables financing?

d)   What is the total annual dollar cost of financing under factoring as compared with receivables financing?

e)   What is the annual effective percentage financing cost paid on the money received under factoring as compared with receivables financing?

f)   Which method of financing should Shandow utilize?

15.11 The Morton Plastics Company manufactures plastic toys. It buys raw materials, manufactures the toys in the spring and summer, and ships them to a large number of department stores and toy stores by late summer or early fall. The company factors its receivables. If it did not, Morton's balance sheet would have appeared as follows:

Morton Company
Pro Forma Balance Sheet as of March 31, 19X0

Cash	$ 40,000	Accounts payable	$1,200,000
Receivables	1,200,000	Notes payable	800,000
Inventory	800,000	Accruals	80,000
Total current assets	$2,040,000	Total current debt	$2,080,000
		Mortgages	200,000
		Common stock	400,000
Fixed assets	800,000	Retained earnings	160,000
Total assets	$2,840,000	Total claims	$2,840,000

Morton provides dating on its sales; thus, its receivables are not due for payment until 90 days after purchase. Also, the company would have been overdue on some $800,000 of its accounts payable if the above situation actually existed.

Morton has an agreement with a finance company to factor the receivables for the quarterly periods. The factoring company charges a flat commission of 1.5 percent, plus interest at 3 points over the prime rate (15 percent) on the outstanding balance. It deducts a reserve of 15 percent for returned and damaged materials. Interest and commission are paid in advance. No interest is charged on the reserved funds or on the commission.

a)   Show the balance sheet of Morton on March 31, 19X0, giving effect to the purchase of all the receivables by the factoring company and the use of the funds to pay accounts payable.

b)   If the $1.2 million is the average level of outstanding receivables and if they turn over four times a year (hence, the commission is paid four times a year), what are the total dollar costs of financing and the computed annual interest rate?

c)   What are the advantages to Morton Plastics of using factoring, as opposed to discounting its receivables?

Selected References

Barlev, Benzion; Livnat, Joshua; and Yoran, Aharon, "Advance Payments During Inflationary Periods," *Journal of Business Finance & Accounting*, 9 (Autumn 1982), pp. 413-426.

Hill, Ned C.; Wood, Robert A.; and Sorenson, Dale R., "Factors Influencing Credit Policy: A Survey," *Journal of Cash Management*, 1 (December 1981), pp. 38-47.

James, Christopher, "An Analysis of Bank Loan Rate Indexation," *Journal of Finance*, 37 (June 1982), pp. 809-825.

Loosigian, Allan M., "Hedging Commercial Paper Borrowing Costs with Treasury Bill Futures," *Journal of Cash Management*, 2, No. 2, (June 1982), pp. 50-57.

Maier, Steven F., and Vander Weide, James H., "A Practical Approach to Short-Run Financial Planning," *Financial Management*, 7 (Winter 1978), pp. 10-16.

Nelson, Robert E., Jr., "The Practice of Business Liquidity Improvement: A Management Approach," *Business Horizons*, 20 (October 1977), pp. 54-60.

Santomero, Anthony M., "Fixed Versus Variable Rate Loans," *Journal of Finance*, 38 (December 1983), pp. 1363-1380.

Stone, Bernell K., "The Cost of Bank Loans," *Journal of Financial and Quantitative Analysis*, 7 (December 1972), pp. 2077-2086.

Part Five

Decision Making under Uncertainty

Part Five deals with an area that has great practical significance because it introduces more realism into our view of financial management. This involves the necessity of making decisions in the face of uncertainty.

In this section, we seek to summarize the ideas that have been developed for treating uncertainty. In Chapter 16, we lay the foundation for this analysis by viewing the firm as a portfolio of assets. From this, we can develop some fundamental relationships involving the pricing of risk in relation to required returns.

The ideas developed in Chapter 16 are extended in Chapter 17 to develop the Capital Asset Pricing Model, which provides decision makers with a basis for estimating the required return (or cost of capital) on risky securities and on capital budgeting projects.

Chapter 18 discusses options on risky assets. The Option Pricing Model has many useful applications because most financial securities can be viewed as options. The concepts, therefore, have applicability to a wide range of financial decisions, including those on mergers and acquisitions, spinoffs, dividend policy, and the pricing of risky debt. Chapter 19 presents the theory of market efficiency. This deals with the issue of whether security prices reflect the information necessary for resources to be efficiently allocated. Capital market efficiency is central to building models for making rational financial policies and decisions.

Chapter 16 Portfolio Theory: Decision Making under Uncertainty

This chapter introduces the modern theory of decision making under uncertainty. The financial ratios, discussed in Chapter 8, have been used for centuries as rules of thumb to aid in understanding tradeoffs between risk and return, but they only scratch the surface. In this chapter, we view financial decision making in a portfolio context. It may seem strange that portfolio theory is necessary to understand corporate finance. However, the firm is really a portfolio of risky assets and liabilities. The fundamental issue is how can a manager select the best combination of risk and return to maximize the wealth of shareholders.

Introduction

We will begin with a review of the mean and variance as measures of risk and return for a single risky asset. Then, we will explore the effects of portfolio diversification. Combinations of risky assets, in the form of portfolios, provide a set of investment opportunities for investors. Given these investment opportunities, we then look at how risk-averse investors choose among them. If we know the risk and return of the objects of choice (portfolios) and the way investors make their choices (the theory of choice), then we can describe optimal portfolio choices. This is the goal of this chapter.

In Chapter 17, we will turn to a market equilibrium context in order to show that there is a market price of risk just as there is a market price for anything else, apples and oranges, for example. If it is possible to meaningfully measure the risk of an investment project, and if we know what the price of risk is, then we can determine the risk-adjusted rate of return, which can be used for computing the project's net present value. The chapter will present two similar equilibrium theories of the measurement and pricing of risk — the Capital Asset Pricing Model (CAPM) and the Arbitrage Pricing Model (APM). But first, we begin with a discussion of how risk-averse investors choose between different combinations of risk and return.

Risk and Return: The Theory of Choice

Chapter 10 has already introduced the mean and variance of a probability distribution and illustrated how they can be estimated from a sample of data. In this chapter, we shall assume that all decision makers are risk averse and prefer higher mean return and lower variance of return. Furthermore, we assume that nothing other than the mean and variance of return matters to investors.[1] Thus, the mean and variance are objects of choice

---

[1]For example, the skewness of returns is assumed to be irrelevant. This will be true if investors' utility is a function of only the mean and variance of returns or if returns are normally distributed such that they can be completely described by the mean and variance, that is, there is no skewness.

much in the same way that apples and oranges are objects of choice. What we need is a theory of choice which will tell us exactly how investors will choose between alternatives which have different combinations of risk and return.

The assumption of risk aversion is basic to many decision models used in finance. Since this assumption is so important, it is appropriate to discuss why risk aversion generally holds.

In theory, we can identify three possible attitudes toward risk: a desire for risk, an aversion to risk, and an indifference to risk. A *risk seeker* is one who prefers risk. Given a choice between more and less risky investments with identical expected monetary returns, this person would prefer the riskier investment. Faced with the same choice, the *risk averter* would select the less risky investment. The person who is indifferent to risk would not care which investment he or she received. *There undoubtedly are individuals who prefer risk and others who are indifferent to it, but both logic and observation suggest that business managers and stockholders are predominantly risk averters.*

Why does risk aversion generally hold? Given two investments, each with the same expected dollar returns, why would most investors prefer the less risky one? Several theories have been advanced in answer to this question, but perhaps the most logically satisfying one involves *utility theory*.

At the heart of utility theory is the notion of *diminishing marginal utility for wealth*. If, for example, you had no wealth and then received $100, you could satisfy your most immediate needs. If you then received a second $100, you could utilize it, but the second $100 would not be quite as necessary to you as the first $100. Thus, the "utility" of the second, or *marginal*, $100 is less than that of the first $100, and so on for additional increments of wealth. Therefore, we say that the marginal utility of wealth is diminishing.

Figure 16.1 graphs the relationship between wealth and its utility, where utility is measured in arbitrary units called *utils*. Curve A, the one of primary interest, is for someone with positive marginal utility for wealth, but this individual also has marginal utility which increases at a decreasing rate. The investor has diminishing marginal utility of wealth. An individual with $5,000 would have ten utils of "happiness" or satisfaction. With an additional $2,500, the individual's satisfaction would rise to 12 utils, an increase of two units. But with a loss of $2,500, the individual's satisfaction would fall to six utils, a loss of four units.

Most investors (as opposed to people who habitually gamble) appear to have a diminishing marginal utility for wealth, and this directly affects their attitudes toward risk. Our measures of risk estimate the likelihood that a given return will turn out to be above or below the expected return. Someone who has a constant marginal utility for wealth will value each dollar of "extra" returns just as highly as each dollar of "lost" returns and will be indifferent to risk. On the other hand, someone with a diminishing marginal utility for wealth will get more "pain" from a dollar lost than "pleasure" from a dollar gained. Because of the diminishing utility of wealth, the second individual will be very much opposed to risk and will require a very high return on any investment that is subject to much risk. In Curve A of Figure 16.1, for example, a gain of $2,500 from a base of $5,000 would bring two utils of additional satisfaction, but a $2,500 loss would cause a four-util satisfaction loss. Therefore, a person with this utility function and $5,000 would be unwilling to make a bet with a 50-50 chance of winning or losing $2,500. However, the risk-indifferent individual with Utility Curve B would be indifferent to the bet, and the risk lover (with Utility Curve C) would be eager to make it. Why?

Diminishing marginal utility leads directly to risk aversion, and this risk aversion is reflected in the capitalization rate investors apply when determining the value of a firm. To make this clear, let us assume that government bonds are riskless securities and that

Figure 16.1   Relationship between Wealth and Its Utility

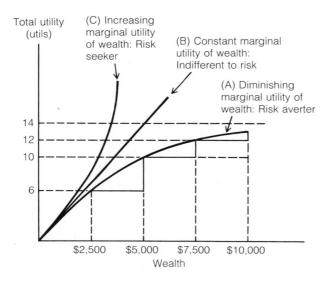

such bonds currently offer a 5 percent rate of return.[2] Thus, someone who bought a $5,000 U.S. Treasury bond and held it for one year would end up with $5,250, a profit of $250. Suppose the same investor had an alternative investment opportunity that called for the $5,000 to be used to back a wildcat oil-drilling operation. If the drilling operation is successful, the investment will be worth $7,500 at the end of the year. If it is unsuccessful, the investor can liquidate the holdings and recover $2,500. There is a 60 percent chance that oil will be discovered and a 40 percent chance of a dry hole. If our investor has only $5,000 to invest, would the riskless government bond or the risky drilling operation be the wiser choice?

Let us first calculate, in Table 16.1, the expected monetary values of the two investments. The calculation for the oil venture shows that its expected value is $5,500, higher than that of the bond, which has an expected value of $5,250. [Also, the expected return on the oil venture is 10 percent (calculated as $500 expected profit/$5,000 cost) versus 5 percent for the bond.] Does this mean that our investor should put the $5,000 in the wildcat well? Not necessarily—it depends on the investor's utility function. If this individual's marginal utility for money is sharply diminishing, then the potential loss of utility that would result from a dry hole, or no oil, might not be fully offset by the potential gain in utility that would result from the development of a producing well. If the utility function

---

[2]We shall not consider in this discussion any risk of declines in bond prices caused by increases in the level of interest rates. Thus, the risk with which we are concerned at this point is *default risk*, the risk that principal and interest payments will not be made as scheduled.

Table 16.1   Expected Returns from Two Projects

States of Nature	Drilling Operation			Government Bond		
	Probability (1)	Outcome (2)	(1) × (2) (3)	Probability (1)	Outcome (2)	(1) × (2) (3)
Oil	0.6	$7,500	$4,500	1.0	$5,250	$5,250
No oil	0.4	2,500	1,000			
		Expected value =	$5,500			$5,250

that is shown in Curve A of Figure 16.1 is applicable, this is exactly the case. To show this, we modify the expected monetary value calculation to reflect utility considerations. Reading from Figure 16.1, Curve A, we see that this particular risk-averse investor would have approximately 12 utils if he or she invests in the wildcat venture and oil is found, 6 utils if this investment is made and no oil is found, and 10.5 utils with certainty if the investor chooses the government bond. This information is used in Table 16.2 to calculate the *expected utility* for the oil investment. No calculation is needed for the government bond; we know its utility is 10.5 regardless of the outcome of the oil venture.

Since the *expected utility* from the wildcat venture is only 9.6 utils versus 10.5 from the government bond, we see that for this investor the government bond is the preferred investment. Thus, even though the *expected monetary value* for the oil venture is higher, *expected utility* is higher for the bond. Risk considerations, therefore, lead us to choose the safer government bond.

Mean-Variance Indifference Curves

Assuming that risk can be measured by the variance of return [or by the square root of the variance, which is called the standard deviation, $\sigma(R)$] and that return is measured by the expected return, $E(R)$, we can map out all combinations of mean and standard deviation which give a risk-averse investor the same total utility. For example, in Figure 16.2, Points A, B, and C all have the same total utility. They lie on an investor's *indifference curve*. The risk-averse investor is indifferent between Point A, which has no risk and low return, and Point C, which has high risk and return. The higher return offered by Point C is sufficient to compensate our investor for the extra risk. A risk-neutral investor would have a family

Table 16.2   Expected Utility of Oil Drilling Project

States of Nature	Probability (1)	Monetary Outcome (2)	Associated Utility (3)	(1) × (3) (4)
Oil	0.6	$7,500	12.0	7.2
No oil	0.4	2,500	6.0	2.4
			Expected utility =	9.6 utils

Figure 16.2   Mean-Variance Indifference Curves

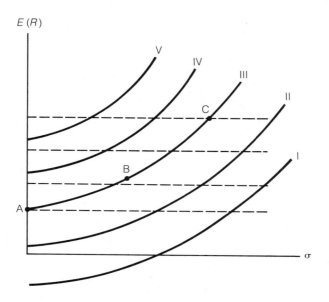

of indifference curves like the horizontal lines in Figure 16.2. Point C would be preferred to Point A because it has higher return, regardless of its risk.

An infinite number of indifference curves (such as those in Figure 16.2) could be drawn to represent the risk-return tradeoff for different levels of total utility for a given risk-averse individual. For a given level of σ, a greater $E(R)$ is received as the curves move farther out to the left. Each point on Curve V represents a higher level of satisfaction, or greater utility, than any point on IV, and III represents more utility than II. Also, different individuals are likely to have different sets of curves, or different risk-return tradeoffs. This is illustrated in Figure 16.3. Since the curves of B start from the same point and have a greater slope in the risk-return plane than the curves of A, this indicates that Investor B requires a higher return for the same amount of risk. Then, similarly for Investor B, as the curves move to the left, they represent higher levels of satisfaction.

The sets of mean-variance indifference curves are literally a theory of choice. The only assumptions necessary to draw the indifference curves for risk-averse investors are (1) that people prefer more wealth to less (this was true for all utility functions in Figure 16.1) and (2) that they have diminishing marginal utility of wealth. These assumptions, if valid, imply that all decision makers are risk averse and will require higher return to accept greater risk.

As illustrated in Figures 16.2 and 16.3, investors' indifference curves represent a complete *theory of choice*. They tell us how risk-averse investors will behave when confronted with risk-return tradeoffs. Next, we focus our attention on the *objects of choice*: risk and return. How are they measured, first for single risky assets and then for portfolios of risky assets?

Figure 16.3   Family of Indifference Curves for Individuals A and B

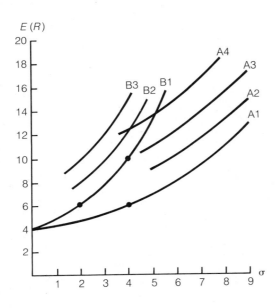

Risk and Return: Objects of Choice

Before turning to the risk and return for portfolios of assets, let us review measures of risk and return for single assets in isolation. Table 16.3 gives hypothetical expected rates of return for a steel company and a residential construction firm. Note that we are focusing on future rate of return projections. Hence, the data in Table 16.3 are not sample statistics. Rather, they are forecasts which are possibly subjectively determined. First, we will look at the mean and standard deviation of each firm separately. Then, we will study the effects of combining them into various portfolios.

Table 16.3   Hypothetical Expected Rates of Return for Two Firms

	Economic Conditions	Probability	Steel	Construction	Combined (50% each)
I	Horrid	.2	−5.5%	35%	14.75%
II	Bad	.2	.5	23	11.75
III	Average	.2	4.5	15	9.75
IV	Good	.2	9.5	5	7.25
V	Great	.2	16.0	−8	4.00

The Mean and Variance of Single Assets

The mean, or average, return is defined as the probability of observing each rate of return, p_i, multiplied by the rate of return, R_i, and then summed across all possible returns. Mathematically, the mean return is defined as

$$E(R) = \sum_{i=1}^{N} p_i R_i. \tag{16.1}$$

Assuming that each economic condition in Table 16.3 is equally likely, the probability of each is $p_i = 1/5 = .2$ and the expected return computation for steel is

$$E(R) = .2(-.055) + .2(.005) + .2(.045) + .2(.095) + .2(.16)$$

$$= -.011 + .001 + .009 + .019 + .032$$

$$= .05, \text{ or } 5\%.$$

Similar calculations for residential construction reveal a 14 percent expected return.[3]

The variance of return (given that we have subjective probability estimates and not sampling statistics) is defined as the average of the mean squared error terms. A mean squared error is simply the square of the difference between a given return, R_i, and the average of all returns, $E(R)$:

$$\text{Mean squared error} = [R_i - E(R)]^2.$$

The variance is the expectation (or average) of these terms; in other words, each mean squared error is multiplied by the probability, p_i, that it will occur and then all terms are summed. The mathematical expression for the variance of returns is

$$\text{VAR}(R) = E\{[R_i - E(R)]^2\}$$

$$= \sum_{i=1}^{N} p_i [R_i - E(R)]^2. \tag{16.2}$$

Substituting in the numbers for the steel firm, we compute the variance of returns as follows:

$$\text{VAR}(R) = .2(-.055 - .05)^2 + .2(.005 - .05)^2 + .2(.045 - .05)^2$$

$$+ .2(.095 - .05)^2 + .2(.16 - .05)^2$$

$$= .2(.011025) + .2(.002025) + .2(.000025) + .2(.002025) + .2(.0121)$$

$$= .002205 + .000405 + .000005 + .000405 + .00242$$

$$= .00544.$$

[3]Note that in Chapter 10, when we were using sampling statistics, it was always true that, given N observations, the probability of any observation was $p_i = 1/N$. With subjectively estimated forecasts, this is no longer necessarily true. Different events can have different probabilities.

Usually, we express risk in terms of the standard deviation, $\sigma(R)$, rather than the variance of returns. The standard deviation is just the square root of the variance.

$$\sigma(R) = \sqrt{\text{VAR}(R)}. \tag{16.3}$$

For the steel firm, the standard deviation of returns is

$$\sigma(R) = \sqrt{.00544} = .0737564, \text{ or } 7.38\%.$$

Similar calculations will show that the variance of returns for the residential construction firm is $\text{VAR}(R) = .02176$ and that the standard deviation is $\sigma(R) = .1475127$, or 14.8 percent.[4]

Figure 16.4 plots the mean and standard deviation of returns for both firms. Because construction has a higher mean and standard deviation than steel it is possible for a risk-averse investor to be indifferent between the two alternatives, as shown by the indifference curve in Figure 16.4.

Figure 16.4 Risk and Return for Hypothetical Steel and Residential Construction Firms

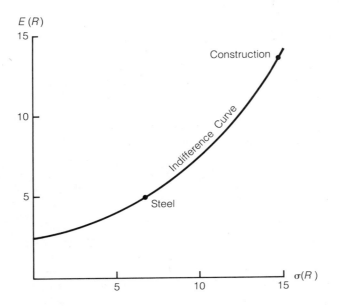

The Mean and Variance of Portfolios of Assets

Portfolios of assets usually offer the advantage of reducing risk through diversification. To illustrate, our steel company may decide to diversify into residential construction materials. We know that when the economy is booming, the demand for steel is high, and the returns from the steel mill are large. Residential construction, on the other hand, may be countercyclical: When the economy is strong, the demand for construction materials may be weak.[5] Because of these divergent cyclical patterns, a diversified firm with investments in both steel and construction could expect to have a more stable pattern of revenues than would a firm engaged exclusively in either steel or residential construction. In other words, the standard deviation of the returns on the *portfolio of assets*, $\sigma(R_p)$, may be less than the sum of the standard deviations of the returns from the individual assets.[6]

This point is illustrated in Figure 16.5. Panel (a) of the figure shows the rate of return variations for the steel plant; Panel (b), the fluctuations for the residential construction division; and Panel (c), the rate of return for the combined company, assuming that the separate firms are of equal size. When the returns from steel are large, those from residen-

---

Figure 16.5   Hypothetical Relationship between Steel and Residential Construction Companies (Data from Table 16.3)

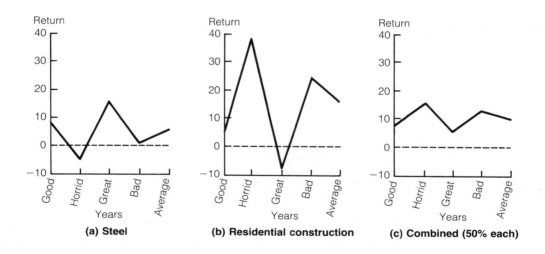

(a) Steel   (b) Residential construction   (c) Combined (50% each)

---

[5]The reason for the countercyclical behavior of the residential construction industry has to do with the availability of credit. When the economy is booming, interest rates are high. High interest rates seem to discourage potential home buyers more than they do other demanders of credit. As a result, the residential construction industry has historically shown countercyclical tendencies.

[6]These conclusions obviously hold also for portfolios of financial assets — stocks and bonds. In fact, the basic concepts of portfolio theory were developed specifically for common stocks by Markowitz [1952]. The logical extension of portfolio theory to capital budgeting calls for considering firms as having "portfolios of tangible assets."

tial construction are small, and vice versa. As a consequence, the combined rate of return is relatively stable. In fact, we shall show later on that there is one combination of steel and construction which results in no risk at all.

The Expected Return on a Portfolio of Assets

A portfolio is defined as a combination of assets. Portfolio theory deals with the selection of optimal portfolios; that is, portfolios that provide the highest possible return for any specified degree of risk or the lowest possible risk for any specified rate of return. Since portfolio theory has been developed most thoroughly for *financial assets* — stocks and bonds — we shall, for the most part, restrict our discussion to these assets.[7] However, extensions of financial asset portfolio theory to physical assets are readily made, and certainly the concepts are relevant in capital budgeting.

The rate of return on a portfolio is always a weighted average of the returns of the individual securities in the portfolio. Let us assume that instead of combining a steel firm and a residential construction firm, that we invest in various combinations of their shares of stock. For example, suppose 50 percent of the portfolio is invested in a steel security with a 5 percent expected return (Security S), and 50 percent in a construction security with a 14 percent expected return (Security C). In general, we can write the return on a portfolio of two assets as

$$R_p = wR_S + (1 - w)R_C,\qquad(16.4)$$

where w is the percentage invested in Security S and $(1 - w)$ is the remainder of the portfolio. The expected rate of return on the portfolio is

$$E(R_p) = wE(R_S) + (1 - w)E(R_C)\qquad(16.5)$$
$$= w(5\%) + (1 - w)(14\%)$$
$$= 0.5(5\%) + 0.5(14\%) = 9.5\%.$$

Here, $E(R_p)$ is the *expected* return on the portfolio. If all of the portfolio is invested in S, the expected return is 5 percent. If all is invested in C, the expected return is 14 percent. If the portfolio contains some of each, the expected portfolio return is a linear combination of the two securities' expected returns — for example, 9.5 percent in our present case. Therefore, given the expected returns on the individual securities, the expected return on the portfolio depends upon the amount of funds invested in each security.

Figure 16.6 illustrates the possible returns for our two-asset portfolio. Line SC represents all possible expected returns when Securities S and C are combined in different proportions. Note that when 50 percent of the portfolio is invested in each asset, the expected return on the portfolio is seen to be 9.5 percent, just as we calculated above.

[7]Financial assets are easily divisible and available in large numbers, and a great deal of data is available on such assets. Capital assets such as plant and equipment, on the other hand, are "lumpy," and the data needed to apply portfolio theory to such assets are not readily available.

Figure 16.6   Rates of Return on a Two-Asset Portfolio

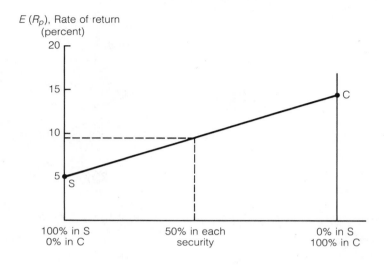

$E(R_p)$, Rate of return
(percent)

100% in S	50% in each	0% in S
0% in C	security	100% in C

The Variance of a Portfolio

A fundamental aspect of portfolio theory is the idea that the riskiness inherent in any single asset held in a portfolio is different from the riskiness of that asset held in isolation. As we shall see, it is possible for a given asset to be quite risky when held in isolation, but not very risky if held in a portfolio. The impact of a single asset on a portfolio's riskiness — which is the riskiness of the asset when it is held in a portfolio — is discussed later in this chapter. But first, how shall we calculate the variance of a portfolio of assets?

According to Equation 16.2, the definition of variance is

$$VAR(R) = \sum_{i=1}^{N} p_i [R_i - E(R)]^2, \tag{16.2}$$

and the return and expected return on a two-asset portfolio are defined as

$$R_p = wR_S + (1 - w)R_C \tag{16.4}$$

$$E(R_p) = wE(R_S) + (1 - w)E(R_C). \tag{16.5}$$

By squaring the terms in brackets and rearranging terms, we have[8]

$$\text{VAR}(R_p) = \sum_{i=1}^{N} p_i w^2 [R_S - E(R_S)]^2$$

$$+ \sum_{i=1}^{N} 2p_i w(1 - w)[R_S - E(R_S)] \ [R_C - E(R_C)]$$

$$+ \sum_{i=1}^{N} p_i (1 - w)^2 [R_C - E(R_C)]^2.$$

The first term of this equation is w-squared times the variance of the first asset, S.

$$w^2 \text{VAR}(R_S) = w^2 \sum_{i=1}^{N} p_i [R_S - E(R_S)]^2.$$

The third term is $(1 - w)$-squared times the variance of the second asset, C.

$$(1 - w)^2 \text{VAR}(R_C) = (1 - w)^2 \sum_{i=1}^{N} p_i [R_C - E(R_C)]^2.$$

The middle term, the cross-product term, is defined as the product of the portfolio weights, $w(1 - w)$, times twice the covariance between the returns on the two assets,

$$2w(1 - w)\text{COV}(R_S, R_C) = 2w(1 - w)\sum_{i=1}^{N} p_i [R_S - E(R_S)][R_C - E(R_C)],$$

[8]In order to find the correct expression for the variance of a two-asset portfolio, we can substitute Equations 16.4 and 16.5 into the definition of variance, Equation 16.2:

$$\text{VAR}(R_p) = \sum_{i=1}^{N} p_i \{wR_S + (1 - w)R_C - [wE(R_S) + (1 - w)E(R_C)]\}^2.$$

In order to simplify this expression, we can rearrange terms as follows

$$\text{VAR}(R_p) = \sum_{i=1}^{N} p_i \{[wR_S - wE(R_S)] + [(1 - w)R_C - (1 - w)E(R_C)]\}^2.$$

In order to simplify further, if we let

$$a = wR_S - wE(R_S)$$

$$b = (1 - w)R_C - (1 - w)E(R_C),$$

the expression is seen to be a binomial equation:

$$\text{VAR}(R_p) = \sum_{i=1}^{N} p_i (a + b)^2$$

$$= \sum_{i=1}^{N} p_i [a^2 + 2ab + b^2].$$

Finally, by substituting back the values of a and b, we have the expression for the variance of a portfolio of two risky assets.

and the definition of covariance is simply[9]

$$COV(R_S,R_C) \equiv \sum_{i=1}^{N} p_i[R_S - E(R_S)] [R_C - E(R_C)]. \tag{16.6}$$

Thus, the variance of a portfolio of two risky assets is not merely the sum of their separate variances. It also includes the covariance between them. The expression for the variance of a portfolio of two risky assets is

$$VAR(R_p) = w^2 VAR(R_S) + 2w(1 - w)COV(R_S,R_C) + (1 - w)^2 VAR(R_C). \tag{16.7}$$

In Figure 16.4, we illustrated the risk and return of a steel and a residential construction firm, and in Figure 16.5, we saw that by combining them, it was possible to reduce risk. Now, let us use the definitions of portfolio mean and variance to compute the return and risk of the merged firm. Since the firms were assumed to be the same size, they each will represent 50 percent of the merged firm; thus, our weights are $w = .5$ and $1 - w = .5$. Using the definition of the mean return of a two-asset portfolio, Equation 16.2, we have

$$E(R_p) = wE(R_S) + (1 - w)E(R_C)$$
$$= .5(.05) + (1 - .5)(.14)$$
$$= .025 + .07 = .095, \text{ or } 9.5\%.$$

Note that a return of 9.5 percent is half-way between the return on the steel firm (5 percent) and the construction firm (14 percent). In order to compute the portfolio variance, we need to know the variance of the steel firm (already calculated as [$VAR(R_S) = .00544$]) and the variance of the construction firm [$VAR(R_C) = .02176$] and the covariance between them. Table 16.4 uses the definition of covariance (Equation 16.6) to perform the necessary

Table 16.4   The Covariance between Two Risky Assets*

State of Nature	Probability	Return on Steel = R_S	Return on Construction = R_C	$R_S - E(R_S)$	$R_C - E(R_C)$	$p_i[R_S - E(R_S)] [R_C - E(R_C)]$
Horrid	.2	−5.5%	35%	−.105	.210	.2(−.105)(.210) = −.00441
Bad	.2	.5	23	−.045	.090	.2(−.045)(.090) = −.00081
Average	.2	4.5	15	−.005	.010	.2(−.005)(.010) = −.00001
Good	.2	9.5	5	.045	−.090	.2(.045)(−.090) = −.00081
Great	.2	16.0	−8	.110	−.220	.2(.110)(−.220) = −.00484
Sum	1.0					$COV(R_S,R_C)$ = −.01088

*We had already calculated that $E(R_S)$ = 5% and $E(R_C)$ = 14%.

[9]The definition of covariance was also introduced in Chapter 10, where it was part of the definition of the slope in a linear regression. We shall use this fact later in this chapter.

calculations. The sum of the numbers in the last column is the covariance between returns on the steel and construction companies. The negative covariance ($-.01088$) reflects the fact that the returns of the two companies are offsetting.

We can now calculate the portfolio variance assuming the two companies are merged. From Equation 16.7, the definition of portfolio variance is

$$VAR(R_p) = w^2 VAR(R_S) + 2w(1 - w)COV(R_S, R_C) + (1 - w)^2 \, VAR(R_C) \qquad \textbf{(16.7)}$$

$$= (.5)^2(.00544) + 2(.5)(1 - .5)(-.01088) + (1 - .5)^2(.02176)$$

$$= .25(.00544) + .5(-.01088) + .25(.02176)$$

$$= .00136 - .00544 + .00544$$

$$= .00136,$$

and the portfolio standard deviation is

$$\sigma(R_p) = \sqrt{VAR(R_p)} = \sqrt{.00136} = .036878, \text{ or } 3.69\%.$$

Note that the standard deviation of return for the merged companies is less than either of their separate standard deviations. This result is shown in Figure 16.7. Also illustrated are the indifference curves of a risk-averse investor, who would prefer the merged firm to the alternatives of owning each firm separately. Note that no risk-averse investor would prefer to invest 100 percent in the steel firm (Point S) because the merged firm (Point M) has higher return and lower risk. However, this does not mean that no one will hold shares of

Figure 16.7   The Risk of a Merged Firm

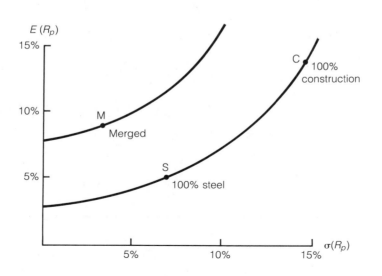

Table 16.5   The Portfolio Mean-Standard Deviation Opportunity Set

	Percent in Steel	Percent in Construction	$E(R_p)$	$\sigma(R_p)$
A	−50.0%	150.0%	18.50%	25.81%
C	0.0	100.0	14.00	14.75
D	25.0	75.0	11.75	9.22
M	50.0	50.0	9.50	3.69
E	66.7	33.3	8.00	0.00
S	100.0	0.0	5.00	7.38
G	150.0	−50.0	0.50	18.44

the steel firm. It only means that the steel firm will always be held as part of a diversified portfolio.

Although merger is one way of reducing risk, it is not necessarily the best way because the relative sizes of the merging firms determine their weight in the resulting portfolio. In our example, the steel and construction firms were of equal size, so that each contributed 50 percent to the new merged firm. Investors who purchase the common stock of steel and construction have an advantage because they can choose any portfolio weights they desire. Table 16.5 shows the expected returns and standard deviations of return for various portfolio combinations of steel and construction. The set of all mean-standard deviation choices is called the *portfolio opportunity set* because it is a list of all possible opportunities available to the investor. Notice that there is one special portfolio (with approximately two-thirds in steel and one-third in construction) where there is no risk at all. This possibility was not obtainable by simply merging the steel and construction firms. However, it becomes possible by holding a portfolio of their securities. Panel (a) of Figure 16.8 graphs

Figure 16.8   The Mean-Standard Deviation Opportunity Set (Steel and Construction)

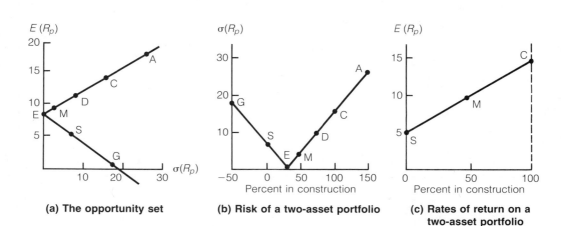

(a) The opportunity set

(b) Risk of a two-asset portfolio

(c) Rates of return on a two-asset portfolio

the opportunity set of risk-return combinations for the portfolios in Table 16.5. Panel (b) shows the standard deviation as a function of the portfolio weights, and Panel (c) shows the expected return as a function of the portfolio weights.

The sample opportunity set shown in Figure 16.8 is unusual because the rates of return for steel and construction were chosen to be perfectly negatively correlated, something which almost never happens in the real world.[10] What we need to do now is generalize our understanding of the portfolio opportunity set to include all possible correlations between assets.

Correlation and Covariance

Chapter 10 introduced the coefficient of determination, r^2, for a linear regression. It measures the percentage of the variance of the dependent variable, which is explained by the independent variable. The square root of the coefficient of determination is called the *correlation coefficient*, ρ. It is defined as the covariance between the dependent and independent variables, divided by the product of their standard deviations,

$$\rho_{xy} = \frac{\text{COV}(x,y)}{\sigma_x \sigma_y}. \qquad (16.8)$$

Figure 16.9 shows asset returns which are perfectly correlated, $\rho_{xy} = 1.0$; which are independent of each other, $\rho_{xy} = 0$; and which are perfectly inversely correlated, $\rho_{xy} = -1.0$. The returns on the steel and construction firms in our earlier example were perfectly

---

Figure 16.9   Examples of Different Correlation Coefficients

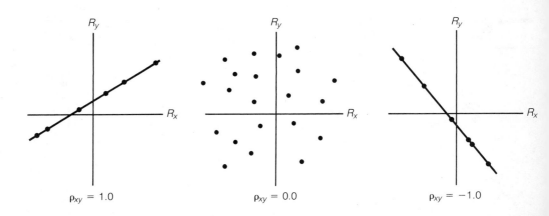

$\rho_{xy} = 1.0$ $\rho_{xy} = 0.0$ $\rho_{xy} = -1.0$

---

[10]The equation used was:

Return on construction = 24% − 2(Return on steel).

inversely correlated and had a negative covariance. When assets have zero correlation with each other, they are unrelated in any way and have zero covariance. Positive correlation implies positive covariance.

We can use the relationship between correlation and covariance to rewrite the equation for the variance of a portfolio. From Equation 16.8, we see that

$$COV(x,y) = \rho_{xy}\sigma_x\sigma_y. \tag{16.9}$$

This relationship can be substituted into the expression for the variance of a portfolio of two assets, Equation 16.7, to give

$$VAR(R_p) = w^2 VAR(R_x) + 2w(1-w)\rho_{xy}\sigma_x\sigma_y + (1-w)^2 VAR(R_y). \tag{16.10}$$

In order to illustrate the usefulness of this new definition, suppose that we have two securities, X and Y. We can allocate our investment funds between the securities in any proportion. Security X has an expected rate of return $E(R_x) = 5\%$ and a standard deviation $\sigma_x = 4\%$. For Security Y, the expected return is $E(R_y) = 8\%$ and the standard deviation is $\sigma_y = 10\%$.

Our ultimate task is to determine the optimal portfolio, that is, the optimal percentage of our available funds to invest in each security. Intermediate steps include (1) determining the opportunity set of attainable portfolios, (2) determining the best or efficient set from among all those which are attainable, and (3) selecting the optimal portfolio from the efficient set.

There is not yet sufficient information to select the best portfolio — we need data on the correlation between the two securities' returns (ρ_{xy}) in order to construct the portfolio opportunity set. Let us examine three different degrees of correlation, $\rho_{xy} = +1.0$, $\rho_{xy} = 0$, and $\rho_{xy} = -1.0$, and then develop the portfolio's expected return, $E(R_p)$, and standard deviation of return, $\sigma(R_p)$, for each case.

Equation 16.5 gives the expected return and 16.10 gives the standard deviation for a portfolio of two risky assets. They are repeated below:[11]

$$E(R_p) = wE(R_x) + (1-w)E(R_y) \tag{16.5}$$

$$\sigma(R_p) = \sqrt{w^2\sigma_x^2 + 2w(1-w)\rho_{xy}\sigma_x\sigma_y + (1-w)^2\sigma_y^2}. \tag{16.10}$$

We may now substitute in the given values of the asset means and standard deviations for a given correlation and then observe how the portfolio mean and standard deviation (return and risk characteristics) are affected by changing the weights which we choose for each asset. For example, when the asset returns are independent, they have zero correlation, $\rho_{xy} = 0$. If we choose to put 75 percent of our wealth in Asset X (and the remainder in Asset Y), then $w = .75$ and $(1-w) = .25$. The resulting portfolio mean and standard deviation are

$$E(R_p) = .75(5\%) + .25(8\%) = 5.75\%$$

$$\sigma(R_p) = \sqrt{.75^2(4\%)^2 + 2(.75)(.25)(0)(4\%)(10\%) + .25^2(10\%)^2}$$

$$= \sqrt{.5625(.0016) + 0 + .0625(.01)}$$

$$= \sqrt{.001525} = 3.9051\%.$$

---

[11]We have written the portfolio variance as the square of the standard deviation, that is, $VAR(R_x) = \sigma_x^2$.

Table 16.6   Portfolio Mean-Standard Deviation Combinations for Different Correlations between Two
Risky Assets

Percent in X Value of w	Percent in Y Value of $(1 - w)$	$\rho_{xy} = +1.0$		$\rho_{xy} = 0$		$\rho_{xy} = -1.0$	
		$E(R_p)$	$\sigma(R_p)$	$E(R_p)$	$\sigma(R_p)$	$E(R_p)$	$\sigma(R_p)$
100%	0%	5.00%	4.00%	5.00%	4.00%	5.00%	4.00%
75	25	5.75	5.50	5.75	3.91	5.75	.50
50	50	6.50	7.00	6.50	5.39	6.50	3.00
25	75	7.25	8.50	7.25	7.57	7.25	6.50
0	100	8.00	10.00	8.00	10.00	8.00	10.00

Similar calculations can be made for any choice of portfolio weights. The results are shown
in Table 16.6 and illustrated in Figure 16.10. In both the table and the graphs, note the
following points:

1.   The portfolio mean return, $E(R_p)$, is a linear function of w, the percentage of wealth
     invested in Asset X. It is the same straight line in the left-most column of the graphs.
     This serves to illustrate that the relationship between $E(R_p)$ and w is unaffected by
     the degree of correlation between the two risky assets.
2.   The portfolio standard deviation, $\sigma(R_p)$, is a function of the correlation, ρ_{xy}, between
     the risky assets. In Case 1, where $\rho_{xy} = 1.0$, it is a straight line. There is a proportion-
     ate tradeoff between risk and return. In Case 2, the assets are uncorrelated and the
     relationship between $\sigma(R_p)$ and w is nonlinear. Finally, when the assets are perfectly
     inversely correlated, $\rho_{xy} = -1.0$, risk can be completely diversified away.
3.   Panels (a.3), (b.3), and (c.3) show the attainable risk-return tradeoffs for various
     portfolios. Panels (a.3) and (c.3) represent the most extreme possibilities when $\rho_{xy} =$
     $+1.0$ or $\rho_{xy} = -1.0$. Panel (b.3) is typical of the general shape of a portfolio opportu-
     nity set.

The Portfolio Opportunity Set and the Efficient Set

Figure 16.11 illustrates the general relationship between return and risk for portfolios of
two risky assets. We know that the correlation coefficient can never be larger than $+1.0$
nor smaller than -1.0 ($-1.0 \le \rho_{xy} \le 1.0$). Line XY shows the return-risk combinations
which are attainable if $\rho_{xy} = +1.0$. This was also illustrated in Figure 16.10, Panel (a.3). At
the other extreme, line XZY shows the return-risk tradeoffs when $\rho_{xy} = -1.0$. This was
illustrated in Figure 16.10, Panel (c.3). The triangle XYZ bounds the set of possibilities. It
was also the shape of the opportunity set for our steel and construction example. The
general case occurs when the risky assets are not perfectly correlated and is illustrated by
the curved line XMY, which is called the *minimum variance portfolio opportunity set*. It is the
combination of portfolios which provide the minimum variance (or standard deviation) for
a given rate of return. It will always have a shape similar to line XMY.

    If there are many risky assets, instead of just two, the general shape of the portfolio
opportunity set is unaltered; however, there are an infinite number of attainable points in
the interior of the set. They are illustrated by the shaded region in Figure 16.12. The solid
line, AC, which starts with the minimum variance portfolio at Point A, is called the *efficient*

Figure 16.10   Illustrations of Portfolio Returns, Risks, and the Attainable Sets of Portfolios

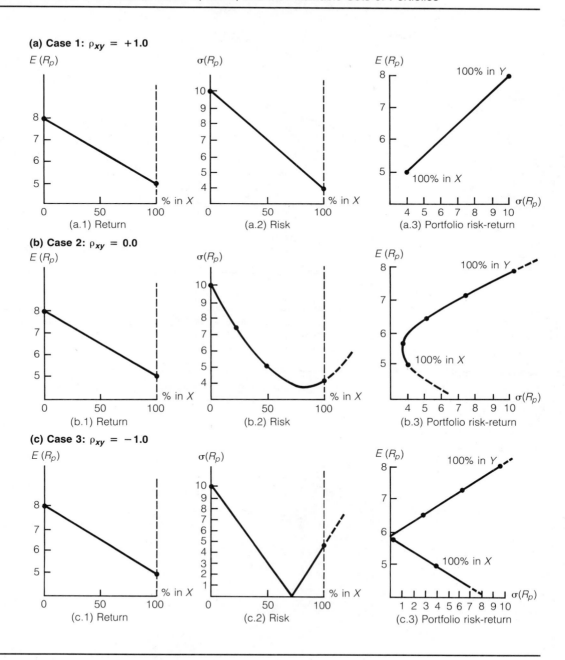

(a) Case 1: $\rho_{xy} = +1.0$

(a.1) Return

(a.2) Risk

(a.3) Portfolio risk-return

(b) Case 2: $\rho_{xy} = 0.0$

(b.1) Return

(b.2) Risk

(b.3) Portfolio risk-return

(c) Case 3: $\rho_{xy} = -1.0$

(c.1) Return

(c.2) Risk

(c.3) Portfolio risk-return

Figure 16.11   The General Shape of the Portfolio Opportunity Set

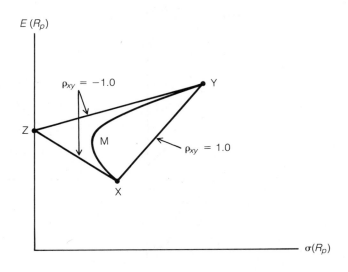

Figure 16.12   The Portfolio Opportunity Set and the Efficient Set with Many Risky Assets

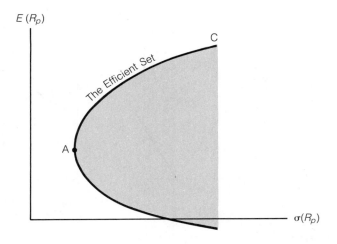

set. It represents the locus of all portfolios which have the highest return for a given level of risk. Risk-averse investors will choose only those portfolios which lie on the efficient set. Why? Assets which lie in the interior of the opportunity set are said to be inefficient and must be held as part of a diversified portfolio in market equilibrium.

Market Equilibrium: The Capital Market Line

So far, we have discussed the theory of choice (that is, indifference curves) and the objects of choice (that is, the portfolio opportunity set). Now we seek to put these concepts together in a market equilibrium setting. In order to do so, we must recognize that the opportunity set, up to this point, has been composed of only risky assets. We have not discussed what opportunity set might result if there is a riskless asset. There has been no opportunity for investors to trade among themselves by borrowing and lending. By introducing borrowing and lending at the risk-free rate of interest, we can characterize a market equilibrium with many market participants. First, we will look at the opportunity set which results from combining one risky asset (or portfolio) with one riskless asset. Then, we will extend the analysis to a full market equilibrium with one riskless and many risky assets.

The Opportunity Set with One Risky and One Riskless Asset

The return on a portfolio composed of a% of our wealth in a risky Asset X and $(1 - a)$% in a riskless asset with return R_F can be written as

$$R_p = aX + (1 - a)R_F. \tag{16.11}$$

The expected return on this portfolio is

$$E(R_p) = aE(X) + (1 - a)R_F. \tag{16.11a}$$

Note that it is unnecessary to calculate the mean (or expectation) for the riskless return because a risk-free asset has the same return in every state of nature. The standard deviation of return for this portfolio is

$$\sigma(R_p) = a\sigma_x. \tag{16.11b}$$

There is no covariance term because the covariance between a riskless asset and a risky asset is zero. Furthermore, the variance of a riskless asset is also zero.

Figure 16.13 shows the linear mean-standard deviation portfolio opportunity set which results from combinations of the risky and riskless assets. At Point X, you have 100 percent of your wealth in the risky asset. To the right of Point X (along XY), you have more than 100 percent of your wealth in X. This is accomplished by borrowing (sometimes called buying a stock on margin). In other words, you have a negative weight in the riskless asset. In effect, borrowing is the same thing as selling the riskless asset short. You are receiving cash now in return for issuing a certificate (a bond) which promises to pay back the loan plus interest at the end of the year. Between Points X and R_F, you have part

Figure 16.13   Opportunity Set for One Risky and One Riskless Asset

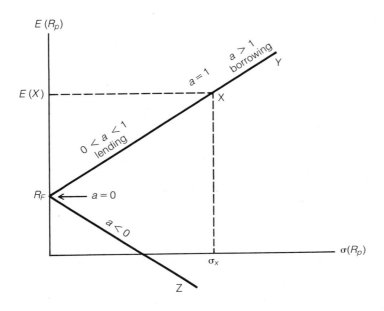

of your wealth in the risky asset (that is, $0 < a < 1$), and the rest has been lent out at the riskless rate. At Point R_F, you have 100 percent of your wealth invested at the riskless rate. And finally, between R_F and Z, you have sold the risky asset short (that is, $a < 0$) in order to invest more than 100 percent of your wealth in the riskless asset. Note however, that no risk-averse investor would do this because points along $R_F Z$ are dominated by any point along $R_F XY$. An investor can always achieve a higher return for the same risk (standard deviation) along $R_F XY$.

The Opportunity Set with One Riskless and Many Risky Assets

If we extend the analysis to a world with riskless borrowing and lending and N risky assets, we can explain market equilibrium. Line $R_F X$ in Figure 16.14 shows all of the feasible portfolios made up of the riskless asset, R_F, and risky asset (or portfolio), X. Clearly, all risk-averse investors will prefer portfolios along line $R_F Y$ because they have higher return for a given risk. But, best of all are portfolios along line $R_F M$. They provide the highest expected return for each level of risk. Line $R_F M$ is given a special name. It is called the *Capital Market Line* (CML) because it represents the market equilibrium tradeoff between risk and return. It exists because of opportunities for investors to borrow and lend at the riskless rate, R_F. Thus, in equilibrium, all risk-averse investors will choose their optimal portfolios from combinations of the riskless asset, R_F, and the risky Portfolio M.

Figure 16.14   The Capital Market Line

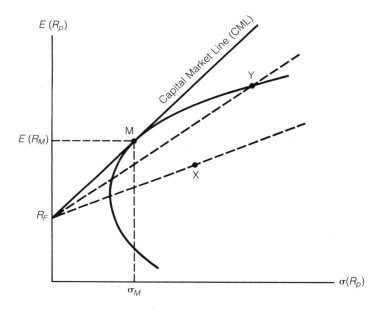

This fact is illustrated in Figure 16.15. Here, for the first time, we combine the theory of choice, as described by investor indifference curves, with the objects of choice, which are represented by the portfolio combinations along the Capital Market Line. Investor I would have chosen Point A as his or her optimal portfolio in a world without opportunities to borrow or lend. This point represents the tangency between his or her indifference curve and the opportunity set of risky assets only. Without a capital market and without opportunities to borrow and lend, Point A would represent the utility maximizing portfolio for Investor I. But if this investor moves to Point M and then borrows to reach Point B, it is possible to reach a higher indifference curve (that is, curve Ib). Hence, Investor I is better off if the capital market exists. Investor II is also better off in a world with opportunities to borrow and lend. If he or she were initially at Point X, it would be possible to achieve greater utility by moving along the opportunity set to Point M and then lending to reach Point Y, which is on a higher indifference curve.

In fact, almost every risk-averse investor is better off in a world where there are opportunities to exchange wealth by borrowing and lending. The only investor who would not have higher expected utility is the individual whose original tangency was at Point M, and he or she would be equally well off, holding Portfolio M in both worlds (with exchange and without). The important conclusion is that opportunities to freely exchange in capital markets by borrowing and lending increase welfare at the expense of no one. An economy with free exchange is better than one without.

Point M is a very special portfolio. It is the portfolio of risky assets held by all investors in equilibrium. By definition, it is the *market portfolio* of risky assets. The market portfolio is

Figure 16.15   All Risk-Averse Investors Choose Optimal Portfolios along the Capital Market Line

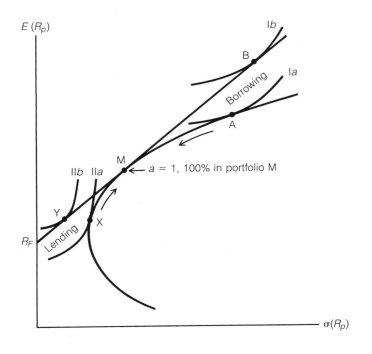

defined as a portfolio made up of all assets in the economy held according to their market value weights. The weight of the ith asset in the market portfolio is

$$w_i = \frac{\text{Market value of the } i^{th} \text{ asset}}{\text{Market value of all assets in the economy}}. \tag{16.12}$$

Point M in Figures 16.14 and 16.15 must be the market portfolio for two reasons. First, we assume that all investors have the same information about the risk-return characteristics of all assets and, therefore, perceive the same investment opportunity set. All investors will then seek to hold portfolios with the highest return for a given level of risk. In equilibrium, all assets will be held according to their market value weights because that is how equilibrium is defined. Therefore, the market portfolio must be one of those along the upper half of the minimum variance opportunity set. Second, the market Portfolio M must be the tangency portfolio in Figures 16.14 and 16.15 because all individuals will seek to hold the best efficient portfolio, that is, the one which maximizes their utility. The best portfolio is the tangency portfolio and it must be the market portfolio. To see why, suppose that Portfolio Y in Figure 16.14 was the market portfolio. Then it would be clearly dominated by Portfolio M because everyone could attain higher utility by choosing to hold combinations of M and the riskless asset, R_F. But the market portfolio cannot be dominated because all assets must be held according to their market value weights in equilibrium. Therefore, Portfolio M, the tangency portfolio, must also be the market portfolio.

The Equilibrium Price of Risk

Perhaps the most important aspect of the Capital Market Line (CML) is that it describes the market price of risk which will be used by all individuals who make decisions in the face of uncertainty. As shown in Figure 16.16, the intercept of the CML is R_F and its slope is $(E(R_M) - R_F)/\sigma_M$; therefore, the equation of the CML is

$$E(R_p) = R_F + \left[\frac{E(R_M) - R_F}{\sigma_M}\right]\sigma(R_p), \qquad (16.13)$$

where

$E(R_p) =$ the expected rate of return for portfolios along the CML, that is, combinations of R_F and R_M

$R_F =$ the riskless borrowing and lending rate

$E(R_M) =$ the expected rate of return on the market Portfolio M

Figure 16.16   The CML and the Equilibrium Price of Risk

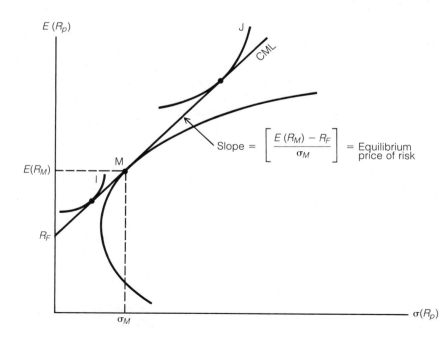

σ_M =   the standard deviation of return on the market Portfolio M
$\sigma(R_p)$ =   the standard deviation of portfolios along the CML.

The term in brackets in Equation 16.13 measures the market rate of exchange between risk and return in equilibrium. It is the market equilibrium price of risk. The *marginal rate of substitution* for each investor is his or her rate of exchange between return and risk; in other words, it is the price of risk. The marginal rate of substitution for Investor I in Figure 16.16 is the slope of the line tangent to his or her indifference curve, but the tangent line is the CML. Therefore, Investor I will use the market price of risk (the slope of the CML) in making tradeoffs between risk and return. The same thing can be said for Investor J. He or she will also use the market price of risk as the appropriate marginal rate of substitution. The CML is also tangent to the portfolio opportunity set; thus, the slope of the CML is equal to the objectively determined rate of exchange between risk and return in equilibrium. This is called the *marginal rate of transformation*. We have the result that, in equilibrium, the marginal rate of substitution for Individuals I and J is equal to the marginal rate of transformation, which, in turn, equals the slope of the CML.

$$\text{Slope of CML} = \text{Market price of risk} = \frac{E(R_M) - R_F}{\sigma_M} \qquad (16.14)$$

$$= \text{MRS}_I = \text{MRS}_J = \text{MRT}.$$

Equation 16.14 is the usual equilibrium result familiar to economics students. All individuals, regardless of the shape of their indifference curves, look to the market price in making decisions. Here, we look to the market price of risk in order to determine our optimal portfolios. An important implication for managers is that it is unnecessary to know the risk preferences of individual shareholders. They will unanimously agree that the market-determined price of risk is the correct rate of exchange between risk and return for decision making under uncertainty.

Suppose you know that the riskless rate is $R_F = 6\%$, the expected rate of return on the market portfolio is $E(R_M) = 14\%$, and the standard deviation of the market portfolio is $\sigma_M = 3\%$. You want to earn an expected rate of return of 22 percent. How can you do it? What percentage of your wealth should you put into the market portfolio and what percentage into the riskless asset?[12] And what amount of risk will you be taking?

From Equation 16.11a, we know that the return for any portfolio along the Capital Market Line is

$$E(R_p) = aE(R_M) + (1 - a)R_F. \qquad (16.11a)$$

If we want an expected return of 22 percent, we have, by substituting in the correct numbers,

$$22\% = a(14\%) + (1 - a)6\%$$

$$a = \frac{22\% - 6\%}{8\%} = 2 \text{ and } 1 - a = -1.$$

---

[12]Investment vehicles called "index" funds provide their clients with the desired amount of risk by investing part of their portfolios in a well-diversified index, such as the Standard & Poor's 500, and the remainder in U.S. Treasury bills.

This implies that if we borrow an amount of money equal to 100 percent of our original wealth and invest the proceeds plus our wealth (that is, $a = 200\%$) in the market portfolio, we will achieve an expected return of 22 percent.[13] The risk associated with this portfolio can be computed from Equation 16.11b, which tells us the standard deviation of portfolios along the CML.

$$\sigma(R_p) = a\ \sigma_M \qquad\qquad\qquad\qquad \textbf{(16.11b)}$$
$$= 2(3\%) = 6\%.$$

In other words, we must expose ourselves to twice as much risk as the market portfolio in order to earn a 22 percent expected return.

Pricing Inefficient Portfolios

Unfortunately, the Capital Market Line tells us only how to evaluate the risk-return combinations of the market portfolio and the riskless asset. All points along the CML are combinations of two "mutual funds," namely, the market portfolio and the riskless asset. We would like to know more. For example, what is the equilibrium relationship between risk and return for inefficient assets and portfolios such as Points B, C, and D which do not lie on the CML in Figure 16.17? They all have the same expected return as Point A, which does lie on the CML, but they are inefficient because none are as well diversified as the market portfolio, which is used in combination with the riskless asset to form Portfolio A. In order to see how to price inefficient assets in equilibrium, we need to understand more about portfolio diversification. In particular, we shall see that the total risk (the variance) of any inefficient asset or portfolio can be partitioned into two parts: diversifiable and undiversifiable risk. Because diversifiable risk can be eliminated at virtually no cost, the market will not offer a risk premium to avoid it. Thus, we shall see that only undiversifiable risk is relevant in pricing inefficient assets. This fact shall lead to a theory which tells us how to price all risky securities in equilibrium — the subject of Chapter 17.

Diversification

An empirical study by Wagner and Lau [1971] can be used to demonstrate the effects of diversification. They divided a sample of 200 NYSE stocks into six subgroups based on the Standard and Poor's quality ratings as of June 1960. Then, they constructed portfolios from each of the subgroups, using one to 20 randomly selected securities and applying equal weights to each security. Table 16.7 can be used to summarize some effects of diversification for the first subgroup (A+ quality stocks). As the number of securities in the portfolio increases, the standard deviation of portfolio returns decreases, but at a decreasing rate, with further reductions in risk being relatively small after about 10 securities are included in the portfolio. More will be said about the third column of the table, correlation with the market, shortly.

These data indicate that even well-diversified portfolios possess some level of risk that cannot be diversified away. Indeed, this is exactly the case, and the general situation is

---

[13]Borrowing to invest in risky assets is called "buying on margin." For example, you might put up $500 to buy $1,000 worth of stock. The brokerage house lends you the rest. If the maximum margin is 50 percent and if the stock price falls, you will receive a "margin call" and be asked to put more cash into the deal. Buying on margin is risky.

Figure 16.17   Portfolios with Different Standard Deviations but Equal Expected Returns

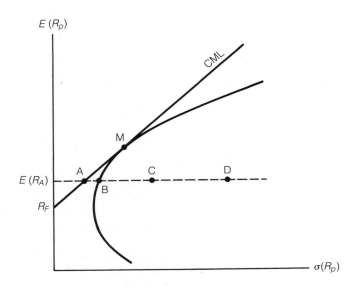

illustrated graphically in Figure 16.18. The risk of the portfolio, σ_p, has been divided into two parts. The part that can be reduced through diversification is defined as *unsystematic* risk, while the part that cannot be eliminated is defined as *systematic*, or market-related, risk.

Now refer back to the third column of Table 16.7. Notice that as the number of securities in each portfolio increases, and as the standard deviation decreases, the correlation be-

Table 16.7   Reduction in Portfolio Risk through Diversification

Number of Securities in Portfolio	Standard Deviation of Portfolio Returns (σ_p) (Percent per Month)	Correlation with Return on Market Index[a]
1	7.0%	0.54
2	5.0	0.63
3	4.8	0.75
4	4.6	0.77
5	4.6	0.79
10	4.2	0.85
15	4.0	0.88
20	3.9	0.89

[a]The "market" here refers to an unweighted index of all NYSE stocks.

Figure 16.18   Reduction of Risk through Diversification

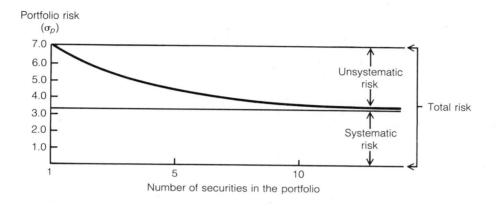

tween the return on the portfolio and the return on the market index increases. Thus, a broadly diversified portfolio is highly correlated with the market, and its risk (1) is largely systematic and (2) arises because of general market movements. In fact, the portfolios along the Capital Market Line (CML) are all perfectly correlated with each other because they contain nothing more than different proportions of the market portfolio and the riskless asset. Furthermore, the market portfolio has the maximum possible diversification. Any combination of the market portfolio and the riskless asset will be perfectly correlated with the market portfolio and with each other.

We can summarize our analysis of risk to this point as follows:

1. The risk of a portfolio can be measured by the standard deviation of its rate of return, σ_p.
2. The risk of an individual security is its contribution to the portfolio's risk, namely, its covariance with the portfolio.
3. A stock's standard deviation reflects both unsystematic risk that can be eliminated by diversification and systematic, or market-related, risk; only the systematic component of security risk is relevant for the well-diversified investor, so only this element is priced in the market place.
4. A stock's systematic risk is measured by the covariance between its returns and the general market.

Table 16.8 provides 11 years of data for the Standard and Poor's 500 stock index, which is a value weighted index of 500 of the largest companies. We shall assume that this index is a good proxy for the true market portfolio. Table 16.8 also contains data for General Motors stock. We would like to use these data for two purposes: (1) to find out how General Motors stock relates to the market index and (2) to partition the variance of General Motors returns into diversifiable and undiversifiable risk.

Table 16.8   Standard and Poor's Stock Index

Year	S&P 500 Price Index	S&P 500 Dividend Yield	S&P 500 Total Return	GM Price	GM Dividend Yield	GM Total Return
19X0	55.85	—	—	48	—	—
19X1	66.27	.0298	.2164	49	.05	.0708
19X2	62.38	.0337	−.0250	52	.06	.1212
19X3	69.87	.0317	.1518	74	.05	.4731
19X4	81.37	.0301	.1947	90	.05	.2662
19X5	88.17	.0300	.1136	102	.05	.1833
19X6	85.26	.0340	.0010	87	.05	−.0971
19X7	91.93	.0320	.1102	78	.05	−.0534
19X8	98.70	.0307	.1043	81	.05	.0885
19X9	97.84	.0324	.0237	74	.06	−.0264
19X0	83.22	.0383	−.1111	70	.05	−.0041

Suppose we assume that GM returns are linearly related to the market index. The linear regression equation would be[14]

$$\tilde{R}_{i,t} = a + b\,\tilde{R}_{M,t} + \tilde{\epsilon}_{i,t},\qquad\qquad (16.15)$$

where

$\tilde{R}_{i,t} =$ the return on GM in Year t
$a =$ the intercept term, a constant
$b =$ the slope term which measures the average relationship between GM and the market index. Recall (from Chapter 10) that $b = \text{COV}(R_i, R_M)/\text{VAR}(R_M)$
$\tilde{R}_{M,t} =$ the return on the market index in Time t
$\tilde{\epsilon}_{i,t} =$ a random error term, that is, the part of GM returns which are uncorrelated with the market index.

Figure 16.19 plots the relationship between GM and the market index. Note that each return is the sum of capital gains and dividends. For example, the return on General Motors for 19X1 was

$$R = \frac{P_t - P_{t-1} + d_t}{P_{t-1}} = \frac{49 - 48 + .05(48)}{48} = .0708.$$

Each point in Figure 16.19 represents a pair of returns, one for GM and one for the market, in the same year. Figure 16.19 makes it obvious that there is a positive covariance between General Motors stock and the market. Much of the total variance (about 25.2 percent) of GM returns is explained by the market.

---

[14]The reader is referred to Chapter 10 for a description of linear regression.

Figure 16.19   The Joint Distribution of GM and the S&P 500 Index

---

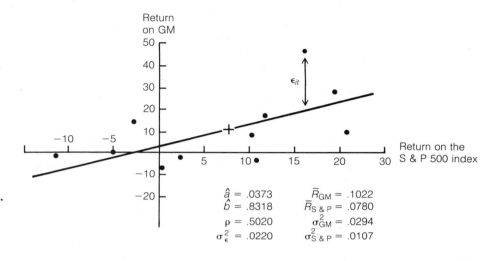

$$\hat{a} = .0373 \qquad \bar{R}_{GM} = .1022$$
$$\hat{b} = .8318 \qquad \bar{R}_{S\,\&\,P} = .0780$$
$$\rho = .5020 \qquad \sigma^2_{GM} = .0294$$
$$\sigma^2_\epsilon = .0220 \qquad \sigma^2_{S\,\&\,P} = .0107$$

Equation 16.15 gives the return on GM as a linear function of the market index. The general expression for the variance of $R_{i,t}$ is much like the variance of a portfolio of two risky assets,

$$\mathrm{VAR}(R_{i,t}) = b^2\mathrm{VAR}(R_{M,t}) + 2b\,\mathrm{COV}(R_{M,t}, \epsilon_{i,t}) + \mathrm{VAR}(\epsilon_{i,t}).$$

But we know that the random error term, $\epsilon_{i,t}$, is independent of the market return, $R_{M,t}$. In other words, $\mathrm{COV}(\epsilon_{i,t}, R_{M,t}) = 0$. Therefore, the variance of $R_{i,t}$ is

$$\mathrm{VAR}(R_{i,t}) = b^2\mathrm{VAR}(R_{M,t}) + \mathrm{VAR}(\epsilon_{i,t}) \qquad\qquad \textbf{(16.16)}$$

Total risk = Undiversifiable risk + Diversifiable risk.

Equation 16.16 has partitioned the total variance of return on the ith security into two parts, undiversifiable risk and diversifiable risk.[15]

Diversifiable risk can, in principle, be completely eliminated simply through costless diversification. All we need to do is combine a large number of assets into a portfolio so that their independent error terms cancel each other out.[16] A good analogy is that the

---

[15]Later on, we shall refer to the slope coefficient, b, as "beta," a "measure of" undiversifiable risk. Although not exactly the same as $b^2\mathrm{VAR}(R_M)$, which is the exact definition of undiversifiable risk, beta is a measure of undiversifiable risk because, for a given $\mathrm{VAR}(R_M)$, it provides a one-for-one correspondence.

[16]In fact, the error terms estimated from Equation 16.15 are not cross-sectionally independent. For this, and other reasons, one might suspect that the market index, by itself, does not provide a complete explanation of individual asset returns. In the next chapter, we shall see that a multi-factor model called the Arbitrage Pricing Model does better.

physicists tell us that every molecule in this page is in constant random motion, called Brownian motion. Yet, the page does not move. Why? The reason is that the molecules are all moving independently of each other. Consequently, their independent random movements cancel out and the page appears to be stationary. If all of the molecules were to move in the same direction at the same time, the page would move violently. There are, however, so many molecules that the probability of the page actually moving is lower than the probability of a nearby star going supernova.

The theoretically correct measure of risk for a single asset is its contribution to the market portfolio of all assets, that is, its covariance with the market portfolio. All other risk can be diversified away at no cost, at least in a world with no transactions costs. Equation 16.16 demonstrates that the total risk of an asset can be separated into two parts, undiversifiable, or systematic, risk and diversifiable, or unsystematic, risk.

$$\text{VAR}(R_{i,t}) = b^2 \text{VAR}(R_{M,t}) + \text{VAR}(\epsilon_{i,t}) \tag{16.16}$$

Total risk = Undiversifiable risk + Diversifiable risk.

Because of costless diversification, investors will only care about the undiversifiable risk of individual assets.

To add more substance to the argument, we note that the slope coefficient, b, in a linear regression is defined as[17]

$$b = \frac{\text{COV}(R_i, R_M)}{\text{VAR}(R_M)}.$$

In our General Motors example (Table 16.8), we suggested that General Motors stock returns could be regressed against a proxy for the market portfolio (the S&P 500 index). When this is done, we find the slope coefficient to be .8318. This is a measure of the undiversifiable risk of General Motors. It tells us that when the market rises (or falls) by 10 percent, General Motors will rise (or fall) by roughly 8.32 percent. In other words, General Motors is less volatile than the market portfolio when one considers only undiversifiable risk. Of course, the total risk of GM [$\text{VAR}(R_i) = .0294$] is greater than the total risk of the S&P 500 index [$\text{VAR}(R_M) = .0107$], but a great portion of GM's total risk is completely uncorrelated with the market. This uncorrelated, or idiosyncratic, risk may be diversified away (completely) at no cost. When applied to the GM example, Equation 16.16 becomes

Total risk = Undiversifiable risk + Diversifiable risk

$$\text{VAR}(R_i) = b^2 \text{VAR}(R_M) + \text{VAR}(\epsilon)$$

$$.0294 = (.8318)^2 (.0107) + .0220$$

$$.0294 = .0074 + .0220.$$

---

[17]Refer to Chapter 10 for the definition of the slope coefficient in a linear regression.

The undiversifiable risk of General Motors is only 25.2 percent of its total risk. In the next chapter, we shall see that the slope coefficient, b, can be used as an equilibrium measure of risk for individual assets.

There are many synonyms for the two components of total risk. For example, diversifiable risk is variously referred to as idiosyncratic risk, unsystematic risk, or firm specific risk. However, no matter how you look at it, this risk is unrelated to whatever else is going on in the economy. That is why it can be diversified away. On the other hand, undiversifiable risk is often called systematic risk (or beta) to reflect the fact that it is related to general economic conditions.

Summary

We began with the theory of choice in the face of uncertainty. We saw that if investors have diminishing marginal utility of wealth, they will be risk averse. They will require higher returns to compensate them for increased risk. Next, we studied the objects of choice. Return and risk were measured by the mean and variance of security returns. When assets were combined into portfolios, their covariances were seen to be important for determining portfolio risk. We defined the portfolio minimum variance opportunity set as the portfolios of securities which have the lowest variance for a given rate of return.

Market equilibrium was introduced by allowing opportunities to borrow and lend at the riskless rate of return. The result was the Capital Market Line, which consisted of various combinations of riskless borrowing (and lending) and the market portfolio. The slope of the Capital Market Line was the equilibrium price of risk. All investors, regardless of their attitudes towards risk, will use this price of risk to determine the risk premia required to take on extra risk.

Finally, by studying the effects of diversification, we saw that the total risk (or variance) of any asset can be separated into two parts: diversifiable and undiversifiable risk. Undiversifiable risk is a function of its covariance with the market portfolio of all assets, divided by the variance of the market portfolio.

In the next chapter, we shall see that in equilibrium, the only risk which counts is undiversifiable risk. This fact will allow us to develop a model (called the Capital Asset Pricing Model) which uniquely relates an asset's undiversifiable risk (or beta) to the rate of return which will be required of it in equilibrium.

Questions

16.1 Define the following terms, using graphs whenever feasible to illustrate your answer.

a)   risk
b)   expected value
c)   standard deviation
d)   marginal rate of substitution between return and risk
e)   marginal rate of transformation between return and risk
f)   the market price of risk

16.2 Assume that the residential construction industry is countercyclical to the economy in general and to steel in particular. Does this negative correlation between construction and steel necessarily mean that a savings and loan association, whose profitability tends to vary with residential construction levels, would be less risky if it diversified by acquiring a steel distributor?

16.3 If Firm A merges with Firm B, which is of equal size, and if there are no economic synergies,
   a) how would you estimate the total risk of the merged Firm AB?
   b) how would you estimate the undiversifiable risk of the merged Firm AB?

16.4 Define the minimum variance opportunity set and the efficient set in a world with only risky assets. How does your definition of the efficient set change if there are opportunities to borrow and lend at the riskless rate?

16.5 Define diversifiable and undiversifiable risk. How can you use linear regression to estimate the undiversifiable risk of an asset?

16.6 What are the advantages of diversification? What is the most diversified portfolio?

16.7 As you add more and more randomly selected securities to your portfolio,
   a) what happens to the portfolio's variance?
   b) what conditions are necessary for the variance to diminish to zero as the number of securities becomes very large?
   c) what usually happens to the variance of the portfolio if the number of securities becomes very large?

16.8 Suppose you can choose a portfolio from among ten assets, all with the same expected return, $E(R)$, and the same standard deviation, $\sigma(R)$. Graph the opportunity set and the efficient set.

16.9 How would the Capital Market Line change if expected inflation suddenly increased by 10 percent?

16.10 Why don't all risky assets lie exactly on the Capital Market Line?

16.11 Why will all investors choose combinations of riskless borrowing and lending and the market portfolio, but not hold other risky assets (except according to their market values)?

16.12 What is the relationship between correlation and covariance?

16.13 Why is the market portfolio the tangency portfolio for the Capital Market Line?

16.14 Why does diminishing marginal utility imply risk aversion?

16.15 In Figure 16.7, why would no risk averse investor put 100 percent of his or her wealth into steel? How will steel be held in equilibrium?

Problems

16.1 Figure 16.1 shows the utility curve of a risk neutral investor. Graph the mean-standard deviation indifference curves for a risk neutral investor.

16.2 Figure P16.2 shows the indifference curves for a risk-averse investor.
   a) Point A has a higher expected return than Point B. Is it preferred to Point B? Why or why not?
   b) Point C has lower risk (standard deviation) than Point B. Is it preferred? Why or why not?
   c) Draw an indifference curve for a risk-averse investor who would be indifferent between Points B and C.
   d) Draw an indifference curve for a risk-averse investor who would be indifferent between Points A and C.
   e) Which of the two investors whose indifference curves you drew for Parts (c) and (d) is the more risk averse? Why?

Figure P16.2   Indifference Curves for a Risk-Averse Investor

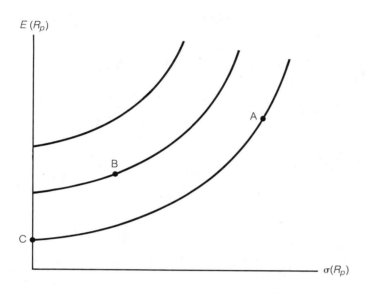

16.3   Based on the following historical market data, calculate the expected return on the market, the variance of the returns on the market, the standard deviation of the returns on the market, and the expected risk-free returns.

Year	S&P 500 Price Index	Dividend Yield	R_F
1	55.85		0.035
2	66.27	0.0298	0.032
3	62.38	0.0337	0.035
4	69.87	0.0317	0.039
5	81.37	0.0301	0.042
6	88.17	0.0300	0.051
7	85.26	0.0340	0.049
8	91.93	0.0320	0.056
9	98.70	0.0307	0.068
10	97.84	0.0324	0.065
11	83.22	0.0383	0.064
12	98.29	0.0314	0.086
13	109.20	0.0284	0.099
14	107.43	0.0306	0.119

16.4   Assuming the following probability distribution of market returns, calculate the $E(R_M)$, $VAR(R_M)$, and σ_M.

State	Probability	Market Return (R_M)
1	0.12	−0.10
2	0.26	0.15
3	0.44	0.20
4	0.18	0.25

16.5 The Barfield Company has a new investment project. The project returns are esti-mated as follows:

Year	Project Return (R_j)
19X1	0.10
19X2	0.17
19X3	0.24
19X4	0.20
19X5	0.14

Calculate:
a)   The expected return on the investment.
b)   The variance of returns.
c)   The standard deviation of returns.

16.6 The McCoy Company has developed the following data regarding a project to add new production facilities.

State (s)	Probability (p_j)	Market Return (R_M)	Project Return (R_j)
1	0.05	−0.20	−0.30
2	0.25	0.10	0.05
3	0.35	0.15	0.20
4	0.20	0.20	0.25
5	0.15	0.25	0.30

Calculate:
a)   The expected return on the project.
b)   The variance of the project returns.
c)   The standard deviation of project returns.
d)   The covariance of the project returns with the market returns.
e)   The correlation coefficient between the project returns and the market returns.

16.7 The expected returns for two firms, A and B, are as follows:

State of Nature	Probability $= p_i$	Return of Firm A	Return of Firm B
Great	.1	−.05	−.10
Good	.4	.10	.15
Average	.3	.25	.10
Bad	.2	.30	.18

Firm A has a total investment in assets of $75 million, three times the size of Firm B.
   Assume that a new Firm, C, is formed through a merger between Firms A and B. The share of A and B in the portfolio represented by the new Firm C is based on the ratio of their total assets prior to merger. Calculate:

a)   The expected return and standard deviation of Firms A and B before the merger.

b)   The covariance and the correlation between the returns for Firms A and B before the merger.

c)   The expected return of Firm C.

d)   The standard deviation of return for Firm C.

16.8   You are planning to invest $100,000. Two securities, A and B, are available. The expected return for A is 9 percent and its standard deviation is 4 percent. For B, the expected return and standard deviations are 10 percent and 5 percent respectively. The correlation between the two assets is $\rho_{AB} = .5$.

a)   Construct a table giving the portfolio expected return and standard deviation for 100 percent, 75 percent, 50 percent, 25 percent, and 0 percent in Security A.

b)   Use your calculated values of $E(R_p)$ and $\sigma(R_p)$ to graph the minimum variance portfolio opportunity set and the efficient set.

c)   Using hypothetical indifference curves, show how an investor might choose his or her optimal portfolio.

16.9   You are planning to invest $100,000. Two securities, I and J, are available, and you can invest in either of them or in a portfolio with some of each. You estimate that the following probability distributions of returns are applicable:

Probability	Security I	Security J
0.1	−5%	0%
0.2	0	5
0.4	11.25	8.75
0.2	15	10
0.1	20	15

The expected returns are 9 percent and 8 percent for I and J, respectively. Also, $p_{ij} = .96$, $\sigma_i = 7.56$ percent and $\sigma_j = 3.76$ percent.

a)   Graph the *opportunity* set of portfolios and identify the *efficient* section of the opportunity set.

b)   Suppose your risk-return tradeoff function, or indifference curve, is a linear family of lines with a slope of 0.40. Use this information, plus the graph constructed in Part (a), to locate (approximately) your optimal portfolio. Give the percentage of your funds invested in each security and the optimal portfolio's σ_p and $E(R_p)$. (Hint: Estimate σ_p and $E(R_p)$ graphically and then use the equation for $E(R_p)$ to determine w.) What is the probability that your optimal portfolio will, in fact, yield less than 4.15 percent?

c)   Demonstrate why a graph of the efficient set such as the one you constructed in Part (a) above is always linear if portfolios are formed between a riskless security (a bond) and a risky asset (a stock or perhaps a portfolio of stocks).

16.10   You are planning to invest $200,000. Two securities, C and D, are available, and you can invest in either of them or in a portfolio with some of each. You estimate that the following probability distributions of returns are applicable:

Probability	Security C	Security D
0.2	−4%	2%
0.3	0	−2
0.3	12	−3
0.2	26	4

The expected returns are 8 percent and $-.3$ percent for C and D, respectively; that is, $E(R_c) = 8$ percent, and $E(R_d) = -.3$ percent; $\sigma_c = 10.84$ percent, and $\sigma_d = 2.795$ percent.

a)   Calculate $E(R_p)$ and $\sigma(R_p)$ for portfolios having 150 percent, 100 percent, 50 percent, 0 percent, and -50 percent in Security C.

b)   Graph the minimum variance opportunity set and the efficient set.

c)   Suppose your indifference curves are a linear family of lines with a slope of .90. Use this information, plus the graph constructed in Part (b), to locate (approximately) your optimal portfolio. Give the percentage of your funds invested in each security and the mean and standard deviation for your optimal portfolio. (Hint: Estimate $E(R_p)$ and $\sigma(R_p)$ graphically and then use the equation for $E(R_p)$ to determine the optimal percent of your wealth in Security C.)

d)   What is the probability that your optimal portfolio will yield less than 1.15 percent?

e)   Demonstrate *why* a graph of the efficient set such as the one you constructed in Part (b) above is always linear if portfolios are formed from a riskless security and a risky security.

16.11 Given that the risk-free rate is 10 percent, the expected return on the market portfolio is 20 percent, and the standard deviation of returns on the market portfolio is $\sigma(R_M) = .2$,

a)   What is the equilibrium price of risk?

b)   What percentage of your wealth would you have to put into the riskless asset and into the market portfolio in order to have a 25 percent expected rate of return?

c)   What would be the variance of the portfolio in Part (b)?

d)   What is the correlation between the portfolio in Part (b) and the market portfolio?

16.12 Table P16.12 gives the rates of return for Security J and the market portfolio.

Table P16.12

Probability	Return on Security J	Return on the Market Portfolio
1/7	15%	20%
1/7	22	16
1/7	-5	9
1/7	0	-6
1/7	2	-8
1/7	12	12
1/7	-8	-5

a)   Estimate the undiversifiable risk of Security J using linear regression.

b)   What is the correlation between Security J and the market portfolio?

c)   What percentage of the total risk of Security J is undiversifiable?

Selected References

Black, F., "Capital Market Equilibrium with Restricted Borrowing," *Journal of Business*, 45 (July 1972), pp. 444-454.

———; Jensen, M. C.; and Scholes, M., "The Capital Asset Pricing Model: Some Empirical Tests," in *Studies in the Theory of Capital Markets*, Edited by M. C. Jensen, New York: Praeger, 1972.

Bowman, Robert G., "The Theoretical Relationship Between Systematic Risk and Financial (Accounting) Variables," *Journal of Finance*, 34 (June 1979), pp. 617-630.

Brennan, M. J., "Capital Market Equilibrium with Divergent Borrowing and Lending Rates," *Journal of*

Financial and Quantitative Analysis, 6 (December 1971), pp. 1197-1205.

Evans, J. L., and Archer, S. H., "Diversification and the Reduction of Dispersion: An Empirical Analysis," *Journal of Finance*, 23 (December 1968), pp. 761-767.

Fama, E. F., "Risk, Return, and Equilibrium," *Journal of Political Economy*, 79 (January-February 1971), pp. 30-55.

Fama, E. F., and MacBeth, J., "Risk, Return and Equilibrium: Empirical Tests," *Journal of Political Economy*, 81 (May-June 1973), pp. 607-636.

Fama, E. F., and Miller, M. H., *The Theory of Finance*, New York: Holt, Rinehart and Winston, 1972.

Ibbotson, Roger G., and Sinquefield, Rex A., "Stocks, Bonds, Bills, and Inflation: Simulations of the Future (1976-2000)," *Journal of Business*, 49 (July 1976), pp. 313-338.

Jacob, N., "The Measurement of Systematic Risk for Securities and Portfolios: Some Empirical Results," *Journal of Financial and Quantitative Analysis*, 6 (March 1971), pp. 815-834.

Jensen, M. C., "Capital Markets: Theory and Evidence," *Bell Journal of Economics and Management Science*, 3 (Autumn 1972), pp. 357-398.

————, ed., *Studies in the Theory of Capital Markets*, New York: Praeger, 1972.

————, "Risk, the Pricing of Capital Assets, and the Evaluation of Investment Portfolios," *Journal of Business*, 42 (April 1969), pp. 167-247.

Lintner, J., "Security Prices, Risk, and Maximal Gains from Diversification," *Journal of Finance*, 20 (December 1965), pp. 587-616.

————, "The Valuation of Risk Assets and the Selection of Risky Investments in Stock Portfolios and Capital Budgets," *Review of Economics and Statistics*, 47 (February 1965), pp. 13-37.

Markowitz, H. M., *Portfolio Selection: Efficient Diversification of Investments*, New York: Wiley, 1959.

————, "Portfolio Selection," *Journal of Finance*, 7 (March 1952), pp. 77-91.

Modigliani, Franco, and Pogue, Gerald A., "An Introduction to Risk and Return," *Financial Analysts Journal*, 30 (March-April 1974), pp. 68-80; 30 (May-June 1974), pp. 69-86.

Mossin, J., "Security Pricing and Investment Criteria in Competitive Markets," *American Economic Review*, 59 (December 1969), pp. 749-756.

————, "Equilibrium in a Capital Asset Market," *Econometrica*, 34 (October 1966), pp. 768-783.

Robichek, Alexander A., and Cohn, Richard A., "The Economic Determinants of Systematic Risk," *Journal of Finance*, 29 (May 1974), pp. 439-447.

Ross, Stephen A., "A Simple Approach to the Valuation of Risky Streams," *Journal of Business*, 51 (July 1978), pp. 453-475.

Schall, Lawrence D., "Asset Valuation, Firm Investment, and Firm Diversification," *Journal of Business*, 45 (January 1972), pp. 11-28.

Sharpe, W. F., *Portfolio Theory and Capital Markets*, New York: McGraw-Hill, 1970.

————, "Capital Asset Prices: A Theory of Market Equilibrium under Conditions of Risk," *Journal of Finance*, 19 (September 1964), pp. 425-442.

————, "A Simplified Model for Portfolio Analysis," *Management Science*, 9 (January 1963), pp. 277-293.

Thompson, Donald J., II, "Sources of Systematic Risk in Common Stocks," *Journal of Business*, 49 (April 1976), pp. 173-188.

Tobin, J., "Liquidity Preference as Behavior toward Risk," *Review of Economic Studies*, 25 (February 1958), pp. 65-86.

Wagner, W. H., and Lau, S. C., "The Effect of Diversification on Risk," *Financial Analysts Journal*, 27 (November-December 1971), pp. 48-53.

Chapter 17 Risk and Return: Theory, Evidence, and Applications

The Capital Asset Pricing Model (CAPM) and the Arbitrage Pricing Model (APM) are theories of how risky assets are priced in market equilibrium. They provide decision makers with useful estimates of the required rates of return on risky securities and on capital budgeting projects. This chapter introduces the theories and shows how they may be used in a variety of applications, such as capital budgeting, the cost of capital, and security valuation. Empirical tests of the validity of the CAPM and the APM are also discussed.

Introduction

In Chapter 16, we developed the basics of decision making under uncertainty in a portfolio theory context. Figure 17.1 summarizes market equilibrium as the Capital Market Line. Equation 17.1 is the algebraic expression for the CML.

$$E(R_p) = R_F + \left[\frac{E(R_M) - R_F}{\sigma_M}\right]\sigma(R_p). \tag{17.1}$$

It allows us to predict the expected return for all portfolios along the Capital Market Line. Unfortunately, this result is of limited usefulness because points along the CML are various combinations of the riskless asset and the market portfolio, and, consequently, they are all perfectly correlated. The CML cannot be used to predict the return for inefficient securities which lie in the interior of the portfolio opportunity set (these securities are represented by dots in Figure 17.1). For example, if we learn that a security has a standard deviation of σ_1, we cannot predict the rate of return which the market will require. Points B, C, and D in Figure 17.1 all have a total risk of σ_1, but they have different expected returns. Thus, there is no unique relationship between the standard deviations of inefficient securities and their required rates of return. We have to find a better measure of risk.

Near the end of Chapter 16, we saw that the total risk of an asset can be separated into two parts: undiversifiable and diversifiable risk,

$$\text{Total risk} = \text{Undiversifiable risk} + \text{Diversifiable risk} \tag{17.2}$$

$$\text{VAR}(R_j) = b^2\text{VAR}(R_M) + \text{VAR}(\epsilon),$$

where

$\text{VAR}(R_j) =$ the variance of return on the jth asset
$b =$ the slope from a linear regression of return on the jth asset against return on the market portfolio $= \text{COV}(R_j, R_M)/\text{VAR}(R_M)$

Figure 17.1   The Capital Market Line

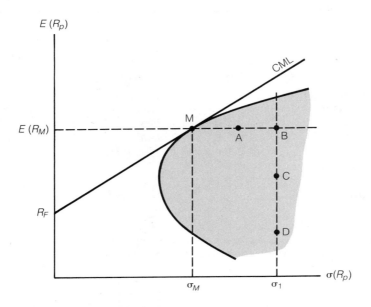

VAR(ϵ) =   the variance of error terms from the linear regression. The error terms are uncorrelated with the market return.

This result is important because we know that the diversifiable risk is made up of error terms which are uncorrelated with the market portfolio. They are sometimes called the idiosyncratic risk of the asset. Since they have zero correlation with the market portfolio and with each other, the error terms can be completely eliminated through costless diversification. If diversifiable risk can be eliminated at zero cost, no risk premium will be associated with it, and it will be irrelevant in determining the risk-adjusted rate of return on individual assets. The only risk relevant for individual securities is their undiversifiable risk. This measure of risk, called beta, β, is at the heart of the Capital Asset Pricing Model, CAPM. It is the better measure of risk which we are seeking.

The CAPM and the Security Market Line

The significant contribution of the Capital Asset Pricing Model (CAPM) is that it provides a measure of the risk of an individual security which is consistent with portfolio theory. It enables us to estimate the undiversifiable risk of a single asset and compare it with the undiversifiable risk of a well-diversified portfolio. Originally developed by Sharpe, Treynor, Mossin, and Lintner, the CAPM equation, or Security Market Line (SML), is usually written as[1]

$$E(R_j) = R_F + [E(R_M) - R_F]\beta_j, \qquad\qquad (17.3)$$

where

$E(R_j) =$ the expected or *ex ante* return on the jth risky asset
$R_F =$ the rate of return on a riskless asset
$E(R_M) =$ the expected or *ex ante* return on the market portfolio
$\beta_j =$ $\text{COV}(R_j, R_M)/\text{VAR}(R_M)$ = a measure of the undiversifiable risk of the jth security.[2]

The CAPM is graphed in Figure 17.2, Panel (b), where it is called the *Security Market Line* (*SML*). In equilibrium, all securities must be priced so that they fall on the Security Market Line. Assets A, B, C, and D in Panel (a) all have different variances but the same expected return. In Panel (b), they all fall on the Security Market Line at Point X. They all have the same undiversifiable risk, that is, $\beta_A = \beta_B = \beta_C = \beta_D$, and the same expected return. The fact that they have different total risk (that is, different variances) is irrelevant for determining their expected return, because total risk contains a diversifiable component which is not priced in market equilibrium.

Figure 17.2   Comparison of the Capital Market Line (CML) and the Security Market Line (SML)

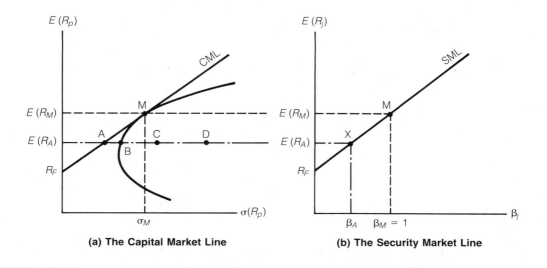

(a) The Capital Market Line   (b) The Security Market Line

---

[1]See Appendix A for the derivation.

[2]Note that β_j, a measure of the undiversifiable risk of the jth security, is exactly the same as the slope, b, of a linear regression of the returns on the jth asset against the returns on the market portfolio. See Equation 17.2.

The Capital Market Line (CML) and the Security Market Line (SML) are merely different pictures of the same market equilibrium. The CML may be used for determining the required return only for those efficient portfolios which are perfectly correlated with the market portfolio because they fall on the CML, but the SML may be used to explain the required rate of return on all securities whether or not they are efficient. The SML provides a unique relationship between undiversifiable risk (measured by β) and expected return. Hence, if we can accurately measure the beta of a security, we can estimate its equilibrium risk-adjusted rate of return.

The relationship between the CML and the SML can be seen by writing the two equations, one underneath the other.

$$\text{CML: } E(R_p) = R_F + \left[\frac{E(R_M) - R_F}{\sigma_M}\right]\sigma(R_p). \tag{17.4}$$

$$\text{SML: } E(R_j) = R_F + [E(R_M) - R_F]\beta_j. \tag{17.5}$$

Rewriting the SML by using the definition of β_j, we have

$$\text{SML: } E(R_j) = R_F + [E(R_M) - R_F]\frac{\text{COV}(R_j, R_M)}{\text{VAR}(R_M)}, \tag{17.6}$$

and since $\text{VAR}(R_M) = \sigma_M^2$,

$$\text{SML: } E(R_j) = R_F + \left[\frac{E(R_M) - R_F}{\sigma_M}\right]\frac{\text{COV}(R_j, R_M)}{\sigma_M}. \tag{17.7}$$

The above equation shows that the market price of risk per unit of risk is the same for the SML and for the CML.

$$\text{Market price of risk} = \frac{E(R_M) - R_F}{\sigma_M}.$$

Also, if we recall that $\text{COV}(R_j, R_M) \equiv \rho_{jM}\sigma_j\sigma_M$, where ρ_{jM} is the correlation between the return on asset j and the market rate of return, we can rewrite the SML as

$$\text{SML: } E(R_j) = R_F + \left[\frac{E(R_M) - R_F}{\sigma_M}\right]\frac{\rho_{jM}\sigma_j\sigma_M}{\sigma_M} \tag{17.8}$$

$$= R_F + \left[\frac{E(R_M) - R_F}{\sigma_M}\right]\rho_{jM}\sigma_j.$$

This equation shows that the undiversifiable risk of each asset can be thought of as having two parts: the asset's standard deviation of returns, σ_j, and its correlation with the market portfolio, ρ_{jM}. If we recall that all points along the CML are perfectly correlated with the market portfolio, $\rho_{jM} = 1$, then Equation 17.8 for the SML reduces to be equal to Equation 17.4, the CML. Hence, for portfolios which are made up of the riskless asset and the market portfolio, the CML and the SML are identical. Equations 17.8, 17.7, and 17.5 are merely different ways of writing the Security Market Line, but the reader should be familiar with all of them.

The Capital Asset Pricing Model (the SML) is an equilibrium theory of how to price and measure risk. As we shall soon see, it has many applications for decision making under uncertainty. We will show how to use it for (1) capital budgeting, (2) asset valuation, (3) determining the cost of equity capital, and (4) explaining risk in the structure of interest rates.

The logic of the Security Market Line equation is that the required return on any investment is the risk-free return plus a risk adjustment factor. The risk adjustment factor is obtained by multiplying the risk premium required for the market return by the riskiness of the individual investment. If the returns on the individual investment fluctuate by exactly the same degree as the returns on the market as a whole, the beta for the security is one. In this situation, the required return on the individual investment is the same as the required return on the total market. If the undiversifiable (or systematic) risk in the return of an individual investment is greater than for the market portfolio, then the beta of the individual investment is greater than one, and its risk adjustment factor is greater than the risk adjustment factor for the market as a whole. The relationship between the riskiness of an individual investment, as measured by its beta, and the risk adjustment factor is illustrated in Figure 17.3. The risk-free return is given as 6 percent. If we use 11 percent as the long-term average return on the market, the market risk premium is 11 percent minus 6

Figure 17.3   Graph of the Security Market Line

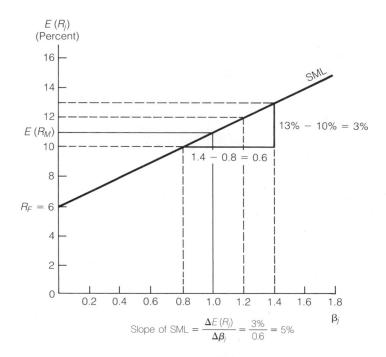

$$\text{Slope of SML} = \frac{\Delta E(R_j)}{\Delta \beta_j} = \frac{3\%}{0.6} = 5\%$$

percent, which is 5 percent, the slope of the SML. If the risk-free return is 6 percent, the required return on the market is 6 percent plus a risk adjustment factor of 5 percent, totaling 11 percent.

The required return on an individual investment depends on the size of its beta, which measures the covariation of its returns in relation to the returns on the market. If the beta of an individual investment is 1.2, its risk adjustment factor is 1.2 times the market risk adjustment factor of 5 percent. The risk adjustment factor for the individual investment, therefore, is 6 percent, and its required return is 12 percent. If the beta measure of an investment is 1.4, its risk adjustment factor is 7 percent, and its required return is 13 percent. An investment with a beta of 0.8 has a risk adjustment factor of 4 percent and a required return of 10 percent.

The advantages of the Security Market Line approach to measuring the risk adjustment factor and the required return on an investment are that the relationships can be quantified and that they have been subjected to considerable statistical testing. The empirical evidence on the validity of the CAPM will be reviewed later on in this chapter.

Applications of the CAPM

One of the most useful properties of the CAPM is that the beta of a portfolio, β_p, of securities (or assets) is the weighted average of the betas of the individual securities, β_i. The weights, w_i, are the value of the ith security divided by the value of the portfolio.

$$\beta_p = \sum_{i=1}^{N} w_i \beta_i. \tag{17.9}$$

For example, if a steel company with total assets of $100 million and a β_s of 1.5 were to merge with a construction company worth $50 million and having a β_c of .7, then (in the absence of any synergy) the resulting firm would be worth $150 million and have a β of

$$\beta = w_s \beta_s + w_c \beta_c$$

$$= \frac{100,000,000}{150,000,000}(1.5) + \frac{50,000,000}{150,000,000}(.7)$$

$$= 1.00 + .23 = 1.23.$$

We can think of a firm as being nothing more than a portfolio of risky assets. The undiversifiable risk of the firm (its beta) is simply the weighted average of the betas of all of its projects.

Required Return on Securities

Equation 17.3 states that the expected return on an individual security or productive investment is represented by a risk-free rate of interest plus a risk premium. Earlier literature did not provide a theory for the determination of the risk premium. Capital market theory shows the risk premium to be equal to the market risk premium, $E(R_M) - R_F$, weighted by the index of the systematic risk, β, of the individual security or productive investment.

The β for an individual security reflects industry characteristics and management policies that determine how returns fluctuate in relation to variations in overall market returns. If the general economic environment is stable, if industry characteristics remain unchanged and management policies have continuity, the measure of β will be relatively stable when calculated for different time periods. However, if these conditions of stability do not exist, the value of β will vary.

The great advantage of Equation 17.3 is that all of its parameters other than β are market-wide constants. If β's are stationary across time, the measurement of expected returns is straightforward. For example, the returns on the market for long periods have been shown by the studies of Fisher and Lorie [1964] and Ibbotson and Sinquefield [1982] to be at the 9 to 11 percent level. The level of R_F has been characteristically at the 4 to 6 percent level. Thus, the expected return on an individual investment, using the lower of each of the two numbers and a β of 1.2, would be

$$E(R_j) = 4\% + (9\% - 4\%)1.2 = 10\%.$$

The higher of each of the two figures gives an $E(R_j)$ of 12%:

$$E(R_j) = 6\% + (11\% - 6\%)1.2 = 12\%.$$

Thus, we have numerical measures of the amount of the risk premium that is added to the risk-free return to obtain a risk-adjusted discount rate. The risk-free rate and the market risk premium (the excess of the market return over the risk-free rate) are economy-wide measures. They vary for different time periods but provide a basis for measurements that can be used in making judgmental decisions. In the numerical illustrations above, if a firm has a beta of 1.2 (and if the risk-free rate is currently in the 4 to 6 percent range), we would expect its required return, according to the Security Market Line, to be between 10 and 12 percent. This provides us with a relatively narrow boundary of returns within which managerial judgments may be exercised.

In Chapter 7, we discussed the issue of how the market determines interest rates. The nominal rate of return on any security was seen to be determined as a function of four variables: the expected real rate of return over the life of the security, expected inflation, a liquidity premium, and a risk premium. Earlier, we had to defer any discussion of the risk premium, but now we know that it is determined by the Capital Asset Pricing Model. From Equation 17.3, the CAPM is

$$E(R_j) = R_F + [E(R_M) - R_F]\beta_j. \tag{17.3}$$

The second term is the risk premium. The risk-free rate includes

$$R_F = f \text{ (expected real rate, expected inflation, liquidity).}$$

In this way, we see that the CAPM includes all four elements of the nominal rate.

Figure 17.4 shows how expected inflation affects the CAPM. Both the risk-free rate and the expected return on the market portfolio include expected inflation, i. Suppose we write the real riskless rate as R_F^* and the real rate of return on the market portfolio as $E(R_M^*)$. Then, if we are specific, the CAPM can be written:

$$E(R_j) = R_F^* + i + [E(R_M^*) + i - (R_F^* + i)]\beta_j$$
$$= R_F^* + i + [E(R_M^*) - R_F^*]\beta_j.$$

Figure 17.4   The CAPM and Expected Inflation

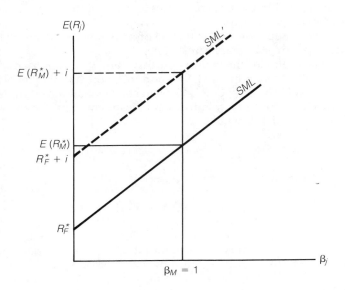

Note that changes in expected inflation do not change the slope of the Security Market Line (SML). Rather, they cause parallel shifts in the SML.[3]

The CAPM and the Market Return on Risky Debt

Usually, the yield to maturity on bonds is computed by finding the internal rate of return which equates the promised payments (coupons and face value) with the current market value of the bond. For example, suppose a bond is currently selling for $952. It promises to pay $100 at the end of each year for three years and a face value of $1,000 at the end of the third year. We would find its promised yield by solving for r in the following equation:

$$B_0 = \sum_{t=1}^{3} \frac{\text{Coupon}_t}{(1 + r)^t} + \frac{\text{Face value}}{(1 + r)^3}. \tag{17.10}$$

The promised yield is $r = 12\%$. But suppose the bond has some default risk, so that 8 percent of the time it goes into bankruptcy and only pays $700 instead of the promised face value of $1,000. There is a difference between its expected payments and its promised payments. The expected payment of the face value is

$$E(\text{face value}) = .92(\$1000) + .08(\$700)$$

$$= \$976.$$

Given this fact, the logical thing to do is find the interest rate which discounts the *expected* payments so that they equal the present value of the bond. This rate is the market-determined, risk-adjusted rate, $E(R_j) = k_b$. Now Equation 17.10 becomes

$$B_0 = \sum_{t=1}^{N} \frac{E(\text{Coupon})_t}{(1 + k_b)^t} + \frac{E(\text{Face value})}{(1 + k_b)^N} \qquad \textbf{(17.11)}$$

$$\$952.00 = \sum_{t=1}^{3} \frac{\$100}{(1 + k_b)^t} + \frac{\$976}{(1 + k_b)^3}.$$

By trial and error, we find that $k_b = 11\%$. But what is this rate? How can it be interpreted? Remember that the market prices only the undiversifiable risk of securities. If default risk is completely independent of the rest of the economy, then it will be uncorrelated with the market portfolio. Any investor or institution which holds well-diversified portfolios of risky bonds may find that default risk, being uncorrelated with the market, cancels out so that the portfolio earns the risk-free rate of return. Although any one firm may default on its debt, if we hold a well-diversified portfolio, we know with certainty that exactly $X\%$ of the firms will default this year. In this case, the 11 percent rate on our bond is the riskless rate. If the beta of risky bonds is positive because default risk is somewhat correlated with the economy, then 11 percent is above the riskless rate. Suppose we know that the risk-free rate is 10 percent and the expected return on the market portfolio is 17 percent. Then, we can use the CAPM to determine the beta of our risky bond.

$$E(R_j) = R_F + [E(R_M) - R_F]\beta_j$$

$$11\% = 10\% + [17\% - 10\%]\beta_j$$

$$\beta_j = \frac{11\% - 10\%}{7\%} = .14286.$$

The purpose of this example is to illustrate that (1) the promised yield to maturity on risky bonds is biased upward from the market equilibrium rate, (2) the market equilibrium rate is calculated by discounting the *expected* cash flows on the bond until their discounted value equals their market price, and (3) a great deal of default risk is diversifiable. Risky bonds have low risk relative to common stock.

The market required rate of return on risky bonds is the before-tax cost of debt to corporations. The cost of debt is a necessary component of the weighted average cost of capital for levered firms. It can be estimated in one of two equivalent ways: Either (1) compute the beta (undiversifiable risk) of the risky bond and use the CAPM to estimate the cost of debt, or (2) use the *expected* cash payments and the current market value of the bond to compute its market yield to maturity.[4]

---

[4]Because quoted bond prices are infrequent and sometimes inaccurate, it is difficult to estimate the CAPM beta for corporate bonds. Hence, the second method, which requires an estimate of expected cash flows, is usually the preferred technique.

Figure 17.5   The CAPM and the Cost of Equity

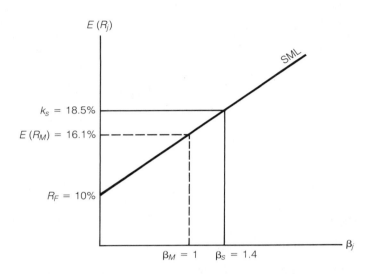

The CAPM and the Cost of Equity

Stock prices for publicly held firms are readily available, making it relatively easy to estimate the beta of a firm's equity. In fact, there are a large number of companies that are in
the business of selling statistical estimates of beta for thousands of firms listed on the New
York and American Stock exchanges. Once you have a good estimate of a firm's equity
beta, β_s, you can use the CAPM (Equation 17.3) to estimate the cost of equity capital. This
is illustrated in Figure 17.5.

Suppose that in 19X4, Spectra Physics, a manufacturer of laser instruments, had a β_s of
1.4. If the risk-free rate was 10 percent and the market risk premium, $[E(R_M - R_F]$, was 6.1
percent, then using the CAPM, we would estimate the cost of equity as

$$E(R_j) = k_s = R_F + [E(R_M) - R_F]\beta_s \tag{17.12}$$

$$= 10\% + [16.1\% - 10\%]1.4$$

$$= 18.54\%.$$

The cost of equity for Spectra Physics was approximately 18.5 percent. This estimate takes
into account such company-specific information as business risk and financial risk, industry-wide risk, and such conditions of the economy as expected inflation and the real rate of
interest. If any of these factors should change, then the cost of equity for Spectra Physics
will also change.

The CAPM and the Weighted Average Cost of Capital

Estimating the weighted average cost of capital (WACC) is a simple matter once the market required rates of return on a firm's debt and equity have been estimated as shown in the previous two sections. There are only two things to keep in mind. First, the market required rates of return, as estimated by the CAPM, are before-tax rates. Hence, the WACC must be written to reflect the fact that interest payments on debt are tax deductible, but payments to equity holders are not. The after-tax WACC is

$$\text{WACC} = k_b(1 - T)\frac{B}{B + S} + k_s\frac{S}{B + S}. \tag{17.13}$$

When k_b and k_s in Equation 17.13 are estimated using the CAPM, then the WACC is a risk-adjusted rate which takes into account the undiversifiable risk of debt and equity.

The second thing to remember is that the WACC uses the company's target capital structure, expressed in market value weights rather than book value weights.

$\dfrac{B}{B + S}$ = the target market value of debt divided by the market value of the firm

$\dfrac{S}{B + S}$ = the target market value of equity divided by the market value of the firm.

Once the risk-adjusted WACC is known, the expected cash flows of the firm can be discounted at this rate in order to estimate the total value of the firm, V. We then get the consistent result that $V = B + S$, as found in the market. Also, note that the WACC is the opportunity cost of capital for the firm. It is the rate used to discount cash flows for capital budgeting purposes in order to determine the net present value of projects.

The CAPM and Capital Budgeting

The risk-return tradeoff given by the Capital Asset Pricing Model requires that all capital budgeting projects earn at least the rate of return required by the market on projects of equivalent risk. The implication is that each project has its own WACC because each project has different risk. The corporate WACC is only an average cost of capital appropriate for the entire portfolio of corporate assets. It may not be (and usually is not) appropriate for an individual project.

In order to illustrate this important concept, let us consider the Morton Company case. The Morton Company is considering four projects in a capital expansion program. The economics staff has projected the future course of the market portfolio over the estimated life span of the projects under each of four states-of-the-world (Column 3 in Table 17.1). State 1 represents a relatively serious recession, State 2 is a mild recession, State 3 is a mild recovery, and State 4 is a strong recovery. The probabilities of these alternative future states-of-the-world are set forth in Column 2 of Table 17.1. Estimates of the project rates of return conditional on the state-of-the-world are set forth in Columns 4 through 7. It is recommended that a risk-free rate of 5 percent be used. Each project requires the same dollar amount of capital outlay. The Morton Company has a WACC of 10 percent and a corporate beta of 1.0. Assuming that the projects are independent (as opposed to mutually exclusive) and that the firm can raise sufficient funds to finance all four projects, which projects should be accepted?

Table 17.1   Summary of Information—Morton Case

State of World (s) (1)	Subjective Probability (P_s) (2)	Market Return (R_M) (3)	Project Rates of Return			
			Project 1 (4)	Project 2 (5)	Project 3 (6)	Project 4 (7)
1	0.1	−0.15	−0.30	−0.30	−0.09	−0.05
2	0.3	0.05	0.10	−0.10	0.01	0.05
3	0.4	0.15	0.30	0.30	0.05	0.10
4	0.2	0.20	0.40	0.40	0.08	0.15

In Table 17.2, the data provided by market relationships are utilized to calculate the expected return on the market along with its variance and standard deviation. The probabilities of the future states-of-the-world are multiplied by the associated market returns and their products are summed to obtain the expected market return $E(R_M)$ of 10 percent.

The expected market return, $E(R_M)$, is used in calculating the variance and standard deviation of the market returns. This is shown in columns 4 through 6 of Table 17.2. The expected return is deducted from the return under each state, and deviations from $E(R_M)$ in Column 4 are squared in Column 5. In Column 6, the squared deviations are multiplied by the probabilities of each expected future state (which appear in Column 1). These projects are summed to give the variance of the market return. The square root of the variance is its standard deviation.

A similar procedure is followed in Table 17.3 for calculating the expected return and the covariance for each of the four individual projects. The expected return is obtained by multiplying the probability of each state times the associated forecasted return. The deviations of the return under each state from the expected return are next calculated in Column 4. The deviations of the market returns from their mean are repeated for convenience in Column 5, and the products of these two are calculated in Column 6. Finally, these products are multiplied by the probability factors and summed to determine the covariance for each of the four projects (Column 7).

In Table 17.4, the beta for each project is calculated as the ratio of its covariance to the variance of the market return, and they are employed in Table 17.5 to estimate the re-

Table 17.2   Calculation of Market Parameters

s	P_s (1)	R_M (2)	$P_s R_M$ (3)	$(R_M - \overline{R}_M)$ (4)	$(R_M - \overline{R}_M)^2$ (5)	$P_s(R_M - \overline{R}_M)^2$ (6)
1	0.1	−0.15	−0.015	−0.25	0.0625	0.00625
2	0.3	0.05	0.015	−0.05	0.0025	0.00075
3	0.4	0.15	0.060	0.05	0.0025	0.00100
4	0.2	0.20	0.040	0.10	0.0100	0.00200
			$E(R_M) = \overline{R}_M = 0.10$			$VAR(R_M) = 0.01$
						$\sigma_{R_M} = 0.1$

Table 17.3 Calculation of Expected Returns and Covariances for the Four Hypothetical Projects

s	P_s (1)	R_j (2)	$P_s R_j$ (3)	$(R_j - \overline{R}_j)(R_M - \overline{R}_M)$ (4) (5) (6)	$P_s(R_j - \overline{R}_j)(R_M - \overline{R}_M)$ (7)
1	0.1	−0.30	−0.03	$(-0.50)(-0.25) = 0.125$	0.0125
2	0.3	0.10	0.03	$(-0.10)(-0.05) = 0.005$	0.0015
3	0.4	0.30	0.12	$(+0.10)(+0.05) = 0.005$	0.0020
4	0.2	0.40	0.08	$(+0.20)(+0.10) = 0.020$	0.0040
		$\overline{R}_1 =$	0.20		$\text{COV}(R_1, R_M) = 0.0200$
1	0.1	−0.30	−0.03	$(-0.44)(-0.25) = 0.110$	0.0110
2	0.3	−0.10	−0.03	$(-0.24)(-0.05) = 0.012$	0.0036
3	0.4	0.30	0.12	$(+0.16)(+0.05) = 0.008$	0.0032
4	0.2	0.40	0.08	$(+0.26)(+0.10) = 0.026$	0.0052
		$\overline{R}_2 =$	0.14		$\text{COV}(R_2, R_M) = 0.0230$
1	0.1	−0.09	−0.009	$(-0.12)(-0.25) = 0.030$	0.0030
2	0.3	0.01	0.003	$(-0.02)(-0.05) = 0.001$	0.0003
3	0.4	0.05	0.020	$(+0.02)(+0.05) = 0.001$	0.0004
4	0.2	0.08	0.016	$(+0.05)(+0.10) = 0.005$	0.0010
		$\overline{R}_3 =$	0.030		$\text{COV}(R_3, R_M) = 0.0047$
1	0.1	−0.05	−0.005	$(-0.13)(-0.25) = 0.0325$	0.00325
2	0.3	0.05	0.015	$(-0.03)(-0.05) = 0.0015$	0.00045
3	0.4	0.10	0.040	$(+0.02)(+0.05) = 0.0010$	0.00040
4	0.2	0.15	0.030	$(+0.07)(+0.10) = 0.0070$	0.00140
		$\overline{R}_4 =$	0.080		$\text{COV}(R_4, R_M) = 0.00550$

Table 17.4 Calculation of the Betas

$\beta_1 = 0.0200/0.01 = 2.00$
$\beta_2 = 0.0230/0.01 = 2.30$
$\beta_3 = 0.0047/0.01 = 0.47$
$\beta_4 = 0.0055/0.01 = 0.55$

Table 17.5 Calculation of Excess Returns

Project Number (1)	$E(R_j)$ Measurement of Required Return (2)	R_j^o Estimated Return (3)	Excess Return (Percent) (4)
P1	$E(R_1) = 0.05 + 0.05(2.0) = 0.150$	0.200	5.00
P2	$E(R_2) = 0.05 + 0.05(2.3) = 0.165$	0.140	−2.50
P3	$E(R_3) = 0.05 + 0.05(0.47) = 0.0735$	0.030	−4.35
P4	$E(R_4) = 0.05 + 0.05(0.55) = 0.0775$	0.080	0.25

Figure 17.6   Application of the CAPM Investment Criterion

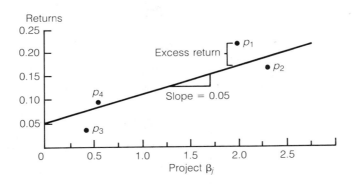

quired return on each project in terms of the market line relationship. The risk-free rate of return is assumed to be 5 percent; consequently, the market risk premium is $(E(R_M) - R_F)$ = 10% − 5% = 5%. Required returns, as shown in Column 2 of Table 17.5, are deducted from the estimated returns for each individual project to derive the "excess returns." These relations are depicted graphically in Figure 17.6.

Recall that the Morton Company had a WACC of 10 percent and a beta of 1.0. If it uses its WACC as the project hurdle rate, it will erroneously reject Project 4, which has an estimated return of 8 percent, and will erroneously accept Project 2, which has a 14 percent estimated return. These decisions are wrong because none of the four projects has the same risk (that is, the same β) as the firm. Projects 3 and 4 are less risky than the firm as a whole while Projects 1 and 2 are riskier.

The correct decision rule is to accept all projects which have positive excess rates of return — those projects which fall above the Security Market Line in Figure 17.6. Thus, Project 4 should be accepted even though it earns less than the firm's WACC of 10 percent. The reason is that Project 4 is less risky than the firm as a whole. Given the β of Project 4, the market requires a return of 7.75 percent for projects of equivalent risk, but Project 4 is estimated to earn 8 percent. Thus, it has an excess return of 0.25 percent and should be accepted. Project 2, on the other hand, is much riskier than the firm, and although it is estimated to earn more than the WACC, it does not earn enough to compensate investors for the risk. With a negative excess return of −2.5 percent it should be rejected.

The Relationship between Risk and Time

The Morton Company example was a very simple one-period situation where project returns were compared with a risk-adjusted opportunity cost of capital in order to evaluate four independent projects. Now, we want to look into the implications of using risk-adjusted discount rates for projects whose cash flows extend across multiple time periods. We will begin by showing how the CAPM can be used, in a one-period framework, to determine project net present values using either of two techniques: (1) the risk-adjusted discount rate or (2) the certainty equivalent approach. Then, we will discuss the multiperiod implications.

The present value, PV, of a one-period project can be found by discounting its expected cash flow, $E(CF)$, at a *risk-adjusted rate*, $E(R_j)$.

$$PV = \frac{E(CF)}{1 + E(R_j)}. \tag{17.14}$$

The correct risk-adjusted rate is given by the CAPM as

$$E(R_j) = R_F + [E(R_M) - R_F]\beta_j. \tag{17.3}$$

Substituting the CAPM, Equation 17.3, into the risk-adjusted present value formula, we have

$$PV = \frac{E(CF)}{1 + R_F + [E(R_M) - R_F]\beta_j}. \tag{17.15}$$

If the project's expected cash flows are \$1,000, the risk-free rate is 10 percent, the expected market return is 17 percent, and the project's beta is 1.5, then its present value is

$$PV = \frac{\$1,000}{1 + .10 + [.17 - .10]1.5}$$

$$= \frac{\$1,000}{1.205} = \$829.88.$$

If the investment outlay for the project, I, is \$800, then its net present value is

$$NPV = PV - I = \$829.88 - \$800.00 = \$29.88,$$

and the project should be accepted.

The *certainty equivalent method* is an equivalent approach for a one-period project. Rather than adjusting for risk by raising the discount rate, the certainty equivalent method (CEM) subtracts a risk premium from the expected cash flows and then discounts this certainty equivalent at the risk-free rate. The CEM can be derived from Equation 17.15. First note that the definition of β_j is

$$\beta_j = \frac{COV(R_j, R_M)}{\sigma_M^2},$$

and the one-period return on the project is

$$R_j = \frac{CF - PV}{PV} = \frac{CF}{PV} - 1.$$

Substituting the project return definition into the definition of undiversifiable risk, we have

$$\beta_j = \frac{COV\left[\dfrac{CF}{PV} - 1, R_M\right]}{\sigma_M^2}.$$

Note that risky end-of-period cash flows are multiplied by $1/PV$, which is a constant that does not covary with the return on the market; therefore, it can be factored out. Also, the minus one which is subtracted from CF/PV has no effect on the covariance. Therefore, the beta becomes

$$\beta_j = \frac{1}{PV}\,\frac{COV(CF,R_M)}{\sigma_M^2}. \tag{17.16}$$

Substituting Equation 17.16 into Equation 17.15, we have

$$PV = \frac{E(CF)}{1 + R_F + [E(R_M) - R_F](1/PV)\left[\dfrac{COV(CF,R_M)}{\sigma_M^2}\right]}.$$

Note that the expression $[E(R_M) - R_F]/\sigma_M^2$ is the market price of risk which we discussed in Chapter 16. If we let λ be the market price of risk and solve for PV, we get the certainty equivalent model (CEM),

$$PV = \frac{E(CF) - \lambda COV(CF,R_M)}{1 + R_F}, \tag{17.17}$$

where

$$\lambda = [E(R_M) - R_F]/\sigma_M^2.$$

In Equation 17.17, the CEM adjusts for risk by subtracting a certainty equivalent risk premium from the expected cash flow and then discounts at the risk-free rate. It is the same as asking the question, what cash flow with no risk at all would make the market indifferent to the project's risky cash flows? Once the certainty equivalent cash flow has been found, we can then discount at the risk-free rate.

By equating (17.15) and (17.17), we can find the dollar amount of the certainty equivalent risk premium for our example.

$$PV = \frac{E(CF)}{1 + R_F + [E(R_M) - R_F]\beta_j} = \frac{E(CF) - \lambda COV(CF,R_M)}{1 + R_F}$$

$$\$829.88 = \frac{\$1,000}{1.205} = \frac{\$1,000 - \lambda COV(CF,R_M)}{1.100}.$$

Solving for the certainty equivalent risk premium, we see that it is

$$\lambda COV(CF, R_M) = \$87.13.$$

Thus, we are indifferent between $\$1,000 - \$87.13 = \$912.87$ with no risk and a risky cash flow whose expected cash flow is $\$1,000$ with a beta of 1.5.

The certainty equivalent method and the risk-adjusted return are equivalent for a one-period project. But how can they be compared for a multiple-period project? Suppose our example specified that the $\$1,000$ cash flow was expected two years hence instead of just one. What are the consequences of using the two approaches?

By its nature, the risk-adjusted discount rate allows for both the time value of money and the relative riskiness of a project's returns. Both *time* and *risk* are accounted for by one adjustment process. Since time and risk are really separate variables, we must be very careful about how we combine them if the risk-adjusted discount rate is to be used for its intended purpose. If $E(R_j)$ is the one-period risk-adjusted discount rate and if the $\$1,000$ cash flow is received two years hence, then the risk-adjusted discount rate method would compute its present value as

$$PV = \sum_{t=0}^{N} \frac{E(CF_t)}{[1 + E(R_j)]^t}$$

$$= \frac{\$1,000}{(1.205)^2} = \frac{\$1,000}{1.452} = \$688.70.$$

If the investment outlay is $\$800$, the net present value of the project would be $\$688.70 - \$800.00 = -\$111.30$, and it would be rejected.

If we use the certainty equivalent method on the same project, we can obtain the same answer only if we make a certainty equivalent adjustment which takes two periods of risk into account. Subtracting a one-period certainty equivalent risk premium of $\$87.13$ will not do the trick. In order to make the two methods equivalent, we can *multiply* the expected cash flows in the certainty equivalent model by a certainty equivalent factor, cef, which is the ratio of the one-period certainty equivalent cash flow to the one-period expected cash flow.

$$\text{cef} = \frac{E(CF) - \lambda COV(CF, R_M)}{E(CF)} \quad\quad\quad (17.18)$$

$$= \frac{\$1,000 - \$87.13}{\$1,000} = .91287.$$

The multiperiod versions of the two models become

$$PV = \sum_{t=0}^{N} \frac{E(CF_t)}{[1 + E(R_j)]^t} = \sum_{t=0}^{N} \frac{(\text{cef})^t E(CF_t)}{(1 + R_F)^t}. \quad\quad\quad (17.19)$$

Using the multiperiod certainty equivalent model and our numerical example, we have

$$PV = \frac{(.91287)^2 \$1,000}{(1.1)^2} = \frac{.8333(\$1,000)}{1.21} = \$688.70.$$

Figure 17.7   An Example with Risk Changing Over Time

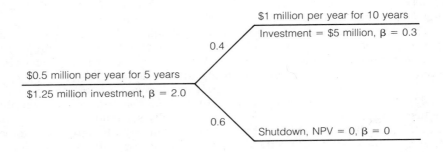

The fact that the two models can be made to give the same answer begs the fundamental question of how risk and time are interrelated. If we discount by using the same risk-adjusted discount rate over the life of a project, we are implicitly assuming that it has the same systematic risk (the same beta) each year of its life.[5] This may be an invalid assumption, particularly for new products, which tend to be highly sensitive to the health of the economy during their initial years and much less sensitive as they mature. For example, consider the 15-year oil shale project outlined in Figure 17.7.

The project has two phases. The five-year pilot study has expected net operating income of $.5 million a year and an initial outlay of $1.25 million. After the pilot phase, uncertainty will be reduced and the project will either be shut down or continued with further investment of $5 million and expected net operating income of $1 million per year for ten years. The project has a beta of 2.0 during the pilot phase. If the risk-free rate is 10 percent and the expected return on the market portfolio is 20 percent, then the risk-adjusted rate of return on the project can be determined from the CAPM as

$$E(R_j) = R_F + [E(R_M) - R_F]\beta_j$$
$$= .10 + [.20 - .10]2.0 = 30\%.$$

If management uses 30 percent as the project hurdle rate for the entire life of the project, the NPV will be[6]

$$\text{NPV} = \sum_{t=0}^{15} \frac{E(CF_t)}{[1 + E(R_j)]^t}$$

---

[5]See Bogue and Roll [1974], Fama [1977], and Myers and Turnbull [1977] for more on the validity of the CAPM in a multiperiod framework.

[6]Note that the pilot phase, when considered alone, has a negative NPV of $32,215. It is not unusual for pilot studies to lose money based on their operating income. The actual value of the pilot study is its NPV plus the value of information which it supplies. It provides the option of shutdown if the project fails or increased scale if it succeeds. This option is valuable. See Chapter 18 for the economics of option pricing, and Appendix 18A for abandonment value.

$$= -1,250,000 + \sum_{t=1}^{5} \frac{500,000}{(1.3)^t} + \sum_{t=6}^{15} \frac{1,000,000}{(1.3)^t} - \frac{5,000,000}{(1.3)^5}$$

$$= -1,250,000 + 1,217,785 + 832,641 - 1,346,645$$

$$= -546,219.$$

The problem with this approach is that it falsely assumes the project is high risk over its entire life. The reason for the pilot project is to reduce uncertainty. There is a 40 percent chance that the project will be successful after the pilot and a 60 percent chance it will not. If the project is shut down, the cash flows are known with certainty to be zero and the NPV = 0. If the project is successful, the beta continues from years 6 through 15 at a level of .3. Therefore, the risk-adjusted discount rate is 13 percent and the NPV of the cash flows, if the project is successful, is:[7]

$$NPV = \sum_{t=6}^{15} \frac{1,000,000}{(1.13)^t} - \frac{5,000,000}{(1.13)^5}$$

$$= \$2,945,148 - \$2,713,800 = \$231,348.$$

Now the NPV of the project is the NPV of the pilot plus the expected NPV of the remainder of the project:

$$NPV \text{ (pilot)} = \$1,217,785 - \$1,250,000 = \$-32,215$$

$$NPV \text{ (remainder)} = .6 \text{ (NPV if shut down)} + .4 \text{ (NPV if successful)}$$

$$= .6(0) + .4(\$231,348)$$

$$= \$92,539$$

$$NPV \text{ (project)} = NPV \text{ (pilot)} + NPV \text{ (remainder)} = \$-32,215 + \$92,539$$

$$= \$60,324.$$

Now our analysis shows that the project should be accepted. The example illustrates that when the risk of a project changes during its life, it is necessary to discount the expected cash flows by a risk-adjusted rate which changes when the risk of the project does. The certainty equivalent method will provide equivalent results.

Managers often express the opinion that because distant cash flows are "riskier," they should be discounted at higher rates. They are forgetting that any risk-adjusted discount rate automatically recognizes that more distant cash flows have more risk. Higher discount rates should be applied to more distant cash flows only if there is good reason to believe that the project's beta will be higher in the distant future.

---

[7]The discount rate is determined from the CAPM; given $R_F = 10\%$, $E(R_M) = 20\%$, and $\beta = .3$,

$$E(R_j) = R_F + [E(R_M) - R_F]\beta_j$$

$$= 10\% + [20\% - 10\%].3 = 13\%.$$

Table 17.6   Risky Cash Outflows for Mutually Exclusive Projects

---

State of Nature	Probability	End-of-Period Outflows		Market Return
		Project A	Project B	
Great	1/3	$500	$600	20%
Average	1/3	400	400	10
Horrid	1/3	300	200	0

Discounting Project Cost Streams

Among the most common types of capital budgeting proposals are equipment replacement projects. The usual assumption is that revenues and output will be unaffected by the investment but that costs will be reduced. Cash flow data are usually limited to costs without any revenue projections. Should "riskier" cost streams be discounted at a higher or a lower rate?

Consider the data in Table 17.6. Projects A and B both have the same end-of-period revenues (assumed to be $1,500), and they both cost $1,000. Their end-of-period cash flows, however, are different. Although both projects have an expected end-of-period outflow of $400, Project A has a low cost variance ($\sigma_A^2 = 81.65$) compared to Project B ($\sigma_B^2 = 163.30$). Which project has the greater NPV? What risk-adjusted discount rate should be used for the risky cost streams?

The CAPM requires that we compute the betas for each project in order to find the risk-adjusted discount rate. The one-period return for Project A in the "great" state is

$$1 + R_A = \frac{\$1,500 - \$500}{\$1,000} = 1$$

$$R_A = 0\%.$$

The project rates of return in each state of nature are given in Table 17.7. From the rates of return, R_i, and the probabilities, p_i, we can calculate, for each project, the expected rates of return,

$$\overline{R}_A = \Sigma \, p_i R_{Ai} = \frac{30}{3} = 10\%$$

$$\overline{R}_B = \Sigma \, p_i R_{Bi} = \frac{30}{3} = 10\%,$$

the covariances with the market portfolio,

$$COV(R_A, R_M) = \Sigma \, p_i (R_{Ai} - \overline{R}_A)(R_M - \overline{R}_M) = \frac{-200}{3}$$

$$COV(R_B, R_M) = \Sigma \, p_i (R_{Bi} - \overline{R}_B)(R_M - \overline{R}_M) = \frac{-400}{3},$$

Table 17.7   Returns Data for Two Risky Projects

State of Nature	Probability	R_A	R_B	$R_A - \overline{R}_A$	$R_B - \overline{R}_B$	R_M	$R_M - \overline{R}_M$
Great	1/3	0%	−10%	−10%	−20%	20%	10%
Average	1/3	10	10	0	0	10	0
Horrid	1/3	20	30	10	20	0	−10

		$(R_A - \overline{R}_A)(R_M - \overline{R}_M)$	$(R_B - \overline{R}_B)(R_M - \overline{R}_M)$	$(R_M - \overline{R}_M)^2$
Great	1/3	−10(10) = −100	−20(10) = −200	10(10) = 100
Average	1/3	0(0) = 0	0(0) = 0	0(0) = 0
Horrid	1/3	10(−10) = −100	20(−10) = −200	−10(−10) = 100

and the betas,

$$\beta_A = \frac{\text{COV}(R_A, R_M)}{\text{VAR}(R_M)} = \frac{-200/3}{200/3} = -1$$

$$\beta_B = \frac{\text{COV}(R_B, R_M)}{\text{VAR}(R_M)} = \frac{-400/3}{200/3} = -2.$$

Our results indicate that the project with greater variance in costs (Project B) has lower systematic risk for the project as a whole. The reason is that the absolute value of the cost stream is positively correlated with the market portfolio. This means that, in favorable states of the economy, the project rates of return will be lower than they might have been had costs been less correlated with the economy and that, in unfavorable states, the returns will be higher than otherwise. For example, if costs go up in a booming economy due to excessive amounts of overtime paid to labor, profits will be lower than they otherwise might have been. But in a slack economy, profits will be relatively higher because of layoffs. The overall effect is to reduce the variability of total returns on the project and to reduce the covariance between the project's total returns and the market portfolio returns. In our example, the more variable cost stream should be discounted at a lower rate (regardless of the variability of the revenue stream), because it reduces the project's beta.

Which project has the greater net present value? The risk-adjusted discount rate method for evaluating projects is

$$\text{NPV} = -I + \frac{E(CF)}{1 + E(R_j)},$$

where $E(R_j)$ is the risk-adjusted rate. Since Project B has the lower beta, it will also have the lower risk-adjusted rate. If the risk-free rate is 8 percent, then the risk-adjusted rates for the two projects are

$$E(R_A) = R_F + [E(R_M) - R_F]\beta_j$$

$$= 8\% + [10\% - 8\%](-1) = 6\%$$

$$E(R_B) = 8\% + [10\% - 8\%](-2) = 4\%,$$

and their net present values are

$$\text{NPV(A)} = -1{,}000 + \frac{1{,}500 - 400}{1.06} = 37.74$$

$$\text{NPV(B)} = -1{,}000 + \frac{1{,}500 - 400}{1.04} = 57.69.$$

As long as the absolute value of the cost stream is positively correlated with the economy, more variable costs will be discounted at a lower risk-adjusted rate.[8]

Factors Affecting Beta

Practical use of the CAPM requires that estimates of beta for stock, bonds, divisions of corporations, or even of individual projects be good enough to be reliable. If estimates of beta based on historical data are unrelated to actual risk, now or in the future, then the CAPM is not a good tool for decision making.

There are dozens of companies that currently estimate (with different levels of statistical sophistication) market betas for virtually every common stock listed on the New York or American Stock exchanges and many of the stocks on the over-the-counter or NASDAQ markets.[9] Those companies that use sophisticated econometrics techniques produce reliable estimates of beta. But what should you do if you are trying to come up with a ball park estimate of the risk of a division within your firm or if you want to know how a financial maneuver will change the beta of your equity? What are the underlying factors which affect beta?

Perhaps the most fundamental factor determining a company's beta is its line of business. Its business risk includes both the cyclical nature of revenues and the firm's operating leverage. Table 17.8 shows the betas for various industry groups and for the highest and lowest beta stocks. The lowest beta industries are railroads and utilities, whose rates of return are regulated. Their profits depend on boards of commissioners and, consequently, are not as sensitive to general movements in the economy. On the other hand, the highest beta group was the brokerage industry with an average beta of 1.55. Brokerage firms are highly sensitive to the economy because their commission revenues go up on high trading volume when the economy is strong and fall on low volume when it is weak. Table 17.8 also shows that the ten lowest beta firms are mostly in regulated industries.

Another strong factor is the amount of financial leverage undertaken by each firm. The beta of the firm's common stock will increase linearly as the firm's financial leverage increases. To prove that this is true, recall that earlier, we discussed the fact that the beta of a firm's portfolio of assets was equal to the weighted average of its liability betas.

$$\beta(\text{assets}) = \beta(\text{debt}) \frac{B}{B+S} + \beta(\text{equity}) \frac{S}{B+S}. \tag{17.20}$$

---

[8]For more on this topic, see Booth [1982].

[9]When attempting to buy "better betas," the old rule of *caveat emptor* applies. The econometric difficulties of obtaining good beta estimates are many, and the quality of estimated betas differs greatly. The nonsynchronous trading problem is one of the most important issues. For example, see Scholes and Williams [1977], Dimson [1979], Fowler and Rorke [1983], and Cohen, Hawawini, Maier, Schwartz, and Whitcomb [1983].

Table 17.8   Betas Estimated from Weekly Data June 75 to June 77

Industry	Beta	Company	Beta
Brokerage	1.55	Ten Highest Betas:	
Restaurants	1.41		
Hotels	1.36	Child World	2.49
Building and construction	1.32	Centronics Data	2.28
Electrical machinery	1.26	Rite Aid Corp.	2.15
Scientific instruments	1.25	Lin Broadcasting	2.15
Airlines	1.24	Soundesign Corp.	2.14
Machinery (excl. electric)	1.18	Centex Corp.	2.11
Motion pictures	1.16	Rollins Inc.	2.09
Retail stores	1.16	Gelco	2.08
Textile mill products	1.14	Congoleum	2.04
Real estate	1.14	Ramada Inns	2.03
Chemicals	1.09		
Food and kindred products	1.04	Ten Lowest Betas:	
Banks	1.01		
Dow Jones Index	.99	ASA Ltd.	.19
Paper and allied products	.98	Hudson Pulp and Paper	.19
Food stores	.96	Standard Prudential	.17
Metal mining	.88	First Banc Group, Ohio	.14
Petroleum refining	.86	Heritage Bancorp.	.13
Electric and gas utilities	.73	Wolf Corp.	.12
Railroads	.71	Connelly Containers	.11
		Washington Scientific	.10
		Cincinnati Gas and Electric	.06
		Midwestern N. Life Insurance	−.11

Source: Wilshire Associates Inc., *Capital Market Equilibrium Statistics*, Santa Monica, Calif., June 30, 1977.

Equation 17.20 can be rearranged to solve for the equity beta as a function of the firm's debt to equity ratio.

$$\beta(\text{equity}) = \beta(\text{assets}) + [\beta(\text{assets}) - \beta(\text{debt})] \frac{B}{S}. \qquad (17.21)$$

If we assume that the undiversifiable risk of the debt is invariant to the debt-equity ratio, then Equation 17.21 can be plotted in Figure 17.8 as a straight line. The equity beta increases with higher financial leverage because shareholders are residual claimants to the firm's cash flows. If the firm's use of debt increases, then more of its asset risk is shifted to the shareholders.

In addition to business risk and financial leverage, there are many other factors which may affect equity betas. Dividend payout, liquidity, firm size, and rate of growth have all been suggested as possibilities.[10] But suppose you are interested in estimating the risk of a new project rather than the beta for an entire firm. In this case, you have no way to statistically estimate the level of risk. What can you do? Our advice is that you try to

---

[10]For example, see Beaver, Kettler, and Scholes [1970] or Rosenberg and Marathe [1975].

Figure 17.8   Equity Betas Increase with Greater Financial Leverage

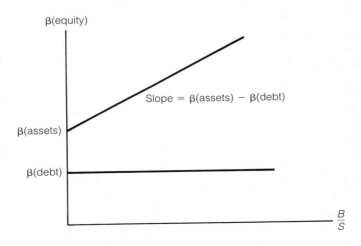

compare your subjective estimate of the project's systematic risk with that of known entities such as the industries or firms mentioned in Table 17.8. Once you are satisfied you
have a valid comparison, then you can use the estimated risk of the comparison firm or
industry as the best guess for the risk of your project.

Empirical Evidence on the Capital Asset Pricing Model

Any practitioner who wishes to employ the CAPM for managerial decision making naturally wants to know whether or not the CAPM theory is empirically valid. As we shall
shortly see, the evidence on the CAPM is mixed. It fits the data fairly well, but there are
some anomalies — phenomena which are not explained by the CAPM.

In order to test the CAPM, we need to know what predictions it makes. The empirical
analog of the CAPM is

$$R_{jt} = R_{Ft} + (R_{Mt} - R_{Ft})\beta_j + \epsilon_{jt}. \tag{17.22}$$

The three differences between Equation 17.22 and the theoretical CAPM (Equation 17.3)
are that (1) time subscripts have been added to the variables, (2) the expectations operator,
E, has been dropped because we use *ex post* data to test the *ex ante* CAPM, and (3) an error
term, ϵ_{jt}, has been added. The model is usually tested in the following form:

$$R_{jt} - R_{Ft} = a + b\beta_j + \epsilon_{jt}. \tag{17.23}$$

This is exactly the same as Equation 17.22 except that the risk-free rate has been subtracted from both sides and an intercept term, a, has been added. If the CAPM is true, then[11]

1.   The intercept term, a, should not be significantly different from zero. If it is different from zero, then there may be something "left out" of the CAPM which is captured in the empirically estimated intercept term.

2.   Beta should be the only factor which explains the rate of return on a risky asset. When other terms (such as residual variance, dividend yield, firm size, price-earnings ratios, or beta squared) are added to the regression, they should have no explanatory power.

3.   The relationship should be linear in beta.

4.   The coefficient of beta, b, should be equal to $R_{Mt} - R_{Ft}$.

5.   When the equation is estimated over long time intervals, the rate of return on the market portfolio should be greater than the risk-free rate. Because the market portfolio is riskier, on average, it should have a higher rate of return.

There have been literally hundreds of published papers which test the CAPM.[12] Most of them use monthly total returns (dividends are reinvested) on listed common stocks as their data base. Some, such as Black, Jensen, and Scholes [1972] and Fama and MacBeth [1973], group individual stocks into portfolios chosen to provide the maximum dispersion in systematic risk. And others, such as Litzenberger and Ramaswamy [1979] and Gibbons [1982], use individual security regressions. With few exceptions, the empirical studies agree on the following conclusions:

1.   The intercept term, a, is significantly different from zero, and the slope, b, is less than the difference between the return on the market portfolio and the risk-free rate. The implication is that low beta securities earn more than the CAPM predicts while high beta securities earn less.

2.   Versions of the model which include a squared beta term or unsystematic risk find that at best these explanatory factors are useful only in a small number of the time periods sampled. Beta dominates them as a measure of risk.

3.   The simple linear model (Equation 17.22) fits the data best. It is linear in beta. Also, over long periods of time, the rate of return on the market portfolio is greater than the risk-free rate (that is, $b > 0$).

4.   Factors other than beta are successful in explaining that portion of security returns not captured by beta. Basu [1977] found that low price/earnings portfolios have rates of return higher than could be explained by the CAPM. Banz [1981] and Reinganum [1981] found that the size of a firm is important. Smaller firms tend to have higher rates of return. Litzenberger and Ramaswamy [1979, 1982] found that the market requires higher rates of return on equities with high dividend yields. Keim [1983] finds evidence that stock returns are seasonal.

In sum, the empirical evidence leads to the conclusion that the CAPM must be rejected. There are two primary reasons. First, the intercept term is significantly different from zero. Second, much of the returns unexplained by the CAPM can be explained by various anomalies such as firm size, dividend yield, price-earnings ratios, or seasonality.

---

[11]Any test of the CAPM is also a joint test of capital market efficiency because the CAPM is derived under the assumption that capital markets are efficient. For more on market efficiency, see Chapter 19.

[12]A partial list of empirical tests of the CAPM includes Blume and Friend [1970, 1973], Black, Jensen, and Scholes [1972], Miller and Scholes [1972, 1982], Blume and Husick [1973], Fama and MacBeth [1973], Basu [1977], Reinganum [1981], Litzenberger and Ramaswamy [1979, 1982], Banz [1981], Stambaugh [1982], Gibbons [1982], and Keim [1983].

Figure 17.9   The Empirical Market Line

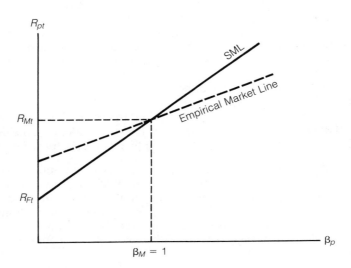

Although the empirical evidence requires that we reject the CAPM as a theoretical construct, it does not mean that expected returns are unrelated to beta. As shown in Figure 17.9, the results show that the *empirical market line* (represented by the dashed line) is linear in beta. Hence, if you have an estimate of beta, you can predict its required return from the empirical market line. The primary difference between the empirical market line (EML) and the theoretical CAPM is that the EML has a higher intercept and a lower slope.

The Arbitrage Pricing Model (APM)

One of the problems with using the CAPM is that only a single factor, the market portfolio, is used to explain security returns. It is a little like flying a private plane and being lost in the clouds. When you call the airport tower to ask for your location, suppose they respond by saying, "You are 100 miles away." Such a message is not of much help. Obviously, you would like to have a little more information. Altitude, longitude, and latitude would also be useful.

The Arbitrage Pricing Model allows us to use many factors, not just one, to explain security returns. First derived by Ross [1976], the APM starts out by assuming that the rate of return on any security is a linear function of the movement of a set of fundamental factors, $\tilde{F}_k$, common to all securities,

$$\tilde{R}_j = E(\tilde{R}_j) + b_{j1}\tilde{F}_1 + b_{j2}\tilde{F}_2 + \ldots + b_{jk}\tilde{F}_k + \tilde{\varepsilon}_j, \qquad \textbf{(17.24)}$$

where

$\tilde{R}_j$ = the stochastic rate of return on the jth asset
$E(\tilde{R}_j)$ = the expected rate of return on the jth asset
b_{jk} = the sensitivity of the jth asset's returns to the kth factor
$\tilde{F}_k$ = the mean zero k^{th} factor common to the returns of all assets under consideration
$\tilde{\epsilon}_j$ = a random, mean zero, noise term for the jth asset.

In the CAPM, the single factor underlying all asset returns is the rate of return on the market portfolio. Each asset's beta, or sensitivity, was estimated by regressing its return on the market portfolio rate of return. The Arbitrage Pricing Model does not allow us to simply regress an asset's returns against arbitrarily determined factors. Instead, factor analysis must be employed to extract the fundamental factors underlying all security returns. Although it is mathematically impossible to use factor analysis to unambiguously identify the underlying factors, Chen, Roll, and Ross [1983] have correlated various macroeconomic variables with the returns on five portfolios which mimic the underlying factors. Their conclusions provide some insight into what the underlying factors might be. Four macroeconomic variables were significant:[13]

1.   Industrial production (or the market portfolio)
2.   Changes in a default risk premium (measured by the differences in promised yields to maturity on AAA versus Baa corporate bonds)
3.   Twists in the yield curve (measured by the differences in promised yields to maturity on long- and short-term government bonds)
4.   Unanticipated inflation.

The economic logic underlying these variables seems to make sense. Common stock prices are the present values of discounted cash flows. The industrial production index is obviously related to profitability. The remaining variables are related to the discount rate. Although more research remains to be done to understand the factors which underlie asset prices, the work of Chen, Roll, and Ross [1983] is a good start and provides intuition for what the common factors might be.

The logic behind the APM is much the same as that for the CAPM. Diversifiable, or idiosyncratic, risk is not priced by the marketplace because it can be eliminated at virtually no cost simply by spreading one's wealth among a large number of assets in a portfolio. All that counts is systematic risk. It cannot be diversified away. Consequently, a risk premium must be paid in order to compensate investors for bearing systematic risk. The measure of systematic risk is the sensitivity of an asset's returns to various factors which affect all assets. In the CAPM, the single underlying factor was the return on the market portfolio. In the APM, the underlying factors may be thought of as industrial production (or the market index), a default risk premium, twists in the yield curve, and unanticipated inflation. These are all economy-wide risks which cannot be diversified away. In order to show how these systematic risks are priced in equilibrium, Ross [1976] used the concept of arbitrage portfolios to derive market equilibrium.

An *arbitrage portfolio* is one which has no risk, which requires no capital investment, and which earns a positive return. Much like the mythical unicorn, an arbitrage portfolio is a nice idea, but it should not exist in equilibrium. No one should be able to earn arbitrage

---

[13]It is also interesting to note some of the variables which were not significant — for example, oil price changes and innovations in real per capita consumption.

profits. In fact, we rely on the nonexistence of arbitrage opportunities to establish capital market equilibrium.[14]

Ross [1976] has shown that if no arbitrage opportunities exist, then the Arbitrage Pricing Model (APM) can be written as

$$E(R_j) = R_F + [\bar{\delta}_1 - R_F]b_{j1} + \ldots + [\bar{\delta}_k - R_F]b_{jk}, \qquad (17.25)$$

where

$E(R_j) =$ the expected return on the jth asset
$R_F =$ the return on the riskless asset
$\bar{\delta}_k =$ the expected return on a mimicking portfolio which has unitary sensitivity to the kth factor and zero sensitivity to all other factors[15]
$b_{jk} =$ the sensitivity of the jth asset to the kth factor.

The APM is very similar to the CAPM. It says (in Equation 17.25) that the expected return on any security in equilibrium will be equal to the risk-free rate plus a set of risk premia. The risk premium for each asset is the market price of risk for the kth factor, $\bar{\delta}_k - R_F$, times the sensitivity of the jth asset to the kth factor, b_{jk}. Under some simplifying assumptions, the factor sensitivities may be interpreted in the same way as beta in the CAPM.[16]

$$b_{jk} = \frac{\text{COV}(\tilde{R}_j, \tilde{\delta}_k)}{\text{VAR}(\tilde{\delta}_k)} \qquad (17.26)$$

This implies that the CAPM is simply a special case of the APM where only one factor, the expected return on the market portfolio, is used to explain asset returns.

The APM: Applications and Empirical Evidence

A detailed discussion of APM applications would be redundant with the CAPM applications discussed earlier in this chapter. The APM can be used in exactly the same way as the CAPM for determining the cost of capital, for valuation, and for capital budgeting. The only difference between them is that the CAPM is a single-factor and the APM is a multiple-factor model.[17]

The question which everyone asks is how much of an improvement can be obtained if one uses the APM rather than the CAPM for various applications? Bower, Bower, and Logue [1984] and Roll and Ross [1983] find that the APM gives improved estimates for the cost of equity in the electric utilities industry. Chen [1983] finds that the CAPM anomaly known as the size effect is largely eliminated by the APM, and that the APM can explain CAPM residuals but not vice versa. These studies seem to suggest that the APM is an improvement over the CAPM, particularly when security returns contain some CAPM

---

[14]See Appendix A of this chapter for a derivation of the Arbitrage Pricing Theory.

[15]Think of the CAPM as a single factor APM and then recall that the beta of the market portfolio is one, $\beta_M = 1$. This is an example of unitary sensitivity. Just as the market portfolio in the CAPM has unitary sensitivity to itself, so too each APM factor (mimicking) portfolio has unitary sensitivity to itself and zero sensitivity to all other factor portfolios.

[16]Assuming that the vectors of asset returns have a joint normal distribution and that the factors have been linearly transformed so that their transformed vectors are orthonormal.

[17]For an interesting application of the APM to multiperiod capital budgeting, see Gehr [1981].

anomaly. On the other hand, portfolio performance studies by Brown and Weinstein [1983] and Chen, Copeland, and Mayers [1983] find no difference between the APM and the CAPM. However, the lack of difference is probably attributable to the fact that the portfolios they were studying contained no CAPM anomalies.

Finally, papers by Gehr [1975], Roll and Ross [1980], Reinganum [1981], Chen [1983], and Dhrymes, Friend, and Gultekin [1984] have tested the APM. In general, the findings indicate that there are at least three or four underlying factors which are important in explaining security returns. This is enough to encourage further research into the APM. Only time will tell whether the APM replaces the CAPM as a central paradigm for understanding risk and return in equilibrium.

Summary

The APM and the CAPM are equilibrium models of asset pricing which focus on systematic or undiversifiable risk as the appropriate measures of risk. Total risk, as measured by the variance of an asset's returns, is not necessarily related to the equilibrium rate of return. In order to illustrate, consider the risk faced by an entrepreneur who owns and captains his own ship. If the ship goes down in a storm, the owner/captain loses everything. If he is risk averse, he will be willing to pay a relatively large fee for insurance. From his point of view, he is bearing a great deal of risk. If we look at the same problem from an insurance company's point of view, Lloyds of London, for example, the picture changes. Lloyds doesn't care about the specific risk faced by a single ship owner. It focuses on the riskiness of all shipping worldwide. If shipping mishaps are independent of each other and if there are many ships, then Lloyds can predict with relative certainty the total damage from sinkings each year. Consequently, Lloyds can charge the risk-free rate on its shipping insurance policies. Individual ship owners will sensibly buy insurance from Lloyds because the cost of insurance is well below what they would be willing to pay in order to avoid their specific risks. The point of this story is that the individual wealth variance faced by a sea captain is irrelevant in determining the market price of shipping insurance. All that counts is the covariance among shipping catastrophes. In our example, the covariance was implicitly assumed to be zero, and, therefore, the insurance companies could charge the risk-free rate.

Once we have estimated the covariance (or systematic) risk of an asset, either in the CAPM where the only factor is the market portfolio or in the APM where many factors may be relevant, then we can estimate the equilibrium risk-adjusted return required by the marketplace. This is a powerful and useful tool for decision making under uncertainty. The CAPM or the APM can be used for capital budgeting, for determining the cost of capital for debt and equity, and for valuation of securities. Empirical evidence indicates that although the CAPM must be rejected on statistical grounds, there does appear to be a linear relationship between beta and expected returns. The APM is an improvement over the CAPM because it appears to correct for some well-known CAPM anomalies, such as the firm size effect.

Questions

17.1 Why is the beta of the market portfolio equal to 1.0?

17.2 Suppose that inflation causes the nominal risk-free return and the market return to rise by an equal amount. How will the market risk premium be affected?

Figure Q17.6

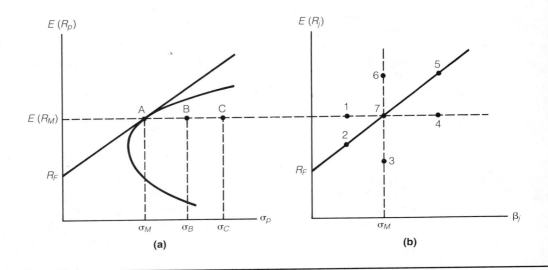

17.3 Why is total risk, as measured by the variance of returns, unrelated to the market required rate of return on a project?

17.4 Consider two firms which are alike in every way except that Firm A has fixed rate debt in its capital structure and Firm B has variable rate debt. Which firm has riskier equity? Why?

17.5 Firms X and Y have exactly the same ratio of debt to total assets. However, Firm X employs short-term debt and rolls it over each year at the existing interest rate while Firm Y has just issued fixed rate long-term debt. Which firm has riskier equity? Why?

17.6 Where do Points A, B, and C in Panel (a) of Figure Q17.6 plot in Panel (b) of Figure Q17.6? Why?

17.7 **a)** Why do firms in the same industry tend to have similar betas?
      b) Why is the average beta of brokerage firms high (that is, 1.55) and the beta of railroads low (that is, .71)?

17.8 What empirical facts have caused researchers to reject the Capital Asset Pricing Model?

17.9 What is the empirical market line, and how does it differ from the Security Market Line?

17.10 What are the four factors which Chen, Ross, and Roll have determined to be common to all asset returns?

17.11 What is an arbitrage portfolio? What role do arbitrage portfolios play in market equilibrium?

Problems

17.1 Prove that β_M (the beta of the market portfolio) equals 1.0.

17.2 Prove that

$$\beta_p = \sum_{i=1}^{N} w_i \beta_i$$

for a two asset case.

17.3 The Rowan Company is faced with two mutually exclusive investment projects. Each project costs $4,500, and each has an expected life of three years. Annual net cash flows from each project begin one year after the initial investment is made and have the probability distributions given in Table P17.3.

Table P17.3

Project A		Project B	
Probability	Cash Flow	Probability	Cash Flow
0.2	$4,000	0.2	$ 0
0.6	4,500	0.6	4,500
0.2	5,000	0.2	12,000

Rowan has decided to evaluate the riskier project at a 12 percent rate and the less risky project at a 10 percent rate.

a) What is the expected value of the annual net cash flows from each project?

b) What is the risk-adjusted NPV of each project?

c) If it were known that Project B was negatively correlated with other cash flows of the firm while Project A was positively correlated, how should this knowledge affect the decision?

17.4 The risk-free rate is 4 percent, and the market risk premium is 5 percent. Under consideration for investment outlays are Projects A, B, and C, with estimated betas of 0.8, 1.2, and 2, respectively. What will be the required rates of return on these projects based on the Security Market Line approach?

17.5 The risk-free rate of return is 6 percent, and the market risk premium is 5 percent. The beta of the project under analysis is 1.8, with expected net cash flows after taxes estimated at $600 for five years. The required investment outlay on the project is $1,800.

a) What is the required risk-adjusted return on the project?

b) Should the project be accepted?

17.6 The McWilliams Company is considering two investment projects, A and B, for which the following information in Table P17.6 has been calculated.

Table P17.6

	Investment A	Investment B
Investment outlay required (I)	$20,000	$20,000
Expected return [$E(R)$]	0.20	0.20
Standard deviation of returns (σ)	0.40	0.60
Coefficient of variation of returns (CV)	2.0	3.0
Beta of returns (β)	1.8	1.2

The vice president of finance has formulated a risk adjustment relationship based on the coefficient of variation, CV, which is defined as the standard deviation of return divided by the mean:

$$\text{Required return on a project} = \text{Risk-free return} + 0.04CV.$$

He also takes into consideration the Security Market Line relationship, using 6 percent as the estimate of the risk-free return and 5 percent as the market risk premium.

a) What is the required return on each project, using alternative methods of calculating the risk adjustment factor?

b) If the two projects are independent, should they both be accepted?

c) If the projects are mutually exclusive, which one should be accepted?

d) Depending upon the approach to risk measurement used, why might the two investments have different risks?

e) What additional analysis might be performed before a final decision is made?

17.7 You are given the following information for an investment project: $P = \$3$ per unit; $VC = \$2$ per unit; $FC = \$300$. The risk-free rate is 5 percent $= R_F$. (Use VAR $R_M = 0.01$.) Also,

Probability	R_M	Q
0.2	−0.05	0
0.5	0.10	600
0.3	0.20	1,000

where

$$
\begin{aligned}
P &= \text{Selling price per unit sold} \\
VC &= \text{Variable costs per unit sold} \\
c &= (P - VC) = \text{Contribution margin per unit} \\
Q &= \text{Units of output sold} \\
FC &= \text{Total fixed costs.}
\end{aligned}
$$

a) What is the price of risk, that is, $[E(R_M) - R_F]/\sigma_M^2$?

b) What is the value of the investment project?

c) What is the required return on the investment project?

17.8 Given the data in Table P17.8 (the investment cost of each project is $1,000), calculate

Table P17.8

S	Probability	R_{MS}	Return to Project 1	Return to Project 2
1	0.1	−0.3	−0.4	−0.4
2	0.2	−0.1	−0.2	−0.2
3	0.3	0.1	0	0.6
4	0.4	0.3	0.7	0

a) The three means, the variances, the standard deviations, and the covariance of Project 1 with the market, covariance of Project 2 with the market, covariance of Project 1 with Project 2, the correlation coefficients ρ_{1M}, ρ_{2M}, and the correlation coefficient of Project 1 with Project 2.

b) If Projects 1 and 2 were to be combined into a portfolio with 40 percent in Project 1 and 60 percent in Project 2, what would be the expected return on that portfolio and its standard deviation?

    c) $R_F = 0.04$. Calculate the Security Market Line. On a graph:
        1)   Plot the Security Market Line.
        2)   Plot points for Project 1 and for Project 2.
    d)   If you had to choose between the two projects, which would you select?

17.9 Consider two projects with different risk. The risky project has a risky rate of 12 percent. The riskless project has a riskless rate of 6 percent.
    a)   Calculate the certainty equivalent factor, $(\text{cef})^t$, for each project for Years 0, 1, 5, 10, 20, and 30.
    b)   What are the implications of your results?

17.10 We have the following data on market parameters. The risk-free rate is 6 percent, the expected return on the market is 11 percent, and the variance on the market is 1 percent. The covariance of the net operating income of the firm with the market returns is $40. The expected net operating income of the firm (X) is $320.
    a)   Calculate the value of the firm, using a certainty equivalent amount in the numerator and the risk-free rate in the denominator.
    b)   Calculate the value of the firm using risk-adjusted measures.
    c)   How do your results compare?

17.11 The Pierson Company is considering two mutually exclusive investment projects, P and Q. The risk and return estimates for these two investment projects are given in Table P17.11.

Table P17.11

	Project P	Project Q
Expected return [$E(R)$]	0.15	0.18
Standard deviation (σ)	0.50	0.75
Beta (β)	1.80	1.40

Assume that the risk-free rate is 10 percent and the expected market return is 14 percent. What would be the firm's decision if the SML analysis is used?

17.12 The Magic Manufacturers Corporation has risky debt with a β_d of .2 and its stock has a beta of 1.6.
    a)   If MMC has 60 percent debt to total assets, what is the beta of the firm as a whole?
    b)   If MMC reduces its debt to total assets ratio to 40 percent debt, without changing the risk of debt, what will its equity beta become?

17.13 The expected return on the market portfolio is 16.2 percent and the risk-free rate is 10 percent. A risky bond is selling for $942.02. Its coupon rate is 10 percent and its face value is $1,000. It has three years to maturity. Although you expect all of its coupons to be paid with certainty, you believe that there is a 10 percent chance it will default on its face value and pay only $700. What is the beta of this bond?

17.14 Given the facts in Table P17.14,

Table P17.14

Year	McNichols Corporation Equity Return	Market Return
19X9	2%	−12%
19X0	13	18
19X1	10	5
19X2	5	15
19X3	−8	10
19X4	−2	12
19X5	6	26

a)   Estimate the historical beta for the equity of McNichols Corporation.

b)   If the risk-free rate is currently 10 percent and the expected return on the market portfolio is 18 percent, what is the cost of equity for the McNichols Corporation?

c)   What assumption do you have to make in order to use a historical estimate of beta to compute a current cost of equity?

17.15   The Jacquier Company has three divisions, each of approximately the same size. The financial staff has estimated the rates of return for different states of nature as given in Table P17.15.

Table P17.15

State of World	Subjective Probability	Market Return	Division Rate of Return		
			Division 1	Division 2	Division 3
Great	.25	.35	.40	.60	.20
Good	.25	.20	.36	.30	.12
Average	.25	.13	.24	.16	.08
Horrible	.25	−.08	.00	−.26	−.02

a)   If the risk-free rate is 9 percent, what rate of return does the market require for each division?

b)   What is the beta of the entire company?

c)   If the company has 30 percent of its funds provided by riskless debt and the remainder by equity, what is the equity beta for the company?

d)   Which of the divisions should be kept? Which should be spun off?

e)   What will the company's beta be if the actions in Part (d) are undertaken?

17.16   Projects A and B are mutually exclusive equipment replacement proposals. Both require an immediate cash outlay of $1,000, both last one year, and both have end-of-year revenues of $3,000 with certainty. Cash outflows at the end of the year, however, are risky. They are given in Table P17.16 along with the market rate of return, R_M.

Table P17.16

State of Nature	Probability	End-of-Period Outflows		R_M
		Project A	Project B	
Great	.333	$1,000	$1,200	30%
Average	.333	800	800	15
Horrid	.333	600	400	0

Since you are given the cash flows, there is no need to worry about taxes, depreciation, or salvage value. Note that the cash outflows of Project B have a higher variance than those of Project A. Which project has the higher net present value?

Selected References

Aggarwal, Raj, "Corporate Use of Sophisticated Capital Budgeting Techniques: A Strategic Perspective and a Critique of Survey Results," *Interfaces*, 10 (April 1980), pp. 31-34.

Banz, Ralph, "The Relationship Between Return and the Market Value of Common Stocks," *Journal of Financial Economics*, (March 1981), pp. 3-18.

Bar-Yosef, Sasson, and Mesnick, Roger, "On Some Definitional Problems with the Method of Certainty Equivalents," *Journal of Finance*, 32 (December 1977), pp. 1729-1737.

Basu, S., "Investment Performance of Common Stocks in Relation to Their Price-Earnings Ratios: A Test of the Efficient Markets Hypothesis," *Journal of Finance*, (June 1977), pp. 663-682.

Beaver, W.; Kettler, P.; and Scholes, M., "The Association Between Market-Determined and Accounting-Determined Risk Measures," *Accounting Review*, (October 1970), pp. 654-682.

Black, Fisher; Jensen, Michael; and Scholes, Myron, "Capital Market Equilibrium with Restricted Borrowing," *Journal of Business*, (July 1972), pp. 444-455.

Blume, Marshall, "Portfolio Theory: A Step Toward Its Practical Application," *Journal of Business*, (April 1970), pp. 152-173.

————, and Friend, Irwin, "A New Look at the Capital Asset Pricing Model," *Journal of Finance*, (March 1973), pp. 19-34.

Blume, Marshall, and Husick, Frank, "Price, Beta and Exchange Listing," *Journal of Finance*, (May 1973), pp. 283-299.

Bogue, Marcus C., and Roll, Richard, "Capital Budgeting of Risky Projects with 'Imperfect' Markets for Physical Capital," *Journal of Finance*, 29 (May 1974), pp. 601-613.

Booth, L., "Correct Procedures for the Evaluation of Risky Cash Outflows," *Journal of Financial and Quantitative Analysis*, (June 1982), pp. 287-300.

Bower, D.; Bower, R.; and Logue, D., "Arbitrage Pricing Theory and Utility Stock Returns," *Journal of Finance*, (September 1984), pp. 1041-1054.

Chen, Nai-Fu, "Some Empirical Tests of the Theory of Arbitrage Pricing," *Journal of Finance*, (December 1983), pp. 1393-1414.

————; Copeland, T. E.; and Mayers, D., "A Comparison of APM, CAPM and Market-Model Portfolio Performance Methodologies: The Value Line Case," working paper #13-83, UCLA, Graduate School of Management, 1983.

Chen, N. F.; Roll, R. W.; and Ross, S. A., "Economic Forces and the Stock Market: Testing the APT and Alternative Asset Pricing Theories," UCLA Working Paper #20-83, December 1983.

Cohen, K.; Hawawini, G.; Maier, S.; Schwartz, R.; and Whitcomb, D., "Friction in the Trading Process and the Estimation of Systematic Risk," *Journal of Financial Economics*, (August 1983), pp. 263-278.

Dhrymes, P.; Friend, I.; and Gultekin, B., "A Critical Reexamination of the Empirical Evidence on the Arbitrage Pricing Theory," *Journal of Finance*, (June 1984), pp. 323-346.

Dimson, E., "Risk Measurement When Shares are Subject to Infrequent Trading," *Journal of Financial Economics*, (June 1979), pp. 197-226.

Fama, Eugene F., "Risk-Adjusted Discount Rates and Capital Budgeting under Uncertainty," *Journal of Financial Economics*, 5 (August 1977), pp. 3-24.

————, and MacBeth, James, "Risk, Return and Equilibrium: Empirical Test," *Journal of Political Economy*, (May/June 1973), pp. 607-636.

Fisher, Lawrence, and Lorie, James, "Rate of Return on Investments in Common Stocks," *Journal of Business*, (January 1964), pp. 1-17.

Fowler, D., and Rorke, H., "Risk Measurement When Shares are Subject to Infrequent Trading: Comment," *Journal of Financial Economics*, (August 1983), pp. 279-283.

Gehr, Adam, "Risk-Adjusted Capital Budgeting Using Arbitrage," *Financial Management*, (Winter 1981), pp. 14-19.

————, "Some Tests of the Arbitrage Pricing Theory," *Journal of the Midwest Finance Association*, (1975), pp. 91-105.

Gibbons, Michael, "Multivariate Tests of Financial Models: A New Approach," *Journal of Financial Economics*, (March 1982), pp. 3-28.

Ibbotson, R., and Sinquefield, R., *Stocks, Bonds, Bills and Inflation: the Past and the Future*, The Financial Analysts Research Foundation, Charlottsville, Virginia, 1982.

Keim, D., "Size-Related Anomalies and Stock Return Seasonality: Further Empirical Evidence," *Journal of Financial Economics*, (June 1983), pp. 13-32.

Litzenberger, Robert H., and Ramaswamy, Krishna, "The Effects of Dividends on Common Stock Prices: Tax Effects or Information Effects?" *Journal of Finance*, (May 1982), pp. 429-444.

————, "The Effect of Personal Taxes and Dividends on Capital Asset Prices: Theory and Empirical Evidence," *Journal of Financial Economics*, (June 1979), pp. 163-195.

Miller, Merton, and Scholes, Myron, "Rates of Return in Relation to Risk: A Re-examination of Some Recent Findings," in M. C. Jensen, Ed., *Studies in the Theory of Capital Markets*, New York: Praeger, 1972, pp. 47-78.

Myers, Stewart C., "Procedures for Capital Budgeting under Uncertainty," *Industrial Management Review*, 9 (Spring 1968), pp. 1-15.

————, and Turnbull, Stuart M., "Capital Budgeting and the Capital Asset Pricing Model: Good News and Bad News," *Journal of Finance*, 32 (May 1977), pp. 321-332.

Reinganum, Mark, "The Arbitrage Pricing Theory: Some Empirical Results," *Journal of Finance*, (May 1981), pp. 313-321.

————, "Misspecification of Capital Asset Pricing: Empirical Anomalies Based on Earnings Yields and Market Values," *Journal of Financial Economics*, (March 1981), pp. 19-46.

Roll, R., and Ross, S., "A Critical Reexamination of the Empirical Evidence on the Arbitrage Pricing Theory: A Reply," *Journal of Finance*, (June 1984), pp. 347-350.

————, "Regulation, the Capital Asset Pricing Model, and the Arbitrage Pricing Theory," *Public Utilities Fortnightly*, (May 26, 1983), pp. 22-28.

———, "An Empirical Investigation of the Arbitrage Pricing Theory," *Journal of Finance*, (December 1980), pp. 1073-1103.

Rosenberg, B., and Marathe, V., "The Prediction of Investment Risk," Proceedings of the CRSP Seminar, University of Chicago, November 1975.

Ross, S., "Return, Risk and Arbitrage," in Friend, I. and Bicksler, I. (Eds.), *Risk and Return in Finance*, Cambridge, Mass.: Ballinger Press, 1977.

———, "The Arbitrage Theory of Capital Asset Pricing," *Journal of Economic Theory*, (December 1976), pp. 341-361.

Scholes, M., and Williams, J., "Estimating Beta from Non-Synchronous Data," *Journal of Financial Economics*, (December 1977), pp. 309-327.

Stambaugh, Robert, "On the Exclusion of Assets from Tests of the Two-Parameter Model: A Sensitivity Analysis," *Journal of Financial Economics*, (November 1982), pp. 237-268.

Weston, J. Fred, "Investment Decisions Using the Capital Asset Pricing Model," *Financial Management*, 2 (Spring 1973), pp. 25-33.

———, and Chen, Nai-fu, "A Note on Capital Budgeting and the Three Rs," *Financial Management*, 9 (Spring 1980), pp. 12-13.

Appendix A to Chapter 17
Derivations of the CAPM and the APT

For students who seek a more complete understanding of the origin of the Capital Asset Pricing Model (CAPM) and the Arbitrage Pricing Theory (APT), this appendix presents derivations of the theories. These are not the only derivations nor even the easiest, but perhaps they are the most intuitive.

Derivation of the Capital Asset Pricing Model

The CAPM is developed in a hypothetical world, where the following assumptions are made about investors and the portfolio opportunity set:

1. Investors are risk-averse individuals who maximize the expected utility of their end-of-period wealth.
2. Investors are price takers and have homogeneous expectations about asset returns which have a joint normal distribution.
3. There exists a risk-free asset such that investors may borrow or lend unlimited amounts at the risk-free rate.
4. The quantities of all risky assets are fixed. Also, all assets are marketable and perfectly divisible.
5. Asset markets are frictionless and information is costless and simultaneously available to all investors.
6. There are no market imperfections such as taxes, regulations, or restrictions on short selling.

Although these assumptions are unrealistic, most have been relaxed without changing the important properties of the CAPM.

Figure 17A.1 shows the expected return and standard deviation of the market portfolio, M, the risk-free asset, R_F, and an inefficient risky asset, I. The straight line connecting the risk-free asset and the market portfolio is the Capital Market Line. We know that if an equilibrium is to exist, the prices of all assets must adjust until all are held by investors. There can be no excess demand. In other words, prices must be established so that the supply of all assets equals the demand for holding them. Consequently, in equilibrium, the market portfolio will consist of all assets held in proportion to their value weights, with

$$w_i \equiv \frac{\text{Market value of individual asset } i}{\text{Market value of all assets}}. \qquad \textbf{(17A.1)}$$

A portfolio consisting of $a\%$ invested in risky Asset I and $(1 - a)\%$ in the market portfolio will have the following mean and standard deviation:

Figure 17A.1   The Opportunity Set Provided by Combinations of the Inefficient
Risky Asset I and the Market Portfolio M

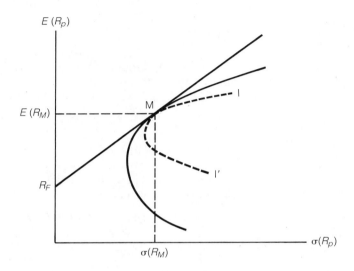

$$E(R_p) = aE(R_i) + (1 - a)E(R_M) \tag{17A.2}$$

$$\sigma(R_p) = [a^2\sigma_i^2 + 2a(1 - a)\sigma_{iM} + (1 - a)^2\sigma_M^2]^{1/2}, \tag{17A.3}$$

where

$\sigma_i^2 =$ the variance of the risky Asset I
$\sigma_M^2 =$ the variance of the market Portfolio M
$\sigma_{iM} =$ the covariance between Asset I and the market portfolio.

It is important to note that the market portfolio already contains Asset I held according to its market value weight. The opportunity set provided by various combinations of the risky asset and the market portfolio is the line IMI' in Figure 17A.1. The change in the mean and standard deviation with respect to the percent of the portfolio, a, invested in Asset I is determined by taking the partial derivatives of Equations 17A.2 and 17A.3 with respect to a:

$$\frac{\partial E(R_p)}{\partial a} = E(R_i) - E(R_M) \tag{17A.4}$$

$$\frac{\partial \sigma(R_p)}{\partial a} = \frac{1}{2}[a^2\sigma_i^2 + 2a(1 - a)\sigma_{iM} + (1 - a)^2\sigma_M^2]^{-1/2} \tag{17A.5}$$

$$\times [2a\sigma_i^2 + 2\sigma_{iM} - 4a\sigma_{iM} - 2\sigma_M^2 + 2a\sigma_M^2].$$

The insight which allows us to use the above facts to determine a market equilibrium price for risk, is that, in equilibrium, the market portfolio already has the weight, w_i percent, invested in the risky Asset I. Therefore, the percent a in the above equations may be interpreted as the excess demand for an individual risky asset. But we know that in equilibrium, the excess demand for any asset must be zero (that is, $a = 0$ in equilibrium). Prices will adjust until all assets are held according to their market value weights. Therefore, we can evaluate Equations 17A.4 and 17A.5 where excess demand, a, equals zero. The result will be the equilibrium pricing relationship:

$$\left. \frac{\partial E(R_p)}{\partial a} \right|_{a = 0} = E(R_i) - E(R_M)$$

$$\left. \frac{\partial \sigma(R_p)}{\partial a} \right|_{a = 0} = \frac{1}{2}[\sigma_M^2]^{-1/2}[-2\sigma_M^2 + 2\sigma_{iM}] = \frac{\sigma_{iM} - \sigma_M^2}{\sigma_M}.$$

The slope of the risk-return tradeoff, evaluated at Point M, in market equilibrium, is

$$\left. \frac{\partial E(R_p)/\partial a}{\partial \sigma(R_p)/\partial a} \right|_{a = 0} = \frac{E(R_i) - E(R_M)}{(\sigma_{iM} - \sigma_M^2)/\sigma_M}. \tag{17A.6}$$

The final insight is to realize that the slope of the opportunity set IMI' (in Figure 17A.1) at Point M must be equal to the slope of the Capital Market Line (CML).

The Capital Market Line is also a description of the same market equilibrium. Recall that the slope of the CML (derived in the body of Chapter 16) was

$$\text{Slope of CML} = \frac{E(R_M) - R_F}{\sigma_M}. \tag{17A.7}$$

Equations 17A.6 and 17A.7 are different but equivalent definitions of the slope of lines tangent to the opportunity set IMI' at Point M. Equating them, we have

$$\frac{E(R_M) - R_F}{\sigma_M} = \frac{E(R_i) - E(R_M)}{(\sigma_{iM} - \sigma_M^2)/\sigma_M}.$$

This relationship can be arranged to solve for $E(R_i)$ as follows:

$$E(R_i) = R_F + [E(R_M) - R_F]\frac{\sigma_{iM}}{\sigma_M^2}. \tag{CAPM}$$

This is the Capital Asset Pricing Model. The required equilibrium rate of return on any asset is equal to the risk-free rate plus a risk premium which is a function of σ_{iM}, the covariance (or sensitivity) of the ith asset to variations in the market index portfolio.

Derivation of the Arbitrage Pricing Model

The Arbitrage Pricing Model, first formulated by Ross [1976], is a more general approach to asset pricing because it allows for the possibility that many factors may be used to explain asset returns. Also, it makes fewer assumptions than the CAPM.

The Arbitrage Pricing Theory (APT) begins by assuming that the rate of return on any security is a linear function of K factors as shown below:

$$\tilde{R}_i = E(\tilde{R}_i) + b_{i1}\tilde{F}_1 + \ldots + b_{ik}\tilde{F}_k + \tilde{\epsilon}_i, \qquad \text{(17A.8)}$$

where

$\tilde{R}_i = $ the stochastic rate of return on the ith asset

$E(\tilde{R}_i) = $ the expected rate of return on the ith asset

$b_{ik} = $ the sensitivity of the ith asset's returns to the kth factor

$\tilde{F}_k = $ the mean zero k^{th} factor common to the returns of all assets under consideration

$\tilde{\epsilon}_i = $ a random zero mean noise term for the ith asset.

As we shall see later on, the CAPM may be viewed as a special case of the APT when the market rate of return is assumed to be the single relevant factor.

The APT is derived under the usual assumptions of perfectly competitive and frictionless capital markets. Furthermore, individuals are assumed to have homogeneous beliefs that the random returns for the set of assets being considered are governed by the linear k-factor model given in Equation 17A.8. The theory requires that the number of assets under consideration, n, be much larger than the number of factors, K, and that the noise term, $\tilde{\epsilon}_i$, be the unsystematic risk component for the ith asset. It must be independent of all factors and all error terms for other assets.

The most important feature of the APT is reasonable and straightforward. In equilibrium, all portfolios which can be selected from among the set of assets under consideration and which satisfy the conditions of (1) using no wealth and (2) having no risk, must earn no return on average. These portfolios are called *arbitrage portfolios*. To see how they can be constructed, let w_i be the *change* in the dollar amount invested in the ith asset as a percentage of an individual's total invested wealth. In order to form an arbitrage portfolio which requires no change in wealth, the usual course of action would be to sell some assets and use the proceeds to buy others. Portfolios of this type are said to be self-financing. Mathematically, the zero change in wealth is written as

$$\sum_{i=1}^{n} w_i = 0. \qquad \text{(17A.9)}$$

If there are n assets in the arbitrage portfolio, then the additional portfolio return gained is

$$\tilde{R}_p = \sum_{i=1}^{n} w_i \tilde{R}_i \qquad \text{(17A.10)}$$

$$= \sum_i w_i E(\tilde{R}_i) + \sum_i w_i b_{i1}\tilde{F}_1 + \ldots + \sum_i w_i b_{ik}\tilde{F}_k + \sum_i w_i \tilde{\epsilon}_i.$$

In order to obtain a riskless arbitrage portfolio, it is necessary to eliminate both diversifiable (that is, unsystematic) and undiversifiable (that is, systematic) risk. This can be done by meeting three conditions: (1) selecting percentage changes in investment ratios, w_i, which are small, (2) diversifying across a large number of assets, and (3) choosing changes, w_i, so that for each factor, k, the weighted sum of the systematic risk components, b_k, is zero. Mathematically, these conditions are

$$w_i \approx 1/n \qquad \text{(17A.11a)}$$

$$n \text{ chosen to be a large number,} \qquad \text{(17A.11b)}$$

$$\sum_i w_i b_{ik} = 0 \text{ for each factor.} \qquad \text{(17A.11c)}$$

Because the error terms, $\tilde{\varepsilon}_i$, are independent, the law of large numbers guarantees that a weighted average of many of them will approach zero in the limit as n becomes large. In other words, costless diversification eliminates the last term (the unsystematic risk) in Equation 17A.10 above. Thus, we are left with

$$\tilde{R}_p = \sum_i w_i E(\tilde{R}_i) + \sum_i w_i b_{i1} \tilde{F}_1 + \ldots + \sum_i w_i b_{ik} \tilde{F}_k. \qquad \text{(17A.12)}$$

At first glance, the return on our portfolio appears to be a random variable, but we have chosen the weighted average of the systematic risk components for each factor to be equal to zero $(\sum_i w_i b_{ik} = 0)$. This eliminates all systematic risk. One might say that we have selected an arbitrage portfolio with zero beta in each factor. Consequently, the return on our arbitrage portfolio becomes a constant. Correct choice of the weights eliminates all uncertainty, so that R_p is not a random variable. Therefore, Equation 17A.12 becomes

$$R_p = \sum_i w_i E(\tilde{R}_i). \qquad \text{(17A.12a)}$$

Recall that the arbitrage portfolio, so constructed, has no risk (of any kind) and requires no new wealth. If the return on the arbitrage portfolio were not zero, then it would be possible to achieve an infinite rate of return with no capital requirements and no risk. Such an opportunity is clearly impossible if the market is to be in equilibrium. In fact, if the individual arbitrageur is in equilibrium (hence content with his or her current portfolio), then the return on any and all arbitrage portfolios must be zero. In other words,

$$R_p = \sum_i w_i E(\tilde{R}_i) = 0. \qquad \text{(17A.13)}$$

Equations 17A.9, 17A.11c, and 17A.13 are really statements in linear algebra. Any vector which is orthogonal to the constant vector, that is,

$$\left(\sum_i w_i\right) \cdot 1 = 0, \qquad \text{(17A.9)}$$

and to each of the coefficient vectors, that is,

$$\sum_i w_i b_{ik} = 0 \text{ for each } k, \tag{17A.11c}$$

must also be orthogonal to the vector of expected returns, that is,

$$\sum_i w_i E(\tilde{R}_i) = 0. \tag{17A.13}$$

An algebraic consequence of this statement is that the expected return vector must be a linear combination of the constant vector and the coefficient vectors. Algebraically, there must exist a set of $K + 1$ coefficients, $\lambda_0, \lambda_1, \ldots, \lambda_k$ such that

$$E(\tilde{R}_i) = \lambda_0 + \lambda_1 b_{i1} + \ldots + \lambda_k b_{ik}. \tag{17A.14}$$

Recall that the b_{ik} are the "sensitivities" of the returns on the ith security to the kth factor. If there is a riskless asset with a riskless rate of return, R_F, then $b_{0k} = 0$ and

$$R_F = \lambda_0.$$

Hence, Equation 17A.14 can be rewritten in "excess returns form" as

$$E(R_i) - R_F = \lambda_1 b_{i1} + \ldots + \lambda_k b_{ik}. \tag{17A.15}$$

Figure 17A.2 illustrates the arbitrage pricing relationship (17A.15) assuming that there is only a single stochastic factor, k. In equilibrium, all assets must fall on the *Arbitrage Pricing Line*. A natural interpretation for λ_k is that it represents the risk premium (that is, the price of risk), in equilibrium, for the kth factor. Because the arbitrage pricing relationship is linear, we can use the slope-intercept definition of a straight line to rewrite Equation 17A.15 as

$$E(R_i) = R_F + [\bar{\delta}_k - R_F]b_{ik},$$

where $\bar{\delta}_k$ is the expected return on a portfolio with unit sensitivity to the kth factor and zero sensitivity to all other factors. Therefore, the risk premium, λ_k, is equal to the difference between (1) the expectation of a portfolio which has unit response to the kth factor and zero response to the other factors and (2) the risk-free rate, R_F.

$$\lambda_k = \bar{\delta}_k - R_F.$$

In general, the Arbitrage Pricing Theory can be rewritten as

$$E(R_i) - R_F = [\bar{\delta}_1 - R_F]b_{i1} + \ldots + [\bar{\delta}_k - R_F]b_{ik}. \tag{17A.16}$$

If Equation 17A.16 is interpreted as a linear regression equation (assuming that the vectors of returns have a joint normal distribution and that the factors have been linearly

Figure 17A.2 The Arbitrage Pricing Line

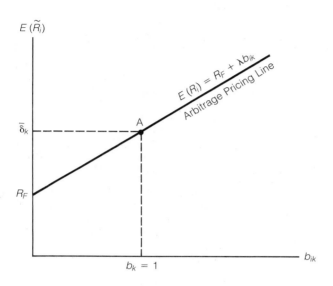

transformed so that their transformed vectors are orthonormal) then the coefficients, b_{ik}, are defined in exactly the same way as beta in the Capital Asset Pricing Model, that is,

$$b_{ik} = \frac{\text{COV}(\tilde{R}_i, \tilde{\delta}_k)}{\text{VAR}(\tilde{\delta}_k)}, \qquad \text{(17A.16a)}$$

where

$\text{COV}(R_i, \tilde{\delta}_k) = $ the covariance between the ith asset's returns and the linear transformation of the kth factor

$\text{VAR}(\tilde{\delta}_k) = $ the variance of the linear transformation of the kth factor.

Hence, the CAPM is seen to be a special case of the APT (where asset returns are assumed to be joint normal).

The Arbitrage Pricing Theory is much more robust than the Capital Asset Pricing Model for several reasons:

1. The APT makes no assumptions about the empirical distribution of asset returns.
2. The APT makes no strong assumptions about individuals' utility functions (at least nothing stronger than greed and risk aversion).
3. The APT allows the equilibrium returns of assets to be dependent on many factors, not just one more (for example, beta).
4. The APT yields a statement about the relative pricing of any subset of assets; hence, one need not measure the entire universe of assets in order to test the theory.

5.   There is no special role for the market portfolio in the APT, whereas the CAPM requires that the market portfolio be efficient.

6.   The APT is easily extended to a multiperiod framework [see Ross (1976)].

We fully expect that future generations of finance students will be taught the Arbitrage Pricing Theory, and the CAPM, if it is mentioned at all, will be taught as a special case of the APT. The main reason for our prediction is that the APT is more closely tied to the fundamental concept of arbitrage. If assets with equivalent risk are not priced to earn the same expected return, then simple arbitrage — buy low and sell high — will force expected returns into equilibrium.

Selected References

Grinblatt, M., and Titman, S., "Factor Pricing in a Finite Economy," *Journal of Financial Economics*, (December 1983), pp. 497-508.

Lintner, J., "The Aggregation of Investors' Diverse Judgements and Preferences in Purely Competitive Security Markets," *Journal of Financial and Quantitative Analysis*, (December 1969), pp. 347-400.

Merton, R., "An Intertemporal Capital Asset Pricing Model," *Econometrica*, (September 1973), pp. 867-888.

Mossin, J., "Equilibrium in a Capital Asset Market," *Econometrica*, (October 1966), pp. 768-783.

Ross, Steve, "The Arbitrage Theory of Capital Asset Pricing," *Journal of Economic Theory*, (December 1976), pp. 343-362.

Sharpe, W. F., "Capital Asset Prices: A Theory of Market Equilibrium Under Conditions of Risk," *Journal of Finance*, (September 1964), pp. 425-442.

Treynor, J., "Toward a Theory of the Market Value of Risky Assets," unpublished manuscript, 1961.

Appendix B to Chapter 17

Sensitivity Analysis of Risky Projects

The capital budgeting process requires estimates of expected cash flows over the life of a project and an accurate estimate of the appropriate risk-adjusted cost of capital. The expected cash flows are then discounted in order to compute the net present value of the project. It sounds simple — right? Actually, there is nothing simple about capital budgeting decisions. A major problem is that cash flows and costs of capital are estimated with error. Sometimes the errors are huge. Consequently, it is wise to undertake a sensitivity analysis of project NPV's in order to gain a better appreciation of the potential errors involved in the decision-making process.

The NPV of a project will, in the final analysis, depend upon such factors as quantity of sales, sales prices, input costs, the opportunity cost of capital, and so on. If these values turn out to be favorable — that is, output and sales prices are high and costs are low — then profits, the realized rate of return, and the actual NPV will be high, and the converse if these values are unfavorable. Recognizing these causal relationships, managers often calculate project NPV's under alternative assumptions and then see just how sensitive NPV is to changing conditions. One example that recently came to the authors' attention involves a fertilizer company that was comparing two alternative types of phosphate plants. Fuel represented a major cost, and one plant used coal, which may be obtained under a long-term, fixed-cost contract, while the other used oil, which must be purchased at current market prices. Considering present and projected future prices, the oil-fired plant looked better — it had a considerably higher NPV. However, oil prices are volatile, and if prices rose by more than the expected rate, this plant would have been unprofitable. The coal-fired plant, on the other hand, had a lower NPV under the expected conditions, but this NPV was not sensitive to changing conditions in the energy market. The company finally selected the coal plant because the sensitivity analysis indicated that there was less potential error in its NPV estimates.

Monte Carlo Simulation Analysis

Sensitivity analysis, as practiced by the fertilizer company described above, is informal in the sense that no probabilities are attached to the likelihood of various outcomes. *Monte Carlo simulation analysis* represents a refinement that does employ probability estimates. In this section, we first describe how *decision trees* can be used to attach probabilities to different outcomes, and then we illustrate how full-scale computer simulation can be employed to analyze major projects.

Decision Trees

Most important decisions are not made once and for all at one point in time. Rather, decisions are made in stages. For example, a petroleum firm considering the possibility of expanding into agricultural chemicals might take the following steps:

1.   Spend $100,000 for a survey of supply-demand conditions in the agricultural chemical industry.
2.   If the survey results are favorable, spend $500,000 on a pilot plant to investigate production methods.
3.   Depending on the costs estimated from the pilot study and the demand potential from the market study, either abandon the project, build a large plant, or build a small one.

Thus, the final decision actually is made in stages, with subsequent decisions depending on the results of previous decisions.

The sequence of events can be mapped out like the branches of a tree, hence the name *decision tree*. As an example, consider Figure 17B.1. There it is assumed that the petroleum company has completed its industry supply-demand analysis and pilot plant study and has determined that it should proceed to develop a full-scale production facility. The firm must decide whether to build a large plant or a small one. The estimated probabilities of demand levels for the plant's products are 50 percent for high demand, 30 percent for medium demand, and 20 percent for low demand. Depending on demand, net cash flows

Figure 17B.1   Illustrative Decision Tree

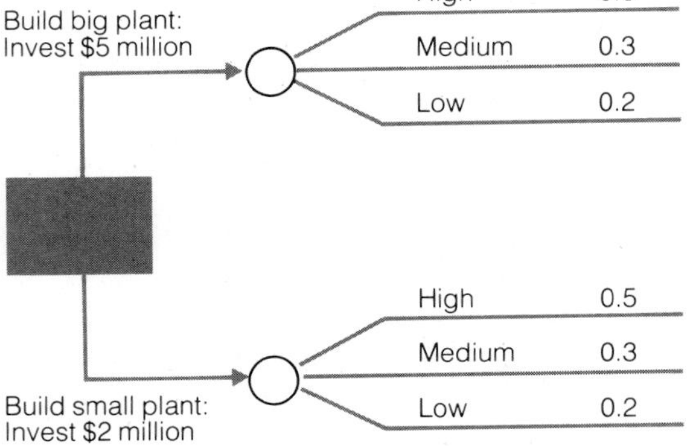

Action (1)	Demand Conditions (2)	Probability (3)	Present Value of Cash Flows (4)	Less Initial Cost (5)	Possible NPV (4) - (5) (6)	Probable NPV (3) × (6) (7)
Build big plant: Invest $5 million	High	0.5	$8,800,000	$5,000,000	$3,800,000	$1,900,000
	Medium	0.3	$3,500,000	$5,000,000	($1,500,000)	($450,000)
	Low	0.2	$1,400,000	$5,000,000	($3,600,000)	($720,000)
					Expected NPV	$730,000
Build small plant: Invest $2 million	High	0.5	$2,600,000	$2,000,000	$600,000	$300,000
	Medium	0.3	$2,400,000	$2,000,000	$400,000	$120,000
	Low	0.2	$1,400,000	$2,000,000	($600,000)	($120,000)
					Expected NPV	$300,000

(sales revenues minus operating costs, all discounted to the present) will range from $8.8 million to $1.4 million if a large plant is built and from $2.6 million to $1.4 million if a small plant is built.

The initial costs of the large and small plants are shown in Column 5 of the figure; when these investment outlays are subtracted from the PV of cash flows, the result is the set of possible NPV's shown in Column 6. One, but only one, of these NPV's will actually occur. Finally, we multiply Column 6 by Column 3 to obtain Column 7, and the sums in Column 7 give the expected NPV's of the large and small plants.

Because the expected NPV of the larger plant ($730,000) is larger than that of the small plant ($300,000), should the decision be to build the large plant? Perhaps, but not necessarily. Notice that the range of outcomes is greater if the large plant is built, with the actual NPV's (Column 6 in Figure 17B.1) varying from $3.8 million to *minus* $3.6 million. However, a range of only $600,000 to minus $600,000 exists for the small plant.

The decision tree illustrated in Figure 17B.1 is quite simple; in actual use, the trees are frequently far more complex and involve a number of sequential decision points. As an example of a more complex tree, consider Figure 17B.2. The boxes numbered 1, 2, and so on are *decision points*, that is, instances when the firm must choose between alternatives, while the circles represent the possible actual outcomes, one of which will follow these decisions. At Decision Point 1, the firm has three choices: to invest $3 million in a large plant, to invest $1.3 million in a small plant, or to spend $100,000 on market research. If the large plant is built, the firm follows the upper branch, and its position has been fixed — it can only hope that demand will be high. If it builds the small plant, then it follows the lower branch. If demand is low, no further action is required. If demand is high, Decision Point 2 is reached, and the firm must either do nothing or else expand the plant at a cost of another $2.2 million. (Thus, if it obtains a large plant through expansion, the cost is $500,000 greater than if it had built the large plant in the first place.)

If the decision at Point 1 is to pay $100,000 for more information, the firm moves to the center branch. The research modifies the firm's information about potential demand. Initially, the probabilities were 70 percent for high demand and 30 percent for low demand. The research survey will show either favorable (positive) or unfavorable (negative) demand prospects. If they are positive, we assume that the probability for high final demand will be 87 percent and that for low demand will be 13 percent; if the research yields negative results, the odds on high final demand are only 35 percent and those for low demand are 65 percent. These results will, of course, influence the firm's decision as to whether to build a large or a small plant.

If the firm builds a large plant and demand is high, then sales and profits will be large. However, if it builds a large plant and demand is weak, sales will be low, and losses, rather than profits, will be incurred. On the other hand, if it builds a small plant and demand is high, sales and profits will be lower than they could have been had a large plant been built, but the chances of losses in the event of low demand will be eliminated. Thus, the decision to build the large plant has greater variability than the one to build the small plant. The decision to commission the research is, in effect, an expenditure to reduce the degree of uncertainty in the decision on which plant to build; the research provides additional information on the probability of high versus low demand, thus lowering the level of uncertainty.

The decision tree in Figure 17B.2 is incomplete in that no dollar outcomes are assigned to the various situations. If this step were taken, along the lines shown in the last two columns of Figure 17B.1, then expected values could be obtained for each of the alternative actions. These expected values could then be used to aid the decision maker in choosing among the alternatives.

Figure 17B.2 Decision Tree with Multiple Decision Points

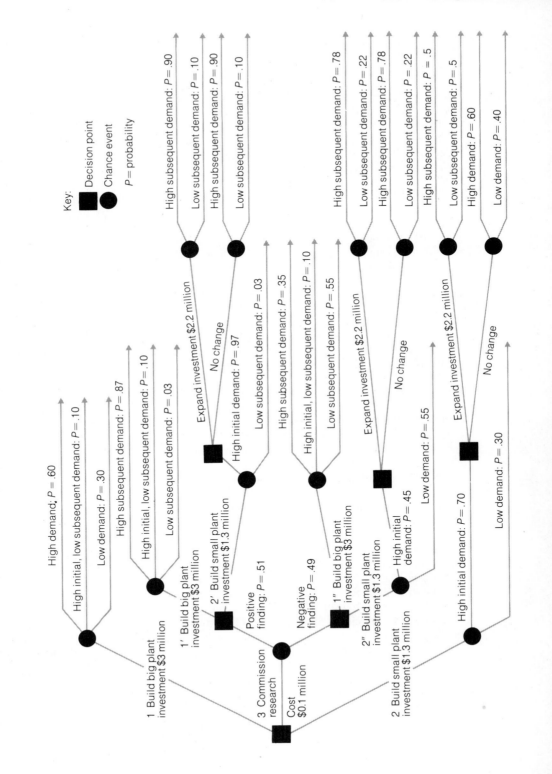

Computer Simulation

The concepts embodied in decision tree analysis can be extended to computer simulation. To illustrate the technique, let us consider a proposal to build a new textile plant. The cost of the plant is not known for certain, although it is expected to run about $150 million. If no problems are encountered, the cost can be as low as $125 million, while an unfortunate series of events — strikes, unprojected increases in materials costs, technical problems, and the like — could result in the investment outlay running as high as $225 million.

Revenues from the new facility, which will operate for many years, will depend on population growth and income in the region, competition, developments in synthetic fabrics research, and textile import quotas. Operating costs will depend on production efficiency, materials, labor cost trends, and the like. Since both sales revenues and operating costs are uncertain, annual profits are also uncertain.

Assuming that probability distributions can be assigned to each of the major cost and revenue determinants, a computer program can be constructed to simulate what is likely to happen. In effect, the computer selects one value at random from each of the relevant distributions, combines it with other values selected from the other distributions, and produces an estimated profit and net present value or rate of return on investment.[1] This particular profit and rate of return occur, of course, only for the particular combination of values selected during this trial. The computer goes on to select other sets of values and to compute other profits and rates of return repeatedly, for perhaps several hundred trials. A count is kept of the number of times each rate of return is computed, and when the computer runs are completed, the frequency with which the various rates of return occurred can be plotted as a frequency distribution.

The procedure is illustrated in Figures 17B.3 and 17B.4. Figure 17B.3 is a flowchart outlining the simulation procedure described above, while Figure 17B.4 illustrates the frequency distribution of rates of return generated by such a simulation for two alternative projects, X and Y, each with an expected cost of $20 million. The expected rate of return on Investment X is 15 percent and that of Investment Y is 20 percent. However, these are only the *average* rates of return generated by the computer; simulated rates range from -10 percent to $+45$ percent for Investment Y and from 5 to 25 percent for Investment X. The standard deviation generated for X is only 4 percentage points — 68 percent of the computer runs had rates of return between 11 and 19 percent — while that for Y is 12 percentage points. Clearly, then, Investment Y has greater potential for estimation errors than Investment X.

The computer simulation has provided us with both an estimate of the expected internal rates of return on the two projects and an estimate of their relative estimation errors. A decision about which alternative should be chosen can now be made.

Very little literature has been written on how to adjust NPV calculations so that known estimation errors can be taken into account. However, the interested reader is referred to Smidt [1979] for an analysis of the issue. If the true cash flows and true risk-adjusted discount rate are known without error, then the NPV of the project is all that is needed to make a correct decision. However, if errors are made in estimating these inputs, then it is necessary to take any potential bias and error into account. Smidt [1979] gives an example where management believes that projects of a given type are drawn from a normal distribution where the mean is -50 and the standard deviation is $33.33. This implies that 93.3

---

[1]If the variables are not independent, then conditional probabilities must be employed. For example, if demand is weak, then both sales in units and sales prices are likely to be low, and these interrelationships must be taken into account in the simulation.

Figure 17B.3   Simulation for Investment Planning

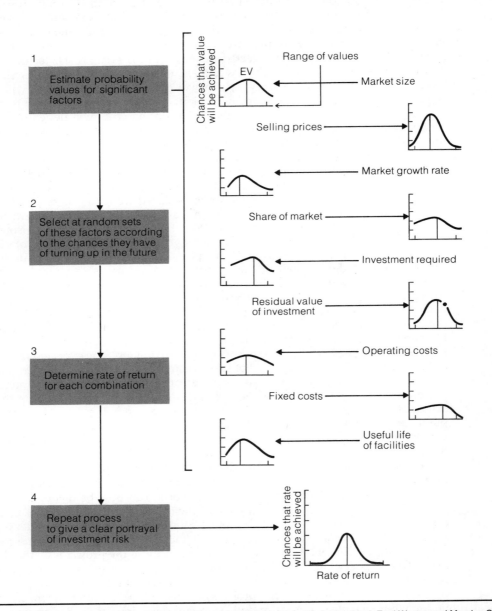

Source: Adapted from David B. Hertz, "Uncertainty and Investment Selection," in J. Fred Weston and Maurice Goudzwaard, eds., *The Treasurer's Handbook* (Homewood, Ill.: Dow Jones-Irwin, 1976), p. 408. © 1976 by Dow Jones-Irwin.

Figure 17B.4   Expected Rates of Return on Investments X and Y

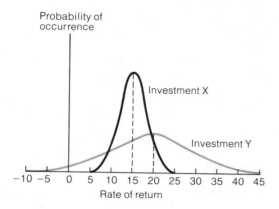

percent of the project proposals are considered to have negative NPV's. Management also believes that project analysts have a routine bias of $+25 in their forecasts of NPV and that the standard deviation of their forecasts is $25. Smidt then shows that the *minimum* acceptable NPV for projects under these circumstances is not $0, but rather is $53. Thus, in our example illustrated by Figure 17B.4, it is not immediately obvious that Investment Y should be favored over Investment X. Although Investment Y has a higher expected internal rate of return, it also has higher estimation errors.

Problems

17B.1 In computer simulation, the computer makes a large number of trials to show what the various outcomes of a particular decision might be if the decision could be made many times under the same conditions. In practice, the decision will be made only once, so how can simulation results be useful to the decision maker?

17B.2 Your firm is considering the purchase of a tractor. It has been established that this tractor will cost $32,000, will produce revenues in the neighborhood of $10,000 (before tax), and will be depreciated via straight line to zero in eight years. The board of directors, however, is having a heated debate as to whether the tractor can be expected to last eight years. Specifically, Wayne Brown insists that he knows of some that have lasted only five years. Tom Miller agrees with Brown but argues that it is more likely that the tractor will give eight years of service. Brown agrees. Finally, Laura Evans says she has seen some last as long as ten years. Given the discussion, the board asks you to prepare a sensitivity analysis to ascertain how important the uncertainty about the life of the tractor is. Assume a 40 percent tax rate on both income and capital loss, zero salvage value, and a cost of capital of 10 percent.

17B.3 You have an investment opportunity for which the outlay and cash flows are uncertain. Analysis has produced the subjective probability assessments given in Table

P17B.3. Let the cost of capital be 12 percent, life expectancy be ten years, and salvage value be zero.

Table P17B.3

Subjective Probability Estimates

Outlay		Annual Cash Flow	
Probability	Amount	Probability	Amount
0.4	$ 80,000	0.2	$14,000
0.3	100,000	0.5	16,000
0.2	120,000	0.3	18,000
0.1	140,000		

a) Construct a decision tree for this investment to show probabilities, payoffs, and expected NPV.
b) Calculate the expected NPV, again using expected cash flow and expected outlay.
c) What is the probability of and the NPV of the worst possible outcome?
d) What is the probability of and the NPV of the best possible outcome?
e) Compute the probability that this will be a good investment.

Selected References

Brumelle, Shelby L., and Schwab, Bernhard, "Capital Budgeting with Uncertain Future Opportunities: A Markovian Approach," *Journal of Financial and Quantitative Analysis*, 7 (January 1973), pp. 111-122.

Hillier, Frederick S., "The Derivation of Probabilistic Information for the Evaluation of Risky Investments," . *Management Science*, 9 (April 1963), pp. 443-457.

Kryzanowski, Lawrence; Lusztig, Peter; and Schwab, Bernhard, "Monte Carlo Simulation and Capital Expenditure Decisions — A Case Study," *Engineering Economist*, 18 (Fall 1972), pp. 31-48.

Smidt, Seymour, "A Bayesian Analysis of Project Selection and of Post Audit Evaluations," *Journal of Finance*, 34 (June 1979), pp. 675-688.

Chapter 18 Options on Risky Assets

Introduction to Options

Options are contracts that give their holder the right to buy (or sell) an asset at a predetermined price, called the *striking* or *exercise price*, for a given period of time. For example, on December 6, 19X6, a call option on Dow Chemical common stock gave its holder the right to buy one share of common at an exercise price of $45 until July 19X7. The price of a share of Dow was $39½ and the call option sold for $1.75. This would be referred to as an *out-of-the-money option* — the exercise price was more than the current price of the common stock. An *in-the-money option* has an exercise price that is less than the current price of the common stock. An option to buy the Dow common stock at $35 when the common was selling at $39½ would be an in-the-money option; it would sell for ($39½ − $35) = $4½ plus the aforementioned premium of about $1.75, or at about $6.25.

In recent years, Option Pricing Models (OPM) have been derived which enable us to predict the market prices of options with a great deal of accuracy.[1] These models are applicable to a wide range of option-type contracts, including the warrants and convertibles discussed in Chapter 28.

The considerable increase in interest in options and option pricing has been associated with the development of new options markets and important new theoretical developments. In April 1973, organized trading in call options began on the Chicago Board Options Exchange (CBOE), followed by call option trading on the American Stock Exchange (AMEX options). The path-breaking paper by Black and Scholes [1973] appeared at about the same time. In addition to deriving the general equilibrium option pricing equation and conducting empirical tests, Black and Scholes suggested implications of option pricing that have significance for many other important aspects of business finance.

Black and Scholes observed that option pricing principles can be used to value other complex contingent claim assets, such as the equity of a levered firm. From this viewpoint, the shareholders of a firm have a call that gives them the right to buy back the firm from the bondholders by paying the face value of the bonds at maturity. A number of important applications of the Option Pricing Model were then made. As observed by Smith [1976] in his comprehensive review article, "the model is also applied by Merton [1974] to analyze the effects of risk on the value of corporate debt; by Galai and Masulis [1976] to examine the effect of mergers, acquisitions, scale expansions, and spin-offs on the relative values of the debt and equity claims of the firm; by Ingersoll [1976] to value the shares of dual purpose funds; and by Black [1976] to value commodity options, forward contracts, and future contracts."[2]

---

[1]Black and Scholes [1973]; Merton [1973].

[2]Smith [1976], p. 5.

Because of the large number of additional areas on which the option pricing model provides new insights, it is useful to develop an understanding of the basic ideas involved. First, some of the fundamental characteristics of options contracts will be developed. Second, some of the basic relationships will be developed in an intuitive way as a background for the presentation and application of the binomial Option Pricing Model. Third, the relationship between the OPM and the CAPM will be developed. Fourth, empirical tests of the OPM will be reviewed. And, finally, applications of the OPM for corporate finance will be discussed.

Four Building Blocks of Financial Contracts

All financial contracts can be constructed with various combinations of only four basic building blocks: stocks, risk-free bonds, call options, and put options. Figure 18.1 shows payoffs for put and call options. The vertical axis measures your change in wealth after T years. The horizontal axis measures the change in the price of the underlying asset (a share of common stock).

Suppose you buy a one-year call option on a share of du Pont stock. The stock sells for $S_0 = \$30$ and the exercise price is $X = \$30$. So, $S_0 = X$ and the option is said to be "at-the-money." A *call option* is a contract which pays its holder nothing if the option expires with the stock price less than the exercise price (if $S \leq X$), or the difference between the stock price and the exercise price if the option finishes in-the-money (that is, if $S > X$). Mathematically, we can write the option value at maturity as[3]

$$C_T = \text{MAX} [0, S_T - X]. \tag{18.1}$$

Figure 18.1   Payoffs from Put and Call Options where $S_0 = X$

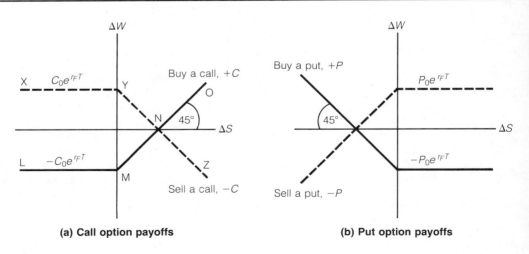

(a) Call option payoffs

(b) Put option payoffs

---

[3]Whenever we want to denote the current value of a security, we will use a subscript zero, S_0. The value at maturity will have a subscript T, S_T; and the value at intermediate dates (or the general value) will have no subscript, S.

Suppose that the call option on du Pont stock costs $3. If the change in the stock price, ΔS, in Figure 18.1(a), is negative, then the change in your wealth, ΔW, measured at the end of one year is[4]

$$\Delta W = -C_0 e^{r_F T}.$$

If the risk-free rate, r_F, is 10 percent and the time interval, T, is one year, then the change in your wealth is the loss of the future value of the $3 which you paid for the call option.

$$\Delta W = -(\$3)e^{.1(1)} = -\$3(1.10517) = -\$3.32.$$

In other words, if your option expires out-of-the-money, you will lose the future value of what you originally paid to buy the option. This is shown as line segment LM in Figure 18.1(a).

If the stock price rises, your wealth will rise $1.00 for each dollar increase in the stock price, ΔS. For example, if the stock price rises $3.32, then your end-of-period gain, that is, $3.32, exactly equals the future value of the price you paid for the option, and your net change in wealth is zero. This is Point N in Figure 18.1(a). Line segment MNO has a slope of 45° because $\Delta W = \Delta S$ whenever $\Delta S > 0$. The entire line LMNO represents your end-of-period wealth if you buy one call option.

The line XYNZ in Figure 18.1(a) represents the payoffs from writing (that is, selling) a call option. These payoffs are exactly the opposite of those from buying a call.

A *put option* is the mirror image of a call. Buying a put option gives you the right to sell one share of stock at the exercise price. If the stock price falls (that is, if $\Delta S < 0$), a put option finishes in-the-money and your payoff is $X - S_T$. If the stock price rises, the put will expire worthless. Mathematically, the end-of-period payoffs for a put contract are

$$P_T = \text{MAX } [0, X - S_T]. \tag{18.2}$$

The end-of-period payoffs from buying a put are illustrated by the solid line in Figure 18.1(b), and the payoffs from selling a put are shown by the dotted line.

Put and call options are two of the building blocks from which all financial contracts are constructed. The other two are stocks and riskless bonds. Their end-of-period payoffs are illustrated in Figure 18.2. The solid line in Panel (a) shows that if you own the stock, your change in wealth increases dollar for dollar with the stock price change. If you go short (that is, sell) the stock, your wealth falls for each dollar increase in the stock price. Figure 18.2(b) illustrates the payoffs for a pure discount riskless bond. "Riskless" means that the bond pays off its face value in every state of nature, and "pure discount" implies that there are no interest payments during the life of the bond. If the face value of a pure discount risk-free bond is $\$B_T$, then its present value is

$$B_0 = B_T e^{-r_F T}. \tag{18.3}$$

The solid line in Figure 18.2(b) gives your end-of-period payoff if you lend $\$B_0$ (that is, if you buy a riskless bond). The dashed line is your payoff if you sell a bond (that is, if you

---

[4]We are using continuous compounding. Therefore, the future value factor is $E^{r_F T}$ instead of $(1 + r_F)^T$. See Chapter 5 if you need to brush up on continuous compounding.

Figure 18.2   End-of-Period Payoffs for Common Stock and Riskless Bonds

---

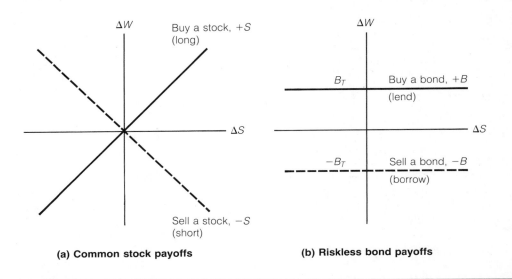

(a) **Common stock payoffs**   (b) **Riskless bond payoffs**

---

borrow). Note that these payoffs are represented by horizontal lines because the bond price is independent of changes in the stock price.

Now that we have covered the four basic building blocks, we can put them together according to the following relationship:

$$S + P = B + C. \tag{18.4}$$

A long position in one share of stock and one put option (with an exercise price of X) written on that stock gives exactly the same payoff as a bond (with face value X) and a call option (with exercise price X) written on the same stock.

Equation 18.4 is valid no matter how it is rearranged. For example, suppose we wish to create a riskless position out of one share of stock, a call, and a put option. Rearranging Equation 18.4, we have

$$B = S + P - C.$$

We own one share of stock, one put option, and we have sold one call option. The resulting portfolio is shown in two steps in Figure 18.3. Panel (a) combines a long position in one share of stock and one put option, assuming that $S_0 = X$. The dashed line is the vertical sum of the two solid lines. For example, when the stock price change is zero, the change in wealth resulting from the stock is Point 0, and for the put option, it is Point X. The sum of the two is $0 + X = X$. Figure 18.3(b) combines the $S + P$ position with a short position in one call contract $(-C)$. The solid line is the vertical sum of the two, and we can

Figure 18.3 Graphical Proof that $B = S + P - C$

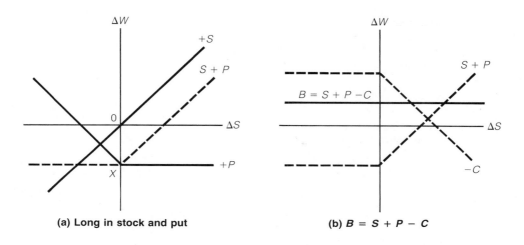

(a) Long in stock and put

(b) $B = S + P - C$

see that the result is a constant payout no matter how the stock price changes. Hence, a perfectly riskless position can be obtained by buying a share of stock, buying a put, and selling a call.

Put-Call Parity

If we restrict our analysis to *European* options, which may be exercised only at maturity, rather than *American* options, which may be exercised any time at all, then we can use Equation 18.4 to develop *put-call parity*. This relationship, derived by Stoll [1969], shows that for European options, there is a fixed relationship between the market price of put and call options written on the same security and with the same maturity date and exercise price.

As in the previous section of this chapter, suppose we have a portfolio where we purchase one share of stock and one put option and then sell one call option. Both options are written on a share of du Pont stock, which sells for $30. Also, they have the same maturity date, T, and the same exercise price, X, which is equal to the stock price, $30. We already know from Equation 18.4 that this portfolio is equivalent to a riskless bond. No matter what the stock price is at time T (maturity of the options), the portfolio will pay off $X (which is also equal to B_T, the face value of the bond).

At maturity, all states-of-the-world can be divided into those where the stock price is less than the exercise price, $S < X$, and those where it is greater than or equal to the exercise price, $S \geq X$. If the stock price is less than the exercise price, the portfolio payoff is

If $S < X$:

		If $S = \$25$
1. You hold the stock and, therefore, receive	S	25.00
2. the call option is worthless and	0	0.00
3. the put option is worth	$X - S$	5.00
4. therefore, your net payoff is	X	30.00

Alternatively, if $S \geq X$:

		If $S = \$35$
1. You hold the stock and receive	S	35.00
2. your short position in the call is worth	$-(S - X)$	−5.00
3. and the put option is worthless	0	0.00
4. therefore, your net payoff is	X	30.00

No matter what state-of-the-world occurs at maturity, the portfolio will be worth X. Consequently, the payoff from the portfolio is completely risk free, and we can discount its value at the risk-free rate. Using continuous discounting, this is

$$S_0 + P_0 - C_0 = Xe^{-r_F T} = B_0,$$

or

$$C_0 - P_0 = S_0 - Xe^{-r_F T}. \tag{18.5}$$

If $T = 1$ year and $r_F = 10\%$, then the current value of a pure discount bond with a $30 face value is

$$B_0 = Xe^{-r_F T}$$

$$= \$30.00 \, e^{-.1(1)}$$

$$= \$30.00(.9048)$$

$$= \$27.15.$$

But this is also equal to $S_0 + P_0 - C_0$. We can use the numbers in our example to solve for the difference between the call and put values:

$$C_0 - P_0 = S_0 - Xe^{-r_F T}$$

$$= \$30.00 - \$27.15$$

$$= \$2.85,$$

and if the call is worth $3.00, the American put must be valued at $3.00 − $2.85 = $.15.

Equation 18.5 is called the *put-call parity* relationship for European options. It is particularly useful because once we have derived an expression which allows us to price European calls, then we can use put-call parity to automatically price European puts as well. No separate derivation of a European put pricing formula is necessary.

A special case of the put-call parity relationship occurs when the exercise price is set equal to the stock price when the options are written. As long as $S_0 = X$, Equation 18.5 reduces to

$$C_0 - P_0 = S_0(1 - e^{-r_F T}) > 0.$$

Thus, when $S_0 = X$ (as was assumed when drawing Figure 18.3), the call price must be greater than the put price.

Valuing a Call Option

A call option is a contingent claim security which depends on the value and riskiness of the underlying security on which it is written. We do not need an equilibrium theory of option pricing. All we need to know are the terms of the call contract and the stochastic process which describes the behavior of stock prices over time.

Intuition behind Five Factors Affecting a Call Option

Suppose that on October 4, 1977, you bought a call option written on the common stock of Digital Equipment. The option was to expire on the third Friday in April 1978 (199 days from the date of purchase).[5] Its exercise price was $45.00 and the price of one share of Digital Equipment was $46.75. What are the five factors which lead you to pay $6.00 (the actual closing price) for the call option?

When you buy the call for $6.00 on October 4, you are betting that the stock will be worth more than $45.00 on the third Friday in April. The current stock price is $46.75. If it were higher, say $50.00, you would be willing to pay more for the call option. Clearly, the call value increases with the stock price. In fact, we can use this intuition to establish some boundaries for the value of a call option. If the option is still alive, it must have a positive value because there is always some chance (however slim) that it will mature in-the-money. Therefore, one boundary is

$$C \geq 0. \tag{18.6a}$$

Next, the call price cannot exceed the value of the underlying stock.

$$C \leq S. \tag{18.6b}$$

And finally, the call price can never be less than its value if exercised, that is, the difference between the stock price and the exercise price.

$$C \geq S - X. \tag{18.6c}$$

---

[5]All Chicago Board of Option (CBOE) contracts expire on the third Friday of their month of maturity and may be exercised until noon on Saturday.

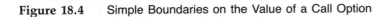

Figure 18.4   Simple Boundaries on the Value of a Call Option

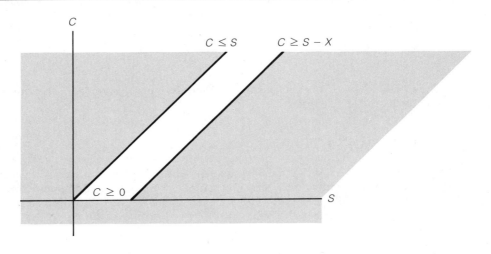

These three boundaries are illustrated in Figure 18.4. The value of the call option must lie in the unshaded area. Note that the value of the call option is graphed on the vertical axis and the value of the underlying stock along the horizontal axis.

The next most obvious factor affecting the call value is the exercise price. The lower it is, the more valuable the call will be. In the most extreme case, the exercise price would be zero and the call would be worth as much as the stock because the boundaries represented by Equations 18.6b and 18.6c would collapse to a single line with $C = S$.

Investors always prefer longer-lived options. The reason is that with more time to maturity, there is a greater chance that the stock price will climb higher above the exercise price. In fact, a call option with an infinite maturity date will have the same value as the stock, regardless of the option's exercise price.

In addition to the stock price, the exercise price, and the time to maturity, there are two other important (but less obvious) factors which affect the option's value: the variance across time of the price of the underlying asset (the common stock) and the risk-free rate of return. The holder of a call option will prefer more variance to less in the price of the stock. The greater the variance, the greater will be the probability that the stock price will exceed the exercise price on the upside while on the downside the minimum option (and stock) value is zero. Hence, a greater variance increases the probability of winning with a call option but does not affect the downside loss.

The value of a higher variance is illustrated in the example given in Table 18.1. Payoffs to the option on the low-variance stock are $0, $5, and $15 (if the exercise price is $45). Payoffs to the option on the high-variance stock are $0, $5, and $35. No matter what exercise price is given, the two options will be worthless when $S \leq X$, but the call option on the high-variance stock will be worth more when $S > X$. Even a risk-averse investor

---

Table 18.1   The Value of Higher Variance to a Call Option Holder

State of Nature	Probability	Low-Variance Stock	Payoff if $X = \$45$	High-Variance Stock	Payoff if $X = \$45$
Horrid	.2	$40	$ 0	$20	0
Average	.6	50	5	50	5
Great	.2	60	15	80	35

---

will prefer the option on the high-variance stock because its payoffs are always greater than or equal to the payoffs to the option on the low-variance stock.

The final factor determining the value of a European call is the risk-free rate of interest. Of all the factors, it is the least intuitive. It was not until Black and Scholes [1973] proved that it is possible to create a risk-free hedge portfolio consisting of a long position in the common stock and a short position in call options written on it that the role of the risk-free rate was fully understood.

Another way of understanding the effect of the risk-free rate on the value of a call option is to prove the following theorem.[6]

> *Theorem*: An American call on a nondividend-paying stock will not be exercised before the call expiration date.[7]

An *American call* may be exercised, at the discretion of its holder, at any time up to and including maturity.[8] It will, however, not be exercised until maturity because it is worth more in the marketplace than if it were exercised. To prove this, let us compare two portfolios. As shown in Table 18.2, Portfolio A is composed of one European call option

---

Table 18.2

		Portfolio Value Given Stock Price at T	
Portfolio	Current Value	$S_T \leq X$	$S_T > X$
A	$C_0 + X B_0$	$0 + X$	$S_T - X + X$
B	S_0	S_T	S_T
Relationship between the terminal values of A and B		$V_A > V_B$	$V_A = V_B$

---

[6]This proof is attributable to Merton [1973].

[7]The theorem applies only to nondividend-paying stocks because American options on the CBOE are not dividend protected. A dividend payment represents a discrete jump in the stock price. When the stock goes ex-dividend, its price falls by (approximately) the value of the dividend, and, consequently, the value of a call option will also fall. If you know that your option will fall in price on the day the stock goes ex-dividend, your only protection is to exercise your option today. See Roll [1977] and Geske [1979b] for details on how to price options on dividend-paying stocks.

[8]We shall adopt the convention that European puts and calls are denoted with an uppercase P or C while American options are written with a lowercase p or c.

(written on one share of stock and having an exercise price X and a maturity date T) plus one zero coupon bond for each dollar of exercise price. For example, if the exercise price is $45.00, then the portfolio will have 45 pure discount bonds. Each bond pays off $1 with certainty at its maturity date, T. Portfolio B is simply one share of stock with a current value, S_0.

The third line in Table 18.2 shows that Portfolio A has a payout greater than or equal to Portfolio B in all states of nature. If the stock price is less than or equal to the exercise price ($S_T \leq X$) at maturity, the call is worthless and the bonds pay off $X. Since $X > S_T$, Portfolio A is worth more than Portfolio B. Alternately, if the option finishes in-the-money (that is, $S_T > X$), then the option is worth $S_T - X$, the bonds are worth X, and adding these together, we see that Portfolio A is worth S_T. But Portfolio B is worth exactly the same amount; hence, whenever $S_T > X$, the two portfolios have the same value.

If Portfolio A has a future payoff which is always greater than or equal to that of Portfolio B, then the current value of A must be greater than the value of B.

$$C_0 + X B_0 \geq S_0.$$

If we subtract $X B_0$ from both sides and recognize that a call option cannot have a negative value (see Equation 18.6a), then we can rewrite the above restriction as

$$C_0 \geq \text{MAX } [0, S_0 - X B_0]. \tag{18.7}$$

We also know, from Equation 18.3, that a bond which pays off a face value of ($B_T = \$1$) will have a present value which is

$$B_0 = B_T e^{-r_F T} = (\$1)e^{-r_F T}.$$

Substituting this into 18.7, we have

$$C_0 \geq \text{MAX } [0, S_0 - Xe^{-r_F T}]. \tag{18.8}$$

Equation 18.8 says that the market value of a European call option must be no less than the current stock price minus the discounted value of the exercise price. An American call must be worth at least as much because it can be exercised anytime, not just at maturity. Consequently, if we designate an American call with a lowercase c_0 and a European call with an uppercase C_0, we can write

$$c_0 \geq C_0 \geq \text{MAX } [0, S_0 - Xe^{-r_F T}]. \tag{18.9}$$

There are three important conclusions to be drawn from Equation 18.9. First, an American option on a nondividend-paying stock will never be exercised early because its value if exercised is only $S_0 - X$ while its value if sold in the marketplace must be at least as great as $S_0 - Xe^{-r_F T}$. For example, using the numbers given earlier for the Digital Equipment stock, the value if exercised was

$$S_0 - X = \$46.75 - \$45.00 = \$1.75,$$

Figure 18.5   Further Limitation of the Feasible Set of Call Option Prices

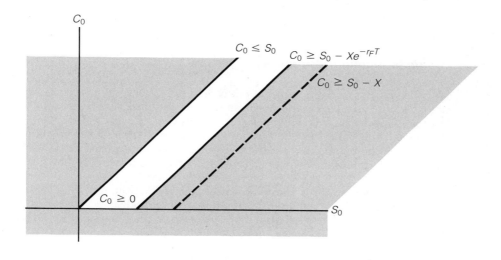

and the lower bound on the market value was[9]

$$S_o - Xe^{-r_FT} = \$46.75 - \$45(.96676) = \$3.25.$$

Clearly, the option was worth more if it is not exercised—it was actually worth $6.00.

The second important result from Equation 18.9 is that it shifts the lower bound on the value of a call option to the left, so that the value of a call option is higher for a given stock price, S. This is illustrated in Figure 18.5 by the solid line labeled $C_0 \geq S_0 - Xe^{-r_FT}$. If you ever find a call option on a nondividend-paying stock which is priced so that it violates one of these boundary conditions, then you have an opportunity to make an easy arbitrage profit.

Finally, the third result from Equation 18.9 is the relationship between the present value of a call option and the risk-free rate. The call must be worth more than the current stock price, S_0, minus the discounted value of the exercise price, Xe^{-r_FT}. If the risk-free rate increases (and nothing else changes), then the call must be worth more because the discounted present value of the exercise price declines.

We can now summarize the five factors which affect the value of a call option. Its value increases with an increase in the price of the underlying common stock, with the time to maturity, with the variance of the underlying security, and with the risk-free rate. It decreases with an increase in the exercise price. These relationships are shown in

[9]The risk-free interest rate was 6.2 percent, and 199 days to maturity translates into 199/365 = .5452 years.

Equation 18.10:

$$C_0 = f(\overset{+}{S_0},\ \overset{-}{X},\ \overset{+}{T},\ \overset{+}{\sigma_S^2},\ \overset{+}{r_F}).$$ **(18.10)**

A Simple Binomial Approach

We shall discuss two different but equivalent approaches to an exact formula for pricing call options. Historically, the first was derived by Black and Scholes [1973], but a more intuitive approach was later developed by Cox, Ross, and Rubinstein [1979] and Rendleman and Bartter [1979]. Besides being easier to understand, the binomial approach provides solutions not only for the European call option price but also for more difficult American put option prices, which (until recently) had to be solved by numerical approximation.

   Before developing the analysis, it is useful to spell out in detail the assumptions which have been used while developing the option pricing model. As we shall point out later on, they are somewhat less restrictive than those used (in Chapter 17) to derive the CAPM. We assume

- Frictionless capital markets with no transactions costs or taxes and with information simultaneously and costlessly available to all individuals.
- No restrictions on short sales.
- Asset prices obey stationary stochastic processes across time.
- The risk-free rate is constant across time.
- Underlying assets pay no dividends (or cash disbursements of any kind).

Most of these assumptions can be relaxed without changing the basics of the Option Pricing Model (OPM).

   In order to develop the binomial model, assume a one-period world where the stock price can move up or down from its current level. This is illustrated in Figure 18.6. In order

---

Figure 18.6   A One-Period Binomial Stochastic Process

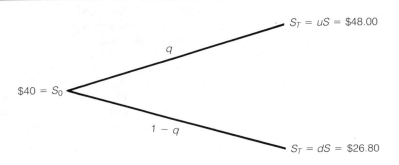

to provide a concrete example, suppose that

$$
\begin{aligned}
S_0 &= \ \$40 = \text{the current stock price} \\
q &= \ .5 = \text{the probability that the stock price will move up} \\
1 + r_F &= \ 1.1 = \text{one plus the risk-free rate of interest} \\
u &= \ 1.2 = \text{the multiplicative upward movement in the stock price } (u > 1 + r_F > 1) \\
d &= \ .67 = \text{the multiplicative downward movement in the stock price } (d < 1).
\end{aligned}
$$

At the end of one time period, the stock price may increase to uS (that is, $48.00) with probability $q = .5$ or decrease to dS (that is, $26.80) with probability $1 - q = .5$. Note that the downward multiplier for the stock, d, must be less than one, and that it need not be related to the upward movement (that is, $d \neq 1/u$). If $d < 1$, then the stock price cannot fall below zero no matter how many time periods are eventually added. If there are n periods, then

$$
\lim_{n \to \infty} d^n = 0 \text{ if } 0 \le d < 1.
$$

The upward stock price movement, u, and the downward movement, d, are defined so that there is no upper limit to the stock price, but its lower limit is zero. This reflects the limited liability feature of common stock. If you buy a share of stock, you can lose what you paid but not more than that. We also require that $u > (1 + r_F) \ge 1 > d$. If these inequalities did not hold, then riskless arbitrage opportunities would exist.

Now, imagine a call option, C, with an exercise price of $X = \$38$ which is written on the stock. The payoffs for the call are shown in Figure 18.7. There is a 50-50 chance of ending up with $10 or $0. The question is, how much would we pay for the call right now?

In order to answer this question, we begin by constructing a risk-free hedge portfolio composed of one share of stock, S_0, and m units of a call option written against the stock.[10]

Figure 18.7   Payoffs for a One-Period Call Option

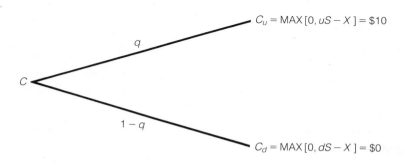

$C_u = \text{MAX}[0, uS - X] = \$10$

q

C

$1 - q$

$C_d = \text{MAX}[0, dS - X] = \$0$

---

[10]The hedge portfolio could also consist of a long position in m units of the call and a short position in one share. The analytical results would not change.

Figure 18.8   The Payoffs for a Risk-Free Hedge

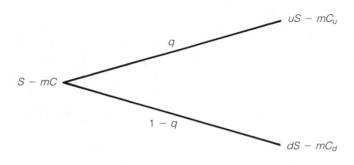

Figure 18.8 shows the payoffs for the hedge portfolio. We can find the correct hedge ratio, m, by equating the end-of-period payoffs,

$$uS - mC_u = dS - mC_d,$$

and then solving for m, the number of call options to be written against the share of stock.

$$m = \frac{S(u - d)}{C_u - C_d}. \tag{18.11}$$

Substituting the numbers from our example, we see that the proper hedge ratio is

$$m = \frac{\$40(1.2 - .67)}{\$10 - \$0} = 2.12.$$

Thus, the riskless hedge portfolio consists of buying one share of stock and writing 2.12 call options against it. Table 18.3 uses our numerical example to show that the hedge portfolio has the same payoff in either state of nature.

    Because the hedge portfolio is constructed to be riskless, we can multiply the current value of the portfolio by one plus the risk-free rate in order to obtain the end-of-period

Table 18.3   Hedge Portfolio Payoffs

State of Nature	Portfolio	Payoff
Favorable	$uS - mC_u$	$1.2(\$40) - 2.12(\$10) = \$26.80.$
Unfavorable	$dS - mC_d$	$.67(\$40) - 2.12(\$0) = \$26.80.$

payoff. Mathematically, this is

$$(1 + r_F)(S - mC) = uS - mC_u.$$

Solving for C, the value of the call option, we have

$$C = \frac{S(1 + r_F - u) + mC_u}{m(1 + r_F)}.$$

Substituting the hedge ratio, m, into the equation and rearranging terms, we can rewrite the value of the call option as

$$C = \left[C_u\left(\frac{1 + r_F - d}{u - d}\right) + C_d\left(\frac{u - 1 - r_F}{u - d}\right)\right] \div (1 + r_F). \tag{18.12}$$

If we let

$$p = \frac{1 + r_F - d}{u - d}, \quad \text{and} \quad 1 - p = \frac{u - 1 - r_F}{u - d},$$

Equation 18.12 can be simplified to be

$$C = [pC_u + (1 - p)C_d] \div (1 + r_F). \tag{18.13}$$

We shall call p the *hedging probability*. It is always greater than or equal to zero and less than or equal to one, so it has all of the properties of a probability.[11] Continuing with our numerical example, we can use Equation 18.13 to value the call option.

$$C = [pC_u + (1 - p)C_d] \div (1 + r_F).$$

$$= \left[\left(\frac{1 + .1 - .67}{1.2 - .67}\right)\$10 + \left(\frac{1.2 - 1 - .1}{1.2 - .67}\right)\$0\right] \div (1 + .1)$$

$$= [(.8113)\$10 + (.1887)\$0] \div (1.1) = \$7.38.$$

If the call is worth \$7.38 and the hedge portfolio required that we buy one share of stock for \$40 and sell 2.12 call options, our net investment was

$$S - mC = \$40 - 2.12(\$7.38) = \$24.35.$$

---

[11]In fact, p is the value that q would have if all investors were risk neutral. A risk-free investor would require only the risk-free rate on an investment in the common stock. Thus, the expected return would be $r_F S$, where

$$(1 + r_F)S = quS + (1 - q)dS.$$

Solving for q, we have

$$q = \frac{1 + r_F - d}{u - d}.$$

Thus, $p = q$ for a risk-neutral investor.

From Table 18.3, we know that the hedge portfolio earns $26.80 in either state of nature. Therefore, one plus the rate of return on our hedge portfolio is

$$1 + r_F = \frac{\$26.80}{\$24.35} = 1 + .1.$$

This confirms that the option is correctly priced and that the hedge portfolio earns the risk-free rate of 10 percent.

The preceding derivation of the value of a call option depends critically on the existence of a hedge portfolio and on the fact that the call must be priced so that the risk-free hedge earns exactly the risk-free rate of return. If the call had a higher (or lower) price, the hedge would earn more (or less) than the riskless rate and opportunities to earn risk-free arbitrage profits would exist. Arbitrage would force the call price back into line because traders can always form riskless hedges which will earn more than the riskless rate if prices are out of line.

The binomial OPM provides insight into three interesting features of option pricing.

1. The option price does not depend on q, the probability of an upward movement in the stock price. Consequently, even though investors may have heterogeneous expectations about future stock prices, they will still agree on the call value relative to its parameters, namely, S_0, u and d, X, r_F and T (where $T = 1$ in the one-period model).
2. Individuals' attitudes toward risk are irrelevant in deriving the call option formula. All that is required is that people prefer more wealth to less, so that arbitrage profits are eliminated.
3. The only random variable on which the call value depends is the stock price. The call value does not depend, for example, on the market portfolio of all securities.

These features serve to emphasize that the OPM is based on fewer assumptions than equilibrium models, for example, the CAPM. An option is merely a contingent claim on a risky asset. Once we observe the equilibrium value of the asset, we know that the option value must move in concert with it.

The binomial model can be extended into a multiperiod framework and used for solving such realistic problems as the value of an American call on a dividend-paying stock or the value of an American put.[12] In the limit, as the number of binomial jumps per unit time becomes infinite, the binomial model approaches the Black-Scholes OPM. Therefore, we shall move on to discuss the Black-Scholes model, which assumes that stock prices follow a (geometric) Brownian motion process through time.

The Black-Scholes Model

The advantage of the Black-Scholes [1973] OPM over the binomial model is that it provides a closed-form solution for option prices. The Black-Scholes formula is given below:

$$C = S\,N(d_1) - Xe^{-r_F T}\,N(d_2), \tag{18.14}$$

---

[12]See Cox, Ross, and Rubinstein [1979] or Rendleman and Bartter [1979].

Figure 18.9   The Unit Normal Distribution, Panel (a), and the Cumulative Unit
Normal Distribution, Panel (b)

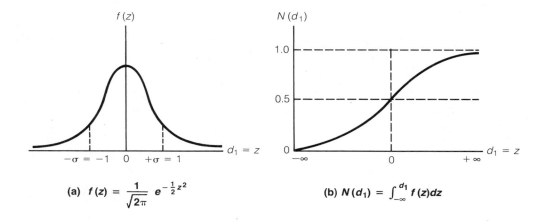

(a) $f(z) = \dfrac{1}{\sqrt{2\pi}}\ e^{-\frac{1}{2}z^2}$

(b) $N(d_1) = \int_{-\infty}^{d_1} f(z)dz$

where

$$d_1 = \frac{ln(S/X) + r_F T}{\sigma\sqrt{T}} + \frac{1}{2}\ \sigma\sqrt{T}$$

$$d_2 = d_1 - \sigma\sqrt{T}.$$

The terms $N(d_1)$ and $N(d_2)$ are the cumulative probabilities for a unit normal variable z. Recall that a unit normal variable has a mean of zero and a standard deviation of one.[13] The unit normal distribution and the cumulative normal distribution are illustrated in Figure 18.9, Panels (a) and (b) respectively.

A quick inspection of the Black-Scholes formula shows that the value of a call option is a function of the stock price, S, the exercise price, X, the time to maturity, T, the instantaneous variance, σ^2, and the risk-free rate, r_F. In order to show how to use the Black-Scholes formula, suppose we want to price an option written on Digital Equipment stock (which had a policy of paying no dividends in 19X7). Table 18.4 provides most of the information needed to value the call. The stock price, the exercise price, and the number of days to maturity are given for each option. The risk-free rate is estimated by using the average of the bid and ask quotes on U.S. Treasury bills of approximately the same maturity as the option. The only missing piece of information is the instantaneous variance of the stock price. Several different techniques have been suggested for estimating it (for example, see Latane and Rendleman [1976] or Parkinson [1977]).

---

[13]Refer to Chapter 10, Appendix A, for a review of the unit normal distribution.

Table 18.4 Data Needed to Price Digital Equipment Calls

	Call Prices as of October 4, 19X7, for Calls Maturing in:			
Exercise Price	October	January	April	Closing Stock Price
35	$11\frac{7}{8}$	$12\frac{7}{8}$	NA	$46\frac{3}{4}$
40	$6\frac{7}{8}$	8	NA	$46\frac{3}{4}$
45	$2\frac{15}{16}$	$4\frac{1}{4}$	6	$46\frac{3}{4}$
50	$\frac{1}{4}$	$1\frac{3}{4}$	3	$46\frac{3}{4}$
Maturity date	21 October	20 January	21 April	
Days to maturity	17	108	199	

	Treasury Bill Rates on October 4, 19X7			
Maturity Date	Bid	Ask	Average	r_F
20 October 19X7	6.04	5.70	5.87	5.9%
19 January 19X8	6.15	6.07	6.11	6.1
4 April 19X8	6.29	6.21	6.25 ⎱	6.2
2 May 19X8	6.20	6.12	6.16 ⎰	

The implicit variance is calculated by simply using the actual call price and the four known exogenous parameters (S,X,T, and r_F) in Equation 18.14 to solve for an estimate of the instantaneous variance. We did this, using the January 45's on Digital Equipment, which were priced at $4\frac{1}{4}$ on October 4.[14] The estimate of instantaneous variance was approximately 7.84 percent (which is a standard deviation of 28 percent).

We can now substitute our estimates of the five parameters into Equation 18.14 in order to estimate the value of any of the other 11 options on Digital Equipment. For example, let us value the April 45's. The parameters are

$$r_F = 6.2\%, \ T = 199/365, \ S = \$46.75, \ X = \$45, \text{ and } \sigma = .28.$$

First, we have to compute $N(d_1)$ and $N(d_2)$, which are the cumulative unit normal probabilities. The first unit normal probability is

$$d_1 = \frac{ln(S/X) + r_FT}{\sigma\sqrt{T}} + \frac{1}{2}\sigma\sqrt{T}$$

$$= \frac{ln(46.75/45) + .062(199/365)}{.28\sqrt{199/365}} + \frac{1}{2}(.28)\sqrt{199/365}$$

$$= \frac{ln(1.03889) + .062(.54521)}{.28\sqrt{.54521}} + .5(.28)\sqrt{.54521}$$

---

[14]It is necessary to use trial-and-error to converge on the estimate of the standard deviation which equates the right-hand side of Equation 18.14 with the observed call price.

$$= \frac{.03815 + .03380}{.28(.73838)} + .5(.28)(.73838)$$

$$= .34801 + .10337 = .45138.$$

Given that $d_1 = .45138$, we can use Appendix D at the end of the book. It gives the areas under a unit normal curve, as shown in Figure 18.10. We know that when $d_1 = .45138$, the unit normal variable lies .45138 standard deviations above its mean (which is equal to zero). Hence, the cumulative probability is the sum of (1) the area from $(-\infty)$ to zero, which equals .5, plus (2) the area from zero to .45138, which equals .17401, when read from Appendix D.[15] Consequently,

$$N(d_1) = .5 + .17401 = .67401.$$

In a similar fashion, we can solve for $N(d_2)$. First, we solve for

$$d_2 = d_1 - \sigma\sqrt{T}$$

$$= .45138 - (.28)\sqrt{199/365}$$

$$= .24463.$$

From Appendix D, we see that

$$N(d_2) = .5 + .09661 = .59661.$$

Figure 18.10   Illustration of the Cumulative Normal Probability $N(d_1)$

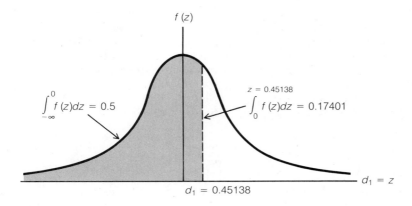

---

[15]The value of .17401 was attained via linear interpolation between the values given for $z = .45$ and $z = .46$ in the table. Linear interpolation is not exact in this case but is a close approximation.

Substituting the parameter values into Equation 18.14, we have

$$C = S\ N(d_1) - Xe^{-r_F T}N(d_2)$$

$$= \$46.75(.67401) - \$45\ e^{-.062(199/365)}(.59661)$$

$$= \$31.51 - \$45(.96676)(.59661)$$

$$= \$31.51 - \$25.96 = \$5.55.$$

The estimated call price turns out to be $5.55 while the actual call price is $6.00, an error of 7.5 percent. If we repeat the procedure for the October 45's (now $r_F = .059$ and $T = 17/365$), the estimated call price is $2.28 while the actual price is $2.94. Since both of the estimated prices are lower than the actual prices, our estimate of the instantaneous variance is probably too low.

The above examples show how the Black-Scholes valuation model may be used to price call options on nondividend-paying stocks. Roll [1977] and Geske [1979b] have solved the problem of valuing American calls when the common stock is assumed to make known dividend payments before the option matures. The binomial Option Pricing Model may be used for this purpose as well.

Hedge Portfolios

In order to provide a little more intuition for the Black-Scholes formula, we have rewritten Equations 18.9 and 18.14 below. Recall that Equation 18.9 was a boundary condition derived earlier.

$$C_0 \geq \text{MAX}\ [0,\ S_0 - Xe^{-r_F T}]. \tag{18.9}$$

$$C = S\ N(d_1) - Xe^{-r_F T}N(d_2). \tag{18.14}$$

The two equations are very similar. The main difference is that in Equation 18.14, the stock price is multiplied by $N(d_1)$ and the discounted exercise price is multiplied by $N(d_2)$. Figure 18.11 shows the call price as a function of the stock price. As predicted earlier, the call value increases with the stock price until, when the call is deep in-the-money (that is, S is much greater than X), the call price is nearly equal to the stock price minus the discounted exercise price.

An intuitive explanation for $N(d_1)$ is provided by taking the partial derivative of the call price (Equation 18.14) with respect to the stock price.[16]

$$\frac{\delta C}{\delta S} = N(d_1) \tag{18.15}$$

Thus, $N(d_1)$ is equal to the change in the call price with respect to a change in the stock price. It is the slope of a line drawn tangent to the call function (for example at Point Z) in Figure 18.11.

---

[16]Equation 18.15 is the exact solution even though the derivative is complicated by the fact that $N(d_1)$ is a function of S. The curious reader is referred to Galai and Masulis [1976] for the math.

Figure 18.11   The Call Pricing Function

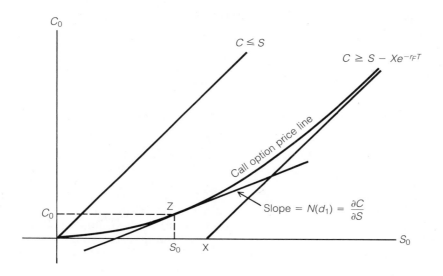

Given a stock price, S_0, we can construct a riskless hedge portfolio by purchasing one share of stock and writing m call options against it. The concept of a hedge portfolio here is exactly the same as that discussed earlier when we covered binomial option pricing. The value of the hedge portfolio, V_H, is

$$V_H = S - mC,$$

and its change per unit time is

$$\frac{dV_H}{dt} = \frac{dS}{dt} - m\frac{dC}{dt}. \tag{18.16}$$

If we let

$$m = \frac{dS}{dC} = \frac{1}{N(d_1)},$$

then the hedge will be riskless for the next increment in time, dt. Substituting the value of m into Equation 18.16, we have

$$\frac{dV_H}{dt} = \frac{dS}{dt} - \frac{dS}{dC}\frac{dC}{dt} = 0.$$

This proves that the hedge is riskless if we hold one share of stock and write $m = 1/N(d_1)$ call options against it. Intuitively, $N(d_1)$ may be thought of as the inverse of the hedge ratio, m.

If we use the Digital Equipment April 45's to hedge against 100 shares of Digital Equipment common stock, then we would have to write 100 times $1/N(d_1)$ options. We earlier computed the value of $N(d_1)$ to be .67401. Therefore,

$$m = \frac{1}{N(d_1)} = \frac{1}{.67401} = 1.48366,$$

and we should write 100 times m, or 148.37, call options in order to hedge against 100 shares.

It is important to bear in mind that this type of hedge is riskless only for small changes in the stock price. The hedge ratio must be adjusted whenever the stock price changes. For example, in Figure 18.11, if the stock price falls below S_0, then the slope of a line tangent to the call function decreases in value, that is, $N(d_1)$ decreases. And if $N(d_1)$ decreases, then the hedge ratio, which is the inverse of $N(d_1)$, will increase. Hence, it takes more out-of-the-money call options to hedge against one share of stock than in-the-money options.

$N(d_2)$, in Equation 18.14, also has an intuitive explanation, although it is difficult to show the logic without a much longer discourse on the binomial option pricing formula. We can interpret $N(d_2)$ as the probability that the option will finish in-the-money. Thus, for our Digital Equipment example, when the stock price is $46.75, the exercise price is $45.00, and 199 days are left until the option matures, we see that the probability of finishing in-the-money is $N(d_2) = .59661$.

Applications of the OPM to Corporate Finance

So far, the major application of the OPM model in this chapter has been an introduction to how option prices are predicted by the OPM. Now, we turn our focus to the financial management of a levered firm. Black and Scholes [1973] were the first to provide the insight that the equity in a firm which has debt in its capital structure (a levered firm) is really a call option on the value of the firm. Later, articles by Galai and Masulis [1976], Myers [1977], Merton [1974], Shastri [1981], and others have further developed the implications of option pricing theory for corporate finance. Also, the option model has been applied to the pricing of convertible debt and warrants by Ingersoll [1977].

Equity as a Call Option

In order to keep the discussion as simple as possible, assume that the firm has only two sources of capital: equity and *risky* debt. The debt is a pure discount bond which pays no coupons, has a face value D, and matures T years from now. It is secured by the assets of the firm, but bondholders may not force the firm into bankruptcy until the maturity date of the bond.

We saw, from Equation 18.4 (which is rewritten below), that any risky portfolio can be constructed from four basic building blocks.

$$S + P = B + C. \tag{18.4}$$

Earlier in the chapter, the underlying risky asset was a share of stock, S. Now it is the value of the firm, V. The equity in a levered firm, S, is really a call option on the value of the firm. If, on the maturity date, the value of the firm, V, exceeds the face value of the bonds, D, the shareholders will exercise their call option by paying off the bonds and keeping the excess. On the other hand, if the value of the firm is less than the face value of the bonds, the shareholders will default on the debt by failing to exercise their option. Therefore, at maturity, the shareholders' wealth, S, is

$$S = \text{MAX } [0, V - D]. \tag{18.17}$$

If we substitute V for S and S for C in Equation 18.4, we have

$$V = (B - P) + S. \tag{18.18}$$

Equation 18.18 tells us that the value of a risky asset, the levered firm, can be partitioned into two parts. The equity position, S, is a call option, and the risky debt position $(B - P)$, is equivalent to the present value of risk-free debt, B, minus the value of a European put option, P. At maturity, the bondholders receive

$$B - P = \text{MIN } [V, D]. \tag{18.19}$$

Table 18.5 shows how the payoffs to equity and risky debt add up to equal the value of the firm at maturity.[17] The table also illustrates the bondholders' position. If the firm is successful, that is, if $V > D$, the bondholders receive the face value of the riskless bond, D, and the put option is worthless. If the firm is bankrupt, they still receive the face value of the riskless bond, but a put option has, in effect, been exercised against them because they lose the difference between the face value of the riskless debt, D, and the market value of the firm, V. They gain D but lose $(D - V)$; therefore, their net position is V, the market value of the firm in bankruptcy.

Table 18.5   Stakeholders' Payoffs at Maturity

	Payoffs at Maturity	
	If $V \leq D$	If $V > D$
Shareholders' position:		
call option, S	0	$V - D$
Bondholders' position:		
risk-free bond, B	D	D
put option, P	$-(D - V)$	0
Total for bondholders	V	D
Sum of shareholders' and bondholders' positions	$0 + V = V$	$V - D + D = V$

---

[17]We are implicitly assuming that there are no taxes and that there are no bankruptcy costs paid to third parties (for example, lawyers and the courts). The entire value of the firm at maturity goes to bondholders and shareholders.

Once we see that the market value of a levered firm is easily partitioned into equity and risky debt positions which can be formulated in an option-pricing framework, then we can use our understanding of the OPM to analyze such corporate finance decisions as risky investments, dividend policy, spinoffs, equity repurchases, subordinated debt, and mergers.

The OPM and Investment Decisions

One of the surprising implications of considering equity in a levered firm as a call option is that investments which increase the idiosyncratic, or diversifiable, risk of a firm without changing its expected return will benefit shareholders at the expense of bondholders even though the value of the firm is unaffected. Because idiosyncratic risk is independent of the market portfolio, an increase in idiosyncratic risk will increase the variance of return for the firm without changing the firm's beta or its expected rate of return. Therefore, the value of the firm will not change. However, there will be a redistribution of wealth to shareholders away from bondholders. The reason is that higher variance will increase the value of the call option held by shareholders. Simultaneously, it will increase the value of the put written by bondholders so that their net position, $B - P$, will fall in value.

We can illustrate this result with an example. Assume the following: The current value of the firm, V, is \$3 million; the face value of debt, D, is \$1 million; and the debt will mature in $T = 4$ years. The variance of returns on the value of the firm, σ^2, is .01, and the riskless rate, r_F, is 5 percent. We can use the OPM, Equation 18.14, to calculate the value of the equity position, S_0. Substituting S for C, D for X, and V for S in Equation 18.14, we have

$$S = V\,N(d_1) - De^{-r_F T}N(d_2)$$

$$d_1 = \frac{ln(V/D) + r_F T}{\sigma\sqrt{T}} + \frac{1}{2}\,\sigma\sqrt{T}$$

$$d_2 = d_1 - \sigma\sqrt{T}.$$

First, solving for d_1 and $N(d_1)$, we have

$$d_1 = \frac{ln(3{,}000{,}000/1{,}000{,}000) + .05(4)}{.1\sqrt{4}} + .5(.1)\sqrt{4}$$

$$= 6.593,$$

and from Appendix D,

$$N(d_1) \cong 1.$$

The solution for d_2 is

$$d_2 = 6.593 - .1\sqrt{4} = 6.393,$$

and from Appendix D,

$$N(d_2) \cong 1.$$

Second, we calculate the value of the common stock,

$$S = \$3,000,000(1) - \$1,000,000e^{-.05(4)}(1)$$
$$= \$3,000,000 - \$818,731 = \$2,181,269.$$

The market value of debt is

$$(B - P) = V - S = \$3,000,000 - \$2,181,269 = \$818,731.$$

It is interesting to note that since $N(d_2) \cong 1$, the probability that the call option (that is, the equity position) will finish in-the-money is nearly 100 percent. This means that there is virtually no probability of default on the bond.[18]

Next, assume that the firm changes the idiosyncratic risk in its investment program so that the firms' variance rises from .01 to .16. Recalculating the market value of equity, we obtain

$$d_1 = \frac{ln(3/1) + .05(4)}{.4\sqrt{4}} + .5(.4)\sqrt{4} = 2.0233$$

and

$$N(d_1) = .9785.$$

Also,

$$d_2 = 1.2233$$

and

$$N(d_2) = .8894.$$

The revised market value of equity is

$$S = \$3,000,000(.9785) - \$1,000,000e^{-.05(4)}(.8894)$$
$$= \$2,935,500 - \$728,178 = \$2,207,322,$$

and the market value of debt becomes

$$(B - P) = V - S = \$3,000,000 - \$2,207,322$$
$$= \$792,678.$$

---

[18]In fact, $818,731 is just the present value of a risk-free pure discount bond which pays a face value of $1 million four years hence.

$$B_0 = De^{-r_F T}$$
$$= \$1,000,000e^{-.05(4)} = \$818,731.$$

In this case, $B - P = B$. The market value of the put is zero.

The increased risk of the investment program has raised the market value of equity by ($2,207,322 − $2,181,269 = $26,053). The market value of risky debt has fallen by an equal amount. The debt moves from being relatively default free [where $1 - N(d_2) = 0$] to an 11.06 percent chance of default [that is, $1 - N(d_2) = .1106$].

We can calculate the promised yield to maturity, k_b, that bondholders would require on the riskier debt by solving for the discount rate which equates the payoff four years hence with the current market value of the risky debt, $\tilde{B}_0$, which has been determined to be $792,678.[19]

$$\tilde{B}_0 = De^{-k_b T} \qquad\qquad (18.20)$$

$$\$792,678 = \$1,000,000e^{-k_b T}$$

$$\frac{\$792,678}{\$1,000,000} = e^{-k_b(4)}$$

$$ln(.792678) = -k_b(4)$$

$$-.23234 = -4k_b$$

$$k_b = .05808.$$

In order to compensate them for their increased default risk, the bondholders would require a 5.808 percent yield to maturity instead of the 5 percent they require on a default-free bond.

Because increasing the riskiness of the firm's production operations increases the value of equity and decreases the value of debt, there is an inherent divergence of interests between shareholders and creditors of the firm. Since the shareholders possess voting control of the firm, they may take actions that may be adverse to the interests of the creditors. It is for this reason that various protective covenants are written into the bond indentures of most debt instruments. While actual restrictions on investment policy are relatively uncommon, one often finds restrictions on dividend policy, subordinated debt, and merger activity.

The Cost of Risky Debt

We can use the OPM to show the relationship between the yield to maturity, which bondholders will require for holding risky debt, and the amount of financial leverage employed by the firm. Using the same set of numbers as before, and assuming that the variance of returns on the value of the firm, σ^2, is .09, we can solve the OPM (repeatedly) for the market value of debt and equity implied by different ratios of the face value of debt to total assets. Then we can use Equation 18.20 to compute the required yield to maturity on the risky debt.[20] The results are shown in Table 18.6 and Figure 18.12. The yield to maturity required by bondholders who invest in risky debt rises quickly with financial leverage. We shall bear this result in mind, because later in the text (Chapter 21), we examine the cost of capital.

---

[19]We use the symbol tilde (∼) to differentiate between risky debt, $\tilde{B}$, and riskless debt, B.

[20]Recall, from Chapter 7, that the yield to maturity is really the "promised" yield to maturity because it is the yield which discounts the face value of the bond rather than its expected value.

Table 18.6   The Promised Yield to Maturity on Risky Debt

Face Value of Debt	Firm Value	D/V	Market Value of Debt	Equity	Yield to Maturity = k_b	B/V
0	3,000,000	0	0	3,000,000	5.00%	0
500,000	3,000,000	.167	408,547	2,591,453	5.05	.136
1,000,000	3,000,000	.333	814,350	2,185,650	5.13	.271
1,500,000	3,000,000	.500	1,195,409	1,804,591	5.67	.398
2,000,000	3,000,000	.667	1,531,108	1,468,892	6.68	.510
2,500,000	3,000,000	.833	1,815,595	1,184,405	8.00	.605
3,000,000	3,000,000	1.000	2,054,483	945,517	9.47	.685

Mergers and Spinoffs

A conglomerate merger is defined as one where there is no economic synergy of any kind — no economies of scale; no increase in managerial effectiveness; no complementarities between research, marketing and production; no tax advantages; and so on. In a pure conglomerate merger, the market value of the combined entities is the same as the sum of their separate values. Thus, if two firms, A and B, propose to merge, the value of

Figure 18.12   The Relationship between the Yield to Maturity on Risky Debt and Financial Leverage

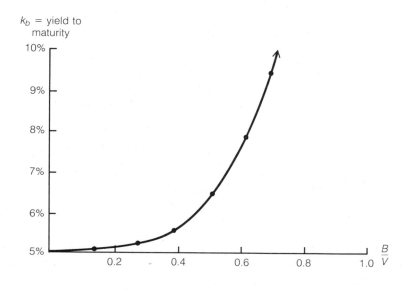

the merged firm, V_{AB} will be

$$V_{AB} = V_A + V_B.$$

No new value is created by a conglomerate merger as we have chosen to define it.

There will, however, be a portfolio diversification effect if the cash flows of the two levered firms are less than perfectly correlated. Because the cash flows of the two firms tend to offset each other, the effect of the merger will be to decrease the probability of bankruptcy. This benefits debtholders, and the market value of debt will rise due to lower risk. Conversely, shareholders' wealth will decline because they hold a call option on the merged firm, which has a lower variance.

The redistribution of wealth from shareholders to debtholders in a conglomerate merger occurs because *a call option written on a portfolio of assets is worth less than a portfolio of call options* (as long as the assets are less than perfectly correlated).

Because the option pricing approach to mergers and acquisitions is thoroughly discussed in Chapter 30, we shall not provide any numerical examples here. However, it is worth mentioning a few related issues in passing. For example, if conglomerate mergers can result in a decrease in shareholders' wealth, why do they take place at all? One possible explanation is that the greater debt capacity created in a conglomerate merger is utilized immediately. Greater financial leverage may raise the value of equity back to its premerger level by providing an additional tax shield due to increased interest payments.

It is often implicitly assumed that merging firms have equal return variances, equal amounts of debt outstanding and that the debt issues of both firms have the same maturity. If these assumptions are relaxed, it is possible for a merger to be detrimental to the bondholders of one of the firms.[21] For example, suppose both firms have the same amount of debt outstanding, but the debt of Firm A matures in one year while the debt of Firm B matures in four years. These circumstances dictate that upon merger, the bonds of Firm B become subordinate to those of Firm A; hence, Firm B bonds will decrease in value and Firm A bonds will appreciate.[22] If both debt issues have the same maturity but Firm A has a larger amount of debt than Firm B, then A's bondholders experience a decrease in risk after the merger because they have equal claim on the combined assets of both firms. Firm A's debt will benefit while B's debt becomes riskier and declines in value. Finally, even though both debt issues may have the same size and maturity, it is possible for debtholders in Firm A to gain relative to those in Firm B if Firm A has a greater variance. After the merger, Firm A's bondholders are exposed to much less risk and Firm B's bondholders may even experience an increase in risk if Firm A had a high variance.

Debtholders can never be sure what effect a merger might have on their claim on the assets of the firm. They have no vote in whether or not a merger is consummated. And they have no way to be compensated for a loss in wealth after a merger takes place. Consequently, one often finds bond indenture provisions which restrict merger in one way or another.[23] Smith and Warner [1979] examined a random sample of 87 public issues of debt registered with the Securities and Exchange Commission between January 1974 and December 1975. Merger activity was restricted by covenants in 39.1 percent of the bonds.

---

[21]For a complete exposition of the effects of a conglomerate merger on all parties, see Shastri [1982].

[22]It is more accurate to say that Firm B's bonds decrease in value *relative* to Firm A's bonds. Because of the portfolio variance effect, which was discussed earlier, both bonds may increase in value, but Firm B's bonds will not increase as much as Firm A's bonds and may even decline in value.

[23]For more on bond covenants, see the American Bar Association, *Commentaries on Model Debenture Indenture Provisions* [1971].

Spinoffs are the opposite of mergers. When a firm spins off a division, the result is a newly created, independent firm. If a spinoff divides a large firm into two smaller firms of equal size and with equal debt amounts and maturities, then the effect (in the absence of any negative synergies) should be to benefit shareholders at the expense of debtholders. Of course, the spinoff may not result in firms with equal size and financial structure. In the extreme, it is possible for shareholders to "strip" the parent firm by spinning off valuable assets paid in the form of shares in the spinoff firm. The parent firm becomes a shell and keeps all of the debt. In this way, shareholders can expropriate wealth from bondholders (but not without a lawsuit). Spinoffs of this type are analytically similar to dividend payments.

Empirical Evidence on the OPM

It is important to understand that there are many different option pricing models. The Black-Scholes model was the first, but there are others which are better tailored to specific situations. For example, if the equity in a levered firm is a call option on the value of the firm's assets, then a CBOE call option written on the equity is really an option on an option. The model which solves this problem was derived by Geske [1977,1979a]. He shows that a CBOE call written on a levered firm depends on the firm's financial leverage and the time to maturity of the firm's debt as well as the five parameters found in the Black-Scholes model (that is, the value of the underlying asset, the exercise price, the variance of return on the underlying asset, the time to maturity for the option, and the risk-free rate). Also, the Black-Scholes model makes no provision for dividend payments. This problem was solved by Roll [1977] and Geske [1978,1979b].

There have been many empirical tests of the Option Pricing Model since its publication in 1973. Studies which have used different versions of the Option Pricing Model to try to find economically exploitable biases have been unsuccessful in doing so when transactions costs were deducted from trading rule profits. From this, one can conclude that the Option Pricing Models fit observed prices well in an economic sense. Also, the results are consistent with semi-strong-form market efficiency (which is described in Chapter 19).

On the other hand, some studies have discovered statistically significant biases in the Black-Scholes model. Black and Scholes [1972] were the first to report that their model underpriced options on low-variance stocks and overpriced options on high-variance stocks. Black later [1975] reported that the model also underpriced out-of-the-money options and near-maturity options, while it overpriced in-the-money options. MacBeth and Merville [1979] and Rubinstein [1981] found similar results but noted that the bias for in- and out-of-the-money options reversed itself around 1977.

The biases with respect to the time to maturity and the exercise price (that is, in- or out-of-the-money) have been explained by Whaley [1982] and Sterk [1982], who used the dividend-adjusted model of Roll [1977] and Geske [1979b]. The volatility bias has been explained by Geske and Roll [1984b], who use a superior variance estimator (called the "Stein shrinker"). Of course, much work remains to be done before we can be sure which Option Pricing Model provides the best fit to the data.

The Relationship between the OPM and the CAPM

At first, it is easy to become confused when trying to compare the Option Pricing Model (OPM) with the Capital Asset Pricing Model (CAPM). The Option Pricing Model implies that option prices increase as the variance of the underlying asset increases. This does not

Figure 18.13   Lognormal Distribution of Stock Values

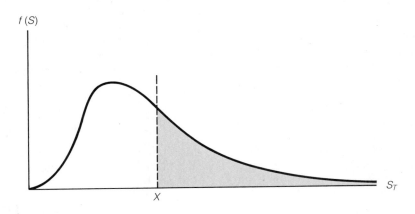

mean that investors prefer greater risk. It only means that an option is a contingent claim on an underlying asset. To price the underlying asset, we need to use such equilibrium models as the CAPM or the APM (Arbitrage Pricing Model). The OPM prices contingent claims while the CAPM prices the underlying assets. The two models are perfectly consistent with each other.

Figure 18.13 helps to give an intuitive feel for the relationship between the CAPM and the OPM. The horizontal axis represents the (lognormal) distribution of stock prices at the maturity of a European option. The CAPM exploits the covariance between the stock and the market portfolio to estimate the stock's systematic risk, and its beta and to determine its equilibrium return. Hence, *the CAPM uses the entire distribution* in order to determine the equilibrium expected return on the stock. *The OPM, on the other hand, uses only a portion of the distribution.* For example, a European call option with an exercise price of X, pays off only when $S_T \geq X$. Hence, as illustrated in Figure 18.13, the OPM "prices" only the shaded region of the stock price distribution, the area to the right of the exercise price, X.

The relationship between the CAPM beta of a stock, β_S, and the beta of a European call option written on that stock, β_C, is given in Equation 18.21.

$$\beta_C = N(d_1)\, \frac{S}{C}\, \beta_S. \tag{18.21}$$

The beta of the call is a function of the common stock beta, β_S, the ratio of the stock price to the call price, S/C, and the inverse of the hedge ratio, $N(d_1)$. While common stock betas are relatively stationary through time, option betas change rapidly. For example, an out-of-the-money call option will have a high beta and a high expected return. If the stock price rises, the option beta will rapidly fall and so too will its expected return.

The partial derivatives of call option betas are[24]

$$\frac{\delta \beta_C}{\delta S} < 0, \ \frac{\delta \beta_C}{\delta X} > 0, \ \frac{\delta \beta_C}{\delta r_F} < 0, \ \frac{\delta \beta_C}{\delta \sigma^2} < 0, \ \frac{\delta \beta_C}{\delta T} < 0.$$

The call becomes less risky if the stock price goes up, if the riskless rate increases, if the variance of the underlying asset increases, or if the option has greater time to maturity. The option's risk rises when the exercise price rises, all other things being held constant.

The equilibrium rate of return, $E(r_C)$, which is expected on a call option can be found by using β_C and the Capital Asset Pricing Model.

$$E(r_C) = r_F + [E(r_M) - r_F]\beta_C.$$

One of the most interesting things about a call option is that its risk (and its expected rate of return) changes every day simply because it is closer to maturity.

Summary

The Option Pricing Model is an extremely useful tool because so many financial assets are options. A partial list includes stocks, risky bonds, warrants, convertible debt, call options, and put options. We have discussed two types of option pricing formulae: the binomial model and the Black-Scholes model. There are, of course, many more. We have also shown that literally any risky asset can be replicated by some combination of the four basic building blocks of finance theory: stocks, riskless bonds, call options, and put options. For example, a risky bond can be thought of as a combination of a pure discount riskless bond and a put option.

The Option Pricing Model is perfectly consistent with the equilibrium theories of asset pricing which were discussed in Chapter 17, the Capital Asset Pricing Model, and the Arbitrage Pricing Model. Empirical evidence indicates that the Black-Scholes OPM explains actual market prices of options so well that it is impossible to make an economic profit by trying to arbitrage when the model price is different from the observed market price. The statistically significant biases in the Black-Scholes model can be explained if one uses slightly more complicated option pricing models which were not discussed here.

In sum, the Option Pricing Model is a powerful and useful tool which provides great insight into an enormous variety of financial assets.

Questions

18.1 What are the five factors which affect the value of a call option? Describe how an increase in each one will affect the call option's price.

18.2 What is put-call parity? Why is it important?

18.3 Why will an American call option on a nondividend-paying stock never be exercised before its maturity date?

---

[24]See Galai and Masulis [1976] for proof.

18.4   Why is it true that investors' subjective estimates of the probability of up or down movements in the value of a common stock are irrelevant for pricing a call option on that stock?

18.5   Why is the equity in a levered firm considered to be a call option on the value of the firm's assets?

18.6   Why is risky debt in a levered firm considered to be a combination of a risk-free bond and a put option on the value of the firm's assets?

18.7   How is the market value of equity affected by a conglomerate merger between two firms of equal size and identical financial leverage?

18.8   How is the market value of equity in a levered firm affected if the shareholders decide to take on riskier projects which increase the variance of the firm's assets? How is the market value of debt affected?

18.9   What is the relationship between the beta of a call option and the beta of the common stock on which it is written? What happens to the beta of the call option if the stock price goes up? What happens to the beta of the call option as it gets closer to its expiration date?

18.10 After a call contract is created, the outcome must be a zero-sum game; that is, the call writer may win or lose N, but the call buyer will experience an opposite return of exactly N, and, consequently, their aggregate payoff is zero. Given this fact, can you explain how they both could enter into the contract anticipating a positive return?

Problems

18.1   A straddle is a combination of a put and a call option in the same contract where both options are written on the same stock and where both have the same exercise price and maturity date. Graph the payoffs at maturity for a straddle.

18.2   Show graphically how one can use a riskless bond and a put and a call in order to duplicate the payoffs on a share of stock.

18.3   Using the simple one-period binomial OPM, determine the value of a call option which has an exercise price of $30, given that the stock price is $28, that $u = 1.4$, that $d = .8$ and that $r_F = 10\%$.

18.4   Given that the price of a nondividend-paying stock is $25, the instantaneous variance on the stock is 64 percent, and the risk-free rate is 20 percent, what is the value of a call option which has an exercise price of $23 and 160 days to maturity?

18.5   Using the facts for Problem 18.4, how many call options must you write (that is, sell short) in order to create a riskless hedge, given that you own 100 shares of stock?

18.6   Estimate the instantaneous variance for a common stock, given the following facts: a call written on the stock sells for $3.50, the stock price is $50.00, the call has an exercise price of $51.00 and has 120 days to maturity, and the risk-free rate is 12 percent.

18.7   The Monarch Company is currently valued at $500,000. Seventy percent of current value is the face value of pure discount debt, all of which will mature in four years. The variance of percentage returns is 56.25 percent. The risk-free rate is 10 percent.
   a)   Determine the market value of the equity.
   b)   Determine the market value of the debt.
   c)   What is the yield to maturity on the debt?

18.8   Itex Distributing Company is currently valued at $4 million. Twenty percent of current value is the face value of pure discount debt, all of which matures in four years. The variance of percentage returns is 42.25 percent. The risk-free rate is 10 percent.

a) Determine the value of the equity.
b) Determine the value of the debt.
c) What is the yield to maturity on the debt?

18.9 Stacy Johnston plans to invest in the newly issued call option of the Remington Corporation. The call option has an exercise price of $50 and a maturity date three months from now. The stock price is $32, the instantaneous variance of the stock price is 0.64, and the risk-free rate is 8 percent. Remington Corporation pays no dividends. What is the value of the call option?

18.10 The Perry Company has a market value of $25 million and outstanding debt of $16 million, which matures in nine years. The variance of the firm's rate of return is 0.49. The firm pays no cash dividends and pays out the interest at maturity only. If the rate of inflation is expected to rise by 4 percent (thus raising the riskless nominal interest rate from 6 percent to 10 percent), use what you know about the OPM to determine which class of Perry's security holders benefits from the rise in r_F. (No calculations are necessary.)

18.11 The Lansing Corporation has $30 million of pure discount debt, which will mature in one year. In the market, the firm has a current value of $100 million. The total risk of Lansing's assets is $\sigma = 1.44$. The expected market rate of return is 15 percent. The riskless rate is 10 percent. The beta of Lansing's equity is 1.4, and the beta of its debt is 0.3.
a) Determine the market value of the firm's debt and equity.
b) Determine the cost of debt and equity capital (assuming a world without taxes).
c) If nothing else changes, what will the beta of Lansing's equity be six months from now?

18.12 The Sandvik Company and the Weller Corporation have the same market value of $75 million. Both firms have the following identical parameters:

$$D_S = D_W = \$25 \text{ million} \quad \text{Face value of debt}$$
$$T_S = T_W = 4 \text{ years} \quad \text{Maturity of debt}$$
$$\sigma_S = \sigma_W = 0.36 \quad \text{Instantaneous standard deviation}$$
$$r_F = 0.11 \quad \text{Risk-free rate.}$$

a) What is the initial market value of debt and equity for Sandvik and Weller?
b) The correlation between the two firms' cash flows is 0.5. If the two firms merge, the surviving firm will be worth $150 million. What will the market value of debt and equity in the merged firm be? If there were no other merger effects, would shareholders agree to the merger?

18.13 Suppose a firm has three classes of securities: senior debt, subordinated debt, and equity. Both debt issues are pure discount debt which mature at the same time, and the common stock pays no dividends. Use the OPM to write equations for the values of each of the three classes of securities. Use the following notation:

$V =$ market value of the firm
$S =$ market value of the stock
$B_S =$ market value of the senior debt with face value D_S
$B_J =$ market value of the junior (subordinated) debt which has face value D_J.

18.14 Suppose the government passes a usury law which prohibits lending at more than 8 percent interest, but normal market rates are much higher due to inflation. You have a customer who is willing to borrow at a 25 percent rate and can put up his business, which has been appraised at $100,000, for collateral. Rather than refusing to lend, you decide to create a ten-year contract with the following terms. You hold title to the business assets and receive the right to sell back the business for $X at the end of ten years. If you decide to sell, the borrower *must* buy. In return, you lend $80,000 in cash (the amount he wants to borrow), and you give the borrower the right to buy the store from you for $X at the end of ten years. What value must $X be in order to provide you with a riskless 25 percent annual rate of return?

Selected References

American Bar Association, *Commentaries on Model Debenture Indenture Provisions*, Chicago, Illinois, 1971.

Ball, Clifford A., and Torous, Walter N., "The Maximum Likelihood Estimation of Security Price Volatility: Theory, Evidence, and Application to Option Pricing," *Journal of Business*, 57 (January 1984), pp. 97-112.

Beckers, S., "The Constant Elasticity of Variance Model and Its Implications for Option Pricing," *Journal of Finance*, 35 (June 1980), pp. 661-673.

Black, Fisher, "The Pricing of Commodity Contracts," *Journal of Financial Economics*, 3 (January-March 1976), pp. 167-179.

——, "Fact and Fantasy in the Use of Options," *Financial Analysts Journal*, (July-August 1975), pp. 61-72.

——, and M. Scholes, "The Pricing of Options and Corporate Liabilities," *Journal of Political Economy*, 81 (May-June 1973), pp. 637-654.

Black, Fisher, and Scholes, Myron, "The Valuation of Option Contracts and a Test of Market Efficiency," *The Journal of Finance*, (May 1972), pp. 399-418.

Bookstaber, Richard M., "Observed Option Mispricing and the Nonsimultaneity of Stock and Option Quotations," *Journal of Business*, 54 (January 1981), pp. 141-155.

Chiras, Donald P., and Manaster, Steven, "The Information Content of Option Prices and a Test of Market Efficiency," *Journal of Financial Economics*, 6 (June-September 1978), pp. 213-234.

Courtadon, Georges, "The Pricing of Options on Default-Free Bonds," *Journal of Financial and Quantitative Analysis*, 17 (March 1982), pp. 75-100.

Cox, John C., and Ross, Stephen A., "The Valuation of Options for Alternative Stochastic Processes," *Journal of Financial Economics*, 3 (January-March 1976), pp. 145-166.

——; and Rubinstein, Mark, "Option Pricing: A Simplified Approach," *Journal of Financial Economics*, 7 (September 1979), pp. 229-263.

Emanuel, David D., and MacBeth, James D., "Further Results on the Constant Elasticity of Variance Call Option Pricing Model," *Journal of Financial and Quantitative Analysis*, 17 (November 1982), pp. 533-554.

Galai, Dan, "Tests of Market Efficiency of the Chicago Board Options Exchange," *Journal of Business*, 50 (April 1977), pp. 167-197.

——, and Masulis, R. W., "The Option Pricing Model and the Risk Factor of Stock," *Journal of Financial Economics*, 3 (January-March 1976), pp. 53-82.

Geske, Robert, "The Valuation of Compound Options," *Journal of Financial Economics*, 7 (March 1979a), pp. 63-81.

——, "A Note on the Analytical Valuation Formula for Unprotected American Call Options on Stocks with Known Dividends," *The Journal of Financial Economics*, (December 1979b), pp. 375-380.

——, "The Pricing of Options with Stochastic Dividend Yield," *Journal of Finance*, 33 (May 1978), pp. 617-625.

——, "The Valuation of Corporate Liabilities as Compound Options," *Journal of Financial and Quantitative Analysis*, 12 (November 1977), pp. 541-552.

——, and Roll, R., "On Valuing American Call Options with the Black-Scholes European Formula," *Journal of Finance*, (June 1984a).

——, "Isolating the Observed Biases in American Call Option Pricing: An Alternative Variance Estimator," Working Paper #4-84, Graduate School of Management, UCLA, February 1984b.

Ingersoll, Jonathan E., Jr., "A Contingent-Claims Valuation of Convertible Securities," *Journal of Financial Economics*, 4 (May 1977), pp. 289-322.

——, "A Theoretical and Empirical Investigation of the Dual Purpose Funds: An Application of Contingent-Claims Analysis," *Journal of Financial Economics*, 3 (January-March 1976), pp. 83-124.

Johnson, H. E., "An Analytic Approximation for the American Put Price," *Journal of Financial and Quantitative Analysis*, 18 (March 1983), pp. 141-148.

Latane, Henry A., and Rendleman, Richard J., Jr., "Standard Deviations of Stock Price Ratios Implied in Option Prices," *Journal of Finance*, 31 (May 1976), pp. 369-381.

MacBeth, James D., and Merville, Larry J., "Tests of the Black-Scholes and Cox Call Option Valuation Models," *Journal of Finance*, (May 1980), pp. 285-300.

———, "An Empirical Examination of the Black-Scholes Call Option Pricing Model," *Journal of Finance*, 34 (December 1979), pp. 1173-1186.

Margrabe, William, "The Value of an Option to Exchange One Asset for Another," *Journal of Finance*, 33 (March 1978), pp. 177-198.

Merton, Robert C., "On the Pricing of Corporate Debt: The Risk Structure of Interest Rates," *Journal of Finance*, 29 (May 1974), pp. 449-470.

———, "The Theory of Rational Option Pricing," *The Bell Journal of Economics and Management Science*, 4 (Spring 1973), pp. 141-183.

Myers, S., "Determinants of Corporate Borrowing," *Journal of Financial Economics*, (November 1977), pp. 147-175.

Parkinson, M., "Option Pricing: The American Put," *Journal of Business*, (January 1977), pp. 21-36.

Phillips, Susan M., and Smith, Clifford W., Jr., "Trading Cost for Listed Options: The Implications for Market Efficiency," *Journal of Financial Economics*, 8 (June 1980), pp. 179-201.

Rendleman, Richard J., Jr., and Bartter, Brit J., "Two-State Option Pricing," *Journal of Finance*, 34 (December 1979), pp. 1093-1110.

Roll, Richard, "An Analytic Valuation Formula for Unprotected American Call Options on Stocks with Known Dividends," *Journal of Financial Economics*, 5 (November 1977), pp. 251-258.

Rubinstein, Mark, "Displaced Diffusion Option Pricing," *Journal of Finance*, 38 (March 1983), pp. 213-217.

———, "Nonparametric Tests of Alternative Option Pricing Models," Working Paper No. 117, University of California at Berkeley, 1981.

———, "The Valuation of Uncertain Income Streams and the Pricing of Options," *Bell Journal of Economics*, 7 (Autumn 1976), pp. 407-425.

Scholes, Myron, "Taxes and the Pricing of Options," *Journal of Finance*, 31 (May 1976), pp. 319-322.

Shastri, K., "Valuing Corporate Securities: Some Effects of Mergers by Exchange Offers," University of Pittsburgh, WP-517, revised January 1982.

———, "Two Essays Concerning the Effects of Firm Investment/Financing Decisions on Security Values: An Option Pricing Approach," unpublished Ph.D. thesis, UCLA, 1981.

Smith, C., Jr., "Option Pricing: A Review," *Journal of Financial Economics*, (January-March 1976), pp. 1-51.

———, and Warner, J. B., "On Financial Contracting: An Analysis of Bond Covenants," *Journal of Financial Economics*, (June 1979), pp. 117-161.

Sterk, W., "Comparative Performance of the Black-Scholes and the Roll-Geske-Whaley Option Pricing Models," *Journal of Financial and Quantitative Analysis*, (September 1983), pp. 345-354.

———, "Tests of Two Models for Valuing Call Options on Stocks with Dividends," *Journal of Finance*, 37 (December 1982), pp. 1229-1237.

Stoll, Hans R., "The Relationship Between Put and Call Option Prices," *Journal of Finance*, (December 1969), pp. 802-824.

Whaley, R., "Valuation of American Call Options on Dividend-Paying Stocks: Empirical Tests," *Journal of Financial Economics*, 10 (March 1982), pp. 29-58.

———, "On the Valuation of American Call Options on Stocks with Known Dividends," *Journal of Financial Economics*, 9 (June 1981), pp. 207-211.

Appendix A to Chapter 18

The Abandonment Decision

At some future time, usually because of unforeseen problems, it may become more profitable to abandon a project than to continue its operation, even though its economic life has not yet ended. Taking this possibility into consideration in the capital budgeting process may increase the project's expected net present value and reduce its standard deviation of returns. In this discussion we first show how to include *abandonment value* in the analysis when making accept-reject decisions, and then we look at criteria for actually abandoning a project after it has been accepted.

When a project is abandoned its tangible assets are usually liquidated. The expected liquidation value sets a lower bound on the value of the project and may be thought of as the exercise price in an American put option. When the present value of the asset falls below the liquidation value, the act of abandoning the project is equivalent to exercising the put. Because the option to liquidate is valuable, a project that can be liquidated is worth more than the same project without the possibility of abandonment. To illustrate this principle, let us use a numerical example. First, we will solve the problem using decision trees, then using option pricing.

Abandonment Analysis Using Decision Trees

The Palmer Corporation has invested $300 in new machinery with expected cash flows over two years. This is shown in Table 18A.1.

Table 18A.1   Expected Cash Flows

Year 1		Year 2	
Initial Probability P(1)	Cash Flow	Conditional Probability P(2|1)	Cash Flow
(0.3)	$200	(0.3)	$100
		(0.5)	200
		(0.2)	300
(0.4)	300	(0.3)	200
		(0.5)	300
		(0.2)	400
(0.3)	400	(0.3)	300
		(0.4)	400
		(0.3)	500

Two sets of probabilities are associated with the project. The initial probabilities should be interpreted as probabilities of particular cash flows from the first year only; the conditional probabilities are the probabilities of particular cash flows in the second year, given that a specific outcome has occurred in the first year. Thus, the results in the second year are *conditional* upon the results of the first year. If high profits occur in the first year, chances are that the second year will also bring high profits. To obtain the probability that a particular first-year outcome and a particular second-year outcome will both occur, we must multiply the initial probability by the conditional probability to obtain what is termed the *joint probability*.

These concepts are applied to the data of Table 18A.1 to construct Table 18A.2. The project is not expected to have any returns after the second year. The cost of capital relevant to the project is assumed to be 12 percent. To indicate the role of abandonment value, we first calculate the expected net present value of the investment and the expected standard deviation of the project's internal rate of return without considering abandonment value. In the calculation made in Table 18A.2, we find the expected NPV to be $201.

Next, in Table 18A.3, we calculate the standard deviation of the project's rate of return, finding that $\sigma = 33.5\%$. Next, we can expand this analysis to take abandonment value into account. Suppose the abandonment value of the project at the end of the first year is estimated to be $250. This is the amount that can be obtained by liquidating the project after the first year, and the $250 is independent of actual first-year results.[1] If the project is abandoned after one year, then the $250 will replace any second-year returns. In other

---

Table 18A.2 Calculation of Expected Net Present Value

Year 1			Year 2			Probability Analysis				
Cash Flow (1)	PV Factor (2)	Present Value: (1) × (2) (3)	Cash Flow (4)	PV Factor (5)	Present Value: (4) × (5) (6)	Present Value of Total Cash Flow: (3) + (6) (7)	Initial Probability (8)	Conditional Probability (9)	Joint Probability: (8) × (9) (10)	Expected Value: (7) × (10) (11)
$200	0.8929	179	$100	0.7972	80	$259		0.3	0.09	$ 23
			200	0.7972	159	338	0.3	0.5	0.15	51
			300	0.7972	239	418		0.2	0.06	25
300	0.8929	268	200	0.7972	159	427		0.3	0.12	51
			300	0.7972	239	507	0.4	0.5	0.20	101
			400	0.7972	319	587		0.2	0.08	47
400	0.8929	357	300	0.7972	239	596		0.3	0.09	54
			400	0.7972	319	676	0.3	0.4	0.12	81
			500	0.7972	399	756		0.3	0.09	68
									1.00	$501

Expected present value = $501
Expected net present value = $201

---

[1] In other words, we assume that the exercise price of the put option at the end of the first year is known with certainty. It is not a random variable.

Table 18A.3   Calculation of Rate of Return Standard Deviation

Cash Flow		IRR	IRR − $\overline{\text{IRR}}$	(IRR − $\overline{\text{IRR}}$)²	×	Joint Probability	=	p_i(IRR − $\overline{\text{IRR}}$)²
Year 1	Year 2							
$200	$100	0.0%	−.594	.352		.09		.0318
200	200	21.5	−.379	.144		.15		.0215
200	300	38.7	−.207	.043		.06		.0026
300	200	45.7	−.137	.019		.12		.0023
300	300	61.8	.024	.001		.20		.0001
300	400	75.8	.164	.027		.08		.0022
400	300	86.9	.275	.076		.09		.0068
400	400	100.0	.406	.165		.12		.0198
400	500	112.0	.526	.277		.09		.0249
Sum						1.00		VAR(IRR) = .1120

Note: $\overline{\text{IRR}} = \Sigma p_i \text{IRR}_i$, where p_i = joint probability, $\overline{\text{IRR}}$ = 59.4%
$[\text{VAR(IRR)}]^{1/2} = \sigma(\text{IRR}) = .3347$ or 33.47%.

words, if the project is abandoned at the end of Year 1, then Year 1 returns will increase by $250 and Year 2 returns will be zero. The present value of this estimated $250 abandonment value is, therefore, compared with the expected present values of the cash flows that would occur during the second year if abandonment did not take place. To make the comparison valid, however, we must use the second year flows based on the conditional probabilities only, rather than the joint probabilities that were used in the preceding analysis. This calculation is shown in Table 18A.4.

Table 18A.4   Expected Present Values of Cash Flow during the Second Year

Cash Flow	PV Factor	PV	Conditional Probability		Expected Present Value
$100	0.7972	80	0.3		$ 24
200	0.7972	159	0.5		80
300	0.7972	239	0.2		48
				Branch total	$152
200	0.7972	159	0.3		$ 48
300	0.7972	239	0.5		120
400	0.7972	319	0.2		64
				Branch total	$232
300	0.7972	239	0.3		$ 72
400	0.7972	319	0.4		128
500	0.7972	399	0.3		120
				Branch total	$320

Table 18A.5   Expected Net Present Value with Abandonment Value Included

Year 1 Cash Flow (1)	×	PV Factor (2)	=	PV (3)	Year 2 Cash Flow (4)	×	PV Factor (5)	=	PV (6)	Present Value of Total Cash Flow (7)	×	Joint Prob-ability (8)	=	Expected Value (9)
$450		0.8929		$402	$ 0		0.7972		$ 0	$402		0.30		$121
300		0.8929		268	200		0.7972		159	427		0.12		51
					300		0.7972		239	507		0.20		101
					400		0.7972		319	587		0.08		47
400		0.8929		357	300		0.7972		239	596		0.09		54
					400		0.7972		319	676		0.12		81
					500		0.7972		399	756		0.09		68

                                                                           1.00
                                            Expected present value   = $523
                                            Expected net present value = $223

We next compare the present value of the $250 abandonment value, $250 × 0.8929 = $223, with the branch expected present values for each of the three possible cash flow patterns (branches) depicted in Table 18A.4. If the $223 present value of abandonment exceeds one or more of the expected present values of the possible branches of cash flows, taking abandonment value into account will improve the indicated returns from the project. The $223 does exceed the $152 expected PV shown in Table 18A.4 for second-year cash flows when the first year cash flow is $200. In Table 18A.5, therefore, abandonment after Year 1 is assumed for the $200 case and the new NPV is calculated; the $250 abandonment value is added to the $200 cash flow to obtain a $450 Year 1 cash flow, and the Year 2 cash flow becomes $0. The new calculation of the standard deviation of returns is shown in Table 18A.6.

We may now compare the results when abandonment value is taken into account with the results when it is not considered. Including abandonment value in the calculations increases the expected net present value from $201 to $223, or by about 10 percent. It reduces the expected standard deviation of returns from 33.5 percent to 22.3 percent. Thus, for this problem, abandonment value improves the attractiveness of the investment.

Abandonment value is important in another aspect of financial decision making: the reevaluation of projects in succeeding years after they have been undertaken. The decision to continue the project or to abandon it sometime during its life depends on which branch occurs during each time period. For example, suppose that during Year 1 the cash flow actually obtained was $200. Then the three possibilities associated with Year 2 are the three that were conditionally dependent upon a $200 outcome in Year 1. The other six probabilities for Year 2, which were considered in the initial evaluation, were conditional upon other first-year outcomes and are thus no longer relevant. A calculation (Table 18A.7) is then made of the second-year net cash flows, discounted back one year.

At the end of the first year the abandonment value is $250. This is compared with the expected present value of the second-year net cash flow series discounted one year. This value is determined to be $171, so the abandonment value of $250 exceeds the net present

Table 18A.6 Calculation of Rate of Return Standard Deviation with Abandonment Value Included

Cash Flow								
Year 1	Year 2	IRR	IRR − $\overline{\text{IRR}}$	(IRR − $\overline{\text{IRR}}$)^2	×	Joint Probability	=	p_i(IRR − $\overline{\text{IRR}}$)^2
$450	$ 0	50.0%	−.188	.035		.09		.0032
450	0	50.0	−.188	.035		.15		.0053
450	0	50.0	−.188	.035		.06		.0021
300	200	45.7	−.231	.053		.12		.0064
300	300	61.8	−.070	.005		.20		.0010
300	400	75.8	.070	.005		.08		.0004
400	300	86.9	.181	.033		.09		.0030
400	400	100.0	.312	.097		.12		.0116
400	500	112.0	.432	.187		.09		.0168
Sum						1.00	VAR(IRR) =	.0498

Note: $\overline{\text{IRR}} = \sum_i p_i \text{IRR}_i$, where p_i = joint probability, $\overline{\text{IRR}}$ = 68.8%

$[\text{VAR(IRR)}]^{1/2} = \sigma(\text{IRR}) = .2232$ or 22.32%.

value of returns for the second year. Therefore, the project should be abandoned at the end of the first year.

In summary, it is sometimes advantageous to abandon a project even though the net present value of continued operation is positive. The basic reason is that the present value of abandonment after a shorter time may actually be greater than the present value of continued operation.

Another, perhaps better way to analyze the abandonment decision is to compute the NPV of the project without the option to abandon, and then add to it the value of the abandonment put option. Thus, we have

NPV (with abandonment) = NPV (without abandonment)

+ Value of abandonment put option

Table 18A.7 Calculation of Expected Net Cash Flow for Second Period when $200 Was Earned during the First Year

Cash Flow	×	PV Factor	=	PV	×	Probability Factor	=	Discounted Expected Cash Flow
$100		0.8929		$ 89		0.3		$ 27
200		0.8929		179		0.5		90
300		0.8929		268		0.2		54
						Expected present value =		$171

The greater the variance of returns on the project, the greater will be the value of the abandonment option. In Table 18A.3 we saw that the standard deviation of returns was 33.5 percent for the project without the abandonment option. This is the correct standard deviation to use in the Black-Scholes formula because it is an estimate of the standard deviation of returns on the underlying asset. The way our example has been structured, we also know that the put option may be exercised only at the end of the first year. Therefore it is a European put option with one year to maturity and an exercise price of $250. The present value of the underlying asset is the present value of the project without abandonment, that is, $501. We assume the risk-free rate is 5 percent.

Note that if the project is abandoned at the end of the first year, we will abandon it only after receiving the first year's cash flows. Therefore, we must compute the asset value *without* these cash flows in order to value the abandonment put option. The calculation is shown in Table 18A.8.

The value of the abandonment put option can be found by using the Black-Scholes formula to value the corresponding call, then put-call parity to compute the put value. The Black-Scholes call value is

$$C = SN(d_1) - Xe^{-r_F T}N(d_2),$$

where

$$d_1 = \frac{ln(S/X) + r_F T}{\sigma\sqrt{T}} + \frac{1}{2}\sigma\sqrt{T}$$

$$d_2 = d_1 - \sigma\sqrt{T}.$$

Substituting in the numbers from our example we have

$$d_1 = \frac{ln(233.57/250) + .05(1)}{.335\sqrt{1}} + \frac{1}{2}(.335)\sqrt{1}$$

Table 18A.8 Present Value of the Project Excluding First-Year Cash Flows

Year 2 Cash Flow	Joint Probability	PV Factor	PV
$100	.09	.7972	$ 7.17
200	.15	.7972	23.92
300	.06	.7972	14.35
200	.12	.7972	19.13
300	.20	.7972	47.83
400	.08	.7972	25.51
300	.09	.7972	21.52
400	.12	.7972	38.27
500	.09	.7972	35.87
Sum	1.00		233.57

$$d_1 = \frac{ln(.9343) + .05}{.335} + .168$$

$$= \frac{-.068 + .05}{.335} + .168$$

$$= -.0537 + .168 = .1143$$

$$d_2 = .1143 - .335 \sqrt{1} = -.2207.$$

Using Appendix D at the end of the book, we find that

$$N(d_1) = .5 + .0455 = .5455, \text{ and}$$

$$N(d_2) = .5 - .0874 = .4126.$$

Thus, the value of the call option is

$$C = 233.57(.5455) - 250(.4126)e^{-.05(1)}$$

$$= 127.41 - 250(.4126)(.9512)$$

$$= 127.41 - 98.12 = 29.29.$$

Finally, we can use Equation 18.5, put-call parity, to find the value of the European put that is implied by the option to abandon.

$$C_0 - P_0 = S_0 - Xe^{-r_F T}$$

$$P_0 = C_0 - S_0 + Xe^{-r_F T}$$

$$= 29.29 - 233.57 + 250e^{-.05(1)}$$

$$= 29.29 - 233.57 + 250(.9512)$$

$$= 29.29 - 233.57 + 237.80$$

$$= \$33.52$$

The decision tree approach gave an abandonment value equal to $22 (that is, $223, the value with abandonment, minus $201, the value without abandonment). The option pricing approach gave an abandonment value of $33.52. We obtained different answers because the assumptions of the Black-Scholes OPM and the decision tree approach are different. For example, Black-Scholes assumes a log-normal distribution of outcomes whereas the decision tree only crudely approximates the continuum of possibilities. It is hard to say which assumption is more realistic for project abandonment decisions.

Further Developments in Abandonment Decision Rules

The traditional abandonment decision rule is that the project should be abandoned in the first year that abandonment value exceeds the present value of remaining expected cash flows from continued operation. More recently it has become evident that this decision rule may not result in the optimal abandonment decision.[2] Abandonment at a later date may result in an even greater net present value. For example, consider a truck with two years of remaining useful life. The present value of continued use is, say, $900, but the current market value of the truck is $1,000. Clearly, if the proceeds from the sale can be invested to earn at least the applicable cost of capital, the better decision would be to sell the truck now. However, there is one option that has not been considered, which is to operate the truck for another year and collect the cash flow from one year's operations (which have a present value of $500) and then abandon it (assuming the present value of abandonment in a year is $600). Thus, the present value of this alternative is $1,100. In this case, the truck should be used for one year and then sold.

The optimal abandonment decision rule is to determine the combination of remaining operating cash flows and future abandonment that has the maximum expected net present value. This decision rule is, unfortunately, difficult to implement, especially when the project life is long and there are numerous opportunities for abandonment over time.[3] If a piece of equipment can be used for 20 years or abandoned at the end of any year, then 20 different net present value calculations might be required to determine the optimum pattern that will result in maximum expected net present value.

It is argued that this approach is too cumbersome and all that is required is to find at least one pattern of cash flows that yields an expected net present value greater than the value of abandonment. Thus the rule becomes an accept-reject decision: Continue to operate the project as long as expected present value of continued operation and abandonment at any later period is greater than the value of abandonment now. Under this system, there is no need ever to determine the maximum expected net present value. Furthermore, since it is impossible to predict accurately future abandonment value, whatever the expected net present value is, it will surely be inaccurate.

The accept-reject decision has one shortcoming, however. It does not provide a means of selecting between mutually exclusive investments or of making capital rationing decisions. To return to our truck example, we have shown that the present value is $1,100 when the truck is operated for another year. Using the accept-reject rule, we would continue to operate the truck. But suppose a truck could be leased for $1,000 for one year and would produce cash flows worth $1,200 at net present value. If only one truck is required (mutually exclusive choice decision), or if the only source of the $1,000 to lease the truck is the sale of the old truck (capital rationing), then the value to the firm is maximized if the truck is sold and the new truck leased.

It is evident that both rules (the maximum net present value rule and the accept-reject rule) have merit. Maximum net present value should be used whenever capital rationing or mutually exclusive choices are involved. Accept-reject can be used to reduce the cumbersomeness of the problem whenever one decision is independent of all others.

Selected References

Brennan, M., and Schwartz, E., "Evaluating Natural Resource Investments," *Journal of Business*, 58 (1985), pp. 135-155.

Copeland, T. E., and Weston, J. F., "A Note on the Evaluation of Cancellable Operating Leases," *Financial Management*, (Summer 1982), pp. 60-67.

Dyl, E. A., and Long, H. W., "Abandonment Value and Capital Budgeting: Comment," *Journal of Finance*, (March 1969), pp. 88-95.

Joy, O. Maurice, "Abandonment Values and Abandonment Decisions: A Clarification," *Journal of Finance*, 31 (September 1976), pp. 1225-1228.

[2]See Dyl and Long [1969]; Robichek and Van Horne [1969]; Joy [1976].

[3]If we were using an option pricing approach, we would have to value an American put option on a dividend paying stock. Although there are numerical solutions to this type of problem, they are beyond the scope of this text.

Myers, S. C., and Majd, S., "Calculating Abandonment Value Using Option Pricing Theory," working paper, Sloan School of Management, MIT, 1983.

Pappas, James L., "The Role of Abandonment Value in Capital Asset Management," *Engineering Economist*, 22 (Fall 1976), pp. 53-61.

Robichek, A. A., and Van Horne, J. C., "Abandonment Value and Capital Budgeting," *Journal of Finance*, 22 (December 1967), pp. 577-590.

————, "Abandonment Value and Capital Budgeting: Reply," *Journal of Finance*, 24 (March 1969), pp. 96-97.

Chapter 19 Market Efficiency and Financial Decisions

At the heart of free market systems is the issue of whether or not prices accurately reflect all the information necessary for scarce resources to be efficiently allocated among an infinite variety of alternate and competing uses. This chapter focuses on the response of securities market prices to the arrival of new information. The theory of capital market efficiency is presented along with some of the empirical evidence.

Capital market efficiency is also implicit in many of the models involved in financial decision making. Hence, the concept is central to building a conceptual framework required for making rational financial policies and choices. We shall discuss the characteristics of securities markets as they really are and attempt to dispel some of the widely held myths.

The Theory of Market Efficiency

At the outset, we should emphasize that we will be talking about the efficiency of *securities* markets. We will not consider more general issues such as whether or not markets for goods and services are efficient. Even if there is a monopoly producer, our only concern here is whether or not the market price of the monopolist's common stock accurately reflects all information known about the monopoly.

Research into the efficiency of securities markets has been aided greatly by large data bases of accurate security transactions prices. For example, the University of Chicago Center for Research in Securities Prices (CRSP) has produced a computer-readable file of monthly returns for all New York Stock Exchange (NYSE) listed securities from 1926 to present and another file with daily returns for all NYSE and AMEX (American Stock Exchange) securities from 1962 to present. This wealth of data has allowed extensive empirical testing of various theories in finance, including the hypothesis of market efficiency. In fact, finance is one of the few social sciences where the data is good enough to allow researchers to reject a theory if it proves unfounded. As we shall see, market efficiency is a theory which has stood up well to empirical testing.

Information and Market Efficiency

A security market is said to be efficient if the price instantaneously and fully reflects all relevant available information. For the time being, we shall assume that information is costless and focus on questions such as (1) What is information? (2) What do we know about the availability of information? (3) What information is relevant? (4) What is meant by prices which "fully reflect" information? and (5) How fast do prices respond to new information?

The issue of what is or is not information and the issue of how to value information are the bases for a separate field of study called information economics.[1] We can only scratch the surface here. Information is a set of messages (for example, a newspaper) which may be used to alter the actions of the recipient in a way to change his or her welfare. The ability to take action is critical. For example, a wheat farmer might be willing to pay a high price for accurate weather forecasts, but an underground coal miner would pay nothing because his activities are unaffected by the weather. Also, in order to have value, a message must be correlated with actual events as they later occur. An uncorrelated message is useless. For example, if you ask an undiscriminating friend about the quality of a movie you want to view, the answer might be "I liked it" regardless of whether or not it was really good. If the message is always the same, it has no value. On the other hand, inversely correlated messages can be just as valuable as those which are positively correlated. If the stock market index always goes up when we forecast a decline (and vice versa), then our forecasts are valuable because you can do the opposite of what we say. As we shall see, some types of messages about common stock actually contain little or no information because they are uncorrelated with changes in the price of the stock. Corporate name changes and annual reports, for example, seem to fall into this category.

The Fair Game Model

The theory which best expresses the efficient markets hypothesis is called the *fair game model*. It says that on average there will be no difference between the actual change in security prices and the expected change in security prices across an interval of time. The appropriate mathematical expression is

$$\epsilon_{j,t+1} = \frac{P_{j,t+1} - P_{j,t}}{P_{j,t}} - \frac{E(P_{j,t+1}|\text{Info}_t) - P_{j,t}}{P_{j,t}}, \tag{19.1}$$

where

$$\begin{aligned}
P_{j,t+1} &= \text{the actual price of Security } j \text{ next period} \\
P_{j,t} &= \text{the price of Security } j \text{ this period} \\
E(P_{j,t+1}|\text{Info}_t) &= \text{the predicted (or expected) security price next period, given a current} \\
& \quad \text{amount of information, Info}_t \\
\epsilon_{j,t+1} &= \text{the difference between actual and predicted returns.}
\end{aligned}$$

Note that the fair game model (19.1) is really written in returns form. If we let the one-period return be defined as

$$r_{j,t+1} = \frac{P_{j,t+1} - P_{j,t}}{P_{j,t}}, \tag{19.2}$$

then (19.1) can be rewritten as

$$\epsilon_{j,t+1} = r_{j,t+1} - E(r_{j,t+1}|\text{Info}_t). \tag{19.3}$$

---

[1] For an excellent review article, see Hirshleifer and Riley [1979].

The fair game model says that, on average, across a large number of observations, the expected return on an asset, given an information set, Info$_t$, will equal its actual return. If we take the expectation of Equation 19.3, the price pattern will be a fair game if the expected difference between the actual and predicted returns is equal to zero.

$$E(\epsilon_{j,t+1}) = E(r_{j,t+1} - E(r_{j,t+1}|\text{Info}_t)) = 0. \tag{19.4}$$

The stock market is a fair game if expected price increases, given available information, are, on average, equal to actual price increases.[2]

Various examples of fair games can help to clarify the concept. Suppose you are asked to bet on the flip of a coin. If your prior information leads you to believe that there is a 50-50 chance of heads or tails, and if the coin actually has a 60 percent chance of heads, then from your perspective, the coin flip will *not* be a fair game. It is not fair because the actual percentage of heads is not equal to the percentage which you expected. Next, suppose you go to a gambling resort (Las Vegas, Atlantic City, or Monte Carlo). You know, before arriving, that the house will take an average of $X\%$ from your winnings. If the house actually takes $X\%$ on average, then gambling at the resort *is* a fair game from your perspective because, on average, you lose what you expected to lose.

Fama [1970] partitioned the fair game model of market efficiency into three useful categories, each based on the type of information set used in making decisions.

1. *Weak-form* market efficiency hypothesizes that today's security prices fully reflect all information contained in historical security prices. This implies that no investor can earn excess returns by developing trading rules based on historical price or return information.
2. *Semi-strong-form* market efficiency says that security prices fully reflect all publicly available information. Thus, no investor could earn excess returns using publicly available sources such as corporate annual reports, NYSE ticker tape information, or published investment advisory reports.
3. *Strong-form* market efficiency hypothesizes that security prices fully reflect all information whether it is publicly available or not.

This categorization is extremely useful because it allows us to empirically test the fair game model of market efficiency with respect to different sets of information.

Implications for Managerial Decision Making

If securities markets are efficient (at least in the semi-strong form), the implications for financial managers are profound. If security prices reflect all publicly available information, then managers can watch their company stock price to find out what the market thinks of recently announced decisions. For example, Ruback [1982] analyzed the much publicized takeover of Conoco by du Pont in 1981, when du Pont offered to pay a total of $7.54 billion for Conoco. It was the largest merger ever. On July 6, 1981, the day the du Pont bid was announced, du Pont shares fell in value by 8.05 percent and Conoco shares

---

[2]A special case of a fair game, called a *submartingale*, occurs when the expected returns are strictly positive, that is,

$$E(r_{j,t+1}|\text{Info}_t) > 0.$$

The stock market is actually a submartingale, with positive expected returns. Returns are positive because of risk and the positive time value of money.

rose by 11.87 percent.[3] The wealth of du Pont shareholders fell by approximately $642 million in a single day. The message to du Pont managers was unavoidable. The market felt they had made a mistake. The moral of the story is simple — trust market prices.

Market efficiency is one of the most important themes in finance. The rapid adjustment of securities prices to new information has many implications for managers. Among them are the following:

1. All securities are perfect substitutes (at least before taxes). The implication is that *the net present value of any securities investment is zero*. For example, if you pay $850 for a bond with a promised yield of 8 percent, you expect to receive cash flows whose present value is exactly $850. The NPV is zero because your investment outlay (the $850 you pay out) is exactly equal to the discounted cash inflows (also $850). This is true for all securities. A common stock which costs $35 per share has discounted cash flows of $35 and a zero NPV. The expected yield on the stock will be higher than the bond because the stock is riskier. But its higher cash flows (dividends and capital gains) exactly offset its higher risk. The result is a zero NPV. The NPV of a securities investment is positive only when the investor has access to information which is not publicly available. For example, if management possesses inside information and believes the shares of its firm are undervalued, then there may be good reason to repurchase the firm's shares.[4]

2. If securities are perfect substitutes, then investors can effortlessly duplicate a wide variety of management decisions. They can either undo management errors or can manufacture results left undone by management. *Homemade financial decision making is a low-cost alternative to corporate financial decision making.* Consider conglomerate mergers as a possibility. It is not unusual to hear a chief executive officer announce a conglomerate merger campaign because the resulting diversification across product lines will benefit shareholders.[5] We question the wisdom of such remarks because investors can create a homemade conglomerate merger simply by holding a portfolio of the firms prior to merger. They do not need management to do it for them. Consequently, the NPV of a pure conglomerate merger should be zero. In 1984, when Bell Telephone was split into many geographically different operating companies, it was possible to buy a mutual fund (called a Humpty Dumpty fund) which consisted of a portfolio recombining the split-up companies, thus undoing the split-up — at least from a financial point of view.

3. *There are no illusions in securities markets.* Securities prices are based on discounted expected cash flows. Cosmetic changes which have no effect on the perceived risk of a firm or on its expected cash flows will have no effect on its security prices in an efficient market. For example, changing your company name will usually have no effect on your stock price. Moving publicly available information (such as lease commitments or pension fund liabilities) from the footnotes of your accounting statement onto the balance sheet will have no effect. Stock splits and stock dividends, which are merely paper transactions, will have little or no effect.[6]

---

[3]These are "abnormal" returns which have removed general stock market movement on the announcement date.

[4]For a detailed discussion of share repurchase, see Chapter 22.

[5]Remember, a conglomerate merger, by definition, is assumed to have no economic synergies (such as economies of scale or better management coordination). It is merely a combination of two disparate firms under the same legal roof. In Chapter 18, we saw that, at best, conglomerate mergers would have no effect on shareholders' wealth if both firms had no debt. If either firm is levered, conglomerate merger is likely to reduce shareholders' wealth. See Chapter 30 for the empirical evidence on conglomerate mergers.

[6]See Chapter 22 for a detailed discussion of the empirical evidence on stock splits and stock dividends.

4.   *Today's securities prices are the best estimate of future prices.* Why? Because thousands of investors are continuously gathering information in order to outguess each other. It pays handsomely to win in the securities market game. If you have information which is not available to the general public and if you can analyze it correctly, you should be able to make the correct investment decision. This is the position in which many financial officers find themselves. But how should they use their knowledge of their firm when issuing new securities (debt or equity) in order to raise capital? Take a new debt issue for example. There are two important considerations. First, will market interest rates rise or fall? Market efficiency tells us that the chief financial officer (CFO) will not have any special knowledge in this arena. Today's bond prices (the forward rate of interest) are the best predictors of future interest rates. No mathematical model or team of experts can do better. The second consideration is that the CFO probably does know whether his firm's risk will go up or down in the future, and he knows this better than the market does. It would pay to issue debt before the market learns of the risk. But wait. If CFOs systematically issue debt prior to an increase in their firm's risk, the market will discount their actions and charge a higher interest rate anyway. The resolution of the market's response to better-informed CFOs is a complicated issue which we cannot answer here. However, the implication of market efficiency is clear. If you think you can beat the market by predicting market interest rates or future stock price movements, you should consider the lesson of market efficiency. What do you know that thousands of other investors do not?

In the next section, we begin to examine the empirical evidence on market efficiency in each of its three forms: weak, semi-strong, and strong. Not all of the examples involve decisions by financial managers. However, they do represent behavior of financial markets to which financial managers must relate in order to make sound financial decisions. The examples are chosen to reflect the best evidence on market efficiency per se. Do prices instantaneously and fully reflect all publicly available information? The implications of market efficiency for corporate finance have been discussed above and will be brought up throughout the remainder of the text.

Evidence on Weak-Form Efficiency

Technical trading rules are a common form of investment strategy. Advocates claim that the pattern of past prices can be used to predict future price movements and thereby make trading profits. The weak form of market efficiency claims the opposite, namely, that *it is impossible to use technical trading rules to earn excess returns because current prices already reflect all information in past price patterns.*

A common source of confusion is that some securities seem to have definite price patterns. The steel and residential construction industries, for example, seem to have recognizable business cycles. Why then can't clever investors make excess returns by buying low and selling high? The answer has to do with the difference between returns and prices (not to mention that the exact timing of the cycles is uncertain). In order to illustrate the relationship between price patterns and security returns, let us take a simple example. Suppose that we know *with certainty* that a firm follows a (rather extreme) two-year cycle. Every two years it will pay a $10 per share dividend, but during the intervening years it will pay nothing. If the risk-free interest rate is a constant 10 percent, how will the security

Figure 19.1   The Security Return Is Constant Even Though Its Price Follows a Definite Pattern

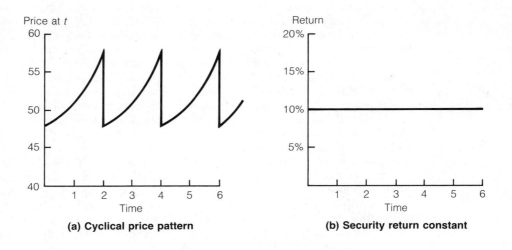

(a) Cyclical price pattern   **(b) Security return constant**

price change through time? The answer is illustrated in Figure 19.1(a).[7] The day before the stock pays its biannual $10 dividend, it is worth $57.62. The next day, the dividend is paid and the stock is said to have gone *ex dividend*. At that time, its market price falls by $10 to $47.62. During the following two years, the stock price rises until, once again, the day before it goes *ex dividend*, it is worth $57.62. One would think that an excess profit could be earned if you buy at $47.62, hold for two years, and sell for $57.62. You can certainly earn a profit, but it is not an *excess* profit. You can earn only the *expected* 10 percent rate of return.[8] Although the price follows a predictable pattern, the expected rate of return is constant.[9] This is illustrated in Figure 19.1(b).

Technical Trading Rules

Direct tests of the fair game model and of the weak form of market efficiency were provided by Alexander [1961] and Fama and Blume [1966]. They used a technical trading filter rule which attempts to exploit historical price patterns in an effort to earn excess returns. Because the rule uses only past prices as the relevant information set, it is a direct test of the weak form of market efficiency. The rule states: Buy a stock if its current price has risen

---

[7]The exact equation for an infinite annuity paid in advance every N years is given in Chapter 6, Equation 6.9. Using the facts of our example, we have

$$PV(2,\infty) = \$10[(1.1)^2 \div (1.1^2 - 1)] = \$57.62.$$

[8]At a 10 percent discount rate, the present value of $57.62 received two years hence is $47.62 today.

[9]See Samuelson [1965] for an eloquent discussion of this concept.

$X\%$ from its previous low, hold it until the price falls $X\%$ from its high, and then sell and go short. Maintain the short position until the price rises $X\%$, and then cover the short position and establish a long position. This process is repeated for a fixed time interval, and the profits from the filter rule are then compared with a buy-and-hold strategy in the same security. Because each security is compared with itself, there is no need to adjust for risk.

Filter rules are designed to make an investor a profit if there are any systematic patterns in the movement of prices over time. It is only a matter of trying enough different filters until one of them picks up price runs and makes a profit which exceeds that of the simple buy-and-hold strategy. Figure 19.2 illustrates the execution of a 10 percent filter rule on IBM during the interval September 1982 through September 1983. The buy-and-hold strategy earned a 72.7 percent return while the filter rule completed eight transactions with a gross return of only 19.5 percent. Of course, a sample of one company does not prove anything. The empirical studies of Alexander and Fama and Blume used hundreds of different securities.

The filter rule tests have three important results. First, even before subtracting transactions costs, filters greater than 1.5 percent cannot beat a simple buy-and-hold strategy. Second, filters below 1.5 percent, on the average, make very small profits which, because of frequent trading, actually outperform the buy-and-hold strategy. However, this is not necessarily evidence of market inefficiency. First, one must subtract from gross profits the cost of transacting. Fama and Blume [1966] show that even a floor trader (the owner of a seat on the NYSE) must pay at least .1 percent per transaction. Once these costs are deducted from the profits of filters that are less than 1.5 percent, the profits vanish. This is clear evidence that capital markets are efficient in their weak form because the return on a portfolio managed with price-history information is the same as a buy-and-hold strategy which uses no information. Therefore, the value of information provided by stock price patterns is zero. Technical trading does not work.

The third inference which can be drawn from filter rule tests is that the market appears to be a fair game with positive expected returns (that is, a submartingale). All the securities had positive average returns. This makes sense because risky assets are expected to yield positive returns to compensate investors for the risk they undertake.

Weak-form market efficiency means that security prices have no memory. Historical patterns in stock prices are of no use in predicting future price movements. A chief financial officer who claims to have no inside information and who refuses to issue new equity simply because the company's price has fallen is using bad logic. A recent price decline does not mean a price rise can be predicted, and it does not mean a further decline can be predicted either.

Evidence on Semi-Strong-Form Efficiency

The semi-strong form of the market efficiency hypothesis says that current security prices fully reflect all publicly available information. There is an infinite variety of different types of publicly available information, and hundreds of empirical tests of the semi-strong efficiency hypothesis have been published. While only a few of these studies will be reviewed here, the preponderance of evidence supports the conclusion that capital markets are indeed efficient in their semi-strong form (although there are some anomalies which have been reported).

If capital markets are semi-strong-form efficient, then when new information becomes public, security prices should respond quickly by adjusting to a new level. Anyone at-

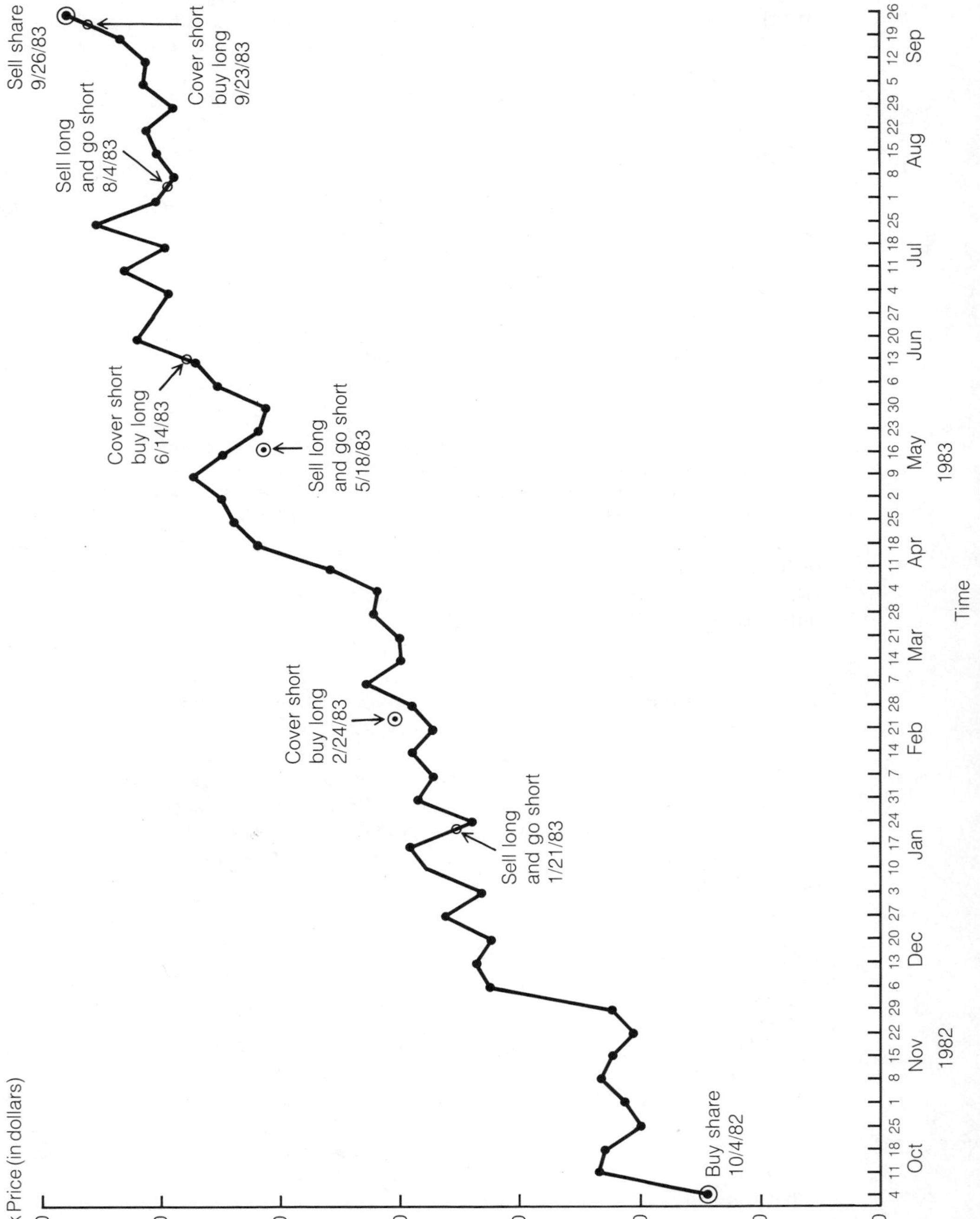

Figure 19.2   Implementing a 10 Percent Filter Rule on IBM during 1982-1983

tempting to utilize published information in a trading strategy will fail to earn excess returns because security prices will have already adjusted, and no further predictable price changes can be expected.

The semi-strong model of market efficiency can also be used to test whether a type of message is relevant. If securities prices do not change when "news" is published or at any time thereafter, then we can argue that the "news" contained no relevant information.

Accounting Earnings Reports

Annual and quarterly earnings reports are obvious examples of information which is made publicly available. We can test semi-strong-form efficiency by measuring security price responses when these reports are released. Remember, there are two things to look for:

1.   If securities prices respond by adjusting to a new level when news is published, then the news message contains relevant information. If there is no price adjustment, then the news contains no information.
2.   If there is no further price adjustment after the initial announcement, then it is impossible to construct a profitable trading rule based on publicly available information, and the market is semi-strong-form efficient.

Ball and Brown [1968] were the first to study market responses to the release of accounting information. They used monthly returns data for a sample of 261 firms between 1946 and 1965. First, they separated the sample into companies which had earnings that were either higher or lower than those predicted by a time-series model. Next, predicted earnings changes were compared with actual earnings changes. If the actual change was greater than predicted, the company was put into a "good news" portfolio and vice versa. The rationale for studying *unanticipated* earnings changes is straightforward. In order for the annual report to contain favorable news, it must announce not only increased earnings but also earnings which are higher than expected. Or if earnings are down, they must be down less than expected.

Figure 19.3 plots an abnormal performance index (API), which represents the excess return earned on $1 invested in a portfolio 12 months before an annual report and held for T months (where $T = 1,2, \ldots ,18$). For example, if you were omniscient, you could have invested in the portfolio of firms which earned more than predicted and done so 12 months before the actual earnings announcement (Month -12). Figure 19.3 shows that between Month -12 and Month 0, the month of the annual report, the API recorded approximately a 7 percent excess rate of return (above what it otherwise would have been expected to return, given its risk).

In order to measure *excess* returns, it is first necessary to have a benchmark to predict expected returns. The difference between actual and predicted returns is an excess return. The *market model* (really an unspecified version of the CAPM) is the usual benchmark. The expected return on a security is estimated in two stages. First, the actual return of a security (or portfolio of securities), R_{jt}, is regressed against the market portfolio, R_{Mt} (for example, the NYSE index) as follows:

$$R_{jt} = \hat{a}_j + \hat{b}_j R_{Mt} + \epsilon_{jt}, \tag{19.5}$$

where

$\hat{a}, \hat{b} = $ the estimated intercept and slope terms
$\epsilon_{jt} = $ the random error terms around the regression line.

Figure 19.3   Abnormal Performance Index of Portfolios Chosen on the Basis of Differences between Actual and Predicted Accounting Income

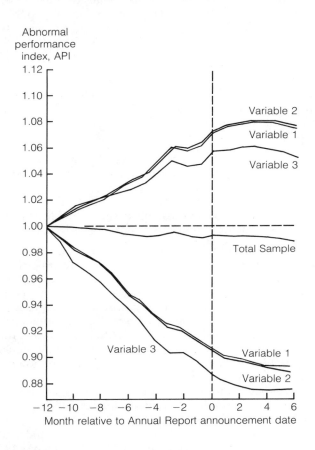

Source: R. Ball and P. Brown, "An Empirical Evaluation of Accounting Income Numbers." Reprinted with permission of *The Journal of Accounting Research*, Autumn 1968, p. 169.

For example, Ball and Brown estimated Equation 19.5 using monthly returns data for each security taken from an interval before the experimental period. The second step is to predict the expected return, $\hat{R}_{jt}$, by using the coefficients estimated in Equation 19.5 and the actual market return, R_{Mt}.

$$\hat{R}_{jt} = \hat{a}_j + \hat{b}_j R_{Mt}. \tag{19.6}$$

Once the expected return has been estimated, it can be subtracted from the actual return in order to obtain the excess return, ϵ_{jt}.

$$\epsilon_{jt} = R_{jt} - \hat{R}_{jt}. \tag{19.7}$$

Ball and Brown estimated excess returns from 12 months before the release of the annual report until 6 months afterward. Having estimated the excess return for each security during each month, they then constructed their abnormal performance index (API) by multiplying the monthly returns together for a given security and then averaging across securities.

$$\text{API} = \frac{1}{N} \sum_{j=1}^{N} \prod_{t=1}^{T} (1 + \epsilon_{jt}), \tag{19.8}$$

where,

$N =$ the number of companies in the sample
$T =$ the number of months over which the abnormal performance is measured ($T = 1$, $2, \ldots, 18$).

The API will be zero if a security earns only its expected return over a given time interval. For example, suppose IBM was expected to return 18 percent during the year prior to the publication of its annual report. If it fell into the "good news" portfolio of Ball and Brown, it had an API of 7 percent, which meant that it earned 25 percent, that is, 7 percent more than expected.

Figure 19.3 shows that when earnings are higher than predicted, returns prior to the annual report month (Month 0) are abnormally high. Furthermore, returns appear to move upward gradually until, by the time of the annual report, almost all of the adjustment has occurred. Most of the information contained in the annual report is anticipated by the market *before* the annual report is released. In fact, anticipation is so accurate that the actual income number does not appear to cause any unusual jumps on the API in the annual report month. Most of the content of the annual report (about 85 percent to 90 percent) is captured by more timely sources of information. Apparently, market prices adjust continuously to new information as it becomes publicly available throughout the year. The annual report has little new information to add.

These results suggest that prices in the market place continuously adjust in an unbiased manner to new information. Two implications for corporate treasurers are (1) significant new information, which will affect the future cash flows of the firm, should be announced as soon as it becomes available so that shareholders can use it without the (presumably greater) expense of discovering it from alternate sources, and (2) it probably does not make any difference whether the cash flow effects are reported in the balance sheet, the income statement, or footnotes — the market can evaluate the news as long as it is publicly available, whatever form it may take.

The final conclusion which can be drawn from the Ball and Brown study is that the market does appear to be semi-strong-form efficient. By the time of the annual report, all of the upward price adjustment for the good news and all of the downward adjustment for the bad news firms has taken place. After the annual report, the API is flat (from Month 0 to Month +6). This means that prices have fully responded to all of the information in the annual report and it is impossible to form a profitable trading rule based on this publicly available information. It might well be the case that if a firm has a good year this year, it will also have a good year next year. However, in an efficient market, investors have already taken this possibility into account and the information is already reflected in today's price. Future price changes are unpredictable; hence, the predicted return from Month 0 forward will be equal to the actual return on average. The excess return will be zero.

One of the troublesome conclusions of the Ball and Brown study was that there seemed to be little or no market response to the annual report. Hence, from the market's point of view, the annual report is irrelevant. It contains no new information. Does this mean that accounting information in general is useless? More recent studies by Aharony and Swary [1980], Joy, Litzenberger, and McEnally [1977], and Watts [1978] have focused on quarterly earnings reports, where information revealed to the market is (perhaps) more timely than that in annual reports.[10] They typically use a time series model to predict quarterly earnings and then form two portfolios of equal risk, one consisting of firms with earnings higher than predicted and the other of firms with lower than expected earnings. The combined portfolio, which is long in the higher than expected earnings firms and short in the lower than expected earnings firms, is a zero beta (that is, zero systematic risk), well-diversified portfolio which requires no investment because the funds provided from short selling are used to buy the securities held in the long position. A portfolio having no risk and requiring no net investment is an arbitrage portfolio and should have zero expected return. Watts [1978] finds a statistically significant return in the quarter of the earnings announcement — a clear indication that quarterly earnings reports contain new information. Hence, we have evidence that accounting information is relevant to the market place. However, he also finds a statistically significant return in the following quarter and concludes that "the existence of those abnormal returns is evidence that the market is (semi-strong-form) inefficient."

Quarterly earnings reports are sometimes followed by announcements of dividend changes which also affect stock prices. To separate the effect of the quarterly earnings report from the effect of the dividend announcement, Aharony and Swary [1980] use daily returns data to examine all dividend and earnings announcements within the same quarter which are at least 11 trading days apart. They conclude that both quarterly earnings announcements and dividend change announcements have statistically significant effects on the stock price. But more important, they find no evidence of market inefficiency when the two types of announcement effects are separated. They used daily data and Watts [1978] used weekly data, so we cannot be sure that the conclusions of the two studies regarding market efficiency are inconsistent. All we can say is that unexpected changes in quarterly dividends and quarterly earnings both have significant effects on the value of the firm. More research needs to be done on possible market inefficiencies following the announcement of unexpected earnings changes.

Block Trading

During a typical day for an actively traded security on a major stock exchange, thousands of shares will be traded, usually in round lots ranging between 100 and several hundred shares. However, occasionally a large block, say 10,000 shares or more, is brought to the floor for trading. The behavior of security prices around large block sales provides answers to the following questions: (1) Do block sales contain information so that there is a permanent change in the security price? (2) Once the block sale becomes publicly available information is it possible to construct a trading rule to make excess returns (that is, is the market place semi-strong-form efficient)? (3) Is there any temporary price pressure effect caused by block sales? (4) How fast does the market price respond to the announcement of a block sale? and (5) If you can participate in a block sale before it becomes publicly

---

[10]See also articles by Brown [1978], Griffin [1977], and Foster [1977].

Figure 19.4   Competing Hypotheses of Price Behavior around the Sale of a Large Block

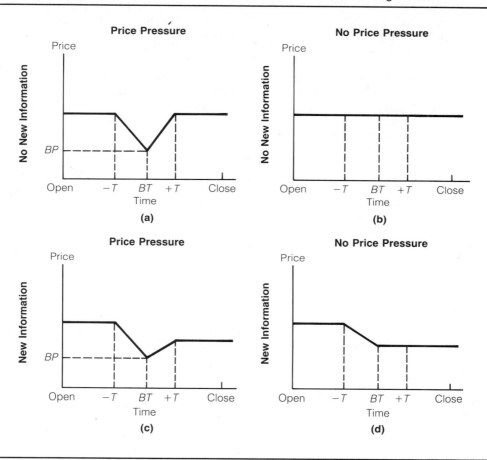

available information, can you make an abnormal return (that is, is the market strong-form efficient)? The first two questions are the same that were studied when we looked at accounting information. The last three introduce new areas of interest and shall be discussed in turn.

Many scholars have argued that the phenomenon of price pressure (Question 3 above) should not exist because all securities of equal risk are perfect substitutes for each other. The number of shares traded should have no effect on a security price because all individuals are assumed to possess the same information. Hence, if a large number of shares in the XYZ company are to be sold as a block, even the smallest price decline would attract investment capital and prevent any temporary price pressure effect. Both the (temporary) price pressure effect and the (permanent) information effect are shown in Figure 19.4, which illustrates four different intraday price patterns. Panel (b) shows what should be observed if there is no price pressure effect and no information in large blocks. The price should remain unaffected throughout the day. Panel (a) illustrates a price pressure effect only. The price drops for a period of time, $-T$ to $+T$, but recovers to its original level by the end of trading. Panel (c) shows both effects. Not only does the price temporarily drop, but also it does not return to its original level. This indicates that the block contained information which caused the security price to permanently adjust to a new level.

Kraus and Stoll [1972] examined price effects for all block trades of 10,000 shares or more carried out on the NYSE between July 1, 1968, and September 30, 1969. They had prices for the close the day before the block trade, the price immediately prior to the transaction, the block price (BP), and the closing price the day of the block trade. Abnormal performance indices based on daily data indicated that by the end of the trading day, prices had fully adjusted to a new equilibrium level.[11] More interesting were intraday price effects, which are shown in Figure 19.5. There is clear evidence of a price pressure effect. The stock price recovers substantially from the block transaction price (BP) by the end of the trading day. The recovery averages .713 percent. For example, a stock which sold for $50.00 before the block transaction would have a block price (BP) of $49.43, but by the end of the day, the price would have recovered to $49.79. The end-of-day price is a new permanent price level. On average, there are no excess returns for a month following the

---

Figure 19.5   Intraday Impacts of Block Trading

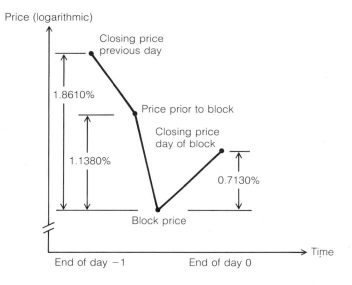

Source: A. Kraus and H. R. Stoll, "Price Impacts of Block Trading on the New York Stock Exchange." Reprinted with permission of *The Journal of Finance*, June 1972, p. 575.

---

[11]Scholes [1972] attained similar results for a sample of secondary distributions (large blocks registered with the SEC underwritten by investment bankers).

block trade. Note that the price pattern in Figure 19.5 is like Figure 19.4(c). The empirical evidence is consistent with both an information effect and a price pressure effect in block trading.

Dann, Mayers, and Raab [1977] extend the analysis of block trading by collecting continuous transaction data during the day of a block trade. Their sample was 298 blocks between July 1968 and December 1969, which had an open-to-block price decline of at least 4.56 percent. The reason for restricting the sample to blocks with large price declines was to provide the strongest test of market efficiency. If an individual or a group of investors can establish a trading rule which allows them to buy a block whose open-to-block price decline is at least 4.56 percent and then sell at the end of the day, they may be able to earn abnormal profits. This would be evidence of capital market inefficiency.

Testing a trading rule of this type takes great care. Normally, news of block trade is not made publicly available until the trade has already been consummated and the transaction is recorded on the ticker tape. The semi-strong form of market efficiency is based on the set of publicly available information. Therefore, a critical issue is: Exactly how fast must we react after we observe that our -4.56 percent trading rule has been activated by the first publicly available announcement which occurs on the ticker tape? Figure 19.6 shows annualized rates of return using the -4.56 percent rule, with the purchase made x minutes after the block and the stock then sold at the close of trading. Returns are net of actual commissions and New York State transfer taxes. For both time periods which are reported, we would have to react in less than 5 minutes in order to earn a positive return. Such a rapid reaction is, for all practical purposes, impossible. It seems that, even when we examine intraday data, no abnormal returns are available to individuals who trade on publicly available information about block trades because prices react so quickly. In no more than 15 minutes after the block trade, transactions prices have completely adjusted to unbiased estimates of closing prices. This gives some idea of how fast market prices adjust to new, unexpected information such as a block trade. The main implication for financial managers is that prices fully reflect new information very quickly—usually in less than one trading day.

What about people who can transact at the block price which, at the time of transaction, is not publicly available information? Usually, the specialist, the floor trader (a member of the NYSE), brokerage houses, and favored customers of the brokerage houses can participate at the block price. Dann, Mayers, and Raab show that with a -4.56 percent trading rule, an individual participating in every block with purchases of $100,000 or more could have earned a *net* annualized return of 203 percent for the 173 blocks which activated their filter rule. Even after adjusting for risk, transactions costs, and taxes, it was possible to earn rates of return in excess of what any existing theory would call "normal." This may be interpreted as evidence that capital markets are inefficient in their strong form. Individuals who are notified of the pending block trade and who can participate at the block price before the information becomes publicly available do, in fact, appear to earn excess profits. However, Dann, Mayers, and Raab caution us that we may not properly understand all the costs which a buyer faces in a block trade. One possibility is that the floor trader (or anyone else) who buys part of a block is doing so with full knowledge that the seller may have better information about the "true" value of the stock. If so, the buyer will offer a low price in order to protect himself. In this way, what appear to be abnormal returns may actually be fair, competitively determined fees for a service rendered—the service of providing liquidity to a seller.

The research on block trading has determined that (1) block sales do contain information so that the postblock price is permanently lower, (2) the market is semi-strong-form efficient because no profits are attainable even shortly after news of a block trade is made

Figure 19.6   Annualized Rates of Return on the −4.56 Percent Rule

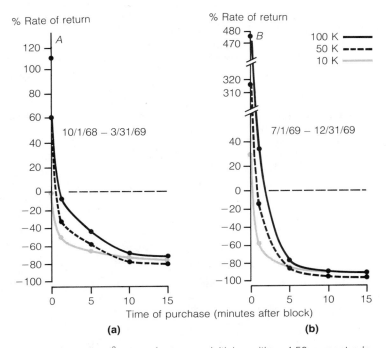

Annualized[a] rates of return on initial wealth, −4.56 percent rule; purchase at first price at least x minutes after block, sell at close[b] (using only first block per day). Gross returns less actual commissions and NY State transfer taxes (curves represent levels of initial wealth).

[a]Annualized rates of return are calculated by squaring the quantity one plus the respective six-month return.

[b]Blocks occurring within x minutes of the close were assumed not to have been acted upon.

publicly available, (3) there is a temporary price pressure effect associated with block trades, (4) the market price adjusts almost instantaneously after news of a block is made public with complete price adjustment occurring in 15 minutes or less, and (5) it is possible to make abnormal returns if you can participate at the block price. This *may* be evidence of strong-form market inefficiency.

Evidence on Strong-Form Efficiency

In order for markets to be strong-form efficient, prices must fully and instantaneously reflect all information whether it is publicly available or not. This is a difficult hypothesis to test because observations of trading behavior based on privately available information are difficult to obtain.

Insider Trading

A direct test of strong-form efficiency is whether or not insiders with access to information which is not publicly available can earn abnormal returns.[12] Jaffe [1974] collected data on insider trading from the *Official Summary of Security Transactions and Holdings,* published by the Security and Exchange Commission. He then defined an intensive trading month as one during which there were at least three more insiders selling than buying or vice versa. If a stock was intensively traded during a given month, it was included in an intensive trading portfolio. Jaffe then calculated risk-adjusted cumulative average residuals in order to measure excess returns earned by the intensive trading portfolios. If the stock had intensive selling, its residual (which would presumably be negative) was multiplied by -1 and added to the portfolio returns of the intensive buying sample. For 861 observations during the 1960s, the residuals rose approximately 5 percent in eight months following the intensive trading event, with 3 percent of the rise occurring in the last six months. These returns are statistically significant and are greater than transactions costs. The findings suggest that insiders do earn abnormal returns and that the strong-form hypothesis of market efficiency should be rejected.

A study by Finnerty [1976] corroborates Jaffe's conclusions. The major difference is that Finnerty's data were not restricted to an intensive trading group. By testing the entire population of insiders, the empirical findings allow an evaluation of "average" insider returns. The data include over 30,000 individual insider transactions between January 1969 and December 1972. Abnormal returns computed from the market model (Equation 19.5) indicate that insiders are able to "beat the market" on a risk-adjusted basis when selling and when buying.[13]

Information Averaging and Aggregation

The efficient markets hypothesis says that prices should fully reflect all relevant information, but it does not say anything about how this process might take place. Suppose that market participants have heterogeneous information sets. For example, suppose that Mr. Smith knows for sure that a Republican will be elected president but knows nothing else. At the same time, Miss Jones knows that both houses of Congress will be Democratic but

---

[12]The Securities and Exchange Commission defines insiders as members of the board of directors, corporate officers, and any beneficial owner of more than 10 percent of any class of stock. They must disclose, on a monthly basis, any changes in their stock holdings.

[13]Most readers know that trading to take advantage of insider trading is illegal and that violators have been successfully prosecuted by the SEC (for example, the Cady-Roberts decision in November 1961 and the Texas Gulf Sulphur case in August 1966). However, the SEC has been able to prosecute only the most flagrant violations. An outright ban on all insider transactions is the only way to prevent all insider trading profits. But such a law would not be advisable because it would very likely destroy a major management incentive for revealing new information on a timely basis.

knows nothing else. The question is this: Will market prices reflect the full impact of both pieces of information as though the market were fully informed, or will prices reflect only some average of the impact of both pieces of information? If prices reflect all information, the market is said to be *fully aggregating*; otherwise, it is only *averaging* information.

A fully aggregating market is consistent with Fama's [1970] definition of strong-form market efficiency. Because prices reflect the full impact of all diverse pieces of information in a fully aggregating market, even insiders who possess private information would not be able to profit by it. One possible mechanism for aggregation has been suggested by Grossman and Stiglitz [1976] and by Grossman [1976].[14] In a market with two types of traders, "informed" and "uninformed," informed traders will acquire better estimates of payoffs in future states of nature and take trading positions based on their superior information. When all informed traders do this, current prices are affected. Uninformed traders invest no resources in collecting information, but they can infer the information of informed traders by observing what happens to prices. Thus, the market prices may aggregate information so that all traders (both informed and uninformed) become informed.

One of the interesting implications of the empirical work on insider trading is that it is consistent with the point of view that markets do *not* fully aggregate information. In a fully aggregating market, an insider should not be able to make abnormal returns because his trading activity would reveal his information to the market. It seems much more likely that market prices are based on averages of diverse information held by market participants.

Efficient Markets with Transactions Costs and Costly Information

If capital markets are efficient, then no one can earn abnormal returns because prices reflect all available information. But without the hope of abnormal returns, investors have no strong incentive to acquire information. Why bother to try to beat the market by doing securities analysis when one can do equally well by simply randomly choosing stocks from *The Wall Street Journal*? This is an argument that one often hears from critics of the efficient markets hypothesis. They ignore two things—private information is valuable and it is costly to obtain.

Costly Information

The above argument may have some merit in a world with costless information because all investors would have zero abnormal returns. However, it is probably premature to predict the demise of the security analysis industry or to argue that prices are uninformative. Grossman and Stiglitz [1976, 1980] and Cornell and Roll [1981] have shown that a sensible efficient market equilibrium must leave some room for security analysis.

The basic argument is simple. If good information is costly to obtain, then investors who bear the expense of seeking it out must earn abnormal rates of return large enough to cover their expenses. However, when we net out their costs, then their net return is the same as the net return for investors who randomly selected their portfolios. The trick is to

---

[14]Actually, this idea can be traced back to Hayek's classic article, "The Use of Knowledge in Society" (1945).

explain how investors who use no information at all can survive in competition with analysts who use costly information.[15]

Imagine a world where all investors purchase costly information for 4 percent of the security's price. Also, transactions costs are another 4 percent. If traders all have the same information, they have no competitive advantage when trading with each other. If the normal rate of return is 6 percent, their net return is $6\% - 8\% = -2\%$. Hence, the expenditures for acquiring information have been wasted. Suppose that one of them decides to spend nothing on information. He will be at a competitive disadvantage when trading with an informed trader, but he doesn't bear the cost of information. Suppose the normal rate of return is halved, so that he earns only 3 percent. Then his net return is $3\% - 4\% = -1\%$, and he is absolutely certain to earn this rate of return because every other trader has purchased the costly information. Since -1 percent is better than -2 percent, uninformed traders will begin to proliferate in a world with mostly informed traders.

Suppose we start with the opposite scenario. All traders are uninformed, and there is no competitive disadvantage, so their payoff is the normal rate of return, 6 percent, less transactions costs of 4 percent. Their net return is 2 percent. Now suppose one of them buys costly information. Because he has superior information, his payoff is doubled (that is, $2 \times 6\% = 12\%$). Subtracting out the 4 percent cost of information and the 4 percent transactions cost, we see that his net return is 4 percent. Since this is greater than the net payoff to uninformed traders, informed traders will proliferate in a world of uninformed traders.

Because we cannot have an equilibrium with 100 percent informed traders or with 100 percent uninformed traders, there must be a stable equilibrium where the two strategies coexist — a mixed strategy stable equilibrium. This equilibrium will occur when the expected net payoff to both strategies is equal. For the numbers we have been using, an equilibrium will exist if two-thirds of the traders buy information and one-third do not. Furthermore, it turns out that the net profit to both kinds of traders is zero, which is the standard equilibrium condition for competitive markets.

This example is important because it explains how uninformed investors can coexist in equilibrium with sophisticated investors who sometimes go to considerable expense to acquire information which gives them a competitive edge. In equilibrium, more and more investors will seek out costly information until their net returns are the same as the returns earned by investors who use no information at all. But most important of all, market prices will reflect the information of informed traders.

Mutual Fund Performance

Mutual funds frequently spend a great deal on security analysis and on management fees. If they invest resources on costly information, do they earn abnormal returns large enough to cover their expenses? This is an empirical question, and many papers have studied mutual fund performance. Among them are articles by Friend and Vickers [1965], Sharpe [1966], Treynor [1965], Farrar [1962], Friend, Blume, and Crockett [1970], Jensen [1968], Mains [1977], Henricksson [1984], and Grinblatt and Titman [1984]. We will focus on the Jensen and Mains studies.

---

[15]See Cornell and Roll [1981] for a detailed description of the Nash equilibrium conditions necessary for equilibrium in a market with pair-wise competition.

Jensen [1968] used the Capital Asset Pricing Model (CAPM) to test the abnormal performance of 115 mutual funds, using annual data between 1955 and 1964.[16] The average abnormal return, *net* of research costs, management fees, and brokerage commissions was −1.1 percent per year over the ten-year period. This suggests that, on the average, the funds were not able to forecast future security prices well enough to cover their expenses. When the returns were measured "gross of expenses" (excepting brokerage commissions), the average abnormal return was −.4 percent per year. Apparently, the gross returns were not sufficient to recoup even brokerage commissions.

More recently, Mains [1977] has reexamined the issue of mutual fund performance. He criticizes Jensen's work on two accounts: (1) The rates of return were underestimated (a) because dividends were assumed to be reinvested at year's end rather than during the quarter they were received, and (b) because expenses were added back at year's end instead of continuously throughout the year to obtain gross returns. By using monthly data instead of annual data, Mains is able to better estimate both net and gross returns. (2) Jensen assumed that mutual fund betas (measures of systematic risk) were stationary over long periods of time. Using monthly data, Mains obtains lower estimates of mutual fund risk and argues that Jensen's estimates were too high.

The abnormal performance results calculated for a sample of 70 mutual funds indicate that as a group the mutual funds had neutral risk-adjusted abnormal returns on a net return basis. On a gross return basis (that is, before operating expenses and transactions costs), 80 percent of the funds had positive abnormal returns. This suggests that mutual funds are able to outperform the market well enough to earn back their operating expenses. It is also consistent with the theory of efficient markets, given costly information. Investors who utilize costly information must have higher gross rates of return if they are to survive. This is just what Mains' work shows. Mutual funds' gross rates of return are greater than the rate on a randomly selected portfolio of equivalent risk, but when transactions costs and management fees are subtracted, the net performance of mutual funds is the same as that for a naive investment strategy.

The Value Line Investor Survey

Hundreds of investment advisory services sell predictions of the future performance of various types of assets. Perhaps the largest is the Value Line Investor Survey. Employing over 200 people, it ranks about 1,700 securities each week. Securities are ranked 1 to 5 (with 1 being highest), based on their expected price performance relative to the other stocks covered in the survey. Security rankings result from a complex filter rule which uses four criteria all based on publicly available information: (1) the earnings and price rank of each security relative to all others, (2) a price momentum factor, (3) year-to-year relative changes in quarterly earnings, and (4) an earnings "surprise" factor. Roughly 42 percent of the securities are ranked third, 22 percent are ranked second or fourth, and 7 percent are ranked first or fifth.

A Value Line subscription costs approximately $400 per year. The question is whether enough abnormal performance results from using Value Line recommendations to pay for the cost of a subscription. Value Line rankings are also a test of semi-strong-form efficiency and, consequently, have been the subject of many academic studies.[17]

---

[16]See Chapter 17 for details on how the CAPM can be employed to measure portfolio performance.

[17]A partial list of Value Line related studies is Shelton [1967], Hausman [1969], Black [1971], Kaplan and Weil [1975], Brown and Rozeff [1978], Holloway [1981], Copeland and Mayers [1982], and Chen, Copeland, and Mayers [1983].

Black [1971] performed the first systematic study using the CAPM to measure risk-adjusted abnormal performance. His results indicated statistically significant abnormal performance for equally weighted portfolios formed from stocks ranked 1, 2, 4, and 5 by Value Line and rebalanced monthly. Before transactions costs, Portfolios 1 and 5 had risk-adjusted abnormal rates of return of +10 percent and −10 percent respectively. Even with round-trip transactions costs of 2 percent, the net rate of return for a long position in Portfolio 1 would still have been positive, thereby indicating economically significant performance. One of the problems with Black's study was his use of the CAPM methodology for measuring abnormal performance. It has been criticized by Roll [1977, 1978], who argues that any methodology based on the CAPM will measure either (1) no abnormal performance if the market index is *ex post* efficient or (2) a meaningless abnormal performance if the index portfolio is *ex post* inefficient.

Copeland and Mayers [1982] and Chen, Copeland, and Mayers [1983] measured Value Line portfolio performance by using a *future benchmark technique* which avoids selection bias problems associated with using historic benchmarks as well as the known difficulties of using CAPM benchmarks.[18] Table 19.1 and Figure 19.7 present abnormal performance results which use a five-factor Arbitrage Pricing Model (APM) as the future benchmark.[19] Results using a single factor market model were similar.

The results show that no Value Line portfolio had statistically signifcant abnormal performance at the 5 percent confidence level, although Portfolio 5 was significant at the 10 percent level. Perhaps the most interesting result was that the measured excess rates of return "lined up" pretty well. Portfolios 1 and 2 did better than Portfolio 3 while Portfolios 4 and 5 did worse. The difference between Portfolios 1 and 5 was 3.42 percent for six months, or 6.96 percent for a year — much less than Black's estimate of a 20 percent difference between Portfolios 1 and 5. For most trading strategies, the Value Line recommendations earn barely enough to pay for transactions costs (brokerage fees and bid-ask spreads).

Table 19.1   Excess Rate of Return Performance for Five Value Line Rankings Portfolios for 24 Six-Month Holding Periods during the Interval November 26, 1965, through February 3, 1978

	Value Line Portfolio Number				
	1	**2**	**3**	**4**	**5**
Average cumulative return	.0053	.0058	−.0005	−.0071	−.0289
Average weekly return	.0002	.0002	−.0000	−.0003	−.0012
t-statistic	.3603	.6704	−.0699	−.8054	−1.9640

Note: Portfolio numbers correspond to the Value Line rankings of the securities in the portfolio. The average cumulative return is the 26-week rate of return averaged over 24 holding periods. The average weekly return is the geometric average. The *t*-statistic tests the null hypothesis that the average cumulative returns are zero. Any *t*-statistic greater than 2.069 is significant at the 5 percent level.

---

[18]Using historic benchmarks creates a selection bias problem because Value Line uses a variant of the "relative strength" criterion to choose rankings. Portfolio 1 stocks tend to have abnormally high *historic* rates of return; thus subtracting these rates from test period returns would tend to bias the results against Value Line.

[19]See Chapter 17 for a brief summary of the Arbitrage Pricing Model.

Figure 19.7   Excess Rate of Return Performance: Average Cumulative Residuals for 26
                    Weeks after the Ranking Date using a Five-Factor Arbitrage Model

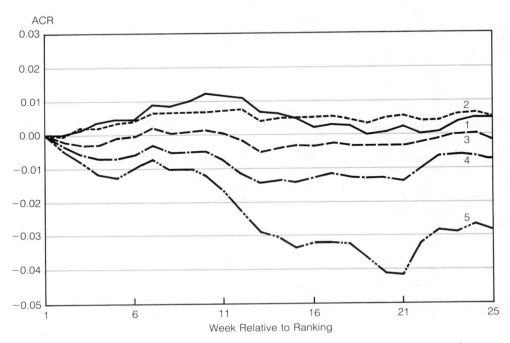

Note: The ACR are the average (across 24 periods) of the weekly excess rates of return
cumulated to the designated week relative to the ranking date in the test period (week
zero). The numbers 1 to 5 correspond to the Value Line rankings of the securities in
the portfolios.

Source: N. F. Chen, T. E. Copeland, and D. Mayers, "A Comparison of APM, CAPM, and the Market-Model Portfolio Performance Methodologies: The Value Line Case (1965-1978)," Working Paper No. 13-83, Graduate School of Management,
UCLA, 1983.

There are two lessons to be drawn from the research on Value Line: (1) Before concluding that capital markets are inefficient, it is wise to carefully examine the rate of return
benchmark against which abnormal performance is measured, and (2) even though some
evidence of abnormal performance shows up on the statistics, it is necessary to examine
performance net of transactions costs before economic significance can be assessed.

Transactions Costs and Operational Efficiency

The empirical evidence on filter rules, on mutual fund performance, on block trading, and
on the Value Line Investor Survey all illustrate that it is often possible to find statistically
significant market inefficiencies but that once transactions costs are considered the inefficiencies prove to be economically unimportant. Investors who wish to use publicly available information to buy or sell so that prices can be brought into line can carry out their

arbitrage activities only up to the limits set by brokerage commissions and bid-ask spreads.[20] Within these limits, economic arbitrage is not possible.

An *operationally* efficient market is one where transactions costs are competitively determined and set at the lowest possible level (usually determined to be the minimum long-run average cost). To date, little research has been devoted to the topic of operational efficiency, but it is no less important than *allocational* efficiency, which is the question of whether or not prices reflect information.

Summary

We have seen that most of the research on capital markets supports the conclusion that they are weak- and semi-strong-form efficient but are probably not strong-form efficient. A semi-strong-form efficient market is one where prices instantaneously and fully reflect all publicly available information. In order for a message to contain relevant information, there must be a security price change when the news is released. This test allows us to separate meaningful information (for example, quarterly earnings reports) from immaterial information such as corporate name changes. The evidence on block trading showed that block sales contain negative information but, even more important, that prices have fully adjusted to their new permanent level within 15 minutes after the block transaction becomes publicly available information. Perhaps prices do not react instantaneously, but they certainly adjust very rapidly. When we say that prices "fully reflect" information, we mean that they reflect an average of investor expectations. The fact that the market is not strong-form efficient implies that prices are not fully aggregating. Finally, we saw that if information is costly, then there is every reason to believe that costly securities analysis pays off well enough to recover its expense. Equilibrium in efficient securities markets allows room for informed and uninformed investors to coexist.

It would be surprising if securities markets were not semi-strong-form efficient. After all, the payoffs to investors who can piece together or ferret out useful information is simply too high. Because it pays to search for new information about the future cash flows from securities, it makes sense that current securities prices can and do reflect all publicly available information. Markets are semi-strong-form efficient.

Questions

19.1 Given that securities markets are semi-strong-form efficient
    a) How can an investor systematically earn a gross abnormal rate of return?
    b) How can an investor systematically earn a net abnormal rate of return?

19.2 As treasurer of a large corporation, you find yourself with $10 million in excess cash, which you can invest in low-risk short-term government bonds or in a risky common stock portfolio.
    a) How would you compare the net present value of these two alternatives?
    b) Suppose another alternative is to invest the money in your own company's common stock by repurchasing it on the open market. How would the net present value of this alternative compare with the other two alternatives?

---

[20]The bid-ask spread is the difference between the highest price a buyer (or the specialist) will pay and the lowest price a seller will accept.

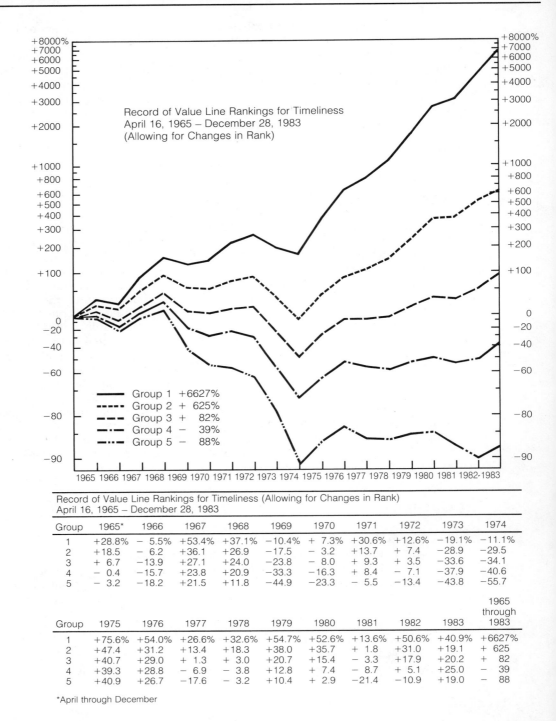

Record of Value Line Rankings for Timeliness
April 16, 1965 – December 28, 1983
(Allowing for Changes in Rank)

Group	——	Group 1	+6627%
	----	Group 2	+ 625%
	– –	Group 3	+ 82%
	–·–	Group 4	– 39%
	–··–	Group 5	– 88%

Record of Value Line Rankings for Timeliness (Allowing for Changes in Rank)
April 16, 1965 – December 28, 1983

Group	1965*	1966	1967	1968	1969	1970	1971	1972	1973	1974
1	+28.8%	− 5.5%	+53.4%	+37.1%	−10.4%	+ 7.3%	+30.6%	+12.6%	−19.1%	−11.1%
2	+18.5	− 6.2	+36.1	+26.9	−17.5	− 3.2	+13.7	+ 7.4	−28.9	−29.5
3	+ 6.7	−13.9	+27.1	+24.0	−23.8	− 8.0	+ 9.3	+ 3.5	−33.6	−34.1
4	− 0.4	−15.7	+23.8	+20.9	−33.3	−16.3	+ 8.4	− 7.1	−37.9	−40.6
5	− 3.2	−18.2	+21.5	+11.8	−44.9	−23.3	− 5.5	−13.4	−43.8	−55.7

Group	1975	1976	1977	1978	1979	1980	1981	1982	1983	1965 through 1983
1	+75.6%	+54.0%	+26.6%	+32.6%	+54.7%	+52.6%	+13.6%	+50.6%	+40.9%	+6627%
2	+47.4	+31.2	+13.4	+18.3	+38.0	+35.7	+ 1.8	+31.0	+19.1	+ 625
3	+40.7	+29.0	+ 1.3	+ 3.0	+20.7	+15.4	− 3.3	+17.9	+20.2	+ 82
4	+39.3	+28.8	− 6.9	− 3.8	+12.8	+ 7.4	− 8.7	+ 5.1	+25.0	− 39
5	+40.9	+26.7	−17.6	− 3.2	+10.4	+ 2.9	−21.4	−10.9	+19.0	− 88

*April through December

Source: Record of Value Line Portfolio Performance (From Bernhard, A., "The Value Line Investment Survey," *Investing in Common Stock*, Value Line, Inc., reprinted with permission.)

19.3   You are approached by salespersons from two competing mutual funds. The first fund earned an 18 percent rate of return last year while the second earned only 14 percent.

a)   What questions do you need to ask the salesperson to determine which fund really did better?

b)   What can be said about the expected future performance of the two funds?

19.4   You are told that the market for options is a fair game but that four out of five options expire worthless. How can these two statements be true?

19.5   If empirical evidence indicates that the stock market is not strong-form efficient, then the market cannot be perfectly aggregating information. Why or why not?

19.6   If the stock market is semi-strong-form efficient, then you cannot hope to earn abnormal profits; consequently, it does not pay to try. True or false. Why?

19.7   Using the fair game model, explain the difference between normal and abnormal returns.

19.8   What empirical evidence confirms the fact that, on average, large block trades contain information?

19.9   What is the difference between operational efficiency and allocational efficiency of capital markets?

19.10 Figure Q19.10 is a chart of the price gains which could have been earned between 1965 and 1983 if you had rebalanced your portfolio weekly in accordance with Value Line recommendations. Note that Portfolio 1 had a price gain of 6,627 percent. What questions would you have to ask in order to determine whether or not this is evidence of capital market inefficiency?

19.11 Suppose that a research team has tried many different multiple regression models on data collected for the years 1950 through 1983 and has found that the following model gives statistically significant results for predicting stock prices (t-statistics are given in parentheses):

$$P_{j,t} = 1.07P_{j,t-1} + .12(D/E)_{j,t-1} - .02\text{Size}_{j,t-1} + \epsilon_{j,t} \qquad r^2 = .78$$

$$(10.3) \qquad (4.6) \qquad\qquad (-12.2) \qquad\qquad F = 17.5,$$

where

$$P_{j,t} = \text{the price of the } j^{th} \text{ stock during year } t$$
$$P_{j,t-1} = \text{the price of the } j^{th} \text{ stock during the previous year, } t-1$$
$$(D/E)_{j,t-1} = \text{the debt to equity ratio of the firm last year}$$
$$\text{Size}_{j,t-1} = \text{the size of the firm last year (measured by sales revenue in billions of dollars)}$$
$$\epsilon_{j,t} = \text{the mean zero error term.}$$

What, in your opinion, does the ability of this model to predict stock prices tell you about market efficiency?

Selected References

Aharony, J., and Swary, I., "Quarterly Dividend and Earnings Announcements and Stockholders' Returns: An Empirical Analysis," *Journal of Finance*, (March 1980), pp. 1-12.

Alexander, S. S., "Price Movements in Speculative Markets: Trends or Random Walks," *Industrial Management Review*, (May 1961), pp. 7-26.

Ball, R., and Brown, P., "An Empirical Evaluation of Accounting Income Numbers," *Journal of Accounting Research*, (Autumn 1968), pp. 159-178.

Black, F., "Yes, Virginia, There is Hope: Tests of the Value Line Ranking System," Graduate School of Business, University of Chicago, May 1971.

Brennan, Michael J., and Schwartz, Eduardo S., "Bond Pricing and Market Efficiency," *Financial Analysts Journal*, 38 (September/October 1982), pp. 49-56.

Brown, L., and Rozeff, M., "The Superiority of Analysts Forecasts as Measures of Expectations: Evidence From Earnings," *Journal of Finance*, (March 1978), pp. 1-16.

Chen, N. F.; Copeland, T. E.; and Mayers, D., "A Comparison of APM, CAPM and the Market-Model Portfolio Performance Methodologies: The Value Line Case (1965-1978)," Working Paper No. 13-83, Graduate School of Management, UCLA, 1983.

Copeland, T. E., and Mayers, D., "The Value Line Enigma (1965-1978): A Case Study of Performance Evaluation Issues," *Journal of Financial Economics*, (December 1982), pp. 289-321.

Cornell, B., and Roll, R., "Strategies for Pairwise Competitions in Markets and Organizations," *Bell Journal of Economics*, (Spring 1981), pp. 201-213.

Dann, Larry; Mayers, David; and Raab, Robert, "Trading Rules, Large Blocks and the Speed of Adjustment," *Journal of Financial Economics*, (January 1977), pp. 3-22.

Fama, Eugene F., "Efficient Capital Markets: A Review of Theory and Empirical Work," *Journal of Finance*, (May 1970), pp. 383-417.

Fama, Eugene F., and Blume, Marshall, "Filter Rules and Stock Market Trading Profits," *Journal of Business*, (January [spec. supp.] 1966), pp. 226-241.

Farrar, D. E., *The Investment Decision Under Uncertainty*, Englewood Cliffs, N. J.: Prentice-Hall, 1962.

Finnerty, J. E., "Insiders and Market Efficiency," *Journal of Finance*, (September 1976), pp. 1141-1148.

Foster, G., "Quarterly Accounting Data: Time Series Properties and Predictive Ability Results," *Accounting Review*, (January 1977), pp. 1-21.

Friend, I., and Vickers, D., "Portfolio Selection and Investment Performance," *Journal of Finance*, (September 1965), pp. 391-415.

Friend, I.; Blume, M.; and Crockett, J., *Mutual Funds and Other Institutional Investors*, New York: McGraw-Hill, 1970.

Griffin, P., "The Time-Series Behavior of Quarterly Earnings: Preliminary Evidence," *Journal of Accounting Research*, (Spring 1977), pp. 71-83.

Grinblatt, M., and Titman, S., "No Need for Beta Shlunk," UCLA Working Paper, March 1984.

Grossman, S. J., "On the Efficiency of Competitive Stock Markets Where Traders Have Diverse Information," *Journal of Finance*, (May 1976), pp. 573-586.

Grossman, S. J., and Stiglitz, J., "The Impossibility of Informationally Efficient Markets," *American Economic Review*, (June 1980), pp. 393-408.

———, "Information and Competitive Price Systems," *American Economic Review*, (May 1976), pp. 246-253.

Hausman, W., "A Note on the Value Line Contest: A Test of the Predictability of Stock Price Changes," *Journal of Business*, (July 1969), pp. 317-320.

Henricksson, R. D., "Market Timing and Mutual Fund Performance: An Empirical Investigation," *Journal of Business*, (January 1984), pp. 73-96.

Hirshleifer, J., and Riley, J., "The Analytics of Uncertainty and Information—An Expository Survey," *Journal of Economic Literature*, (December 1979), pp. 1375-1421.

Holloway, C., "A Note on Testing an Aggressive Investment Strategy Using Value Line Ranks," *Journal of Finance*, (June 1981), pp. 711-719.

Jaffe, J., "The Effect of Regulation Changes on Insider Trading," *Bell Journal of Economics and Management Science*, (Spring 1974), pp. 93-121.

Jensen, M., "Risk, the Pricing of Capital Assets, and the Evaluation of Investment Portfolios," *Journal of Business*, (April 1969), pp. 167-247.

———, "The Performance of Mutual Funds in the Period 1945-64," *Journal of Finance*, (May 1968), pp. 389-416.

Joy, M.; Litzenberger, R.; and McEnally, R., "The Adjustment of Stock Prices to Announcements of Unanticipated Changes in Quarterly Earnings," *Journal of Accounting Research*, (Autumn 1977), pp. 207-225.

Kaplan, Robert, and Weil, Roman, "Risk and the Value Line Contest," *Financial Analysts Journal* (July/August 1975), pp. 56-60.

Kraus, Alan, and Stoll, Hans, "Price Impacts of Block Trading on the New York Stock Exchange," *Journal of Finance*, (June 1972), pp. 569-588.

Mains, N. E., "Risk, the Pricing of Capital Assets, and the Evaluation of Investment Portfolios: Comment," *Journal of Business*, (July 1977), pp. 371-384.

Plott, C. R., and Sunder, S., "Efficiency of Experimental Security Markets with Insider Information: An Application of Rational Expectations Models," *Journal of Political Economy*, (August 1982), pp. 663-698.

Roll, Richard, "Ambiguity When Performance is Measured by the Securities Market Line," *Journal of Finance*, (September 1978), pp. 1051-1069.

———, "A Critique of the Asset Pricing Theory's Tests," *Journal of Financial Economics*, (March 1977), pp. 129-176.

Ruback, R., "The Conoco Takeover and Stockholder Returns," *Sloan Management Review*, (Winter 1982), pp. 13-32.

Samuelson, Paul A., "Proof that Properly Anticipated Prices Fluctuate Randomly," *Industrial Management Review*, (Spring 1965), pp. 41-49.

Scholes, Myron, "The Market for Securities: Substitution versus Price Pressure and the Effects of Information on Share Prices," *Journal of Business*, (April 1972), pp. 179-211.

Schwert, G. William, "The Adjustment of Stock Prices to Information About Inflation," *Journal of Finance*, 36 (March 1981), pp. 15-29.

Sharpe, W. F., "Mutual Fund Performance," *Journal of Business*, (January 1966), pp. 119-138.

Shelton, J., "The Value Line Contest: A Test of the Predictability of Stock Price Changes," *Journal of Business*, (July 1967), pp. 251-269.

Treynor, J. L., "How to Rate Mutual Fund Performance," *Harvard Business Review*, (January/February 1965), pp. 63-75.

Watts, R., "Systematic 'Abnormal' Returns After Quarterly Earnings Announcements," *Journal of Financial Economics*, (June/September 1978), pp. 127-150.

Part Six   Cost of Capital and Valuation

Part Six provides the basis for determining the relevant cost of capital and how it is influenced by financial decisions. The chapters in this section examine financing decisions in the broad categories of debt versus equity, and attempt to determine the optimal financial structure—the financial structure that simultaneously minimizes the firm's cost of capital and maximizes its market value. Financing decisions and investment decisions are interdependent—the optimal financing plan and the optimal level of investment must be determined simultaneously. Therefore Part Six also serves the important function of integrating the theory of capital budgeting with the theory of capital structure.

    Chapter 20 analyzes the influence of capital structure decisions on the riskiness of the returns of a firm and hence on its required return. Chapter 21 discusses how the firm may move toward its goals of minimizing its cost of capital and maximizing its value. Chapter 22 considers whether dividend policy influences the cost of capital and the value of the firm. Chapter 23 deals with factors determining the value of the firm and how the patterns of future revenue streams affect valuation.

Chapter 20 Financial Structure and the Use of Leverage

We have previously seen that operating leverage refers to the extent to which fixed operating costs are part of a firm's total operating costs. If all costs were variable (such as 80 percent of sales), the firm's pretax profits would equal 20 percent of sales. But, if some costs are fixed, the firm suffers a loss until it achieves a volume of sales to cover both variable costs and the fixed costs. As volume increases beyond this breakeven point, profits increase because the fixed costs become smaller per unit of volume of sales made by the firm. So, operating leverage increases the volatility of profitability.

Financial leverage, similar in concept, refers to the use of debt in financing the firm. If all funds were supplied by owners in the form of common stock, the firm would have no fixed periodic contractual cash payments for financing. But, the interest on debt that is sold to obtain financing is usually a fixed financial charge that must be paid regardless of the level of the firm's earnings. The greater the use of debt, the greater the financial leverage and the greater the extent to which financial fixed costs are added to operating fixed costs.

The addition of more fixed costs increases the volatility of net returns to the common stockholders, and greater volatility means greater dispersion in their returns, or increased risk. Quantifying the degrees of risk depends upon how risk is measured. We shall use both the coefficient of variation and beta as measures of risk.

Financial Leverage

Some basic terms will be defined and will mean the same thing in all of the subsequent discussion. *Financial structure* refers to the way the firm's assets are financed. Financial structure is represented by the entire right-hand side of the balance sheet. It includes short-term debt and long-term debt as well as shareholders' equity. *Capital structure* or the *capitalization* of the firm is the permanent financing represented by long-term debt, preferred stock, and shareholders' equity. Thus, a firm's capital structure is only part of its financial structure. The book value of shareholders' equity (E) includes common stock, paid-in or capital surplus, and the accumulated amount of retained earnings. If the firm has preferred stock, it is added to the shareholders' equity, and the two together may be termed the firm's *net worth*.

The key concept for this chapter is financial leverage, or the leverage factor. The *leverage factor* is the ratio of the book value of total debt (D) to total assets (TA) or to the total value (V) of the firm. When we refer to total assets (TA) we are referring to the total accounting book value of assets. Total value (V) refers to the total market value of all of the components of the firm's financial structure. While market values are used predominantly in developing financial theory, the leverage factor will also be defined with reference to accounting book values. For example, a firm having book value total assets of $100 million and total debt of $50 million would have a leverage factor of 50 percent. When we set forth the leverage relationships based on the ratio of debt to total assets, this necessarily implies what the ratio of debt to shareholders' equity (or in brief, the debt-to-equity ratio) will be. If we define the debt-to-equity ratio as D/E, we can see that it is equal to D/TA ÷ (1 − D/TA). Thus, if the ratio of debt to total assets is 50 percent, this means that the amount of debt is exactly equal to the amount of (shareholders') equity and the D/E ratio is equal to one. Or D/TA = 0.5, and, therefore, D/E = [0.5 ÷ (1 − 0.5)] = 1.

Finally, we should distinguish between business risk and financial risk. *Business risk* is the variability of expected pretax returns (EBIT) on the firm's total assets. *Financial risk* is the additional risk induced by the use of financial leverage and is reflected in the variability of the net income stream, NI.

The Nature of Financial Leverage

To convey the nature of financial leverage, we first analyze its impact on profitability and fluctuations in profitability under a range of leverage conditions. As an example, consider four alternative financial structures for the Universal Machine Company, a manufacturer of equipment used by industrial firms. The alternative balance sheets are displayed in Table 20.1.

Structure 1 uses no debt and, consequently, has a leverage factor of zero; Structure 2 has a leverage factor of 20 percent; Structure 3, 50 percent; and Structure 4, 80 percent.

The Impact of Financial Leverage

To understand the impact of financial leverage on the risk of the firm, we first have to understand its impact on the degree of fluctuations in profitability. It will be demonstrated algebraically and by example that greater leverage will produce greater volatility in the firm's net income stream. Table 20.2 and Figure 20.1 provide the basic data and a graphical presentation of the relationships. Table 20.2 begins by considering a range of possible

---

Table 20.1   Four Alternative Financial Structures, Universal Machine Company, Based on Book Values

Structure 1 (D/E = 0%; D/TA = 0%)

		Total debt	$ 0
		Common stock ($10 par)	10,000
Total assets	$10,000	Total claims	$10,000

Structure 2 (D/E = 25%; D/TA = 20%)

		Total debt	$ 2,000
		Common stock ($10 par)	8,000
Total assets	$10,000	Total claims	$10,000

Structure 3 (D/E = 100%; D/TA = 50%)

		Total debt	$ 5,000
		Common stock ($10 par)	5,000
Total assets	$10,000	Total claims	$10,000

Structure 4 (D/E = 400%; D/TA = 80%)

		Total debt	$ 8,000
		Common stock ($10 par)	2,000
Total assets	$10,000	Total claims	$10,000

Table 20.2   Universal Machine, Financial Leverage, and Stockholders' Returns

Before-tax Return on Total Assets	EBIT or NOI to Total Assets		
	-20%	20%	60%
Capital structure 1: D/TA = 0%			
EBIT or NOI	-$2,000	$2,000	$6,000
Less: interest (rD)	0	0	0
Earnings before taxes	-2,000	2,000	6,000
Less: income taxes (@ 40%)[a]	-800	800	2,400
Net income (NI)	-1,200	1,200	3,600
Return on stockholders' equity (ROE)	-12%	12%	36%
EPS on 1,000 shares	-$1.20	$1.20	$3.60
Capital structure 2: D/TA = 20%			
EBIT or NOI	-$2,000	$2,000	$6,000
Less: interest (@ 10%)	200	200	200
EBT	-2,200	1,800	5,800
Less: tax (@ 40%)[a]	-880	720	2,320
Net income (NI)	-1,320	1,080	3,480
Return on $8,000 equity (ROE)	-16.5%	13.5%	43.5%
EPS on 800 shares	-$1.65	$1.35	$4.35
Capital structure 3: D/TA = 50%			
EBIT or NOI	-$2,000	$2,000	$6,000
Less: interest (@ 14%)	700	700	700
EBT	-2,700	1,300	5,300
Less: tax (@ 40%)[a]	-1,080	520	2,120
Net income (NI)	-1,620	780	3,180
Return on $5,000 equity (ROE)	-32.4%	15.6%	63.6%
EPS on 500 shares	-$3.24	$1.56	$6.36
Capital structure 4: D/TA = 80%			
EBIT or NOI	-$2,000	$2,000	$6,000
Less: interest (@ 20%)	1,600	1,600	1,600
EBT	-3,600	400	4,400
Less: tax (@ 40%)[a]	-1,440	160	1,760
Net income (NI)	-2,160	240	2,640
Return on $2,000 equity (ROE)	-108%	12%	132%
EPS on 200 shares	-$10.80	$1.20	$13.20

[a]The tax calculations assume that losses are carried back or forward or otherwise utilized to produce tax credits.

ratios of EBIT or NOI to total assets. Different levels of profitability as measured by the ratios of EBIT (or NOI) to total assets have effects which vary with alternative capital structures. Four different levels of financial leverage are illustrated in Table 20.2, the degree of financial leverage (D/TA) ranging from 0 to 80 percent. With zero leverage, the return on total assets after taxes [EBIT$(1 - T)$/TA] is 60 percent of the pretax rate of return on total assets because of the 40 percent corporate tax rate. With no leverage, the after-tax return on total assets is equal to the ratio of net income to shareholders' equity (NI/E = ROE).

Figure 20.1   Financial Leverage Magnifies Variations in the Return on Equity

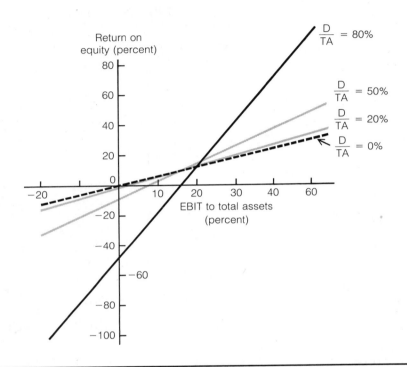

With leverage, the amount of interest paid affects the relation between the after-tax return on total assets and the return on equity. The numerators of the two ratios have the following relationship:

$$(EBIT)(1 - T) = NI + (1 - T) \text{ Interest paid.}$$

The amount of interest paid is rD, the coupon rate (r) times the amount of debt outstanding (D). The rate of interest paid by Universal Machine is assumed to begin at 10 percent for the leverage factor of 20 percent. It is further assumed that the increased risk of rising leverage causes interest rates to rise. The increases in interest rates shown are purely illustrative.[1]

Table 20.2 shows that the higher the ratio of financial leverage employed, the greater is the dispersion of returns. The pattern for the return on equity is summarized in Table 20.3. With no leverage, the range (the spread between the high and low values) of the ROE is

---

[1]The relation between financial leverage and the cost of debt and equity capital is discussed in the following chapter.

Table 20.3   Relation between Leverage Factors and Range of Returns

Leverage Factor	Range of Returns on Equity
0%	48%
20	60
50	96
80	240

---

48 percent. With an 80 percent leverage factor, the range of the ROE is 240 percent. Financial leverage magnifies the volatility of returns whether measured by net income, return on equity, or earnings per share. These results are depicted in Figure 20.1. When none of the total assets are financed by debt, the ratio of the return on shareholders' equity to the return on total assets is a relatively flat line. But when the debt ratio D/TA equals 80 percent, the line becomes steeper. This means that a small change in the ratio of EBIT to total assets produces a very large change in the ratio of net income to shareholders' equity. Thus, greater financial leverage produces greater volatility in the return to equity.

Relationship of Financial Leverage to Operating Leverage

To some degree, but not completely, a firm can influence its level of operating leverage. For example, if it owns a building, it has a fixed depreciation cost. It could lease the building for a 10- to 20-year period, but its lease costs would be fixed for the duration of the lease. Or it could rent the building in the extreme on a monthly basis; this would reduce the extent to which its costs were fixed. However, the extreme example of leasing a factory or a building on a monthly basis is inefficient. The landlord would need a very high rent to compensate him for the risk that the tenant might move out on very short notice. Hence, efficiency considerations, along with the fundamental economic and business characteristics of the products and services that the firm sells, will have a high degree of influence upon the degree of operating leverage to which the firm will be subject.

If a firm has a high degree of operating leverage, its breakeven point is at a relatively high sales level, and changes in the sales level have a magnified (or "leveraged") impact on profits. Notice that financial leverage has exactly the same kind of effect on profits; the higher the leverage factor, the higher the breakeven sales volume and the greater the impact on profits from a given change in sales volume.

In Chapter 9, the *degree of operating leverage* was defined as the ratio of percentage change in net operating income (NOI = EBIT) associated with a given percentage change in sales volume as shown in Equation 20.1:

$$\text{Degree of operating leverage (DOL)} = \frac{\%\ \text{change in EBIT}}{\%\ \text{change in sales}} = \frac{C}{X}. \qquad \textbf{(20.1)}$$

In earlier tables, the measure of earnings before interest and taxes (EBIT) reflected Universal Machine's total cost function. Its fixed costs are $6,000 and its variable costs are 20 percent of sales. The selling price per unit is $100. We can illustrate the second expression for DOL by the data in Table 20.4, which uses the data from Table 20.2 for Universal Machine with a leverage factor of 80 percent, at an output of 100 units and an EBIT of $2,000. At sales of 100 units, C, the contribution margin, is sales minus variable operating expenses, or $8,000. Earnings before interest and taxes (EBIT or X) is $2,000. Since DOL is the ratio of the two, DOL at sales of 100 units is 4. Thus, a 10 percent increase in sales would result in a 40 percent increase in EBIT or NOI. This degree of operating leverage is relatively high.

Degree of Financial Leverage (DFL)

Financial leverage takes over where operating leverage leaves off, further magnifying the effects on earnings per share of changes in the level of sales. For this reason, operating leverage is sometimes referred to as *first-stage leverage* and financial leverage as *second-stage leverage*. The *degree of financial leverage* is defined as the ratio of the percentage change in net income available to common stockholders that is associated with a given percentage change in earnings before interest and taxes (EBIT):

$$\text{Degree of financial leverage (DFL)} = \frac{\% \text{ change in net income}}{\% \text{ change in EBIT}}. \qquad \textbf{(20.2)}$$

The expression for the degree of financial leverage shown in Equation 20.2 can also be expressed in a simplified form as shown in Equation 20.2a:[2]

$$\text{DFL} = \frac{\text{EBIT}}{\text{EBIT} - rD} = \frac{X}{X - rD}. \qquad \textbf{(20.2a)}$$

---

[2]The equation is developed as follows:

1. Notice that EBIT $= Q(P - v) - F$.
2. Net income (NI) $= (\text{EBIT} - rD)(1 - T)$,

    where

    $\text{EBIT} =$ earnings before interest and taxes
    $rD =$ interest paid
    $T =$ corporate tax rate.

3. The expression rD is a constant, so ΔNI, the change in NI, is

    $$\Delta\text{NI} = \Delta\text{EBIT}(1 - T).$$

4. The percentage increase in NI is the change in NI over the original NI, or

    $$\frac{\Delta\text{EBIT}(1 - T)}{(\text{EBIT} - rD)(1 - T)} = \frac{\Delta\text{EBIT}}{\text{EBIT} - rD}.$$

5. The degree of financial leverage is the percentage change in NI over the percentage change in EBIT, so

    $$\text{Financial leverage} = \frac{\dfrac{\Delta\text{EBIT}}{\text{EBIT} - rD}}{\dfrac{\Delta\text{EBIT}}{\text{EBIT}}} = \frac{\text{EBIT}}{\text{EBIT} - rD} = \frac{X}{X - rD}.$$

Table 20.4   Illustration of Operating Leverage, UM Company

The total cost structure of the firm: Total costs = $6,000 + 0.2 Sales.

	Sales in Units		
	50	100	150
Sales in dollars @ $100 per unit	$ 5,000	$10,000	$15,000
Fixed operating expenses	6,000	6,000	6,000
Variable operating expenses	1,000	2,000	3,000
Earnings before interest and taxes	−2,000	2,000	6,000
Less: interest expense	1,600	1,600	1,600
Income before taxes	−3,600	400	4,400
Less: taxes @ 40%	−1,440	160	1,760
Net income	$−2,160	$ 240	$2,640

Using the data from Table 20.4 for the Univeral Machine (UM) Company, for an output of 100 units, the degree of financial leverage is

$$DFL = \frac{\$2,000}{\$2,000 - \$1,600} = 5.$$

Thus, a 10 percent increase in EBIT would result in a 50 percent increase in net income.[3] If the leverage factor were only 20 percent, we see from the data in Table 20.2 that the degree of financial leverage based on an EBIT of $2,000 and a capital structure of 20 percent would be

$$DFL = \frac{\$2,000}{\$2,000 - \$200} = 1.11.$$

Thus, the degree of financial leverage drops to 111 percent. Note that if there were no debt, the degree of financial leverage would be exactly one. The use of debt will cause the degree of financial leverage to rise above 1.0 or above 100 percent. If the degree of financial leverage is exactly one, or 100 percent, the multiplication factor is 1.0, and there is no degree of magnification in net income, return on equity, or earnings per share. Thus, the degree of financial leverage measures the magnification factor.

Combining Operating and Financial Leverage

Operating leverage causes a change in sales volume to have a magnified effect on EBIT. If financial leverage is superimposed on operating leverage, changes in EBIT have a magnified effect on NI, on ROE, and on EPS. Therefore, if a firm uses a considerable amount of

---

[3]The degree of financial leverage is unchanged whether it is measured by net income, return on equity, or earnings per share as the measure in the numerator.

both operating leverage and financial leverage, even small changes in the level of sales will produce wide fluctuations in NI, ROE, and EPS.

Equation 20.1 for the degree of operating leverage (DOL) can be combined with Equation 20.2 for the degree of financial leverage (DFL) to obtain the degree of combined leverage (DCL).

$$\text{DCL} = \left(\frac{\%\ \text{change in EBIT}}{\%\ \text{change in sales}}\right)\left(\frac{\%\ \text{change in net income}}{\%\ \text{change in EBIT}}\right) \tag{20.3}$$

$$= \frac{\%\ \text{change in net income}}{\%\ \text{change in sales}}.$$

We could also obtain DCL by multiplying expressions for point estimates of DOL and DFL. We would then have

$$\text{DCL} = \frac{C}{X}\left(\frac{X}{X - rD}\right) = \frac{C}{X - rD}. \tag{20.3a}$$

To obtain DCL, we could use the expression in Equation 20.3a, but since this represents the multiplication of DOL times DFL and we have already calculated 4 as the DOL and 5 as the DFL, the degree of combined leverage is 20. This is a very high degree of leverage; it indicates that a 10 percent change in sales would cause a 200 percent change in net income, return on equity, or earnings per share. The DOL of 4 combined with a DFL of 1.11 for the leverage factor of 20 percent would result in a degree of combined leverage of 4.44 times. In this case, a 10 percent change in sales would result in a 44.4 percent change in NI, ROE, or EPS.

A number of different combinations of operating and financial leverage could produce the same combined leverage factor. Hence, to some degree, firms can make tradeoffs between operating and financial leverage. A firm with a high degree of operating leverage is likely to use financial leverage to a lesser extent. However, if its DOL is very high, the use of a lower DFL (or using no debt at all which would produce a DFL of one) might not bring the firm's degree of combined leverage down as low as other firms whose DOL was low to start with. Alternatively, a firm with a low degree of operating leverage might seek a high degree of financial leverage, but its degree of combined leverage might still be lower than other firms which started with a high DOL.

Financial Leverage and Risk

We now examine the impact of different degrees of financial leverage on risk. The first step is a consideration of possible alternative levels of sales and the appropriate probability assessments of each. The probability distribution for future sales, constructed by Universal's marketing department in cooperation with representatives from the general staff group of top management, was based on their knowledge of present supply and demand conditions, along with estimates for future economic conditions and sales. The probable conditions range from "very poor" (due to a labor strike resulting from some very difficult labor negotiations currently under way) to "very good" (under an optimistic assessment of the future outlook).

The best judgments of the probabilities of alternative levels of future sales are presented in Row 1 of Table 20.5. In addition, the cost structure from Table 20.4 is used to obtain the

---

Table 20.5   Probabilities Associated with Alternative Sales Levels, UM Company

	0.2	0.5	0.3
Probabilities	0.2	0.5	0.3
Sales	$5,000	$10,000	$15,000
Costs:			
Fixed costs	6,000	6,000	6,000
Variable costs (0.2S)	1,000	2,000	3,000
Total costs	7,000	8,000	9,000
Earnings before interest and taxes (EBIT)	−$2,000	$ 2,000	$ 6,000
Return on total assets	−20%	20%	60%

---

pretax return on total assets for each level of sales with its associated probability. The return on total assets in the last row of Table 20.5 is identical to the return on total assets in the top row of Table 20.2. Hence, the measurements in Table 20.2 of the effects of alternative capital structures can be utilized in the subsequent analysis. The data will be used to calculate the two basic risk measures: the coefficient of variation (CV) and the beta (β).[4]

In Table 20.6, the expected returns on total assets and the standard deviation of those returns are calculated to obtain the coefficient of variation reflecting operating leverage alone. The result is a coefficient of variation in the returns on total assets of 1.167, which indicates a high probability that the return on assets could either be wiped out or doubled. Hence, operating risk is high.

Table 20.7 utilizes the results of the return on equity calculations from Table 20.2 to measure the effects of financial leverage on risk as measured by the coefficient of variation. For Financial Structure 1, the return on equity has an expected return and standard deviation which is $(1 - T)$ times the corresponding measures for the return on assets. The resulting coefficient of variation for the return on equity with no leverage is exactly equal to the CV for the return on total assets. Thus, with no leverage, the CV risk measure is no different for the ROE than for the ROA.

However, with increased leverage, the CV is magnified. The expected ROE also is increased. Thus, both the expected ROE and its dispersion measures are increased by increased leverage.

Table 20.6   Calculation of Risk Measures for UM

S	P_s	ROA	P_sROA	(ROA − $\overline{\text{ROA}}$)	(ROA − $\overline{\text{ROA}}$)^2	P_s(ROA − $\overline{\text{ROA}}$)^2
1	0.2	−0.20	−0.04	−0.44	0.1936	0.03872
2	0.5	0.20	0.10	−0.04	0.0016	0.00080
3	0.3	0.60	0.18	0.36	0.1296	0.03888
			$\overline{\text{ROA} = 0.24}$			$\sigma^2 = \overline{0.07840}$

$$CV = \frac{\sigma}{\overline{\text{ROA}}} = \frac{0.28}{0.24} = 1.167 \qquad \sigma = 0.280$$

---

[4]The coefficient of variation was introduced in Chapter 10, and beta was introduced in Chapter 17.

Table 20.7　　　Effects of Leverage on UM's Risk Measures

	S	P_s	ROE	P_sROE	(ROE $-$ $\overline{\text{ROE}}$)	P_s(ROE $-$ $\overline{\text{ROE}}$)^2
Financial Structure 1	1	0.2	−0.12	−0.024	−0.264	0.0139
	2	0.5	0.12	0.060	−0.024	0.0003
	3	0.3	0.36	0.108	0.216	0.0140
				$\overline{\text{ROE}} = 0.144$		$\sigma^2 = 0.0282$
			$\text{CV} = \dfrac{\sigma}{\overline{\text{ROE}}} = \dfrac{0.168}{0.144} = 1.167$			$\sigma = 0.168$
Financial Structure 2	1	0.2	−0.165	−0.0330	−0.330	0.0218
	2	0.5	0.135	0.0675	−0.030	0.0005
	3	0.3	0.435	0.1305	0.270	0.0219
				$\overline{\text{ROE}} = 0.165$		$\sigma^2 = 0.0442$
			$\text{CV} = \dfrac{0.21}{0.165} = 1.273$			$\sigma = 0.210$
Financial Structure 3	1	0.2	−0.324	−0.0648	−0.528	0.0558
	2	0.5	0.156	0.0780	−0.048	0.0012
	3	0.3	0.636	0.1908	0.432	0.0560
				$\overline{\text{ROE}} = 0.204$		$\sigma^2 = 0.1130$
			$\text{CV} = \dfrac{0.336}{0.204} = 1.647$			$\sigma = 0.336$
Financial Structure 4	1	0.2	−1.08	−0.216	−1.320	0.3485
	2	0.5	0.12	0.060	−0.120	0.0072
	3	0.3	1.32	0.396	1.080	0.3499
				$\overline{\text{ROE}} = 0.240$		$\sigma^2 = 0.7056$
			$\text{CV} = \dfrac{0.84}{0.24} = 3.500$			$\sigma = 0.840$

The second basic measure of risk is the beta coefficient. Suppose that for the Universal Machine Company, one of the financial services had calculated a beta of 1.568. This was associated with the degree of leverage for Universal Machine that resulted in a ratio of debt to equity of 20 percent based on market values. Assume further that the same financial services suggested that the appropriate Security Market Line to apply is shown by Equation 20.4:

$$E(R_j) = 0.09 + (0.05)\beta_j. \tag{20.4}$$

From the data provided, some estimates of the effect of changing leverage can be made. The following basic relationship between the unlevered beta and the levered beta can be employed.[5]

$$\beta_L = \beta_u[1 + (B/S)(1 - T)], \tag{20.5}$$

[5]Rubinstein [1973].

where β_u is the unlevered beta, β_L is the levered beta, and B/S is the debt to equity ratio measured at market values.[6] From the information provided, we can calculate the unlevered beta using the above expression. We would have

$$1.568 = \beta_u[1 + .2(.6)] \tag{20.5a}$$

$$\beta_u = 1.4.$$

With this result of β_u equal to 1.4, we use the information in Table 20.8 to calculate the levered betas. The ratios of debt to equity at book values for Universal Machine are shown in Column (2). These are the alternative levels of leverage at book value that we have been using before.

In Column (3), some estimated debt to equity market relationships are set forth that correspond to the financial structures measured at book value in Column (2). For financial structures 2 and 3, it is assumed that more leverage increases the market value of equity so that the ratio of debt to equity measured at market is lower than the ratio of debt to equity measured at book. For Financial Structure 4, where there is $4 of debt at book value to $1 of equity at book value, we judge that this degree of leverage is excessive. Because it is excessive, it results in a decline in the market value of equity. As a consequence, the ratio of debt to equity at market values is shown to be greater than the ratio of debt to equity at book values.[7]

Column (4) provides the factors by which the unlevered beta of 1.4 is multiplied in order to obtain the levered betas. The resulting levered betas in Column (5) are plausible for the first three financial structures illustrated. The levered beta of 5.6 for Financial Structure 4 may seem to be unusually high. On the other hand, a leverage ratio of $4 of debt to $1 of equity is also extremely high. From a practical standpoint, we would probably not actually observe a beta as high as 5.6 nor would we observe a debt ratio of $4 of debt to $1 of equity. The analysis is realistic and practical in indicating that such high debt ratios would not be observed because they would represent unduly high levels of financial risk.

Table 20.8   Calculations of Leveraged Betas (Assuming that $T = 40\%$)

(1)	(2)	(3)	(4)	(5)
		Ratio of Debt to Equity		Levered Betas
Financial Structure	At Book	At Market	$[1 + (B/S)(1 - T)]$	β_j
1	0.00	0.00	1.00	1.400
2	0.25	0.20	1.12	1.568
3	1.00	0.60	1.36	1.904
4	4.00	5.00	4.00	5.600

---

[6]This relationship was derived in Chapter 17, for a world without taxes.

[7]The numbers used here are purely illustrative. We need the material in the next chapter to explain the calculations which we defer to Chapter 21.

Table 20.9   Relations between Expected and Required Returns for Alternative Beta Levels of UM

Financial Structure	β_L	$E(R_j)$	$\overline{ROE}$
1	1.400	0.1600	0.1440
2	1.568	0.1684	0.1650
3	1.904	0.1852	0.2040
4	5.600	0.3700	0.2400

SML: $E(R_j) = .09 + .05\beta_L$.

In Table 20.9, the leveraged betas that have been calculated are applied to the Security Market Line to obtain the required rates of return. The required rates of return range from the 16 percent for an unlevered firm to 37 percent for the financial structure that we have indicated to be excessively top-heavy with debt. Under the assumptions reflected in the data patterns that we have employed, the results in Table 20.9 suggest at least a tentative conclusion. For the leverage factors of Financial Structures 1, 2, and 4, the required return on equity is greater than the expected return on equity. For Financial Structure 3, with the debt to equity book ratio of one, the expected return is greater than the required return. These results would indicate that Financial Structure 3 would be preferred to the alternatives.

Financial Leverage with Additional Investment

Thus far in the analysis, we have varied leverage, holding constant the total amount of investment by the firm. In real-world decision making, it is often necessary to perform an analysis in which alternative leverage structures are considered along with financing that increases the firm's amount of investment and size of total assets. This aspect of combining the financing and leverage decisions will be developed by a continuation of the Universal Machine Company example. Universal's latest balance sheet is set forth in Table 20.10. Universal manufactures equipment used in industrial manufacturing. Its major product is a lathe used to trim the rough edges off sheets of fabricated steel. As is typically the case for producers of durable capital assets, the company's sales fluctuate widely, far

Table 20.10   Universal Machine Company: Balance Sheet for Year Ended December 31, 1984 (Thousands of Dollars)

Cash	$ 300	Total liabilities having an average cost of 10%	$ 5,000
Receivables (net)	1,200		
Inventories	1,400		
Plant (net)	3,000	Common stock ($10 par)	5,000
Equipment (net)	4,100		
Total assets	$10,000	Total claims on assets	$10,000

more than does the overall economy. For example, during 9 of the preceding 25 years, the company's sales have been below the breakeven point, so losses have been relatively frequent. Although future sales are uncertain, current demand is high and appears to be headed higher. Thus, if Universal is to continue its sales growth, it will have to increase capacity. A capacity increase involving $2 million of new capital is under consideration. James Watson, the financial vice president, learns that he can raise the $2 million by selling bonds with a 12 percent coupon or by selling 100,000 shares of common stock at a market price of $20 per share. Fixed costs after the planned expansion will be $6.4 million a year. Variable costs excluding interest on the debt will be 20 percent of sales.[8] The probability distribution for alternative future states-of-the-world is the same as was set forth in the previous section analyzing the pure leverage decision for Universal.

Although Watson's recommendation will be given much weight, the final decision for the method of financing rests with the company's board of directors. Procedurally, the financial vice president analyzes the situation, evaluates all reasonable alternatives, comes to a conclusion, and then presents the alternatives with his recommendations to the board. For his own analysis, as well as for presentation to the board, Watson prepares the materials shown in Table 20.11.

The top third of the table calculates earnings before interest and taxes (EBIT) for different levels of sales ranging from $5 million to $20 million. The firm suffers an operating loss until sales are $8 million, but beyond that point, it enjoys a rapid rise in gross profit.[9]

The middle third of the table shows the financial results that will occur at the various sales levels if bonds are used. First, the $840,000 annual interest charges ($600,000 on existing debt plus $240,000 on the new bonds) are deducted from the earnings before interest and taxes. Next, taxes are taken out; and if the sales level is so low that losses are incurred, the firm receives a tax credit. Then, net profits after taxes are divided by the 500,000 shares outstanding to obtain earnings per share (EPS) of common stock.[10] The various EPS figures are multiplied by the corresponding probability estimates to obtain an expected EPS of $3.79.

The bottom third of the table calculates the financial results that will occur with stock financing. Net profit after interest and taxes is divided by 600,000 — the original 500,000 shares plus the 100,000 new shares ($20 × 100,000 = $2,000,000) — to find earnings per share. Expected EPS is computed in the same way as for the bond financing.

Figure 20.2 shows the probability distribution of earnings per share. Stock financing has the tighter, more peaked distribution. We know from Table 20.3 that it will also have a smaller coefficient of variation than bond financing. Hence, stock financing is less risky than bond financing. However, the expected earnings per share are lower for stock financing than for bond financing, so we are again faced with the kind of risk-return tradeoff that characterizes most financial decisions. What choice should Watson recommend to the board? How much leverage should Universal Machine use? These questions cannot be answered at this point; the answers must be deferred until the effects of leverage on the cost of both debt and equity capital have been examined in the following chapter.

---

[8]The assumption that variable costs will be a constant percentage of sales over the entire range of output is not valid, but variable costs are relatively constant over the output range likely to be actually experienced.

[9]The breakeven sales are $S^* = \$6,400,000 + 0.2S^*$. Hence, $S^* = \$8,000,000$.

[10]The number of shares initially outstanding can be calculated by dividing the $5 million common stock figure given on the balance sheet by the $10 par value.

Table 20.11   Profit Calculations at Various Sales Levels, Universal Machine
Company (Thousands of Dollars)

	0.2	0.5	0.3
Probability of indicated sales	0.2	0.5	0.3
Sales	$5,000	$12,000	$20,000
Costs:			
Fixed	6,400	6,400	6,400
Variable (0.2S)	1,000	2,400	4,000
Total costs	7,400	8,800	10,400
Earnings before interest and taxes (EBIT)	−$2,400	$3,200	$9,600
Financing with bonds			
Earnings before interest and taxes	−$2,400	$3,200	$9,600
Less: interest (12% × $7,000)[a]	840	840	840
Earnings before taxes	−3,240	2,360	8,760
Less: income taxes (40%)	−1,296	944	3,504
Net income (NI)	−1,944	1,416	5,256
EPS on 500,000 shares[b]	−3.89	2.83	10.51
Return on equity	−38.9%	28.3%	105.1%
Expected EPS = $3.79			
Financing with stock			
Earnings before interest and taxes	−$2,400	$3,200	$9,600
Less: interest (10% × $5,000)	500	500	500
Earnings before taxes	−2,900	2,700	9,100
Less: income taxes (40%)	−1,160	1,080	3,640
Net income (NI)	−1,740	1,620	5,460
EPS on 600,000 shares[b]	−2.90	2.70	9.10
Return on equity	−24.8%	23.14%	78%
Expected EPS = $3.50			

[a]With higher leverage, the cost of debt rises to 12 percent on the new debt, and 12 percent represents the opportunity cost of the old debt as well. Some would argue for using 10 percent on the existing $5 million of debt, since this is the actual interest that would be paid until it matures. For cost of capital calculations or effects on earnings, we use the opportunity cost. For interest coverage, we will use actual interest outlays.
[b]The EPS figures can also be obtained using the following formula:

$$EPS = \frac{(\text{Sales} - \text{Fixed costs} - \text{Variable costs} - \text{Interest})(1 - \text{Tax rate})}{\text{Shares outstanding}}.$$

For example, at sales = $12 million:

$$EPS_{Bonds} = \frac{(12 - 6.4 - 2.4 - 0.84)(0.6)}{0.5} = \$2.83$$

$$EPS_{Stock} = \frac{(12 - 6.4 - 2.4 - 0.5)(0.6)}{0.6} = \$2.70.$$

Crossover Analysis

At a low level of sales, the EPS using stock is much higher than the EPS when debt is used. (See Figure 20.3.) The debt line has a steeper slope and rises faster, however, showing that earnings per share will go up faster with increases in sales if debt is used. The two lines cross at sales of $11.175 million. Below that sales volume, the firm will be better off issuing

Figure 20.2   Probability Curves for Stock and Bond Financing

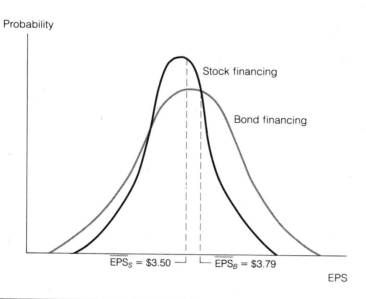

Probability

Stock financing

Bond financing

$\overline{EPS}_S = \$3.50$ $\overline{EPS}_B = \$3.79$

EPS

common stock; above that level, debt financing will produce higher earnings per share.[11] If Watson and his board of directors know with certainty that sales will never again fall below \$11.175 million, bonds are the preferred method of financing the asset increase. But, if any detrimental long-run events occur, future sales may again fall well below \$11.175 million.

Watson's recommendation and the directors' decision will depend on each person's (1) appraisal of the future and (2) psychological attitude towards risk. The pessimists and risk averters will prefer to employ common stock, while the optimists and those less sensitive to risk will favor bonds. This example, which is typical of many real-world situations, suggests that the major disagreements over the choice of forms of financing are likely to reflect uncertainty about the future levels of the firm's sales. The uncertainty, in turn, reflects the characteristics of the firm's environment — general business conditions, industry trends, and quality and aggressiveness of management.

---

[11]Since the equation in this case is linear, the breakeven or indifference level of sales (S) can be found as follows:

$$EPS_S = \frac{(S - 6.4 - 0.2S - 0.5)(0.6)}{0.6} = \frac{(S - 6.4 - 0.2S - 0.84)(0.6)}{0.5} = EPS_B$$

$$S = \$11.175 \text{ million, and EPS} = \$2.04.$$

Figure 20.3   Earnings per Share for Stock and Debt Financing

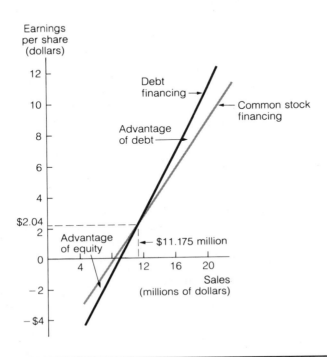

Effects of Fluctuating Interest Rates

Another aspect of leverage is the impact of fixed rate debt while general interest rates are fluctuating. In general, with fixed rate debt, rising interest rates will cause the market value of the firm's debt to decline. But with fixed rate debt, a rise or fall in interest rates may also have an impact on the firm's asset values. For example, if interest rates rise, for some firms, such as automobile manufacturers, the value of their assets may fall, other things being equal. This is because at higher interest rates, fewer automobiles may be sold because most automobiles are bought with credit, so that the monthly cost increases with higher interest rates. On the other hand, if the economy is stronger when interest rates are higher, the favorable income outlook for consumers may offset the negative impact of higher interest rates.

   If the value of the firm's assets declines with higher interest rates, then a type of "immunization" has occurred. The values of the firm's assets have declined, but the market value of its debt has also decreased. Hence, these are offsetting changes.

   On the other hand, if the values of the firm's assets are positively correlated with interest rate levels, a disparity is created. With high interest rates, the market value of liabilities falls and the market value of assets rises. With lower interest rates, the market value of liabilities rises and the market value of assets declines. Hence, if interest rate movements are positively correlated with asset values, this has a destabilizing impact on the firm. If interest rate levels are negatively correlated with asset values, this provides the firm with a form of "immunization" of the relationship between the value of its assets and the value of its liabilities.

Effects of Floating Rate Debt

The preceding analysis has been based on debt with a fixed interest rate coupon, or fixed rate debt. With increased economic uncertainty and interest rate volatility of recent years, both borrowers and lenders have agreed on using variable or floating rate debt. In some general sense, floating rate debt is fair to everybody. In effect, it says the borrower pays whatever current interest rate conditions call for, and similarly for the lender.

The effect on the borrower, whose viewpoint we are taking primarily here, depends upon the covariation of interest rates with general economic conditions, the revenues of the borrower, the costs of the borrower, and hence the level of the borrower's operating income. If interest rates are positively correlated with the borrower's net operating income, floating rate coupons will reduce financial risks to borrowers. This is because when interest rates are high, operating income is high. When interest rates are low, operating income is low. Hence, net income will tend to be relatively stable.

If interest rate levels are negatively correlated with the borrower's operating income, the opposite effects will occur. Fluctuating interest rates will increase the volatility of the borrower's net income and thereby increase the equity risk of the borrower.

But whether interest rates represent fixed coupons or fluctuating coupons, interest costs remain a fixed charge. They must be paid regardless of the level of the operating income of the firm. Hence, the increased use of floating rate debt does not fundamentally affect the general propositions developed in this chapter. If interest rates are positively correlated with operating income, the floating rate debt may mitigate to some degree the leverage effects. If interest rate levels are negatively correlated with the firm's net operating income, the leverage effects will be magnified.

The remainder of the chapter will discuss the key variables that influence judgments about the degree of financial leverage to employ. Adding consideration of these qualitative factors provides a more complete basis for decisions on the use of debt versus equity financing.

Factors Influencing Financial Structure

The more important of the financial structure determinants are (1) growth rate of future sales, (2) stability of future sales, (3) industry characteristics, (4) asset structure of the firm, (5) control position and attitudes towards risk of owners and management, and (6) lenders' attitudes towards the firm and the industry.

Growth Rate of Sales

The future growth rate of sales is a measure of the extent to which the earnings per share of a firm are likely to be magnified by leverage. If sales and earnings grow at a rate of 8 to 10 percent a year, for example, financing by debt with limited fixed charges should magnify the returns to owners of the stock.[12] This can be seen from Figure 20.1. However, the common stock of a firm whose sales and earnings are growing at a favorable rate commands a high price; this favors equity financing. The firm must weigh the benefits of using leverage against the opportunity of broadening its equity base when its common stock prices are high.

Sales Stability

Sales stability and debt ratios are directly related. With greater stability in sales and earnings, a firm can incur the fixed charges of debt with less risk than when its sales and earnings are subject to substantial declines. When earnings are low, the firm may have difficulty meeting its fixed interest obligations.

Industry Characteristics

Debt-servicing ability is dependent on the profitability, as well as the volume, of sales. Hence, the stability of profit margins is as important as the stability of sales. The ease with which new firms can enter the industry and the ability of competing firms to expand capacity both influence profit margins. A growth industry promises higher profit margins, but such margins are likely to narrow if the industry is one in which the number of firms can be easily increased through additional entry. For example, the franchised fast-service food companies were a very profitable industry in the early 1960s, but it was relatively easy for new firms to enter the business and compete with the older firms. As the industry matured during the late 1960s and early 1970s, the capacity of the old and the new firms grew at an increased rate. As a consequence, profit margins declined.

Asset Structure

Asset structure influences the sources of financing in several ways. Firms with long-lived fixed assets, especially when demand for their output is relatively assured (for example, public utilities), use long-term mortgage debt extensively.[13] Firms that have their assets mostly in receivables and in inventories whose value is dependent on the continued profitability of the individual firm (for example, those in wholesale and retail trade) rely less on long-term debt financing and more on short-term financing.

Management Attitudes

The management attitudes that most directly influence the choice of financing are those concerning control of the enterprise and risk. Large corporations whose stock is widely owned may choose additional sales of common stock because such sales will have little influence on the control of the company.

In contrast, the owners of small firms may prefer to avoid issuing common stock in order to be assured of continued control. Because they generally have confidence in the

---

[12]Such a growth rate is also often associated with a high profit rate.

[13]But, the returns allowed on the assets by regulators of public utilities are also critical. In recent decades, the inadequate returns allowed caused the securities of many public utility companies to be considered to involve relatively high risks.

prospects of their companies and because they can see the large potential gains to themselves resulting from leverage, managers of such firms are often willing to incur high debt ratios.

The converse can, of course, also hold; the owner-manager of a small firm may be more conservative than the manager of a large company. If the net worth of the small firm is, say, $1 million, and if it all belongs to the owner-manager, that individual may well decide to limit the use of debt, which increases risks of losing a substantial portion of his wealth.

Lender Attitudes

Regardless of managements' views, lenders' attitudes determine financial structures. The corporation discusses its financial structure with lenders and gives much weight to their advice. But, if management seeks to use leverage beyond norms for the industry, lenders may be unwilling to accept such debt increases. They emphasize that excessive debt reduces the credit standing of the borrower and the credit rating of the securities previously issued. The lenders' point of view has been expressed by a borrower (a financial vice president), who stated, "Our policy is to determine how much debt we can carry and still maintain an Aa bond rating, then use that amount less a small margin for safety."

Financial Structure in Practice

In this final section of the chapter, we shall indicate how the factors influencing the degree of financial leverage are reflected in actual practice among industries and firms. Wide variations in asset structures and capital structure proportions are observed in practice. This generalization is supported by the data presented in Table 20.12. First, the patterns for wholesale trade, retail trade, and all manufacturing are compared. The ratio of current assets to total assets declines from 65 percent for wholesale trade to 42 percent for all manufacturing. Current liabilities are almost one-half of total assets for wholesale trade but only about one-fourth for all manufacturing. The ratio of shareholders' equity to total assets rises from 36 percent for wholesale trade to 47 percent for all manufacturing. These variations reflect, of course, the differences in the nature of wholesaling, retailing, and manufacturing activities.

Table 20.12   Asset and Capital Structure Proportions as a Percentage of Total Assets, 1984

	Current Assets	Short-Term Debt*	Current Liabilities	Long-Term Debt	Total Liabilities	Equity
Wholesale trade	65	17	45	16	64	36
Retail trade	52	7	31	20	59	41
All manufacturing	42	5	27	18	53	47
Individual manufacturing industries:						
Instruments	50	4	22	10	38	62
Drugs	36	8	24	12	41	59
Iron and steel	38	4	24	30	67	33
Aircraft and guided missiles	68	3	56	6	67	33

*Includes current installment of long-term debt.
Source: Bureau of the Census. *Quarterly Financial Reports.*

Table 20.13   Capital Structures, Electric and Gas Utilities, 1985

	Percent of Total Capitalization*	
	Electric Utilities**	Gas Utilities**
Long-term debt	49%	41%
Preferred stock	11	6
Common equity	39	53

*Defined as sum of long-term debt, preferred stock, and common equity.
**Investor owned.
Source: Estimates by authors based on company financial data and industry composites.

For example, among individual manufacturing industries depicted in the lower part of the table, the highest and lowest industries in the ratio of shareholders' equity to total assets are shown. In addition to variation in asset structures, the ratio of shareholders' equity to total assets ranges from 62 percent for "instruments" down to 33 percent for "aircraft and guided missiles." Variations in forms of debt are also observed. The ratio of long-term debt to total assets for aircraft and guided missiles was only 6 percent, while it was 30 percent for iron and steel. These variations among individual industries reflect a complex of considerations discussed previously as well as historical practices that are changing.

In Table 20.13, the capital structures of investor-owned electric and gas utilities are set forth. The capital structures of gas utilities are similar to those of manufacturing companies. The electric utilities, however, have a much lower ratio of common equity to total capitalization.

Even lower ratios of equity to total assets are found among financial institutions. In recent years, commercial banks have had a ratio of common stock shareholders' equity to total assets of less than 5 percent. This ratio for savings and loans has been under 10 percent. For finance companies, it has averaged around 20 percent.

Thus, wide ranges in leverage ratios are observed among different industries and even among individual companies within a given industry. These large differences, in turn, reflect a wide range of historical, managerial, and other factors influencing financial leverage decisions. In the following chapters, we shall consider in greater depth the major influences (such as relative costs, risk, and control) in determining a basis for choosing among alternative forms and sources of financing.

Summary

Financial leverage is the use of debt. Whenever the return on assets exceeds the cost of debt, leverage is favorable, and the return on equity is raised by using it. However, leverage is a two-edged sword, and if the returns on assets are less than the cost of debt, then leverage reduces the returns on equity. The more leverage a firm employs, the greater is this reduction. As a result, leverage may be used to increase stockholder returns, but it is used at the risk of increasing losses under adversity. Thus, gains and losses are magnified by leverage; and the higher the leverage employed by a firm, the greater will be the volatility of its returns.

This chapter analyzed the effects of financial leverage by demonstrating the relationship between leverage and alternative risk measures. With increased financial leverage, the measures of risk increase as well. Using the Security Market Line from the Capital Asset Pricing Model, a set of quantitative relationships between risk and required return can be demonstrated. To the extent that the assumptions of the theory are applicable, a basis is provided for measuring how beta increases with financial leverage. The beta is used with the SML to calculate the required rates of return. These could then be compared with the expected returns to develop a basis for a decision on how much financial leverage to use.

Using the coefficient of variation approach, we do not have a precise set of quantitative relationships between risk and required return. However, this measure of risk is consistent with the beta measure of risk in that both increase with increased financial leverage. The Capital Asset Pricing Model provides a precise set of relationships. The problem in applying the Capital Asset Pricing Model is that the parameters of the relationships are difficult to measure without error and may not be stable. As in capital budgeting analysis, we recommend the calculation of alternative measures of risk. They are useful in providing a first-step basis for a quantitative analysis of a capital budgeting or financial structure decision. Ultimately, qualitative factors and judgments will have to be used to arrive at a final decision.

In the following chapter, the concepts developed to this point will be extended to the formal theory of the cost of capital. The way investors appraise the relative desirability of increased returns versus higher risks is seen to be a most important consideration — one that, in general, invalidates the theory that firms should strive for maximum earnings per share regardless of the risks involved.

Questions

20.1 How will each of the occurrences listed below affect a firm's financial structure, capital structure, and net worth?
    a) The firm retains earnings of $100 during the year.
    b) A preferred stock issue is refinanced with bonds.
    c) Bonds are sold for cash.
    d) The firm repurchases 10 percent of its outstanding common stock with excess cash.
    e) An issue of convertible bonds is converted.

20.2 From an economic and social standpoint, is the use of financial leverage justifiable? Explain by listing some advantages and disadvantages.

20.3 Financial leverage and operating leverage are similar in one very important respect. What is this similarity, and why is it important?

20.4 How does the use of financial leverage affect the firm's breakeven point?

20.5 Would you expect risk to increase proportionately, more than proportionately, or less than proportionately with added financial leverage? Explain.

20.6 What are some reasons for variations of debt ratios among the firms in a given industry?

20.7 Why is the following statement true? "Other things being the same, firms with relatively stable sales and profits are able to incur relatively high debt ratios."

20.8 Why do public utility companies usually pursue a different financial policy from that of trade firms?

20.9 The use of financial ratios and industry averages in the financial planning and analysis of a firm should be approached with caution. Why?

Problems

20.1 The Bonner Company and the Kirkeby Company are identical except for their leverage ratios and the interest rate on debt. Each has $10 million in assets, each earned $2 million before interest and taxes in 1984, and each has a 40 percent corporate tax rate. Bonner, however, has a leverage ratio (D/TA) of 30 percent and pays 10 percent interest on its debt, while Kirkeby has a 50 percent leverage ratio and pays 12 percent interest on debt.

a) Calculate the rate of return on equity (net income/equity) for each firm.

b) Observing that Kirkeby has a higher return on equity, Bonner's treasurer decides to raise the leverage ratio from 30 to 60 percent. This will increase Bonner's interest rate on debt to 15 percent. Calculate the new rate of return on equity for Bonner.

20.2 The Tarko Company wishes to calculate next year's return on equity under different leverage ratios. Tarko's total assets are $10 million and its tax rate is 40 percent. The company is able to estimate next year's earnings for three possible states-of-the-world. It estimates that 1986 earnings before interest and taxes will be $3 million with a 0.2 probability, $2 million with a 0.5 probability, and $500,000 with a 0.3 probability. Calculate Tarko's expected return on equity, the standard deviation, and the coefficient of variation for each of the following leverage ratios:

Leverage (Debt/Total Assets)	Interest Rate
0%	—
10	10%
50	12
60	15

20.3 The beta for the Hume Company is 0.8 if it employs no leverage, and its tax rate is 40 percent. The financial manager of Hume uses the following expression to calculate the influence of leverage on beta:

$$\beta_L = \beta_u[1 + (B/S)(1 - T)].$$

a) Several alternative target leverage ratios are being considered. What will be the beta on the common stock of Hume Company if the following alternative leverage ratios are employed — that is, B/S = 0.4? 0.8? 1.0? 1.2? 1.6?

b) If the financial manager of Hume uses the SML to estimate the required return on equity, what are the required rates of return on equity at each of the above leverage ratios? (The estimated risk-free return is 6 percent, and the market risk premium is 5 percent.)

c) The financial manager wants to keep the beta at 1.5 or below. What is the maximum leverage ratio which can be employed? What is the required rate of return on equity at this leverage ratio?

20.4 The Shuman Company plans to raise a net amount of $240 million for new equipment financing and working capital. Two alternatives are being considered. Common stock may be sold to net $40 per share, or debentures yielding 10 percent may be issued. The balance sheet and income statement of the Shuman Company prior to financing follow on page 575.

The Shuman Company Balance Sheet as of December 31, 1985 (Millions of Dollars)

Current assets	$ 800	Accounts payable	$ 150
Net fixed assets	400	Notes payable to bank	250
		Other current liabilities	200
		Total current liabilities	$ 600
		Long-term debt	250
		Common stock, $2 par	50
		Retained earnings	300
Total assets	$1,200	Total claims	$1,200

The Shuman Company Income Statement for Year Ended December 31, 1985
(Millions of Dollars)

Sales	$2,200
Earnings before interest and taxes (10%)	$ 220
Interest on debt	40
Earnings before taxes	$ 180
Tax (40%)	72
Net income after tax	$ 108

Annual sales are expected to be distributed according to the following probabilities:

Annual Sales	Probability
$2,000	0.30
2,500	0.40
3,200	0.30

a) Assuming that earnings before interest and taxes remain at 10 percent of sales, calculate earnings per share under both the stock financing and the debt financing alternatives at each possible level of sales.

b) Calculate expected earnings per share under both debt and stock financing.

20.5 CME Corporation produces one product, a small calculator. Last year, 50,000 calculators were sold at $20 each. CME's income statement is shown below.

CME Corporation Income Statement for Year Ended December 31, 1985

Sales		$1,000,000
Less: variable costs	$400,000	
fixed costs	200,000	600,000
EBIT		$ 400,000
Less: interest		125,000
Net income before tax		$ 275,000
Less: income tax ($T = 0.40$)		110,000
Net income		$ 165,000
EPS (100,000 shares)		$1.65

a) Calculate the following for CME's 1985 level of sales:
   1. the degree of operating leverage
   2. the degree of financial leverage
   3. the combined leverage effect.
b) CME is considering changing to a new production process for manufacturing the calculators. Highly automated and capital intensive, the new process will double fixed costs to $400,000 but will decrease variable costs to $4 a unit. If the new equipment is financed with bonds, interest will increase by $70,000; if it is financed by common stock, total stock outstanding will increase by 20,000 shares. Assuming that sales remain constant, calculate for each financing method:
   1. earnings per share
   2. the combined leverage effect.
c) Under what conditions would you expect CME to want to change its operations to the more automated process?
d) If sales are expected to increase, which alternative will have the greatest impact on EPS? Illustrate with an example.

20.6 You are given the following information about the Richardson Company, which manufactures small hot plates:

Price	$35
Variable costs	$19 per unit
Fixed costs	$200,000
Debt (B)	$300,000
Interest rate	12%
T	40%

In 1985, Richardson's net income was $600,000.
a) How many hot plates were sold in 1985?
b) Calculate the degrees of operating, financial, and combined leverage for Richardson.
c) Suppose that Richardson restructures its balance sheet, increasing debt to $1 million. Prepare a pro forma income statement and calculate degree of the combined leverage assuming the same level of sales calculated in Part (a).

20.7 The Lewis Corporation plans to expand assets by 50 percent. To finance the expansion, it is choosing between a straight 11 percent debt issue and common stock. Its current balance sheet and income statement are shown below. If Lewis Corporation finances the $350,000 expansion with debt, the rate on the incremental debt will be 11 percent, and the price-earnings ratio of the common stock will be 8 times. If the expansion is financed by equity, the new stock can be sold at $25. The price-earnings ratio of all the outstanding common stock will remain at 10 times.

Lewis Corporation Balance Sheet as of December 31, 1985

		Debt (at 8%)	$140,000
		Common stock, $10 par	350,000
		Retained earnings	210,000
Total assets	$700,000	Total claims	$700,000

Lewis Corporation Income Statement for Year Ended December 31, 1985

Sales	$2,100,000	
Total costs		Earnings per share: $\dfrac{\$103,600}{35,000} = \$2.96$
(excluding interest)	1,881,600	
Earnings before interest and taxes	$ 218,400	Price/earnings ratio: $10\times$[a]
Debt interest	11,200	
Income before taxes	$ 207,200	Market price: $10 \times \$2.96 = \$29.60$
Taxes (at 50%)	103,600	
Net income	$ 103,600	

[a]The price/earnings ratio is the market price per share divided by earnings per share. It represents the amount of money an investor is willing to pay for $1 of current earnings. The higher the riskiness of a stock, the lower its P/E ratio, other things held constant.

a) Assuming that earnings before interest and taxes (EBIT) is 10 percent of sales, what are the earnings per share at sales levels of $0; $700,000; $1,400,000; $2,100,000; $2,800,000; $3,500,000, and $4,200,000, when financing is with common stock? When financing is with debt? (Assume no fixed costs of production.)

b) Make a chart for EPS indicating the crossover point in sales (where EPS using bonds = EPS using stock).

c) Using the price/earnings ratio, calculate the market value per share of common stock for each sales level for both the debt and the equity financing.

d) Using data from Part (c), make a chart of market value per share for the company indicating the crossover point.

e) Which form of financing should be used if the firm follows the policy of seeking to maximize
   1. EPS?
   2. market price per share?

f) Now assume that the following probability estimates of future sales have been made: 5 percent chance of $0, 7.5 percent chance of $700,000, 20 percent chance of $1,400,000, 35 percent chance of $2,100,000, 20 percent chance of $2,800,000, 7.5 percent chance of $3,500,000, and 5 percent chance of $4,200,000. Calculate expected values for EPS and market price per share under each financing alternative.

g) What other factors should be taken into account in choosing between the two forms of financing?

h) Would it matter if the presently outstanding stock was all owned by the final decision maker (the president) and that this represented his entire net worth? Would it matter if he was compensated entirely by a fixed salary? If he had a substantial number of stock options?

Selected References

Altman, Edward I., "Corporate Bankruptcy Potential, Stockholder Returns, and Share Valuation," *Journal of Finance*, 24 (December 1969), pp. 887-900.

Barnea, Amir; Haugen, Robert A.; and Senbet, Lemma W., "Market Imperfections, Agency Prob-

lems, and Capital Structure: A Review," *Financial Management*, 10 (Summer 1981), pp. 7-22.

Castanias, Richard, "Bankruptcy Risk and Optimal Capital Structure," *Journal of Finance*, 38 (December 1983), pp. 1617-1635.

Chambers, Donald R.; Harris, Robert S.; and Pringle, John J., "Treatment of Financing Mix in Analyzing Investment Opportunities," *Financial Management*, 11 (Summer 1982), pp. 24-41.

Chen, Andrew H., and Kim, E. Han, "Theories of Corporate Debt Policy: A Synthesis," *Journal of Finance*, 34 (May 1979), pp. 371-384.

Cooper, Ian, and Franks, Julian R., "The Interaction of Financing and Investment Decisions When the Firm has Unused Tax Credits," *Journal of Finance*, 38 (May 1983), pp. 571-583.

Cordes, Joseph J., and Sheffrin, Steven M., "Estimating the Tax Advantage of Corporate Debt," *Journal of Finance*, 38 (March 1983), pp. 95-105.

Harris, John M., Jr.; Roenfeldt, Rodney L.; and Cooley, Philip L., "Evidence of Financial Leverage Clienteles," *Journal of Finance*, 38 (September 1983), pp. 1125-1132.

Heinkel, Robert, "A Theory of Capital Structure Relevance under Imperfect Information," *Journal of Finance*, 37 (December 1982), pp. 1141-1150.

Hong, Hai, "Inflation and the Market Value of the Firm: Theory and Tests," *Journal of Finance*, 32 (September 1977), pp. 1031-1048.

Huffman, Lucy, "Operating Leverage, Financial Leverage, and Equity Risk," *Journal of Banking and Finance*, 7 (June 1983), pp. 197-212.

Kim, E. Han, "Miller's Equilibrium, Shareholder Leverage Clienteles and Optimal Capital Structure," *Journal of Finance*, 37 (May 1982), pp. 301-319.

———, "A Mean-Variance Theory of Optimal Capital Structure and Corporate Debt Capacity," *Journal of Finance*, 33 (March 1978), pp. 45-63.

Kim, E. Han; Lewellen, Wilbur G.; and McConnell, John J., "Financial Leverage Clienteles: Theory and Evidence," *Journal of Financial Economics*, 7 (March 1979), pp. 83-109.

Kim, E. Han; McConnell, John J.; and Greenwood, Paul R., "Capital Structure Rearrangements and Me-First Rules in an Efficient Capital Market," *Journal of Finance*, 32 (June 1977), pp. 789-810.

Krainer, Robert E., "Interest Rates, Leverage, and Investor Rationality," *Journal of Financial and Quantitative Analysis*, 12 (March 1977), pp. 1-16.

Kraus, Alan, and Litzenberger, Robert, "A State-Preference Model of Optimal Financial Leverage," *Journal of Finance*, 28 (September 1973), pp. 911-922.

Litzenberger, Robert H., and Sosin, Howard B., "A Comparison of Capital Structure Decisions of Regulated and Non-Regulated Firms," *Financial Management*, 8 (Autumn 1979), pp. 17-21.

Marsh, Paul, "The Choice Between Equity and Debt: An Empirical Study," *Journal of Finance*, 37 (December 1982), pp. 121-144.

Masulis, Ronald W., "The Impact of Capital Structure Change on Firm Value: Some Estimates," *Journal of Finance*, 38 (March 1983), pp. 107-126.

———, "The Effects of Capital Structure Change on Security Prices: A Study of Exchange Offers," *Journal of Financial Economics*, 8 (June 1980), pp. 139-177.

Morris, James R., "Taxes, Bankruptcy Costs and the Existence of an Optimal Capital Structure," *Journal of Financial Research*, 5 (Fall 1982), pp. 285-299.

Myers, Stewart C., "Determinants of Corporate Borrowing," *Journal of Financial Economics*, 5 (November 1977), pp. 147-175.

Phillips, Paul D.; Groth, John C.; and Richards, R. Malcolm, "Financing the Alaskan Project: The Experience at Sohio," *Financial Management*, 8 (Autumn 1979), pp. 7-16.

Rubinstein, M. E., "A Mean-Variance Synthesis of Corporate Financial Theory," *Journal of Finance*, 28 (March 1973), p. 178.

Scott, David F., Jr., and Johnson, Dana J., "Financing Policies and Practices in Large Corporations," *Financial Management*, 11 (Summer 1982), pp. 51-59.

Scott, David F., Jr., and Martin, John D., "Industry Influence on Financial Structure," *Financial Management*, 4 (Spring 1975), pp. 67-73.

Senbet, Lemma W., and Taggart, Robert A., Jr., "Capital Structure Equilibrium under Market Imperfections and Incompleteness," *Journal of Finance*, 39 (March 1984), pp. 93-103.

Taggart, Robert A., Jr., "A Model of Corporate Financing Decisions," *Journal of Finance*, 32 (December 1977), pp. 1467-1484.

Turnbull, Stuart M., "Debt Capacity," *Journal of Finance*, 34 (September 1979), pp. 931-940.

———, "Debt Capacity: Erratum," *Journal of Finance*, 37 (March 1981), p. 197.

Chapter 21 Capital Structure and the Cost of Capital

Chapter 21 builds on the fundamental theories of risk and return developed in Chapter 17. In that chapter, the underlying determinants of the cost of debt and equity were developed. In this chapter we consider how these costs are influenced by the degree of leverage employed. In addition, the costs of hybrid forms of securities that combine elements of debt and equity (for example, preferred stock) will be discussed. This provides a basis for discussing the determination of the optimal degree of financial leverage or the optimal financing mix by reference to minimizing the firm's cost of capital, which is equivalent to maximizing the market value of the firm. The implications of capital restructuring for seeking the optimal financing mix are also considered. We then seek to pull the various threads together by showing how the cost of capital could be measured in practice. Finally, the implications of the foregoing for guiding the firm in setting its overall capital budget are set forth.

Leverage and the Cost of Capital — Theory

An extensive literature has developed related to the influence of leverage on the costs of debt and equity. In seeking to summarize the best theory and practice in this area, we must begin with the classic 1958 Modigliani-Miller (MM) article on the cost of capital since all subsequent developments in finance have been related to what are called the "MM propositions." Initially MM discuss a no growth firm with no net new investments in a world of no taxes. Consistent with our discussion in Chapter 6 on capital budgeting, the value of such a firm (or project) would be:

$$V = \frac{\overline{NOI}}{k} = \frac{\overline{X}}{k}. \tag{21.1}$$

This is MM's Proposition I. It states that the market value of any firm (or project) "is given by capitalizing its expected return at the rate k appropriate to its class." This is what MM were referring to when they stated that firms in a given risk class would have the same applicable discount rate. In their discussions they stated that firms of different sizes would differ only by a "scale factor" and pointed out that the expected cash flows from two firms of different size or scale (or projects) would be perfectly correlated.

The measurement of k depends upon the riskiness of the firm, project, or activity. Thus, if the expected net operating income, $\overline{NOI}$ or $\overline{X}$, in the numerator were \$200,000 and the activity were of relatively low risk, the discount factor, k, might be 10 percent. The value of the firm would then be \$2 million. If the activity of the firm was highly risky, the discount rate might be 20 percent. If so, the value of the firm would be \$1 million.

We now consider the influence of leverage. Under the assumptions to this point MM argue that the expression in Equation 21.1 would be unaffected by financial leverage. This is their Proposition I, which states that the market value of any firm is independent of its capital structure (that is, the percentage of debt-to-total assets, expressed in market value terms) and is obtained by discounting its expected return (net operating income) at a rate appropriate to its risk class. They obtain this result from an arbitrage process involving "homemade leverage," which can be formulated simply.[1] Consider two investment alternatives with the following patterns of investments and returns:

Decision	Investment	Dollar Return
A. Buy α of the equity of levered firm, L	αS_L	$\alpha(X - k_b B)$
B. Buy α of unlevered firm, U		
Borrow αB	$\alpha S_U - \alpha B$	$\alpha(X) - \alpha k_b B = \alpha(X - k_b B)$

In the above, the symbols have the following meanings:

L = levered
U = unlevered
S = market value of common stock (equity)
B = market value of debt (bonds)
k_b = marginal cost of debt
X = net operating income (also assumed to be equal to earnings before interest and taxes, EBIT)
α = a fraction, that is, $0 \leq \alpha \leq 1$.

Investment A is to buy a fraction of the common equity of a levered firm. Investment B is to buy the same fraction of the common equity of an unlevered firm and to create an amount of homemade leverage equivalent to that represented by the investment of the α fraction of equity of the levered firm. Since the returns from the two investments are equal, their investment market values will also be equal. Hence we set the two investment values equal to each other:

$$\alpha S_L = \alpha S_U - \alpha B \qquad \text{Divide by } \alpha.$$
$$S_L = S_U - B \qquad \text{Regroup terms.}$$
$$S_L + B = S_U \qquad \text{Since } S_L + B = V_L \text{ and } S_U = V_U, \text{ we have } V_L = V_U.$$

Thus, under the conditions we have specified, the value of the levered firm is equal to the value of the unlevered firm.[2] This is the famous capital structure irrelevance or leverage irrelevance of Proposition I of Modigliani-Miller. We can also rewrite Equation 21.1 by solving for k to obtain Equation 21.2:

$$k = k_U = \frac{\overline{X}}{V}. \qquad \textbf{(21.2)}$$

This is a restatement of Proposition I in terms of the cost of capital (or return on assets). It states that the cost of capital to any firm is independent of its capital structure and is equal to the capitalization rate of a pure equity stream of its risk class. The foregoing was under

---

[1]Remember that $B = rD/k_b$ so that $k_b B = rD$. Recall that r is the coupon rate on debt and D is the book value of debt.

[2]Note that the argument implicitly assumes that individuals can borrow at the same rate as the firm, k_b. This is a valid assumption in a world without transactions costs.

the assumptions of a no-tax world. We will now consider successively the introduction of various types of taxes. We start with a proportional corporate tax rate that we will initially refer to as T. We will start with an unlevered firm. The net operating income available for distribution to claimants must now be expressed net of the corporate income tax. We, therefore, have Equation 21.3:

$$V_U = \frac{\overline{X}(1 - T)}{k_U}.$$

(21.3)

A simple rearrangement gives us the cost of capital of an unlevered firm in Equation 21.4:

$$k_U = \frac{\overline{X}(1 - T)}{V_U}.$$

(21.4)

We repeat the simple arbitrage process. Based on two decision alternatives described below, some associated investment and returns patterns follow:

Decision	Investment	Dollar Return
A. Buy α of levered firm, L	αS_L	$\alpha(X - k_b B)(1 - T)$
B. Buy α of unlevered firm, U		
Borrow $\alpha(1 - T)B$	$\alpha S_U - \alpha(1 - T)B$	$\alpha(X)(1 - T) - \alpha(1 - T)k_b B =$
		$\alpha(X - k_b B)(1 - T).$

Decision A is to buy a fraction of the common equity of a levered firm. Decision B is to buy the same fraction of the common equity of an unlevered firm and to create an amount of homemade leverage equivalent to that represented by the investment in the equity of the levered firm by selling $\alpha(1 - T)B$ of debt. The return from the investment in the equity of the levered firm is the α percent of its income after deduction of debt interest, and taxes. For Decision B, the return is given as a fraction of the after-tax income of the unlevered firm less the interest (after taxes) paid on the homemade borrowings. The returns from the two investments are equal; consequently their market values will also be equal. It follows that

$$\begin{aligned}
\alpha S_L &= \alpha S_U - \alpha(1 - T)B & &\text{Divide through by } \alpha. \\
S_L &= S_U - (1 - T)B & &\text{Expand the last term.} \\
S_L &= S_U - B + TB & &\text{Regroup terms.} \\
S_L + B &= S_U + TB. & &\text{Since } S_L + B = V_L \text{ and } S_U = V_U,
\end{aligned}$$

then

$$V_L = V_U + TB.$$

(21.5)

Equation 21.5 conveys an important implication of the MM relations.[3] Because of the tax subsidy represented by the tax deductibility of interest on debt, the value of a levered firm

---

[3]For later use, note that from Equations 21.4 and 21.5 that

$$k_U = \frac{\overline{X}(1 - T)}{V_L - TB}.$$

Hence

$$\overline{X}(1 - T) = k_U V_L - k_U TB.$$

(21.6)

will be greater than the value of an unlevered firm by the amount of debt multiplied by the applicable corporate tax rate. Since the value of the common equity, S, is equal to the value of a levered firm less the value of debt, the effects of leverage decisions on the market behavior of the common equity are predictable on the basis of the Equation 21.5 relations. This leads to MM's Proposition II, which deals with the cost of equity capital. We start with the definitions of the cost of equity and net income. For a perpetual income stream, we know that the stock value is

$$S = \frac{\overline{NI}}{k_s}.$$

Therefore the cost of equity is

$$k_s = \frac{NI}{S}. \tag{21.7}$$

Next, the accounting definition of net income is

$$NI = (X - k_bB) - (X - k_bB)T$$

This is NOI after debt interest, and taxes.
We multiply through in the term with T.

$$= X - k_bB - XT + k_bBT$$
$$= X(1 - T) - k_bB(1 - T)$$

We then regroup terms.
Use Equation 21.6 to substitute for $X(1 - T)$.

$$= k_UV_L - k_UBT - k_bB(1 - T).$$

Let $V_L = S + B$ and divide by S.

$$\frac{NI}{S} = k_s = \frac{k_US}{S} + \frac{k_UB}{S} - \frac{k_UBT}{S} - \frac{k_bB}{S}(1 - T)$$

Regroup terms.

$$k_s = k_U + k_U\frac{B}{S}(1 - T) - k_b\frac{B}{S}(1 - T)$$

Factor $B/S(1 - T)$ from last two terms.

$$k_s = k_U + (k_U - k_b)(1 - T)(B/S). \tag{21.8}$$

This is MM's Proposition II with corporate taxes, which states that the cost of equity is equal to the cost of capital of an unlevered firm plus the after-tax difference between the cost of capital of an unlevered firm and the cost of debt, weighted by the leverage ratio. Proposition II states that the cost of equity rises with the debt-to-equity ratio in a linear fashion, with the slope of the line equal to $(k_U - k_b)(1 - T)$, as shown in Figure 21.1. It makes sense that the cost of equity increases with greater financial leverage because shareholders are exposed to greater risk.

Next the weighted average (marginal) cost of capital (WACC) can be formulated in three versions. We start with the descriptive buildup of the cost of capital as the weighted costs of the market values of debt and equity. This traditional definition of the cost of capital is

$$k = \text{WACC} = k_b(1 - T)\frac{B}{V_L} + k_s\frac{S}{V_L}. \tag{21.9}$$

A major difficulty with this traditional definition is that although it can be used to compute the WACC given the currently observable costs of debt and equity, it cannot be

Figure 21.1   Cost of Equity Capital as a Function of Leverage

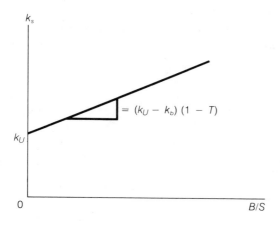

used to tell us how the WACC changes as the financial leverage of the firm is changed. In order to see how the firm's WACC changes with leverage we will have to answer the basic question — How does the value of the firm change as a new investment is undertaken? The weighted average cost of capital is the return on assets that the firm must earn, given its leverage level, in order to increase shareholders' wealth.

If a new investment, ΔI, is undertaken, it will be financed with some combination of new debt, ΔB^n, and new equity, ΔS^n. Therefore, by definition,

$$\Delta I = \Delta B^n + \Delta S^n.$$

Furthermore, the accompanying change in the value of the levered firm, ΔV_L, must arise from one of four sources: original debt, ΔB^o, original shareholders' wealth, ΔS^o, new debt, or new equity. Hence, we know that

$$\Delta V_L = \Delta B^o + \Delta B^n + \Delta S^o + \Delta S^n.$$

Dividing through by the amount of new investment, ΔI, gives the change in the value of the firm with respect to new investment:

$$\frac{\Delta V_L}{\Delta I} = \frac{\Delta B^o}{\Delta I} + \frac{\Delta B^n}{\Delta I} + \frac{\Delta S^o}{\Delta I} + \frac{\Delta S^n}{\Delta I}.$$

If we assume that the new investment does not affect original bondholders' wealth so that

$$\frac{\Delta B^o}{\Delta I} = 0,$$

and if we rearrange terms, we have

$$\frac{\Delta V_L}{\Delta I} = \frac{\Delta S^o}{\Delta I} + \frac{\Delta B^n + \Delta S^n}{\Delta I}.$$

Finally, because $\Delta B^n + \Delta S^n = \Delta I$ (because all new investment dollars are provided by either new debt or new equity)

$$\frac{\Delta V_L}{\Delta I} = \frac{\Delta S^o}{\Delta I} + 1$$

$$\frac{\Delta S^o}{\Delta I} = \frac{\Delta V_L}{\Delta I} - 1. \tag{21.10}$$

We now have an expression for the change in original shareholders' wealth when new investment is undertaken. Since original shareholders completely control this decision, it is reasonable to make the behavioral assumption that the change in original shareholders' wealth must be positive, that is,

$$\frac{\Delta S^o}{\Delta I} = \frac{\Delta V_L}{\Delta I} - 1 > 0.$$

Another expression showing how the value of a levered firm changes with new investment is derived by substituting Equation 21.3 into Equation 21.5:

$$\dot{V}_L = \frac{\overline{X}(1 - T)}{k_U} + TB.$$

Here the value of the levered firm is shown to be the sum of two parts. First is the discounted present value of the perpetual expected after-tax net operating income stream,

$$\frac{\overline{X}(1 - T)}{k_U},$$

and the second is the gain from leverage, TB. If the firm takes on a new investment with the same risk as the portfolio of projects already held by the firm, the change in the firm's value would be

$$\frac{\Delta V_L}{\Delta I} = \frac{\Delta X(1 - T)}{k_U \Delta I} + T \frac{\Delta B^n}{\Delta I}. \tag{21.11}$$

Substituting Equation 21.11 into 21.10, we have

$$\frac{\Delta S^o}{\Delta I} = \frac{\Delta \overline{X}(1 - T)}{k_U \Delta I} + T \frac{\Delta B^n}{\Delta I} - 1 > 0,$$

and rearranging terms gives,

$$\frac{\Delta \overline{X}(1 - T)}{\Delta I} > k_U \left(1 - T \frac{\Delta B^n}{\Delta I} \right). \tag{21.12}$$

The left-hand side of this expression is the change in the firm's after-tax operating income brought about by the new investment, ΔI. It is literally the after-tax return on assets that the firm would have if it had no debt. Remember that in Chapter 6 we carefully defined the cash flow for capital budgeting projects in exactly the same way. This definition appears again here in the derivation of the weighted average cost of capital because the expected cash flows for capital budgeting purposes are discounted by the weighted average cost of capital in order to determine the change in the value of shareholders' wealth. In other words,

$$V_L = \frac{\overline{X}(1 - T)}{k}.$$

Hence,

$$k = \text{WACC} = \frac{\overline{X}(1 - T)}{V_L}. \tag{21.13}$$

The right-hand side of Inequality 21.12 is the Modigliani-Miller definition of the weighted average cost of capital.

$$k = \text{WACC} \equiv k_U\left(1 - T\,\frac{\Delta B^n}{\Delta I}\right).$$

We know that $\Delta I = \Delta B^n + \Delta S^n$. If we further assume that the firm issues new financing in proportion to its target capital structure, then the definition of WACC becomes

$$k = \text{WACC} \equiv k_U\left(1 - T\,\frac{B}{B + S}\right). \tag{21.14}$$

The Modigliani-Miller definition of the weighted average cost of capital not only tells us how the WACC changes with increasing leverage, it also ties together other aspects of finance, namely

1. When firms undertake projects that earn more than their WACC, they must be increasing shareholders' wealth because $\Delta S^o/\Delta I > 0$.
2. All of the increase in the firm's value accrues to original shareholders. Bondholders merely maintain their original claim, that is, $\Delta B^o/\Delta I = 0$.
3. When cash flows from new investment are discounted at the weighted average cost of capital, they are defined as the after-tax operating cash flows that the firm would have if it had no debt, that is, cash flows are $CF = \overline{X}(1 - T)$.

Three formulations of the WACC have been shown to be mathematically equivalent. For convenience, the three measures of the weighted cost of capital can be summarized as follows:

1. $k = k_b(1 - T)(B/V) + k_s(S/V)$ **(21.15 or 21.9)**

2. $k = \dfrac{\overline{X}(1 - T)}{V_L}$ **(21.16 or 21.13)**

3. $k = k_U(1 - TL)$, where $L = B/V$.   **(21.17 or 21.14)**

Figure 21.2   The Cost of Capital as a Function of the Ratio of Debt to Equity;
(a) Assuming $T = 0$; (b) Assuming $T > 0$

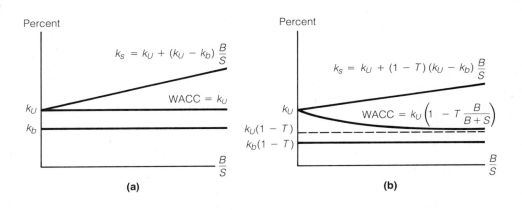

$$k_s = k_U + (k_U - k_b)\frac{B}{S}$$

WACC $= k_U$

$$k_s = k_U + (1 - T)(k_U - k_b)\frac{B}{S}$$

$$\text{WACC} = k_U\left(1 - T\frac{B}{B+S}\right)$$

(a)   (b)

Figure 21.2 is a graphical representation of the cost of capital and its components as a function of the ratio of debt to equity. In a world without corporate taxes, the weighted average cost of capital is a constant. With taxes, the weighted average cost of capital declines as the ratio of debt to equity increases. In both panels of Figure 21.2, the cost of equity capital rises linearly with higher proportions of debt. The reason is that increasing financial leverage causes the residual claims of shareholders to become more variable, as described in Chapter 20. Shareholders require a higher rate of return to compensate them for this additional risk. The cost of debt is assumed to be constant in both panels because the debt is assumed to be riskless. In a world with taxes, the cost of debt remains constant, but at a lower level. (Note: From this point on, V is understood to be V_L, and the value of an unlevered firm will be designated as V_U.)

It will be useful to give content to the MM propositions with corporate taxes by the use of an illustrative case study for the Stevens Company. We consider two alternative capital structures for the Stevens Company:

Stevens Company Balance Sheet, Unlevered

Total assets	$1,000,000	Stockholders' equity	$1,000,000

Stevens Company Balance Sheet, Levered

Total assets	$1,000,000	Debt at 10%	$ 500,000
		Stockholders' equity	500,000
		Total claims	$1,000,000

The applicable corporate tax rate is 40 percent. The income statements for Stevens would reflect the two different capital structures.[4]

Stevens Company Income Statements	Unlevered	Levered
Net operating income (X)	$200,000	$200,000
Interest on debt ($k_bB = rD$)	—	50,000
Income before taxes ($X - k_bB$)	$200,000	$150,000
Taxes at 40% $T(X - k_bB)$	80,000	60,000
Net income ($X - k_bB)(1 - T)$	$120,000	$ 90,000

With the above accounting information, which represents data generally available in financial reports and financial manuals, we can apply the MM propositions. For an unlevered firm of similar characteristics to Stevens, we obtain a measure of the cost of capital for the unlevered cash flows, k_U, which we will assume to be 12 percent. All other relationships can now be computed.

Stevens' value as an unlevered firm would be

$$V_U = \frac{\overline{X}(1 - T)}{k_U} = \frac{(\$200,000)0.6}{0.12} = \$1,000,000.$$

We find that without leverage, Stevens' market value is equal to the book value of its total assets. Next, consider Stevens as a levered firm. Its new value becomes

$$V_L = V_U + TB = \$1,000,000 + 0.4(\$500,000) = \$1,200,000.$$

Now the market value of Stevens exceeds the book value of its total assets. The market value of the equity, S, is

$$S = V_L - B = \$1,200,000 - \$500,000 = \$700,000.$$

The cost of equity capital of Stevens, unlevered, is equal to k_U, or 12 percent. The cost of equity capital for Stevens, as a levered firm, can be calculated by two relationships:

$$k_s = k_U + (k_U - k_b)(1 - T)B/S \qquad \text{or} \qquad k_s = NI/S.$$

The first formulation is MM's Proposition II (our Equation 21.8). The second can be calculated directly. We illustrate both:

$$k_s = 0.12 + (0.12 - 0.10)(0.6)(5/7) \qquad k_s = \$90,000/\$700,000$$

$$= 0.12 + 0.0086 \qquad\qquad\qquad = 12.86\%.$$

$$= 12.86\%.$$

---

[4]Recall that the firm pays rD, which we have shown is also equal to k_bB.

The SML formulation of the cost of equity capital is shown by Hamada [1969] to be

$$k_s = R_F + (\overline{R}_M - R_F)\beta_U[1 + (B/S)(1 - T)].$$

He also demonstrates that $\beta_U[1 + (B/S)(1 - T)] = \beta_L$. Recall that β is the systematic risk of a security. Thus, β_U is the riskiness of the unlevered cash flows of the firm, and β_L is the riskiness of the net income (levered equity) stream. For the Stevens example, let

$$R_F = 0.10, \overline{R}_M = 0.16, \text{ and } \beta_U = 0.333 \text{ and}$$

$$k_s = 0.10 + (0.16 - 0.10)0.333[1 + (5/7)(0.6)] = 0.1286 = 12.86\%.$$

With leverage, the cost of equity capital has risen from 12 percent to 12.86 percent. What happens to the weighted cost of capital? We can employ all three formulations:

1. $k = k_b(1 - T)(B/V) + k_s(S/V)$ $\qquad$ $k = 0.10(0.6)(5/12) + 0.1286(7/12)$
$\qquad\qquad\qquad\qquad\qquad\qquad\qquad\qquad\qquad\qquad = 0.025 + 0.075 = 10\%.$

2. $k = \dfrac{\overline{X}(1 - T)}{V_L}$ $\qquad\qquad\qquad\qquad$ $k = \dfrac{\$120,000}{\$1,200,000} = 10\%.$

3. $k = k_U(1 - TL)$ $\qquad\qquad\qquad\qquad$ $k = 0.12[1 - 0.4(5/12)] = 0.12(5/6)$
$\qquad\qquad\qquad\qquad\qquad\qquad\qquad\qquad\qquad\qquad = 10\%.$

Each formulation gives a weighted cost of capital of 10 percent. The example illustrates that the use of leverage has increased the value of the firm from \$1,000,000 to \$1,200,000. The weighted cost of capital has been reduced from 12 percent to 10 percent. Thus, under the MM propositions, with corporate taxes only, the influence of the tax subsidy on debt is to increase the value of the firm and decrease its weighted cost of capital.

The Cost of Capital with Personal as Well as Corporate Taxes

In our discussion of the cost of capital with corporate taxes, we obtain the result in Equation 21.5 that $V_L = V_U + TB$. A further implication of this result is that the weighted average cost of capital for a levered firm is below the cost of capital for an unlevered firm. This was most clearly seen in the expression for Equation 21.17:

$$k = k_U(1 - TL). \tag{21.17}$$

An implication of these results is the more debt the better. Indeed it implies that firms would have 100 percent debt in their capital structures. We don't observe leverage ratios anywhere near this high, which suggests that the original MM model with taxes requires modification.

One possible extension is to consider personal taxes in addition to corporate taxes. We will use the following symbols:

T_c = corporate tax rate
T_{pb} = ordinary personal income tax rate (paid on debt interest)
T_{ps} = tax rate paid by persons who receive income or capital gains from stock. It is an "average" of the capital gains tax rate and the ordinary rate on dividends received, and is less than T_{pb}

We can analyze the effects of the two types of personal taxes by use of the simple arbitrage framework employed in our previous discussions of the MM models. We have

Decision	Investment	Dollar Return
1. Buy α of the equity of levered firm L	$\alpha S_L = \alpha(V_L - B_L)$	$\alpha(X - R_F B)(1 - T_c)(1 - T_{ps})$
2. Buy α of the equity of unlevered firm V_U	$\alpha S_U - \alpha\left[\dfrac{(1 - T_c)(1 - T_{ps})}{(1 - T_{pb})}\right]B_L$	$\alpha X(1 - T_c)(1 - T_{ps}) - \alpha\left[\dfrac{(1 - T_c)(1 - T_{ps})}{(1 - T_{pb})}\right]$
Sell bonds $\alpha\left[\dfrac{(1 - T_c)(1 - T_{ps})}{(1 - T_{pb})}\right]B_L$		$R_F B_L(1 - T_{pb}) =$ $\alpha(X - R_F B_L)(1 - T_c)(1 - T_{ps})$

The analysis proceeds similar to that for the world of corporate taxes alone. The two alternatives are purchasing the equity of a levered firm versus purchasing the equity of an unlevered firm, and selling bonds in an amount such that the resulting dollar returns will be equal to the dollar returns when the alternative is the purchase of equity of a levered firm. The analysis proceeds as before with the result that since the dollar returns are equal, the investment values are equal. Therefore, we set the two investment values equal to each other. Hence we have

$$\alpha(V_L - B_L) = \alpha S_U - \alpha\left[\frac{(1 - T_c)(1 - T_{ps})}{(1 - T_{pb})}\right]B_L.$$

We cancel the α's and rearrange terms. We obtain

$$V_L = V_U + B_L - \left[\frac{(1 - T_c)(1 - T_{ps})}{(1 - T_{pb})}\right]B_L = V_U + \left[1 - \frac{(1 - T_c)(1 - T_{ps})}{(1 - T_{pb})}\right]B_L. \quad \textbf{(21.18)}$$

Suppose we designate G as the gain from leverage and use B for B_L,

$$G = \left[1 - \frac{(1 - T_c)(1 - T_{ps})}{(1 - T_{pb})}\right]B. \quad \textbf{(21.19)}$$

The right-hand side of (21.19) is the tax benefit of corporate debt with three types of taxes. This expression has also been referred to as the gain from leverage. Let us do some sensitivity analysis of this gain to understand better its properties and implications. If the tax on common stock income, T_{ps}, is the same as the tax on bond income, T_{pb}, we would have

$$V_L = V_U + (1 - 1 + T_c)B_L = V_U + T_c B.$$

This is the same as Equation 21.5, the expression that we had before for a world with corporate taxes alone. We obtain this result because the two types of personal taxes would cancel out. This indicates that the expression for the gain from corporate leverage is consistent with the previous analysis. Another way to analyze the implications of the gain term is to assume a tax rate on stock holdings of $T_{ps} = 20$ percent and investigate the effect of the level of the marginal ordinary personal income tax rate on the tax benefit of corporate debt. Assuming a corporate tax rate of 50 percent and a capital gains tax rate of 20 percent, we would have

$$G = \left[1 - \frac{(.5)(.8)}{(1 - T_{pb})}\right]$$

$$= \frac{1 - T_{pb} - .4}{1 - T_{pb}} = \frac{.6 - T_{pb}}{1 - T_{pb}}.$$

We can use this simple expression for the gain from corporate leverage factor to develop the data in Table 21.1. With a zero ordinary personal income tax rate, the tax benefit of corporate debt would be even greater than the corporate tax rate. At a personal income tax rate of 60 percent, the tax benefit of corporate debt would be eliminated. This implies a corporate leverage clientele effect. Individual taxpayers in low tax brackets would benefit from investing in highly levered corporations. Investors in high tax brackets would benefit more from investing in corporations with low degrees of leverage. But this is not the end of the story. Let us consider some further possibilities.

Miller [1977] developed the framework of our Equation 21.19. Furthermore, in a later paper by Miller and Scholes [1978], procedures were described under which taxes on dividends received on common stock may be reduced to zero. The methods they describe are discussed in Chapter 22 on dividend policy. If the tax rate on dividends received on corporate stock or the capital gains from the sale of the stock of companies who retain earnings can be reduced to zero, the gain from leverage would become

$$G = \left[1 - \frac{(1 - T_c)}{(1 - T_{pb})}\right]B. \tag{21.20}$$

This expression was used by Miller to analyze the aggregate supply and demand for corporate debt as illustrated in Figure 21.3.

In Figure 21.3 the pretax rate of returns on bonds supplied by corporations is $r_b = r_o/(1 - T_c)$. This represents the aggregate supply of corporate bonds shown as the horizon-

Table 21.1   Tax Gain from Debt

T_{pb}	G = Tax Benefit of Corporate Debt
.0	.60
.2	.50
.3	.43
.4	.33
.5	.20
.6	.00
.7	−.33

Figure 21.3   Aggregate Supply and Demand for Corporate Bonds (Before-Tax Rates)

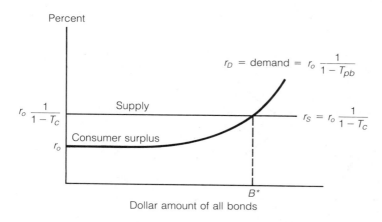

tal line in Figure 21.3. The supply curve is assumed to be horizontal because all corporations are assumed to have the same tax rate. The demand for corporate bonds starts with the intercept point r_o. This is the acceptable rate paid on the debt of tax-free institutions (municipal bonds, for example). If all corporate bonds paid only r_o, they would not be held by anyone except tax-free institutions. Other investors would require that their return be grossed up to $r_o/(1 - T_{pb})$. The personal income tax rate is progressive so that the demand curve for corporate bonds by taxable investors at some point begins to rise as shown in Figure 21.3. Where the demand and supply curves for corporate bonds intercept, we have

$$\text{Supply} = \text{Demand}$$

$$\frac{r_o}{1 - T_c} = \frac{r_o}{1 - T_{pb}}.$$

If corporations offered more than the equilibrium quantity of bonds (B^*), interest rates would be driven above their supply price and firms would find leverage unprofitable. The supply of bonds would decline until the equilibrium quantity (B^*) was again reached. If the volume initially supplied were below B^*, interest rates would be lower. Firms would increase borrowing and this would proceed until the equilibrium quantity B^* was again reached. Thus, we have an equilibrium where the gain from leverage is (once again) zero. As long as all corporations have the same effective tax rate, the value of each firm will be unaffected by its choice of financial leverage.

The Effect of Multiple Tax Shields

DeAngelo and Masulis [1980] further develop the analysis. They consider the role of corporate tax shields in addition to interest payments on debt. Not all corporations pay the same effective tax rate. Corporate tax shields include investment tax credits, depreciation

Figure 21.4   Possible Declining Benefit of Interest Tax Shields

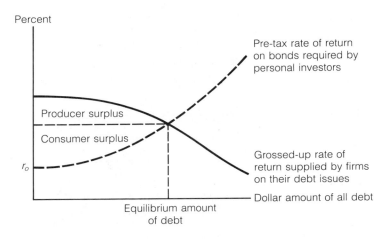

allowances, and oil depletion allowances. The DeAngelo and Masulis model predicts that firms will select a level of debt that is negatively related to the level of other tax shield substitutes such as investment tax credits, depreciation, or depletion. They also point out that as more and more debt is utilized the probability of having insufficient earnings to utilize fully all available interest tax shields will increase. Thus, the expected value of interest tax shields will decline. The supply curve for corporate debt would, therefore, have a downward slope as depicted in Figure 21.4. In these circumstances there would be an optimal amount of debt for the firm. Thus, the existence of multiple forms of tax shields may produce an optimal debt structure. In addition, if there are significant bankruptcy costs, this will reinforce conditions producing an optimal capital structure. The marginal expected benefit of interest tax shields will be related to the marginal expected cost of bankruptcy to produce an optimal degree of financial leverage. This concept will be developed further in a later section.

Evidence from Exchange Offers

Some aspects of influences on capital structure were tested in a study of exchange offers by Masulis [1980]. He studied exchanges of debt for common stock, debt for preferred stock, and preferred stock for common stock. The advantage of studying exchange offers is that financial leverage is changed with no simultaneous change in the amount of investments or assets of the firm. Hence the influence of a relatively pure financial event can be analyzed. The period covered was between 1962 and 1976. The influence of general market movements was removed and adjustments were made for risk. For 106 leverage-increasing announcements, the common stock portfolio two-day announcement period return was 7.6 percent. The *t*-value was almost 15, so the result was highly significant. For the portfolio of decreasing leverage, the two-day announcement period return was -5.4 percent. The t-value was 6.1, again, a highly significant result.

It is difficult to choose between alternative theories when interpreting these results. If debt is issued to retire equity, existing bondholders may suffer a wealth loss if the claim of the new debt is not subordinated. The reason is that the existing debt is riskier with a smaller equity base. Hence the market value of the debt claim would be expected to fall. Shareholders would benefit from this redistribution effect. Another possibility, however, is that the value of the equity increases because of the tax benefit of the additional debt. A third possibility is that an exchange offer that increases leverage may be interpreted as favorable information (a signal) about a change for the better in the firm's future prospects. Thus, the findings are consistent with three possible explanations.

Option Pricing Implications for Capital Structure

Black and Scholes [1973] made a suggestion that Merton [1974] developed further. They pointed out that the equity ownership in a firm with outstanding debt can be regarded as a call option. When bonds are sold by a firm, from the equity holders' point of view they receive the cash proceeds from the sale of the bonds plus a call option. At the maturity date of the debt, if the value of the firm, V, exceeds the face value of the bonds, D, the equity holders will exercise the call option by paying off the bonds. The payoff to the bondholders will be the face value of the debt at maturity if the value of the firm exceeds the debt obligation. If the value of the firm is less than the face value of the debt, the shareholders will not exercise their option to pay off the debt and the debtholder will receive the value of the firm, which will be less than the face value of the debt. From our previous discussion of options this is seen as equivalent to selling a covered call option.

Viewing the sale of debt as equivalent to creating options yields a number of implications. These examples depend on the Modigliani-Miller proposition that, in the absence of transactions costs or taxes, the value of the firm is not affected by financial decisions. To illustrate, current bondholders will experience a loss of wealth if new debt is issued and used to retire equity. The assets of the firm will remain unchanged, but the new debt has an equal claim on the assets with the original bondholders. The original bondholders would then have a smaller proportionate claim to the same assets of the firm than they had before the new debt was issued. This change places the original bondholders in a riskier position.

The Influence of Agency Problems on Capital Structure

The preceding discussion illustrates a divergence of interest between equity holders and bondholders. Jensen and Meckling [1976] discuss a number of ways in which agency problems of this kind may influence financial decisions. We have just described how selling more debt and using it to retire equity reduces the equity cushion for bondholders. Another way that equity holders can cause the position of bondholders to be affected adversely is to shift to more risky investment programs. Consider the two investment programs in Table 21.2. Program 1 has a 50/50 probability of achieving an end-of-period cash flow of $40,000 or $60,000. The second program has a 50/50 probability of returning $10,000 or $90,000. The expected value of each is $50,000, and the investment cost assumed is $40,000 so they are both positive NPV investments. If the firm borrows $20,000 to finance the investment, the lenders are assured of being repaid under Program 1, but only have a 50/50 probability of being paid under Program 2. Furthermore, they do not

Table 21.2   Investment Programs of Different Risks

Probability	Program 1	Program 2
.5	$40,000	$10,000
.5	$60,000	$90,000

benefit if the $90,000 return is realized because they would still receive only $20,000, the face value of the bond, while the equity holders would receive the benefit of the difference.

The problem would be especially troublesome if bondholders had the expectation that the firm was going to follow Program 1, which is less risky, and then the firm actually follows Program 2, which involves greater risk. Such a shift would represent a transfer of wealth from bondholders to shareholders. This example illustrates another reason why bondholders require various types of agreements in the bond contract to protect their position. Agency costs refer to the costs of writing and enforcing such agreements. These expropriation costs are likely to increase with the percentage of financing provided by bondholders and the costs of protection against agency problems are likely to increase with leverage as well.

In addition agency problems are associated with the use of outside equity. Consider a firm initially owned entirely by one individual. All actions taken by the individual affect his position alone. If the original owner-manager sells a portion of the equity interest to outsiders, conflicts of interest arise. Extra consumption benefits paid to the original owner-manager by the firm are now entirely consumed by him, but paid for in part by the new outside owners. If the original owner-manager indulges in perquisites such as an expensive company car entirely for his own use, lavish furniture and rugs in his own spacious office, short working days to play more golf, etc., he doesn't bear the entire costs as he did when he was the sole owner. The new outside shareholders will have to incur monitoring costs of one kind or another to be sure that the original owner-manager acts fully in their interest.

As shown in Figure 21.5, there are increasing agency costs with the use of higher proportions of outside equity as well as with higher proportions of debt. There is an optimum combination of outside equity and debt that may minimize total agency costs. This would result in a desired or optimum capital structure even in a world without taxes or bankruptcy costs.

There are other considerations that also may be regarded as agency costs with implications for capital structure. Titman [1981] points out that customers who buy durable products such as automobiles, washing machines, or refrigerators, need to have future services such as parts and repair. When a customer buys a durable good he is paying for the product itself, but also for the availability of follow-up parts and repair services. If a firm goes bankrupt and is liquidated, customers are unable to obtain the parts and services they had expected. Hence the agency problem in this relationship is the assurance that the future required parts and services will be forthcoming. Consumers must judge the probability that a seller of durable goods may fail and be liquidated. Hence firms that produce and sell durable goods run the risk that if they use higher leverage which will increase their probability of bankruptcy, it may reduce the demand for their products. Hence we would expect, other things being equal, that durable goods producers would carry less debt than producers of nondurable goods such as food.

Figure 21.5   Optimal Capital Structure with Agency Costs of Equity and Debt

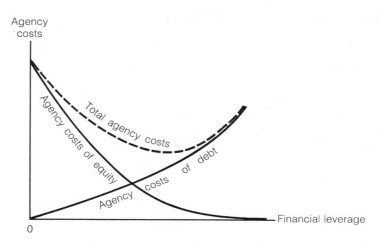

Similarly agency factors are involved in labor contracts. Under competitive labor markets, workers will charge lower wages to work for firms that have a lower probability of bankruptcy. In some industries, a firm's labor force develops specialized skills that may not be used easily in other industries. For example, some aspects of producing steel might have little use in other industries. Another example would be the air traffic controllers who lost their jobs and found it difficult to use their skills in other work. Thus, firms and industries that involve the development of a considerable degree of job-specific human capital would tend to carry less debt than firms and industries in which workers can readily enter into and out of employment.

Still another related aspect is suggested by Scott [1976], who demonstrates that optimal leverage may be related to the collateral value of the firm's assets. If a firm fails and is liquidated, tangible nonspecific physical assets of the firm may have only a small decline in value, which should reduce losses upon bankruptcy. Collateral value also reduces the need for monitoring costs to protect the position of bondholders.

All of these aspects of agency considerations may have an influence on the degree of use of outside equity and the use of outside debt. All of these aspects are candidates for additional empirical research to test the propositions involved. Another subtle aspect of financial structure has been suggested by the concept of signaling, which is described in the next section.

Information Asymmetry and Signaling

Ross [1977] describes how signaling and manager compensation arrangements can be used to deal with information asymmetry. Ross postulates that manager-insiders have information about their own firms not possessed by outsiders. Ross demonstrates that the capital structure decision is not irrelevant and in some cases a unique interior optimal capital structure exists if (1) the nature of the firm's investment policy is signaled to the market through its capital structure decision and (2) the manager's compensation is tied to the truth or falsity of the capital structure signal. In Ross's model a manager may not trade in the financial instruments of his own firm. This avoids the moral hazard problem as well as violation of the incentives structure that he develops. The essence of Ross's model can be expressed verbally.[5] Investors use the face amount of the debt or dividends the manager decides to issue as a signal of the firm's probable performance. Ross analyzes two types of firms. Type A is a firm that will be successful, whereas Type B is a firm that will be unsuccessful. With reference to a critical level of debt, D^*, the market perceives the firm to be Type A if it issues debt greater than this amount and Type B if it issues debt less than this amount. In order for the management of a Type B firm to have the incentive to signal that the firm will be unsuccessful, the payoff from telling the truth must be greater than that produced by telling lies. This is achieved by assessing a substantial penalty against the manager if his firm experiences bankruptcy.

A signaling equilibrium is achieved if "A" managers choose debt financing levels above the critical amount and "B" managers choose debt levels below that amount. An "A" manager will have no incentive to change because the compensation system maximizes his return under the true signal. The "B" manager will not have an incentive to signal falsely because the penalty built into the incentive structure would reduce his compensation.

Haugen and Senbet [1979] seek to implement Ross's penalty function through the use of contingent claims. They require that the manager simultaneously sell a combination of calls and puts so that the manager of an "A" firm is completely hedged, suffering no penalty if the firm turns out to be successful. If the firm turns out to be unsuccessful, prior to the expiration of the contingent claims, the holders of the puts will exercise them with a consequent penalty for management compensation. This design also provides a control on agency problems. If the manager consumes an excessive amount of perquisites, the value of the firm will decline. In effect, he causes an "A" firm to become a "B" firm. If so, the puts will be exercised and the manager will suffer the consequences of his having caused a decline in the value of the firm.

Leland and Pyle [1977] use information asymmetry influences to rationalize the existence of financial intermediation institutions. They find informational asymmetries to be a primary explanation for the existence of intermediaries and rely on signaling as a significant aspect of the operations of financial intermediaries. For assets, particularly those related to individuals, such as mortgages or insurance, information is not publicly available and can be developed only at some cost. Since such information is valuable to potential lenders, if there are economies of scale, firms will be developed to assemble the information and to sell it.

Two problems would arise if such firms sought to sell the information directly to investors. One is the "public good" aspect of information. Individual purchasers of information could resell it to others without diminishing its usefulness to themselves. The second problem is the reliability of the information. It would be difficult for potential users to make a judgment of the likelihood that they are receiving good versus bad information. Thus, the price of information will reflect its average value and the average value of information offered for sale will be lower than what potentially could be available.

Both these problems in obtaining a return on information are overcome by a financial intermediary that buys and holds assets on the basis of accumulated information. The value of the firm's information is reflected in a private good, the returns from its portfolio. Potential buyers of the intermediary's claim can judge whether the intermediary has de-

---

[5]See Chapter 22 for an algebraic development of the same issue in the context of dividend policy.

veloped valuable information by observing the extent to which the entrepreneurs or organizers of the financial intermediary have been willing to invest in their own firm's equity shares. In general, the degree to which owners are willing to invest in their own projects will serve as a signal of project quality. Thus, a firm's value will be related positively to the fraction of its equity held by its organizers. This higher value will also give the firm greater debt capacity and lead it to use greater amounts of debt. While debt is not a signal in this model, its use will be correlated positively with the firm's value.

The Effects of Bankruptcy Costs

To this point we have established that the cost of equity rises with financial leverage. The cost of debt may also rise with leverage. Even if the debt is risky, it has been established that the MM propositions still hold [Rubinstein, 1973] as long as there are no bankruptcy costs. But with bankruptcy costs, we have another basis for arriving at an optimal degree of leverage for a firm.

Bankruptcy costs take several forms. The most obvious are the legal, accounting, and other administrative costs associated with financial readjustments and legal proceedings. In addition to these direct costs, some costs of bankruptcy arise before the actual legal procedures of bankruptcy take place. As the operating performance of the firm deteriorates in relation to its fixed contractual obligations, or as the amount of debt increases in relation to the firm's equity for a given level of operating performance, the financial markets may become increasingly reluctant to provide additional financing. A number of costs arise as a result of increased evidence of financial inadequacy or failure on the part of the firm. These costs, in order of seriousness, include the following:

1. Financing under increasingly onerous terms, conditions, and rates.
2. Loss of key employees. If the firm's prospects are unfavorable, able employees and executives will seek alternative employment.
3. Loss of suppliers of the most salable types of goods. The suppliers may fear that they will not be paid or that the customer will not achieve sales growth in the future.
4. Loss of sales due to lack of confidence on the part of customers that the firm will be around to stand behind the product.
5. Lack of financing under any terms, conditions, and rates to carry out favorable but risky investments because the overall prospects of the firm are not favorable in relation to its existing obligations.
6. Need to liquidate fixed assets to meet working capital requirements (forced reduction in the scale of operations).
7. Formal bankruptcy proceedings, with the incurrence of legal and administrative costs. In addition, a receiver will be appointed to conduct the firm's operations, and this may involve a disruption of operations.

The costs of building up new organizations after old ones have been broken up represent substantial transaction costs in the creation and destruction of organizations.

In Chapter 20, we used the Universal Machine Company case to demonstrate that for any given degree of business risk, the higher the debt ratio, the larger the measures of variability in earnings per share and return on equity. The higher the level of debt, the higher the fixed charges and the higher the probability of not being able to cover them. The inability to meet fixed charges may trigger a number of penalty clauses in the debt indentures (agreements) and lead to reorganization or bankruptcy (see Chapter 31), with attendant costs of attorneys and court proceedings. Even before such legal difficulties, the increasing risk of financial difficulties may result in the loss of key employees (who find positions with firms whose financial outlook is safer), in the reduced availability of goods from key suppliers, and in reduced financing.

Empirical studies to date suggest that the direct costs of bankruptcy are small but significant (Warner [1977]; Altman [1984]). When indirect as well as direct bankruptcy costs are taken into account, they may be substantial, as much as 20 percent of the value of the firm (Altman [1984]).

Bankruptcy costs could affect the component elements of a firm's cost of capital in alternative ways. In our previous discussion of agency costs we indicated that the return to equity is MAX $[0, V - D]$. The return to the debtholders is MIN $[V, D]$. Under the assumption that all firms draw from the same bankruptcy distribution *ex ante*, it can be argued that even with bankruptcy costs the outcome for the equity holders is unchanged. Because of limited liability they can lose nothing more than their original investment; this is not affected by bankruptcy costs. However, the outcome for the debtholders with bankruptcy costs becomes MIN $[V - \theta V, D]$. The theta represents the magnitude of bankruptcy costs as some proportion of the value of the firm. Thus, the outcome for debtholders is diminished. The required return to debtholders will, therefore, increase as the probability of bankruptcy increases with increased leverage.

Thus, if firms go bankrupt in the same states with or without bankruptcy costs, the required returns to equity holders would appear to be unaffected. But since the costs of bankruptcy are charged to debtholders, they will take this into account when debt is initially issued. So bondholders will require higher returns to compensate them for bearing the costs of bankruptcy. For the firm to receive the same dollars when selling debt now, they will have to promise a higher dollar amount of payment at maturity. Therefore, the firm will go bankrupt in more states of nature because the size of D is higher for a given V. Shareholders will, therefore, require compensation in the form of higher required returns to compensate them for the increased probability of bankruptcy. Hence the effect of bankruptcy will require higher rates of return both to debtholders and shareholders, as depicted in Figure 21.6.

Figure 21.6 Effects of Bankruptcy Costs on Cost of Capital

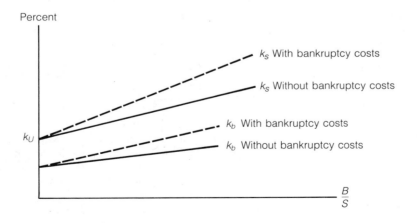

The Capital Structure Decision

In the previous sections, we explained why more leverage may increase the costs of both debt and equity financing. We now illustrate how the rising financing costs with increased leverage lead to the determination of a preferred amount of leverage to employ. Both the criteria of a minimum cost of capital and a maximum value of the firm will be employed.

Leverage and the Cost of Capital—Numerical Illustration

We continue with the Universal Machine example. In Table 21.3, we illustrate the conditions under which the cost of debt rises with leverage and the cost of equity rises even more rapidly. The resulting weighted cost of capital is calculated in the final column of Table 21.3.

Table 21.3   Calculation of the Weighted Cost of Capital for Different Capital Structures for Universal Machine Company

	Percent of Total (1)	Component Costs (2)	Weighted Cost $k = (1) \times (2) \div 100$ (3)[a]
Debt	0%	5.00%	0.0%
Equity	100	12.00	12.00
	100		12.00
Debt	10	5.10	0.51
Equity	90	12.30	11.07
	100		11.58
Debt	20	5.40	1.08
Equity	80	12.75	10.20
	100		11.28
Debt	30	5.50	1.65
Equity	70	13.29	9.30
	100		10.95
Debt	35	5.70	2.00
Equity	65	13.50	8.78
	100		10.78
Debt	40	6.00	2.40
Equity	60	15.00	9.00
	100		11.40
Debt	50	8.00	4.00
Equity	50	18.00	9.00
	100		13.00
Debt	60	13.50	8.10
Equity	40	24.00	9.60
	100		17.70

[a]We multiply by 100 to obtain percentages; figures are rounded to the nearest hundredth.

Figure 21.7   Cost of Capital Curves for Universal Machine Company

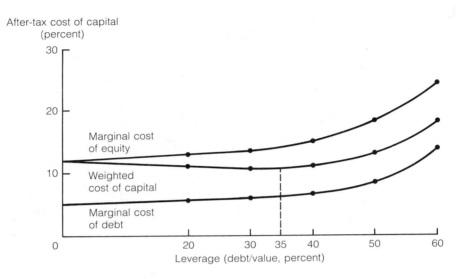

The individual component costs of financing and the weighted cost of capital are plotted in Figure 21.7. We can now see graphically what is conveyed by the data. With small amounts of leverage, both the component costs of debt and equity are relatively flat. The weighted cost of capital in this range is falling because lower cost debt is substituted for equity as leverage increases. As debt rises beyond 20 percent of the value of the firm, the cost of equity begins to rise. As the debt ratio is further increased, the cost of debt begins to rise and the cost of equity rises even more sharply.

At a debt ratio of about 35 percent, the rising costs of debt and equity cause the weighted cost of capital to rise. Hence under the pattern of costs depicted, Universal Machine's weighted cost of capital is minimized when its debt ratio is approximately 35 percent. So the optimal capital structure of UM would be approximately 35 percent debt and 65 percent equity.

Note that the average cost of capital curve is relatively flat over a fairly broad range. If Universal Machine's debt ratio is in the range of 20 to 40 percent, the average cost of capital cannot be lowered very much by moving to the optimal point. This appears to be a fairly typical situation, since almost any "reasonable" schedule for the component costs of debt and equity will produce a saucer-shaped average cost of capital schedule similar to the one shown in Figure 21.7. This gives financial managers a large degree of flexibility in planning their financing programs, permitting them to sell debt one year and equity the next in order to take advantage of capital market conditions and to avoid high flotation costs associated with small security issues.

Table 21.3 and Figure 21.7 are based on the assumption that the firm is planning to raise a given amount of new capital during the year. For a larger or smaller amount of new capital, some other cost figures may be applicable; the optimal capital structure may call for a different debt ratio, and the minimum weighted cost of capital (k) may be higher or lower.

Leverage and the Value of the Firm

With increased leverage, the value of the firm first increases, reaches a maximum, and then begins to decline. Thus, the valuation criterion provides guidance on the preferred capital structure of the firm.

We now explain the individual influences which cause the value of the firm to rise and then to fall. The first factor is the tax shelter benefits of using leverage. Since interest on debt is deductible for tax purposes, the use of debt provides a tax shelter for some of the firm's cash flows. Hence the value of a firm increases with increases in debt if the only influence operating is the tax shelter effect of increased debt. However, a second factor to take into account is the possibility of significant bankruptcy costs. The risks of the increased probabilities of bankruptcy will cause the value of a firm to fall at some level of increased leverage. Agency costs may also rise with leverage.

The existence of tax shelter benefits of corporate debt and increased risks of bankruptcy and agency costs with increased leverage will cause the value of the firm to behave as depicted in Figure 21.8. As the amount of debt in the financial structure increases, the present value of tax savings will initially cause the market value of the firm to rise. (The slope of the line will reflect the corporate tax rate.) However, at some point, bankruptcy and agency costs will cause the market value of the firm to be less than what it would have been if the only influence were corporate income taxes (Point B in Figure 21.8). Possible bankruptcy and agency costs may become so large that the indicated market value of the firm actually begins to turn down (Point C in Figure 21.8). This point represents the target leverage ratio at which the market value of the firm is maximized — the optimal financial structure. We next turn to a consideration of some issues involved in the calculations of the cost of capital in actual practice.

Costs of External Equity Funds versus Retained Earnings

It is useful to recognize and to avoid a fallacy that is sometimes encountered. This is the argument that retained earnings in a given year or accumulated retained earnings have no cost. This view is wrong. Retained earnings represent capital invested in the firm just as much as funds obtained externally do. So retained earnings definitely have a cost. The question is, how is their cost measured?

The traditional approach has been to begin with the dividend growth valuation model to illustrate the difference between the cost of internal versus external equity financing. If we let k_r represent the cost of retained earnings, and consider an all equity financed firm to set aside the leverage issue, we could express its determinants either on a per share basis (that is, dividends per share, d_1, divided by price per share, p_o) or for the firm as a whole, (for example, total dividends, D_1, divided by total value, V_o) as shown in Equation 21.21

$$k_r = \frac{d_1}{p_o} + g = \frac{D_1}{V_o} + g. \qquad \textbf{(21.21)}$$

Figure 21.8   Influence of Debt on Market Value of the Firm

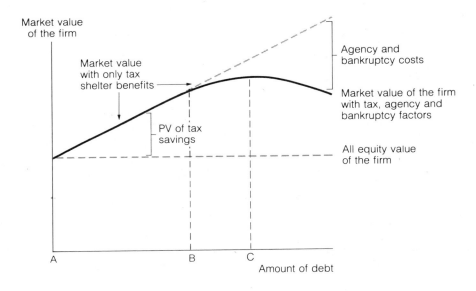

The g should be interpreted as the growth in dividends per share or in total dividends for the company, given the assumptions of the dividend valuation model. A weakness in this approach is that the value of the firm or its value per share depends upon the growth rate. Hence it is not valid to treat the growth term as though it were independent of the current price per share or value of the firm.

Setting aside these problems, the traditional approach in using the dividend valuation model is to argue that flotation costs reduce the net proceeds from any external equity offering. If we express the flotation costs as a percentage of the gross proceeds on any particular offering, it would reduce the denominator in the dividend yield expression by a factor of $(1 - f)$ where f represents the equity flotation costs percentage. We would have the expression shown in Equation 21.22 for the cost of external equity financing.

$$k_s = \frac{d_1}{p_o(1 - f)} + g = \frac{D_1}{V_o(1 - f)} + g. \tag{21.22}$$

We can illustrate the application of the expression in Equation 21.22 using the per share relationship. For example, if p_o is $20, d_1 is $2, and f is 10 percent, then the firm receives $18 for each new share sold. Hence the net proceeds are $18 per share. Assuming a constant future growth in dividends per share of 5 percent, the cost of new outside equity would be

$$k_s = \frac{\$2}{\$20(1 - 0.10)} + 5\% = 16.11\%.$$

Without the influence of flotation costs, the required return would be 15 percent. However, because of flotation costs, the required return on external equity financing would be 16.11 percent. Since the cost of equity capital is defined as the rate of return that must be earned to prevent the price of the stock from falling, we observe that the company's cost of external equity financing is 16.11 percent.[6]

If this approach is used to calculate the cost of external equity financing, we would have the situation depicted in Figure 21.9. The flotation costs factor is used to gross up the cost of internal equity funds to arrive at the cost of equity funds obtained externally. This also provides a basis for determining the availability of dividends. In Figure 21.9(a), the marginal efficiency of the firm's investment schedule crosses the marginal cost of capital function at a point where internal equity funds available are not fully used. Hence dividends could be paid equal to the total internal equity funds available less the amount required for investment. In Figure 21.9(b), the marginal efficiency of investment schedule intersects the marginal cost of capital schedule at a point beyond funds available from internal sources. A firm characterized by the situation in Panel (b) would not pay dividends, but would only be raising external funds. Or if the firm paid dividends it would have to raise external funds to meet investment needs plus whatever amount of dividends were paid.

Another view holds that flotation costs should not affect the opportunity costs of funds supplied to the firm. It is proposed that the costs of investment projects be grossed up by the weighted average flotation costs on all sources of financing (cf. Copeland and Weston [1983] pp. 469-470). This approach is reflected in Equation 21.23:

$$\text{NPV} = \sum_{t=1}^{N} \frac{CF_t}{(1 + k)^t} - \frac{\Delta I}{(1 - f)}. \tag{21.23}$$

In Equation 21.23 the standard NPV expression in capital budgeting has the investment term grossed up by the $(1 - \text{flotation cost})$ factor.

If the tax deductibility of flotation costs is taken into account, then the burden of flotation costs is reduced by the factor of $(1 - T)$. This is illustrated in Equation 21.24:

$$\text{NPV} = \sum_{t=1}^{N} \frac{CF_t}{(1 + k)^t} - \frac{\Delta I}{[1 - f(1 - T)]}. \tag{21.24}$$

If the tax deductions can all be taken at the time of the outlay, then Equation 21.24 expresses the tax influence correctly. If, however, some of the tax deductions have to be amortized over the life of the project, then the tax benefits for reducing flotation costs would also have to be amortized over time. If the assumptions that flotation costs and their tax effects are associated with the time period over which the investment outlays for

---

[6]The cost of external equity is sometimes defined as

$$k_s = \frac{k_r}{1 - f}.$$

This equation is correct only if the firm's expected growth rate is zero. In other cases it overstates k_s.

Figure 21.9   Cost of Internal versus External Funds

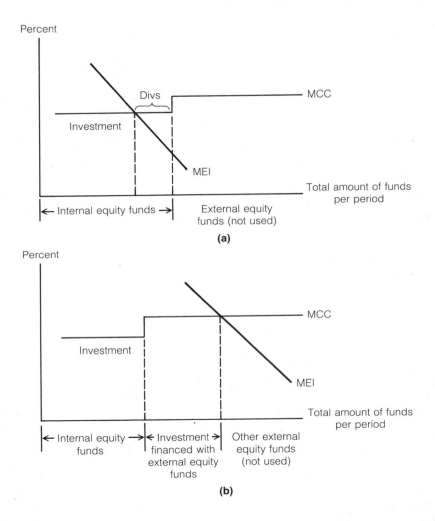

(a)

(b)

projects are made, the newer approach is correct. An argument that has been made in support of the older method is that it may be difficult for a going concern to associate individual projects with their sources of financing. The business firm represents a pool of funds used to finance a stream of project activities. Thus, although applying the gross-up factor to the investment outlay may be correct theoretically, as a practical matter it may be more appropriate to apply the gross-up factor for flotation costs to the relevant cost of capital.

Cost of Depreciation-Generated Funds

The first increment of cash flow used to finance any year's capital budget is depreciation-generated funds. In their statements of changes in financial position, corporations generally show depreciation charges to be a very substantial noncash charge. For capital budgeting purposes, should depreciation be considered free capital, should it be ignored completely, or should a charge be assessed against it? The answer is that a charge should be assessed against these funds, and that this cost is the weighted cost of capital before outside equity is used.

The reasoning here is that the firm could, if it so desired, distribute the depreciation-generated funds to its creditors and stockholders, the parties who financed the assets in the first place. For example, if $10 million of depreciation-generated funds were available, the firm could either reinvest them or distribute them. If the funds are to be distributed, the distribution must be to both bondholders and stockholders in proportion to their shares of the capital structure; otherwise, the capital structure will change. Obviously, this distribution should take place if the funds cannot be invested to yield the cost of capital. However, retention should occur if the internal rate of return exceeds the cost of capital. Since the cost of depreciation-generated funds is equal to the weighted cost of capital, depreciation does not enter the calculation of the weighted cost of capital.

Depreciation may, however, affect the cost of capital *schedule*. If we are concerned with gross capital expenditures — including replacement as well as expansion investments — then the cost of capital schedule that includes depreciation is the relevant one. The flat part of the marginal cost of capital curve, before it is increased by using external equity funds at higher rates, would be extended by the inclusion of depreciation. But if we are concerned with the effects of *net increases* in assets, then the schedule without depreciation is appropriate.

Calculating the Component Financing Costs

The following case study illustrates how the cost of capital can actually be measured for a firm. The concepts previously developed will now be put to practical application. Although we shall attempt to make the procedures specific and numerically precise, we must recognize that considerable judgment must be exercised. Because of the crucial role of cost of capital measurements in guiding a firm's investment decisions, and because the valuation of a firm is highly sensitive to the applicable cost of capital employed, the judgments must be arrived at with great care. We shall use a stylized case example to keep the presentation within reasonable bounds. Our own experience in making such calculations for individual firms has involved reports that are quite lengthy. Final judgments involve comparisons with firms similar to the one for which the analysis is made. To make the comparisons, the same cost of capital calculations have to be made for the 7 to 10 other firms for which the comparisons may be made. The purpose of the example is to provide a road map of the main procedures that should be employed.

We shall illustrate calculations of the cost of capital of the three major types of financing — debt, preferred stock, and common equity.

We shall employ the following symbols throughout the discussion:

k_b = the before-tax opportunity cost of debt
k_{ps} = the before- and after-tax opportunity cost of preferred stock
k_s = the before- and after-tax return required by the market for equity capital

$k_r =$ the before- and after-tax cost of internally generated equity capital

WACC = the weighted average cost of capital, represents a weighted marginal cost of capital

Our ultimate objective is to obtain the firm's marginal cost of capital for use in capital budgeting decisions and for application in valuation analysis. The firm's marginal cost of capital is a weighted average of the opportunity costs of its financing sources. In calculating WACC, all costs are expressed on an after-tax basis. This provides consistency with the after-tax cash flows utilized in our previous capital budgeting analysis. In using the marginal cost of capital for decision-making purposes, we are assuming that the risks of individual projects are similar to the riskiness of the firm's present portfolio of assets. This is required for utilization of the WACC in both capital budgeting and valuation analysis.

In this illustrative case study we will use data for a company we shall call the United Corporation (UC). Because we are only providing the main guidelines for determining a cost of capital measurement, we will not use a specific company. Space does not permit discussion of all the actual detailed considerations that would be taken into account in arriving at a final judgment. The calculations will be assumed to be those representative for early 1984.

Cost of Debt

The cost of debt should be on an after-tax basis because interest payments are tax deductible. Therefore, the cost of debt capital is calculated as follows:

$$k_b(1 - T) = \text{the after-tax cost of debt.}$$

Here T is the corporate tax rate as used previously. Thus, if the before-tax cost of debt were 15 percent and the firm's effective corporate tax rate were 40 percent, the after-tax cost of debt would be 9 percent.

We start with the firm's before-tax cost of debt and multiply it by the $(1 - T)$ factor to obtain the relevant after-tax cost. How do we obtain the before-tax cost of debt in practice for an actual firm? Two main procedures may be used. We can look in any of the investment manuals to determine the rating of the firm's outstanding publicly held bonds. Various government agencies and investment banking firms periodically publish promised yields to maturity of debt issues by rating categories.

For our United Corporation example, its bonds were rated AA. In the publications of Salomon Brothers at the time, we find that seasoned AA industrial debt issues of 10-year maturity (the remaining years to maturity of most of UC's long-term corporate debt) are 13.5 percent.

We can check this by calculating the promised yield to maturity on the cash flows from UC's long-term debt in relation to its current price. For its major issue of long-term debt, UC pays a coupon of 10 percent based on $1,000 par value per bond. Coupons are paid semiannually. UC's bonds are rated AA rather than Aaa, so there is some very slight risk associated with them. We can obtain the current price of the UC bonds by looking in the daily newspaper or various quote machines. We find that the price is $810.95. We can estimate the promised yield to maturity of UC's bonds by solving for k_b in Equation 21.25:

$$\$810.95 = \sum_{t=1}^{20} \frac{50}{\left(1 + \frac{k_b}{2}\right)^t} + \frac{(1,000)}{\left(1 + \frac{k_b}{2}\right)^{20}}. \tag{21.25}$$

When we make the calculation, we find that the k_b that solves this equation is very close to the 13.5 percent cost of AA seasoned industrial bond issues. We shall, therefore, use 13.5 percent as the before-tax cost of long-term debt. Let us postulate that the firm's effective corporate tax rate is 40 percent. The after-tax cost of long-term debt would, therefore, be as follows:

$$k_b(1 - T) = .135(.6) = .081.$$

Thus, the after-tax cost of debt would be 8.1 percent. We had indicated that the coupon payment actually promised by the long-term debt of UC was 10 percent. But the coupon rate simply indicates what the cost was at the time the debt was issued. What is relevant for present decision making is the current cost of the debt, which we calculated.

Cost of Preferred Stock

Preferred stock is a hybrid between debt and common stock. Like debt, preferred stock carries a fixed commitment on the part of the corporation to make periodic payments; in liquidation, the claims of the preferred stockholders take precedence over those of the common stockholders. However, failure to make the preferred dividend payments does not result in bankruptcy as nonpayment of interest on bonds does. Thus, to the firm, preferred stock is somewhat less risky than common stock but riskier than bonds. To the investor, preferred stock is also less risky than common but riskier than bonds.

From the standpoint of the issuing firm, preferred stock has the disadvantage that its dividend is not deductible for tax purposes. On the other hand, the tax law provides that 85 percent of all dividends received by one corporation from another are not taxable. This 85 percent dividend exclusion makes preferred stock a potentially attractive investment to other corporations such as commercial banks and stock insurance companies. This attractiveness on the demand side pushes the yields on preferred stock to slightly below yields on bonds of similar companies. Although preferred issues may be callable and may be retired, most are perpetuities. If the preferred issue is a perpetuity, then its yield is calculated as follows:

$$\text{Preferred yield} = \frac{\text{Preferred dividend}}{\text{Price of preferred stock}} = \frac{d_{ps}}{p_{ps}}. \tag{21.26}$$

Returning to our example for United Corporation, we find that its only preferred stock issue outstanding carries a $9 dividend. The current price of the preferred stock obtained from newspapers or other sources is $69.23. Hence, the preferred stock yield or its cost will be

$$\frac{d_{ps}}{p_{ps}} = \frac{\$9}{\$69.23} = .13 = 13\%.$$

The result is 13 percent. Since preferred stock dividends paid by the issuing corporation are not deductible for tax purposes, this 13 percent is therefore already on an after-tax basis. No further tax adjustment need be made. It stands on the same basis as the 8.1 percent after-tax cost of long-term debt whose before-tax cost was 13.5 percent.

Cost of Common Equity

The cost of common equity is the most difficult of the major sources of financing to be determined. Four major methods will be employed. They are

1. The Capital Asset Pricing Model (CAPM)
2. The bond yield plus equity risk premium
3. Realized investor yield
4. The dividend growth model

The first three are based fundamentally on financial market data. The fourth, the dividend growth model, has some theoretical problems but is so widely used that we include it as one of the inputs.

Capital Asset Pricing Model (CAPM) Approach.   Recall that the CAPM approach states that the investors' required rate of return on common stock is equal to a risk-free rate plus a risk premium. The risk premium is the market risk premium (which is the market return minus a risk-free rate) multiplied by the applicable beta of the firm. The Security Market Line equation is

$$k_s = R_F + (\overline{R}_M - R_F)\beta_j.$$

The market risk premium has been calculated in a number of studies. Over long periods of time it appears to average out for the United States between 6 and 8 percent. We will use 7.5 percent in our calculations here. Theory calls for using the short-term treasury bill rate as an estimate of the risk-free rate. For our example we can readily determine that the short-term treasury bill rate is 10 percent. The only information specific to the firm that is required in the use of the CAPM is the beta or the risk measure. Various investment advisory services publish beta estimates for a large number of companies. Drawing on these we find that the beta for the common stock of United Corporation is 1.05. The Security Market Line for UC is, therefore, $k_s = 10 + 7.5(1.05) = 17.875$ percent. Thus, our initial estimate of the cost of equity capital for UC is 17.875 percent.

Short-term interest rates fluctuate with greater volatility than longer-term interest rates. This is true of short-term T-bill rates as well as other short-term interest rates. Some analysts, therefore, find it useful to use a longer-term treasury bond rate as a check in developing a CAPM estimate of the firm's cost of equity capital. For the early 1984 period we would find that the 10-year T-bill rate was 12.5 percent so that we would have

$$k_s = 12.5 + 7.875 = 20.375 \text{ percent.}$$

For early 1984 use of the 10-year T-bill rate would yield a somewhat higher cost of equity capital. For some prior periods such as early 1982, the reverse would have been true. Thus, we have some initial estimates of the firm's cost of equity capital, but we need to test these estimates by using other procedures as well.

Bond Yield Plus Equity Risk Premium.   Under the CAPM method described, the required return on equity represents a premium over the risk-free rate measured by yields on government securities. This second method also involves a risk premium. However, in this case it represents a premium over the firm's own long-term debt cost. This method provides a logical test check since the cost of common equity should be greater than the cost of debt. Debt represents a fixed legal claim giving bondholders a senior position over preferred stock or common stock. The beta of long-term debt for a firm is typically much lower than the beta of its common stock. Hence we would expect a premium over the debt return in the required return to common stock.

This method is in the same spirit as the CAPM placing both the debt and the equity on a Security Market Line with the debt having a lower beta. If we had a good estimate of the beta of the debt, the differential between the required yield on the debt and the required yield on the equity would be given by the Security Market Line. The premium of the required equity return over the long-term debt return would represent the indicated risk premium. We have estimated this to be 4.5 percent for the United Corporation. Hence given the cost of long-term debt that we have calculated to be 13.5 percent, the indicated required return to common equity by this method would be 18 percent.

Realized Investor Yield. The realized investor yield is the average dividend yield plus the average capital gain over some prior period such as 10 years. This measure represents what investors have, in fact, required as a return from this company's common stock. This method captures the readjustments that investors make in the price of the firm's stock to take account of changes in the outlook for the firm. However, the measure for an individual firm may be unstable. To make the measure more reliable, another test check is to make the calculation for a group of similar firms, where random individual firm instabilities may be averaged out.

This calculation of the average dividend yield plus the average capital gain represents the average return realized by investors. This can be related to the Security Market Line, which gives us the required return on equity. In the long run we would expect the average return to equal the required return since stock prices will be adjusted to move the two toward equality. For the previous 10 years for United Corporation we have calculated the average dividend yield to be 4.1 percent and the average capital gain to be 14.1 percent. Thus, by this method the indicated required return on equity is 18.2 percent.

Dividend Growth Model. The dividend valuation model can be expressed as follows:

$$p_o = \frac{d_1}{k_s - g} = \frac{d_o(1 + g)}{k_s - g} = \frac{\text{EPS}_o(1 + g)(1 - b)}{k_s - br}. \tag{21.27}$$

The required return on equity can be derived from this dividend valuation expression. In Equation 21.27, b is the percent of earnings retained by the firm, and r is the internal profitability rate. The other terms have already been defined. A number of assumptions underlying the dividend valuation model should be noted to understand how it may be used to estimate the required return on equity for a firm. The growth rate (g) refers to the growth in dividends. Since g is the product of the retention rate times the internal profitability rate, this indicates that the model is an all internal equity financing model. Retained earnings is the only source of financing investment in this model. Furthermore, constant growth is required. There is no period of supernormal or subnormal growth and the constant growth continues through infinity.

The logic of the model indicates that the g refers to the growth rate in dividends, but under the assumptions of the model everything else also grows at the same rate. If dividends grow at 12 percent, and the payout ratio and retention rate are constant, earnings must be growing at the same 12 percent. Since retained earnings are the only source of growth, the total assets of the firm will also be growing at 12 percent. And over time, the value of the firm or the price of its common stock will be growing at a 12 percent rate as well. Clearly there is a relationship between p, the price of the common stock, and the growth rate in earnings, dividends, and the total assets of the firm. Thus, the model does not provide an unambiguous basis for estimating k_s.

Nevertheless, the dividend valuation model is widely used in practice both for valuing common stock and for estimating the cost of equity capital. In estimating the cost of equity capital for United Corporation the valuation expression is solved for k_s as shown in Equation 21.28

$$k_s = \frac{d_1}{p_o} + g. \tag{21.28}$$

Equation 21.28 states that the required return on equity is the expected dividend yield plus the expected growth rate in dividends. The expected dividend is obtained by taking the current dividend, d_o, and applying the expected growth rate. For United Corporation the current dividend is $2.75. It is difficult to arrive at a reliable figure for the expected growth rate. One approach is to begin with the growth over some previous period. But the position of the firm is likely to be affected by developments of the economy as a whole as well as in its own industry. Nevertheless, various financial services provide estimates of expected growth in earnings and dividends for individual firms. In addition, an independent analysis can be made by the analyst attempting to make a calculation of the cost of capital for the firm. Suppose that by a combination of all of these methods we arrive at an expected growth rate in dividends for the firm of 12 percent. Then d_1 would be $2.75 multiplied by 1.12 to give us a d_1 or expected next year's dividend of $3.08. The current price of UC's stock is $62.44. The $3.08 divided by $62.44 represents a 4.9 percent dividend yield. When this is added to the 12 percent expected growth rate, we obtain a 16.9 percent estimate of the required return on equity.

Summarizing our results thus far we have the following results for the four methods:

1. CAPM — 17.9 percent
2. Bond yield plus equity risk premium — 18.0 percent
3. Realized investor yield — 18.2 percent
4. Dividend growth model — 16.9 percent

Note that the first three methods of estimating the cost of equity capital use information generated by the financial markets. Therefore they may be reasonably regarded as the required rates of return on equity by external investors. Hence they represent an estimate of the cost of external equity funds. Since the dividend valuation model is an all internal equity financing model it may be reasonably regarded as providing the cost of internal funds. It is interesting to note that the three methods that provide estimates of external equity financing cluster at approximately 18 percent, whereas the dividend valuation model gives a somewhat lower figure at approximately 17 percent as a cost of internal equity financing. Hence we may conclude that for the United Corporation the cost of external financing is 18 percent and the cost of internal equity financing is 17 percent. One view is that this differential results from taxation effects as described by the Masulis-Trueman model discussed in Chapter 22. Adherents to the older view of charging financing with costs of flotation explain the difference by flotation costs.

We now have estimates of all of the costs of the individual components in financing. We next consider how we can pull all of this information together to calculate the weighted marginal cost of capital for the firm as a whole, an expression that is referred to as WACC or MCC.

Table 21.4   Balance Sheet for United Corporation

Assets		Liabilities and Stockholders' Equity	
Current assets	$2,080	Accounts payable	$ 360
Fixed assets	2,490	Accruals	400
		Notes payable @ 12%	400
		Deferred taxes	110
		Minority interests	120
		Long-term debt @ 10%	1,000
		Preferred stock	200
		Stockholders' equity	1,980
Total	$4,570	Total	$4,570

Calculating the Firm's Cost of Capital

We have the costs of the individual financing components. We next need to determine the proportions of each of the financing components to calculate a weighted cost. We begin with the accounting balance sheet of the United Corporation, which is shown in Table 21.4. In the balance sheet we focus on the right-hand side, which represents liabilities and stockholders' equity.

Among the liabilities we observe that some carry an interest cost explicitly while others do not. Since there are no "free lunches" in this world, we know that all of the liabilities that do not carry an explicit cost must surely have an implicit cost. For example, accounts payable typically represent the largest single category of current liabilities and carry no interest charge explicitly. To the firm extending credit, the loss of interest on funds tied up in receivables represents a cost of doing business. It is likely that the costs of carrying accounts receivable are reflected in the prices charged by supplier firms. Hence accounts payable does not represent "free financing" but rather a source of financing whose costs have already been levied and reflected in the income statement. We will, therefore, focus only on those liabilities and equity claims for which an explicit cost can be calculated. This is the starting point for the analysis in Table 21.5.

Column (1) in Table 21.5 represents the book value of the liabilities and stockholders' equity accounts for which an explicit charge can be calculated. The first item is notes payable on a short-term basis. Short-term notes payable would carry an interest cost relatively close to current interest rate levels. Hence their market value would approximate their face value. Therefore, in Column (2), the market price factor of the notes payable is shown at 100 percent. In calculating the effective cost of long-term debt we indicated that with a coupon rate of 10 percent and a current required market rate of 13.5 percent on United Corporation's AA debt, the current price per $1,000 bond for United Corporation would be approximately $800. Hence the market price would be about 80 percent of their maturity value. We made a similar calculation for preferred stock arriving at a 70 percent factor. For common equity we would employ the price of $62.44 previously used, which is 120% of the $52.04 book value per share.

Applying the market prices to the book value figures, we obtain the indicated market values shown in Column (3). When we sum the market value figures we obtain $3,716 million as compared with book values of the four items of a somewhat smaller amount.

Table 21.5   Calculation of Market Value Weights and Proportions for United Corporation

	Book Value (millions) (1)	Market Price Factor (2)	Market Value (millions) (3)	Proportions (4)	Targets (5)
Notes payable	$ 400	100%	$ 400	.108	10%
Long-term debt	1,000	80%	800	.215	20%
Preferred stock	200	70%	140	.038	5%
Common equity*	1,980	120%	2,376	.639	65%
	$3,580		$3,716	1.000	

*38.05 million shares.

From the market value figures we can calculate the proportions of financing, shown in Column (4). These are proportions at market values. The use of book value weights would have been inappropriate because they are less likely to indicate what the proportions would be in the future financing of the firm. Market proportion weights provide a better estimate of the target financing mix of the firm than book value weights. In the financial planning models of the firm, target financing proportions would be employed. These would be the best indicator of the appropriate proportions to use in calculating the firm's weighted cost of capital. In Column (5) we assume that we have access to such information. The figures are closely related to the current market proportions. It is assumed that the target proportion of common equity financing would increase slightly with the expected future rise in the price of the firm's common equity shares.

We now have the component costs of financing and the target proportions. We can bring these together to calculate the marginal cost of capital or the WACC (see Table 21.6). In Table 21.6 we assume that for a relatively small investment program the firm can finance its needs entirely from internal equity financing. We, therefore, use 17 percent as the cost of common equity financing. Recall that we assumed a 40 percent tax rate for United Corporation so that the after-tax cost of notes payable and the after-tax cost of long-term debt represent their before-tax cost multiplied by $(1 - .40)$. We obtain a weighted average marginal cost of financing of 14.04 percent for United Corporation as of the early part of 1984.

Table 21.6   United Corporation's Cost of Capital with Internal Equity Financing

	Before-Tax Cost	After-Tax Cost	Target Proportions	Weighted Cost
Notes payable	12%	7.2%	.10	.72%
Long-term debt	13.5%	8.1%	.20	1.62%
Preferred stock	13%	13.0%	.05	.65%
Common equity	17%	17.0%	.65	11.05%
			WACC =	14.04%

Cost of Capital for Projects or a Division

Calculating the cost of capital for a project or for a division encounters some common problems. First, the data are in dollars rather than rates of return. Second, different projects and different divisions are likely to have different risks, risks different from those of the firm as a whole. Fortunately we can solve both types of problems based on relationships derived from the basic Security Market Line. We shall illustrate the procedure.[7] We start with the Security Market Line as repeated in Equation 21.29:

$$E(R_j) = R_F + \lambda \text{COV}(R_j, R_M), \qquad (21.29)$$

where

$$\lambda = \frac{\overline{R}_M - R_F}{\sigma_M^2}.$$

We then recognize that

$$E(R_j) = \frac{E(X_j)}{V_j}. \qquad (21.30)$$

We substitute Equation 21.30 in the SML and solve for V_j, which gives us Equation 21.31:

$$V_j = \frac{E(X_j) - \lambda \text{COV}(X_j, R_M)}{R_F}. \qquad (21.31)$$

We now have a relationship between the covariance expressed in terms of the net operating income (after taxes) of an unlevered activity. This we can obtain from the available data for an individual division of a firm or for a firm even if its securities are not traded publicly. If the division or nonpublicly traded firm has a historical record, we could develop a calculation of $\text{COV}(X_j, R_M)$ as described in some of the problems at the end of Chapters 16 and 17. Even if we had no historical record or sometimes as a check on historical data we may also formulate subjective estimates of net operating income under alternative future states-of-the-world. Using either the historical data or subjective estimates under alternative future states-of-the-world we are thereby enabled to calculate the expected net operating income and its covariance. Suppose we have made these calculations and obtain the following:

$$\overline{X}_j = \$240$$

$$\text{COV}(X_j, R_M) = \$11.60.$$

We postulate further the market parameters, which are

$$R_F = 10\%$$

$$\lambda = 8 \qquad \text{VAR}(R_M) = .01.$$

[7]This procedure was described in Weston and Lee [1977], pp. 1779-1780.

We can now use these data inputs in Equation 21.31:

$$V_j = \frac{\$240 - 8(11.60)}{.10}$$

$$V_j = \$1,472.$$

We thus obtain an estimate of the value of the division or the firm whose securities are not publicly traded of $1,472. We can now express the covariance in rate of return form using the following relationship:

$$COV(R_j, R_M) = \frac{COV(X_j, R_M)}{V_j}.$$

Inserting the numbers, we have

$$COV(R_j, R_M) = \frac{\$11.60}{\$1,472} = .0079.$$

Since the variance of the market has been given as 1 percent, we can readily express the risk relationship in the form of beta.

$$\beta_U = \frac{COV(R_j, R_M)}{VAR(R_M)} = \frac{.0079}{.01} = .79$$

To this point we have assumed no leverage, so the beta of .79 we have obtained represents an unlevered beta. Let us postulate further that after careful assessment of the operations of the division under analysis we determine the applicable leverage to be applied is a ratio of debt to equity of one-half and that the effective corporate tax rate that would be applicable to this division's activities is 40 percent. We can then calculate the indicated levered beta.

$$\beta_j = \beta_U[1 + B/S(1 - T)] \qquad \text{(21.32)}$$

Inserting the numerical values calculated, we would have

$$\beta_j = .79[1 + .5(.6)]$$

$$\beta_j = 1.027 \approx 1.03.$$

We have thus obtained a levered beta of 1.03 that would be applicable to the activities of the division. Before utilizing the beta calculated in the Security Market Line to obtain the cost of equity capital and related measures, we check the number we have obtained. One way to do so would be to observe the betas of publicly traded companies whose activities are similar to the individual division we have under analysis. Suppose we find a publicly traded company that is very similar. We observe that it has a beta of .85. But we also observe that for a long period of time this company has had a leverage ratio measured by the market value of debt to the market value of equity of .1. This is much lower than the .5 target leverage ratio of our division. We, therefore, have to releverage the comparable company to see what its beta would be at the target leverage for our division. First, we calculate its unlevered beta based on our knowledge of its current leverage. We solve Equation 21.32 for β_U to obtain Equation 21.33:

$$\beta_U = \frac{\beta_j}{[1 + B/S(1 - T)]}. \tag{21.33}$$

Inserting our numerical values we have

$$\beta_U = \frac{.85}{1.06} = .80.$$

We obtain an unlevered beta of .80, which is very close to the .79 we estimated for our particular division. This gives us some assurance that the company that we have chosen as similar in its activities to our division is indeed comparable since its unlevered beta is approximately the same as the unlevered beta we have calculated for our division. We now releverage the external similar company. We would then have

$$\beta_k = .80[1 + .5(.6)]$$

$$= 1.04.$$

We obtain a levered beta for our comparable company of 1.04. This is very close to the 1.03 that we had calculated using internal data. Giving greater weight to the market determined number, we will use the beta of 1.04 in the subsequent analysis. First, we apply this to the Security Market Line parameters. Since we know that the variance of the market is 1 percent, Equation 21.29 can be rewritten in beta form as shown in Equation 21.34:

$$E(R_j) = R_F + [E(R_M) - R_F]\beta_j. \tag{21.34}$$

We now have all the information we need to solve Equation 21.34 to estimate the cost of equity capital for the division or for the nonpublicly traded firm. This would be

$$E(R_j) = 10\% + 8\%(1.04)$$

$$= 18.32\%.$$

We obtain a cost of equity capital for our division of 18.32 percent. We can now proceed finally to calculate an applicable weighted marginal cost of capital that would represent the appropriate investment hurdle rate for projects undertaken by the division. Recall that in calculating the levered beta we indicated that the appropriate debt-equity ratio was 50 percent. This means that the leverage ratio expressed in terms of the total value of the firm is one-third debt and two-thirds equity. For this division the applicable cost of debt is 15 percent. We can, therefore, proceed to calculate the weighted marginal cost of capital.

Source	After-Tax Cost	Financing Proportions	Marginal Cost of Capital
Debt	9%	.33	3.00%
Equity	18.32%	.67	12.27%
		Divisional Cost of Capital	15.27%

We find that the cost of capital for this division would be slightly more than 15 percent. This is the appropriate investment hurdle rate to use for new projects of the division that are not greatly different from its existing product market mix. In a similar fashion we could calculate the cost of capital for each of the divisions of the firm. In addition to the application of these divisional investment hurdle rates in capital budgeting, these estimates would provide a check on the firm's overall beta and cost of capital. This is because the firm's beta is simply a value-weighted average of the betas of its individual divisions. Therefore, the value-weighted average of the betas of the individual divisions should be reasonably close to the publicly available estimates of the beta for the firm as a whole.[8]

The same problems are involved in analyzing a project. Indeed, in the foregoing analysis we could always substitute "project" for "division." The results are estimates of investment hurdle rates by division or project for use in capital budgeting decisions. Without these estimates of investment hurdle rates for individual projects or divisions, highly risky activities would be allocated too much financing and less risky activities would not receive the requisite funds. If a single marginal weighted cost of capital were applied to all risky activities, some projects that should not be financed would be adopted. For less risky activities, projects that should be accepted would be rejected.

Developing the Firm's Overall Capital Budget

Either a falling marginal efficiency of investment schedule or a rising marginal cost of capital schedule will provide a basis for arriving at the size of the firm's overall capital budget for a forthcoming time period. The marginal efficiency of investment schedule declines because at any given point in time the investment opportunities of the firm are likely to be limited. We have shown here in addition a rising marginal cost of capital schedule. Possible reasons are flotation costs or differential tax rates.

The marginal cost of financing may rise from an additional cause. If the firm attempts to grow at a high rate, the marginal cost of financing curve may begin to rise sharply. For example, if a firm sought to obtain financing for a 50 percent growth rate in one year, the market might require a substantial financing cost premium.

This is not a "pricing pressure" argument which says that the market is unwilling to absorb a particular firm's securities if its supply increases substantially. There is little empirical evidence to support the pricing pressure argument since securities differ only in their risks and returns. Firms of different size, but identical risk, plot at the same point on the Security Market Line.

Another view holds that whether a premium for financing a high percent rate of growth is required depends upon how well the funds will be used. Thus, a growth firm with very good investment prospects may be able to raise even larger amounts of funds on favorable rather than unfavorable costs and terms. This view has an element of validity. However, the financing premium argument relies on more general principles. It states that when a firm grows at a very high rate, such as 50 percent, it is likely to encounter difficulties from two sources. One, although it may have been successful in developing its organization to that point, an additional 50 percent increase may involve substantial risks. It may be difficult to find qualified people. Even if qualified people are found it may be difficult to fit them into an effectively functioning organization. It is this organizational development

[8]This has actually been done for a sample of multi-division firms using the "pure-play technique," which involves matching each division of a multi-division firm with a publicly traded company having only one business line. See Fuller and Kerr [1981].

aspect that represents an additional source of risk when a firm seeks to achieve a very rapid rate of growth.[9]

Another strand of the argument is that in an enterprise system success attracts imitation. A firm that has been growing at a very rapid rate with high profitability provides an example for the world to see that it has uncovered a very attractive product-market area. Existing firms are likely to expand in those directions and a large number of new firms are likely to be formed to imitate successful firms and exploit similar opportunities. Thus, the risks of being able to sustain a high rate of growth increase over time. It is these additional and rising risks that may cause investors to require larger premiums for financing continued high rates of growth.

But even if the risks of organizational development and competitive reactions are real and present in the markets, some argue that they should not be reflected in a rising marginal cost of capital schedule. Rather they argue that these risks indicate that the marginal efficiency of investment schedule is not as attractive as it had been thought to be. This view holds that the marginal efficiency of investment schedule should be shifted to the left rather than having the marginal cost of capital curve rise more rapidly. Whichever set of curves is affected, the result will be that the size of the capital budget contemplated by the firm will have to be reduced. Shifting the marginal efficiency of investment schedule to the left will reduce the planned capital budget. Alternatively, causing the marginal cost of capital curve to rise more sharply for a given marginal efficiency of investment schedule is also likely to cause the size of the capital budget to be reduced. Regardless of which point of view is followed, the framework presented here provides a basis for a rational assessment of the outlook necessary for developing the overall financial plan for a firm.

Summary

Under the Modigliani and Miller assumptions, a firm's cost of capital is not affected by leverage when there are no taxes. However, even without taxes, the firm's cost of equity capital rises linearly. With taxes, the firm's cost of equity capital still rises linearly but at a reduced rate. The firm's marginal weighted cost of capital under the MM theory would decline, implying that firms would all be highly leveraged. However, we do not observe this in actuality. A number of factors could limit leverage, including agency problems, information asymmetry and signaling, and bankruptcy costs. Any of these could result in limiting the amount of leverage employed so that a firm would have an "optimal capital structure." The foregoing framework provided a basis for analyzing the influence of leverage on the cost of capital of a firm, the subject of the remainder of the chapter.

The rate of return required or expected on any security, $E(R_j)$, is the minimum rate of return necessary to induce investors to buy or to hold the security; it is a function of the riskless rate of interest and the investment's risk characteristics:

$$E(R_j) = R_F + [E(R_M) - R_F]\beta_j.$$

This equation is called the Security Market Line (SML). Because investors generally dislike risk, the required rate of return is higher on riskier securities. As a class, bonds are less risky than preferred stocks; and preferred stocks, in turn, are less risky than common stocks. The result is that the required rate of return is lowest for bonds, higher for pre-

---

[9]This has also been called the *Penrose effect* first set forth in the book by Penrose [1959].

ferred stocks, and highest for common stocks. Within each of these security classes there are variations among the issuing firms' risks; hence, required rates of return vary among firms.

The *cost of debt* is defined as the required yield to maturity on new increments of debt capital, k_b, multiplied by (1 − Tax rate). The *cost of preferred stock* with no maturity date is the required yield. It is found as the annual expected preferred dividend divided by the preferred stock price. The cost of common equity is the return required to prevent the price of the common stock from declining from its current levels. The cost of common equity may be calculated by at least four methods. One is the use of the Security Market Line — the risk-free rate plus the product of the market risk premium and the firm's beta. A second is the cost of the firm's long-term debt plus an equity risk premium. A third is consideration of the return (dividend yield plus realized capital gains yield) required by investors in this and similar companies over representative prior periods. A fourth is the widely used dividend valuation model — the expected dividend yield plus the expected growth in dividends.

Internal financing is generally recognized to cost less than external financing. Some argue that this is due to avoidance of flotation costs; others would assign flotation costs to investment outlays on new projects. Differential effective personal income tax rates and differential effective tax rates on dividends and on capital gains could also account for lower internal equity financing costs.

Increasing the leverage ratio in a firm will make the debt and equity riskier because it increases the probability of bankruptcy. If bankruptcy costs are substantial, then with increasing leverage the value of the firm will rise, reach a peak, and then fall. The maximum point on this curve indicates a target debt or leverage ratio.

The first step in calculating the weighted cost of capital, k, is to determine the cost of the individual capital components. The next step is to establish the proper set of weights to be used in the averaging process. The basic issues are whether to use the actual historical financing costs of the firm and whether to use book or market value in calculating the proportions or weights of each source of financing. Financing costs must represent current opportunity costs, so the actual historical financing costs (reflected in the books) are not relevant. With regard to weights or proportions of each source of financing, theory calls for the use of target capital structure. However, current market values may not represent the target equilibrium values, so we do not necessarily apply the market values that we observe at a particular time. We should use those proportions or weights that represent the debt capacity of the firm appropriate for use in formulating the firm's target leverage proportions. A wide range of factors would have to be considered by a firm's management in formulating its target leverage ratio.

The *marginal cost of capital schedule*, defined as the cost of incremental funds raised during a period of time, is of interest for two reasons. First, the firm should finance in a manner that minimizes the MCC schedule; therefore, it must measure the MCC. Second, the MCC is the rate that should be used in the capital budgeting process. The firm should take on new capital projects only if the net present values are positive when evaluated at the marginal cost of capital.

The marginal cost of capital is constant over a range, then may begin to rise. If a rise takes place, it is because investors judge that a firm that is expanding rapidly may encounter organizational problems and stir up competitive reactions from its rivals. But even with a flat marginal cost of capital schedule, the declining investment opportunities schedule will guarantee that it intersects the marginal cost of capital schedule. This intersection will provide a guide to the determination of the amount of the firm's annual capital budget.

Questions

21.1 Suppose that basic business risks to all firms in any given industry are similar.
    a) Would you expect all firms in the industry to have approximately the same cost of capital?
    b) How would the averages differ among industries?

21.2 Are internally generated retained earnings less expensive than equity raised by selling stock? Why or why not?

21.3 Prior to the 1930s, the corporate income tax was not very important because the rates were fairly low. Also prior to the 1930s, preferred stock was much more important than it has been since that time. Is there a relationship between the rise of corporate income taxes and the decline in importance of preferred stock?

21.4 The firm's covariance is 0.014, the risk-free rate is 10 percent, the market risk premium $(\bar{R}_M - R_F)$ is 5 percent, and the variance of the market returns is 1 percent.
    a) With no bankruptcy costs, what is the cost of capital for this unlevered firm?
    b) What is the beta of the firm?

21.5 Assume that the information in Question 21.4 is all on an after-tax basis, that the corporate tax rate is 50 percent, and that the firm now has a debt-to-equity ratio of 50 percent, with a debt cost of 10 percent.
    a) What is the new beta of the firm?
    b) What is its return on equity?
    c) What is the cost of capital for the levered firm?

21.6 An unlevered firm has a beta of 0.8. How much leverage can it employ if its corporate tax rate is 50 percent and it aims to have a beta of 1.2?

21.7 The formula $k_r = (d_1/p_o) + g$, where d_1 = expected current dividend, p_o = the current price of a stock, and g = the past rate of growth in dividends, is sometimes used to estimate k_r, the cost of equity capital. Explain the implications of the formula.

21.8 What factors operate to cause the cost of debt to increase with financial leverage?

21.9 Explain the relationship between the required rate of return on common equity (k_s) and the debt ratio.

21.10 How will the various component costs of capital and the average cost of capital be likely to change if a firm expands its operations into a new, riskier industry?

21.11 The stock of XYZ Company is currently selling at its low for the year, but management feels that the stock price is only temporarily depressed because of investor pessimism. The firm's capital budget this year is so large that the firm is contemplating the use of new outside equity. However, management does not want to sell new stock at the current low price and is considering a temporary departure from its "optimal" capital structure by borrowing the funds it would otherwise have raised in the equity markets. Does this seem to be a wise move? Explain.

21.12 Explain the following statement: The marginal cost of capital is an average in some sense.

Problems

21.1 Companies U and L are identical in every respect except that U is unlevered while L has $10 million of 5 percent bonds outstanding. Assume (1) that all of the MM assumptions are met, (2) that the tax rate is 40 percent, (3) that EBIT is $2 million, and (4) that the equity capitalization rate for Company U is 10 percent.
    a) What value would MM estimate for each firm?

b)   Suppose $V_U = \$8$ million and $V_L = \$18$ million. According to MM, do these represent equilibrium values? If not, explain the process by which equilibrium will be restored. No calculations are necessary.

21.2   You are provided the following information: The firm's expected net operating income (X) is $600. Its value as an unlevered firm (V_U) is $2,000. The tax rate is 40 percent. The cost of debt is 10 percent. The ratio of debt to equity for the levered firm, when it is levered, is 1. Use the MM propositions to:

a)   Calculate the after-tax cost of equity capital for both the levered and the unlevered firm.

b)   Calculate the after-tax weighted average cost of capital for each.

c)   Why is the cost of equity capital higher for the levered firm, but the weighted average cost of capital lower?

21.3   The Gorman Company is unlevered. Its balance sheet can be summarized as follows:

Gorman Company
Balance Sheet, 12/31/X0 (Millions of Dollars)

Total assets	$500	Common stock (par value = $1)	$100
		Paid-in capital	100
		Retained earnings	300
		Total claims	$500

Net operating earnings for the year ending December 31, 19X0 were $100 million and the effective tax rate was 50 percent. The common stock has a market price of $5 per share. To finance additional projects, $100 million of long-term debt is sold at par with an 8 percent coupon rate. Earnings rise to $120 per year. Alternatively, the expansion may be financed by the sale of an additional 20 million shares of common stock. Use the Modigliani-Miller model to answer the following questions.

a)   Before the new financing,
  1.   What are earnings per share of common stock?
  2.   What is the price earnings ratio on the common stock?
  3.   What is the relationship between book value and market value?
  4.   What is the cost of capital?

b)   After the new financing by debt,
  5.   What is the new value of the firm?
  6.   What are the new earnings per share?
  7.   What is the new price per share of common stock?
  8.   What is the new price/earnings ratio on the common stock?
  9.   What is the new required return on the common equity?
  10.   What is the new cost of capital for the firm?
  11.   What is the market/book relationship?

c)   After financing by equity,
  12-18. Answer Questions 5 through 11 for Part (c).

d)   Interpretation:
  19.   Comment on the implications of the above analysis.

21.4   The earnings, dividends, and stock price of the Abbott Company are expected to grow at 9 percent per year. Abbott's common stock sells for $30 per share, and the company will pay a year-end dividend of $2.40 per share. What is its cost of retained earnings?

21.5 The Crothers Company has a beta of 1.5. It has no debt in its capital structure.
   a) The expected market rate of return is 14 percent and the risk-free rate is 6 percent. What is the cost of equity capital for Crothers?
   b) Should Crothers accept a project that earns a rate of return of 15 percent and has a beta of 0.9?

21.6 The Graham Company's financing plans for next year include the sale of long-term bonds with a 9 percent coupon. The company believes it can sell the bonds at a price that will give a yield to maturity of 10 percent. If the tax rate is 40 percent, what is Graham's after-tax cost of debt?

21.7 The Brandon Company plans to issue 20-year bonds that have a 10 percent coupon, a par value of $1,000, and can be sold for $920. Interest is paid semiannually. Brandon's tax rate is 40 percent.
   a) What is the after-tax cost of this debt to Brandon?
   b) What would be the after-tax cost if this were a perpetual bond issue?

21.8 Infinity Industries has just issued some $100 par preferred stock with a 10 percent dividend. The stock is selling on the market for $96.17, and Infinity must pay flotation costs of 6 percent of the market price. What is the cost of the preferred stock for Infinity?

21.9 The Iversen Company earns $5 per share. The expected year-end dividend is $1.60, and price per share is $40. Iversen's earnings, dividends, and stock price have been growing at 8 percent per year, and this growth rate is expected to continue indefinitely. New common stock can be sold to net $38. What is Iversen's cost of retained earnings?

21.10 The Longwell Company is expected to pay a year-end dividend of $4.40. Longwell earns $7.70 per share, and its stock sells at $55 per share. Stock price, earnings, and dividends are expected to grow 6 percent per year indefinitely.
   a) Calculate the stockholders' rate of return.
   b) If the firm has a zero growth rate and pays out all its earnings as dividends, what is the stockholders' rate of return?

21.11 The Riley Company has $200 million in total net assets at the end of 19X0. It plans to increase its production machinery in 19X1 by $50 million. Bond financing, at an 11 percent rate, will sell at par. Preferred will have an 11.5 percent dividend payment and will be sold at a par value of $100. Common stock currently sells for $50 per share and can be sold to net $45 after flotation costs. There is $10 million of internal funding available from retained earnings. Over the past few years, dividend yield has been 6 percent and the firm's growth rate 8 percent. The tax rate is 40 percent. The present capital structure shown below is considered optimal:

Debt:		
4% coupon bonds	$40,000,000	
7% coupon bonds	40,000,000	$ 80,000,000
Preferred stock		20,000,000
Common stock ($10 par)	$40,000,000	
Retained earnings	60,000,000	
Equity		100,000,000
		$200,000,000

   a) How much of the $50 million must be financed by equity capital if the present capital structure is to be maintained?
   b) How much of the equity funding must come from the sale of new common stock?

c)   Calculate the component cost of:
    1.   New debt
    2.   New preferred stock
    3.   Retained earnings
    4.   New equity
d)   What is Riley's average cost of equity for 19X1?
e)   What would be Riley's weighted average cost of capital if only retained earnings were used to finance additional growth — that is, if only $20 million were raised?
f)   What is the weighted average cost of capital when $50 million is raised?
g)   What is the weighted average cost of capital on the $30 million raised over the $20 million?

21.12 The Tanner Company's cost of equity is 18 percent. Tanner's before-tax cost of debt is 12 percent, and its tax rate is 40 percent. Using the following balance sheet, calculate Tanner's after-tax weighted average cost of capital. (Assume that this accounting balance sheet also represents Tanner's target capital structure.)

Assets		Liabilities	
Cash	$ 100	Accounts payable	$ 200
Accounts receivable	200	Accrued taxes due	200
Inventories	300	Long-term debt	400
Plant and equipment, net	1,800	Equity	1,600
Total assets	$2,400	Total liabilities	$2,400

21.13 Parnelli Products' stock is currently selling for $45 a share. The firm is earning $5 per share and is expected to pay a year-end dividend of $1.80.
    a)   If investors require a 12 percent return, what rate of growth must be expected for Parnelli?
    b)   If Parnelli reinvests retained earnings to yield the expected rate of return, what will be next year's EPS?

21.14 You are planning to form a new company, and you can use several different capital structures. Investment bankers indicate that debt and equity capital will cost the following under different debt ratios (debt/total assets):

Debt Ratio	20% and below	21 to 40%	41 to 50%	51 to 65%
Before-tax cost of debt	8%	9%	11%	14%
Cost of equity capital	12	13	18	25

a)   Assuming a 40 percent tax rate, what is the after-tax weighted cost of capital for the following capital structures?

	(1)	(2)	(3)	(4)	(5)	(6)	(7)	(8)
Debt	0%	20%	21%	40%	41%	50%	51%	65%
Equity	100	80	79	60	59	50	49	35

b)   Which capital structure minimizes the weighted average cost of capital?

21.15 On January 1, 19X0, the total assets of the Rossiter Company were $60 million. By the end of the year total assets are expected to be $90 million. (Assume there is no short-term debt.) The firm's capital structure, shown below, is considered to be optimal:

Debt (10% coupon bonds)	$24,000,000
Preferred stock (at 10.5%)	6,000,000
Common equity	30,000,000
	$60,000,000

New bonds will have an 11 percent coupon rate and will be sold at par. Preferred stock will have an 11.5 percent rate and will also be sold at par. Common stock, currently selling at $30 a share, can be sold to net the company $27 a share. Stockholders' required rate of return, estimated to be 12 percent, consists of a dividend yield of 4 percent and an expected growth of 8 percent. Retained earnings are estimated to be $3 million (ignoring depreciation). The marginal corporate tax rate is 40 percent.

a) Assuming all asset expansion (gross expenditures for fixed assets plus related working capital) is included in the capital budget, what is the dollar amount of the capital budget (ignoring depreciation)?

b) To maintain the present capital structure, how much of the capital budget must be financed by equity?

c) How much of the new equity funds needed must be generated internally? How much externally?

d) Calculate the cost of each of the equity components.

e) At what level of capital expenditures will there be a break in the MCC schedule?

f) Calculate the MCC both below and above the break in the schedule.

g) Plot the MCC schedule. Also, draw in an IRR or MEI schedule that is consistent with the MCC schedule and the projected capital budget.

Selected References

Aivazian, Varouj, and Callen, Jeffrey L., "Investment, Market Structure, and the Cost of Capital," *Journal of Finance*, 34 (March 1979), pp. 85-92.

Alberts, William W., and Hite, Gailen L., "The Modigliani-Miller Leverage Equation Considered in a Product Market Context," *Journal of Financial and Quantitative Analysis*, 18 (December 1983), pp. 425-437.

Altman, Edward I., "A Further Empirical Investigation of the Bankruptcy Cost Question," *Journal of Finance*, 39 (September 1984), pp. 1067-1089.

Arditti, Fred D., "The Weighted Average Cost of Capital: Some Questions on Its Definition, Interpretation and Use," *Journal of Finance*, 28 (September 1973), pp. 1001-1007.

———, "Risk and the Required Return on Equity," *Journal of Finance*, 22 (March 1967), pp. 19-36.

Arditti, Fred D., and Pinkerton, John M., "The Valuation and the Cost of Capital of the Levered Firm with Growth Opportunities," *Journal of Finance*, 33 (March 1978), pp. 65-73.

Arditti, Fred D., and Tysseland, Milford S., "Three Ways to Present the Marginal Cost of Capital," *Financial Management*, 2 (Summer 1973), pp. 63-67.

Auerbach, Alan J., "Wealth Maximization and the Cost of Capital," *Quarterly Journal of Economics*, 43 (August 1979), pp. 433-446.

Beranek, William, "The Weighted Average Cost of Capital and Shareholder Wealth Maximization," *Journal of Financial and Quantitative Analysis*, 12 (March 1977), pp. 17-32.

Black, F., and Scholes, M., "The Pricing of Options and Corporate Liabilities," *Journal of Political Economy*, 81 (May-June 1973), pp. 637-654.

Boness, A. James, and Frankfurter, George M., "Evidence of Non-homogeneity of Capital Costs within 'Risk-Classes,'" *Journal of Finance*, 32 (June 1977), pp. 775-787.

Brennan, M. J., and Schwartz, E. S., "Corporate Income Taxes, Valuation, and the Problem of Optimal

Capital Structure," *Journal of Business*, 51 (January 1978), pp. 103-114.

Chen, Andrew, "Recent Developments in the Cost of Debt Capital," *Journal of Finance*, 33 (June 1978), pp. 863-883.

Constantinides, George M., and Ingersoll, Jonathan E., Jr., "Tax Effects and Bond Prices," *Journal of Finance*, 37 (May 1982), pp. 349-352.

Copeland, Thomas E., and Weston, J. Fred, *Financial Theory and Corporate Policy*, 2nd Ed., Reading, Mass.: Addison-Wesley, 1983.

Davidson, Wallace N., III., "The Effect of Rate Cases on Public Utility Stock Returns," *Journal of Financial Research*, 7 (Spring 1984), pp. 81-93.

DeAngelo, H., and Masulis, R., "Optimal Capital Structure under Corporate and Personal Taxation," *Journal of Financial Economics*, 8 (March 1980), pp. 3-30.

Draper, Dennis W., and Findlay, M. Chapman, III., "A Note on Vickers' Marginal Cost of Debt Capital," *Journal of Business Finance & Accounting*, 9 (Winter 1982), pp. 579-582.

Dyl, Edward A., and Joehnk, Michael D., "Sinking Funds and the Cost of Corporate Debt," *Journal of Finance*, 34 (September 1979), pp. 887-893.

Ezzell, John R., and Porter, R. Burr, "Flotation Costs and the Weighted Average Cost of Capital," *Journal of Financial and Quantitative Analysis*, 11 (September 1976), pp. 403-414.

Fama, Eugene F., "Risk, Return, and Equilibrium: Some Clarifying Comments," *Journal of Finance*, 23 (March 1968), pp. 29-40.

Fama, Eugene F., and Miller, Merton H., *The Theory of Finance*, New York: Holt, Rinehart and Winston, 1972.

Feldstein, Martin; Green, Jerry; and Sheshinski, Eytan, "Corporate Financial Policy and Taxation in a Growing Economy," *Quarterly Journal of Economics*, 43 (August 1979), pp. 411-431.

———, "Inflation and Taxes in a Growing Economy with Debt and Equity Finance," *Journal of Political Economy*, 86 (April 1978), pp. S53-S70.

Fuller, Russell J., and Kerr, Halbert S., "Estimating the Divisional Cost of Capital: An Analysis of the Pure-Play Technique," *Journal of Finance*, 36 (December 1981), pp. 997-1009.

Gordon, M. J., "Leverage and the Value of a Firm Under a Progressive Personal Income Tax," *Journal of Banking and Finance*, 6 (December 1982), pp. 483-493.

Gordon, M. J., and Kwan, Clarence C. Y., "Debt Maturity, Default Risk, and Capital Structure," *Journal of Banking and Finance*, 3 (December 1979), pp. 313-329.

Grier, Paul, and Strebel, Paul, "An Implicit Clientele Test of the Relationship Between Taxation and Capital Structure," *Journal of Financial Research*, 6 (Summer 1983), pp. 163-174.

Gup, Benton E., and Norwood, Samuel W., III., "Divisional Cost of Capital: A Practical Approach," *Financial Management*, 11 (Spring 1982), pp. 20-24.

Hamada, Robert S., "Portfolio Analysis, Market Equilibrium and Corporation Finance," *Journal of Finance*, 24 (March 1969), pp. 13-32.

Haugen, R. A., and Senbet, L. W., "New Perspectives on Informational Asymmetry," *Journal of Financial and Quantitative Analysis*, 14 (November 1979), pp. 671-694.

Higgins, Robert C., "Growth, Dividend Policy and Capital Costs in the Electric Utility Industry," *Journal of Finance*, 29 (September 1974), pp. 1189-1201.

Hirshleifer, Jack, "Investment Decisions under Uncertainty: Applications of the State-Preference Approach," *Quarterly Journal of Economics*, 83 (May 1966), pp. 252-277.

Hite, Gailen L., "Leverage, Output Effects, and the M-M Theorems," *Journal of Financial Economics*, 4 (March 1977), pp. 177-202.

Hsia, Chi-Cheng, "Optimal Debt of a Firm: An Option Pricing Approach," *Journal of Financial Research*, 4 (Fall 1981), pp. 221-231.

Ibbotson, Roger G.; Diermeier, Jeffrey J.; and Siegel, Laurence B., "The Demand for Capital Market Returns: A New Equilibrium Theory," *Financial Analysts Journal*, 40 (January/February 1984), pp. 22-33.

Jensen, M. C., and Meckling, W., "Theory of the Firm: Managerial Behavior, Agency Costs and Capital Structure," *Journal of Financial Economics*, 3 (October 1976), pp. 11-25.

Keenan, Michael, "Models of Equity Valuation: The Great Serm Bubble," *Journal of Finance*, 25 (May 1970), pp. 243-273.

Krouse, Clement G., "Optimal Financing and Capital Structure Programs for the Firm," *Journal of Finance*, 27 (December 1972), pp. 1057-1072.

Lee, Wayne Y., and Barker, Henry H., "Bankruptcy Costs and the Firm's Optimal Debt Capacity: A Positive Theory of Capital Structure," *Southern Economic Journal*, 43 (April 1977), pp. 1453-1465.

Leland, H. E., and Pyle, D. H., "Informational Asymmetries, Financial Structure, and Financial Intermediation," *Journal of Finance*, 32 (May 1977), pp. 371-387.

Lewellen, Wilbur G., "A Conceptual Reappraisal of Cost of Capital," *Financial Management*, 3 (Winter 1974), pp. 63-70.

———, *The Cost of Capital*, Belmont, Calif.: Wadsworth, 1969, Chapters 3-4.

Lewellen, Wilbur G., and Ang, James S., "Inflation, Security Values, and Risk Premia," *Journal of Financial Research*, 5 (Summer 1982), pp. 105-123.

Lewellen, Wilbur G., and McConnell, John J., "Utility Rate Regulation," *Journal of Business Research*, 7, no. 2 (1979), pp. 117-138.

Masulis, R. W., "The Effects of Capital Structure Change on Security Prices: A Study of Exchange Offers," *Journal of Financial Economics*, 8 (June 1980), pp. 139-177.

Merton, Robert C., "On the Pricing of Corporate Debt: The Risk Structure of Interest Rates," *Journal of Finance*, 29 (May 1974), pp. 449-470.

Miller, Merton H., "Debt and Taxes," *Journal of Finance*, 32 (May 1977), pp. 261-275.

Miller, Merton H., and Modigliani, Franco, "Cost of Capital to Electric Utility Industry," *American Economic Review*, 56 (June 1966), pp. 333-391.

Modigliani, Franco, and Miller, Merton H., "The Cost of Capital, Corporation Finance and the Theory of Investment," *American Economic Review*, 48 (June 1958), pp. 261-297.

Myers, Stewart C., "The Capital Structure Puzzle," *Journal of Finance*, 39 (July 1984), pp. 575-592.

———, "Interactions of Corporate Financing and Investment Decisions — Implications for Capital Budgeting," *Journal of Finance*, 29 (March 1974), pp. 1-25.

Penrose, E. T., *The Theory of the Growth of the Firm*, New York: John Wiley and Sons, 1959.

Petry, Glenn H., "Empirical Evidence on Cost of Capital Weights," *Financial Management*, 4 (Winter 1975), pp. 58-65.

———, "An Unidentified Corporate Risk — Using the Wrong Cost of Funds," *MSU Business Topics*, Graduate School of Business Administration, Michigan State University, (Autumn 1975), pp. 57-65.

Petry, Glenn H., and Fuller, Russell J., "Inflation and Stock Prices," *American Association of Individual Investors Journal*, VI (January 1984), pp. 11-15.

Pettway, Richard H., and Jordon, Bradford D., "Diversification, Double Leverage, and the Cost of Capital," *Journal of Financial Research*, 6 (Winter 1983), pp. 289-300.

Protopapadakis, Aris, "Some Indirect Evidence on Effective Capital Gains Tax Rates," *Journal of Business*, 56 (April 1983), pp. 127-138.

Reilly, Raymond R., and Wecker, William E., "On the Weighted Average Cost of Capital," *Journal of Financial and Quantitative Analysis*, 8 (January 1973), pp. 123-126.

Reinganum, Marc R., "Abnormal Returns in Small Firm Portfolios," *Financial Analysts Journal*, 37 (March/April 1981), pp. 52-56.

Robichek, Alexander A., and Myers, Stewart C., *Optimal Financial Decisions*, Englewood Cliffs, N. J.: Prentice-Hall, 1965.

Ross, S. A., "The Determination of Financial Structure: The Incentive-Signalling Approach," *Bell Journal of Economics*, 8 (Spring 1977), pp. 23-40.

Rubinstein, Mark E., "A Mean-Variance Synthesis of Corporate Financial Theory," *Journal of Finance*, 28 (March 1973), pp. 167-181.

Scott, J. H., "Bankruptcy, Secured Debt, and Optimal Capital Structure," *Journal of Finance*, 32 (March 1977), pp. 1-19.

———, "A Theory of Optimal Capital Structure," *Bell Journal of Economics*, 7 (Spring 1976), pp. 33-54.

Shiller, Robert J., and Modigliani, Franco, "Coupon and Tax Effects on New and Seasoned Bond Yields and the Measurement of the Cost of Debt Capital," *Journal of Financial Economics*, 7 (September 1979), pp. 297-318.

Sosin, Howard B., "Neutral Recapitalizations: Predictions and Tests Concerning Valuation and Welfare," *Journal of Finance*, 33 (September 1978), pp. 1228-1234.

Stapleton, R. C., and Subrahmanyam, M. G., "Market Imperfections, Capital Market Equilibrium, and Corporation Finance," *Journal of Finance*, 32 (May 1977), pp. 307-319.

Thompson, H., "Estimating the Cost of Equity Capital for Electric Utilities: 1958-1976," *Bell Journal of Economics*, 10 (Autumn 1979), pp. 619-635.

Titman, S., "The Effect of Capital Structure on a Firm's Liquidation Decision," unpublished Ph.D. thesis, Graduate School of Industrial Administration, Carnegie-Mellon University, 1981.

Vickers, Douglas, "The Cost of Capital and the Structure of the Firm," *Journal of Finance*, 25 (March 1970), pp. 35-46.

Warner, J., "Bankruptcy Costs: Some Evidence," *Journal of Finance*, 32 (May 1977), pp. 337-348.

Weinstein, Mark, "The Systematic Risk of Corporate Bonds," *Journal of Financial and Quantitative Analysis*, 16 (September 1981), pp. 257-278.

Weston, J. Fred, "A Test of Cost of Capital Propositions," *Southern Economic Journal*, 30 (October 1963), pp. 105-112.

Weston, J. Fred, and Lee, Wayne Y., "Cost of Capital for a Division of a Firm: Comment," *Journal of Finance*, 32 (December 1977), pp. 1779-1780.

Wippern, Ronald F., "Financial Structure and the Value of the Firm," *Journal of Finance*, 21 (December 1966), pp. 615-634.

Appendix A to Chapter 21

The Modigliani-Miller Propositions: Some Extensions

Cost of Capital for Finite Lives

Three equivalent formulas were set forth in Chapter 21 for measuring the weighted cost of capital. The one that brings out most clearly the effect of the tax benefits of using debt is Equation 21.17:

$$k = k_U(1 - TL). \tag{21.17}$$

Thus, if $T = .4$ and $L = .5$, then $TL = .2$. Hence the weighted average cost of capital would be .8 of the unlevered cost of capital or

$$k = .8k_U.$$

Thus, if k_U were 15 percent, the weighted cost of capital would be 12 percent. The three percentage points by which the weighted cost of capital is below the unlevered cost of capital represent the tax benefit of the leverage employed. The expressions in Equation 21.17 and in the related MM valuation relationships are based on constant or unchanging cash flows, a perpetuity. Alternatively these could be considered one-period models. The question arises with respect to uneven cash flows from year to year in the setting of a finite project life. A number of materials have been developed on the subject. They are brought together very well in an analysis by Miles and Ezzell (ME) [1980]. Making no assumptions with regard to either the time pattern or the duration of the unlevered cash flows, ME developed the relationship between the unlevered cost of capital and the weighted cost of capital. The relationship depends on maintaining a constant leverage ratio throughout the project life. This means that as the value of the firm changes as a consequence of the investments made, the amount of debt outstanding has to be readjusted to maintain the constant leverage ratio. When these conditions are met, we obtain Equation 21A.1:

$$k = k_U - rTL\left(\frac{1 + k_U}{1 + r}\right), \tag{21A.1}$$

where

$$r = k_b = \text{cost of debt.}$$

Thus, the original MM relationship is modified somewhat. Let us explore its characteristics. For a corporate tax rate equal to .4 and a leverage ratio of .5 as before, TL is again .2.

The expression then becomes

$$k = k_U - .2r\left(\frac{1 + k_U}{1 + r}\right).$$

In the previous example we had assumed k_U to be 15 percent. If the cost of debt were also 15 percent, then the last expression becomes 1 and the weighted cost of capital would again be 12 percent. This is a very special case, however. Normally we would expect the unlevered cost of equity capital to be somewhat higher than the cost of debt. If so, the ratio expression would be greater than 1. Continuing the previous example but with a cost of debt of 10 percent, we would have

$$k = k_U - .2(.1)\left(\frac{1.15}{1.10}\right)$$

$$= .1291.$$

In this case the weighted cost of capital would be somewhat higher than the weighted cost of capital under the infinite horizon case. On the other hand, if the cost of debt were greater than the unlevered cost of capital we would have

$$k = k_U - .2(.20)\left(\frac{1.15}{1.20}\right)$$

$$= .11167 \approx .112.$$

In this case the weighted cost of capital would be lower than the weighted cost of capital under the infinite horizon example. For finite project lives, the weighted cost of capital would be somewhat different from the result under the infinite horizon case. The advantage of the ME procedure is that the cash flow for each year of the finite life project would be discounted by the weighted cost of capital based on that year's data as calculated by the expression that ME have developed.

The MM Propositions with Depreciable Assets

Levy and Arditti (LA) [1973] presented an analysis which argued that MM propositions must be modified to recognize a reduction in the value of the firm when assets are depreciable. The issue of leverage is not involved, so we will focus on their unlevered firm case. In the basic LA equation for the unlevered firm, the firm's annual post-tax cash flows are

$$X^t = (1 - T)X + K - K, \tag{21A.2}$$

where $-K$ is the annual investment and $+K$ the depreciation charge, assumed to be equal in LA's model.

LA then state, "We claim that one cannot cancel the $+K$ and $-K$ terms and then apply the appropriate discount rates to the expected value of the resulting cash flow expression. The reason is that while the replacement outlay $(-K)$ is a certain amount, only a part of the

$+K$ term is certain."[1] They reformulate Equation 21A.2 as

$$X^t = (1 - T)C + TK - K, \tag{21A.3}$$

where C is the annual pretax flow before depreciation and interest.
They observe:

> Thus, X^t is separated into two distinct components: (a) an uncertain stream equal
> to $(1 - T)C$, and (b) a certain stream equal to . . . $TK - K$ in the unlevered
> case. . . . So TK is a certain stream and should be capitalized by the riskless rate
> r. The annual investment flow, $-K$, must also be treated as a certain amount,
> since our model requires the firm to invest an amount equal to its depreciation
> expense in order to assure perpetual asset lives. Hence $TK - K$ may be treated as
> a certain stream.[2]

Their resulting valuation relationship is

$$V_U = \frac{(1 - T)\overline{C}}{\rho^t} - \frac{(1 - T)K}{r}, \tag{21A.4}$$

where "C denotes the expected cash flow . . . and ρ^t denotes . . . the required rate of
return on a pure equity stream." They point out that their resulting valuation expression is
smaller than the MM values by

$$\frac{1}{r} - \frac{1}{\rho^t}(1 - T)K,$$

and that the MM valuation expressions must be correspondingly reduced for the case of
depreciable assets.

Paul [1975] commented that the LA results assume that their ρ^t is the same ρ^t used by
MM to discount the unlevered firm's EBIT. All of LA's modifications assume that the same
rate would be used to discount both the expected pretax operating cash flow $(\overline{C})$ and the
expected EBIT $(\overline{X})$. Paul demonstrates the basic LA assumption cannot be made, consistent with the underlying nature of the models under analysis. The example she presents is
reproduced in Table 21A.1.

Since the two firms have the same EBIT, they must have the same value. But if 10
percent is the applicable discount rate for Firm A, it has a value of $1,500. Using LA
Equation 3, reproduced as Equation 21A.4, not changing ρ^t and using a 5 percent riskless
rate gives a value of $1,050 for Firm B. This suggests that the discount rate for discounting
$\overline{C}$ is not the same discount rate applicable to $\overline{X}$. Paul then demonstrates this analytically,
using the symbol $\hat{\rho}^t$ (rho with a hat) to indicate the appropriate capitalization rate for $\overline{C}$.
For the firms to have the same value, it follows that

$$\frac{(1 - T)\overline{C}_b}{\hat{\rho}^t} = \frac{(1 - T)\overline{C}_a}{\rho^t} + \frac{(1 - T)K}{r}. \tag{21A.5}$$

---

[1]See Levy and Arditti [1973], p. 688.
[2]Ibid., pp. 688-689.

Table 21A.1   Comparisons of Two Firms with Equal EBIT

Distribution of Annual Flows for Firm A with No Depreciable Assets

P	C = Pretax Operating Cash Flow	K = Depreciation	X = EBIT	Y^a = Net Cash Flow
0.2	150	0	150	90
0.5	200	0	200	120
0.3	400	0	400	240
1.0	$\overline{C}$ = 250	K = 0	$\overline{X}$ = 250	$\overline{Y}$ = 150

Distribution of Annual Flows for Firm B with Depreciable Assets

P	C = Pretax Operating Cash Flow	K = Depreciation	X = EBIT	Y^a = Net Cash Flow
0.2	225	75	150	90
0.5	275	75	200	120
0.3	475	75	400	240
1.0	$\overline{C}$ = 325	K = 75	$\overline{X}$ = 250	$\overline{Y}$ = 150

$^a Y = [X(1 - T) + K] - K$, where the bracketed term represents after-tax operating cash flow and the $-K$ represents the capital outflow necessary to maintain the operating cash flow at its present level.
Source: R. S. Paul, "Comment," *Journal of Finance* 30 (March 1975), p. 212. Used by permission.

But C_a is the same as X_b with the same probability distributions, so with substitution we have the following relationship for any Firm B with depreciable assets:

$$\frac{(1 - T)\overline{C}_b}{\hat{\rho}^t} = \frac{(1 - T)\overline{X}_b}{\rho^t} + \frac{(1 - T)K}{r}. \qquad \textbf{(21A.6)}$$

When we solve Equation 21A.6 for the first term on the right-hand side, we have the following result:

$$V_U = \frac{(1 - T)\overline{X}_b}{\rho^t} = \frac{(1 - T)\overline{C}_b}{\hat{\rho}^t} - \frac{(1 - T)K}{r}. \qquad \textbf{(21A.7)}$$

The first equality is MM's original Proposition I. The second equality is LA's Equation 3 for depreciable assets, shown to be the same as MM's expression if $\hat{\rho}^t$ is changed appropriately. The basic point is that once $\overline{C}_b$ contains both the uncertain and certain cash flow stream components, it would be capitalized by a lower discount rate than $\overline{X}_b$, which contains only the uncertain cash flow streams. In their reply, LA acknowledged that $\hat{\rho}^t$ had to be 0.081 (below 0.10) for the equality to hold.[3] In so doing, they acknowledged the validity of the clarification presented by Paul. It appears that LA misinterpreted Paul's analysis since they concluded their reply to her as follows:

[3]See Levy and Arditti [1975].

"It appears that Paul believes that the discount rate (in her example, 10 percent) is independent of the probability distribution of returns. Why else would she apply the same discount rate of 10 percent to stream C_a as well as stream C_b?"[4]

But Paul did this only to emphasize that it resulted in unequal values for the two firms, which could not be the case, given the underlying facts and assumptions. In doing so, she established that $\hat{\rho}^t$ has to be lower than ρ^t. When this is recognized, MM's Proposition I applies as fully to the valuations of firms with depreciable assets as to firms with nondepreciable assets.

The Weighted Average Cost of Capital as a Cutoff Rate

Another criticism is that the application of the weighted average cost of capital as derived in the MM propositions is incorrectly specified as an investment hurdle rate or for deriving the value of the firm. The expression we developed from the MM materials and now generally referred to as the "traditional textbook theory" is

$$V_L = \frac{\overline{X}(1 - T)}{k_s(S/V) + (1 - T)r(B/V)}. \tag{21A.8}$$

Here we again use r for k_b. But in developing other relationships, MM also have

$$V = \frac{\overline{X}(1 - T)}{k_U} + TB = \frac{\overline{X}(1 - T)}{k_U} + \frac{TrB}{r}. \tag{21A.9}$$

Building on the Equation 21A.9 relationship, Arditti and Levy (AL) [1977] proposed that the true valuation formula is

$$V_L^* = \frac{(\overline{X} - rB)(1 - T) + rB}{k(S/V) + r(B/V)} = \frac{\overline{X}(1 - T) + rBT}{k^*}. \tag{21A.10}$$

In the AL expression, the capitalization factor uses the before-tax cost of debt rather than the after-tax cost of debt and adds the interest tax shelter to the cash flows in the numerator to be capitalized. We shall demonstrate that the AL formulation is actually the same as the "traditional textbook" formulation and that when appropriately applied to projects gives the same results.[5]

We shall develop a proof that

$$V_L^* = V_L.$$

[4]Ibid., p. 222.

[5]See similar demonstrations in the group of articles on the "Weighted Average Cost of Capital" in *Financial Management*, 8 (Summer 1979) by Boudreaux and Long; Ezzell and Porter; Ben-Horim, and Shapiro.

As before, let

$$L = B/V_L.$$

Then

$$k = rL(1 - T) + k_s(1 - L)$$
$$= rL - rLT + k_s(1 - L).$$

AL define k^* as

$$k^* = rL + k_s(1 - L).$$

Thus,

$$k^* = k + TrL$$
$$V_L^* = \frac{\overline{X}(1 - T) + rTLV_L^*}{k + rTL}. \tag{21A.11}$$

Multiply by the denominator of the right-hand side of Equation 21A.11:

$$V_L^*(k + rTL) = \overline{X}(1 - T) + rTLV_L^*$$
$$kV_L^* + rTLV_L^* = kV_L + rTLV_L^*. \tag{21A.12}$$

Cancel common terms on each side of Equation 21A.12:

$$V_L^* = V_L.$$

Therefore it has been established that the AL expression in Equation 21A.10 is identical to the MM formulation.

A numerical illustration can be provided from the example in Chapter 21 where:

$\overline{X} = \$200,000$
$T = 40\%$
$k_s = 12.8571\%$
$k_b = r = 10\%$
$B = \$500,000$
$S = \$700,000$
$V_L = B + S = \$1,200,000$
$k_U = 12\%$
$k = 10\%$

For k^* we would have

$$k^* = k + \frac{rBT}{V_L} = 0.10 + \frac{0.10(500,000)0.4}{1,200,000} = 0.10 + \frac{20,000}{1,200,000}$$
$$= 0.10 + 0.01667 = 0.11667 = 11.667\%.$$

Using the AL expression for V_L:

$$V_L^* = \frac{\overline{X}(1 - T) + rBT}{k^*} = \frac{120{,}000 + 0.10(500{,}000)0.4}{0.11667}$$

$$= \frac{120{,}000 + 20{,}000}{0.11667} = \frac{140{,}000}{0.11667} = \$1{,}200{,}000.$$

This is, of course, the same as the V_L we obtained before.

Project Evaluation

AL next evaluate a project with an investment cost, I, and an earnings annuity of Y in perpetuity. The standard NPV approach states:

$$\text{NPV} = \frac{\overline{Y}(1 - T)}{k} - I. \tag{21A.13}$$

AL state that the actual net present value is NPV^* defined as:

$$\text{NPV}^* = \frac{\overline{Y}(1 - T) + Tr(B/V)I}{k^*} - I. \tag{21A.14}$$

But this NPV^* formulation is inconsistent in shifting to a book (investment) basis for leverage, while the market value of the firm increases by $(I + \text{NPV}^*)$. To maintain a constant leverage ratio, the firm must increase debt by an amount equal to $(I + \text{NPV}^*)(B/V)$. When we make the necessary adjustment to the NPV^* formulations, we obtain Equation 21A.14a:

$$\text{NPV}^* = \frac{\overline{Y}(1 - T) + Tr(B/V)(I + \text{NPV}^*)}{k^*} - I. \tag{21A.14a}$$

Multiply through numerator:

$$\text{NPV}^* = \frac{\overline{Y}(1 - T)}{k^*} + \frac{rT(B/V)I}{k^*} + \frac{rT(B/V)(\text{NPV}^*)}{k^*} - I.$$

Move NPV^* term to left side of equation and factor out NPV^*.

$$\text{NPV}^*\left(1 - \frac{rTB}{k^*V}\right) = \frac{\overline{Y}(1 - T) + rT(B/V)I}{k^*} - I.$$

Multiply both sides by k^*.

$$NPV^*\left(k^* - \frac{rTB}{V}\right) = \overline{Y}(1 - T) + rT(B/V)I - k^*I.$$

But the last two terms in the above equation are equal to kI, since $[k^* - rT(B/V)] = k$. Then we have

$$kNPV^* = \overline{Y}(1 - T) - kI.$$

Next divide by k to obtain:

$$NPV^* = \frac{\overline{Y}(1 - T)}{k} - I = NPV.$$

Thus, when the target leverage ratio is maintained by applying it to the increase in the market value of the firm, instead of to the book value of the new investment, NPV^* is equal to the traditional NPV.

We can continue our previous numerical example to illustrate the formal proof. Let I be $10,000 and $\overline{Y} = \$2,500$. Using the traditional measure of NPV, we have

$$NPV = \frac{\$2,500(0.6)}{0.10} - \$10,000 = \frac{1,500}{0.10} - \$10,000 = \$5,000.$$

The same data can be applied to the NPV^* formulation as corrected in Equation 21A.14a. The value of NPV^* that satisfies the corrected equation is $5,000:

$$NPV^* = \frac{\$1,500 + 0.4(0.10)(5/12)(15,000)}{0.116667} - \$10,000$$

$$= \$12,857 + \frac{5/12(600)}{0.116667} - \$10,000$$

$$= \$12,857 + \frac{250}{0.116667} - \$10,000$$

$$= \$5,000 = NPV.$$

Again, the proposed reformulation actually reinforces the MM relationships when used in a manner consistent with the underlying theory.

Selected References

Arditti, F. D., and Levy, H., "The Weighted Average Cost of Capital as a Cutoff Rate: A Critical Analysis of the Classical Textbook Weighted Average," *Financial Management*, 6 (Fall 1977), pp. 24-34.

Boudreaux, K. J., et al., "The Weighted Average Cost of Capital: A Discussion," *Financial Management*, 8 (Summer 1979), pp. 7-14.

Hite, Gailen L., "Leverage, Output Effects, and the M-M Theorems," *Journal of Financial Economics*, 4 (March 1977), pp. 177-202.

Levy, H., and Arditti, F. D., "Valuation, Leverage,

and the Cost of Capital in the Case of Depreciable Assets," *Journal of Finance*, 28 (June 1973), pp. 687-693.

———, "Reply," *Journal of Finance*, 30 (March 1975), pp. 221-223.

Martin, John D.; Scott, David F., Jr.; and Vandell, Robert F., "Equivalent Risk Classes: A Multidimensional Examination," *Journal of Financial and Quantitative Analysis*, 14 (March 1979), pp. 101-118.

Miles, J. A., and Ezzell, J. R., "The Weighted Average Cost of Capital, Perfect Capital Markets, and Project Life: A Clarification," *Journal of Financial and Quantitative Analysis*, 15 (September 1980), pp. 719-729.

Miller, Merton H., "Debt and Taxes," *Journal of Finance*, 32 (May 1977), pp. 261-275.

Miller, Merton H., and Modigliani, Franco, "Cost of Capital to Electric Utility Industry," *American Economic Review*, 56 (June 1966), pp. 333-391.

Modigliani, Franco, and Miller, Merton H., "The Cost of Capital, Corporation Finance and the Theory of Investment," *American Economic Review*, 48 (June 1958), pp. 261-297.

————, "Taxes and the Cost of Capital: A Correction," *American Economic Review*, 53 (June 1963), pp. 433-443.

Paul, R. S., "Comment," *Journal of Finance*, 30 (March 1975), pp. 211-213.

Stiglitz, Joseph E., "A Re-examination of the Modigliani-Miller Theorem," *American Economic Review*, 59 (December 1969), pp. 784-793.

Appendix B to Chapter 21
The State-Preference Model[1]

Three important recent developments in finance are the Capital Asset Pricing Model (CAPM), the State-Preference Model (SPM), and the Option Pricing Model (OPM). The Capital Asset Pricing Model is presented in Chapter 17. The Option Pricing Model is set forth in Chapter 18. In this appendix we describe the State-Preference Model to conclude the discussion of financial leverage.

Alternative Future States-of-the-World

The State-Preference Model provides a useful way of looking at the world and the nature of securities. One way of describing uncertainty about the future is to say that one of a set of possible states-of-the-world will occur. Definition of a set of states provides a means of describing characteristics of securities, since any security can be regarded as a contract to pay an amount that depends on the state that actually occurs.

For example, the decision to invest in the securities of a machinery manufacturer or the decision of a machinery manufacturer to issue securities under a favorable set of conditions will depend on the potential future states of the economy. Will the economy be sufficiently strong that the demand for capital goods will provide favorable demand factors for a machinery manufacturer? Similarly, in the production plans of an automobile manufacturer, or in an investor's decision to buy securities of an automobile company, will the future state of the economy be sufficiently strong to stimulate consumer optimism, resulting in a high volume of automobile purchases? Some of the main factors influencing the future states-of-the-world that will influence the sales of a firm or the prospects for investments in a firm are set forth in Table 21B.1.

As a practical matter, a person will explicitly consider only a small number of factors in making a decision. Hence individual decision makers are likely to select those variables judged to be most critical for influencing the payoff possibilities of securities in which a position or investment is contemplated. For practical reasons, therefore, alternative future states-of-the-world might be summarized into forecasts of alternative levels or rates of growth in the gross national product. Ultimately, a wide variety of the factors listed in Table 21B.1 are likely to be reflected in levels of gross national product. Furthermore, the rate of growth and the performance of most individual industries in the economy are greatly influenced by movements in gross national product. Thus, alternative future states-of-the-world may be characterized in terms of four possibilities with respect to gross national product: a strong rate of growth, a moderate rate of growth, a moderate decline, or a substantial decline.

---

[1]This section was written with the valuable counsel of Professor Harry DeAngelo.

Table 21B.1   Central Factors Influencing Estimates of Future States-of-the-World
for Use in Forecasting the Sales of the Firm

    A. Economy
       1. Growth rate of GNP — real terms
       2. Growth rate of GNP — inflation
       3. Growth rate of monetary base (availability)
       4. Long-term interest rates
       5. Short-term interest rates

    B. Competition
       1. Prices of rival products
       2. New products by rivals
       3. Changes in products by rivals
       4. New advertising campaigns by rivals
       5. Salesperson and other selling efforts by rivals
       6. Prices of industry-substitute products
       7. Quality of industry-substitute products

    C. Cultural and political factors
       1. Externalities and their influences on sales of our products
       2. Product liabilities

While for practical problems we might limit the number of alternative future states-of-the-world, from another standpoint — that of personal portfolio construction — we would like to provide for all possible future states-of-the-world. If we could always find a security that provided some payoff under one of the many possible future states-of-the-world, we could hedge by combining a large number of securities so that regardless of the future state-of-the-world that occurs, we would receive some payoff. The securities we encounter in the real world are complex securities in the sense that their payoffs are generally different under alternative states-of-the-world. If we could obtain some payoff for every possible future state-of-the-world by appropriately combining long and short positions in actual complex securities, we could create a pure, or primitive, security.

The Concept of a Pure Security

A pure, or primitive, security is one that pays off $1 if one particular future state-of-the-world occurs and pays off nothing if any other state-of-the-world occurs. This seems like an abstract concept, so let us develop the idea further by means of an example. We shall take the case of the Mistinback Company, which sells baskets of fruit. This particular company limits its sales to only two types of baskets. Basket 1 is composed of 10 bananas and 20 apples and sells for $8. Basket 2 is composed of 30 bananas and 10 apples and sells for $9. The question is posed: What is the price of one banana or one apple only? The situation may be summarized by the payoffs set forth in Table 21B.2.
To calculate the value of a banana or an apple, we set up two equations:

$$10\ V_b + 20\ V_a = \$8.$$

$$30\ V_b + 10\ V_a = \$9.$$

Table 21B.2   Payoffs in Relation to Prices of Baskets of Fruit

	Bananas	Apples	Prices
Basket #1	10	20	$8
Basket #2	30	10	$9

Solving simultaneously, we obtain:

$$V_a = \$.30.$$

$$V_b = \$.20.$$

We may now apply this same analysis to securities. Any individual security is similar to a mixed basket of goods with regard to alternative future states-of-the-world. Recall that a pure security is a security that pays $1 if a specified state occurs and nothing if any other state occurs.[2]

We can determine the price of a pure security in a manner analogous to that used for the fruit baskets. Consider Security j, which pays $10 if State 1 occurs and $20 if State 2 occurs. The current price of Security j is $8. Security k pays $30 if State 1 occurs and $10 if State 2 occurs. Its current price is $9. Note that State 1 might be a GNP growth during the year of 8 percent in real terms, while State 2 might represent a growth in real national product of only 1 percent. In Table 21B.3 the payoff for the two securities is set forth. Here, F_{j1} is the payoff in State 1 to Security j, F_{k1} is the payoff in State 1 to Security k, and so on. The equations for determining the prices for the two pure securities related to the situation described are

$$p_1 F_{j1} + p_2 F_{j2} = p_j.$$

$$p_1 F_{k1} + p_2 F_{k2} = p_k.$$

Table 21B.3   Payoff Table for Securities 1 and 2

	State 1	State 2	
Security j	$F_{j1} = \$10$	$F_{j2} = \$20$	$p_j = \$8$
Security k	$F_{k1} = \$30$	$F_{k2} = \$10$	$p_k = \$9$

---

[2]Observe that this is a clear form of nondiversification. It represents putting all of one's financial resources into one state-basket.

Proceeding analogously to the situation for the fruit baskets, we insert the value of security payoffs into the two equations to obtain the price of Pure Security 1 as $.20 and the price of Pure Security 2 as $.30.

$$10p_1 + 20p_2 = \$8$$

$$30p_1 + 10p_2 = \$9$$

$$p_1 = \$.20$$

$$p_2 = \$.30.$$

It should be emphasized that the p_1 of $.20 and the p_2 of $.30 are not assigned to Securities j and k.

In sum, Securities j and k represent bundles of returns under alternative future states. Any actual security provides different payoffs for different future states. But under appropriately defined conditions, the prices of pure securities can be determined from the prices of actual securities. The concept of a pure security is useful for analytical purposes as well as for providing a useful point of view in financial analysis as illustrated in the following section, which provides an application of the State-Preference Model to leverage decisions.

Use of the SPM to Determine the Optimal Financial Leverage

The State-Preference Model has been used to analyze the question of optimal financial leverage.[3] The ideas will be conveyed by a specific example. It is assumed that there are four possible states-of-the-world and that the capital markets are complete in that there exists at least one security for every possible state-of-the-world such that there is a full set of primitive securities. The symbols that will be utilized are listed in Table 21B.4, and the data that will be analyzed in this example are summarized in Table 21B.5.

In Table 21B.5 we have ordered the states by the size of the EBIT that the firm will achieve under alternative states. Column (3) of the table lists the prices of primitive securi-

---

Table 21B.4   Symbols Used in the SPM Analysis of Optimal Financial Leverage

p_s = Market price of the primitive security that represents a claim on one dollar in State s and zero dollars in all other states

X_s = Earnings before interest and taxes that the firm will achieve in State s (EBIT)

B = Nominal payment to debt, representing a promise to pay Fixed Amount B, irrespective of the state that occurs

$S(B)$ = Market value of the firm's equity as a function of the amount of debt issued by the firm

$V(B)$ = Market value of the firm as a function of the amount of debt issued

f_s = Costs of failure in State s; $0 < f_s \leq X_s$

T = Corporate tax rate = 50%

---

[3]See Kraus and Litzenberger [1973].

Table 21B.5   Data for SPM Analysis of Optimal Financial Leverage

s	X_s	p_s	f_s
(1)	(2)	(3)	(4)
1	$ 100	$0.30	$ 100
2	500	0.50	400
3	1,000	0.20	500
4	2,000	0.10	1,200

---

ties for each of the four states. In Column (4) we list the failure or bankruptcy costs associated with the inability to meet debt obligations.

In this state-preference framework, let us analyze the position of debtholders and equity holders. Table 21B.6 analyzes the amounts received under alternative conditions. Under Condition 1 the EBIT is equal to or exceeds the debt obligation. Under that condition, debtholders will receive B and equity holders will receive the income remaining after deduction of B and of taxes. Under Condition 2, the EBIT is positive but less than the amount of the debt obligation, B. The debtholders will receive whatever EBIT remains after payment of the failure or bankruptcy costs. Equity holders will receive nothing. If the EBIT is negative, neither the debtholders nor equity holders receive anything. These relationships are quite logical and straightforward.

The amounts received under alternative conditions as outlined in Table 21B.7 are multiplied by the prices of the primitive securities to obtain the value of debtholders' receipts and of equity holders' receipts as well as the value of the firm under alternative conditions. The value of debtholders' receipts is obtained by simply multiplying what the debtholders receive by p_s and similarly for the value of equity holders' receipts. The value of the firm is obtained by adding the value of the debtholders' receipts to the value of the equity holders' receipts.

In Table 21B.8 we utilize the preceding information to calculate the value of the firm under alternative debt levels. On the left-hand side of the table we begin by specifying the amount of debt and the resulting relationships between X_s, the EBIT under alternative states, and the promised debt payment. The subsequent lines on the left then set forth the applicable formulas for calculating the state contingent value of the firm depending upon the level of debt utilized. For example, when the firm is unlevered, its value is equal to

---

Table 21B.6   Amounts Received under Alternative Conditions

Condition	Amount of X_s in Relation to B (1)	Debtholders Receive (2)	Equity Holders Receive (3)
1	$X_s \geq B$	B	$(X_s - B)(1 - T)$
2	$0 \leq X_s < B$	$(X_s - f_s)$	0
3	$X_s < 0$	0	0

Table 21B.7   Formulas for the Value of the Firm under Alternative Conditions

Condition	Amount of X_s in Relation to B (1)	Debt-holders Receive (2)	Value of Debtholders' Receipts in State s (3)	Equity Holders Receive (4)	Value of Equity Holders' Receipts in State s (5)	Value of the Firm in State s (6)
1	$X_s \geq B$	B	Bp_s	$(X_s - B)(1 - T)$	$(X_s - B)(1 - T)p_s$	$Bp_s + (X_s - B)(1 - T)p_s$
2	$0 \leq X_s < B$	$(X_s - f_s)$	$(X_s - f_s)p_s$	0	0	$(X_s - f_s)p_s$
3	$X_s < 0$	0	0	0	0	0

EBIT times (1 minus the tax rate) times the price of the primitive security for each state summed over all the states. Using the illustrative data from Table 21B.5, we obtain the amounts on the right-hand column of Table 21B.8.

When debt is 100, EBIT is equal to or greater than debt for all states-of-the-world. The formula employed, therefore, is set forth in Table 21B.7 under Condition 1 and shown in Column (6). Again, the numbers from Table 21B.5 are inserted to obtain a current market value of the firm, V(100), of $395 for Debt Level 2 in Table 21B.8.

We shall discuss the pattern for debt of $1,000 as illustrative of the remaining sections of Table 21B.8. When B is equal to $1,000 the EBIT is less than the promised debt payment for States 1 and 2 and equal to or greater than debt for States 3 and 4. As Table 21B.7 indicates, Condition 2, therefore, obtains for States 1 and 2, while Condition 1 obtains for States 3 and 4. The applicable formulas are therefore utilized to obtain a V(1,000) of $400, as shown in Table 21B.8.

An analysis of Table 21B.8 shows that the highest value of the firm is obtained when debt leverage of $500 is employed by the firm. For any other level of debt obligations the value of the firm is lower. This example illustrates that with taxes and bankruptcy costs, there exists an optimal amount of leverage.[4]

Implications for Leverage Decisions

Our use of the State-Preference Model has enabled us to analyze some conditions under which an optimal capital leverage exists.[5] This result is, of course, not perfectly general since it was based on a specific illustration. Some more general relationships will now be set forth. First, we need to introduce the concept of complete capital markets. *Complete capital markets* are those in which a security exists for every possible state-of-the-world, so that it is possible to create a full set of primitive securities. In complete capital markets, in the absence of such imperfections as taxes, agency costs, and bankruptcy costs, capital structure would not matter (the Modigliani-Miller propositions would obtain).

[4]Kraus and Litzenberger conclude with regard to their analysis as follows: "Contrary to the traditional net income approach to valuation, if the firm's debt obligation exceeds its earnings in some states the firm's market value is not necessarily a concave (from below) function of its debt obligation." Ibid., p. 918. However, this result follows only from their formulation of the problem in discontinuous terms. The problem could equally well be formulated with continuous functions in such a way that the resulting value of the firm would be a continuous and concave (from below) function of B.

[5]Problems 21B.4 and 21B.5 illustrate that the production decisions and capital structure decisions of the firm can be interdependent, given the presence of imperfections.

Table 21B.8   Calculations of the Value of the Firm under Alternative Debt Levels

---

Condition	State	Value of Firm's State s Payoff
1. $B = 0, X_s > B$ for all s $V_s(0) = \sum_{s=1}^{4} X_s(1 - T)p_s$	1 2 3 4	$100(0.5)0.3 = \quad 15$ $500(0.5)0.5 = \quad 125$ $1,000(0.5)0.2 = \quad 100$ $2,000(0.5)0.1 = \quad 100$ $V(0) = \$340$
2. $\quad B = 100, X_s \geq B$ for all s $V_s(100) = \sum_{s=1}^{4} Bp_s + \sum_{s=1}^{4}(X_s - B)(1 - T)p_s$	1 2 3 4	$100(0.3) + (100 - 100)(0.5)0.3 = \quad 30$ $100(0.5) + (500 - 100)(0.5)0.5 = \quad 150$ $100(0.2) + (1,000 - 100)(0.5)0.2 = \quad 110$ $100(0.1) + (2,000 - 100)(0.5)0.1 = \quad 105$ $V(100) = \$395$
3. $\quad B = 500, X_s < B$ for $s = 1$ $\quad\quad X_s \geq B$ for $s = 2, 3, 4$ $V_s(500) = (X_s - f_s)p_s$ for $s = 1$ $V_s(500) = \sum_{s=2}^{4} Bp_s + \sum_{s=2}^{4}(X_s - B)(1 - T)p_s$	1 2 3 4	$(100 - 100)0.3 = \quad 0$ $500(0.5) + (500 - 500)(0.5)0.5 = \quad 250$ $500(0.2) + (1,000 - 500)(0.5)0.2 = \quad 150$ $500(0.1) + (2,000 - 500)(0.5)0.1 = \quad 125$ $V(500) = \$525$
4. $\quad B = 1,000, X_s < B$ for $s = 1, 2$ $\quad\quad X_s \geq B$ for $s = 3, 4$ $V_s(1,000) = \sum_{s=1}^{2}(X_s - f_s)p_s$ $V_s(1,000) = \sum_{s=3}^{4} Bp_s + \sum_{s=3}^{4}(X_s - B)(1 - T)p_s$	1 2 3 4	$(100 - 100)0.3 = \quad 0$ $(500 - 400)0.5 = \quad 50$ $1,000(0.2) + (1,000 - 1,000)(0.5)0.2 = \quad 200$ $1,000(0.1) + (2,000 - 1,000)(0.5)0.1 = \quad 150$ $V(1,000) = \$400$
5. $\quad B = 2,000, X_s < B$ for $s = 1, 2, 3$ $\quad\quad X_s \geq B$ for $s = 4$ $V_s(2,000) = \sum_{s=1}^{3}(X_s - f_s)p_s$ $V_s(2,000) = Bp_s + (X_s - B)(1 - T)p_s$ for $s = 4$	1 2 3 4	$(100 - 100)0.3 = \quad 0$ $(500 - 400)0.5 = \quad 50$ $(1,000 - 500)0.2 = \quad 100$ $2,000(0.1) + (2,000 - 2,000)(0.5)0.1 = \quad 200$ $V(2,000) = \$350$

The leverage policy of a firm consists of repackaging the claims on its EBIT. The only reason why repackaging of claims on the firm's EBIT would have an effect on the value of the firm would be that the firm had thereby provided investors with a new set of market opportunities for forming portfolios or taking a position with regard to future states-of-the-world. But if the capital markets are already complete, the firm has added nothing by a repackaging of claims on EBIT since no new independent investment opportunities can be provided. All possible future states-of-the-world have already been covered by existing securities.

The proof of the Modigliani-Miller independence thesis does not depend on the assumption that the firm will always meet its debt obligations. For some debt levels the firm may not meet its debt obligations in some states-of-the-world and would be bankrupt. If there are no bankruptcy penalties or bankruptcy costs (the situation in a perfect market), the *nature* of the claims on the firm's EBIT have been fundamentally unaltered. Thus, the value of the firm remains unchanged.

Thus, complete and perfect capital markets constitute sufficient conditions for the Modigliani-Miller propositions to hold. But as the foregoing example illustrated, the taxation of corporate profits and the existence of bankruptcy-agency penalties represent market imperfections under which the capital structure choice will affect the value of the firm. We conclude that Modigliani and Miller are correct under properly specified conditions.

Furthermore, it is the absence of complete and perfect capital markets that makes capital structure matter. It is not clear whether the actual number of securities approximates the condition of completeness of the capital markets. However, without question there are corporate income taxes as well as agency and bankruptcy costs. The extent to which agency and bankruptcy costs significantly affect capital structure is an empirical matter.

Problems

21B.1 Security A pays $30 if State 1 occurs and $10 if State 2 occurs. Security B pays $20 if State 1 occurs and $40 if State 2 occurs. The price of Security A is $5 and the price of Security B is $10.
    a)   Set up the payoff table for Securities A and B.
    b)   Determine the prices of pure Securities 1 and 2.

21B.2 The common stock of GM will pay $70 if State 1 occurs, in which the U.S. economy is in an upswing and GM's production volume of small cars causes the volume of imports to decline. In State 2, the U.S. economy experiences stagflation, with real growth at 1 percent per year and inflation near the two-digit rate. In State 2, the common stock of GM pays $35. In State 2, Control Data pays $68. In State 1, Control Data pays $55. The current price of GM is $53, and the current price of Control Data is $60.
    a)   Set up the payoff tables for GM and Control Data.
    b)   Determine the prices of the two pure securities.

21B.3 The Sand Corporation is evaluating alternatives for financing its production. There are essentially three possible levels of production, depending on which state-of-the-world occurs. Costs of failure and earnings before interest and taxes are different for each state. The company is considering use of debt in the amount of $0, $1,000, $3,000, or $6,000 and would like to know which alternative will maximize the expected value of the firm, given the primitive security prices associated with each state. The tax rate is 40 percent.

State (s)	Planned Production EBIT (X_s)	Price of Primitive Security (p_s)	Cost of Failure (f_s)
1	2,000	0.30	500
2	4,000	0.50	1,500
3	8,000	0.20	4,000

21B.4 The Kendrick Company is evaluating three alternative production plans (X_s, Y_s, and Z_s), as follows. Cost of failure is the same for each plan. Prices of primitive securities for the four possible states are as indicated.

State (s)	Price of Primitive Security (p_s)	Cost of Failure (f_s)	Planned Production EBIT		
			(X_s)	(Y_s)	(Z_s)
1	0.10	100	200	600	100
2	0.40	600	1,200	1,500	800
3	0.30	1,500	3,000	2,800	3,200
4	0.20	2,000	3,500	3,000	3,800

Assuming the production will be financed with funds including $3,000 of debt, which of the three production plans would maximize the value of the firm? The tax rate is 40 percent.

21B.5 Under production Plan A, the EBIT of the firm for alternative states-of-the-world is indicated by the X_s column. The price of the primitive pure securities in State s is p_s. The failure or bankruptcy costs are f_s. Under production Plan B, the EBIT of the firm is indicated by X'_s. Production Plan B involves giving up $300 in State 3 to add $300 in State 2. Since the prices of pure securities and bankruptcy costs are given by the market, they remain unchanged under production Plan B. The tax rate is 40 percent.

s	X_s	p_s	f_s	X'_s
1	$ 500	0.20	100	$ 500
2	600	0.40	300	900
3	1,400	0.30	500	1,100
4	2,000	0.10	800	2,000

a) What is the optimal financial leverage for production Plan A by the criterion of maximizing the value of the firm? Calculate the value for debt levels of $0, $500, $600, $1,400, and $2,000.

b) Is the optimal financial leverage changed by new production Plan B? Answer for debt levels of $0, $500, $900, $1,100, and $2,000.

c) What implications do the results under Plans A and B have for the interdependence between production plans and financial structure?

Selected References

Arrow, K. J., "The Role of Securities in the Optimal Allocation of Risk-Bearing," *Review of Economic Studies*, 31 (April 1964), pp. 91-96.

Dyl, Edward A., "A State Preference Model of Capital Gains Taxation," *Journal of Financial and Quantitative Analysis*, 14 (September 1979), pp. 529-535.

Hirshleifer, J., "Investment Decisions under Uncertainty: Application of the State-Preference Approach," *Quarterly Journal of Economics*, 80 (May 1966), pp. 262-277.

Kraus, Alan, and Litzenberger, Robert, "A State-Preference Model of Optimal Financial Leverage," *Journal of Finance*, 28 (September 1973), pp. 911-922.

Chapter 22 Dividend Policy

Dividend policy determines the division of earnings between payments to stockholders and reinvestment in the firm. Retained earnings are one of the most significant sources of funds for financing corporate growth, but dividends constitute the cash flows that accrue to stockholders. This chapter analyzes the factors that influence the allocation of earnings to dividends or retained earnings. It also discusses the relationship between dividend payouts and share prices.

Dividend Payments

Dividends are normally paid quarterly. For example, suppose Liggett Group pays annual dividends of $2.50. In financial parlance we say that Liggett Group's regular quarterly dividend is 62.5 cents, or that its regular annual dividend is $2.50. The management of a company such as Liggett Group conveys to stockholders, sometimes by an explicit statement in the annual report and sometimes by implication, an expectation that the regular dividend will be maintained if at all possible. Furthermore, management conveys its belief that earnings will be sufficient to maintain the dividend.

Many variables influence dividends, however. For example, a firm's cash flows and investment needs may be too volatile for it to set a very high regular dividend. Yet, it may desire a high dividend payout to distribute funds not necessary for reinvestment. In such a case, the directors can set a relatively low regular dividend — low enough that it can be maintained even in low profit years or in years when a considerable amount of reinvestment is needed — and supplement it with an extra dividend in years when excess funds are available. General Motors, whose earnings fluctuate widely from year to year, has long followed the practice of supplementing its regular dividend with an extra dividend paid in addition to the regular fourth quarter dividend.

Payment Procedure

The actual payment procedure is of some importance, and the following is an outline of the payment sequence.

1. *Declaration date*. The directors meet, say, on November 15 and declare the regular dividend. On this date, they issue a statement similar to the following: "On November 15, 19X0, the directors of the XYZ Company met and declared the regular quarterly dividend of 50 cents a share, plus an extra dividend of 75 cents a share, to holders of record on December 15, payment to be made on January 2, 19X1."
2. *Holder-of-record date*. On December 15, the *holder-of-record date*, the company closes its stock transfer books and makes up a list of the shareholders as of that date. If XYZ Company is notified of the sale and transfer of some stock before December 16, the

new owner receives the dividend. If notification is received on or after December 16, the old stockholder gets the dividend.

3.   *Ex-dividend date.* Suppose Irma Jones buys 100 shares of stock from Robert Noble on December 13. Will the company be notified of the transfer in time to list her as new owner and pay her the dividend? To avoid conflict, the brokerage business has set up a convention of declaring that the right to the dividend remains with the stock until four days prior to the holder-of-record date; on the fourth day before the record date, the right to the dividend no longer goes with the shares. The date when the right to the dividend leaves the stock is called the *ex-dividend date*. In this case, the ex-dividend date is four days prior to December 15, or December 11. Therefore, if Jones is to receive the dividend, she must buy the stock by December 10. If she buys it on December 11 or later, Noble will receive the dividend. The total dividend, regular plus extra, amounts to $1.25, so the ex-dividend date is important. Barring fluctuations in the stock market, we would normally expect the price of a stock to drop by approximately the amount of the dividend on the ex-dividend date.

4.   *Payment date.* The company actually mails the checks to the holders of record on January 2, the payment date.

Factors Influencing Dividend Policy

What factors determine the extent to which a firm will pay out dividends instead of retaining earnings? As a first step toward answering this question, we shall consider some of the factors that influence dividend policy.

Legal Rules

Although some statutes and court decisions governing dividend policy are complicated, their essential nature can be stated briefly. The legal rules provide that dividends must be paid from earnings — either from the current year's earnings or from past years' earnings as reflected in the balance sheet account "retained earnings."

State laws emphasize three rules: (1) the net profits rule, (2) the capital impairment rule, and (3) the insolvency rule. The *net profits rule* provides that dividends can be paid from past and present earnings. The *capital impairment rule* protects creditors by forbidding the payment of dividends from capital. (Paying dividends from capital would be distributing the investment in a company rather than earnings.)[1] The *insolvency rule* provides that corporations cannot pay dividends while insolvent. (*Insolvency* is defined here, in the bankruptcy sense, as liabilities exceeding assets. To pay dividends under such conditions would mean giving stockholders funds that rightfully belong to creditors.)

Legal rules are significant in that they provide the framework within which dividend policies can be formulated. Within their boundaries, however, financial and economic factors have a major influence on policy.

---

[1]It is possible, of course, to return stockholders' capital; when this is done, however, the procedure must be clearly stated as such. A dividend paid out of capital is called a *liquidating* dividend.

Liquidity Position

Profits held as retained earnings (which show up on the right-hand side of the balance sheet) are generally invested in assets required for the conduct of the business. Retained earnings from preceding years are already invested in plant and equipment, inventories, and other assets; they are not held as cash. Thus, even if a firm has a record of earnings, it may not be able to pay cash dividends because of its liquidity position. Indeed, a growing firm, even a very profitable one, typically has a pressing need for funds. In such a situation the firm may elect not to pay cash dividends.

Need to Repay Debt

When a firm has sold debt to finance expansion or to substitute for other forms of financing, it is faced with two alternatives. It can refund the debt at maturity by replacing it with another form of security, or it can make provisions for paying off the debt. If the decision is to retire the debt, this will generally require the retention of earnings.

Restrictions in Debt Contracts

Debt contracts, particularly when long-term debt is involved, frequently restrict a firm's ability to pay cash dividends. Such restrictions, which are designed to protect the position of the lender, usually state that (1) future dividends can be paid only out of earnings generated *after* the signing of the loan agreement (that is, they cannot be paid out of past retained earnings) and (2) that dividends cannot be paid when net working capital (current assets minus current liabilities) is below a specified amount. Similarly, preferred stock agreements generally state that no cash dividends can be paid on the common stock until all accrued preferred dividends have been paid.

Rate of Asset Expansion

The more rapidly a firm is growing, the greater its needs for financing asset expansion. The greater the future need for funds, the more likely the firm is to retain earnings rather than pay them out. If a firm seeks to raise funds externally, natural sources are the present shareholders, who already know the company. But if earnings are paid out as dividends and are subjected to high personal income tax rates, only a portion of them will be available for reinvestment.

Profit Rate

The expected rate of return on assets determines the relative attractiveness of paying out earnings in the form of dividends to stockholders (who will use them elsewhere) or using them in the present enterprise.

Stability of Earnings

A firm that has relatively stable earnings is often able to predict approximately what its future earnings will be. Such a firm is therefore more likely to pay out a higher percentage of its earnings than is a firm with fluctuating earnings. The unstable firm is not certain that in subsequent years the hoped-for earnings will be realized, so it is likely to retain a high proportion of current earnings. A lower dividend will be easier to maintain if earnings fall off in the future.

Access to the Capital Markets

A large, well-established firm with a record of profitability and stability of earnings has easy access to capital markets and other forms of external financing. A small, new, or venturesome firm, however, is riskier for potential investors. Its ability to raise equity or debt funds from capital markets is restricted, and it must retain more earnings to finance its operations. A well-established firm is thus likely to have a higher dividend payout rate than is a new or small firm.

Control

Another important variable is the effect of alternative sources of financing on the control situation in the firm. As a matter of policy, some corporations expand only to the extent of their internal earnings. This policy is defended on the ground that raising funds by selling additional common stock dilutes the control of the dominant group in that company. At the same time, selling debt increases the risks of fluctuating earnings to the present owners of the company. Reliance on internal financing in order to maintain control reduces the dividend payout.

Tax Position of Stockholders

The tax position of a corporation's owners greatly influences the desire for dividends. For example, a corporation closely held by a few taxpayers in high income tax brackets is likely to pay a relatively low dividend. The owners prefer taking their income in the form of capital gains rather than as dividends, which are subject to higher personal income tax rates. However, the stockholders of a large, widely held corporation might prefer a high dividend payout.

At times there is a conflict of interest in large corporations between stockholders in high income tax brackets and those in low tax brackets. The former may prefer to see a low dividend payout and a high rate of earnings retention in the hope of an appreciation in the capital stock of the company. The latter may prefer a relatively high dividend payout. The dividend policy in such firms may be a compromise between a low and a high payout—an intermediate payout ratio. If one group comes to dominate the company and sets, say, a low payout policy, those stockholders who seek income are likely to sell their shares over time and shift into higher-yielding stocks. Thus, to at least some extent, a firm's payout policy determines the type of stockholders it has—and vice versa. This has been called the "clientele influence" on dividend policy.

Tax on Improperly Accumulated Earnings

To prevent wealthy stockholders from using the corporation as an "incorporated pocketbook" by which they can avoid high personal income tax rates, tax regulations applicable to corporations provide for a special surtax on improperly accumulated income. However,

Section 531 of the Revenue Act of 1954 places the burden of proof on the Internal Revenue Service to justify penalty rates for accumulation of earnings. That is, earnings retention is justified unless the IRS can prove otherwise.

General Dividend Patterns in the Economy

Table 22.1 presents after-tax profits, dividends, and dividend payouts for the postwar years 1946 to 1983. Payouts for selected time periods are also calculated. From 1947 to 1955, the postwar adjustment and the time of the Korean conflict, the payout was about 50 percent. It declined slightly to a 45 percent rate during the 1955 to 1966 period of price stability. During the first part of the inflationary period that started in 1966, the dividend payout averaged 47 percent. However, during the period of continued inflation and the rise in oil prices from 1973 on, the dividend payout has risen, to 58 percent for the period 1980 to 1983.

Table 22.1   Dividend Payout Patterns, 1946-1983 (Billions of Dollars)

Year	After-Tax Profits	Dividends	Dividend Payout	Year	After-Tax Profits	Dividends	Dividend Payout
1946	$ 7.5	$ 5.6	0.75	1965	49.1	19.1	0.39
1947	11.0	6.3	0.57	1966	51.4	19.4	0.38
1948	17.0	7.0	0.41	1967	49.9	20.2	0.40
1949	16.9	7.2	0.43	1968	50.0	22.0	0.44
1950	16.0	8.8	0.55	1969	45.6	22.5	0.49
1951	16.1	8.5	0.53	1970	37.2	22.5	0.60
1952	16.7	8.5	0.51	1971	45.7	22.9	0.50
1953	16.0	8.8	0.55	1972	55.0	24.4	0.44
1954	17.5	9.1	0.52	1973	59.3	27.0	0.46
1955	23.4	10.3	0.44	1974	43.3	29.9	0.69
1956	21.8	11.1	0.51	1975	59.9	30.8	0.51
1957	21.8	11.5	0.53	1976	74.3	37.4	0.50
1958	19.5	11.3	0.58	1977	94.6	40.8	0.43
1959	26.0	12.2	0.47	1978	109.1	47.0	0.43
1960	24.9	12.9	0.52	1979	107.2	52.7	0.49
1961	25.8	13.3	0.52	1980	90.6	58.6	0.65
1962	32.6	14.4	0.44	1981	109.5	64.7	0.59
1963	35.9	15.5	0.43	1982	105.6	68.7	0.65
1964	41.2	17.3	0.42	1983	150.6	73.3	0.49

	Dividend Payout		
1947-1955	150.6	74.5	0.49
1956-1966	350.0	158.0	0.45
1967-1972	283.4	134.5	0.47
1973-1979	547.7	265.6	0.48
1980-1983	456.3	265.3	0.58

Note: The second column shows corporate profits with inventory valuation and capital consumption adjustments.
Sources: President's Council of Economic Advisers, *Economic Report of the President*, (Washington, D. C.: Government Printing Office, 1983), Tables B-1, B-52, B-82; and U.S. Department of Commerce, Bureau of Economic Analysis, *Survey of Current Business* (Washington, D. C.: Government Printing Office, December 1983).

Table 22.2   Compound Annual Growth Rates in Selected Series, 1948-1983

	1948-1966	1966-1972	1972-1979	1979-1983
GNP	6.12%	7.79%	10.71%	8.16%
After-tax profits	6.34	1.13	10.00	8.87
Dividends	5.83	3.90	11.63	8.60
CPI	1.67	4.32	8.19	8.24

Source: President's Council of Economic Advisers, *Economic Report of the President*, (Washington, D. C., Government Printing Office, 1983), Tables B-1, B-52, B-82.

Another perspective is obtained by examining growth rate patterns for selected time periods, as shown in Table 22.2. The postwar period, 1948 to 1966, was characterized by relative price stability in which the consumer price index (CPI) increased by less than 2 percent annually. The GNP, after-tax profits, and dividends all grew at about a 6 percent rate. From 1966 to 1972, the CPI increased at an annual rate of 4.32 percent, and GNP in nominal terms was growing at a 7.79 percent rate. After-tax profits were virtually flat, while dividends did not quite keep up with the inflation rate — the real dividend growth rate was slightly negative.

For the period 1972 to 1979, the CPI increased at over 8 percent per year. The GNP in nominal terms grew at a rate of 10.71 percent per year but at less than 2.6 percent per year in real terms. After-tax profit growth surpassed the inflation rate, while dividend growth was 11.63 percent annually, representing a margin of 3.44 percent over the inflation rate. Hence the dividend payout rate increased from 44 percent in 1972 to 65 percent in 1980. From 1979 to 1983, the CPI continued to grow at better than 8 percent per year. In nominal terms, GNP gained 8.16 percent per year, but remained virtually unchanged in real terms (actually dropping .08 percent per year). After-tax profits edged slightly ahead of inflation, as did dividend growth. Over these four years, the dividend payout ratio averaged nearly 60 percent. Because of the impact of inflation since 1966, it is useful to deflate both after-tax profits and dividends by the CPI. We find that deflated dividends increased at a 1.14 percent rate from 1966 to 1983, while deflated after-tax profits were decreasing at a rate of .43 percent per year for the same time period. In spite of slowly declining real profits, real dividends have been relatively stable. This is also shown by Figure 22.1, which presents deflated after-tax profits and deflated dividends for the 1946 to 1983 period. Deflated dividends remained at about $20 billion from 1965 through 1975. Dividends moved up to about $24 billion for 1978 and 1979. But considerable stability in deflated dividends is exhibited for most of the 1966 to 1983 period. With the background of dividend patterns for the economy as a whole, we next turn to an examination of dividend policy at the level of the individual firm.

Dividend Policy Behavior

Most corporations seek to maintain a target dividend per share. However, dividends increase with a lag after earnings rise. That is, they are increased only after an increase in earnings appears clearly sustainable and relatively permanent. When dividends have been increased, strenuous efforts are made to maintain them at the new level. If earnings de-

Figure 22.1   Corporate Earnings after Taxes and Dividends (CPI Deflated), 1946-1983

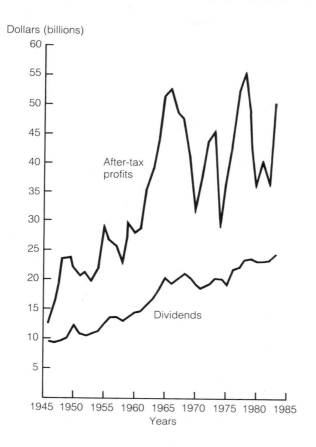

cline, the existing dividend generally is maintained until it is clear that an earnings recovery will not take place.

Figure 22.2 illustrates these ideas by showing the earnings and dividend patterns for the Walter Watch Company over a 30-year period. Initially, earnings are $2 and dividends $1 a share, providing a 50 percent payout ratio. Earnings rise for four years, while dividends remain constant; thus, the payout ratio falls during this period. During 1955 and 1956, earnings fall substantially; however, the dividend is maintained, and the payout ratio rises above the 50 percent target. During the period between 1956 and 1960, earnings experience a sustained rise. Dividends are held constant for a time, while management seeks to determine whether the earnings increase is permanent. By 1961, the earnings gains seem permanent, and dividends are raised in three steps to reestablish the 50 percent target payout. During 1965 a strike causes earnings to fall below the regular dividend; expecting the earnings decline to be temporary, management maintains the dividend. Earnings fluc-

---

Figure 22.2   Dividends and Earnings Patterns for the Walter Watch Company

---

tuate on a fairly high plateau from 1966 through 1972, during which time dividends remain constant. A new increase in earnings induces management to raise the dividend in 1973 to reestablish the 50 percent payout ratio.

Different Dividend Payout Schemes

Even though most firms seem to have a policy of paying stable dollar dividends, this is not the only policy. The three major types of dividend payout schemes are:

1. *Stable dollar amount per share.* The policy of a stable dollar amount per share, followed by most firms, is the policy implied by the words *stable dividend policy.*
2. *Constant payout ratio.* Very few firms follow a policy of paying out a constant percentage of earnings. Since earnings fluctuate, following this policy necessarily means that the dollar amount of dividends will fluctuate. This policy is not likely to maximize the value of a firm's stock because it results in unreliable signals to the market about the future prospects of the firm and because it may interfere with investment policy. Before its bankruptcy, Penn Central Railroad followed the policy of paying out half its earnings — "A dollar for the stockholders and a dollar for the company," as one director put it.
3. *Low regular dividend plus extras.* The low regular dividend plus extras policy is a compromise between the first two. It gives the firm flexibility, but it leaves investors somewhat uncertain about what their dividend income will be. If a firm's earnings are quite volatile, however, this policy may well be its best choice.

In addition to these policies that describe how a target payout is achieved across the years, there is also the question of what the target payout should be in the first place. Should a firm's target dividend payout be 10 percent of earnings or 50 percent? We turn to this question next.

Theories of Dividend Policy

The central issue of dividend policy is whether it is possible to affect shareholders' wealth by changing the firm's target dividend payout ratio — its dividend policy. If we compare two firms that are alike in every way, except for their current dividend payout, will the shares of the firms be valued differently? If so, then dividend policy matters. To answer this question we begin in the simplest possible world — one with no taxes. Then we move to a more realistic world of personal and corporate taxes. Finally, we consider the relationship between investment policy (capital budgeting) and dividend policy.

Dividend Policy in a World without Taxes

Consider two firms that are alike in every way except for their dividend policies. They have the same portfolio of risky assets, the same cash flows, and the same earnings each year. In addition, assume they have no debt at all so that we don't confuse the effect of capital structure (the mixture of debt and equity financing) with dividend policy. Finally, assume a world without taxes, just to keep things simple. Miller and Modigliani [1961] formalized these assumptions in a multiperiod model as follows:

$$\text{NOI}_1(t) = \text{NOI}_2(t) \qquad t = 0,1, \ldots ,\infty \qquad \textbf{(22.1a)}$$

$$I_1(t) = I_2(t) \qquad t = 0,1, \ldots ,\infty \qquad \textbf{(22.1b)}$$

$$d_1(t) = d_2(t) \qquad t = 1, \ldots ,\infty \qquad \textbf{(22.1c)}$$

$$d_1(0) \neq d_2(0) \qquad t = 0. \qquad \textbf{(22.1d)}$$

Assumptions (22.1a) and (22.1b) say that the cash flows from operations, $\text{NOI}(t)$, as well as both firms' investment plans, $I(t)$, are identical in every time period from now, $t = 0$, to infinity, $t = \infty$.[2] They imply that each firm's investment decisions are separate from its dividend policy (and other financing decisions). No matter what level of current cash flows are paid out in the form of dividends, the firm will make the same investment decisions. As we shall see later on, this assumption is absolutely critical. If the firm were to forego positive net present value projects because it wanted to pay high dividends, then the value of the firm would surely be affected not by dividend policy per se, but by the refusal to take profitable investments. Assumptions (22.1c) and (22.1d) state that current dividend payout will be different for the two firms, that is, $d_1(0) \neq d_2(0)$, but all future dividends will be identical.

The important question is whether or not the two firms will have different values if their current dividend payouts are different. To supply an answer we need a simple valuation model. Start by noting that the two firms have the same risk because their streams of operating cash flows are identical. Hence the cash flows of the two firms can be discounted at the same risk-adjusted rate, k_U, the cost of capital for an unlevered firm. The

---

[2]Net operating income, NOI, is defined as earnings from operations before interest and taxes. If there are no nonrecurring items on the income statement, then NOI equals EBIT, earnings before interest and taxes. We have also previously used the symbol X to designate operating income. For this chapter, we assume that NOI = EBIT = X.

one-period rate of return, k_U, for a share of stock is

$$k_U(t + 1) = \frac{d_i(t + 1) + p_i(t + 1) - p_i(t)}{p_i(t)},$$ (22.2)

where

$k_U(t + 1) = $ the cost of capital for an unlevered firm in time period t
$d_i(t + 1) = $ dividends per share paid at the end of time period t
$p_i(t + 1) = $ the price per share at the end of time period t
$p_i(t) = $ the price per share at the beginning of period t

If the numerator and denominator of Equation 22.2 are multiplied by the current number of shares outstanding, $n_i(t)$, and if we rearrange terms, we obtain

$$n_i(t)p_i(t) = S_i(t) = \frac{D_i(t + 1) + n_i(t)p_i(t + 1)}{1 + k_U(t + 1)},$$ (22.3)

where

$D_i(t + 1) = $ total dollar dividend payment $= n_i(t)d_i(t + 1)$
$S_i(t) = $ the market value of the all-equity firm

The value of the firm is seen to be equal to the discounted sum of two cash flows: dividends paid out, $D_i(t + 1)$, and the end-of-period value of the firm, $S_i(t + 1) = n_i(t)p_i(t + 1)$.

The key to understanding why dividend payout does not affect the value of the firm, given our current set of assumptions, is the firm's sources and uses of funds. The major sources are internal funds provided by cash flows from operations, $NOI_i(t + 1)$; and external funds provided by issuing new shares, $m_i(t + 1)p_i(t + 1)$, where $m_i(t + 1)$ is the number of new shares. The major uses of funds are investment expenditures, $I_i(t + 1)$, and dividends, $D_i(t + 1)$.[3] By definition, sources and uses must be equal, therefore we can write the following:

$$NOI_i(t + 1) + m_i(t + 1)p_i(t + 1) \equiv I_i(t + 1) + D_i(t + 1).$$ (22.4)

The sources and uses identity shows why investment decisions can be independent of dividend policy. For example, suppose a firm has $100 in cash flow from operations, wishes to invest $80, and to pay $40 in dividends. Equation 22.4 becomes

$$\$100 + m_i(t + 1)p_i(t + 1) = \$80 + \$40$$

$$m_i(t + 1)p_i(t + 1) = \$20.$$

The firm must issue enough new shares to raise $20. On the other hand, suppose the firm wishes to invest only $20. The sources and uses equation becomes

$$\$100 + m_i(t + 1)p_i(t + 1) = \$20 + \$40$$

$$m_i(t + 1)p_i(t + 1) = \$-40.$$

---

[3]We have assumed, for the sake of convenience, that sources and uses of funds from the balance sheet (for example, changes in inventory, accounts payable, etc.) are negligible.

In this case the firm uses its excess cash flow to repurchase \$40 worth of its outstanding stock. These two examples serve to illustrate that external sources and uses of funds (sale or repurchase of equity) can be used to balance the sources and uses equation without affecting planned investments.

To continue the proof of dividend policy irrelevancy, solve the sources and uses identity (Equation 22.4) for dividend payments:

$$D_i(t + 1) = \text{NOI}_i(t + 1) - I_i(t + 1) + m_i(t + 1)p_i(t + 1),$$

then substitute the result into the numerator of our one-period valuation equation (Equation 22.3).

$$S_i(t) = \frac{\text{NOI}_i(t + 1) - I_i(t + 1) + m_i(t + 1)p_i(t + 1) + n_i(t)p_i(t + 1)}{1 + k_U(t + 1)}$$

Next, we know that if new shares are issued, the total number of shares outstanding at the end of the period, $n_i(t + 1)$, will be the sum of current shares, $n_i(t)$, and new shares $m_i(t + 1)$:

$$n_i(t + 1) = n_i(t) + m_i(t + 1).$$

Rearranging this expression, the current number of shares is

$$n_i(t) = n_i(t + 1) - m_i(t + 1).$$

Finally, substituting this into our valuation equation we have

$$
\begin{aligned}
S_i(t) &= \frac{\text{NOI}_i(t + 1) - I_i(t + 1) + m_i(t + 1)p_i(t + 1) + n_i(t + 1)p_i(t + 1) - m_i(t + 1)p_i(t + 1)}{1 + k_U(t + 1)} \\
&= \frac{\text{NOI}_i(t + 1) - I_i(t + 1) + n_i(t + 1)p_i(t + 1)}{1 + k_U(t + 1)} \\
&= \frac{\text{NOI}_i(t + 1) - I_i(t + 1) + S_i(t + 1)}{1 + k_U(t + 1)}.
\end{aligned}
\tag{22.5}
$$

It is no accident that dividends do not appear in the valuation equation 22.5. The firm can choose any dividend policy whatsoever without affecting the stream of cash flows available to shareholders. Because we have assumed that there are no taxes, shareholders are indifferent as to whether they receive their cash flows as dividends, if the cash is paid out, or as capital gains if the cash is kept as retained earnings. The firm could, as illustrated earlier, elect to pay current dividends in excess of cash flows from operations and still be able to undertake any planned investment. The extra funds needed are supplied by issuing new equity. It is the availability of external financing in a world without transactions costs that makes the value of the firm independent of dividend policy, because all profitable investments can be undertaken regardless of the extent of dividend payout.

Note that Equation 22.5 has four variables. All are identical for both firms even though they have different current dividend payouts. First, the market-determined cost of equity for the unlevered firms, k_U, must be the same because both firms have identical risk.

Second, current cash flows from operations and current investment outlays for the two firms have been assumed to be identical:

$$\text{NOI}_1(1) = \text{NOI}_2(1); \ I_1(1) = I_2(1).$$

Finally, the end-of-period values of the two firms depend only on *future* investments, dividends, and cash flows, which have also been assumed to be identical. Therefore, the end-of-period values of the two firms must be the same

$$S_1(1) = S_2(1).$$

Consequently, the present values of the two firms must be identical regardless of their current dividend payout. Dividend policy is irrelevant in a world without taxes or transactions costs.

Dividend Policy in a World with Taxes

As before, we want to assume that the firm's investment policy is unaffected by its dividend policy and that there are no transactions costs associated with raising external capital. However, the analysis is made more realistic if we allow taxes to enter the picture. Assume there are three different tax rates. First there is a proportional corporate tax, T_c. Second is a personal tax rate on income from bonds, dividends and wages, T_p. And finally there is a tax on capital gains, T_g. Furthermore, assume that all firms and all investors actually pay these tax rates, that is, there are no loopholes.

As long as the personal tax rate on income received in the form of dividends is greater than the personal tax rate on capital gains ($T_p > T_g$), then shareholders will prefer that the firm pay no dividends. They would be better off if the funds remained in the firm or were paid out via repurchase of shares.[4] Either way, the stock price per share would be higher than it would be had dividends been paid out. If dividends are not paid out, shareholders who need cash can always sell off a fraction of their holdings. In doing so, they pay capital gains taxes that are lower than the ordinary income taxes they would have paid had they received dividends.

Formal analysis of this idea was provided in a partial equilibrium context by Farrar and Selwyn [1967] and in a market equilibrium framework by Brennan [1970]. The idea is that shareholders maximize their after-tax income. They have two choices. They can own shares in an all equity firm and borrow to provide personal leverage, or they can buy shares in a levered firm. Either way they have the same risk. Their first choice is the amount of personal versus corporate leverage that is desired. The second choice is the form of payment to be made by the firm. It can pay out earnings as dividends or it can retain earnings and allow shareholders to take their income in the form of capital gains.

Let's consider two cases as they relate to dividend policy. Either the firm pays out all of its income as dividends (Case 1) or it pays out no dividends at all (Case 2).

---

[4]Later on we shall see that the repurchase of shares is an important alternative to paying out cash dividends — so important that the Internal Revenue Service can declare regular stock repurchases (on a pro rata basis) to be taxable as dividends.

Case 1. If a firm pays out all of its cash flows as dividends, the ith shareholder will receive the following after-tax income, Y_{di}:

$$Y_{di} = [(\text{NOI} - rD_c)(1 - T_c) - rD_{pi}](1 - T_{pi}), \qquad (22.6)$$

where

Y_{di} = after-tax stream of income to the ith individual if all corporate income is paid out as dividends

NOI = cash flows from operations of the firm (net operating income) = \$1,000

r = borrowing rate that is assumed identical for individual and firms = 10%

D_c = corporate debt = \$6,000

D_{pi} = personal debt held by the ith individual = \$2,000

T_c = corporate tax rate = 40%

T_p = personal tax rate on income (wages, rents, interest received, and dividends) received by the ith individual = 30%

The first term within the brackets in Equation 22.6 is the after-tax cash flow of the firm, which is $(\text{NOI} - rD_c)(1 - T_c) = \$240$. All of this is assumed to be paid out as dividends. The before-tax income to the shareholder is the dividends received minus the interest on debt used to buy shares, $(\text{NOI} - rD_c)(1 - T_c) - rD_{pi} = \$40$. After subtracting personal income taxes, $\$40T_{pi} = \$12$, we are left with after-tax income, \$28.

Case 2. Alternatively, the firm can decide to pay no dividends, in which case we assume that all capital gains are realized *immediately* by investors and taxed at the capital gains rate.[5] In this case, the after-tax income of a shareholder is

$$Y_{gi} = (\text{NOI} - rD_c)(1 - T_c)(1 - T_{gi}) - rD_{pi}(1 - T_{pi}), \qquad (22.7)$$

where

Y_{gi} = after-tax income to the ith individual if the firm pays no dividends

T_{gi} = capital gains rate for the ith individual = 15%

Now the individual pays a capital gains tax rate on the firm's income and deducts after-tax interest expenses on personal debt. The capital gain after taxes is

$$(\text{NOI} - rD_c)(1 - T_c)(1 - T_{gi}) = (\$1,000 - \$600)(1 - .4)(1 - .15) = \$204.$$

From this we subtract the after-tax cost of interest on personal debt, $rD_{pi}(1 - T_{pi}) = \$140$. Altogether the individual's after-tax income is \$64. Clearly, the individual is better off if the firm pays no dividends. If the firm pays dividends the individual's after-tax income is $Y_{di} = \$28$. If the firm retains the cash flows or uses them to repurchase shares, the individual realizes a capital gain and an after-tax income of $Y_{gi} = \$64$, which is better than if the firm pays no dividends at all. This result will be true as long as the personal tax rate on dividends is higher than the capital gains rate $(T_{pi} > T_{gi})$.

---

[5]Obviously there is the third possibility that earnings are translated into capital gains and the capital gains are deferred to a later date. This possibility is considered in Farrar and Selwyn [1967]. It does not change their conclusions.

Miller and Scholes [1978] modified the preceding argument by demonstrating that even with existing tax laws (where the tax on ordinary personal income is greater than the capital gains tax) many individuals need not pay more than the capital gains rate on dividends. The implication is that many individuals may be indifferent between payments in the form of dividends or capital gains. Thus, the firm's value may be unrelated to its dividend policy even in a world with taxes.

The Miller and Scholes argument can be illustrated with an example. Suppose we have an initial net worth of $25,000, which is represented wholly by an investment in 2,500 shares worth $10 each in a company that earns $1.00 per share. At the end of the year the company pays $.40 per share in dividends and retains $.60. Consequently, its end-of-year price per share is $10.60. In order to neutralize dividend income for tax purposes, we borrow $16,667 at 6 percent and invest the proceeds in a risk-free project (such as life insurance or a Keogh account), which pays 6 percent of tax-deferred interest. Our opening and closing balance sheets and our income statement are shown in Table 22.3. Note that by investing in risk-free assets we have not increased the risk of our wealth position. The riskless cash inflows from insurance exactly match the required payments on debt. Our true economic income would be $1,500 in *unrealized* capital gains plus the $1,000 of tax-deferred interest from life insurance or our Keough account.

Of course, federal tax laws are complex and tax sheltering investments cannot be carried out without some transactions costs. Also, Feenberg [1981] has shown that the maximum amount of dividends or interest income that can be sheltered in this way is $10,000. Nevertheless, the above argument is a clever way to demonstrate the fact that ordinary income taxes on dividends can be legally avoided.

In a world with personal and corporate taxes, dividends are undesirable to most taxpaying shareholders, or at best shareholders are indifferent between dividends and capital gains. Of course there are also many institutional investors, such as pension funds, which pay no taxes on either dividends or capital gains; or corporations that pay taxes on only 15 percent of the dividends they receive. There is nothing in the theory to suggest that dividends are desirable. Why, then, do corporations pay any dividends at all?

Table 22.3   A Technique for Sheltering Dividend Income

Opening Balance Sheet				Closing Balance Sheet				
Assets		**Liabilities**		**Assets**			**Liabilities**	
2500 shares at $10	= $25,000	Loan	$16,667	2500 shares at $10.60	=	$26,500	Loan accrued	= $16,667
Insurance	= 16,667	Net worth	25,000	Accrued dividends	=	1,000	Accrued interest	= 1,000
	$41,667		$41,667	Insurance	=	16,667	Net worth	= 26,500
						$44,167		$44,167

Ordinary Income		**Capital Gains**	
Dividends received	$1,000	Sale of 2500 shares at $10.60 =	$26,500
Less: interest expense	1,000	Less: original basis	25,000
	0	Capital gain	$ 1,500
Nontaxable income	$1,000		
	$1,000		

Ingredients for Optimal Dividend Policy

For an optimal dividend policy to exist, there must be benefits from paying dividends as well as costs due to their payment. There are three different approaches to optimal dividend policy that identify benefits as well as costs. The first two theories work as well in a world without as in a world with taxes. The third extends our intuition of how taxes affect dividend policy.

Dividends, Agency Costs, and External Financing

Rozeff [1982] suggests that optimal dividend policy may exist even without considering tax implications. Systematic patterns in corporate dividend payout ratios may be explained by a trade-off between the flotation costs of raising external capital and the benefit of reduced agency costs when the firm increases its dividend payout.

The more dividends a firm chooses to pay, the greater the probability that the supply of retained earnings (internally generated capital) will be exhausted, thus making it necessary to seek external funds (debt or equity) in order to undertake new investment. But the flotation costs associated with raising external capital make it a more expensive source of financing. Consequently, dividend payout is costly because it increases the probable need to raise more expensive external capital.

A possible benefit of dividend payments is that they may reduce agency costs between owner-managers and outside owners of a firm. To see how agency costs might arise (in an all equity firm) let's begin with an owner-managed firm. Because the owner-manager (Mr. Jones) owns all of the firm's common stock, any decision he makes will maximize his utility. For example, if he decides to play golf on Wednesday afternoons he bears all of the costs and benefits of that decision. If he sells part of his common stock to some outsiders, the situation changes. Now, if he plays golf, the outsiders share in the cost of his actions. This creates an agency problem. The owner-manager can shirk his duties or pay himself more perquisites at the expense of outsiders. Consequently, the outsiders must charge, *ex ante*, for the potential agency problem that owner-managers may increase their personal wealth in lieu of maximizing the wealth of all shareholders. They do this by demanding a higher rate of return on the equity capital that they invest in the firm. To decrease this *ex ante* charge, owner-managers find it in their own interest to agree to incur monitoring or bonding costs if such costs are less than the *ex ante* charge that outsiders would be forced to request. Thus, a wealth-maximizing firm will adopt an optimal monitoring/bonding policy that minimizes agency costs.

Dividend payments may well serve as a means of monitoring or bonding management performance. Although greater dividend payout results in costly external financing, the very fact that the firm must go to the capital markets implies that it will come under greater scrutiny. For example, banks will require a careful analysis of the credit-worthiness of the firm and the Securities and Exchange Commission will require prospectus filings for new equity issues. Thus, outside suppliers of capital help to monitor the owner-manager on behalf of outside equity owners. Of course, audited financial statements are a substitute means for supplying the same information, but they may not be a perfect substitute for the "adversary" relationship between the firm and new suppliers of capital.

Because of the transactions costs of external financing, Rozeff also argues that the variability of a firm's cash flows will affect its dividend payout. Consider two firms with the same average cash flows across time but different variability. The firm with greater volatil-

Table 22.4   Cross-Sectional Dividend Payout Regressions

	CONSTANT	INS	GROW1	GROW2	BETA	STOCK	R^2	D.W.	F-statistic
(1)	47.81	−0.090	−0.321	−0.526	−26.543	2.584	0.48	1.88	185.47
	(12.83)	(−4.10)	(−6.38)	(−6.43)	(−17.05)	(7.73)			
(2)	24.73	−0.068	−0.474	−0.758	—	2.517	0.33	1.79	123.23
	(6.27)	(−2.75)	(−8.44)	(−8.28)		(6.63)			
(3)	70.63	—	−0.402	−0.603	−25.409	—	0.41	1.88	231.46
	(40.35)		(−7.58)	(−6.94)	(−15.35)				
(4)	39.56	−0.116	—	—	−33.506	3.151	0.39	1.80	218.10
	(10.02)	(−4.92)			(−21.28)	(8.82)			
(5)	1.03	−0.102	—	—	—	3.429	0.12	1.60	69.33
	(0.24)	(−3.60)				(7.97)			

t-statistics are shown in parentheses under estimated values of the regression coefficients. R^2 is adjusted for degrees of freedom.
D.W. is Durbin-Watson statistic.
Source: Rozeff, M., "Growth, Beta, and Agency Costs as Determinants of Dividend Payout Ratios," Working Paper series no. 81-11, University of Iowa, June 1981. Reprinted with permission of the author.

ity will borrow in bad years and repay in good. It will need to finance externally more often. Consequently, it will have a lower payout ratio.

Rozeff [1982] selected a sample of 1,000 nonregulated firms in 64 different industries and examined their average dividend payout ratios during the years 1974-1980. Five proxy variables were used in a multiple regression equation to test his theory. The results are shown in Table 22.4. The independent variables GROW1 and GROW2 are an attempt to measure the effect of costly external financing. Firms that grow faster can reduce their need to use external financing by paying lower dividends. GROW1 measures the growth rate in revenues between 1974 and 1979, while GROW2 is Value Line's forecast of the growth in sales revenue over the five-year period 1979-1984. Both variables are negatively related to dividend payout and are statistically significant. The variables INS and STOCK are proxies for the agency relationship. INS is the percentage of the firm held by insiders. Dividend payout is negatively related to the percentage of insiders because given a lower percentage of outsiders there is less need to pay dividends to reduce agency costs.[6] On the other hand, if the distribution of outsider holdings is diffuse, then agency costs will be higher, hence one would expect STOCK, the number of stockholders, to be positively related to dividend payout. Both INS and STOCK are statistically significant and of the predicted sign. Finally, the variable BETA measures the systematic risk of the firm. The prediction that riskier firms have lower dividend payout is verified by the regression.

The best regression in Table 22.4 explains 48 percent of the cross-sectional variability on dividend payout across individual firms. All of the explanatory variables are statistically significant with the predicted signs. Although the results cannot be used to distinguish among various theories of optimal dividend policy, they are consistent with Rozeff's predictions. Furthermore, the very existence of strong cross-sectional regularities suggests that there is an optimal dividend policy.

[6]This relationship is also consistent with the tax argument that assumes high tax bracket insiders prefer to take their return in the form of capital gains rather than dividends.

Dividends as Signals

Dividend signaling is more a story about how information may be transmitted to the marketplace than it is a theory about optimal dividend policy. The announcement that a firm has decided to increase dividends per share may be interpreted by investors as good news because higher dividends per share imply that the firm believes future cash flows will be large enough to support the higher dividend level.

Managers, as insiders who have monopolistic access to information about the firm's cash flows, will choose to establish unambiguous signals about the firm's future if they have the proper incentive to do so. Ross [1977] proved that an increase in dividends paid out (or in the usage of debt) can represent an inimitable and unambiguous signal to the marketplace that a firm's prospects have improved. In order for a signal to be useful, four conditions must be met:

1. Management must always have the right incentive to send a truthful signal, even if the news is bad.
2. The signal of a successful firm cannot be easily mimicked by less successful competitors.
3. The signal must be significantly correlated with observable events (for example, higher dividends today must be correlated with higher future cash flows).
4. There cannot be a more cost effective way of sending the same message.

To show how these conditions are met by Ross' [1977] signaling equilibrium, assume a one-period world. Managers' compensation, M, paid at the end of the period, depends on the market's current assessment of the value of the firm, V_0, and on its end-of-period value, V_1. In general, managers' compensation can be expressed as

$$M = (1 + r)\gamma_0 V_0 + \gamma_1 \begin{cases} V_1 & \text{if } V_1 \geq D \\ V_1 - L & \text{if } V_1 < D, \end{cases} \tag{22.8}$$

where

$\gamma_0, \gamma_1 =$ positive fractions of the value of the firm which are paid to managers
$r =$ the one-period interest rate
$V_0, V_1 =$ the current and future value of the firm
$D =$ the face value of debt
$L =$ a penalty paid by managers if bankruptcy occurs, that is, if $V_1 < D$

The first term in Equation 22.8 is the end-of-period value of the managers' fraction of the current price of the firm. The second term is the managers' fraction of the end-of-period value. Note that if the firm goes bankrupt (because its value is less than the face value of debt obligations), managers experience a decrease, L, in the value of their human capital.

Suppose we have two firms that have the same size and the same amount of debt, D, but have different earnings prospects, which are known by management, but not by the marketplace in general. The successful firm (which will have higher future cash flows) can pay out greater dividends today and still have enough cash left at the end of the period to pay off its debt obligations ($V_1 \geq D$).[7] The unsuccessful firm cannot pay high current

[7]Miller and Rock [1984] have suggested that D may be interpreted as *net* dividends, the difference between cash dividends and borrowing. Thus, a firm that borrows $1 million to pay $1 million in dividends will have a net dividend of $0. This interpretation links dividend and debt signals into a unified concept.

dividends without going bankrupt at the end of the period ($V_1 < D$). Assume that div^* is the maximum amount of dividends that the unsuccessful firm can pay out without going bankrupt. If a firm elects to pay out current dividends greater than div^*, then the market perceives the firm to be successful and vice versa.

To show that managers have the incentive to provide truthful signals to the market, begin by assuming the end-of-period value of the successful firm is V_{1a} and V_{1b} is the value of the unsuccessful firm. Compensation of the management of the successful firm depends on the type of dividend signal they send to the market. If they tell the truth they will signal $div > div^*$ and the market will assign a current market value that is

$$V_0 = \frac{V_{1a}}{1 + r}.$$

If the successful firm wants to lie, the managers will signal $div < div^*$ and the market will assign a current value

$$V_0 = \frac{V_{1b}}{1 + r} < \frac{V_{1a}}{1 + r}.$$

For the successful firm, we can summarize the managers' compensation using Equation 22.8 as follows:

$$M_a = \begin{cases} \gamma_0(1 + r)\dfrac{V_{1a}}{1 + r} + \gamma_1 V_{1a} & \text{if } div \geq div^* \text{ (tell the truth)} \\[2ex] \gamma_0(1 + r)\dfrac{V_{1b}}{1 + r} + \gamma_1 V_{1b} & \text{if } div < div^* \text{ (lie).} \end{cases}$$

Clearly, the management of the successful firm has the incentive to pay a high level of dividends ($div > div^*$) to earn maximum compensation. Therefore, it will give the correct signal. But what about the management of the unsuccessful firm? Doesn't it have an incentive to lie by falsely signaling with high dividends? The answer is found by looking at the management incentive scheme:

$$M_b = \begin{cases} \gamma_0(1 + r)\dfrac{V_{1a}}{1 + r} + \gamma_1(V_{1b} - L) & \text{if } div \geq div^* \text{ (lie)} \\[2ex] \gamma_0(1 + r)\dfrac{V_{1b}}{1 + r} + \gamma_1(V_{1b}) & \text{if } div < div^* \text{ (tell the truth).} \end{cases}$$

In order for management of an unsuccessful firm to have incentive to signal that the firm will be unsuccessful, the payoff from telling the truth must be greater than that produced by telling lies. Mathematically,

$$\gamma_0 V_{1a} + \gamma_1(V_{1b} - L) < \gamma_0 V_{1b} + \gamma_1 V_{1b},$$

which can be rewritten as

$$\gamma_0(V_{1a} - V_{1b}) < \gamma_1 L.$$

This condition says that management will provide a truthful signal if the marginal gain from a false signal, $V_{1a} - V_{1b}$, weighted by management's share γ_0, is less than the penalty paid by management, $\gamma_1 L$, if the firm goes bankrupt. Managers of unsuccessful firms who falsely signal success by paying a higher current dividend can benefit because the market assigns a higher current value to the firm, but they ultimately lose because the value of their human capital declines (by $\gamma_1 L$) when the firm goes bankrupt due to cash flow insufficiency.

The incentive-signaling approach suggests that management might choose real financial payouts such as dividends (or debt payments) as a means of sending unambiguous signals to the public about the future performance of the firm. These signals cannot be mimicked by unsuccessful firms because such firms do not have sufficient cash flow to back them up and because managers have correct incentives to tell the truth.

Bhattacharya [1979] develops a dividend signaling model closely related to that of Ross [1977], which can be used to explain why firms may use dividends for signaling despite the tax disadvantages of doing so. If investors believe that firms that pay greater dividends per share have higher values, then an unexpected dividend increase will be taken as a favorable signal. Presumably dividends convey information about the value of the firm that cannot be fully communicated by other means such as annual reports, earnings forecasts, or presentations before security analysts. It is expensive for less successful firms to mimic the signal because they must incur extra costs associated with raising external funds in order to pay the cash dividend. Hence, the signaling value of dividends is positive and can be traded off against the tax loss associated with dividend income (as opposed to capital gains).

If dividend changes are to have an impact on share values, it is necessary that they convey information about future cash flows, but it is not sufficient. The same information may be provided to investors via other sources. Therefore, it becomes an empirical question whether or not announcements of dividend changes actually affect share value.

There have been many studies of the effect of the announcement of an unexpected change in dividends.[8] Most of the results strongly support the conclusion that unanticipated changes in dividends are, indeed, interpreted by the marketplace as signals about the future prospects of the firm. Figure 22.3 shows the dividend announcement effects for a sample of firms studied by Aharony and Swary [1980]. Because firms often announce earnings and dividends at about the same time, Aharony and Swary were careful to select only those dividend announcements that were separated from earnings announcements by at least ten trading days. Figure 22.3 shows the average residual rates of return attributable to the announced dividend changes taken from a sample of 2,610 dividend announcements that were preceded by earnings announcements (representative of 149 firms over the period January 1963 to December 1976). Even though the dividend change announcements were preceded by earlier announcements of earnings changes, there was a strong market reaction to dividend signals. When dividends decreased, the average stock price decrease was −3.76 percent and when they rose the stock price increased .72 percent. Both results were statistically significant. These findings strongly support the hypothesis that dividend changes contain information about changes in management's assessment of the future prospects of the firm. Furthermore, dividend announcements contain useful information beyond that already provided by earnings announcements.

---

[8]For example, see Fama, Fisher, Jensen, and Roll [1969], Pettit [1972], Watts [1973], Kwan [1981], and Aharony and Swary [1980].

Figure 22.3   Daily Cumulative Average Abnormal Returns:
                   Cases Where Earnings Announcements Precede Dividend Announcements

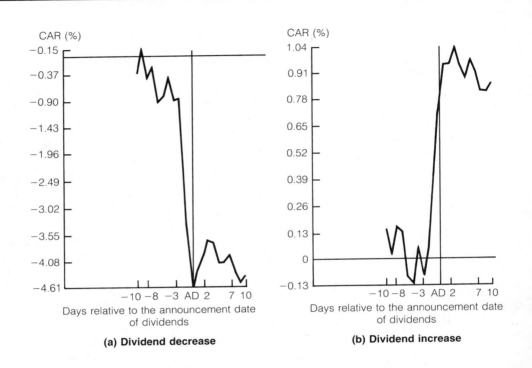

(a) Dividend decrease   (b) Dividend increase

Source: Aharony, J., and I. Swary, "Quarterly Dividend and Earnings Announcements and Stockholder Returns: An Empirical Analysis," *Journal of Finance*, (March 1980), p. 8.

Dividends, Investment, and Taxes

The complex individual and corporate tax system in the United States may be an important part of the dividend puzzle. Masulis and Trueman [1983] model the investment and dividend decision under fairly realistic assumptions and show that the costs of deferring dividends may be large enough to induce firms to optimally pay cash dividends. The tax system that they model assumes:

1. Corporations pay an effective marginal tax rate, T_c.
2. Individuals pay different personal tax rates on dividend income, T_{di}.
3. There are no capital gains taxes, $T_g = 0$.
4. The IRS taxes regular corporate repurchases and equity in the same way as dividend payments.
5. There is an 85 percent dividend exclusion from taxes on all dividends paid by one corporation to another.

In addition, to keep capital structure questions separate from dividend policy, they assume no debt.

Figure 22.4 illustrates the effect of taxes on the supply and demand for investment funds. Internal capital (retained earnings) and external equity capital (proceeds from new issues) have different costs to the firm. If retained earnings are not reinvested, then the ith shareholder receives the following after-tax return for each dollar paid out as dividends:

$$r_b(1 - T_c)(1 - T_{di}) = \text{cost of internal funds,} \qquad (22.9)$$

where r_b = the pretax return on investments in real assets.

For example, if the pretax return required on investments of equal risk is $r_b = 15\%$, the corporate tax rate is $T_c = 50\%$, and the individual's tax rate is 40 percent, then the individual will be indifferent between (1) earning 9.0 percent before taxes on a corporate investment and (2) receiving dividends.[9] If the individual's tax rate is 20 percent, a 12 percent before-tax rate on investment will be required. The higher an individual's tax bracket, the more likely he is to want the firm to invest cash flows internally instead of paying divi-

Figure 22.4   Corporate Investment and Dividend Decisions with Differing Personal Tax Rates

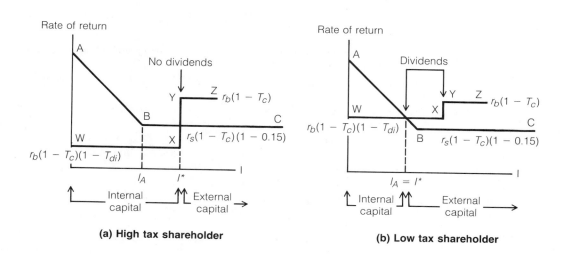

(a) High tax shareholder   **(b) Low tax shareholder**

Source: Rozeff, M., "Growth, Beta, and Agency Costs as Determinants of Dividend Payout Ratios," *Journal of Financial Research*, Vol. 5, No. 3, Fall 1982, pp. 249-259. Reprinted with permission.

[9]Given an individual tax rate of 40 percent, and a 15 percent before-tax rate on investment, the after-tax rate on a dollar paid out as dividends would be

$$r_b(1 - T_c)(1 - T_{di}) = .15(1 - .5)(1 - .4) = .045.$$

If the money is kept in the firm, the before-tax return can fall to 9.0 percent and should give the same after-tax yield:

$$r_b(1 - T_c) = .09(1 - .5) = .045.$$

See Equation 22.10 for the cost of external equity capital.

dends, even when investment returns decline with more investment. The line segment WX in Figure 22.4 represents the cost of capital to current shareholders in different tax brackets. In Panel (a) it represents a high tax bracket shareholder and in Panel (b), a low tax bracket shareholder. At Point Y are shareholders who pay no personal taxes at all (for example, pension funds). They are indifferent between earnings retention and dividend payout because their opportunity cost is the same as the cost of external capital to the firm.

$$r_b(1 - T_c) = \text{cost of external funds} \tag{22.10}$$

External funds are more expensive to the firm because investors do not pay double taxes (corporate and personal) on funds put to other uses. It is assumed that alternative investments earn capital gains only and are not taxed at the personal level. The cost of external capital is illustrated by the horizontal line segment YZ in Figure 22.4 (both panels).

The firm has two categories of investment opportunity. First are investments in real assets, represented by line segment AB, and assumed to have diminishing returns to scale. Second are investments in securities of other firms. These securities investments have constant returns to scale as illustrated by line segment BC. The before-tax return on investments in securities of other firms is defined as r_s. There is a virtually infinite amount of security investments (in assets of equivalent risk) but their after-tax rate of return to the firm is affected by the fact that we have to pay corporate taxes on 15 percent of the dividends paid to us by other firms. Thus, the after-tax return on security investments is

$$r_s(1 - T_c)(1 - .15). \tag{22.11}$$

To reach its optimal investment/dividend decision the firm in Figure 22.4(a), uses internal funds to undertake all investments in real assets, I_A, and then invests in securities of other firms up to an amount I^*. At this point it stops because the after-tax return on investing in securities is less than the opportunity cost of capital for externally supplied equity, and we see that the investment in real assets, I_A, is less than total investment, I^*. Since all internal funds have been used, dividends will not be paid out. The high tax bracket shareholders, in Panel (a), prefer low (or zero) dividend payout.

In Panel (b), however, low tax bracket shareholders have a higher opportunity cost for internally generated funds. They will want investment in real assets to stop at $I_A = I^*$. At this point, not all internally generated capital has been spent on real investment and dividends are paid out. For low tax bracket shareholders the cost of deferring dividends is sufficiently high that they prefer dividend payout.

One of the implications of this model is that shareholders with different tax rates, T_{di}, will not unanimously agree on the firm's investment/dividend decision. High tax bracket shareholders would prefer the firm to invest more and low tax bracket shareholders would prefer less investment. This lack of unanimity can be diminished somewhat if investors self-select into clienteles with low tax bracket individuals purchasing shares of high dividend firms and vice versa.[10]

There are five other implications of the Masulis-Trueman model. (1) Firms are predicted not to externally finance security purchases for investment purposes. However, they are likely to purchase stocks with the internally generated funds which remain after financing their own profitable production opportunities. (2) Firms with many profitable production opportunities (high growth firms) will use up all of their internally generated funds with-

[10]See Appendix 22A for empirical evidence on dividend clientele effects.

out paying dividends, but older more mature firms will pay dividends because not all internally generated funds will be exhausted by investment opportunities. (3) Mergers are predicted between firms where one is internally financing its profitable investments and the other is externally financing. (4) While a decrease in current earnings should leave unchanged the investment expenditures of externally financed firms, it is likely to decrease investment expenditures of firms that initially planned to internally finance all of their investments rather than to make up the shortfall of funds through external financing. (5) Shareholder disagreement over internally financed investment policy will be more likely the greater the amount of internally generated funds relative to the firm's investment opportunities. In these cases, firms are more likely to experience takeover attempts, proxy fights, and efforts to "go private." Given these tax-induced shareholder conflicts, diffuse ownership is more likely for externally financed firms than internally financed firms.

Stock Dividends, Stock Splits, and Repurchases

Another aspect of dividend policy is stock dividends and stock splits. A *stock dividend* is paid in additional shares of stock instead of in cash and simply involves a bookkeeping transfer from retained earnings to the capital stock account.[11] In a *stock split* there is no change in the capital accounts; instead, a larger number of shares of common stock is issued. In a two-for-one split, stockholders receive two shares for each one previously held. The book value per share is cut in half; and the par, or stated, value per share of stock is similarly changed.

From a practical standpoint there is little difference between a stock dividend and a stock split. The New York Stock Exchange considers any distribution of stock totaling less than 25 percent of outstanding stock to be a stock dividend and any distribution of 25 percent or more a stock split. Since the two are similar, the issues outlined below are discussed in connection with both stock splits and stock dividends.

Stock Splits and Stock Dividends

Many hypotheses have been put forth to explain why corporations have stock splits. The most common story is that, by some miracle, a paper transaction that doubles the number of shares outstanding without changing the firm in any other way can create shareholder wealth out of thin air. The exact effect of stock splits on shareholder wealth has been studied extensively. The pioneering study by Fama, Fisher, Jensen, and Roll [1969] measured unexpected stock price changes around split ex dates. Monthly data for 940 splits between 1927 and 1959 revealed no significant changes in shareholder wealth in the split month. However, for a subsample of firms that split and increased their dividends, they found an increase in shareholders' wealth in the months following the split. For a dividend decrease subsample they found a decrease in shareholders' wealth. These results are consistent with the idea that splits are interpreted as messages about dividend increases.

---

[11]The transfer from retained earnings to the capital stock account must be based on market value. In other words, if a firm's shares are selling for $100 and it has 1 million shares outstanding, a 10 percent stock dividend requires the transfer of $10 million (100,000 × $100) from retained earnings to capital stock. Stock dividends are thus limited by the size of retained earnings. The rule was put into effect to prevent the declaration of stock dividends unless the firm has had earnings.

A more recent study by Grinblatt, Masulis, and Titman [1984] used daily data and looked at shareholder returns on the split announcement date as well as the split ex date. They examined a special subsample of splits where no other announcements were made in the three-day period around the split announcement and where no cash dividends had been declared in the previous three years.[12] For this sample of 125 "pure" stock splits they found a statistically significant announcement return of 3.44 percent. They interpret stock split announcements as favorable signals about the firm's future cash flows. Surprisingly, they also find statistically significant returns (for their entire sample of 1,360 stock splits) on the split ex date. There is no good explanation for this result.

In the same study, Grinblatt, Masulis, and Titman [1984] confirm earlier work on stock dividends by Foster and Vickrey [1978] and Woolridge [1983a, 1983b]. The announcement effects for stock dividends are large, 4.90 percent for a sample of 382 stock dividends and 5.89 percent for a smaller sample of 84 stock dividends with no other announcements in a three-day period around the stock dividend announcement. One possible reason for the larger announcement effect of a stock dividend is that retained earnings must be reduced by the dollar amount of the stock dividend. Only those companies that are confident they will not run afoul of debt restrictions that require minimum levels of retained earnings will willingly announce a stock dividend. As with stock splits, there was a statistically significant positive return on the stock dividend ex date (and the day before). No explanation is offered for why the ex-date effect is observed.

One often hears that stocks split because there is an "optimal" price range for common stocks. Moving the security price into this range is alleged to make the market for trading in the security "wider" or "deeper," hence there is more trading liquidity. Copeland [1979] reports that contrary to the above argument, market liquidity is actually lower following a stock split. Trading volume is proportionately lower than its presplit level, brokerage revenues (a major portion of transactions costs) are proportionately higher, and bid-ask spreads are higher as a percentage of the bid price.[13] Taken together, these empirical results point to lower post-split liquidity.

Table 22.5, from a study by Barker [1958], shows the effect of stock dividends and stock splits on common stock ownership during a four-year period. Stock splits resulted in the largest percentage increases in stock ownership. For companies and industries that did not offer stock splits or stock dividends, the increase was only 5 percent. Furthermore, the

Table 22.5   Effect of Stock Dividends on Stock Ownership

	Percentage Increase in Ownership, 1950-1953
Stock split, 5 for 4 or higher	30
Stock dividend, 5-25%	17
No stock dividends or splits	5

Source: C. Austin Barker, "Evaluation of Stock Dividends," *Harvard Business Review*, 36 (July/August 1958), pp. 99-114.

[12]However, 11 percent of the pure samples declared a dividend within one year of the stock split.

[13]The bid price is the price that a potential buyer offers, say $20, and the ask price is what the seller requires, suppose it's $20\frac{1}{4}$. The bid-ask spread is the difference, specifically, $\frac{1}{4}$.

degree of increase itself increased with the size of the stock dividend or split. This evidence suggests that regardless of the effect on the total market value of the firm, the use of stock dividends and stock splits effectively increases the number of shareholders by lowering the price at which shares are traded to a more popular range. Perhaps this change in ownership is a reason for stock splits and dividends.

Stock Repurchases

A corporation's repurchase of its own stock can serve as a tax advantageous substitute for dividend payout. Repurchases have the effect of raising share prices so that shareholders can be taxed at the capital gains rate instead of the ordinary dividend rate on cash dividends.[14]

Corporations can repurchase their own shares in two ways: on the open market or via tender offer. Open market repurchases usually (but not always) involve gradual programs to buy back shares over a period of time. In a tender offer, the company usually specifies the number of shares it is offering to repurchase, a tender price, and a period of time during which the offer is in effect. If the number of shares actually tendered by shareholders exceeds the maximum number specified by the company, then purchases are usually made on a *pro rata* basis.[15] Alternatively, if the tender offer is undersubscribed the firm may decide to cancel the offer or extend the expiration date. Shares tendered during the extension may be purchased on either a *pro rata* or first-come, first-served basis.

Tender offers are usually significant corporate events. Dann [1981] reports that for a sample of 143 cash tender offers by 122 different firms between 1962 and 1976, the average cash distributions proposed by the tender represented almost 20 percent of the market value of the company's pre-tender equity value. The announcement effects of tender offers on the market values of corporate securities have been studied by Masulis [1980], Dann [1981], and Vermaelen [1981].[16] Share repurchases are not just a simple alternative to cash dividends. Tender offers for repurchase are related to (at least) five separate, but not mutually exclusive, hypotheses:

1. *The information or signaling hypothesis.* The cash disbursed to shareholders in a tender offer may represent a signal that the firm is expected to have increased future cash flows but it may also imply that the firm has exhausted profitable investment opportunities. Therefore, the signal may be interpreted as either good or bad news by shareholders.

2. *The leverage hypothesis.* If the repurchase is financed by issuing debt rather than paying out cash, the leverage of the firm may increase — and if there is a gain to leverage as suggested by Modigliani and Miller [1963], then shareholders may benefit.

3. *The dividend tax avoidance hypothesis.* The tender for share repurchase will be taxed as a capital gain rather than a dividend if the distribution is "essentially not equivalent to paying a dividend" (according to Section 302 of the U.S. Internal Revenue Code) or if the redemption is "substantially disproportionate" to the extent that the individual shareholder must have sold more than 20 percent of his or her holdings in the

---

[14]The following material is similar to Copeland and Weston [1983] pp. 520-524.

[15]To avoid taxation of repurchases as dividends, the repurchase usually excludes corporate officers, directors, and other insiders. Hence, most repurchases are not *strictly pro rata*.

[16]The reader is also referred to studies by Woods and Brigham [1966], Bierman and West [1966], Young [1967], Elton and Gruber [1968], Stewart [1976], Coates and Fredman [1976], and Lane [1976].

tender.[17] These criteria are rarely violated, consequently there may be a tax incentive for repurchases as opposed to large extraordinary dividends.

4. *The bondholder expropriation hypothesis.* If the repurchase unexpectedly reduces the asset base of the company, then bondholders are worse off because they have less collateral. Of course, bond indentures serve to protect against this form of expropriation. A direct test of this hypothesis is to look at bond price changes on the repurchase announcement date.

5. *Wealth transfers among shareholders.* Wealth transfers between tendering and nontendering stockholders may occur when there are differential constraints and/or costs across groups of owners. Even when the tender price is substantially above the pre-tender stock price, some shareholders may voluntarily decide not to tender their shares.

A great deal can be learned about these hypotheses if we focus on the price effects on shares, bonds, and preferred stock. Figure 22.5 shows the average pattern of share price changes around the tender announcement date and the expiration date. More or less the same results were reported by Masulis [1980], Dann [1981], and Vermaelen [1981]. The average tender price, p_T, is roughly 23 percent above the announcement price, p_0. If all shares tendered were actually purchased by the firm, then the tender price, p_T, would

---

Figure 22.5   Schematic Representation of Average Price Changes
                    Surrounding Tender Offers for Repurchase

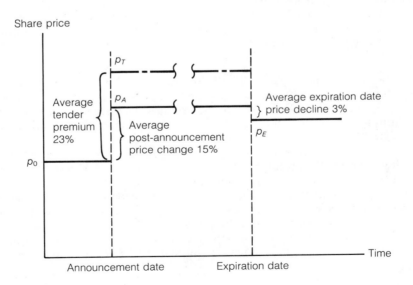

[17]According to Vermaelen [1981] only three out of 105 tender offers which he studied actually were subject to ordinary income taxes.

equal the average post-announcement price, p_A. But because of *pro rata* repurchases given oversubscribed tenders we observe that on average $p_A < p_T$. The post-announcement price, p_A, averages 15 percent above the pre-announcement price, p_0. Finally, note that the average post-expiration price, p_E, is only 3 percent below the average post-announcement price, p_A, and is above the pre-announcement price, p_0. This suggests that the tender offer may have increased the market value of the firm's equity.

Unfortunately, the difference between the pre-announcement price and the post-expiration price does not measure the information effect of the tender offer. We have to look deeper. Begin by noting that the market value of the firm's equity after expiration, $p_E n_E$, is equal to the pre-announcement value, $p_0 n_0$, minus the cash paid out in the tender, $p_T(n_0 - n_E)$, plus the tender offer effect, ΔW:

$$p_E n_E = p_0 n_0 - p_T(n_0 - n_E) + \Delta W, \qquad (22.12)$$

where

$p_E =$ the post-expiration share price
$n_E =$ the number of shares outstanding after repurchase
$p_0 =$ the pre-announcement share price
$n_0 =$ the pre-announcement number of shares outstanding
$p_T =$ the tender price
$\Delta W =$ the shareholder wealth effect attributable to the tender offer

Note that the change in value attributable to the tender, ΔW, may be caused by (1) personal tax savings, (2) a leverage effect, (3) expropriation of bondholder wealth, or (4) the reassessment of the firm's earnings prospects.

If we define the fraction of shares repurchased, F_P, as

$$F_P = 1 - \frac{n_E}{n_0}, \qquad (22.13)$$

and divide Equation 22.12 by n_0, we have

$$p_E(1 - F_P) = p_0 - p_T F_P + \frac{\Delta W}{n_0}. \qquad (22.14)$$

Solving for $\Delta W/n_0$ and dividing by p_0 gives

$$\frac{\Delta W}{n_0 p_0} = (1 - F_P)\frac{p_E - p_0}{p_0} + F_P\frac{p_T - p_0}{p_0}. \qquad (22.15)$$

Thus, the rate of return created by the tender offer has two components. First is the rate of return received by nontendering shareholders weighted by the percent of untendered shares, $1 - F_P$; and second is the rate of return received by tendering shareholders weighted by the percent of shares purchased, F_P.

Vermaelen [1981] found that the average wealth effect, $\Delta W/n_0 p_0$, was 15.7 percent and that only 10.7 percent of the tender offers experienced a wealth decline. On average, both nontendered shares and tendered shares experienced a wealth increase, although not by equal amounts.

What causes the average 15.7 percent wealth gain from tender offers? Personal tax savings are a possibility but seem too small to explain the large wealth gain. For example, if 20 percent of the value of the firm is repurchased and if the marginal investor's tax rate is 40 percent, then the tax savings would imply a 4 percent rate of return. This is too small to explain the wealth gain.

The leverage hypothesis suggests that if the repurchase is financed with debt, and if there is a tax gain from leverage, then the shareholders will benefit. Both Masulis [1980] and Vermaelen [1981] find evidence consistent with a leverage effect. Masulis divided his sample into offers with more than 50 percent debt financing where the average announcement return was 21.9 percent, and offers with less than 50 percent debt where the average announcement return was only 17.1 percent. Vermaelen finds similar results and concludes that while it is not possible to reject the leverage hypothesis outright, it is possible to conclude that it is not the predominant explanation for the observed abnormal returns following the tender offer. Also, if leverage is a signal, then it is not possible to separate the leverage signaling effect from the leverage tax effect.

The best explanation for the shareholder wealth gain from the tender offer is that the offer represents a favorable signal. Vermaelen [1981] finds that the per-share earnings of tendering firms are above what would have been predicted by a time series model using pre-announcement data. Thus, the tender offer may be interpreted as an announcement of favorable earnings prospects. Also, the size of the tender premium, the fraction of shares repurchased, and the fraction of insider holdings are all positively related to the wealth gain, ΔW, and explain roughly 60 percent of its variance. These results are also consistent with interpreting the tender offer as a signal.

Evidence on the bondholder wealth expropriation hypothesis is provided by looking at bond price changes around the announcement date. Dann [1981] found 122 publicly traded debt and preferred stock issues for 51 tender offers. There were 41 issues of straight debt, 34 issues of convertible debt, 9 issues of straight preferred stock, and 38 issues of convertible preferred stock. An analysis of abnormal returns around the announcement date revealed significant positive rates of return for the convertible securities and rates that were insignificantly different from zero for straight debt and preferred. Furthermore, the correlation between common stock returns and straight debt (and preferred) returns was positive. Thus, the evidence seems to contradict bondholder expropriation as the dominant effect.

Repurchases via tender offer represent an interesting and significant corporate event. The empirical evidence, although not rejecting leverage effects or dividend tax avoidance effects, seems to most strongly support the hypothesis that the tender offer for repurchase is interpreted by the marketplace as favorable information regarding future prospects of the firm.

Summary

Dividend policy remains a puzzle. The earliest model of dividend policy, by Miller and Modigliani [1961], shows that, in a world without taxes, dividends have no effect on shareholders' wealth. Later models, which include corporate and individual taxes (Farrar and Selwyn [1967] and Brennan [1970]), suggest that the best policy is to pay no dividends at all — that shareholders are better off selling their shares a few at a time and paying the lower capital gains rate.

Corporations do pay dividends and their payout patterns seem to have a great deal of cross-sectional regularity (as shown by Rozeff [1981]). Theories of optimal dividend policy include signaling (Ross [1978], Bhattacharya [1979], Hakansson [1982]), agency costs (Rozeff [1981]), and taxation (Masulis and Trueman [1983]). As yet, none of these theories is completely satisfactory, but together they seem to shed some light on why corporations pay dividends.

The empirical evidence on dividends, which has been voluminous, suggests that the following conclusions are warranted.

1. On average, shareholders require higher risk-adjusted returns for those firms that have higher dividend yields. These results (which are reported in Appendix 22A) have to be tempered somewhat by the fact that the studies have looked at average effects and have not attempted to look at departures from "optimal" dividend policy.

2. Dividend *changes* are clearly interpreted as signals about the future prospects of the firm. The market reacts strongly and immediately to announcements of positive dividend increases.

3. Repurchases, and to a lesser extent stock dividends and stock splits, are interpreted by the market as good news.

4. There is evidence that shareholders do self-select into clienteles, with high tax bracket shareholders migrating toward low payout firms and low tax bracket shareholders selecting high payout firms. (See Appendix A to this chapter for more on clientele effects.)

Questions

22.1 As an investor, would you rather invest in a firm with a policy of maintaining a constant payout ratio, a constant dollar dividend per share, or a constant regular quarterly dividend plus a year-end extra when earnings are sufficiently high or corporate investment needs are sufficiently low? Explain your answer.

22.2 How would each of the following changes probably affect aggregate payout ratios? Explain your answer.
   a) An increase in the personal income tax rate
   b) A liberalization in depreciation policies for federal income tax purposes
   c) A rise in interest rates
   d) An increase in corporate profits
   e) A decline in investment opportunities

22.3 Discuss the pros and cons of having the directors formally announce what a firm's dividend policy will be in the future.

22.4 Most firms would like to have their stock selling at a high price-earnings ratio with extensive public ownership (many different shareholders). Explain how stock dividends or stock splits may be compatible with these aims.

22.5 What is the difference between a stock dividend and a stock split? As a stockholder, would you prefer to see your company declare a 100 percent stock dividend or a two-for-one split?

22.6 In theory, if we had perfect capital markets, we would expect investors to be indifferent about whether cash dividends were issued or an equivalent repurchase of stock outstanding were made. What factors might in practice cause investors to value one over the other?

22.7 Discuss this statement. The cost of retained earnings is less than the cost of new outside equity capital. Consequently, it is totally irrational for a firm to sell a new issue of stock and to pay dividends during the same year.

22.8   Would it ever be rational for a firm to borrow money to pay dividends? Explain.

22.9   Unions have presented arguments similar to the following: "Corporations such as General Foods retain about half their profits for financing needs. If they financed by selling stock instead of by retaining earnings, they could cut prices substantially and still earn enough to pay the same dividend to their shareholders. Therefore, their profits are too high." Evaluate this statement.

22.10   If executive salaries are tied more to the size of the firm's sales or its total assets rather than to profitability, how might managers' policies be adverse to the interests of stockholders?

Problems

22.1   The Bane Engineering Company has $2 million of backlogged orders for its patented solar heating system. Management plans to expand production capacity by 30 percent with a $6 million investment in plant machinery. The firm wants to maintain a 45 percent debt-to-total-asset ratio in its capital structure; it also wants to maintain its past dividend policy of distributing 20 percent of after-tax earnings. In 19X0 earnings were $2.6 million. How much external equity must the firm seek at the beginning of 19X1?

22.2   Lifton Company expects next year's after-tax income to be $5 million. The firm's current debt-equity ratio is 80 percent. If Lifton has $4 million of profitable investment opportunities and wishes to maintain its current debt-equity ratio, how much should it pay out in dividends next year?

22.3   After a three-for-one stock split, Novak Company paid a dividend of $4. This represents an 8 percent increase over last year's pre-split dividend. Novak Company's stock sold for $80 prior to the split. What was last year's dividend per share?

22.4   The following is an excerpt from a 1977 *Wall Street Journal* article:

> General Motors Corp., confident of its outlook for auto sales and profit, boosted its quarterly dividend to $1 a share from 85 cents and declared a special year-end dividend of $2.25 a share. Both the quarterly and the special are payable Dec. 10 to stock of record Nov. 17.
>
> The sizeable fourth quarter payout, totaling $3.25 a share, is a record for any GM dividend in the final quarter. Last year, the No. 1 auto maker, buoyed by strong sales and sharply improved earnings, paid $3 a share in the fourth quarter.
>
> The $3.25-a-share fourth quarter will bring GM's total cash dividend on common stock for 1977 to a record $6.80 (*sic*) a share, up from the previous record, set last year, of $5.55 a share.
>
> Yesterday's action by GM directors underscored the wave of higher profit that most of the auto makers have been riding for almost two years. Moreover, in raising its quarterly dividend to $1 a share, GM indicated that it expects strong sales and earnings to continue into 1978. In announcing the board's action, Thomas A. Murphy, Chairman, and Elliott M. Estes, President, said the dividends "reflect GM's strong earnings and capital position and our confidence in the fundamental strength of the U.S. economy and the automotive market."

The 85-cents-a-share quarterly dividend was instituted by GM in 1966; it was scaled back in 1974 when the auto industry entered a prolonged slump. The 85-cent rate was restored in the third quarter of 1976.[18]

a) Did GM appear to be following a stable dividend payout ratio or a policy of a stable dollar amount of dividends per quarter? What role did the fourth-quarter year-end "extras" perform in this policy?

b) Some authors have suggested that dividends have "announcement effects," performing the role of signaling investors that a change in underlying earning power has taken place. Is there anything in the article relevant to the concept that dividend changes convey information to investors?

22.5 In 19X0 the Odom Company paid dividends totaling $1,125,000. For the past ten years, earnings have grown at a constant rate of 10 percent. After-tax income was $3,750,000 for 19X0. However, in 19X1, earnings were $6,750,000 with investment of $5,000,000. It is predicted that Odom Company will not be able to maintain this higher level of earnings and will return to its previous 10 percent growth rate. Calculate dividends for 19X1 if Odom Company follows each of the following policies.

a) Its dividend payment is stable and growing.

b) It continues the 19X0 dividend payout ratio.

c) It uses a pure residual dividend policy (30 percent of the $5,000,000 investment was financed with debt).

d) The investment in 19X1 is financed 90 percent with retained earnings and 10 percent with debt. Any earnings not invested are paid out as dividends.

e) The investment in 19X1 is financed 30 percent with external equity, 30 percent with debt, and 40 percent with retained earnings. Any earnings not invested are paid out as dividends.

22.6 Raffer Company stock earns $7 per share, sells for $30, and pays a $4 dividend per share. After a two-for-one split, the dividend will be $2.70 per share. By what percentage has the payout increased?

22.7 Barnes Company has 500,000 shares of common stock outstanding. Its capital stock account is $500,000, and retained earnings are $2 million. Barnes is currently selling for $10 per share and has declared a 10 percent stock dividend. After distribution of the stock dividend, what balances will the retained earnings and capital stock accounts show?

22.8 The directors of Northwest Lumber Supply have been comparing the growth of their market price with that of one of their competitors, Parker Panels. Their findings are summarized in Table P22.8 on the following page.

---

[18]"General Motors Boosts Payout to $1 a Share," *The Wall Street Journal*, November 8, 1977. Reprinted by permission of *The Wall Street Journal*, Dow Jones & Company, Inc., 1977. All rights reserved.

Table P22.8

Northwest Lumber Supply and Parker Panels: Comparative Statements

Northwest Lumber Supply

Year	Earnings	Dividend	Payout	Price	P-E
1978	$4.30	$2.58	60%	$68	15.8
1977	3.85	2.31	60	60	15.6
1976	3.29	1.97	60	50	15.2
1975	3.09	1.85	60	42	13.6
1974	3.05	1.83	60	38	12.5
1973	2.64	1.58	60	31	11.7
1972	1.98	1.19	60	26	13.1
1971	2.93	1.76	60	31	10.6
1970	3.48	2.09	60	35	10.1
1969	2.95	1.77	60	30	10.2

Parker Panels

Year	Earnings	Dividend	Payout	Price	P-E
1978	$3.24	$1.94	60%	$70	21.6
1977	2.75	1.79	65	56	20.4
1976	2.94	1.79	61	53	18.0
1975	2.93	1.73	59	48	16.4
1974	2.90	1.65	57	44	15.2
1973	2.86	1.57	55	41	14.3
1972	2.61	1.49	57	35	13.4
1971	1.66	1.50	97	20	12.9
1970	2.24	1.50	67	34	15.2
1969	2.19	1.49	68	30	13.7

Both companies are in the same markets, and both are similarly organized (approximately the same degree of operating and financial leverage). Northwest has been consistently earning more per share; yet for some reason, it has not been valued at as high a P-E ratio as Parker. What factors would you point out as possible causes for this lower market valuation of Northwest's stock?

22.9 Associated Engineers has experienced the sales, profit, and balance sheet patterns found in Table P22.9. Identify the financial problem that has developed, and recommend a solution for it.

Table P22.9

Associated Engineers Financial Data, 1970-1979 (Millions of Dollars)

Income Statements	1970	1971	1972	1973	1974	1975	1976	1977	1978	1979
Sales	$100	$140	$180	$200	$240	$400	$360	$440	$480	$680
Profits after tax	10	14	18	20	24	40	36	44	48	68
Dividends	8	10	12	12	14	20	20	28	36	48
Retained earnings	$ 2	$ 4	$ 6	$ 8	$ 10	$ 20	$ 16	$ 16	$ 12	$ 20
Cumulative retained earnings	$ 2	$ 6	$ 12	$ 20	$ 30	$ 50	$ 66	$ 82	$ 94	$114

Balance Sheets	1970	1971	1972	1973	1974	1975	1976	1977	1978	1979
Current assets	$ 20	$ 30	$ 40	$ 50	$ 60	$100	$ 80	$110	$120	$160
Net fixed assets	30	40	50	50	60	100	100	110	120	180
Total assets	$ 50	$ 70	$ 90	$100	$120	$200	$180	$220	$240	$340
Trade credit	$ 8	$ 12	$ 16	$ 18	$ 20	$ 36	$ 30	$ 40	$ 40	$120
Bank credit	8	12	20	20	26	58	28	40	40	40
Other	2	10	12	12	14	16	16	18	16	16
Total current liabilities	$ 18	$ 34	$ 48	$ 50	$ 60	$110	$ 74	$98	$ 96	$176
Long-term debt	0	0	0	0	0	10	10	10	20	20
Total debt	$ 18	$ 34	$ 48	$ 50	$ 60	$120	$ 84	$108	$116	$196
Common stock	30	30	30	30	30	30	30	30	30	30
Retained earnings	2	6	12	20	30	50	66	82	94	114
Net worth	$ 32	$ 36	$ 42	$ 50	$ 60	$ 80	$ 96	$112	$124	$144
Total claims on assets	$ 50	$ 70	$ 90	$100	$120	$200	$180	$220	$240	$340

22.10 Babco Industries has earnings this year of $16.5 million, 50 percent of which is required to take advantage of the firm's excellent investment opportunities. The firm has 206,250 shares outstanding, selling currently at $320 a share. Ralph Miller, a major stockholder (18,750 shares), has expressed displeasure with a great deal of managerial policy. Management has approached him with the prospect of selling his holdings back to the firm, and he has expressed a willingness to do this at a price of $320 a share. Assuming that the market uses a constant P-E ratio of 4 in valuing the stock, answer the following questions.

a) Should the firm buy Miller's shares? Assume that dividends will not be paid on them if they are repurchased.

b) How large a cash dividend should be declared?

c) What is the final value of Babco Industries' stock after all cash payments to shareholders?

22.11 Consider two firms in a world without taxes. They both initially have $100 of assets and both can earn 10 percent on assets with certainty. Both are all equity firms with a 10 percent cost of equity capital. One pays out all of its earnings in dividends while the other has a 50 percent dividend payout.

a) What is the market value of equity for each firm?

b) What does your answer to Part (a) tell you about the effect of dividend policy decisions on the market value of the firm in a world without taxes?

22.12 Firms A and B carry no debt, have the same current earnings before interest and taxes (EBIT = $1,000), the same tax rate ($T = 40\%$), and the same unlevered cost of capital ($k_U = 10\%$). However, their growth rates and dividend policies are dramatically different. Firm A retains 80 percent of its net income for future investment and its dividends grow (forever) at 8 percent per year ($g = .08$). Firm B retains only 20 percent of its net income and its dividends grow at 4 percent per year ($g = .04$).

a) Which firm is worth more?

b) Explain the intuition behind your answer to Part (a).

Selected References

Aharony, J., and Swary, I., "Quarterly Dividend and Earnings Announcements and Stockholders' Returns: An Empirical Analysis," *Journal of Finance*, (March 1980), pp. 1-12.

Asquith, Paul, and Mullins, David W., Jr., "The Impact of Initiating Dividend Payments on Shareholders' Wealth," *Journal of Business*, 56 (January 1983), pp. 77-96.

Barker, C. Austin, "Evaluation of Stock Dividends," *Harvard Business Review*, (July/August, 1958), pp. 99-114.

Bhattacharya, S., "Imperfect Information, Dividend Policy, and 'The Bird in the Hand' Fallacy," *Bell Journal of Economics*, 10 (Spring 1979), pp. 259-270.

Bierman, Harold, Jr., and West, Richard, "The Acquisition of Common Stock by the Corporate Issuer," *Journal of Finance*, 21 (December 1966), pp. 687-696.

Black, F., "The Dividend Puzzle," *Journal of Portfolio Management*, (Winter 1976), pp. 5-8.

Blume, M., "Stock Returns and Dividend Yields: Some More Evidence," *Review of Economics and Statistics*, (1980), pp. 567-577.

Brennan, Michael, "Taxes, Market Valuation and Corporate Financial Policy," *National Tax Journal*, (December 1970), pp. 417-427.

Brickley, James A., "Shareholder Wealth, Information Signaling and the Specially Designated Dividend: An Empirical Study," *Journal of Financial Economics*, 12 (August 1983), pp. 187-209.

Brittan, J. A., *Corporate Dividend Policy*, Washington, D. C.: Brookings Institute, 1966.

Charest, Guy, "Dividend Information, Stock Returns and Market Efficiency, I, II," *Journal of Financial Economics*, 6 (June-September 1978), pp. 265-296, 297-330.

Coates, C., and Fredman, A., "Price Behavior Associated With Tender Offers to Repurchase Common Stock," *Financial Executive*, (April 1976), pp. 40-44.

Copeland, Thomas E., "Liquidity Changes Following Stock Splits," *Journal of Finance*, 34 (March 1979), pp. 115-141.

Dann, Larry Y., "Common Stock Repurchases: An Analysis of Returns to Bondholders and Stockholders," *Journal of Financial Economics*, 9 (June 1981), pp. 113-138.

Eades, Kenneth M., "Empirical Evidence on Dividends as a Signal of Firm Value," *Journal of Financial and Quantitative Analysis*, 17 (November 1982), pp. 471-502.

————; Hess, P.; and Kim, E. H., "On Interpreting Security Returns During the Ex-Dividend Period," *Journal of Financial Economics*, (March 1984), pp. 3-34.

Elton, Edwin J., and Gruber, Martin J., "The Cost of Retained Earnings — Implications of Share Repurchase," *Industrial Management Review*, 9 (Spring 1968), pp. 68-74.

Fama, Eugene F., "The Empirical Relationships between the Dividend and Investment Decisions of Firms," *American Economic Review*, 64 (June 1974), pp. 304-318.

————, and Babiak, Harvey, "Dividend Policy: An Empirical Analysis," *Journal of the American Statistical Association*, 63 (December 1968), pp. 1132-1161.

Fama, Eugene F.; Fisher, Lawrence; Jensen, Michael; and Roll, Richard, "The Adjustment of Stock Prices to New Information," *International Economic Review*, 10 (February 1969), pp. 1-21.

Farrar, D., and Selwyn, L., "Taxes, Corporate Financial Policy and Return to Investors," *National Tax Journal*, (December 1967), pp. 444-454.

Feenberg, Daniel, "Does the Investment Interest Limitation Explain the Existence of Dividends?", *Journal of Financial Economics*, 9 (September 1981), pp. 265-269.

Foster, T., and Vickrey, D., "The Information Content of Stock Dividend Announcements," *The Accounting Review*, (1978), pp. 360-370.

Friend, Irwin, and Puckett, Marshall, "Dividends and Stock Prices," *American Economic Review*, 54 (September 1964), pp. 656-682.

Grinblatt, M.; Masulis, R.; and Titman, S., "The Valuation Effects of Stock Splits and Stock Dividends," *Journal of Financial Economics*, (December 1984), pp. 461-490.

Hakansson, Nils H., "To Pay or Not to Pay," *Journal of Finance*, (May 1982), pp. 415-428.

Handjinicolaou, G., and Kalay, A., "Wealth Redistributions or Changes in Firm Value: An Analysis of Returns to Bondholders and Stockholders Around Dividend Announcements," *Journal of Financial Economics*, (March 1984), pp. 35-64.

Hess, P., "The Ex-Dividend Behavior of Stock Returns: Further Evidence on Tax Effects," *Journal of Finance*, 37 (May 1982), pp. 445-456.

Kalay, Avner, "Stockholder-Bondholder Conflict and Dividend Constraints," *Journal of Financial Economics*, 10 (June 1982), pp. 211-233.

————, "Signaling, Information Content, and the Reluctance to Cut Dividends," *Journal of Financial and Quantitative Analysis*, 15 (November 1980), pp. 855-870.

Khoury, N., and Smith, K., "Dividend Policy and the Capital Gains Tax in Canada," *Journal of Business Administration*, (Spring 1977).

Kim, E. H.; Lewellen, W.; and McConnell, J., "Financial Leverage Clienteles: Theory and Evidence," *Journal of Financial Economics*, (March 1979), pp. 83-110.

Kwan, C., "Efficient Market Tests of the Informational Content of Dividend Announcements: Critique and Extension," *Journal of Financial and Quantitative Analysis*, 16 (June 1981), pp. 193-206.

Lane, W., "Repurchase of Common Stock and Managerial Discretion," unpublished Ph.D. dissertation, University of North Carolina, Chapel Hill, N.C. (1976).

Lintner, John, "Distribution of Incomes of Corporations among Dividends, Retained Earnings, and Taxes," *American Economic Review*, 46 (May 1956), pp. 97-113.

Long, John B., Jr., "Efficient Portfolio Choice with Differential Taxation of Dividends and Capital Gains," *Journal of Financial Economics*, 5 (August 1977), pp. 25-53.

Masulis, R., "Stock Repurchase via Tender Offer: An Analysis of the Causes of Common Stock Price Changes," *Journal of Finance*, 35 (May 1980), pp. 305-318.

————, and Trueman, B., "Corporate Investment and Dividend Decisions Under Differential Personal Taxation," working paper #22-83, UCLA Graduate School of Management (February 1983).

Miller, Merton H., and Modigliani, Franco, "Dividend Policy, Growth, and the Valuation of Shares," *Journal of Business*, 34 (October 1961), pp. 411-433.

————, "Dividend Policy and Market Valuation: A Reply," *Journal of Business*, 36 (January 1963), pp. 116-119.

Miller, Merton H., and Rock, Kevin, "Dividend Policy under Asymmetric Information," working paper, University of Chicago, 1984.

Miller, Merton H., and Scholes, Myron S., "Dividends and Taxes," *Journal of Financial Economics*, 6 (December 1978), pp. 333-364.

Penman, Stephen H., "The Predictive Content of Earnings Forecasts and Dividends," *Journal of Finance*, 38 (September 1983), pp. 1181-1199.

Peterson, Pamela P., and Benesh, Gary A., "A Reexamination of the Empirical Relationship between Investment and Financing Decisions," *Journal of Financial and Quantitative Analysis*, 18 (December 1983), pp. 439-453.

Pettit, R. Richardson, "The Impact of Dividend and Earnings Announcements: A Reconciliation," *Journal of Business*, 49 (January 1976), pp. 86-96.

————, "Dividend Announcements, Security Performance, and Capital Market Efficiency," *Journal of Finance*, 27 (December 1972), pp. 993-1007.

Ross, S. A., "Some Notes on Financial Incentive-Signalling Models, Activity Choice and Risk Preferences," *Journal of Finance*, 33 (June 1978), pp. 777-792.

————, "The Determination of Financial Structure: The Incentive-Signalling Approach," *Bell Journal of Economics*, (Spring 1977), pp. 23-40.

Rozeff, Michael S., "Growth, Beta and Agency Costs as Determinants of Dividend Payout Ratios," *Journal of Financial Research*, 5 (Fall 1982), pp. 249-259.

Shefrin, Hersh M., and Statman, Meir, "Explaining Investor Preference for Cash Dividends," *Journal of Financial Economics*, (June 1984), pp. 253-282.

Stewart, Samuel S., Jr., "Should a Corporation Repurchase Its Own Stock?", *Journal of Finance*, 31 (June 1976), pp. 911-921.

Vermaelen, Theo, "Common Stock Repurchases and Market Signalling: An Empirical Study," *Journal of Financial Economics*, 9 (June 1981), pp. 139-183.

Watts, Ross, "The Information Content of Dividends," *Journal of Business*, 46 (April 1973), pp. 191-211.

West, Richard R., and Brouilette, Alan B., "Reverse Stock Splits," *Financial Executive*, 38 (January 1970), pp. 12-17.

Woods, Donald H., and Brigham, Eugene F., "Stockholder Distribution Decisions: Share Repurchase or Dividends," *Journal of Financial and Quantitative Analysis*, 1 (March 1966), pp. 15-28.

Woolridge, J. Randall, "Ex-Date Stock Price Adjustment to Stock Dividends: A Note," *Journal of Finance*, (1983a), pp. 247-255.

————, "Stock Dividends as Signals," *Journal of Financial Research*, (1983b), pp. 1-12.

Young, Allan E., "The Performance of Common Stock Subsequent to Repurchase," *Financial Analysts Journal*, (September-October 1967), pp. 117-121.

Appendix A to Chapter 22

Dividend Policy: Stock Prices and Clientele Effects

The chapter on dividend policy covered most managerial decisions. However, there are two important related issues. First is the matter of how stock prices are affected by dividend policy. Do firms with higher dividend yields have higher or lower stock prices? This question is different from whether or not changes in dividends have signaling effects. The issue is whether a firm with 50 percent of its earnings paid out in dividends has a higher stock price than the same firm with a 20 percent dividend payout. The second issue is whether or not dividend policy affects the type of shareholder who is attracted to hold the firm's stock. We might guess that low dividend firms attract high tax bracket investors and that high dividend firms attract widows and orphans with low tax brackets, and the empirical evidence seems to support this supposition.[1]

Dividends and Value

In a world with no taxes, Miller and Modigliani [1961] proved that dividend payout has no effect on shareholders' wealth. When corporate and personal taxes are introduced into the model, Farrar and Selwyn [1967] and Brennan [1970] proved that shareholders' wealth decreases when dividends are paid out. Finally, Chapter 22 gave three possible arguments for optimal dividend policies: agency costs, signaling, and taxes. The empirical research on the relationship between dividend yields and common stock prices has, in most cases, not looked at the effect of departures from an optimal dividend payout. All of the studies mentioned below are tests of the general question — do investors require higher rates of return on common stocks with high dividend yields? They are based on various versions of Brennan's [1970] model:

$$E(R_{jt}) - R_{ft} = a_1 + a_2\beta_j + a_3(d_{jt} - R_{ft}), \qquad (22A.1)$$

where

$E(R_{jt}) =$ the expected before-tax return on the jth security
$R_{ft} =$ the before-tax return on the risk-free asset
$\beta_j =$ the systematic risk of the jth security (its "beta")
$a_1 =$ the constant term
$a_2 =$ the marginal effect of systematic risk
$a_3 =$ the marginal effective tax differences between ordinary income and capital gains rates
$d_{jt} =$ the dividend yield, that is, the dividend divided by the price of the jth security

---

[1]This appendix is similar to material found in Copeland and Weston [1983] pp. 506-509 and 515-518.

Equation 22A.1 is analogous to the standard Capital Asset Pricing Model discussed in Chapter 17, except that the last term looks at the possibility of a dividend effect. If a_3 is significantly positive, then we can conclude that investors do not like dividends and therefore require higher before-tax returns, R_{jt}, in order to compensate them. All other things held constant, stocks with greater dividend payout would have lower prices.

Black and Scholes [1974] tested for the relationship between security returns and dividend yield by forming well-diversified portfolios and ranking them on the basis of their systematic risk (their "beta") and then by dividend yields within each risk class. They concluded that dividend yield had no effect on security returns.

Litzenberger and Ramaswamy [1979, 1980 and 1982] also test the relationship between dividends and security returns. Using the Brennan model, Equation 22A.1, they conclude that risk-adjusted returns are higher for securities with higher dividend yields. The implication is that dividends are undesirable, hence higher returns are necessary to compensate investors in order to induce them to hold high dividend yield stocks.

There are (at least) three serious problems with testing for the dividend effect predicted by Equation 22A.1. The first is that investors use dividend announcements to estimate expected returns, $E(\tilde{R}_{jt})$, that is, there is an information effect. The second is that measures of systematic risk, $\hat{\beta}_j$, are subject to a great deal of error. And the third is that individual security returns (rather than portfolio returns) are needed to obtain statistically powerful results. Litzenberger and Ramaswamy [1979] largely solved the second and third problems, but were criticized by Miller and Scholes [1983] for their handling of the information effect of dividend announcements. When using monthly data, about two-thirds of the firms in the sample will have a zero yield because most firms pay dividends on a quarterly basis. Of the firms that pay their dividend (that is, go ex dividend) in month t, about 30 to 40 percent also announce the dividend in the same month. When the announcement date and the ex-dividend date occur in the same month, the monthly return will contain both the information effect and the tax effect (if any). In order to avoid confusing these effects, Litzenberger and Ramaswamy computed dividend yields in the following way:

- If a firm declared its dividend prior to month t and went ex dividend in month t, then the dividend yield, d_{jt}, was computed using the actual dividend paid in t divided by the share price at the end of month $t - 1$.
- If a firm both declared and went ex dividend in month t, then the yield, d_{jt}, was computed using the last regular dividend, going back as far as one year.

Table 22A.1 shows the results of regressions run by Miller and Scholes [1983] using Equation 22A.1. Regressions using the actual dividend yield in month t show that the dividend variable has a coefficient of .317 and is highly significant, but recall that the actual yield confuses announcement effects with dividend tax effects. When the Litzenberger-Ramaswamy measure of dividend yield (called the level-revised yield) was duplicated by Miller and Scholes, the dividend coefficient dropped from .317 to .179 and also dropped in significance.

The third regression in Table 22A.1 corrects for a bias not contemplated in the two prior regressions. Namely, some firms are expected to pay a dividend in month t but, for some reason, the board of directors suspends the dividend. Miller and Scholes call this the case of the "dog that didn't bark." Suppose that a $10 stock has a 50-50 chance of either announcing a $2 dividend (in which case the stock price doubles to $20) or suspending the dividend (thereby causing the stock price to fall to $5). The *ex ante* rate of return (and the

Table 22A.1   Cross-Sectional Estimates of the Dividend Yield Effect (Equation 22A.1) 1940-1978

Definition of Expected Dividend Yield	Regression Coefficients		
	a_1	a_2	a_3
Actual dividend yield	.0059	.0024	.3173
	(4.5)	(1.6)	(10.2)
Level-revised monthly	.0065	.0022	.1794
dividend yield	(4.9)	(1.4)	(6.1)
Dividend yield of 12	.0038	.0019	.0376
months ago	(2.9)	(1.3)	(1.3)
Only firms with dividends	.0043	.0035	.0135
declared in advance	(2.5)	(2.2)	(0.1)

t-Statistics in parentheses.
Source: Miller, M., and M. Scholes, "Dividends and Taxes: Some Empirical Evidence," *The Journal of Political Economy*, (December 1983), pp. 1118-1141.

average *ex post* return) is 35 percent, and the *ex ante* dividend yield is 10 percent.[2] However, if the level-revised measure of dividend yield is used, then if the firm actually pays the $2 dividend the yield is 20 percent and the return is 120 percent. But if the dividend is passed, the yield is 0 percent and a −50 percent return is recorded. Thus, the regressions with the level-revised measure tend to show what appears to be a positive association between returns and dividend yields. However, the correlation is spurious. A simple way to correct for the problem is to use the dividend yield of 12 months ago. Shown in the third regression in Table 22A.1, the results indicate a small, statistically insignificant, relationship between dividend yields and returns.

Another approach, shown in the fourth regression in Table 22A.1, is to drop from the sample all firms except those that both paid dividends in month *t* and announced them in advance. Again the dividend coefficient is insignificant.

Litzenberger and Ramaswamy [1982] have responded to the Miller-Scholes criticism by rerunning their regressions. Table 22A.2 shows their results. The level-revised dividend yield gave the highest coefficient (a_3) and it is slightly higher than the Miller-Scholes estimate. Instead of using a dividend 12 months ago Litzenberger and Ramaswamy built a more sophisticated model to predict dividends. Their "predicted dividend yield" model avoids the Miller-Scholes criticism and continues to give a statistically significant estimate of the dividend effect. So, too, does a restricted subsample designed to avoid the Miller-Scholes criticism. Thus, the empirical evidence, at this point in time, points toward the

[2]The *ex ante* return is computed as

$$.5\left(\frac{20-10}{10} + \frac{2}{10}\right) + .5\left(\frac{5-10}{10}\right) = .35,$$

and the *ex ante* dividend yield is

$$.5\left(\frac{2}{10}\right) + .5\left(\frac{0}{10}\right) = .10.$$

Table 22A.2   Pooled Time Series and Cross-Section Test of the Dividend Effect, 1940-1980

Definition of expected dividend yield	a_1	a_2	a_3
Level-revised monthly	.0031	.0048	.233
dividend yield	(1.81)	(2.15)	(8.79)
Predicted dividend yield	.0034	.0047	.151
	(1.95)	(2.08)	(5.39)
Restricted subsample	.0010	.0053	.135
	(0.52)	(2.33)	(4.38)

Source: Litzenberger, R., and K. Ramaswamy, "The Effects of Dividends on Common Stock Prices: Tax Effects or Information Effects?", *Journal of Finance*, (May 1982), p. 441.

conclusion that shareholders express their displeasure with corporate dividend payments by requiring a higher risk-adjusted return (that is, by paying a lower price) for those stocks that have higher dividend yields.[3]

Dividend Clientele Effects

The clientele effect was originally suggested by Miller and Modigliani [1961]:

> *If, for example, the frequency distribution of corporate payout ratios happened to correspond exactly with the distribution of investor preferences for payout ratios, then the existence of these preferences would clearly lead ultimately to a situation whose implications were different, in no fundamental respect, from the perfect market case. Each corporation would tend to attract to itself a "clientele" consisting of those preferring its particular payout ratio, but one clientele would be as good as another in terms of the valuation it would imply for firms.*

The clientele effect is a possible explanation for management reluctance to alter established payout ratios because such changes might cause current shareholders to incur unwanted transactions costs.

Elton and Gruber [1970] attempt to measure clientele effects by observing the average price decline when a stock goes ex dividend. If we were current shareholders and sold our stock the instant before it went ex dividend, we would receive its price, p_B, and pay the capital gains rate, T_g, on the difference between the selling price and the price at which it was purchased, p_C. Alternatively, we could sell the stock after it went ex dividend. In this case we would receive the dividend, d, and pay the ordinary tax rate, T_0, on it. In addition, we would pay a capital gains tax on the difference between its ex-dividend price, p_A, and the original purchase price, p_C. To prevent arbitrage profits, our gain from either course of

---

[3]The only empirical study that has found evidence shareholders prefer dividends is a paper by Long [1978], which carefully examines the case of Citizens Utilities, a company that has two classes of stock that are alike in every way except one pays cash dividends and the other pays stock dividends.

action must be the same, namely,

$$p_B - T_g(p_B - p_C) = p_A - T_g(p_A - p_C) + d(1 - T_0). \tag{22A.2}$$

Rearranging (22A.2), we obtain

$$\frac{p_B - p_A}{d} = \frac{1 - T_0}{1 - T_g}. \tag{22A.3}$$

Therefore the ratio of the decline in stock price to the dividend paid becomes a means of estimating the marginal tax rate of the average investor if we assume that the capital gains rate is half the ordinary tax rate.

Using 4,148 observations between April 1, 1966 and March 31, 1967, Elton and Gruber discovered that the average price decline as a percent of dividend paid was 77.7 percent. This implied that the marginal tax bracket of the average investor was 36.4 percent. They continued by arguing

> . . . the lower a firm's dividend yield the smaller the percentage of his total return that a stockholder expects to receive in the form of dividends and the larger the percentage he expects to receive in the form of capital gains. Therefore, investors who hold stocks that have high dividend yields should be in low tax brackets relative to stockholders who hold stocks with low dividend yield.

Table 22A.3 shows the dividend payout ranked from the lowest to highest deciles along with (1) the average drop in price as a percent of dividends and (2) the implied tax bracket. Note that the implied tax bracket decreases when dividend payout increases. Elton and Gruber conclude that the evidence suggests that Miller and Modigliani were right in hypothesizing a clientele effect.

Table 22A.3   Dividend Yield Statistics Ranked by Decile

		$(p_B - p_A)/d$*				
Decile	d/p Mean	Mean	Standard Deviation	Z Value	Probability: True Mean Is One or More	Implied Tax Bracket
1	.0124	.6690	.8054	.411	.341	.4974
2	.0216	.4873	.2080	2.465	.007	.6145
3	.0276	.5447	.1550	2.937	.002	.5915
4	.0328	.6246	.1216	3.087	.001	.5315
5	.0376	.7953	.1064	1.924	.027	.3398
6	.0416	.8679	.0712	1.855	.031	.2334
7	.0452	.9209	.0761	1.210	.113	.1465
8	.0496	.9054	.0691	1.369	.085	.1747
9	.0552	1.0123	.0538	.229	.591	**
10	.0708	1.1755	.0555	3.162	.999	**

*Spearman's rank correlation coefficient between d/p and $(p_B - p_A)/d$ is .9152, which is significant at the 1 percent level.
**Indeterminate.
Source: Elton, E. J., and M. J. Gruber, "Marginal Stockholders' Tax Rates and the Clientele Effect," reprinted from *The Review of Economics and Statistics*, (February 1970), p. 72.

A possible counterargument to this interpretation is that arbitrage may also be carried out by traders who do not own the stock initially. They would not receive favored capital gains treatment but would have to pay ordinary income taxes on short-term gains. Their arbitrage profit, Π, may be stated mathematically as

$$\Pi = -p_B + d - T_0 d + p_A + T_0(p_B - p_A). \qquad \textbf{(22A.4)}$$

They spend p_B to acquire the stock before it goes ex dividend, then receive the dividend and pay ordinary income taxes on it, and finally sell the stock after it goes ex dividend (receiving p_A dollars) and receive a tax shield from their short-term loss. Rearranging Equation 22A.4, we see that their profit is

$$\Pi = (1 - T_0)[p_A - p_B + d]. \qquad \textbf{(22A.5)}$$

To prevent arbitrage profits, the price decline must equal the amount of dividend payout, that is, $p_B - p_A = d$.

The above condition is completely different from Equation 22A.3 proposed by Elton and Gruber. Of course, neither model has taken transactions costs into account, nor have we considered other classes of investors, such as tax-free investors. Therefore no strong conclusion can be made regarding the existence of a clientele effect.

More recently, Pettit [1977] has tested for clientele effects by examining the portfolio positions of approximately 914 individual accounts handled by a large retail brokerage house between 1964 and 1970. He argues that stocks with low dividend yields will be preferred by investors with high income, by younger investors, by investors whose ordinary and capital gains tax rates differ substantially, and by investors whose portfolios have high systematic risk. His model is

$$DY_i = a_1 + a_2\beta_i + a_3 AGE_i + a_4 INC_i + a_5 DTR_i + \epsilon_i, \qquad \textbf{(22A.6)}$$

where

$DY_i =$ dividend yield for the ith individual's portfolio in 1970
$\beta_i =$ the systematic risk of the ith individual's portfolio
$AGE_i =$ the age of the individual
$INC_i =$ the gross family income averaged over the last three years
$DTR_i =$ the difference between the income and capital gains tax rates for the ith individual
$\epsilon_i =$ a normally distributed random error term

He finds that[4]

$$DY_i = \quad .042 \quad - \quad .021\beta_i \quad + \quad .031 AGE_i \quad - \quad .037 INC_i \quad + \quad .006 DTR_i.$$

$$(11.01) \quad (-16.03) \quad (6.15) \quad (-2.25) \quad (1.57)$$

The evidence suggests that there is a clientele effect because a significant portion of the observed cross-sectional variation in individual portfolio dividend yields can be explained.

---

[4]The numbers in parentheses are t-statistics. The r^2 was .3 for 914 observations.

However, the study in no way suggests that the market price of a security is determined by the dividend policy followed by the firm.

A second study by Lewellen, Stanley, Lease, and Schlarbaum [1978] was drawn from the same data base as the Pettit study, but reached different conclusions. They ran a multiple regression to explain the dividend yields of investor portfolios as a function of various investor characteristics. Although the tax rate variable was negatively related to dividend yield and was statistically significant, it implied that a 10 percent increase in an investor's marginal (imputed) tax bracket was associated with only a .1 percent decline in the yield of securities held. This suggests only a very weak clientele effect.

Finally, the Litzenberger-Ramaswamy study [1982] reports results that may be interpreted as consistent with dividend clienteles. They ranked all NYSE stocks on the basis of their dividend yield and then divided the entire sample into quantities based on market value. Companies in the first quintile comprised the one-fifth of total market value with the lowest dividend yield, and so on. They then ran a regression based on Equation 22A.1. The results are given in Table 22A.4. Note that the dividend yield coefficient, a_3, decreases as the dividend yield in each quintile becomes larger. The lowest dividend yield stocks had the most severe return penalty for dividend payments and the highest yield stocks had no statistically significant penalty at all. These results are consistent with the interpretation that high tax bracket clientele hold low yield stocks while low bracket clientele hold high yield stocks.

Summary

The empirical evidence on the relationship between dividends and share prices is mixed. Some researchers such as Litzenberger and Ramaswamy [1979, 1980, 1982] report that investors dislike dividends and that they require higher returns to compensate them for dividend taxes. However, Miller and Scholes [1983] find no dividend effect. Only one study by Long [1978] provides evidence for shareholder preference for dividends.

Although the empirical evidence on dividend clientele effects is also mixed, most studies do find evidence in support of a clientele effect. High tax bracket investors seem to prefer low dividend stocks, presumably because they pay lower taxes when receiving their return in the form of capital gains.

Table 22A.4   Pooled Time Series and Cross-Section Test of Tax Clientele, 1940-1980, Using Predicted Dividends

Dividend Yield Group	a_1	$t(a_1)$	a_2	$t(a_2)$	a_3	$t(a_3)$
1 (low yield)	.0048	(2.22)	.0050	(2.06)	.555	(2.83)
2	.0021	(1.01)	.0047	(1.97)	.486	(4.18)
3	.0034	(1.69)	.0043	(1.78)	.339	(5.32)
4	.0018	(0.98)	.0067	(2.70)	.212	(4.74)
5 (high yield)	.0037	(1.94)	.0062	(2.62)	.022	(0.65)

Source: Litzenberger, R., and K. Ramaswamy, "The Tax Effects of Dividends on Common Stock Prices: Tax Effects or Information Effects?", *Journal of Finance*, (May 1982), p. 438.

Selected References

Black, F., and Scholes, M., "The Effects of Dividend Yield and Dividend Policy on Common Stock Prices and Returns," *Journal of Financial Economics*, 1 (May 1974), pp. 1-22.

Brennan, Michael, "Taxes, Market Valuation and Corporate Financial Policy," *National Tax Journal*, (December 1970), pp. 417-427.

Copeland, Thomas E., and Weston, J. Fred, *Financial Theory and Corporate Policy*, 2nd Ed., Reading, Mass.: Addison-Wesley, 1983.

Elton, Edwin J., and Gruber, Martin J., "Marginal Stockholder Tax Rates and the Clientele Effect," *Review of Economics and Statistics*, 52 (February 1970), pp. 68-74.

Farrar, D., and Selwyn, L., "Taxes, Corporate Financial Policy and Return to Investors," *National Tax Journal*, (December 1967), pp. 444-454.

Lewellen, Wilbur G.; Stanley, Kenneth L.; Lease, Ronald C.; and Schlarbaum, Gary G., "Some Direct Evidence on the Dividend Clientele Phenomenon," *Journal of Finance*, 33 (December 1978), pp. 1385-1399.

Litzenberger, R., and Ramaswamy, K., "The Effects of Dividends on Common Stock Prices: Tax Effects or Information Effects?", *Journal of Finance*, 37 (May 1982), pp. 429-444.

——, "Dividends, Short-Selling Restrictions, Tax-Induced Investor Clienteles and Market Equilibrium," *Journal of Finance*, 35 (May 1980), pp. 462-482.

——, "The Effect of Personal Taxes and Dividends on Capital Asset Prices: Theory and Empirical Evidence," *Journal of Financial Economics*, (June 1979), pp. 163-196.

Long, John B., Jr., "The Market Valuation of Cash Dividends: A Case to Consider," *Journal of Financial Economics*, 6 (June-September 1978), pp. 235-264.

Miller, Merton H., and Modigliani, Franco, "Dividend Policy, Growth, and the Valuation of Shares," *Journal of Business*, 34 (October 1961), pp. 411-433.

Miller, Merton H., and Scholes, Myron S., "Dividends and Taxes: Some Empirical Evidence," *Journal of Political Economy*, (December 1983), pp. 1118-1141.

Pettit, R. Richardson, "Taxes, Transactions Costs and the Clientele Effect of Dividends," *Journal of Financial Economics*, 5 (December 1977), pp. 419-436.

Chapter 23 Valuation

In Chapter 1, we noted that the goal of financial management is to maximize the value of the firm. Now, having discussed the time dimension, risk factors, cash flow patterns, capital structure and cost of capital, and dividend policy, we are prepared to consider how these inputs affect valuation.

Definitions of Value

While it may be difficult to ascribe monetary returns to certain kinds of assets — works of art, for instance — the fundamental characteristic of business assets is that they give rise to income flows. Sometimes these flows are easy to determine and measure; the interest return on a bond is an example. At other times, the cash flows attributable to the asset must be estimated, as was done in Chapter 6 on capital budgeting. Regardless of the difficulties of measuring income flows, it is the prospective income from business assets that gives them value.

Liquidating Value versus Going-Concern Value

Several different definitions of *value* exist in the literature and in practice; different definitions are appropriate at different times. The first distinction that must be made is that between liquidating value and going-concern value. *Liquidating value* is the amount that can be realized if an asset or a group of assets (the entire assets of a firm, for example) is sold separately from the organization that has been using them. If the owner of a machine shop decides to retire, he may auction off his inventory and equipment, collect his accounts receivable, and sell his land and buildings to a grocery wholesaler for use as a warehouse. The sum of the proceeds from each category of assets is the liquidating value of the assets. If the owner's debts are subtracted from this amount, the difference represents the liquidating value of his ownership in the business.

The *going-concern value* of a company is its worth, as an operating business, to another firm or individual. If this value exceeds the liquidating value, the difference represents the market value of the organization as distinct from the book value of the assets.[1]

Book Value versus Market Value

Book value, the accounting value at which an asset is carried, must also be distinguished from *market value*, the price at which the asset can be sold. If the asset in question is a firm,

---

[1]Accountants have termed this difference "goodwill," but "organization value" would be a more appropriate description.

it actually has two market values — a liquidating value and a going-concern value. Only the higher of the two is generally referred to as the market value.

For stocks, book value per share is the firm's total common equity — common stock, capital or paid-in surplus, and accumulated and retained earnings — divided by shares outstanding. Market value, what people will actually pay for a share of the stock, can be above or below book value. Since market value depends on earnings while book value reflects historical cost, it is not surprising to find deviations between book and market values in a dynamic, uncertain world.

Market Value versus Fair or Reasonable Value

The concept of fair or reasonable value (sometimes called *intrinsic value*) is widespread in the literature on stock market investments. Although the market value of a security is known at any given time, the security's fair value as viewed by different investors can differ. Graham, Dodd, and Cottle, authors of a leading investments text, define *fair value* as "that value which is justified by the facts; for example, assets, earnings, dividends. . . . The computed (fair) value is likely to change at least from year to year, as the factors governing that value are modified."[2]

Although Graham, Dodd, and Cottle have developed this concept for security (that is, stock and bond) valuation, the idea applies to all business assets. It basically involves estimating the future net cash flows attributable to an asset; determining an appropriate capitalization, or discount, rate; and then finding the present value of the cash flows. This, of course, is exactly what was done in Chapter 6, where the concept of reasonable value was developed to help find the present value of investment opportunities.

The procedure for determining an asset's value is known as the *capitalization-of-income method of valuation* — a fancy name for the present value of a stream of earnings, discussed at length in Chapter 6. In going through the present chapter, keep in mind that *value, or the price of securities, is exactly analogous to the present value of assets* as determined in Chapter 6. From this point on, whenever the word *value* is used, it means the present value found by capitalizing expected future cash flows.

The next section applies these concepts to bond valuation; the two following sections treat the valuation of preferred and common stocks.

Valuation of Financial Instruments

Different financial instruments are characterized by varying cash flow patterns as shown in Table 23.1. In this overview, we shall distinguish between bonds and common stocks. We discuss two basic categories for bonds — Consols with infinite maturities and other bonds with finite maturities.

Bond Valuation

For fixed rate bonds, the expected cash flows are the annual interest payments plus the principal due when the bond matures. Depending on differences in the risk of default on interest or principal, the appropriate capitalization (or discount) rate applied to different

---

[2]Graham, Dodd, and Cottle [1961].

Table 23.1   Patterns of Future Cash Net Inflows

Pattern of Growth	Duration of Receipts	Examples
No growth	Infinite or perpetual	Consols, preferred stock, common stock
No growth	Finite time period	Notes and bonds
Constant growth	Infinite or perpetual	Common stock
Temporary growth	Finite time period for growth, followed by a subsequent pattern to infinity	Common stock

bonds varies. A U.S. Treasury security, for example, has less risk than a security issued by a corporation; consequently, a lower discount (or capitalization) rate is applied to its interest payments. The actual calculating procedures employed in bond valuation are illustrated by the following examples.

Perpetual Bond

After the Napoleonic Wars (1814), England sold a huge bond issue, which it used to pay off many smaller issues that had been floated in prior years to pay for the war. Since the purpose of the new issue was to consolidate past debts, the individual bonds were called Consols. Suppose the bonds paid $100 interest annually to perpetuity. (Actually, interest was stated in pounds.) What would the bonds be worth under current market conditions?

First, note that the value v_b of any perpetuity is computed as follows:[3]

---

[3]A perpetuity is a bond that never matures; that is, it pays interest indefinitely. Equation 23.1 is simply the present value of an infinite series; its proof is demonstrated below. Rewrite Equation 23.1 as follows:

$$v_b = c\left[\frac{1}{(1 + k_b)^1} + \frac{1}{(1 + k_b)^2} + \ldots + \frac{1}{(1 + k_b)^n}\right]. \tag{1}$$

Multiply both sides of Equation (1) by $(1 + k_b)$:

$$v_b(1 + k_b) = c\left[1 + \frac{1}{(1 + k_b)^1} + \frac{1}{(1 + k_b)^2} + \ldots + \frac{1}{(1 + k_b)^{n-1}}\right]. \tag{2}$$

Subtract Equation (1) from Equation (2), obtaining

$$v_b(1 + k_b - 1) = c\left[1 - \frac{1}{(1 + k_b)^n}\right]. \tag{3}$$

As $n \to \infty$,

$$\frac{1}{(1 + k_b)^n} \to 0,$$

so Equation (3) approaches

$$v_b k_b = c,$$

and

$$v_b = \frac{c}{k_b}.$$

$$v_b = \frac{c}{(1 + k_b)^1} + \frac{c}{(1 + k_b)^2} + \cdots$$

$$= \frac{c}{k_b}. \tag{23.1}$$

Here c is the constant annual interest in dollars and k_b is the appropriate interest rate (or required rate of return) for the bond issue. Equation 23.1 is an infinite series of $\$c$ a year, and the value of the bond is the discounted sum of the infinite series.

We know that the Consol's annual interest payment is \$100; therefore, the only other thing we need in order to find its value is the appropriate interest rate. This is commonly taken as the going interest rate, or yield, on bonds of similar risk. Suppose we find such bonds to be paying 8 percent under current market conditions. Then the Consol's value is determined as follows:

$$v_b = \frac{c}{k_b} = \frac{\$100}{0.08} = \$1,250.$$

If the going rate of interest rises to 10 percent, the value of the bond falls to \$1,000 (\$100/0.10). If interest rates continue rising, when the rate goes as high as 12 percent, the value of the Consol will be only \$833.33. Values of this perpetual bond for a range of interest rates are given in Table 23.2.

Short-Term Bond

Suppose the British government issues bonds with the same risk of default as the Consols but with a three-year maturity. The new bonds also pay \$100 interest and have a \$1,000 maturity value. What will the value of these new bonds be at the time of issue if the going rate of interest is 8 percent? To find this value, we must solve Equation 23.2:

$$v_b = \frac{c_1}{(1 + k_b)^1} + \frac{c_2}{(1 + k_b)^2} + \frac{c_3 + M}{(1 + k_b)^3}. \tag{23.2}$$

Table 23.2   Valuation of a Consol

Current Market Interest Rate	Current Market Value
4%	$2,500.00
6	1,666.67
8	1,250.00
10	1,000.00
12	833.33
14	714.29
16	625.00

Table 23.3   Valuation of a Three-Year Bond at 8 Percent

Year	Receipt	8 Percent Discount Factors	Present Value
1	$100	0.9259	$ 92.59
2	$100	0.8573	85.73
1	$100 + $1,000	0.7938	873.18
		Bond value =	$1,051.50

Here M is the maturity value of the bond. The solution is given in Table 23.3.[4] At the various rates of interest used in the perpetuity example, this three-year bond will have the values as shown in Table 23.4.

Interest-Rate Risk

Figure 23.1 shows how the values of the long-term bond (the Consol) and the short-term bond change in response to changes in the going market rate of interest. Note how much less sensitive the short-term bond is to changes in interest rates. At a 10 percent interest rate, both the perpetuity and the short-term bond are valued at $1,000. When rates rise to 16 percent, the long-term bond falls to $625, while the short-term bond falls only to $865. A similar situation occurs when rates fall below 10 percent. *This differential responsiveness to changes in interest rates depends on the required yield levels.* At the lower yields depicted in

---

Table 23.4   Valuation of a Three-Year Bond at Different Interest Rates

Current Market Interest Rate	Current Market Value
4%	$1,166.51
6	1,106.90
8	1,051.50
10	1,000.00
12	951.99
14	907.17
16	865.30

---

[4]If the bond has a long maturity, 20 years for example, we would calculate its present value by finding the present value of a 20-year annuity and adding to it the present value of the $1,000 principal received at maturity. Special bond tables have been devised to simplify the calculation procedure. Note also that k_b frequently differs for the long- and short-term bonds; as we saw in Chapter 7, unless the yield to maturity curve is flat, long- and short-term rates differ.

Figure 23.1   Values of Long-Term and Short-Term Bonds, 10 Percent Coupon Rate, at Different Market Interest Rates

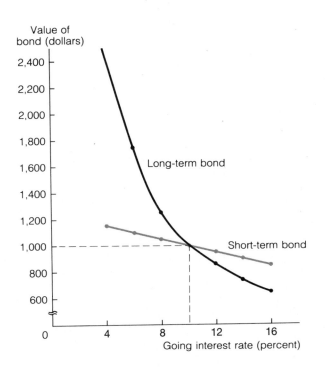

Figure 23.1, the longer the maturity of a security, the greater is its price change in response to a given change in interest rates. This helps explain why corporate treasurers are reluctant to hold their near-cash reserves in the form of long-term debt instruments. These reserves are held at moderate interest levels for precautionary purposes, and treasurers are unwilling to sacrifice safety for a little higher yield on a long-term bond. However, for deep discount bonds at required yields of 10 percent or more, the further decline in price with higher required yields is at a lesser rate for longer-term bonds than for shorter-term bonds. This is depicted in Figure 23.2, where the value of the 30-year bond falls less rapidly than the value of a 20-year bond as required yields rise from 10 to 25 percent.

Preferred Stock Valuation

Most preferred stocks entitle their owners to regular, fixed dividend payments similar to bond interest. Although many preferred issues are eventually retired, some are perpetuities whose value is found as follows:

$$v_{ps} = \frac{d_{ps}}{k_{ps}}.$$

(23.3)

Figure 23.2   Values of 20-Year and 30-Year Bonds at Required Yields of 10 to 25 Percent

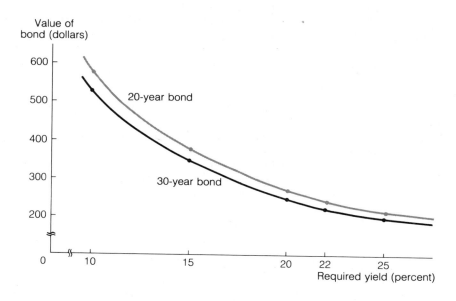

In this case, d_{ps} is the dividend on the preferred stock, and k_{ps} is the appropriate capitalization rate for investments of this degree of risk. For example, a General Motors $3.75 no par preferred stock issue was originally sold at 100 to yield 3.75 percent. On August 7, 1984, the $3.75 preferred stock of General Motors closed at $35.00. The yield on a preferred stock is similar to that on a perpetual bond and is found by solving Equation 23.3 for k_{ps}. Thus, the yield is 10.7 percent, calculated as follows:

$$k_{ps} = \frac{d_{ps}}{v_{ps}} = \frac{\$3.75}{\$35} = 10.7\%.$$

The valuation relationship expressed by Equation 23.3 is also implied. If we know the promised dividend payment on the preferred stock and its current yield, we can determine its value:

$$v_{ps} = \frac{\$3.75}{0.107} = \$35.$$

Common Stock Returns and Valuation

While the same principles apply to the valuation of common stocks as to bonds or preferred stocks, two features make their analysis more difficult. First is the degree of certainty with which receipts can be forecast. For bonds and preferred stocks, this presents little difficulty, since the interest payments or preferred dividends are known with relative certainty. However, in the case of common stocks, forecasting future earnings, dividends, and stock prices can be difficult. The second complicating feature is that, unlike interest and preferred dividends, common stock earnings and dividends are generally expected to grow, not remain constant. Hence, while standard annuity formulas can be applied, more difficult conceptual schemes must also be used.

Estimating the Value of a Stock: The Single-Period Case

The price today of a share of common stock, p_o, depends on the return investors expect to receive if they buy the stock, and the riskiness of these expected cash flows. The expected returns consist of two elements: (1) the dividend expected in each Year t, defined as d_t, and (2) the price investors expect to receive when they sell the stock at the end of Year n, defined as p_n. The price includes the return of the original investment plus a capital gain (or minus a capital loss). If investors expect to hold the stock for one year, and if the stock price is expected to grow at the rate g, the valuation equation is

$$p_o = \frac{\text{Expected dividend} + \text{Expected price (Both at end of Year 1)}}{1.0 + \text{Required rate of return}}$$

$$= \frac{d_1 + p_1}{(1 + k_s)} = \frac{d_1 + p_o(1 + g)}{(1 + k_s)}, \tag{23.4}$$

which results in Equation 23.5 after simplification.[5]

$$p_o = \frac{d_1}{k_s - g}. \tag{23.5}$$

Equations 23.4 and 23.5 represent the present value of the expected dividends and the year-end stock price, discounted at the required rate of return. Solving Equation 23.5 gives the expected or intrinsic price for the stock. To illustrate: Suppose you are thinking of buying a share of United Rubber common stock and holding it for one year. You note that United Rubber earned $2.86 per share last year and paid a dividend of $1.90. Earnings and dividends have been rising at about 5 percent a year, on the average, over the last 10 to 15 years, and you expect this growth to continue. Further, if earnings and dividends grow at the expected rate, you think the stock price will likewise grow by 5 percent a year.

The next step is to determine the required rate of return on United Rubber stock. The current rate of interest on U.S. Treasury securities, R_F, is about 9 percent. But, United Rubber is clearly more risky than government securities. Competitors can erode the company's market; labor problems can disrupt operations; an economic recession can cause sales to fall below the breakeven point; auto sales can decline, pulling down United Rubber's own sales and profits; and so on. Further, even if sales, earnings, and dividends meet projections, the stock price can still fall as a result of a generally weak market.

---

[5]Notice that this equation is developed for a one-year holding period. In a later section, we will show that it is also valid for longer periods, provided the expected growth rate is constant.

Given all these risk factors, you conclude that a 7 percent risk premium is justified, so you calculate your required rate of return on United Rubber's stock, k_s, as follows:[6]

$$k_s = R_F + \rho = 9\% + 7\% = 16\%.$$

Next, you estimate the dividend for the coming year, d_1, as follows:

$$d_1 = d_0(1 + g) = \$1.90(1.05) = \$2.$$

Now you have the information necessary to estimate the fair value of the stock by the use of Equation 23.5:

$$p_0 = \frac{d_1}{k_s - g}$$

$$= \frac{\$2}{0.16 - 0.05} = \$18.18. \tag{23.5}$$

To you, $18.18 represents a reasonable price for United Rubber's stock. If the actual market price is less, you will buy it; if the actual price is higher, you will not buy it, or you will sell if you own it.[7]

Factors Leading to Changes in Market Prices

Assume that United Rubber's stock is in equilibrium, selling at a price of $18.18 per share. If all expectations are exactly met, over the next year, the price will gradually rise to $19.09 (5 percent). However, many different events can occur to cause a change in the equilibrium price of the stock. To illustrate the forces at work, consider again the stock price model, the set of inputs used to develop the price of $18.18, and a new set of assumed input variables shown in Table 23.5.

The first three variables influence k_s, which declines from 16 to 15.2 percent as a result of the new set of variables.

$$\text{Original: } k_s = 9\% + (5\%)(1.4) = 16\%.$$

$$\text{New: } \quad k_s = 8\% + (6\%)(1.2) = 15.2\%.$$

Using these values, together with the new d and g values, we find that p_0 rises from $18.18 to $21.85.

$$\text{Original: } p_0 = \frac{\$1.90(1.05)}{0.16 - 0.05} = \frac{\$2}{0.11} = \$18.18.$$

$$\text{New: } \quad p_0 = \frac{\$1.90(1.06)}{0.152 - 0.06} = \frac{\$2.01}{0.092} = \$21.85.$$

[6]This is really an application of the Capital Asset Pricing Model, which was introduced in Chapter 17. To obtain a 7 percent risk premium, we assume that the expected return on the market portfolio is 14 percent and that United Rubber has a beta of 1.40.

[7]Notice the similarity between this process and the NPV method of capital budgeting described in Chapter 6. In the earlier chapter, we (1) estimated a cost of capital for the firm, which compares with estimating k_s, our required rate of return; (2) discounted expected future cash flows, which are analogous to dividends plus the future stock price; (3) found the present value of future cash flows, which corresponds to the fair value of the stock; (4) determined the initial outlay for the project, which compares to finding the actual price of the stock; and (5) accepted the project if the PV of future cash flows exceeded the initial cost of the project, which is similar to comparing the fair value of the stock to its market price.

Table 23.5   Influences on Stock Prices

	Variable Value	
	Original	New
Riskless rate, R_F	9%	8%
Market risk premium, $E(R_M) - R_F$	5%	6%
Index of stock's risk, β	1.4	1.2
Expected growth rate, g	5%	6%

We can obtain the expected return by solving Equation 23.5 for k_s as shown in Equation 23.6.

$$k_s = \frac{d_1}{p_o} + g \qquad (23.6)$$

At the new price, the expected return, k_s^o, and the required return, k_s, are equal:

$$k_s^o = \frac{\$2.01}{\$21.85} + 6\% = 9.2\% + 6\% = 15.2\% = k_s,$$

as found above.

As we saw in Chapter 19 on market efficiency, securities adjust rapidly to disequilibrium situations. Consequently, equilibrium ordinarily exists for any given stock, and, in general, the required and expected returns are equal. Stock prices certainly change, sometimes violently and rapidly, but this simply reflects changing conditions and expectations. There are, of course, times when a stock continues to react for several months to a favorable or unfavorable development, but this does not signify a long adjustment period; it merely shows that as more information about the situation becomes available, the market adjusts to the new information.

Valuation under Alternative Growth Patterns

To this point, we have treated a single-period model of stock valuation, in which investors hold the stock for one year, receive one dividend, and then sell the stock at the end of the year. We now take up multiperiod stock valuation models.

According to generally accepted theory, stock prices are determined as the present value of a stream of cash flows. In other words, the capitalization of income procedure applies to stocks as well as to bonds and other assets. What are the cash flows that corporations provide to their stockholders? What flows do the markets in fact capitalize? A number of different models have been formulated, of which we shall illustrate the stream of dividends approach and the free cash flow model.

The Stream of Dividends Approach

In the stream of dividends approach, a share of common stock is regarded as similar to a perpetual bond or a share of perpetual preferred stock, and its value is established as the present value of its stream of dividends.

$$\text{Value of stock} = p_o = \text{PV of expected future dividends}$$

$$= \frac{d_1}{(1 + k_s)^1} + \frac{d_2}{(1 + k_s)^2} + \cdots$$

$$= \sum_{t=1}^{\infty} \frac{d_t}{(1 + k_s)^t}. \tag{23.7}$$

Unlike bond interest and preferred dividends, common stock dividends are not generally expected to remain constant in the future; hence, the convenient annuity formulas cannot be used. This fact, combined with the much greater uncertainty about common stock dividends than about bond interest or preferred dividends, makes common stock valuation a more complex task than bond valuation or preferred stock valuation.

Equation 23.7 is a general stock valuation model in the sense that the time pattern of d_t can be anything; that is, d_t can rise, fall, remain constant, or even fluctuate randomly, and Equation 23.7 will still hold. For many purposes, however, it is useful to estimate a particular time pattern for d_t and then develop a simplified (easier to evaluate) version of the stock valuation model expressed in Equation 23.7. The following sections consider the special cases of zero growth, constant growth, and supernormal growth.

Stock Values with Zero Growth

Suppose the rate of growth is measured by the rate at which dividends are expected to increase. If future growth is expected to be zero, the value of the stock reduces to the same formula as that developed for a perpetual bond.

$$\text{Price} = \frac{\text{Dividend}}{\text{Capitalization rate}}$$

$$p_o = \frac{d_1}{k_s}. \tag{23.8}$$

Normal, or Constant, Growth

Year after year, the earnings and dividends of most companies have been increasing. In general, this growth is expected to continue in the foreseeable future at about the same rate as the GNP. Thus, if such a company's current dividend is d_0, its dividend in any future Year t will be $d_t = d_0(1 + g)^t$, where g = the expected rate of growth. For example, if United Rubber just paid a dividend of \$2.00 (d_0 = \$2.00) and its investors expect an 8 percent growth rate, the estimated dividend one year hence is $d_1 = (\$2.00)(1.08) = \$2.16$; two years hence, \$2.33; and five years hence,

$$d_t = d_0(1 + g)^t$$

$$= \$2.00(1.08)^5$$

$$= \$2.94.$$

Using this method of estimating future dividends, the current price, p_o, is determined as follows:

$$p_o = \frac{d_1}{(1 + k_s)^1} + \frac{d_2}{(1 + k_s)^2} + \frac{d_3}{(1 + k_s)^3} + \cdots$$

$$= \frac{d_0(1 + g)^1}{(1 + k_s)^1} + \frac{d_0(1 + g)^2}{(1 + k_s)^2} + \frac{d_0(1 + g)^3}{(1 + k_s)^3} + \cdots$$

$$= \sum_{t=1}^{\infty} \frac{d_0(1 + g)^t}{(1 + k_s)^t}. \tag{23.9}$$

If g is constant, Equation 23.9 can be simplified as follows:[8]

$$p_o = \frac{d_1}{k_s - g}. \tag{23.10}$$

Notice that the constant growth model expressed in Equation 23.10 is identical to the single-period model, Equation 23.5, developed in an earlier section.

A necessary condition for the constant growth model is that k_s be greater than g; otherwise, Equation 23.10 gives nonsense answers. If k_s equals g, the equation blows up, yielding an infinite price; if k_s is less than g, a negative price results. Since neither infinite nor negative stock prices make sense, it is clear that in equilibrium, k_s must be greater than g.

Note that Equation 23.10 is sufficiently general to encompass the no growth case described above. If growth is zero, this is simply a special case, and Equation 23.10 is equal to Equation 23.8.[9]

---

[8]The proof of Equation 23.10 is as follows. Rewrite Equation 23.9 as

$$p_o = d_0\left[\frac{(1 + g)}{(1 + k_s)} + \frac{(1 + g)^2}{(1 + k_s)^2} + \frac{(1 + g)^3}{(1 + k_s)^3} + \cdots + \frac{(1 + g)^n}{(1 + k_s)^n}\right]. \tag{1}$$

Multiply both sides of Equation (1) by $(1 + k_s)/(1 + g)$:

$$p_o\left[\frac{(1 + k_s)}{(1 + g)}\right] = d_0\left[1 + \frac{(1 + g)}{(1 + k_s)} + \frac{(1 + g)^2}{(1 + k_s)^2} + \cdots + \frac{(1 + g)^{n-1}}{(1 + k_s)^{n-1}}\right]. \tag{2}$$

Subtract Equation (1) from Equation (2) to obtain

$$p_o\left[\frac{(1 + k_s)}{(1 + g)} - 1\right] = d_0\left[1 - \frac{(1 + g)^n}{(1 + k_s)^n}\right]$$

$$p_o\left[\frac{(1 + k_s) - (1 + g)}{(1 + g)}\right] = d_0\left[1 - \frac{(1 + g)^n}{(1 + k_s)^n}\right].$$

Assuming $k_s > g$, as $n \to \infty$, the term in brackets on the right side of the equation $\to 1.0$, leaving

$$p_o\left[\frac{(1 + k_s) - (1 + g)}{(1 + g)}\right] = d_0,$$

which simplifies to

$$p_o(k_s - g) = d_0(1 + g) = d_1$$

$$p_o = \frac{d_1}{k_s - g}.$$

[9]The logic underlying the analysis implicitly assumes that investors are indifferent between dividend yield and capital gains. Empirical work has not conclusively established whether or not this is true. See the appendix to Chapter 22 for a review of the empirical evidence.

Figure 23.3   A Comparison of Four Companies' Dividend Growth Rates

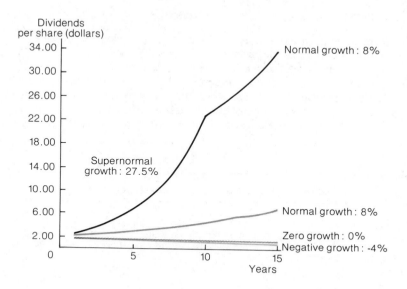

Supernormal Growth

Firms typically go through life cycles; during part of these cycles, their growth is much faster than that of the economy as a whole. Automobile manufacturers in the 1920s and computer and office equipment manufacturers in the 1960s are examples. Figure 23.3 illustrates such supernormal growth and compares it with normal growth, zero growth, and negative growth.[10]

A hypothetical supernormal growth firm is expected to grow at a 27.5 percent rate for ten years and then to have its growth rate fall to 8 percent. The value of the firm with this growth pattern is determined by the following equation:

Present price = PV of dividends during supernormal growth period

+ Value of stock price at end of supernormal growth period discounted back to present

$$p_0 = \sum_{t=1}^{n} \frac{d_0(1 + g_s)^t}{(1 + k_s)^t} + \left(\frac{d_{n+1}}{k_s - g}\right)\left(\frac{1}{(1 + k_s)^n}\right), \qquad (23.11)$$

[10] A negative growth rate represents a declining company (for example, a mining company whose profits are falling because of a declining ore body). Note that the market will assess a negative value to growth whenever a firm earns less than its weighted average cost of capital. Hence, it is possible for accounting earnings to grow (slowly) and for the market to place a negative value on a firm's growth. This will be explained fully later in the chapter when we look at a cash flow model of valuation.

where

g_s =   the supernormal growth rate
g =   the normal growth rate
n =   the period of supernormal growth.

Working through an example will help make this clear. Consider a supernormal growth firm whose current dividend is $2.00 ($d_0$ = 2.00), with the dividend expected to increase by 27.5 percent a year for ten years and thereafter at 8 percent a year indefinitely. If stockholders' required rate of return is 16 percent on an investment with this degree of risk, what is the value of the stock? On the basis of the calculations in Table 23.6, the value is $104.41, the present value of the dividends during the first ten years plus the present value of the stock at the end of the tenth year, discounted back to the present.

Table 23.6   Method of Calculating the Value of a Stock with Supernormal Growth

---

Assumptions:
1. Stockholders' capitalization rate is 16 percent (k_s = 16%).
2. Growth rate is 27.5 percent for ten years, 8 percent thereafter (g_s = 27.5%, g = 8%, and n = 10).
3. The current dividend is $2.00 ($d_0$ = 2.00).
Step 1. Find present value of dividends during rapid growth period.

(1) Year	(2) Amount of Dividend $2(1.275)^t$	(3) PVIF Factor $1/(1.16)^t$	(4) Present Value (2) × (3)
1	2.55	0.8621	2.20
2	3.25	0.7432	2.42
3	4.15	0.6407	2.66
4	5.29	0.5523	2.92
5	6.74	0.4761	3.21
6	8.59	0.4104	3.53
7	10.96	0.3538	3.88
8	13.97	0.3050	4.26
9	17.81	0.2630	4.68
10	22.71	0.2267	5.15

Present value of ten years' dividends $34.91

Step 2. Find present value of Year 10 stock price.
a. Find value of stock at end of Year 10:

$$p_{10} = \frac{d_{11}}{k_s - g} = \frac{\$22.71(1.08)}{0.08} = \$306.59.$$

b. Discount p_{10} back to present:

$$PV = p_{10}\left(\frac{1}{1 + k}\right)^{10} = \$306.59(0.2267) = \$69.50.$$

Step 3. Sum to find total value of stock today:

$$p_0 = \$34.91 + \$69.50 = \$104.41.$$

Table 23.7   Prices, Dividend Yields, and Price-Earnings Ratios under Different Growth Assumptions

		Price	Dividend Yield (d_1/p_0)	P-E Ratio[a]
Declining firm:	$p_0 = \dfrac{d_1}{k_s - g} = \dfrac{\$1.92}{0.16 - (-0.04)}$	$ 9.60	20.0%	2.40
No growth firm:	$p_0 = \dfrac{d_1}{k_s} = \dfrac{\$2.00}{0.16}$	12.50	16.0	3.13
Normal growth firm:	$p_0 = \dfrac{d_1}{k_s - g} = \dfrac{\$2.16}{0.16 - 0.08}$	27.00	8.0	6.75
Supernormal growth firm:	$p_0 = $ (See Table 23.6)	104.41	2.4	26.10

[a]The beginning of this example assumed that each company is earning $4.00 initially. Divided into the various prices, this $4.00 gives the indicated P-E ratios.

Comparing Companies with Different Expected Growth Rates

A comparison of four companies' illustrative dividend growth rates graphed in Figure 23.3 will help summarize this section. Using the valuation equations developed in this chapter, the conditions assumed in the preceding examples, and the additional assumptions that each firm had earnings per share of $4 (EPS$_0$ = $4) during the preceding reporting period and paid out 50 percent of its reported earnings (therefore, that dividends per share, d_0, are $2 for each company), we show prices, dividend yields, and price-earnings (P-E) ratios in Table 23.7.

Investors require and expect a return of 16 percent on each of the stocks. For the declining firm, this return consists of a relatively high current dividend yield combined with a capital loss amounting to 4 percent a year. For the no growth firm, there is neither a capital gain nor a capital loss expectation, so the 16 percent return must be obtained entirely from the dividend yield. The normal growth firm provides a relatively low current dividend yield but an 8 percent per year capital gain expectation. Finally, the supernormal growth firm has the lowest current dividend yield but the highest capital gain expectation.

What is expected to happen to the prices of the four firms' stocks over time? Three of the four cases are straightforward. The no growth firm's price is expected to be constant $(p_t = p_{t+1})$; the declining firm is expected to have a falling stock price; and the normal growth firm's stock is expected to grow at a constant rate, 8 percent. The supernormal growth case is more complex, but what is expected can be seen from the data in Table 23.6.

In Table 23.6, the present value of dividends during the rapid growth period was calculated on a year-by-year basis. The same result can be obtained more directly by use of the compound sum formula. The multiplier present value of dividends during the growth period in Equation 23.11 can be evaluated as follows:

$$\sum_{t=1}^{n} \frac{(1 + g_s)^t}{(1 + k_s)^t} = (1 + h)\left[\frac{(1 + h)^n - 1}{h}\right] = (1 + h)\text{FVIFA}_{h,n}$$

where

$$\frac{(1 + g_s)}{(1 + k_s)} = (1 + h).$$

We have an extra term in front of the compound future sum of an annuity formula because we started with an immediate annuity instead of a deferred annuity. The value of the $(1 + h)$ term for the example in Table 23.6 is

$$1 + h = \frac{(1 + g_s)}{(1 + k_s)} = \frac{1.275}{1.16} = 1.099138.$$

The period of supernormal growth is ten years, so we have

$$(1 + h)^{10} = (1.099138)^{10} = 2.5735.$$

We can now finish the calculation of the future value of an annuity.

$$(1 + h)^{10} - 1 = 1.5735$$

$$\frac{(1 + h)^{10} - 1}{h} = \frac{1.5735}{.099138} = 15.87 = \text{FVIFA}(9.9138\%, 10 \text{ yrs.}).$$

We next multiply by the extra $(1 + h)$ as well as the initial dividend:

$$d_0(1 + h)(15.87) = \$2.00(1.099138)(15.87) = \$34.89.$$

This is the present value of the first ten years' dividends and, comparing it to the result obtained by the long way in Table 23.6 of \$34.91, is approximately the same result. We then proceed as in Table 23.6 to pick up Steps (2) and (3), which represent adding the present value of the price of the stock in Year 10 to the present value of the first ten years' dividends that we have just calculated.[11]

The relationships among the P-E ratios, shown in the last column of Table 23.7, are similar to what can be intuitively expected — the higher the expected growth (all other things being equal), the higher the P-E ratio.[12]

The underlying determinants of the kind of growth in earnings, dividends, and value that will be experienced by a firm should be noted. The key relationship goes back to the discussion of capital budgeting in Chapter 6. If the earnings rate on new investments is greater than the firm's cost of capital, net present value will be added to the firm. Its value will increase and it will be a growth company.

For a declining company, the earnings rate on new investments is less than its cost of capital. For a no growth company, the earnings rate on new investment is just equal to the

---

[11]An even more general formula approach for performing calculations under a wider range of assumptions about the patterns of growth is presented in Fuller and Hsia [1984].

[12]Differences in P-E ratios among firms can also arise from differences in the rate of return, k_s, that investors use in capitalizing the future dividend streams. If one company has a higher P-E ratio than another, this could be caused by a higher g, a lower k_s, or a combination of these two factors.

firm's cost of capital. This sometimes creates confusion in the minds of even experienced financial executives. If the earnings rate on new investments is exactly equal to the firm's cost of capital, it can be demonstrated that the firm's earnings per share and value per share will not increase. Of course, the accounting measures of total assets and net income will increase, but no increase in market value per share can be expected to take place.

For the constant growth company, the earnings rate on new investments will exceed the firm's cost of capital. For the supernormal growth company, the excess rate will be very high for a period of time before settling to some lower level.

So, valuation is associated with how well the firm budgets its capital and how well it manages its cost of capital. The key to value growth is an earnings rate in excess of the firm's cost of capital. In the next section of this book, we will take up in greater detail how financing decisions can help hold down the firm's cost of capital and thereby contribute to the increases in value that represent a fundamental goal of financial management.

The Free Cash Flow Approach to Common Stock Valuation

An alternative approach to the stream of dividends is the more general free cash flow model. While the dividend model focuses on the value of a single share of stock (or, on an aggregate level, on the total value of equity), the free cash flow model may be extended from the valuation of common stock to the valuation of any firm.

To derive the free cash flow model, we shall first consider firms financed entirely by equity, using no debt in their capital structure. Our point of view is that of a stockholder analyzing the value of the firm's earnings. Table 23.8 provides the opportunity to consider a concrete example of a company's balance sheet and income statement.

We focus on the results of the operating activity of the firm as measured by its net operating income (NOI). For brevity, this is also referred to as X. For a firm whose net operating income, X, does not grow, the valuation model is similar to that for any uniform amount in perpetuity. The formula is the same as shown in Equation 23.1; however, the

---

Table 23.8   Financial Statements, Marshall Company

Balance Sheet, December 31, 19X0			
Total assets	$3,500,000	Stockholders' equity	$3,500,000

Income Statement for the Year Ended December 31, 19X0	
Sales	$7,000,000
Cost of goods sold	4,900,000
Gross profit margin	$2,100,000
Other operating expenses	1,500,000
Net operating income (NOI, X)	$ 600,000
Income taxes at 40%	240,000
Net income	$ 360,000

discount factor is that associated with common stock rather than with bonds. The valuation formula for common stock with no growth is shown in Equation 23.12:

$$V_U = \frac{X(1-T)}{k_U} = S,$$ (23.12)

where

$V_U =$ value of an unlevered firm
$X =$ net operating income of the firm
$k_U =$ cost of capital of an unlevered firm
$S =$ value of the stockholders' equity in the firm
$T =$ applicable corporate tax rate.

Since the firm uses no debt, $S = V_U$, because the total value of the firm is represented by the value of the stockholders' equity. The capitalization factor is the cost of capital for an unlevered firm; that is, $k_U = k_s =$ the cost of equity for the unlevered firm.

In the model expressed in Equation 23.12, taxes are taken into account, whereas taxes were not considered in the bond valuation model. A difference in the viewpoint reflected in bond valuation models as compared with stock valuation models is the reason this happens. In the bond valuation models, the point of view is that of the bondholders who have received the dollars represented by the coupon on the bond. The firm does not have to pay taxes on its income until bond interest has been deducted. But in valuing the equity or common stock of the firm, we begin with the net operating income, X, of the firm. We must take into account what portion of this income flow is available to the owners of the firm, and, therefore, provision for payment of taxes must be taken into account.

We can illustrate the valuation model shown in Equation 23.12 by using the balance sheet and income statement data in Table 23.8. From that data, we know that $X = \$600,000$ and $T = 40$ percent; we assume that $k_U = 15$ percent.

Using Equation 23.12, the value of the common stock equity of the firm would be

$$V_U = S = \frac{\$600,000(0.6)}{0.15} = \frac{\$360,000}{0.15} = \$2,400,000.$$ (23.12a)

We next consider a firm whose net operating income, X, is growing at some rate. The valuation model for a firm whose net operating income is growing at a constant rate forever is

$$V = \frac{X_0(1-T)(1-b)(1+g)}{k_U - g},$$ (23.13)

where

$b =$ ratio of net investment, I, in period t to the after-tax NOI in period $t = I_t/X_t(1-T)$
$g =$ growth rate of $X(1-T) = br$
$r =$ profitability rate of new investment in the firm $= \Delta X(1-T)/I$.

Since the firm is growing, the source of its growth must be taken into account. The source of the firm's growth is represented by a combination of its investment activity and its favorable profitability rate.

In the model expressed in Equation 23.13, it can be shown that $g = br$. The growth in X or $X(1 - T)$ is exactly the product of the investment rate times the profitability rate. Since this model is for an infinite time period, g must not equal or exceed k_U. Otherwise, the firm would grow to infinite size and value or have a meaningless negative value. Also, r must exceed k_U for investment and growth to occur. In order to show why the relationship between r and k_U is so important, we can revise Equation 23.13 as follows:

$$
\begin{aligned}
V &= \frac{X(1 - T)(1 - b)(1 + g)}{k_U - g} \\[6pt]
&= \frac{X(1 - T)(1 + g) - bX(1 - T)(1 + g)}{k_U - g} \\[6pt]
&= \frac{k_U X(1 - T)(1 + g) - k_U bX(1 - T)(1 + g)}{k_U(k_U - g)} \\[6pt]
&= \frac{X(1 - T)(1 + g)(k_U - bk_U)}{k_U(k_U - g)} \\[6pt]
&= \frac{X(1 - T)(1 + g)(k_U - g + g - bk_U)}{k_U(k_U - g)} \\[6pt]
&= \frac{X(1 - T)(1 + g)(k_U - g)}{k_U(k_U - g)} + \frac{X(1 - T)(1 + g)(g - bk_U)}{k_U(k_U - g)} \\[6pt]
&= \frac{X(1 - T)(1 + g)}{k_U} + \frac{X(1 - T)(1 + g)}{k_U} \cdot \frac{(br - bk_U)}{k_U - g} \\[6pt]
&= \frac{X(1 - T)(1 + g)}{k_U} + \frac{X(1 - T)(1 + g)}{k_U}\left[\frac{b(r - k_U)}{k_U - g}\right].
\end{aligned}
\tag{23.13a}
$$

The first term is the value of assets in place assuming no growth. The second term is the value of perpetual growth. Note that growth depends on b, the retention rate, and $(r - k_U)$, the amount of excess return over the cost of capital.

We now have the background for using the constant growth stock valuation model. Let us assume the same values as before for X, T, and k_U. In addition, let $b = 0.5$ and $r = 16$ percent. Note that in the numbers we are using, r exceeds k_U, and $br = g = 8$ percent, which is less than a k_U of 15 percent. The resulting valuation is shown by using Equation 23.13:

$$
V_U = \frac{\$600,000(0.6)(0.5)(1.08)}{0.15 - 0.08} = \frac{\$194,400}{0.07} = \$2,777,143.
\tag{23.13b}
$$

The value of the firm and the value of the shareholders' equity which represents the firm's total ownership now rises from the previous \$2,400,000 to \$2,777,143.

Equation 23.13a emphasizes that r must be greater than k_U in order for growth to be possible. For example, suppose that r is .14 instead of .16. Let b rise to .8. Now g becomes 11.2 percent, higher than the 8 percent in the previous example. We now have the pattern shown in Equation 23.13c:

$$
V_U = \frac{600,000(.6)(.2)(1.112)}{.15 - .112} = \frac{80,064}{0.038} = \$2,106,947.
\tag{23.13c}
$$

Thus, the value falls to $2,106,947, despite the increase in growth. When r is greater than k_U, the more investment the better. When r is less than k_U, more investment is worse since we are investing to obtain a return lower than our cost of capital.

Valuation—Temporary Supernormal Growth

We next consider valuation when supernormal growth occurs for a finite time period. Let us first develop the background of this type of growth situation. In a competitive economy, each firm tries to develop some areas of investment with above-average profitability. But such success is likely to stimulate imitation by other firms. Hence, the probable duration of investment activities that achieve above-average profitability is only a limited number of years. This is the economic rationale behind the model for valuing firms financed entirely by common stock whose earnings grow at an above-average rate for a limited number of years.

To develop the model for *temporary supernormal growth*, we must also specify what occurs at the end of the period of supernormal earnings. A wide range of plausible earnings patterns could be imagined, and the nature of the assumptions in each pattern could be reflected in the resulting model. For present purposes, it is convenient to make only two assumptions, both of which have been covered in the earlier part of this chapter. We will assume either no growth or growth at a constant rate, for which formulas have already been developed. In Equation 23.14, we present the model for the valuation of temporary supernormal growth followed by no growth:

$$V_U = X_0(1 - T)(1 - b)\sum_{t=1}^{n} \frac{(1 + g_s)^t}{(1 + k_U)^t} + \frac{X_0(1 - T)(1 + g_s)^n}{k_U(1 + k_U)^n}, \qquad (23.14)$$

where

$g_s =$ rate of supernormal growth
$n =$ years of supernormal growth.

Equation 23.14 is composed of two terms. The first term covers the period of supernormal growth. In front of the summation term is the after-tax *free cash flow* (FCF), which represents the NOI after taxes and after provision for investment requirements. This initial free cash flow grows each year at g_s and is discounted at k_U. The numerator in Equation 23.13 also contains this FCF term [multiplied by $(1 + g_s)$ to begin discounting at the end of Period 0].

The second term on the right-hand side of Equation 23.14 brings together a number of pieces, each of them already discussed. We begin with the after-tax net operating income, $X(1 - T)$. This has grown for n years at g_s. The product, therefore, is the level of net operating income after the n years of supernormal growth. This level of income is discounted at k_U, exactly as in Equation 23.12. Finally, the resulting value is discounted back to the present by the present value factor $1/(1 + k_U)^n$.

In supernormal growth, there are no restrictions on the relationship between g and k_U. This is in contrast to the constant growth formula, for which a number of restrictions were noted. We can now proceed to apply Equation 23.14. The only new data required are g_s and n. Let us assume that g_s equals 30 percent and n equals five years. We then proceed to place all of the appropriate numbers in Equation 23.14 to obtain the firm's value.

$$V_U = \$600,000(0.6)(0.5)\sum_{t=1}^{5}\frac{(1.30)^t}{(1.15)^t} + \frac{\$600,000(0.6)(1.30)^5}{.15(1.15)^5}. \qquad \textbf{(23.14a)}$$

We begin the computations with the term

$$\sum_{t=1}^{5}\frac{(1.30)^t}{(1.15)^t} \cong \sum_{t=1}^{5}(1.13)^t = (1.13)^1 + (1.13)^2 + \ldots + (1.13)^5.$$

Let $\left(\dfrac{1 + g_s}{1 + k_U}\right) = (1 + h)$. We can then make use of the relationship involved for a geometric series expressed most generally by the following:

$$\sum_{t=1}^{n}(1 + h)^t = (1 + h) \times \text{FVIFA}_{h,n}.$$

For our data,

$$(1 + h)\text{FVIFA}_{13\%,5 \text{ yrs.}} = (1.13)(6.4803).$$

Similarly, in the second term for $(1.30)^5$ divided by $(1.15)^5$, we have $(1.13)^5$. Because the FVIF (the compound sum factor) is found by $(1 + h)^t$, our result of $(1.13)^5$ is equal to FVIF$_{13\%,5 \text{ yrs.}}$, or 1.8424. We now have all the numbers needed to complete the calculations initially expressed in Equation 23.14a.

$$V_U = \$180,000(1.13)(6.4803) + \$2,400,000(1.8424)$$
$$= \$1,318,093 + \$4,421,760$$
$$= \$5,739,853. \qquad \textbf{(23.14b)}$$

The first term starts with the $180,000, the free cash flow that first appeared in Equation 23.13b. We then multiply by $(1 + h)$ times FVIFA$_{h,n}$, where $h = 0.13$ and $n = 5$. The second term is the valuation result for the no growth case multiplied by the compound sum factor for the supernormal growth rate of 30 percent for five years discounted at 15 percent. Thus, the value of the firm with five years of supernormal growth at 30 percent with no growth thereafter rises to over $5.7 million.

An alternative assumption for the period following the limited duration of supernormal growth is the assumption of continued growth at a constant rate of 8 percent under the restrictions previously set forth. The general expression for this situation is set forth in Equation 23.15. All the elements of Equation 23.15 have been previously discussed.

$$V_U = X_0(1 - T)(1 - b)\sum_{t=1}^{n}\frac{(1 + g_s)^t}{(1 + k_U)^t} + \frac{X_0(1 - T)(1 - b)(1 + g)}{k_U - g} \times \frac{(1 + g_s)^n}{(1 + k_U)^n}$$
$$= \$1,318,093 + \$2,777,143(1.8424) = \$6,434,701. \qquad \textbf{(23.15)}$$

Table 23.9   Effects of Growth on Price-Earnings Ratios and Market to Book Relations

	Valuation of the Firm and Valuation of Shareholders' Equity[a] (1)	Price to Earnings Ratio[b] (2)	Market to Book Ratio[c] (3)
1. No growth	$2,400,000	6.7X	0.69 to 1
2. Constant growth ($g = 0.08$)	2,777,143	7.7X	0.79 to 1
3. Temporary super growth ($g_s = 0.3$)			
A. Subsequent no growth	5,739,853	15.9X	1.6 to 1
B. Subsequent constant growth ($g = 0.08$)	6,434,701	17.9X	1.8 to 1

[a]The cost of capital, k_U, is 15 percent for all these examples.
[b]Recall that initial earnings after tax were $360,000.
[c]Recall that the accounting book value of total assets is $3,500,000.

The first term in the valuation model is exactly what we had in Equation 23.14. The second term simply utilizes materials from the constant growth formula set forth in Equation 23.13. The second term takes the valuation result of the constant growth case and multiplies it by the compound sum factor. The resulting value is $6.435 million.

This overview of the influence of growth on valuation provides a basis for establishing some other relationships, illustrated in Table 23.9. In the table, we first summarize for the four categories of growth the valuation of the firm that we previously developed for each of the growth situations. These valuations can then be related to the initial after-tax earnings, which were $360,000. The resulting price to earnings ratios are shown in Column (2). Clearly, there is a relationship between these ratios and the underlying growth pattern of the earnings. The higher the growth, the higher the ratio. However, a higher price-earnings ratio does not necessarily mean that the firm's cost of capital is lower or higher. The cost of capital that was employed for the unlevered firm throughout all these examples was 15 percent.

In Column (3), we utilize the valuations of Column (1) and relate them to the accounting book value of total assets stated in Table 23.8, which was $3.5 million. Again, the more favorable the underlying growth pattern, the more favorable is the resulting market to book ratio. When net operating income is assumed to have no growth, the firm is likely to have a market value less than its book value. For more favorable growth assumptions, the market to book ratio rises above one.

Thus, we have developed a basis for judging how effectively the management of a firm has achieved favorable valuation performance for the firm. One measure of favorable valuation performance is the price-earnings ratio. Another is the market to book relationship. The market to book relationship indicates that value can be created above the initial investment outlay. This favorable increase in value rises with growth.

Because our focus thus far has been the valuation of common stock, we have developed the cash flow model using the example of an unlevered firm in which the value of equity is equivalent to the value of the firm. However, the cash flow model can be extended to the valuation of any firm, regardless of capital structure, simply by substituting k (the firm's weighted average cost of capital) for k_U in Equations 23.12 through 23.15. The result will be the value of the firm.

To illustrate the use of the free cash flow model to find the value of the levered firm, assume the same facts as above except that the target leverage ratio of debt to equity is 100 percent with a debt cost, $k_b = 12\%$.

Using the facts that we know, we can use the Modigliani-Miller model to calculate the cost of equity of the levered firm and the weighted average cost of capital. We begin with Equation 21.8 from Chapter 21.

$$k_s = k_U + (k_U - k_b) \frac{B}{S} (1 - T)$$

$$= .15 + (.15 - .12) \frac{1}{1} (.6)$$

$$= .15 + .03(.6)$$

$$= .168.$$

We can now calculate the marginal cost of capital.

$$\text{WACC} = k_b(1 - T) \frac{B}{B + S} + k_s \left(\frac{S}{B + S} \right)$$

$$= .12(.6)(.5) + .168(.5)$$

$$= .036 + .084$$

$$= .12.$$

We shall first illustrate the relationships for the no growth firm. We now have

$$V_L = B + S = \frac{\$600,000(0.6)}{0.12} = \frac{\$360,000}{0.12} = \$3,000,000.$$

Recall that the value of the unlevered firm was ($360,000/.15 = $2,400,000). Thus, an increase of $600,000 has taken place. This is in the framework of the MM propositions as can be seen from the relationship

$$V_L = V_U + TB.$$

Since $B/V_L = .5$ and $V_L = 3,000,000$, we know that $B = \$1,500,000$. So $TB = \$600,000$, which, added to $2,400,000, gives us the new value of the firm. The value of the new equity is $.5 V_L = \$1,500,000$. This is less than the value of the old equity of $2,400,000, but the decline in value is only $900,000, while $1,500,000 of debt has been sold. This gain of $1,500,000 less $900,000 is the same $600,000 by which the value of the firm has increased. Shareholders keep this value.

Next assume a growth pattern as above of five years of supernormal growth at 30 percent followed by no growth. The value of the levered firm is found by applying Equation 23.14, using k, the weighted average cost of capital, instead of k_U:

$$V_L = X_0(1 - T)(1 - b)\sum_{t=1}^{n} \frac{(1 + g_s)^t}{(1 + k)^t} + \frac{X_0(1 - T)(1 + g_s)^n}{k(1 + k)^n}$$

$$= \$600,000(.6)(.5)(1 + h)(\text{FVIFA}_{h\%,5 \text{ yrs.}}) + \frac{\$600,000(.6)}{.12}\text{FVIF}_{h\%,5 \text{ yrs.}},$$

where

$$1 + h = \frac{1.30}{1.12} = 1.16$$

$$V_L = \$180,000(1.16)(6.8771) + \$3,000,000(2.1003)$$

$$= \$1,435,938 + \$6,300,900$$

$$= \$7,736,838.$$

Recall that the value of equity alone for the unlevered firm was \$5,739,853. The use of leverage has increased the value of the firm by \$1,996,985.

Similar results will follow for the case where supernormal growth is followed by constant growth.

Summary

The different types of value defined are (1) liquidating value versus going-concern value, (2) book value versus market value, and (3) fair value versus current market price. The market value, or price, of a security is found by the capitalization-of-income method, which finds the present value of the security's stream of earnings in the same way that an asset's cash flows are discounted in capital budgeting. For bond valuation, the relevant cash flows are the periodic interest payments and the principal repaid at maturity, discounted by the required yield on the bond given its risk and maturity. The earnings stream for preferred stock consists of the regular fixed dividend payments discounted at the required rate of return. In terms of valuation, preferred stock is similar to a perpetual bond.

The valuation of common stock involves the same principles, but the returns to common stock consist of both the dividend yield and a capital gain expectation based on expected growth. Another complicating feature of common stock is the degree of uncertainty involved. Bond and preferred stock payments are relatively predictable, but forecasting common stock dividends and, even more, capital gains, is highly uncertain.

Two models of common stock valuation were demonstrated: the stream of dividends approach, and the more generalized free cash flow approach, which can also be used to value both unlevered and levered firms. Both models can incorporate the effect on value of alternative patterns of growth: no growth, constant growth, temporary supernormal growth followed by no growth, and temporary supernormal growth followed by constant growth.

Questions

23.1 What are the different kinds of growth that are likely to have an influence on the valuation relationship?

23.2 Explain why a share of no growth common stock is similar to a share of preferred stock. Use one of the equations developed in the chapter as part of your explanation.

23.3 Explain the importance in common stock valuation of
a) dividend policy
b) net operating income
c) current market price
d) the expected future growth rate
e) the market capitalization rate.

23.4 What are the main components influencing the value of a bond with a finite maturity date?

23.5 Describe the factors that determine the market rate of return on a particular stock at a given point in time.

23.6 Explain how the following influence stock and bond prices:
a) interest rates
b) investors' aversion to risk.

Problems

23.1 The Kubler Company has two issues of bonds outstanding. Both bear coupons of 7 percent, and the effective yield required on each is 12 percent. Bond A has a maturity of 10 years and Bond B a maturity of 20 years. Both pay interest annually and pay $1,000 at maturity.
a) What is the price of each bond?
b) If the effective yield on each bond rises to 14 percent, what is the price of each bond?
c) Explain why the price of one bond falls more than the price of the other when the effective yield rises.

23.2 The Rush Company has two issues of bonds outstanding. Both bear coupons of 10 percent, and the effective yield required on each is 18 percent because of the uncertain future of the company. Bond C has a maturity of 20 years and Bond D a maturity of 30 years. Both pay interest annually and pay $1,000 at maturity.
a) What is the price of each bond?
b) If the effective yield on each bond rises to 24 percent, what is the price of each bond?
c) Explain why the price of one bond falls more than the price of the other when the effective yield rises.
d) Compare the results in this problem with the results in the previous problem.

23.3 What will be the yield to maturity of a perpetual bond with a $1,000 par value, an 8 percent coupon rate, and a current market price of $800? Of $1,000? Of $1,200? Assume that interest is paid annually.

23.4 Assume that a bond has four years remaining to maturity and that interest is paid annually.
a) What will be the yield to maturity on the bond with a $1,000 maturity value, an 8 percent coupon interest rate, and a current market price of $825? Of $1,107?
b) Would you pay $825 for the bond if your required rate of return for securities in the same risk class was 10 percent ($k_b = 10\%$)? Explain.

23.5 The bonds of the Stanroy Corporation are perpetuities bearing a 9 percent coupon. Bonds of this type yield 8 percent. The par value of the bonds is $1,000.
a) What is the price of the Stanroy bonds?
b) Interest rate levels rise to the point where such bonds now yield 12 percent. What is the price of the Stanroy bonds now?
c) Interest rate levels drop to 9 percent. At what price do the Stanroy bonds sell?

d) How would your answers to Parts (a), (b), and (c) change if the bonds had a definite maturity date of 19 years?

23.6 Prosun Engineering has just developed a solar panel capable of generating 200 percent more electricity than any solar panel currently on the market. As a result, Prosun is expected to experience a 30 percent annual growth rate for the next 15 years. By the end of 15 years, other firms will have developed comparable technology, and Prosun's growth rate will slow to 8 percent per year indefinitely. Stockholders require a return of 12 percent on Prosun stock. The most recent annual dividend (d_0) was $1.50 per share. What is the current price of Prosun stock?

23.7 The Olson Company has a beta of 1.4. The expected return on the market is 12 percent, the risk-free rate is 7 percent, and the market variance is 1 percent. The net operating income of the Olson Company for the year just completed was $5 million, with an applicable corporate tax rate of 40 percent.

a) Assuming no growth in Olson's NOI is expected, what would be the value of the firm?

b) Next, assume that the profitability rate, r, of Olson is 18 percent and that b, the ratio of investment to after-tax net operating income, averages 0.50. What would be the value of Olson under these new assumptions?

c) Compare the price to after-tax earnings ratios under no growth and constant growth.

23.8 The Pelman Company has a required return of 15 percent. Its net operating income, now $4 million, is expected to grow at a rate of 26.5 percent for the next eight years, with a ratio of investment to after-tax net operating income of 0.20. The applicable tax rate is 40 percent.

a) If, after the period of supernormal growth, the net operating income of Pelman has zero growth, what is the current value of the firm?

b) If, after the period of supernormal growth, the net operating income of Pelman grows at 10 percent per year, what is the current value of the firm?

c) Compare the price to after-tax earnings ratios for the two alternative assumptions with respect to the growth of net operating earnings after the period of supernormal growth.

23.9 After six years as vice president of a New York bank, Henry Thorson has decided to simplify his lifestyle and become a small-town shopkeeper. He has found an apparently successful variety store in rural Pennsylvania for sale at a price of $120,000. The most recent balance sheet is given in Table P23.9.

Table P23.9

Assets		Liabilities	
Cash	$ 18,000	Notes payable, bank	$ 6,000
Receivables, net	6,000	Accounts payable	12,000
Inventories	39,000	Accruals	3,000
Net fixed assets	42,000	Net worth	84,000
		Total liabilities and	
Total assets	$105,000	net worth	$105,000

Annual pre-tax earnings (after rent, interest, and salaries) have averaged $24,000 for the preceding three years. The store has been in business in the same community for 20 years and has 6 years remaining on a 10-year lease. The purchase price includes all assets, except for cash, and Thorson would have to assume all debts.

a) Is the price of $120,000 reasonable?

b) What other factors should be considered in arriving at a purchase price?

c) What is the significance, if any, of the lease?

23.10 The Ellis Company is a small jewelry manufacturer. The company has been success-ful and has grown. Now, Ellis is planning to sell an issue of common stock to the public for the first time, and it faces the problem of setting an appropriate price on its common stock. The company feels that the proper procedure is to select firms similar to it, with publicly traded common stock, and to make relevant comparisons.

The company finds several jewelry manufacturers similar to it with respect to product mix, size, asset composition, and debt/equity proportions. Of these, Bonden and Seeger are most similar, with data as shown in Table P23.10.

Table P23.10

Relationships	Bonden	Seeger	(Ellis Totals)
Earnings per share, 19X6	$ 5.00	$ 8.00	$ 1,500,000
Average, 19X0-X6	4.00	5.00	1,000,000
Price per share, 19X6	48.00	65.00	—
Dividends per share, 19X6	3.00	4.00	700,000
Average, 19X0-X6	2.50	3.25	500,000
Book value per share	45.00	70.00	12,000,000

a) Calculate the per share data for Ellis assuming that 500,000 shares of stock will be sold.

b) Calculate the P-E, dividend yield, and market to book relations for Bonden and Seeger.

c) Apply the relationships in Part (b) to the Ellis per share data to establish boundaries for the indicated market price for the Ellis stock.

d) Using the boundaries, and taking trend patterns into account, what is your recommendation for an issuing price for the Ellis stock?

23.11 An investor requires a 20 percent return on the common stock of the M Company. During its most recent complete year, the M Company stock earned $4 and paid $2 per share. Its earnings and dividends are expected to grow at a 32 percent rate for five years, after which they are expected to grow at 8 percent per year. At what value of the M Company stock would the investor earn a required 20 percent return?

23.12 The Rowe Company is contemplating the purchase of the Colima Company. During the most recent year, Colima had earnings of $2 million and paid dividends of $1 million. The earnings and dividends of Colima are expected to grow at an annual rate of 30 percent for five years, after which they will grow at an 8 percent rate per year. The required return on an investment with the risk characteristics of the Colima Company is 16 percent.

What is the maximum that the Rowe Company could pay for the Colima Company to earn at least a 16 percent return on its investment?

23.13 The Stoll Company has a beta of 1.2. The expected return on the market is 12 per-cent, the risk-free rate is 7 percent, and the market variance is 1 percent. The net operating income of the Stoll Company for the year just completed was $8 million, with an applicable corporate tax rate of 40 percent.

a) Assuming no growth in Stoll's NOI is expected, what would be the value of the firm?

b) Next assume that the profitability rate of Stoll is 15 percent and that the ratio of investment to net operating income averages 0.60. What would be the value of Stoll under these new assumptions?

Selected References

Banz, Rolf W., "The Relationship Between Return and Market Value of Common Stocks," *Journal of Financial Economics*, 9 (March 1981), pp. 3-18.

Basu, Sanjoy, "The Relationship Between Earnings' Yield, Market Value and Return for NYSE Common Stocks: Further Evidence," *Journal of Financial Economics*, 12 (June 1983), pp. 129-156.

Brennan, Michael, "A Note on Dividend Irrelevance and the Gordon Valuation Model," *Journal of Finance*, 26 (December 1971), pp. 1115-1123.

Fuller, Russell J., and Hsia, Chi-Cheng, "A Simplified Common Stock Valuation Model," *Financial Analysts Journal*, 40 (September-October 1984), pp. 49-56.

Graham, B.; Dodd, D. L.; and Cottle, S., *Security Analysis*, New York: McGraw-Hill, 1961, p. 28.

Haugen, Robert A., "Expected Growth, Required Return, and the Variability of Stock Prices," *Journal of Financial and Quantitative Analysis*, 5 (September 1970), pp. 297-308.

Hakansson, Nils H., "Changes in the Financial Market: Welfare and Price Effects and the Basic Theorems of Value Conservation," *Journal of Finance*, 37 (September 1982), pp. 977-1004.

Holt, Charles C., "The Influence of Growth Duration on Share Prices," *Journal of Finance*, 17 (September 1962), pp. 465-475.

Malkiel, Burton G., "Equity Yields, Growth, and the Structure of Share Prices," *American Economic Review*, 53 (December 1963), pp. 467-494.

Miller, Merton H., and Modigliani, Franco, "Dividend Policy, Growth, and the Valuation of Shares," *Journal of Business*, 34 (October 1961), pp. 411-433.

Modigliani, Franco, "Debt, Dividend Policy, Taxes, Inflation and Market Valuation," *Journal of Finance*, 37 (May 1982), pp. 255-273.

Morris, James R., "The Role of Cash Balances in Firm Valuation," *Journal of Financial and Quantitative Analysis*, 18 (December 1983), pp. 533-545.

Robichek, Alexander A., and Bogue, Marcus C., "A Note on the Behavior of Expected Price/Earnings Ratios over Time," *Journal of Finance*, 26 (June 1971), pp. 731-736.

Salmi, Timo, "Estimating the Internal Rate of Return from Published Financial Statements," *Journal of Business Finance & Accounting*, 9 (Spring 1982), pp. 63-74.

Senbet, Lemma W., and Thompson, Howard E., "Growth and Risk," *Journal of Financial and Quantitative Analysis*, 17 (September 1982), pp. 331-340.

Stapleton, Richard C., "Portfolio Analysis, Stock Valuation, and Capital Budgeting Decision Rules for Risky Projects," *Journal of Finance*, 26 (March 1971), pp. 95-118.

Stone, B. K., "The Conformity of Stock Values Based on Discounted Dividends to a Fair-Return Process," *Bell Journal of Economics*, 6 (Autumn 1975), pp. 698-702.

Turnbull, Stuart M., "Market Value and Systematic Risk," *Journal of Finance*, 32 (September 1977), pp. 1125-1142.

Walter, James E., *Dividend Policy and Enterprise Valuation*, Belmont, Calif.: Wadsworth, 1967.

Wendt, Paul F., "Current Growth Stock Valuation Methods," *Financial Analysts Journal*, 33 (March-April 1965), pp. 3-15.

Part Seven

The Treasurer's Point of View: Policy Decisions

Part One covered the fundamental concepts of managerial finance. Part Two developed the time value of money and its application in capital budgeting. In Part Three, we developed materials for the analysis, planning, and control of the firm as a whole and for the control of decentralized divisions within the firm. Part Four considered the top half of the balance sheet, analyzing current assets, current liabilities, and the interactions between the two. In Part Five, we treated decision making under uncertainty to provide a basis for pricing risk. With the guidance of the concepts developed in Part Six on the cost of capital and valuation, we can now evaluate individual financing decisions.

Part Seven takes the point of view of the treasurer of the firm. It covers mainly the lower right side of the balance sheet, considering the various types of funds available to the firm when it seeks long-term, external capital. Within the framework of the relationship between financial structure and the cost of capital, decisions on individual financing episodes can be made to help the firm towards its objective of achieving an optimal mix of financing.

Chapter 24 presents an overview of the institutional material essential to an understanding of the use of the financial markets by business firms. Chapter 25 analyzes the conditions under which common stock financing is used. Chapter 26 describes the nature of long-term debt and preferred stocks and their role in the financing of the firm. Chapter 27 analyzes leasing decisions, which involve the issue of choosing the applicable discount rate. Chapter 28 discusses the nature of warrants, convertibles, and options and describes how their use helps resolve the problem of pricing the uncertain risk of corporate debt. Chapter 29 deals with pension fund management, with emphasis on decision making about alternative types of pension plans, performance evaluation, and tax aspects.

Chapter 24 External Financing: Institutions and Behavior

With a background of investment plans related to the value-maximizing cost of capital, we now turn to the objective of an optimal mix of financing that will result from individual financing decisions. The present chapter deals with a number of aspects of the institutions and behavior of the capital markets which business firms use in financing. We begin with an overview of the main sources of funds used by business corporations. We examine the important practice of financing directly from such institutions as insurance companies and banks. We then turn to the investment banking mechanism by which the funds of individual investors are mobilized for use by business firms. We analyze the relative costs of different methods of sale of new issues, with particular attention to competitive versus negotiated securities offerings. We summarize and discuss the implications of the securities laws for financing by business firms. Finally, recent trends in financing practices are summarized.

Sources of Business Financing

Statistics on the three broad sources of funds used by business corporations are presented in Table 24.1. The sources are internal cash flows, short-term external funds, and long-term external funds. The first two categories of financing were discussed in previous chapters. The third is the subject of the present chapter, which provides an overview of the market mechanisms for raising long-term funds. This overview is intended as a framework for the discussion of individual forms of long-term financing, which are presented in the remaining chapters of this section.

The data in Table 24.1 show that internal financing has provided 73 percent of the sources of funds for business corporations in recent years. External financing has averaged 27 percent of total sources. Generally, long-term financing exceeds short-term external financing, except when the cost of long-term debt appears cyclically high.

In making decisions about where and how to raise long-term funds, one important choice is between private sources and the public markets. Private financing represents funds obtained directly from one or a few individuals or financial institutions, such as banks, insurance companies, or pension funds. Public financing uses investment bankers to sell securities to a large number of investors—both individuals and financial institutions. In the 1800s, before the development of broad financial markets, business firms were financed by a few wealthy individuals. One of the economic contributions of investment banking was to bring the general public into such financing by assembling smaller amounts of funds from larger numbers of sources and making the total available to business firms. By the 1930s, large pools of funds had been accumulated in insurance companies, pension funds, and commercial banks. This resulted in an increase in direct financing that bypassed to some degree the use of investment banking. Since direct financing is less complicated than public financing, it will be covered first in the chapter. Then, the nature of investment banking will be discussed.

Table 24.1   Sources of Funds for Business Corporations, 1977-1984 (Billions of Dollars)

	Total Sources	Internal Cash Flow		Short-Term External Funds		Long-Term External Funds		Other	
		Amount	Percent	Amount	Percent	Amount	Percent	Amount	Percent
1978	$ 289	$ 200	69%	$ 30	10%	$ 45	16%	$14	5%
1979	332	232	70	48	14	37	11	16	5
1980	329	232	71	24	7	58	18	14	4
1981	369	254	69	51	14	48	13	16	4
1982	322	249	77	18	6	60	19	−4	−1
1983 (est.)	380	290	76	27	7	51	13	12	3
1984 (proj.)	440	337	77	39	9	53	12	11	3
1978-84	$2,461	$1,794	73%[a]	$237	10%[a]	$352	14%[a]	$79	3%[a]

[a]%'s are weighted averages.
Source: Summarized from Bankers Trust Company, *Credit and Capital Markets, 1984*, p. T26.

Direct Financing

Two major forms of direct long-term financing are term lending by commercial banks and insurance companies and the private placement of securities with insurance companies and pension funds. *Term loans* are direct business loans with a maturity of more than one year but less than 15 years, with provisions for systematic repayment (amortization during the life of the loan). *Private placements* are direct business loans with a maturity of more than 15 years. The distinction is, of course, arbitrary. Private placement differs from the term loan only in its arbitrary maturity length; this distinction becomes even fuzzier when we discover that some private placements call for repayment of a substantial portion of the principal within 5 to 10 years. Thus, term loans and private placements represent about the same kind of financing arrangements.

Characteristics of Term Loans and Private Placements

Amortization. Most term loans are repayable on an amortized basis. The purpose of amortization, of course, is to have the loan repaid gradually over its life rather than fall due all at once; this protects both the lender and the borrower against the possibility that the borrower will not make adequate provisions for retirement of the loan during its life. Amortization is especially important for a loan used to purchase a specific item of equipment; here, the schedule of repayment will be geared to the productive life of the equipment, and payments will be made from cash flows resulting from use of the equipment. The mechanics of preparing an amortization schedule were illustrated in Chapter 5.

Maturity. For commercial banks, the term loan runs 5 years or less (typically 3 years). For insurance companies, typical maturities have been 5 to 15 years. This difference reflects the fact that liabilities of commercial banks are shorter term than those of insurance companies. Banks and insurance companies occasionally cooperate in their term lending. For example, if a firm (usually a large one) seeks a 15-year term loan, a bank may take the loan for the first 5 years and an insurance company for the last 10 years.

Collateral. Commercial banks require security on about 60 percent of the volume and 90 percent of the number of term loans made. They take as security mainly stocks, bonds, machinery, and equipment. Insurance companies also require security on nearly one-third of their loans, frequently using real estate as collateral on the longer term ones.

Options. In recent years, institutional investors have increasingly taken compensation in addition to fixed interest payments on directly negotiated loans. The most popular form of additional compensation is an option to buy common stock, the option being in the form of detachable warrants permitting the purchase of the shares at stated prices over a designated period. (See Chapter 28 for more details on warrants.)

Terms of Loan Agreements

A major advantage of a term loan is that it assures the borrower of the use of the funds for an extended period. On a 90-day loan, since the commercial bank has the option to renew or not renew, it has frequent opportunities to reexamine the borrower's situation. If it has deteriorated unduly, the loan officer simply does not renew the loan. On a term loan, however, the bank or insurance company has committed itself for a period of years. Because of this long-term commitment, restrictive provisions are incorporated into the loan agreement to protect the lender for the duration of the loan. The most important of these provisions (though by no means all of them) are listed below:

1. *Current ratio.* The current ratio must be maintained at some specified level — $2\frac{1}{2}$ to 1; 3 to 1; $3\frac{1}{2}$ to 1, depending on the borrower's line of business. Net working capital must also be maintained at some minimum level.
2. *Additional long-term debt.* Typically, there are prohibitions against (a) incurring additional long-term indebtedness, except with the permission of the lender; (b) the pledging of assets; (c) the assumption of any contingent liabilities, such as guaranteeing the indebtedness of a subsidiary; and (d) the signing of long-term leases beyond specified amounts.
3. *Management.* The loan agreement may require that (a) any major changes in management personnel be approved by the lender; (b) life insurance be taken out on the principals, or key people, in the business; and (c) a voting trust be created or proxies be granted for a specified period to ensure that the management of the company will be under the control of the group on which the lender has relied in making the loan.
4. *Financial statements.* The lender will require the borrower to submit periodic financial statements for review.

Costs

As with other forms of lending, the interest rate on term loans varies with the level of interest rates generally, the size of the loan, and the quality of the borrower. Surveys show that on small term loans, the effective interest rate may run up to as much as six to eight percentage points above the prime rate. On loans of $1 million and more, term loan rates have been close to the prime rate.

The interest rate may be fixed for the life of the loan, or it may vary. Often the loan agreement specifies that the interest rate will be based on the average of the rediscount rate in the borrower's Federal Reserve district during the previous three months —

generally 1 or 2 percent above the rediscount rate.[1] It may also be geared to the published prime rate charged by New York City banks.

Hays, Joehnk, and Melicher [1979] analyzed risk premiums when corporate debt was issued in public offerings versus private placements during the 1970-75 time period. Risk premiums were measured for 376 public issues and 314 private placements by relating their yields to maturity to the yield to maturity on U.S. Treasury securities of comparable maturities. On public offerings, risk premiums were smaller when the issue size was large, the issue was secured, the EBIT trend was favorable, and the times interest earned ratio was favorable. Risk premiums were larger when the years to maturity were longer and the long-term debt-to-total-asset ratio higher. For private placements, only the issue size and times interest earned ratio were significant and negatively related to risk premiums. For both public and private offerings, risk premiums were negatively related to the level of economic activity as measured by industrial production. They were also negatively related to market factors such as the level of free reserves. In addition, for private placements, the risk premium was positively related to plant and equipment expenditure expectations and negatively related to the amount of life insurance funds available for direct placements.

While the model was able to explain approximately 50 percent of the variation in risk premiums, the variables that were important in doing so differed. Risk premiums for public offerings were largely explained by default risk measures in the form of issue and issuing firm characteristics. Risk premiums in the private market were explained more by economic and market-related factors. The authors conclude that investors in the public market used different measures to assess investment attractiveness than did investors in the private placement market.

On private placements, the interest rate generally runs from about 10 to 50 basis points higher than that on comparable public issues. In the Hays-Joehnk-Melicher study, the yield to maturity on the private placements was 46 basis points higher than on the public offerings. Thus, to some extent, the economies of using private placements are offset by their somewhat higher interest rates.

Evaluation of Direct Financing

From the standpoint of the borrower, the advantages of direct financing are

1. Much seasonal short-term borrowing can be dispensed with, thereby reducing the danger of nonrenewal of loans.
2. The borrower avoids the expenses of SEC registration and investment bankers' distribution.
3. Less time is required to complete arrangements for obtaining a loan than is involved in a bond issue.
4. Since only one lender is involved, rather than many bondholders, it is possible to modify the loan indenture.

The disadvantages to a borrower of direct financing are

1. The interest rate may be higher on a term loan than on a short-term loan because the lender is tying up money for a longer period and, therefore, does not have the opportunity to review the borrower's status periodically (as is done whenever short-term loans are renewed).

---

[1]The rediscount rate is the rate of interest at which a bank can borrow from a Federal Reserve bank.

2. The cash drain is large. Since the loans provide for regular amortization or sinking fund payments, the company experiences a continuous cash drain. From this standpoint, direct loans are less advantageous than equity funds (which never have to be repaid), a preferred stock without maturity, or even a bond issue without a sinking fund requirement.

3. Since the loan is a long-term commitment, the lender employs high credit standards, insisting that the borrower be in a strong financial position and have a good current ratio, a low debt-equity ratio, good activity ratios, and good profitability ratios.

4. Because of the long-term exposure of the lender, the loan agreement has restrictions that are not found in a 90-day note.

5. Investigation costs may be high. The lender stays with the company for a longer period. Therefore, the longer term outlook for the company must be reviewed, and the lender makes a more elaborate investigation than would be done for a short-term note. For this reason, the lender may set a minimum on any loan (for example, $50,000) in order to recover the costs of investigating the applicant.

In addition, there are some advantages to the public distribution of securities that are not achieved by term loans or private placement, including

1. The firm establishes its credit and achieves publicity by having its securities publicly and widely distributed. Because of this, it will be able to engage in future financing at lower rates.

2. The wide distribution of debt or equity may enable its repurchase on favorable terms at some subsequent date if the market price of the securities falls.

Thus, direct long-term financing has both advantages and limitations. Its use has declined somewhat in recent years.

Recent Trends in the Use of Direct Financing

Table 24.2 presents data on recent trends in the relative use of publicly sold versus privately placed long-term debt. As interest rates declined in the second half of 1982, the sales of long-term debt in the public markets rose to a record $43.3 billion annual rate. However, the sales of privately placed bonds declined from a peak of almost $18 million in 1977 to slightly under $11 billion for the first half of 1983. Thus, private financing, which represented about 60 percent of public sales of debt in the late 1970s, declined to nearly one-half that level by the early 1980s.

The reason for the decline in the private placement market appears to be due primarily to the decreased participation by life insurance companies. During the tight money conditions from 1980 through the first half of 1982, insurance sales (which, in part, represent a form of saving) decreased, and policyholders borrowed against the cash surrender values of their existing policies. This decreased the availability of lendable funds by life insurance companies. Although the funds available to insurance companies increased as monetary conditions changed in the second half of 1982, the pressures that the life insurance companies had faced led to a preference to maintain more liquid portfolios. By investing more in publicly traded bond issues, the insurance companies can raise funds as needed by resales in the publicly traded markets. In addition, the demand for private financing decreased, since the greater availability of funds in the public markets for lower quality issuers reduced their need to seek funds in the private market.

In the private placement market, a shift has taken place towards the shorter intermediate-term maturities. In part, this is because real interest rates (the nominal interest rates

Table 24.2   Sales of Public vs. Private Debt

(1)	(2)	(3)	(4)
	Sale of Notes and Bonds	Private Placement of Bonds	Percent Private to Public Sales
Year			
1977	29.6	17.9	60%
1978	28.8	17.5	61
1979	27.3	16.4	60
1980	37.6	11.9	32
1981	35.5	13.2	37
1982H1[a]	24.7		
1982H2[a]	43.3		
1982	34.0	12.7	37
1983H1[a]	31.8	10.8	34
1983	24.4		

[a]Seasonally adjusted annual rates for H1, or first half of year, and H2, or second half of year.
Source: Michael J. Moran, "Recent Financing Activity of Nonfinancial Corporations," *Federal Reserve Bulletin,* 70 (May 1984), pp. 403-405.

less the inflation rate actually experienced) have remained high. Also insurance companies have entered into contracts for annuities and pension funds under which they guarantee a fixed rate of return for periods of time that have usually ranged from three to ten years. Insurance companies have sought to reduce their interest rate risk by matching the duration of their bond portfolios with the duration of their guaranteed investment contracts.

Thus, the use of private or direct financing in recent years has declined. Public financing of long-term debt still predominates and is likely to continue to do so. Therefore, the institutions for long-term public financing are discussed next.

Investment Banking

In the U.S. economy, saving is done by one group of persons and investing by another. (*Investing* is used here in the sense of actually putting money into plant, equipment, and inventory, and not in the sense of buying securities.) Savings are placed with financial intermediaries, who, in turn, make the funds available to firms wishing to acquire plants and equipment and to hold inventories.

One of the major institutions performing this channeling role is the *investment banking* institution. The term *investment banker* is somewhat misleading, since investment bankers are neither investors nor bankers. That is, they do not invest their own funds permanently, nor are they repositories for individuals' funds, as are commercial banks or savings banks. What, then, is the nature of investment banking?

The many activities of investment bankers can be described first in general terms and then with respect to specific functions. The traditional function of the investment banker has been to act as the middleman in channeling individuals' savings and funds into the purchase of business securities. The investment banker does this by purchasing and distributing the new securities of individual companies while performing the functions of underwriting, distribution of securities, and advice and counsel.

Underwriting

Underwriting is the insurance function of bearing the risks of adverse price fluctuations during the period in which a new issue of securities is being distributed. The nature of the investment banker's underwriting function can best be conveyed by example: A business firm needs $10 million. It selects an investment banker, holds conferences, and decides to issue $10 million of bonds. An underwriting agreement is drawn up. On a specific day, the investment banker presents the company with a check for $10 million (less commission). In return, the investment banker receives bonds in denominations of $1,000 each to sell to the public.

The company receives the $10 million before the investment banker has sold the bonds. Between the time the firm is paid the $10 million and the time the bonds are sold, the investment banker bears all the risk of market price fluctuations in the bonds. Conceivably, it can take the investment banker days, months, or longer to sell bonds. If the bond market collapses in the interim, the investment banker carries the risk of loss on the sale of the bonds.

There have been dramatic instances of bond market collapses within one week after an investment banker has bought $50 million or $100 million of bonds. For example, in the spring of 1974, an issue of New Jersey Sporting Arena bonds dropped $140 per $1,000 bond during the underwriting period, costing the underwriters an estimated $8 million. The issuing firm, however, does not need to be concerned about the risk of market price fluctuations while the investment banker is selling the bonds, since it has received its money. One fundamental economic function of the investment banker, then, is to underwrite the risk of a decline in the market price between the time the money is transmitted to the firm and the time the bonds are placed in the hands of their ultimate buyers. For this reason, investment bankers are often called underwriters; they underwrite risk during the distribution period.

Distribution

The second function of the investment banker is marketing new issues of securities. The investment banker is a specialist with a staff and organization to distribute securities and, therefore, the capacity to perform the physical distribution function more efficiently and more economically than can an individual corporation. A corporation that wished to sell an issue of securities would find it necessary to establish a marketing or selling organization—a very expensive and ineffective method of selling securities. The investment banker has a permanent, trained staff and dealer organization available to distribute securities. In addition, the investment banker's reputation for selecting good companies and pricing securities fairly builds up a broad clientele over time, and this further increases the efficiency with which securities can be sold.

Advice and Counsel

The investment banker, engaged in the origination and sale of securities, through experience becomes an expert adviser about terms and characteristics of securities that will appeal to investors. This advice and guidance is valuable. Furthermore, the person's reputation as a seller of securities depends on the subsequent performance of the securities.

Therefore, investment bankers often sit on the boards of firms whose securities they have sold. In this way, they can provide continuing financial counsel and increase the firm's probability of success.

Investment Banking Operations

Probably the best way to gain a clear understanding of the investment banking function is to trace the history of a new issue of securities.[2] Accordingly, this section describes the steps necessary to issue new securities.

Preunderwriting Conferences

First, the members of the issuing firm and the investment banker hold preunderwriting conferences, at which they discuss the amount of capital to be raised, the type of security to be issued, and the terms of the agreement. Memoranda describing proposals suggested at the conferences are written by the treasurer of the issuing company to the firm's directors and other officers. Meetings of the board of directors of the issuing company are held to discuss the alternatives and to attempt to reach a decision.

At some point, the issuer and the investment banker enter an agreement that a flotation will take place. The investment banker then begins to conduct an underwriting investigation. If the company is proposing to purchase additional assets, the underwriter's engineering staff may analyze the proposed acquisition. A public accounting firm is called upon to make an audit of the issuing firm's financial situation and also helps prepare the registration statements in connection with these issues for the SEC.

A firm of lawyers is called in to interpret and judge the legal aspects of the flotation. In addition, the originating underwriter (who is the manager of the subsequent underwriting syndicate) makes an exhaustive investigation of the company's prospects.

When the investigations are completed, but before registration with the SEC is made, an underwriting agreement is drawn up by the investment banker. Terms of the tentative agreement may be modified through discussions between the underwriter and the issuing company, but the final agreement will cover all underwriting terms except the price of the securities.

Registration Statement

A registration statement containing all relevant financial and business information on the firm then is filed with the SEC. The statutes set a 20-day waiting period (which, in practice, may be shortened or lengthened by the SEC), during which the SEC staff analyzes the registration statement to determine whether there are any omissions or misrepresentations of fact. During the examination period, the SEC can file exceptions to the registration statement or can ask for additional information from the issuing company or the under-

---

[2]The process described here relates primarily to situations where the firm doing the financing picks an investment banker and then negotiates over the terms of the issue. An alternative procedure, used extensively only in the public utility industry, is for the selling firm to specify the terms of the new issue and then to have investment bankers bid for the entire new issue with sealed bids. The very high fixed costs that an investment banker must incur to thoroughly investigate the company and its new issue rule out sealed bids except for the largest issues. The operation described in this section is called *negotiated underwriting*. Competition is keen among underwriters, of course, to develop and maintain working relations with business firms.

writers. Also during this period, the investment bankers are not permitted to offer the securities for sale, although they can print a preliminary prospectus with all the customary information except the offering price.

Pricing the Securities

The actual price the underwriter pays the issuer is not generally determined until the end of the registration period. There is no universally followed practice, but one common arrangement for a new issue of stock calls for the investment banker to buy the securities at a prescribed number of points below the closing price on the last day of registration. For example, in October 1977, the stock of Wilcox Chemical Company had a current price of $38.00 and had traded between $35.00 and $40.00 a share during the previous three months. The firm and the underwriter agreed that the investment banker would buy 200,000 new shares at $2.50 below the closing price on the last day of registration. The stock closed at $36.00 on the day the SEC released the issue, so the firm received $33.50 a share. Typically, such agreements have an escape clause that provides for the contract to be voided if the price of the securities falls below some predetermined figure. In the case of Wilcox, this *upset price* was set at $34.00 a share. Thus, if the closing price of the shares on the last day of registration had been $33.50, Wilcox would have had the option of withdrawing from the agreement.

This arrangement holds, of course, only for additional stock offerings of firms whose old stock was previously traded. When a company goes public for the first time, the investment banker and the firm negotiate a price in accordance with the valuation principles described in Chapters 17 and 23.

The investment banker has an easier job if the issue is priced relatively low, but the issuer of the securities naturally wants as high a price as possible. Some conflict on price, therefore, arises between the investment banker and the issuer. If the issuer is financially sophisticated and makes comparisons with similar security issues, the investment banker is forced to price close to the market.

Underwriting Syndicate

The investment banker with whom the issuing firm has conducted its discussions does not typically handle the purchase and distribution of the issue alone, unless the issue is a very small one. If the sums of money involved are large and the risks of price fluctuations are substantial, the investment banker forms a syndicate in an effort to minimize the amount of personal risk. A *syndicate* is a temporary association for the purpose of carrying out a specific objective. The nature of the arrangements for a syndicate in the underwriting and sale of a security through an investment banker can best be understood with the aid of Figure 24.1.

The managing underwriter invites other investment bankers to participate in the transaction on the basis of their knowledge of the particular kind of offering to be made and their strength and dealer contacts in selling securities of this type. Each investment banker has business relationships with other investment bankers and dealers and thus has a selling group composed of these people.

Some firms combine all these characteristics. For example, Merrill Lynch, Pierce, Fenner & Smith underwrites some issues and manages the underwriting of others. On still other flotations, it is invited by the manager to join in the distribution of the issue. It also purchases securities as a dealer, carries an inventory of those securities, and publishes

Figure 24.1   Diagram of Sales of $100 Million of Bonds through Investment Bankers

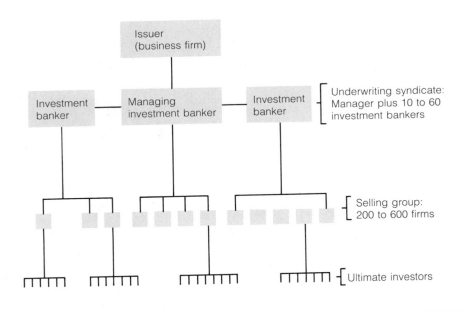

lists of securities it has for sale. In addition to being a dealer, Merrill Lynch, of course, carries on substantial activity as a broker. Any other individual investment firm may also carry on all these functions.

There are also firms with a narrower range of functions — specialty dealers, specialty brokers, and specialty investment counselors. Thus, in the financial field, there is often specialization of financial functions. A *dealer* purchases securities outright, holds them in inventory, and sells them at whatever price can be gotten. The dealer may benefit from price appreciation or may suffer a loss on declines, as any merchandiser does. A *broker*, on the other hand, takes orders for purchases and transmits them to the proper exchange; the gain is the commission charged for the service.

Syndicates are used in the distribution of securities for three reasons:

1. A single investment banker may be financially unable to handle a large issue alone.
2. The originating investment banker may desire to spread the risk even if it is financially able to handle the issue alone.
3. The utilization of several selling organizations (as well as other underwriters) permits an economy of selling effort and expense and encourages nationwide distribution.

Participating underwriters and dealers are provided with full information on all phases of these financing transactions, and they share in the underwriting commission. Suppose that an investment banker buys $10 million worth of bonds to be sold at par, or $1,000 each. If this banker receives a two-point spread, the banker pays the issuer $9.8 million. Typically, on a two-point spread, the managing underwriter receives the first one-quarter of one percent for originating and managing the syndicate. Next, the entire underwriting group receives about 0.75 percent. Members of the selling group receive about 1 percent as a sales commission.

The manager of the underwriting group who makes a sale to an ultimate purchaser of the securities receives the 0.25 percent as manager, 0.75 percent as underwriter, and 1 percent as seller — the full 2 percent. If the manager wholesales some of the securities to members of the selling group who make the ultimate sale, they receive the 1 percent selling commission and the manager receives the other 1 percent for managing and underwriting the issue. Variations take place around these patterns.

Ordinarily, each underwriter's liability is limited to the agreed-upon commitment. For example, an investment banker who participates in a $20 million offering and agrees to see to it that $5 million of the securities are sold no longer is responsible after that firm sells the $5 million of securities.

Selling Group

The selling group is formed primarily for the purpose of distributing securities; it consists of dealers, who take relatively small participations from the members of the underwriting group. The underwriters act as wholesalers; members of the selling group act as retailers. The number of investment banking houses in a selling group depends partly on the size of the issue. A selling group may have as many as 300 to 400 dealers. The operation of the selling group is controlled by the *selling group agreement*, which usually covers the following major points.

1. *Description of the issue.* The description is set forth in a report on the issue — the prospectus — which fully describes the issue and the issuer.
2. *Concession.* Members of the selling group subscribe to the new issue at a public offering price less the *concession* given to them as a commission for their selling service. The selling commission is generally greater than the sum of the managing and underwriting fees.
3. *Handling purchased securities.* The selling group agreement provides that no member of the selling group will be permitted to sell the securities below the public offering price. The syndicate manager invariably "pegs" the quotation in the market by placing continuous orders to buy at the public offering price. A careful record is kept of bond or stock certificate numbers, so that repurchased securities can be identified with the member of the selling group who sold them. The general practice is to cancel the commission on such securities. Repurchased securities are then placed with other dealers for sale.[3]
4. *Duration of selling group.* The most common provision in selling group agreements is that the group has an existence of 30 days, subject to earlier termination by the manager. The agreement may be extended, however, for an additional 80 days by members representing 75 percent of the selling group.

---

[3]Without these repurchase arrangements, members of the selling group could sell their share of the securities on the market instead of soliciting new purchasers. Since the pegging operation is going on, there will be a ready market for the securities; consequently, a penalty is necessary to avoid thwarting the syndicate operation.

Offering and Sale

After the selling group has been formed, the actual offering takes place. Publicity for the sale is given in advance of the offering date. Advertising material is prepared for release as soon as permitted. The actual day of the offering is chosen with a view to avoiding temporary congestion in the security market and other unfavorable events or circumstances.

The formal public offering is called *opening the books*, an archaic term reflecting ancient customs of the investment banking trade. When the books are opened, the manager accepts subscriptions to the issue from both selling group participants and outsiders who wish to buy. If the demand is great, the books may be closed immediately and an announcement made that the issue is oversubscribed; the issue is said to "fly out the window." If the reception is weak, the books may remain open for an extended period.

Market Stabilization

During the period of the offering and distribution of securities, the manager of the underwriting group typically stabilizes the price of the issue. The duration of the price-pegging operation is usually 30 days. The price is pegged by placing orders to buy at a specified price in the market. The pegging operation is designed to prevent a cumulative downward movement in the price, which would result in losses for all members of the underwriting group. Since the manager of the underwriting group has the major responsibility, that person assumes the task of pegging the price.

If the market deteriorates during the offering period, the investment banker carries a substantial risk. For this reason, the pegging operation may not be sufficient to protect the underwriters. In one Pure Oil Company issue of $44 million convertible preferred stock, only $1 million of shares were sold at the $100 offering price. At the conclusion of the underwriting agreement, initial trading took place at $74, incurring for the investment bankers a loss of over $11 million ($43 million × 26 percent). In the Textron issue of June 1967, the offering was reduced from $100 million to $50 million because of market congestion, and 5 percent of the bonds still were unsold after the initial offering. More recent examples were described in a *Wall Street Journal* article of December 13, 1984, stating that "investment bankers are stuck with a lot of unsold bonds on their shelves and $40 million of potential losses." As one investment banker expressed it: "There's a lot of blood on the floor." Reference was also made to the craters that the offering bombs had made on the corporate finance landscape.

It has been charged that pegging the price during the offering period constitutes a monopolistic price-fixing arrangement. Investment bankers reply, however, that not to peg the price would increase the risk and, therefore, the underwriting cost to the issuer. On balance, it appears that the pegging operation has a socially useful function. The danger of monopolistic pricing is avoided, or at least mitigated substantially, by competitive factors. If an underwriter attempts to set a monopolistic price on a particular issue of securities, the investor can turn to thousands of other securities. The degree of control over the market by the underwriter in a price-pegging operation seems negligible.

IBM's October 1979 Debt Offering

The IBM debt offering of October 1979 provides an informative case study of the nature of modern investment banking and underwriting.[4] IBM's debt offering was called the largest in U.S. corporate history. It represented a combined offering by IBM of $500 million in seven-year notes and $500 million in 25-year debentures (unsecured long-term debt) for a total of $1 billion. IBM's customary investment banker had been Morgan Stanley & Co. For this offering, IBM requested separate proposals from Morgan Stanley and from Salomon Brothers. It was reported that IBM's financial management was of the opinion that two managers would provide better execution of the sale and back it up with a larger amount of capital. John H. Gutfreund, Salomon Brothers' managing partner, is quoted as stating, "A major corporation is best served by two sets of eyes and ears." Robert H. B. Baldwin, president of Morgan Stanley, is said to have responded, "You need only one brain surgeon." Morgan Stanley dropped out as manager and Merrill Lynch became the co-manager, with an underwriting group totaling 227 members.

The Salomon and Morgan Stanley proposals had been presented to IBM early in September 1979. The ensuing discussions during that month took place during a period when the prime rate was increased five times, reaching a level of 13.5 percent by September 28. The planned date for the offering was moved up from October 15 to the first week in October. A pricing meeting took place on October 3, 1979, with rapidly rising yields taking place in the money market. Discussions centered around prices based on a yield of 7 basis points above Treasury notes for the IBM notes and 12 basis points above Treasury bonds for the IBM debentures. Taking the small price discounts into account, IBM was paying 9.62 percent for the seven-year notes and 9.41 percent for the 25-year debentures. The underwriting spread or commission on the notes was five-eighths of 1 percent, or $6.25 per note. The underwriter fee on the debentures was seven-eighths of 1 percent, or $8.75 per debenture.

October 3 was a Wednesday. After the pricing meeting, which ended at 12:40 p.m., the market yield of Treasury bonds moved up during the afternoon by five basis points. The IBM offering began on Thursday, October 4. Also on Thursday, the Treasury auctioned $2.5 billion of four-year notes yielding 9.79 percent, higher than the 9.62 percent for the IBM seven-year notes.

On Saturday, October 6, the Federal Reserve System announced an increase in its discount rate from 11 percent to 12 percent. A number of other credit-tightening policies, called "Draconian" in their severity, were implemented. As a result of the Fed's actions, by Tuesday, October 9, an additional increase in the prime rate was announced, with a rise of one full percent — to 14.5 percent. On Wednesday morning, October 10, the underwriting syndicate was disbanded. The price of both the notes and the debentures fell by about $5 each, with yields rising to 10.65 percent per note and 10.09 percent for the debentures.

When the syndicate was disbanded, it was estimated that $600 million to $700 million of the issue had been sold. Using the midfigure of $650 million and applying the underwriting fees indicated revenues of about $5 million. When the market quotations dropped after the syndicate was disbanded, the losses on the $350 million sold at lower prices were estimated at around $15 million. The potential losses to individual underwriters were substantial. The two managers, Salomon and Merrill Lynch, each underwrote over $124

---

[4]This summary is based on contemporaneous accounts in the financial press.

million. Morgan Stanley took $40 million. First Boston and Goldman Sachs each took $20 million.

Underwriting exposure must also take the practice of *swapping* into account. To sell institutional buyers a new issue, the seller takes in exchange (swaps) some other bonds that the institutions already own. The value placed on the bonds taken in exchange may have a substantial effect on the actual price received. Another aspect is the practice of hedging. When in a long position on bonds while interest rates are rising, the underwriter can take self-protective action by selling other issues short.

A controversy remains over whether the IBM issue pricing was "too tight." During the month of September preceding the actual offering, the Federal funds rate, the prime rate, and the discount rate had all been increasing. The financial markets during the week of October 3, when the pricing decision was made, were hectic if not chaotic. Undoubtedly, the severe measures taken by the Federal Reserve System on Saturday, October 6, 1979, were in the air during the week.[5] For example, the October 5 *Wall Street Journal* reported, "Another negative development was the apparent decision by the Federal Reserve System to tighten its credit reins further and to push key short-term interest rates still higher." Whether the underwriters should have given themselves more cushion to avoid a subsequent price decline is a matter of judgment. From one standpoint, the price decline of $4 to $5 after disbanding the underwriting syndicate was relatively modest, given the sharply rising interest rates during the period and the Fed announcement on Saturday, October 6. Differences in judgment on this matter are likely, but such differences in judgment are what make markets.

The IBM offering illustrates a number of basic characteristics of investment banking. First, the risks are real. Second, competition among investment bankers continues to be vigorous and tough. Third, a corporate issue of a well-managed, prestigious firm which is taking on debt for the first time (and in moderate quantity in relation to its total assets) will be rated Aaa and priced close to Treasury issues. Fourth, the turbulence of the financial markets during the week of the offering made the task of the underwriters and the company a supremely difficult one. It demonstrated the great risk-taking and judgment required to make decisions in the face of an extremely turbulent financial environment. Fifth, the episode illustrates the high drama, the considerable financial sophistication, and the continued great challenges that exist in the field of financial decision making.

Costs of Flotation

The cost of selling new issues of securities is put into perspective in Table 24.3. The table summarizes recent data on costs of flotation compiled by the SEC. Two important generalizations can be drawn from these data:

1. The cost of flotation as a percentage of the gross proceeds is greater for small issues than for large ones.
2. Rights offerings appear to cost much less than fully underwritten issues.

Other studies find that the cost of flotation for common stock is greater than for preferred stock, and the costs of both are greater than the cost of flotation for bonds. The explanations for these relationships are found in the amount of risk involved and in the job of physical distribution. Bonds are generally bought in large blocks by relatively few

---

[5]"Prices Drop Further as Record IBM Offer Encounters Surprising Buyer Resistance," *Wall Street Journal*, October 5, 1979, p. 37.

Table 24.3 Costs of Flotation as a Percentage of Proceeds for Common Stock Issues, 1971-75[a]

Size of Issue (millions of dollars)	Underwriting				Rights with Standby Underwriting				Rights	
	Number	Compensation as a Percentage of Proceeds	Other Expenses as a Percentage of Proceeds	Total Cost as a Percentage of Proceeds	Number	Compensation as a Percentage of Proceeds	Other Expenses as a Percentage of Proceeds	Total Cost as a Percentage of Proceeds	Number	Total Cost as a Percentage of Proceeds
Under 0.50	0	—	—	—	0	—	—	—	3	8.99
0.50–0.99	6	6.96	6.78	13.74	2	3.43	4.80	8.24	2	4.59
1.00–1.99	18	10.40	4.89	15.29	5	6.36	4.15	10.51	5	4.90
2.00–4.99	61	6.59	2.87	9.47	9	5.20	2.85	8.06	7	2.85
5.00–9.99	66	5.50	1.53	7.03	4	3.92	2.18	6.10	6	1.39
10.00–19.99	91	4.84	0.71	5.55	10	4.14	1.21	5.35	3	0.72
20.00–49.99	156	4.30	0.37	4.67	12	3.84	0.90	4.74	1	0.52
50.00–99.99	70	3.97	0.21	4.18	9	3.96	0.74	4.70	2	0.21
100.00–500.00	16	3.81	0.14	3.95	5	3.50	0.50	4.00	9	0.13
Total/Average	484	5.02	1.15	6.17	56	4.32	1.73	6.05	38	2.45

Source: Clifford W. Smith, Jr., "Substitute Methods for Raising Additional Capital: Rights Offerings versus Underwritten Issues." Original version appeared in *Journal of Financial Economics*, Vol. 5:3, December 1977. Copyright North-Holland 1977.
[a]Issues are included only if the company's stock was listed on the NYSE, AMEX, or regional exchanges prior to the offering; any associated secondary distribution represents less than 10 percent of the total proceeds of the issue, and the offering contains no other types of securities.

institutional investors, whereas stocks are bought by millions of individuals. For this reason, the distribution job for common stock is harder and the expenses of marketing it are greater. Similarly, stocks are more volatile than bonds, so underwriting risks are larger for stock than for bond flotations.

Reasons for the variation in cost with the size of issue are also easily found. First, certain fixed expenses are associated with any distribution of securities: the underwriting investigation, the preparation of the registration statement, legal fees, and so on. Since these expenses are relatively large and fixed, their percentage of the total cost of flotation runs high on small issues. Second, small issues are typically those of relatively less well-known firms, so underwriting expenses may be larger than usual because the danger of omitting vital information is greater. Furthermore, the selling job is more difficult; salespeople must exert greater effort to sell the securities of less well-known firms. For these reasons, the underwriting commission, as a percentage of the gross proceeds, is relatively high for small issues.

Flotation costs for common stock issued on a rights offering with standby underwriting are at about the same level as fully underwritten issues.[6] But, pure rights offerings have much lower flotation costs. Yet, during the five-year period studied, only 38 of 578 common stock issues were pure rights offerings. Smith [1977], who compiled the data in Table 24.3, considered a wide range of explanations for preferring underwriting to rights offerings but reached the conclusion that none have validity. An additional possibility is that it was only some special circumstances of the rights offerings that resulted in their lower costs and that absent these characteristics, the costs of flotation of pure rights offerings would not be greatly different from underwritten issues.

Flotation Costs on Negotiated versus Multiple-Bidding Underwritings

The general practice is for a long-term relationship to develop between a business firm and its investment banker. The investment banking firm builds up a cumulative background of knowledge and understanding through its continuous counseling with the firm over a period of years. On a particular financing, the firm's historical investment banker already has considerable background knowledge. It takes much more time and expense for another investment banking firm to develop a comparable fund of knowledge. The business firm, therefore, is likely to look to its traditional investment banker on any new financing requirement. The terms and arrangements on any particular issue will be worked out in direct negotiations between the firm and its investment banker. These are called "negotiated underwritings."

However, for public utility firms, more than one investment banker is likely to be competing for the business of underwriting a particular issue. The SEC Rule U-50 makes competitive bidding mandatory on new issues of securities by public utility holding companies. Whether required by law or not, it is more likely that competitive bidding will be used by public utilities than by industrial firms. The characteristics of public utilities are more uniform, with fewer special circumstances than for industrial firms in a wide variety of business activities. Also, as regulated industries, the utilities have long been required to provide substantial amounts of information on a relatively uniform basis. Hence, the kinds of information that the historical investment banker develops for an industrial firm

---

[6]Rights offerings involve the sale of stock to existing stockholders. The topic is discussed extensively in Chapter 25.

over a longer period of time are more easily developed for utility firms. The question of the relative costs of negotiated versus "competitive" underwritings has been raised.

The terms *negotiated* and *competitive* are sometimes misleading. Negotiated underwritings are as fully competitive as underwritings with bidding by more than one investment banker. The performance of the historical investment banker must assure the firm that no other investment banker could do the job better. Hence, the potential competition from others waiting in the wings for the opportunity of displacing the historical investment banker assures that competition is as effective on single bids as on multiple bidding. Thus, the empirical studies are measuring not only the effects of multiple bidding on the costs of underwriting but also the characteristics of the firms and the nature of the general financial market conditions that are likely to result in negotiated versus multiple bidding underwritings in particular cases.

Several recent articles have studied the relative costs of negotiated versus multiple-bidding underwritings. In their studies, Tallman, Rush, and Melicher (TRM) [1974] concluded that "competitive offerings appeared to be less costly during stable market conditions, but that negotiated offerings might be more advantageous during unstable markets." Their empirical results indicated that underwriter compensation was a positive function of "default risk" and a negative function of "market preference for utility bonds" in the case of competitive issues only. In their paper on utility debt, Dyl and Joehnk [1976] found that competitive offerings result in lower underwriting charges, attempting to hold all other factors constant. But they also found a significant fixed cost element in the flotation charges for competitive issues. With different data sets, Ederington [1976] reached conclusions similar to TRM: Competitive offerings might be more desirable during stable markets and negotiated offerings superior during troubled markets. Ederington found that the negotiated offering variable was significant in explaining yield spreads and implied a yield eight basis points higher than a similar competitive issue. He came to the conclusion that some relaxation of SEC Rule U-50, at least during periods of great market uncertainty, might be appropriate.

A more recent study was made by Findlay, Johnson, and Morton (FJM) [1979]. The independent variables used in their study were (1) issuer size, (2) type of utility, (3) seasoning, (4) maturity, (5) sinking fund, (6) type of offering, (7) issue size, (8) stock market ebullience, (9) bond market interest rate, (10) volume conditions, (11) AT&T ownership, and (12) S&P's rating class. The dependent variable employed was the ratio of total direct issuance cost (underwriter fees plus other direct expenses) to gross total dollar amount raised in the issue. Regressions were run on the total sample of 628 issues and on the subsamples of 135 communications and 493 electric, gas, and water issues.

A low bond rating had a positive influence on flotation costs, while a high bond rating had a negative influence. These results would seem to be a proxy for selling effort and/or risk effect. The implication is that even after taking account of the yield differential, Aaa utility bonds were viewed as fast or easy sales, and Bbb bonds were seen as slow or hard sales. These results are consistent with earlier studies, which found default risk premium to be the most important influence on issuing costs.

The next variable to enter the regression was issuer size, which had a negative impact on flotation costs. This variable undoubtedly acts as a proxy for any economies of scale in the underwriting process. Besides that, issuer size may also proxy a repeat business effect from the underwriter's perspective. Finally, the level of interest rates, as depicted by the Aaa utility bond average, had a significantly positive influence on flotation costs.

The FJM study demonstrates that the traditional competitive-negotiated issue question is far more complex than it would appear. At least four reasons why high interest rates might lead to high flotation costs were discussed — higher inventory carrying costs, reduction in underwriter competition, higher interest rate risk, and negotiated offerings.

Only the last is related to the mode of issue, and it had perhaps the least convincing economic rationale. Where the firm and its situation are standard, this facilitates a competitive bidding process. Where the situation is more complex, a negotiated transaction is more likely. As the previous studies indicate, even where competitive bids have been used, a shift may be made to a negotiated transaction when the markets themselves become unsettled. Apparently, it is for this reason that the FJM study concludes that "the data and methodology employed in all studies to date are simply too crude to determine whether an inefficiency exists with respect to mode of banker compensation which can be exploited by a purchaser of intermediation services."

Regulation of Security Trading

The operations of investment bankers, exchanges, and over-the-counter markets are significantly influenced by a series of federal statutes enacted during and after 1933. The financial manager is affected by these laws for several reasons:

1. Corporate officers are subject to personal liabilities.
2. The laws affect the ease and costs of financing and the behavior of the money and capital markets in which the corporation's securities are sold and traded.
3. Investors' willingness to buy securities is influenced by the existence of safeguards provided by these laws.

Securities Act of 1933

The first of the securities acts, the Securities Act of 1933, followed congressional investigations of the stock market collapse of 1929-32. Motivating the act were (1) the large losses to investors, (2) the failures of many corporations on which little information had been provided, and (3) the misrepresentations that had been made to investors.

The basic objective of the Securities Act of 1933 is to provide for both *full disclosure* of relevant information and a *record of representations*. The act seeks to achieve these objectives by the following means:

1. It applies to all interstate offerings to the public in amounts of $1.5 million or more. (Some exemptions are government bonds and bank stocks.)
2. Securities must be registered at least 20 days before they are publicly offered. The registration statement provides financial, legal, and technical information about the company. A prospectus summarizes this information for use in selling the securities. If information is inadequate or misleading, the SEC will delay or stop the public offering. (Obtaining the information required to review the registration statement may result in a waiting period that exceeds 20 days.)
3. After the registration has become effective, the securities can be offered if accompanied by the prospectus. Preliminary, or "red herring," prospectuses can be distributed to potential buyers during the waiting period.
4. If the registration statement or prospectus contains misrepresentation or omissions of material facts, any purchaser who suffers a loss can sue for damages. Liabilities and severe penalties can be imposed on the issuer and its officers, directors, accountants, engineers, appraisers, and underwriters and on all others who participated in preparing the registration statement.

Securities Exchange Act of 1934

The Securities Exchange Act of 1934 extends the disclosure principle applied to new issues by the Securities Act of 1933 to trading in already issued securities (the secondhand securities market). It seeks to accomplish this by the following measures:

1. It establishes the Securities and Exchange Commission. (The Federal Trade Commission had been administering the Securities Act of 1933.)
2. It provides for registration and regulation of national securities exchanges. Companies whose securities are listed on an exchange must file reports similar to registration statements with both the SEC and the stock exchange and must provide periodic reports as well.
3. It establishes control over corporate "insiders." Officers, directors, and major stockholders of a corporation must file monthly reports of changes in holdings of the corporation's stock. Any short-term profits from such transactions are payable to the corporation.
4. It gives the SEC the power to prohibit manipulation by such devices as pools (aggregations of funds used to affect prices artificially), wash sales (sales among members of the same group to record artificial transaction prices), and pegging the market other than during stock flotations.
5. It gives the SEC control over the proxy machinery and practices.
6. It establishes control over the flow of credit into security transactions by giving the board of governors of the Federal Reserve System the power to control margin requirements.

The Securities Acts Amendments of 1975

The Securities Acts Amendments of 1975 were passed after four years of research and investigation into the changing nature of securities markets. Secondary markets were seen as being under stress due to overall increased trading volume and increased dominance by large institutional investors. In particular, the NYSE system of fixed minimum percentage rate brokerage commissions was seen as inequitable, resulting in unreasonably high transactions costs on a per-share basis when applied to large block trades. This system had led many large traders to move away from the NYSE to the over-the-counter market and the regional exchanges, resulting in market fragmentation and nondisclosure of significant trading on the NYSE tape. The study recommended the abolition of fixed minimum brokerage commissions and increased automation of trading by utilizing electronic communication and data processing technology to link markets. The wording of the amendments is general, speaking of fostering efficiency, enhancing competition, increasing available information, and so forth. The Securities and Exchange Commission was mandated to work with the securities industry to develop an operational framework for a national market system to achieve the goal of nationwide competition in securities trading, with centralized reporting of price quotations and transactions and a central order routing system to find the best available price. (The development of this system was discussed in Chapter 3.)

Empirical studies have demonstrated that both higher trading volume and more dealer competition result in narrower bid-ask spreads in stock trading. Among the benefits to corporate financial managers which might be expected from the new securities legislation are

1.   Broader exposure to the public, since both listed and unlisted firms would be in-
     cluded in the national market system.
2.   Stronger secondary markets, which should encourage individual investors to com-
     mit capital on new issues.
3.   More liquid securities markets, leading to lower costs of capital.

Recent Changes in SEC Rules

The mechanisms of selling securities in the public markets have been greatly influenced by
some recent changes in the rules of the Securities and Exchange Commission. In 1978, the
SEC began to streamline the securities registration process. Large well-known corporations were permitted to abbreviate registration statements, to disclose information by reference to other documents that had already been made public, and to be subject to only
selective reviews of documents by the SEC staff. Before these changes, the registration
process sometimes took several weeks to be completed. With the changes made after 1978,
a registration statement can be approved in as short a time as two days.

A further development took place in March 1982, when the Securities and Exchange
Commission authorized shelf registration. Larger corporations (with stock outstanding
exceeding $150 million in market value) can register the full amount of debt or equity they
plan to sell over a two-year period. After this initial registration has been completed, the
firm can sell up to the specified amount of debt or equity without further delay. The firm
can choose the time when the funds are needed or when market conditions appear favorable. With the increased volatility in financial markets in recent years, shelf registration
gives firms the flexibility to act quickly when market conditions appear favorable. Shelf
registration reduces the costs of issuing securities because of the savings achieved on
accounting, legal, and printing expenses. It appears to have introduced increased competition among investment bankers, and this, in turn, may lower underwriting fees. But the
method of distribution may also be involved. When securities are sold from a shelf registration, a large investment banking firm often quickly places them with a relatively small
number of buyers. Thus, extensive syndication, as described earlier in the chapter, does
not take place, and the securities are not as broadly distributed, at least initially.

The use of shelf registration thus far has been quite different in the bond market as
compared with the issue of new equity shares. Shelf registration has been very popular in
the sale of bonds. Since 1982, on average, 50 to 60 percent of all debt sales made use of
shelf registration. It has been noted that financial firms such as commercial banks have
made use of shelf registration to a greater degree than have manufacturing corporations,
for example. Financial firms have traditionally raised funds quickly in a number of receptive markets. Hence, shelf registration permits them to extend their traditional financing
practices.

In contrast to the very considerable use of shelf registration in the bond market, in the
equity market less than 10 percent of total issuance has been accounted for by shelf
registration. The reason for the smaller use of shelf registration by equity issuers has not
been fully studied. One possible explanation is that equity issuers prefer broader distribution, which is achieved through the use of investment banking syndicates but not through
shelf registration. Another hypothesis offered is that unissued equity shares in shelf registration may be viewed as over-hanging the market by potential investors. They may view
the unissued equity shares as potentially coming on the market and, hence, take this
increased number into account in calculating earnings per share and other measures of
firm performance that may be employed.

Streamlined registrations and shelf registration appear to represent attempts to reduce the transactions costs of issuing securities. Some people have argued that these reduced costs come at the expense of diminished services performed. These developments are so new that more experience will be required to make an informed assessment of what their full impacts will be over the years.

Appraisal of Regulation of Security Trading

Why should security transactions be regulated? It can be argued that a great body of relevant knowledge is necessary to make an informed judgment of the value of a security. Moreover, security values are subject to many gyrations that influence stability and business conditions generally. Hence, social well-being requires that orderly markets be promoted. There are three primary objectives of regulation:

1.   To protect investors from fraud and to provide them with a basis for informed judgments.
2.   To control the volume of bank credit to finance security speculation.
3.   To provide orderly markets in securities.

Progress has been made on all three counts. There has been some cost in the increased time and expense involved in new flotations by companies, although the benefits seem worth their costs. The regulations are powerless to prevent investors from investing in unsound ventures or to prevent stock prices from skyrocketing during booms and plummeting during periods of pessimism. Still, requirements for increased information have been of value in preventing fraud and gross misrepresentations.

From the standpoint of the financial manager, regulation has a twofold significance. It affects both the costs of issuing securities and the riskiness of securities, and hence the rate of return investors require when they purchase stocks and bonds. As previous chapters have shown, these two factors have an important bearing on the firm's cost of capital and, through the capital budgeting process, on its investment decisions. Further, since business investment is a key determinant of employment and production in the economy, efficient capital markets have an important impact on all of society.

Recent Trends in Business Financing

The sharp fluctuations in interest rate levels and shifts in the availability of financing in recent years have brought about significant changes in financing patterns.[7] In Table 24.4, some recent trends in external financing are depicted. After a negative use of net funds raised from equity financing during the period 1977 through 1981, the use of equity financing sharply increased. By the first half of 1983, $38.2 billion of net equity funds were raised in the external publicly traded markets. The rise in equity prices between August 1982 and June 1983 was 68.4 percent for the New York Stock Exchange Composite and over 100 percent for both the AMEX Composite and the NASDAQ Composite. This increase in stock prices stimulated new issues by firms whose stock was already traded publicly. In addition, as is typical of strong equity markets, the market for firms going public for the

---

[7]This section is based in part on Moran [1984].

Table 24.4　　Net Funds Raised in Markets by Nonfinancial Corporations, 1977-83 (Billions of Dollars)

Type of Instrument	1977	1978	1979	1980	1981	1982[a] H1	1982[a] H2	1983[a] H1	1983[a] H2
Total, long-term	**35.8**	**32.8**	**20.9**	**52.5**	**22.5**	**31.7**	**58.7**	**74.6**	**36.7**
Equity	2.7	−.1	−7.8	12.9	−11.5	7.0	15.8	38.2	18.4
Notes and bonds[b]	29.6	28.8	27.3	37.6	35.5	24.7	43.3	31.8	17.0
Mortgages	3.5	4.1	1.4	2.0	−1.5	.0	−.4	4.6	1.3
Total, short-term	**36.6**	**47.7**	**67.3**	**38.5**	**69.7**	**64.6**	**13.2**	**.2**	**60.2**
Bank loans[c]	20.9	32.3	47.1	30.6	44.1	55.3	31.4	3.9	30.5
Commercial paper	1.6	2.7	9.0	4.0	14.7	8.7	−18.2	−8.7	7.8
Finance company loans	13.5	11.5	10.2	3.1	8.7	1.7	−2.6	8.8	18.8
Acceptances	.6	1.2	1.0	.8	2.2	−1.1	2.6	−3.8	3.1

[a]Seasonally adjusted annual rate.
[b]Includes notes and bonds sold in foreign markets by U.S. nonfinancial corporations and tax-exempt bonds issued by state or local governments for the benefit of a corporation.
[c]Includes a small amount of U.S. government loans.
Source: Moran, Michael J., "Recent Financing Activity of Nonfinancial Corporations," *Federal Reserve Bulletin*, 70 (May 1984), pp. 403–405.

first time was also very favorable. It is estimated that during 1983, over $7 billion of initial public offerings by companies took place.

As noted earlier in this chapter, the use of debt financing also increased sharply during the second half of 1982 and the first half of 1983. This was accompanied by a number of other related developments. In addition to increasing the total volume of bond financing during this period, business firms also sought to lengthen the maturities of their borrowing. In the years before 1982, only about one-third of bond offerings had maturities of 20 years or longer. By the first half of 1983, the proportion of longer-term bonds had reached almost 50 percent.

Another shift in financing patterns by U.S. firms has been the increased use of foreign markets. For example, in 1977 and 1978, the use of offshore financing by U.S. firms was only slightly over $1 billion. For the years 1982 through the first half of 1984, the annual rate of foreign financing rose to $13 billion. Larger, well-known firms have made increased use of the Euromarket. Another influence of the Euromarket activity is in the pricing of term business loans. In earlier years, commercial banks priced term loans at some spread above the U.S. prime rate. In recent years, competition has forced banks to permit borrowers to choose among alternative bases for setting the floating rates. Included among the alternatives is the London Interbank Offer Rate (LIBOR).

Most Eurobond issues have maturities in the five to ten year range and carry interest rates lower than would be obtained in the U.S. market. A differential in interest costs between two markets can exist only if they are segmented. One reason was that the U.S. market was unattractive to foreign investors because the interest payments on bonds sold in the U.S. were subject to a 30 percent withholding tax. This provision was repealed by the Deficit Reduction Act of 1984, signed into law in July 1984. Another plus for the Euromarket was that investors could achieve a greater degree of anonymity since the bonds are generally issued in bearer form, which does not require the use of the purchaser's name. Also, some U.S. investment bankers have been selling bearer bonds abroad based on portfolios of U.S. securities. It appears that the segmentation is being reduced.

Because of the extreme financial pressures before monetary policy was changed in the summer of 1982, U.S. firms have adopted other measures to increase their access to financing and to improve the condition of their balance sheets. Since 1977, the volume of unused loan commitments made available to business firms has nearly tripled to some $350 billion. In the middle of the decade of the 1970s, only about 500 business firms had access to the commercial paper market, with a volume outstanding of about $13 billion. By early 1984, the number of firms issuing commercial paper had increased to about 1,800, with an outstanding volume of $50 billion. A recent innovation has helped firms use the commercial paper market. There is an increasing practice of having commercial banks issue letters of credit specifically backing the commercial paper issued by business firms. This not only gives them access to the commercial paper market but also improves the terms on which they can sell commercial paper.

Another innovation has helped business firms improve the appearance of their balance sheets. This technique is called "in-substance defeasance," approved by both the Financial Accounting Standards Board (FASB) and the Securities and Exchange Commission (SEC). The procedure involves having the firm place in an irrevocable trust such risk-free assets as cash or U.S. government obligations to generate sufficient cash flows to service a portion of its debt. Since the principal and interest payments on the debt can be made from the assets placed in trust, the firm is permitted to remove the debt and the assets from its balance sheet. In addition, if low coupon debt with a market value below par is removed from the balance sheet, the firm can report as current income an amount roughly the difference between the book values of the defeased debt and the assets placed in trust.

Still another development since 1982 is the "interest rate swap." Two firms issue debt, one bearing a fixed interest rate and the other a floating interest rate. They then exchange their interest rate obligations. If each issuer has a comparative advantage in a particular type of debt or in a particular market, the swap enables each party to service its preferred type of debt at an interest cost lower than otherwise. This extends an earlier practice utilized by multinational corporations. The "currency swaps" by multinational corporations involve swapping interest obligations denominated in different currencies. The currency swaps arose because, in seeking to minimize foreign exchange risk, firms wanted to shift from one foreign currency position to another.

In general, the use of interest rate swaps and currency swaps enables corporations to reposition the characteristics of their debt and reduce their exposure to risks associated with fluctuating interest rates and exchange rates. The development of financial futures, options, and forward contracts also have permitted business firms to reduce their exposure to interest rate and currency value fluctuations. As a part of this trend, some commercial banks have devised foreign interest rate contracts that enable their borrowers to fix the rates on loans or deposits before the actual transaction date. Firms are now able to hedge their interest rate risks for up to about two years and to limit their exchange rate risks for periods up to one year.

Institutional Developments

Important new developments are taking place in the financial markets, in commercial banking, and in investment banking. Some of these developments result from legislative changes, and others from fundamental shifts in the nature of international economic and financial relationships.

A major legislative change took place in the United States when the Depository Institutions Deregulation and Monetary Control Act of 1980 was passed. The new law directs the Federal Reserve to set reserve requirements, not only for its member banks, but for all commercial banks, savings banks, and savings and loan associations. The new reserve requirements will be phased in over three years for member banks and over seven years for other financial institutions. All deposit interest ceilings (such as the regulation limiting the interest rate that may be paid on time and savings deposits) will be phased out over six years. Under the law, depository institutions are permitted to offer interest-bearing checking accounts or negotiable order of withdrawal (NOW) accounts. Federally chartered savings and loan associations and savings banks are given new lending and investing powers, including the ability to make more types of consumer loans, offer credit cards, and invest in commercial paper and corporate debt.

In 1982, the Garn-St. Germain Depository Institutions Act was enacted by Congress. It further broadened the lending powers of savings and loan associations as well as other thrift institutions, allowed acquisitions across state lines, and permitted thrift institutions to establish money market deposit accounts to compete with money market funds.

The full impact of this legislation will not be apparent for some time. It can be predicted that competition among the different types of financial institutions will increase. The barriers to national operations by commercial banks also appear to be on their way toward relaxation and perhaps even elimination. Foreign banks have had greater flexibility than domestic banks in operating in the United States. The International Banking Act of 1978 established some guidelines for foreign banks operating in the United States and called upon the president of the United States to investigate whether U.S. banks have been under a competitive disadvantage with respect to foreign banks.

Revolutionary developments also have occurred in investment banking. Investment banking has moved from its traditional business base in underwriting and brokerage activities towards insurance and commercial banking. Half the revenues of the large investment banking firms used to come from commissions until the Securities and Exchange Commission in 1975 ordered the end of fixed commission schedules. This was followed by competition for the big accounts of the institutional investors (insurance companies, pension funds, mutual funds, and so forth). Commission rates were driven down and commission income dropped to less than 40 percent of revenues. Investment bankers have become more like commercial banks in that, for the larger firms, net interest revenues have ranged upwards from 70 percent of pretax earnings.

Additional new sources of income for investment banking firms include credit cards and money market funds as well as counseling on corporate financing, ranging from cash management to mergers. Other important new activities that generate revenues are equity-based insurance policies; tax shelter programs in oil, real estate, and so forth; stock options; commodities trading commissions; and participation in the interest rate futures markets.

Much of this new activity is facilitated by computer-assisted analysis; additionally, the tasks of office record keeping and reporting to customers have been computerized. As a result, the degree of operating leverage (DOL) of the investment banking firms has increased. (Here is another practical illustration of the importance of the concept discussed in both Chapters 9 and 20.) This has occurred because the firms were shifting from the partly fixed costs of clerical workers to the almost completely fixed costs of computers. With higher operating leverage, recall that declines in volume have a greater adverse impact on profitability. As a consequence, the lower commission income (resulting from the abolition of fixed commission schedules), coupled with higher DOL, places severe financial pressures on investment banking firms during periods of low income activity. To avoid financial disaster, numerous "mergers of necessity" have taken place, as evident in the compound names of some of the surviving firms: Merrill Lynch White Weld Capital Markets Group; Blyth Eastman Paine Webber; Dean Witter Reynolds Inc.; and Smith Barney, Harris Upham & Co. In addition to mergers within the investment banking and brokerage business, mergers between different types of financial institutions have taken place. Bache and Co., once the eighth largest investment banking firm, was taken over by the Prudential Insurance Company of America. The American Express Company merged with Shearson Loeb Rhoades, the second largest investment banking firm in terms of brokerage business. The Bechtel consulting engineering company bought Dillon Read, an investment banking firm.

The traditional barriers between banking and other financial services are disappearing. Brokerage houses, retail department stores, credit card agencies, and securities companies are all taking business from the traditional bankers' role as intermediary between borrowers and lenders. Commercial banks are moving into other institutions' areas — brokerage, insurance, corporate finance, real estate, securities trading, and even esoteric fields such as barter trade and venture capital. This has taken place in the United States despite the Glass-Steagall Act of 1932 (which separated commercial from investment banking) and the McFadden Act of 1927 (which prohibited interstate banking).

Cash management systems initiated through terminals on the corporate treasurer's desk, remote disbursement accounts, and nationwide loan production offices mean that in corporate banking, state boundaries are not much more than a minor irritation. In consumer banking, banks have taken over ailing savings and loan associations. Citicorp's acquisitions, including the First Federal Savings & Loan Association of Chicago and the Biscayne Federal Savings & Loan Association of Miami, make Citicorp one of the largest operators of S&L's. In July 1983, Bank of America took over Seafirst, parent of the ailing Seattle First National Bank of Washington state. Big American commercial banks have also become investment bankers. Under the Rule 415 "shelf registration" procedure, by which corporations can register future security issues in advance, commercial banks effectively act as underwriters. Instead of the formal underwriting process of buying the securities and then selling them (prohibited by Glass-Steagall), they simply act as agents, placing the paper privately with large institutional investors.

The distinction between commercial banks and other financial services is being eroded in another fundamental way. Banks traditionally think of themselves as principals, taking risk directly onto their own balance sheets — in contrast to brokers, who act as agents. But banks are moving into the brokerage business. In 1983, Bank of America paid $52 million for the discount stock broker Charles Schwab.

Banks are having their own toes trampled on by so-called "nonbank banks." Insurance companies, brokerage firms, money market funds, retailers, and so forth, are not allowed to own a commercial bank as defined under the Bank Holding Company Act. However, if they strip a commercial bank of either its commercial lending functions or its deposit functions, the bank no longer falls under the act's definition of a commercial bank. These "nonbank banks" are then free to get into all other aspects of the banking business without being subject to the Fed. For example, Merrill Lynch offers checking facilities through its cash management account. Customers do not deposit money with Merrill Lynch, but they buy shares in a money market mutual fund, against which checks can be drawn and loans made. Dean Witter, acquired by Sears Roebuck in 1981, has a similar scheme. Nearly one-half of America's 83 million households have a relationship with Sears, through either a credit card, the catalog list, or policies with Sears' insurance subsidiary, Allstate Insurance.

Traditionally, banks have been good at selling the services they have. But their grasp of marketing in the broader sense of finding out what customers really want and designing a product to suit their needs has been poor. This is where retailing firms such as Sears have a head start over banks. The big growth in retail financial services is customer-driven.

Charles Moran, head of Sears' corporate planning, says, "This is not new to us. We didn't invent the lawn mower and tell our customers to use it to cut the grass. People came along, and said they needed to cut the grass, so we supplied the lawn mower." It's exactly the same in financial services. Sears' strategy is based on the theory that they have identified middle income customers as the big growth area for its financial services — insurance through Allstate Insurance, real estate through Coldwell Banker, and brokerage through Dean Witter. In addition, Sears has a large savings and loan association operation. Sears found through market research that the average Dean Witter investor earned only marginally more than the average Sears charge card holder. While most brokerage firms continued to concentrate their marketing on the wealthy, Sears has been successfully exploiting the new middle income market for financial services by selling "stocks and socks," virtually side by side, in its department stores.

Many describe this trend as a movement towards financial services conglomerates. They point to other manifestations of these developments as well. It is commonplace for large industrial firms such as General Electric, Ford, or IBM to have a financial or credit affiliate or subsidiary. The National Steel Corporation owns the fourth largest publicly owned (rather than mutually owned) savings and loan holding company in the United States. By 1979, more than half the earnings of Household Finance Corporation (traditionally a consumer finance firm) came from sources other than financial operations.

Truly, the financial markets are experiencing fundamental changes. Laws are changing, but more important, the underlying economic and financial forces are exploding in many different directions. From the standpoint of managerial finance, these changes profoundly influence the characteristics and terms of external funds obtained by business firms.

Summary

Longer-term obligations are sold directly to investors or through the investment banking distribution systems. Two major forms of direct financing are term lending by commercial banks and the private placement of securities with insurance companies and pension funds. Term loans and private placements represent similar financing arrangements. Their advantages are avoidance of SEC registration procedures, flexibility in renegotiation of terms, and the assurance of availability of financing provided by long-term arrangements as compared with short-term bank borrowing.

Ordinarily, direct loans are retired by systematic repayments (amortization payments) over the life of the loan. Security, generally in the form of a chattel mortgage on equipment, is often employed, although the larger, stronger companies are usually able to borrow on an unsecured basis. Commercial banks typically make smaller, shorter-term loans; life insurance companies and pension funds grant larger, longer-term loans.

Like rates on other credits, the cost of direct loans varies with general interest rate levels, the size of the loan, and the strength of the borrower. For small loans to small companies, rates may be as high as six to eight percentage points above the prime lending rate; for large loans to large, stable firms, they will probably be close to the prime rate. Since these loans run for long periods, during which interest rates can change radically, many of them have variable interest rates, with the rate set at a certain level in relation to the domestic prime rate or above the Federal Reserve rediscount rate or an international rate such as the LIBOR. Often, direct loans include a "kicker" in the form of warrants to purchase the borrower's equity securities near the price prevailing at the time of the loan transaction.

Another aspect of direct loans is the series of *protective covenants* contained in most loan agreements. The lender's funds are tied up for a long period, and during this time, the borrower's situation can change markedly. For self-protection, the lender includes in the loan agreement stipulations that the borrower will maintain the current ratio at a specified level, limit acquisitions of additional fixed assets, keep the debt ratio below a stated amount, and so on. These provisions are necessary from the lender's point of view, but they restrict the borrower's actions.

The investment banker provides middleman services to both the seller and the buyer of new securities, helping plan the issue, underwriting it, and handling the job of selling the issue to the ultimate investor. The cost of this service to the issuer is related to the magnitude of the total job that must be performed to place the issue. The investment banker must also look to the interests of the brokerage customers; if these investors are not satisfied with the banker's products, they will deal elsewhere.

Flotation costs are lowest for bonds, higher for preferred stock, and highest for common stock. For each type of security, flotation costs are lower for larger companies than for smaller ones, and most companies can cut their stock flotation costs by issuing the new securities to stockholders through rights offerings. (These offerings are discussed in Chapter 25.)

The financial manager should be familiar with the federal laws regulating the issuance and trading of securities, because they influence liabilities and affect financing methods and costs. Regulation of securities trading seeks (1) to provide information that investors can utilize as a basis for judging the merits of securities, (2) to control the volume of credit used in securities trading, and (3) to provide orderly securities markets. The laws do not, however, prevent either purchase of unsound issues or wide price fluctuations. They raise the costs of flotation somewhat, but they also probably decrease the cost of capital by increasing public confidence in the securities markets. Recent SEC rule changes, such as the use of shelf registration, have sought to lower the time and costs of SEC regulation.

In the increasingly dynamic environment of the 1970s and 1980s, a number of innovations were developed to increase investor interest in new issues while attempting to control the costs of long-term financing for issuers. These include increased use of the external debt and equity markets, increased use of foreign financing markets, removal of debt from the balance sheet by "in-substance defeasance," increased use of interest rate swaps, currency swaps, and the hedging of interest rate risks.

Questions

24.1 Define these terms: *brokerage firm, underwriting group, selling group,* and *investment banker.*

24.2 Before entering a formal agreement, investment bankers carefully investigate the companies whose securities they underwrite; this is especially true of the issues of firms going public for the first time.

    a) Since the bankers do not themselves plan to hold the securities but intend to sell them to others as soon as possible, why are they so concerned about making careful investigations?

    b) Does your answer to the question have any bearing on the fact that investment banking is a very difficult field to break into? Explain.

24.3 Since investment bankers price new issues in relation to outstanding issues, should a spread exist between the yields on the new and the outstanding issues? Discuss this matter separately for stocks and bonds.

24.4 **a)** If competitive bidding were required on all security offerings, would flotation costs be higher or lower?

b)   Would the size of the issuing firm be material in determining the effects of required competitive bidding?

24.5   Each month, the Securities and Exchange Commission publishes a report of the transactions made by the officers and directors of listed firms in their own companies' equity securities. Why do you suppose the SEC makes this report?

24.6   Prior to 1933, investment banking and commercial banking were both carried on by the same firm. In that year, however, the Banking Act required that these functions be separated. Discuss the pros and cons of this forced separation.

24.7   Suppose two similar firms are each selling $10 million of common stock. The firms are of the same size, are in the same industry, have the same leverage, and so on — except that one is publicly owned and the other is closely held.

   a)   Will their costs of flotation be the same?

   b)   If the issue were $10 million of bonds, would your answer be the same?

24.8   Evaluate the following statement: The fundamental purpose of the federal security laws dealing with new issues is to prevent investors, principally small ones, from sustaining losses on the purchase of stocks.

24.9   What issues are raised by the increasing purchase of equities by institutional investors?

Problems

24.1   As the chief financial officer of XTZ Corporation, you are planning to sell $100 million of ten-year bonds to finance the construction of a hot-tub factory. The market rate of interest on debt of this quality and maturity is 12 percent. However, the total costs of the underwriting have been estimated to be 10.5 percent of the gross proceeds.

   a)   Calculate the effective cost of debt of this debt to your firm, before taxes. (Hint: Let the coupon rate be 12 percent, so that the bonds will sell at face value; then solve for the IRR, which will make the future payments on the bond equal to the face value less 10.5 percent — that is, to $895 per bond.)

   b)   Your investment banker advises you that a 10 percent interest rate may be obtained by establishing a sinking fund provision whereby one-tenth of the debt principal will be retired at the end of each year. What is the effective cost of debt for this issue? (Underwriting costs remain at 10.5 percent.)

   c)   Why would an investment banker prefer you to finance by (b) rather than (a)?

24.2   If your firm sells preferred stock in the amount of $100 million, the total flotation expense will be about 11.5 percent of gross proceeds. If the going rate on preferred stock of the same quality as your firm's is 12 percent, what is the effective cost of the preferred stock issue? (Assume the stock will remain outstanding in perpetuity.)

24.3   The Fairmont Drilling Company was planning to issue $5 million of new common stock. In reaching the decision as to the form of offering, two alternatives were considered:

   1.   A rights offering, with out-of-pocket cost as a percentage of new capital at 1.4 percent.

   2.   An underwriting, with out-of-pocket cost as a percentage of new capital at 7.0 percent.

Fairmont chose the second alternative. Given the difference in cost, this choice seems paradoxical.

   a)   From Table 24.3, what proportion of issues this size are made by rights offerings instead of by underwriters?

b) Discuss the influence of other factors (in addition to direct costs cited) that must be taken into account in choosing between the two alternative methods of offering. In your answer, consider the following as well as other factors that may occur to you:
1. Timing of receipt of flows
2. Risk
3. Other internal benefits and costs
4. Distribution
5. Effect on stock price.

24.4 Alfred Cognac is a senior partner of a prominent investment banking firm. He has the opportunity to invest in a potential acquisition candidate, which will provide him with a $1 million profit if successful. He anticipates that there is a .90 probability of the acquisition occurring and that he will suffer no trading loss if it does not.

  Mr. Cognac would be considered an insider by the SEC. If he profits from the transaction *and* the SEC finds out about it, he will be forced to resign his position and return all of his profits to the acquired company. He estimates that there is a .25 probability that he will be discovered. The loss of his job would cost him $400,000 per year for the next ten years. His discount rate is 10 percent.

a) If Mr. Cognac's only concern is the maximization of his wealth, should he make the investment?
b) At what discount rate would Mr. Cognac be indifferent to his two alternatives?
c) What probability of SEC discovery would make him indifferent?

24.5 Three executives of the Hughes Aircraft Company, one of the largest privately owned corporations in the world, have decided to break away from Hughes and to set up a company of their own. The principal reason for this decision was capital gains; Hughes Aircraft stock is all privately owned, and the corporate structure makes it impossible for executives to be granted stock purchase options. Hughes's executives receive substantial salaries and bonuses, but this income is all taxable at normal tax rates, and no capital gains opportunities are available.

  The three men, Jim Adcock, Robert Goddard, and Rick Aiken, have located a medium-size electronics manufacturing company available for purchase. All the stock of this firm, Baynard Industries, is owned by the founder, Joseph Baynard. Although the company is in excellent shape, Baynard wants to sell it because of his failing health. A price of $5.7 million has been established, based on a price/earnings ratio of 12 and annual earnings of $475,000. Baynard has given the three prospective purchasers an option to purchase the company for the agreed price; the option is to run for six months, during which time the three men are to arrange financing with which to buy the firm.

  Adcock has consulted with Jules Scott, a partner in the New York investment banking firm of Williams Brothers and an acquaintance of some years' standing, to seek his assistance in obtaining the funds necessary to complete the purchase. Adcock, Goddard, and Aiken each have some money available to put into the new enterprise, but they need a substantial amount of outside capital. There is some possibility of borrowing part of the money, but Scott has discouraged this idea. His reasoning is, first, that Baynard Industries is already highly leveraged, and if the purchasers were to borrow additional funds, there would be a very severe risk that they would be unable to service this debt in the event of a recession in the electronics industry. Although the firm is currently earning $475,000 a year, this figure could quickly turn into a loss in the event of a few cancelled defense contracts or cost miscalculations.

Scott's second reason for discouraging a loan is that Adcock, Goddard, and Aiken plan not only to operate Baynard Industries and seek internal growth but also to use the corporation as a vehicle for making further acquisitions of electronics companies. This being the case, Scott believes that it would be wise for the company to keep any borrowing potential in reserve for use in later acquisitions. Scott proposes that the three partners obtain funds to purchase Baynard Industries in accordance with the figures shown in Table P24.5.

Table P24.5

Baynard Industries			
Price paid to Joseph Baynard			$5,700,000
(12 × $475,000 earnings)			
Authorized shares		5,000,000	
Initially issued shares		1,125,000	
Initial distribution of shares:			
Adcock	100,000 shares at $1		$ 100,000
Goddard	100,000 shares at $1		100,000
Aiken	100,000 shares at $1		100,000
Williams Brothers	125,000 shares at $7		875,000
Public stockholders	700,000 shares at $7		4,900,000
	1,125,000		$6,075,000
Underwriting costs: 5% of $4,900,000		$ 245,000	
Legal fees, and so on, associated with issue		45,000	290,000
			$5,785,000
Payment to Joseph Baynard			5,700,000
Net funds to Baynard Industries			$ 85,000

Baynard Industries would be reorganized with an authorized 5,000,000 shares, with 1,125,000 to be issued at the time the transfer takes place and the other 3,875,000 to be held in reserve for possible issuance in connection with acquisitions. Adcock, Goddard, and Aiken would each purchase 100,000 shares at a price of $1 a share, the par value. Williams Brothers would purchase 125,000 shares at a price of $7. The remaining 700,000 shares would be sold to the public at a price of $7 a share.

Williams Brothers' underwriting fee would be 5 percent of the shares sold to the public, or $245,000. Legal fees, accounting fees, and other charges associated with the issue would amount to $45,000, for a total flotation cost of $290,000. After deducting the underwriting charges and the payment to Baynard from the gross proceeds of the stock sale, the reorganized Baynard Industries would receive funds in the amount of $85,000, which would be used for internal expansion purposes.

As a part of the initial agreement, Adcock, Goddard, and Aiken each would be given options to purchase an additional 80,000 shares at a price of $7 a share for one year. Williams Brothers would be given an option to purchase an additional 100,000 shares at $7 a share in one year.

a)   What is the total flotation cost, expressed as a percentage of the funds raised by the underwriter? Does this charge seem reasonable in the light of published statistics on the cost of floating new issues of common stock?

b)   Suppose that the three men estimate the following probabilities for the firm's stock price one year from now:

Price	Probability
$ 1	0.05
5	0.10
9	0.35
13	0.35
17	0.10
21	0.05

Assuming Williams Brothers exercises its options, calculate the following ratio based on the expected stock price (ignore time-discount effects):

$$\frac{\text{Financial benefits to Williams Brothers}}{\text{Funds raised by underwriter}}.$$

Disregard Williams Brothers's profit on the 125,000 shares it bought outright at the initial offering. Comment on the ratio.

c) Are Adcock, Goddard, and Aiken purchasing their stock at a "fair" price? Should the prospectus disclose the fact that they would buy their stock at $1 a share whereas public stockholders would buy their stock at $7 a share?

d) Would it be reasonable for Williams Brothers to purchase its initial 125,000 shares at a price of $1?

e) Do you foresee any problems of control for Adcock, Goddard, and Aiken?

f) Would the expectation of an exceptionally large need for investment funds next year be a relevant consideration in deciding on the amount of funds to be raised now?

Selected References

Baron, David P., "A Model of the Demand for Investment Banking and Advising and Distribution Services for New Issues," *Journal of Finance*, 37 (September 1982), pp. 955-976.

Baron, David P., and Holmstrom, Bengt, "The Investment Banking Contract for New Issues Under Asymmetric Information: Delegation and the Incentive Problem," *Journal of Finance*, 35 (December 1980), pp. 1115-1138.

Brown, J. Michael, "Post-Offering Experience of Companies Going Public," *Journal of Business*, (January 1970), pp. 10-18.

Cohen, Kalman J.; Maier, Steven F.; Schwartz, Robert A.; and Whitcomb, David K., "Limit Orders, Market Structure, and the Returns Generation Process," *Journal of Finance*, 33 (June 1978), pp. 723-736.

Dyl, Edward, and Joehnk, Michael, "Competitive versus Negotiated Underwriting of Public Utility Debt," *Bell Journal of Economics*, 7 (Autumn 1976), pp. 680-689.

Ederington, Louis, "Negotiated versus Competitive Underwritings of Corporate Bonds," *Journal of Finance*, 31 (March 1976), pp. 17-28.

Fabozzi, Frank J., and West, Richard R., "Negotiated versus Competitive Underwritings of Public Utility

Bonds: Just One More Time," *Journal of Financial and Quantitative Analysis*, 16 (September 1981), pp. 323-339.

Findlay, M. Chapman, III; Johnson, Keith B.; and Morton, T. Gregory, "An Analysis of the Flotation Cost of Utility Bonds, 1971-76," *Journal of Financial Research*, 2 (Fall 1979), pp. 133-142.

Furst, Richard W., "Does Listing Increase the Market Price of Common Stock," *Journal of Business*, 43 (April 1970), pp. 174-180.

Goulet, Waldemar M., "Price Changes, Managerial Actions and Insider Trading at the Time of Listing," *Financial Management*, 3 (Spring 1974), pp. 30-36.

Hays, Patrick A.; Joehnk, Michael D.; and Melicher, Ronald W., "Differential Determinants of Risk Premiums in the Public and Private Corporate Bond Markets," *Journal of Financial Research*, 2 (Fall 1979), pp. 143-152.

Ibbotson, Roger G., and Jaffe, Jeffrey F., "'Hot Issue' Markets," *Journal of Finance*, 30 (June 1975), pp. 1027-1042.

Joehnk, Michael, and Kidwell, David S., "Comparative Costs of Competitive and Negotiated Underwritings in the State and Local Bond Market," *Journal of Finance*, 34 (June 1979), pp. 725-731.

Johnson, Keith; Morton, T. Gregory; and Findlay, M. Chapman, III, "An Analysis of the Flotation Cost of Utility Bonds," *Journal of Financial Research*, 2 (Fall 1979), pp. 133-142.

———, "An Empirical Analysis of the Flotation Cost of Corporate Securities, 1971-1972," *Journal of Finance*, 30 (June 1975), pp. 1129-1133.

Logue, Dennis E., and Jarrow, Robert A., "Negotiation vs. Competitive Bidding in the Sale of Securities by Public Utilities," *Financial Management*, 31 (Autumn 1978), pp. 31-39.

Logue, Dennis E., and Lindvall, John R., "The Behavior of Investment Bankers: An Econometric Investigation," *Journal of Finance*, 29 (March 1974), pp. 203-215.

Malkiel, Burton G., "The Capital Formation Problem in the United States," *Journal of Finance*, 34 (May 1979), pp. 291-306.

Moor, Roy E., "The Timing of Financial Policy," in *The Treasurer's Handbook*, edited by J. Fred Weston and Maurice B. Goudzwaard, Homewood, Ill.: Dow Jones-Irwin, 1976, pp. 43-67.

Moran, Michael J., "Recent Financing Activity of Nonfinancial Corporations," *Federal Reserve Bulletin*, 70 (May 1984), pp. 401-410.

Parker, George G. C., and Cooperman, Daniel, "Competitive Bidding in the Underwriting of Public

Utilities Securities," *Journal of Financial and Quantitative Analysis*, 13 (December 1978), pp. 885-902.

Smith, Clifford W., Jr., "Substitute Methods for Raising Additional Capital: Rights Offerings versus Underwritten Issues," *Journal of Financial Economics*, 5 (December 1977).

Sorensen, Eric H., "The Impact of Underwriting Method and Bidder Competition upon Corporate Bond Interest Cost," *Journal of Finance*, 34 (September 1979), pp. 863-870.

Stapleton, R. C., and Subrahmanyam, M. G., "Marketability of Assets and the Price of Risk," *Journal of Financial and Quantitative Analysis*, 14 (March 1979), pp. 1-10.

Stoll, Hans R., "The Supply of Dealer Services in Securities Markets," *Journal of Finance*, 33 (September 1978), pp. 1133-1151.

Stover, Roger D., "The Interaction between Pricing and Underwriting Spread in the New Issue Convertible Debt Market," *Journal of Financial Research*, 6 (Winter 1983), pp. 323-332.

Tallman, Gary; Rush, David; and Melicher, Ronald, "Competitive versus Negotiated Underwriting Costs for Regulated Industries," *Financial Management*, 3 (Summer 1974), pp. 49-55.

Van Horne, James C., "New Listings and Their Price Behavior," *Journal of Finance*, 25 (September 1970), pp. 783-794.

Chapter 25   Common Stock Financing

Common equity, or, if unincorporated firms are being considered, partnership or proprietorship interests, constitute the first source of funds to a new business and the base of support for borrowing by existing firms. Accordingly, our discussion of specific forms of long-term financing will begin with an analysis of common stock.

Apportionment of Income, Control, and Risk

The nature of equity ownership depends on the form of the business or organization. The central problem of such ownership revolves around an apportionment of certain rights and responsibilities among those who have provided the funds necessary for the operation of the business. The rights and responsibilities attaching to equity consist of positive considerations (income potential and control of the firm) and negative considerations (loss potential, legal responsibility, and personal liability).

General Rights of Holders of Common Stock

The rights of holders of common stock in a business corporation are established by the laws of the state in which the corporation is chartered and by the terms of the charter granted by the state. Charters are relatively uniform on many matters, including collective and specific rights.

Collective Rights.   Certain collective rights are usually given to the holders of common stock. Some of the more important rights allow stockholders to (1) amend the charter with the approval of the appropriate officials in the state of incorporation, (2) adopt and amend bylaws, (3) elect the directors of the corporation, (4) authorize the sale of fixed assets, (5) enter into mergers, (6) change the amount of authorized common stock, and (7) issue preferred stock, debentures, bonds, and other securities.

Specific Rights.   Holders of common stock also have specific rights as individual owners: (1) the right to vote in the manner prescribed by the corporate charter, (2) the right to sell their stock certificates (their evidence of ownership) and, in this way, to transfer their ownership interest to other persons, (3) the right to inspect the corporate books,[1] and (4) the right to share residual assets of the corporation on dissolution. (However, the holders of common stock are last among the claimants to the assets of the corporation.)

---

[1]Obviously, a corporation cannot have its business affairs disturbed by allowing every stockholder to go through any records the stockholder wants to inspect. Furthermore, a corporation cannot wisely permit a competitor who buys shares of its common stock to look at all the corporation records. There must be, and there are, practical limitations to this right.

Apportionment of Income

Two important positive considerations are involved in equity ownership: income and control. The right to income carries the risk of loss. Control also involves responsibility and liability. In an individual proprietorship that uses funds supplied only by the owner, the owner has a 100 percent right to income and control and to loss and responsibility. As soon as the proprietor incurs debt, however, he or she has entered into contracts that limit the freedom to control the firm and to apportion the firm's income. In a partnership, these rights are apportioned among the partners in an agreed-upon manner. In the absence of a formal agreement, a division is made by state law. In a corporation, more significant issues arise concerning the rights of the owners.

Apportionment of Control

Through the right to vote, holders of common stock have legal control of the corporation. As a practical matter, however, in many corporations, the principal officers constitute all, or a majority, of the members of the board of directors. In this circumstance, the board may be controlled by the management rather than by the owners. However, numerous examples demonstrate that stockholders can reassert their control if they are dissatisfied with the corporation's policies. In recent years, proxy battles with the aim of altering corporate policies have occurred fairly often, and firms whose managers are unresponsive to stockholders' desires are subject to takeover bids by other firms.

Apportionment of Risk

Another consideration involved in equity ownership is risk: On liquidation, holders of common stock are last in the priority of claims. Therefore, the portion of capital they contribute provides a cushion for creditors, if losses occur on dissolution. The equity-to-total-assets ratio indicates the percentage by which assets may shrink in value on liquidation before creditors will incur losses.

For example, compare two corporations, A and B, whose balance sheets are shown in Table 25.1. The ratio of equity to total assets in Corporation A is 80 percent. Total assets, therefore, will have to shrink by 80 percent before creditors will lose money. By contrast, in Corporation B, the extent to which assets will have to shrink in value on liquidation before creditors lose money is only 40 percent.

Table 25.1   Balance Sheets for Corporations A and B

Corporation A				Corporation B			
		Debt	$ 20			Debt	$ 60
		Equity	80			Equity	40
Total assets	$100	Total claims	$100	Total assets	$100	Total claims	$100

Common Stock Financing

Before undertaking an evaluation of common stock financing, more of the important characteristics of such stock will be described: (1) the nature of voting rights, (2) the nature of the preemptive right, and (3) variations in the forms of common stock.

Nature of Voting Rights

For each share of common stock owned, the holder has the right to cast one vote at the annual meeting of stockholders or at such special meetings as may be called.

Proxy. Provision is made for the temporary transfer of the right to vote by an instrument known as a *proxy*. The transfer is limited in its duration; typically, it applies only to a specific occasion, such as the annual meeting of stockholders.

The SEC supervises the use of the proxy machinery and frequently issues rules and regulations to improve its administration. SEC supervision is justified for at least two reasons:

1. If the proxy machinery is left wholly in the hands of management, there is a danger that the incumbent management will be self-perpetuated.
2. If it is made easy for minority groups of stockholders and opposition stockholders to oust management, there is a danger that they will gain control of the corporation for temporary advantages to place themselves or their friends in management positions.

Dodd and Warner [1983] find that proxy contests perform a useful economic function. In 96 proxy contests over a 16-year sample period beginning in 1962, they observed that the challenges were often lead by former company insiders, suggesting that proxy contests, to some degree, are an outgrowth of competition in the managerial labor market. They found that the challenges obtained a majority of seats on the board of directors in about one-fifth of the 96 contests. Dissidents gain some board representation in over half the sample contests. Our own experience is that dissidents feel that they have "won" if they obtain two seats on the board — one person to make motions and another to second them, so that the resulting discussion is included in the board minutes.

Dodd and Warner find that proxy contests stimulate expectations of improved corporate performance. During the 40-day period prior to the date of the initial public contest announcement, their estimate of the average positive abnormal performance is 10.5 percent. They find that a portion of the positive share price changes taking place in early stages of proxy contests is not permanent. Dodd and Warner found some price declines just after record date, which establishes who has the right to vote shares. Thus, negative excess returns found in the later stages of proxy contests are at least partially attributable to declines in the market value of the vote.

Cumulative Voting. A method of voting that has come into increased prominence is cumulative voting. Cumulative voting for directors is required in 22 states, including California, Illinois, Michigan, Ohio, and Pennsylvania. It is permissible in 18, including Delaware, New Jersey, and New York. Ten states make no provision for it.

Cumulative voting permits multiple votes for a single director. For example, suppose six directors are to be elected. The owner of 100 shares can cast 100 votes for each of the six openings. Cumulatively, then, the stockholder has 600 votes. When cumulative voting is permitted, the stockholder can accumulate the votes and cast all of them for one director, instead of 100 each for six directors. Cumulative voting is designed to enable a minority group of stockholders to obtain some voice in the control of the company by electing at least one director to the board.

The nature of cumulative voting is illustrated by use of the following formula:

$$\text{req.} = \frac{\text{des.}(N)}{\# + 1} + 1, \tag{25.1}$$

where

req. = number of shares required to elect a desired number of directors
des. = number of directors stockholder desires to elect
N = total number of shares of common stock outstanding and entitled to be voted[2]
\# = total number of directors to be elected.

The formula can be made more meaningful by an example. The ABC Company will elect six directors. There are 15 candidates and 100,000 shares entitled to be voted. If a group desires to elect two directors, how many shares must it have?

$$\text{req.} = \frac{2 \times 100,000}{6 + 1} + 1 = 28,572.$$

Observe the significance of the formula. Here, a minority group wishes to elect one-third of the board of directors. It can achieve its goal by owning less than one-third the number of shares of stock.[3]

Alternatively, assuming that a group holds 40,000 shares of stock in the company, how many directors can it elect following the rigid assumptions of the formula? The formula can be used in its present form or can be solved for des. and expressed as

$$\text{des.} = \frac{(\text{req.} - 1)(\# + 1)}{N}. \tag{25.2}$$

Inserting the figures, the calculation is

$$\text{des.} = \frac{39,999 \times 7}{100,000} = 2.8.$$

The 40,000 shares can thus elect 2.8 directors. Since directors cannot exist as fractions, the group can elect only two directors.

As a practical matter, suppose that, in the above situation, the total number of shares is 100,000; hence, 60,000 shares remain in other hands. The voting of all 60,000 shares may not be concentrated. Suppose the 60,000 shares (cumulatively 360,000 votes) not held by

---

[2]An alternative that may be agreed to by the contesting parties is to define N as the number of shares *voted*, not *authorized to be voted*. This procedure, which in effect gives each group seeking to elect directors the same percentage of directors as their percentage of the voted stock, is frequently followed. When it is used, a group that seeks to gain control with a minimum investment must estimate the percentage of shares that will be voted and then obtain control of more than 50 percent of that number.

[3]Note also that at least 14,286 shares must be controlled to elect one director.

the minority group are distributed equally among ten candidates, with 36,000 shares held by each candidate. If the minority group's 240,000 votes are distributed equally among each of six candidates, it can elect all six directors even though it does not have a majority of the stock.

Actually, it is difficult to make assumptions about how the opposition votes will be distributed. What is shown here is a good example of game theory. One rule in this theory is to assume that your opponents will do the worst they can do to you and to counter with actions to minimize the maximum loss. This is the kind of assumption followed in the formula. If the opposition concentrates its votes in the optimum manner, what is the best you can do to work in the direction of your goal? Other plausible assumptions can be substituted if there are sufficient facts to support alternative hypotheses about the opponents' behavior.

Preemptive Right

The preemptive right gives holders of common stock the first option to purchase additional issues of common stock. In some states, the right is made part of every corporate charter; in others, it is necessary to insert the right specifically in the charter.

The purpose of the preemptive right is twofold. First, it protects the power of control of present stockholders. If it were not for this safeguard, the management of a corporation under criticism from stockholders could prevent stockholders from removing it from office by issuing a large number of additional shares at a very low price and purchasing these shares itself. Management would thereby secure control of the corporation to frustrate the will of the current stockholders.

The second, and by far the more important, protection that the preemptive right affords stockholders concerns dilution of value. For example, assume that 1,000 shares of common stock, each with a price of $100, are outstanding, making the total market value of the firm $100,000.[4] An additional 1,000 shares are sold at $50 a share, a total of $50,000, thereby raising the market value of the firm to $150,000. When the total market value is divided by the new total shares outstanding, a value of $75 a share is obtained. Thus, selling common stock at below market value will enable new shareholders to buy stock on terms more favorable than those that had been extended to the old shareholders. The preemptive right prevents such occurrences. (This point is discussed at length later in the chapter.)

Forms of Common Stock

Classified. Classified common stock was used extensively in the late 1920s, sometimes in ways that misled investors. During that period, Class A common stock was usually nonvoting and Class B was usually voting. Thus, promoters could control companies by selling large amounts of Class A stock while retaining Class B stock.

In more recent years, there has been a revival of Class B common stock for sound purposes. It is used by small, new companies seeking to acquire funds from outside sources. Class A common stock is sold to the public and typically pays dividends; its holders have full voting rights. Class B common stock is retained by the organizers of the

---

[4]What is relevant is market value not par value, which is a purely arbitrary designation, nor book value, which reflects only historical accounting numbers.

company, but dividends are not paid on it until the company has established its earning power. By the use of this classified stock, the public can take a position in a conservatively financed growth company without sacrificing income. More recently, General Motors has been making very imaginative use of its Class E stock issued in acquiring EDS and Class H stock issued in buying Hughes Aircraft Co.

Founders' Shares.   Founders' shares are somewhat like Class B stock except that they carry *sole* voting rights and typically do not confer the right to dividends for a number of years. Thus, the organizers of the firm are able to maintain complete control of the operations in the firm's crucial initial development. At the same time, other investors are protected against excessive withdrawals of funds by owners.

Evaluation of Common Stock as a Source of Funds

We will now appraise common stock from the viewpoint of the issuer and from a social viewpoint.

From the Viewpoint of the Issuer

Advantages.   There are several advantages to the issuer of financing with common stock:

1. Common stock does not entail fixed charges. If the company generates the earnings, it can pay common stock dividends. In contrast to bond interest, however, there is no legal obligation to pay dividends.
2. Common stock carries no fixed maturity date.
3. Since common stock provides a cushion against losses of creditors, the sale of common stock increases the credit-worthiness of the firm.
4. Common stock can, at times, be sold more easily than debt. It appeals to certain investor groups because (a) it typically carries a higher expected return than does preferred stock or debt; and (b) since it represents the ownership of the firm, it provides the investor with a better hedge against inflation than does straight preferred stock or bonds. Ordinarily, common stock increases in value when the value of real assets rises during an inflationary period.[5]
5. Returns from common stock in the form of capital gains are subject to the lower personal income tax rates on capital gains. Hence, the effective personal income tax rates on returns from common stock may be lower than the effective tax rates on the interest on debt.

Disadvantages.   Disadvantages to the issuer of common stock include the following:

1. The sale of common stock may extend voting rights or control to the additional stock owners who are brought into the company. For this reason, among others, additional equity financing is often avoided by small and new firms, whose owner-managers may be unwilling to share control of their companies with outsiders.
2. Common stock gives more owners the right to share in income. The use of debt may enable the firm to utilize funds at a fixed low cost, whereas common stock gives equal rights to new stockholders to share in the net profits of the firm.

---

[5]During the inflation of the last decade, the lags of product price increases behind the rise of input costs have depressed corporate earnings and increased the uncertainty of earnings growth, causing price-earnings multiples to fall.

3.   As we saw in Chapter 24, the costs of underwriting and distributing common stock are usually higher than those for underwriting and distributing preferred stock or debt. Flotation costs for selling common stock are characteristically higher because (a) costs of investigating an equity security are higher than that of investigating the feasibility of a comparable debt security; and (b) stocks are more risky, which means equity holdings must be diversified, which, in turn, means that a given dollar amount of new stock must be sold to a greater number of purchasers than the same amount of debt.

4.   As we saw in Chapter 21, if the firm has more equity or less debt than is called for in the optimum capital structure, the average cost of capital will be higher than necessary.

5.   Common stock dividends are not deductible as an expense for calculating the corporation's income subject to the federal income tax, but bond interest is deductible. The impact of this factor is reflected in the relative cost of equity capital vis-à-vis debt capital.

The leading study of unseasoned new issues of common stock made by companies going public for the first time was made by Ibbotson [1975]. The estimated systematic risk (beta) in the month of the issue was 2.26. Since betas generally average about one, this indicates that stocks are regarded as highly risky when new issues are in the process of being brought to the market. The positive abnormal return on new issues was 11.4 percent. Even after transactions costs, this is a statistically significant positive abnormal return. Hence, either the offering price is set too low or investors systematically overvalue new issues at the end of the first month of seasoning. Other evidence demonstrates that the after-market is efficient, which suggests that investment bankers may systematically price the security below its fair market value. A related piece of evidence was developed by Korwar [1981]. He found that, on average, when seasoned firms announce a new stock issue which increases the number of shares outstanding, the stock price falls by a statistically significant −3.3 percent for industrial firms. Masulis [1983] found that when a stock repurchase is announced, stock prices rise on average. Some writers regard this evidence as suggesting that managers may have inside information, and when their company's common stock is overvalued, they sell more of it; when it is undervalued, they buy it back. The market believing this takes the announcement of a seasoned new issue as a signal that the stock is overvalued; the market takes the announcement of a share repurchase as evidence that the stock is undervalued.

From a Social Viewpoint

From a social viewpoint, common stock is a desirable form of financing because it renders business firms (a major segment of the economy) less vulnerable to the consequences of declines in sales and earnings. Common stock financing involves no fixed charges, the payment of which might force a faltering firm into reorganization or bankruptcy.

Use of Rights in Financing

If the preemptive right is contained in a firm's charter, then the firm must offer any new common stock to existing stockholders. If the charter does not prescribe a preemptive right, the firm has a choice of making the sale to its existing stockholders or to an entirely new set of investors. If it sells to the existing stockholders, the stock flotation is called a *rights offering.* Each stockholder is issued an option to buy a certain number of the new shares, and the terms of the option are contained on a piece of paper called a *right*. Each stockholder receives one right for each share of stock owned. The advantages and disadvantages of rights offerings are described in the following section.

The value of rights amendments *per se* was investigated by Bhagat [1983]. For a sample of 211 proposals to remove charter provisions which required rights offerings, he found that (1) in only four instances did shareholders turn down the proposal and that (2) stock prices declined by an average of $-.34$ percent when the proposal was announced (statistically significant at the 10 percent confidence level). The evidence indicates that removal of the rights provision from corporate charters has the effect of decreasing shareholders' wealth but leaves the puzzle of why shareholders would vote in favor of the removal in the first place.

Theoretical Relationships of Rights Offerings

Several issues confront the financial manager who is deciding on the details of a rights offering. The various considerations can be shown by the use of illustrative data on the Southeast Company, whose balance sheet and income statement are given in Table 25.2. Southeast earns $4 million after taxes and has 1 million shares outstanding, so earnings per share are $4. The stock sells at 25 times earnings, or for $100 a share. The company plans to raise $10 million of new equity funds through a rights offering and decides to sell the new stock to shareholders for $80 a share. This present analysis will not take into account the NPV from the new investment. A positive NPV would increase the value of the firm. We here consider only the pure "stock split" effects of the use of rights. Under these assumptions, the questions posed to the financial manager are

1. How many rights will be required to purchase a share of the newly issued stock?
2. What is the value of each right?
3. What effect will the rights offering have on the price of the existing stock?

Table 25.2   Southeast Company Financial Statements before Rights Offering

---

Partial Balance Sheet

		Total debt (at 5%)	$ 40,000,000
		Common stock	10,000,000
		Retained earnings	50,000,000
Total assets	$100,000,000	Total liabilities and capital	$100,000,000

Partial Income Statement

Total earnings	$10,000,000
Interest on debt	2,000,000
Income before taxes	$ 8,000,000
Taxes (50% assumed)	4,000,000
Earnings after taxes	$ 4,000,000
Earnings per share (1 million shares)	$4
Market price of stock (price-earnings ratio of 25 assumed)	$100

Number of Rights Needed to Purchase a New Share

As already mentioned, Southeast plans to raise $10 million in new equity funds and to sell the new stock at a price of $80 a share. Dividing the subscription price into the total funds to be raised gives the number of shares to be issued:

$$\text{Number of new shares} = \frac{\text{Funds to be raised}}{\text{Subscription price}} = \frac{\$10,000,000}{\$80}$$

$$= 125,000 \text{ shares.}$$

The next step is to divide the number of new shares into the number of previously outstanding shares to get the number of rights required to subscribe to one share of the new stock. Note that stockholders always receive one right for each share of stock they own:

$$\frac{\text{Number of rights needed to}}{\text{buy a share of the stock}} = \frac{\text{Old shares}}{\text{New shares}} = \frac{1,000,000}{125,000} = 8 \text{ rights.}$$

Therefore, a stockholder will have to surrender eight rights plus $80 to receive one of the newly issued shares. If the subscription price had been set at $95 a share, 9.5 rights would have been required to subscribe to each new share; if the price had been set at $10 a share, only one right would have been needed. If the number of new shares exceeds the number of old shares, the number of rights required to subscribe to each new share would be a fraction of one. For example, if the number of old shares is 1 million and 1.6 million new shares are to be issued, the number of rights required to subscribe to each new share would be five-eighths of one right. Trading in the rights would take place so that exact, not fractional, numbers of new shares could be purchased by the exercise of rights plus the required cash.

Value of a Right

It is clearly worth something to be able to pay less than $100 for a share of stock selling for $100. The right provides this privilege, so it must have a value. To see how the theoretical value of a right is established, we continue with the example of the Southeast Company, assuming that it will raise $10 million by selling 125,000 new shares at $80 a share.

Notice that the *market value* of the old stock was $100 million: $100 a share times 1 million shares. (The book value is irrelevant.) When the firm sells the new stock, it brings in an additional $10 million. As a first approximation, assume that the market value of the common stock increases by exactly this $10 million. Actually, the market value of all the common stock will go up by more than $10 million if investors think the company will be able to invest these funds at a yield substantially in excess of the cost of equity capital, but it will go up by less than $10 million if investors are doubtful of the company's ability to put the new funds to work profitably in the near future.

Under the assumption that market value exactly reflects the new funds brought in, the total market value of the common stock after the new issue will be $110 million. Dividing this new value by the new total number of shares outstanding, 1.125 million, gives a new market value of $97.78 a share. Therefore, after the financing has been completed, the price of the common stock will have fallen from $100 to $97.78.

Since the rights give the stockholders the privilege of paying only $80 for a share of stock that will end up being worth $97.78, thereby saving them $17.78, is $17.78 the value of each right? The answer is no, because eight rights are required to buy one new share. The $17.78 must be divided by 8 to get the value of each right. In the example, each one is worth $2.22.

Ex Rights

The Southeast Company's rights have a very definite value, and this value accrues to the holders of the common stock. But what happens if stock is traded during the offering period? Who will receive the rights — the old owners or the new? The standard procedure calls for the company to set a *holder of record date* and for the stock to go *ex rights* after that date. If the stock is sold prior to the ex rights date, the new owner receives the rights; if it is sold on or after the ex rights date, the old owner receives them. For example, on October 15, Southeast Company announces the terms of the new financing; the company states that rights will be mailed out on December 1 to stockholders of record as of the close of business on November 15. Anyone buying the old stock on or before November 15 will receive the rights; anyone buying the stock on or after November 16 will *not* receive them. Thus, November 16 is the *ex rights date*; before November 16, the stock sells *rights-on*. In the case of Southeast Company, the rights-on price is $100, and the ex rights price is expected to be $97.78.

Formula Value of a Right

Rights On. Equations have been developed for determining the value of rights without going through all the procedures described above. While the stock is still selling rights-on, the value at which the rights will sell when they are issued can be found by use of the following formula:

$$\text{Value of one right} = \frac{\text{Market value of stock, rights-on} - \text{Subscription price}}{\text{Number of rights required to purchase 1 share} + 1}$$

$$v_r = \frac{p_o - p^s}{\# + 1}, \tag{25.3}$$

where

p_o = rights-on price of the stock
p^s = subscription price
$\#$ = number of rights required to purchase a new share of stock
v_r = value of one right.

Substituting the appropriate values for the Southeast Company:

$$v_r = \frac{\$100 - \$80}{8 + 1} = \frac{\$20}{9} = \$2.22.$$

This agrees with the value of the rights found by the step-by-step analysis.

Ex Rights. Suppose you are a stockholder in the Southeast Company. When you return to the United States from a trip to Europe, you read about the rights offering in the newspaper. The stock is now selling ex rights for $97.78 a share. How can you calculate the theoretical value of a right? By using the following formula, which follows the logic described in preceding sections, you can determine the value of each right:

$$\text{Value of one right} = \frac{\text{Market value of stock, ex rights} - \text{Subscription price}}{\text{Number of rights required to purchase 1 share}}$$

$$v_r = \frac{p_e - p^s}{\#}$$

$$= \frac{\$97.78 - \$80}{8} = \frac{\$17.78}{8} = \$2.22. \tag{25.4}$$

Here, p_e is the ex rights price of the stock.[6]

To this point, we have developed the value of a right under some simplifying assumptions, which we shall now relax. First we took a static approach. We assumed that the total value of the equity was increased only by the amount of additional funds raised from the rights offering. If we take a longer-term view, and postulate that the additional funds will be used in positive net present value investments, then the value of equity would increase by more than the new funds raised. If so, the value of the rights would be above the level we had illustrated in the example of $2.22.

Another approach would be to treat each right as a call option. This is because a right is an option to buy the stock of the company at the subscription price (the exercise price) for a specified period of time. The main difference between a right and a warrant is that the maturity of a right is typically around 30 days while the maturity of a warrant is more

---

[6]We developed Equation 25.4 directly from the verbal explanation given in the immediately preceding section. Equation 25.3 can be derived from Equation 25.4 as follows:

$$p_e = p_o - v_r. \tag{25.5}$$

Substituting Equation 25.5 into Equation 25.4:

$$v_r = \frac{p_o - v_r - p^s}{\#}. \tag{25.6}$$

Simplifying Equation 25.6:

$$v_r = \frac{p_o - p^s}{\#} - \frac{v_r}{\#}$$

$$v_r + \frac{v_r}{\#} = \frac{p_o - p^s}{\#}$$

$$v_r\left(\frac{\# + 1}{\#}\right) = \frac{p_o - p^s}{\#}$$

$$v_r = \frac{p_o - p^s}{\#} \cdot \frac{\#}{\# + 1}$$

$$v_r = \frac{p_o - p^s}{\# + 1}.$$

The result is Equation 25.3.

likely to be two to ten years. But the valuation methodology would be the same for both. Galai and Schneller [1978] have shown that a right or a warrant is valued exactly as a call divided by $(1 + q)$, where q is the ratio of the additional rights or warrants issued to the number of shares previously outstanding. (See proof in Chapter 28.) In our symbols, q would be equal to $1/\#$. We can now illustrate this procedure. Recall that the relevant option pricing equations we will need to evaluate are the following:

$$C_o = S_o N(\text{dist. } 1) - X_o e^{-R_F T} N(\text{dist. } 2)$$

$$\text{dist. } 1 = \frac{\ln(S_o/X_o) + [R_F + (\sigma^2/2)]T}{\sigma\sqrt{T}}$$

$$\text{dist. } 2 = \text{dist. } 1 - \sigma\sqrt{T}.$$

To utilize the above expressions, we already were given that S, the stock price before the rights offering, was \$100 and that the subscription price (exercise price) is \$80. We will further assume that the risk-free rate is 10 percent, the variance of the returns on equity is 16 percent, and the time to maturity is 0.1 of a year. We can then make the calculations as follows:

$$d_1 = \frac{.223 + [.10 + .08].1}{.4(.316)} = \frac{.223 + .018}{.1264} = \frac{.241}{.1264} = 1.9066$$

$$N(d_1) = .9719$$

$$d_2 = 1.9066 - .1264 = 1.7802 = 1.78$$

$$N(d_2) = .9625$$

$$C = 100(.9719) - 80(.9625).99$$

$$= 97.19 - 76.23$$

$$= 20.96.$$

The value of the rights as a call is \$20.96. Since eight rights are required to purchase one share of stock, the value per right will be \$20.96 ÷ 8, which is \$2.62. We now apply the dilution factor effect on the value of the right, so we divide further by $(1 + q)$, which is 1.125 here. We obtain \$2.33 for the value of each right. This is somewhat above the \$2.22 obtained when the right is valued in the traditional way. Although these numbers are only illustrative, the order of the relationships is plausible. This is because we would expect that the value of a right, when its call value properties are taken into account, should be higher than when the call privilege has not been considered.

Effects on Position of Stockholders

Stockholders have the choice of exercising their rights or selling them. If they have sufficient funds and want to buy more shares of the company's stock, they will exercise the rights. If they do not have the money or do not want to buy more stock, they will sell the rights. In either case, provided the formula value of the rights holds true, stockholders will neither benefit nor lose by the rights offering. This statement can be made clear by considering the position of an individual stockholder in the Southeast Company.

The stockholder has eight shares of stock before the rights offering. Each share has a market value of $100, so the stockholder has a total market value of $800 in the company's stock. If, after the rights offering, a shareholder exercises the rights, this individual will be able to purchase one additional share at $80—a new investment of $80. With a total investment of $880, the stockholder will own nine shares of the company's stock, which now has a value of $97.78 a share. The value of this stock will be $880, exactly what was invested in it.

Alternatively, by selling the eight rights, which have a value of $2.22 each, the holder will receive $17.76 and will thus have the original eight shares of stock plus $17.76 in cash. But, the original eight shares of stock now have a market price of $97.78 a share. The $782.24 market value of this stock plus the $17.76 in cash is the same as the $800 market value of stock with which the investor began.

Oversubscription Privilege

Even though the rights are very valuable and should be exercised, some stockholders neglect to do so. Still, all the stock is sold because of the *oversubscription privilege* contained in most rights offerings. This privilege gives subscribing stockholders the right to buy, on a pro rata basis, all shares not taken in the initial offering. To illustrate: If Jane Doe owns 10 percent of the stock in Southeast Company, and if 20 percent of the rights offered by the company are not exercised (or sold) by the stockholders to whom they were originally given, then she can buy an additional 2.5 percent of the new stock.[7] Since this stock is a bargain—$80 for stock worth $97.78—Jane Doe and other stockholders will use the oversubscription privilege, thereby assuring the full sale of the new stock issue.

Relationship between Market Price and Subscription Price

We can now investigate the factors influencing the use of rights and, if they are used, the level at which the subscription price is set. The Southeast Company's articles of incorporation permit the firm to decide whether to use rights, depending on whether their use is advantageous to the firm and its stockholders. The financial vice president of the company is considering three methods of raising the sum of $10 million:

1. The company could sell to the public, through investment bankers, additional shares at approximately $100 a share. The company would net approximately $96 a share; thus, it would need to sell approximately 105,000 shares in order to cover the underwriting commission.
2. The company could sell additional shares through rights, using investment bankers and paying a commission of 1 percent on the total dollar amount of the stock sold plus an additional 3/4 percent on all shares unsubscribed and taken over by the investment bankers. Also with the usual market pressure when common stock is sold, the new shares would be sold at a 20 percent discount, or at $80. Thus, 125,000 additional shares would be offered through rights. With eight rights, an additional

[7]Eighty percent of the stock was subscribed. Since Jane Doe subscribed to 10/80, or 12.5 percent, of the stock that was taken, she can obtain 12.5 percent of the unsubscribed stock. Therefore, her oversubscription allocation is 12.5 percent × 20 = 2.5 percent of the new stock.

share could be purchased at $80. Since stockholders are given the right to subscribe to any unexercised rights on a pro rata basis, only those shares not subscribed to on the original or secondary level are sold to the underwriters and subjected to the 3/4 percent additional commission.

3. The company could sell additional shares through rights, at $10 a share, and not use investment bankers. The number of additional shares of common stock to be sold would be 1 million. For each right held, existing stockholders would be permitted to buy one share of the new common stock.

Method 1 uses investment bankers and no rights at all. In this circumstance, the underwriting commission, or flotation cost, is approximately 4 percent. In Method 2, where rights are used with a small discount, the underwriting commission is reduced, because the discount removes much of the risk of not being able to sell the issue. The underwriting commission consists of two parts—1 percent on the original issue and an additional 3/4 percent commission on all unsubscribed shares the investment bankers are required to take over and sell. Thus, the actual commission ranges somewhere between 1 percent and $1\frac{3}{4}$ percent. Under Method 3, the subscription price is $10 a share. With such a large concession, the company does not need to use investment bankers at all, because the rights are certain to have value and to be either exercised or sold. Which of the three methods is superior?

Method 1 can provide a wider distribution of the securities sold, particularly if the underwriting agreement specifies that efforts will be made to sell to new shareholders. The use of investment bankers assure that the company will receive the $10 million involved in the new issue, and they give the firm on-going financial counsel. The company pays for these services in the form of underwriting charges. After the issue, the stock price should be approximately $100.

Under Method 2, by utilizing rights, the company reduces its underwriting expenses and the unit price per share (from $100 to $97.78). Some stockholders may suffer a loss because they neither exercise nor sell their rights. Existing stockholders will buy some of the new shares, so the distribution is likely to be narrower than under Method 1. Because of the underwriting contract, the firm is assured of receiving the funds sought. Finally, investors often like the opportunity to purchase additional shares through rights offerings; thus, their use may increase stockholder loyalty.

Method 3 involves no underwriting expense and results in a substantial decrease in the unit price of shares. Initially, however, the shares are less widely distributed than under either of the other two methods. Method 3 also has a large stock-split effect, which results in a much lower final stock price per share than under either of the other two methods.[8] Many people feel that there is an optimal stock price—one that will produce a maximum total market value of the shares—and that this price is generally in the range of $30 to $60 a share. If this is the feeling of Southeast's directors, they may believe that Method 3 will permit them to reach the more desirable price range while at the same time reducing flotation costs on the new issue. However, since the rights have a substantial value, any stockholder who fails either to exercise or to sell them will suffer a serious loss. The three methods are summarized in Table 25.3.

The most advantageous method depends on the company's needs. For a company strongly interested in wide distribution of its securities, Method 1 is preferable. For a firm most interested in reducing the unit price of its shares and confident that the lower unit

---

[8] Stock splits were discussed in Chapter 22. Basically, a *stock split* is simply the issuance of additional shares to existing stockholders for *no* additional funds. Stock splits divide the "pie" into more pieces.

Table 25.3 Summary of Three Methods of Raising Additional Money

	Advantages	Disadvantages
Method 1 Underwritten offering	1. Wide distribution 2. Certainty of receiving funds	1. High underwriting costs
Method 2 Rights with a standby agreement	1. Small underwriting costs 2. Lower unit price of shares 3. Certainty of receiving funds 4. Increased stockholder loyalty	1. Narrow distribution 2. Losses to forgetful stockholders
Method 3 Pure rights offering	1. No underwriting costs 2. Substantial decrease in unit price of shares 3. Increased stockholder loyalty	1. Narrow distribution 2. Severe losses to forgetful stockholders

price will induce wide distribution, Method 3 is preferable. For a company whose needs are moderate in both directions, Method 2 may offer a satisfactory compromise. Whether rights will be used and the level of the subscription price both depend on the company's needs at a particular time.

Exercise of Rights

Interestingly enough, it is expected that a small percentage of stockholders will neglect to exercise or to sell their rights. In a recent offering, the holders of $1\frac{1}{2}$ percent of General Motors common stock did not exercise their rights. The loss experienced by these stockholders was $1.5 million. In a recent AT&T issue, the loss to shareholders who neglected to exercise their rights was $960,000.

Market Price and Subscription Price

Measured from the registration date for the new issue of the security, the average percentage by which the subscription prices of new issues were below their market prices has been about 15 percent in recent years. Examples of price concessions of 40 percent or more can be observed in a small percentage of issues, but the most frequently encountered discounts are from 10 to 20 percent.

Effect on Subsequent Behavior of Market Price

It is often said that issuing new stock through rights will depress the price of the company's existing common stock. To the extent that a subscription price, in connection with the rights offering, is lower than the market price, there will be a "stock-split effect" on the market price of the common stock. With the prevailing market price of Southeast Company's stock at $100 and a $10 subscription price, the new market price will probably drop to about $55.

But whether, because of the rights offering, the actual new market price will be $55 or lower or higher is unknown. Again, empirical analysis of the movement in stock prices during rights offerings indicates that generalization is not practical. What happens to the market prices of the stock ex rights and after the rights trading period depends on the future earnings prospects of the issuing company.

Advantages of Use of Rights in New Financing

The preemptive right gives shareholders the protection of preserving their pro rata share in the earnings and control of the company. It also benefits the firm. By offering new issues of securities to existing stockholders, the firm increases the likelihood of a favorable reception for the stock. By their ownership of common stock in the company, investors have already evaluated the company favorably. They, therefore, may be receptive to the purchase of additional shares.

Other factors can offset the tendency towards a downward pressure on the price of the common stock occurring at the time of a new issue.[9] With the increased interest in (and advantages afforded by) the rights offering, the "true" or "adjusted" downward price pressure may actually be avoided.

A related advantage is that the issuer's flotation costs associated with a rights offering are lower than the cost of a public flotation. The costs referred to here are cash costs. For example, Smith [1977] found that the flotation costs of common stock issues during the period 1971 to 1975 were 6.17 percent on public issues compared with 2.45 percent on the rights offerings.

The financial manager can obtain positive benefits from underpricing. Since a rights offering is a stock split to a certain degree, it causes the market price of the stock to fall to a level lower than it otherwise would be. But stock splits can increase the number of shareholders in a company by bringing the price of a stock down to a more attractive trading level. Furthermore, a rights offering may be associated with increased dividends for the stock owners.[10]

In general, a rights offering can stimulate an enthusiastic response from stockholders and from the investment market as a whole, with the result that opportunities for financing become more attractive to the firm. Thus, the financial manager may be able to engage in common stock financing at lower costs and under more favorable terms.

Choosing among Alternative Forms of Financing

A pattern of analysis can be formulated for choosing among alternative forms of financing. This framework applies to the decision choices involved in evaluating the other major forms of financing covered: various forms of debt, preferred stock, lease financing, and

---

[9]The downward pressure develops because of an increase in the supply of securities without a necessarily equivalent increase in the demand. Generally, it is a temporary phenomenon, and the stock tends to return to the theoretical price after a few months. Obviously, if the acquired funds are invested at a very high rate of return, the stock price benefits; if the investment does not turn out well, the stock price suffers.

[10]The increased dividends may convey information that the prospective earnings of the firm have improved and may result in a higher market price for the firm's stock.

Table 25.4   Chemical Industry Financial Ratios

Current ratio: 2.0 times
Sales to total assets: 1.6 times
Current debt to total assets: 30%
Long-term debt to net worth: 40%
Total debt to total assets: 50%
Coverage of fixed charges: 7 times
Cash flow coverage: 3 times
Net income to sales: 5%
Return on total assets: 9%
Net income to net worth: 13%

financing in international markets, among others. Thus, the pattern of analysis has broad applications.

To make the application of the concepts more concrete, a case will be used to illustrate and exemplify the procedures involved. Stanton Chemicals, having estimated that it will need to raise $200 million for an expansion program, discusses with its investment bankers whether it should raise the $200 million through debt financing or through selling additional shares of common stock. The bankers are asked to make their recommendation to Stanton's board of directors using the information on industry financial ratios and the company's 1984 balance sheet and income statement found in Tables 25.4, 25.5, and 25.6, respectively.

Stanton's dividend payout has averaged about 30 percent of net income. At present, its cost of debt is 10 percent (with an average maturity remaining of ten years), and its cost of equity is 14 percent. If the additional funds are raised by debt, the cost of debt will rise to 12 percent, and the cost of equity will rise to 16 percent. If the funds are raised by equity, the cost of debt will remain at 10 percent, and the cost of equity will fall to 12 percent; new equity will initially be sold at $9 per share.

Stanton's common stock is widely held; there is no strong control group. The market parameters are a risk-free rate of 6 percent and an expected return on the market of 11

Table 25.5   Stanton Chemicals Company Balance Sheet as of December 31, 1984 (Millions of Dollars)

Assets		Liabilities		
Total current assets	$1,000	Notes payable (at 10%)	$300	
Net fixed assets	800	Other current liabilities	400	
		Total current liabilities		$ 700
		Long-term debt (at 10%)		300
		Total debt		$1,000
		Common stock, par value $1		100
		Paid-in capital		300
		Retained earnings		400
Total assets	$1,800	Total claims on assets		$1,800

Table 25.6   Stanton Chemicals Company Income Statement for Year Ended December 31, 1984 (Millions of Dollars)

	1984	Pro Forma after Financing
Total revenues	$3,000	$3,400
Depreciation expense	200	220
Other costs	2,484	2,820
Net operating income	$ 316	$ 360
Interest expense	60	
Net income before taxes	$ 256	
Income taxes (at 50%)	128	
Net income	$ 128	

percent. The debt will carry a maturity of ten years and will require a sinking fund of $20 million per year in addition to the present $20 million annual sinking fund requirement.

In their analysis of which form of financing should be chosen, the investment bankers consider the following factors:

A. Risk
  1. Financial structure
  2. Fixed charge coverage
  3. Coverage of cash flow requirements
  4. Level of systematic risk (beta)
B. Relative costs
  1. Effects on market value per share of common stock
  2. Effects on cost of capital
C. Effects on control

The solution proceeds as follows. First, the two forms of financing are examined with reference to the firm's risk as measured by its financial structure (see Table 25.7). Stanton

Table 25.7   Stanton Financial Structure (Millions of Dollars)

	Present		Pro Forma				Industry Standard
			Debt		Equity		
	Amount	Percent	Amount	Percent	Amount	Percent	Percent
Current debt	$ 700	39	$ 700	35	$ 700	35	30
Long-term debt	300	17	500	25	300	15	20
Total debt	$1,000	56	$1,200	60	$1,000	50	50
Equity	800	44	800	40	1,000	50	
Total assets	$1,800	100	$2,000	100	$2,000	100	
Long-term debt to net worth		38		63		30	40

Table 25.8   Stanton's Fixed Charge Coverage (Millions of Dollars)

| | Present | Pro Forma | | Industry Standard |
		Debt	Equity	
Net operating income	$316	$360	$360	
Interest expenses	60	90[a]	60	
Coverage ratio	5.27	4.00	6.00	7.00

[a]See Table 25.10 and related discussion.

fails to meet the industry standards on both the short-term and total debt ratios. If it finances with debt, its financial structure ratios will be further deficient. If it finances with equity, its long-term debt to net worth ratio will be strengthened, and it will meet the industry standard for the total debt to total assets ratio. Stanton, therefore, should seek to fund some short-term debt into longer-term debt in the future, and it should try to build up its equity base further from retained earnings.

Stanton's fixed charge coverage is analyzed next, in Table 25.8. The table shows that the company's fixed charge coverage is below the industry standard. The use of debt financing will further aggravate the weakness in this area. The use of equity financing will move the company towards the industry standard.

Stanton's cash flow coverage is analyzed in Table 25.9. To obtain the cash inflow, depreciation expense is added to net operating income. To obtain the cash outflow requirements, the before-tax sinking fund payment is added to the interest expenses. The sinking fund payments must be placed on a before-tax basis because they are not a tax-deductible expense.

The resulting cash flow coverage ratios appear satisfactory when measured against the industry standard of 3.00. However, this result has to be qualified by the recognition that a full analysis of cash flow coverage must consider other cash outflow requirements. These will include scheduled principal repayments on debt obligations, preferred stock dividends, payments under lease obligations, and probably some capital expenditures that are

Table 25.9   Stanton's Cash Flow Coverage (Millions of Dollars)

| | Present | Pro Forma | | Industry Standard |
		Debt	Equity	
Net operating income	$316	$360	$360	
Depreciation expense	200	220	220	
Cash inflow	$516	$580	$580	
Interest expense	60	90	60	
Sinking fund payments	20	40	20	
Before-tax sinking fund payments	40	80	40	
Cash outflow requirements	$100	$170	$100	
Cash flow coverage ratio	5.16	3.41	5.80	3.00

regarded as essential for the continuity of the firm. Within the broader definition of cash outflow requirements, Stanton's cash flow coverage would undoubtedly be lowered.

The next consideration is the effect of the various forms of financing on the level of the firm's systematic risk, that is, its beta. As indicated earlier, Stanton's cost of equity is 14 percent at present. Using the Security Market Line and additional data on the market parameters already provided, Stanton's present level of beta can be determined as follows:

$$k_s = R_F + [E(R_M) - R_F]\beta$$

$$0.14 = 0.06 + (0.11 - 0.06)\beta$$

$$\beta_s = 1.6 \text{ at present.}$$

Stanton's present equity beta is 1.6. As stated earlier, if the additional funds are raised by debt, the cost of equity will rise to 16 percent. The implied new equity beta, therefore, will be

$$0.16 = 0.06 + (0.05)\beta$$

$$\beta = 2.0.$$

Stanton's beta will rise to 2 with debt financing. With equity financing, the cost of equity will fall to 12 percent. The implied new beta will thus be 1.2.

Four measures of risk have been used to assess the effect of choosing between equity financing and debt financing. Each measure has covered different aspects of risk, and the results for Stanton have all pointed in the same direction. If debt financing is used, the financial structure ratios will be above the industry standards, the deficiency in the fixed charge coverage ratio will be further aggravated, and the cash flow coverage will decline toward the industry standard (and, by a broader measure, may even fall below it). The existing 1.6 beta level is relatively high. The use of debt financing will push the beta level to 2, which is high for an industrial firm. The use of equity financing will move the beta level toward the average beta level of the market, which is one. Clearly, therefore, from the standpoint of the four different measures of risk, equity financing is the more favorable.

The next consideration is the relative costs of the different forms of financing. Relative costs are measured by the effects of each form of financing on the market value per share of common stock and by the effects on the firm's cost of capital. To apply these two criteria, it is first necessary to calculate the amount of interest expense (in Table 25.10) for use in the income statements (Table 25.11).

The total amount of interest expense without expansion is $60 million. Interest expense will remain unchanged if the expansion is financed by equity funds. If the expansion is financed by long-term debt, the facts of the problem state that the cost of debt will rise to 12 percent. The opportunity cost of all debt funds, therefore, is 12 percent, and an argument can be made that all forms of debt should bear the higher 12 percent rate. However, the actual rate paid on the long-term debt will remain at 10 percent, while the short-term notes payable must be renewed periodically at the higher 12 percent rate (as shown in Table 25.10). If the expansion is financed by debt, the total interest expense will be $90 million. The total interest expense amounts needed for the income statements in Table 25.11 are now available. With the information developed in the income statements, the market value of equity can be calculated (see Table 25.12).

Table 25.10   Calculation of the Amount of Debt Interest for Stanton (Millions of Dollars)

Form of Debt	No Expansion		Expansion with Debt		Expansion with Equity	
	Amount	Rate	Amount	Rate	Amount	Rate
$300 million short-term notes payable	$30	10%	$36	12%	$30	10%
$300 million existing long-term debt[a]	30	10	30	10	30	10
$200 million new long-term debt			24	12		
Total interest expense	$60		$90		$60	

[a]If debt financing is used, the current market value of the debt (with an average life of ten years remaining), when the interest rate rises from the coupon rate of 10 percent to a market rate of 12 percent, would become $885 per bond, or for the 300,000 bonds outstanding, it would become $265.5 million. Note that the interest payment would be .12 × $265.5, which equals $31.86 million. This is approximately the same as the 10 percent interest on the $300 million existing long-term debt, illustrating that $rD = k_bB$.

The net income under each alternative is capitalized by the applicable cost of equity to obtain the total market value of equity. The price per share can also be determined. The total number of shares of common stock outstanding remains unchanged with no expansion or with expansion financed by debt. The facts of the case stated that if equity were sold, the price would be $9 per share; the $200 million of new financing divided by the $9 equals 22.2 million shares. Thus, the total number of shares is 122.2 million (the original 100 million plus the additional 22.2 million). The indicated new price per share of common stock is obtained by dividing the total value of equity by the total number of shares of common stock outstanding. The resulting new price per share declines with expansion by debt financing and increases with expansion by equity financing — which means that equity financing is more favorable than debt financing. If debt financing were used, the criterion of maximizing share price would recommend that the expansion program not be adopted.

This result can be checked further by calculating the total market value of the firm (see Table 25.13). The total market value is obtained by adding the amount of interest-bearing

Table 25.11   Stanton's Income Statements (Millions of Dollars)

	No Expansion	Expansion with Debt	Expansion with Equity
Net operating income	$316	$360	$360
Interest expense	60	90	60
Net income before taxes	$256	$270	$300
Income taxes (at 50%)	128	135	150
Net income	$128	$135	$150

Table 25.12   Stanton's Market Value of Equity (Millions of Dollars)

	No Expansion	Expansion with Debt	Expansion with Equity
Net income (NI)	$128	$135	$150
Cost of equity (k_s)	0.14	0.16	0.12
Value of equity (S)	$914	$844	$1,250
Number of shares	100	100	122.2
Price per share	$9.14	$8.44	$10.23

debt to the market value of equity. It is increased by expansion with either debt or equity. However, as shown in Table 25.12, the market price per share of common stock is decreased by expansion with debt.

We calculate the total market value of the firm to determine the firm's capital structure proportions for use in the cost of capital calculations. In the process, we also find that the value of the firm is greatest when expansion is financed with equity funds. The leverage ratios are calculated in Table 25.14. The leverage ratio is increased if debt is employed but decreased if equity financing is employed. Using the capital structure proportions from Table 25.14, the weighted average cost of capital can be calculated:

$$k_b(1 - T)(B/V) + k_s(S/V) = k$$

No expansion $\quad$ $0.10(0.5)(0.40) + 0.14(0.60) = 10.4\%$

Expansion with debt $\quad$ $0.12(0.5)(0.48) + 0.16(0.52) = 11.2\%$

Expansion with equity $\quad$ $0.10(0.5)(0.32) + 0.12(0.68) = 9.8\%$.

Expansion with debt will raise Stanton's cost of capital from 10.4 percent to 11.2 percent. Expansion with equity will lower the company's cost of capital from 10.4 percent to 9.8 percent. These results are consistent with the findings for the market value per share of common stock, where debt financing caused a decrease and equity financing an increase. Thus, the cost of capital and market price per share of common stock criteria provide

Table 25.13   Stanton's Market Value (Millions of Dollars)

	No Expansion	Expansion with Debt	Expansion with Equity
Market value of equity	$ 914	$ 844	$1,250
Amount of debt[a]	600	766	600
Value of the firm	$1,514	$1,610	$1,850

[a]Since the market value of the long-term debt has fallen by $34 million, the total amount of debt is $800 million less $34 million, or $766 million, as shown in the table.

Table 25.14   Calculation of Stanton's Leverage Ratios

	No Expansion	Expansion with Debt	Expansion with Equity
Total debt	$ 600	$ 766	$ 600
Market value of the firm	$1,514	$1,610	$1,850
Debt to value ratio	0.40	0.48	0.32

consistent findings.[11] For example, we could also obtain the value of the firm using:

$$V_L = \frac{X(1 - T)}{k_U} + TB.$$

For the no expansion case, we have

$$k = k_b(1 - T)(L) + k_s(1 - L), \text{ where } L = B/V$$

$$= 0.10(0.5)(0.4) + 0.14(0.6)$$

$$= 0.02 + 0.084 = 0.104.$$

Since $k = k_U(1 - TL)$,

$$0.104 = k_U(1 - 0.2),$$

and

$$k_U = 0.13.$$

Hence,

$$V_L = \frac{\$316(0.5)}{0.13} + 0.5(\$600)$$

$$= \$1,515.$$

The final item on the checklist of factors for evaluating alternative forms of financing is "effects on control." The problem states that the common stock is already widely held so that there is no control problem to militate against the use of equity financing.

The investment bankers summarize the evidence with respect to the two forms of financing as follows. Risks are already high and will be further increased if debt financing is used. As a result of this substantial increase in risk, the costs of both debt and equity funds will rise. With equity financing, the value per share of common stock is increased and the

---

[11]We are here using the Modigliani and Miller valuation framework and the three equations for calculating the weighted cost of capital developed in Chapter 21 on capital structure and the cost of capital.

cost of capital reduced. There is no control issue. On the basis of all the factors considered, the common stock financing is recommended.

The Stanton case illustrates the application of a checklist of key factors to evaluate alternative forms of financing. Four measures of risk and several measures of costs to the firm (returns to investors) are employed. Relative costs of financing can be evaluated by reference to effects on market value per share of common stock, on the cost of capital, and on control of the firm. Thus, the analysis is essentially a risk-return evaluation and reflects a basic theme that runs through all of the chapters of this book.

Summary

The explanations of common stock financing and of the advantages and disadvantages of external equity financing compared with the use of preferred stock and debt provide a basis for making sound decisions when a firm is considering common stock financing.

Rights offerings can be used effectively by financial managers. If the new financing associated with the rights represents a sound decision — one likely to result in improved earnings for the firm — a rise in stock values will probably result. The use of rights will permit shareholders to preserve their positions or improve them. However, if investors feel that the new financing is not well advised, the rights offering may cause the price of the stock to decline by more than the value of the rights. Because rights offerings are directed to existing shareholders, their use can reduce the costs of floating the new issue.

A major decision for financial managers in a rights offering is where to set the subscription price, or the amount of the concession from the existing market price of the stock. Formulas reflecting the static effects of a rights offering indicate that neither the company nor the stockholders gain or lose from the price changes. The rights offering has the effect of a stock split; that is, the level set for the subscription price reflects, to a great degree, the objectives and effects of a stock split.

The subsequent price behavior of the rights and the common stock in the associated new offering reflects the earnings and dividends prospects of the company as well as underlying developments in the securities markets. The new financing associated with the rights offering can be an indicator of prospective growth in the company's sales and earnings. The stock-split effects of the rights offering can be used to alter the company's dividend payments. The effects of these developments on the market behavior of the rights and the securities before, during, and after the rights trading period reflect the expectations of investors toward the outlook for the earnings of the firm.

A framework for decisions on choosing among various forms of financing is applied to the evaluation of common stock financing and can also be applied to the other forms of financing discussed in subsequent chapters.

Questions

25.1 By what percentage could total assets shrink in value on liquidation before creditors incur losses in each of the following cases:
  a) Equity-to-total-asset ratio of 50 percent
  b) Debt-to-equity ratio of 50 percent
  c) Debt-to-total-asset ratio of 40 percent?

25.2 How many shares must a minority group own in order to assure election of two directors if nine new directors will be elected and 200,000 shares are outstanding? Assume cumulative voting exists.

25.3 Should the preemptive right entitle stockholders to purchase convertible bonds before they are offered to outsiders?

25.4 What are the reasons for not letting officers and directors of a corporation make short sales in their company's stock?

25.5 It is frequently stated that the primary purpose of the preemptive right is to allow individuals to maintain their proportionate share of the ownership and control of a corporation.

    a) Just how important do you suppose this consideration is for the average stockholder of a firm whose shares are traded on the New York or American Stock Exchange?

    b) Is the preemptive right likely to be of more importance to stockholders of closely held firms? Explain.

25.6 How would the success of a rights offering be affected by a declining stock market?

25.7 What are some of the advantages and disadvantages of setting the subscription price on a rights offering substantially below the current market price of the stock?

25.8 **a)** Is a firm likely to get wider distribution of shares if it sells new stock through a rights offering or directly to underwriters?

    b) Why would a company be interested in getting a wider distribution of shares?

Problems

25.1 The common stock of McLean Development Company is selling for $32 a share on the market. Stockholders are offered one new share at a subscription price of $20 for every three shares held. What is the value of each right?

25.2 United Appliance Company common stock is priced at $40 a share on the market. Notice is given that stockholders can purchase one new share at a price of $27.50 for every four shares held.

    a) At approximately what market price will each right sell?

    b) Why will this be the approximate price?

    c) What effect will the issuance of rights have on the original market price?

25.3 Adele Jackson's total assets consist of 490 shares of Collingwood Corporation and $2,000 in cash. Collingwood now offers stockholders one additional share at a price of $20 for each five shares held. The current market price of the stock is $35.

    a) What is the value of each right?

    b) Prepare statements showing Jackson's total assets after the offering for each of these alternative courses of action.

        1. She exercises all her rights.

        2. She sells all her rights.

        3. She sells 400 rights and exercises 90 rights.

        4. She neither sells nor exercises the rights.

25.4 The Fuller Company has the balance sheet and income statement in Table P25.4.

Table P25.4

The Fuller Company Balance Sheet before Rights Offering

		Total debt (6%)	$ 7,000,000
		Common stock (100,000 shares)	3,000,000
		Retained earnings	4,000,000
Total assets	$14,000,000	Total liabilities and capital	$14,000,000

The Fuller Company Income Statement

Earnings rate: 10.5% on total assets	
Total earnings	$1,470,000
Interest on debt	420,000
Income before taxes	$1,050,000
Taxes (40% rate assumed)	420,000
Earnings after taxes	$ 630,000
Earnings per share	$6.30
Dividends per share (56% of earnings)	$3.53
Price-earnings ratio	15 times
Market price per share	$94.50

The company plans to raise an additional $5 million through a rights offering; the additional funds will continue to earn 10.5 percent. The price-earnings ratio is assumed to remain at 15 times, the dividend payout will continue to be 56 percent, and the 40 percent tax rate will remain in effect. (Do not attempt to use the formula given in the chapter. Additional information is given here that violates the "other things constant" assumption inherent in the formula.)

a) Assuming subscription prices of $25, $50, and $80 a share:
  1. How many additional shares of stock will have to be sold?
  2. How many rights will be required to purchase one new share?
  3. What will be the new earnings per share?
  4. What will be the new market price per share?
  5. What will be the new dividend per share if the dividend payout ratio is maintained?
b) Suppose you hold 100 shares of Fuller stock before the rights offering. After you exercise your rights, what is the value of your position?

25.5 The Marpole Company common stock is selling for $60 per share. With its investment bankers the company has formulated a plan to raise additional funds through a common stock rights offering at $50 per share, with 4 rights needed to buy one share at the subscription price.

a) Using the traditional formula (Equation 25.3), what is the value of each right?
b) Assume that the risk-free rate is 9 percent, the variance of returns on equity is 16 percent and the time to maturity of the rights is 0.1 of a year. Calculate the value of a right using the option pricing approach plus consideration of the dilution factor.

25.6 As one of the minority shareholders of the Keane Corporation, you are dissatisfied with the current operations of the company. You feel that if you could gain membership on the company's board of directors, you could persuade the company to make improvements. The problem is that current management controls 75 percent of the stock, you control only 7 percent, and the balance is held by other minority shareholders. There is a total of 500,000 voting shares. Ten directors will be elected at the next annual stockholder meeting.

a) If voting is noncumulative, can you elect yourself director?
b) Suppose you are able to persuade all the minority shareholders that you should be elected. If voting is noncumulative, can they elect you?
c) If voting is cumulative, can you elect yourself director?
d) What percent of the minority shares other than your own will you need to have voted for you to be certain of election?

e)   What is the number of directors the minority shareholders can elect with certainty?

25.7 The Frost Crop Food Company is engaged principally in the business of growing, processing, and marketing a variety of frozen vegetables. A major company in this field, it produces and markets high quality food at premium prices.

During each of the past several years, the company's sales have increased and the needed inventories have been financed from short-term sources. The officers have discussed the idea of refinancing their bank loans with long-term debt or common stock. A common stock issue of 310,000 shares sold at this time (present market price $72 a share) will yield $21 million after expenses. The same sum can be raised by selling 12-year bonds with an interest rate of 8 percent. (See financial ratios and statements in Tables P25.7a, P25.7b, and P25.7c.)

a)   Should Frost Crop Food refinance the short-term loans? Why?

b)   If the bank loans should be refinanced, what factors should be considered in determining which form of financing to use?

Table P25.7a

Food Processing Industry Financial Ratios

Current ratio: 2.2 times
Sales to total assets: 2.0 times
Sales to inventory: 5.6 times
Average collection period: 22.0 days
Current debt/total assets: 25-30%
Long-term debt/total assets: 10-15%
Preferred/total assets: 0.5%
Net worth/total assets: 55-65%
Profits to sales: 2.3%
Net profits to total assets: 4.0%
Profits to net worth: 8.4%
Expected growth rate of earnings and dividends: 6.5%

Table P25.7b

Frost Crop Food Company Consolidated Balance Sheet as of March 31, 19X3 (Millions of Dollars)[a]

Current assets	$141	Accounts payable	$12	
Fixed plant and equipment	57	Notes payable	36	
Other assets	12	Accruals	15	
		Total current liabilities		$ 63
		Long-term debt (at 5%)		63
		Preferred stock		9
		Common stock (par $6)	$12	
		Retained earnings	63	
		Shareholders' equity		75
Total assets	$210	Total claims on assets		$210

[a]The majority of harvesting activities do not begin until late April or May.

Table P25.7c

Frost Crop Food Company Consolidated Income Statement for Year Ended March 31
(Millions of Dollars)

	19X0	19X1	19X2	19X3
Net sales	$225.0	$234.6	$292.8	$347.1
Cost of goods sold	146.1	156.6	195.3	230.4
Gross profit	$ 78.9	$ 78.0	$ 97.5	$116.7
Other expenses	61.8	66.0	81.0	88.5
Operating income	$ 17.1	$ 12.0	$ 16.5	$ 28.2
Interest expense	3.3	4.2	5.7	9.3
Earnings before tax	$ 13.8	$ 7.8	$ 10.8	$ 18.9
Taxes	7.2	3.3	5.4	9.6
Net profit	$ 6.6	$ 4.5	$ 5.4	$ 9.3
Preferred dividend	0.3	0.3	0.3	0.3
Earnings available to common stock	$ 6.3	$ 4.2	$ 5.1	$ 9.0
Earnings per share	$3.15	$2.10	$2.55	$4.50
Cash dividends per share	$1.29	$1.44	$1.59	$1.80
Price range for common stock:				
High	$66.00	$69.00	$66.00	$81.00
Low	$30.00	$42.00	$51.00	$63.00

25.8 Inland Steel is planning an expansion program. It estimates that it will need to raise
an additional $200 million. Inland discussed with its investment banker whether to
raise the $200 million through debt financing or through selling additional shares
of common stock. The banker's recommendation was based on the following
background information. The dividend payout has averaged about 50 percent
of net income. The cost of debt is 10 percent, and the cost of equity is 14 percent. If the additional funds are raised by debt, the cost of debt will be 12 percent
and the cost of equity will rise to 16 percent. If the additional funds are raised by
equity, the cost of debt will remain at 10 percent, and the cost of equity will fall to
12 percent. Equity will be sold at $9 per share. (See also the steel industry stand-
ards in Table P25.8a and Inland's balance sheet and income statement in Table
P25.8b.)

Table P25.8a

Steel Industry Standards

Long-term debt to shareholder's equity: 30%
Shareholders' equity to total assets: 55%
Fixed charge coverage: 7 times
Current ratio: 2.1 times
Return on net worth: 11%

Table P25.8b

Inland Steel Balance Sheet as of December 31, 19X0 (Millions of Dollars)

Assets		Liabilities		
Total current assets	$ 600	Notes payable (at 10%)	$100	
Net fixed assets	1,200	Other current liabilities	100	
		Total current liabilities		$ 200
		Long-term debt (at 10%)		500
		Other liabilities		300
		Total debt		$1,000
		Common stock, par value $1		100
		Paid-in capital		300
		Retained earnings		400
Total assets	$1,800	Total claims on assets		$1,800

Inland Steel Income Statement for Year Ended December 31, 19X0 (Millions of Dollars)

	Current Year	With Expansion, Pro Forma
Total revenues	$2,000	$2,400
Net operating income	231	260
Interest expense	60	—
Net income before taxes	$ 171	—
Income taxes (at 25%)	43	—
Net income to equity	$ 128	—

a) Make a financial risk analysis using financial structure ratios.

b) Complete the pro forma income statements under the two forms of financing and compare fixed charge coverage under the two alternatives.

c) Calculate the market value of equity and the indicated market price per share before and after financing by the two methods.

d) Calculate the value of the firm and the B/S, B/V, and S/V percentages.

e) Calculate the weighted cost of capital at present and under the two financing alternatives.

f) Recommend the best form of financing for Inland.

Selected References

Bacon, Peter W., "The Subscription Price in Rights Offerings," *Financial Management*, 1 (Summer 1972), pp. 59-64.

Bhagat, Sanjai, "The Effect of Preemptive Right Amendments on Shareholder Wealth," *Journal of Financial Economics*, (November 1983), pp. 289-310.

Dodd, P., and Warner, J. B., "On Corporate Governance: A Study of Proxy Contests," *Journal of Financial Economics*, 11 (April 1983), pp. 401-438.

Duvall, Richard M., and Austin, Douglas V., "Predicting the Results of Proxy Contests," *Journal of Finance*, 20 (September 1965), pp. 467-471.

Galai, D., and Schneller, M., "The Pricing of Warrants and the Value of the Firm," *Journal of Finance*, 33 (December 1978), pp. 1333-1342.

Ibbotson, R. R., "Price Performance of Common Stock New Issues," *Journal of Financial Economics*, 2 (September 1975), pp. 235-272.

Johnson, Ramon E.; Pratt, Richard T.; and Stewart, Samuel S., Jr., "The Economic Consequences of ESOPs," *Journal of Financial Research*, 5 (Spring 1982), pp. 75-83.

Korwar, A. N., "The Effect of New Issues of Equity: An Empirical Examination," working paper, University of California, Los Angeles, 1981.

Masulis, R. W., "The Impact of Capital Structure Change on Firm Value," *Journal of Finance*, 38 (March 1983), pp. 107-126.

———, "The Effects of Capital Structure Change on Security Prices: A Study of Exchange Offers," *Journal of Financial Economics*, 8 (June 1980), pp. 139-177.

Smith, Clifford W., Jr., "Alternative Methods for Raising Capital: Rights versus Underwritten Offerings," *Journal of Financial Economics*, 5 (December 1977), pp. 273-307.

Chapter 26 Debt and Preferred Stock

There are many classes of fixed-income securities: long-term and short-term, secured and unsecured, marketable and nonmarketable, participating and nonparticipating, senior and junior, and so on. Financial managers, with the counsel of investment bankers and other financial advisers, seek to package securities with characteristics that will make them attractive to the widest range of different types of investors. By relating the design of securities effectively to the tastes and needs of potential investors, financial managers can hold the firm's cost of financing to the lowest possible levels. This chapter deals with the two most important types of long-term, fixed-income securities — bonds and preferred stocks.

Instruments of Long-Term Debt Financing

An understanding of long-term forms of financing requires some familiarity with technical terminology. The discussion of long-term debt, therefore, begins with an explanation of several important instruments and terms.

Bond

Most people have had some experience with short-term promissory notes. A *bond* is simply a long-term promissory note.

Mortgage

A *mortgage* represents a pledge of designated property for a loan. Under a *mortgage bond*, a corporation pledges certain real assets as security for the bond. A mortgage bond, therefore, is secured by real property.[1] The pledge is a condition of the loan.

Debenture

A *debenture* is a long-term bond that is *not* secured by a pledge of any specific property. However, like other general creditor claims, it is secured by any property not otherwise pledged.

---

[1]There is also the *chattel mortgage*, which is secured by personal property; but this is generally an intermediate-term instrument. *Real property* is defined as real estate — land and buildings. *Personal property* is defined as any other kind of property, including equipment, inventories, and furniture.

Indenture

The long-term relationship between the borrower and the lender of a long-term promissory note is established in a document called an *indenture*. In the case of an ordinary 60- or 90-day promissory note, few developments that will endanger repayment are likely to occur in the life or affairs of the borrower. The lender looks closely at the borrower's current position, because current assets are the main source of repayment. A bond, however, is a long-term contractual relationship between the bond issuer and the bondholder; over this extended period, the bondholder has cause to worry that the issuing firm's position may change materially.

In the ordinary common stock or preferred stock certificate or agreement, the details of the contractual relationship can be summarized in a few paragraphs. The bond indenture, however, can be a document of several hundred pages that discusses a large number of factors important to the contracting parties, such as: (1) the form of the bond and the instrument; (2) a complete description of property pledged; (3) the authorized amount of the bond issue; (4) detailed protective clauses, or *covenants*; (5) a minimum current ratio requirement; and (6) provisions for redemption or call privileges.

Bond covenants can be divided into four broad categories: (1) those restricting the issuance of new debt, (2) those with restrictions on dividend payments, (3) those with restrictions on merger activity, and (4) those with restrictions on the disposition of the firm's assets. A good description of the multitude of specific provisions in debt contracts can be found in the American Bar Association compendium called *Commentaries on Model Indenture Provisions* [1971]. Smith and Warner [1979] examined a random sample of 87 public issues of debt registered with the Securities and Exchange Commission between January 1974 and December 1975. They observed that fully 90.8 percent of the bonds restricted the issuance of new debt, 23 percent restricted dividend payments, 39.1 percent restricted merger activity, and 35.6 percent constrained the firm's disposition of assets.

Bond covenants that restrict subsequent financing are by far the most common type. The covenant provisions are usually stated in terms of accounting numbers and consequently are easy to monitor. The issuance of debt may carry restrictions that require all new debt to be subordinate or prohibit the creation of new debt with a higher priority unless existing bonds are upgraded to have an equal priority. All these restrictions are designed to prevent the firm from increasing the riskiness of outstanding debt by issuing new debt with a superior or equal claim on the firm's assets. Alternate restrictions may prohibit the issuance of new debt unless the firm maintains minimum prescribed ratios between net tangible assets and funded (long-term) debt, capitalization and funded debt, tangible net worth and funded debt, income and interest charges, or current assets and current liabilities (working capital tests). There may also be "clean-up" provisions that require the company to be debt-free for limited periods.

If there is any advantage to the firm that holds debt in its capital structure, then bondholders can benefit by allowing new debt but only under the condition that acquiring this obligation does not increase the riskiness of their position. Hence, an outright prohibition of new debt under any condition is rare.

Other techniques that are used to protect bondholders against subsequent financing include restrictions on rentals, leases, and sale-leaseback agreements; sinking fund requirements (which roughly match the depreciation of the firm's tangible assets); required purchase of insurance; required financial reports and specification of accounting techniques; and required certifications of compliance by the officers of the firm.

Bond covenants that restrict dividend payments are necessary if for no other reason than to prohibit the extreme case of shareholders voting to pay themselves a liquidating dividend that would leave the bondholders holding an empty corporate shell. Kalay [1979] reported that in a random sample of 150 firms, every firm had a dividend restriction in at least one of its debt instruments. Restrictions on dividend policy are relatively easy to monitor, and they protect debtholders against the unwarranted payout of the assets that serve as collateral. Appropriately, most indentures refer not only to cash dividends but to all distributions in respect to capital stock, whether they be dividends, redemptions, purchases, retirements, partial liquidations, or capital reductions, and whether in cash, in kind, or in the form of debt obligations to the company. Without such general provisions, the firm could, for example, use cash to repurchase its own shares. From the bondholders' point of view, the effect would be the same as payment of cash dividends. No matter what the procedure is called, once cash is paid out to shareholders, it is no longer available for collateral in the event of reorganization or bankruptcy.

Most restrictions on the payout of the firm's assets require that dividends increase only if the firm's earnings are positive, if the firm issues new equity capital, or if dividends paid out since the bonds were issued have been kept below a predefined maximum level. Mathematically, the "inventory" of funds allowable for dividend payment, Div_t^*, in quarter t, can be expressed as

$$Div_t^* = K\sum_{t=0}^{T} NI_t + \sum_{t=0}^{T} S_t + F - \sum_{t=0}^{T-1} Div_t,$$

where

$$NI_t = \text{net earnings in quarter } t$$
$$K = \text{predetermined constant, } 0 \le K \le 1$$
$$S_t = \text{net proceeds from issue of new equity}$$
$$F = \text{number fixed over life of bonds, known as the "dip"}$$
$$Div_t = \text{dividends paid out in quarter } t$$

Thus, the dividend covenant does not restrict dividends per se; rather, it restricts the financing of the payment of dividends with new debt or by sale of the firm's existing assets. This arrangement is in the interest of stockholders because it does not restrict the payment of earned income. It is also in the interest of bondholders because it prevents any dilution of their claim on the firm's assets.

Bond covenants that restrict merger activity prohibit many mergers. More often, though, they will allow mergers, provided certain conditions are met. The effect of a merger on bondholders can be beneficial if the cash flows of the merged firms are not perfectly correlated. Offsetting cash flow patterns can reduce the risk of default, thereby bettering the positions of the bondholders of both firms. Merger can also be detrimental to bondholders. For example, if Firm A has much more debt in its capital structure than Firm B, the bondholders of B will suffer increased risk after the merger. Or if the maturity of debt in Firm A is shorter than for Firm B, the bondholders of B will, for all practical purposes, become subordinate to those of Firm A after the merger.

To protect against the undesirable effects that can result from a merger, it is possible to require bond covenants that allow merger only if the net tangible assets of the firm, calculated on a postmerger basis, meet a certain dollar minimum or are at least a certain fraction of long-term debt. The merger can also be made contingent on the absence of default of any indenture provision after the transaction is completed.

Bond covenants that restrict production or investment policies are numerous. They are frequently difficult to enforce, however, given the impossibility of effectively monitoring the investment opportunities that the managers of the firm decide not to undertake. Myers [1977] suggests that a substantial portion of the value of a firm is composed of intangible assets in the form of future investment opportunities. A firm with outstanding debt may have the incentive to reject projects that have a positive net present value if the benefit from accepting the project accrues to the bondholders without also increasing shareholders' wealth.

Direct restrictions on investment-disinvestment policy take the following forms: (1) restrictions on common stock investments, loans, extensions of credit, and advances that cause the firm to become a claimholder in another business enterprise, (2) restrictions on the disposition of assets, and (3) covenants requiring the maintenance of assets. Secured debt is an indirect restriction on investment policy. Assets that provide surety cannot be disposed of under the provisions of the indenture agreement. Collateralization also reduces foreclosure expenses because the lender already has established title via the bond covenant.

Even though covenants are designed to protect bondholders from various actions which can diminish the surety of their position, no set of covenants can eliminate all risk. Consequently, there is considerable interest in accurate information about changes in the riskiness of corporate debt on a firm-by-firm basis.

The usual method for determining the default risk of corporate long-term debt is to refer to the bond ratings supplied by various agencies. Major bond rating agencies are Moody's Investors Service, Inc., Standard & Poor's Corp., and Fitch Investor Service. Moody's bond rating has seven classifications, ranging from Aaa, which is the highest quality bond, down to Caa, the lowest quality. Weinstein [1978] collected data on 179 new bond issues between 1962 and 1974. Table 26.1 shows the distribution by risk class. About 40 percent of the new bonds qualified for the two highest quality ratings. Figure 26.1 shows the yields on bonds of different risk. Just as expected, the high-quality, low-risk bonds have lower promised yields to maturity than do the low-quality, high-risk bonds. A common-sense way of estimating the marginal cost of new debt for a firm (assuming that the new debt will not change the firm's bond rating) is to compute the yield to maturity on other bonds with maturities and bond ratings similar to the new issue.

Of the roughly 2,000 major corporations that are evaluated by the agencies, approximately 500 are rerated quarterly because they issue commercial paper, another 500 are rerated annually (most of the utilities), and the remaining 1,000 have no established review date but are usually reviewed annually.

Table 26.1   Sample of New Issues by Moody's Rating of Issue

Rating	Industrials	Percent of Total	Utilities	Percent of Total
Aaa	29	26.1%	14	20.6%
Aa	18	16.2	14	20.6
A	38	34.3	18	26.5
Baa	20	18.0	20	29.4
Ba	1	0.9	2	2.9
B	5	4.5	0	0
	111	100.0	68	100.0

Source: Adapted from Mark Weinstein, "The Effect of a Rating Change Announcement on Bond Price," *Journal of Finance,* December 1978.

Figure 26.1   Comparison of Bond Yields for Bonds of Different Risks

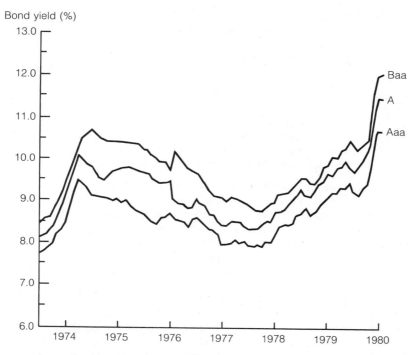

Source: From the *Federal Reserve Bulletin*, Board of Governors of the Federal Reserve System, various issues.

From an investor's point of view, one might ask the following question: Do the agencies determine the prices and interest rates paid for bonds or do investors in the capital markets? The evidence collected by Wakeman [1978] and Weinstein [1977] shows that changes in bond ratings are not treated as new information by capital markets. In fact, changes in ratings usually occur several months after the capital markets have already reacted to the fundamental change in the bond's quality. Changes in agency ratings do not cause changes in required yields to maturity. It is the other way around. However, this does not imply that bond ratings are without value. On average, the ratings provide unbiased estimates of bond risk and are, therefore, a useful source of information.

Trustee

Bonds are not only of long duration but also, usually, of substantial size. Before the rise of large aggregations of savings through insurance companies or pension funds, no single buyer was able to buy an issue of such size. Bonds, therefore, were issued in denominations of $1,000 each and were sold to a large number of purchasers. To facilitate communication between the issuer and the numerous bondholders, a trustee was appointed to represent the bondholders. The trustee is still presumed to act at all times for the protection of the bondholders and on their behalf.

Any legal person, including a corporation, is considered competent to act as a trustee. Typically, however, the duties of the trustee are handled by a department of a commercial bank.

Trustees have three main responsibilities:

1. They certify the issue of bonds. This duty involves making certain that all the legal requirements for drawing up the bond contract and the indenture have been carried out.
2. They police the behavior of the corporation in its performance of the responsibilities set forth in the indenture provisions.
3. They are responsible for taking appropriate action on behalf of the bondholders if the corporation defaults on payment of interest or principal.

It is said that in many corporate bond defaults in the early 1930s, trustees did not act in the best interests of the bondholders. They did not conserve the assets of the corporation effectively, and often they did not take early action, thereby allowing corporation executives to continue their salaries and to dispose of assets under conditions favorable to themselves but detrimental to the bondholders. In some cases, assets pledged as security for the bonds were sold, and thus specific security was no longer available. The result, in many instances, was that holders of mortgage bonds found themselves more in the position of general creditors than of secured bondholders.

As a consequence of such practices, Congress passed the Trust Indenture Act of 1939 in order to give more protection to bondholders. The act provides that (1) trustees must be given sufficient power to act on behalf of bondholders; (2) the indenture must fully disclose rights and responsibilities and must not be deceptive; (3) bondholders may make changes in the indenture; (4) prompt, protective action be taken by the trustee for bondholders if default occurs; (5) an arm's-length relationship exist between the issuing corporation and the trustee; and (6) the corporation must make periodic reports to its trustee to enable that person to carry out the protective responsibilities.

Call Provision

A *call provision* gives the issuing corporation the right to call in the bond for redemption. The provision generally states that the company must pay an amount greater than the par value of the bond; this additional sum is defined as the *call premium*. The call premium is typically equal to one year's interest if the bond is called during the first year, and it declines at a constant rate each year thereafter. For example, the call premium on a $1,000 par value, 20-year, 6 percent bond is generally $60 if called during the first year, $57 if called during the second year (calculated by reducing the $60, or 6 percent, premium by one-twentieth), and so on.

The call privilege is valuable to the firm but potentially detrimental to the investor, especially if the bond is issued in a period when interest rates are thought to be cyclically high. The problem for investors is that the call privilege enables the issuing corporation to substitute bonds paying lower interest rates for bonds paying higher ones. Consider a simple example of consols (bonds with no maturity). Suppose consols are sold to yield 10 percent when interest rates are high. If interest rates drop so that the consols yield 8 percent, the value of the bond, theoretically, could rise to $1,250. Suppose the issuing firm can call the bond by paying a $100 premium. The investor receives $1,100 for a bond whose market value will otherwise be $1,250. The callability of the bond will probably prevent its rising to the full $1,250 in the marketplace.

This disadvantage of the call privilege to the investor is supported by empirical data. Studies indicate that when interest rate levels are high, new issues of callable bonds must bear yields from one-quarter to one-half of 1 percent higher than the yields of noncallable bonds. If callability is deferred for five years (that is, if the issuer cannot exercise the call privilege until the bond has been outstanding for at least five years), in periods of relatively high interest rates, the yields for long-term bonds with five years of call deferment are about 0.13 percent lower than the yields for similar bonds that can be called immediately. During periods of relatively low interest rates, the discount for five years of deferment drops to about 0.04 percent from yields on fully callable bonds.[2] (The procedures for calculating when it is advantageous for the corporation to call or refund a bond or preferred stock issue are presented later in the chapter.)

Sinking Fund

A *sinking fund* is a provision that facilitates the orderly retirement of a bond issue (or, in some cases, preferred stock issue). Typically, it requires the firm to buy and retire a portion of the bond issue each year. Sometimes, the stipulated sinking fund payment is tied to the current year's sales or earnings, but usually it is a mandatory fixed amount. If it is mandatory, a failure to meet the payment causes the bond issue to be thrown into default and can lead the company into bankruptcy. Obviously, then, a sinking fund can constitute a dangerous cash drain on the firm.

In most cases, the firm (through the bond trustee) is given the right to handle the sinking fund in either of two ways:

1. It can call a certain percentage of the bonds at a stipulated price each year (for example, 2 percent of the original amount at a price of $1,050). The serial numbers of the actual bonds to be called are determined by a lottery.
2. To retire the required face amount of the bonds, it can buy the bonds on the open market.

The firm will do whichever results in the required reduction of outstanding bonds for the smallest outlay. Therefore, if interest rates have risen (and the price of the bonds has fallen), the firm will choose the open market alternative. If interest rates have fallen (and bond prices have risen), it will elect the option of calling bonds.

The call provision of the sinking fund, at times, works to the detriment of bondholders. If, for example, the bond carries a 7 percent interest rate, and if yields on similar securities are 4 percent, the bond will sell for well above par. A sinking fund call at par thus greatly disadvantages some bondholders.

On balance, securities that provide for a sinking fund and continuing redemption are likely to be offered initially on a lower yield basis than are securities without such a fund. Since sinking funds provide additional protection to investors, sinking fund bonds are likely to sell initially at higher prices; hence, they have an interest rate to the issuer.

---

[2] See Jen and Wert [1967] and Pye [1967].

Funded Debt

Funded debt is simply long-term debt. A firm planning to "fund" its floating debt will replace short-term securities by long-term securities. *Funding* does not imply placing money with a trustee or other repository; part of the jargon of finance, it simply means long-term.[3]

Secured Bonds

Secured long-term debt can be classified according to (1) the priority of claims, (2) the right to issue additional securities, and (3) the scope of the lien.

Priority of Claims

A senior mortgage has prior claims on assets and earnings. Senior railroad mortgages, for example, have been called the "mortgages next to the rail," implying that they have the first claim on the land and assets of the railroad corporations. A junior mortgage is a subordinate lien, such as a second or third mortgage. It is a lien or claim junior to others.

Right to Issue Additional Securities

Mortgage bonds can also be classified with respect to the right to issue additional obligations pledging already encumbered property.

In the case of a *closed-end mortgage*, a company cannot sell additional bonds (beyond those already issued) secured by the property specified in the mortgage. For example, assume that a corporation with plant and land worth $5 million has a $2 million mortgage on these properties. If the mortgage is closed-end, no more bonds having first liens on this property can be issued. Thus, a closed-end mortgage provides security to the bond buyer. The ratio of the amount of the senior bonds to the value of the property is not increased by subsequent issues.

If the bond indenture is silent on this point, it is called an *open-end mortgage*. Its nature can be illustrated by referring to the example cited above. Against property worth $5 million, bonds of $2 million are sold. If an additional first mortgage bond of $1 million is subsequently sold, the property has been pledged for a total of $3 million of bonds. If, on liquidation, the property sells for $2 million, the original bondholders will receive 67 cents on the dollar. If the mortgage had been closed-end, they would have been fully paid.

Most characteristic is the *limited open-end mortgage*. Its nature can be indicated by continuing the example. A first mortgage bond issue of $2 million, secured by the property worth $3 million, is sold. The indenture provides that an additional $1 million worth of bonds — or an additional amount of bonds to bring the total to 60 percent of the original cost of the property — can be sold. Thus, the mortgage is open only to a certain point.

---

[3]Tampa Electric Company provides a good example of funding. This company has a continuous construction program. Typically, it uses short-term debt to finance construction expenditures. However, once short-term debt has built up to about $75 million, the company sells a stock or bond issue, uses the proceeds to pay off its bank loans, and starts the cycle again. The high flotation costs of small security issues make this process desirable.

Scope of the Lien

Bonds can also be classified with respect to the scope of their lien. A lien is granted on certain specified property. When a *specific lien* exists, the security for a first or second mortgage is a specifically designated property. On the other hand, a *blanket mortgage* pledges all real property currently owned by the company. Real property includes only land and those things affixed thereto; thus, a blanket mortgage is not a mortgage on cash, accounts receivables, or inventories, which are items of personal property. A blanket mortgage gives more protection to the bondholder than does a specific mortgage because it provides a claim on all real property owned by the company.

Unsecured Bonds

Debentures

The reasons for a firm's use of unsecured debt are diverse. Paradoxically, the extremes of financial strength and weakness may give rise to its use. Also, tax considerations and great uncertainty about the level of the firm's future earnings have given rise to special forms of unsecured financing. A *debenture* is an unsecured bond and, as such, provides no lien on specific property as security for the obligation. Debenture holders, therefore, are general creditors whose claim is protected by property not otherwise pledged. The advantage of debentures from the issuer's standpoint is that the property is left unencumbered for subsequent financing. However, in practice, the use of debentures depends on the nature of the firm's assets and its general credit strength.

A firm whose credit position is exceptionally strong can issue debentures; it simply does not need specific security. However, the credit position of a company may be so weak that it has no alternative to the use of debentures; all its property may already be encumbered. The debt portion of American Telephone & Telegraph's vast financing program since the end of World War II has been mainly through debentures. AT&T is such a strong institution that it does not have to provide security for its debt issues.

Debentures are also issued by companies in industries where it is not practical to provide a lien through a mortgage on fixed assets. Examples of such companies are large mail order houses and finance companies, which characteristically do not have large fixed assets in relation to their total assets. The bulk of their assets is in the form of inventory or receivables, neither of which is satisfactory security for a mortgage lien.

Subordinated Debentures

The term *subordinate* means below or inferior. Thus, *subordinated debt* has claims on assets after unsubordinated debt in the event of liquidation. Debentures can be subordinated to designated notes payable — usually bank loans — or to any or all other debt. In the event of liquidation or reorganization, the debentures cannot be paid until senior debt *as named in the indenture* has been paid. Senior debt, typically, does not include trade accounts payable. How the subordination provision strengthens the position of senior debtholders is shown in Table 26.2.

In Table 26.2, where $200 is available for distribution, the subordinated debt has a claim on 25 percent of $200, or $50. However, this claim is subordinated to the bank debt (the

Table 26.2   Illustration of Bankruptcy Payments to Senior Debt, Other Debt, and Subordinated Debt

Financial Structure	Book Value (1)	Percent of Total Debt (2)	Initial Allocation (3)	Actual Payment (4)	Percent of Original Claim Satisfied (5)
$200 available for claims on liquidation					
Bank debt	$200	50%	$100	$150	75%
Other debt	100	25	50	50	50
Subordinated debt	100	25	50	0	0
Total debt	$400	100%	$200	$200	50%
Net worth	300				0
Total	$700				29%
$300 available for claims on liquidation					
Bank debt	$200	50%	$150	$200	100%
Other debt	100	25	75	75	75
Subordinated debt	100	25	75	25	25
Total debt	$400	100%	$300	$300	75%
Net worth	300				0
Total	$700				43%

Steps:
1. Express each type of debt as a percentage of total debt (Column 2).
2. Multiply the debt percentages (Column 2) by the amount available to obtain the initial allocations (Column 3).
3. The subordinated debt is subordinate to bank debt. Therefore, the initial allocation to subordinate debt is added to the bank debt allocation until it has been exhausted or until the bank debt is finally paid off (Column 4).

only senior debt) and is added to the $100 claim of the bank. As a consequence, 75 percent of the bank's original claim is satisfied.

Where $300 is available for distribution, the $75 allocated to the subordinated debt is divided into two parts; $50 goes to the bank, and the other $25 remains for the subordinated debtholders. In this situation, the senior bank debtholders are fully paid off, 75 percent of other debt is paid, and only 25 percent of subordinated debt is paid.

Subordination is frequently required. Alert credit managers of firms supplying trade credit or commercial bank loan officers typically insist on subordination, particularly where debt is owed to the principal stockholders or officers of a company. Often, subordinated debentures are also convertible into the common stock of the issuing company.

In comparison to subordinated debt, preferred stock suffers from the disadvantage that its dividends are not deductible as an expense for tax purposes. Subordinated debentures have been referred to as being like a special kind of preferred stock, the dividends of which *are* deductible as an expense for tax purposes. Subordinated debt has, therefore, become an increasingly important source of corporate capital.

The reasons for the use of subordinated debentures are clear. They offer a great tax advantage over preferred stock; yet, they do not restrict the borrower's ability to obtain senior debt, as would be the case if all debt sources were on an equal basis.

The use of subordinated debentures is further stimulated by periods of tight money, when commercial banks tend to require a greater equity base for short-term financing. These debentures provide a greater equity cushion for loans from commercial banks or other forms of senior debt. Their use also illustrates the development of hybrid securities that emerge to meet the changing situations that develop in the capital market.

Income Bonds

Income bonds provide that interest must be paid only if the earnings of the firm are sufficient to meet the interest obligations. The principal, however, must be paid when due. Thus, the interest itself is not a fixed charge. Income bonds, historically, have been issued because a firm has been in financial difficulties and its history suggests that it may be unable to meet a substantial level of fixed charges in the future. More generally, however, income bonds simply provide flexibility to the firm in the event that earnings do not cover the amount of interest that would otherwise have to be paid. Income bonds are like preferred stock in that the firm will not be in default if current payments on the obligations are not made. They have an additional advantage over preferred stock in that the interest is a deductible expense for corporate income tax computations, while the dividends on preferred stock are not.

The main characteristic and distinct advantage of the income bond is that interest is payable only if the company achieves earnings. Since earnings calculations are subject to differing interpretations, the indenture of the income bond carefully defines income and expenses. If it did not, litigation might result. Some income bonds are cumulative indefinitely (if interest is not paid, it accumulates, and it must be paid at some future date); others are cumulative for the first three to five years, after which they become noncumulative.

Income bonds usually contain sinking fund provisions to provide for their retirement. The annual payments to the sinking funds range between 1/2 and 1 percent of the face amount of the original issue. Because the sinking fund payment requirements are typically contingent on earnings, a fixed cash drain on the company is avoided. Typically, income bondholders do not have voting rights when the bonds are issued. Sometimes, bondholders are given the right to elect some specified number of directors if interest is not paid for a certain number of years.

Sometimes, income bonds are convertible; there are sound reasons for convertibility if the bonds arise out of a reorganization. Creditors who receive income bonds in exchange for defaulted obligations have a less desirable position than they had previously. Since they have received something based on an adverse and problematical forecast of the company's future, it is appropriate that if the company does prosper, income bondholders are entitled to participate. When income bonds are issued in situations other than reorganization, the convertibility feature is likely to make the issue more attractive to prospective bond buyers.

Floating-Rate Notes

When inflation forces interest rates to high levels, borrowers are reluctant to commit themselves to long-term debt. Yield curves are typically inverted at such times, with short-term interest rates higher than long-term. One factor is that borrowers would rather pay a premium for short-term funds than lock themselves into high long-term rates for two or three decades.

Two risks are faced by those who defer long-term borrowing in hope that interest rates will soon fall. First, there is no assurance that rates will not rise even higher and remain at unexpectedly high levels for an indefinite period. If long-term rates rise to 15 percent, for example, debt that looked expensive at 12 percent will seem like a bargain to a borrower who passed it up in the hope of waiting out the rate crisis. Second, the short-term money may simply become unavailable.

The floating-rate note (FRN) was developed to decrease the risks of interest rate volatility at high levels.[4] In an FRN, the coupon rate varies at a given percentage above prevailing short- or long-term Treasury debt yields. The FRN rate is typically either fixed or guaranteed to exceed a stated minimum for an initial period and then adjusted at specified intervals to movements in the Treasury rates.

FRN's were first issued in the United States by Citicorp in 1974. The rate was set at a minimum of 9.7 percent for ten months and then adjusted semiannually to 1 percent above the current three-month Treasury bill rate. Other firms followed Citicorp's lead. These early issues carried rates based on T-bill yields, and most allowed investors to "put" the FRN to the issuer at face value after a given date.[5] Initial rates on the notes were well below the going rate on such short-term borrowing as commercial paper. In July 1974, the rate on three-month prime commercial paper was 11.9 percent, while Treasury bills of comparable maturity were yielding 7.6 percent. Because interest rates were generally expected to decline, borrowers hoped that FRN's would also cost less over the life of the notes than fixed-rate long-term debt.

Rates declined as predicted during the following two years, justifying the use of FRN's rather than fixed-rate debentures. Many holders exercised their put options when other investments became more profitable, however, a situation which forced the borrowers to seek new funds after just a few years.

When borrowers began to issue FRN's again in 1978, the put option was far less common. For that reason, and because high-yield certificates were newly available from savings institutions, the second round of FRN's was less well-suited to individual investors. Institutional investors found FRN's a valuable hedge against declines in the value of their bond portfolios, however. Because FRN's carry rates that vary with the market, their value tends to stay stable near the original price. This is another way of saying that they are less risky from the lender's point of view.

The terms of FRN's are not fixed by law. A variety of features have been employed by issuing companies during the relatively short period FRN's have been available. Typical characteristics are

1. *Convertibility.* Either to common stock or to fixed-rate notes or to both, at either the issuer's option, the holder's option, or both. The note may state particular dates or time periods when conversion is allowed and may set other conditions, such as a given Treasury bill rate at the time of conversion. The rate on the fixed-rate note may be preset or may depend on Treasury rates at conversion.
2. *Put option.* This feature allows the holder to redeem the note at face value, generally at stated times or under other given conditions.

---

[4]See the survey by Marks and Law [1980].

[5]Remember that a *call* gives the holder the option to buy at a specified price. For example, a security may be selling for $50, but you may have a call to buy it for $45. By symmetry, a *put* gives the owner the option to sell the security to the issuer at a specified price. For example, a bond may have a market price of $900, but you may own a put to sell the bond to the issuing corporation for $1,050.

3. *Minimum rate.* This feature prevents the note rate from floating below a stated minimum.
4. *Drop-lock rate.* If the note rate has dropped to a stated rate, it becomes locked at that rate until maturity.
5. *Sinking fund provision.* Permits the issuer to repay stated portions of the principal amount before maturity.
6. *Declining spread.* The spread between the note rate and the Treasury rate decreases by given amounts at specified times.
7. *Declining minimum rate.* The minimum rate decreases in a similar manner.
8. *Call option.* The issuer has the right to call the note, usually at a moderate premium, and sometimes within a short time after issuance.

Since certain features benefit the issuer while others favor potential buyers, the choice of terms for a particular offering influences the market value of the note. For example, convertibility at the issuer's option gives the issuer control over the cost of debt should Treasury rates remain at high levels; lenders will charge a premium for this right. Conversely, convertibility by the holder allows lenders to lock into higher rates of return if Treasury rates begin to fall. Lenders will accept a lower mark-up, or spread, over Treasury rates in return for this option. One important consideration for issuers is the complexity of the offering. If the FRN includes too many options, investors may conclude they are unable to evaluate it accurately and reduce the amount they are willing to pay.

The floating-rate note makes it possible for borrowers to obtain long-term funds when interest rates are generally high without locking into high rates for the entire life of the loan. The cost of debt will automatically fall when Treasury rates drop, and the issuer-convertibility features can be included as a hedge against the possibility that Treasury rates may continue to rise.

FRN's are particularly useful for financial institutions, which often hold a large percentage of assets bearing floating-rate returns. These institutions can issue FRN's to establish a constant spread between their return on investments and cost of debt. Nonfinancial companies whose revenues tend to vary more than their costs with the rate of inflation can also use FRN's to stabilize their cost-revenue spread. Capital-intensive companies, whose depreciation expenses vary little with inflation, are one example.

FRN's give investors two important guarantees during periods of high and unpredictable inflation:

1. Returns on investment will follow changes in Treasury rates.
2. Because FRN rates vary with the market, the market value of the note will remain relatively stable.

The convertibility and minimum rate features found in most FRN's give investors additional assurance and flexibility in an unstable investment environment.

When yield curves are inverted, the immediate costs of issuing FRN's based on short-term Treasury rates can be higher than ordinary fixed-rate, long-term borrowing. In such periods, however, FRN's have tended to remain less expensive initially than short-term bank loans or commercial paper.

The long-term cost of selling FRN's depends on the movement of interest rates during the life of the notes. Borrowers issue FRN's when they expect current high rates to decline significantly within a short time and then remain at lower levels. If this occurs, the total cost of funding with FRN's falls below the cost for long-term, fixed-rate notes. When rates have declined, the issuer can use the issuer-convertibility feature to ensure that total FRN costs remain low despite possible future rate increases.

While most FRN's have been tied to short-term T-bill rates, a few have been based on long-term Treasury bonds. One advantage of long-term-based FRN's is that long-term rates vary less than short-term rates. Borrowers may be willing to pay a premium for greater predictability of costs.

Floating-rate notes provide another illustration of the flexibility of financial markets and instruments. The increased volatility of fluctuations in interest rates has brought forth debt instruments with new types of provisions. Additional new efforts by lenders to achieve protection against inflation include a provision that the principal will also float — that it will be tied to the value of real assets such as oil or silver. Other inflation hedges by lenders include such claims on equity as warrants, convertibility into common stock, or add-on contingent interest fees based on some measure of company performance such as sales or income. Such hedges are added to a fixed interest rate that will be lower than it would otherwise have to be to provide protection against uncertain inflation. Thus, the lender trades off some inflation protection against some near-term interest income.

Bond Values and Their Fluctuations

In Chapter 21, we presented materials on the cost of capital for both long-term debt and short-term debt. In Chapter 23, we examined the discounted cash flow valuation of bonds. Their fluctuations are one aspect of the risk of bond investments and, therefore, affect the ability of the issuing firm to sell bonds to potential buyers. The cost of debt is, of course, implicit in the bond valuation formulas. We saw that bond values are relatively easy to determine. The expected cash flows are the annual interest payments plus the principal due when the bond matures. Depending on differences in the risk of default on interest or principal, the appropriate capitalization (or discount) rate applied to different bonds varies. A U.S. Treasury security, for example, has less risk than a security issued by a corporation; consequently, a lower discount (or capitalization) rate is applied to its interest payments. The actual calculating procedures employed in bond valuation were illustrated in Chapter 23 and need not be repeated at great length here.

However, it is worth studying bond risk in greater detail. In Chapter 23, we saw (Figure 23.1) that for a given change in the interest rate, short-term bond prices fluctuated less than long-term bonds. This insight needs to be extended in two ways. First, short- and long-term interest rates rarely fluctuate by the same amount at the same time. Usually, short-term rates are much more volatile than long-term rates. Hence, a money supply announcement which increases short-term rates by 1 percent might only increase long-term rates (ten years or more) by .1 percent or .2 percent. Consequently, although it is true that for a given change in the interest rate, long-term bond prices will fluctuate more than short-term bonds, it is rarely true that the term structure of interest rates moves by the same amount for bonds of different maturities. The second major insight is that the sensitivity of bond prices to interest rates will depend not only on their time to maturity but also on the exact pattern of cash flows which they promise the investor. This concept is called duration.

Duration

A more sophisticated definition of interest rate risk is called *duration*. It is a statistic which measures the sensitivity of bond prices to changes in interest rates rather than the relationship between yields and maturity. For example, it is possible for two bonds with the same maturity, say five years, to have very different sensitivity to interest rate changes. Let us

Table 26.3   Cash Flows for Two Bonds with Equal Maturity

	Fully Amortized Bond			Balloon Bond		
Year	(1) Payment	(2) Interest	(3) Principal	(4) Payment	(5) Interest	(6) Principal
19X4	$263.80	$100.00	$163.80	$ 100.00	$100.00	$ 0
19X5	263.80	83.62	180.18	100.00	100.00	0
19X6	263.80	65.60	198.20	100.00	100.00	0
19X7	263.80	45.78	218.02	100.00	100.00	0
19X8	263.80	23.98	239.82	1,100.00	100.00	1,000.00
Total	$1,319.00	$318.98	$1,000.02	$1,500.00	$500.00	$1,000.00

compare a fully amortized five-year bond with a balloon payment bond of the same maturity. Suppose they both yield 10 percent and the market rate of interest is also 10 percent. Their cash flows are shown in Table 26.3. They both have a present value of $1,000. But suppose market rates of interest fall to 5 percent. The market values of both bonds increase, but the fully amortized bond increases less. Its price goes from $1,000 to $1,142 while the balloon bond increases from $1,000 to $1,216. Why? The answer is duration. The balloon bond pays its cash flows in the more distant future than does the fully amortized bond. Therefore, it has greater duration and is more sensitive to unexpected changes in interest rates.

Duration is formally defined as the percent change in a bond's price with respect to a percent change in interest rates; thus, it is a measure of price elasticity.

$$\text{dur}_i = -\frac{dB/B}{d(1 + k_b)/(1 + k_b)} \tag{26.1}$$

where

$\text{dur}_i =$ the measure of duration for the ith bond
$B =$ the present value of the bond
$k_b =$ the market rate of return on bonds of equivalent risk.

Although Equation 26.1 defines duration, we can develop a measure of duration by starting with Equation 26.2, the present value of a bond with T years to maturity, where c_t are the annual coupons, and M is the face value promised at maturity.

$$B = \frac{c_1}{(1 + k_b)^1} + \frac{c_2}{(1 + k_b)^2} + \cdots + \frac{c_T}{(1 + k_b)^T} + \frac{M}{(1 + k_b)^T}. \tag{26.2}$$

Next, take the derivative of the bond value with respect to the change in the market yield rate:

$$\frac{dB}{d(1 + k_b)} = -c_1(1 + k_b)^{-2} - 2c_2(1 + k_b)^{-3} - \cdots - Tc_T(1 + k_b)^{-(T+1)} - TM(1 + k_b)^{-(T+1)}$$

$$= -\left[\frac{c_1}{(1 + k_b)^2} + \frac{2c_2}{(1 + k_b)^3} + \cdots + \frac{Tc_T}{(1 + k_b)^{T+1}} + \frac{TM}{(1 + k_b)^{T+1}}\right].$$

If we divide both sides by B and multiply by $(1 + k_b)$, we have a measure of duration equal to Equation 26.1:

$$\frac{dB/B}{d(1 + k_b)/(1 + k_b)} = -\frac{1}{B}\left[\frac{c_1}{(1 + k_b)} + \frac{2c_2}{(1 + k_b)^2} + \cdots + \frac{Tc_T}{(1 + k_b)^T} + \frac{TM}{(1 + k_b)^T}\right]$$

If we let CF_t represent the appropriate cash flows in Year t (where $t = 1, \ldots, T$) and express the result in summation form, we have

$$\text{dur}_i = -\frac{\displaystyle\sum_{t=1}^{T}\frac{tCF_t}{(1 + k_b)^t}}{B}. \tag{26.3}$$

Duration, as measured by Equation 26.3, is not the same as the maturity of the bond. Instead, duration weights each cash flow by a time factor, t. Higher weights are given to more distant cash flows because their present value is more sensitive to changes in interest rates.

If we apply the duration statistic in Equation 26.3 to the two bonds mentioned earlier, we find that the duration of the fully amortized bond, dur_1, given that the current market rate is 10 percent and the value of the bond is \$1,000, is

$$\text{dur}_1 = -\frac{\left(\dfrac{263.80}{(1.1)^1} + (2)\dfrac{263.80}{(1.1)^2} + (3)\dfrac{263.80}{(1.1)^3} + (4)\dfrac{263.80}{(1.1)^4} + (5)\dfrac{263.80}{(1.1)^5}\right)}{1000.00}$$

$$= -\frac{(239.82 + 436.03 + 594.59 + 720.72 + 819.00)}{1000.00}$$

$$= -\frac{2810.16}{1000.00} = -2.810.$$

Alternately, the duration of the balloon bond, dur_2, is

$$\text{dur}_2 = -\frac{\left(\dfrac{100}{(1.1)^1} + (2)\dfrac{100}{(1.1)^2} + (3)\dfrac{100}{(1.1)^3} + (4)\dfrac{100}{(1.1)^4} + (5)\dfrac{100}{(1.1)^5} + (5)\dfrac{1000}{(1.1)^5}\right)}{1000.00}$$

$$= -\frac{(90.91 + 165.29 + 225.39 + 273.21 + 310.46 + 3104.61)}{1000.00}$$

$$= -\frac{4169.87}{1000.00} = -4.170.$$

Thus, we see that even though both bonds have the same maturity date, five years hence, the balloon bond is much more sensitive to changes in the interest rates, as indicated by its greater duration. The fact that the duration measure is preceded by a minus sign simply means that bond prices move in the direction opposite to changes in the interest rate.

The implication of duration for financial managers is that it is necessary to consider not only the maturity of bonds but also their cash flow pattern in order to obtain an accurate assessment of their sensitivity to changes in the interest rate.

The Cost of Long-Term Debt

In calculating bond values, the discount rate we use is the required rate of return on the bond, representing the cost of long-term debt. If we have the bond value — that is, what we are required to pay to purchase the bond — we can turn the problem around and solve for the bond's yield to maturity as a measure of the cost of long-term debt. For example, suppose a perpetuity has a stated par value of $1,000 and a 5 percent coupon (that is, it pays 5 percent, or $50 annually, on this stated value) and that it is currently selling for $625. We can solve Equation 26.4 for k_b to find the yield on the bond:

$$B = \frac{c}{k_b}$$ (26.4)

$$\text{Yield on a perpetuity} = k_b = \frac{c}{B} = \frac{\$50}{\$625} = 8\%.$$

If the bond sells for $1,250, the formula shows that the yield is 4 percent. For the three-year bond paying $50 interest a year, if the price of the bond is $922.66, the yield to maturity is found by solving for k_b in Equation 26.2. The solution PVIF is the one for 8 percent:[6]

$$\$922.66 = \$50(\text{PVIF}) + \$50(\text{PVIF}) + \$1,050(\text{PVIF})$$

$$= \$50(0.9259) + \$50(0.8573) + \$1,050(0.7938)$$

$$= \$46.30 + \$42.87 + \$833.49 = \$922.66.$$

The interest factors are taken from the 8 percent column of Table A.2 in Appendix A at the end of the book. The solution procedure is exactly like that for finding the internal rate of return in capital budgeting. Also, note that the yield to maturity calculation in the above example assumes that the bond will make its promised payments on time. If there is any default risk, then we would have to use the expected payments rather than the promised payments. For more on this, refer back to Chapter 17.

Characteristics of Long-Term Debt

From the viewpoint of long-term debtholders, debt is less risky than preferred or common stock, has limited advantages in regard to income, and is weak in regard to control. To elaborate:

1. In the area of risk, debt is favorable (relative to preferred or common stock) because it gives the holder priority both in earnings and in liquidation. Debt also has a definite maturity and is protected by the covenants of the indenture.
2. In the area of income, the bondholder has a fixed return, except in the case of income bonds or floating rate notes. Interest payments are not contingent on the company's

---

[6]We first tried the PVIF's for 6 percent and found that the equation did not work. Then, we raised the PVIF to 8 percent, where the equation did work. This indicated that 8 percent was the yield to maturity on the bond. In practice, specialized interest tables (called *bond tables*) generated by a computer are available to facilitate determination of the yield to maturity on bonds with different stated interest rates and on bonds selling for various discounts below or premiums above their maturity values. The results can also be obtained directly on a programmable hand calculator.

level of earnings or current market rates of interest. However, debt does not participate in any superior earnings of the company, and gains are limited in magnitude. Bondholders actually suffer during inflationary periods. A 20-year, 6 percent bond pays $60 of interest each year. Under inflation, the purchasing power of this $60 is eroded, causing a loss in real value to the bondholder.[7] Frequently, long-term debt is callable. If bonds are called, the investor receives funds that must be reinvested to be kept active.

3.   In the area of control, the bondholder usually does not have the right to vote. However, if the bonds go into default, then bondholders, in effect, take control of the company.

From the viewpoint of long-term debt issuers, there are several advantages and disadvantages to bonds. The advantages are

1.   The cost of debt is definitely limited. Bondholders do not participate in superior profits (if earned).
2.   Not only is the cost limited, but, typically, the expected yield is lower than that of common stock.
3.   The owners of the corporation do not share their control when debt financing is used.
4.   The interest payment on debt is deductible as a tax expense.
5.   Flexibility in the financial structure of the corporation can be achieved by inserting a call provision in the bond indenture.

The disadvantages are

1.   Debt is a fixed charge; if the earnings of the company fluctuate, it may be unable to meet the charge.
2.   As seen in Chapter 17, higher financial leverage brings higher required rates of return on equity earnings. Thus, even though leverage may be favorable and may raise earnings per share, the higher required rates attributable to leverage may drive the common stock value down. An indirect cost of using more debt is possibly a higher cost of equity.
3.   Debt usually has a fixed maturity date, and the financial officer must make provision for repayment of the debt.
4.   Since long-term debt is a commitment for a long period, it involves risk. The expectations and plans on which the debt was issued may change, and the debt may prove to be a burden. For example, if income, employment, the price level, and interest rates all fall greatly, the prior assumption of a large amount of long-term debt may have been an unwise financial policy. The railroads are always given as an example in this regard. They were able to meet their ordinary operating expenses during the 1930s but were unable to meet the heavy financial charges they had undertaken earlier, when their prospects looked more favorable than they turned out to be.
5.   In a long-term contractual relationship, the indenture provisions are likely to be much more stringent than they are in a short-term credit agreement. Hence, the firm may be subject to much more disturbing and crippling restrictions than if it had borrowed on a short-term basis or had issued common stock.
6.   There is a limit on the extent to which funds can be raised through long-term debt. Generally accepted standards of financial policy dictate that the debt ratio shall not exceed certain limits. When debt goes beyond these limits, its cost rises rapidly.

---

[7]Recognizing this fact, investors demand higher interest rates during inflationary periods.

Decisions on the Use of Long-Term Debt

Financial managers are often faced with the following decisions regarding the use of debt capital:

1.   What is the optimal ratio of total debt to total assets?
2.   What is the best mixture of short- versus long-term debt?
3.   Should the interest rate be fixed or variable?
4.   Should the debt be secured or unsecured?

These are difficult decisions. The first of them was discussed at length in Chapters 20 and 21 when we covered the capital structure decision. Firms have optimal capital structures, or perhaps optimal ranges, and the average cost of capital is higher than it need be if the firm uses other than the optimal amount of debt.

   Whenever the firm contemplates raising new external capital and chooses between debt and equity, it implicitly makes a judgment about its actual debt ratio in relation to its optimal ratio. For example, consider Figure 26.2, which shows the assumed shape of the Longstreet Company's average cost of capital schedule. If Longstreet plans to raise external capital, it must make a judgment about whether it is presently at Point A or Point B. If it decides it is at Point A, it should issue debt. If it believes it is at Point B, it should sell new common stock or retain more earnings. This is, of course, a judgment decision based on the factors analyzed in Chapter 21.

   In addition to the decision of how much debt to use, there is also the question of the mixture of short- and long-term debt. Generally, the conservative policy is to continuously roll over short-term debt. This is a low-risk strategy because operating revenues and market rates of interest both tend to be high during favorable economic conditions and low during recessions. Hence, profits tend to be more stable because revenues and interest costs are correlated. Alternately, use of long-term, fixed-rate debt is more aggressive be-

Figure 26.2   The Longstreet Company's Average Cost of Capital Schedule

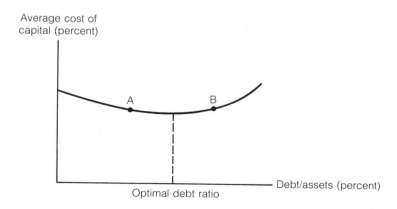

cause profits are higher in good economies and lower in bad. This results in greater systematic risk (that is, a greater beta) for shareholders.

The choice of fixed- versus variable-rate debt has much the same effect as short- versus long-term debt. Variable rate debt is a more conservative instrument so long as interest rates are positively correlated with general market conditions. Of course, a firm may find that its revenues are always down when interest rates are up. Given this negative correlation between revenues and interest rates, then variable rate debt will be the riskier strategy.

The choice of secured versus unsecured debt usually depends on the type of assets held by the firm. If the assets can be liquidated near to their market value, then the firm can successfully use secured debt. But, if the assets are worth only scrap value (as in the case of most chemical companies), then the debt will usually remain in the form of unsecured debentures.

Nature of Preferred Stock

Preferred stock has claims and rights ahead of common stock but behind all bonds. The preference may be a prior claim on earnings, a prior claim on assets in the event of liquidation, or a preferential position with regard to both earnings and assets.

The hybrid nature of preferred stock becomes apparent when we try to classify it in relation to bonds and common stock. The priority feature and the (generally) fixed dividend indicate that preferred stock is similar to bonds. Payments to preferred stockholders are limited in amount, so that common stockholders receive the advantages (or disadvantages) of leverage. However, if the preferred dividends are not earned, the company can forego paying them without danger of bankruptcy. In this characteristic, preferred stock is similar to common stock. Moreover, failure to pay the stipulated dividend does not cause default of the obligation, as does failure to pay bond interest.

In some types of analysis, preferred stock is treated as debt. This occurs, for example, when the analysis is being made by a *potential stockholder* considering the earnings fluctuations induced by fixed charge securities. Suppose, however, that the analysis is by a *bondholder* studying the firm's vulnerability to failure brought on by declines in sales or income. Since the dividends on preferred stock are not a fixed charge (in the sense that failure to pay them represents a default of an obligation), preferred stock represents a cushion; it provides an additional equity base. For *stockholders*, it is a leverage-inducing instrument much like debt. For *creditors*, it constitutes additional net worth. Preferred stock, therefore, can be treated as either debt or equity, depending on the nature of the problem under consideration.[8]

The dividend stream on preferred stock which is not convertible into common stock or callable represents a perpetuity. Therefore, the valuation and cost of preferred stock measures are based on the perpetuity formulation.

$$k_{ps} = \frac{d_{ps}}{p_{ps}} \tag{26.5}$$

[8]Accountants generally include preferred stock in the equity portion of the capital structure. But preferred is very different from common equity.

Major Provisions of Preferred Stock Issues

Because the possible characteristics, rights, and obligations of any specific security vary so widely, a point of diminishing returns is quickly reached in a descriptive discussion of the different kinds of securities. As economic circumstances change, new kinds of securities are manufactured. Their number and variety are limited chiefly by the imagination and ingenuity of the managers formulating the terms of the issues. It is not surprising, then, that preferred stock can be found in many forms. The following sections will look at the main terms and characteristics in each case and examine the possible variations in relation to the circumstances in which they could occur.[9]

Priority in Assets and Earnings

Many provisions in a preferred stock certificate are designed to reduce the purchaser's risk in relation to the risk carried by the holder of common stock. Preferred stock usually has priority with regard to earnings and assets. Two provisions designed to prevent undermining this priority are often found. The first states that, without the consent of the preferred stockholders, there can be no subsequent sale of securities having a prior or equal claim on earnings. The second seeks to keep earnings in the firm. It requires a minimum level of retained earnings before common stock dividends are permitted. In order to assure the availability of liquid assets that can be converted into cash for the payment of dividends, the maintenance of a minimum current ratio may also be required.

Par Value

Unlike common stock, preferred stock usually has a par value which is a meaningful quantity. First, the par value establishes the amount due the preferred stockholders in the event of liquidation. Second, the preferred dividend is frequently stated as a percentage of the par value. For example, J. I. Case's preferred stock outstanding has a par value of $100 and a stated dividend of 7 percent of par. (It would, of course, be just as appropriate for the Case preferred stock to state simply that the annual dividend is $7; on many preferred stocks, the dividends are stated in this manner rather than as a percentage of par value.)

Cumulative Dividends

A high percentage of preferred stock issues provide for cumulative dividends — that is, all past preferred dividends must be paid before common dividends can be paid. The cumulative feature, therefore, is a protective device. If the preferred stock were not cumulative, preferred and common stock dividends could be passed by for a number of years. The company could then vote a large common stock dividend but only the stipulated payment to preferred stock. Suppose that preferred stock with a par value of $100 carried a 7 percent dividend and that the company did not pay dividends for several years, thereby accumulating funds that would enable it to pay in total about $50 in dividends. It could

---

[9]Much of the data in this section are taken from a study by Fischer and Wilt [1968].

pay a single $7 dividend to the preferred stockholders and a $43 dividend to the common stockholders. Obviously, this device could be used to evade the preferred position that the holders of preferred stock have tried to obtain. The cumulative feature prevents such evasion.[10]

Large arrearages on preferred stock make it difficult to resume dividend payments on common stock. To avoid delays in beginning common stock dividend payments again, a compromise arrangement with the holders of preferred stock is likely to be worked out. A package offer is one possibility; for example, a recapitalization plan may provide for an exchange of shares. The arrearage will be wiped out by the donation of common stock with a value equal to the amount of the preferred dividend arrearage, and the holders of preferred stock will thus be given an ownership share in the corporation. Alternately, resumption of current dividends on the preferred may be promised. Whether these provisions are worth anything depends on the future earnings prospects of the company.

The advantage to the company of substituting common stock for dividends in arrears is that it can start again with a clear balance sheet. If earnings recover, dividends can be paid to the holders of common stock without making up arrearages to the holders of preferred stock. The original common stockholders, of course, will have given up a portion of their ownership of the corporation.

Convertibility

Approximately 40 percent of the preferred stock that has been issued in recent years is convertible into common stock. For example, one share of a particular preferred stock could be convertible into 2.5 shares of the firm's common stock at the option of the preferred shareholder. (The nature of convertibility will be discussed in Chapter 28.)

Some Infrequent Provisions

Some of the other provisions occasionally encountered in preferred stocks include the following:

1. *Voting rights.* Sometimes preferred stockholders are given the right to vote for directors. When this feature is present, it generally permits the preferred stockholders to elect a *minority* of the board, say three out of nine directors. The voting privilege becomes operative only if the company has not paid the preferred dividend for a specified period, say six, eight, or ten quarters.

2. *Participating.* A rare type of preferred stock is one that participates with the common stock in sharing the firm's earnings. The following factors generally relate to participating preferred stocks: (a) the stated preferred dividend is paid first — for example, $5 a share; (b) next, income is allocated to common stock dividends up to an amount equal to the preferred dividend — in this case, $5; and (c) any remaining income is shared equally between the common and preferred stockholders.

---

[10]Note, however, that compounding is absent in most cumulative plans. In other words, the arrearages themselves earn no return.

3.   *Sinking fund*. Some preferred issues have a sinking fund requirement. When they do, the sinking fund ordinarily calls for the purchase and retirement of a given percentage of the preferred stock each year.

4.   *Maturity*. Preferred stocks almost never have maturity dates on which they must be retired. However, if the issue has a sinking fund, this effectively creates a maturity date.

5.   *Call provision*. A call provision gives the issuing corporation the right to call in the preferred stock for redemption, as for bonds. If it is used, the call provision states that the company must pay an amount greater than the par value of the preferred stock, the additional sum being defined as the *call premium*. For example, a $100 par value preferred stock might be callable at the option of the corporation at $108 a share.

6.   *Adjustable-rate preferred*. If the economy experiences a great deal of unexpected inflation, preferred stock with fixed dividend rates becomes undesirable from the investor's point of view because of the risk that the market value of the preferred will fall. In order to share the risk, and in order to make preferred issues more attractive to investors, many companies, particularly utilities, have begun to issue preferred stock with dividends tied to rates on various U.S. government obligations. Adjustable-rate preferred is especially attractive to utilities because the higher preferred dividend costs in inflationary economies can be passed on to their customers.

Evaluation of Preferred Stock

There are both advantages and disadvantages to selling preferred stock. Among the advantages are

1.   In contrast to bonds, the obligation to make fixed interest payments is avoided.
2.   A firm wishing to expand because its earning power is high can obtain higher earnings for the original owners by selling preferred stock with a limited return rather than by selling common stock.
3.   By selling preferred stock, the financial manager avoids the provision of equal participation in earnings that the sale of additional common stock would require.
4.   Preferred stock also permits a company to avoid sharing control through participation in voting.
5.   In contrast to bonds, it enables the firm to conserve mortgageable assets.
6.   Since preferred stock typically has no maturity and no sinking fund, it is more flexible than bonds.

Among the disadvantages are

1.   Characteristically, preferred stock must be sold on a higher yield basis than that for bonds.[11]

---

[11]Historically, a given firm's preferred stock generally carried higher rates than its bonds because of the preferred's greater risk from the holder's viewpoint. However, as is noted below, the fact that preferred dividends are largely exempt from the corporate income tax has made preferred stock attractive to corporate investors. In recent years, high-grade preferreds, on average, have sold on a lower yield basis than have high-grade bonds. As an example, on March 27, 1973, AT&T sold a preferred issue that yielded 7.28 percent to an investor. On that same date, AT&T bonds yielded 7.55 percent, or 0.27 percent more than the preferred. The tax treatment accounted for this differential; the *after-tax* yield was greater on the preferred stock than on the bonds.

2.   Preferred stock dividends are not deductible as a tax expense, a characteristic that makes their cost differential very great in comparison with that of bonds.
3.   As shown in Chapter 21, the after-tax cost of debt is approximately half the stated coupon rate for profitable firms. The after-tax cost of preferred, however, is frequently the full percentage amount of the preferred dividend.[12]

In fashioning securities, the financial manager needs to consider the investor's point of view. Frequently, it is asserted that preferred stocks have so many disadvantages to both the issuer and the investor that they should never be issued. Nevertheless, preferred stock is issued in substantial amounts. Preferred stock provides the following advantages to the investor:

1.   It provides reasonably steady income.
2.   Preferred stockholders have a preference over common stockholders in liquidation; numerous examples can be cited where the preference position of holders of preferred stock saved them from losses incurred by holders of common stock.
3.   Many corporations (for example, insurance companies) like to hold preferred stocks as investments because 85 percent of the dividends received on these shares is not taxable.

Preferred stock also has some disadvantages to investors:

1.   Although the holders of preferred stock bear a substantial portion of ownership risk, their returns are limited.
2.   Price fluctuations in preferred stock are far greater than those in bonds; yet, yields on bonds are frequently higher than those on preferred stock.
3.   The stockholders have no legally enforceable right to dividends.
4.   Accrued dividend arrearages are seldom settled in cash comparable to the amount of the obligation that has been incurred.

Recent Trends

Because of the nondeductibility of preferred stock dividends as a tax expense, many companies have retired their preferred stock. Often, debentures or subordinated debentures are offered to preferred stockholders in exchange, since the interest on the debentures is deductible as a tax expense.

When the preferred stock is not callable, the company must offer terms of exchange sufficiently attractive to induce the preferred stockholders to agree to the exchange. Characteristically, bonds or other securities in an amount somewhat above the recent value of the preferred stock are issued in exchange. Sometimes, bonds equal in market value to the preferred stock are issued along with additional cash or common stock to provide an extra inducement to the preferred stockholders. At other times, the offer is bonds equal to only a portion of the current market value of the preferred, with an additional amount represented by cash or common stock that will bring the total offered the preferred stockholder to something over the preferred market value as of a recent date.

---

[12]By far the most important issuers of nonconvertible preferred stocks are the utility companies. For these firms, taxes are an expense for rate-making purposes — that is, higher taxes are passed on to the customers in the form of higher prices — so tax deductibility is not an important issue. This explains why utilities issue about 85 percent of all nonconvertible preferreds.

U.S. Steel's replacement of its 7 percent preferred stock in 1965 is a classic illustration of these exchange patterns. U.S. Steel proposed that its 7 percent preferred stock be changed into 4⅝ percent 30-year bonds at a rate of $175 principal amount of bonds for each preferred share. On August 17, 1965, when the plan was announced, the preferred stock was selling at $150. U.S. Steel also announced that the conversion would increase earnings available to common stock by $10 million yearly, or 18 cents a share at 1965 federal income tax rates; this was sufficient inducement to persuade the company to give the preferred stockholders the added $25 a share.

Decision Making on the Use of Preferred Stock

As a hybrid security, preferred stock is favored by conditions that fall between those favoring common stock and those favoring debt. When a firm's profit margin is high enough to more than cover preferred stock dividends, it is advantageous to employ leverage. However, if the firm's sales and profits are subject to considerable fluctuation, the use of debt with fixed interest charges may be unduly risky. Preferred stock can offer a happy compromise. Its use is strongly favored if the firm already has a debt ratio that is high in relation to the reference level maximum for the line of business. Preferred stock may also be the desired form of financing whenever the use of debt will involve excessive risk, but the issuance of common stock will result in problems of control for the dominant ownership group in the company.

Rationale for Different Classes of Securities

At this point, the following questions are likely to come to mind: Why are there so many different forms of long-term securities? Why is anybody ever willing to purchase subordinated bonds or income bonds? The answers to both questions can be made clear by reference to Figure 26.3. The now-familiar tradeoff function is drawn to show the risk and expected returns for the various securities of the Longstreet Company. Longstreet's first mortgage bonds are slightly more risky than U.S. Treasury bonds and sell at a slightly higher expected return. The second mortgage bonds are yet more risky and have a still higher expected return. Subordinated debentures, income bonds, and preferred stocks all are increasingly risky and have increasingly higher expected returns. Longstreet's common stock, the riskiest security the firm issues, has the highest expected return of any of its offerings.

Why does Longstreet issue so many different classes of securities? Why not just offer one type of bond plus common stock? The answer lies in the fact that different investors have different risk-return tradeoff preferences, so if the company's securities are to appeal to the broadest possible market, Longstreet must offer as many as investors seem to want. Used wisely, a policy of selling differentiated securities can lower a firm's overall cost of capital below what it would be if it issued only one class of debt and common stock.

Refunding Debt or Preferred

In an era of falling interest rates, a firm may find itself with bonds or preferred stock outstanding which pay a coupon rate higher than the prevailing market rate. A net present value analysis will reveal whether the outstanding securities should be called or, if

Figure 26.3   The Longstreet Company's Risk and Expected Returns on Different Classes of Securities

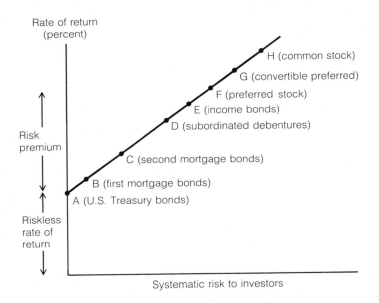

they are not callable, repurchased on the open market.[13] Almost all public bond issues and many preferred stock issues have a call provision allowing the firm to force recall of the security at a call premium. Although the following example is for a bond refinancing, the same analysis applies equally well to a preferred stock refinancing.

To provide a focus for the analysis, consider the following facts. The L and S Company has a $10 million bond issue outstanding with five years to maturity, a coupon rate of 16 percent, and with annual interest payments. The current market rate on debt of equivalent risk is 10 percent. The call price on the $1,000 face value debt is $1,050, and the firm has a 40 percent tax rate. What is the net present value of calling the outstanding bonds and replacing them with new bonds of equivalent maturity and risk? Assume no transactions costs.

This is a capital budgeting decision and the usual procedures apply. The changes in the after-tax cash flows should be discounted at the appropriate after-tax discount rate. In this case, the appropriate rate is the after-tax rate on debt of equivalent risk, that is, $(1 - T_c)k_b = (1 - .4).10 = .06$. We use the after-tax rate because all refunding costs (such as

---

[13]The accounting treatment of bond repurchase when bonds are selling at a discount can cause extremely perverse behavior. Suppose that interest rates have risen, thereby causing fixed-rate outstanding debt to sell at a discount. Repurchase of this debt at market value has no economic gain or loss before taxes because the firm is paying the fair market price. However, the accounting treatment allows the firm to record the difference between the face value and the market value as profit. Therefore, firms that desire to increase their reported earnings per share may decide to repurchase discounted debt. Unfortunately, this is a negative present value decision because the firm has to pay (1) ordinary income taxes on its paper gain and (2) higher coupons on replacement debt.

the call premium) are assumed to be financed with debt capital. This debt provides an interest tax shield; hence, the relevant discount rate is the after-tax rate.

The after-tax cash flows have three components (in a world without transactions costs).

1. The *call premium* will cost $500,000. It is deductible as an expense; therefore, its after-tax cost is $500,000(1 − .4) = $300,000. We assume that the cash flow from the tax shield is available immediately.

2. The new debt issue will have to be $10,300,000, and it will pay a 10 percent coupon (r_2 = 10%); thus, the new interest will be $1,030,000 per year. The old interest was 16 percent (r_1 = 16%) of $10,000,000, or $1,600,000 per year. Therefore, the *after-tax interest saving* amounts to $(1 − T_c)(r_1 − r_2)D − (1 − T_c)r_2 \Delta D$, where D is the original book value and ΔD is the change in book value. Numerically, the annual interest savings is

$$(1 − .4)(.16 − .10)(10,000,000) − (1 − .4)(.10)(300,000) = 342,000.$$

3. *Incremental principal* on the new debt, namely $300,000, must be paid off at maturity.

The net present value of these components is

$$\text{NPV} = \sum_{t=1}^{n} \frac{(1 − T_c)(r_1 − r_2)D}{[1 + (1 − T_c)k_b]^t} − \sum_{t=1}^{n} \frac{(1 − T_c)r_2 \Delta D}{[1 + (1 − T_c)k_b]^t} − \frac{\Delta D}{[1 + (1 − T_c)k_b]^n}$$

$$= \sum_{t=1}^{5} \frac{(1 − .4)(.16 − .10)10,000,000}{[1 + (1 − .4)(.10)]^t} − \sum_{t=1}^{5} \frac{(1 − .4).10(300,000)}{[1 + (1 − .4)(.10)]^t} − \frac{300,000}{[1 + (1 − .4)(.10)]^5}$$

$$= 1,516,464 − 75,823 − 224,190$$

$$= 1,216,451.$$

Therefore, the debt should be refunded.

Two additional issues are pertinent. First, we should consider the fact that the debt refinancing may slightly alter the capital structure of the firm because the market value of the new debt issue exceeds the market value of the outstanding debt. This may create a tax gain from leverage.[14] The second issue is that callable debt should never sell for more than the call price plus a small premium approximately equal to the flotation costs of exercising the call. No investor would rationally pay $1,100 for a bond which might be called (any minute) at $1,050.

Summary

A *bond* is a long-term promissory note. A *mortgage bond* is secured by real property. An *indenture* is an agreement between the firm issuing the bond and the numerous bondholders, represented by a *trustee*.

Secured long-term debt differs with respect to (1) the priority of claims, (2) the right to issue additional securities, and (3) the scope of the lien provided. These characteristics determine the amount of protection provided to the bondholder by the terms of the secu-

---

[14]For more on this topic, see Ofer and Taggart [1977].

rity. Giving investors more security will induce them to accept a lower yield but will restrict the future freedom of action of the issuing firm.

The main classes of unsecured bonds are (1) *debentures*, (2) *subordinated debentures*, and (3) *income bonds*. Holders of debentures are unsecured general creditors. Subordinated debentures are junior in claim to bank loans. Income bonds are similar to preferred stock in that interest is paid only when earned.

The characteristics of long-term debt determine the circumstances under which it will be used when alternative forms of financing are under analysis. The cost of debt is limited, but it is a fixed obligation. Bond interest is an expense deductible for tax purposes. Debt carries a maturity date and may require sinking fund payments to prepare for extinguishing the obligation. Indenture provisions are likely to include restrictions on the freedom of action of the firm's management.

The nature of long-term debt encourages its use under the following circumstances:

1. Sales and earnings are relatively stable.
2. Profit margins are adequate to make leverage advantageous.
3. A rise in profits or in the general price level is expected.
4. The existing debt ratio is relatively low.
5. Common stock price-earnings ratios are low in relation to the levels of interest rates.
6. Control considerations are important.
7. Cash flow requirements under the bond agreement are not burdensome.
8. Restrictions of the bond indenture are not onerous.

Even if seven of the eight factors favor debt, the remaining factor can swing the decision to the use of equity capital. Thus, the list of factors is simply a checklist of things to be considered when deciding on bonds versus stock; the actual decision is based on a judgment about the relative importance of the several factors.

The characteristics of preferred stock vary with the requirements of the situation under which it is used. However, certain patterns tend to remain. Preferred stocks usually have priority over common stocks with respect to earnings and claims on assets in liquidation. Preferred stocks are usually cumulative; they have no maturity but are sometimes callable. They are typically nonparticipating and offer only contingent voting rights.

The advantages to the issuer are limited dividends and no maturity. These advantages may outweigh the disadvantages of higher cost and nondeductibility of the dividends as an expense for tax purposes. But their acceptance by investors is the final test of whether they can be sold on favorable terms.

Companies sell preferred stock when they seek the advantages of financial leverage but fear the dangers of the fixed charges on debt in the face of potential fluctuations in income. If debt ratios or the cost of common stock financing are relatively high, the advantages of preferred stock are reinforced.

The use of preferred stock has declined significantly since the advent of the corporate income tax because preferred dividends are not deductible for income tax purposes, while bond interest payments are deductible. In recent years, however, there has been a strong shift back to a new kind of preferred stock—convertible preferred, used primarily in connection with mergers. If the stockholders of the acquired company receive cash or bonds, they are required to pay capital gains taxes on any gains they realize. If convertible preferred stock is given to the selling stockholders, this constitutes a tax-free exchange of securities. The selling stockholders can obtain a fixed income security and, at the same time, postpone the payment of capital gains taxes.

If a bond or preferred stock issue was sold when interest rates were higher than they are at present, and if the issue is callable, it may be profitable to call the old issue and refund it with a new, lower-cost issue. An analysis similar to capital budgeting is required to determine whether a refunding operation should be undertaken.

Questions

26.1   Explain what is meant by the term *yield to maturity* in reference to (a) bonds and (b) preferred stocks. Is it appropriate to talk of a yield to maturity on a preferred stock that has no specific maturity date?

26.2   Explain why bonds with longer maturities sometimes experience wider price movements from a given change in interest rates than do shorter maturity bonds. Answer first in words and then mathematically.

26.3   A sinking fund is set up in one of two ways:

a)   The corporation makes annual payments to the trustee, who invests the proceeds in securities (frequently government bonds) and uses the accumulated total to retire the bond issue on maturity.

b)   The trustee uses the annual payments to retire a portion of the issue each year, either calling a given percentage of the issue by a lottery and paying a specified price per bond or buying bonds on the open market, whichever is cheaper.

Discuss the advantages and disadvantages of each procedure from the viewpoint of both the firm and the bondholders.

26.4   Since a corporation often has the right to call bonds at will, do you believe individuals should be able to demand repayment at any time they so desire? Explain.

26.5   What are the relative advantages and disadvantages of issuing a long-term bond during a recession versus during a period of prosperity?

26.6   Missouri Pacific's $4\frac{3}{4}$ percent income bonds due in 2020 are selling for $770, while the company's $4\frac{1}{4}$ percent first mortgage bonds due in 2005 are selling for $945. Each has a $1,000 par value. Why do the bonds with the lower coupon sell at a higher price?

26.7   When a firm sells bonds, it must offer a package of terms acceptable to potential buyers. Included in this package are such features as the issue price, the coupon interest rate, the term to maturity, and sinking fund provisions. The package itself is determined through a bargaining process between the firm and the investment bankers who handle the issue. What particular features would you, as a corporate treasurer, be especially interested in having, and which would you be most willing to give ground on, under each of the following conditions:

a)   You believe that the economy is near the peak of a business cycle.

b)   Long-run forecasts indicate that your firm may have heavy cash inflows in relation to cash needs during the next five to ten years.

c)   Your current liabilities are presently low, but you anticipate raising a considerable amount of funds through short-term borrowing in the near future.

26.8   Bonds are less attractive to investors during periods of inflation because a rise in the price level reduces the purchasing power of the fixed interest payments and of the principal. Discuss the advantages and disadvantages to a corporation of using a bond whose interest payments and principal would increase in direct proportion to increases in the price level (a floating rate bond).

26.9   If preferred stock dividends are passed for several years, the preferred stockholders are frequently given the right to elect several members of the board of directors. In the case of bonds that are in default on interest payments, this procedure is not followed. Why does the difference exist?

26.10 Preferred stocks are found in almost all industries, but one industry is the really dominant issuer of preferred shares. What is this industry, and why are firms in it so disposed to using preferred stock?

26.11 If the corporate income tax were abolished, would this raise or lower the amount of new preferred stock issued?

26.12 Investors buying securities have some expected or required rate of return in mind. Which would you expect to be higher — the required rate of return (before taxes) on preferred stocks or that on common stocks?

26.13 Do you think the before-tax required rate of return is higher on very high-grade preferred stocks or on bonds in the following instances:
a)   for individual investors?
b)   for corporate investors?

26.14 For purposes of measuring a firm's leverage, should preferred stock be classified as debt or as equity? Does it matter if the classification is being made by (a) the firm itself, (b) creditors, or (c) equity investors?

26.15 A firm is seeking a term loan from a bank. Under what conditions would it want a fixed interest rate, and under what conditions would it want the rate to fluctuate with the prime rate?

Problems

26.1 Three years ago, your firm issued some 18-year bonds with 10.5 percent coupon rates and a 10 percent call premium. You have called these bonds. The bonds originally sold at their face value of $1,000.
a)   Compute the realized rate of return for investors who purchased the bonds when they were issued.
b)   Given the rate of return in Part (a), did investors welcome the call? Explain.

26.2 A fully amortized bond, a balloon payment bond, and a pure discount bond, each with five years to maturity were newly issued today. Each has a 12 percent promised yield to maturity. Their annual cash flows and current market values are provided in Table P26.2.
a)   If current market yields are 12 percent, what is the duration of each bond?
b)   If current market yields were 20 percent, what would the duration of each bond be? (Don't forget that their current values decrease if the interest rate rises from 12 percent to 20 percent.)

Table P26.2

Cash Flows on Three Bonds with Five-Year Maturities

Year	Fully Amortized	Balloon	Pure Discount
Current value	$1,000.00	$1,000.00	$1,000.00
1	277.41	120.00	0
2	277.41	120.00	0
3	277.41	120.00	0
4	277.41	120.00	0
5	277.41	1,120.00	1,762.34

26.3 Carson Electronics, a leading manufacturer in its field, is planning an expansion program. It has estimated that it will need to raise an additional $100 million. Carson is discussing with its investment banker the alternatives of raising the $100 million through debt financing or through selling additional shares of common stock.

The prevailing cost of Aaa debt is 8 percent, while the prevailing cost of Baa debt is 9.6 percent. New equity would be sold at $10 per share. The corporate tax rate is 40 percent. The industry's financial ratios, followed by Carson's balance sheet and income statement, are provided in Table P26.3.

Table P26.3

Electronics Industry Financial Ratios

Current ratio: 2.1 times
Sales to total assets: 1.8 times
Current debt to total assets: 30%
Long-term debt to net worth: 40%
Total debt to total assets: 50%
Coverage of fixed charges: 7 times
Net income to sales: 5%
Return on total assets: 9%
Net income to net worth: 12%

Carson Electronics Balance Sheet as of December 31, 19X0 (Millions of Dollars)

Assets		Liabilities		
Total current assets	$ 600	Total current liabilities	$200	
Net fixed assets	400	Long-term debt (at 8%)	100	
		Total debt		$ 300
		Common stock, par value $1		100
		Additional paid-in capital		200
		Retained earnings		400
Total assets	$1,000	Total claims on assets		$1,000

Carson Electronics Income Statement for Year Ended December 31, 19X0 (Millions of Dollars)

Total revenues	$2,000
Net operating income	208
Interest expense	8
Net income before taxes	$ 200
Income taxes (at 40%)	80
Net income to equity	$ 120

a) Estimate Carson Electronics' cost of equity capital by using the Security Market Line. The risk-free rate is 6 percent, the expected return on the market is 11 percent, and the beta based on Carson's present leverage is 1.2.

b) What is the value of Carson's total equity? What is its indicated price per share?

c) On the basis of a cost of debt of 8 percent and the cost of equity that you have calculated, determine the weighted average cost of capital for Carson at the present time. (The company has no short-term interest bearing debt.)

d) If Carson finances its expansion by the use of debt, calculate the new financial structure and coverage relationships and present your conclusion on whether the new debt issue will be risky or relatively risk-free. (Assume that the same percentage of net operating income is earned on the increase in assets as was earned on the total assets before the financing.)

e) If Carson finances with debt, the cost of debt will be 8 percent, while the cost of equity will reflect the rise in beta to 1.25. If the company finances with equity, the cost of debt will be 8 percent, while the cost of equity will reflect a drop in beta to 1.19. Compare the cost of equity under the two methods of financing.

f) Under each of the two methods of financing, what will be the total value of the equity, and what will be the new value per share of common stock?

g) Under the same assumptions as in the preceding questions, calculate the value of the firm under the two methods of financing.

h) Compare the weighted cost of capital under the two methods of financing.

i) Summarize your recommendation about which form of financing Carson should employ for raising the additional $100 million.

26.4 In late 19X8, the Coaltown Gas & Electric Company sought to raise $6 million for expansion of facilities and services. The company could have sold additional debt at 9 percent, preferred stock at 8.84 percent, or common stock at $50 a share. Growth in earnings and dividends was expected to be 4.5 percent. How should the company have raised the money? Relevant financial information is provided in Table P26.4.

Table P26.4

Public Utilities Financial Ratios

Current ratio: 1.0 times
Interest earned (before taxes): 4.0 times
Sales to total assets: 0.3 times
Average collection period: 28.0 days
Current debt/total assets: 5-10%
Long-term debt/total assets: 45-50%
Preferred/total assets: 10-15%
Common equity/total assets: 30-35%
Earnings before interest and taxes to total assets: 8.9%
Profits to common equity: 12.1%

Coaltown Gas & Electric Company Balance Sheet as of July 31, 19X8 (Thousands of Dollars)

Assets		Liabilities	
Cash	$ 750	Current liabilities	$ 3,000
Receivables	1,500	Long-term debt (at 8%)	30,000
Materials and supplies	1,200	Preferred stock (at 10%)	3,000
Total current assets	$ 3,450	Common stock, $25 par value	11,250
Net property	56,550	Capital surplus	6,600
		Retained earnings	6,150
Total assets	$60,000	Total claims	$60,000

Coaltown Gas & Electric Company Income Statement for Year Ended July 31, 19X8 (Thousands of Dollars)

Operating revenues	$18,900
Operating expenses	12,000
Earnings before interest and taxes	$ 6,900
Interest deduction	2,400
Earnings before taxes	$ 4,500
Income taxes (at 40%)	1,800
Earnings after taxes	$ 2,700
Preferred dividends	300
Net income available to common	$ 2,400

$$\text{Earnings per share} = \$5.33$$
$$\text{Expected dividends per share} = \$4.25$$

26.5 The Ellis Corporation plans to expand assets by 25 percent. It can finance the expansion with straight debt or with common stock. The interest rate on the debt would be 12 percent. Ellis's current balance sheet and income statement are given in Table P26.5.

Table P26.5

Ellis Corporation Balance Sheet as of December 31, 19X0 (Thousands of Dollars)

Assets		Liabilities	
		Debt (at 10%)	$300
		Common stock, $1 par (100,000 shares outstanding)	100
		Retained earnings	400
Total assets	$800	Total claims	$800

Ellis Corporation Income Statement for Year Ended December 31, 19X0 (Thousands of Dollars)

Sales	$2,300
Total costs (excluding interest)	2,070
Net operating income	$ 230
Debt interest	30
Income before taxes	$ 200
Taxes (at 50%)	100
Net income	$ 100

Earnings per share: $\dfrac{\$100,000}{100,000} = \$1$.

Price-earnings ratio = 10.[a]

Market price = P-E × EPS = 10 × 1 = $10.

[a]The P-E ratio is the market price per share divided by earnings per share. It represents the amount of money an investor is willing to pay for $1.00 of current earnings. The higher the riskiness of a stock, the lower its P-E ratio, other things held constant.

If Ellis Corporation finances the $200,000 expansion with debt, the rate on the incremental debt will be 12 percent, and the price-earnings ratio of the common stock will drop to nine times. If the expansion is financed with equity, the new stock will sell for $8 per share, the rate on debt will be 10 percent, and the price-earnings ratio will remain at ten times. (The opportunity cost of debt is 12 percent. However, use the 10 percent rate on the debt already on the balance sheet, because this is the rate actually being paid.)

a) Assume that the net income before interest and taxes (EBIT) is 10 percent of sales. Calculate EPS at sales levels of $0, $600,000, $2,400,000, $2,800,000, $3,000,000, $3,600,000 and $4,800,000 for financing with (1) debt and (2) common stock. Assume no fixed costs of production.

b) Make a companion chart for EPS and indicate the crossover point in sales (that is, where EPS using bonds equals EPS using stock).

c) Using the price-earnings ratio, calculate the market value per share of common stock for each sales level for both the debt and the equity financing.

d) Using data from Part (c), plot market value per share against level of sales and indicate the crossover point.

e) If the firm follows the policy of seeking to maximize (1) EPS or (2) market price per share, which form of financing should be used?

f) The probability estimates of future sales are the following: 5 percent chance of $0; 10 percent chance of $600,000; 20 percent chance of $2,400,000; 30 percent chance of $2,800,000; 20 percent chance of $3,000,000; 10 percent chance of $3,600,000; and 5 percent chance of $4,800,000. Calculate expected values for EPS, market price per share, the standard deviation, and the coefficient of variation for each alternative.

g) What other factors should be taken into account in choosing between the two forms of financing?

h) Would it matter if the presently outstanding stock were all owned by the final decision maker — the president — and that this represented that individual's entire net worth? Would it matter if the president were compensated entirely by a fixed salary? If the president had a substantial number of stock options?

26.6 a) A manufacturing firm with $60 million of assets judges that it is at the beginning of a three-year growth cycle. It has a total debt-to-assets ratio of 16 percent, and it expects sales and net earnings to grow at a rate of 10 percent a year and stock prices to rise 30 percent a year over the three-year period. The firm will need $6 million at the beginning of the three-year period and another $3 million by the middle of the third year. It is at the beginning of a general business upswing, when money and capital costs are what they generally are after about a year of recession and at the beginning of an upswing. By the middle of the third year, money and capital costs will show their characteristic pattern near the peak of an upswing. How should the firm raise the $6 million and the $3 million?

b) An aerospace company with sales of $25 million a year needs $5 million to finance expansion. It has a debt-to-total-assets ratio of 65 percent; and its common stock, which is widely held, is selling at a price-earnings ratio of 25 times. It is comparing the sale of common stock and convertible debentures. Which do you recommend? Explain.

c) A chemical company has been growing steadily. To finance a growth of sales from $40 million a year to $50 million over a two-year period, it needs $2 million in additional equipment. When additional working capital needs are taken into account, the total additional financing required during the first year is $5 million. Profits will rise by 50 percent after the first ten months. The stock is currently selling at 20 times earnings. The company can borrow on straight debt at $7\frac{1}{2}$ percent or with a convertibility or warrant "sweetener" for $\frac{3}{4}$ percent less. The present debt to total assets ratio is 25 percent. Which form of financing should it employ?

26.7   The Rubik Company is trying to decide whether or not it should call its outstanding debt. It has a $25,000,000 bond issue outstanding which has eight years to maturity and pays a 14 percent annual coupon. The call price on each $1,000 face value bond is $1,100, and the firm has a 40 percent tax rate. If the current market rate on bonds of equivalent risk is 9 percent, what is the net present value of calling the bonds and financing the deal with new bonds of equivalent risk and maturity?

Selected References

Agmon, T.; Ofer, A. R.; and Tamir, A., "Variable Rate Debt Instruments and Corporate Debt Policy," *Journal of Finance*, 36 (March 1981), pp. 113-125.

American Bar Association, *Commentaries on Model Debenture Indenture Provisions*, Chicago, 1971.

Ang, James S., "The Two Faces of Bond Refunding," *Journal of Finance*, 30 (June 1975), pp. 869-874.

Bierwag, G. O., "Measures of Duration," *Economic Inquiry*, 16 (October 1978), pp. 497-507.

———, "Immunization, Duration and the Term Structure," *Journal of Financial and Quantitative Analysis*, 12 (December 1977), pp. 701-742.

Bodie, Zvi, and Taggart, Robert A., "Future Investment Opportunities and the Value of the Call Provision on a Bond," *Journal of Finance*, 33 (September 1978), pp. 1187-1200.

Boyce, W. M., and Kalotay, A. J., "Tax Differentials and Callable Bonds," *Journal of Finance*, 34 (September 1979), pp. 825-838.

Brennan, M., and Schwartz, E., "The Case for Convertibles," *Chase Financial Quarterly*, (Spring 1982), pp. 27-46.

———, "Convertible Bonds: Valuation and Optimal Strategies for Call and Conversion," *Journal of Finance*, (December 1977), pp. 1699-1715.

Cox, John C.; Ingersoll, Jonathan E., Jr.; and Ross, Stephen A., "Duration and the Measurement of Basis Risk," *Journal of Business*, 52 (January 1979), pp. 51-61.

Dyl, Edward A., and Joehnk, Michael D., "Sinking Funds and the Cost of Corporate Debt," *Journal of Finance*, 34 (September 1979), pp. 887-893.

Dyl, Edward A., and Spahr, Ronald W., "Taxes and the Refunding of Discount Bonds," *Journal of Financial Research*, 6 (Winter 1983), pp. 265-273.

Ederington, Louis H., "Negotiated versus Competitive Underwritings of Corporate Bonds," *Journal of Finance*, 31 (March 1976), pp. 17-26.

———, "The Yield Spread on New Issues of Corporate Bonds," *Journal of Finance*, 29 (December 1974), pp. 1531-1543.

Emanuel, David, "A Theoretical Model for Valuing Preferred Stock," *Journal of Finance*, 38 (September 1983), pp. 1133-1155.

Fischer, Donald E., and Wilt, Glenn A., Jr., "Nonconvertible Preferred Stock as a Financing Instrument, 1950-1965," *Journal of Finance*, 23 (September 1968), pp. 611-624.

Fisher, Lawrence, "Determinants of Risk Premiums on Corporate Bonds," *Journal of Political Economy*, 67 (June 1959), pp. 217-237.

Fong, H. Gifford, and Vasicek, Oldrich, "The Tradeoff Between Return and Risk in Immunized Portfolios," *Financial Analysts Journal*, 39 (September/October 1983), pp. 73-78.

Galai, Dan, "Pricing of Optional Bonds," *Journal of Banking and Finance*, 7 (September 1983), pp. 323-337.

Hsia, Chi-Cheng, and Weston, J. Fred, "Price Behavior of Deep Discount Bonds," *Journal of Banking and Finance*, 5 (September 1981), pp. 357-361.

Ingersoll, Jonathan E., Jr., "A Contingent-Claims Valuation of Convertible Securities," *Journal of Financial Economics*, (May 1977), pp. 289-321.

———, "An Examination of Corporate Call Policies on Convertible Securities," *Journal of Finance*, (May 1977), pp. 463-478.

———; Skelton, Jeffrey; and Weil, Roman L., "Duration and Security Risk," *Journal of Financial and Quantitative Analysis*, 13 (November 1978), pp. 627-650.

Jen, Frank C., and Wert, James E., "The Effects of Call Risk on Corporate Bond Yields," *Journal of Finance*, 22 (December 1967), pp. 637-652.

Kalay, A., "Toward a Theory of Corporate Dividend Policy," unpublished Ph.D. thesis, University of Rochester, Rochester, New York, 1979.

Lanstein, Ronald, and Sharpe, William F., "Duration and Security Risk," *Journal of Financial and Quantitative Analysis*, 13 (November 1978), pp. 653-668.

Marks, Kenneth R., and Law, Warren A., "Hedging against Inflation with Floating-Rate Notes," *Harvard Business Review*, 58 (March-April 1980), pp. 106-112.

McConnell, J., and Schlarbaum, G., "The Income Bond Puzzle," *Chase Financial Quarterly*, (Summer 1982), pp. 8-28.

——, "Returns, Risks and the Pricing of Income Bonds, 1956-1976 (Does Money Have an Odor?)," *Journal of Business*, 54 (January 1981), pp. 33-63.

Mikkelson, W., "Convertible Calls and Security Returns," *Journal of Financial Economics*, 9 (September 1981), pp. 237-264.

Morris, James R., "A Model for Corporate Debt Maturity Decisions," *Journal of Financial and Quantitative Analysis*, 11 (September 1976), pp. 339-358.

Myers, S., "Determinants of Corporate Borrowing," *Journal of Financial Economics*, (November 1977), pp. 147-176.

Ofer, Ahron R., and Taggart, Robert A., Jr., "Bond Refunding: A Clarifying Analysis," *Journal of Finance*, 32 (March 1977), pp. 21-30.

——, "'Bond Refunding Reconsidered': Reply," *Journal of Finance*, 35 (March 1980), pp. 197-200.

Pinches, George E., and Singleton, J. Clay, "The Adjustment of Stock Prices to Bond Rating Changes," *Journal of Finance*, 33 (March 1978), pp. 29-44.

Pye, Gordon, "The Value of Call Deferment on a Bond: Some Empirical Results," *Journal of Finance*, 22 (December 1967), pp. 623-636.

Smith, Clifford W., and Warner, Jerold B., "On Financial Contracting: An Analysis of Bond Covenants," *Journal of Financial Economics*, 7 (June 1979), pp. 117-161.

Wakeman, L., "Bond Rating Agencies and Capital Markets," working paper, Graduate School of Management, University of Rochester, Rochester, New York, 1978.

Weinstein, Mark I., "The Seasoning Process of New Corporate Bond Issues," *Journal of Finance*, 33 (December 1978), pp. 1343-1354.

——, "The Effect of a Rating Change Announcement on Bond Price," *Journal of Financial Economics*, (December 1977), pp. 329-350.

Yawitz, Jess B., and Marshall, William J., "The Shortcomings of Duration as a Risk Measure for Bonds," *Journal of Financial Research*, 4 (Summer 1981), pp. 91-101.

Appendix A to Chapter 26

Refunding Decisions

Since 1974, many articles have appeared on bond refunding, as indicated by the Selected References to this appendix. These articles — and the current broad interest in refunding — were stimulated by large fluctuations in the interest rates during the 1970s and 1980s. This appendix discusses the debate about whether the appropriate discount rate is the before- or after-tax cost of debt. It also discusses debt refunding in an era of rising interest rates.

Choosing a Discount Rate for the Bond Refunding Decision

Bond refunding, which takes place when interest rates have fallen, may yield future cash benefits to the firm as the result of the reduction in bond interest payments. Once the contractual terms under which the new bonds will be sold have been established, the interest saving is known with certainty. Therefore, it is generally agreed that the discount rate should be the cost of debt. However, disagreement has arisen on whether the before-tax cost of debt or the after-tax cost of debt should be used, and this is a central question to be addressed in the materials which follow.

The net present value from a bond refunding can be expressed logically by Equation 26A.1:

$$\text{NPV} = \overset{(1)}{\sum_{t=1}^{n} \frac{(1 - T)(r_1 - r_2)D}{(1 + r_2)^t}} - \overset{(2)}{\sum_{t=1}^{n} \frac{(1 - T)r_2\Delta D}{(1 + r_2)^t}}$$

$$- \overset{(3)}{\frac{\Delta D}{(1 + r_2)^n}} - \overset{(4)}{[(1 - T)RC - \Delta D]}, \tag{26A.1}$$

where

$T =$ corporate income tax rate
$RC =$ cost of refunding
$r_1 =$ coupon rate on old issue
$r_2 =$ coupon rate on new issue (also assumed to be the current yield on bonds of equivalent risk)
$D =$ par value (or face value) of debt
$n =$ remaining years to maturity on the old issue
$\Delta D =$ the incremental debt needed to pay for refunding costs.

The four numbered terms on the right-hand side of the equation represent the following:

1. present value of after-tax interest savings on the old bond issue
2. present value of interest that will be paid on incremental debt
3. present value of repayment of the incremental debt at maturity
4. present value of financing issued, the difference between after-tax refunding costs (such as the call premium and flotation costs) and the new financing issued to cover these costs. Later on, we shall assume that all new financing is via new debt.

The sense of each of the terms can also be readily explained. In the first term, the difference in the expression $(r_1 - r_2)(1 - T)$ is the after-tax interest savings, which is multiplied times the value of the old bonds and discounted to arrive at the present value of the interest savings (PVS). In the second term, the after-tax cost of whatever increase in debt is used to finance the refunding costs is also discounted back to the present. The third term is the present value of the incremental debt. In the fourth term, we start with the after-tax refunding costs and deduct the incremental debt. The difference must be the amount of financing needed to refund the debt issue. We have not thus far discussed the discount factor used in the present value calculations. We shall do that in the following analysis.

We begin by simplifying the second term, with the results shown in Equation 26A.2:

$$\sum_{t=1}^{n} \frac{(1 - T)(r_2)\Delta D}{(1 + r_2)^t} = \left[\frac{(1 - T)(r_2)\Delta D}{(1 + r_2)} \right] \sum_{t=0}^{n-1} \frac{1}{(1 + r_2)^t}$$

$$= \left[\frac{(1 - T)r_2\Delta D}{(1 + r_2)} \right] \frac{1 - \dfrac{1}{(1 + r_2)^n}}{1 - \dfrac{1}{(1 + r_2)}}$$

$$= (1 - T)\Delta D[1 - (1 + r_2)^{-n}]. \tag{26A.2}$$

First, we factored a $1/(1 + r_2)$ from the denominator. We were then able to evaluate the denominator, using a standard geometric series, to arrive at the results shown. Having the second term in this simplified form permits the equation to be simplified still further. By multiplying through and regrouping terms, we arrive at the results shown in Equation 26A.3:

$$NPV = PVS - \Delta D(1 - T)[1 - (1 + r_2)^{-n}] - \Delta D(1 + r_2)^{-n} - [(1 - T)RC - \Delta D]$$

$$= PVS - \Delta D + \Delta D(1 + r_2)^{-n} + T \Delta D[1 - (1 + r_2)^{-n}] - \Delta D(1 + r_2)^{-n}$$

$$-[(1 - T)RC] + \Delta D$$

$$= PVS + T \Delta D[1 - (1 + r_2)^{-n}] - (1 - T)RC. \tag{26A.3}$$

If the net present value expression is to be greater than zero, then the after-tax refunding costs must be exceeded by the sum of the other terms in the expression. To show this relationship, we formulate the inequality shown in Equation 26A.4:

$$\sum_{t=1}^{n} \frac{(1 - T)(r_1 - r_2)D}{(1 + r_2)^t} + T \Delta D[1 - (1 + r_2)^{-n}] > (1 - T)RC. \tag{26A.4}$$

Thus far, the analysis has been within the framework of debt with a finite time to maturity. If we let n go to infinity, Equation 26A.4 becomes 26A.5:

$$\frac{(1 - T)(r_1 - r_2)D}{r_2} + T \, \Delta D > (1 - T)RC. \tag{26A.5}$$

The first term represents the standard capitalization of an infinite stream. In the second term, the value of $1/(1 + r_2)^n$ becomes zero.

Additionally, if the total after-tax refunding costs are financed by debt so that we have $\Delta D = (1 - T)RC$, we obtain Equation 26A.6:[1]

$$\frac{(1 - T)(r_1 - r_2)D}{r_2} > (1 - T)RC - T(1 - T)RC$$

$$\frac{(1 - T)(r_1 - r_2)D}{r_2} > (1 - T)RC(1 - T)$$

$$\frac{(1 - T)(r_1 - r_2)D}{(1 - T)r_2} > (1 - T)RC. \tag{26A.6}$$

The result in 26A.6 is the same as that obtained by Ofer and Taggart [1977] when all new financing is via incremental debt. The significance of this result is that if the refunding costs are financed entirely by debt, the incremental debt generates a tax shelter on the full amount of the financing. Hence, the relevant cost becomes the after-tax cost of debt.[2]

Gordon [1974] argued for the use of after-tax cash flows with the before-tax cost of debt as the discount factor. However, his proof is flawed by the use of the valuation model for risky returns in his analysis of nonrisky returns. Also, when bonds are used to finance the refunding costs, additional tax shelter is achieved so that the discount rate is the after-tax rate on the refunding bonds.

Livingston [1980] criticizes the Ofer and Taggart results as well as equivalent textbook procedures developed under the same financing assumptions. To view the nature of the criticism, first define the gain in the value of shareholders' equity as the excess of the gains from refunding over the after-tax refunding costs, as shown in Equation 26A.7:

$$\frac{(1 - T)(r_1 - r_2)D}{(1 - T)r_2} - (1 - T)RC = \Delta S. \tag{26A.7}$$

Next, cancel the $(1 - T)$ expressions in the first term and separate the elements of the numerator.

$$\left(\frac{r_1 D}{r_2} - D\right) - (1 - T)(RC) = \Delta S. \tag{26A.8}$$

Livingston argues that the gain from refunding appears to be the market value of the old bond less the par value of the new bond. But, he objects that the old bond cannot sell for more than its call price plus other (relatively small) refunding costs. Technically, Living-

---

[1]See Laber [1979b].

[2]Note, however, that 26A.6 is also equivalent to discounting the before-tax cash flows at the before-tax cost of debt.

ston is correct. But, the $D(r_1 - r_2)/r_2$ term still measures the value of the interest "saving" from refunding the old bond. The original r_1 and the new r_2 on callable bonds are higher than the rates on noncallable bonds since the issuer must compensate investors for the call option.

Refunding When Interest Rates Have Risen

Widely fluctuating interest rates give rise to opportunities for bond refunding. Bonds sold at high interest rates in the late sixties and early seventies provided opportunities for refunding when interest rates fell in the mid-1970s. The resumption of the sharp rise in interest rates caused those bonds which were sold at lower interest levels to go to a discount by the late 1970s. This raised questions about the profitability of advanced refunding of discounted bonds. The early 1980s also saw a large decline in interest rates.

Interest rate fluctuations in which interest rates go either lower or higher are said to provide opportunities for bond refunding. Lower interest rates may provide opportunities for interest rate savings. Higher interest rates may provide opportunities for buying in bonds at a discount. Before becoming immersed in the details of the following analysis, we should like first to present as an overview some general principles that should be kept in mind as a framework for the subsequent detailed computations.

In the absence of special characteristics or restrictions, neither falling interest rates nor rising interest rates provide an obvious basis for savings to corporate financial managers. Lower or higher interest rates simply represent the costs of funds at a particular time, and without special restrictions provide no opportunities for gains or losses. What makes refunding at lower interest rates advantageous is the call option that is inserted in corporate bond indentures. For example, if the bond is issued at a 9 percent interest rate and if interest rates subsequently fall to 6 percent, a noncallable perpetual bond issued at a par value of 100 would sell at 150 at the lower 6 percent interest yield basis. If the company has a call option which permits it to buy in the bond at 105, for example, the firm can achieve interest savings with a substantial present value.

On the other hand, if the market had accurately priced the value of the call privilege, then the bond refunding would not represent a net gain. In such a case, the bond refunding would represent only the interest savings that the company would have to realize in order to be compensated for the higher yield it was required to offer on callable bonds.

With respect to bonds that sell at a discount because interest rates have risen substantially, there is no special privilege analogous to the call option. The firm simply goes into the market and buys its bonds at a discount because the going yield is higher than the coupon rates paid on its existing bonds. One attractive feature to business firms is that the difference between the value of the bond shown on its books and the market price at which the bonds are purchased can be recorded as a realized profit from the standpoint of reporting income. The firm is thus able to report higher income than it otherwise would. However, from a cash flow standpoint, this is a disadvantage, not an advantage. The reported profit is subject to income taxation. The gain is simply a paper gain. It has not produced an increment of positive cash flows for the company. The net effect of reporting the income and the taxation of it is to reduce the cash flows for the firm, not to increase them. Thus, unless the taxation can be avoided, net cash flows are reduced by buying in the discount bonds.

Consider the situation where interest rates have risen substantially above the coupon rates on the firm's outstanding bonds. For example, suppose that Firm F had sold ten $1,000 perpetual bonds at 6 percent, but the prevailing yield on such bonds is now 10 percent. The old bonds now sell for $600 each. Firm F can retire the bonds at $6,000, reporting a profit of $4,000. The interest paid on the old bonds is $600. The total interest on the $6,000 of new bonds issued at 10 percent to buy up the old bonds would also be $600. Thus, Firm F experiences no change in interest costs. If the gain of $4,000 is taxed at, say, 40 percent, the net cash flow to the firm is reduced by $1,600. Thus, from a pure cash flow standpoint, all that has really happened is that the firm has an additional cash outflow required by the amount of taxes it has to pay on the increase in reported income.

The Internal Revenue Code provides that a corporation may elect to have excluded from gross income the gain when it buys its own bond at a discount.[3] But, if a corporation does make this election, the basis of the property against which the obligations were issued is reduced by the amount of the gain.[4] This may more than offset the advantage of not reporting the gain from the repurchase of the discount bond, since the depreciation basis is reduced and the basis for determining the gain or loss on a subsequent sale is also reduced. Thus, it is difficult to envisage how the negative effects of the tax payments on the actual cash flows of the firm can be avoided.

A superior strategy would be to buy a bond of the same quality at par that pays 10 percent. The interest income will just cancel with the interest expense of the old bond, but there will be no tax liability. From a cash flow standpoint, the firm avoids the $1,600 cash tax payment.

An article in *Business Week* of November 12, 1979, described the very active operations of investment bankers in arranging for helping clients buy up bonds at a discount. The context of this presentation was that the firms were going to have to make purchases for bond sinking funds in one, two, three, or five years anyhow: In other words, the firms had decided that it was a good strategy to make anticipatory purchases, since when the purchases would have to be made in subsequent years, the bonds might not be at such deep discounts. The bonds could be purchased at a saving and used to meet future sinking fund requirements as they became effective.

We believe that this analysis also requires qualification. By buying its own bonds at a discount, a firm would have reported profits and taxable income. The basis for the anticipatory bond purchases appears to be the expectation that interest rates would be lower in the future. If the firm really believed that interest rates were going to be lower, it could buy bonds of equal quality (or a portfolio of bonds) and then hold them until it was required to purchase bonds for its own sinking fund. If interest rates fell in the meantime, the firm would have realized capital gain on the bonds that it had purchased. It would have an equal paper loss on its own bonds that it did not purchase. At the same time, it would be receiving a higher yield on the bonds that it purchased at the market when interest rates were higher. Furthermore, it would have obtained protection against a rise in the required yield on its own bonds through quality deterioration. But, the fundamental point is that at a minimum, it would defer the taxes on the capital gain involved in the interest rate change by buying bonds other than its own.

These general observations provide the foundation for a key to understanding some of the literature in this area. Ang [1975] made a presentation in which he sought to demonstrate that refunding was advantageous not only when current interest rates fall below interest rates at issue but also possibly when current interest rates rise above the interest rate at issue. Single-period and multiperiod models were used along with the hypothetical application using dynamic programming.

However, Mayor and McCoin [1978] demonstrate (following the general logic set forth in this analysis) that refunding when interest rates have risen cannot be profitable unless

---

[3]Internal Revenue Code, Secs. 108(a); 1.108(a)-1.
[4]Ibid., Secs. 1017; 1.1017-1.

implementation costs are negative. Implementation costs are measured by brokerage commissions plus the difference between the average purchase price and the current market
price. Implementation costs cannot be reasonably assumed to be negative. In the multiperiod model, refunding when interest rates have risen, again depends upon very extreme assumptions. First, implementation costs are assumed to be very small. Second,
implicit in the analysis is that interest rates will subsequently fall, and the firm will realize
a capital gain from the interest rate change. This second assumption then means that the
firm is able to forecast future interest rates correctly, and part of the gain from refunding is
to buy the bonds when interest rates are high and sell them when interest rates are lower.
If the firm is able to forecast future interest rates, it does not have to engage in refunding
to make a profit. It will simply buy bonds when interest rates are high and sell them when
interest rates have fallen.

This general result for refunding criteria when interest rates have risen can be made
more explicit with reference to the general points made by employing the framework
developed by Kalotay [1978]. The most general expression for the advanced refunding of
discounted debt is set forth by Kalotay in Equation 26A.9, where NPV is expressed as a
percentage of the debt issue.

$$NPV = -p + \sum_{t=1}^{n} \frac{(1-T)r_1}{[1+(1-T)r_2]^t} + \frac{1}{[1+(1-T)r_2]^n}$$

$$- \sum_{t=0}^{M} \frac{T(1-p)}{M+1} \times \frac{1}{[1+(1-T)r_2]^t} - (1-T)RC'. \qquad (26A.9)$$

The symbols are the same as defined earlier, with the exception of p and M; p is the price at
which the discounted bond can be purchased, expressed as a decimal ratio of its par value.
M is the number of years over which the taxable gain can be amortized. The second term
on the right-hand side of the equation is the discounted interest payments. The third term
is the discounted principal payment. The fourth term is represented by the tax obligations
associated with the gain $(1-p)$. The RC' term represents other refunding costs that have
not been explicitly dealt with to this point. In Equation 26A.10, the same equation is
rewritten with the summation expressions carried out.

$$NPV = -p + \frac{r_1}{r_2}\left\{1 - [1+(1-T)r_2]^{-n}\right\} + [1+(1-T)r_2]^{-n} - \frac{T(1-p)}{M+1}$$

$$\times \left\{\frac{[1+(1-T)r_2] - [1+(1-T)r_2]^{-(M-1)}}{(1-T)r_2}\right\} - (1-T)RC'. \qquad (26A.10)$$

The nature of the expressions in the above equation can be shown by using illustrative
values for the variables involved. Let $p = 0.57$, $r_1 = 0.0425$, $r_2 = 0.11$, $n = 18$, $RC' = 0.02$,
$T = 0.5$, and $M = 18$. Under the assumptions in the illustration, the value of the discounted interest payments and the discounted principal payments was 0.62, while the
purchase price of the bond was assumed to be 0.57. This represented a gain of 0.05. The
taxable income, however, is the difference between the par value of the bond at one and
the purchase price of 0.57. Thus, the taxable gain is 0.43. The present value of the tax
obligations then turns out to be −0.13. The difference between the 0.05 gain from buying a
bond with a value of 0.62 at 0.57 is offset by the additional tax obligations of 0.13. The
result is a negative 9 percent ($-0.57 + 0.24 + 0.38 - 0.13 - 0.01 = -0.09$).

Kalotay emphasizes that profitable refunding when interest rates have risen is probably plausible only if for some reason there are no tax obligations or if the tax obligations are amortized over an extremely long period of time. To illustrate this, Kalotay takes the extreme case where the firm discounts interest payments and principal payments at the after-tax cost of debt while the individual investor in the market uses the before-tax rate of interest as the discount factor. This results in an even lower value of p. Under the numerical values previously assumed, the value of p becomes 0.48. Or, alternatively, the underlying determinants of p are shown in Equation 26A.11. Suppose

$$p = \sum_{t=1}^{n} \frac{r_1}{(1 + r_2)^t} + \frac{1}{(1 + r_2)^n} = \frac{r_1}{r_2} [1 - (1 + r_2)^{-n}] + \frac{1}{(1 + r_2)^n}. \qquad \textbf{(26A.11)}$$

If these underlying determinants of p are substituted in Equation 26A.10, and if we use the numerical values previously assumed plus the assumption that p is determined by the before-tax cost of debt, the NPV becomes -2 percent ($-0.48 + 0.24 + 0.38 - 0.15 - 0.01 = -0.02$). Kalotay comments that the assumption that p is determined by discounting at the before-tax cost of debt is more favorable to the refunding decision at higher interest rates. Yet, under plausible relationships, the NPV is still negative.

The thrust of the logic set forth above and the concrete framework presented by Kalotay is this: To initiate the possibility of favorable refunding requires that the price at which the bond can be purchased be lower than the appropriately discounted interest payments plus the discounted principal payment. Second, the difference between the par value of the bond and its purchase price is taxable income. Profitable refunding requires either that this differential is for some reason not taxable or, alternatively, that the amortization period for the taxable income be extremely long.

Summary

We reiterate our general conclusions. When declines in the general level of interest rates have occurred, the call privilege appears to provide an opportunity for reducing interest expenses. But, if the call privilege had been correctly priced, then, on average, the exercise of this option simply compensates the firm for the higher interest rates that it paid by having the call provision in the indenture of the bonds it sold. The firm paid a higher interest rate differential that it can recoup only by exercising the option it has purchased. The refunding operation then is required to "balance the books" in some sense.

The other face of bond refunding is considered when interest rates have risen. Unless the taxes on the gain from buying back the bonds can be avoided, the net cash flow effects are negative. The absolute amount of interest costs would be essentially unchanged. Therefore, unless the taxes can be avoided without other disadvantages, the effects of refunding when interest rates have risen would appear to be unfavorable. The conclusion seems to be that bond refunding has but one face, not two.

Selected References

Ang, James S., "The Two Faces of Bond Refunding," *Journal of Finance*, 30 (June 1975), pp. 869-874.

———, "The Two Faces of Bond Refunding: Reply," *Journal of Finance*, 33 (March 1978), pp. 354-356.

Bierman, Harold, "The Bond Refunding Decision," *Financial Management*, 1 (Summer 1972), pp. 22-29.

Gordon, M. J., "A General Solution to the Buy or Lease Decision: A Pedagogical Note," *Journal of Finance*, 29 (March 1974), pp. 245-250.

Kalotay, A. J., "On the Advanced Refunding of Discounted Debt," *Financial Management*, 7 (Summer 1978), pp. 7-13.

Kolodny, Richard, "The Refunding Decision in Near Perfect Markets," *Journal of Finance*, 29 (December 1974), pp. 1467-1477.

Laber, Gene, "The Effect of Bond Refunding on Shareholder Wealth: Comment," *Journal of Finance*, 34 (June 1979a), pp. 795-799.

———, "Implications of Discount Rates and Financing Assumptions for Bond Refunding Decisions," *Financial Management*, 8 (Spring 1979b), pp. 7-12.

Livingston, Miles, "Bond Refunding Reconsidered: Comment," *Journal of Finance*, 35 (March 1980), pp. 191-196.

———, "The Effect of Bond Refunding on Shareholder Wealth: Comment," *Journal of Finance*, 34 (June 1979), pp. 801-804.

Mayor, Thomas H., and McCoin, Kenneth G., "Bond Refunding: One or Two Faces?" *Journal of Finance*, 33 (March 1978), pp. 349-353.

Ofer, Ahron R., and Taggart, Robert A., Jr., "Bond Refunding: A Clarifying Analysis," *Journal of Finance*, 32 (March 1977), pp. 21-30.

———, "'Bond Refunding Reconsidered': Reply," *Journal of Finance*, 35 (March 1980), pp. 197-200.

Chapter 27 Lease Financing

Firms are generally interested in using buildings and equipment. One way of obtaining their use is to buy them, but an alternative is to lease them. Prior to the 1950s, leasing was most often associated with real estate — land and buildings — but today, it is possible to lease virtually any kind of fixed asset. We estimate that from 15 to 20 percent of all new capital equipment put in use by business each year is leased. In many cases, our analysis will show that leasing is a perfect substitute for borrowing. Hence, managers should think of the lease/ borrow decision rather than the lease/buy decision.

Leasing simultaneously provides for the use of assets and their financing. One advantage over debt is that the lessor has a better position than a creditor if the user firm experiences financial difficulties. If the lessee does not meet the lease obligations, the lessor has a stronger legal right to take back the asset, because the lessor still legally owns it. A creditor, even a secured creditor, encounters costs and delays in recovering assets that have been directly or indirectly financed. Since the lessor has less risk than other financing sources used in acquiring assets, the riskier the firm seeking financing, the greater is the reason for the supplier of financing to formulate a leasing arrangement rather than a loan. The relative tax positions of lessors and users of assets may also affect the lease versus own decision.

Types of Leases

Leases take several different forms, the most important of which are sale and leaseback, service or operating leases, and straight financial leases. These three major types of leases are described below.

Sale and Leaseback

Under a sale and leaseback arrangement, a firm owning land, buildings, or equipment sells the property to a financial institution and simultaneously executes an agreement to lease the property back for a certain period under specific terms.

Note that the seller, or *lessee*, immediately receives the purchase price put up by the buyer, or *lessor*. At the same time, the seller-lessee retains the use of the property. This parallel is carried over to the lease payment schedule. Under a mortgage loan arrangement, the financial institution receives a series of equal payments just sufficient to amortize the loan and to provide the lender with a specified rate of return on investment. Under a sale and leaseback arrangement, the lease payments are set up in the same manner. The payments are sufficient to return the full purchase price to the financial institution in addition to providing it with some return on its investment.

Operating Leases

Operating, or service, leases include both financing and maintenance services. IBM is one of the pioneers of the service lease contract. Computers and office copying machines, together with automobiles and trucks, are the primary types of equipment covered by operating leases. The leases ordinarily call for the lessor to maintain and service the leased equipment, and the costs of this maintenance are either built into the lease payments or contracted for separately.

Another important characteristic of the service lease is that, frequently, it is not fully amortized. In other words, the payments required under the lease contract are *not* sufficient to recover the full cost of the equipment. Obviously, however, the lease contract is written for considerably less than the expected life of the leased equipment, and the lessor expects to recover the cost either in subsequent renewal payments or on disposal of the equipment.

A final feature of the service lease is that, frequently, it contains a cancellation clause, giving the lessee the right to cancel the lease and return the equipment before the expiration of the basic agreement. This is an important consideration for the lessee, who can return the equipment if technological developments render it obsolete or if it simply is no longer needed.

Financial Leases

A strict financial lease is one that does not provide for maintenance services, is not cancellable, and is fully amortized (that is, the lessor contracts for rental payments equal to the full price of the leased equipment). The typical arrangement involves the following steps:

1. The firm that will use the equipment selects the specific items it requires and negotiates the price and delivery terms with the manufacturer or distributor.
2. Next, the user firm arranges with a bank or leasing company for the latter to buy the equipment from the manufacturer or distributor, simultaneously executing an agreement to lease the equipment from the financial institution. The terms call for full amortization of the financial institution's cost, plus a return on the lessor's investment. The lessee generally has the option to renew the lease at a reduced rental on expiration of the basic lease but does not have the right to cancel the basic lease without completely paying off the financial institution.

Financial leases are almost the same as sale and leaseback arrangements, the main difference being that the leased equipment is new and the lessor buys it from a manufacturer or a distributor instead of from the user-lessee. A sale and leaseback can thus be thought of as a special type of financial lease.

Internal Revenue Service Requirements for a Lease

The full amount of the annual lease payments is deductible for income tax purposes, provided the Internal Revenue Service agrees that a particular contract is a genuine lease, and not simply an installment loan called a lease. This makes it important that the lease contract be written in a form acceptable to the IRS. Following are the major requirements for bona fide lease transactions from the standpoint of the IRS.

1. The term must be less than 30 years; otherwise, the lease is regarded as a form of sale.
2. The rent must represent a reasonable return to the lessor — in the range of 7 to 12 percent on the investment.
3. The renewal option must be bona fide, and this requirement can best be met by giving the lessee the first option to meet an equal bona fide outside offer.
4. There must be no repurchase option; if there is, the lessee should merely be given parity with an equal outside offer.

Accounting for Leases

In November 1976, the Financial Accounting Standards Board issued its Statement of Financial Accounting Standards No. 13, *Accounting for Leases*. Like other FASB statements, the standards set forth must be followed by business firms if their financial statements are to receive certification by auditors. FASB Statement No. 13 has implications both for the utilization of leases and for their accounting treatment. The elements of FASB Statement No. 13 most relevant for financial analysis of leases are summarized below.

For some types of leases, this FASB statement requires that the obligation be capitalized on the asset side of the balance sheet with a reduced lease obligation on the liability side. The accounting treatment depends on the type of lease. The classification is more detailed than the two categories of operating and financial leases described above.

From the standpoint of the lessee:
1. Capital leases
2. Operating leases (all leases other than capital leases)

From the standpoint of the lessor:
1. Sales-type leases
2. Direct financing leases
3. Leveraged leases
4. Operating leases (all leases other than the first three)

A lease is classified in Statement No. 13 as a capital lease if it meets one or more of four Paragraph 7 criteria:

1. The lease transfers ownership of the property to the lessee by the end of the lease term.
2. The lease gives the lessee the option to purchase the property at a price sufficiently below the expected fair value of the property that the exercise of the option is highly probable.
3. The lease term is equal to 75 percent or more of the estimated economic life of the property.
4. The present value of the minimum lease payments exceeds 90 percent of the fair value of the property at the inception of the lease. The discount factor to be used in calculating the present value is the implicit rate used by the lessor or the lessee's incremental borrowing rate, whichever is lower. (Note that the lower discount factor represents a higher present value factor and, therefore, a higher calculated present value for a given pattern of lease payments. It thus increases the likelihood that the 90 percent test will be met and that the lease will be classified as a capital lease.)

From the standpoint of the lessee, if a lease is not a capital lease, it is classified as an operating lease. From the standpoint of the lessor, four types of leases are defined: (1)

sales-type leases, (2) direct financing leases, (3) leveraged leases, and (4) operating leases representing all leases other than the first three types. Sales-type leases and direct financing leases meet one or more of the four Paragraph 7 criteria and both of the Paragraph 8 criteria, which are

1. Collectibility of the minimum lease payments is reasonably predictable.
2. No important uncertainties surround the amount of unreimbursable costs yet to be incurred by the lessor under the lease.

Sales-type leases give rise to profit (or loss) to the lessor — the fair value of the leased property at the inception of the lease is greater (or less) than its cost of carrying amount. Sales-type leases normally arise when manufacturers or dealers use leasing in marketing their products. Direct financing leases are leases other than leveraged leases for which the cost-of-carrying amount is equal to the fair value of the leased property at the inception of the lease. Leveraged leases are direct financing leases in which substantial financing is provided by a long-term creditor on a nonrecourse basis with respect to the general credit of the lessor.

Accounting by Lessees

For operating leases, rentals must be charged to expense over the lease term, with disclosures of future rental obligations in total as well as by each of the following five years. For lessees, capital leases are to be capitalized and shown on the balance sheet both as a fixed asset and a noncurrent obligation. Capitalization represents the present value of the minimum lease payments minus that portion of lease payments representing executory costs such as insurance, maintenance, and taxes to be paid by the lessor (including any profit return in such charges). The discount factor is as described in Paragraph 7(4) — the lower of the implicit rates used by the lessor and the incremental borrowing rate of the lessee.

The asset must be amortized in a manner consistent with the lessee's normal depreciation policy for owned assets. During the lease term, each lease payment is to be allocated between a reduction of the obligation and the interest expense to produce a constant rate of interest on the remaining balance of the obligation. Thus, for capital leases, the balance sheet includes the items in Table 27.1.

In addition to the balance sheet capitalization of capital leases, substantial additional footnote disclosures are required for both capital and operating leases. These include a description of leasing arrangements, an analysis of leased property under capital leases by major classes of property, a schedule by years of future minimum lease payments (with

Table 27.1   Company X Balance Sheet

Assets	December 31, 1986	December 31, 1987	Liabilities	December 31, 1986	December 31, 1987
			Current:		
Leased property under capital leases, less accumulated amortization	XXX	XXX	Obligations under capital leases	XXX	XXX
			Noncurrent:		
			Obligations under capital leases	XXX	XXX

executory and interest costs broken out for capital leases), and contingent rentals for operating leases.

FASB Statement No. 13 sets forth requirements for capitalizing capital leases and for standardizing disclosures by lessees for both capital leases and operating leases. Lease commitments, therefore, do not represent "off-balance-sheet" financing for capital assets, and standard disclosure requirements make general the footnote reporting of information on operating leases. Hence, the argument that leasing represents a form of off-balance-sheet financing that lenders may not take into account in their analysis of the financial position of firms seeking financing is simply invalid.

It is unlikely that sophisticated lenders were ever fooled by off-balance-sheet leasing obligations. However, the capitalization of capital leases and the standard disclosure requirements for operating leases will make it easier for general users of financial reports to obtain additional information on firms' leasing obligations. Hence, the requirements of FASB Statement No. 13 are useful. Probably, the extent or use of leasing will remain substantially unaltered, since the particular circumstances that have provided a basis for its use in the past are not likely to be greatly affected by the increased disclosure requirements.

The Financing Decision: Lease versus Borrow

We next consider the framework for the analysis of the cost of owning with the cost of leasing. The form of leasing to be analyzed initially will be a pure financial lease which is fully amortized, noncancellable, and without provision for maintenance services. Furthermore, we assume that the asset's salvage value is zero and that there is no investment tax credit.

In concept, the first screening test is whether, from a capital budgeting standpoint, the project passes the investment hurdle rate. The second question is then whether leasing or some other method of financing, namely borrowing, is the least expensive method of financing the project.

Alternatively, it could be argued that we do not know what the cost of capital (and, therefore, the investment screening rate) is until we have determined the least expensive method of financing. Having determined this method, we can determine the applicable investment screening hurdle rate for the decision of whether to undertake the project from a capital budgeting standpoint.

To lay a foundation for the leasing versus owning cost comparison, the lessor's point of view will first be considered. The leasing company, or lessor, could be a commercial bank, a subsidiary of a commercial bank, or an independent leasing company. These various types of lessors are considered to be providing financial intermediation services of essentially the same kind. Each form of financial intermediary is considered to be providing a product, which represents a form of senior debt financing to the company that uses the equipment. Since the product that is being sold by the financial intermediary is a debt instrument, the income to that intermediary is considered to be a return on debt which earns the intermediary's cost of capital. This is equivalent to the judgment that the financial intermediary's cost of capital, composed of both debt and equity capital, is approximately equal to the rate charged on the debt (or equivalent) instruments that comprise its assets (the assets of the lessor in our analysis).

We can then proceed to calculate the required lease-rental charge that must be made by the lessor to obtain a fair rate of return for a lending position. To illustrate the analysis, assume the following data:

$$
\begin{aligned}
I_0 &= \text{cost of an asset} = \$20{,}000 \\
\text{Dep} &= \text{annual economic and tax depreciation charge} \\
k_b &= \text{before-tax cost of debt} = 8\% \\
T &= \text{lessor's corporate tax rate} = 40\% \\
n &= \text{economic life and tax depreciation life of the asset} = 5 \text{ years} \\
\text{NPV}_{LOR} &= \text{net present value of the lease-rental income from the assets to the lessor}
\end{aligned}
$$

With the above facts, the equilibrium lease-rental rate in a competitive market of lessors can be calculated. What has been posed is a standard capital budgeting question: What cash flow return from the use of an asset will earn the applicable cost of capital? The investment in the capital budgeting project, is $-I_0$. The return is composed of two elements: the cash inflow from the lease rental and the tax shelter from depreciation. The discount factor is the lessor's weighted cost of capital, which, as we have indicated, will be equal to the applicable rate on debt instruments of the risk of the cash flows involved. As Myers, Dill, and Bautista [1976] have pointed out, the weighted average cost of capital of the financial intermediary is

$$
k_L = k_{UL}(1 - \lambda T). \tag{27.1}
$$

For the financial intermediary, the lambda (λ) is the debt per dollar of assets leased. In other words, it is the capital structure employed in the leasing project. Equation 27.1 is the Modigliani-Miller definition of the weighted average cost of capital, which was discussed in Chapter 21. For the data assumed in the example, we can compute the cost of capital of the lessor by using Equation 27.1 as shown below. Here we postulate that the all-equity financing rate for the lessor (k_{UL}) is 8.57 percent and that the debt to assets ratio, λ, is 0.75.

$$
\begin{aligned}
k_L &= k_{UL}(1 - \lambda T) \\
&= 8.57\%[1 - 0.75(0.4)] \\
&= 6\%.
\end{aligned}
$$

The after-tax weighted cost of capital to the lessor is 6 percent. In other words, the bank or leasing company has to earn at least 6 percent after taxes in order for the lease to have a positive net present value. Note that the before-tax rate of return, which is the lessor's lending rate, will be

$$
k_b = \frac{k_L}{1 - T} = \frac{.06}{1 - .4} = 10\%.
$$

Next, we can compute the minimum competitive lease fee which would be charged by the lessor. Equation 27.2 discounts the lease cash flows at the lessor's after-tax cost of capital. The cash flows are the after-tax lease payments received plus the depreciation tax shield provided because the lessor owns the asset. The NPV of the lease to the lessor is

$$
\begin{aligned}
\text{NPV}_{LOR} &= -I_0 + \sum_{t=1}^{n} \frac{L_t(1 - T) + T\text{Dep}_t}{(1 + k_L)^t} \\
&= -I_0 + \text{PVIFA}(6\%, 5 \text{ yrs.})[L_t(1 - T) + T\text{Dep}_t], \tag{27.2}
\end{aligned}
$$

where

L_t = periodic lease payment (assumed to be paid at the end of each period)
Dep_t = amount of depreciation expense in Period t. Using straight line depreciation, $Dep_t = \$4{,}000$.

We can now solve for the equilibrium lease-rental rate required by the lessor by utilizing the data inputs we have provided.[1] The NPV of the lease is set equal to zero so that we can compute the minimum lease payment required by the lessor. The minimum fee will also be the competitive fee if the leasing industry is perfectly competitive.

$$0 = -\$20{,}000 + (4.2124)[0.6L_t + 0.4(\$4{,}000)]$$

$$L_t = \$5{,}246.$$

Presented with a lease-rental rate of $5,246, the user firm takes the lease fee as an input in making a comparison of the cost of leasing with the cost of borrowing. The analysis of the possible benefits of leasing as compared with borrowing involves the analysis of the following cash flows:

1. A cash savings equal to the dollar amount of the investment outlay, I_0, which the firm does not have to incur if it leases.
2. A cash outflow amounting to the present value of the after-tax lease dollars which must be paid out, $PV[L_t(1 - T)]$.
3. The present value of the opportunity cost of the lost depreciation tax shield, $PV(T\,Dep_t)$.
4. The present value of the *change* in the interest tax shield on debt which is displaced by the lease financing, $PV[T\Delta(k_bB_t)]$.

These four terms are presented in Equation 27.3, which gives the net advantage of leasing, NAL, as compared with borrowing in present value terms:

$$\text{NAL} = I_0 - PV[L_t(1 - T)] - PV[T\,Dep_t] + PV[T\Delta(k_bB_t)]. \qquad \textbf{(27.3)}$$

We shall assume that from the standpoint of the user firm, debt and lease financing are perfect substitutes. This is certainly true for strict financial leases. Therefore, the fourth term in Equation 27.3 reflects a dollar-for-dollar substitution of debt tax shield for leasing tax shield applied to the portion of the asset which would be debt-financed at the project's optimal capital structure.

Since both the lease payments and the foregone depreciation tax shields have the same risk for the lessee as for the lessor, they can be discounted at the before-tax cost of debt, that is, 10 percent. Alternatively, as shown by Myers, Dill, and Bautista [1976], we can discount the cash flows exclusive of interest tax shields at the after-tax cost of capital (which is 6 percent). In order to see why, note that the fourth term in Equation 27.3 is the opportunity cost of the interest tax shield which is lost because the firm decides to lease rather than borrow to finance ownership. Throughout the text, we have explicitly excluded interest costs from our definition of cash flows because the effect of these costs as

---

[1]We have assumed that all lease payments are made in arrears, that is, at the end of each year. However, most actual lease contracts require lease payments to be made at the beginning of each time period.

well as their tax shield is accounted for by discounting at the after-tax cost of capital. Given our assumptions, discounting the first three terms in Equation 27.3 at the after-tax cost of debt is the same as discounting all four terms at the before-tax cost of debt. Therefore, we can write the NPV of the lease from the lessee's point of view as

$$\text{NAL} = I_0 - \sum_{t=1}^{n} \frac{L_t(1 - T) + T\text{Dep}_t}{[1 + (1 - T)k_b]^t}. \tag{27.4}$$

Note that Equation 27.4 is exactly the same as Equation 27.2, the value of the lease from the lessor's point of view, if two conditions are met: (1) The lessee and the lessor have the same tax rate, T, and (2) the after-tax weighted average cost of capital to the lessor, k_L, is equal to the after-tax cost of borrowing to the lessee. For the time being, we have assumed the tax rates of the lessee and lessor are equal, but they need not be. The discount rates have to be the same because the cash flows in the numerators of Equations 27.2 and 27.4 are identical and have the same risk. The rate earned by the lessor is the rate paid by the lessee. Substituting the numbers from our example into Equation 27.4, we have

$$\text{NAL} = I_0 - \text{PVIFA}(6\%,5 \text{ yrs.})[L_t(1 - T)] - \text{PVIFA}(6\%,5 \text{ yrs.})[T\text{Dep}_t]$$

$$= 20,000 - 4.2124(5,246)(1 - 0.4) - 4.2124(0.4)(4,000)$$

$$= 20,000 - 13,259 - 6,740$$

$$= 20,000 - 19,999 \cong 0.$$

This result tells us that the firm is indifferent between the two methods of financing the project, namely leasing or borrowing. The first and last terms on the right-hand side of the equation represent the costs of borrowing in order to own the asset. The investment outlay is $\$I$ and the lost depreciation tax shield is $T\text{Dep}_t$. The second term is the cost of leasing.

$$\text{Cost of borrowing} = I_0 - \text{PVIFA}(6\%,5 \text{ yrs.})[T\text{Dep}_t] = 20,000 - 6,740$$

$$= 13,260.$$

$$\text{Cost of leasing} = \text{PVIFA}(6\%,5 \text{ yrs.})[L_t(1 - T)]$$

$$= 13,259.$$

In our example, the cost of borrowing equals the cost of leasing; hence, the net advantage of leasing is zero. Thus, there is equilibrium between the lessor market and the user market. The lessor earns its cost of capital, which determines the lease-rental charge that it must make. At this lease-rental rate, and given that the lessee and lessor have identical tax rates, then the lessee is indifferent between borrowing to own the asset or leasing it.

Note that in determining the lessor's cost of capital, we started with the all-equity financing rate for the lessor, k_{UL}, that would be applicable to the debt instrument portfolio, or lease portfolio, of the financial intermediary. Given the appropriate leverage ratio for the lessor, λ, we arrived at the after-tax cost of capital of the lessor. When this is placed on a before-tax basis, it represents the cost of debt borrowing or the implicit capital cost in the lease financing contract. All the required conditions for indifference between leasing and borrowing are obtained.

Whenever the lessor has a higher tax rate than the lessee, there is a possibility (but not necessity) of a financial advantage of leasing over borrowing in order to finance a project. In order to illustrate this result, let us assume that the numbers from the lessor's point of view are unchanged. With a 40 percent tax rate, the lessor would require a lease fee of $L_t = \$5,246$ in order to earn 6 percent after taxes. But, suppose the lessee's tax rate is 20 percent rather than 40 percent as assumed earlier. If so, the after-tax cost of debt to the lessee increases from $(1 - T)k_b = (1 - .4).10 = 6\%$ to $(1 - .2).10 = 8\%$. Substituting the lease fee and depreciation opportunity costs into Equation 27.4, along with the lower 20 percent tax rate and the higher after-tax borrowing rate (8 percent), we have

$$\text{NAL} = I_0 - \text{PVIFA}(8\%,5 \text{ yrs.})[L_t(1 - T)] - \text{PVIFA}(8\%,5 \text{ yrs.})T\text{Dep}_t$$

$$= 20,000 - 3.9927(5,246)(1 - .2) - 3.9927(.2)(4,000)$$

$$= 20,000 - 16,757 - 3,194$$

$$= 49.$$

Now the net advantage of leasing is positive because the cost of borrowing is greater than the cost of leasing. The lease has a positive NPV. Therefore, from the lessee's point of view, leasing is preferred to borrowing as a means of financing the project. The increased value to the lessee results from the fact that the lessor can take better advantage of the tax shelters (depreciation, interest expenses, and investment tax credits) because of the lessor's higher tax rate.

The Investment Decision

So far, we have analyzed leasing as a perfect substitute for borrowing. The issue has been how to finance the project. But now, we must turn to the central issue, namely, whether the investment should be undertaken in the first place. If the project has a large negative net present value, it will not make any difference how we finance it. Any value added by financing can be easily outweighed by unfavorable cash flows from the project itself. Also, remember that the strict financial leases we have been analyzing are not cancellable, except via bankruptcy.

Owning an asset exposes one to more risk than simply taking a lending or a lease position. Owning and operating a project involves the total risk of its cash flows, not merely the relatively secure risk of a debt position. Suppose we define k_U as the all-equity financing rate of return required on the project. We know that the risk-adjusted rate of return on the project, k_U, is greater than the before-tax borrowing rate, k_b, and that, in turn, this is greater than the lessor's after-tax cost of capital, k_L (that is, $k_U > k_b > k_L$). Suppose that the all-equity financing rate, given the operating risks of the project, is $k_U = 13.33\%$, that the project can carry 50 percent debt to total assets, and that the firm's tax rate is 20 percent. Given these facts, we can use the Modigliani-Miller definition of the weighted average cost of capital, Equation 27.1, to compute the discount rate for the project's cash flows:

$$k(\text{project}) = k_U(1 - \lambda T)$$

$$= .1333(1 - .5(.2))$$

$$= 12\%.$$

Suppose that the project costs $20,000 as before, that it has a five-year life, that the firm uses straight line depreciation, that the project increases annual revenues by $10,000 and costs by $4,068. Using the capital budgeting techniques of Chapter 6, the NPV of the project is

$$NPV = -I_0 + \sum_{t=1}^{n} \frac{(R - C)(1 - T) + T\text{Dep}}{[1 + k(\text{project})]^t}$$

$$= -20,000 + \text{PVIFA}(12\%,5 \text{ yrs.})[(10,000 - 4,068)(1 - .2) + .2(4,000)]$$

$$= -20,000 + 3.6048[(5,932)(.8) + .2(4,000)]$$

$$= -20,000 + 19,991$$

$$= -9.$$

Under our assumptions, the project should be rejected. However, since an additional $49 is added if we lease, the value added by lease financing is enough to raise the project to a positive NPV. Note, however, that if there were other projects which are mutually exclusive with the one under consideration and which can be leased, then one of them should be accepted if its NPV is higher.

Alternative Computation Procedures in the Leasing Analysis

Thus far, we have made the leasing versus owning analysis using compact equations. The same results can be obtained when the flows are tabulated by years. To illustrate, we shall use data similar to the previous example. The cost of the asset is $20,000, and the required lease-rental rate is calculated to be $5,246 under straight line depreciation. The earlier analysis treated leasing and borrowing as substitutes; so under the ownership scenario, the $20,000 is assumed to be borrowed at a 10 percent before-tax cost of debt by the user of the asset.[2]

It is assumed that the loan of $20,000 is paid off at a level annual amount that covers annual interest charges plus amortization of the principal. The amount is an annuity that can be determined by the use of the present value of an annuity formula, shown in Equation 27.5:

$$\$20,000 = \sum_{t=1}^{n} \frac{a_t}{(1 + k_b)^t}$$

$$a_t = \frac{\$20,000}{(\text{PVIFA})(10\%,5 \text{ yrs.})}$$

$$= \frac{\$20,000}{3.7908} = \$5,276. \tag{27.5}$$

[2]The implicit assumption here is that the entire investment amount, $I_0 = \$20,000$, is financed with the lease and that this is not a change in the firm's target capital structure. This assumption is valid if one compares the firm's balance sheet when financing the project with debt with the alternative of financing the project with leasing. For example, suppose the firm had $100,000 in assets and a 50 percent debt to total assets ratio before the project. If the $20,000 investment is financed with debt and equity, assets will increase to $120,000 and debt to $60,000. If the project is leased, debt will fall to $40,000 and leasing increase from zero to $20,000. Equity will be $60,000 either way. Comparing the two balance sheets, we see that debt is $20,000 less if the asset is leased.

Table 27.2   Schedule of Debt Payments

End of Year (1)	Balance of Principal Owed at End of Year (2)	Principal plus Interest Payments (3)	Annual Interest 10% × (2): (4)	Reduction of Principal (5)
1	$20,000	$5,276	$2,000	$ 3,276
2	16,724	5,276	1,672	3,604
3	13,120	5,276	1,312	3,964
4	9,156	5,276	916	4,360
5	4,796	5,276	480	4,796
Totals		$26,380	$6,380	$20,000

Solving Equation 27.5 for the level annual annuity results in $5,276, which represents the principal plus interest payments set forth in Column (3) of Table 27.2. The sum of these five annual payments is shown to be $26,380, which represents repayment of the principal of $20,000 plus the sum of the annual interest payments. The interest payments of each year are determined by multiplying Column (2), the balance of principal owed at the end of the year, by 10 percent, the assumed cost of borrowing. The sum of the annual interest payments does, in fact, equal the total interest of $6,380, obtained by deducting the principal of $20,000 from the total of the five annual payments shown in Column (3).

A schedule of cash outflows for the borrow-own alternative is then developed to determine the present value of the after-tax cash flows. This is illustrated in Table 27.3.

The analysis of cash outflows begins with a listing of the loan payments, as shown in Column (2). Next, the annual interest payments from Table 27.2 are listed in Column (3). Since straight line depreciation is assumed, the annual depreciation charges are $4,000 per year, as shown in Column (4). The tax shelter to the owner of the equipment is the sum of the annual interest plus depreciation multiplied by the tax rate. The amounts of the annual

Table 27.3   Costs of Borrowing

End of Year (1)	Loan Payment (2)	Annual Interest (3)	Depreciation (4)	Tax Shield: [(3) + (4)]0.4 (5)	Cash Flows after Taxes: (2) − (5) (6)	Present Value Factor (at 6%) (7)	Present Value of Costs (8)
1	$ 5,276	$2,000	$ 4,000	$ 2,400	$ 2,876	0.9434	$ 2,713
2	5,276	1,672	4,000	2,269	3,007	0.8900	2,676
3	5,276	1,312	4,000	2,125	3,151	0.8396	2,646
4	5,276	916	4,000	1,966	3,310	0.7921	2,622
5	5,276	480	4,000	1,792	3,484	0.7473	2,603
Totals	$26,380	$6,380	$20,000	$10,552	$15,828		$13,260

tax shield are shown in Column (5). Column (6) is cash flow after taxes, obtained by deducting Column (5) from Column (2).

Since the cost of borrowing is 10 percent, its after-tax cost with a 40 percent tax rate is 6 percent. The present value factors at 6 percent are listed in Column (7). They are multiplied by the after-tax cash flows to obtain Column (8), the present value of the after-tax costs of owning the asset.

The costs of leasing the asset can be obtained in a similar manner, as shown in Table 27.4. The uniform annual lease payments are shown in Column (2). By multiplying 0.6 times the Column (2) figures, the after-tax cost of leasing is obtained and shown in Column (3). The present value factors for 6 percent are listed in Column (4) and multiplied times the figures in Column (3). Column (5) presents the after-tax costs of leasing by year, which total to $13,260.

The result is the same as for the costs of borrowing in order to own the asset. Thus, in formulating the problem to make the positions of the lessors and users symmetrical, indifference between the costs of borrowing and the costs of leasing is obtained once again. A number of factors could change this result: differences in costs of capital, differences in applicable tax rates or usability of tax subsidies, differences in patterns of payments required under leasing versus owning, and so on. But in order to measure the effects of factors which cause the costs of leasing and owning to be different, it is helpful to start with an equality relation to understand better what is causing a divergence.

Cost Comparison for Operating Leases

Under an operating lease, the lessor must bear the risk involved in the use of the asset because the lease is cancellable and, therefore, may be returned by the lessee. Operating leases are virtually equivalent to having the lessor own the equipment and operate it. In these circumstances, the required rate of return is not the rate on a portfolio of assets of loaned funds. Rather, it is something higher. The operating lease, from the lessor's point of view, has three elements: (1) the cash flows received from the lease contract, (2) the expected market or salvage value of the asset, and (3) the value of an American put option. The put option captures the present value of the lessee's right to cancel the lease and return the asset whenever the value of the economic rent on the asset falls below the lease fee. This may happen if the asset wears out faster than anticipated or if the asset (for

---

Table 27.4   Costs of Leasing

End of Year (1)	Lease Payments (2)	After-Tax: 0.6 × (2) (3)	Present Value Factor (at 6%) (4)	Present Value of Costs: (3) × (4) (5)
1	$ 5,246	$ 3,147.6	0.9434	$ 2,970
2	5,246	3,147.6	0.8900	2,802
3	5,246	3,147.6	0.8396	2,643
4	5,246	3,147.6	0.7921	2,493
5	5,246	3,147.6	0.7473	2,352
Totals	$26,230	$15,738.0		$13,260

example, a computer) becomes obsolete faster than expected. Equation 27.6 shows how the NPV of the lease to the lessor must be adjusted for operating leases:

$$\text{NPV}_{LOR} = -I_0 + \sum_{t=1}^{n} \frac{L_t(1 - T) + T\text{Dep}_t}{[1 + (1 - T)k_b]^t} + \frac{E(MV)}{(1 + k_1)^n} - P, \tag{27.6}$$

where

$$
\begin{aligned}
\text{NPV}_{LOR} &= \text{present value to the lessor} \\
L_t &= \text{lease rental fee without the cancellation feature} \\
E(MV) &= \text{expected market value of the asset} \\
k_1 &= \text{the risk-adjusted discount rate for the salvage value} \\
P &= \text{the value of the American put implied by the cancellation feature.}
\end{aligned}
$$

Because the lessor is giving up something when he allows the lease to be cancelled, it is necessary to charge a higher lease fee. How much higher depends on the value of the American put, P.[3] As the risk of obsolescence increases so does the value of the put option held by the lessee. Since there are no free lunches, the lease fee charged by the lessor will rise to reflect the extra risk being undertaken. An internal rate of return analysis of a cancellable operating lease which uses only the first three terms of Equation 27.6, thereby leaving out the put option, will show that the lessor sets the lease fee such that a high rate of return is being charged. The lessee would be badly mistaken to compare the rate required on a cancellable operating lease with the rate required on a straight (noncancellable) financial lease (or comparable debt financing).

Additional Influences on the Leasing versus Owning Decision

A number of other factors can influence the user firm's costs of leasing versus owning capital assets. These include (1) different costs of capital for the lessor versus the user firm; (2) financing costs higher in leasing; (3) differences in maintenance costs; (4) the benefits of residual values to the owner of the assets; (5) the possibility of reducing obsolescence costs by the leasing firms; (6) the possibility of increased credit availability under leasing; (7) more favorable tax treatment, such as more rapid write-off; and (8) possible differences in the ability to utilize tax reduction opportunities. A number of arguments exist with respect to the advantages and disadvantages of leasing, given these factors. Many of the arguments carry with them implicit assumptions, thus their applicability to real-world conditions is subject to considerable qualification.

Different Costs of Capital for the Lessor versus the User Firm

If the lessor has a lower cost of capital than the user, the cost of leasing is likely to be lower than the cost of owning to the user. But is it realistic to assume that the cost of capital would be different? To answer this question, the basic risks involved in using capital assets must be considered. It has been demonstrated that two broad types of risks are present.

---

[3]See Copeland and Weston [1982] for an analysis of cancellable operating leases and Lee, Martin, and Senchack [1982] for an analysis of the salvage value problem.

One risk is that an asset's economic rate of depreciation and obsolescence will vary, in some systematic way with the level of the economy, from the rate expected when the lease-rental rate was determined. That is, the risk is that the agreed-upon lease payments, which are based on expected depreciation, will be insufficient to cover the subsequent realized depreciation. This risk is borne by the owner, whether it is a leasing firm or a user-buyer.

The other risk is associated with the uncertain future net cash flows to be derived from employing the capital services of the asset. This risk is borne by the leasing company if the lease contract is cancellable at any time with no penalty, borne by the user firm if the lease contract is noncancellable over the life of the asset, and shared by them under any contractual arrangement between these two extremes. But, competitive capital markets will ensure that the implicit discount rate in the leasing arrangement, as negotiated, will reflect the allocation of the risks under the particular sharing arrangement specified. Under the standard price equals marginal cost condition of competitive markets, it is the project's cost of capital that is the relevant discount rate. Hence, it is difficult to visualize why the risk in use of a capital asset will be different whether the asset is owned by a leasing company or by the user firm.[4]

Another possibility is that the user firm may have a lower cost of capital than the leasing company. This possibility has been evaluated as follows: "It is true that such a company, looking only at the conventional formulas, might find it profitable to buy rather than rent. But it would find it even more profitable, under those circumstances, to enter the leasing business."[5] This would eliminate any divergence.

Under competitive market conditions, it is unlikely that the disequilibrium conditions implied by the different costs of capital will long persist. The supply of financial intermediaries as lessors will either increase or decrease to restore equilibrium in the benefits to a user firm from leasing versus owning an asset.

Financing Costs Higher in Leasing

A similar view is that leasing always involves higher implicit financing costs. This argument is also of doubtful validity. First, when the nature of the lessee as a credit risk is considered, there may be no difference. Second, it is difficult to separate the money costs of leasing from the other services embodied in a leasing contract. If, because of its specialized operations, the leasing company can perform nonfinancial services such as maintenance of the equipment at a lower cost than the lessee or some other institution can perform them, then the effective cost of leasing may be lower than the cost of funds obtained from borrowing or other sources. The efficiencies of performing specialized services may thus enable the leasing company to operate by charging a lower total cost than the lessee would have to pay for the package of money plus services on any other basis.

Differences in Maintenance Costs

Another argument frequently encountered is that leasing may be less expensive because no explicit maintenance costs are involved. But, this is because the maintenance costs are included in the lease-rental rate. The key question is whether the maintenance can be

---

[4]Miller and Upton [1976].
[5]Ibid., p. 767.

performed at a lower cost by the lessor or by an independent firm that specializes in performing maintenance on capital assets of the type involved. Whether the costs will differ if supplied by one type of specialist firm rather than another is a factual matter, depending on the industries and particular firms involved.

Residual Values

One important point that must be mentioned in connection with leasing is that the lessor owns the property at the expiration of the lease. The value of the property at the end of the lease is called the *residual value*. Superficially, it appears that where residual values are large, owning is less expensive than leasing. However, even this apparently obvious advantage of owning is subject to substantial qualification. On leased equipment, the obsolescence factor may be so large that it is doubtful whether residual values will be of a great order of magnitude. If these values appear favorable, competition between leasing companies and other financial sources, as well as competition among leasing companies themselves, will force leasing rates down to the point where the potentials of residual values are fully recognized in the leasing contract rates. Thus, the existence of residual values is unlikely to result in materially lower costs of owning.

However, in decisions about whether to lease or to own land, the obsolescence factor is involved only to the extent of deterioration in areas with changing population or use patterns. In a period of optimistic expectations about land values, there may be a tendency to overestimate their rates of increase. As a consequence, the current purchase of land may involve a price so high that the probable rate of return on owned land will be relatively small. Under this condition, leasing may well represent the more economical way of obtaining the use of land. Conversely, if the probable increase in land values is not fully reflected in current prices, it will be advantageous to own the land.

Thus, it is difficult to generalize about whether residual value considerations are likely to make the effective cost of leasing higher or lower than the cost of owning. The results depend on whether the individual firm has opportunities to take advantage of overoptimistic or overpessimistic evaluations of future value changes by the market as a whole and whether the firm or market is correct on average.

Obsolescence Costs

Another popular notion is that leasing costs will be lower because of the rapid obsolescence of some kinds of equipment. If the obsolescence rate on equipment is high, leasing costs must reflect that rate. Thus, in general terms, it can be argued that neither residual values nor obsolescence rates can basically affect the relative cost of owning versus leasing.

However, it is possible that certain leasing companies are well equipped to handle the obsolescence problem. For example, the Clark Equipment Company is a manufacturer, reconditioner, and specialist in materials handling equipment, with its own sales organization and system of distributors. This may enable Clark to write favorable leases for equipment. If the equipment becomes obsolete to one user, it may be satisfactory for other users with different materials handling requirements, and Clark is well situated to locate the other users. The situation is similar in computer leasing.

This illustration indicates how a leasing company, by combining lending with other specialized services, may reduce the social costs of obsolescence and increase effective residual values. By such operations, the total cost of obtaining the use of such equipment is reduced. Possibly other institutions that do not combine financing and specialist functions (such as manufacturing, reconditioning, servicing, and sales) may, in conjunction with financing institutions, perform the overall functions as efficiently and at as low a cost as do integrated leasing companies. However, this is a factual matter depending on the relative efficiency of the competing firms in different lines of business and different kinds of equipment.

Increased Credit Availability

Two possible situations that give leasing an advantage to firms seeking the maximum degree of financial leverage may exist. First, it is frequently stated that firms wishing to purchase a specific piece of equipment can obtain more money for longer terms under a lease arrangement than under a secured loan agreement. Second, leasing may not have as much of an impact on future borrowing capacity as does borrowing to buy the equipment.

This point is illustrated by the balance sheets of two hypothetical firms, A and B, in Table 27.5. Initially, the balance sheets of both firms are identical, with both showing debt ratios of 50 percent. Next, each company decides to acquire assets costing $100. Firm A borrows $100 to make the purchase, so an asset and a liability go on its balance sheet, and its debt ratio is increased to 75 percent. Firm B leases the equipment. The lease may call for fixed charges as high as or even higher than the loan, and the obligations assumed under the lease can be equally (or more) dangerous to other creditors; but the fact that its reported debt ratio is lower may enable Firm B to obtain additional credit from other lenders. The amount of the annual rentals is shown as a note to Firm B's financial statements, so credit analysts are aware of it; but many of them may still give less weight to Firm B's lease than to Firm A's loan.

This illustration indicates quite clearly a weakness of the debt ratio. If two companies are being compared, and if one leases a substantial amount of equipment, then the debt ratio as calculated here does not accurately show their relative leverage positions.[6]

Table 27.5   Balance Sheet Effects of Operating Leases

Before Asset Increase Firms A and B				After Asset Increase Firm A				Firm B			
		Debt	$ 50			Debt	$150			Debt	$ 50
		Equity	50			Equity	50			Equity	50
Total assets	$100	Total	$100	Total assets	$200	Total	$200	Total assets	$100	Total	$100

[6]Three comments are appropriate here. First, financial analysts frequently attempt to reconstruct the balance sheets of firms such as B by capitalizing the lease payments — that is, estimating the value of both the lease obligation and the leased assets and transforming B's balance sheet into one comparable to A's. Second, as indicated in Chapter 8, lease charges are included in the fixed charge coverage ratio; and this ratio is approximately equal for Firms A and B, thereby revealing the true state of affairs. Thus, it is unlikely that lenders will be fooled into granting more credit to a company with a lease than to one with a conventional loan having terms similar to those of the lease. Third, FASB Statement No. 13 provides for including capital leases in the firm's balance sheet.

Rapid Write-Off

If the lease is written for a period that is much shorter than the depreciable life of the asset (with renewals at low rentals after the lessor has recovered costs during the basic lease period), then the deductible depreciation which the lessee could take if the asset were owned is small in relation to the deductible lease payment in the early years. In a sense, this amounts to a very rapid write-off, which is advantageous to the lessee. However, the Internal Revenue Service disallows the deductibility of lease payments that provide for an unduly rapid amortization of the lessor's costs and have a relatively low renewal or purchase option.

Differences in Tax Rates or Tax Subsidies

An advantage to leasing or to buying may occur when the tax rates of lessors and user firms are different. But, even here, unambiguous predictions are not always possible. The effects of differential taxes depend upon the relationships among earnings from the capital assets and their interactions with differential tax rates and tax subsidies.

But, the inability of a user firm to utilize tax benefits such as the investment tax credit or accelerated depreciation may make it advantageous for it to enter a lease arrangement. In this situation, the lessor (a bank or a leasing company) can utilize the credit, and competition with other lessors may result in lower leasing rates.

For example, the investment tax credit (discussed in Chapter 4) can be taken only if the firm's profits and taxes exceed a certain level. If a firm is unprofitable, or if it is expanding so rapidly and generating such large tax credits that it cannot use them all, then it may be profitable for it to enter a lease arrangement. In this situation, the lessor (a bank or a leasing company) can take the credit and give the lessee a corresponding reduction in lease charges. In recent years, railroads and airlines have been large users of leasing for this reason, as have industrial companies faced with similar situations. Anaconda, for example, financed most of the cost of a $138 million aluminum plant built in 1973 through a lease arrangement.[7] Anaconda had suffered a $365 million tax loss when Chile expropriated its copper mining properties, and the carry-forward of this loss would hold taxes down for years. Thus, the firm could not use the tax credit associated with the new plant. By entering a lease arrangement, the company was able to pass the tax credit on to the lessors, who, in turn, gave it lease payments lower than would have existed under a loan arrangement. Anaconda's financial staff estimated that financial charges over the life of the plant would be $74 million less under the lease arrangement than under a borrow-and-buy plan.

Incidentally, the Anaconda lease was set up as a leveraged lease.[8] A group of banks and Chrysler Corporation provided about $38 million of equity and were the owner-lessors. They borrowed the balance of the required funds from Prudential, Metropolitan, and Aetna, large life insurance companies. The banks and Chrysler received not only the investment tax credit but also the tax shelter associated with accelerated depreciation on

---

[7]Vanderwicken [1973].

[8]Technically, a *leveraged lease* is one in which the financial intermediary (a bank or other lessor) uses borrowed funds to acquire the assets it leases.

the plant. Such leveraged leases, often with wealthy individuals seeking tax shelters acting as owner-lessors, are an important part of the financial scene today and help explain why leasing has reached a total volume of over $100 billion.

Summary

Leasing has long been used in connection with the acquisition of equipment by railroad companies. In recent years, it has been extended to a wide variety of equipment, such as computers and airplanes.

The most important forms of lease financing are (1) sale and leaseback, in which a firm owning land, buildings, or equipment sells the property and simultaneously executes an agreement to lease it for a certain period under specific terms; (2) service leases or operating leases, which include both financing and maintenance services and are often cancellable and call for payments under the lease contract that may not fully recover the cost of the equipment; and (3) financial leases, which do not provide for maintenance services, are not cancellable, and do fully amortize the cost of the leased asset during the basic lease contract period.

It is important to remember that lease financing is a substitute for debt. There is no such thing as a company which is 100 percent lease financed. Lease financing, like debt financing, requires an equity base. The first step in a lease versus buy analysis is to discount the cash flows of the project under consideration at the appropriate weighted average cost of capital. Then, if the project makes sense, the second step is to decide whether it should be financed with a mixture of debt and equity or with a lease. As shown in Equation 27.4, the net present value of the lease is determined by discounting the after-tax lease fees and the lost depreciation tax shield at the lessee's after-tax cost of debt. If the NPV of the lease is positive, then leasing is preferred to borrowing as a means of financing the project. Always be sure that the NPV of the project plus the NPV of the lease is positive.

In the absence of major tax advantages and other "market imperfections," there should be no advantage to either leasing or owning. A wide range of factors that may influence the indifference result can be introduced. These possible influences include tax differences, differences in maintenance costs, different costs of capital for the lessor and the user firm, differences in obsolescence, and differences in the contractual positions in leasing versus other forms and sources of financing. Whether these other factors will actually give an advantage or disadvantage to leasing depends on the facts and circumstances of each transaction analyzed.

Questions

27.1   Discuss this statement: The type of equipment best suited for leasing has a long life in relation to the length of the lease; is a removable, standard product that could be used by many different firms; and is easily identifiable. In short, it is the kind of equipment that could be repossessed and sold readily. However, we would be quite happy to write a ten-year lease on paper towels for a firm such as Eastman Kodak or Owens-Illinois.

27.2   Leasing is often called a hedge against obsolescence. Under what conditions is this actually true?

27.3   Is leasing in any sense a hedge against inflation for the lessee? For the lessor?

27.4   One alleged advantage of leasing is that it keeps liabilities off the balance sheet, thus making it possible for a firm to obtain more leverage than it otherwise could. This raises the question of whether both the lease obligation and the asset involved should be capitalized and shown on the balance sheet. Discuss the pros and cons of capitalizing leases and related assets.

Problems

27.1 a)   The Clarkton Company produces industrial machines, which have five-year lives. Clarkton is willing to either sell the machines for $30,000 or to lease them at a rental that, because of competitive factors, yields an after-tax return to Clarkton of 6 percent — its cost of capital. What is the company's competitive lease-rental rate? (Assume straight line depreciation, zero salvage value, and an effective corporate tax rate of 40 percent.)

b)   The Stockton Machine Shop is contemplating the purchase of a machine exactly like those rented by Clarkton. The machine will produce net benefits of $10,000 per year. Stockton can buy the machine for $30,000 or rent it from Clarkton at the competitive lease-rental rate. Stockton's cost of capital is 12 percent, its cost of debt 10 percent, and $T = 40$ percent. Which alternative is better for Stockton?

c)   If Clarkton's cost of capital is 9 percent and competition exists among lessors, solve for the new equilibrium rental rate. Will Stockton's decision be altered?

27.2   The Nelson Company is faced with the decision of whether it should purchase or lease a new forklift truck. The truck can be leased on an eight-year contract for $4,641.44 a year or it can be purchased for $26,000. The salvage value (Z_n) of the truck after eight years is $2,000. The company uses straight line depreciation. The discount rate applied is its after-tax cost of debt. The company can borrow at 15 percent and has a 40 percent marginal tax rate and a 12 percent cost of capital.

a)   Analyze the lease versus purchase decision using the firm's after-tax cost of debt as the discount factor.

b)   Discuss your results.

27.3   The Bradley Steel Company seeks to acquire the use of a rolling machine at the lowest possible cost. The choice is either to lease one at $21,890 annually or to purchase one for $54,000. The company's cost of capital is 14 percent, its cost of debt is 10 percent, and its tax rate is 40 percent. The machine has an economic life of six years and no salvage value. The company uses straight line depreciation. The discount rate applied is the after-tax cost of debt. Which is the less costly method of financing?

27.4   The Scott Brothers Department Store is considering a sale and leaseback of its major property, consisting of land and a building, because it is 30 days late on 80 percent of its accounts payable. The recent balance sheet of Scott Brothers is as shown in Table P27.4.

Profit before taxes is $36,000; after taxes, $20,000. Annual depreciation charges are $57,600 on the building and $72,000 on the fixtures and equipment. The land and building could be sold for a total of $2.8 million. The annual net rental will be $240,000.

a)   How much capital gains tax will Scott Brothers pay if the land and building are sold? (Assume all capital gains are taxed at the capital gains tax rate, 30 percent; disregard such items as recapture of depreciation, tax preference treatment, and so on.)

Table P27.4

Scott Brothers Department Store Balance Sheet as of December 31, 19X0
(Thousands of Dollars)

Assets		Liabilities	
Cash	$ 288	Accounts payable	$1,440
Receivables	1,440	Bank loans (at 8%)	1,440
Inventories	1,872	Other current liabilities	720
Total current assets	$3,600	Total current debt	$3,600
Land	1,152	Common stock	1,440
Building	720	Retained earnings	720
Fixtures and equipment	288		
Net fixed assets	2,160		
Total assets	$5,760	Total claims	$5,760

b) Compare the current ratio before and after the sale and leaseback if the after-tax net proceeds are used to clean up the bank loans and to reduce accounts payable and other current liabilities.

c) If the lease had been in effect during the year shown in the balance sheet, what would Scott Brothers' profit for that year have been?

d) What are the basic financial problems facing Scott Brothers? Will the sale and leaseback operation solve them?

Selected References

Abdel-Khalik, A. R., "The Economic Effects on Lessees of FASB No. 13 — Accounting for Leases," Stanford: FASB, 1981.

Ang, James, and Peterson, Pamela, "The Leasing Puzzle," *Journal of Finance*, (September 1984), pp. 1055-1066.

Athanasopoulos, Peter J., and Bacon, Peter W., "The Evaluation of Leveraged Leases," *Financial Management*, 9 (Spring 1980), pp. 76-80.

Bowman, R. G., "The Debt Equivalence of Leases: An Empirical Investigation," *Accounting Review*, (April 1980), pp. 237-253.

Copeland, Thomas E., and Weston, J. Fred, "A Note on the Evaluation of Cancellable Operating Leases," *Financial Management*, 11 (Summer 1982), pp. 60-67.

Flath, D., "The Economics of Short-Term Leasing," *Economic Inquiry*, (April 1980), pp. 247-259.

Johnson, Robert W., and Lewellen, Wilbur G., "Analysis of the Lease-or-Buy Decision," *Journal of Finance*, 27 (September 1972), pp. 815-823.

Kim, E. Han; Lewellen, Wilbur G.; and McConnell, John J., "Sale-and-Leaseback Agreements and Enterprise Valuation," *Journal of Financial and Quantitative Analysis*, 13 (December 1978), pp. 871-883.

Lee, Wayne Y.; Martin, John D.; and Senchack, Andrew J., "The Case for Using Options to Evaluate Sal-

vage Values in Financial Leases," *Financial Management*, 11 (Autumn 1982), pp. 33-41.

Levy, Haim, and Sarnat, Marshall, "Leasing, Borrowing, and Financial Risk," *Financial Management*, 8 (Winter 1979), pp. 47-54.

Lewellen, Wilbur G.; Long, Michael S.; and McConnell, John J., "Asset Leasing in Competitive Capital Markets," *Journal of Finance*, 31 (June 1976), pp. 787-798.

McConnell, John J., and Schallheim, James S., "Valuation of Asset Leasing Contracts," *Journal of Financial Economics*, 12 (August 1983), pp. 237-261.

Miller, Merton H., and Upton, Charles W., "Leasing, Buying and the Cost of Capital Services," *Journal of Finance*, 31 (June 1976), pp. 761-786.

Myers, Stewart C.; Dill, David A.; and Bautista, Alberto J., "Valuation of Financial Lease Contracts," *Journal of Finance*, 31 (June 1976), pp. 799-819.

Schall, Lawrence D., "The Lease-or-Buy and Asset Acquisition Decisions," *Journal of Finance*, 29 (September 1974), pp. 1203-1214.

Vanderwicken, P., "Powerful Logic of the Leasing Boom," *Fortune*, (November 1973), pp. 136-140.

Chapter 28 Warrants and Convertibles

In Chapter 18, the theory of options was set forth. In the present chapter, we discuss two particular forms of options: warrants and convertibles. The ordinary options discussed in Chapter 18 do not directly raise funds for the firm. Indeed, the firm may not be involved in the purchase and sale of call and put options. But, warrants and convertibles are used to assist in raising additional funds for the firm. Warrants are used in connection with the sale of other securities in order to make their purchase more attractive. Convertibles give the holder the right to exchange a form of debt or preferred stock for common stock. Since both warrants and convertibles are used to facilitate financing by the firm, they are discussed here in Part Seven, which deals with alternative methods of raising funds as a part of the responsibilities of financial managers.

Warrants

A *warrant* is an option to buy a stated number of shares of common stock at a specified exercise price. Warrants are similar to the call options we discussed in Chapter 18, except that they are issued by the firm itself and, typically, have longer maturities. When debt, preferred stock, or common stock is issued, it may be sold in units, which include one or more warrants to purchase common stock or other securities. Warrants, thus, are often used as "sweeteners" to make it easier to sell the associated security.

Characteristics

A warrant is in the nature of an option. Hence, it states an exercise price at which the common stock may be purchased and the number of shares of common stock which may be purchased per warrant. In Table 28.1, the characteristics of an illustrative group of warrants are listed. In Column (1), the name of the issuing company is set forth. Column (2) lists the expiration date. The warrants in this random sample all have a maturity of greater than one year, and some have maturities of almost ten years. Some warrants have no expiration date and so may be exercised without a time limit. For example, the Atlas Corp. has warrants outstanding to purchase its common at $31.25 with no expiration date.

In Column (3), the exercise price per share for each of the warrants is set forth. This may be compared in Column (4) with the current market price of the common stock that the warrant may be used to acquire. Column (5) lists the number of common shares that each warrant enables the holder to obtain. The remaining columns of the table will be discussed in connection with the valuation of warrants.

Warrants may be nondetachable from the security they accompany (for example, bonds) or detachable so that they can be traded separately. Since a warrant is an option to buy common stock, it does not carry the rights of common stockholders until it is exercised.

Table 28.1   Characteristics of Warrants

(1)	(2)	(3)	(4)	(5)	(6)	(7)	(8)
		Exercise	Current	Number	Formula Value	Actual	
Company Name	Expiration Date	Price per Share	Common Price	of Common	of Warrant	Warrant Price	Percent Premium*
American Express	2/28/87	$27.50	$26.25	2.00	0	$14.00	27%
Apache Petroleum	7/15/86	18.00	18.63	1.00	.63	2.38	9
Bally Mfg.	1/4/88	40.00	19.50	1.00	0	5.25	27
Caesar's World	8/1/85	24.50	11.13	1.00	0	1.25	11
Eastern Air Lines	6/1/87	10.00	4.63	1.00	0	1.50	32
Genesco	10/15/93	11.75	7.25	1.00	0	2.63	36
Harnischfeger Corp.	4/14/89	13.38	11.63	1.00	0	3.75	32
Int'l. Harvester	12/15/93	5.00	6.38	1.00	1.38	4.25	45
MCI Communications	8/1/88	27.50	7.88	1.00	0	1.50	19
Orion Pictures	2/1/89	20.50	11.63	1.00	0	3.50	30
Square D	10/1/88	44.38	34.25	.50	0	3.13	18

$$\text{*Percent premium} = \frac{\text{Actual price of warrant} - \text{Formula value}}{\text{(Price of common stock)(Number of common)}} = \frac{(7) - (6)}{(4)(5)}.$$

Source: Various financial publications for the date of June 18, 1984.

Thus, cash dividends are not paid on warrants. Warrants do not have voting power. If the position of the underlying common stock is altered through a stock dividend or through a stock split, provision is usually made to adjust the exercise price of the warrant appropriately.

Generally accepted accounting principles now require that a company with warrants outstanding (this applies to convertibles also) report its earnings per share in two ways. The first method is called the *primary* earnings per share, which is simply the total earnings available to shareholders divided by the actual number of common shares of stock outstanding. The second method of reporting is on a *fully diluted* basis. This represents earnings available to common shareholders divided by the total number of shares actually outstanding plus the additional number of shares that would come into being if all warrants were exercised or all convertible securities were converted. This makes it possible to take into account the impact on the company's earnings per share if all of the options were exercised.

Valuation of Warrants

Since a warrant is fundamentally an option, its value can be determined by exactly the same methods described in Chapter 18. However, rather than a relatively short time to maturity such as three to six months, the time to maturity used in the formula would be the longer number of years typically found in warrants. In the publications of various financial services, a "percent premium" is usually calculated for the warrant. This percent premium is calculated by reference to the so-called formula value of the warrant. Warrants have a formula value, and they have an actual value that is observed in the marketplace.

The formula value is found by use of the following expression:

$$\text{Formula value} = \left(\begin{array}{c}\text{Market price}\\\text{of common stock}\end{array} - \begin{array}{c}\text{Exercise}\\\text{price}\end{array}\right) \times \left(\begin{array}{c}\text{Number of shares each warrant}\\\text{entitles owner to purchase}\end{array}\right).$$

The calculation of the formula value starts by comparing the exercise price of the warrant with the current price of the common stock. By reference to Table 28.1, this would represent subtracting Column (3), the exercise price of the warrant, from Column (4), the current market price of the stock. If the exercise price of the warrant is greater than the current market price of the common stock, in the terminology of Chapter 18, the warrant is "out-of-the-money," and the formula value would be defined as zero. To illustrate, we will use the American Express warrants, which are in the first row of Table 28.1. The exercise price is $27.50 while the price of the common stock on the date of analysis (June 18, 1984) was $26.25. Hence, the warrant was "out-of-the-money" and its formula value was zero. The actual warrant price at the close of trading on June 18, 1984, was $14.00. The percent premium is then calculated by deducting the formula value from the actual price and dividing by the price of the common stock in Column (4). This results in a 27 percent premium in Column (8) of Table 28.1 for the American Express warrants expiring February 28, 1987. Note that in making this calculation, since one warrant enabled the holder to buy two shares of American Express at $27.50, the actual warrant price relates to two shares of common stock. Hence, in calculating the percent premium, the $14.00 is divided by 2 and then divided by $26.25 to obtain the 27 percent. Or alternatively, one could divide the $14.00 by the value of two shares of common stock, which would be $52.50, giving the same 27 percent premium.

The percent premium of the actual price of a warrant in excess of its formula value relates to the elements that give value to any option as discussed in Chapter 18. Hence, the size of the percent premium will reflect the five underlying determinants of the value of an option. Other things being equal, the value of an option will be higher (the percent premium of a warrant larger) if (1) the price of the underlying common stock is higher, (2) the exercise price of the option is lower, (3) the variance of the returns of the underlying asset is higher, (4) the time to maturity of the option is longer, and (5) the risk-free interest rate is higher. Thus, the percent premium of the actual price of a warrant in relation to its formula value reflects the underlying determinants of the warrant value as an option.

Use of Warrants in Financing

Warrants are often used as sweeteners to improve the terms of financing by the issuing firm. They are used by firms of different sizes in different circumstances. The list of firm names in Table 28.1 represents relatively large and well-known firms. Large, strong corporations may sell bonds with warrants, for example, in order to be able to sell the bonds at an interest rate lower than otherwise would be required. The amount of interest saved would depend upon the circumstances of the firm as well as the state of the financial markets at the time of issues. Firms as large as AT&T have sold bonds with warrants to obtain lower interest rates.

Firms that are relatively new and still in their development stage have uncertain futures. Since their outlook is uncertain, investors would be reluctant to purchase straight debt issues without extremely high, burdensome rates of interest. The high rates of interest can be moderated by selling debt with warrants, which give the purchaser the opportunity to obtain a higher rate of return if the small, rapidly growing firm succeeds and the value of its common stock increases. The warrant is especially attractive to investors in high-income tax brackets because they can take part of their return on the bonds in the form of capital gains rather than interest subject to ordinary personal income tax rates. Warrants are also used as additional compensation to investment bankers to induce them to risk their reputation in bringing out an issue of common stock for a new firm whose track record has not been firmly established.

Another characteristic of warrants is that when they are exercised, the firm receives additional funds. This can be shown by an illustrative example. Consider the situation of the ABC Company. Its situation before financing is depicted in Column (2) of Table 28.2. It has 4 million shares of common stock outstanding at $1 par value. Its paid-in capital is $16 million and its retained earnings are $80 million. Its net worth is $100 million and its total capitalization is the same.

Column (3) then depicts the results of selling $25 million of debentures with warrants. Column (3) is the same as Column (2), except that we add the $25 million of debentures, so that total capitalization increases to $125 million. The debentures carry a 10 percent coupon interest rate, with each debenture of $1,000 face value carrying 40 warrants permitting the purchase of one share of common stock at $5 per share. Since 25,000 debentures are outstanding, each carrying 40 warrants, one million new shares would be sold if the warrants were exercised. With a par value of $1, $1 million would be added to common stock and $4 million to paid-in capital. Net worth would increase from $100 million to $105 million. The total capitalization would rise to $130 million.

The example in Table 28.2 illustrates how warrants can be used to facilitate the sale of a security. A further advantage of the use of the warrants is that when they are exercised, additional funds flow into the corporation. All this, of course, depends upon the company growing and prospering so that the market price of its stock goes up. This is because the exercise price set when the warrants are issued is typically from 15 to 25 percent higher than the prevailing market price of the common stock.

The value of a warrant, or in its short maturity form, a right, has been developed under simplifying conditions by Galai and Schneller [1978]. They postulate a one-period model for a 100 percent equity-financed firm which distributes the proceeds from issuing warrants as dividends to the old shareholders and the warrants are assumed to be exercised as a block. The following summarizes the symbols and illustrative magnitudes for the variables in the analysis.

Table 28.2 Use of Warrants in Financing (Thousands of Dollars)

Financing Source (1)	Before Financing (2)	Sale of Debentures (3)	Exercise Warrants (4)
Debentures		$ 25,000	$ 25,000
Common stock ($1 par value)	$ 4,000	4,000	5,000
Paid-in capital	16,000	16,000	20,000
Retained earnings	80,000	80,000	80,000
Net worth	100,000	100,000	105,000
Total capitalization	$100,000	$125,000	$130,000

$V =$ value of the firm without warrants = $1 million
$N =$ current number of shares = 10,000
$q =$ ratio of warrants to shares = .25
$X =$ exercise price of warrant = $80
$S =$ price per share without warrants = $100
$S_x =$ price per share warrants exercised
$W =$ value of a right or a warrant.

The price per share of the stock without warrants will be

$$S = \frac{V}{N} = \frac{\$1,000,000}{10,000} = \$100.$$

Next, postulate that warrants are issued and that they are exercised. The resulting price per share is

$$S_x = \frac{V + NqX}{N(1 + q)} = \frac{\$1,000,000 + 10,000(.25)\$80}{10,000(1 + .25)} = \frac{1,200,000}{12,500} = \$96.$$

The alternative formulation also produces the same result:

$$S_x = \frac{S + qX}{1 + q} = \frac{100 + .25(80)}{1.25} = \frac{120}{1.25} = \$96.$$

Two other relationships can also be calculated:

$$NqX = \text{Cash received} = 10,000(.25)\$80 = \$200,000$$

$$N(1 + q) = \text{Total shares if warrants are exercised} = 10,000(1.25) = 12,500.$$

The warrants will be exercised if their value after conversion is greater than the exercise price. But, it must also be true that the firm's end-of-period stock price without the warrants must exceed the warrant exercise price as well. Hence, the warrant will be exercised in the same states of nature as a call option with the same exercise price. When we analyze the end-of-period payoffs, we observe the following relationships:

	End-of-Period Payoffs	
	If $S \leq X$	If $S > X$
Call on firm without warrants, C	0	$S - X$
Warrant on firm with warrants, W	0	$\dfrac{S + qX}{1 + q} - X = \dfrac{1}{1 + q}(S - X)$

We see that the payoffs to the warrant are a constant proportion of the payoffs to a call written on a firm without warrants. The returns on the warrant, therefore, are perfectly correlated with the returns on a call option written on the firm without warrants. Hence, the value of a right or a warrant will be related to the value of the call in the following way:

$$W = \frac{1}{1 + q}C.$$

In addition, because the right or the warrant and the call are perfectly correlated, they will have the same systematic risk and, consequently, the same required rate of return.

We have now described the characteristics of warrants. We shall next treat the nature of convertibles, which are similar in functions performed. The rationale for the use of these options sold by the firm will then be discussed.

Convertibles

Convertible securities are bonds or *preferred stocks* that are exchangeable into common stock at the option of the holder and under specified terms and conditions. The most important of the special features relates to how many shares of stock a convertible holder receives by converting. This feature is defined as the *conversion ratio*, and it gives the number of shares of common stock the holder of the convertible receives on surrender of the security. Related to the conversion ratio is the *conversion price* — the effective price paid for the common stock when conversion occurs. In effect, a convertible is similar to a bond with an attached warrant.

Some illustrative convertible debt issues are listed in Table 28.3. In Column (1) is the company name. Column (2) sets forth the coupon rates. These vary widely. One influence on the coupon rate is the conversion premium at the time the security is issued. The conversion premium is the percent by which the conversion price at the time of issue exceeds the prevailing price of the common stock into which the debt or preferred stock will be converted. Other influences on the coupon level will be discussed below.

Column (3) contains the maturity dates, which also vary. On convertible preferred stocks, often there will be no maturity. Column (4) is the conversion ratio, the number of shares of common stock received on conversion. Column (5) is the prevailing price of the common stock as of the date of the analysis, which was June 18, 1984. Column (6) is the product of the previous two columns, since the conversion ratio times the current price of the common stock gives the current conversion value per $100 of the convertible bond. For

Table 28.3   Characteristics of Convertible Debt

(1)	(2)	(3)	(4)	(5)	(6)	(7)	(8)
					Current		Conversion
			Conversion	Price	Conversion	Price of	Price
Company Name	Coupon	Maturity	Ratio	of Common	Value	Convertible	Premium
Alaska Airlines	9%	11/15/2003	55.172	$12.25	$ 67.59	$ 92.00	36%
Atlantic Research	8	5/1/2008	22.386	28.75	64.36	86.50	34
Castle & Cooke Inc.	5.375	3/1/94	59.101	12.13	71.66	84.00	17
GTE Corp.	4	3/15/90	22.476	36.88	82.88	81.25	−2
McGraw-Hill Inc.	3.875	5/1/92	32.00	41.38	132.40	132.00	0
Oak Industries	10.5	2/1/2002	29.740	4.13	12.27	52.50	328
Owens Corning	8.25	12/1/2007	26.229	27.88	73.11	90.00	23
Rockwell Int'l.	4.25	2/15/91	86.957	26.88	233.70	231.25	−1
GD Searles & Co.	5.25	8/1/89	22.748	43.75	99.52	104.00	4
Viacom Int'l.	9.25	10/15/2007	29.762	28.25	84.08	105.00	25
Wang Labs	7.75	6/1/2008	19.171	25.50	48.89	80.00	64

Source: Various financial publications for the date of June 18, 1984.

example, for the first bond in the list, the Alaska Airlines' 9 percent coupon convertible bonds maturing on November 15, 2003, the conversion ratio was 55.172. This multiplied times the applicable current price of the common stock gives $675.86, divided by 10, to give the current conversion value shown in Column (6) of $67.59. The price of the convertible bond per $100 of par value of the bond was $92.00 on June 18, 1984. The conversion price premium on the date of analysis was 36 percent. This is the percent by which the current price of the convertible exceeds its current conversion value. Note that there is a distinction between the conversion price and the current conversion value. The conversion price is established at the time of the design of the issue of the convertible bond. It is, of course, determined by the conversion ratio. Thus, for Alaska Airlines, the conversion price would be

$$\text{Conversion price} = \frac{\text{Par value of bond}}{\text{Shares received}} = \frac{\$1,000}{55.172} = \$18.125.$$

The conversion price and conversion ratio are established at the time the convertible bond is sold. Generally, these values are fixed for the life of the bond, although sometimes a stepped-up conversion price is used. Litton Industries' convertible debentures, for example, were convertible into 12.5 shares until 1972, into 11.76 shares from 1972 until 1982, and into 11.11 shares from 1982 until maturity in 1987. The conversion price thus started at $80, rose to $85, and then to $90. Litton's convertibles, like most, are callable at the option of the company.

Another factor that may cause a change in the conversion price and ratio is a standard feature of almost all convertibles — the clause protecting the convertible against dilution from stock splits, stock dividends, and the sale of common stock at low prices (as in a rights offering). The typical provision states that no common stock can be sold at a price below the conversion price and that the conversion price must be lowered (and the conversion ratio raised) by the percentage amount of any stock dividend or split. For example, if Alaska Airlines had a two-for-one split, the conversion ratio would be adjusted to 110.344 and the conversion price lowered to $9.0626. If this protection were not contained in the contract, a company could completely thwart conversion by the use of stock splits and dividends. Warrants are similarly protected against dilution.

Like warrant exercise prices, the conversion price is characteristically set from 15 to 20 percent above the prevailing market price of the common stock at the time the convertible issue is sold. How the conversion price is established can best be understood after considering the rationale for the use of convertibles.

The Rationale for the Use of Convertibles

The traditional reasons for selling convertibles were that the coupon rate was low and that the conversion price represented a premium over the current price of the common stock. But, our previous discussion of options in Chapter 18 should indicate that this older view is incomplete at best. The convertible bond may be viewed as a package of straight debt plus an associated option. This is equivalent to straight debt plus a warrant, discussed in the first part of this chapter.

Since a convertible bond is a hybrid between straight debt and equity, its cost must be a weighted average of the cost of straight debt and the cost of equity. More precisely, it is a weighted average of the explicit interest charges on straight debt and the value of the associated option.

Recall from Chapter 21 on capital structure and the cost of capital that the value of straight debt would decline with risk as depicted in Figure 28.1. The cost of debt would, of course, rise with risk, also shown in Figure 28.1. Since the assessment of risk is uncertain, both the value of straight debt and the cost of debt are also uncertain. Hence, the value of straight debt is depicted as varying within some range. In contrast, we established in Chapter 18 that the value of an option rises with the variance or the riskiness of the underlying security into which the option is exercised. This relationship is depicted in Figure 28.2. Again, the value of the option is shown as a band since both the assessment of the risk and the related value would be uncertain.

High uncertainty would decrease the value and increase the cost of straight debt. With high risk or uncertainty for a company or project, the likelihood of establishing a value or cost that is fair both to the issuer and the buyer is improved by attaching an option. Combining an option with a straight debt security makes its value and cost less sensitive to the uncertainty associated with the outlook for a firm or a project.

The foregoing provides a basis for predictions of the characteristics of firms and the circumstances under which convertibles or securities with warrants are likely to be employed. These are listed below:

1.   Firms with uncertain operating risks characterized by low stock and bond ratings
2.   Concern about agency problems
     a.   Uncertain investment programs
     b.   Other divergences of interest between shareholders and bondholders
3.   Periods of general uncertainty in the economy
4.   Firms with investment activities in international markets or other environments of high uncertainty
5.   Firms with less need for tax shelter.

Figure 28.1   Debt Value and Risk

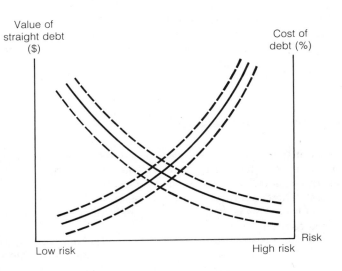

Figure 28.2   Option Value and Risk

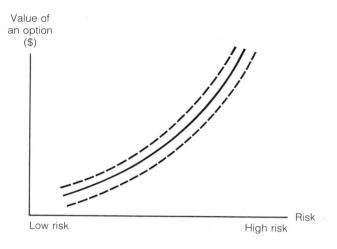

Low risk

High risk

Value of an option ($)

Risk

The reasons why options may perform a useful role by combining them with other securities under the conditions listed above will next be briefly summarized.

Low stock and bond ratings indicate a high uncertainty with regard to the outlook for the firm. Hence, when such firms sell debt, we would expect to find some form of option associated with it. With regard to agency problems, the managers of a company with straight debt outstanding may have an incentive to increase the riskiness of the firm's investment programs. Increasing the risk of the firm hurts the bondholders and helps the common stockholders. This is because if risky projects turn out well, the bondholders do not receive any more than the fixed return originally promised, and the stockholders reap all of the rewards. The buyers of straight debt must take this possibility into account and require compensation in the form of a higher promised coupon rate. The higher cost of straight debt can be avoided by attaching an option which enables bondholders to participate in any actions which increase the value of the common stock.

This is an example of the agency problem reflecting the divergence of interest with respect to investment programs. A wide range of divergent interests may be present. For example, a high dividend payout or selling off the assets of the company reduces the asset security for the bondholders. All of these potentially adverse actions by shareholders will be taken into account by bondholders and cause the cost of straight debt to be higher. One way of avoiding these higher costs is to use bond covenants or bond agreements which restrict the discretion of shareholders. But, this represents a cost also in that it restricts the flexibility and freedom of action of the firm. Hence, using options instead of bond covenants may be a way of reducing the cost of dealing with agency problems.

Periods of general uncertainty in the economy are likely to be particularly adverse to bondholders. For example, a severe recession will decrease the ability of a firm to pay the interest on its debt. At the other extreme, a high rate of inflation will reduce the purchasing power of the fixed return provided by straight debt. Thus, periods of high uncertainty are likely to be associated with the increased use of debt with some form of options such as warrants or convertibility.

For similar reasons, firms with considerable activity in international markets or other environments of high uncertainty impose greater risks on bondholders. International activities involve new risks such as adverse policies by foreign governments, including, in the extreme, the possibility of expropriation. Fluctuating exchange rates impose additional risks.

Finally, there is also a tax aspect. When an option feature is included in straight debt, the nominal interest expense is lowered. Hence, the tax shield provided by interest payments is reduced for the firm. This is a disadvantage unless the firm has less need for interest-type shields because of previous losses or large tax shields in the form of investment tax credits or accelerated depreciation. Hence, firms with less need for interest tax shields are more likely to use the lower interest bearing debt with options in the form of warrants or convertibility.

Empirical Evidence Consistent with the Foregoing Rationale for the Use of Convertibles

In his early study, Brigham [1966] found that firms using convertible debt, on average, had lower bond ratings relative to firms generally. In a more recent study, Mikkelson [1980] found that firms with high debt leverage and high growth companies were active users of convertibles. High leverage increases financial risks. High growth is subject to the risks of building an effective organization, competitive reactions by rivals, and changes in investment programs. Longer maturities were also found to increase the likelihood of adding convertibility to a debt issue. Investment programs are subject to change over longer periods, and, in addition, it is simply more difficult to forecast the outlook for a firm over longer periods of time.

The basic rationale for associating options with straight debt is that while greater uncertainty increases the cost of debt, it increases the value of an associated warrant. Brennan and Schwartz [1982] provide a numerical illustration of the nature of this benefit. Table 28.4 conveys the nature of their example. Table 28.4 suggests that the rate on the straight debt of a firm of high risk might be three percentage points higher than the rate a firm of average risk would pay. The use of convertible debt, however, would reduce the coupon for both firms. But, it would be reduced relatively more for the firm of high risk. The suggested spread is only one-fourth of 1 percent for the high-risk firm over the firm of average risk. These numerical relationships, of course, are purely illustrative. The actual figures would depend upon the state of the security markets and the terms of the individual issues.

Table 28.4   Illustrative Benefit of Convertible Debt

	Company Risk	
	Average	High
Straight debt	13%	16%
Convertible debt	10%	10.25%

It should be emphasized that these nominal coupon rates do not represent the cost of convertible debt. Since convertible debt is a hybrid between straight debt and equity, the cost of convertible debt must necessarily be higher than the cost of straight debt. The 10 percent coupon on convertible debt shown for the firm of average risk is only part of the compensation to the investor. The other portion is the value of the option that he has received through the convertibility feature.

Furthermore, the total cost of convertible debt to the firm of high risk is not the one-fourth of 1 percent differential shown in Table 28.4. In the high-risk firm, the convertible debt will necessarily have a cost higher than that for the firm of average risk. Since the nominal coupon is only slightly higher for the firm of higher risk, the value of the option attached to its convertible debt must be even greater than for the firm of average risk. Thus, the investor in the convertible debt of the high-risk firm will be taking an even larger portion of his compensation in the form of the value of the option that he receives.

Nevertheless, there is still a rationale for the use of convertible debt. Necessarily, a high-risk company must pay more for financing than a firm of average risk. By combining straight debt with an option, the penalty of the higher risk is mitigated to some degree, so the differential cost is somewhat lower than it otherwise would be.

The Valuation of Convertibles

In concept, a *convertible bond* is a combination of a straight bond plus an option. Thus, in one sense, a convertible bond could be valued by calculating the value of the option expressed in the convertibility features. This would represent an oversimplification, however. In practice, additional factors must be taken into account. In their seminal work in this area, Brennan and Schwartz [1977, 1980] included consideration of call provisions, bankruptcy risk, and relations between the value of the underlying stock and the convertible bond value near maturity. Their formula involves a system of partial differential equations solved by numerical methods on the computer.

The Duplicating Portfolio Approach to the BOP

The complex model used by Brennan and Schwartz does not permit an easy numerical illustration of the valuation of convertible bonds. However, the binomial option pricing model (BOP), discussed in Chapter 18, permits a straightforward explanation. To demonstrate the versatility of option pricing, we shall employ a slight variation on the BOP described in Chapter 18. [See Courtadon and Merrick, 1983.]

Here, the main organizing idea is the use of a duplicating portfolio whose payoffs are identical to the payoff of the portfolio of call options alone. Since the payoffs are the same, the value of the calls will be equal to the value of the duplicating portfolio. To illustrate the use of the duplicating portfolio to value calls, we shall use the same data employed in Chapter 18 and illustrated by Figure 18.6. We will first summarize the facts from that previous example.

$$S_o = \$40.00 = \text{the current stock price}$$
$$X = \$38.00 = \text{the exercise price}$$
$$1 + R_F = 1.1 = 1 \text{ plus the risk-free rate of interest}$$
$$u = 1.2 = \text{the multiplicative upward movement in the stock price}$$
$$d = .67 = \text{the multiplicative downward movement in the stock price}$$
$$S^h = \$48$$

S^L =   \$26.80
C^h = $S^h - X = 10$
C^L = $\text{MAX}[0, S^L - X] = 0$
h =   the hedge ratio, defined as the ratio of *number of stock shares* divided by number of calls sold. (In Chapter 18, the symbol for the hedge ratio was *m*, where it was the *number of calls* per share of stock.)
B =   the beginning-of-the-period borrowings required in addition to the long position in stock (from h) to duplicate the 100 share option contract.

We shall next set forth three simple formulas whose results we will use to illustrate the formation of the duplicating portfolio.

$$h = \frac{C^h - C^L}{S^h - S^L} = \frac{\$10 - 0}{\$48 - \$26.80} = \frac{\$10}{21.2} = .4717 \tag{28.1}$$

$$B = \frac{100}{1 + R_F}[hS^L - C^L] = \frac{100}{1.1}[.4717(\$26.80) - 0] = \$1{,}149.23 \tag{28.2}$$

$$C = 100hS_o - B = 100(.4717)\$40 - \$1{,}149.23 = \$737.57. \tag{28.3}$$

The value of the 100 calls is \$737.57. Hence, the value for one call is \$7.38. With the above data, we can now illustrate the concept of the duplicating portfolio and some other relevant relationships. Recall that we begin with a portfolio of calls for 100 shares of stock. The hedge ratio we have calculated guides us to form a duplicating portfolio which consists of a long position in 47.17 shares of stock levered by a one-period borrowing of \$1,149.23. The current value of the duplicating portfolio is

Current value of stock: 47.17 × \$40	\$1,886.80
Less: borrowing	1,149.23
Current value of the duplicating portfolio	\$ 737.57

This is consistent with our formula calculation of the value of 100 calls at \$737.57. We shall next demonstrate that the payoffs for the duplicating portfolio are exactly the same as the end-of-period payoffs of the original portfolio of 100 calls. If the high value of the stock occurs, we have \$48 × 47.17 = \$2,264.16. From this, we deduct the amount borrowed multiplied by 1.1, the risk-free interest rate, to determine the amount of loan to be repaid. This would be \$1,264.16. The net value of the duplicating portfolio, therefore, if the high value of the stock occurs, is \$1,000. The value of the call would be \$10 × 100 = \$1,000. So the payoffs, if the high price of the stock occurs, are equal.

If the low price of the stock occurs, the stock is worth \$26.80 × 47.17 shares, giving a total of \$1,264.16. We have already calculated that the loan plus interest to be repaid at the end of the period is exactly this amount, so the net value of the portfolio is \$0. And, since the low value of the stock is \$26.80, the call which carries the exercise price of \$38 is worthless. So again, the payoff to the call portfolio is exactly the same as the payoff to the duplicating portfolio. This is why, with identical payoffs, the current value of the duplicating portfolio also provides a correct measure of the current value of the portfolio of calls.

We can also construct Table 28.5 (analogous to Table 18.3) which shows the payoffs from holding the portfolio of calls and the perfect hedge provided by holding the duplicating portfolio. If the call is worth \$7.38 and the hedge portfolio required that we buy h times one share of stock for \$40.00 and sell one call option, our net investment was

$$hS_o - C = (.4717)(\$40.00) - \$7.38 = \$11.488.$$

Table 28.5   Hedge Portfolio Payoffs (Variation of Table 18.3)

State of Nature	Portfolio	Payoff
Favorable	$hS^h - C^h$	$(.4717)(\$48) - \$10 = \$12.64$
Unfavorable	$hS^L - C^L$	$(.4717)(\$26.80) - \$0 = \$12.64$

From Table 28.5, we know that the hedge portfolio earns $12.64 in either state of nature. Therefore, one plus the rate of return on our hedge portfolio is

$$1 + R_F = \frac{\$12.64}{\$11.488} = 1.1.$$

This confirms that the option is correctly priced and that the hedge portfolio earns the risk-free rate of 10 percent.

Additionally, we need to be able to value a put option for use in subsequent analysis. Previously, we had indicated that having valued a call, the put-call parity relationship enables us to value a put. In the binomial option pricing model, we can value a put option directly.

A put option contract confers the right (which does not have to be exercised) to sell shares of stock at the put exercise price on or before a specified expiration date. The put will be "in-the-money" whenever the stock price is less than the exercise price; its value will be the difference between the exercise price of the put and (lower) stock price. Of course, if the stock price is greater than the exercise price of the put, the put will be "out-of-the-money" and would not be exercised. Formulas corresponding to those of the call can now be set forth for a put.

$$P^h = \text{MAX}[0,(X - S^h)]$$
$$P^L = X - S^L.$$

The other terms are defined by analogy to the call. We will assume the same facts as before, except that the exercise price of $38 applies to a put rather than a call. The three formulas that we will use are set forth below. (We use L^P for required beginning-of-period lending.)

$$h^P = \frac{P^h - P^L}{S^h - S^L} \tag{28.4}$$

$$L^P = \frac{100}{1 + R_F}[P^L - h^P S^L] \tag{28.5}$$

$$P = 100 h^P S_o + L^P \tag{28.6}$$

We now proceed to use the facts given to calculate the values of h^P, L^P, and the value of a put.

$$h^P = \frac{0 - \$11.20}{\$48 - \$26.80} = \frac{\$-11.20}{\$21.20} = -.5283 \qquad\qquad (28.4a)$$

$$L^P = \frac{100}{1.1}[\$11.20 - (-.5283)(\$26.80)] = \$2{,}305.31 \qquad\qquad (28.5a)$$

$$P = 100(-.5283)(\$40) + \$2{,}305.31 = \$-2{,}113.20 + \$2{,}305.31 \qquad (28.6a)$$

$$= \$192.11.$$

The result is $192.11. This is for 100 puts, so the value per put is $1.92.

We can also verify that the duplicating portfolio has the same payoff as our original portfolio of 100 puts. We can see from Equation 28.4a that the duplicating portfolio consists of a short position in 52.83 shares of the stock plus one period lending of $2,305.31. If the stock declines in value to $26.80, the value of a put is that figure subtracted from $38.00, which is $11.20 times 100 shares to give the value of a put portfolio of $1,120. The value of the duplicating portfolio is

Receive on the loan: 1.1 × $2,305.31	$ 2,536
Less: Buy 52.83 shares @ $26.80	−1,416
Value of the duplicating portfolio	$ 1,120

Thus, we see that the payoff of the duplicating portfolio is exactly equal to the payoff of the put portfolio.

If the value of the stock rises to $48, the value of each put is zero because we would not exercise the right to force someone to buy our stock for $38 when it could be sold in the open market for more than that. The value of the duplicating portfolio is

Receive on the loan: 1.1 × $2,305.31	$2,536
Buy in stock: 52.83 shares @ $48	2,536
Value of the duplicating portfolio	−0−

Thus, the payoffs of the put portfolio are the same as the payoffs of the duplicating portfolio. Hence, the current value of the duplicating portfolio can be used to measure the current value of the put portfolio. This value was shown in Equation 28.6a as $192.11.

Use of the Binomial Option Pricing to Value Straight Debt and Convertible Debt

We first consider the situation of straight debt. We start with the valuation of straight debt as a basis for moving on to the valuation of convertible debt. Straight debt carries with it an implicit option from the standpoint of the equity holders and from the standpoint of the bondholders. The equity shareholders have a call option on the value of the firm's assets with an exercise price equal to the par value of the debt. If, at the maturity of the debt, the value of the firm is greater than the face value of the debt, the call will be exercised. If less, the call will not be exercised and the bondholders will receive the value of the firm (which will be below the face value of their claim). The bondholders may view their position as a riskless, one-period claim on the face value of debt and a short-position in a one-period put option contract on the value of the firm's assets with an exercise price equal to the face value of the debt. Through the limited liability provision for stockholders, they have the right to put to the bondholders the assets of the firm regardless of its value to satisfy the face value claim of the debt. Since the market value of the debt reflects what bondholders are willing to pay for it, we take the view of bondholders. Hence, we need to use the put option formulas just developed but modified to relate to the bond claims. The resulting equations are

$$h = \frac{C_u - C_d}{V_u - V_d} \tag{28.7}$$

$$L = \frac{1}{1 + R_F}(h\ V_d - C_d) \tag{28.8}$$

$$C_f = h\ V - L, \tag{28.9}$$

where

$V =$ current market value of the firm = \$10 million
$V_u =$ upper value of the firm, end of the period = \$20 million
$V_d =$ lower value of the firm, end of the period = \$5 million
$D_1 =$ aggregate face value of the firm's debt, end of period = \$8 million
$C_u =$ upper value of the contingent claim, end of period = \$8 million
$C_d =$ lower value of the contingent claim, end of period = \$5 million
$R_F =$ risk-free rate of interest = 10 percent.

So that all symbols will be in one place, the symbols used in the discussion are collected here.

$h =$ proper hedge ratio; proper proportion of the firm's assets in the duplicating portfolio
$L =$ proper current riskless money market position in the duplicating portfolio (positive value indicates borrowing; negative value indicates lending)
$D_o =$ one-period discounted beginning-of-period value of the firm's debt = $D_1/(1.1)$
$C_f =$ current fair value of the contingent claim represented by nonconvertible debt $\equiv B_o =$ market value of a straight bond
$C_{fc} =$ current fair value of the contingent claim represented by convertible debt $\equiv B_{oc} =$ market value of a convertible bond
$N =$ current number of shares of common stock outstanding = 1,000,000
$n =$ additional shares upon conversion
$CP =$ conversion price
$CV =$ conversion value
$TCV =$ total conversion value.

Using the data included in the definition of symbols, we use the binomial option pricing model for a put to obtain the current market value of the straight bond. The resulting values are

$$h = \frac{\$8 - \$5}{\$20 - \$5} = \frac{\$3}{\$15} = .2 \tag{28.7a}$$

$$L = \frac{1}{1.1}[.2(\$5) - \$5] = -\frac{\$4}{1.1} = \$-3.636\ (-\text{ is lend, } +\text{ is borrow}) \tag{28.8a}$$

$$C_f = .2(\$10) - (\$-3.636) = \$2 + \$3.636 = \$5.636 = B_o. \tag{28.9a}$$

The results we have obtained represent the valuation of the straight debt by a duplicating portfolio whose value can be directly calculated. The hedge ratio of .2 represents the portion of the firm's assets held by purchasing 20 percent of the firm's debt and equity. In addition, the duplicating portfolio includes one-period riskless lending whose present value is $3.636 million. Since the pure debt position and the value of the duplicating portfolio have the same end-of-period payoffs, they must have the same current market values to avoid arbitrage opportunities. The fair value of the debt (viewed as a contingent claim) as shown by Equation 28.9a is the 20 percent of the current value of the firm plus the present value of the lending, giving a total of $5.636 million.

But, the end-of-period payoff of the debt is $8 million, which discounted back to the present at the 10 percent rate is $7.273 million, which exceeds the current market value of the debt of $5.636 by $1.637 million. This represents the premium necessary to compensate a current buyer of the firm's debt for the loss if the end-of-period asset value turns out to be only $5 million. It represents the fair price for writing a put with one year to expiration on the value of the firm's assets with an exercise price of $8 million.

BOP Valuation of Convertible Debt

We next analyze the valuation of convertible debt employing the same basic logic. We assume that the debt has a convertibility feature with a conversion price of $11. If conversion of the debt takes place, the number of new shares would be

$$n = D_1/CP = \$8,000,000/\$11 = 727,273 \text{ shares.}$$

Since $N = 1,000,000$, $(n + N)$ would be 1,727,273. If the higher value of the firm occurred at the end of the period, the conversion value per share would be

$$CV = V_u/(n + N) = \$20,000,000/1,727,273 = \$11.58.$$

The total conversion value of the bond (TCV) can be obtained by simply multiplying the $11.58 just calculated by the number of shares obtained on conversion:

$$TCV = CV(n) = \$11.58(727,273) = \$8,421,821.$$

Hence, if V_u occurs, the bondholders should convert since $8.42 million is greater than the face value of $8 million. We can then calculate the current value of the convertible bond. We use the same formulas, except that the C_u value is now the $8.42 million. The resulting equations are

$$h = \frac{\$8.42 - \$5}{\$20 - \$5} = \frac{\$3.42}{\$15} = .228 \qquad\qquad \textbf{(28.7b)}$$

$$L = \frac{1}{1.1}[.228(\$5) - \$5]$$

$$= .909(\$1.14 - \$5) = .909(\$-3.86) = \$-3.509 \qquad\qquad \textbf{(28.8b)}$$

$$C_{fc} = .228(\$10) + \$3.509 = \$2.28 + \$3.509 = \$5.789. \qquad\qquad \textbf{(28.9b)}$$

The hedge ratio rises to .228; the lending decreases to $3.509 million; and C_{fc} = $5.789. Thus, a portfolio that duplicates the cash flows of the convertible debt combines .228 of the firm's debt plus equity plus riskless one-period lending of $3.509 million. Since this portfolio is currently valued at $5.789 million, it is also the fair value of the convertible issue.

Recall that the value of the straight debt was $5.636 million. We had observed that a convertible could be regarded as the combination of straight debt plus a warrant. Hence, the value of the implicit warrant is

$$\text{Value of ``warrant''} = C_{fc} - C_f = \$5.789 - \$5.636$$

$$= \$.153 \text{ million.}$$

The convertible debt is a straight debt plus a call option. Hence, convertible debt is a risk-free bond, plus a short put option position and a long call option position. We, therefore, have the following relationships:

Face value of the debt at maturity	$8.000 million
Current discounted value of the straight debt = 8/1.1	$7.273 million
Current market value of straight debt (Equation 28.9a)	$5.636 million
Difference: Fair value of selling a put with an exercise price of $8 million when value might fall to $5 million	$1.637 million
Current market value of convertible debt	$5.789 million
Current market value of straight debt	$5.636 million
Difference: Fair value of holding a call on the common stock with an exercise price of $11	$ .153 million

Thus, the binomial option pricing model enables us to convey the logic of option pricing applied to valuing both straight debt and convertible debt. We had observed in Chapter 18 that the Black and Scholes option pricing model is one of the limiting cases of the binomial option pricing model. The logic of the two approaches is the same, but the principles can be conveyed more simply by use of the binomial option pricing model.

Call Policy on Convertible Bonds

The call policy on convertible bonds performs a critical role. The effective return to the investor depends on how much the issuer permits the market price of a convertible bond to rise before calling it. For example, suppose that a convertible bond with a face value of $1,000 can be converted into 40 shares of common stock. The conversion price is, therefore, $25. If the market price of the common stock were $20, there would be no immediate incentive to convert into the common stock. However, as the common stock rises above $25, there will be some incentive to convert. For example, if the common stock were to rise in value to $35, the market value of the stock into which the bond can be converted is $1,400, which is 40 percent above the face value of the bond. Suppose that the bond carries a call provision which gives the company the right to call the bond at $105, or a value of $1,050. When the market price of the stock rises sufficiently above $25 to give the bond a value of more than $1,050, the company is in a position to call the bond at the $1,050.

Purchasers of convertible bonds would obviously prefer to have the company permit the price of the stock to rise well above the $25 before the company forced conversion.

Otherwise, the holders of the convertible bonds would be faced with the choice of exercising their conversion privilege or accepting the $1,050 call price for their bond. A number of alternative company policies would be possible. Companies could establish the reputation for calling convertibles as soon as the market value of the convertible rises a small amount above the call price. Other companies might seek to establish a reputation for waiting until the market price of the stock is substantially above its conversion price to allow more generous returns to investors in their convertibles. Or a company might follow a pattern which made it difficult to discern whether or not it had a definite policy on conversion. These are the kinds of issues that have stimulated a literature on the optimal call policy for a company to follow.

Ingersoll [1977a] has set forth the optimal call point. He defines the expression for conversion terms by Equation 28.10:

$$q \equiv n/(n + N). \tag{28.10}$$

In the above expression, q represents the conversion terms, n is the number of shares of common stock into which the convertible issue can be exchanged, and N is the number of shares of common stock already outstanding. He defines the conversion value of the issue as qV, where V is the value of the firm, assuming that the common stock and convertible are the only financial claims issued by the company. Ingersoll states, "Under the optimal call policy, the bond is called when its conversion value equals its call price, K." (pp. 465-466). Thus,

$$qV = K. \tag{28.11}$$

From a practical standpoint, Ingersoll observes that bondholders must be given 30-day notice of a call. During this delayed period, there is some risk of price fluctuations. The firm will want to have some margin of safety that conversion will take place rather than having to use cash to redeem the bonds. Ingersoll suggests that a cushion of about 6 to 8 percent above the call price would be prudent. This will give management reasonable assurance that fluctuations in the stock price after notice has been given will not create incentives for redemption rather than conversion.

The actual call policies of companies diverge widely from the theoretical boundaries. Ingersoll found that for the period between 1968 and 1975, the average ratio of conversion value of the bonds was 43.9 percent above the call price. For convertible preferreds, on average, the conversion value exceeded the call price by 38.5 percent.

The prevailing literature has found it difficult to provide a satisfactory explanation of this wide divergence between theory and practice with respect to call policy. One possible explanation is that management seeks to avoid dilution in reported earnings per share. But this is not plausible since earnings must be reported on both a diluted and undiluted basis. If management compensation is tied to undiluted reported earnings, this, of course, would make a difference.

Another possible explanation has been termed "fair play" by some and "market memory" by others. The idea that management imposes self-restrictions on call policy out of some notion of fair play has not received much support. A more plausible view is that on successive issues of convertibles, the market will form an expectation of the company's call policies by its past behavior. Anecdotal evidence can be found in the financial press that companies have had to pay a somewhat higher interest rate on a new issue of convertibles because of a past history of calling convertibles as soon as their conversion value has risen modestly above their call price. The market will penalize erratic behavior; what appears optimal is the adoption by the company of a consistent call policy. Whether the policy is to call at a conversion value substantially above call price or at a conversion value close to call price will be "priced out" by the market. This is not a matter of "fairness" or self-imposed restrictions. It is a matter of providing investors with a basis for forming expectations.

The reason that the call policy of a company takes on significance is that it has a major influence on what investors will earn by purchasing a convertible (which also, of course, represents the cost to the issuing firm). But, the convertible is a straight bond plus an option. The idea behind an option is that there will be variations in the price of the underlying stock. Upside fluctuations provide opportunities for converting into the common stock. One way of portraying these relationships is expressed in Equation 28.12:

$$C_t = p_o(1 + g)^t q, \tag{28.12}$$

where

$C_t =$ the conversion value of the bond at Time t
$p_o =$ the initial price of the underlying common stock = \$44.02
$g =$ the growth rate in the price of the common stock = .06
$q =$ the conversion ratio = 18.52.

Equation 28.12 is an oversimplification in a number of respects. The idea of an option is that there are fluctuations in both directions. Equation 28.12 ignores the downside fluctuations and postulates upside movements expressed as a constant rate of growth. Also, the formula implies certainty, but a number of uncertainties are involved. The actual rate of growth is uncertain, its duration is not known, and the call policy of the company may not be clear.

But, Equation 28.12 is a useful oversimplification for illustrating how the return to the investor and the cost to the issuing firm depend upon the price of the underlying stock which is obtained if the option is exercised. In the present illustration, the convertible bond was not callable until five years after issuance. Let us consider some possibilities of what the conversion value of the bond might be after five years have elapsed. Suppose that during the five-year period, the stock averaged a growth rate of 6 percent and that the call price at the end of five years is \$1,080. First, calculate the conversion value as shown in Equation 28.12a:

$$C_5 = \$44.02(1 + .06)^5 18.52$$
$$= \$44.02(1.3382)(18.52) \tag{28.12a}$$
$$= \$1,090.97.$$

Suppose the call value at the end of five years is \$1,080. The conversion value is only about 1 percent above its call value. On the other hand, if the underlying stock price had grown at an average rate of 12 percent for the five years, we would have the situation depicted in Equation 28.12b:

$$C_5 = \$44.02(1 + .12)^5 18.52$$
$$= \$44.02(1.7623)(18.52) \tag{28.12b}$$
$$= \$1,436.72.$$

Here, the conversion value would be $1,436.72, which is about 33 percent above the $1,080 call value.

The return that investors actually realize on a convertible, therefore, is heavily dependent on the performance of the stock price in relation to the exercise price, which is, of course, implicit in the conversion ratio used in Equation 28.12. For example, using the data assumed for Equation 28.12b, we can calculate the return realized by the investor if the company followed the policy of calling a convertible as soon as callability is permitted when its conversion value is substantially above the call price. We shall define the expected rate of return on a convertible, k_c, by solving for k_c in Equation 28.13:

$$B_{co} = \sum_{t=1}^{n} \frac{c}{(1 + k_c)^t} + \frac{C_n}{(1 + k_c)^n}. \tag{28.13}$$

The equation is purely definitional; it simply states that if an investor pays B_{co} dollars for a convertible bond, holds it for n years, and receives a series of interest payments plus a conversion value, then the return on the investment will be equal to k_c.[1]

The *ex ante* yield on a convertible (k_c) is probabilistic — dependent on a set of variables subject to probability distributions and, hence, itself a random variable. It is possible, however, to define each of the determinants of k_c in terms of its mean expected value; $E(g)$, for example, is the expected value of the growth rate in the stock's price over n years. For simplicity, $E(g)$ and other random variables are shortened to g, C_n, and so on.

For example, we have a bond paying a coupon of $80 a year and we are analyzing the effect if the company calls the bond as soon as possible at the end of five years when the provisions of the bond indenture permit the company to do so. Using semiannual compounding, we can express the relationships in Equation 28.13a:

$$B_{co} = \sum_{t=1}^{10} \frac{40}{(1 + .07)^t} + \frac{1,436.72}{(1 + .07)^{10}} \tag{28.13a}$$

$$997 = 7.0236(40) + .5083(1,436.72)$$

$$= 280.94 + 730.28$$

$$997 \approx 1,011.22.$$

With semiannual compounding, the coupon would be $40 at each semiannual payment for ten periods. We find that using a semiannual rate of 7 percent, we obtain a bond value approximating the assumed price paid for the convertible bond, $997. Hence, the effective yield to the investor and the effective cost to the issuer is slightly over 14 percent. This represents 2.5 percentage points higher than the then-prevailing market rate on straight debt of otherwise similar characteristics. This illustrates how the effective return on a convertible bond is likely to be greater than the return on straight debt. The relationships depicted here are purely illustrative. What is actually realized depends upon the resolution of a wide range of uncertainties that are involved as to the performance of the company and its common stock during the time period under analysis.

---

[1] Three simplifications are made in this analysis. First, taxes are ignored. Second, the problem of reinvestment rates is handled by assuming that all reinvestment is made at the internal rate of return. Third, it is assumed that bondholders do not hold stock after conversion; they cash out, as do some institutional investors precluded from holding common stock.

Studies of convertible bond calls find a negative effect on market prices [Mikkelson, 1981]. Convertible bond calls are associated with an average 2 percent decline in stock prices. Forced conversions of preferred stock issues are associated with an average market decline of 0.33 percent. One possible explanation for this negative market reaction to forced conversion is that debt leverage has been decreased and some of the firm's interest tax shelter has been lost. However, if only a pure tax effect were involved, then managers would not be acting in the best interest of shareholders to reduce the tax advantage from which they had been benefiting. This suggests that management had been pressured by some other developments or factors which caused it to sacrifice some tax shelter. Thus, forced conversions may convey an "information effect." The market may interpret forced conversions as a judgment by management that less-favorable developments are facing the firm. This activity by managers in reducing the amount of debt on the balance sheets may be regarded as getting the firm ready to meet some future adversity. Thus, forced conversion may be viewed as a harbinger of unfavorable things to come and cause the market price of the firm's common stock to decline.

The relationships among the coupon, purchase price, call policy, and investor cash-out policy determine the return on an investment in a convertible security. This represents the cost of convertible debt. The required return or cost of convertible debt is composed of two parts. One is the interest return based on the coupon on the convertible debt. This is, typically, lower than the return on straight debt. The second component of return is based on the expected rise in the price of the common stock into which a conversion may be made. This component of return carries risk associated with a security junior to straight debt. Hence, the required return on convertibles would, on average, be higher than the cost of straight debt.

Summary

Both warrants and convertibles are forms of options used in financing business firms. When warrants are exercised, they bring in additional funds to the firm. When convertibles are exchanged for common stock, no increase in funds is provided to the firm. Only the form of its financing has been changed. The time to maturity on warrants issued by a company is usually much longer than the maturity of puts and calls traded on the options exchanges. A warrant is a call option plus a provision for the issuance of more securities for cash. The return and risk of a warrant are correlated with the return and risk of a call. The value of a warrant is the value of the equivalent call divided by the dilution factor $(1 + q)$, where q is the ratio of warrants to shares.

In concept, a convertible bond represents straight debt plus a warrant. Hence, the value of a convertible bond may be viewed as a package of straight debt plus the value of the associated option. Since a convertible bond usually includes a call feature which is adjusted over time, and since the maturity characteristics as well as bankruptcy possibilities must be taken into account, the precise calculation of the value of a convertible can be quite complex.

But, the rationale for both warrants and convertibles has now been well established. The value of straight debt falls with risk, or, equivalently, its required cost rises with risk. But, the value of the associated warrant or option rises with risk. Hence, it is easier for sellers and buyers of a security which combines both features to arrive at a mutually agreeable price. Thus, warrants and convertibles perform a particularly useful role in selling the securities of firms with high or uncertain operating risks. They also provide control of agency problems with respect to the possibility of changing investment programs and other areas where there may be a divergence of interests between shareholders and bondholders. Warrants and convertibles are also likely to be used to an increased degree during periods of high uncertainty in the economy.

In theory, convertibles should be called when the conversion value of the bond equals its call price plus a cushion of about 6 to 8 percent above the call price. However, the practice is much different. On average, companies call convertibles when they are about 40 percent above their call price. The reasons for this divergence are still in dispute.

It is clear, however, that a call policy which delays until a substantial premium of conversion value over call price has developed increases the return to holding a convertible. The basic reason is that the value of any option is increased as its maturity is increased. Delaying the call until a substantial premium has developed will generally involve a longer time for investors to exercise the conversion option. The expected return on a convertible can be calculated from Equation 28.13. The cost of a convertible will generally be found to be above the cost of straight debt. It will represent a weighted average between the cost of straight debt and the cost of equity capital.

In brief, warrants and convertibles may perform a useful role in reducing monitoring costs of controlling agency problems. Also, combining an option with a straight debt security makes its value and cost less sensitive to the uncertainty associated with a firm or a project. Thus, warrants and convertibles are likely to be used when agency problems may be of high concern and when uncertainty due either to external economy factors or to conditions specific to the firm may be particularly large.

Questions

28.1   Why do warrants typically sell at prices greater than their formula values?

28.2   Why do convertibles typically sell at prices greater than straight debt with the same coupon, maturity, and call provisions?

28.3   What effect does the trend in stock prices (subsequent to issue) have on a firm's ability to raise funds through convertibles? Through warrants?

28.4   If a firm expects to have additional financial requirements in the future, would you recommend that it use convertibles or bonds with warrants? Why?

28.5   Evaluate the following statement: Issuing convertible securities represents a means by which a firm can sell common stock at a price above the existing market.

28.6   Why do corporations often sell convertibles on a rights basis?

28.7   Why might an investor prefer a bond with a warrant attached, over a convertible bond?

Problems

28.1   A convertible bond has a face value of $1,000 and a 10 percent coupon rate. It is convertible into stock of $50; that is, each bond can be exchanged for 20 shares. The current price of the stock is $43 per share.

    a)   If the price per share grows at 6 percent per year for five years, what will the approximate conversion value be at the end of five years?

    b)   If dividends on the stock are presently $2 per share, and if these also grow at 6 percent per year, will bondholders convert after five years, or will they tend to hold onto their bonds? Explain.

    c)   If the bonds are callable at a 10 percent premium, about how much would you lose per bond if the bonds were called before you converted? (Assume the same conversion value as in Part (a) above, at the end of five years.)

28.2 Warrants attached to a bond entitle the bondholder to purchase one share of stock at $10 per share. Compute the approximate value of a warrant if

a) The market price of the stock is $9 per share
b) The market price of the stock is $12 per share
c) The market price of the stock is $15 per share
d) Each warrant entitles you to purchase two shares at $10, and the current price of the stock is $15 per share.

28.3 The Schuller Chemical Company's net income for 1984 was $2,450,000. Schuller's capital stock consists of 500,000 shares of common stock, and 175,000 warrants, each good for buying two shares of common stock at $25. The warrants are protected against dilution; that is, the exercise price must be adjusted downward in the event of a stock dividend or if Schuller sells common stock at less than the $25 exercise price. On June 1, 1985, Schuller issued rights to buy one new share of common stock for $15 for every four shares held. The market price of Schuller stock on June 1 was $45 per share.

a) Compute primary and fully diluted EPS as of December 31, 1984.
b) What is the theoretical value of the rights before the stock sells ex rights?
c) What is the adjusted exercise price of the warrants after the rights offering? (Hint: Adjust the exercise price of the warrant so that the formula value of the warrant based on the ex rights stock price is the same as the formula value before the rights offering.)
d) Net income for 1985 is $2,800,000. All of the rights and none of the warrants have been exercised. Compute primary and fully diluted EPS for 1985.

28.4 The Ironhill Manufacturing Company was planning to finance an expansion in the summer of 1985. The principal executives of the company were agreed that an industrial company such as theirs should finance growth by means of common stock rather than debt. However, they felt the price of the company's common stock did not reflect its true worth, so they were desirous of selling a convertible security. They considered a convertible debenture but feared the burden of fixed interest charges if the common stock did not rise in price to make conversion attractive. They decided on an issue of convertible preferred stock.

The common stock was selling at $48.00 a share. Management projected earnings for 1986 at $3.60 a share and expected a future growth rate of 12 percent a year. It was agreed by the investment bankers and management that the common stock would sell at 13.3 times earnings, the current price-earnings ratio.

a) What conversion price should be set by the issuer?
b) Should the preferred stock include a call price provision? Why?

28.5 The Durham Forge has the following balance sheet:

Balance Sheet 1

Current assets	$125,000	Current debt (free)	$ 50,000
Net fixed assets	125,000	Common stock, par value $2	50,000
		Retained earnings	150,000
Total assets	$250,000	Total claims	$250,000

Durham plans to sell $150,000 of debentures in order to finance its expected sales growth. It is trying to decide whether to sell convertible debentures or debentures with warrants. With spontaneous financing and retained earnings, next year's balance sheet is projected as follows:

Balance Sheet 2

Current assets	$250,000	Current debt	$100,000
Net fixed assets	250,000	Debentures	150,000
		Common stock, par value $2	50,000
		Retained earnings	200,000
Total assets	$500,000	Total claims	$500,000

The convertible debentures will pay 7 percent interest and will be convertible into 40 shares of common stock for each $1,000 debenture. The debentures with warrants will carry an 8 percent coupon and entitle each holder of a $1,000 debenture to buy 25 shares of common stock at $50.

a)   Assume that convertible debentures are sold and that all are later converted. Show the new balance sheet, disregarding any changes in retained earnings.

Balance Sheet 3

		Current debt	____
		Debentures	____
		Common stock, par value $2	____
		Paid-in capital	____
		Retained earnings	____
Total assets	____	Total claims	____

b)   Assume that instead of convertibles, debentures with warrants were issued. Assume further that the warrants were all exercised. Show the new balance sheet figures:

Balance Sheet 4

		Current debt	____
		Debentures	____
		Common stock, par value $2	____
		Paid-in capital	____
		Retained earnings	____
Total assets	____	Total claims	____

c)   Durham's earnings before interest and taxes are 30 percent of total assets, its P-E ratio is 16, and its corporate tax rate is 40 percent. Prepare income statements corresponding to balance sheets 3 and 4. What is the effect of each alternative on Durham's EPS and market price per share?

d)   Should Durham choose convertible debentures or debentures with warrants?

28.6   On July 2, 1984, it was announced that the Dana Corporation was issuing $150 million face amount of debt at $500 for each $1,000 face amount of securities. The debentures carry a 5⅞ percent coupon, maturing in 2009. They are convertible until December 15, 1996, at $75.64 face amount of debentures for each common share. The common closed on July 2, 1984, at $32.

a)   How many shares of common stock would be received upon conversion?

b)   What is the conversion price based on the $500 issuing price of the bonds?

c)   What percentage premium does this represent over the $32 common stock price?

d) What is the yield to maturity of the bonds based on the data given? (Assume semiannual compounding.)

e) Assume that the common stock of Dana increases in price by 10 percent per year and that the bonds sell at the higher of 12 percent above their conversion value or at their "intermediate face value," which is the $500 issue price increased by 4 percent per year. Assume that for a number of reasons, a purchaser of the bonds sells the bonds at the end of ten years. Based on the higher of the two prices, what return has the investor earned?

28.7 The Printomat Company has grown rapidly during the past five years. Recently, its commercial bank has urged the company to consider increasing permanent financing. Its bank loan under a line of credit has risen to $175,000, carrying 15 percent interest. Printomat has been 30 to 60 days late in paying trade creditors.

Discussions with an investment banker have resulted in the suggestion to raise $350,000 at this time. Investment bankers have assured the company that the following alternatives will be feasible (ignoring flotation costs):

1. Sell common stock at $7.
2. Sell convertible bonds at a 7 percent coupon, convertible into common stock at $8.
3. Sell debentures at a 7 percent coupon, each $1,000 bond carrying 125 warrants to buy common stock at $8.

Additional information is given in the company's balance sheet and income statement below:

Printomat Company Balance Sheet

		Current liabilities	$315,000
		Common stock, par $1	90,000
		Retained earnings	45,000
Total assets	$450,000	Total liabilities and capital	$450,000

Printomat Company Income Statement

Sales	$900,000
All costs except interest	810,000
Net operating income	$ 90,000
Interest	26,250
Income before taxes	$ 63,750
Taxes (at 40%)	25,500
Net income	$ 38,250
Shares	90,000
Earnings per share	$0.43
Price-earnings ratio	17 times
Market price of stock	$7.31

Mary Anderson, the president, owns 70 percent of Printomat's common stock and wishes to maintain control of the company; 90,000 shares are outstanding.

a) Show the new balance sheet under each alternative. For alternatives 2 and 3, show the balance sheet after conversion of the debentures or exercise of warrants. Assume that half the funds raised will be used to pay off the bank loan and half to increase total assets.

b)   Show Anderson's control position under each alternative, assuming that she does not purchase additional securities.

c)   What is the effect on earnings per share of each alternative if it is assumed that profits before interest and taxes will be 20 percent of total assets?

d)   What will be the debt ratio under each alternative?

e)   Which of the three alternatives would you recommend to Anderson? Explain.

28.8   Vaught Engineering plans to sell a 6 percent coupon, $1,000 par value, 20-year convertible bond issue. The bond is callable at $1,050 in the first year, and the call price declines by $2.50 each year thereafter. The bond may be converted into 18 shares of stock with a current market price of $46 per share. The stock price is expected to grow at a rate of 7 percent per year. Nonconvertible bonds of the same risk as Vaught's would yield 9 percent. In the past, Vaught's policy has been to call convertible securities when the conversion value exceeds the call price by 20 percent.

a)   Determine the straight debt value (B_t) at $t = 0$, $t = 6$, and $t = 10$. Use these three points and the maturity value (M) to graph the straight debt value of the convertible.

b)   Graph the conversion value (C_t) on the same graph for $t = 0$, $t = 6$, and $t = 10$.

c)   What is the minimum the convertible can sell for at $t = 0$? At $t = 6$? At $t = 10$? Assume the stock value increases as predicted.

d)   Show the call price, D_{ct}, of the debt on the same graph at $t = 0$, $t = 5$, $t = 6$, and $t = 10$.

e)   In what year is the debt expected to be called?

f)   On the graph, locate on C_t the point where the expected call policy forces conversion (M'). Draw a curve between the issue price B_{co} and M' with curvature similar to the C_t curve.

g)   What would debtholders do if the bond was called at $t = 0$? At $t = 5$? At $t = 6$?

h)   What return on investment is earned by bondholders who purchased the convertibles at par value on the date they were issued if the bonds are called in four years?

28.9   Olympic Lumber Company is planning to raise $10 million by selling convertible debentures. It recently sold an issue of nonconvertible debentures yielding 10 percent. Investment bankers have informed the treasurer that she can sell convertibles at a lower interest yield; they have offered her these two choices:

A. $p_c = \$55.55$ $(q = 18)$
       $c = \$70$ (7% coupon yield)
       $M = \$1,000$
       25-year maturity

B. $p_c = \$58.82$ $(q = 17)$
       $c = \$80$ (8% coupon yield)
       $M = \$1,000$
       25-year maturity

In each case, the bonds are not callable for two years; but, thereafter, they are callable at $1,000. Investors do not expect the bonds to be called unless $C_t = \$1,354$; but they do expect the bonds to be called if $C_t = \$1,354$.

Olympic's current stock price (p_o) is $50, and its growth is expected to continue at an annual rate of 6 percent. Olympic's current dividend is $4.50 per share, so investors appear to have an expected (and required) rate of return of 15 percent $(k = d/p_o + g = \$4.50/\$50 + 6\%)$ on investments as risky as the company's common stock. Olympic's tax rate is 40 percent.

a) Determine the expected yield on Bond A and on Bond B.

b) Do the terms offered by the investment bankers seem consistent? Which bond would an investor prefer? Which would Olympic's treasurer prefer?

c) Suppose the company decided on Bond A but wanted to step up the conversion price from $55.55 to $58.82 after ten years. Should this stepped-up conversion price affect the expected yield and the other terms on the bonds?

d) Suppose, contrary to investors' expectations, Olympic called the bonds after two years. What would the *ex post* (after-the-fact) effective yield be on Bond A? Would this early call affect the company's credibility in the financial markets?

e) What would happen to the wealth position of an investor who bought Olympic bonds the day before the announcement of the unexpected two-year call?

f) Suppose the expected yield on the convertible had been less than that on straight debt (actually, it was higher). Would this appear logical? Explain.

28.10 The Wright Corporation has a current market value of $40 million with 1 million shares of common stock outstanding. If the firm's current investment policy is successful, its value at the end of one period is expected to be $60 million; if unsuccessful, end-of-period value is expected to be $20 million. The firm has debt outstanding on which the face value of $25 million must be repaid at the end of the period. The risk-free rate is 10 percent.

a) Use the BOP model to find the present value of Wright's debt if the debt is nonconvertible.

b) If the debt is convertible with a conversion price of $25 per share, what is the present value of the convertible debt?

Selected References

Alexander, Gordon J., and Stover, Roger D., "The Effect of Forced Conversion on Common Stock Prices," *Financial Management*, 9 (Spring 1980), pp. 39-45.

———, "Pricing in the New Issue Convertible Debt Market," *Financial Management*, 6 (Fall 1977), pp. 35-39.

———, and Kuhnau, David B., "Market Timing Strategies in Convertible Debt Financing," *Journal of Finance*, 34 (March 1979), pp. 143-155.

Black, Fischer, and Scholes, Myron, "The Valuation of Option Contracts and a Test of Market Efficiency," *Journal of Finance*, 27 (May 1972), pp. 399-417.

Brennan, M. J., "The Pricing of Contingent Claims in Discrete Time Models," *Journal of Finance*, 24 (March 1979), pp. 53-68.

———, and Schwartz, E., "The Case for Convertibles," *Chase Financial Quarterly*, 1 (1982), pp. 27-46.

———, "Analyzing Convertible Bonds," *Journal of Financial and Quantitative Analysis*, 15 (November 1980), pp. 907-929.

———, "Convertible Bonds: Valuation and Optimal Strategies for Call and Conversion," *Journal of Finance*, 32 (December 1977), pp. 1699-1715.

Brigham, Eugene F., "An Analysis of Convertible Debentures: Theory and Some Empirical Evidence," *Journal of Finance*, 21 (March 1966), pp. 35-54.

Courtadon, G. R., and Merrick, J. J., "The Option Pricing Model and the Valuation of Corporate Securities," *Chase Financial Quarterly*, 1 (Fall 1983), pp. 43-56.

Emanuel, David C., "Warrant Valuation and Exercise Strategy," *Journal of Financial Economics*, 12 (August 1983), pp. 211-235.

Frankle, A. W., and Hawkins, C. A., "Beta Coefficients for Convertible Bonds," *Journal of Finance*, 30 (March 1975), pp. 207-210.

Galai, Dan, and Schneller, Mier I., "Pricing of Warrants and the Value of the Firm," *Journal of Finance*, 33 (December 1978), pp. 1333-1342.

Hettenhouse, G. W., and Puglisi, D. J., "Investor Experience with Options," *Financial Analysts Journal*, 31 (July-August 1975), pp. 53-58.

Ingersoll, J., "An Examination of Corporate Call Policies on Convertible Securities," *Journal of Finance*, (May 1977a), pp. 463-478.

———, "A Contingent-Claims Valuation of Convertible Securities," *Journal of Financial Economics*, (May 1977b), pp. 289-322.

Loy, L. David, and Toole, Howard R., "Accounting for Discounted Convertible Bond Exchanges: A Survey of Results," *Journal of Accounting, Auditing and Finance*, 3 (Spring 1980), pp. 227-243.

Mikkelson, Wayne H., "Convertible Calls and Security Returns," *Journal of Financial Economics*, 9 (September 1981), pp. 237-264.

————, "Convertible Debt and Warrant Financing: A Study of the Agency Cost Motivation and the Wealth Effects of Calls of Convertible Securities," MERC monograph and theses series MT-80-03, University of Rochester, Rochester, N. Y., 1980.

Schwartz, Eduardo S., "The Valuation of Warrants: Implementing a New Approach," *Journal of Financial Economics*, 4 (January 1977), pp. 79-93.

Stone, Bernell K., "Warrant Financing," *Journal of Financial and Quantitative Analysis*, 11 (March 1976), pp. 143-154.

Chapter 29 Pension Fund Management

Corporate pension plan liabilities have grown rapidly during the last three decades. For many companies, pension plan liabilities are larger than the book value of all long-term assets. This chapter describes various types of pension plans, publicly accepted accounting principles which govern pension plan reporting, the regulation of pension plans by ERISA, and management decision making about various pension plan problems, such as how to evaluate the performance of pension fund assets and how to use pension fund assets to reduce taxes.

Pension Plan Overview: Historical Data and Financial Statements

A *pension plan* is a promise by an employer to provide benefits to employees upon their retirement. Contractual pension fund commitments are a liability of the employer and must be disclosed in the firm's financial statements. A pension fund is established on behalf of the employees and is managed by a trustee, who collects cash from the firm, manages the assets owned by the fund, and makes disbursements to retired employees. The firm is able to expense pension fund contributions for tax purposes. The fund pays no taxes on its earnings. However, beneficiaries must pay personal taxes upon receiving retirement payments from the fund. Hence, pension funds are a tax-favored form of employee compensation because taxes are deferred until retirement.

Table 29.1 shows the rapid growth of pension fund assets in the United States over the past three decades. Private pension plans have grown at a rate of 12.5 percent per year and government plans at 8.4 percent per year. The rapid growth of private plans is explained, in part, by the fact that corporate contributions are tax deductible while employee benefits are tax deferred until retirement, when payments are then taxed at the individual's ordinary tax rate. Table 29.1 also shows that in 1980, $712.3 billion was invested in pension funds, with 59.3 percent of this total in the private sector. Pension fund management involves huge sums of money. Corporations often make their pension contributions to insurance companies, which then guarantee the benefits, or else firms manage their own funds. In 1980, 39.2 percent of the private pension fund assets were with insurance companies, but the majority, 60.8 percent, was controlled by the corporation via a pension fund trustee. It is also worth noting that in 1980, there were 30.3 million people who were members of pension plans. They represent roughly 30 percent of the work force.

Table 29.2 shows the format of a pension fund income statement and balance sheet. Cash inflows to the fund are provided by corporate contributions, employee contributions, dividends and interest earned by the fund's stocks and bonds, and capital gains. Cash outflows are management fees, brokerage expenses, disbursements to beneficiaries, and capital losses. The change in the net fund balance is the difference between inflows and outflows. The fund's profit is not taxable.

Table 29.1   Assets and Reserves of Major Pension and Retirement Programs in the United States
(Billions of Dollars)

	1950	1960	1970	1980
Private Plans				
With life insurance companies	$ 5.6	$ 18.8	$ 41.1	$165.8
Other private plans	6.4	33.1	97.0	256.9
Government Plans				
Railroad retirement	2.5	3.7	4.4	2.1
Federal civilian employees	4.3	10.8	23.9	75.8
State and local employees	5.2	19.6	58.2	185.2
Old-age, survivors', and				
disability insurance	13.7	22.6	38.1	26.5
Total	$37.7	$108.6	$262.7	$712.3

Sources: Railroad Retirement Board, Social Security Administration, U.S. Department of Health and Human Services, Securities and Exchange Commission, and the American Council of Life Insurance.

Turning to the balance sheet in Table 29.2, most pension funds hold their assets in the form of marketable securities: money market accounts, bonds, and stock. Because pension fund earnings are not taxed, it never pays to hold municipal bonds because their low tax-exempt interest rates are always dominated by the higher interest paid by taxable bonds. Direct investment in real estate (with the possible exception of undeveloped land) is also not advisable because most real estate investments are priced such that the investor must be in a relatively high tax bracket in order to receive a positive after-tax return. Pension funds are in a zero tax bracket. Although the pension fund can profitably hold taxable securities, it is not immediately clear what percentage of the fund's investment should be held in the form of interest-bearing securities (money market funds and bonds) or common stock. This choice will be discussed later in the chapter. Meanwhile, Table 29.3 shows the actual portfolio composition of private pension plans not held with insurance

Table 29.2   Format for Pension Fund Income Statement and Balance Sheet

Pension Fund Income Statement	Pension Fund Balance Sheet
Funds Received	Assets
From employer(s)	Marketable securities (market value)
From employees	Cash (money market accounts)
From dividends, interest, and capital gains (losses)	Bonds
	Stock
Funds Expended	PV of future contributions
Management fees and brokerage costs	Deficit (surplus)
Disbursements to beneficiaries	
Change in net fund balance	Liabilities
	PV of benefits for past service
	PV of benefits for future service

Table 29.3   Distribution of Assets of Noninsured Pension Funds (Percent of the Book Value of Total Assets Invested)

	1950	1960	1970	1980
U.S. Government Securities	30.5%	8.1%	3.1%	11.0%
Corporate bonds	43.8	47.4	30.6	24.9
Stocks	17.1	34.7	55.1	50.5
Mortgages	1.6	3.9	4.3	1.6
Cash, deposits, other	7.0	5.9	6.9	12.0
Total	100.0%	100.0%	100.0%	100.0%

Source: U.S. Securities and Exchange Commission.

companies at the end of each of the last four decades. The most striking change in portfolio composition is the decline in the proportion invested in bonds from 74.3 percent in 1950 to 35.9 percent in 1980 and the increase in stocks (common and preferred) from 17.1 percent in 1950 to 50.5 percent in 1980.

Returning to the pension fund balance sheet in Table 29.2, marketable securities is the only item which is not the result of a present value calculation. The present value of future contributions to the fund is the other major asset. Contributions are received in two forms: cash from the firm and earnings on the fund's assets. A major issue is: What rate of return will be generated from the fund's assets? If the return is high, then the firm can reduce the amount of cash which it puts into the fund. As we shall see, later in the chapter, the rate of return assumption is a tricky decision.

Liabilities are subdivided into two categories. The present value of benefits from past service is handled one of two ways. Some companies calculate the present value of *vested benefits* only. These are the benefits which would be paid if all employees left the firm immediately. However, it is typical that employees become vested in the pension plan only after accumulating a minimum period of seniority, say five years. If they leave prior to five years, they receive none of their promised pension benefits. An alternative procedure is to calculate the present value of all benefits accrued for past service whether employees are fully vested or not. Hence, *accrued benefits* will usually be larger than vested benefits because not all employees are fully vested. Regardless of how the present value of benefits from past service is handled, total pension liabilities remain unchanged. If only vested benefits are included in the present value of benefits for past service, then unvested benefits are included in the second liability category.

The second major liability item is the present value of benefits for future service. Its computation is complex and depends on actuarial assumptions about the amount of employee turnover, the age and seniority of retiring employees, their life expectancy, and the choice of a discount rate for present value computations.

Of major concern to all parties is the size of the pension fund deficit or surplus. An unfunded deficit is an asset of the pension fund (as shown in Table 29.2) and a liability of the firm, and it can be enormous. For example, had the pension liabilities of du Pont been included, its balance sheet for the end of its 1984 fiscal year would have looked like Table 29.4. The $7.6 billion pension liability represents the vested liabilities of du Pont, that is, the liability which would be incurred if all of the employees left the firm at the end of 1984. Du Pont's pension was overfunded by $800 million. In principle, this money "belongs" to shareholders. Even though the pension was overfunded, the addition of pension assets

Table 29.4 Hypothetical 1984 Consolidated Year-End Balance Sheet for du Pont Showing Vested Pension Liabilities (Billions of Dollars)

Assets		Liabilities	
Pension fund	$ 8.4	Pension liability	$ 7.6
Plant and equipment	14.4	Long-term debt	3.4
Other long-term assets	1.0	Equity	13.0
Current assets	8.7	Other long-term liabilities	3.3
		Current liabilities	5.2
Total assets	$32.5	Total liabilities	$32.5

and liabilities to the balance sheet raised du Pont's debt-to-total-assets ratio from 49 percent to 60 percent.[1] Clearly, pension fund liabilities are important enough to require full disclosure.

Pension Fund Regulations: ERISA, FASB 36, and the IRS

With the rapid growth of pensions as a form of deferred compensation (as documented in Table 29.1), it became more and more important that firms fully disclose their pension commitments in their financial statements and that various pension practices become regulated by law. The Financial Accounting Standards Board (FASB) has established the generally accepted accounting practices for reporting by pension funds (FASB No. 35, issued in 1980) and by firms (APB No. 8, issued in 1966, and FASB No. 36, issued in 1980). In September 1974, President Ford signed into law the Employment Retirement Income Security Act (ERISA), which regulates various aspects of pension plans, including eligibility, vesting, funding, fiduciary responsibility, reporting and disclosure, and plan termination insurance.

There are two types of pension plans. *Defined contribution plans* consist of funds built up over time via employee and employer contributions, but benefits are not predetermined. Employees are simply paid out the market value of their portion of the pension fund when they retire. The firm has no responsibilities other than paying its share of the contributions and prudent management of the pension fund assets. The second, and more common type, is a *defined benefit plan*. Corporations are required to pay a contractual benefit upon the retirement of a vested employee. When ERISA was signed, defined benefit pensions were converted from corporate promises to liabilities enforceable by law.

The provisions of ERISA are many. No employee older than 25 years and with more than one year of service with a company, or hired more than five years before normal retirement age, may be excluded from participation in that company's pension plan. Prior to ERISA, unusual vesting practices resulted in many injustices. For example, some plans

---

[1]The effect of the pension fund on the balance sheet is to increase assets by $8.4 billion, to increase pension liabilities by $7.6 billion, and to increase equity by $.8 billion (the amount of the overfunding). Note that Table 29.4 is purely hypothetical and does not conform to the generally accepted accounting practices which are discussed later in the chapter.

required 20 or more years of uninterrupted service before an employee became vested. Sometimes, workers would be fired in their nineteenth year simply to prevent vesting them in a pension plan. With the advent of ERISA, all plans must choose from one of three vesting schedules for the corporate portion of the contributions to the pension plan:

1. Ten-year vesting: 100 percent vesting after ten years of service.
2. Graded vesting: 25 percent vesting after 5 years of service and then increasing by 5 percent per year to 50 percent vesting after 10 years of service; thereafter, increasing by 10 percent a year up to 100 percent vesting after 15 years.
3. Rule of 45: 50 percent vesting when a participant's age and years of service add up to 45 and then increasing by 10 percent a year up to 100 percent vesting 5 years later.

All employee contributions to a pension fund, and investment returns on such contributions, are fully vested from the beginning.

ERISA legislates minimum corporate funding of defined benefit plans while the IRS (Internal Revenue Service) sets limits on the maximum corporate contribution. According to ERISA, the minimum contribution is determined as follows: (1) All *normal costs* attributable to benefit claims deriving from employee services in a given year must be paid that year; (2) any *experience losses* (caused by a decline in the value of the securities in the fund, by unexpected changes in employee turnover, or by changes in actuarial assumptions about the discount rate) must be amortized over a period not to exceed 15 years; and (3) *supplemental liabilities* resulting from increased benefits or unfunded past service costs must be amortized over a period not to exceed 30 years (40 years for companies with pre-ERISA supplemental liabilities). On the other hand, the IRS defines the maximum corporate pension contribution as the actuarially determined normal cost of the plan plus any amount necessary to amortize supplemental and experience losses over a 10-year period. The ERISA and IRS restrictions limit corporate discretion over the amount of funds contributed to a plan.

One of the most important provisions of ERISA was the creation of the Pension Benefit Guaranty Corporation (PBGC). It is a pension insurance fund operated under the supervision of the U.S. Department of Labor. Corporations must pay the PBGC a fixed annual premium (currently $2.60) for each employee in a pension plan. This central fund is then used to guarantee pension benefits even if a plan fails. A pension plan may be terminated voluntarily by the corporation or involuntarily by the PBGC upon court order. The PBGC may terminate a plan (1) if the plan fails to meet minimum funding standards, (2) if the plan is unable to pay benefits when due, (3) if the plan is administered improperly, or (4) if the liability of the PBGC for fulfilling claims deriving from the plan is likely to increase unreasonably.

If a plan is terminated because it is underfunded, the company is liable for 100 percent of the deficit up to 30 percent of the company's net worth. Furthermore, the PBGC may place a lien on corporate assets which has the same priority as federal taxes. Hence, unfunded pension liabilities are equivalent to the most senior debt. A bankrupt firm may have few assets to pay to the PBGC; hence, a worthy public policy question is whether the PBGC has enough resources of its own to adequately insure the pensioneers in a major corporate bankruptcy.

Perhaps the best way to understand corporate pension accounting is to use a realistic example. Assume that a 52-year-old worker is fully vested, has already accumulated 20 years of work experience, and is expected to retire after 10 additional years. We want to illustrate the calculations for how the normal cost of her defined benefits will increase for each additional year that she works. Her annual salary, which is currently $30,000 per year, is expected to increase at a rate of 10 percent per year. The formula for her annual pension, starting when she reaches age 62, is

$$\text{Annual pension} = (.25 + .01N)[\text{MAX } S],$$

where N is the number of years worked and MAX S is her maximum salary. Table 29.5 shows the pension calculations, assuming that her life expectancy is 20 years when she retires. Column (3) shows her expected salary each year. Column (4) is her annual pension, starting at the end of Year 10 but assuming she stops work after only N years of seniority. For example, if she only works two additional years (if she stops work after her twenty-second year of seniority, that is, $N = 22$), her expected maximum salary is $33,000 and her annual pension will be

$$\text{Annual pension} = (.25 + .01(22))[\$33,000]$$
$$= (.47)(\$33,000) = \$15,510.$$

Column (5) is the present value, at the end of Year 10, of the assumed 20 annual pension payments. The discount rate is assumed to be 6 percent. Therefore, Column (5) is the present value of an annuity (her annual pension) discounted at 6 percent for 20 years. The annuity factor is PVIFA = 11.4699. Hence, the present value of her pension, as of the end of Year 10, is

$$\text{PV of benefits at the end of Year 10} = (\text{Annual pension})\text{PVIFA}$$
$$= \$15,510(11.4699) = \$177,898.$$

Column (6), the accumulated benefits, is computed as the present value in the current year of the amount in Column (5). For example, in Year 2, the accumulated benefits are

$$\text{Accumulated benefits (Year 2)} = \$177,898(1.06)^{-8}$$
$$= \$177,898(.6274)$$
$$= \$111,615.$$

Finally, the normal cost, Column (7), represents the amount by which the present value of the accumulated benefits increased because the employee worked for the year just ended. In our example, the normal cost in current Year 2 is $111,615 − $93,689 = $17,926. Normal costs increase with employee seniority because (1) her salary has increased; (2) another 1 percent has been added to her pension formula; and (3) the pension is one year closer to being paid, so that its present value increases.

Remember that ERISA requires that firms must contribute (at least) normal costs [Column (7)] into the pension fund each year and that the IRS allows these costs to be expensed on the firm's income statement. There are a variety of techniques for computing projected pension fund benefits. The technique used in Table 29.5 is called the *accrued benefit* method. Other methods are the entry age normal method, the attained age normal

Table 29.5   Defined Benefit Pension Cost Computations

Current Year (1)	N (2)	Expected Salary (3)	Annual Pension Starting at End of Year 10 (4)	PV of Benefits at End of Year 10 (5)	Accumu- lated Benefits (6)	Normal Cost (7)
1	21	$30,000	$13,800	$158,285	$ 93,689	$15,084[a]
2	22	33,000	15,510	177,898	111,615	17,926
3	23	36,300	17,424	199,852	132,913	21,298
4	24	39,930	19,565	224,409	158,199	25,286
5	25	43,923	21,962	251,902	188,236	30,037
6	26	48,315	24,641	282,630	223,869	35,633
7	27	53,147	27,636	316,982	266,144	42,275
8	28	58,462	30,985	355,396	316,301	50,157
9	29	64,308	34,726	398,304	375,758	59,457
10	30	70,738	38,906	446,249	446,249	70,491

[a]Accumulated benefits for Year 0 are assumed to be $78,605.

method, the aggregate cost method, and the individual level premium method.[2] All four of these methods have the effect of accelerating corporate contributions to the pension fund at a rate faster than the accrued benefit method. They are analogous to accelerated depreciation methods, except pension contributions involve cash flows while depreciation does not. In the next section of this chapter, we will discuss the economic implications of accelerated cost methods and of changes in the assumed discount rate.

Accounting regulations (APB No. 8 and FASB No. 36) require that companies with defined benefit plans provide the following information:

1.   The actuarial present value of vested accumulated plan benefits, [Column (6) in Table 29.5, assuming 100 percent vesting].
2.   The actuarial present value of nonvested accumulated plan benefits [a fraction of Column (6) in Table 29.5 if not 100 percent vesting].
3.   The plan's net assets available for benefits.
4.   The assumed actuarial rates of return used in determining the actuarial present values of vested and nonvested accumulated plan benefits.
5.   The date as of which the benefit information was determined.

The actuarial present value of plan benefits was explained by the previous example (Table 29.5). The plan's net assets available for benefits are computed from the records of the pension fund. If the firm is contributing to the fund more rapidly than pension expenses accumulate, then the plan's net assets available for benefits will be positive and vice versa if contributions build slower than expenses.[3]

---

[2]See Dreher [1967] for a complete discussion. Note that the pension plan administrator *must* use the accrued benefit method when computing the liabilities of the pension plan.

[3]For details on the computation of net assets available for benefits, see Davidson, Stickney, and Weil [1980], pp. 19.18 through 19.22.

Managerial Decisions

Most of the foregoing discussion has been descriptive in nature. We have discussed the rapid growth of pension funds, their asset composition, the pension plan financial statements, pension fund regulation by ERISA, the IRS, and the FASB, and we have looked at a simple pension fund example. Now, it is time to ask what types of pension fund decisions confront financial managers and how will these decisions affect the value of shareholders' wealth. Listed by order of presentation, the decisions are

1.   What are the effects of changing the actuarial assumptions of a pension plan?
2.   What is the optimal mix of pension plan investments?
3.   How should pension fund investment performance be measured?
4.   When, if ever, is it optimal to voluntarily terminate a pension plan? How can termination legally be accomplished?
5.   Should the firm manage its pension plan or enter into a contract with an insurance company?

These are common pension plan problems, and every chief financial officer should understand the impact which pension plan decisions will have on the corporation's shareholders.

Changing the Actuarial Assumptions

In 1973, U.S. Steel increased its reported profits by $47 million by "reducing" its pension costs. This was accomplished by recognizing some appreciation in its $2 billion pension fund. Presumably, cash was then diverted from pension contributions to other uses. In the fourth quarter of 1980, Chrysler changed its assumed discount rate on its employee pension plan from 6 percent to 7 percent. Pension costs were reduced, and $50 million was added to profits. Also in 1980, Bethlehem Steel changed the assumed discount rate for its pension benefits [similar to Column (6) in Table 29.5] to 10 percent from 7 percent.[4] This 3 percent increase had the effect of decreasing accumulated pension plan benefits by $713 million (22.5 percent of the total benefits). Before the change, pension plan net assets totaled $1.952 billion and the plan was underfunded by $1.215 billion. After the change, underfunding fell to $502 million, a 58.7 percent decline. *Accounting Trends and Techniques*, an annual survey of reporting practices of 600 companies, showed that roughly 30 percent of the companies sampled voluntarily changed their pension fund accounting assumptions at least once between 1975 and 1980.

The economic effect on shareholders' wealth depends on how the accounting changes revised shareholders' expectations about the level and riskiness of the future cash flows of the firm. The value of shareholders' wealth is equal to the market value of the firm, V, minus the market value of its liabilities. For convenience, we shall divide liabilities into pension fund liabilities, PFL, and all other debt, B. When ERISA was signed, defined pension liabilities became senior debt of the firm. Equation 29.1 shows, S, the value of shareholders' wealth.

$$S = V - \text{PFL} - B. \tag{29.1}$$

---

[4]FASB Statement No. 36 allows companies to use different interest rate assumptions for disclosure in the annual report and for funding purposes; for example, Bethlehem used 7 percent for funding and 10 percent for disclosure. See Regan [1982].

We are interested in the market value of pension fund liabilities and how they are affected by accounting changes. The market value is the way the marketplace will view the true pension fund deficit and does not have any necessary relationship to the accounting or book value deficit. The market value of the pension fund deficit (or surplus) is given in Equation 29.2:

$$\text{PFL} = - \text{ Market value of pension fund assets} \qquad (29.2)$$
$$- [\text{PV(Expected contributions)}](1 - T)$$
$$+ \text{PV(Expected pension fund benefits from past and future service)}.$$

There are two major pension fund assets. First is the current market value of the stocks, bonds, mortgages, and so forth, held by the pension fund. Second is the present value of the expected pension fund contributions, which are multiplied by one minus the corporate tax rate $(1 - T)$ in order to reflect the fact that pension fund contributions are tax deductible by the firm. As long as the firm is making profits, then pension contributions are "shared" with the government because more contributions mean lower taxes.[5] Expected contributions, as we have discussed earlier, include (1) normal costs [for example, Table 29.5, Column (7)], (2) experience costs (caused by a decline in the market value of securities in the fund, by unexpected changes in employee turnover, or by changes in actuarial assumptions about the discount rate) which are amortized over a period not to exceed 15 years, and (3) supplemental liabilities (resulting from increased benefits or unfunded past service costs) which must be amortized over a period not to exceed 30 years. Balancing the pension fund assets is the pension fund liability, the present value of expected pension fund benefits to be paid to employees. Column (6) in Table 29.5 showed how this number is calculated by the actuaries.

The main difference between the book value of the pension fund deficit and its market value, or true economic value, PFL, is reflected in the rates of return. Equation 29.3 further elaborates Equation 29.2 by showing the present value of the pension fund along with the appropriate market-determined discount rates.

$$\text{PFL} = - \text{ Market value of pension fund assets} \qquad (29.3)$$
$$- \sum_{t=1}^{n} \frac{E(\text{Contributions in Year } t)(1 - T)}{[1 + k_b(1 - T)]^t}$$
$$+ \sum_{t=1}^{n} \frac{E(\text{Benefits in Year } t)}{(1 + k_b)^t}$$

The expected pension benefits are discounted at the pre-tax cost of senior debt, k_b, because ERISA has made the payment of pension benefits a senior obligation of the firm, second

---

[5]If one considers Social Security to be a pension plan, then recent changes in the Social Security tax law which requires nonprofit organizations to pay Social Security for their employees are burdensome. Because nonprofit organizations have no tax shelter, they must bear the full cost of Social Security expenses.

only to tax liabilities.[6] Pension contributions are also discounted at the rate, k_b, but on an after-tax basis. Prior to ERISA, the expected benefits would have been discounted at the cost of junior, or subordinated debt, k_J, which is higher than k_b, the cost of senior debt. One of the major effects of ERISA was to transfer wealth from shareholders to pension beneficiaries by increasing the present value of pension deficits, PFL. The transfer was especially large for plans which were seriously underfunded.

The real effect of a change in pension plan actuarial assumptions depends on the cash flow consequences. If the *actuarial* discount rate assumption is raised, then the present value of accumulated benefits in book value terms [Column (6) of Table 29.5] decreases, as do the normal costs which have to be paid into the fund. This has the effect of decreasing the annual expected contributions into the fund and, hence, decreasing their present value in Equation 29.3 because expected contributions decrease while the *market-determined* discount rate, k_b, does not change. The present value of expected benefits, however, remains unchanged. The net effect is to increase the market value of pension liabilities, PFL. There is usually no effect on the firm as a whole because the cash flow not put into pension fund contributions may be used either to decrease other liabilities or to increase assets. Either way, the increased pension liability is exactly offset.[7] Thus, we see that, from the shareholders' point of view, changing the actuarial assumptions in order to change pension contributions is usually an exercise in futility. Even worse, if the funds generated by cutting pension contributions are used for a purpose which is not expensed (for example, repaying the principal on debt), the effect is to increase taxable income and decrease net cash flows to shareholders. Accounting profits have increased, but the firm has sacrificed the pension contribution tax shield. The net effect (assuming the firm is paying taxes) is to benefit the IRS at the expense of shareholders. Finally, changing actuarial assumptions for disclosure in the annual report but not for funding purposes is chicanery at best and stupid at worst. If taxes are based on income reported in the annual report, the effect of such a maneuver is to increase tax liabilities without decreasing cash contributions to the pension fund. If taxes are based on actual contributions, then, at best, managers think they can somehow fool the marketplace.

The Mix of Pension Plan Assets

As with any other portfolio decision, the choice of assets for a pension plan involves a selection of risk and return. Furthermore, tax considerations and pension fund insurance through ERISA are paramount.

A World without Taxes and without ERISA

Before turning to the effect of ERISA and taxes on pension fund investments, let us build a more complete understanding of their risk and return characteristics. Before the passage of ERISA, corporate pension liabilities were analogous to risky debt, and the shareholders'

[6]Some have argued that promised pension benefits are subordinated to other debt claims in spite of ERISA because other debt comes due before pension obligations. Pension beneficiaries cannot force the firm into bankruptcy while debtholders can. The existence of large unfunded pension deficits will, in our opinion, cause debtholders to force bankruptcy sooner than they might if there were no pension obligations. Nevertheless, pension liabilities will still be senior claims at the time of bankruptcy.

[7]One sometimes hears that pension contributions can be legitimately cut if the funds are alternatively used to invest in positive net present value projects. This argument confuses the investment decision (take the profitable project) with the way it is financed (cut pension fund contributions). The project can be financed either by cutting pension contributions, which increases pension liabilities, or by borrowing, which increases debt liabilities. Either way, the effect on shareholders' wealth is the same.

position was equivalent to a call option on a levered firm.[8] To illustrate this, assume a one-period framework, an all-equity firm which has an uncertain end-of-period market value, V_1, and a world with no taxes. The pension fund holds some risky assets with an end-of-period value, A_1, and the pension beneficiaries have been promised an end-of-period benefit, B.

Figure 29.1 shows the end-of-period payoffs to the pension beneficiaries, assuming that the pension fund is uninsured. Along the horizontal axis, we have the market value of the firm plus the market value of the pension assets, $V + A$, while dollars of end-of-period payoff are graphed along the vertical axis. The pension beneficiaries will receive the full promised amount if the market value of total assets, $V + A$, exceeds the promised benefits, B. But, if not, the pension beneficiaries receive $V + A < B$. The solid line OXB in Figure 29.1 shows the pension beneficiaries' payoff. Because we have assumed the firm has no debt, the shareholders' payoff is simply the residual, as shown in the equation below:

$$\text{Shareholders' payoff} = \text{MAX}[0,(V + A) - B]. \tag{29.4}$$

Referring back to Chapter 18 on options on risky assets, we see that the shareholders' payoff is identical to a call option on a levered firm. The pension beneficiaries' position is equivalent to owning a risk-free bond with an end-of-period value equal to the promised pension benefits, B, and selling a put option, P, on the assets of the firm.[9] In other words,

---

Figure 29.1   End-of-Period Pension Fund Payoffs

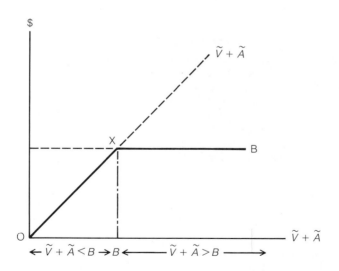

---

[8]For a more complete presentation of pension fund liabilities as options, see Sharpe [1976] and Treynor, Priest, and Regan [1976].

[9]Given that this is a one-period model and that pension benefits are not payable until employees retire at the end of the period, all options in the model are European options. They cannot be exercised before maturity.

Figure 29.2   The Pension Beneficiaries' Position Is Equivalent to Risky Debt (Long in a Riskless Bond and Short in a Put Option)

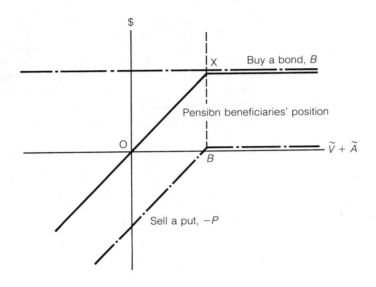

they have a risky debt claim. Figure 29.2 shows that if we vertically sum the payoff from holding a riskless bond and selling a put option (at no cost to shareholders), we do, indeed, arrive at the pension beneficiaries' position.

The claims of all parties can be summarized by referring to the put-call parity equation (discussed in Chapter 18). Put-call parity said that the current market value of an underlying risky asset plus the value of a put option written on it (with maturity T periods hence and X as the exercise price) is equal to the value of a riskless bond plus a call option on the risky asset (with the same maturity and exercise price as the put). Using our current notation, the put-call parity expression becomes

$$(V_0 + A_0) + P_0 = B_0 + S_0$$
$$S_0 = (V_0 + A_0) - (B_0 - P_0). \tag{29.5}$$

The shareholders' position, S_0, is equivalent to a call option on a levered firm. On the right-hand side of Equation 29.5, we note that $(V_0 + A_0)$ is the present value of the firm and pension fund assets and that $(B_0 - P_0)$ is the present value of risky debt, that is, the pension benefits.

Considerable insight into pension fund asset mix can be provided by this simple option pricing approach. For example, what happens to shareholders' wealth if the pension trustees change the mix of pension assets from a well-diversified portfolio of equity to being

100 percent invested in shares of the firm?[10] The effect would be to increase the correlation between V, the value of the firm, and A, the value of the pension assets. Consequently, the variance of the underlying portfolio of assets increases and the value of shareholders' wealth, S_0, which is a call option on the assets, will also increase. Thus, the effect of any decision which unexpectedly increases the risk of $(V + A)$ is to shift wealth to shareholders and away from pension beneficiaries. The only mitigating circumstance, which was pointed out by Sharpe [1976], is that employees may be able to demand higher wages to compensate them for the higher risk they must bear when pension assets are invested in the firm's own stock. Or they might require pension fund insurance.[11]

The Effect of ERISA and the PBGC

Now let us look at the effect of government pension fund insurance on the pension fund asset mix but maintain our assumption that there are no taxes. As was mentioned earlier, the Pension Benefit Guarantee Corporation (PBGC) insures pension fund liabilities. Corporations contribute into PBGC a fixed insurance premium per employee each year. In the event that an underfunded pension plan is terminated, the firm is liable up to 30 percent of its net worth and the PBGC guarantees the remainder of the pension liability.

If the PBGC were a privately owned insurance company, it would charge premiums based on the probability of corporate default on a pension fund. However, as a government organization, it charges all firms exactly the same insurance premium regardless of the extent of pension plan underfunding or the likelihood of bankruptcy. One implication, of course, is that firms with overfunded pension funds are paying too much to the PBGC relative to those with badly underfunded pension plans. Another implication is that firms threatened with bankruptcy can decide to change their pension plan asset mix to maximize the value of the call option which represents their shareholders' wealth. If they go bankrupt, shareholders receive nothing, and although the PBGC can claim 30 percent of each firm's net worth, 30 percent of nothing is still nothing. The PBGC claim on equity is worthless in both Chapter 7 bankruptcy or Chapter 11 reorganization (discussed in Chapter 31). Consequently, the optimal strategy from the point of view of shareholders, is to put all of the pension assets into very risky stocks. If they are lucky, the risky portfolio may do well and even result in overfunding of the pension fund. If they are unfortunate, then they end up with nothing, which is where they would have been anyway, and the PBGC has to pay off the pension beneficiaries.

Given that the PBGC undercharges for pension fund insurance for underfunded plans, then there is the distinct possibility that corporations facing potential bankruptcy can game the PBGC by shifting pension plan assets to being 100 percent invested in risky stocks.

An interesting case history of a company in trouble is International Harvester. In May of 1982, *The Wall Street Journal* reported that International Harvester Company's pension fund abruptly switched at least $250 million of stock holdings into bonds, chiefly U.S. government issues. Pension industry executives suggested that the company was pursuing a strategy which would let it reduce pension contributions. As of October 31, 1981, Harvester's combined pension assets totaled $1.35 billion.

[10]This situation is not unusual. For example, at one time, Sears's pension fund had over 50 percent of its assets invested in its stock.

[11]For more on the economics of insuring portfolios of risky assets, see Gatto, Geske, Litzenberger and Sosin [1980].

What are the real economic consequences of Harvester's decision? First, since the company had negative earnings, it is not likely that the tax consequences of the decision were important.[12] Second, by changing the actuarial assumptions of the plan either (1) by realizing gains on the stocks which were sold or (2) by raising the fund rate of return assumption due to the shift from stocks to bonds, Harvester could reduce its planned cash contributions to the fund. We have already seen (in the previous section of this chapter) that the change in actuarial assumptions has no effect on shareholders' wealth at best and a negative effect at worst. Finally, the analysis in this section of the chapter suggests that a shift from stocks to bonds (in the absence of tax benefits) decreases shareholders' wealth and benefits pension beneficiaries (and debtholders of the firm). Although we have insufficient information to draw a definite conclusion about the Harvester decision, it looks like the net effect was to diminish shareholders' wealth.

Tax Effects of the Pension Fund Asset Mix

For most firms, pension fund contributions reduce taxes because they are immediately deductible. At the same time, the pension plan pays no taxes on its earnings. Hence, the rapid growth of pensions is largely attributable to the fact that they are a form of tax-deferred compensation.

The pension assets should be invested in those securities which have the most favorable pre-tax rates of return. Obvious examples of securities which pension managers should *not* invest in are those which are used as tax shelters by investors with high marginal tax rates, such as municipal bonds or real estate with depreciable assets like buildings.

Perhaps the most interesting tax implication for the pension fund asset mix is that pension plans should be fully funded and invested totally in bonds as opposed to equities.[13] The logic is developed in two parts. The first argument is that the return on debt held in a corporate pension fund is passed through the firm to its shareholders in the form of higher share prices because an overfunded pension plan is an asset of the firm.[14] The implication is that the return on debt held in the pension fund is ultimately taxed at the lower personal tax rate on equities. Shareholders will pay less tax than if the debt were held in their personal portfolios. Consequently, shareholders are better off if the pension funds of corporations are invested in bonds while their personal portfolios are invested in equities. This conclusion is based on the fact that pension plan earnings are not taxed and that bond income is taxed at a higher rate than capital gains. It does not depend on any theoretical gain to leverage (for example, Chapter 21).

The second reason for investing pension assets in bonds is the potential value of the tax shelter involved when the firm borrows to invest pension assets in bonds. The following example compares two pension investment strategies, the first with all pension assets in stock and the second with all assets in bonds. For the sake of simplicity, we assume a one-period world with two equally likely states of nature. If the economy is good, stocks will yield a 100 percent rate of return while bonds will yield 10 percent. If the economy is bad, stocks yield −50 percent and bonds yield 10 percent. The risk-free rate is 10 percent.

[12]The next section of this chapter provides the only rational tax explanation for why Harvester shareholders may have benefited from switching pension assets to bonds.

[13]For proof of this proposition, the reader is referred to Tepper and Affleck [1974], Black [1980], and especially to Tepper [1981].

[14]The next section of this chapter discusses ways that shareholders can gain access to the assets of overfunded pension plans.

Table 29.6   Beginning Balance Sheets for Two Pension Investment Strategies

100 Percent Stock Strategy
(Millions of Dollars)

Assets		Liabilities	
Pension Plan		Pension Plan	
Bonds, B	0	PV of Benefits, PFB	200
Stock, S	200	Corporate	
Corporate, A	800	Debt, D	300
		Equity, E	500
	1,000		1,000

100 Percent Bond Strategy
(Millions of Dollars)

Assets		Liabilities	
Pension Plan		Pension Plan	
Bonds, B	200	PV of Benefits, PFB	200
Stock, S	0	Corporate	
Corporate, A	800	Debt, D	400
		Equity, E	400
	1,000		1,000

Note that the expected (or average) return on stocks is 25 percent while bonds are expected to yield only 10 percent. Even so, we will see that the bond investment strategy is better for shareholders.

Table 29.6 shows a beginning-of-period market value balance sheet which combines the firm and pension fund assets and liabilities for each of the two pension investment strategies: all stock and all bonds. The firm's defined benefit pension plan promises to pay $220 million at the end of the period. The present value of this liability is $200 million, and it appears on the liabilities side of the corporate balance sheet. On the assets side, the current market value of pension assets is $200 million (either in bonds or in stocks). The pension plan is fully funded because the present value of its assets equals that of its liabilities.

If we employ the 100 percent stock investment strategy for our pension plan, the end-of-period payoffs are as shown in Table 29.7. Using the "good economy" as an example, we see that the pension fund stocks can be sold for $400 million at the end of the year. After paying the $220 million of pension benefits, shareholders are left with $180 million pretax and $90 million after taxes. In the "bad economy," they suffer a $60 million loss. The expected gain in shareholders' wealth is $15 million, but they are exposed to a great deal of risk.

The alternate pension investment strategy is to invest $200 million in bonds. If that is all we did, the end-of-period payoff would be exactly $220 million in either economy; the pension benefits would be paid off; and there would be no gain or loss to shareholders. Their expected gain is zero, but they take no risk at all.

In order to present a valid comparison of the stock and bond strategies, we need to keep shareholders' risk constant. Then, we can compare after-tax expected returns to see which

Table 29.7   Payoffs for the 100 Percent Stock Pension Investment Strategy (Millions of Dollars)

	State of Nature	
	Good Economy	Bad Economy
Sell stock and receive	$400	$100
Payoff defined benefits	−220	−220
Cash to the firm	180	−120
Less taxes at 50 percent	−90	60
Net cash to shareholders	90	−60

strategy is better, given equivalent risk. Table 29.6 shows balance sheets which have the same risk for shareholders.[15] On the assets side, $200 million of bonds is less risky than $200 million of stock. Therefore, in order to offset the decline in risk caused by the 100 percent bond strategy, we increase the firm's financial leverage by borrowing $100 million and using the proceeds to repurchase $100 million in equity.[16] The resulting payoffs are given in Table 29.8.

In the "good economy," the bonds are sold for $220 million and the proceeds are used to pay off the defined benefits. Next, the $100 million of repurchased equity is reissued for

Table 29.8   Payoffs for the 100 Percent Bond Pension Investment Strategy (Millions of Dollars)

	State of Nature	
	Good Economy	Bad Economy
Sell bonds and receive	$220	$220
Payoff defined benefits	220	220
	0	0
Sell stock (Book value = $100 million)	200	50
Payoff extra bonds	−100	−100
	100	−50
Less interest on bonds	−10	−10
	90	−60
Plus tax shield on interest	5	5
Net cash to shareholders	95	−55

[15]It really does not make any difference, in our example, how risk is measured. Shareholders' risk is equivalent whether you use the range, the variance, or the beta to measure risk.

[16]In practice, it is not necessary for corporations to actually repurchase shares in order to implement the 100 percent bond pension investment plan. What is important is that when pension assets are invested in bonds rather than stock, the risk of the corporate asset portfolio is lower. Hence, from the point of view of lenders, there is greater debt capacity. More borrowing provides a debt tax shield.

$200 million (because the stock has appreciated by 100 percent in the good economy). Half of the $200 million is used to repay the $100 million of borrowing and $10 million pays the required interest. Note that the interest payments are tax deductible. If the firm is in a 50 percent tax bracket, then taxes are reduced $5 million below what they otherwise would have been. Net cash available to shareholders in the favorable state of nature is $95 million with the 100 percent bond investment strategy but was only $90 million with the 100 percent equity strategy. The bond strategy also dominates the equity strategy in the unfavorable state of nature ($−55 million versus $−60 million). Hence, our example demonstrates the superiority of the bond strategy from the shareholders' point of view. We have increased their return in both states of nature without changing their risk, because the range of payoffs is $150 million in either case. Regardless of whether the actual return on stock investments is higher or lower than on bonds, the bond strategy is preferable.

Summarizing, we have seen that investing all pension fund assets in bonds benefits shareholders in two ways. First, the pretax bond rate of return is passed through the firm to its shareholders in the form of higher share prices, which are, in turn, taxed at the lower capital gains rate. This argument applies even if there is no gain to leverage. The second reason for favoring bonds over equity is that there may be a gain to firms which can carry more debt without increasing shareholders' risk — a gain to leverage. We have seen that firms which choose to invest pension assets in bonds actually experience lower total asset risk than firms which put pension assets in stock. The lower risk means a greater debt capacity. If the firm uses this debt capacity and if there is a valuable tax shield created by the deductibility of interest payments, then there is a gain to leverage from investing pension assets in bonds while borrowing to hold shareholders' risk constant.[17]

Measuring Pension Plan Portfolio Performance

If your firm decides to hire a pension plan management firm for a substantial fee, the natural question is what are you getting for your money? The answer comes in two parts. First, how do you calculate the rate of return on monies invested in the pension fund? Second, once you have determined the rate of return, was it higher than could have been expected, given the riskiness of the portfolio of investments? Was it a positive risk-adjusted rate of return?

The first consideration for measuring pension fund return is that it must be a total market value return, which includes all dividends, coupons, and capital gains. Second, it must be a *time-weighted return*, which properly accounts for contributions to and disbursements from the fund.[18] In order to illustrate the difference between time-weighted returns and *dollar-weighted returns*, consider the following example. Two funds have all of their assets continuously invested in the Standard & Poor's 500 Index for a two-year period. They both begin with $10 million. As shown in Table 29.9, Fund A receives an additional $10 million contribution at the beginning of the second year while Fund B disburses $1 million. The only difference between the funds was their pattern of receipts and disbursements, yet, if we use a dollar-weighted return measure, we find that in two years, Fund A

[17]The gain to leverage is most likely to be valuable for those firms which have higher effective tax rates because their tax shelters from other sources (such as investment tax credits, depreciation, research and development expenses, or tax carry-back and carry-forward) are limited.

[18]The recommendations of the Bank Administration Institute have become a standard for performance measurement. In cooperation with the University of Chicago, they have devised two ways for estimating time-weighted returns.

Table 29.9　　Fund Balances for Two Pension Funds

		Fund A			Fund B		
Year	Return on S&P 500	Beginning Cash	Beginning of Year Deposit	Ending Cash	Beginning Cash	Beginning of Year Deposit	Ending Cash
1	−50%	$10MM	—	$ 5	$10MM	—	$5
2	100%	$ 5	$10MM	$30	$ 5	$−1MM	$8

appears to have a 200 percent rate of return,

$$\text{Dollar-weighted return on Fund A} = \frac{\$30MM - \$10MM}{\$10MM} = 200\%,$$

while Fund B appears to have a two-year return of −20 percent,

$$\text{Dollar-weighted return on Fund B} = \frac{\$8MM - \$10MM}{\$10MM} = -20\%.$$

A time-weighted return, similar to that used by many mutual funds, begins by dividing the fund into "shares." In Table 29.10, we have divided the initial $10 million investment into 10 shares, each worth $1 million.[19] By the end of the first year, both funds have declined to $5 million because the S&P 500 went down 50 percent. Each share has declined

Table 29.10　　Time-Weighted-Returns for Two Pension Funds (Millions of Dollars)

		Beginning of Period			Beginning of Year Deposit		End of Period			
Year	S&P Return	Cash	Number of Shares	Price per Share	Cash	Number of Shares	Cash	Number of Shares	Price per Share	Time-Weighted Return
Fund A										
1	−50%	$10	10	$1.0	—	—	$ 5	10	$ .5	−50%
2	+100%	$ 5	10	$ .5	$10	20	$30	30	$1.0	100%
3	+50%	$30	30	$1.0	$10	10	$60	40	$1.5	50%
Fund B										
1	−50%	$10	10	$1.0	—	—	$ 5.0	10	$ .5	−50%
2	+100%	$ 5	10	$ .5	$ −1	−2	$ 8.0	8	$1.0	100%
3	+50%	$ 8	8	$1.0	$ 21	21	$43.5	29	$1.5	50%

[19]The number of "shares" is arbitrary. Usually, the initial investment is divided by enough shares so that each is worth $1.00.

in price to $.5 million. When money is deposited or disbursed, we compute the number of "shares" involved. For example, at the beginning of Year 2, a deposit of $10 million to Fund A represents 20 new shares at $.5 million each. Thus, in Period 2, Fund A has 30 shares and $15 million. When the market goes up 100 percent, Fund A finishes the year with $30 million and 30 shares worth $1 million each. The time-weighted return is computed by using the hypothetical share prices. For example, the Year 2 return for Fund A is

$$\frac{\text{Time-weighted}}{\text{return}} = \frac{(\text{End-of-period share price}) - (\text{Beginning share price})}{\text{Beginning share price}}$$

$$= \frac{1.0\text{MM} - .5\text{MM}}{.5\text{MM}} = 100\%.$$

Since both funds were continuously 100 percent invested in the S&P 500 Index, we know that they must have had exactly the same return. The time-weighted return calculations shown in the last column of Table 29.10 show that the returns for both funds are indeed identical.

Having correctly measured the time-weighted returns, it is necessary to evaluate the risk-adjusted performance of portfolio managers. It is not very hard to invest in the Standard & Poor's 500 Index. The difficult task, the task which should be rewarded, is to select a portfolio which has the same risk but higher returns. The Capital Asset Pricing Model (CAPM) and the Arbitrage Pricing Model (APM) which were discussed in Chapter 17 provide a sound theoretical basis for measuring risk-adjusted returns. The data given in Table 29.11 show the rates of return on a hypothetical pension portfolio and on the S&P 500 Index from 1973 to 1981, a nine-year interval.

Most pension fund managers report their performance by comparing their portfolio with the Standard & Poor's 500 Index regardless of their portfolio's risk.[20] Figure 29.3

Table 29.11   Hypothetical Pension Fund Returns

Year	Hypothetical Pension Fund Returns	S&P 500 Index	90-day T-bill Rate
1973	40.0%	29.1%	7.0%
1974	−15.0	−22.9	7.8
1975	−8.0	4.0	5.8
1976	22.0	18.5	5.0
1977	−10.0	−3.7	5.3
1978	−20.0	−2.2	7.2
1979	10.0	7.1	10.1
1980	25.0	15.5	11.4
1981	7.0	7.9	14.0
Arithmetic average	5.66%	5.92%	8.18%
Standard deviation	20.48%	14.94%	3.05%
Beta	1.22	1.00	.02

[20]Bond portfolios are usually compared with the Lehman Brothers government and corporate bond index, which is a weighted average of the rates of return on government and corporate bonds.

Figure 29.3   Typical Lay Version of Pension Fund Performance Evaluation

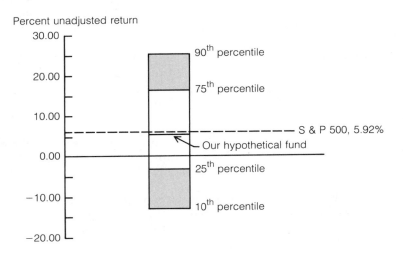

---

illustrates a typical presentation. The gross rates of return (before management fees and brokerage expenses) on a pension fund (5.66 percent in our example) are compared with the distribution of S&P 500 returns or with the actual performance of other managed funds over the same time interval.[21] Our hypothetical pension fund has earned just about the "average" rate of return and is in the 49th percentile.

Unfortunately, it is meaningless to compare gross rates of return, which are unadjusted for risk. In order to illustrate, let us use the Capital Asset Pricing Model, which explains rates of return adjusted for risk. The measure of risk is beta. A perfectly riskless asset has a beta of zero and the market portfolio (in this case, the S&P 500 Index) has a beta which is defined to be $\beta = 1.0$. The *ex post* version of the Capital Asset Pricing Model says that the predicted risk-adjusted rate of return will be equal to the risk-free rate, R_F, plus a risk premium which is equal to the amount of risk, β_j, times a market risk premium which is equal to the difference between the market rate of return, R_M, and the risk-free rate.

$$R_j = R_F + (R_M - R_F)\beta_j. \tag{29.6}$$

Our pension portfolio had a beta of 1.22. In other words, it was 22 percent riskier than the S&P 500 Index. Substituting the appropriate numbers from Table 29.11 into Equation 29.6, we have the predicted return:

$$\hat{R}_j = 8.18\% + (5.92\% - 8.18\%)1.22$$

$$= 5.42\%.$$

---

[21]A. G. Becker Inc. is the usual source for the distribution of managed funds' gross rates of return.

The actual rate of return was 5.66 percent. Hence, our pension fund managers earned a positive risk-adjusted rate of return equal to the difference between the fund's actual return, R_j, and the rate of return which could have been earned in the marketplace for portfolios of equivalent risk, $\hat{R}_j$.

$$\text{Risk-adjusted abnormal return} = R_j - \hat{R}_j$$

$$= 5.66\% - 5.42\% = .24\%.$$

Between 1973 and 1981, the S&P 500 Index actually did worse, on average, than the lower-risk 90-day Treasury Bill portfolio. Those were the breaks of the game. In the long run, we expect riskier stock portfolios to outperform low-risk bond portfolios, and they have (see Chapter 7 for details). However, in shorter time intervals, riskier portfolios can and do underperform bonds. That is what happened in our example. Nevertheless, our pension managers did better than they were expected to do and should be rewarded, even though their gross rate of return was less than the lower-risk S&P 500 Index.[22]

A few rules of thumb for managing and evaluating pension funds are

1. Keep bond and stock funds separate. This makes it easier to evaluate their performance.
2. Keep a record of time-weighted returns.
3. Evaluate pension fund managers' performance by having them first subtract all management and brokerage fees from the fund's gross rate of return and then comparing this net return with the risk-adjusted return expected for portfolios of equivalent risk.
4. You should give the fund manager guidelines for the percentage of the fund which should be invested in bonds or stocks. In so doing, keep in mind the effect your decision will have on the risk of the pension fund and on the value of shareholders' wealth *after taxes*.

Voluntary Termination of Defined Benefit Pension Plans

In June of 1983, Occidental Petroleum voluntarily terminated four defined benefit pension plans for salaried employees in its oil and chemicals divisions, replacing them with defined contribution plans. All employees covered by the terminated plans received a lump sum payment covering their vested benefits. Because the defined benefit plans were overfunded by approximately $294 million (at the end of 1982), the voluntary termination boosted Occidental's after-tax net income by approximately $100 million, or 64 percent of its 1982 earnings.

Fortune magazine (December 26, 1983) reported that since 1980, 128 companies have carried out 138 fund reversions where defined benefit plans were cancelled. The excess assets, which reverted to use in operating and capital budgets, amounted to $515 million. The Pension Benefit Guarantee Corporation (PBGC), which has to approve any cancellations, was considering applications which would free up well over $1 billion more in excess assets. Furthermore, an estimated $150 billion in excess assets sits untapped in other private pension plans.

---

[22]Of course, one year of abnormal performance might be attributable to luck rather than skill.

These examples clearly demonstrate that if underfunded pension plans are liabilities of shareholders, then overfunded plans are assets. Although the firm owns the excess assets in the fund, it is restricted greatly in its ability to use them.[23] ERISA states that any residual assets in a terminated plan revert to the employer only if the pension plan explicitly provides for such a distribution upon termination. In many cases, the PBGC has contended that excess assets should go to plan beneficiaries. Consequently, firms must be careful about the process of terminating overfunded pension plans. It should also be noted that ERISA has made it more difficult to borrow against the assets in the pension fund.

Usually, firms do not consider voluntary termination of underfunded plans because the PBGC can lay claim to 30 percent of their net worth. However, two questions arise. How is net worth to be measured? And, can a subsidiary with negative net worth terminate its pension plan and relinquish the unfunded liabilities to the PBGC? In answer to the second question, the PBGC has denied subsidiaries the right to terminate their plans so long as the parent company shows adequate net worth. Furthermore, the PBGC has argued that in determining net worth, it can look beyond book value and use other information to establish the value of the firm as a going concern. Consequently, voluntary termination of underfunded plans is an unlikely strategy.

Most companies replace their defined benefit with defined contribution plans, thereby shifting the uncertainties of pension performance from themselves to their employees. The company simply promises to pay a fixed percentage of each employee's salary or wages into the defined contribution plan. Benefits upon retirement depend on the return on pension assets. Sometimes, the defined contribution plans are coupled with the 401K tax-deferred savings plan authorized by the Internal Revenue Act of 1978. Employee contributions to the plan reduce their tax liabilities and earn tax-free returns until retirement. One drawback, from the company's perspective, is that its contribution to the 401K plan is vested immediately.

Insurance Company Contracts

As noted in Table 29.1, about 39 percent of all nongovernment pension plans were invested with insurance companies. The usual insurance company contract provides "guaranteed" rates of return for a fixed period of time. For example, you may be guaranteed an 8 percent return for a ten-year period. The insurance companies can provide the guarantee because they invest your pension fund contributions in ten-year government bonds, which, if held to maturity, yield exactly 8 percent. The catch is that you cannot withdraw your pension plan assets if interest rates change. When market rates of interest rose rapidly during the late 1970s and early 1980s, many firms suddenly realized that a guaranteed rate of return was very different from a riskless return. Market rates of interest of 14 percent on long-term bonds were not unusual, but those companies whose pension assets were committed to insurance company contracts found they were locked into an 8 percent return. This is the hard way to learn about opportunity cost.

If your company is large enough to provide its own pension fund accounting for employees, then there is no difference between contributing pension funds to an insurance company plan and directly investing in 8 percent ten-year bonds yourself. Just bear in mind that long-term bonds are riskier than short-term bonds or money market assets.

[23]For a more complete exposition, the reader is referred to Bulow, Scholes, and Manell [1982].

Some companies have decided to immunize their defined benefit pension liabilities by purchasing long-term bonds which mature with the same pattern as employee retirements. They know for sure that the maturing bonds will pay promised benefits.

Summary

The rapid growth of pension funds in the last two decades has made their management one of the primary responsibilities of corporate chief financial officers. CFO's must be familiar with accounting regulations governing pension fund reporting practices, with government regulation of defined benefit plans under ERISA, and with a wide range of managerial decisions. We discussed the economic implications of changing the pension fund actuarial assumptions, the choice of asset mix, the problem of measuring pension fund portfolio performance, the implications of voluntary termination of defined benefit plans, and the economics of investing pension plan assets with guaranteed insurance company plans.

There are still some as yet unanswered questions. For example, why were 50.5 percent of all noninsured pension fund assets invested in common stocks in 1980? The tax advantage of investing in bonds (at least for fully funded plans) seems obvious. Another question is why the industry standard for measuring pension fund portfolio performance is not risk-adjusted? And finally, why are actuarial changes so frequent when they have no impact on shareholders' wealth?

Questions

29.1   What is the difference between accrued benefits and vested benefits?

29.2   What are the differences between defined contribution pension plans and defined benefit plans?

29.3   Why should a pension fund never invest its assets in nontaxable municipal bonds?

29.4   How does a change in the actuarial assumptions of a pension plan affect shareholders' wealth?

29.5   What effect did the implementation of ERISA have on the distribution of wealth between shareholders and employees
   a)   for underfunded defined benefit plans and
   b)   for overfunded defined benefit plans?

29.6   Using an option pricing approach, describe how a firm's shareholders might be affected if a large fraction of its pension assets are shifted
   a)   from bonds to a well-diversified stock portfolio
   b)   from a well-diversified stock portfolio to owning the firm's own stock.

29.7   There are two tax-related reasons why pension fund assets should be invested in bonds rather than stock. What are they?

Problems

29.1   Suppose that Mr. Brandon, a 60-year-old worker, is fully vested in his pension plan and has accumulated 35 years of work experience. He is expected to retire in 5 years at age 65. His current annual salary of $40,000 is expected to increase at the rate of 5 percent per year, and the annual pension formula is

$$\text{Annual pension} = (.25 + .01N)[\text{MAX } S].$$

If his life expectancy is 15 years when he retires, what is the normal pension cost next year and the following year if the company discounts benefits at 8 percent? (The present value of Brandon's accumulated benefits is currently $139,811.)

29.2 Table 29.2 in the text shows a pension fund income statement and balance sheet. Where in the balance sheet would you enter the following items:

a) $500 million in U.S. Government bonds which are held in trust for the members of the pension plan.

b) An amount of $200 per month which the firm plans to put aside to pay the pension of an existing employee.

c) A $15,000 per year pension which you expect to pay to an employee who is currently not vested.

d) A $10,000 per year pension, which the plan is currently paying to a retired employee.

29.3 Table P29.3 shows the cash positions of the Megabucks pension fund over a six-year period. Compute its dollar-weighted and time-weighted returns.

Table P29.3

Fund Balances for the Megabucks Pension (Millions of Dollars)

Year	Beginning Cash	Beginning of Period Deposit	Ending Cash
1	$ 90	$ 0	$ 97
2	$ 97	$−12	$ 85
3	$ 85	$ 10	$100
4	$100	$ 10	$102
5	$102	$ −5	$117
6	$117	$ 0	$121

29.4 Table P29.4 shows the time-weighted rates of return on the Bigload Pension Fund, the S&P 500 Index, and the 90-day T-bill rate (annualized). Did Bigload have a successful investment strategy?

Table P29.4

Returns on the Bigload Fund

Year	Bigload Returns	S&P 500 Returns	90-day T-bill Rate
19X5	8.4%	4.0%	5.8%
19X6	42.1	18.5	5.0
19X7	−1.0	−3.7	5.3
19X8	−10.4	−2.2	7.2
19X9	5.6	7.1	10.1

Selected References

Bagehot, W. (pseud.), "Risk and Reward in Corporate Pension Funds," *Financial Analysts Journal*, (January/ February 1972), pp. 80-84.

Bank Administration Institute, *Measuring the Investment Performance of Pension Funds*, Park Ridge, Illinois, 1968.

Black, F., "The Tax Consequences of Long-run Pension Policy," *Financial Analysts Journal*, (July/August 1980), pp. 21-28.

Bulow, J.; Scholes, M.; and Manell, P., "Economic Implications of ERISA," working paper, Graduate School of Business, University of Chicago, March 1982.

Davidson, S.; Stickney, C.; and Weil, R., *Intermediate Accounting*, Hinsdale, Ill.: Dryden Press, 1980.

Dreher, W., "Alternatives Available under APB Opinion No. 8: An Actuary's View," *The Journal of Accountancy*, (September 1967), pp. 37-51.

Feldstein, M., and Seligman, Stephanie, "Pension Funding, Share Prices and National Savings," *Journal of Finance*, 36 (September 1981), pp. 801-824.

Gatto, M.; Geske, R.; Litzenberger, R.; and Sosin, H., "Mutual Fund Insurance," *Journal of Financial Economics*, (September 1980).

Miller, M., and Scholes, M., "Pension Funding and Corporate Valuation," working paper, Graduate School of Business, University of Chicago, 1981.

Regan, P., "Reasons for the Improving Pension Figures," *Financial Analysts Journal*, (March/April 1982), pp. 14-15.

Sharpe, W., "Corporate Pension Funding Policy," *Journal of Financial Economics*, (June 1976), pp. 183-194.

Tepper, I., "The Future of Private Pension Funding," *Financial Analysts Journal*, (1982), pp. 25-31.

———, "Taxation and Corporate Pension Policy," *Journal of Finance*, 36 (March 1981), pp. 1-13.

———, and Affleck, A. R. P., "Pension Plan Liabilities and Corporate Financial Strategies," *Journal of Finance*, 29 (December 1974), pp. 1549-1564.

Treynor, J., "The Principles of Corporate Pension Finance," *Journal of Finance*, (May 1977), pp. 627-638.

———; Priest, W.; and Regan, P., *The Financial Reality of Pension Funding Under ERISA*, Homewood, Ill.: Dow Jones-Irwin Inc., 1976.

Part Eight

Integrated Topics in Managerial Finance

In the final three chapters, we take up important topics that bring together materials from a number of earlier sections of the book. Chapter 30 discusses the growth of firms through mergers and holding companies and seeks to explain the factors behind these developments. Chapter 31 considers the causes and possible remedies when firms encounter financial difficulties.

Finally, in Chapter 32, we extend the framework of financing into its international dimensions. A number of international aspects have been treated throughout the book, but in this final chapter, we focus specifically on issues of international business finance.

Chapter 30 Mergers and Corporate Control

Growth is vital to the well-being of a firm. Growth is needed to compete for the best managerial talent by offering rapid promotions and broadened responsibilities. Without able executives, the firm is likely to decline and die. Much of the previous material dealing with analysis, planning, and financing has a direct bearing on the financial manager's potential contribution to the firm's growth. This chapter focuses on strategies for promoting growth through mergers and on the role of financial managers in evaluating prospective merger partners and making decisions on which parts of the company to sell off.

Mergers and Acquisitions

From a legal standpoint, there are many distinctions between types of mergers and combinations. Most generally, *mergers* mean any transaction that forms one economic unit from two or more previous ones. Two major forms of combination have been recognized in compiling data — mergers and acquisitions. In fact, the department of an investment banking firm engaged in providing advice on these activities is usually referred to as the "M & A (mergers and acquisitions) department." Another distinction is made, from an accounting standpoint, between a purchase and a pooling of interests (see the appendix to this chapter). A *purchase* generally refers to the acquisition of a much smaller entity which is absorbed into the acquiring firm. A *pooling of interests* represents the joining of two firms of not greatly unequal size, followed by operations in which their identities are continued to a considerable degree. But, this distinction is made mainly from a financial accounting standpoint, while the more general distinction is between mergers and acquisitions.

Examples of large *mergers* in recent years include three instances given in Table 30.1. Examples of large *acquisitions* completed or pending as of September 1984 are given in Table 30.2.

Tender Offers

A recent development in acquisition activity is the increased use of tender offers. In a *tender offer*, one party — generally a corporation seeking a controlling interest in another corporation — asks the stockholders of the firm it is seeking to control to submit, or tender, their shares of stock in the target firm. Tender offers have been used for a number of years, but the pace greatly accelerated after 1965 and peaked in 1978 and 1979 (The W.T. Grimm & Co., Chicago, Ill., *Mergerstat Review 1984*, p. 91).

If one firm wishes to gain control over another, it typically seeks approval for the merger from the other firm's management and board of directors. An alternative approach is the "bear hug." In this approach, a company mails to the directors of the takeover target a letter announcing the acquisition proposal and requiring the directors to make a quick decision on the bid. If approval cannot be obtained, the acquiring company can appeal

Table 30.1   Illustrative Large Mergers

Partners		Combined Market Value (in Billions)
Nabisco	Standard Brands	$2.0
Dart Industries	Kraft	2.4
Schering	Plough	1.4

directly to the stockholders by means of the tender offer, unless the management and the directors of the target firm hold enough stock to retain control. The technique of going directly to the shareholders has been called a *Saturday night special*. The term implies that a gun has been aimed at the directors, since if the shareholders respond favorably to the tender offer, the acquiring company will gain control and have the power to replace the directors who have not cooperated in the takeover effort. (This is also referred to as a *hostile takeover*.) The target firm may seek to avoid being acquired or may seek to join with another firm with which it would rather be associated. The target firm, therefore, may seek to elicit an offer or tender from a partner it considers more desirable—a *white knight*.

The frequency of tender offers in the 1960s resulted in regulatory legislation. The "Williams Act" placing tender offers under full SEC jurisdiction became effective on July 29, 1968. Disclosure requirements written into the statute include the following:

1. The acquiring firm must give the management of the target firm and the SEC 30 days' notice of its intentions to make the acquisition.
2. When substantial blocks are purchased through tender offers or through open market purchases—that is, on the stock exchange—the beneficial owner of the stock

Table 30.2   Illustrative Large Acquisitions

Buyer	Target	Price (in Billions)
Chevron	Gulf	$13.3
Texaco	Getty Oil	10.1
Du Pont	Conoco	7.5
Mobil	Superior Oil	5.7
Royal Dutch/Shell	Shell Oil	5.5
Shell Oil	Belridge Oil	3.7
Beatrice Foods	Esmark	2.7
General Motors	Electronic Data Systems	2.5
Standard Oil (Ohio)	Kennecott	2.3
Fluor Corp.	St. Joe Minerals	2.0
Manufacturers Hanover	CIT Financial	1.5
American General	Gulf United Insurance	1.2
American Stores	Jewel Companies	1.2
Dun & Bradstreet	A.C. Nielsen	1.1

must be disclosed, together with the name of the party putting up the money for the transaction. Usually, the stock is in the "street" name of the brokerage house that acts on behalf of the real (beneficial) owner.

In addition to the powers granted to the SEC to require disclosure of takeover intentions, certain tactics to prevent takeover can be used by the intended target. More than 40 states have adopted antitakeover laws that can delay tender offers so that an alternative can be pursued. The takeover target may also utilize other legal tactics, such as court suits alleging that antitrust laws and other regulatory guidelines are being violated. Such tactics may forestall a takeover. For example, when Anderson, Clayton, & Co. made a bid for Gerber Products Co., the latter instituted a number of legal suits. After five months of legal maneuvers on both sides, Anderson, Clayton, & Co. dropped its bid. In another case, because Marshall Field and Co. threatened antitrust actions and announced its own acquisition program, Carter Hawley Hale dropped its takeover attempt. The Hart-Scott-Rodino Act of 1976, amending the antitrust laws, contains a provision requiring that premerger notification of large mergers be made to the FTC. This provision became effective in July 1978.

As a consequence of the disclosure requirements in connection with intended tender offers, competition among bidders in takeover efforts may cause the acquisition price to rise well above the market price of the stock before the initial tender offer. This is illustrated by the Conoco story.

The Conoco Acquisition

During 1978, Conoco common stock traded in a relatively narrow range of $24 to $32. This range widened to $28-$50 in 1979 and to $41-$73 in 1980. In May 1981, Dome Petroleum made a tender offer of $65 per share for 14 million shares (13 percent) of Conoco common stock; Conoco termed the offer inadequate and took legal action to block the offer. On June 25, 1981, Seagram, the Canadian distiller, made a $73 per share tender offer for 41 percent of Conoco's stock. Conoco also opposed this bid. Conoco found a "white knight" in du Pont, and on July 6, 1981, the firms announced an agreement to merge. The merger terms provided that du Pont would pay $87.50 per share in cash for 40 percent and trade 1.6 shares of du Pont common stock for each of the remaining 60 percent of Conoco shares, representing a total price of $7.3 billion.

On July 12, 1981, Seagram increased its offer to $85 per share for 51 percent of Conoco shares. On July 14, du Pont raised its offer to $85 in cash for the 40 percent and 1.7 du Pont shares for the remaining 60 percent, representing a total bid of $7.4 billion. On July 17, Mobil Oil entered the picture, with a cash offer of $90 a share for half of Conoco's common stock and new Mobil preferred stock or debentures valued at $90 per Conoco common share for the remainder. On July 23, Seagram raised its offer to $92 cash. On July 27, Mobil increased its cash offer to $105 a share. On August 3, Mobil moved the cash offer to $115, and on the following day, to $120 per share. Du Pont countered by raising its cash offer to $98 per share. At 3:45 A.M. on August 5, 1981, du Pont began purchasing the 55 percent of Conoco shares for which it held tenders.

The higher Mobil offer was clouded by investor uncertainty as to whether a Mobil-Conoco merger would lead to a protracted antitrust suit. In contrast, on July 31, 1981, the U.S. Department of Justice stated that the only possible antitrust problem it saw in the Conoco-du Pont merger stemmed from Conoco's joint venture in a petrochemical plant with Monsanto, a du Pont competitor. Du Pont quickly stated that any potential problem could be avoided since it was willing to either sell Conoco's share to Monsanto or to buy out Monsanto's interests; du Pont subsequently did buy out Monsanto.

Other recent dramatic fights for corporate control include the 1983 attempt of The Limited department stores to take over the Carter Hawley Hale department stores. Also in the news in 1984 was the buying program of the common stock of Walt Disney Productions by entrepreneur Saul Steinberg. In order to ward off his possible efforts to buy effective control, his shares were repurchased at a premium over the market. During 1985, Pickens failed to take over Unocal as did Ted Turner in his effort to acquire CBS.

In 1984 and in 1985, takeover attempts in the oil industry resulted in mergers among very large oil companies. This included the acquisition of Gulf Oil by Chevron. Phillips Petroleum warded off the takeover attempts of T. Boone Pickens by its own restructuring program. In March of 1985, Castle & Cooke, one of the original large corporations based in Hawaii, after having paid $71 million to buy back shares from Charles Hurwitz, became the object of a control fight between David Murdoch, through his Flexi-Van Corporation and a stock purchase program by Irwin L. Jacobs, a Minneapolis investor.

The episodes described are but a small sample of the many dramas that filled the pages of the financial press in the late 1970s and early 1980s. Some natural questions are: Why all this merger and acquisition activity? What is its broader significance? These topics are considered next before taking up the discussion of the managerial finance aspects of merger.

Restructuring Business Firms

The above examples of struggles for control suggest a broad range of activities in connection with expanding, shrinking, and otherwise restructuring business firms. To provide an overview of these many kinds of practices, they are summarized in Table 30.3. The grouping is somewhat arbitrary but indicates the direction of the emphasis in these various practices. Each type of activity will be briefly explained.

Expansion

Under expansion, we have listed mergers, tender offers, and joint ventures. Mergers are like a marriage in the romantic tradition. There is a period of courtship leading to the joining of two or more separate entities into one, after which the parties hope to live happily ever after.

In a tender offer, one party takes the initiative in making a monetary offer for the ownership shares of the other party or parties. Joint ventures involve the intersection of only a small fraction of the activities of the companies involved and for limited duration of 10 to 15 years or less. They may represent a separate entity in which each of the parties makes cash and other forms of investments.

Sell-Offs

Distinct types of sell-offs should be distinguished. The two major types are (1) spin-offs and (2) divestitures. A spin-off creates a separate new legal entity, its shares are distributed on a pro rata basis to existing shareholders of the parent company. Thus, existing

---

Table 30.3   Forms of Restructuring Business Firms

    I. **Expansion**
       Mergers and Acquisitions
       Tender Offers
       Joint Ventures

   II. **Sell-offs**
       Spin-offs
         Split-offs
         Split-ups
       Divestitures
         Equity Carve-Outs

  III. **Corporate Control**
       Premium Buy-backs
       Standstill Agreements
       Antitakeover Amendments
       Proxy Contests

  IV. **Changes in Ownership Structure**
       Exchange Offers
       Share Repurchases
       Going Private
       Leveraged Buy-outs

---

stockholders have the same proportion of ownership in the new entity as in the original firm. There is, however, a separation of control, and, over time, the new entity as a separate decision-making unit may develop policies and strategies different from those of the original parent. Note that no cash is received by the original parent. In some sense, a spin-off represents a form of a dividend to existing shareholders. A variation of a spin-off is the split-off, in which a portion of existing shareholders receive stock in a subsidiary in exchange for parent company stock. Still a different variation on the spin-off is a split-up, in which the entire firm is broken up into a series of spin-offs, so that the parent no longer exists and only the new offspring survive.

In contrast to the class of spin-offs in which only shares are transferred or exchanged is another group of transactions in which cash comes in to the firm — divestitures. Basically, a divestiture involves the sale of a portion of the firm to an outside third party. Cash or equivalent consideration is received by the divesting firm. Typically, the buyer is an existing firm, so that no new legal entity results. It simply represents a form of expansion on the part of the buying firm. A variation on divestiture is the equity carve-out. An equity carve-out involves the sale of a portion of the firm via an equity offering to outsiders. In other words, new shares of equity are sold to outsiders which give them ownership of a portion of the previously existing firm. A new legal entity is created. The equity holders in the new entity need not be the same as the equity holders in the original seller. A new control group is immediately created.

The distinctions between these various forms of spin-offs are somewhat arbitrary, and some writers view them all as simply various forms of stock dividends, except for transactions that involve the sale of shares to parties other than existing shareholders.

Corporate Control

The third grouping of activities in Table 30.3 we have referred to as "corporate control." Premium buy-backs represent the repurchase of a substantial stockholder's ownership interest at a premium above the market price (called "greenmail"), as illustrated by the Disney-Saul Steinberg episode described above. Often in connection with such buy-backs, a standstill agreement is written. These represent voluntary contracts in which the stockholder who is bought out agrees not to make further investments in the company in the future. When a standstill agreement is made without a buy-back, the substantial stockholder simply agrees not to increase his ownership which presumably would put him in an effective control position.

Antitakeover amendments are changes in the corporate bylaws to make an acquisition of the company more difficult or more expensive. These include (1) supermajority voting provisions requiring a percentage (for example, 80 percent) of stockholders to approve a merger, (2) staggered terms for directors which can delay change of control for a number of years, and (3) golden parachutes which award large termination payments to existing management if control of the firm is changed and management is terminated.

In a proxy contest, an outside group seeks to obtain representation on the firm's board of directors. The outsiders are referred to as "dissidents" or "insurgents," who seek to reduce the control position of the "incumbents" or existing board of directors. Since the management of a firm often has effective control of the board of directors, proxy contests are often regarded as directed against the existing management.

Changes in Ownership Structure

Changes in ownership structure represent the fourth group of restructuring activities listed in Table 30.3. One form is through exchange offers, which may be the exchange of debt or preferred stock for common stock, or conversely, of common stock for the more senior claims. Exchanging debt for common stock increases leverage; exchanging common stock for debt decreases leverage.

A second form is share repurchase, which simply means that the corporation buys back some fraction of its outstanding shares of common stock. As we described in Chapter 22, tender offers may be made for share repurchase. The percentage of shares purchased may be small or substantial. If the latter, the effect may be to change the control structure in the firm. For example, it has been said that the substantial share repurchase activity by Teledyne, Inc., has increased the effective control position of H. E. Singleton, the chairman and chief executive officer of the company. The company purchased shares from other shareholders, but Mr. Singleton did not reduce his already substantial holdings. The fixed holdings of Mr. Singleton thereby became a larger percentage of the new reduced company total.

In a "going private" transaction, the entire equity interest in a previously public corporation is purchased by a small group of investors. The firm is no longer subject to the regulations of the Securities and Exchange Commission, whose purpose is to protect public investors. Going private transactions typically include members of the incumbent management group, who obtain a substantial proportion of the equity ownership of the newly private company. Usually, a small group of outside investors provides funds and, typically, secures representation on the private company's board of directors. These outside investors also arrange other financing from third party investors. When financing from third parties involves substantial borrowing by the private company, such transactions are referred to as "leveraged buy-outs" (LBO's).

Issues Raised by Restructuring

Clearly, many forms of business and financial activities are covered by Table 30.3. These activities have stirred much controversy. Are they good for the economic health of the nation or are they bad? Do they divert the energies of managers from *bona fide* economic activity to financial manipulation? Do they use up financial resources which otherwise would be employed in "real" investment activities? Why has such heightened merger activity been a phenomenon of the last 20 years? In short, we need a theory or theories to explain the "restructuring of corporate America."

In attempting to provide some explanations for these many activities, it may be useful to treat the first group of activities in Table 30.3 separately from the other groups. The first involves the combining and recombining of real assets. The remaining groups of activities appear to involve rearranging ownership and control structures in business firms.

Theories of Asset Redeployment

Let us first consider the explanations for mergers, tender offers, and joint ventures. We will then consider the divestitures and spin-offs, which represent, at least to some degree, a mirror image of the combining of assets. Theories of mergers, tender offers, and joint ventures can be grouped into five major areas:

1. Efficiency
2. Information
3. Agency problems
4. Market power
5. Taxes

Each of these five groups of theories will be briefly discussed.[1]

1. Efficiency Explanations

We will first take up the efficiency theory, which generally involves improving the performance of incumbent management or achieving some form of synergy. Unfortunately, during the heyday of the conglomerate merger activities of the late 1960s, exaggerated claims were made for synergy which came to be referred to as the "2 + 2 = 7" effect. But, while the claims for synergy achieved through asset deployment were exaggerated, there is a solid basis for achieving positive net present value investments by recombining the activities of business operations. Three forms of synergy may be distinguished:

Operating Synergy. Operating synergy or operating economies may be involved in horizontal and vertical mergers. For horizontal mergers, the source of operating economies must represent some form of economies of scale. These economies, in turn, may reflect indivisibilities and better utilization of capacity after the merger. Or important complementarities in organizational capabilities may be present that result in gains not attainable from internal investments in the short run.

Another area in which operating economies may be achieved is in vertical integration. Combining firms at different stages of an industry may achieve more efficient coordina-

---

[1]This material draws on Weston and Chung, "Some Aspects of Merger Theory," *Journal of the Midwest Finance Association*, Vol. 12, 1983, pp. 1-33.

tion of the different levels. The argument here is that costs of communication and various forms of bargaining and opportunistic behavior can be avoided by vertical integration.

Financial Synergy.   The possible financial synergies involve some unsettled issues of finance theory. Nevertheless, empirical analysis of mergers may shed some light directly or indirectly on the fundamental issues. Financial synergy argues that the cost of capital function may be lowered for a number of reasons. If the cash flow streams of the two companies are not perfectly correlated, bankruptcy probabilities may be lowered; and this consequence may decrease the existing present value of bankruptcy costs.

This debt-coinsurance effect benefits debtholders at the expense of shareholders (Higgins and Schall [1975]). However, this effect can be offset by increasing leverage after the merger, and the result will be increased tax savings on interest payments (Galai and Masulis [1976]). The increase in debt capacity (defined as the maximum amount of debt that can be raised at any given interest rate) due to merger has been explicitly analyzed by Stapleton [1982] in the context of the option-pricing theory. In his theory, the increase in debt capacity does not require the existence of bankruptcy costs.

Another dimension, emphasized by Levy and Sarnat [1970], is economies of scale in flotation and transaction costs that may be realized in conglomerate firms. Arguments may be raised about the potential magnitude of these financial factors. Further questions could be raised as to why joint activities might not be taken by unmerged firms to achieve the same economies of scale in flotation and transaction costs. However, the heterogeneity of firms and the costs of contracting would seem to make such activities prohibitive since such joint activities are not observed in the real world.

Strategic Realignment to Changing Environments.   The literature on long-range strategic planning has exploded in recent years. The emphasis of strategic planning is on areas related to firms' environments and constituencies, and not just their operating decisions.

The strategic planning approach to mergers appears to imply either the possibilities of economies of scale or utilization of some unused capacity in the firm's present managerial capabilities. Another rationale is that by external diversification, the firm acquires management skills for needed augmentation of its present capabilities. This approach still leaves some questions unanswered. New capabilities and new markets could be developed internally. The less-risky strategy may be to buy established organizations, but a competitive market for acquisitions implies that the net present value to acquirers from such investments is likely to be small. Nevertheless, if the changes in the environment call for a rapid adjustment, the combinations of existing firms may have significant positive benefits. Furthermore, if these investments can be used as a base for still additional investments with positive net present values, the strategy may succeed.

Another approach that may be considered in this group is the Hubris Hypothesis [Roll 1984]. Hubris refers to the optimistic animal spirits that appear to drive creative activity, investment decisions, etc. Thus, hubris on the part of bidding firms may explain why bids are made substantially above current market prices. Roll argues that the empirical evidence supports his hubris hypothesis as much as it supports alternative explanations, such as taxes, synergy and inefficient target management.

2. Information and Signaling

The second possible reason for mergers, tender offers, and joint ventures is what has been termed the "information hypothesis." This refers to the revaluation of the ownership shares of firms due to new information that is generated during the merger negotiations, the tender offer process, or the joint venture planning. Alternative forms of the information hypothesis have been distinguished by Bradley, Desai, and Kim [1983]. One is the "kick in the pants" explanation. Management is stimulated to implement a higher-valued operating strategy. A second is the "sitting on a gold mine" hypothesis. The negotiations or tendering activity may involve the dissemination of new information or lead the market to judge that the bidders have superior information. The market may then revalue previously "undervalued" shares.

Undervaluation.   A third aspect of information effects is a variant of the "undervaluation" hypothesis. This variation suggests that firms have stepped up diversification efforts in recent years by entry into new product market areas or by expansion on a bargain basis. The inflation of the 1970s had a double-barrelled impact. For various reasons, stock prices were depressed during the 1970s and did not recover until the latter part of 1982, when the level of inflation dropped and business prospects improved. The second impact of inflation was to cause current replacement costs of assets to be substantially higher than their recorded historical book values. These two economic trends resulted in a decline of what has been called the *q-ratio*. The q-ratio is defined as the market value of equity plus interest-bearing debt divided by the current replacement cost of net assets. Assets are net in the sense that both depreciation reserves and noninterest-bearing debt are deducted from gross total assets.

In recent years, the q-ratio had been running between 0.5 and 0.6. If a company wished to add to capacity in producing a particular product, it could acquire the additional capacity more cheaply by buying a company that produces the product rather than building brick-and-mortar from scratch. If Firm A seeks to add capacity, this activity implies that its marginal q-ratio is greater than one. But, if other firms in its industry have average q-ratios of less than one, it is efficient for Firm A to add capacity by the purchase of other firms. For example, if the q-ratio is 0.6, and if in a merger the premium paid over market value is 50 percent (which is the average figure for recent years), the resulting purchase price is 0.6 times 1.5, which equals 0.9. This outcome would mean that the average purchase price would still be 10 percent below the current replacement costs of the assets acquired. This potential advantage would provide a broad basis for the operation of the undervaluation theory in recent years when the q-ratio was low.

For companies in natural resource industries, q-ratios have been as low as 0.2 because of high estimated values of reserves in the ground used in the denominator. The low q-ratio provided a basis for even more substantial premiums where natural resource firms were involved in mergers. For example, although U.S. Steel paid a substantial premium over market value in the Marathon merger, shareholders threatened suit because they stated that independent appraisals had estimated the current value of Marathon assets at more than double the price paid by U.S. Steel. Of course, these appraisals were subject to considerable uncertainty. Witness the sharp decline in oil prices that began in early 1983.

3. Agency Problems

Jensen and Meckling [1976] formulated the implications of agency problems. An agency problem arises when managers own only a fraction of the ownership shares of the firm. Partial ownership may cause managers to work less vigorously than otherwise and/or to consume more perquisites (such as luxurious offices, company cars, membership in clubs) because the majority owners bear most of the cost. The argument can be made that in large corporations with widely dispersed ownership, individual owners do not have sufficient incentive to expend the substantial resources required to monitor the behavior of managers. A number of compensation arrangements and the market for managers may mitigate the agency problem (Fama [1980]).

Another market mechanism is the threat of takeovers. The threat of a takeover may substitute for individual shareholders' efforts to monitor the managers. The agency explanation of mergers extends the previous work by Manne [1965]. Manne emphasized the market for corporate control and viewed mergers as a threat of takeover if a firm's management lagged in performance either because of inefficiency or because of agency problems.

A variant of the agency problem is the managerialism theory of conglomerate mergers. The "managerialism" explanation for conglomerate mergers was set forth by Mueller [1969]. Mueller hypothesized that managers are motivated to further increase the size of their firms. He assumed that the compensation to managers is a function of the size of the firm and also argued that managers adopt too low an investment hurdle rate in their analysis of merger opportunities. But, in a study critical of earlier evidence, Lewellen and Huntsman [1970] presented findings that managers' compensation is significantly correlated with the firm's profit rate, and not its level of sales. The basic premise of the managerialism theory, therefore, is doubtful.

Agency theory suggests that when the market for managers does not solve the agency problem, the market for firms or merger activity will come into play. This theory suggests, therefore, that merger activity is a method of dealing with the agency problem. The managerialism theory argues that the agency problem is not solved and that merger activity is a manifestation of the agency problems of inefficient, external investments by managers. The empirical evidence presented below will enable us to test these competing theories.

4. Market Power

An objection sometimes raised against permitting a firm to increase its market share by merger is that the result will be "undue concentration" in the industry. Indeed, public policy in the United States has held that when four or fewer firms account for 40 percent or more of the sales in a given market or line of business, an undesirable market structure or "undue concentration" exists. The argument, in brief, is that if four or fewer firms account for a substantial percentage of an industry's sales, these firms will recognize the impact of their actions and policies upon one another. This recognized interdependence will lead to a consideration of actions and reactions to changes in policy that will tend toward "tacit collusion." As a result, the prices and profits of the firms will contain monopoly elements. Thus, if economies from mergers cannot be established, it is assumed that the resulting increases in concentration may lead to monopoly returns. If economies of scale can be demonstrated, then a comparison of efficiencies versus the effects of increased concentration must be made.

In 1982, and again in 1984, the U.S. Department of Justice announced new merger guidelines to supersede those which had been issued in 1968. The new merger guidelines adopt the Herfindahl-Hirschman Index (HHI), which takes into consideration the market shares of all of the firms in the industry. The theory behind the use of the HHI is that if one or more firms have relatively high market shares, this is of even greater concern than the share of the largest four firms. An example presented with the announcement of the new merger guidelines illustrates this point. In one market, four firms each hold a 15 percent market share, and the remaining 40 percent is held by 40 firms, each with a 1 percent market share. Its HHI would be

$$H = 4(15)^2 + 40(1)^2 = 940.$$

In another market, one firm has a 57 percent market share, and the remaining 43 percent is held by 43 firms, each with a 1 percent market share. Like the first market, the four-firm concentration ratio here would be the same 60 percent. However, the HHI would be

$$H = (57)^2 + 43(1)^2 = 3,292.$$

Thus, the HHI registers a concern about inequality as well as degree of concentration. The economic basis for either concern has not been well established. While some economists hold that high concentration, however measured, causes some degree of monopoly, other economists hold that increased concentration is generally the *result* of active and intense competition. They argue further that the intense competition continues among large firms in concentrated industries because the dimensions of decision making over prices, outputs, types of product, quality of product, service, and so forth are so numerous and of so many gradations that collusion simply is not feasible. This is an area where the issues continue to be unresolved.

5. Tax Considerations

Tax considerations also are involved in mergers. One example is the substitution of capital gains taxes for ordinary income taxes by acquiring a growth firm with a small or no dividend payout and then selling it after its growth to realize capital gains. When the growth of a firm has slowed so that earnings retention cannot be justified to the Internal Revenue Service, an incentive for sale to another firm is created. Rather than pay out future earnings as dividends subject to the ordinary personal income tax, future earnings can be capitalized in a sale to another firm.

Another tax factor is the sale of firms with accumulated tax losses. Although a business purpose also must be demonstrated, a firm with tax losses can shelter the positive earnings of another firm with which it is joined. The Economic Recovery Tax Act of 1981 provided for the sale of tax credits from the use of accelerated depreciation (subsequently restricted). These transactions often involved sale and lease-back arrangements. This tactic suggests that whether tax considerations induce mergers depends on the availability of alternative methods of achieving equivalent tax benefits.

Another strong tax incentive is to acquire firms in order to achieve a stepped-up basis for depreciable assets. This motivation represents an attempt to avoid the penalty of depreciation on lower historical costs during a period of inflation.

Still other tax effects are associated with inheritance taxes. A closely held firm may be sold as the owners become older because of the uncertainty of the value placed on the firm in connection with estate taxes. Also, a sale may be made to provide greater liquidity for the payment of estate taxes. A study of mergers in the newspaper industry illustrates the effects of the two previous tax influences (Dertouzos and Thorpe [1982]). The stepped-up basis for depreciable assets leads to competition among bidding firms that results in premiums paid for newspaper companies acquired. These high, demonstrated market values are then used by the income-tax service in setting values on newspaper companies for estate tax purposes. But, the realization of the tax benefits of the higher depreciable values requires actual transactions which stimulate the purchase of individual newspaper companies.

Theories of Restructuring

The first group of activities in Table 30.3 involves combining assets; the remaining groups involve uncombining assets or what some have referred to as "reverse mergers." The synergy theories involve the "2 + 2 = 7" effect, whereas the reverse mergers seem to imply the "5 − 1 = 7" effect. Thus, a new math has evolved to explain both mergers and reverse mergers. The various forms of divestiture can be rationalized as transferring business assets to a higher valued use or to a more efficient user. A divestiture may create value by slicing off a business which was a poor fit with the remaining operations. If so, good divestiture programs may increase the market values of both the buying and selling companies.

There is another aspect of the second to fourth categories of activities in Table 30.3 which deal with corporate control and rearranging the ownership structure. Here, the hypothesis is that improvements in managerial accountability and a strengthening of incentives may be achieved by separating unrelated business activities. Spin-offs may provide managers with greater decision-making authority. Better performance evaluation criteria and measurement may also be achieved. Having publicly traded stock which provides continuing market valuations is useful for performance evaluation. Improvements in profitability may also be achieved by linking managerial compensation more directly to performance tests, including those which track stock price behavior.

The recent literature of finance has provided hypotheses to explain the many types of restructuring activities. Some sophisticated procedures for empirical tests of these hypotheses have also been achieved. The results of this empirical work will next be summarized.

Empirical Studies of Mergers and Other Aspects of Corporate Control

The empirical studies of mergers and other aspects of corporate control use the methodology of testing for residuals or "abnormal returns." This methodology builds on the materials presented in Chapter 17 on the application of the CAPM. It is the methodology used in connection with studies of the impact of alternative accounting procedures, new issues of common stock or of bonds, and particularly in connection with the many aspects of corporate control.

Merger or tender offer studies, for example, generally examine a large number of mergers or tender offers (usually more than 100). In the analysis, the reference date or "event date" is typically the *announcement* of the merger or tender offer under consideration. The statistical analysis is then based on the behavior of the returns before and after the "event." The procedure begins with an adjustment for the market risk premium. The many other influences that might be operating are averaged out over the many different companies and different calendar time periods in the sample.

Thus, the statistical procedures are designed to hold constant the influences of all factors other than the event under analysis. The return predicted by the market line relationship between return and risk is compared with the actual return. The actual return minus the predicted return is called the residual and the procedure is termed residual analysis. The residuals are averaged over all of the firms in the sample for various days or months

---

Table 30.4   Empirical Results from Studies of Residuals

Studies	Returns
A. Merger Studies	
1. Acquired firms	20%
2. Acquiring firms	2–3%[a]
B. Tender Offer Studies	
1. Acquired firms	35%
2. Acquiring firms	3–5%
C. Joint Ventures	
1. Absolute	2.5%
2. Scaled by investment	23%
D. Sell-offs	
1. Spin-offs	2–4%
2. Divestitures	
Sellers	.5–1%
Buyers	.34%
3. Equity carve-outs	2%
E. Premium Buy-backs	
1. Single blocks from outsiders	−2%
2. From insiders or small shareholdings	1.2%
3. Sellers of single blocks	1.5%
F. Standstill Agreements	
(Nonparticipating stockholders)	−4%
G. Antitakeover Amendments	1.5%
H. Proxy Contests	10%
I. Share Repurchases	16%
J. Going Private	20%
K. Leveraged Buy-outs	50%

---

[a]Not statistically significant.

before and after the event. These average residuals are also accumulated over a period of time and called cumulative average residuals, or CAR's. Using the methodology described, a large number of empirical studies have been performed. On every aspect of mergers, tender offers, and corporate control, one or more event studies have been performed. The patterns of results are summarized in Table 30.4.

In mergers, the acquired firms, on average, experience a 20 percent excess or abnormal return. For acquiring firms, the residuals appear to be 2 to 3 percent positive on average but statistically not significant. In tender offers for acquisitions, the excess returns for acquired firms run about 35 percent. Acquiring firms appear to have a small 3 to 5 percent positive return on average that is statistically significant. For joint ventures, there is, on average, for the participating firms a small, 2 to 3 percent, positive return that is significant. However, expressed as a percentage of the dollar investment involved, the returns appear to be 23 percent.

Three types of sell-offs have been distinguished. In spin-offs, the two-day average abnormal return is a positive 2 to 4 percent. For divestitures, the two-day return is also positive and significant but much smaller than for spin-offs, generally under 1 percent. For equity carve-outs, the return is just under 2 percent and significant. It appears also that in the period preceding the interval near the announcement date, the residuals are positive for spin-offs and negative for divestitures. This suggests the possibility that spin-offs are associated with favorable performance which is expected to be continued or enhanced by associating managerial returns with the new equity created in the spin-offs. In contrast, the negative prior returns in divestitures suggest inability of the firm to manage those assets well. The small positive return at the announcement date indicates that the market views with some approval the firm's decision to divest itself of assets that it has been unable to manage effectively. The somewhat better returns on equity carve-outs may be related to improved managerial motivation effects.

Premium buy-backs result in a small negative effect on the residuals. There is a statistically significant 1.5 negative return associated with buying off a corporate "raider." The standstill agreements in which a potential buyer group agrees not to make further investments to achieve control are associated with a negative 4 percent residual return. The announcement of antitakeover amendments to make acquisition of a given company more difficult appears to result in a small positive excess return of about 2 percent. This positive return is statistically significant.

On share repurchases, there is a positive return of about 16 percent associated with the announcement of such programs. On average, when proxy contests are announced, there is a +10 percent excess return. Announcements of going private result in a +20 percent positive residual. Finally, leveraged buy-outs result in a large positive return of about 50 percent upon the announcement of such a program.

In summary, most of the event studies associated with mergers, tender offers, and other aspects of corporate control result in positive gains to shareholders. Only the premium buy-backs and standstill agreements used to buy off potential raiders result in negative returns to shareholders. In connection with mergers, tender offers, and joint ventures, it appears that there may be real value added as a basis for the increase in valuation. The sources of the value increases are some combination of efficiency, information effects or signaling, reduction of agency problems, and/or tax advantages. The empirical studies have been unable to separate the relative importance of these four major factors that lie behind the benefits of buy-outs and sell-offs. The basis for increases in value associated with the other elements of corporate control relates more to organizational aspects of running large business firms. The gains from the various aspects of corporate control described relate to more clearly identifying responsibility for results and the more direct linking of managerial rewards with stock price and performance. But, on average, these various aspects of mergers, tender offers, and corporate ownership and control relationships seem to represent positive net present value activities. It would appear that they supplement other types of investment activity by business firms.

Terms of Mergers

For every merger actually consummated, a number of other potentially attractive combinations fail during negotiations. Negotiations may be broken off when it is revealed that the companies' operations are not compatible or when the parties are unable to agree on the merger terms. The most important of these terms is the price to be paid by the acquiring firm.

Table 30.5   Basic Information for Analysis of Dilution and Appreciation

	Company A	Company B
Total earnings	$20,000	$50,000
Number of shares of common stock	5,000	10,000
Earnings per share of stock	$4	$5
Price-earnings ratio per share	15 times	12 times
Market price per share	$60	$60

Effects on Price and Earnings

A merger carries the potential for either favorable or adverse effects on earnings, on market price of shares, or on both. Previous chapters have shown that investment decisions should be guided by the effects on market values, as predicted by the probable effects on future earnings and dividends. Future events are difficult to forecast, however, so both stockholders and managers attribute great importance to the immediate effects on earnings per share of a contemplated merger. Company directors will often state, "I do not know how the merger will affect the market price of the shares of my company, because so many forces influencing market prices are at work. But the effect on earnings per share can be seen directly."

An example will illustrate the effects of a proposed merger on earnings per share and thus suggest the kinds of problems likely to arise. Assume the facts in Table 30.5 for two companies. Suppose the firms agree to merge, with B, the surviving firm, acquiring the shares of A by a one-for-one exchange of stock. The exchange ratio is determined by the market prices of the two companies. Assuming no increase in earnings, the effects on earnings per share are shown in Table 30.6.

Since total earnings are $70,000, and since a total of 15,000 shares will be outstanding after the merger has been completed, the new earnings per share will be $4.67. Earnings will increase by 67 cents for A's stockholders, but they will decline by 33 cents for B's.

The effects on market values are less certain. If the combined company sells at Company A's price-earnings ratio of 15, the market value per share of the new company will be $70.

Table 30.6   Effects of Differential P-Es When Merger Terms Are at Market Prices

	Shares of Company B Owned after Merger	Earnings per Share	
		Before Merger	After Merger
A's stockholders	5,000	$4	$4.67
B's stockholders	10,000	5	4.67
Total	15,000		

In this case, shareholders of both companies will have benefited. This result comes about because the combined earnings are now valued at a multiplier of 15, whereas prior to the merger, one portion of the earnings was valued at a multiplier of 15 and another portion at a multiplier of 12. If, on the other hand, the earnings of the new company are valued at B's multiplier of 12, the indicated market value of the shares will be $56, and the shareholders of each company will have suffered a $4 dilution in market value.

Because the effects on market value per share are less certain than those on earnings per share, the impact on earnings per share tends to be given great weight in merger negotiations. The following analysis thus illustrates effects on earnings per share while recognizing that maximizing market value is the valid rule for investment decisions.

As shown below, if a merger takes place on the basis of earnings, neither earnings dilution nor earnings appreciation will take place, as shown in Table 30.7. It is clear that the equivalent earnings per share after the merger are the same as before the merger.[2] The effect on market values, however, will depend on the size of the earnings multiplier that prevails.

Quantitative Factors Affecting Terms of Mergers

Five factors have received the greatest emphasis in arriving at merger terms: (1) earnings and the growth of earnings, (2) dividends, (3) market values, (4) book values, and (5) net current assets. Analysis is typically based on the per-share values of the foregoing factors. The relative importance of each factor and the circumstances under which each is likely to be the most influential determinant in arriving at terms will vary. The nature of these influences is described below.

Earnings and Growth Rates.   Both expected earnings and capitalization rates as reflected in P-E ratios are important in determining the values that will be established in a merger. The analysis necessarily begins with historical data on the firms' earnings; their past growth rates, probable future trends, and variability are important determinants of the earnings multiplier, or P-E ratio, that will prevail after the merger.

Table 30.7   Effects of Differential P-Es When Merger Terms Are Based on Earnings

	Shares of Company B Owned after Merger	Earnings per Share	
		Before Merger	After Merger
A's stockholders	4,000	$4	$4
B's stockholders	10,000	5	5
Total	14,000		

[2]On the basis of earnings, the exchange ratio is 4:5. That is, Company A's shareholders receive four shares of B stock for each five shares of A stock they own. Earnings per share of the merged company are $5. But, since A's shareholders now own only 80 percent of the number of their old shares, their equivalent earnings per *old* share are the same $4. For example, if one of A's stockholders formerly held 100 shares, that person will own only 80 shares of B after the merger, and the total earnings will be $80 \times \$5 = \$400$. Dividing the $400 total earnings by the number of shares formerly owned, 100, gives the $4 per *old* share.

The ways in which future earnings growth rates affect the multiplier can be illustrated by extending the preceding example. First, high P-E ratios are commonly associated with rapidly growing companies. Since Company A has the higher P-E ratio, it is reasonable to assume that its earnings will grow more rapidly than those of Company B. Suppose A's expected growth rate is 10 percent and B's is 5 percent. Looking at the proposed merger from the viewpoint of Company B and its stockholders, and assuming that the exchange ratio is based on present market prices, it can be seen that B will suffer a dilution in earnings when the merger occurs. However, B will be acquiring a firm with more favorable growth prospects; hence, its earnings after the merger should increase more rapidly than before. In this case, the new growth rate is assumed to be a weighted average of the growth rates of the individual firms — weighted by their respective total earnings before the merger. In the example, the new expected growth rate is 6.43 percent.

With the new growth rate, it is possible to determine just how long it will take Company B's stockholders to regain the earnings dilution — that is, how long it will take earnings per share to revert to their premerger position as shown in Figure 30.1.[3] Without the

---

Figure 30.1   Effect of Merger on Future Earnings

---

[3]The calculation could also be made algebraically by solving for n in the following equation:

$$E_1(1 + g_1)^n = E_2(1 + g_2)^n,$$

where

E_1 and E_2 = earnings per share before and after the merger, respectively

g_1 and g_2 = growth rates before and after the merger, respectively

n = breakeven number of years.

merger, B will have initial earnings of $5 a share, and these earnings will grow at a rate of 5 percent a year. With the merger, earnings will drop to $4.67 a share, but the rate of growth will increase to 6.43 percent. Under these conditions, the earnings dilution will be overcome after five years; from the fifth year on, B's earnings will be higher, assuming the merger is consummated.

This same relationship can be developed from the viewpoint of the faster growing firm, for which there is an immediate earnings increase but a reduced rate of growth. Working through the analysis shows the number of years before the earnings accretion will be eroded.

It is apparent that the critical variables are (1) the respective rates of growth of the two firms; (2) their relative sizes, which determine the actual amount of the initial earnings per share dilution or accretion, as well as the new weighted average growth rate; (3) the firms' P-E ratios; and (4) the exchange ratio. These factors interact to produce the resulting pattern of earnings per share for the surviving company. It is possible to generalize the relationships somewhat; for the immediate purposes, it is necessary simply to note that in the bargaining process, the exchange ratio is the variable that must be manipulated in an effort to reach a mutually satisfactory earnings pattern.[4]

Dividends.   Because they represent the actual income received by stockholders, dividends can influence the terms of merger. As Chapter 22 suggests, however, dividends are likely to have little influence on the market price of companies with a record of high growth and high profitability. Some companies have not yet paid cash dividends, but they nonetheless command market prices representing a high multiple of current earnings. However, for utility companies and for companies in industries where growth rates and profitability have declined, the dollar amount of dividends paid can have a relatively important influence on the market price of the stock. Dividends, therefore, can influence the terms on which these companies will be likely to trade in a merger.[5]

Market Values.   The price of a firm's stock reflects expectations about its future earnings and dividends, so current market values are expected to have a strong influence on the terms of a merger. However, the value placed on a firm in an acquisition may exceed its current market price for a number of reasons:

1.   The prospective purchaser may be interested in the company for the contribution that it will make to the purchaser's company. Thus, the acquired company may be worth more to an informed purchaser than it is in the general market.
2.   Stockholders are offered more than current market prices for their stock as an inducement to sell.

---

[4]Certain companies, especially the conglomerates, are reported to have used mergers to produce a "growth illusion" designed to increase the prices of their stocks. When a high P-E ratio company buys a low P-E ratio company, the earnings per share of the acquiring firm rise *because* of the merger. Thus, mergers can produce growth in reported earnings for the acquiring firm. This growth by merger, in turn, can cause the acquiring firm to keep its high P-E ratio. With this ratio, the conglomerates can seek new low P-E merger candidates and thus continue to obtain growth through mergers. The chain is broken if (1) the merger activity slows or (2) the P-E ratio of the acquiring firm falls. In 1968 and 1969, several large conglomerates reported profit declines caused by losses in certain of their divisions. This reduced the growth rate in EPS, which, in turn, led to a decline in the P-E ratio. A change in tax laws and antitrust suits against some conglomerate mergers also made it more difficult to consummate favorable mergers. These factors, along with tight money and depressed conditions in some industries, caused a further reduction in the P-E ratio and compounded the firms' problems. The net result was a drastic revaluation of conglomerate share prices, with such former favorites as LTV falling from a high of $169 to $7.50 and Litton Industries from $115 to $6.75.

[5]If a company that does not pay dividends on its stock is seeking to acquire a firm whose stockholders are accustomed to receiving dividends, the exchange can be on a "convertibles for common stock" basis. This will enable the acquired firm's stockholders to continue receiving income.

3. The value of control or ability to realize tax advantages may add values above the current market levels (Lease, McConnell, and Mikkelson [1983]).

For these reasons, the offering price, historically, had been in the range of 10 to 20 percent above the market price before the merger announcement. In recent years, premiums of 50 percent or more have been observed.

Book Value per Share. Book value is generally considered to be relatively unimportant in determining the value of a company, since it represents only the historical investments made in the company—investments that may have little relation to current values or prices. At times, however, especially when it substantially exceeds market value, book value may well have an impact on merger terms. Book value is an index of the amount of physical facilities made available in the merger. Despite a past record of low earning power, it is always possible that, under effective management, a firm's assets may once again achieve normal earning power, in which case, the market value of the company will rise. Because of the potential contribution of physical properties to improved future earnings, book value may have an influence on actual merger terms.

Net Current Assets per Share. Net current assets (current assets minus current liabilities) per share are likely to have an influence on merger terms because they represent the amount of liquidity that can be obtained from a company in a merger. In the postwar textile mergers, net current assets were very high, and this was one of the characteristics making textile companies attractive to the acquiring firms. By buying a textile company, often with securities, an acquiring company was in a position to look for still other merger candidates, paying for new acquisitions with the just-acquired liquidity. Similarly, if an acquired company is debt-free, the acquiring firm may be able to borrow the funds required for the purchase, using the acquired firm's assets and earning power to pay off the loan after the merger or to provide security for renewing or even increasing the borrowing.[6]

Relative Importance of Quantitative Factors. Attempts have been made to determine statistically the relative weights assigned to each of the above factors in actual merger cases. These attempts have been singularly unsuccessful. In one case, one factor seems to dominate; in another, some other determinant appears most important. This absence of consistent patterns among the quantitative factors suggests that qualitative forces are also at work.

Qualitative Influences: Synergy

Sometimes, the most important influence on the terms of a merger is a business consideration not reflected at all in historical quantitative data. A soundly conceived merger is one in which the combination produces what may be called a *synergistic*, or "two-plus-two-equals-five," effect. By the combination, more profits are generated than could be achieved by the sum of the individual firms operating separately.

To illustrate: In the merger between Merck and Company and Sharp and Dohme, it was said that each company complemented the other in an important way. Merck had a good reputation for its research organization, whereas Sharp and Dohme had an effective sales force. The combination of these two pharmaceutical companies added strength to both.

---

[6]By the same token, a firm seeking to *avoid* being acquired may reduce its liquid position and use up its borrowing potential.

Another example is the merger between Carrier Corporation and Affiliated Gas Equipment. The merger enabled the combined company to provide a complete line of air-conditioning and heating equipment. The merger between Hilton Hotels and Statler Hotels led to economies in the purchase of supplies and materials. One Hilton executive estimated that the savings accruing simply from the combined management of the Statler and Hilton hotels in New York amounted to $700,000 a year. The bulk of the savings was in laundry, food, advertising, and administrative costs.

The qualitative factors may also reflect other influences. The merger or acquisition may enable a company that lacks general management ability to obtain it from the other company. Another factor may be the acquisition of a technically competent scientific or engineering staff if one of the companies has fallen behind in the technological race. In such a situation, the company needing the technical competence possessed by the other firm may be willing to pay a substantial premium over previous levels of earnings, dividends, market values, or book values of the acquired firm.

Managerial motives may also be involved. Managers may seek mergers to reduce the diversifiable (unsystematic) risk of the firm. While stockholders can deal with unsystematic risk by diversification (as explained in Chapters 16 and 17), managers are concerned with total risk because a substantial portion of their wealth and their reputations as executives are tied to the performance of one firm. This is another example of agency problems associated with a conflict of interest between stockholders and managers. As a consequence, we have used the coefficient of variation as a measure of risk (which may be important to managers) in addition to the beta that is priced in the CAPM.

The foregoing are the kinds of qualitative considerations that may have an overriding influence on the actual terms of merger, and the value of such contributions is never easy to quantify. The all-encompassing question, of course, is how the factors will affect the contribution of each company to future market value of the combined operation. These historical data and qualitative considerations described, in addition to judgment and bargaining, combine to determine merger terms.

Holding Companies

In 1889, New Jersey became the first state to pass a general incorporation law permitting corporations to be formed for the sole purpose of owning the stocks of other companies. This law was the origin of the holding company. The Sherman Act of 1890, which prohibits combinations or collusion in restraint of trade, gave an impetus to holding company operations as well as to outright mergers, because companies could do as one company what they were forbidden to do as separate companies.

Many of the advantages and disadvantages of holding companies are no more than the advantages and disadvantages of large-scale operations already discussed in connection with mergers and consolidations. Whether a company is organized on a divisional basis or with the divisions kept as separate companies does not affect the basic reasons for conducting a large-scale, multiproduct, multiplant operation. However, the holding company form of large-scale operations has different advantages and disadvantages from those of completely integrated divisionalized operations.

Advantages of Holding Companies

Control with Fractional Ownership. Through a holding company operation, a firm can buy 5, 10, or 50 percent of the stock of another corporation. Such a fractional ownership may be sufficient to give the acquiring company effective working control of or substantial influence over the operations of the company in which it has acquired ownership. Working control is often considered to entail more than 25 percent of the common stock, but it can be as low as 10 percent if the stock is widely distributed. Also, control on a very slim margin can be held through friendship with large stockholders outside the holding company group. Sometimes, holding company operations represent the initial stages of transforming an operating company into an investment company, particularly when the operating company is in a declining industry. When an industry's sales begin to decline permanently and the firm begins to liquidate its operating assets, it may use the liquid funds to invest in industries having a more favorable growth potential.

Isolation of Risks. Because the various operating companies in a holding company system are separate legal entities, the obligations of any one unit are separate from those of the other units. Catastrophic losses incurred by one unit, therefore, are not transmitted as claims on the assets of the other units.

Although this is the customary generalization of the nature of a holding company system, it is not completely valid. In extending credit to one of the units of a holding company system, an astute financial manager or loan officer will require a guarantee or a claim on the assets of all the elements in the system. To some degree, therefore, the assets in the various elements are joined. The advantage remains to the extent that catastrophes occurring to one unit are not transmitted to the others.

Approval Not Required. A holding company group that seeks to obtain effective working control of a number of companies may quietly purchase a portion of their stock. The operation is completely informal, and the permission or approval of the stockholders of the acquired company or companies is not required. Thus, the guiding personalities in a holding company operation are not dependent on negotiations and approval of the other interest groups in order to obtain their objectives. This feature of holding company operations has, however, been limited somewhat by recent state law and SEC rules governing tender offers.

Disadvantages of Holding Companies

Partial Multiple Taxation. Provided the holding company owns at least 80 percent of a subsidiary's voting stock, Internal Revenue Service regulations permit the filing of consolidated returns, in which case, dividends received by the parent are not taxed. However, if less than 80 percent of the stock is owned, returns cannot be consolidated, although 85 percent of the dividends received by the holding company can be excluded. With a tax rate of 46 percent, this means that the effective tax on intercorporate dividends is 6.9 percent. This partial double taxation somewhat offsets the benefits of holding company control with limited ownership, but whether the penalty of 6.9 percent of dividends received is sufficient to offset the advantages is a matter that must be decided in individual situations.[7]

Ease of Enforced Dissolution. In the case of a holding company operation that falls into disfavor with the U.S. Department of Justice, it is relatively easy to require dissolution of the relationship by disposal of stock ownership; for instance, in the late 1950s, du Pont

---

[7]The 1969 Tax Reform Law also empowers the Internal Revenue Service to prohibit the deductibility of debt issued to acquire another firm where the following conditions hold: (1) The debt is subordinated to a "significant portion" of the firm's other creditors; (2) the debt is convertible or has warrants attached; (3) the debt/assets ratio exceeds 67 percent; and (4) on a pro forma basis, the times interest earned ratio is less than 3. The IRS can use discretion in invoking this power.

was required to dispose of its 23 percent stock interest in General Motors Corporation, acquired in the early 1920s. Because there was no fusion between the corporations, there were no difficulties, from an operating standpoint, in requiring the separation of the two companies. However, if complete amalgamation had taken place, it would have been much more difficult to break up the company after so many years, and the likelihood of forced divestiture would have been reduced.

Risks of Excessive Pyramiding.   Financial leverage effects in pyramiding magnify profits if operations are successful, but they also magnify losses. The greater the degree of pyramiding, the greater is the degree of risk involved in any fluctuations in sales or earnings. This potential disadvantage of pyramiding operations through holding companies is discussed in the next section.

Leverage in Holding Companies

The problem of excessive leverage is worthy of further note, for the degree of leverage in certain past instances has been truly staggering. For example, in the 1920s, Samuel Insull and his group controlled electric utility-operating companies at the bottom of a holding company pyramid by a one-twentieth of 1 percent investment. As a ratio, this represents 1/2,000. In other words, $1.00 of capital at the top holding company level controlled $2,000 of assets at the operating level. A similar situation existed in the railroad field. It has been stated that Robert R. Young, with an investment of $254,000, obtained control of the Allegheny system, consisting of total operating assets of $3 billion.

The nature of leverage in a holding company system and its advantages and disadvantages are illustrated by the hypothetical example developed in Table 30.8.[8] As in the previous example, although this case is hypothetical, it illustrates actual situations. Half of the operating company's Class B common stock is owned by Holding Company 1; in fact, it is the only asset of Holding Company 1. Holding Company 2 holds as its total assets half of the Class B common stock of Holding Company 1. Consequently, $1,000 of Class B common stock of Holding Company 2 controls $2 million of assets at the operating company level. Further leverage could, of course, have been postulated in this situation by setting up a third company to own Class B common stock of Holding Company 2.

Table 30.9 shows the effects of holding company leverage on gains and losses at the top level. In the first column, it is assumed that the operating company earns 12 percent before taxes on its $2 million of assets; in the second column, it is assumed that the return on assets is 8 percent. The operating and holding companies are the same as described in Table 30.8.

A return of 12 percent on the operating assets of $2 million represents earnings of $240,000. The debt interest of $40,000 is deducted from this amount, and the 50 percent tax rate applies to the remainder. The amount available to common stock after payment of debt interest, preferred stock dividends, and an 8 percent return to the nonvoting Class A common stock is $40,500. Assuming a $40,000 dividend payout, Holding Company 1, on the basis of its 50 percent ownership of the operating company, earns $20,000. If the same kind of analysis is followed through, the amount available to Class B common stock in Holding Company 2 is $4,455. This return is on an investment of $1,000, and it represents a return on the investment in Class B common stock of Holding Company 2 of about 445 percent. The power of leverage in a holding company system can indeed be great.

---

[8]Corrections in computations were supplied by Dr. Narendra C. Bhandari, University of Baltimore.

Table 30.8   Leverage in a Holding Company System

Operating Company			
Total assets	$2,000,000	Debt	$1,000,000
		Preferred stock	150,000
		Common stock: Class A[a]	650,000
		Common stock: Class B	200,000
	$2,000,000		$2,000,000
Holding Company 1			
Class B common stock of		Debt	$ 50,000
operating company	$100,000	Preferred stock	10,000
		Common stock: Class A[a]	30,000
		Common stock: Class B	10,000
	$100,000		$100,000
Holding Company 2			
Class B common stock of Holding		Debt	$2,000
Company 1	$5,000	Preferred stock	$1,000
		Common stock: Class A[a]	1,000
		Common stock: Class B	1,000
	$5,000		$5,000

[a]Class A common stock is nonvoting.

On the other hand, if a decline in revenues causes the pretax earnings to drop to 8 percent of the total assets of the operating company, the results will be disastrous. The amount earned under these circumstances will be $160,000. After deducting the bond interest, the amount subject to tax will be $120,000, and the tax will be $60,000. The after-tax but before-interest earnings will be $100,000. The total prior charges will be $99,500, leaving $500 available to Class B common stock. If all earnings are paid out in dividends to Class B common stock, the earnings of Holding Company 1 will be $250. This is not enough to meet the debt interest. The holding company system, thus, will be forced to default on the debt interest of Holding Company 1 and, of course, Holding Company 2.

This example illustrates the potential for tremendous gains in a holding company system. It also illustrates that a small earnings decline on the assets of the operating companies will be disastrous.

Leveraged Buy-Outs

Leveraged buy-outs belong to the general class of transactions called "going private." When firms that formerly were publicly held go private, the entire equity interest is purchased by a small group of investors, typically including representation from incumbent management. In some buy-outs, current management obtains 100 percent equity ownership. In other deals, a small group of outside investors will share the equity ownership. In addition to the equity capital they supply, the outside investors arrange other financing for buying out the publicly held stock. The substantial borrowing involved in the outside financing is the basis for the description of such transactions as "leveraged buy-outs."

Table 30.9   Effects of Holding Company Leverage on Gains and Losses

	Earnings before Interest and Taxes	
	at 12%	at 8%
Operating Company		
Earnings before interest and taxes	$240,000	$160,000
Less interest on debt (at 4%)	40,000	40,000
Earnings after interest	$200,000	$120,000
Less tax (at 50%)	100,000	60,000
After-tax earnings available for stockholders	$100,000	$ 60,000
Less: Preferred stock (at 5%)	7,500	7,500
Class A common stock (at 8%)	52,000	52,000
Earnings available to Class B common stock	$ 40,500	$ 500
Dividends to Class B common stock		
(by management decision)	40,000	500
Transferred to retained earnings	$ 500	$ 0
Holding Company 1		
Earnings before interest and taxes (received from the operating company)	$ 20,000	$ 250
Less 85% of dividends received	17,000	212
Intercorporate dividends subject to tax, before interest	$ 3,000	$ 38
Less interest on debt (at 4%)	2,000	2,000
Before-tax earnings	$ 1,000	[a]
Less tax (at 50%)	500	
After-tax earnings	$ 500	
Amount of untaxed dividend	$ 17,000	
After-tax earnings available to stockholders	$ 17,500	
Less: Preferred stock (at 5%)	500	
Class A common stock (at 8%)	2,400	
Earnings available to Class B common stock	$ 14,600	
Less dividends to Class B common stock		
(by management decision)	10,000	
Transferred to retained earnings	$ 4,600	
Holding Company 2		
Earnings before interest and taxes (received from Holding Company 1)	$ 6,000	
Less 85% of dividends received	4,250	
Intercorporate dividends subject to tax, before interest	$ 750	
Less interest on debt (at 4%)	80	
Before-tax earnings	$ 670	
Less tax (at 50%)	335	
After-tax earnings	$ 335	
Amount of untaxed dividends	4,250	
After-tax earnings available to stockholders	$ 4,585	
Less: Preferred stock (at 5%)	50	
Class A common stock (at 8%)	80	
Earnings available to Class B common stock	$ 4,455	
Percentage return on Class B common stock	445.5%	

[a]Loss

The empirical evidence demonstrates that going private transactions result in market value changes in common stock of about 30 percent over the 40-day trading period prior to and including the initial proposal (DeAngelo, DeAngelo, and Rice [1984]). In buy-outs, managers offer cash premiums averaging about 56 percent relative to the open market share price 40 trading days prior to the proposal. Thus, going private transactions benefit the public shareholders. From a formal standpoint, all that is involved is rearranging the ownership structure of the firm. There would appear to be no potential for the synergies that might accompany various forms of business combinations. What, then, is the source of the value increase?

Managers are motivated to arrange going private or leveraged buy-outs because they see the opportunity for substantial gains as a private company. Several factors may be the source of the gains. One is the increased motivation of the managers who have the potential for achieving great increases in wealth. A second is avoiding the expenses and regulatory constraints of a public company. Third, are potential tax advantages. These factors can best be explained by analyzing the nature of leveraged buy-out transactions.

Characteristics Conducive to a Buy-Out Situation

The earnings of the firm must be relatively predictable, so that they will be adequate to cover interest and loan amortization. The company must have potential for growth at rates exceeding the inflation rate. The company must have a strong market position in its industry, so that it will be less vulnerable to economic fluctuations and strategic actions by rivals.

Typically, the firm is a manufacturing company with a large asset base for collateral on financing packages. The existing balance sheet is relatively clean with an abundance of unencumbered assets. The firm has a high degree of liquidity. There is little existing short-term or long-term debt. Future resaleability is also desirable, since the new owners look forward to selling the company after five years or so to others that may be interested or in taking the company public again. Some analysts have referred to leveraged buy-outs as "inventorying" companies for future sale.

To illustrate the nature of a leveraged buy-out transaction, let us consider the B Company, a manufacturer of electronics equipment. Its present sales are $1.8 million per year. Its present earnings before interest and taxes (EBIT) are $150,000, expected to grow 10 percent per year. B Company is purchased by its management and a limited number of outside investors for $500,000. Sixty percent of the purchase price ($300,000) is represented by secured debt bearing an interest rate of 19 percent and requiring amortization over a five-year period. An additional 30 percent of the financing comes from $150,000 of subordinated debt, carrying an interest rate at 21 percent. There is $50,000 of equity, representing 10 percent of the purchase price. The company is clearly highly leveraged with a debt-to-equity ratio of 900 percent.

Why will lenders permit such high leverage? The basic answer is that they have confidence in the managers of the company. The managers are typically in their 50s with their children grown up, are looking for new challenges with the opportunity for wealth gains they could not achieve in a larger company, and have a reputation as able executives. In the leveraged buy-out, they are betting their reputations. The assets they have accumulated outside their highly leveraged purchases of equity in the company they have taken private are not at stake. They have only their equity investments to lose under the typical limited liability position of equity holders. In this sense, the borrowing is on a "nonrecourse" basis. If things do not go well, other equity holders will be brought in and the original management will end up with the minority position in the equity ownership.

Table 30.10   Pro Forma Cash Flows for a Leveraged Buy-Out

	Year 0	Year 1	Year 2	Year 3	Year 4	Year 5
1. EBIT	150.00	165.00	181.5	199.7	219.6	241.6
2. Interest		88.5	76.5	62.2	45.0	24.5
3. EBT		76.5	105.0	137.5	174.6	217.1
4. Taxes @ 40%		30.6	42.0	55.0	69.8	86.8
5. Net Income		45.9	63.0	82.5	104.8	130.3
6. Depreciation		30.0	30.0	30.0	30.0	30.0
7. Cash Flow		75.9	93.0	112.5	134.8	160.3
8. Amortization of Loans		60.9	72.9	87.2	104.4	124.9
9. Cash Flow Cushion		15.0	20.1	25.3	30.4	35.4

An illustrative example of how the B Company transactions might work out is shown in Table 30.10. Table 30.10 shows how the earnings before interest and taxes grow at 10 percent a year. The interest payments reflect the amortization of principal that takes place each year. A 40 percent tax rate is assumed. After deduction of taxes, net income is shown in Row 5. Depreciation is added back to obtain the usual definition of cash flow shown in Row 7. Row 8 illustrates an amortization schedule for the debt. This results in the cash flow cushion depicted in Line 9. With the amortization schedule shown in Row 8, we can also indicate how the debt-equity position changes over time. This is illustrated by Table 30.11.

Table 30.11 reflects the amortization program agreed upon. Over the five-year period, debt is reduced from 90 percent to zero. We then assume that the B Company is sold at its book value at the end of Year 5. This is a conservative assumption because, with the record it has established, the firm might well sell for a premium over book value. The ratio of the price received to the initial equity investment is 476.5/50, which equals 953 percent. This represents a five-year annual compounded rate of return on the initial $50,000 investment of 57 percent. The plausibility of these results is indicated by some published statistics. A *Fortune* magazine article of January 23, 1984, stated that one of the leveraged buy-out specialist companies, Kohlberg, Kravis, Roberts and Co., has earned an average annualized return of 62 percent on the equity it has invested in its transactions. Another buy-out specialist, Carl Ferenbach, has stated that his firm expects an annual return of 50 percent on its equity investment (DeAngelo, DeAngelo, and Rice [1984]).

Table 30.11   The Changing Debt Ratio in a Leveraged Buy-Out

	Year 0	Year 1	Year 2	Year 3	Year 4	Year 5
1. Equity	50.0	95.9	158.9	241.4	346.2	476.5
2. Debt	450.0	389.1	316.2	229.0	124.6	0
3. Total Assets	500.0	485.0	475.1	469.7	470.1	476.5
4. Percent Debt	90%	80%	67%	49%	26%	0%

The driving force behind these spectacular results appears to reflect a number of factors. The managers have a good track record and are highly motivated by the wealth gains they may achieve. Operations of the firm are less subject to government regulatory constraints. Substantial tax advantages may be achieved from writing up the assets of the firm and the high leverage employed. Lenders have confidence in the ability of the executives to achieve their projections. Investors are paid off at interest rates three to five percentage points above the prime rate. The previous public shareholders receive a premium when they sell out. However, the thin equity leaves little room for "surprises" and high risk is involved.

Managerial Policies in a Valuation Framework

In the perspective of alternative merger theories and empirical tests, the foundation has been provided to guide managerial policies with respect to merger and acquisition decisions. From an operational standpoint, mergers and acquisitions should be related to a firm's general planning framework. These requirements have been set forth in detail in other studies [Chung and Weston, 1982]. Here, we focus on merger policies in a capital budgeting valuation framework. We make the concepts explicit by using an illustrative case example to convey the ideas.

The Adams Corporation is a manufacturer of materials handling equipment, with heavy emphasis on forklift trucks. Because of a low internal profitability rate and lack of favorable investment opportunities in its existing line of business, Adams is considering a merger to achieve more favorable growth and profitability opportunities. It·has made an extensive search of a large number of corporations and has narrowed the candidates to two firms, for a number of considerations. The Black Corporation is a manufacturer of agricultural equipment and is strong in research and marketing. It has had high internal profitability and substantial investment opportunities. The Clark Company is a manufacturer of plastic toys. It has a better profitability record than Black. Some relevant data on the three firms are summarized in Table 30.12. Additional information on market parameters includes a risk-free rate, R_F, of 6 percent and an expected return on the market, $E(R_M)$, of 11 percent. Each firm pays a 10 percent interest rate on its debt. The tax rate, T_c, of each is 50 percent. A period of ten years is estimated for the duration of supernormal growth, n. From the information provided, we can first formulate the accounting balance sheets for the three firms (Table 30.13).

Table 30.12   Comparative Statistics for the Year Ended 19X0

	Book Value per Share	Price-Earnings Ratio (P/EPS)	Number of Shares (millions)	Debt Ratio, % (D/E)	Beta for Existing Leverage	Internal Profit-ability Rate (r)	Invest-ment Rate (b)	Growth Rate (g)
Adams	$10	5.40	5	30	1.2	.04	0.1	.004
Black	40	11.70	1	30	1.4	.12	1.5	.18
Clark	40	9.88	1	30	1.6	.14	1.0	.14

Table 30.13   Accounting Balance Sheets (Millions of Dollars)

	Adams	Black	Clark
Debt	$15	$12	$12
Equity	50	40	40
Total assets	$65	$52	$52

Dividing the internal profitability rate r by $(1 - T_c)$ and multiplying by total assets, we get the net operating income. From the net operating income, we can obtain the market price per share and the total market value that would have to be paid for each of the three companies (Table 30.14). We now have earnings per share, market values per share, and total market values of equity for use in the subsequent analysis.

One popular criterion for evaluating the desirability of making acquisitions from the standpoint of the acquiring company is to determine the effect on its earnings per share. Table 30.15 illustrates these effects based on the data in the present example. It can be seen that the merger would cause the earnings per share of Adams to decline. The percentage dilution in the earnings per share of Adams would be 47 percent if Black were acquired and 39 percent if Clark were acquired. We believe that this widely used criterion is in error. The effects on market values are relevant, and not the effects on earnings per share.

Table 30.14   Market Price per Share

	Adams	Black	Clark
1. Total assets (millions)	$65	$52	$52
2. Earning rate, $r \div (1 - T_c)$	.08	.24	.28
3. Net operating income (1) × (2) (millions)	$ 5.2	$12.48	$14.56
4. Interest on debt (millions)	1.5	1.20	1.20
5. Profit before tax (millions)	3.7	11.28	13.36
6. Taxes at 50% (millions)	1.85	5.64	6.68
7. Net income (millions)	1.85	5.64	6.68
8. Number of shares of common stock (millions)	5	1	1
9. Earnings per share of common stock, (7) ÷ (8)	$ .37	$ 5.64	$ 6.68
10. Price-earnings ratio (information provided)	5.4×	11.7×	9.88×
11. Market price per share, (9) × (10)	$ 2.00	$66.00	$66.00
12. Total market value of equity, (11) × (8) (millions)	$10	$66	$66

Table 30.15   Effects of Merger on EPS

	Effects on Adams's Earnings per Share if it Merges:	
	With Black	With Clark
1. Number of new shares (millions)[a]	33	33
2. Existing shares (millions)	5	5
3. Total new shares (millions)	38	38
4. Earnings after taxes (millions of dollars)	5.64	6.68
5. *Add* Adams's after-tax earnings (millions of dollars)	1.85	1.85
6. Total new earnings (millions of dollars)	7.490	8.530
7. New earnings per share, (6) ÷ (3), $	.197	.224
8. *Less* Adams's old earnings per share, $	.370	.370
9. Net effect	(.173)	(.146)
10. Percent dilution [(9 ÷ 8)100]	47%	39%

[a]Each share of Black and Clark has a market value 33 times that of Adams. Hence, 33 shares times the 1 million existing shares of Black and Clark is the total number of new Adams's shares required.

In a valuation framework, it is necessary to make a forecast of the key variables affecting value after the merger has taken place. This requires an in-depth business analysis of each proposed merger in terms of its impact on the key valuation factors. From the background provided, we observe that Adams is a manufacturer of materials handling equipment. Black is a manufacturer of agricultural equipment with strength in research and marketing. Clark is a manufacturer of plastic toys. While Clark has a better profitability record than Black, the toy industry is under the pressure of continuously creating new ideas and concepts if growth and profitability are to continue. In addition, there seems to be less potential for favorable interaction of management capabilities in a merger between Adams and Clark than there would be in a merger between Adams and Black. Black is known to have a strong research organization, which may be able to develop new products in Adams's area of materials handling equipment. This merely sketches the kind of favorable carry-over of capabilities that may be achieved in a merger between Adams and Black. Reflecting these qualitative considerations, the following estimates are made of the new financial parameters of the combined firms.

	NOI	r	b	g_s
Adams/Black (AB)	18	.1556	.9	.14
Adams/Clark (AC)	16	.1444	.9	.13

We can now proceed to evaluate the two alternative acquisition prospects, using a valuation analysis. First, we calculate the new beta for the merged company under the two alternatives. We assume the beta for the combined companies is a market-value weighted average of the betas of the constituent companies. We use the new betas in the Security Market Line equation to obtain the cost of equity capital for each of the two combined firms:

$$\beta_{AB} = 1.2\left(\frac{10}{10 + 66}\right) + 1.4\left(\frac{66}{10 + 66}\right)$$

$$= .1579 + 1.2158 = 1.374 = 1.37$$

$$k_s(AB) = R_F + [E(R_M) - R_F]\beta_{AB}$$

$$= .06 + [.05]1.37 = .1285 = 12.85\%$$

$$\beta_{AC} = 1.2\left(\frac{10}{10 + 66}\right) + 1.6\left(\frac{66}{10 + 66}\right)$$

$$= .1579 + 1.3895 = 1.547 = 1.55$$

$$k_s(AC) = .06 + .05(1.55)$$

$$= .1375 = 13.75\%.$$

Given the debt cost of 10 percent and the cost of equity capital as calculated, we can then proceed to determine the weighted average cost of capital for the two combined firms.

	AB	AC
Debt, B	27	27
Equity, S	76	76
Value, V^L	103	103

We now continue our calculations:

$$WACC = k = k_s(S/V) + k_b(1 - T_c)(B/V)$$

$$k(AB) = .1285\left(\frac{76}{103}\right) + .05\left(\frac{27}{103}\right)$$

$$= .0948 + .0131 = .1079 = 10.8\%$$

$$k(AC) = .1375\left(\frac{76}{103}\right) + .05\left(\frac{27}{103}\right)$$

$$= .1015 + .0131 = .1146 = 11.5\%.$$

We now have all the information required to calculate the valuation of the two alternative combinations.

We use the valuation formula for a period of supernormal growth (10 years in this example) followed by zero growth. From Chapter 23 on valuation, this is Equation 23.14, reproduced below for a leveraged company.

$$V = X_0(1 - T)(1 - b)\sum_{t=1}^{n}\frac{(1 + g_s)^t}{(1 + k)^t} + \frac{X_0(1 - T)(1 + g_s)^n}{k(1 + k)^n} \qquad (23.14)$$

We next insert the numerical values to determine the value of the combined firm if Adams merges with Black (AB) or with Clark (AC). The computations are shown below:

$$V_{AB} = \$18(.5)(.1)\sum_{t=1}^{10}\frac{(1.14)^t}{(1.108)^t} + \frac{\$18(.5)(1.14)^{10}}{.108(1.108)^{10}}$$

$$= .9\sum_{t=1}^{10}(1.029)^t + \frac{9}{.108}(1.029)^{10}$$

$$= .9(1.029)\text{FVIFA}(2.9\%, 10 \text{ yrs.}) + 83.33\text{FVIF}(2.9\%, 10 \text{ yrs.})$$

$$= .9261\left[\frac{1.331 - 1}{.029}\right] + 83.33(1.331)$$

$$= .9261(11.414) + 110.91$$

$$V_{AB} = 10.57 + 110.91 = \$121.48 \text{ million.}$$

$$V_{AC} = \$16(.5)(.1)\sum_{t=1}^{10}\left(\frac{1.13}{1.115}\right)^t + \frac{\$16(.5)(1.13)^{10}}{.115(1.115)^{10}}$$

$$= .8\sum_{t=1}^{10}(1.01345)^t + \frac{8}{.115}(1.01345)^{10}$$

$$= .8(1.01345)\left[\frac{1.14294 - 1}{.01345}\right] + 69.5652(1.14294)$$

$$= .81076(10.63) + 79.51$$

$$V_{AC} = 8.62 + 79.51 = \$88.13 \text{ million.}$$

Using the results obtained, we make a summary comparison of the gains or losses from the two alternative mergers shown in Table 30.16.

The data show that, based on estimates of the key parameters, a gain in value of $18 million would result from a merger between Adams and Black. However, the merger

Table 30.16   Comparison of Two Mergers (Dollars in Millions)

	Adams/Black	Adams/Clark
Postmerger value, V	$121	$88
Less amount of debt, B	27	27
Value of equity, S	94	61
Less Adams's premerger market value	10	10
Gain in equity value	84	51
Cost if acquired at market price	66	66
Gain in value (loss)	18	(15)

between Adams and Clark would result in a loss in valuation amounting to $15 million. The results of this comparison permit some margin of error yet clearly indicate that a merger between Adams and Black is preferable to a merger between Adams and Clark. Indeed, the gain in value of $18 million could be divided between the shareholders of Adams and those of Black. Adams could pay a 10 to 20 percent premium over the current market price of Black and still achieve a gain in net value that would go to its shareholders.

The foregoing example provides a general methodology for the management analysis of merger activity, which utilizes a number of principles: The acquiring firm is considering other firms as alternative merger candidates. To come up with a rational basis for analysis, prospective returns and risk from alternative merger combinations must be estimated. While historical data may be used as inputs, a forecast or estimate must be made of the returns and risk that may arise after alternative merger combinations have taken place.

Thus, the forecast of the variables that measure prospective returns and risk for alternative postmerger combinations is critical to a sound evaluation of merger alternatives. The estimates of net operating earnings and of their potential growth may or may not reflect synergy between the combining firms depending on the nature and potential of the combined operations. Studies in depth of the relevant product markets and the results of combining the organizations of the two firms are required. The resulting forecasts are subject to prediction errors, which are sometimes of substantial magnitude.

We may obtain the measures of risk by market-value weighted averages of the betas (the systematic risk) of the combining firms. With the estimates of the new betas, along with a selection of market parameters, we can calculate the new relevant cost of capital for the merged firm, utilizing the Security Market Line relationship. We must also estimate the effect of alternative merger combinations on the cost of debt. With estimates of the cost of equity capital and the cost of debt, we must formulate appropriate capital structure targets for the combined firm and use these to estimate a cost of capital.

Having obtained an estimate of the applicable cost of capital and the estimates of returns discussed earlier, we can apply valuation principles to formulate estimates of the value of alternative merger combinations. From these, we deduct the value of the acquiring firm in the absence of the merger to determine the total value remaining, which we next compare with the cost of acquiring the firm or firms with which a merger is being considered. If the value contributed by the merger exceeds the cost of the acquisition, the acquiring firm has a basis for making an offer that includes a premium to the shareholders of the acquired firm yet still provides an increase in value for the shareholders of the acquiring firm.

Summary

Mergers have played an important part in the growth of firms, and since financial managers are required both to appraise the desirability of a prospective merger and to participate in evaluating the respective companies involved in it, this chapter has emphasized analysis of the terms of merger decisions.

The gains from corporate combinations may come from

1. Increased efficiency
2. Information and signaling effects
3. Reduction of agency problems
4. Stronger market positions
5. Tax benefits.

In transactions involving the rearrangement of the ownership structures of firms, the sources of increased value may come from stronger managerial incentives, better performance evaluation, and the reduction in government regulatory constraints.

In leveraged buy-outs, experienced managements have the opportunity to achieve large wealth gains by obtaining complete control unfettered by the intervention of public shareholders and less subject to government regulatory agencies. With the backing of outside lenders, they enter into a highly leveraged situation. If the company performs according to projections, the debt is reduced over a period of years and the gains to the equity investors represent a high rate of return.

The most important term to be negotiated in a merger arrangement is the price the acquiring firm will pay for the acquired one. The most important *quantitative* factors influencing the terms of a merger are (1) current earnings, (2) current market prices, (3) book values, and (4) net working capital. Qualitative considerations may suggest that *synergistic*, or "two-plus-two-equals-five," effects may be present to an extent sufficient to warrant paying more for the acquired firm than the quantitative factors suggest. Recently, the current replacement values of corporate assets have exceeded the market values of related corporate securities.

In mergers, one firm disappears. However, an alternative is for one firm to buy all or a majority of the common stock of another and to run the acquired firm as an operating subsidiary. When this occurs, the acquiring firm is said to be a *holding company*. A number of advantages arise when a holding company is formed, among them:

1. It may be possible to control the acquired firm with a smaller investment than necessary for a merger.
2. Each firm in a holding company is a separate legal entity, and the obligations of any unit are separate from the obligations of the other units.
3. Stockholder approval is required before a merger can take place. This may not be necessary in a holding company situation.

There are also some disadvantages to holding companies, among them:

1. If the holding company does not own 80 percent of the subsidiary's stock and does not file consolidated tax returns, it is subject to taxes on 15 percent of the dividends received from the subsidiary.
2. The leverage effects possible in holding companies can subject the company to magnification of earnings fluctuations and related risks.
3. The antitrust division of the U.S. Department of Justice can much more easily force the breakup of a holding company than it can bring about the dissolution of two completely merged firms.

In the perspective of alternative merger theories and tests, we developed a framework for managerial analysis of prospective mergers. Basically, good forecasts of postmerger returns and risks are required as a starting point. Standard capital budgeting procedures, cost of capital analysis, and valuation principles presented in the preceding chapters are then applied. The aim is to determine whether the value of the merged firm exceeds the value of the constituent firms. If it does, the merger has a valid social and private justification.

We have shown that the fundamental basis for valuation in merger transactions represents an extension of basic capital budgeting principles. If there is a positive net present value from an external investment in other companies, sound capital budgeting criteria have been met. If the business combination results in synergies or other sources of increases in value, the incremental net present value will provide a basis for paying a premium to the shareholders of the company acquired. Whether the shareholders of acquiring companies gain depends in part on the intensity of competition in the market for acquisitions and in part on the market's view of what will be achieved by the combined companies. In a well-conceived buy-out or sell-out, increases in value are achieved, which provide a basis for gains to parties on both sides of the transaction.

Questions

30.1 What are some of the potential benefits that can be expected by a firm that merges with a company in a different industry?

30.2 Distinguish between a holding company and an operating company. Give an example of each.

30.3 Which appears to be riskier — the use of debt in the holding company's capital structure or the use of debt in the operating company's capital structure? Explain.

30.4 Is the public interest served by an increase in merger and tender offer activity? Give both pro and con arguments.

30.5 Is the book value of a company's assets considered the absolute minimum price to be paid for a firm? Explain. Is there any value that qualifies as an absolute minimum? Explain.

30.6 Discuss the situation in which Midwest Motors calls off merger negotiations with American Data Labs because the latter's stock price is overvalued. What assumption concerning dilution is implicit in the above situation?

30.7 There are many methods by which a company can raise additional capital. Can a merger be considered a means of raising additional equity capital? Explain.

30.8 Are the negotiations for merger agreements more difficult if the firms are in different industries or in the same industry? If they are about the same size or quite different in size? If the ages of the firms are about the same or if they are very different? Explain.

30.9 How would the existence of long-term debt in a company's financial structure affect its valuation for merger purposes? Could the same be said for any debt account regardless of its maturity? Explain.

30.10 During the merger activity of recent years, cash was used by the acquiring company to a much greater extent than during the height of the conglomerate merger activity during 1967–1969. What are some reasons for the relatively greater use of cash in the acquisitions of the more recent period?

30.11 Why are lenders willing to permit the 9 to 1 debt ratios sometimes found in leveraged buy-outs?

Problems

30.1 The Niles Company has agreed to merge with the Aruba Company. Table P30.1 gives information about the two companies prior to their merger:

Table P30.1

	Aruba	Niles
Total earnings	$1,000,000	$750,000
Shares outstanding	1,000,000	250,000
P/EPS ratio	20 times	18 times

The Aruba Company will buy the Niles Company with a four-for-one exchange of stock. Combined earnings will remain at the premerger level.
a)   What will be the effect on EPS for Aruba stockholders?
b)   What will be the effect on EPS for premerger Niles Company stockholders?

30.2 The Brunner Company has agreed to merge with the Powell Company. The shareholders of Powell have agreed to accept half a share of Brunner for each of their Powell shares. The new company will have a P/EPS ratio of 40. Table P30.2 gives additional information about the merging companies.

Table P30.2

	Brunner	Powell
P/EPS ratio	56	7
Shares outstanding	2,500,000	500,000
Earnings	$1,750,000	$700,000
Earnings per share	$.70	$1.40
Market value per share	$39.20	$9.80

a)   After Brunner and Powell merge, what will the new price per share be, assuming that combined earnings remain the same?
b)   Calculate the dollar and percent accretion in EPS for Brunner.
c)   Calculate the dollar and percent dilution in EPS for Powell.
d)   What is the effect on market price for each?
e)   Assuming that Brunner has been growing at 24 percent per year, and Powell at 8 percent, what is the expected growth rate for the merged firm? (There are no synergistic effects.)
f)   How long will it be before Powell's EPS recovers from the dilution caused by the merger? Illustrate by means of a graph showing premerger and postmerger EPS.

30.3 Dalton Company acquires Cory Company with a three-for-one exchange of stock. Table P30.3 presents data for the two companies:

Table P30.3

	Dalton	Cory
Total earnings	$100,000,000	$1,000,000
Shares outstanding	80,000,000	800,000
Expected growth rate in earnings	10%	25%
P/EPS ratio	8 times	24 times

a)   What is the basis for the three-for-one exchange ratio?
b)   What is the new EPS for the premerger Dalton and Cory stockholders?
c)   If Dalton's P/EPS ratio rises to 15, what is its new market price?
d)   What merger concept does this problem illustrate?

30.4 Hempler Company merges with Rider Company on the basis of market values. Hempler pays one share of convertible preferred stock with a par value of $100 and an interest rate of 6 percent (convertible into two shares of Hempler's common stock) for each four shares of Rider Company. Table P30.4 presents more data:

Table P30.4

	Hempler	Rider
Total earnings	$1,000,000	$400,000
Common shares outstanding	200,000	80,000
Expected growth rate in earnings	18%	6%
Dividends per share	$1.80	$1.80
P/EPS ratio	12 times	6 times
Dividend yield	3%	6%

a) **1.** What are the new EPS and market price of Hempler if the P/EPS ratio remains at 12 times?

2. What are the new EPS and market price on a fully diluted basis?

b) Why might Rider Company shareholders agree to the acquisition?

30.5 You are given the balance sheets in Table P30.5a.

Table P30.5a

Rocky Mountain Services Company Consolidated Balance Sheet (Millions of Dollars)

Cash	$1,500	Borrowings	$1,125
Other current assets	1,125	Common stock	1,875
Net property	1,875	Retained earnings	1,500
Total assets	$4,500	Total claims on assets	$4,500

White Lighting Company Balance Sheet (Millions of Dollars)

Cash	$375	Net worth	$750
Net property	375		
Total assets	$750	Total net worth	$750

a) The holding company, Rocky Mountain, buys the operating company, White Lighting, with "free" cash of $750 million. Show the new consolidated balance sheet for Rocky Mountain after the acquisition.

b) Instead of buying White Lighting, Rocky Mountain buys Conner Company with free cash of $1.125 billion. Conner's balance sheet is shown in Table P30.5b.

Table P30.5b

Conner Company Balance Sheet (Millions of Dollars)

Cash	$ 750	Borrowings	$ 750
Net property	1,125	Net worth	1,125
Total assets	$1,875	Total claims on assets	$1,875

Show the new consolidated balance sheet for Rocky Mountain after acquisition of Conner.

c)   What are the implications of your consolidated balance sheets for measuring the growth of firms resulting from acquisitions?

30.6   Fiscor is a holding company owning the entire common stock of Walter Company and Albright Company. The balance sheet for each subsidiary as of December 31, 1984, is identical to the one in Table P30.6.

Table P30.6

Balance Sheet as of December 31, 1984 (Millions of Dollars)

Current assets	$ 7.50	Current liabilities	$ 1.25
Fixed assets, net	5.00	First mortgage bonds (at 9%)	5.00
		Common stock	5.00
		Retained earnings	1.25
Total assets	$12.50	Total claims on assets	$12.50

Each operating company earns 10 percent annually on total assets, before interest and taxes. The corporate tax rate for each is 40 percent.

a)   What is the annual rate of return on each operating company's net worth (common stock plus retained earnings)?

b)   Construct a balance sheet for Fiscor based on the following assumptions: (1) The only asset of the holding company is the common stock of the two subsidiaries, carried at par (not book) value; and (2) the holding company has $6.2 million of 8 percent coupon debt.

c)   What is the annual rate of return on Fiscor's net worth, assuming a 100 percent payout ratio for the subsidiaries?

d)   If the subsidiaries' earnings rate before interest and taxes drops to 8 percent, what will be Fiscor's rate of return on net worth?

30.7   Every merger agreement is subject to negotiation between the companies involved. One significant indicator of the compensation received by the acquired company is the market price of each company's stock in relation to the merger terms. Some actual merger data are given in Table P30.7.

Table P30.7

Company		Terms	Market Price Two Quarters before Merger		Market Price Immediately Preceding Merger	
			A	B	A	B
1	A Celanese Corporation B Champlain Oil	2 shares of Celanese for every 3 shares of Champlain	62	34	67	42
2	A Cities Service Company B Tennessee Corporation	0.9 shares (2.25 pref.) for each Tenn. Corp. share (common)	65	48	61	55
3	A Ford Motor Company B Philco Corporation	1 share of Ford for every 4½ shares of Philco	81	22	113	25
4	A General Telephone B Sylvania Electric	Share-for-share basis	52	46	69	69

Calculate the percent premium, or discount, received by the acquired company, using market prices as the criterion. Compare the results of your calculations on the basis of the stock prices two quarters previous with that of your results on the basis of the prices immediately preceding the merger. Which is the proper measure of the actual discount or premium received: the one indicated by the earlier stock prices or the one indicated by the stock prices immediately preceding the merger? Explain.

30.8 To meet its growth objectives, Proxmore Manufacturing is planning to expand by acquisition. It has two potential candidates, Apex Corporation and Allied Engineering. The latest balance sheet for Proxmore and the latest income statements for Apex and Allied are given in Table P30.8, along with certain other statistical information. Both Apex and Allied have debt of $50 million, at a before-tax cost of 10 percent. Assume that the weighted average cost of capital is 10 percent for Proxmore, 8 percent for Apex, and 12 percent for Allied. Assume also that the effective tax rate for all three companies is 40 percent.

Table P30.8

Proxmore Manufacturing
Balance Sheet as of December 31, 1984 (Thousands of Dollars)

Current assets	$125,000	Current liabilities	$ 50,000
Net fixed assets	150,000	Long-term debt (at 10%)	75,000
		Common equity	150,000
Total	$275,000	Total	$275,000

Income Statement for the Year Ending December 31, 1984 (Thousands of Dollars)

	Apex	Allied
NOI	$20,000	$30,000
Interest on debt (at 10%)	5,000	5,000
Earnings before taxes	15,000	25,000
Less tax at 40%	6,000	10,000
Net income	$ 9,000	$15,000

	NOI	EPS	Growth Rate (Percent)	Market Price	Shares Outstanding
Proxmore	$32.5M	$3.00	6.0	$45	5,000,000
Apex	20M	4.50	7.5	50	2,000,000
Allied	30M	5.00	2.0	42	3,000,000

a) Based on the above information, determine an appropriate price for Proxmore to pay for each acquisition candidate. Proxmore uses its own weighted average cost of capital in computing the value of an acquisition candidate by capitalizing NOI after tax.

b) Compute the price of each acquisition candidate, using each candidate's own weighted average cost of capital as the capitalization rate.

c) Which capitalization rate is most appropriate in determining the value of an acquisition candidate?

    d)   Given that Proxmore is forced to make a tender offer for the common stock of each of the two candidates at 20 percent above their current market value, compute the following:

        1.   The exchange ratio based on a stock offering.

        2.   Proxmore's new earnings growth rate for next year after the acquisition of each company — Apex and Allied.

        3.   Proxmore's new EPS following each acquisition.

    e)   Chart Proxmore's growth in EPS for the next ten years with and without each acquisition to illustrate the dilution effect of the purchase price computed in Part (d).

30.9 The Johnson Corporation is a manufacturer of heavy-duty trucks. Because of a low internal profitability rate and lack of favorable investment opportunities in the existing line of business, Johnson is considering merger to achieve more favorable growth and profitability opportunities. It has made an extensive search of a large number of corporations and has narrowed the candidates to two firms. The Koslow Corporation is a manufacturer of materials handling equipment and is strong in research and marketing. It has had higher internal profitability than the other firm being considered and has substantial investment opportunities.

    The Landon Company is a manufacturer of food and candies. It has a better profitability record than Koslow. Data on all three firms are given in Table P30.9.

Table P30.9

	Book Value per Share	Price/ Earnings (P/EPS) Ratio	Number of Shares (millions)	Debt Ratio, (D/E)	β for Existing Leverage	Internal Profit- ability Rate, r	Invest- ment Rate, b	Growth Rate, g
Johnson	$20	6	4	1	1.4	.06	0.5	.03
Koslow	20	15	2	1	1.2	.12	1.5	.18
Landon	20	12	2	1	1.5	.15	1.0	.15

Additional information on market parameters includes a risk-free rate of 6 percent and an expected return on the market, $E(R_M)$, of 11 percent. Each firm pays a 10 percent interest rate on its debt. The tax rate, T_c, of each is 40 percent. Ten years is estimated for the duration of supernormal growth.

    a)   Prepare the accounting balance sheets for the three firms.

    b)   If each company earns the before-tax r on total assets in the current year, what is the net operating income for each company?

    c)   Given the indicated price-earnings ratios, what is the market price of the common stock for each company?

    d)   What will be the immediate effects on the earnings per share of Johnson if it acquires Koslow or Landon at its current market price by the exchange of stock based on the current market price of each of the companies?

    e)   Compare Johnson's new beta and required return on equity if it merges with Koslow with the same parameters that would result from its merger with Landon.

    f)   Calculate the new required cost of capital for a Johnson-Koslow combination and for a Johnson-Landon combination, respectively.

    g)   Using valuation Equation 23.14, compare the increase in value of Johnson as a result of a merger at market values with the cost of acquiring either Koslow or Landon if the combined firms have the following financial parameters:

	NOI	WACC	b	g_s
Johnson/Koslow	32	9.3%	.9	.16
Johnson/Landon	36	10%	.9	.13

Selected References

Alexander, Gordon J.; Benson, P. George; and Biebel, Joan K., "Investigating the Valuation Effects of Announcements of Voluntary Corporate Divestitures," University of Minnesota, 1982.

Alexander, Gordon J.; Benson, P. George; and Kampmeyer, Joan M., "Investigating the Valuation Effects of Announcements of Voluntary Corporate Selloffs," *Journal of Finance*, 39 (June 1984), pp. 503-517.

Ashton, D. J., and Atkins, D. R., "A Partial Theory of Takeover Bids," *Journal of Finance*, 39 (March 1984), pp. 167-183.

Asquith, P., and Kim, E. Han, "The Impact of Merger Bids on the Participating Firms' Security Returns," *Journal of Finance*, 37 (December 1982), pp. 1209-1228.

Baron, David P., "Tender Offers and Management Resistance," *Journal of Finance*, 38 (May 1983), pp. 331-343.

Bradley, M., "Interfirm Tender Offers and the Market for Corporate Control," *Journal of Business*, (October 1980), pp. 345-376.

Carleton, William R.; Guilkey, David K.; Harris, Robert S.; and Stewart, John F., "An Empirical Analysis of the Role of the Medium of Exchange in Mergers," *Journal of Finance*, 38 (June 1983), pp. 813-826.

Chung, K. S., and Weston, J. Fred, "Diversification and Mergers in a Strategic Long-Range-Planning Framework," Chapter 13 in M. Keenan and L. J. White, eds., *Mergers and Acquisitions*, Lexington, Mass.: D. C. Heath, 1982.

Dann, L. Y., and DeAngelo, H., "Standstill Agreements, Privately Negotiated Stock Repurchases, and the Market for Corporate Control," *Journal of Financial Economics*, (April 1983), pp. 275-300.

DeAngelo, H., and Rice, E. M., "Antitakeover Charter Amendments and Stockholder Wealth," *Journal of Financial Economics*, (April 1983), pp. 329-359.

DeAngelo, Harry; DeAngelo, Linda; and Rice, Edward M., "Going Private: Minority Freezeouts and Stockholder Wealth," *Journal of Law and Economics*, 27 (October 1984), pp. 367-401.

———, "Going Private: The Effects of a Change in Corporate Ownership Structure," *Midland Corporate Finance Journal*, (Summer 1984), pp. 35-43.

Dertouzos, James N., and Thorpe, Kenneth E., "Newspaper Groups: Economies of Scale, Tax Laws, and Merger Incentives," Santa Monica, California: Rand Corporation, R-2878-SBA, June 1982.

Dodd, P., "Merger Proposals, Management Discretion, and Stockholder Wealth," *Journal of Financial Economics*, (June 1980), pp. 105-137.

———, and Leftwich, Richard, "The Market for Corporate Charters: 'Unhealthy Competition' versus Federal Regulation," *Journal of Business*, 53 (July 1980), pp. 259-284.

Dodd, P., and Ruback, R., "Tender Offers and Stockholder Returns: An Empirical Analysis," *Journal of Financial Economics*, (December 1977), pp. 351-374.

Eger, Carol Ellen, "An Empirical Test of the Redistribution Effect in Pure Exchange Mergers," *Journal of Financial and Quantitative Analysis*, 18 (December 1983), pp. 547-572.

Elgers, P. T., and Clark, J. J., "Merger Types and Shareholder Returns: Additional Evidence," *Financial Management*, (Summer 1980), pp. 66-72.

Ellert, J. C., "Mergers, Antitrust Law Enforcement, and Stockholder Returns," *Journal of Finance*, (May 1976), pp. 715-732.

Fama, E., "Agency Problems and the Theory of the Firm," *Journal of Political Economy*, (April 1980), pp. 288-307.

Gahlon, James M., and Stover, Roger D., "Diversification, Financial Leverage, and Conglomerate Systematic Risk," *Journal of Financial and Quantitative Analysis*, 14 (December 1979), pp. 999-1013.

Galai, D., and Masulis, R. W., "The Option Pricing Model and the Risk Factor of Stock," *Journal of Financial Economics*, (January/March 1976), pp. 53-82.

Ginsburg, Martin D., "Taxing Corporate Acquisitions," *Tax Law Review*, 38 (Winter 1983), pp. 177-319.

Gort, Michael, and Hogarty, Thomas E., "New Evidence on Mergers," *Journal of Law and Economics*, 13 (April 1970), pp. 167-184.

Grossman, S., "The Allocational Role of Takeover Bids in Situations of Asymmetric Information," *Journal of Finance*, (May 1981), pp. 253-270.

Halpern, P. J., "Corporate Acquisitions: A Theory of Special Cases? A Review of Event Studies Applied to Acquisitions," *Journal of Finance*, 38 (May 1983), pp. 297-317.

———, "Empirical Estimates of the Amount and Distribution of Gains to Companies in Mergers," *Journal of Business*, (October 1973), pp. 554-575.

Haugen, Robert A., and Langetieg, Terence C., "An Empirical Test for Synergism in Merger," *Journal of Finance*, 30 (June 1975), pp. 1003-1014.

Higgins, Robert C., "Discussion," *Journal of Finance,* (May 1971), pp. 543-545.

———, and Schall, Lawrence D., "Corporate Bankruptcy and Conglomerate Merger," *Journal of Finance,* 30 (March 1975), pp. 93-113.

Hite, Gailen L., and Owers, James E., "The Restructuring of Corporate America: An Overview," *Midland Corporate Finance Journal,* (Summer 1984), pp. 6-16.

Hong, Hai; Kaplan, Robert S.; and Mandelker, Gershon, "Pooling vs. Purchase: The Effects of Accounting for Mergers on Stock Prices," *The Accounting Review,* 53 (January 1978), pp. 31-47.

Jain, Prem C., "The Effect of Voluntary Sell-off Announcements on Shareholder Wealth," *Journal of Finance,* 40 (March 1985), pp. 209-224.

Jarrell, G., and Bradley, M., "The Economic Effects of Federal and State Regulations of Cash Tender Offers," *Journal of Law and Economics,* (October 1980), pp. 371-407.

Jensen, M. C., and Meckling, W. H., "Theory of the Firm: Managerial Behavior, Agency Costs and Ownership Structure," *Journal of Financial Economics,* 3 (October 1976), pp. 350-360.

Jensen, M. C., and Ruback, R., eds., *Journal of Financial Economics,* (April 1983). The entire volume contains articles on mergers and corporate control.

Keown, Arthur J., and Pinkerton, John M., "Merger Announcements and Insider Trading Activity: An Empirical Investigation," *Journal of Finance,* 36 (September 1981), pp. 855-870.

Kim, E. Han, and McConnell, John J., "Corporate Merger and the Co-insurance of Corporate Debt," *Journal of Finance,* 32 (May 1977), pp. 349-363.

Kummer, Donald R., and Hoffmeister, J. Ronald, "Valuation Consequences of Cash Tender Offers," *Journal of Finance,* 33 (May 1978), pp. 505-516.

Langetieg, Terence C., "An Application of a Three-Factor Performance Index to Measure Stockholder Gains from Merger," *Journal of Financial Economics,* 6 (December 1978), pp. 365-384.

Lease, Ronald C.; McConnell, John J.; and Mikkelson, Wayne H., "The Market Value of Control in Publicly-Traded Corporations," *Journal of Financial Economics,* 11 (April 1983), pp. 439-471.

Levy, H., and Sarnat, M., "Diversification, Portfolio Analysis and the Uneasy Case for Conglomerate Mergers," *Journal of Finance,* (September 1970), pp. 795-802.

Lewellen, Wilbur G., "A Pure Financial Rationale for the Conglomerate Merger," *Journal of Finance,* 26 (May 1971), pp. 521-537.

———, and Huntsman, B., "Managerial Pay and Corporate Performance," *American Economic Review,* (September 1970), pp. 710-720.

Linn, Scott C., and Rozeff, Michael S., "The Corporate Sell-Off," *Midland Corporate Finance Journal,* (Summer 1984), pp. 17-26.

Malatesta, P. H., "The Wealth Effect of Merger Activity and the Objective Functions of Merging Firms," *Journal of Financial Economics,* (April 1983), pp. 155-181.

Mandelker, G., "Risk and Return: The Case of Merging Firms," *Journal of Financial Economics,* (December 1974), pp. 303-335.

Manne, H. G., "Mergers and the Market for Corporate Control," *Journal of Political Economy,* (April 1965), pp. 110-120.

Melicher, Ronald W., and Rush, David F., "Evidence on the Acquisition-Related Performance of Conglomerate Firms," *Journal of Finance,* 29 (March 1974), pp. 141-149.

Miles, James A., and Rosenfeld, James D., "The Effect of Voluntary Spin-off Announcements on Shareholder Wealth," *Journal of Finance,* 38 (December 1983), pp. 1597-1606.

Mueller, Dennis C., "A Theory of Conglomerate Mergers," *Quarterly Journal of Economics,* (November 1969), pp. 643-659.

Reinganum, Marc R., and Smith, Janet Kiholm, "Investor Preference for Large Firms: New Evidence on Economies of Size," *Journal of Industrial Economics,* 32 (December 1983), pp. 213-242.

Reinhardt, Uwe E., *Mergers and Consolidations: A Corporate-Finance Approach,* Morristown, N.J.: General Learning Press, 1972.

Roll, Richard, "The Hubris Hypothesis of Corporate Takeovers," Finance Working Paper #14-83, University of California, Los Angeles, November 1983.

Ruback, Richard S., "The Cities Service Takeover: A Case Study," *Journal of Finance,* 38 (May 1983), pp. 319-330.

Salter, Malcolm S., and Weinhold, Wolf A., "Diversification via Acquisition: Creating Value," *Harvard Business Review,* 56 (July/August 1978), pp. 166-176.

Schipper, Katherine, and Smith, Abbie, "A Comparison of Equity Carve-Outs and Equity Offerings: Share Price Effects and Corporate Restructuring," University of Chicago paper, October 1984.

———, "The Corporate Spin-Off Phenomenon," *Midland Corporate Finance Journal,* (Summer 1984), pp. 27-34.

———, "Effects of Recontracting on Shareholder Wealth: The Case of Voluntary Spin-offs," *Journal of Financial Economics,* 12 (1983), pp. 437-467.

Schipper, Katherine, and Thompson, Rex, "Evidence on the Capitalized Value of Merger Activity for Acquiring Firms," *Journal of Financial Economics,* (April 1983), pp. 85-119.

Shad, John S. R., "The Financial Realities of Mergers," *Harvard Business Review,* 47 (November/December 1969), pp. 133-146.

Shick, Richard A., and Jen, Frank C., "Merger Benefits to Shareholders of Acquiring Firms," *Financial Management,* 3 (Winter 1974), pp. 45-53.

Shrieves, Ronald E., and Stevens, Donald L., "Bankruptcy Avoidance as a Motive for Merger," *Journal of Financial and Quantitative Analysis*, 14 (September 1979), pp. 501-515.

Smith, Keith V., and Weston, J. Fred, "Further Evaluation of Conglomerate Performance," *Journal of Business Research*, 5 (1977), pp. 5-14.

Stapleton, R. C., "Mergers, Debt Capacity, and the Valuation of Corporate Loans," Chapter 2 in M. Keenan and L. J. White, eds., *Mergers and Acquisitions*, Lexington, Mass.: D. C. Heath, 1982.

————, "The Acquisition Decision as a Capital Budgeting Problem," *Journal of Business Finance & Accounting*, 2 (Summer 1975), pp. 187-202.

Stern, Joel, et al., "A Discussion of Corporate Restructuring," *Midland Corporate Finance Journal*, (Summer 1984), pp. 44-79.

Wansley, James W.; Roenfeldt, Rodney L.; and Cooley, Phillip L., "Abnormal Returns from Merger Profiles," *Journal of Financial and Quantitative Analysis*, 18 (June 1983), pp. 149-162.

Weston, J. Fred, *The Role of Mergers in the Growth of Large Firms*, Berkeley: University of California Press, 1953.

————, and Chung, K. S., "Some Aspects of Merger Theory," *Midwest Finance Journal*, 12 (1983), pp. 1-38.

————, "Do Mergers Make Money?" *Mergers & Acquisitions*, (Fall 1983), pp. 40-48.

Weston, J. Fred, and Mansinghka, Surendra K., "Tests of the Efficiency of Conglomerate Firms," *Journal of Finance*, 26 (September 1971), pp. 919-936.

Weston, J. Fred; Smith, Keith V.; and Shrieves, Ronald E., "Conglomerate Performance Using the Capital Asset Pricing Model," *Review of Economics and Statistics*, 54 (November 1972), pp. 357-363.

Appendix A to Chapter 30
Financial Accounting for Mergers

After merger terms have been agreed upon, the financial manager must be familiar with the accounting principles for recording the financial results of the merger and for reflecting the initial effect on the earnings of the surviving firm. The financial statements of the survivor in a merger must follow the SEC's regulations. These regulations follow the recommendations of professional accounting societies on combinations, but interpretations of actual situations require much financial and economic analysis.

On August 2, 1970, the 18-member Accounting Principles Board (APB) of the American Institute of Certified Public Accountants issued Opinion 16 dealing with guidelines for corporate mergers and Opinion 17 dealing with goodwill arising from mergers. The recommendations, which became effective October 31, 1970, modify and elaborate previous pronouncements on the pooling of interests and purchase methods of accounting for business combinations. For reasons that will become clear later in this section, corporate managements generally prefer pooling. Six broad tests are used to determine whether the conditions for the pooling of interest treatment are met. If all of them are met, then the combination is, in a sense, a merger among equals, and the *pooling of interests* method can be employed. The six tests are

1. The acquired firm's stockholders must maintain an ownership position in the surviving firm.
2. The basis for accounting for the assets of the acquired entity must remain unchanged.
3. Independent interests must be combined. Each entity must have had autonomy for two years prior to the initiation of the plan to combine, and no more than 10 percent ownership of voting common stock can be held as intercorporate investments.
4. The combination must be effected in a single transaction; contingent payouts are not permitted in poolings but can be used in purchases.
5. The acquiring corporation must issue only common stock with rights identical to its outstanding voting common stock in exchange for substantially all the voting common stock of the other company (*substantially* is defined as 90 percent).
6. The combined entity must not intend to dispose of a significant portion of the assets of the combining companies within two years after the merger.

In contrast, a *purchase* involves (1) new owners, (2) an appraisal of the acquired firm's physical assets and a restatement of the balance sheet to reflect these new values, and (3) the possibility of an excess or deficiency of consideration given up vis-à-vis the book value of equity. Point 3 refers to the creation of goodwill. In a purchase, the excess of the purchase price paid over the book value (restated to reflect the appraisal value of physical assets) is set up as goodwill, and capital surplus is increased (or decreased).[1] In a pooling

---

[1]Some acquiring companies have paid less than book value and set up "negative goodwill," whose write-off contributed to reported earnings in subsequent years.

of interests, the combined total assets after the merger represent a simple sum of the asset contributions of the constituent companies.

In a *purchase*, if the acquiring firm pays more than the acquired net worth, the excess is associated either with tangible depreciable assets or with goodwill. Asset write-offs are deductible, but goodwill written off is not deductible for tax purposes, even though the new recommendations require that goodwill be written off over some reasonable period but no longer than 40 years. This requires a write-off of at least 2.5 percent a year of the amount of goodwill arising from a purchase. Therefore, if a merger is treated as a purchase, reported profits will be lower than if it is handled as a pooling of interests. This is one of the reasons that pooling is popular among acquiring firms. But, in their analysis of the effects of pooling versus purchase, Hong, Kaplan, and Mandelker [1978] conclude that "investors do not seem to have been fooled . . . into paying higher stock prices even though firms in our sample using pooling-of-interests accounting report higher earnings than if they had used the purchase method." (p. 42)

Previous to the issuance of APB Opinion 16, another stimulus to pooling was the opportunity to dispose of assets acquired at depreciated book values, selling them at their current values and recording subsequent profits on sales of assets. Opinion 16 attempted to deal with this practice by the requirement that sales of major portions of assets not be contemplated for at least two years after the merger has taken place. For example, suppose Firm A buys Firm B, exchanging stock worth $100 million for assets worth $100 million but carried at $25 million. After the merger, A could, before the change in rules, sell the acquired assets and report the difference between book value and the purchase price, or $75 million, as earned income. Thus, mergers could be used in still another way to create an illusion of profits and growth.

Financial Treatment of a Purchase

The financial treatment of a purchase can best be explained by use of a hypothetical example. The Mammoth Company has just purchased the Petty Company under an arrangement known as a *purchase*. The facts are as given in Table 30A.1, which also shows the financial treatment.

The illustration conforms to the general nature of a purchase. Measured by total assets, the Mammoth Company is 20 times as large as Petty, while its total earnings are 15 times as large. The terms of the purchase are one share of Mammoth for two shares of Petty, based on the prevailing market value of their shares of common stock. Thus, in terms of Mammoth's stock, Mammoth is giving to Petty's stockholders $30 of market value and $7 of book value for each share of Petty stock. Petty's market value is $30 a share, and its book value is $3 a share, for a total book value of equity of $6,000.[2] The total market value of Mammoth paid for Petty is $60,000. The goodwill involved can be calculated as in Table 30A.2. The $54,000 goodwill represents a debit in the adjustments column and is carried to the pro forma balance sheet. The pro forma balance sheet is obtained by simply adding the balance sheets of the constituent companies, together with adjustments.

---

[2]Under purchase accounting, the acquiring company "should allocate the cost of an acquired company to the assets acquired and liabilities assumed" (APB Opinion No. 16, p. 318, par. 87). A specific procedure is set forth. First, all identifiable assets acquired should be assigned a portion of the cost of the acquired company, normally equal to their fair (market or appraised) values at date of acquisition. Second, the excess of the cost of the acquired company over the sum of the amounts assigned to net assets should be recorded as goodwill. The sum of fair market values assigned may exceed the cost of the acquired company. If so, values otherwise assignable to noncurrent assets should be reduced by a proportionate part of the excess. If noncurrent assets are reduced to zero, any excess should be set up as a deferred credit.

Table 30A.1   Financial Treatment of a Purchase

	Mammoth Company	Petty Company	Adjustments Debit	Adjustments Credit	Pro Forma Balance Sheet
Assets					
Current assets	$ 80,000	$ 4,000			$ 84,000
Other assets	20,000	2,000			22,000
Net fixed assets	100,000	4,000			· 104,000
Goodwill			$54,000		54,000
Total assets	$200,000	$10,000			$264,000
Liabilities and Net Worth					
Current liabilities	$ 40,000	$ 4,000			$ 44,000
Long-term debt	20,000				20,000
Common stock	40,000	1,000	1,000	4,000	44,000
Capital surplus	20,000			56,000	76,000
Retained earnings	80,000	5,000	5,000		80,000
Total liabilities and net worth	$200,000	$10,000	$60,000	$60,000	$264,000
Explanation					
Par value per share, common stock	$4	$0.50			
Number of shares outstanding	10,000	2,000			
Book value per share	$14	$3			
Net income	$30,000	$2,000			
Earnings per share	$3	$1			
Price-earnings ratio	20 times	30 times			
Market value per share	$60	$30			

A total value of $60,000 has been given by Mammoth for a book value of $6,000. This amount represents, in addition to the debt, a payment of $1,000 for the common stock of Petty, $5,000 for the retained earnings, and $54,000 for goodwill. The corresponding credit is the 1,000 shares of Mammoth given in the transaction at their par value of $4 a share, resulting in a credit of $4,000. The capital surplus of Mammoth is increased by $56,000 ($60,000 paid minus $4,000 increase in common stock). The net credit to the net worth accounts is $54,000, which balances the net debit to the asset accounts. When these adjustments are carried through to the pro forma balance sheet, total assets are increased from the uncombined total of $210,000 to a new total of $264,000. Total tangible assets, however, still remain $210,000.

Table 30A.2

Value given by Mammoth	$60,000
Book value of net worth of Petty purchased	6,000
Goodwill	$54,000

Table 30A.3

Total earnings (before Write-off of Goodwill)	$32,000
Amortization of goodwill	1,350
Total net earnings	$30,650
Total shares	11,000
Earnings per share	$2.79
For Petty shareholders	
New earnings per share	$1.40
Before-purchase earnings per old share	$1.00
Accretion per share	$0.40
For Mammoth shareholders	
Before-purchase earnings per share	$3.00
New earnings per share	2.79
Dilution per share	$0.21

The effects on earnings per share for stockholders in each company are shown in Table 30A.3. Total earnings represent the combined earnings of Mammoth and Petty. Mammoth believes that the value reflected in goodwill will be permanent, but under APB Opinion 17, it is required to write off the goodwill account over a maximum of 40 years. The annual charge of $1,350 is the goodwill of $54,000 divided by 40. The total amount of net earnings is, therefore, $30,650.

The total shares are 11,000 because Mammoth has given one share of stock for every two shares of Petty previously outstanding.[3] The new earnings per share are, therefore, $2.79. The calculation of earnings accretion or dilution proceeds on the same principles as the calculations set forth earlier. The results require two important comments, however.

Although the earnings accretion per share for Petty is 40 cents, the earnings dilution per share for Mammoth is relatively small — only 21 cents a share. The explanation is that the size of Mammoth is large in relation to that of Petty. This example also illustrates a general principle: When a large company acquires a small one, it can afford to pay a high multiple of earnings per share of the smaller company. In the present example, the price-earnings ratio of Petty is 30, whereas that of Mammoth is 20. If the acquiring company is large in relation to the acquired firm, it can pay the higher P-E ratio and yet suffer only small dilution in its earnings per share.

It is, however, unrealistic to assume that the same earnings on total assets will result after the merger. After all, the purpose of the merger is to achieve something that the two companies could not have achieved alone. When Philip Morris & Company purchased Benson & Hedges (the maker of Parliament, a leading filter-tip brand), it was buying the ability and experience of Benson & Hedges. By means of this merger, Philip Morris was able to make an entry into the rapidly growing filter cigarette business more quickly than it could otherwise have done. The combined earnings per share were expected to rise.

In the Mammoth-Petty illustration, the earnings rate on the tangible assets of Mammoth is 15 percent and on the tangible assets of Petty is 20 percent. Assume that the return on

---

[3]After the one-for-two exchange, Petty shareholders have only half as many shares as before the merger.

total tangible assets of the combined companies rises to 20 percent. The 20 percent of tangible assets of $210,000 equals $42,000; less the amortization of goodwill over 40 years at $1,350 per year, the total is $40,650 net earnings. With the same total shares of 11,000 outstanding, the new earnings per share will be $3.70. Thus, there will be an accretion of 85 cents for the Petty shareholders and an accretion of 70 cents for the Mammoth shareholders.

This illustrates another general principle: If the purchase of a small company adds to the earnings of the consolidated enterprise, earnings per share may increase for both participants in the merger. Even if the merger results in an initial dilution in earnings per share of the larger company, it may still be advantageous. The initial dilution can be regarded as an investment that will have a payoff at some future date in terms of increased growth in earnings per share of the consolidated company.

Treatment of Goodwill

In purchase accounting, a goodwill account is likely to be created. The accounting treatment established by APB Opinion 17 is that intangibles must be written off over a period of 40 years or less. It appears that prevailing business practice is to write off goodwill over a 40-year period.

From one standpoint, goodwill should be treated like any other asset. Charges based on the estimated life of the goodwill should be made against income. However, since goodwill accounting does not affect actual cash flows and has no income tax consequences, its accounting treatment should not have material effects on the value of the firm. This suggests that it might be useful to write off goodwill immediately, so that subsequent financial reports reflect the results of current operations only.

Financial Treatment of Pooling of Interests

When a business combination is a pooling of interests rather than a purchase, the accounting treatment is simply to combine the balance sheets of the two companies. Goodwill will not ordinarily arise in the consolidation. The financial treatment can be indicated by another example, which reflects the facts as they are set forth in Table 30A.4. In order to focus on the critical issues, the balance sheets are identical in every respect. However, a difference in the amount and rate of profit after interest of the two companies is indicated.

Book value per share is $10. The amount of profit after interest and taxes is $42,000 for Company A and $21,000 for Company B. Earnings per share are, therefore, $3.50 and $1.75, respectively. The price-earnings ratio is 18 for A and 12 for B, so the market price of stock is $63 for A and $21 for B. The net working capital per share is $4.17 in each instance. The dividends per share are $1.75 for A and $0.875 for B. Assume that the terms of the merger will reflect either (1) earnings or (2) market price per share. In both cases, it is assumed that A is the acquiring and surviving firm. If A buys B on the basis of earnings, it exchanges half of a share of A's common stock for one share of B's common stock. The total number of shares of A common stock that will be outstanding after the acquisition is 18,000, of which 6,000 will be held by the old stockholders of B. The new earnings per share in the now-larger Firm A will be the total earnings of $63,000 divided by 18,000, which equals $3.50 per share. Thus, the earnings for A remain unchanged. The old shareholders of B now hold half a share of A for each share of B held before the acquisition. Hence, their equivalent earnings per share from their present holdings of A shares are

Table 30A.4 Financial Treatment of Pooling of Interests

	Company A	Company B	Net Adjustments on A's Books Debit	Net Adjustments on A's Books Credit	Acquiring Company A's New Balance Sheets and Earnings if the Exchange Basis Is: Earnings 2/1	Acquiring Company A's New Balance Sheets and Earnings if the Exchange Basis Is: Price 3/1
Current assets	$100,000	$100,000			$200,000	$200,000
Fixed assets	100,000	100,000			200,000	200,000
Total assets	$200,000	$200,000			$400,000	$400,000
Current liabilities	$ 50,000	$ 50,000			$100,000	$100,000
Long-term debt	30,000	30,000			60,000	60,000
Total debt	80,000	80,000			160,000	160,000
Common stock, par value $5	60,000	60,000	$30,000[a] $40,000[b]		90,000	80,000
Capital surplus	50,000	50,000		$30,000[a] $40,000[b]	130,000	140,000
Retained earnings	10,000	10,000			20,000	20,000
Total claims on assets	$200,000	$200,000			$400,000	$400,000
			Ratios A/B			
Number of shares of stock	12,000	12,000			18,000	16,000
Book value	$10	$10	1.0			
Amount of profit after interest and taxes	$42,000	$21,000			$63,000	$63,000
Earnings per share	$3.50	$1.75	2.0		$3.50	$3.94
Price-earnings ratio	18	12				
Market price of stock	$63	$21	3.0			
Net working capital per share	$4.17	$4.17	1.0			
Dividends per share	$1.75	$0.875	2.0			
Shareholders' new EPS						
Company A					$3.50	$3.94
Company B					$1.75	$1.31

[a]2/1 ratio basis.
[b]3/1 ratio basis.

$1.75, the same as before the acquisition. The stockholders of both A and B have experienced no earnings dilution or accretion.

When the terms of exchange are based on market price per share, the terms of acquisition will be the exchange of one-third share of A stock for one share of B stock. The number of A shares is increased by the 4,000 exchanged for the 12,000 shares of B. The combined earnings of $63,000 are divided by 16,000 shares to obtain an increase in A's earnings per share to $3.94, which represents an earnings accretion of 44 cents per share for the A shareholders. The old B shareholders now hold one-third share of A for each share of B held before the acquisition. Their equivalent earnings are now $3.94 divided by 3, or $1.31, representing an earnings dilution of 44 cents per share.

When the acquisition is made on the basis of earnings, the adjustment to the common stock account in surviving Firm A's balance sheet reflects the fact that only 6,000 shares of A are used to buy 12,000 shares of B. The net decrease of 6,000 shares times the par value of $5 requires a net debit of $30,000 to the common stock account of A ($60,000 + $60,000 − $30,000 = $90,000), with an offsetting increase of $30,000 in the capital surplus account of Firm A ($50,000 + $50,000 + $30,000 = $130,000). When the exchange is made on the basis of market values, only 4,000 shares of A are needed to acquire the 12,000 shares of B. Hence, the net decrease of 8,000 shares in the combined common stock account is $40,000, with an offsetting increase of the same amount in A's capital surplus.

The general principle is that when the terms of merger are based on the market price per share, and the price-earnings ratios of the two companies are different, earnings accretion and dilution will occur. The company with a higher P-E ratio will have earnings accretion; the company with the lower P-E ratio will suffer earnings dilution. If the sizes of the companies are greatly different, the effect on the larger company will be relatively small, whether in dilution or accretion. The effect on the smaller company will be relatively large.

Problems

30A.1 The Vorno Company has just acquired the Hondo Company in an exchange of stock, treating it as a purchase for merger accounting. Vorno paid a 20 percent premium over the market price of Hondo. Data on the two companies are given in Table P30A.1.

Table P30A.1

	Vorno	Hondo	Adjustments Debit	Adjustments Credit	Pro Forma Balance Sheet
1. Current assets	$ 450,000	$ 7,000			_____
2. Other assets	150,000	5,000			_____
3. Fixed assets	400,000	13,000			_____
4. Intangibles	_____	_____	_____		_____
Total assets	$1,000,000	$25,000			_____
5. Current liabilities	200,000	10,000			_____
6. Long-term debt	150,000	—			_____
7. Common stock	200,000	5,000	_____	_____	_____
8. Capital surplus	150,000	—	_____	_____	_____
9. Retained earnings	300,000	10,000	_____	_____	_____
Total claims	$1,000,000	$25,000			_____
Par value	$5.00	$0.50			
Number of shares	_____	_____			
Earnings available to common stock	$120,000	$10,000			
Book value per share	_____	_____			
Earnings per share	_____	_____			
Price/earnings ratio	10X	25X			
Market price per share	_____	_____			

a) Fill in the blanks, complete the adjustments and pro forma balance sheet columns, and show the journal entries for the stock purchase. Explain your journal entries.

b) Assuming that total earnings are unchanged, calculate whether earnings dilution or accretion occurs for each company.

c) Do the same on the assumption that earnings available to common stock rise to $160,000 for the combined company.

30A.2 You are given data in Table P30A.2 on two companies.

Table P30A.2

	Company I	Company II	Adjustments	Consolidated Statement
Current assets	$56,000	$56,000		_____
Fixed assets	34,000	34,000		_____
Total assets	$90,000	$90,000		_____
Current liabilities	$31,000	$31,000		_____
Long-term debt	19,000	19,000		_____
Total debt, 5%[a]	$50,000	$50,000		_____
Common stock, par value $4	24,000	24,000	_____	_____
Capital surplus	11,000	11,000	_____	_____
Retained earnings	5,000	5,000	_____	_____
Total claims on assets	$90,000	$90,000		_____

				Ratios (I/II)	
1. Number of shares of stock	6,000	6,000			1. _____
2. Book value per share	_____	_____		2. _____	2. _____
3. Amount of profit before interest and taxes[b]	$24,583	$12,917			3. _____
4. Earnings per share	_____	_____		4. _____	4. _____
5. Price/earnings ratio	22.6	12			
6. Market price of stock	_____	_____		6. _____	
7. Working capital per share	_____	_____		7. _____	7. _____
8. Dividends per share, 50% payout	_____	_____		8. _____	8. _____
9. Exchange ratio	_____	_____		9. _____	
10. Equivalent earnings per old share	_____	_____			

[a]Average rate on interest bearing and non-interest bearing debt combined.
[b]Assume a 40 percent tax rate.

a) In your judgment, what would be a reasonable basis for determining the terms at which shares in Company I and in Company II would be exchanged for shares in a new company, III? What exchange ratio would you recommend and why?

b) Use the market price of stock relation as the basis for the terms of exchange of stock in the old company for stock in the new company (two shares of III for one share of I, and one-half share of III for one share of II). Then complete the calculations for filling in all the blank spaces, including the adjustments for making the consolidated statement. Treat this problem as a situation that the SEC and accountants would refer to as a pooling of interests.

Selected References

See references at the end of Chapter 30.

Chapter 31 Reorganization and Bankruptcy

Thus far, the text has dealt with issues associated mainly with a growing, successful enterprise. Not all businesses are so fortunate, however; so this chapter will examine financial difficulties — their causes and their possible remedies. The material is significant for the financial managers of successful, as well as potentially unsuccessful, firms. The successful firm's financial manager must know the firm's rights and remedies as a creditor and must participate effectively in efforts to collect from financially distressed debtors. The financial manager of a less-successful firm must know how to handle the firm's affairs if financial difficulties arise. Such understanding can often mean the difference between loss of ownership of the firm and rehabilitation of the firm as a going enterprise.

Bankruptcy law in the United States was changed considerably by The Bankruptcy Reform Act of 1978. The new law consolidates and streamlines some of the procedures of the previous law, with the objective of concluding the bankruptcy process faster and with less expense.

Some dramatic major bankruptcies have occurred in recent years. Most notable was the huge Penn Central Company, which involved total assets at the end of 1969 of almost $7 billion and total debts outstanding of over $4 billion. The W. T. Grant bankruptcy was also of substantial magnitude, involving $1.2 billion of assets. A number of bankruptcies have raised questions of impropriety, such as the Equity Funding Company bankruptcy, which involved fictitious life insurance policies. In April 1982, Wickes Cos., with sales of $4 billion, filed a petition in the bankruptcy courts listing debts of $2 billion to a list of creditors that was reported to fill thousands of pages of computer printouts. Wickes was one of the largest lumber and furniture retailers with interests also in department stores and home improvement stores, all of which had been adversely affected by the recession. With the economic recovery of 1983, Wickes was able to announce, in February 1984, that its creditors had agreed to a reorganization plan that would enable the company to emerge from bankruptcy proceedings.

The instabilities of the early 1970s involved large commercial banks as well as nonfinancial enterprises. The Franklin National Bank, which failed in 1974, had reached an asset size of $5 billion and was the twentieth largest of the nation's more than 14,000 FDIC-insured banks. In the same year, the Beverly Hills Bancorp went into bankruptcy. Earlier, the U.S. National Bank of San Diego had to be taken over by the FDIC, and questions of fraud were raised in connection with its prior management. Some large foreign banks also ran into difficulties. The 1974 failure of Bankhaus I. D. Herstatt, one of Germany's largest private banks, sent shock waves through the international money markets. In early July 1982, the Penn Square Bank of Oklahoma City, which held loans of over $300 million and which had sold more than $2 billion of energy loans to other banks, was closed by federal regulators. With the boom in the energy business, the bank had expanded rapidly during the 1970s. The recession of 1982 reinforced a shift away from the use of oil and gas, reducing the power of OPEC to push up oil prices, and led to a general collapse of the energy boom. These developments impacted the Continental Illinois Bank of Chicago, which was required to undergo a substantial restructuring during 1984. The collapse of the Home State Savings Bank of Cincinnati in mid-March 1985 led to the emergency closing of 71 state-chartered savings and loan institutions in Ohio.

The banking system has continued to raise serious concerns. Large banks especially have been operating with debt-to-equity ratios as high as 20 to 1. Some banks sought rapid growth by aggressively seeking funds from money brokers. Basic issues have been raised about the operation of federal bank deposit insurance. One proposal has been to establish risk-adjusted insurance premiums for banks instead of the flat one-twelfth of 1 percent of domestic deposits now paid to the Federal Deposit Insurance Corporation (FDIC).

The financial system continues to be vulnerable to shocks. Banks are strained by foreign loans that have been repeatedly extended; the debt obligations of farmers are onerous; and the increased failures among bank and thrift institutions have shaken the confidence upon which stability depends. Thus, the risks of failure involve the giant institutions at one end of the scale as well as the small "Mom and Pop" operations.

Failure

Failure can be defined in several ways, and some failures do not necessarily result in the collapse and dissolution of a firm.

Economic Failure

Failure in an economic sense usually signifies that a firm's revenues do not cover its costs. It can also mean that the rate of earnings on its historical cost of investment is less than the firm's cost of capital. It can even mean that the firm's actual returns have fallen below its expected returns. There is no consensus on the definition of failure in an economic sense.

Financial Failure

Although *financial failure* is a less-ambiguous term than *economic failure*, it has two generally recognized aspects. A firm can be considered a failure if it cannot meet its current obligations as they fall due, even though its total assets may exceed its total liabilities. This is defined as *technical insolvency*. A firm is a failure, or *bankrupt*, if its total liabilities exceed a fair valuation of its total assets (that is, if the "real" net worth of the firm is negative).

We shall use the term *business failure* to refer generally to the inability of a firm to meet its obligations. This would include, therefore, any form of economic failure and any of the definitions of financial failure.

Causes of Failure

Over the years, many studies have been made of the factors which cause firms to be unable to meet their obligations. There is a general consensus that, by far, the major source of business failure is management incompetence. What this means is not always clear. Often, it is a lack of experience in that particular line of business. Or the top management may be familiar with the product-market but have unbalanced experience in one or more of the management functions, such as sales, finance, production, research, or planning. Still another inadequacy ascribed to management is failure to anticipate unfavorable industry developments. If all of these various categories of management problems are grouped under the general heading of managerial inadequacy, over 90 percent of business failures can be attributed to this single broad source. Unanticipated catastrophes such as earthquakes, floods, and fires account for less than 5 percent of business failures. Fraud has accounted for some major and dramatic business failures, but, as a percentage of the total number, it is also quite small.

In one sense, except for unusual general catastrophes, one could argue that the cause of business failure is always attributable to management. It is argued that good management will react promptly to strong competition and prepare for adverse general economic developments so that the firm can adjust to changes in the patterns of growth and decay in individual industries. For this reason, the usual procedure after a business has encountered difficulties is to provide for a change in management as well as an infusion of funds to try to reestablish the economic health of the enterprise.

The Failure Record

How widespread is business failure?[1] Is it a rare phenomenon, or does it occur fairly often? In recent times, about 20,000 to 30,000 firms a year have failed, but they represent less than one-half of 1 percent of all business firms. The failure rate rises during recession periods, when the economy is weakened and credit is tightened.

Often, mergers or government intervention are arranged as alternatives to outright bankruptcy. Thus, in recent years, the Federal Home Loan Bank System has arranged the mergers of several very large "problem" savings and loan associations into sound institutions, and the Federal Reserve System has done the same thing for banks. Several government agencies, principally the U.S. Department of Defense, arranged to bail out Lockheed in 1970 to keep it from failing. The merger of Douglas Aircraft and McDonnell in the late 1960s was designed to prevent Douglas's failure. Similar instances could be cited for the securities brokerage industry in the late 1960s and early 1970s. In 1980 and 1981, loan guarantees were made by the federal government to keep credit flowing to Chrysler Corporation in the effort to keep it in business.

Why do government and industry seek to prevent the bankruptcy of larger firms? Three of the many reasons are (1) to prevent an erosion of confidence (in the case of financial institutions), (2) to maintain a viable supplier, and (3) to avoid disrupting a local community. Also, bankruptcy is an expensive process; so even when the public interest is not at stake, private industry has strong incentives to prevent it.

Alternative Remedies

When a business firm is unable to meet its obligations, alternative remedies may be employed. It will be useful to have an overview of the alternative methods of dealing with business failure. A framework for this overview is provided in Figure 31.1. The procedures take two broad routes — relatively informal or relatively formal legal procedures.

Whichever broad method is used, the firm either continues in existence or it is liquidated. Under the out-of-court procedures, the most informal is simply to postpone the date when payment is required — this is called an *extension*. Or the creditors may agree to

---

[1]This section draws from Altman [1972, 1985].

Figure 31.1   Alternative Remedies when Firms Fail

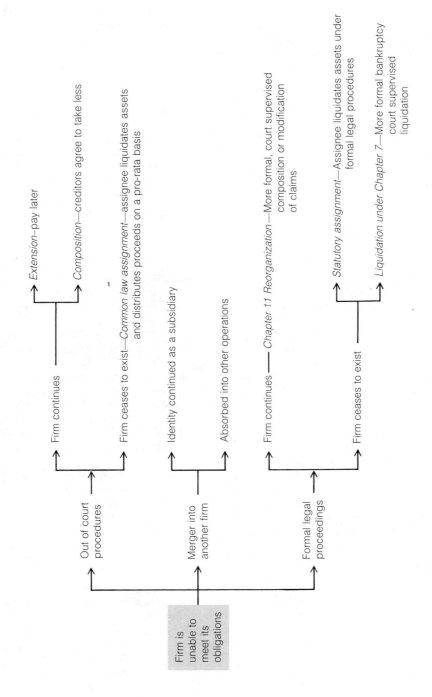

take some fraction of what is owed as full settlement — this is called *composition*. A relatively informal procedure for liquidating the firm is called a common law *assignment*. The assets of the firm are assigned to a trustee who liquidates the assets and distributes the proceeds on a pro rata basis to the creditors.

The other broad path upon business failure involves more formal legal proceedings. Here, there are three alternatives: the firm continues, it is merged into another firm, or the firm is liquidated. Under the Bankruptcy Reform Act of 1978, provision is made for a Chapter 11 reorganization. This represents formal court-supervised procedures for scaling down or modifying the claims of creditors, a form of composition. One of the major functions of merger activity is to provide alternatives to bankruptcy. In a merger, the firm's identity may be continued as a separate subsidiary or its identity may be lost through absorption into other operations. Finally, the firm may cease to exist through an assignment or by liquidation under Chapter 7 of the 1978 federal bankruptcy act. In an assignment, an assignee is designated to liquidate the assets of the failed firm under procedures that are careful to meet certain legal requirements. Under Chapter 7 proceedings, there is much more court supervision involved in the processes for liquidating the assets of the firm which has failed.

With this broad overview of reorganization and bankruptcy procedures, the remainder of the chapter will explain more fully each of these alternatives.

Extension and Composition

Extension and composition are discussed together because they both represent voluntary concessions by creditors. *Extension* postpones the date of required payment of past-due obligations. *Composition* voluntarily reduces the creditors' claims on the debtor. Both are intended to keep the debtor in business and to avoid court costs. Although creditors must absorb a temporary loss, the debtor's rehabilitation is often greater than if one of the formal procedures had been followed; and the hope is that a stable customer will emerge, with long-run benefits to the creditors.

Procedure

A meeting of the debtor and the creditors is held. At the meeting, the creditors appoint a committee consisting of four or five of the largest creditors and one or two of the smaller ones. The meeting is typically arranged and conducted by an adjustment bureau associated with the local credit managers' association or by a trade association.

After the first meeting, if it is judged that the case can be worked out, the bureau assigns investigators to make an exhaustive report. The bureau and the creditors' committee use the facts of the report to formulate a plan for adjustment of the claims. Another meeting between the debtor and the creditors is then held in an attempt to work out an extension or a composition, or a combination of the two. Subsequent meetings may be required to reach final agreements.

Necessary Conditions

At least three conditions are usually necessary to make an extension or a composition feasible:

1. The debtor must be a good moral risk, in the sense of seeking to honor obligations and not diverting the business's assets to personal use and advantage.
2. The debtor must show ability to make a recovery.
3. General business conditions must be favorable to recovery.

Extension

Creditors prefer an extension because it provides for payment in full. The debtor buys current purchases on a cash basis and pays off the past-due balance over an extended time. In some cases, creditors may agree not only to extend the time of payment but also to subordinate existing claims to new debts incurred in favor of vendors extending credit during the period of the extension.

Of course, the creditors must have faith that the debtor will solve the problems. But, because of the uncertainties involved, they will want to exercise controls over the debtor while waiting for their claims to be paid. For example, the creditors' committee may insist that an assignment of assets be executed, to be held in escrow in case of default. If the debtor is a corporation, the committee may require that stockholders transfer their stock certificates into an escrow account until the repayment called for under the extension has been completed. The committee may also designate a representative to countersign all checks, and it may obtain security in the form of notes, mortgages, or assignment of accounts receivable.

Composition

In a composition, a pro rata cash settlement is made. Creditors receive from the debtor a uniform percentage of the obligations — in cash. The cash received is taken as full settlement of the debt, even though the ratio may be as low as 10 percent. Bargaining occurs between the debtor and the creditors over the savings that result from avoiding bankruptcy: administration costs, legal fees, investigating costs, and so on. In addition to avoiding these costs, the debtor avoids the stigma of bankruptcy and thus may be induced to part with most of the savings that result from avoiding the bankruptcy.

Combination Settlement

Often the bargaining process results in a compromise involving both an extension and a composition. For example, the settlement may provide for a cash payment of 25 percent of the debt and six future installments of 10 percent each. Total payment thereby aggregates to 85 percent. Installment payments are usually evidenced by notes, and creditors also seek protective controls.

Appraisal of Voluntary Settlements

The advantages of voluntary settlements are informality and simplicity. Investigative, legal, and administrative expenses are held to a minimum. The procedure is the most economical and results in the largest return to creditors.

One possible disadvantage is that the debtor is left in control of the business. This situation may involve legal complications or erosion of assets still operated by the debtor. However, numerous controls are available to give the creditors protection.

A second disadvantage is that small creditors may take a nuisance role in that they may insist on payment in full. As a consequence, settlements typically provide for payment in full for claims under $50 or $100. If a composition is involved, and all claims under $50 are paid, all creditors will receive a base of $50 plus the agreed-on percentage of the balance of their claims.

On balance, the lower cost and the flexibility of voluntary settlements make them preferable to the alternatives. We next take up the recent changes in the bankruptcy laws, which provide a general framework for the subsequent discussion. We postpone the treatment of out-of-court liquidations, since they are more easily understood in connection with liquidation procedures under the new Chapter 7 of the federal bankruptcy law enacted in 1978.

Federal Bankruptcy Law

The Bankruptcy Reform Act of 1978 (often referred to as "The Code") became the governing law with respect to all cases begun on or after October 1, 1979. Some additional implementation adjustments to the law were made in 1984.[2] Under the bankruptcy laws that prevailed prior to 1979, there were two major types of proceedings—Chapter X and Chapter XI. Proceedings under Chapter X were developed for large corporations with public investors in the bonds and common stock of the firm.

From the creditors' viewpoint, Chapter X proceedings were inflexible and time consuming. The operating control of the debtor firm was placed in a court-appointed trustee, who sometimes did not have the technical knowledge to operate the debtor company successfully. Thus, creditors would suffer losses if the debtor company lost customers and operating efficiency under the trustee arrangement.

In contrast, Chapter XI proceedings were more flexible and informal. Chapter XI proceedings were devised for use with small corporations, partnerships, proprietorships, or individuals in cases involving no public participation in the financing or ownership of the firm. In Chapter XI proceedings, the debtor automatically received the status of debtor in possession. A bankruptcy referee appointed by the court could grant an order of continuance which enabled the debtor to continue operating the business. The referee could enjoin the creditors from legal action to recover debts by obtaining preference over other creditors and by property foreclosure. Payment schedules were worked out between the debtor and creditors, presented to the referee for approval, and ultimately paid out to the creditors. From the creditors' standpoint, Chapter XI proceedings were much less time consuming. The debtors in possession had the opportunity to remain in control of the business, in the hope that they would be more successful than outsiders in reviving the firm and repaying its debts. Creditors were able to exert influence on the debtors. The creditors could even continue to grant credit to the debtor in helping the indebted firm achieve profitability again.

Under the 1978 law that became effective in 1979, Chapters X and XI are blended into a single procedure. Cases can be initiated on either a voluntary or involuntary basis. Invol-

[2]This summary of the new Act is an oversimplification and represents a distortion to some degree. For the "straight stuff," please consult your bankruptcy lawyer.

untary petitions must be commenced only under Chapter 7, which deals with liquidation, or Chapter 11, which deals with reorganization. The debtor company remains in possession of its business and continues to operate it unless the court orders otherwise. Under a Chapter 7 liquidation case, the court may appoint an interim trustee to operate the business to avoid loss. The debtor, however, may regain possession from the trustee by filing an appropriate bond as required by the court. The trustee has very broad powers and discretion if so authorized by the court. The trustee may retain or replace management as well as augment management with additional professionals. The trustee may also obtain additional financing on an unsecured credit basis.

Overall, the new bankruptcy law provides for greater flexibility in the procedures. The major parts of the new bankruptcy law are Chapter 11, which deals with reorganization, Chapter 7, which deals with liquidation, and Chapter 13, which covers personal bankruptcies. Our treatment will not cover the last topic.

Reorganization

Reorganization is a form of extension or composition of the firm's obligations. Regardless of the legal procedure followed, reorganization processes have several features in common:

1. The firm is insolvent either because it is unable to meet cash obligations as they come due or because claims on the firm exceed its assets. Hence, some modifications in the nature or amount of the firm's obligations must be made. A scaling down of terms or amounts must be formulated. This procedure may represent scaling down fixed charges or converting short-term debt into long-term debt or both forms of debt into equity.
2. New funds must be raised for working capital and for property rehabilitation.
3. The operating and managerial causes of difficulty must be discovered and eliminated.

In essence, a reorganization is a composition, a scaling down of claims. In any composition, two conditions must be met:

1. The scaling down must be *fair* to all parties.
2. In return for the sacrifices, successful rehabilitation and profitable future operation of the firm must be *feasible*.

These are the standards of fairness and feasibility, which are the bases for evaluating a reorganization.

Financial Decisions in Reorganization

When a business becomes insolvent, a decision must be made whether to dissolve the firm through liquidation or to keep it alive through reorganization. Fundamentally, this decision depends on a determination of the value of the firm if it is rehabilitated versus the value of the sum of the parts if it is dismembered.

Liquidation values depend on the degree of specialization of the capital assets used in the firm and, hence, their resale value. In addition, liquidation itself involves costs of dismantling, including legal costs. Of course, successful reorganization also involves costs. Typically, better equipment must be installed, obsolete inventories must be disposed of, and improvements in management must be made. Often, the greater indicated value of the firm in reorganization compared with its value in liquidation is used to force a compromise agreement among the claimants, even when they feel that their relative position has not been treated fairly in the reorganization plan.

Both the courts and the SEC are called upon to determine the fairness and feasibility of proposed plans of reorganization.

Standards of Fairness

The basic doctrine of fairness states that claims must be recognized in the order of their legal and contractual priority. Junior claimants, such as common stockholders, can participate only to the extent that they make an additional cash contribution to the reorganization of the firm.

Carrying out this concept of fairness involves the following steps:

1. An estimate of future sales must be made.
2. An analysis of operating conditions must be made so that the future earnings on sales can be estimated.
3. A determination of the capitalization rate to be applied to these future earnings must be made.
4. The capitalization rate must be applied to the estimated future earnings to obtain an indicated value of the company's properties.
5. A determination of the amounts to be distributed to the claimants must be made.

Standards of Feasibility

The primary test of feasibility is that the fixed charges on the income of the corporation after reorganization are amply covered by earnings or, if a value is established for a firm that is to be sold, that a buyer can be found at that price. Adequate coverage of fixed charges for a company that is to continue in operation generally requires an improvement in earnings, a reduction of fixed charges, or both.

Among the actions that have to be taken to improve the earning power of the company are the following:

1. The maturities of debt obligations are often extended, and some unsecured debt is converted into common stock.
2. Where the management has been inefficient and inadequate for the task, new talents and abilities must be brought into the company.
3. If inventories have become obsolete, they must be disposed of and the operations of the company streamlined.
4. Sometimes, the plant and the equipment of the firm must be modernized before it can operate and compete successfully on a cost basis.
5. Reorganization may also require an improvement in production, marketing, advertising, and other functions to enable the firm to compete successfully.
6. It is sometimes necessary to develop new products so the firm can move from areas where economic trends have become undesirable into areas where the growth and stability potential is greater.

The Priority of Claims

In Chapter 5 of the new bankruptcy law, Section 507 sets out the priority of expenses and claims.

1. Secured creditors receive the proceeds from the sales of property pledged. Under Chapter X of the old bankruptcy law, the secured creditor could be forced to accept payment of the depressed collateral value in full satisfaction of his lien, which was appropriately termed a "cram down." In a Chapter XI arrangement, the unsecured deficiency claim would share equally with unsecured creditors. But, the "cram down" effectively caused the secured creditor to lose any benefit from any future appreciation in the value of the collateral which might be retained by the debtor. Under the new bankruptcy code, if the unsecured creditors do not accept the reorganization plan, the secured creditors must receive the full amount of their lien. If the unsecured creditor class accepts the plan (by at least two-thirds in amount and a majority in number), the deficiency claim of the secured creditors receives whatever is provided to the unsecured creditor class in the plan. However, when a secured claim class makes a particular election provided for in Section 1111(b), the secured creditor may receive payment over time of the full amount of its debt, benefiting from future appreciation of the property which remains as collateral for the debt. This essentially eliminates the "cram down" that had existed under Chapters X and XI of the older bankruptcy act.
2. Trustees' costs involved in the proceedings.
3. Expenses after an involuntary case has begun but before a trustee is appointed.
4. Wages due workers if earned within three months prior to filing the petition in bankruptcy; the amount is not to exceed $2,000 per person.
5. Claims for unpaid contributions to employee benefit plans to have been paid within six months prior to the filing. The $2,000 limit in Item 4 covers the sum of both wages and unpaid pension contributions.
6. Unsecured claims for customer deposits, with a maximum of $900 per individual.
7. Taxes due to federal, state, county, and any other governmental agencies.
8. Unfunded pension plan liabilities have a priority over general creditors up to 30 percent of the sum of common and preferred equity; the balance represents a claim on the same level as the general creditors.
9. General or unsecured creditors include trade credit, unsecured loans, debenture bonds, and the unsatisfied portions of the secured loans and unfunded pension plan liabilities described in Items 1 and 8 above. Subordinated debt must first satisfy subordination provisions, as illustrated by the example in the following section.
10. Preferred stockholders can receive up to the par value of the issue.
11. Common stockholders receive anything that remains.

The absolute priority doctrine calls for exactly following the above ordering. The relative priority doctrine is less rigid in view of the uncertainties of estimating the current value of a future stream of cash flows. It seeks to preserve some stake in the company for junior claimants. With the general provisions of the new bankruptcy act having been summarized, we now turn to their applications. We begin with an example of reorganization.

Example of Reorganization

The reorganization procedures are explained by a composite case based on some recent examples. The Braden Company expanded rapidly, both internally and through acquisitions. It began suffering losses, as indicated by the balance sheet and income statement shown in Tables 31.1 and 31.2 respectively.

Before financial readjustment, the Braden Company earned $3.85 million before depreciation, interest, and taxes. Depreciation is 5 percent of the gross value of plant and equip-

Table 31.1   Braden Company, Balance Sheet, March 31, 19X1 (Millions of Dollars)

	Before Financial Readjustment (1)		After Financial Readjustment (2)	
Current assets	$12		$6	
Net property	18		8	
Total assets		$30		$14
Accounts payable	$ 5		$ —	
Taxes	1		1	
Notes payable to banks (9%)	5		5	
Notes payable to trade creditors (10%)	5		—	
Accrued wages	1		1	
Total current liabilities		$17		$ 7
10% first mortgage bonds, due 1990	$ 5		$5	
12% subordinated debentures, due 1990	10		—	
Total long-term debt		$15		$ 5
Common stock ($1 par)	$ 1		$2	
Paid-in capital	4		—	
Retained income	(7)		—	
Net worth		$ (2)		$ 2
Total liabilities and capital		$30		$14

ment of $40 million, which is $2 million. EBIT is, therefore, $1.85 million. The interest expense represents the sum of the following amounts:

Notes payable to banks at 9% times $5 million	$ .45 million
Notes payable at 10% times $5 million	.50
First mortgage bonds at 10% times $5 million	.50
Subordinated debentures at 12% times $10 million	1.20
Total interest expense	$2.65 million

After deducting interest expense, the earnings both before and after taxes represent a loss of $0.8 million. The cumulative losses shown in the balance sheet resulted in a retained income account of a negative $7 million. Tax credits from profits in earlier years have been exhausted. With the continued losses, the firm filed a petition with the federal court for reorganization under the new Chapter 11. The court, in accordance with the law, appointed a disinterested trustee. On May 28, 19X1, the trustee filed a plan of reorganization with the court.

Attempt at Voluntary Readjustment. As shown in Column (2) of Tables 31.1 and 31.2, a number of readjustments were made. Inventories were written down by $6 million, and gross fixed assets were written down by $10 million. Hence, total assets became $14 million. The banks agreed to forego interest on the notes payable loans for five years as part of their contribution to the hoped-for work-out plans and to receive 20 percent of the firm's cash flow in loan repayments beginning in the sixth year. In return for their claims,

Table 31.2   Braden Company, Partial Income Statement, Year Ended December 31, 19X0
(Income Statement Items in Millions of Dollars; Memo Items as Shown)

	Before Financial Readjustment (1)		After Financial Readjustment (2)
Earnings before depreciation, interest, and taxes	$3.85		$3.85
Depreciation (5% of $40)	2.00	(5% of $30)	1.50
EBIT	$1.85		$2.35
Interest expense	2.65		.50
Earnings before taxes	$(.80)		$1.85
Taxes	—		—
Earnings after taxes	$(.80)		$1.85
Memo			
Number of shares	1 million		2 million
Earnings per share	$(.80) per share		$.93 per share

the subordinated debenture holders and the trade creditors are each given 500,000 shares of stock. Thus, they own shares of stock approximately equal in total to those held by the existing stockholders before financial readjustment. The total liabilities and capital therefore become $14 million, equal to total assets as shown in Column (2) of the balance sheet in Table 31.1.

The income statement after readjustment is shown in Column (2) of Table 31.2. Depreciation expense is reduced to $1.5 million and interest expense is the $.50 million due on the mortgage bonds. Hence, the net income of Braden Company will be $1.85 million per year during the first five years, with earnings of $.93 per share.

The trustee found that the company could not be rehabilitated by management changes, and so concluded that the only feasible program was to solicit the interest of a number of companies in related lines of business. One of these was Sandow Company, an established producer of a similar line of products whose characteristics made the combination of operations more efficient.

Formal Reorganization Procedure. Sandow made a formal proposal: (1) to assume the obligations for the 10 percent first mortgage bonds of Braden, (2) to pay its $1 million back wages and $1 million back taxes and, in addition, (3) offered 200,000 shares of Sandow common stock, which had a current market value of $5 per share. Thus, Sandow offered an amount equivalent to the following:

First mortgage bond obligation	$5,000,000
Payment of wages	1,000,000
Payment of taxes	1,000,000
Value of common shares	1,000,000
	$8,000,000

The trustee's plan allocated the claims of the unsecured creditors, as set forth in Table 31.3.

Table 31.3   Trustee's Plan for Braden Company

Prior Claims	Amount	Receives
Wages	$1,000,000	Cash paid by successor
Taxes	1,000,000	Cash paid by successor
First mortgage, 10%, 19X5	5,000,000	Assumed by successor
	$7,000,000	

Trustee's plan for remainder of claims — valuation based on 200,000 shares at $5 = $1 million, or 4 percent of $25 million liabilities.

Claims	Amount	4 Percent × Amount of Claim	Claim After Subordination	Number of Shares of Common Stock
1. Notes payable to banks	$ 5,000,000	$ 200,000	$ 600,000	120,000
2. Notes payable to trade	5,000,000	200,000	200,000	40,000
3. General unsecured creditors	5,000,000	200,000	200,000	40,000
4. Subordinated debentures	10,000,000	400,000	0	0
	$25,000,000	$1,000,000	$1,000,000	200,000

The trustee's plan provides for satisfying the claims with high priority, including full satisfaction of the secured claim represented by the first mortgage bonds. The total remaining claims of the unsecured creditors equal $25 million. For their claims, they are to receive some portion of the 200,000 shares of common stock of Sandow Company. The allocation to them is shown in the lower portion of Table 31.3. Each claimant would be entitled to a portion of the 200,000 shares of stock, with a total current value of $1 million. Before adjustment, the holders of the notes payable to banks would receive 4 percent of their $5 million claim, or $200,000. But, since the debentures are subordinated to the bank loan, their $400,000 is allocated to the bank claim. As a result, the banks will receive 12 percent of their claim, as compared with 4 percent for the other general creditors and nothing for the subordinated debenture holders. The final column shows the number of shares of common stock each of the claimants will receive.

SEC Evaluation. The Securities and Exchange Commission made an evaluation from the standpoint of fairness. On the basis of estimates set forth in Table 31.4, the SEC arrived at an evaluation of net value. First, sales estimates based on the underlying properties of

Table 31.4   Braden Company, SEC Evaluation of Fairness Valuation

Estimated sales of Braden Co. properties	$18,000,000	— $20,000,000 per year
Earnings at 4-5% of sales	720,000	— 1,000,000
P-E ratio of 8 times earnings	5,760,000	— 8,000,000
Cash paid and mortgage assumed	(7,000,000)	— (7,000,000)
Net value	$(1,240,000)	— $ 1,000,000

Braden Company were made. These ranged from $18 million to $20 million. The earnings power of companies in this line of business is 4 to 5 percent of sales. Applying the 4 percent to the $18 million of sales gives an earnings estimate of $720,000; applying the 5 percent estimate to $20 million of sales gives earnings of $1 million. It was agreed that an 8 times price-earnings ratio was reasonable. Utilizing the 8 times price-earnings ratio, the SEC arrived at a total value, less the mortgage assumed plus cash paid, ranging from a negative $1,240,000 to a positive $1,000,000. Thus, the amount paid by Sandow is at the high end of the range of the indicated value of the Braden Company. The SEC, therefore, recommended the approval of the trustee's plan for reorganization as meeting the test of fairness.

With regard to the feasibility test, we now consider Braden as a division of the Sandow Company. With the writedown of the assets (assumed), the depreciation expense would be reduced to $1.5 million per year. The interest on the mortgage bonds assumed by Sandow would represent $0.5 million per year. Hence, the contribution of earnings before taxes that would be made to Sandow from the former Braden operations would be $1.85 million per year. Furthermore, it is expected that the Sandow Company will improve the management policies of Braden so that the underlying earning power of the company will also be improved. So, as a part of the Sandow Company, the Braden entity is expected to contribute to profitability rather than being a drag on the acquiring company.

In addition, the SEC considered the financial strength of the Sandow Company before its acquisition of Braden. A financial ratio analysis was applied by the SEC. The Sandow Company was found to be strong by all of the categories of tests that we had described in Chapter 8. Its liquidity ratios were strong; its activity and profitability ratios were also well above its industry standards. In addition, it had a relatively clean balance sheet with respect to the use of debt. Its own rate of growth had not been spectacular, but solid. Thus, the feasibility tests for both Braden and Sandow were satisfied.

The court, therefore, approved the trustee's plan. In addition, all of the claimants approved the plan because they felt it was the best deal they could obtain under the circumstances. While the shares of common stock that they received represented a relatively small fraction of their claims, they appeared to have no better alternatives. Often in such cases, the value of the common stock may subsequently rise substantially. When that occurs, the market value of the common stock they receive may climb to a relatively favorable percentage of the dollar amount of their original claims. It will be noted that the original common stockholders receive nothing, since the value of the firm was insufficient to meet the claims of unsecured creditors. This illustrates the nature of the risk taken by common stockholders.

Use of Reorganization to Recontract

Labor unions may be among the interested parties in many reorganizations. An important current issue in bankruptcy legislation is whether ailing firms may unilaterally cancel their labor union contracts after filing for bankruptcy protection.

Shortly after Continental Airlines filed for reorganization in September 1983, contracts with several unions were dissolved, salaries were reduced, and the work force was cut in an effort to make the firm a profitable, low-cost airline. In June of 1984, the court upheld the pilots' union contract cancellation (and was expected to rule similarly in cases involving other union contracts). The contract was called burdensome and a threat to Continental's financial health.

Similar issues were raised when Wilson Foods, a large meat packer, filed for bankruptcy in April 1983. Wilson had a positive net worth of over $60 million when it filed. Critics complained that Wilson filed for the main purpose of reducing its labor costs. In a reorganization under Chapter 11, various kinds of existing contracts, including labor contracts, can be modified.

The basic problem appears to be that in a number of industries, including airlines and meat packing, new competitors entered with nonunion, low-cost employees. With this labor cost advantage and competitive price cuts, considerable pressure was placed on firms with higher labor costs under union wage contracts. It has been argued that it is inappropriate to use the bankruptcy laws to break union contracts. One can recognize the problems of firms with high wages competing against firms with nonunion, low wages. On the other hand, it is difficult for the employees to adjust to reductions in family income. The traditional financial approach of providing an equity interest in the company when other claims are scaled down may be applicable here. One way to deal with the labor contract problem would be to compensate the workers who accept lower wages with a share of the equity of the reorganized firm. This would have the dual effect of compensating labor for the cancelled contract, while providing the incentive to work for the renewed profitability of the reorganized firm.

Liquidation Procedures

Liquidation of a business occurs when the firm is worth more dead than alive. Common-law assignment is a liquidation procedure that does not go through the courts, although it can be used to achieve full settlement of claims on the debtor. Bankruptcy is a legal procedure, carried out under the jurisdiction of special courts, in which a firm is formally liquidated and creditors' claims are completely discharged.

Assignment

Assignment (as well as bankruptcy) takes place when the debtor is insolvent and the possibility of restoring profitability is so remote that the enterprise should be dissolved. Assignment is a technique for liquidating a debt and yielding a larger amount to the creditors than is likely to be achieved in formal bankruptcy.

Technically, there are three classes of assignments: (1) common-law assignment, (2) statutory assignment, and (3) assignment plus settlement.

Common-Law Assignment. Common law provides for an assignment whereby a debtor transfers the title to assets to a third person, known as an *assignee* or *trustee*. This person is instructed to liquidate the assets and to distribute the proceeds among the creditors on a pro rata basis.

Typically, an assignment is conducted through the adjustment bureau of the local credit managers' association. The assignee may liquidate the assets through a bulk sale — a public sale through an auctioneer. The auction is preceded by advertising so there will be a number of bids. Liquidation may also be by a piecemeal auction sale conducted on the premises of the assignor by a competent, licensed auctioneer. On-premises sales are particularly advantageous in the liquidation of large machine shops of manufacturing plants.

The common-law assignment, as such, does not discharge the debtor's obligations. If a corporation goes out of business and does not satisfy all its claims, there will still be claims against it; but, in effect, the corporation has ceased to exist. The people who have been associated with it can organize another corporation free of the debts and obligations of the previous one. Under a common-law assignment, the assignee, in drawing up the checks to pay the creditors, should write on each check the requisite legal language to make the payment a complete discharge of the obligation. The legal requirements for this process are technical and best carried out with the aid of a lawyer, but a statement that endorsement of the check represents acknowledgement of full payment for the obligation is essential.

Statutory Assignment.   Statutory assignment is similar in concept to common-law assignment. Legally, it is carried out under state statutes regulating assignment; technically, it requires more formality. The debtor executes an instrument of assignment, which is recorded and thereby provides notice to all third parties. The proceedings are handled under court order; the court appoints an assignee and supervises the proceedings, including the sale of the assets and the distribution of the proceeds. As with the common-law assignment, debtors are not automatically discharged from the balance of the obligations. They can discharge themselves, however, by printing the requisite statement on the settlement checks.

Assignment Plus Settlement.   Both the common-law and the statutory assignment may take place with recognition and agreement beforehand by the creditors that the assignment will represent a complete discharge of obligation. Normally, the debtor communicates with the local credit managers' association. The association's adjustment bureau arranges a meeting of all the creditors, and a trust instrument of assignment is drawn up. The adjustment bureau is designed to dispose of the assets, which are sold through regular trade channels, by bulk sales, by auction, or by private sales. The creditors typically leave all responsibility for the liquidation procedure with the assignee — the adjustment bureau.

Having disposed of the assets and obtained funds, the adjustment bureau then distributes the proceeds pro rata among the creditors, designating on the check that this is in full settlement of the claims on the debtor. Ordinarily, a release is not agreed upon before the execution of the assignment. Instead, after full examination of the facts, the creditors' committee usually recommends granting a release following the execution of the assignment. If releases are not forthcoming, the assignor can, within four months of the date of the assignment, file a voluntary petition in bankruptcy. In this event, the assignment is terminated and the assignee must account for the assets, report to the trustee and the referee in bankruptcy, and deliver to the trustee all assets in the estate. (Usually, by that time, assets have been reduced to cash.)

Assignment has substantial advantages over bankruptcy. Bankruptcy through the courts involves much time, legal formalities, and accounting and legal expenses. Assignment saves the costs of bankruptcy proceedings, and it may save time as well. Furthermore, an assignee usually has more flexibility in disposing of property than does a bankruptcy trustee. Assignees may be more familiar with the normal channels of trade; and since they take action quickly, before the inventories become obsolete, they may achieve better results.

Liquidation in Bankruptcy

The procedures under Chapter 7 of the 1978 Federal Bankruptcy Reform Act achieve at least three things during a liquidation: (1) They provide safeguards against fraud by the debtor during liquidation; (2) simultaneously, they provide for an equitable distribution of the debtor's assets among the creditors; and (3) insolvent debtors can discharge all their obligations and start new businesses unhampered by a burden of prior debt.

Table 31.5   Order of Priority of Claims for the Braden Company

Cash received from sale of current assets		$6,000,000
1. Fees and expenses of bankruptcy proceedings	$ 500,000	
2. Wages due workers earned three months prior to filing of bankruptcy petition	1,000,000	
3. Unpaid taxes	1,000,000	
Total of priority claims from current assets		2,500,000
Available to general claims		$3,500,000
Cash received from sale of net property	$4,000,000	
First mortgage claim	5,000,000	
Unsatisfied portion of first mortgage claim	$1,000,000	

Claims of General Creditors	Claim (1)	Application of 13.5 Percent[a] (2)	After Subordination (3)	Percent of Original Claim Received (4)
Unsatisfied portion of first mortgage	$ 1,000,000	$ 135,000	$ 135,000	82.7%
Notes payable to bank	5,000,000	675,000	2,025,000	40.5
Notes payable to trade	5,000,000	675,000	675,000	13.5
Accounts payable	5,000,000	675,000	675,000	13.5
Subordinated debentures	10,000,000	1,350,000	0	0.0
	$26,000,000	$3,500,000	$3,500,000	

[a]Does not add to total because of rounding.

To illustrate procedures for liquidation under Chapter 7, let us continue with the Braden Company example. Now we consider an alternative set of assumptions. The offer by Sandow was equivalent to $8 million. Here we assume that under a plan of liquidation, $10 million in cash would be realized, representing 25 percent more than the Sandow offer. The trustee recommended acceptance, which resulted in $6 million cash from the sale of current assets and $4 million from the sale of the net property. The order of priority of claims is set forth in Table 31.5.

In Table 31.5, we see that the amount available to general creditors is $3,500,000. The total general claims are $26,000,000. Thus, 13.5 percent of the total claims can be met. Since the debentures are subordinated to the bank notes payable, the full amount of the claim of the subordinated debentures must be transferred to the claim of the notes payable to banks. The total amount realized on liquidation is the first mortgage claim of $4,000,000 plus the $3,500,000 available to the general creditors, a total of $7,500,000. This represents, of course, the $10,000,000 proceeds less the prior claims of $2,500,000 representing bankruptcy fees, wages owed, and taxes owed. Thus, the creditors on total claims of $26,000,000 plus the $4,000,000 first mortgage claim satisfied, have total claims of $30,000,000. For these total claims of $30,000,000, a net of $7,500,000 is available. Thus, the creditors as a group receive 25 cents on the dollar on liquidation.

But, the percentages realized vary among the individual claimants: ranging from 82.7 percent for the first mortgage holders and 40.5 percent for the banks, down to 13.5 percent for the other general creditors and nothing for the subordinated debenture holders. This illustrates the value of the first mortgage security as well as the role of the subordination agreement. It also shows the generally unfavorable position of the general creditors on liquidation. It is for this reason that they are often willing to work out some informal financial readjustment in hope that they may do better than the average of 15 to 20 percent on the dollar received by general creditors. Again, common stockholders receive nothing, illustrating the riskiness of their junior position.

The order of priority can be altered by special subordination agreements. For example, in the W. T. Grant bankruptcy during the mid-1970s, the commercial banks had agreed to subordinate their loans to the amounts payable to trade creditors in order to induce suppliers of W. T. Grant to continue the flow of merchandise to the company. As a consequence, of the $400 million that appeared to be realizable from W. T. Grant, the order of priority was the following. First in line were the holders of the $24 million worth of senior debentures. Second, because of an unusual lien arrangement, came trade creditors, with $110 million owed. Third were the banks, which subordinated to the trade creditors $300 million of their $640 million loan to Grant, along with an additional $90 million loaned after the filing for reorganization. Next came junior debenture holders, with claims of $94 million. Last in line were the holders of unsecured debt, including $300 million in landlord claims and utility bills. In addition, it was estimated that administrative costs of the reorganization would total $30 million. There was also an unresolved Internal Revenue Service claim of $60 million plus interest. Further, there would be legal fees estimated to run into the millions that would assume a priority status.[3]

Bankruptcy Prediction

Experienced credit managers and financial analysts are often able to predict the likelihood of financial difficulties by closely following all aspects of a firm over a long period of time. Their efforts are substantially aided by a formal methodology called "multiple discriminant analysis (MDA)." As we described in Chapter 8, MDA uses financial ratios, which include measures of liquidity such as the current ratio, leverage ratios such as debt-to-equity, and profitability ratios such as net income to net worth or the accumulated retained earnings (positive or negative). It uses financial ratios in statistical relationships in an effort to establish the probabilities for bankruptcy.

Since multiple discriminant analysis makes heavy use of financial ratios, its nature and application were described in Appendix 8B to the chapter on financial ratio analysis. Based on financial ratios, MDA has successfully been used to classify companies into those with a high probability of going bankrupt and those with a low probability of going bankrupt. The leader in the development and application of MDA was Edward Altman (see references at the end of Appendix 8B). He has continuously improved his models so that they are able to predict bankruptcy with a high degree of dependability at least two years ahead of the event.

MDA has also been used successfully by credit analysts to formulate default probabilities for loan applicants and by portfolio managers evaluating stock and bond investments. In some applications, it is called "credit scoring." Thus, the approach is finding applications in a number of areas of financial decision making.

[3]"Dividing What's Left of Grant's," *Business Week*, March 1, 1976, p. 21.

Summary

The major cause of a firm's failure is incompetent management. Bad managers should, of course, be removed as promptly as possible; if failure has occurred, a number of remedies are open to the interested parties.

The first question to be answered is whether the firm is better off dead or alive — whether it should be liquidated and sold off piecemeal or rehabilitated. Assuming the decision is made that the firm should survive, it must be put through what is called a *reorganization*. Legal procedures are always costly, especially in the case of a business failure. Therefore, if it is at all possible, both the debtor and the creditors are better off if matters can be handled on an informal basis rather than through the courts. The informal procedures used in reorganization are (1) extension, which postpones the date of settlement, and (2) composition, which reduces the amount owed.

If voluntary settlement through extension or composition is not possible, the matter is thrown into the courts. If the court decides on reorganization rather than liquidation, it will appoint a trustee (1) to control the firm going through reorganization and (2) to prepare a formal plan of reorganization. The plan, which must be reviewed by the SEC, must meet the standards of fairness to all parties and feasibility in the sense that the reorganized enterprise will stand a good chance of surviving instead of being thrown back into the bankruptcy courts.

The application of standards of fairness and feasibility can help determine the probable success of a particular plan for reorganization. The concept of fairness involves the estimation of sales and earnings and the application of a capitalization rate to the latter to determine the appropriate distribution to each claimant.

The feasibility test examines the ability of the new enterprise to carry the fixed charges resulting from the reorganization plan. The quality of management and the company's assets must be assured. Production and marketing may also require improvement.

Where liquidation is treated as the only solution to the debtor's insolvency, the creditors should attempt procedures that will net them the largest recovery. Assignment of the debtor's property is the cheaper and the faster procedure. Furthermore, there is more flexibility in disposing of the property and thus larger returns. Bankruptcy provides formal procedures in liquidation to safeguard the debtor's property from fraud and to assure equitable distribution to the creditors. The procedures have been streamlined and improved under the new bankruptcy law of 1978.

We also remind the reader of the potential use of multiple discriminant analysis (MDA) in predicting bankruptcy. MDA can be used to evaluate the prospects of individual firms. In addition, MDA can aid in evaluating the fairness and feasibility of reorganization plans and in judging the alternatives of reorganization and liquidation.

Questions

31.1   Discuss this argument, giving both pros and cons: A certain number of business failures is a healthy sign. If there are no failures, this is an indication (a) that entrepreneurs are overly cautious, hence not as inventive and as willing to take risks as a healthy, growing economy requires; (b) that competition is not functioning to weed out inefficient producers; or (c) that both situations exist.

31.2   How can financial analysis be used to forecast the probability of a given firm's failure? Assuming that such analysis is properly applied, will it always predict failure? Explain.

31.3 Why do creditors usually accept a plan for financial rehabilitation rather than demand liquidation of the business?

31.4 Would it be possible to form a profitable company by merging two companies, both of which are business failures? Explain.

31.5 Distinguish between a reorganization and a bankruptcy.

31.6 Would it be a sound rule to liquidate whenever the liquidation value is above the value of the corporation as a going concern? Discuss.

31.7 Why do liquidations usually result in losses for the creditors or the owners or both? Would partial liquidation or liquidation over a period of time limit their losses? Explain.

31.8 Are liquidations likely to be more common for public utility, railroad, or industrial corporations? Why?

Problems

31.1 The final balance sheet of the bankrupt Scotshop Discount Stores is shown in Table P31.1.

Table P31.1

Assets		Liabilities	
Current assets	$12,000,000	Accounts payable	$ 3,000,000
Net fixed assets	1,400,000	Notes payable (bank)	700,000
		Accrued wages (700 at $400 each)	280,000
		Taxes due	720,000
		Current liabilities	$ 4,700,000
		Mortgage	$ 1,000,000
		Subordinated debentures[a]	1,000,000
		Long-term debt	$ 2,000,000
		Preferred stock	$ 815,000
		Common stock	5,000,000
		Retained earnings	885,000
		Net worth	$ 6,700,000
Total assets	$13,400,000	Total claims	$13,400,000

[a]Subordinated to $700,000 notes payable to bank.

Total legal fees and administrative expenses of the bankruptcy proceeding were $1 million. Upon liquidation of the firm's assets, only $5 million was realized:

Current assets	$4,300,000
Net property	700,000
Total assets	$5,000,000

Prepare a schedule showing the distribution of the liquidation proceeds.

31.2 The financial statements of the Nova Publishing Company for 19X0 are shown in Table P31.2.

Table P31.2

Nova Publishing Company Balance Sheet as of December 31, 19X0
(Thousands of Dollars)

Current assets	$130,000	Current liabilities	$ 53,000
Investments	40,000	Advance payments for subscriptions	78,000
Net fixed assets	200,000	Reserves	8,000
Goodwill	14,000	$8 preferred stock, $100 par	
		(1,500,000 shares)	150,000
		$9 preferred stock, no par	
		(100,000 shares, callable at $110)	11,000
		Common stock, $1.50 par	
		(8,000,000 shares)	12,000
		Retained earnings	72,000
Total assets	$384,000	Total claims	$384,000

Nova Publishing Company Income Statement for Year Ended December 31, 19X0
(Thousands of Dollars)

Operating income		$194,400
Operating expenses		174,800
Earnings before income tax		19,600
Income tax (@ 40 percent)		7,840
Income after taxes		11,760
Dividends on $8 preferred stock	$12,000	
Dividends on $9 preferred stock	900	
Income available for common stock		12,900
		$-1,140

A recapitalization plan is proposed in which each share of $8 preferred stock will be exchanged for a share of $2 preferred (stated value $20), plus $80 of stated principal in 8 percent subordinated income debentures with par value $1,000. The $9 preferred will be retired from cash.

a) Show the pro forma balance sheet (in thousands of dollars) giving effect to the recapitalization and showing the new preferred at its stated value and the common stock at par value.

b) Present the pro forma income statement (in thousands of dollars).

c) How much does the firm increase income available to common stock by the recapitalization?

d) How much less are the required pre-tax earnings after the recapitalization compared to before the change? (Required earnings are the amount necessary to meet fixed charges, debenture interest, and preferred dividends.)

e) How is the debt to net worth position of the company affected by the recapitalization?

f) Would you vote for the recapitalization if you were a holder of the $8 preferred stock?

31.3 The Positech Company produces precision instruments. The company's products, designed and manufactured according to specifications set out by its customers, are highly specialized. Declines in sales and increases in development expenses in recent years resulted in a large deficit at the end of 1985 (see the balance sheet and income data in Table P31.3).

Table P31.3

Positech Company Balance Sheet as of December 31, 1985 (Thousands of Dollars)

Current assets	$375	Current liabilities	$450
Fixed assets	375	Long-term debt (unsecured)	225
		Capital stock	150
		Retained earnings (deficit)	−75
Total assets	$750	Total claims	$750

Positech Company Sales and Profits, 1982-1985 (Thousands of Dollars)

Year	Sales	Net Profit after Tax before Fixed Charges
1982	$2,625	$262.5
1983	2,400	225.0
1984	1,425	−75.0
1985	1,350	−112.5

Independent assessment led to the conclusion that the company would have a liquidation value of about $600,000. As an alternative to liquidation, management concluded that a reorganization was possible with the investment of an additional $300,000. Management was confident of the company's eventual success and stated that the additional investment would restore earnings to $125,000 a year after taxes and before fixed charges. The appropriate multiplier to apply is 8 times. Management is negotiating with a local investment group to obtain the additional $300,000. If the funds are obtained, the holders of the long-term debt will be given half the common stock in the reorganized firm in place of their present claims.

Should the creditors agree to the reorganization, or should they force liquidation of the firm?

31.4 During the past several months, the American Industrial Products Company has had difficulty meeting its current obligations. Attempts to raise additional working capital have failed. To add to AIP's problems, its principal lenders, the First National Bank and the General Insurance Company, have been placing increased pressure on it because of its continued delinquent loan payments and apparent lack of fiscal responsibility.

The First National Bank is first mortgage holder on AIP's production facility and has a $1 million, unsecured revolving loan with AIP that is past due and on which certain restrictive clauses have been violated. The General Insurance Company is holding $5 million of AIP's subordinated debentures, which are subordinate to the notes payable.

Because of the bank's increasing concern for the long-term failure of AIP, it has attached $750,000 of AIP's deposits. This action has forced the company into either reorganization or bankruptcy.

General Insurance has located a large manufacturing company that is interested in taking over AIP's operations. This company has offered to assume the $8 million mortgage, pay all back taxes, and pay $4.3 million in cash for the company.

AIP's estimated sales for 1986 are $20 million, its estimated earnings are $1,294,000, and its capitalization factor is 10 times. The company's balance sheet as of December 31, 1985, is shown in Table P31.4.

Table P31.4

American Industrial Products Company Balance Sheet as of December 31, 1985
(Thousands of Dollars)

Assets		Liabilities	
Current assets	$ 3,000	Accounts payable	$ 2,000
Net property, plant,			
and equipment	12,000	Taxes	200
Other assets	2,800	Notes payable to bank	250
		Other current liabilities	1,350
		Total current liabilities	3,800
		Mortgage	8,000
		Subordinated debentures	5,000
		Common stock	1,000
		Paid-in capital	2,000
		Retained earnings	−2,000
		Total liabilities and	
Total assets	$17,800	stockholders' equity	$17,800

a)   Given all the data and the fact that AIP cannot be reorganized internally, show the effect of the reorganization plan on claims of AIP's creditors.

b)   Based on the information in the paragraph preceding the balance sheet, test for the standard of fairness.

c)   Comment on the actions of the bank in offsetting AIP's deposits.

d)   Do you feel the bank and the insurance company were right in not advancing AIP additional money?

31.5   The Massey-Ferguson Company is a Canadian manufacturer of agricultural machinery. For the year ended October 31, 1978, the firm's net income was a negative $262 million (U.S. dollars). An abbreviated balance sheet and income statement for the year ended October 31, 1979, is presented in Table P31.5.

Table P31.5

Massey-Ferguson Company of Canada, Ltd., Income Statement for Year Ended
October 31, 1979 (Thousands of Dollars)

Revenues[a]	$3,125,000
Expenses (except interest)	2,930,000
Interest expense	164,000
Tax	cr 6,000
Net income	$ 37,000

[a]Revenues include an extraordinary item of over $95 million, without which net income would be negative.

Massey-Ferguson Company of Canada, Ltd., Consolidated Balance Sheet as of October 31, 1979 (Thousands of Dollars)

Assets		Liabilities and Net Worth		
Current assets	$1,935,000	Current liabilities	$1,509,000	
Other assets	810,000	Long-term debt	658,000	
		Total debt		$2,167,000
		Preferred stock	$ 96,000	
		Common stock[a]	177,000	
		Retained earnings	305,000	
		Net worth		$ 578,000
Total assets	$2,745,000	Total claims		$2,745,000

[a]18,250,000 shares. Average stock price, 1979, was approximately $11.

Recall from Appendix B to Chapter 8 the Altman model of bankruptcy prediction utilizing discriminant analysis. Altman's discriminant function, Z, was found to be

$$Z = 0.012X_1 + 0.014X_2 + 0.033X_3 + 0.006X_4 + 0.999X_5,$$

where

$X_1 = $ Working capital/Total assets (in percent)
$X_2 = $ Retained earnings/Total assets (in percent)
$X_3 = $ EBIT/Total assets (in percent)
$X_4 = $ Market value of equity/Book value of debt (in percent)
$X_5 = $ Sales/Total assets (times).

a)   Apply the Altman model to the Massey-Ferguson data. What is the Z value for Massey-Ferguson?

b)   Does it appear likely that the firm will go bankrupt?

Selected References

Altman, Edward I., *Corporate Bankruptcy in America*, Lexington, Mass.: Heath Lexington Books, 1972, pp. 19-24.

————, and Nammacher, Scott A., "The Default Rate Experience on High Yield Corporate Debt," New York: Morgan Stanley & Co. Incorporated, 1985.

Altman, Edward I., and Spivack, Joseph, "Predicting Bankruptcy: The Value Line Relative Financial Strength System vs. the Zeta Bankruptcy Classification Approach," *Financial Analysts Journal*, 39 (November/December 1983), pp. 60-67.

Baldwin, Carliss Y., and Mason, Scott P., "The Resolution of Claims in Financial Distress: The Case of Massey Ferguson," *Journal of Finance*, 38 (May 1983), pp. 505-516.

Castagna, A. D., and Matolcsy, Z. P., "The Market Characteristics of Failed Companies: Extensions and Further Evidence," *Journal of Business Finance & Accounting*, 8 (Winter 1981), pp. 467-483.

Clark, Truman A., and Weinstein, Mark I., "The Behavior of the Common Stock of Bankrupt Firms," *Journal of Finance*, 38 (May 1983), pp. 489-504.

Gombola, Michael J., and Ketz, J. Edward, "A Caveat on Measuring Cash Flow and Solvency," *Financial Analysts Journal*, 39 (September/October 1983), pp. 66-72.

Richardson, Frederick M., and Davidson, Lewis F., "An Exploration into Bankruptcy Discriminant Model Sensitivity," *Journal of Business Finance & Accounting*, 10 (Summer 1983), pp. 195-207.

Scapens, Robert W.; Ryan, Robert J.; and Fletcher, Leslie, "Explaining Corporate Failure: A Catastrophe Theory Approach," *Journal of Business Finance & Accounting*, 8 (Spring 1981), pp. 1-26.

White, Michelle J., "Bankruptcy Costs and the New Bankruptcy Code," *Journal of Finance*, 38 (May 1983), pp. 477-488.

Chapter 32 International Business Finance

International financial developments are having an increased effect on people because all parts of the world are now more closely linked together than ever before. Communications throughout the world take place within a matter of minutes or even seconds. Jet airplanes can take people anywhere within a matter of hours. Realignment of the relative values of different countries' currencies is continually occurring. These international financial developments have been helpful to some and harmful to others. Although the relationships are complex, the fundamentals presented here will provide a basis for understanding the new opportunities and threats that result from the increasingly dynamic international environment.

The Importance of International Finance

International finance in recent years has taken on great significance. Widely fluctuating exchange rates have affected not only profits and losses from changes in foreign currency values but also the ability to sell abroad and to meet import competition. For example, suppose that a Japanese auto producer needs to receive 1.2 million yen per car to cover costs plus a required return on equity. At an exchange rate of 200 yen to the dollar, a rate which existed in the late 1970s, the Japanese producer would have to receive $6,000 for an automobile sold in the United States. When the exchange rate is 265 yen to the dollar, as existed in early 1985, dividing the 1.2 million yen by 265 tells us that the dollars required now are $4,528. Thus, the Japanese producer is in a position to either reduce his dollar price by approximately 25 percent and still receive the same number of yen or take higher profit margins on sales in the United States. Of course, the success of Japanese auto companies in the United States has not been completely due to changes in foreign exchange rates alone. Auto producers in Japan have achieved improved production processes that have resulted in greater productivity and high quality cars. But, exchange rate movements have also been a factor, as the above example illustrates.

From the standpoint of American companies selling products abroad, the rising value of the dollar in relation to foreign currencies has the opposite consequences. For example, suppose that an American producer is selling a product in the United Kingdom, and to meet competition, it has to be sold for 500 pounds. When the pound had a value of $2.25, as it did in the late 1970s, the dollar amount received by the U.S. seller would be $1,125. By March 1985, the value of the pound had fallen to $1.07. If the U.S. producer continued to sell the product for 500 pounds, he would now receive $535. If the original $1,125 represented a dollar price necessary to earn its cost of capital, the U.S. firm would find it difficult to survive with a price that had declined by more than 50 percent. Or alternatively, to continue to realize a dollar price of $1,125 at the exchange rate of $1.07 to the pound would require a new selling price of 1,051 pounds, a price increase of over 100 percent expressed in pounds. As a consequence, it is more difficult for U.S. firms to sell abroad, and it is much more attractive for foreign firms to sell in the United States.

These are not just hypothetical examples. They reflect the actual patterns of foreign exchange movements during recent years. One measure of this phenomenon we are describing is the trade-weighted index of the dollar's value measured against 15 major currencies using the 1980–1982 average value as a basis of 100. (The designation of the major currencies and their weights in the index is based on the country's exports.) At the end of 1980, the dollar's value was at an index level of 90. In February 1985, this index value had risen to 136, an increase of over 50 percent. Its consequences are reflected, from an overall standpoint, in the merchandise trade balance in 1983, which was a negative $61 billion. The negative trade balance for 1984 was $123.3 billion and is projected to be between $140 billion and $150 billion for 1985. However, by definition, the U.S. balance of payments must balance. In 1983, there was an offset to the large negative trade balance, represented by the change in foreign private assets in the United States, which increased by over $76 billion.

What appears to have been happening since 1980 is the following scenario: Large government budget deficits had to be financed with substantial amounts of U.S. private savings; the competition for private savings pushed up interest rates; high U.S. interest rates attracted inflows of foreign investments; to transfer funds to the U.S., foreigners had to convert their domestic currencies into U.S. dollars; the increase in the demand for dollars in the foreign exchange markets caused the international value of the dollar to rise; this appreciation in the foreign exchange value of the dollar caused the prices of U.S. products in the international markets to rise and the prices of foreign products in the United States to decline; U.S. exports slowed down and imports of foreign products accelerated; the U.S. trade balance deficit increased, requiring larger inflows of foreign capital to finance it; and budget deficits continued to be large, so the process has continued.

There have been upward and downward fluctuations in the value of the dollar in relation to the currencies of developed countries such as Japan and West Germany. For less developed countries, the movements have represented a one-way street as shown in Table 32.1. From 1954 through 1970, the value of the Mexican peso was stable at 12.5 pesos to

Table 32.1   Number of Foreign Currency Units per U.S. Dollar

	1965	1970	1975	1980	June 20, 1984	March 27, 1985
Japan X	360.90	357.60	305.15	215.45	234.25	255.40
E	0.00277	0.00280	0.00328	0.00464	0.00427	0.003915
Index	100	101	118	168	154	141
W. Germany X	4.00	3.65	2.62	1.76	2.7770	3.2090
E	0.2500	0.2740	0.3817	0.5682	0.3601	0.3116
Index	100	110	153	227	144	125
Mexico X	12.50	12.50	12.50	22.83	191.00	244.00
E	0.08	0.08	0.08	0.0438	.005236	.004098
Index	100	100	100	55	6.5	5.1
Brazil X	0.89	2.47	9.07	51.45	1600.0	4,270
E	1.1236	0.4049	0.1103	0.0194	.000625	.0002342
Index	100	36	10	2	.056	.021

X = Number of FC's (foreign currency units) per dollar.
E = Dollar value of one FC (foreign currency unit).
Index is of dollar value, with 1965 = 100.
Sources: International Monetary Fund, *International Financial Statistics*, monthly issues; and "Foreign Exchange," *Wall Street Journal*, June 21, 1984, p. 52; March 28, 1985, p. 49.

the U.S. dollar. Subsequent devaluations caused a continued erosion, so that by March 1985, 244 pesos were required for one dollar — the peso had declined from 8 U.S. cents in value to less than one-half of one cent. Similarly, for Brazil, the cruziero, which was approximately equal to a dollar in 1965, required by March 27, 1985, 4,270 cruzieros to equal one dollar.

Much concern has been expressed about the rising value of the dollar. Indeed, in early March 1985, the central banks of many of the western European countries aggressively sold dollars in the effort to bring down the dollar's value. They attempted to change the market psychology by making it clear that they were in the market to weaken the strength of the dollar. As one British banker stated it, referring to the Bank of England (which corresponds to our Federal Reserve Bank): "The Old Lady of Threadneedle Street wanted everyone to see her ankles." However, the impact of this intervention was already fading away in mid-March 1985, when the Home State Savings Bank of Cincinnati failed after losing an estimated $150 million when the Florida-based E.S.M. government securities company went bankrupt at least partly because of fraud. This wiped out the $136 million reserve of the Ohio Deposit Guarantee Fund. The governor of Ohio, as an emergency measure, temporarily closed the 71 state privately insured savings and loan associations. These events created uncertainty about the stability of the U.S. banking and financial system. The value of the dollar began to decline, and by March 27, 1985, the value of the British pound had moved up from its low of $1.07 to $1.21, a rise of over 13 percent in less than a month. What the mighty central banks of Europe were unable to achieve, a little Ohio S&L, linked to a relatively obscure Florida government securities firm, was able to do by raising doubts about the soundness of the U.S. economy.

Thus, changes in foreign currency values in relation to the dollar have been both substantial and uncertain. Most business firms, as well as individuals, have experienced some of the effects of these changes in currency values that have taken place and which are likely to continue to take place in the future — with magnitudes and directions of movements subject to considerable uncertainty. These changes have particularly severe effects on a manufacturing firm. Its inputs may include imported materials, and its products may be exported or become part of an exported product. Some large companies have earned more than half their profits abroad. Even for smaller companies, it is not uncommon to find that, if international sales can be developed to about one-fourth of total sales, then earnings from foreign sales or operations are likely to be as high as 40 to 50 percent of total earnings. International operations often enable the smaller firm to achieve better utilization of its investment in fixed plant and equipment.

Impact of Exchange Rate Fluctuations

A difference between international business finance and domestic business finance is that international transactions and investments are conducted in more than one currency. For example, when a U.S. firm sells goods to a French firm, the U.S. firm usually wants to be paid in dollars and the French firm usually expects to pay in francs. Because of the existence of a foreign exchange market in which individual dealers and many banks trade, the buyer can pay in one currency and the seller can receive payment in another.

Since different currencies are involved, a rate of exchange must be established between them. The conversion relationship of the currencies is expressed in terms of their price relationship. If foreign exchange rates did not fluctuate, it would make no difference whether firms dealt in dollars or any other currency. However, since exchange rates do fluctuate, firms are subject to exchange rate fluctuation risks if they have a net asset or net liability position in a foreign currency. When net claims exceed liabilities in a foreign currency, the firm is said to be in a "long" position, because it will benefit if the value of the foreign currency rises. When net liabilities exceed claims in regard to foreign currencies, the firm is said to be in a "short" position, because it will gain if the foreign currency declines in value.

Expressing Foreign Exchange Rates

The foreign exchange rate represents the conversion relationship between currencies and depends on demand and supply relationships between the two currencies. The foreign exchange rate is the price of one currency in terms of another. Exchange rates may be expressed in dollars per foreign currency unit or units of foreign currency per dollar. An exchange rate of $.50 to FC1 shows the value of one foreign currency unit in terms of the dollar. We shall use E_o to indicate the spot rate, E_f to indicate the forward rate at the present time, and E_1 to indicate the actual future spot rate corresponding to E_f.[1] An exchange rate of FC2 to $1 shows the value of the dollar in terms of the number of foreign currency units it will purchase. We will use the symbol X with corresponding subscripts to refer to the exchange rate expressed as the number of foreign currency units per dollar.

Measuring the Percentage of Devaluation or Revaluation

Assume that there has been a devaluation of the French franc from 3 per U.S. dollar to 4 per U.S. dollar. This can be expressed as the percentage change in the number of French francs required to purchase 1 U.S. dollar ($= D_{fd}$).

For example, where $X_o = 3$ and $X_1 = 4$,

$$\% \text{ change} = (X_1 - X_0)/X_0 = (4 - 3)/3 = \tfrac{1}{3}, \text{ or } 33\tfrac{1}{3}\% = D_{fd}.$$

There has been an increase of $33\tfrac{1}{3}$ percent in the number of French francs required to equal one U.S. dollar, which is a $33\tfrac{1}{3}$ percent appreciation in the franc value of the dollar.

To show the percentage change in the dollar value of the franc ($= D_{df}$),

$$E_o = \frac{1}{X_0} = \frac{1}{3} \text{ and } E_1 = \frac{1}{X_1} = \frac{1}{4}.$$

Now the percentage change is given by

$$\% \text{ change} = (E_o - E_1)/E_o = \left(\frac{1}{X_0} - \frac{1}{X_1}\right) \Big/ \frac{1}{X_0}$$

$$= (\tfrac{1}{3} - \tfrac{1}{4})/(\tfrac{1}{3}) = [(4 - 3)/12]/(\tfrac{1}{3}) = \tfrac{1}{4} = 25\% = D_{df}.$$

There has been a 25 percent decrease in the value of the franc in terms of the U.S. dollar, that is, there has been a 25 percent depreciation in the dollar value of the franc.

---

[1]Recall that a forward contract is a purchase or sale at a price specified now (the *forward rate*), with the transaction to take place at some future date.

Summary of Exchange-Rate Relationships

D_{fd} is the change in value in terms of FC/$:

$$D_{fd} = \frac{X_1 - X_0}{X_0} = \frac{\dfrac{1}{E_1} - \dfrac{1}{E_0}}{\dfrac{1}{E_0}} = \frac{E_0}{E_1} - 1 = \frac{E_0 - E_1}{E_1}.$$

D_{df} is the change in value in terms of $/FC:

$$D_{df} = \frac{E_0 - E_1}{E_0} = \frac{\dfrac{1}{X_0} - \dfrac{1}{X_1}}{\dfrac{1}{X_0}} = \frac{X_0}{X_0} - \frac{X_0}{X_1} = \frac{X_1 - X_0}{X_1}.$$

Because of the risks of exchange rate fluctuations, transactions have developed in a forward, or futures, foreign exchange market. This market enables a firm to hedge in an attempt to reduce the risk. Individuals also speculate by means of transactions in the forward market. Forward contracts are normally for a 30-, 60-, or 90-day period, although special contracts for longer periods can be arranged by negotiation.

The cost of this protection is the premium or discount of the forward contract over the current spot rate, which varies from 0 to 2 or 3 percent per year for currencies that are considered reasonably stable. For currencies undergoing devaluation in excess of 4 to 5 percent per year, the required discounts may be as high as 15 to 20 percent per year. When it is probable that future devaluations may exceed 20 percent per year, forward contracts are usually unavailable.

The magnitude of the premium or discount required depends on the forward expectations of the financial communities of the two countries involved and on the supply and demand conditions in the foreign exchange market. Since members of the financial communities are usually well informed about the expected forward exchange values of their respective currencies, the premiums or discounts quoted are very closely related to the probable occurrence of changes in the exchange rates.

Four basic relationships will be treated:

1. Consistent foreign exchange rates
2. The Fisher effect
3. The interest rate parity theorem (IRPT)
4. The purchasing power parity theorem (PPPT).

Consistent Foreign Exchange Rates

Equilibrating transactions take place when exchange rates are not in proper relationship with one another. This will be illustrated by some examples with unrealistically rounded numbers that make the arithmetic of the calculations simple. The right direction of analysis will be obtained if the reader remembers the general maxim that arbitrageurs will seek to sell high and to buy low. First, we will indicate the consistency of spot rates. Suppose the dollar value of the pound is $2 in New York City and $1.90 in London. The following adjustment actions would take place: In New York City, sell £190 for $380. Pounds are sold in New York because the pound value is high there. In London, sell $380 for £200. In London, the dollar value is high in relation to the pound. Thus, £190 sold in New York City for $380 can be used to buy £200 in London, a gain of £10. The sale of pounds in New York causes their value to decline in New York, and the purchase of pounds in London causes their value in London to rise until no further arbitrage opportunities remain. The same foreign exchange prices, assuming minimal transportation costs, would have to prevail in all locations.

The relations between two individual localities can be generalized across all countries. This is referred to as "consistent cross rates." It works in the following fashion: Assume that the equilibrium relation between the dollar and the pound is $2 to £1 and that the dollar to franc rate is $.25 to fr 1. Now, suppose that in New York City £.10 = fr 1. The following adjustment process would take place. Sell $200 for £100 used to obtain fr 1,000. The fr 1,000 will buy $250. This is a $50 profit over the initial $200. Sell dollars for pounds and pounds for francs, since the pound is overvalued with respect to both the dollar to pound and dollar to franc relationships. Dollars will fall in relation to the pound, and the pound will fall in relation to the franc until consistent cross rates obtain. If the relation were fr 1 = £.125, consistent cross rates would obtain. Check using the following relation:

$$\$1 = \pounds.5$$

$$\pounds1 = fr\ 8.00$$

$$fr\ 1 = \$.25.$$

The product of the right-hand sides of the three relationships must equal 1. Checking, we have $0.5 \times 8 \times 0.25 = 1$. We have thus established consistency between foreign exchange rates.

The Fisher Effect

The Fisher effect holds for the relationship between interest rates and the anticipated rate of inflation. While it can also be regarded as purely a relationship for a domestic economy, it is utilized in developing some of the international relationships we will consider. The Fisher effect states that nominal interest rates rise to reflect the anticipated rate of inflation. The Fisher effect can be stated in a number of forms, as shown below:[2]

$$\frac{P_0}{P_1} = \frac{1 + r}{1 + R_n}$$

$$1 + r = (1 + R_n)\frac{P_0}{P_1}$$

$$r = \left[(1 + R_n)\frac{P_0}{P_1}\right] - 1$$

$$R_n = \left[(1 + r)\frac{P_1}{P_0}\right] - 1,$$

---

[2]See Chapter 7 for further material on the Fisher effect.

where

$P_0 =$ initial price level
$P_1 =$ subsequent price level
$\dfrac{P_1}{P_0} =$ rate of inflation

$\dfrac{P_0}{P_1} =$ relative purchasing power of the currency unit

$r =$ real rate of interest
$R_n =$ nominal rate of interest

While the Fisher effect can be stated in a number of forms, its basic idea can be conveyed by a simple numerical example. Over a given period of time, if the price index is expected to rise by 10 percent and the real rate of interest is 7 percent, then the current nominal rate of interest is

$$R_n = [(1.07)(1.10)] - 1$$

$$= 17.7 \text{ percent.}$$

Similarly, if the nominal rate of interest is 12 percent and the price index is expected to rise by 10 percent over a given time period, the current real rate of interest is

$$r = \left[1.12\left(\frac{100}{110}\right)\right] - 1$$

$$= 1.018 - 1 = 0.018 = 1.8 \text{ percent.}$$

The Interest Rate Parity Theorem (IRPT)

The interest rate parity theorem is an extension of the Fisher effect to international markets. It holds that the ratio of the forward and spot exchange rates will equal the ratio of foreign and domestic gross interest rates.[3] The formal statement of the interest rate parity theorem can be expressed as follows:

$$\frac{X_f}{X_0} = \frac{1 + R_{f0}}{1 + R_{d0}} = \frac{E_0}{E_f},$$

where

$X_f =$ current forward exchange rate expressed as FC units per \$1
$E_f =$ current forward exchange rate expressed as dollars per FC1
$X_0 =$ current spot exchange rate expressed as FC units per \$1
$E_0 =$ current spot exchange rate expressed as dollars per FC1
$R_{f0} =$ current nominal foreign interest rate
$R_{d0} =$ current nominal domestic interest rate.

---

[3]These relations are further clarified by Problem 32.14.

Thus, if the foreign interest rate is 15 percent while the domestic interest rate is 10 percent and the spot exchange rate is $X_0 = 10$, the predicted current forward exchange rate will be

<table>
<tr><td>Annual basis:</td><td>Quarterly basis:</td></tr>
<tr><td>$$X_f = \frac{1 + R_{f0}}{1 + R_{d0}}(X_0)$$</td><td>$$X_f = \frac{1 + R_{f0}/4}{1 + R_{d0}/4}(X_0)$$</td></tr>
<tr><td>$$= \frac{1.15}{1.10}(10)$$</td><td>$$= \frac{1.0375}{1.025}(10)$$</td></tr>
<tr><td>$$= 10.45$$</td><td>$$= 10.122.$$</td></tr>
</table>

Thus, the indicated foreign forward rate is 10.45 units of foreign currency per $1, and the foreign forward rate is at a discount of 4.5 percent on an annual basis. If the time period of a transaction is 90 days, we have to rework the problem, first changing the interest rates to a quarterly basis. The discount on the 90-day forward rate would now be 1.22 percent on the quarterly basis, since the 90-day forward rate would be 10.122.

Alternatively, the example could be formulated for the effect on interest rates of expected changes in future foreign exchange rates. Here is a dynamic relationship that needs to be recognized: If the foreign exchange rate is expected to rise over a period of time, relative interest rates will reflect the rate of change expected in the foreign exchange rates. This is illustrated in Figure 32.1.

The figure shows that as the value of the foreign currency falls (the exchange rate expressed in the number of foreign currency units per dollar rises), the ratio of foreign interest rates to domestic interest rates rises. At the inflection point of the rise in the expected number of foreign currency units per dollar, the ratio of foreign interest rates to domestic interest rates peaks. When the expected ratio of the number of foreign currency

Figure 32.1   Illustration of the Interest Rate Parity Theorem

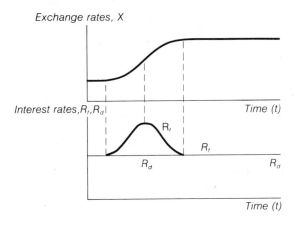

units per domestic currency unit levels off, then the former ratio of foreign interest rates to domestic interest rates is reestablished.

We could also use the interest rate parity theorem to express the results in terms of the interest rate parities required for given relationships between spot and future exchange rates. The transactions that result in interest rate parity are referred to as *covered interest arbitrage*. The basic facts of an *arbitrage outflow* situation are

$$\text{U.S. interest rate} = 5\%$$

$$\text{German interest rate} = 7\%$$

$$\text{Spot exchange rate } \$1 = \text{DM4}$$

$$\text{Forward exchange rate discount} = 1\%.$$

The following arbitrage transaction will take place. In New York, borrow $100,000 for 90 days (one-fourth year) at 5 percent. The loan repayment at the end of 90 days is $100,000 [1 + (0.05/4)] = $101,250. At the spot exchange rate, convert the $100,000 loan into DM400,000. In Germany, invest the DM400,000 for 90 days at 7 percent. Receive at the end of 90 days DM400,000 [1 + (0.07/4)] = DM407,000.

A covering transaction is also made. To insure against adverse changes in the spot rate during the 90-day investment period, sell investment proceeds forward. Since the forward exchange rate discount is 1 percent, then 4[1 + (0.01/4)] = DM4.01 is required to exchange for $1, in 90 days (forward). Sell investment proceeds forward; that is, contract to receive DM407,000 ÷ 4.01 = $101,496.

$$\text{Arbitrage profits} = \text{Investment receipts} - \text{Loan payments}$$

$$= \$101,496 - \$101,250$$

$$= \$246.$$

The arbitrage transaction increases the *demand* for currency in New York and increases the *supply* of funds in Germany. This raises the interest rate in New York and lowers it in Germany, thus narrowing the differential. The covering transaction increases the supply of German forward exchange, while the arbitrage investment action increases the demand for spot funds. Both forces tend to increase the forward exchange discount. The interest rate differential decreases and the forward rate discount increases until both are equalized, and arbitrage profits are eliminated.

An *arbitrage inflow* takes place when the forward exchange rate discount exceeds the interest rate differential. The basic facts are now

$$\text{U.S. interest rate} = 5\%$$

$$\text{German interest rate} = 6\%$$

$$\text{Spot exchange rate DM4} = \$1$$

$$\text{Forward exchange rate discount} = 2\%.$$

The arbitrage transaction involves borrowing in the foreign country. In Germany, borrow DM400,000 for 90 days at 6 percent. The loan repayment at the end of 90 days is DM400,000 [1 + (0.06/4)] = DM406,000. At the spot exchange rate, convert the

DM400,000 loan into $100,000. In New York, invest the $100,000 for 90 days at 5 percent. Receive at the end of 90 days $100,000 [1 + (0.05/4)] = $101,250.

Again, a covering transaction would be made. To insure coverage for the loan repayment, buy DM406,000 forward. At a 2 percent forward exchange rate discount, it costs DM4[1 + (0.02/4)] = DM4.02 to buy $1 forward. Thus, to repay the DM406,000 with a certain amount of dollars requires DM406,000 ÷ 4.02 = $100,995.

$$\text{Arbitrage profits} = \text{Investment receipts} - \text{Loan repayments}$$

$$= \$101,250 - \$100,995$$

$$= \$255.$$

The arbitrage transaction increases the *demand* for DM and increases the *supply* of dollars. The U.S. interest rate decreases and the German rate rises; thus, the differential increases. Covering transactions increase the spot supply of DM, thus decreasing the premium on forward DM. The interest rate differential and the forward exchange rate discount decrease until both rates are equalized.

As a result of the covered interest arbitrage transactions of the types described, the relationships depicted by the interest rate parity theorem would obtain. This relationship determines the home-currency cost that would be involved when a purchase or sale is made and a future payment or receipt is involved.

The Purchasing Power Parity Theorem (PPPT)

The purchasing power parity doctrine states that currencies will be valued for what they will buy. If an American dollar buys the same basket of goods and services as five units of a foreign currency, we have an exchange rate of five foreign currency units to the dollar or 20 cents per foreign currency unit. An attempt to compare price indexes to computed purchasing power parity assumes that it is possible to compile comparable baskets of goods in different countries. As a practical matter, the parity rate is, in general, estimated from changes in the purchasing power of two currencies with reference to some past base period when the exchange rate was theoretically in equilibrium. In formal terms, the PPPT may be stated as follows:

$$CX = \frac{X_1}{X_0} = \frac{P_{f1}/P_{f0}}{P_{d1}/P_{d0}} = RPC$$

where

$$\frac{X_1}{X_0} = \frac{E_0}{E_1},$$

$X_0 = $ FC units per dollar now,

$X_1 = $ FC units per dollar one period later,

$$E_0 = \frac{1}{X_0} = \text{dollars per FC unit now,}$$

$$E_1 = \frac{1}{X_1} = \text{dollars per FC unit one period later,}$$

$$CX = \frac{X_1}{X_0} = \text{change in exchange rate,}$$

$P_{f0} = $ initial price level in the foreign country,

P_{f1} = foreign country price level one period later,
P_{d0} = initial domestic price level,
P_{d1} = domestic price level one period later,

RPC = $\dfrac{P_{f1}/P_{f0}}{P_{d1}/P_{d0}}$ = change in relative prices = ratio of inflation rates.

A few numerical examples will illustrate some of the implications of the purchasing power parity doctrine. Let us assume that for a given period, foreign price levels have risen by 32 percent while domestic price levels have risen by 20 percent. If the initial exchange rate is FC 10 to $1, the subsequent new exchange rate will be

$$\frac{1.32}{1.20} = \frac{X_1}{10}, \qquad X_1 = 1.1(10) = 11.$$

It will now take 10 percent more foreign currency units to equal $1, because the relative inflation rate has been higher in the foreign country. Alternatively, with an exchange rate of FC 10 to $1, let us assume that foreign prices have risen by 17 percent while domestic prices have risen by 30 percent. The new expected exchange rate would be

$$\frac{1.17}{1.30} = \frac{X_1}{10}, \qquad X_1 = .9(10) = 9.$$

In the present instance, the number of foreign currency units needed to buy $1 would drop by 10 percent. Thus, the value of the foreign currency has increased by 10 percent due to the differential rates of inflation in domestic versus foreign prices.

Empirical studies indicate that while the purchasing power parity relationship does not hold perfectly, it tends to hold in the long run. More fundamentally, the doctrine predicts that an equilibrium rate between two currencies will reflect market forces and that random deviations from the central tendency will tend to be self-correcting; that is, it suggests the existence of some strong equilibrating forces. Furthermore, it argues that the relations between exchange rates will not be haphazard but will reflect underlying economic conditions and changes in these conditions. The relationships are not precise because of a number of factors. These include (1) differences in incomes or other endowments between the two countries, (2) differences in government monetary and fiscal policies, (3) large capital movements motivated by changes in relative political risks or differences in prospective economic opportunities, (4) transportation costs, (5) lags in market responses, (6) differences between the two countries in the price ratios of internationally traded goods to domestically traded goods, (7) the impact of risk premium influences.

Risk Position of the Firm in Foreign Currency Units

The risk position of a firm in relation to possible fluctuations in foreign exchange rates can be clarified by referring to expected receipts or obligations in foreign currency units. If a firm is expecting receipts in foreign currency units (if it is "long" in the foreign currency units), its risk is that the value of the foreign currency units will fall (devaluing the foreign currency in relation to the dollar). If a firm has obligations in foreign currency units (if it is "short" in the foreign currency units), its risk is that the value of the foreign currency will rise and it will have to buy the currency to repay the obligations at a higher price.

Methods of Dealing with the Risk of a Decline in Foreign Currency Values

A brief example will illustrate methods of taking protective action against a decline in the value of a foreign currency. On September 1, 1984, the USP Company makes a sale of goods to a foreign firm; it will receive FC 380,000 (payment in local or foreign currency units) on December 1, 1984. The USP Company has incurred costs in dollars and is considering three alternatives to deal with exchange rate fluctuation. The first alternative is to enter the forward market to sell FC 380,000 for dollars at the 90-day forward rate quoted on September 1, 1984. The company can then utilize the FC 380,000 it receives on December 1, 1984, to pay for the dollars it has contracted to buy at the 90-day forward rate. Under this arrangement, the company will receive a definite amount in dollars in December as determined by the forward rate on September 1.

The second alternative is to borrow now from a foreign bank the FC amount such that the principal plus interest will equal what the company will be receiving on December 1. The interest rate paid is 28 percent. By borrowing, the company will receive the FC's immediately, and with them it can immediately purchase dollars at the September spot rate. It can then invest the dollars received in the United States at an 8 percent interest rate. When the company receives the FC 380,000 in December, it can use the funds to liquidate the local currency loan incurred in September. (The effective tax rate in both countries is 40 percent.)

The third alternative is to make no attempt to cover the exchange risk involved in waiting the three months for receipt of the FC 380,000. Under this alternative, the USP Company will convert the FC 380,000 into dollars at whatever spot rate prevails on December 1, 1984.

The three alternatives will be analyzed for a pattern of actual spot and forward exchange rates on September 1, 1984, and the expected spot rate on December 1, 1984. First to be considered is the pattern of rates characteristic of countries subject to currency devaluation:

	September 1, 1984
Spot rate of foreign currency units per $1.00	FC 1.90
90-day forward rate	FC 2.00

	December 1, 1984
Expected future spot rate	FC 2.10

The three alternatives can now be analyzed. The first alternative involves entering a forward contract in which the USP Company sells FC 380,000 for dollars at a rate of 2 FC to $1.00. Therefore, the company has contracted to receive $190,000. At the spot rate, it would have received $200,000, so a reduction of expected sales revenue of $10,000 has been incurred, providing a tax shelter of $4,000. Thus, total receipts and taxes saved amounts to $194,000.

Under the second alternative, the USP Company borrows FC from a bank in the foreign country; the amount of FC plus interest equals the FC 380,000 that will be received in December. The company will have to pay interest at 28 percent on the loan obtained from the foreign bank. Since the loan is for 90 days, or one-fourth of a year, the 28 percent is divided by four to obtain 7 percent, which is then multiplied by $(1 - T)$, for a total of 4.2 percent, the after-tax interest rate. Since the required proceeds, Q, are:

$$1.042Q = FC\ 380,000,$$

$$Q = FC\ 364,683.$$

At the spot exchange rate, the proceeds from the FC 364,683 divided by 1.90 equals $191,938, and this amount can be invested in the United States to earn an 8 percent annual rate for 90 days, or 2 percent times $(1 - T)$, which equals 1.2 percent. The proceeds of $191,938 times 1.012 equal $194,241. On December 1, 1984, USP will receive the FC 380,000, which it will use to repay the FC 380,000 principal plus interest on its FC loan.

Under the third alternative, on December 1, 1984, the FC 380,000 will be converted into dollars at the spot rate then in effect. This represents FC 380,000 divided by 2.10, or $180,952. The expected $180,952 involves a reduction in taxable sales revenue of $19,048, so net proceeds with the tax shelter are $180,952 plus 0.4 times $19,048, which equals $188,571.

The net proceeds received under the three alternatives are

1.	Sell FC in forward market for dollars	$194,000
2.	Borrow FC and repay from FC received in future	194,241
3.	Receive dollars based on spot rate when FC funds received	188,571

Under the assumptions of this example, the second alternative provides the greatest amount of funds. But disequilibrium conditions and different degrees of uncertainty are associated with each of the three alternatives.

Before the fact, it is not possible to state definitely which alternative will yield the largest number of dollars on December 1, 1984. It depends on the future level of the spot rate on that date. Suppose that the actual spot rate on that December 1 turns out to be exactly what it was on September 1, 1984. In this situation, the first two alternatives will be unchanged, but for the third alternative, 380,000 divided by 1.90 equals $200,000— making it the best choice. But, under the original assumptions, the third alternative was the worst choice. Thus, doing nothing under the new set of assumed data turns out to be the best course of action, although it is clearly the riskiest. The use of the forward market or borrowing and investing through the money markets will sometimes yield lower net proceeds than taking no protective actions whatsoever will do, but having an unprotected position with respect to foreign exchange rate fluctuations is the greatest risk.

Using the forward market or borrowing is a form of insurance taken out to protect against unexpected fluctuations in foreign exchange rates. Like other forms of insurance, the protection involves a cost. But, the situation is similar to that of buying fire insurance on your house. You could save the money if you could be sure that a fire were not going to occur. If you have paid fire insurance for several years and no fire has occurred, you could have saved money by not buying the fire insurance. But, you paid the money to protect against the loss that would have taken place if the unexpected fire had occurred. Similarly, the cost of forward hedging or borrowing is a form of insurance premium paid to avoid even larger losses. Note that foreign exchange risk is reduced by using the forward market or by borrowing, but the business risks of changing price and cost relations still remain as well as the purchasing power risk of the domestic currency.

Protection against Rising Values of Foreign Currencies

When a foreign currency is rising in value, the U.S. firm has a risk exposure if it is in a short position with respect to the foreign currency. This means that if the firm has payments to be made in foreign currency or has liabilities outstanding that are expressed in such units, a rise in the value of the foreign currency unit will require that more dollars be used to buy it after it has risen in value. Or, to put it another way, if the firm has future obligations that are expressed in foreign currency units, its risk exposure is from the potential rise in the value of those units. The procedures to deal with the foreign exchange risk of rising foreign currency values would be the opposite of those described in the previous section.

Monetary Balance

Firms must take protective actions not only in regard to future expected receipts or obligations but also against a long or short position in foreign currencies resulting from the balance sheet position of their foreign subsidiaries. In the example of USP Company, the sale of the goods for FC 380,000 represented an account receivable for the three months until the obligation was paid. Suppose, however, that the number of FC's per $1 had risen from 1.90 to 2.00. At 1.90 FC's per $1, the account receivable would have been worth $200,000 in U.S. currency. But, at the lower value of the FC's, 2FC to $1, the account receivable would have been worth only $190,000. This represents a before-tax loss of $10,000 in the dollar value of the receivables.

Conversely, if a firm had an account payable of FC 380,000, an upward change in the FC value from FC 2.00 to FC 1.90 per $1, would result in a loss because the accounts payable expressed in dollars would have increased by $10,000. Hence, the concept of monetary balance comes into consideration. *Monetary balance* involves avoiding either a net receivable or a net payable position. Monetary assets and liabilities are those items whose value, expressed in local currency, does not change with devaluation or revaluation. To illustrate:

Monetary Assets	Monetary Liabilities
Cash	Accounts payable
Marketable securities	Notes payable
Accounts receivable	Tax liability reserve
Tax refunds receivable	Bonds
Notes receivable	Preferred stock
Prepaid insurance	

What is referred to as a firm's monetary position is another way of stating the firm's position with regard to real assets. For example, the basic balance sheet equation can be written as follows:

$$\text{Monetary assets} + \text{Real assets} = \text{Monetary liabilities} + \text{Net worth.}$$

Consider the following pattern of relationships:

	Monetary Assets	+	Real Assets	=	Monetary Liabilities	+	Net Worth
Firm A: Monetary creditor	$6,000		$4,000		$4,000		$6,000
Firm B: Monetary debtor	4,000		6,000		6,000		4,000

Firm A is a monetary creditor because its monetary assets exceed its monetary liabilities; its net worth position is negative with respect to its investment coverage of net worth by real assets. In contrast, Firm B is a monetary debtor because it has monetary liabilities that exceed its monetary assets; its net worth coverage by investment in real assets is positive. Thus, the monetary creditor can be referred to as a firm with a negative position in real assets and the monetary debtor as a firm with a positive position in real assets. From the foregoing, we can see that the following relationships are equivalent:

Firm A	(Long position in foreign currency)	≡	Monetary creditor	≡	Monetary assets exceed monetary liabilities	≡	Negative position in real assets	≡	Balance of receipts in foreign currency less obligations in foreign currency is *positive*
Firm B	(Short position in foreign currency)	≡	Monetary debtor	≡	Monetary liabilities exceed monetary assets	≡	Positive position in real assets	≡	Balance of receipts in foreign currency less obligations in foreign currency is *negative*

Thus, if Firm A has a long position in a foreign currency, on balance, it will be receiving more funds in foreign currency, or it will have a net monetary asset position that exceeds its monetary liabilities in that currency. The opposite holds for Firm B, which is in a short position with respect to a foreign currency.

A firm with net receipts is a net monetary creditor, its foreign exchange rate risk exposure is vulnerable to a decline in value of the foreign currency. Conversely, a firm with net future obligations in foreign currency is in a net monetary debtor position. The foreign exchange risk exposure it faces is the possibility of an increase in the value of the foreign currency. The alternative methods of protection against foreign exchange fluctuations discussed earlier with respect to accounts receivable also apply to the short or long balance sheet position a firm may have with respect to foreign currency.

In addition to the specific actions of hedging in the forward market or borrowing and lending through the money markets, other business policies can help the firm achieve a balance sheet position that minimizes the foreign exchange rate risk exposure to either currency devaluation or currency revaluation upward. Specifically, in countries whose currency values are likely to fall, local management of subsidiaries should be encouraged to follow these policies:

1. Never have excessive idle cash on hand. If cash accumulates, it should be used to purchase inventory or other real assets.
2. Attempt to avoid granting excessive trade credit or trade credit for extended periods. If accounts receivable cannot be avoided, an attempt should be made to charge interest high enough to compensate for the loss of purchasing power.
3. Wherever possible, avoid giving advances in connection with purchase orders unless a rate of interest is paid by the seller on these advances from the time the subsidiary — the buyer — pays them until the time of delivery, at a rate sufficient to cover the loss of purchasing power.

4.   Borrow local currency funds from banks or other sources whenever these funds can be obtained at a rate of interest no higher than U.S. rates adjusted for the anticipated rate of devaluation in the foreign country.
5.   Make an effort to purchase materials and supplies on a trade credit basis in the country in which the foreign subsidiary is operating, extending the final date of payment as long as possible.

The opposite policies should be followed in a country where a revaluation upward in foreign currency values is likely to take place. All these policies are aimed at a monetary balance position in which the firm is neither a monetary debtor nor a monetary creditor. Some firms take a more aggressive position. They seek to have a net monetary debtor position in a country whose exchange rates are expected to fall and a net monetary creditor position in a country whose exchange rates are likely to rise.

Some writers have expressed reservations on whether a firm should try to hedge against foreign currency risk (Cornell and Shapiro [1983], p. 25). Several reasons have been given for this view. First, the real impact of nominal currency changes will be reduced by the offsetting effects of relative inflation. Second, shareholders can reduce foreign exchange risks by holding well-diversified portfolios. Third, shareholders may prefer that a portion of their returns be denominated in a foreign currency since their overall risk will be reduced by having foreign currency inflows to match their foreign currency outflows resulting from the purchase of foreign goods. Fourth, hedging is expensive since the simple strategy of forward hedging in the major currencies costs about 0.65 percent per year. Fifth, borrowing in local currencies is usually even more costly than forward hedging when points and other fees are taken into account. But, local borrowing often is the only alternative available, because active forward markets exist in fewer than a dozen currencies. Sixth, management cannot hedge against *anticipated* movements in exchange rates since they are already reflected in the forward premium and in the interest rate differentials. Hedging may provide partial protection against foreign exchange risks resulting from unanticipated fluctuations in foreign currency values.

Translation of Financial Statements

When the parent company's ownership of a subsidiary exceeds 50 percent and the contribution of the subsidiary is substantial in relation to that parent company, the subsidiary is likely to consolidate its financial statements into those of the parent. When consolidation takes place, the statements of the foreign subsidiary must be translated from the local currency of account into the currency used by the parent.

A number of alternative principles of translation of financial statements from one currency into another have developed over time. The current-noncurrent approach translates current assets and liabilities at current exchange rates. Other accounts are translated at historical exchange rates. The monetary-nonmonetary approach translates monetary items at current exchange rates and nonmonetary items at historical exchange rates. The temporal method was first introduced in Accounting Research Study Number 12 of the American Institute of Certified Public Accountants in 1972. It was also adopted in FASB Statement No. 8 in 1976.

The temporal method modifies the monetary-nonmonetary approach in considering the valuation basis of assets and liabilities. For example, inventories valued on the last-in-first-out (LIFO) principle are likely to be carried on the balance sheet at historical costs, since the most recent movements into inventories are charged to the income statement. Hence, historical foreign exchange rates would be applied to the inventories carried at historical

Table 32.2   Alternative Methods of Currency Translation (Millions of Dollars)

Forsub Company, S. A. Balance Sheet as of December 31, 19X4	In Local Currency Accounts	Current-Noncurrent Method		Monetary-Nonmonetary Method		Temporal Method	
		Exchange Rate	Amount	Exchange Rate	Amount	Exchange Rate	Amount
Cash	FC 400	5	$ 80	5	$ 80	5	$ 80
Accounts receivable	1,000	5	200	5	200	5	200
Inventory[a]	2,000	5	400	4	500	5	400
Total current assets	3,400		$ 680		$ 780		$ 680
Investments, nonmonetary	1,200	4	$ 300	4	$ 300	4	$ 300
Gross plant and equipment	10,000	4	2,500	4	2,500	4	2,500
Reserve for depreciation	4,000	4	1,000	4	1,000	4	1,000
Net plant and equipment	6,000	4	1,500	4	1,500	4	1,500
Total assets	FC 10,600		$2,480		$2,580		$2,480
Accounts payable	FC 400	5	$ 80	5	$ 80	5	$ 80
Notes payable	600	5	120	5	120	5	120
Accruals	400	5	80	5	80	5	80
Total current liabilities	1,400		280		280		280
Bonds outstanding	1,600	4	400	5	320	5	320
Common stock	4,000	4	1,000	4	1,000	4	1,000
Retained earnings	3,600	4	900	4	900	4	900
Revaluation account			(100)		80		(20)
Total liabilities and capital	FC 10,600	·	$2,480		$2,580		$2,480

[a]Assuming the FIFO method of inventory accounting.

costs. This would coincide with the monetary-nonmonetary translation approach. On the other hand, if inventory valuation is based on the first-in-first-out (FIFO) principle, the balance sheet will reflect inventories acquired at the most recent dates. Hence, the temporal method would translate the balance sheet inventory account at current exchange rates rather than historical exchange rates when first-in-first-out inventory accounting is used. The foregoing concepts can be clarified by use of an illustrative case.

The Forsub Company, S. A., a subsidiary of the Multinat Company, a U.S. firm, is operating in an inflationary country. The first column of Table 32.2 presents its balance sheet expressed in local currency units. A year ago, the exchange rate of the host country's currency was FC4 per $1. It is now FC5 per $1. The host government permits write-up of assets on an annual basis. This is accomplished every January in line with the rate of inflation during the prior year. For this reason, the proper historical exchange rate is the one in effect at the beginning of the year. For the sake of simplicity, it is assumed that the firm uses an average rate of FC4.5 per $1 for profit and loss statement purposes.

First, we shall illustrate translation by the current-noncurrent method and then by the monetary-nonmonetary method. The relationship to the temporal method will then be indicated.

Note that the revaluation account is negative under the current-noncurrent and temporal methods but is positive under the monetary-nonmonetary method. While the revaluation account serves as a balancing figure for the balance sheet, it can also be independently derived as follows.

Under the monetary-nonmonetary approach, the net monetary position (NMP) of the firm is equal to monetary assets (MA) less monetary liabilities (ML).

$$NMP = MA - ML$$
$$= 400 + 1,000 - (400 + 600 + 400 + 1,600)$$
$$= 1,400 - 3,000 = -1,600.$$

This net monetary liability position is favorable under the existing conditions of devaluation. The change in value of the monetary assets and liabilities in terms of the U.S. dollar due to translation is therefore calculated as

$$Change = NMP\left(\frac{1}{X_1} - \frac{1}{X_0}\right)$$
$$= -1,600\left(\frac{1}{5} - \frac{1}{4}\right)$$
$$= -1,600\left(-\frac{1}{20}\right) = +80.$$

This represents a net gain of $80 million in net worth due to the decrease in the dollar value of the net monetary liabilities, and it results in this amount being added to the revaluation reserve. The revaluation account can likewise be determined for the current-noncurrent approach.

$$Net\ current\ position = CA - CL$$
$$= 3,400 - 1,400$$
$$= 2,000.$$
$$Change = NCP\left(\frac{1}{X_1} - \frac{1}{X_0}\right)$$
$$= 2,000\left(\frac{1}{5} - \frac{1}{4}\right)$$
$$= -100.$$

The temporal method takes into account the valuation basis of the assets. Forsub uses the FIFO method of inventory accounting. Under this method, the oldest inventories are charged out first, and the balance sheet values will reflect the most current inventory cost. Hence, the current exchange rate would be used for translation. In this way the temporal method modifies the monetary method. Under the temporal method the exposure is $20 million, shown as a negative amount in the revaluation account.

If LIFO had been the method of inventory accounting, the balance sheet value of inventory would reflect historical costs. Hence, the historical exchange rate would be

Table 32.3 Income Statement for the Year Ended December 31, 19X4 (Millions of Dollars)

				Exchange Rate		Dollar Amount
Sales, net			FC 5,400	4.5		$1,200
Cost of sales:						
Inventory charge-outs[a]	FC	400		4	100	
Depreciation		600		4	150	
Other costs		2,025		4.5	450	
Cost of sales			3,025			700
Gross operating profit			2,375			$ 500
Selling, general and						
administrative expense			900	4.5		200
Net operating profit			1,475			$ 300
Interest expense			200	5		40
Earnings before taxes			1,275			$ 260
Income taxes at 40%			510	5		102
Earnings after taxes			FC 765			$ 158

[a]Assuming the FIFO method of inventory accounting.

applicable for translation. Under these circumstances, the temporal method would give the same result as the monetary-nonmonetary method for the facts of this particular case.

Translation of the income statement for the foreign subsidiary is presented in Table 32.3. Sales, selling, general and administrative expenses, and other costs are translated at the average exchange rate in effect during the year, 4.5 foreign currency units to the dollar. Inventory charge-outs are translated at the historical exchange rate, since the FIFO method of inventory accounting is employed. Depreciation is translated at the historical exchange rate that is used to translate the plant and equipment account to which the depreciation item relates. Interest expense is translated at the average rate of 4.5 because, like other categories of revenues and costs, it is developing over the entire period covered by the income statement. Note that where exchange rates are not shown for an item (as in the subtotals), the dollar amount is found merely by summing or subtracting the translated cost and revenue figures. Also, the 40 percent tax rate is applied to the FC earnings before taxes and then translated at the appropriate exchange rate, resulting in a slightly lower than 40 percent rate on earnings expressed in dollars.

Among the alternative methods of financial translation, we believe that accounting practice had been moving in the right direction. The current-noncurrent approach called for translation of long-term debt at the old exchange rates. This procedure involved a logical error because the long-term debt obligation was expressed in foreign currency units. With fluctuations in exchange rates, the current dollar value in relation to the foreign currency has changed from the historical dollars received; therefore, a gain or loss has actually taken place. The temporal method recommended by FASB Statement No. 8 represents a logical extension of the monetary rule. This method of international financial translation provides internally consistent and meaningful financial results.

FASB 8 and FASB 52

In December 1981, the Financial Accounting Standards Board (FASB) issued FASB No. 52, *Foreign Currency Translation*, superseding FASB No. 8, which had been issued in 1976. In general, translation gains or losses are carried directly to the equity account on the balance sheet and do not affect net income. Individual transactions gains or losses net of hedging costs and net of translation gains or losses do enter into the calculations which determine net income. Also, the method of translation is changed from the temporal method to the use of the current exchange rate for all balance sheet items and the use of the average exchange rate for the period for the income statement. However, the temporal method will continue to be applied to operations in highly inflationary economies, defined as those in which the price level doubles within a three-year period of time. The two methods are now illustrated by a numerical example.[4]

In this example, the Canadian subsidiary of a U.S. company with a Canadian dollar functional currency started business and acquired fixed assets at the beginning of the year when the value of the Canadian dollar in U.S. dollars was $.95 (U.S.). The average exchange rate for the period was $.90, the rate at the end of the period was $.85, and the historical rate for inventory was $.91. The LIFO inventory valuation method is employed.

The different methods are illustrated in Table 32.4. The temporal method used in FASB 8 (and for inflationary economies in FASB 52) applies the current (end-of-period) rate to monetary assets and liabilities. It uses the applicable historical rates for the nonmonetary assets and liabilities. Since LIFO is used, the balance sheet inventory account reflects historical costs, and the historical rate for inventories is used. In the income statement, the applicable average rates are applied to all items except cost of goods sold and depreciation. Depreciation expense in the income statement would employ the same rate as fixed assets on the balance sheet.

In contrast, FASB 52 applies the current rate to all balance sheet items except common stock, to which the historical rate is applied. The average rate is applied to all income statement items. The net income figure that results is reflected in the translated retained earnings account. Total assets and claims are brought into balance by a translation adjustment account.

The use of the current method of FASB 52 results in financial ratios that are unchanged from their relationships in the foreign currency before translation. This is claimed to be an advantage of the new method. But, if the underlying reality is a change in the ratios, preserving them is a distortion. The logic of the temporal method captures the underlying economic determinants of exposure, as demonstrated in the previous discussion of the net monetary creditor or debtor position of the foreign subsidiary. It is difficult to discern the economic logic for the application of the current method prescribed by FASB 52.

More fundamentally, exchange risk cannot be really measured by accounting numbers. In an economic sense, exchange risk is measured by the forecasted relation between exchange rates and changes in the patterns of real cash flows to the firm (Cornell and Shapiro [1983]). Exchange rate changes reflect price level and interest rate level changes. Hence, the behavior of a firm's costs in relation to its prices translated to its home currency will have a major influence on its profit position. This is the flow aspect. The stock aspect is the effect of currency value fluctuations on its monetary-nonmonetary balance sheet position.

---

[4]Taken from Peat, Marwick, Mitchell & Co., *Statement of Financial Accounting Standards No. 52, Foreign Currency Translation*, 1981.

Table 32.4   Translation of Canadian Subsidiary Financial Statements — 1981

Balance sheet	Canadian Dollars	FASB 8 Rates Used	FASB 8 U.S. Dollars	FASB 52 Rates Used	FASB 52 U.S. Dollars
Cash and receivables, net	100	.85	$ 85	.85	$ 85
Inventory	300	.91	273	.85	255
Fixed assets, net	600	.95	570	.85	510
	1,000		$928		$850
Current liabilities	180	.85	$153	.85	$153
Long-term debt	700	.85	595	.85	595
Stockholders' equity					
Common stock	100	.95	95	.95	95
Retained earnings	20		85		18
Equity adjustment from foreign currency translation	—		—		(11)
	1,000		$928		$850
Income statement					
Revenue	130	.90	$117	.90	$117
Cost of goods sold	(60)	.93[a]	(56)	.90	(54)
Depreciation	(20)	.95[a]	(19)	.90	(18)
Other expenses, net	(10)	.90	(9)	.90	(9)
Foreign exchange gain	—		70		—
Income before taxes	40		$103		$36
Income taxes	(20)	.90	(18)	.90	(18)
Net income	20		$ 85		$ 18
Ratios					
Net income to revenue	.15		.73		.15
Gross profit	.54		.52		.54
Debt to equity	5.83		3.31		5.83

[a]Historical rates for cost of goods sold and depreciation of fixed assets.
Source: Peat, Marwick, Mitchell and Company, *Statement of Financial Accounting Standards, No. 52, Foreign Currency Translation*, December 1981, p. 52, reprinted with permission. © 1981 by Peat Marwick.

International Financing

The general principles affecting financing decisions are the same for international financing as for domestic financing. However, the variables affecting international financing decisions are expanded, and the number of financing methods and sources is increased. The forms and sources of financing are similar in the different countries of the world, but important differences provide new pitfalls and additional opportunities. A wider range of alternatives must be evaluated in both quantitative and qualitative terms in choosing among alternative sources, forms, and localities of international financing. Financing in an international setting makes use of the increasingly important international financing markets — the Eurocurrency and Eurobond markets. The facilities of private lending institutions are augmented substantially by international lending agencies, national development banks, and other government agencies performing important functions in financing operations and projects.

Some financing operations are distinctive to international business finance. A form of commercial bank financing widely used in Europe is represented by overdrafts. An overdraft agreement permits a customer to draw checks up to some specified maximum limit in excess of the checking account balance. In contrast to U.S. practice, European overdrafts are provided for in previous loan agreements and have widespread use in normal banking relations.

Another form of financing — one that was until recent years much more widespread in Europe than in the United States — is the use of discounted *trade bills* (a time draft, or bill of exchange, drawn by the seller of goods, sold before its due date) in both domestic and foreign transactions. The increased use of bankers' acceptances in the United States has been associated with the growth of the movement of goods in international trade.

A third variation from U.S. financing practices found in Europe is the broad participation of commercial banks in medium- and long-term lending activities. In Europe, commercial banks carry on considerable activities of the kind that would be described as investment banking operations in the United States. This difference results from a legal requirement in the United States. The Banking Act of 1933 required the divestiture of investment banking operations by commercial banks.

A fourth practice distinctive to international financing relates to arbi-loans and link financing, both of which represent forms of equalizing the supply of and demand for loanable funds in relation to sensitive interest rate levels among different countries. Under *arbi-loans*, or international interest arbitrage financing, a borrower obtains loans in a country where the supply of funds is relatively abundant. The borrowed funds are then converted into another foreign currency needed by the firm. Simultaneously, the borrower enters into a forward exchange contract to protect itself on the reconversion of the new foreign currency into the original foreign currency that will be required at the time the loan must be repaid. Commercial banks are typically involved in arbi-loan transactions both as lenders and as intermediaries in the foreign exchange trading.

In *link financing*, the commercial banks take an even more direct role. A lender bank in the United States, for example, deposits funds with a bank in Mexico, the borrower's country, where interest rates are higher. This deposit may be earmarked for the specified borrower. The lender, of course, is expected to hedge its position in the foreign exchange markets, since it will be repaid in the currency of the country in which the bank deposit was made. The U.S. bank receives a rate that provides an interest differential after all additional expenses, such as the cost of hedging, are taken into consideration. The Mexican bank receives a commission for handling the transaction.

Expanding Role of U.S. Commercial Banks and Investment Bankers

Commercial banks have long performed an important role in export and import financing. They have increased the number of their foreign branches and have expanded their foreign operations and lending activities. They have also participated in consortiums with foreign merchant banks (banks that specialize in business lending) and investment banks for the conduct of all forms of international financing services.

Loans and credits to foreign borrowers extended by U.S. banks reached the total outstanding of $357 billion by the end of 1983.[5] Loans to the less-developed countries (LDC's)

---

[5]Federal Reserve Bank of Chicago, *International Letter*, No. 532, August 10, 1984, p. 1.

had reached $107 billion by year-end 1983. Loans to the LDC's have had to be rewritten to extend the repayment dates and to modify interest payments in some cases. This "foreign exposure" of U.S. banks has raised some questions about their financial stability.

Through their Edge Act corporations, by which they can make equity investments, commercial banks have participated for many years in the financing of international operations. Edge Act subsidiaries were provided for by amendments in 1916 and 1919 to the Federal Reserve Act of 1913. The amendments give U.S. commercial banks the authority to enter international markets and engage in certain operations that are prohibited in the United States. Edge Act subsidiaries can conduct all forms of international banking; they can issue or confirm letters of credit, finance foreign trade, engage in spot and foreign exchange transactions, and so on. Through these foreign banking subsidiaries and affiliates, direct investments in the form of both debt and equity can be made in commercial and industrial firms.

U.S. investment banking firms have actively participated in arranging Eurocurrency financing, mainly for their U.S. customers. They have developed joint participation activities with foreign merchant banks and with foreign investment banking houses. They have established offices in foreign countries and have participated in international underwriting groups that have developed the Eurobond market.

Commercial banks have become especially active in international project financing. This type of financing involves large investment projects, usually joint ventures between government and private enterprise that are financed by international and government sources as well as by private sources, often through a Eurodollar bank syndicate. International project financing is characterized by large investments for development activities such as the opening of a new mine, major drilling or exploration, or the establishment of a major chemical or pharmaceutical complex. Normally, there is more than one major equity owner of the project company itself. The equity owners collectively possess or arrange for the requisite operating, technical, marketing, and financial strengths needed for the project's success.

International project financing generally involves relatively high debt leverage. Since the projects provide output for international markets, debt is issued in several currencies. The sources of debt are commercial banks, export credit agencies, suppliers, product purchasers, international lending agencies, regional or national development banks, and local governments.

International investment bankers serve as project financial advisers, fitting together the various types of financing needed to meet the project's requirements. Each transaction typically includes various covenants related directly to the characteristics of the project.[6]

The Eurodollar System

The Eurodollar system, which operates as an international money market, was developed in the early 1950s as banks accepted interest bearing deposits in currencies other than their own. Most of the early activity occurred in Europe, where the predominant foreign currency used was the dollar (whose stability gave it the status of an international currency). Since the system is now worldwide, including many different currencies, it is often called the *Eurocurrency system*.

The flow process of the Eurodollar market can be illustrated as follows. A European firm holds a dollar deposit in a New York bank. It can hold the dollars in the form of a dollar

---

[6]For a more complete discussion, see Huston [1976].

deposit claim on its European bank by drawing a check on the New York bank and making a deposit in the European bank. The European bank can, in turn, make loans to other customers. Except for holding fractional reserves against its dollar deposit liabilities, the European bank has served as an intermediary in transferring the dollar balances in the United States from its depositors to its borrowers. Yet, its depositors still hold claims in dollars.

The Eurobanks, including the foreign branches of many U.S. banks, accept Eurodollar deposits and lend out these funds. The transactions involve large amounts, and the spread between the interest rates on loans and the interest paid on deposits is usually small. This is a fast-action market in which most transactions are arranged over the phone or through cables, with the confirming documents sent later by mail.

Eurodollar loans are typically in multiples of $1 million and have maturities ranging from 30 days to five to seven years. If the borrower is known to the bank, a loan of less than a year can be arranged quickly. Eurodollar loans are typically unsecured, but there may be restrictions of other kinds placed on the borrowing activities of the firm receiving the loan. One form of Eurodollar loan is the floating rate revolving loan, sometimes referred to as a "revolver" or a "roll-over" credit. The rate on the loan is quoted as a percentage above the London interbank offer rate (LIBOR), and it reflects the rates on liquid funds that move among the money markets of the developed nations. The floating rate provision dampens borrowing based on speculation on future interest rates.

An Example of International Financing

A case will illustrate the decision-making process in selecting among alternative currencies to use in financing long-term bonds.[7] Worldcorp operates throughout the world, with facilities in many countries. It is planning a joint venture that includes building a new plant in West Germany. To help meet its financing requirements, Worldcorp is considering an issue of bonds with a ten-year maturity in the equivalent amount of $50 million. Worldcorp is evaluating two alternatives:

1. A dollar issue at 11 percent annual coupon issued at par, with issuing expenses of 2.5 percent of face value.
2. A Deutschemark (DM) issue at 8 percent annual coupon issued at 99, with additional issuing expenses of 2.5 percent of face value. (Therefore, total flotation expense is 3.5 percent of face value.)

The initial exchange rate is DM1 = U.S. $0.5701. The treasurer of Worldcorp forecasts the DM to rise in value in relation to the U.S. dollar by 4.13 percent per year for the ten-year life of the bond. Worldcorp's applicable tax rate is 46 percent. To make the comparison between the two alternatives, we first analyze the DM borrowing. We need four items: the net proceeds of the loan in dollars, the annual after-tax interest expense in dollars, tax savings from the issuing expenses, and after-tax repayment of principal in dollars at the end of ten years.

The Net Proceeds in Dollars.   Flotation expense is 3.5 percent of the face amount, or $0.035 \times \$50,000,000 = \$1,750,000$. The net proceeds are $50,000,000 less $1,750,000 = $48,250,000.

---

[7]This presentation is based on Folks and Advani [1980].

Annual Interest Expense in Dollars. The amount borrowed is $50,000,000, which, expressed in DM by dividing by the current exchange rate of 0.5701, is DM87,703,912. The interest rate on the DM loan is 8 percent, which is multiplied times the DM87,703,912 to obtain DM7,016,313. This is expressed in dollars by multiplying by 0.5701 to obtain $4 million, or $2,160,000 after tax. This after-tax interest expense expressed in dollars increases at the rate of the forecast of the rise in the DM value in relation to the dollar, which is 4.13 percent per year.

Tax Savings from the Issuing Expenses. The issuing expenses in dollars are $1,750,000, or $175,000 per year. This represents a tax shelter of 0.46 × $175,000, which equals $80,500 per year.

After-Tax Repayment of Principal. The net repayment of the principal amount borrowed involves several factors. The value of the DM in dollars is now 0.5701. Its value is expected to grow in relation to the dollar at a rate of 4.13 percent per year. The compound value of one dollar at 4.13 percent in ten years is $(1.0413)^{10}$, which equals 1.49885. Multiplied by 0.5701, this gives the tenth year exchange rate of 0.8545 used in the following calculations:

Repayment of principal = DM87,703,912 at 0.8545 =		$74,942,993
Original principal = DM87,703,912 at 0.5701 =		50,000,000
Exchange loss		$24,942,993
Tax savings at 0.46		11,473,777
After-tax exchange loss		$13,469,216

The net repayment of principal is $74,942,993 less $11,473,777 = $63,469,216.

We now have the basic inputs for determining the after-tax cost of borrowing in DM. It is obtained by solving for r_a (the after-tax interest cost) in the following equation:

$$\$48,250,000 = \sum_{t=1}^{10} \frac{(0.54)(\$4,000,000)(1.0413)^t}{(1 + r_a)^t} - \sum_{t=1}^{10} \frac{\$175,000(0.46)}{(1 + r_a)^t}$$
$$+ \frac{\$63,469,216}{(1 + r_a)^{10}}.$$

The solution is 7.55 percent, which we can verify as follows:

$$\$48,250,000 = \$2,160,000 \times \left(\frac{1.0413}{1.0755}\right)\left[\text{FVIFA}\left(\frac{1.0413}{1.0755} - 1, \; 10 \text{ years}\right)\right]$$

$$- \text{PVIFA}(7.55\%, \; 10 \text{ years}) \times \$80,500$$

$$+ \text{PVIF}(7.55\%, \; 10 \text{ years})\$63,469,216$$

$$= \$2,160,000(0.9682)\text{FVIFA}(-3.18\%, \; 10 \text{ years})$$

$$- \text{PVIFA}(7.55\%, \; 10 \text{ years}) \times \$80,500$$

$$+ \text{PVIF}(7.55\%, \; 10 \text{ years})\$63,469,216$$

$$= \$2,160,000(0.9682)(8.68385) - (6.84844) \times \$80,500$$

$$+ (0.482943) \times \$63,469,216$$

$$= \$18,160,640 - \$551,299 + \$30,652,014$$

$$\cong \$48,261,355.$$

Thus, at an after-tax cost of 7.55 percent, the net proceeds in dollars are equal to the present value of the after-tax interest costs (less the tax savings from the issuing costs) plus the present value of the net repayment of principal.

We next compare the cost of borrowing in DM with the cost of borrowing in dollars. We need the same four basic information inputs.

Net Proceeds in Dollars. Issuing expenses are 2.5 percent of $50,000,000 = $1,250,000. Net proceeds are therefore $48,750,000.

Interest Costs in Dollars. The interest expense is 0.11 times $50,000,000 times $(1 - 0.46)$, which equals $2,970,000 each year.

Tax Savings from the Issuing Expenses. Issuing expenses per year are $125,000. The tax shelter is 0.46 times this amount, which equals $57,500.

After-Tax Repayment of Principal. This is simply the present value of $50,000,000 to be paid ten years hence.

The equation to test for the after-tax cost is

$$\$48,750,000 = (\$2,970,000 - \$57,500)(\text{PVIFA } r_a\%, \text{ 10 years})$$
$$+ \$50,000,000(\text{PVIF } r_a\%, \text{ 10 years}).$$

The solution is 6.17 percent, which can be verified as follows:

$$\$48,750,000 = \$2,912,500(7.3012) + \$50,000,000(0.5495)$$
$$= \$21,264,745 + \$27,475,000$$
$$\cong \$48,739,745.$$

We find that the after-tax cost of using dollar bonds is 6.17 percent, while the after-tax cost of using bonds denominated in DM is 7.55 percent. Several issues are raised by this result. First, the difference is not of great magnitude. Second, the difference reflects the forecast of the future rise in the foreign exchange value of the DM in relation to the dollar. This forecast could be in error. The current interest rate differential on dollars versus DM implies a smaller rise in the exchange value of the DM in relation to the dollar than the 4.13 percent per annum. This forecast by the treasurer of Worldcorp implies that full interest rate parity is not reflected in the current dollar versus DM borrowing rates and that the "market is wrong." (While the market is never wrong, it does change its mind, sometimes frequently.)

Of course, a wide range of economic and political factors in the United States and in West Germany could change the interest parity relation and relative dollar and DM exchange rates over the ten-year life of the loan. The choice among the two alternative sources of financing is subject to uncertainty and error. One set of considerations for the treasurer is to judge the most likely direction of error. Is the most likely possibility that the DM will rise in value in relation to the dollar at a rate even higher than the 4.13 percent forecast? If so, this is a further reason for borrowing in dollars.

Or, alternatively, suppose that Worldcorp has large amounts of future receipts that will be made in DM — particularly near the tenth year maturity of the bond. If so, Worldcorp would be at least partially hedged with respect to a DM bond issue. On the other hand,

Worldcorp may already have future exposure to a rise in the value of the DM in relation to the dollar. This would be a further reason for using the dollar as the denomination of the bond issue rather than the DM.

Working Capital Management in International Enterprise

The general principles that apply to the management of cash on an international basis are very similar to those used successfully by many firms on a domestic basis. Multinational firms try to speed up the collection of cash by having bank accounts in the banking system of each country. In many countries, customers pay their bills by requesting their bank or postal administration to deduct the amount owed from their account and to transfer it to the other firm's account.

Multinational commercial banks, particularly those that have branches or affiliates in a large number of countries, can be very helpful to multinational firms. Several of the larger U.S. multinational commercial banks have foreign departments whose sole purpose is to help U.S. multinational firms solve their problems of international cash management. An international bank can speed the flow of funds of a multinational firm and thereby decrease the exposure of these funds to foreign exchange rate risk. It can suggest the routing of the transfers as well as the national currency to be used. While in the United States, the average time between the initiation and completion of a financial transaction is two to three days, the time interval for foreign transactions can be as long as two to three weeks. The long delays unnecessarily tie up large amounts of funds and should be avoided. In this area, the multinational commercial banks are particularly helpful, since they can transfer funds from one country to another (provided government restrictions do not interfere) on a same-day basis if they have branches or affiliates in the two countries involved.

Increasingly, the arena for business finance is the global market. At the start of each day, the corporate treasurer determines whether to borrow or to lend in the international financial market. The investment activity takes place in both domestic and foreign countries.

The financial manager of the multinational corporate enterprise must consider the form and extent of protection against currency fluctuations on sales and purchases. If the firm has surplus cash, the financial manager must compare the returns from investing in the domestic money market with those from investing in the international market. Similarly, if short-term financing needs arise, the manager must make comparisons between domestic and foreign financing sources. Among the considerations are the advantages and disadvantages of using the impersonal international financial market versus those of developing long-term financing relations with international commercial banks or financial groups in the United States, London, Paris, Zurich, Bonn, and Tokyo.

Summary

Some fundamental exchange rate relationships provide a foundation for decisions with respect to managing the risks of international business finance. Because a different set of relationships is involved, the following key symbols have been used: D = devaluation, E = dollars per foreign currency (FC) unit, X = FC units per dollar, P = price level, R = the nominal interest rate and r = the real rate of interest. D_{fd} is the change in the number of

FC units per dollar:

$$D_{fd} = \frac{X_1 - X_0}{X_0} = \frac{E_0 - E_1}{E_1}$$

Alternatively, D_{df} is the change in the dollar value of a foreign currency unit:

$$D_{df} = \frac{E_0 - E_1}{E_0} = \frac{X_1 - X_0}{X_1}$$

In addition to presenting the requirements for consistent foreign exchange rates, three fundamental exchange rate relationships were explained.

1.   Fisher Effect

$$R_0 = \left[(1 + r)\left(\frac{P_1}{P_0}\right) \right] - 1$$

2.   Interest Rate Parity Theorem

$$\frac{X_f}{X_0} = \frac{1 + R_{f0}}{1 + R_{d0}} = \frac{E_0}{E_f}$$

3.   Purchasing Power Parity Theorem

$$\frac{X_1}{X_0} = \frac{P_{f1}/P_{f0}}{P_{d1}/P_{d0}}$$

With these key relationships as a background, we consider managerial decisions in the setting of the international economy. A firm generally develops its international activities through an evolutionary process. First, it needs to develop a strong competitive product for domestic sales. Then, it may start to export through a broker. When foreign sales increase, it may open a foreign branch sales office. Finally, it may establish a wholly owned manufacturing plant or subsidiary in the foreign country. If the foreign government places restrictions on foreign investments or imports, licensing or joint ventures may be the only feasible ways of doing business in the foreign country.

International business transactions are conducted in more than one currency. If a firm is expecting receipts in foreign currency units, its risk is that the value of the foreign currency units will fall. If it has obligations to be paid in foreign currency units, its risk is that the value of the foreign currency will rise. To reduce foreign exchange risk, firms can engage in transactions in the forward foreign exchange market. They can also borrow at current spot exchange rates the amount of foreign currency needed for future transactions. These two forms of hedging are essentially insurance and, therefore, involve costs.

Firms also take protective action against long or short positions in foreign currencies resulting from the balance sheet position of their foreign subsidiaries. Monetary assets and liabilities are those items whose value, expressed in local currency, does not change with devaluation or revaluation. A firm seeks to have a net monetary creditor position in a country whose exchange rates are expected to rise and a net monetary debtor position in a country whose exchange rates are expected to fall. A monetary debtor position can be created by investing all excess cash, granting as little trade credit as possible, avoiding advances, and borrowing funds. A monetary creditor position can be developed by holding cash or cash equivalents, such as foreign securities, and by having receivables due in the foreign currency.

International financing broadens the range of fund sources. These sources include international and government institutions, Eurocurrency and Eurobond markets, overdrafts from European banks, discounted trade bills, and arbi-loans and link financing. Edge Act subsidiaries permit commercial banks to enter international markets and engage in operations from which they are prohibited in the United States. U.S. commercial banks and investment banking firms have become very active in international financing and related services.

International cash management involves minimizing exposure of foreign-located funds to exchange rate risks and avoiding restrictions on the movement of funds from one country to another. International banks provide many services that facilitate effective international working capital management by multinational firms.

Questions

32.1 What has been the impact of advances in the technology of transportation and communication on international trade and finance?

32.2 Why is the ratio of foreign earnings to a firm's total earnings likely to be greater than the ratio of its foreign sales to total sales?

32.3 If a firm has difficulty developing a product that will sell in the local domestic market, is it likely to have greater success in a foreign market? Explain.

32.4 What are the advantages and disadvantages to a firm of licensing the production of its products to foreign firms?

32.5 What are the pros and cons of engaging in a joint venture rather than establishing a wholly owned foreign subsidiary?

32.6 What are monetary assets and liabilities (as contrasted with "real" or nonmonetary assets and liabilities)?

32.7 What are arbi-loans and link financing?

32.8 What are some of the services provided by U.S. commercial banks to firms engaged in international operations or financing?

32.9 What are some of the services provided by U.S. investment banking firms to U.S. business firms engaged in international operations or financing?

32.10 What is the Eurocurrency system, and what economic functions does it perform?

32.11 Describe some major characteristics of Eurodollar loans.

32.12 In what respects are domestic working capital management and international working capital management similar and different?

32.13 What services can the multinational commercial bank perform to help the U.S. multinational operating firm solve its problems of international cash management?

32.14 What are some of the reasons that U.S. firms engage in financing abroad?

Problems

32.1 In 1978, the number of Japanese yen required to equal one U.S. dollar was 194.60. In March 1981, the U.S. dollar was worth 211 yen.

a) What is X_0 (1978)? What is X_1 (1981)?

b) What is E_0 (1978)? What is E_1 (1981)?

    c)   What was the percentage devaluation or revaluation of the yen in terms of the U.S. dollar?

    d)   What was the percentage devaluation or revaluation of the dollar in terms of the yen?

32.2 If the exchange rate between dollars and francs is fr 5 = \$1.00, and between dollars and pounds is £1 = \$1.60, what is the exchange rate between francs and pounds?

32.3 *The Wall Street Journal*, on March 5, 1981, listed the following information on the exchange rates between the dollar and the German mark:

$$X_0 = 2.1436 \text{ DM/\$}$$

$$E_0 = \$0.4665/\text{DM}$$

$$X_f(90 \text{ days}) = 2.1304 \text{ DM/\$}$$

$$E_f(90 \text{ days}) = \$0.4694/\text{DM}.$$

The prime interest rate on that day was $18\frac{1}{2}$ percent.

    a)   What is implied about the German interest rate?

    b)   If the forward exchange rate was \$0.45/DM, what would be the German interest rate?

    c)   If the German interest rate was 12 percent, what would be the 90-day forward rate on Deutschemarks per dollar?

32.4 The Coret Company's subsidiary has monetary assets of FC 800,000 and monetary liabilities of FC 1,000,000. Calculate the gain or loss of the parent under the following two states of the world:

    a)   There has been a devaluation; the local currency has dropped from 20 FC per \$1 to 25 FC per \$1.

    b)   There has been a revaluation; the local currency has appreciated from 20 FC per \$1 to 15 FC per \$1.

32.5 Debussy Corporation exports a substantial amount of cosmetics each year and, therefore, has a great part of its assets invested in FC receivables. Monetary assets are FC 30,000,000, while monetary liabilities are FC 10,000,000. Calculate any gains or losses under the following two states of the world:

    a)   There is a revaluation from 4 FC per \$1 to 3 FC per \$1.

    b)   There is a devaluation from 4 FC per \$1 to 5 FC per \$1.

32.6 The MNC Corporation has a number of subsidiaries located in various Asian countries. These subsidiaries collect the equivalent of \$500,000 each month, and the funds are transferred to the company's cash center in Hong Kong. The average transfer time has been 14 days. An international bank, eager to solicit business from MNC, has offered to handle the transfer of these funds at a guaranteed average transfer time of not more than 2 days. The company's opportunity cost is 15 percent.

    a)   How much is this service worth to the company?

    b)   What are the advantages and disadvantages of the arrangement?

32.7 Cartell International's principal manufacturing plant in Europe is located in Paris. In-transfer and temporarily idle funds have been routed to and through this office. However, since forward market quotations on the French franc have been weakening lately, the manager of the international division is planning to reroute temporarily idle cash funds to the office of the company's German subsidiary. The company has been protecting itself by entering into forward 90-day contracts to purchase dollars with French francs at an annual discount of 5 to 6 percent. By comparison, 90-day forward contracts can be obtained to buy dollars with Deutschemarks at a premium in relation to the present spot rate of 1.5 percent. Short-term interest rates in France are 7.5 percent and in West Germany approximately 7 percent.

a)   Should West Germany become the transfer center of the firm's international funds flow? What would be the cost or benefit of any change that might be suggested?

b)   What requirements for an international financial center are considered important in locating a cash concentration center in a particular city? Why?

32.8 The treasurer of a company in Mexico borrowed $10,000 in dollars at a 15 percent interest rate when the exchange rate was 22 pesos to the dollar. His company paid the loan plus interest one year later, when the exchange rate was 25 pesos to the dollar.

a)   What rate of interest was paid, based on the pesos received and paid by the treasurer?

b)   Show how your result illustrates the interest rate parity theorem.

32.9 The treasurer of a company in Mexico is comparing two borrowing alternatives for a 180-day loan. He can borrow in U.S. dollars from a U.S. bank at a 15 percent interest rate or from a Mexican bank in pesos at a 25 percent interest rate. The spot exchange rate is 23.5 pesos to the dollar. The 180-day forward exchange rate is 25 pesos to the dollar.

a)   What is the effective interest rate in pesos on the U.S. loan?

b)   Verify your answer by use of the interest rate parity relationship.

32.10 The Kory Company has made a sale of construction equipment to a foreign firm and will receive FC 11,000,000 on May 31, 19X9. The company has incurred all of its expenses in dollars and needs to know the definite dollar amounts that it will receive on May 31, 19X9. The effective tax rate in both countries is 40 percent, and the expected future spot rate is 12 FC per dollar. The director of finance at Kory Company is considering three options to deal with the foreign exchange risk:

a)   To enter the forward market to sell FC 11,000,000 for dollars at the 90-day forward rate quoted on March 1, 19X9, which is 11 FC per dollar. Under this arrangement, the Kory Company will receive a definite amount in dollars in May as determined by the forward rate on March 1, 19X9.

b)   To borrow on March 1, 19X9, from a foreign bank an amount in foreign currency that, with interest, will equal the amount the Kory Company will be receiving on May 31, 19X9. The interest rate on the loan would be 32 percent. By borrowing, the company will receive FC's and, with the FC's received, can immediately purchase dollars at the March 1, 19X9, spot rate, which is FC 10 per dollar. The dollars received can be invested in the United States at an interest rate of 12 percent. When the company receives the FC 11,000,000 on May 31, 19X9, it can liquidate the local currency loan plus interest.

c)   To make no attempt to cover the exchange risk involved in waiting the three months for receipt of the FC 11,000,000. Under the third alternative, the company will convert the FC 11,000,000 into dollars at the spot rate of FC 12 per dollar that is expected to prevail on May 31, 19X9.

Which alternative should be chosen?

32.11 Rework Problem 32.10, assuming a foreign interest rate of 60 percent. Which alternative is the most attractive now? Explain.

32.12 On March 1, 19X9, the Burrows Company bought electronic equipment from a foreign firm that will require the payment of FC 900,000 on May 31, 19X9. The spot rate on March 1, 19X9, is FC 10 per dollar; the expected future spot rate is FC 8 per dollar; and the 90-day forward rate is FC 9 per dollar. The U.S. interest rate is 12 percent, and the foreign interest rate is 8 percent. The tax rate for both countries is 40 percent.

The Burrows Company is considering three alternatives to deal with the risk of exchange rate fluctuations:

a) To enter the forward market to buy FC 900,000 at the 90-day forward rate in effect on March 1, 19X9.

b) To borrow an amount in dollars to buy the FC at the current spot rate. This money is to be invested in government securities of the foreign country; with the interest income, it will equal FC 900,000 on May 31, 19X9.

c) To wait until May 31, 19X9, and buy FC's at whatever spot rate prevails at that time.

Which alternative should the Burrows Company follow in order to minimize its cost of meeting the future payment in FC's? Explain.

32.13 The U.S.-based Polychem Corporation wishes to borrow $1 million for a six-month period. The funds can be borrowed in the United States at a 16 percent annual rate. The financial vice president feels that 16 percent is quite high and finds that he can borrow in Swiss francs at an 8 percent annual rate. The spot value of Swiss francs is $.5120; the forward rate for a 180-day contract is $.5311. Is there an advantage to borrowing in Swiss francs at the 8 percent rate?

32.14 In January 1977 (when DM 3 = $1), it was expected that by the end of 1977, the price level in the United States would have risen by 10 percent and in West Germany by 5 percent. Assume that the real rate of interest in both countries is 4 percent.

a) Use the purchasing power parity theorem (PPPT) to project the expected DM's per $1 at the end of 1977 (the expected future spot rate of DM's per $1).

b) Use the Fisher relation to estimate the nominal interest rates in each country which make it possible for investments in each country to earn its real rate of interest.

c) Use the interest rate parity theorem (IRPT) to estimate the current one-year forward rate of DM's per $1.

d) Compare your estimate of the current forward rate in (c) with your estimate of the expected future spot rate in (a).

e) Prove analytically that the Fisher effect and the IRPT guarantee consistency with the PPPT relation when real interest rates in the different countries are equal. (Assume that all the fundamental relations hold.)

Selected References

Adler, Michael, and Dumas, Bernard, "International Portfolio Choice and Corporation Finance: A Synthesis," *Journal of Finance*, 38 (June 1983), pp. 925-984.

Adler, Michael, and Lehmann, Bruce, "Deviations from Purchasing Power Parity in the Long Run," *Journal of Finance*, 38 (December 1983), pp. 1471-1487.

Aliber, Robert Z., *Exchange Risk and Corporate International Finance*, New York: Wiley, 1978.

Aubey, Robert T., and Lombra, Raymond E., "The Use of International Currency Cocktails in the Reduction of Exchange Rate Risk," *Journal of Economics and Business*, 29 (Winter 1977), pp. 128-134.

Bowditch, Richard L., and Burtle, James L., "The Corporate Treasurer in a World of Floating Exchange Rates," in *The Treasurer's Handbook*, Edited by J. Fred Weston and Maurice B. Goudzwaard, Homewood, Ill.: Dow Jones-Irwin, 1976, pp. 84-112.

Browne, F. X., "Departures from Interest Rate Parity: Further Evidence," *Journal of Banking and Finance*, 7 (June 1983), pp. 253-272.

Calderon-Rossell, Jorge R., "Covering Foreign Exchange Risks of Single Transactions," *Financial Management*, 8 (Autumn 1979), pp. 78-85.

Cornell, Bradford, "Relative Price Changes and Deviations from Purchasing Power Parity," *Journal of Banking and Finance*, 3 (September 1979), pp. 263-279.

——, "Spot Rates, Forward Rates and Exchange Market Efficiency," *Journal of Financial Economics*, 5 (August 1977), pp. 55-65.

——, and Dietrich, J. Kimball, "The Efficiency of the Market for Foreign Exchange under Floating Exchange Rates," *Review of Economics and Statistics*, 60 (February 1978), pp. 111-120.

Cornell, Bradford, and Reinganum, Marc R., "Forward and Futures Prices: Evidence from the Foreign Exchange Markets," *Journal of Finance*, 36 (December 1981), pp. 1035-1045.

Cornell, Bradford, and Shapiro, Alan C., "Managing Foreign Exchange Risk," *Midland Corporate Finance Journal*, 1 (Fall 1983), pp. 16-31.

Dufey, Gunter, "Corporate Finance and Exchange Rate Variations," *Financial Management*, 1 (Summer 1972), pp. 51-57.

Eiteman, David K., and Stonehill, Arthur I., *Multinational Business Finance*, 3rd ed., Reading, Mass.: Addison-Wesley, 1982.

Errunza, Vihang R., and Senbet, Lemma W., "The Effects of International Operations on the Market Value of the Firm: Theory and Evidence," *Journal of Finance*, 36 (May 1981), pp. 401-417.

Feiger, George, and Jacquillat, Bertrand, "Currency Option Bonds, Puts and Calls on Spot Exchange and the Hedging of Contingent Foreign Earnings," *Journal of Finance*, 34 (December 1979), pp. 1129-1139.

Folks, William R., Jr., "Optimal Foreign Borrowing Strategies with Operations in Forward Exchange Markets," *Journal of Financial and Quantitative Analysis*, 13 (June 1978), pp. 245-254.

———, "Decision Analysis for Exchange Risk Management," *Financial Management*, 1 (Winter 1972), pp. 101-112.

Folks, William R., Jr., and Advani, Ramesh, "Raising Funds with Foreign Currency," *Financial Executive*, 48 (February 1980), pp. 44-49.

Fowler, D. J., "Transfer Prices and Profit Maximization in Multinational Enterprise Operations," *Journal of International Business Studies*, 9 (Winter 1978), pp. 9-26.

Geweke, John, and Feige, Edgar, "Some Joint Tests of the Efficiency of the Markets for Forward Foreign Exchange," *Review of Economics and Statistics*, 61 (August 1979), pp. 334-341.

Giddy, Ian H., "Exchange Risk: Whose View?" *Financial Management*, 6 (Summer 1977), pp. 23-33.

———, "An Integrated Theory of Exchange Rate Equilibrium," *Journal of Financial and Quantitative Analysis*, 11 (December 1976), pp. 883-892.

Hill, Joanne, and Schneeweis, Thomas, "The Hedging Effectiveness of Foreign Currency Futures," *Journal of Financial Research*, 5 (Spring 1982), pp. 95-104.

Huston, Robert L., "Project Financing," in J. Fred Weston and Maurice B. Goudzwaard, Eds., *The Treasurer's Handbook*, Homewood, Ill.: Dow Jones-Irwin, 1976.

Ibbotson, Roger G.; Carr, Richard C.; and Robinson, Anthony W., "International Equity and Bond Returns," *Financial Analysts Journal*, 38 (July/August 1982), pp. 61-83.

Kane, Alex; Rosenthal, Leonard; and Ljung, Greta, "Tests of the Fisher Hypothesis with International Data: Theory and Evidence," *Journal of Finance*, 38 (May 1983), pp. 539-551.

Lee, Wayne Y., and Sachdeva, Kanwal S., "The Role of the Multinational Firm in the Integration of Segmented Capital Markets," *Journal of Finance*, 32 (May 1977), pp. 479-492.

Lessard, Donald R., Ed., *International Financial Management, Theory and Application*, New York: Warren, Gorham & Lamont, 1979.

Levi, Maurice, *International Finance*, New York: McGraw-Hill, 1983.

Lewellen, Wilbur G., and Ang, James S., "Inflation, Currency Exchange Rates, and the International Securities Market," *Journal of Business Research*, 12 (March 1984), pp. 97-114.

Logue, Dennis E., and Oldfield, George S., "Managing Foreign Assets When Foreign Exchange Markets Are Efficient," *Financial Management*, 16 (Summer 1977), pp. 16-22.

Logue, Dennis E., and Senbet, Lemma W., "External Currency Market Equilibrium and Its Implications for Regulation of the Eurocurrency Market," *Journal of Finance*, 38 (May 1983), pp. 435-447.

Logue, Dennis E.; Sweeney, Richard James; and Willett, Thomas D., "Speculative Behavior of Foreign Exchange Rates during the Current Float," *Journal of Business Research*, 6 (May 1978), pp. 159-174.

Maldonado, Rita, and Saunders, Anthony, "Foreign Exchange Futures and the Law of One Price," *Financial Management*, 12 (Spring 1983), pp. 19-23.

McFarland, James W.; Pettit, R. Richardson; and Sung, Sam K., "The Distribution of Foreign Exchange Price Changes: Trading Day Effects and Risk Measurement," *Journal of Finance*, 37 (June 1982), pp. 693-715.

Mehra, Rajnish, "On the Financing and Investment Decisions of Multinational Firms in the Presence of Exchange Risk," *Journal of Financial and Quantitative Analysis*, 13 (June 1978), pp. 227-244.

Rodriguez, Rita M., "FASB No. 8: What Has It Done to Us?" *Financial Analysts Journal*, 33 (March-April 1977), pp. 40-47.

———, and Carter, E. Eugene, *International Financial Management*, 2nd ed., Englewood Cliffs, N. J.: Prentice-Hall, 1979.

Schwab, Bernhard, and Lusztig, Peter, "Apportioning Foreign Exchange Risk through the Use of Third Currencies: Some Questions on Efficiency," *Financial Management*, 7 (Autumn 1978), pp. 25-30.

Senbet, Lemma W., "International Capital Market Equilibrium and the Multinational Firm Financing and Investment Policies," *Journal of Financial and Quantitative Analysis*, 14 (September 1979), pp. 455-480.

Shapiro, Alan C., "Nominal Contracting in a World of Uncertainty," *Journal of Banking and Finance*, 7 (March 1983), pp. 69-82.

————, *Multinational Financial Management*, Boston: Allyn and Bacon, 1982.

————, "Financial Structure and Cost of Capital in the Multinational Corporation," *Journal of Financial and Quantitative Analysis*, 13 (June 1978), pp. 211-226.

————, "Capital Budgeting for the Multinational Corporation," *Financial Management*, 7 (Spring 1978), pp. 7-16.

Solnik, Bruno, "International Arbitrage Pricing Theory," *Journal of Finance*, 38 (May 1983), pp. 449-457.

————, "The Relation Between Stock Prices and Inflationary Expectations: The International Evidence," *Journal of Finance*, 38 (March 1983), pp. 35-48.

————, "International Parity Conditions and Exchange Risk: A Review," *Journal of Banking and Finance*, 2 (October 1978), pp. 281-293.

Stehle, Richard, "An Empirical Test of the Alternative Hypotheses of National and International Pricing of Risky Assets," *Journal of Finance*, 32 (May 1977), pp. 493-502.

Stulz, Rene M., "A Model of International Asset Pricing," *Journal of Financial Economics*, 9 (December 1981), pp. 383-406.

Vinso, Joseph D., and Rogalski, Richard J., "Empirical Properties of Foreign Exchange Rates," *Journal of International Business Studies*, 9 (Fall 1978), pp. 69-79.

Weston, J. Fred, and Sorge, Bart W., *International Managerial Finance*, Homewood, Ill.: Richard D. Irwin, 1972, pp. xv and 388.

————, *Guide to International Financial Management*, New York: McGraw-Hill, 1977.

Zecher, J. Richard, "The Effects of the Current Turbulent Times on American Multinational Banking: An Overview," *Journal of Banking and Finance*, 7 (December 1983), pp. 625-637.

Appendix A   Interest Tables

Table A.1   Future Value of $1 at the End of n Periods: $FVIF_{r,n} = (1 + r)^n$

Period	1%	2%	3%	4%	5%	6%	7%	8%	9%	10%	12%	14%	15%	16%	18%	20%	24%	28%	32%	36%
1	1.0100	1.0200	1.0300	1.0400	1.0500	1.0600	1.0700	1.0800	1.0900	1.1000	1.1200	1.1400	1.1500	1.1600	1.1800	1.2000	1.2400	1.2800	1.3200	1.3600
2	1.0201	1.0404	1.0609	1.0816	1.1025	1.1236	1.1449	1.1664	1.1881	1.2100	1.2544	1.2996	1.3225	1.3456	1.3924	1.4400	1.5376	1.6384	1.7424	1.8496
3	1.0303	1.0612	1.0927	1.1249	1.1576	1.1910	1.2250	1.2597	1.2950	1.3310	1.4049	1.4815	1.5209	1.5609	1.6430	1.7280	1.9066	2.0972	2.3000	2.5155
4	1.0406	1.0824	1.1255	1.1699	1.2155	1.2625	1.3108	1.3605	1.4116	1.4641	1.5735	1.6890	1.7490	1.8106	1.9388	2.0736	2.3642	2.6844	3.0360	3.4210
5	1.0510	1.1041	1.1593	1.2167	1.2763	1.3382	1.4026	1.4693	1.5386	1.6105	1.7623	1.9254	2.0114	2.1003	2.2878	2.4883	2.9316	3.4360	4.0075	4.6526
6	1.0615	1.1262	1.1941	1.2653	1.3401	1.4185	1.5007	1.5869	1.6771	1.7716	1.9738	2.1950	2.3131	2.4364	2.6996	2.9860	3.6352	3.9980	5.2899	6.3275
7	1.0721	1.1487	1.2299	1.3159	1.4071	1.5036	1.6058	1.7138	1.8280	1.9487	2.2107	2.5023	2.6600	2.8262	3.1855	3.5832	4.5077	5.6295	6.9826	8.6054
8	1.0829	1.1717	1.2668	1.3686	1.4775	1.5938	1.7182	1.8509	1.9926	2.1436	2.4760	2.8526	3.0590	3.2784	3.7589	4.2998	5.5895	7.2058	9.2170	11.703
9	1.0937	1.1951	1.3048	1.4233	1.5513	1.6895	1.8385	1.9990	2.1719	2.3579	2.7731	3.2519	3.5179	3.8030	4.4355	5.1598	6.9310	9.2234	12.166	15.916
10	1.1046	1.2190	1.3439	1.4802	1.6289	1.7908	1.9672	2.1589	2.3674	2.5937	3.1058	3.7072	4.0456	4.4114	5.2338	6.1917	8.5944	11.805	16.059	21.646
11	1.1157	1.2434	1.3842	1.5395	1.7103	1.8983	2.1049	2.3316	2.5804	2.8531	3.4785	4.2262	4.6524	5.1173	6.1759	7.4301	10.657	15.111	21.198	29.439
12	1.1268	1.2682	1.4258	1.6010	1.7959	2.0122	2.2522	2.5182	2.8127	3.1384	3.8960	4.8179	5.3502	5.9360	7.2876	8.9161	13.214	19.342	27.982	40.037
13	1.1381	1.2936	1.4685	1.6651	1.8856	2.1329	2.4098	2.7196	3.0658	3.4523	4.3635	5.4924	6.1528	6.8858	8.5994	10.699	16.386	24.758	36.937	54.451
14	1.1495	1.3195	1.5126	1.7317	1.9799	2.2609	2.5785	2.9372	3.3417	3.7975	4.8871	6.2613	7.0757	7.9875	10.147	12.839	20.319	31.691	48.756	74.053
15	1.1610	1.3459	1.5580	1.8009	2.0789	2.3966	2.7590	3.1722	3.6425	4.1772	5.4736	7.1379	8.1371	9.2655	11.973	15.407	25.195	40.564	64.358	100.71
16	1.1726	1.3728	1.6047	1.8730	2.1829	2.5404	2.9522	3.4259	3.9703	4.5950	6.1304	8.1372	9.3576	10.748	14.129	18.488	31.242	51.923	84.953	136.96
17	1.1843	1.4002	1.6528	1.9479	2.2920	2.6928	3.1588	3.7000	4.3276	5.0545	6.8660	9.2765	10.761	12.467	16.672	22.186	38.740	66.461	112.13	186.27
18	1.1961	1.4282	1.7024	2.0258	2.4066	2.8543	3.3799	3.9960	4.7171	5.5599	7.6900	10.575	12.375	14.462	19.673	26.623	48.038	85.070	148.02	253.33
19	1.2081	1.4568	1.7535	2.1068	2.5270	3.0256	3.6165	4.3157	5.1417	6.1159	8.6128	12.055	14.231	16.776	23.214	31.948	59.567	108.89	195.39	344.53
20	1.2202	1.4859	1.8061	2.1911	2.6533	3.2071	3.8697	4.6610	5.6044	6.7275	9.6463	13.743	16.366	19.460	27.393	38.337	73.864	139.37	257.91	468.57
21	1.2324	1.5157	1.8603	2.2788	2.7860	3.3996	4.1406	5.0338	6.1088	7.4002	10.803	15.667	18.821	22.574	32.323	46.005	91.591	178.40	340.44	637.26
22	1.2447	1.5460	1.9161	2.3699	2.9253	3.6035	4.4304	5.4365	6.6586	8.1403	12.100	17.861	21.644	26.186	38.142	55.206	113.57	228.35	449.39	866.67
23	1.2572	1.5769	1.9736	2.4647	3.0715	3.8197	4.7405	5.8715	7.2579	8.9543	13.552	20.361	24.891	30.376	45.007	66.247	140.83	292.30	593.19	1178.6
24	1.2697	1.6084	2.0328	2.5633	3.2251	4.0489	5.0724	6.3412	7.9111	9.8497	15.178	23.212	28.625	35.236	53.108	79.496	174.63	374.14	783.02	1602.9
25	1.2824	1.6406	2.0938	2.6658	3.3864	4.2919	5.4274	6.8485	8.6231	10.834	17.000	26.461	32.918	40.874	62.668	95.396	216.54	478.90	1033.5	2180.0
26	1.2953	1.6734	2.1566	2.7725	3.5557	4.5494	5.8074	7.3964	9.3992	11.918	19.040	30.166	37.856	47.414	73.948	114.47	268.51	612.99	1364.3	2964.9
27	1.3082	1.7069	2.2213	2.8834	3.7335	4.8223	6.2139	7.9881	10.245	13.110	21.324	34.389	43.535	55.000	87.259	137.37	332.95	784.63	1800.9	4032.2
28	1.3213	1.7410	2.2879	2.9987	3.9201	5.1117	6.6488	8.6271	11.167	14.421	23.883	39.204	50.065	63.800	102.96	164.84	412.86	1004.3	2377.2	5483.8
29	1.3345	1.7758	2.3566	3.1187	4.1161	5.4184	7.1143	9.3173	12.172	15.863	26.749	44.693	57.575	74.008	121.50	197.81	511.95	1285.5	3137.9	7458.0
30	1.3478	1.8114	2.4273	3.2434	4.3219	5.7435	7.6123	10.062	13.267	17.449	29.959	50.950	66.211	85.849	143.37	237.37	634.81	1645.5	4142.0	10143
40	1.4889	2.2080	3.2620	4.8010	7.0400	10.285	14.974	21.724	31.409	45.259	93.050	188.88	267.86	378.72	750.37	1469.7	5455.9	19426.	66520.	*
50	1.6446	2.6916	4.3839	7.1067	11.467	18.420	29.457	46.901	74.357	117.39	289.00	700.23	1083.6	1670.7	3927.3	9100.4	46890.	*	*	*
60	1.8167	3.2810	5.8916	10.519	18.679	32.987	57.946	101.25	176.03	304.48	897.59	2595.9	4383.9	7370.1	20555.	56347.	*	*	*	*

*FVIF > 99.999.

Table A.2

Present Value of $1 Received at the End of n Periods:

$$PVIF_{r,n} = 1/(1 + r)^n = (1 + r)^{-n}$$

Period	1%	2%	3%	4%	5%	6%	7%	8%	9%	10%	12%	14%	15%	16%	18%	20%	24%	28%	32%	36%
1	.9901	.9804	.9709	.9615	.9524	.9434	.9346	.9259	.9174	.9091	.8929	.8772	.8696	.8621	.8475	.8333	.8065	.7813	.7576	.7353
2	.9803	.9612	.9426	.9246	.9070	.8900	.8734	.8573	.8417	.8264	.7972	.7695	.7561	.7432	.7182	.6944	.6504	.6104	.5739	.5407
3	.9706	.9423	.9151	.8890	.8638	.8396	.8163	.7938	.7722	.7513	.7118	.6750	.6575	.6407	.6086	.5787	.5245	.4768	.4348	.3975
4	.9610	.9238	.8885	.8548	.8227	.7921	.7629	.7350	.7084	.6830	.6355	.5921	.5718	.5523	.5158	.4823	.4230	.3725	.3294	.2923
5	.9515	.9057	.8626	.8219	.7835	.7473	.7130	.6806	.6499	.6209	.5674	.5194	.4972	.4761	.4371	.4019	.3411	.2910	.2495	.2149
6	.9420	.8880	.8375	.7903	.7462	.7050	.6663	.6302	.5963	.5645	.5066	.4556	.4323	.4104	.3704	.3349	.2751	.2274	.1890	.1580
7	.9327	.8706	.8131	.7599	.7107	.6651	.6227	.5835	.5470	.5132	.4523	.3996	.3759	.3538	.3139	.2791	.2218	.1776	.1432	.1162
8	.9235	.8535	.7894	.7307	.6768	.6274	.5820	.5403	.5019	.4665	.4039	.3506	.3269	.3050	.2660	.2326	.1789	.1388	.1085	.0854
9	.9143	.8368	.7664	.7026	.6446	.5919	.5439	.5002	.4604	.4241	.3606	.3075	.2843	.2630	.2255	.1938	.1443	.1084	.0822	.0628
10	.9053	.8203	.7441	.6756	.6139	.5584	.5083	.4632	.4224	.3855	.3220	.2697	.2472	.2267	.1911	.1615	.1164	.0847	.0623	.0462
11	.8963	.8043	.7224	.6496	.5847	.5268	.4751	.4289	.3875	.3505	.2875	.2366	.2149	.1954	.1619	.1346	.0938	.0662	.0472	.0340
12	.8874	.7885	.7014	.6246	.5568	.4970	.4440	.3971	.3555	.3186	.2567	.2076	.1869	.1685	.1372	.1122	.0757	.0517	.0357	.0250
13	.8787	.7730	.6810	.6006	.5303	.4688	.4150	.3677	.3262	.2897	.2292	.1821	.1625	.1452	.1163	.0935	.0610	.0404	.0271	.0184
14	.8700	.7579	.6611	.5775	.5051	.4423	.3878	.3405	.2992	.2633	.2046	.1597	.1413	.1252	.0985	.0779	.0492	.0316	.0205	.0135
15	.8613	.7430	.6419	.5553	.4810	.4173	.3624	.3152	.2745	.2394	.1827	.1401	.1229	.1079	.0835	.0649	.0397	.0247	.0155	.0099
16	.8528	.7284	.6232	.5339	.4581	.3936	.3387	.2919	.2519	.2176	.1631	.1229	.1069	.0930	.0708	.0541	.0320	.0193	.0118	.0073
17	.8444	.7142	.6050	.5134	.4363	.3714	.3166	.2703	.2311	.1978	.1456	.1078	.0929	.0802	.0600	.0451	.0258	.0150	.0089	.0054
18	.8360	.7002	.5874	.4936	.4155	.3503	.2959	.2502	.2120	.1799	.1300	.0946	.0808	.0691	.0508	.0376	.0208	.0118	.0068	.0039
19	.8277	.6864	.5703	.4746	.3957	.3305	.2765	.2317	.1945	.1635	.1161	.0829	.0703	.0596	.0431	.0313	.0168	.0092	.0051	.0029
20	.8195	.6730	.5537	.4564	.3769	.3118	.2584	.2145	.1784	.1486	.1037	.0728	.0611	.0514	.0365	.0261	.0135	.0072	.0039	.0021
25	.7798	.6095	.4776	.3751	.2953	.2330	.1842	.1460	.1160	.0923	.0588	.0378	.0304	.0245	.0160	.0105	.0046	.0021	.0010	.0005
30	.7419	.5521	.4120	.3083	.2314	.1741	.1314	.0994	.0754	.0573	.0334	.0196	.0151	.0116	.0070	.0042	.0016	.0006	.0002	.0001
40	.6717	.4529	.3066	.2083	.1420	.0972	.0668	.0460	.0318	.0221	.0107	.0053	.0037	.0026	.0013	.0007	.0002	.0001	*	*
50	.6080	.3715	.2281	.1407	.0872	.0543	.0339	.0213	.0134	.0085	.0035	.0014	.0009	.0006	.0003	.0001	*	*	*	*
60	.5504	.3048	.1697	.0951	.0535	.0303	.0173	.0099	.0057	.0033	.0011	.0004	.0002	.0001	*	*	*	*	*	*

*The factor is zero to four decimal places.

Table A.3 Sum on an Annuity of $1 Per Period for n Periods:

$$FVIFA_{r,t} = \sum_{t=1}^{n}(1+r)^{t-1} = \frac{(1+r)^n - 1}{r}$$

Number of Periods	1%	2%	3%	4%	5%	6%	7%	8%	9%	10%	12%	14%	15%	16%	18%	20%	24%	28%	32%	36%
1	1.0000	1.0000	1.0000	1.0000	1.0000	1.0000	1.0000	1.0000	1.0000	1.0000	1.0000	1.0000	1.0000	1.0000	1.0000	1.0000	1.0000	1.0000	1.0000	1.0000
2	2.0100	2.0200	2.0300	2.0400	2.0500	2.0600	2.0700	2.0800	2.0900	2.1000	2.1200	2.1400	2.1500	2.1600	2.1800	2.2000	2.2400	2.2800	2.3200	2.3600
3	3.0301	3.0604	3.0909	3.1216	3.1525	3.1836	3.2149	3.2464	3.2781	3.3100	3.3744	3.4396	3.4725	3.5056	3.5724	3.6400	3.7776	3.9184	4.0624	4.2096
4	4.0604	4.1216	4.1836	4.2465	4.3101	4.3746	4.4399	4.5061	4.5731	4.6410	4.7793	4.9211	4.9934	5.0665	5.2154	5.3680	5.6842	6.0156	6.3624	6.7251
5	5.1010	5.2040	5.3091	5.4163	5.5256	5.6371	5.7507	5.8666	5.9847	6.1051	6.3528	6.6101	6.7424	6.8771	7.1542	7.4416	8.0484	8.6999	9.3983	10.146
6	6.1520	6.3081	6.4684	6.6330	6.8019	6.9753	7.1533	7.3359	7.5233	7.7156	8.1152	8.5355	8.7537	8.9775	9.4420	9.9299	10.980	12.135	13.405	14.798
7	7.2135	7.4343	7.6625	7.8983	8.1420	8.3938	8.6540	8.9228	9.2004	9.4872	10.089	10.730	11.066	11.413	12.141	12.915	14.615	16.533	18.695	21.126
8	8.2857	8.5830	8.8923	9.2142	9.5491	9.8975	10.259	10.636	11.028	11.435	12.299	13.232	13.726	14.240	15.327	16.499	19.122	22.163	25.678	29.731
9	9.3685	9.7546	10.159	10.582	11.026	11.491	11.978	12.487	13.021	13.579	14.775	16.085	16.785	17.518	19.085	20.798	24.712	29.369	34.895	41.435
10	10.462	10.949	11.463	12.006	12.577	13.180	13.816	14.486	15.192	15.937	17.548	19.337	20.303	21.321	23.521	25.958	31.643	38.592	47.061	57.351
11	11.566	12.168	12.807	13.486	14.206	14.971	15.783	16.645	17.560	18.531	20.654	23.044	24.349	25.732	28.755	32.150	40.237	50.398	63.121	78.998
12	12.682	13.412	14.192	15.025	15.917	16.869	17.888	18.977	20.140	21.384	24.133	27.270	29.000	30.850	34.931	39.580	50.894	65.510	84.320	108.43
13	13.809	14.680	15.617	16.626	17.713	18.882	20.140	21.495	22.953	24.522	28.029	32.088	34.351	36.786	42.218	48.496	64.109	84.852	112.30	148.47
14	14.947	15.973	17.086	18.291	19.598	21.015	22.550	24.214	26.019	27.975	32.392	37.581	40.504	43.672	50.818	59.195	80.496	109.61	149.23	202.92
15	16.096	17.293	18.598	20.023	21.578	23.276	25.129	27.152	29.360	31.772	37.279	43.842	47.580	51.659	60.965	72.035	100.81	141.30	197.99	276.97
16	17.257	18.639	20.156	21.824	23.657	25.672	27.888	30.324	33.003	35.949	42.753	50.980	55.717	60.925	72.939	87.442	126.01	181.86	262.35	377.69
17	18.430	20.012	21.761	23.697	25.840	28.212	30.840	33.750	36.973	40.544	48.883	59.117	65.075	71.673	87.068	105.93	157.25	233.79	347.30	514.66
18	19.614	21.412	23.414	25.645	28.132	30.905	33.999	37.450	41.301	45.599	55.749	68.394	75.836	84.140	103.74	128.11	195.99	300.25	459.44	700.93
19	20.810	22.840	25.116	27.671	30.539	33.760	37.379	41.446	46.018	51.159	63.439	78.969	88.211	98.603	123.41	154.74	244.03	385.32	607.47	954.27
20	22.019	24.297	26.870	29.778	33.066	36.785	40.995	45.762	51.160	57.275	72.052	91.024	102.44	115.37	146.62	186.68	303.60	494.21	802.86	1298.8
21	23.239	25.783	28.676	31.969	35.719	39.992	44.865	50.422	56.764	64.002	81.698	104.76	118.81	134.84	174.02	225.02	377.46	633.59	1060.7	1767.3
22	24.471	27.299	30.536	34.248	38.505	43.392	49.005	55.456	62.873	71.402	92.502	120.43	137.63	157.41	206.34	271.03	469.05	811.99	1401.2	2404.6
23	25.716	28.845	32.452	36.617	41.430	46.995	53.436	60.893	69.531	79.543	104.60	138.29	159.27	183.60	244.48	326.23	582.62	1040.3	1850.6	3271.3
24	26.973	30.421	34.426	39.082	44.502	50.815	58.176	66.764	76.789	88.497	118.15	158.65	184.16	213.97	289.49	392.48	723.46	1332.6	2443.8	4449.9
25	28.243	32.030	36.459	41.645	47.727	54.864	63.249	73.105	84.700	98.347	133.33	181.87	212.79	249.21	342.60	471.98	898.09	1706.8	3226.8	6052.9
26	29.525	33.670	38.553	44.311	51.113	59.156	68.676	79.954	93.323	109.18	150.33	208.33	245.71	290.08	405.27	567.37	1114.6	2185.7	4260.4	8233.0
27	30.820	35.344	40.709	47.084	54.669	63.705	74.483	87.350	102.72	121.09	169.37	238.49	283.56	337.50	479.22	681.85	1383.1	2798.7	5624.7	11197.9
28	32.129	37.051	42.930	49.967	58.402	68.528	80.697	95.338	112.96	134.20	190.69	272.88	327.10	392.50	566.48	819.22	1716.0	3583.3	7425.6	15230.2
29	33.450	38.792	45.218	52.966	62.322	73.639	87.346	103.96	124.13	148.63	214.58	312.09	377.16	456.30	669.44	984.06	2128.9	4587.6	9802.9	20714.1
30	34.784	40.568	47.575	56.084	66.438	79.058	94.460	113.28	136.30	164.49	241.33	356.78	434.74	530.31	790.94	1181.8	2640.9	5873.2	12940.	28172.2
40	48.886	60.402	75.401	95.025	120.79	154.76	199.63	259.05	337.88	442.59	767.09	1342.0	1779.0	2360.7	4163.2	7343.8	22728.	69377.	*	*
50	64.463	84.579	112.79	152.66	209.34	290.33	406.52	573.76	815.08	1163.9	2400.0	4994.5	7217.7	10435.	21813.	45497.	*	*	*	*
60	81.669	114.05	163.05	237.99	353.58	533.12	813.52	1253.2	1944.7	3034.8	7471.6	18535.	29219.	46057.	*	*	*	*	*	*

*FVIFA > 99,999.

Table A.4   Present Value of an Annuity of $1 Per Period for n Periods:

$$PVIFA_{r,t} = \sum_{t=1}^{n} \frac{1}{(1+r)^t} = \frac{1 - \frac{1}{(1+r)^n}}{r}$$

Number of payments	1%	2%	3%	4%	5%	6%	7%	8%	9%	10%	12%	14%	15%	16%	18%	20%	24%	28%	32%
1	0.9901	0.9804	0.9709	0.9615	0.9524	0.9434	0.9346	0.9259	0.9174	0.9091	0.8929	0.8772	0.8696	0.8621	0.8475	0.8333	0.8065	0.7813	0.7576
2	1.9704	1.9416	1.9135	1.8861	1.8594	1.8334	1.8080	1.7833	1.7591	1.7355	1.6901	1.6467	1.6257	1.6052	1.5656	1.5278	1.4568	1.3916	1.3315
3	2.9410	2.8839	2.8286	2.7751	2.7232	2.6730	2.6243	2.5771	2.5313	2.4869	2.4018	2.3216	2.2832	2.2459	2.1743	2.1065	1.9813	1.8684	1.7663
4	3.9020	3.8077	3.7171	3.6299	3.5460	3.4651	3.3872	3.3121	3.2397	3.1699	3.0373	2.9137	2.8550	2.7982	2.6901	2.5887	2.4043	2.2410	2.0957
5	4.8534	4.7135	4.5797	4.4518	4.3295	4.2124	4.1002	3.9927	3.8897	3.7908	3.6048	3.4331	3.3522	3.2743	3.1272	2.9906	2.7454	2.5320	2.3452
6	5.7955	5.6014	5.4172	5.2421	5.0757	4.9173	4.7665	4.6229	4.4859	4.3553	4.1114	3.8887	3.7845	3.6847	3.4976	3.3255	3.0205	2.7594	2.5342
7	6.7282	6.4720	6.2303	6.0021	5.7864	5.5824	5.3893	5.2064	5.0330	4.8684	4.5638	4.2883	4.1604	4.0386	3.8115	3.6046	3.2423	2.9370	2.6775
8	7.6517	7.3255	7.0197	6.7327	6.4632	6.2098	5.9713	5.7466	5.5348	5.3349	4.9676	4.6389	4.4873	4.3436	4.0776	3.8372	3.4212	3.0758	2.7860
9	8.5660	8.1622	7.7861	7.4353	7.1078	6.8017	6.5152	6.2469	5.9952	5.7590	5.3282	4.9464	4.7716	4.6065	4.3030	4.0310	3.5655	3.1842	2.8681
10	9.4713	8.9826	8.5302	8.1109	7.7217	7.3601	7.0236	6.7101	6.4177	6.1446	5.6502	5.2161	5.0188	4.8332	4.4941	4.1925	3.6819	3.2689	2.9304
11	10.3676	9.7868	9.2526	8.7605	8.3064	7.8869	7.4987	7.1390	6.8052	6.4951	5.9377	5.4527	5.2337	5.0286	4.6560	4.3271	3.7757	3.3351	2.9776
12	11.2551	10.5753	9.9540	9.3851	8.8633	8.3838	7.9427	7.5361	7.1607	6.8137	6.1944	5.6603	5.4206	5.1971	4.7932	4.4392	3.8514	3.3868	3.0133
13	12.1337	11.3484	10.6350	9.9856	9.3936	8.8527	8.3577	7.9038	7.4869	7.1034	6.4235	5.8424	5.5831	5.3423	4.9095	4.5327	3.9124	3.4272	3.0404
14	13.0037	12.1062	11.2961	10.5631	9.8986	9.2950	8.7455	8.2442	7.7862	7.3667	6.6282	6.0021	5.7245	5.4675	5.0081	4.6106	3.9616	3.4587	3.0609
15	13.8651	12.8493	11.9379	11.1184	10.3797	9.7122	9.1079	8.5595	8.0607	7.6061	6.8109	6.1422	5.8474	5.5755	5.0916	4.6755	4.0013	3.4834	3.0764
16	14.7179	13.5777	12.5611	11.6523	10.8378	10.1059	9.4466	8.8514	8.3126	7.8237	6.9740	6.2651	5.9542	5.6685	5.1624	4.7296	4.0333	3.5026	3.0882
17	15.5623	14.2919	13.1661	12.1657	11.2741	10.4773	9.7632	9.1216	8.5436	8.0216	7.1196	6.3729	6.0472	5.7487	5.2223	4.7746	4.0591	3.5177	3.0971
18	16.3983	14.9920	13.7535	12.6593	11.6896	10.8276	10.0591	9.3719	8.7556	8.2014	7.2497	6.4674	6.1280	5.8178	5.2732	4.8122	4.0799	3.5294	3.1039
19	17.2260	15.6785	14.3238	13.1339	12.0853	11.1581	10.3356	9.6036	8.9501	8.3649	7.3658	6.5504	6.1982	5.8775	5.3162	4.8435	4.0967	3.5386	3.1090
20	18.0456	16.3514	14.8775	13.5903	12.4622	11.4699	10.5940	9.8181	9.1285	8.5136	7.4694	6.6231	6.2593	5.9288	5.3527	4.8696	4.1103	3.5458	3.1129
25	22.0232	19.5235	17.4131	15.6221	14.0939	12.7834	11.6536	10.6748	9.8226	9.0770	7.8431	6.8729	6.4641	6.0971	5.4669	4.9476	4.1474	3.5640	3.1220
30	25.8077	22.3965	19.6004	17.2920	15.3725	13.7648	12.4090	11.2578	10.2737	9.4269	8.0552	7.0027	6.5660	6.1772	5.5168	4.9789	4.1601	3.5693	3.1242
40	32.8347	27.3555	23.1148	19.7928	17.1591	15.0463	13.3317	11.9246	10.7574	9.7791	8.2438	7.1050	6.6418	6.2335	5.5482	4.9966	4.1659	3.5712	3.1250
50	39.1961	31.4236	25.7298	21.4822	18.2559	15.7619	13.8007	12.2335	10.9617	9.9148	8.3045	7.1327	6.6605	6.2463	5.5541	4.9995	4.1666	3.5714	3.1250
60	44.9550	34.7609	27.6756	22.6235	18.9293	16.1614	14.0392	12.3766	11.0480	9.9672	8.3240	7.1401	6.6651	6.2492	5.5553	4.9999	4.1667	3.5714	3.1250

Appendix B   Natural Logarithms of Numbers between 1.0 and 4.99

N	0	1	2	3	4	5	6	7	8	9
1.0	0.00000	.00995	.01980	.02956	.03922	.04879	.05827	.06766	.07696	.08618
.1	.09531	.10436	.11333	.12222	.13103	.13976	.14842	.15700	.16551	.17395
.2	.18232	.19062	.19885	.20701	.21511	.22314	.23111	.23902	.24686	.25464
.3	.26236	.27003	.27763	.28518	.29267	.30010	.30748	.31481	.32208	.32930
.4	.33647	.34359	.35066	.35767	.36464	.37156	.37844	.38526	.39204	.39878
.5	.40547	.41211	.41871	.42527	.43178	.43825	.44469	.45108	.45742	.46373
.6	.47000	.47623	.48243	.48858	.49470	.50078	.50682	.51282	.51879	.52473
.7	.53063	.53649	.54232	.54812	.55389	.55962	.56531	.57098	.57661	.58222
.8	.58779	.59333	.59884	.60432	.60977	.61519	.62058	.62594	.63127	.63658
.9	.64185	.64710	.65233	.65752	.66269	.66783	.67294	.67803	.68310	.68813
2.0	0.69315	.69813	.70310	.70804	.71295	.71784	.72271	.72755	.73237	.73716
.1	.74194	.74669	.75142	.75612	.76081	.76547	.77011	.77473	.77932	.78390
.2	.78846	.79299	.79751	.80200	.80648	.81093	.81536	.81978	.82418	.82855
.3	.83291	.83725	.84157	.84587	.85015	.85422	.85866	.86289	.86710	.87129
.4	.87547	.87963	.88377	.88789	.89200	.89609	.90016	.90422	.90826	.91228
.5	.91629	.92028	.92426	.92822	.93216	.93609	.94001	.04391	.94779	.95166
.6	.95551	.95935	.96317	.96698	.97078	.97456	.97833	.98208	.98582	.98954
.7	.99325	.99695	.00063[a]	.00430[a]	.00796[a]	.01160[a]	.01523[a]	.01885[a]	.02245[a]	.02604[a]
.8	1.02962	.03318[a]	.03674	.04028	.04380	.04732	.05082	.05431	.05779	.06126
.9	.06471	.06815	.07158	.07500	.07841	.08181	.08519	.08856	.09192	.09527
3.0	1.09861	.10194	.10526	.10856	.11186	.11514	.11841	.12168	.12493	.12817
.1	.13140	.13462	.13783	.14103	.14422	.14740	.15057	.15373	.15688	.16002
.2	.16315	.16627	.16938	.17248	.17557	.17865	.18173	.18479	.18784	.19089
.3	.19392	.19695	.19996	.20297	.20597	.20896	.21194	.21491	.21788	.22083
.4	.22378	.22671	.22964	.23256	.23547	.23837	.24127	.24415	.24703	.24990
.5	.25276	.25562	.25846	.26130	.26413	.26695	.26976	.27257	.27536	.27815
.6	.28093	.28371	.28647	.28923	.29198	.29473	.29746	.30019	.30291	.30563
.7	.30833	.31103	.31372	.31641	.31909	.32176	.32442	.32708	.32972	.33237
.8	.33500	.33763	.34025	.34286	.34547	.34807	.35067	.35325	.35584	.35841
.9	.36098	.36354	.36609	.36864	.37118	.37372	.37624	.37877	.38128	.38379
4.0	1.38629	.38879	.39128	.39377	.39624	.39872	.40118	.40364	.40610	.40854
.1	.41099	.41342	.41585	.41828	.42070	.42311	.42552	.42792	.43031	.43270
.2	.43508	.43746	.43984	.44220	.44456	.44692	.44927	.45161	.45395	.45629
.3	.45862	.46094	.46326	.46557	.46787	.47018	.47247	.47476	.47705	.47933
.4	.48160	.48387	.48614	.48840	.49065	.49290	.49515	.49739	.49962	.50185
.5	.50408	.50630	.50851	.51072	.51293	.51513	.51732	.51951	.52170	.52388
.6	.52606	.52823	.53039	.53256	.53471	.53687	.53902	.54116	.54330	.54543
.7	.54756	.54969	.55181	.55393	.55604	.55814	.56025	.56235	.56444	.56653
.8	.56862	.57070	.57277	.57485	.57691	.57898	.58104	.58309	.58515	.58719
.9	.58924	.59127	.59331	.59534	.59737	.59939	.60141	.60342	.60543	.60744

a. Add 1.0 to indicated figure.

Appendix C
Tables of Accelerated Depreciation Factors

Sum-of-Years'-Digits Method (SYD) at Different Costs of Capital

Period	6%	8%	10%	12%	14%	15%	16%
1	—	—	—	—	—	—	—
2	—	—	—	—	—	—	—
3	0.908	0.881	0.855	0.831	0.808	0.796	0.786
4	0.891	0.860	0.830	0.802	0.776	0.763	0.751
5	0.875	0.839	0.806	0.775	0.746	0.732	0.719
6	0.859	0.820	0.783	0.749	0.718	0.703	0.689
7	0.844	0.801	0.761	0.725	0.692	0.676	0.661
8	0.829	0.782	0.740	0.702	0.667	0.650	0.635
9	0.814	0.765	0.720	0.680	0.643	0.626	0.610
10	0.800	0.748	0.701	0.659	0.621	0.604	0.587
11	0.786	0.731	0.683	0.639	0.600	0.582	0.565
12	0.773	0.715	0.665	0.620	0.581	0.562	0.545
13	0.760	0.700	0.648	0.602	0.562	0.543	0.526
14	0.747	0.685	0.632	0.585	0.544	0.525	0.508
15	0.734	0.671	0.616	0.569	0.527	0.508	0.491
16	0.722	0.657	0.601	0.553	0.511	0.492	0.475
17	0.711	0.644	0.587	0.538	0.496	0.477	0.460
18	0.699	0.631	0.573	0.524	0.482	0.463	0.445
19	0.688	0.618	0.560	0.510	0.468	0.449	0.432
20	0.677	0.606	0.547	0.497	0.455	0.436	0.419

Double Declining Balance Method (DDB) at Different Costs of Capital

Period	6%	8%	10%	12%	14%	15%	16%
1	—	—	—	—	—	—	—
2	—	—	—	—	—	—	—
3	0.920	0.896	0.873	0.851	0.831	0.821	0.811
4	0.898	0.868	0.840	0.814	0.789	0.777	0.766
5	0.878	0.843	0.811	0.781	0.753	0.739	0.727
6	0.858	0.819	0.783	0.749	0.718	0.704	0.689
7	0.840	0.796	0.756	0.720	0.687	0.671	0.656
8	0.821	0.774	0.731	0.692	0.657	0.641	0.625
9	0.804	0.753	0.708	0.667	0.630	0.614	0.597
10	0.787	0.733	0.685	0.643	0.605	0.588	0.571
11	0.771	0.714	0.664	0.620	0.582	0.564	0.547
12	0.755	0.696	0.644	0.599	0.559	0.541	0.524
13	0.740	0.678	0.625	0.579	0.539	0.521	0.504
14	0.725	0.661	0.607	0.560	0.520	0.501	0.484
15	0.711	0.645	0.590	0.542	0.502	0.483	0.466
16	0.697	0.630	0.573	0.526	0.485	0.466	0.450
17	0.684	0.615	0.558	0.510	0.469	0.451	0.434
18	0.671	0.601	0.543	0.495	0.454	0.436	0.419
19	0.659	0.587	0.529	0.480	0.440	0.422	0.405
20	0.647	0.574	0.515	0.467	0.427	0.409	0.392

Appendix D   Table of Areas under the Normal Curve

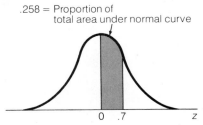

.258 = Proportion of total area under normal curve

0   .7   z

Graph of an Appendix Table D Value

z	.00	.01	.02	.03	.04	.05	.06	.07	.08	.09
0.0	.0000	.0040	.0080	.0120	.0160	.0199	.0239	.0279	.0319	.0359
0.1	.0398	.0438	.0478	.0517	.0557	.0596	.0636	.0675	.0714	.0753
0.2	.0793	.0832	.0871	.0910	.0948	.0987	.1026	.1064	.1103	.1141
0.3	.1179	.1217	.1255	.1293	.1331	.1368	.1406	.1443	.1480	.1517
0.4	.1554	.1591	.1628	.1664	.1700	.1736	.1772	.1808	.1844	.1879
0.5	.1915	.1950	.1985	.2019	.2054	.2088	.2123	.2157	.2190	.2224
0.6	.2257	.2291	.2324	.2357	.2389	.2422	.2454	.2486	.2517	.2549
0.7	.2580	.2611	.2642	.2673	.2704	.2734	.2764	.2794	.2823	.2852
0.8	.2881	.2910	.2939	.2967	.2995	.3023	.3051	.3078	.3106	.3133
0.9	.3159	.3186	.3212	.3238	.3264	.3289	.3315	.3340	.3365	.3389
1.0	.3413	.3438	.3461	.3485	.3508	.3531	.3554	.3577	.3599	.3621
1.1	.3643	.3665	.3686	.3708	.3729	.3749	.3770	.3790	.3810	.3830
1.2	.3849	.3869	.3888	.3907	.3925	.3944	.3962	.3980	.3997	.4015
1.3	.4032	.4049	.4066	.4082	.4099	.4115	.4131	.4147	.4162	.4177
1.4	.4192	.4207	.4222	.4236	.4251	.4265	.4279	.4292	.4306	.4319
1.5	.4332	.4345	.4357	.4370	.4382	.4394	.4406	.4418	.4429	.4441
1.6	.4452	.4463	.4474	.4484	.4495	.4505	.4515	.4525	.4535	.4545
1.7	.4554	.4564	.4573	.4582	.4591	.4599	.4608	.4616	.4625	.4633
1.8	.4641	.4649	.4656	.4664	.4671	.4678	.4686	.4693	.4699	.4706
1.9	.4713	.4719	.4726	.4732	.4738	.4744	.4750	.4756	.4761	.4767
2.0	.4772	.4778	.4783	.4788	.4793	.4798	.4803	.4808	.4812	.4817
2.1	.4821	.4826	.4830	.4834	.4838	.4842	.4846	.4850	.4854	.4857
2.2	.4861	.4864	.4868	.4871	.4875	.4878	.4881	.4884	.4887	.4890
2.3	.4893	.4896	.4898	.4901	.4904	.4906	.4909	.4911	.4913	.4916
2.4	.4918	.4920	.4922	.4925	.4927	.4929	.4931	.4932	.4934	.4936
2.5	.4938	.4940	.4941	.4943	.4945	.4946	.4948	.4949	.4951	.4952
2.6	.4953	.4955	.4956	.4957	.4959	.4960	.4961	.4962	.4963	.4964
2.7	.4965	.4966	.4967	.4968	.4969	.4970	.4971	.4972	.4973	.4974
2.8	.4974	.4975	.4976	.4977	.4977	.4978	.4979	.4979	.4980	.4981
2.9	.4981	.4982	.4982	.4983	.4984	.4984	.4985	.4985	.4986	.4986
3.0	.4987	.4987	.4987	.4988	.4988	.4989	.4989	.4989	.4990	.4990

Appendix E
Answers to Selected End-of-Chapter Problems

We list below answers to selected end-of-chapter problems. The primary limitation, which must be kept in mind, is that some questions may have more than one solution, depending upon which of several equally plausible assumptions are made in working the problem. Also, many of the problems involve some verbal discussion as well as numerical calculations. We have not presented any of this discussion material here.

2.1 ΔCash = $\$-5,000$.
2.2 ΔCash = $\$-20$.

4.1   a) $11,250; b) 30%; c) 18.75%.
4.2   a) $9,750; b) 30%; c)17.73%.
4.3   a) $27,820; b) 21.40%; c) 46%.
4.5   1980: $0; 1981: $0; 1982: $4,650; 1983: $14,250; 1984: $$-18,900$.
4.6   a) 1. 1984: $7,825; 1985: $15,130; 1986: $23,526; 2. 1984: $6,290; 1985: $9,440; 1986: $13,040.
4A.1   a) $1,000; b) Year 1: $1,560; Year 2: $1,092; Years 3–5: $782.7; c) Year 1: $1,666.7; Year 2: $1,333.3; Year 3: $1,000; Year 4: $666.7; Year 5: $333.3.

5.1 $1,000 today is worth less.
5.2   5.60 million tons.
5.3   8 years.
5.4 $34,030.
5.5 $885,180.
5.6 $10,066.
5.7   Year 1: $1,180,000; Year 2: $1,392,400; Year 3: $1,643,000; Year 4: $1,938,800; Year 5: $2,287,800; Year 6: $2,699,600.
5.8 $56,472.36.
5.9   a) $6,447.78; b) $59,931.78.
5.10   b) $748.51; c) $906.15.
5.11   12%.
5.12   14%.
5.13   7%.
5.15   a) $PV_A = \$4,788.36$, $PV_B = \$5,216.10$.
5.16 $22,366.72.
5.17   a) 11.57%; b) $490.
5.19   a) $875.39; b) $1,000.01; c) $1,297.58.
5.21   c) $PV = \$10$; d) $16.
5A.1   10.52%.
5A.3   6%.
5A.6 $5,000.

6.1   a) NPV = $100,338; b) IRR = 18%.
6.2   a) NPV = $24,306; b) Cash flow = $28,000.
6.3   b) NPV = $23,490.
6.4   a) NPV = $17,235; b) NPV = $20,477.
6.5   NPV = $44,166.
6.6   d) Yes, NPV = $94,106.
6.7   a) Cash flow = $46,200; NPV = $70,317.2; b) Cash flow = $31,200;
        NPV = $733.7; c) NPV = $5,752.8.
6.8   a) NPV = $ − 1,251.59; b) NPV = $58.66; c) NPV = $2,458.66;
        d) NPV = $6,188.47.
6.9   b) IRR_O = 12.87%, IRR_M = 15.78%.
6.10 a) NPV = $341; b) NPV = $9,148.
6.11 a) NPV = $ − 243; b) NPV = $ − 183.36.
6.12 a) 28%.
6.13 $NPV_\infty(F)$ = $14,481.56, $NPV_\infty(H)$ = $67,404.96.
6.14 $NPV_\infty(E)$ = $4,678, IRR_E = 17.3%, $NPV_\infty(F)$ = $1,503.58, IRR_F = 13.69%.
6.15 Project A: NPV_∞ = $903.09, PI = 1.7341; Project B: NPV_∞ = $2,079.99,
        PI = 1.7124; Project C: NPV_∞ = $2,733.64, PI = 1.5943.
6.16 NPV at 8% = $ − 185,070; NPV at 14% = $660,940.

7.1   a) I_A^* = 2, I_B^* = 10; b) r = 5.83%, B_A = 5/6, B_B = − 5/6.
7.4   a) A = 6%, B = 6%, C = 7%, D = 7%; b) A = 5.99%, B = 5.99%, C = 6.92%,
        D = 6.99%.
7.5   a) 12.03%; b) 25.49%.
7.6   NPV = $ − 630.
7.7   NPV = $67,939.
7.8   a) NPV = $8,711; b) NPV = $ − 1,779.
7.9   a) NPV_A = $8.54, NPV_B = $8.21; b) NPV_A = $5.09, NPV_B = $5.21.
7.11 a) r_A = 5.079%, r_B = 8.422%; c) p = .14817.

8.1 $500,000.
8.3   a) Current assets/Current liabilities = 3.5, Debt/Total assets = 46%, Times
        interest earned = 3.1×, Sales/Inventory = 3.0×, Average collection period =
        49 days, Sales/Total assets = 1.6×, Net income/Sales = 2.2%, EBIT$(1 − T)$/Total
        assets = 5.1%, Net income/Net worth = 6.4%.

9.1   a) Loss on 175,000 units = $ − 75,000, Gain on 300,000 units = $300,000; b) S^* =
        $2,000,000 or Q^* = 200,000 units; c) DOL (225,000 units) = 9, DOL (300,000
        units) = 3.
9.2   b) S^* = $280,000, Q^* = 8,000 units; c) DOL (6,000 units) = − 3, DOL (9,000 units)
        = 9; d) S^* = $256,000 or Q^* = 6,400 units; e) S^* = $320,000 or Q^* = 8,000 units.
9.3   b) Q^* = 5,000 units; c) Cash break-even point = 1,000 units.
9.4   b) Loans outstanding: July—$0; August—$0; September—$151,750;
        October—$26,500; November—$0; December—$0.
9.5   a) Current = 2.6×, Quick = 1.5×, Debt/Assets = 50%, Times interest earned
        = 3.8×, Inventory turnover = 5.2×, Average collection period = 90 days,
        Fixed asset turnover = 5.49×, Total asset turnover = 1.55×, Cost of goods
        sold/Sales = 76.1%, Net operating income/Sales = 7.42%, Net income/Sales =
        3.02%, Net operating income/Total assets = 11.50%, Net income/Net worth =
        9.30%.

10.1 $262,500.
10.2   Cash = $3,000,000, Accounts receivable = $12,000,000, Inventory = $25,000,000, Fixed assets = $40,000,000, Accounts payable = $8,000,000, Notes payable = $6,900,000, Accruals = $20,000,000, Common stock = $20,000,000, Retained earnings = $25,100,000.
10.4   a) Additional financing needed = $150,000, Total assets = $13,500,000.
10.5   a) Total assets = $9,600,000; b) Funds needed = $1,214,400; d) (1)(i) Funds needed = $1,041,600; (ii) $1,387,200 increase needed; (2)(i) $1,444,800 increase needed; (ii) Decreases needs $1,099,200; (3) $720,000 increase.
10.6   a) 12.4%; b) 22%; c) 3.2%; d) 13%; e) g = 19.0%.
10.7   Total assets = $7.2 million, Net income = $.7 million.
10.8 $E(Y) = 353.7$, VAR $(Y) = 53,188.13$.
10.9   Slope = .3568, Intercept = −708.42, Coefficient of determination = .9832.
10.10 a) $r^2 = .9496$, $r^2 = .9604$.
10A.1 b) $E(X) = \$15$; c) $\sigma_X = 2.9326$; d) CV = .1955; e) 36.65%; f) 24.75%; g) 38.6%; h) 24.75%.
10A.2 a) E(Gain) = $6,500.

11.2   a) Return on equity: Aggressive = 11.8%, Average = 10.6%, Conservative = 8.7%; b) No.
11.3   Net income: Strong economy: A = $81,600, B = $76,800, C = $41,400; Average economy: A = $27,600, B = $34,800, C = $29,400; Weak economy: A = $−8,400, B = $−7,200, C = $5,400.

12.1   a) 23.45%.
12.2   a) $2,450,000; b) $196,000; c) $16,333.
12.4 $S^* = \$5,833$.
12.5   a) $C^* = \$50,000$; b) $25,000; c) 75.

13.1   a) For 70 units: 40 orders, Average inventory = 35, Carrying cost = $210; Order cost = $210, Total cost = $420; b) EOQ = 70 units.
13.2   a) EOQ = 12,000 units; b) 15 orders; c) Reorder point = 13,600 units.
13.4   a) 5,000 units; b) 100; c) Reorder point = 15,000 units; d) Elasticity = .41; e) Elasticity = −.29.
13.5   c) EOQ(A) = 141.42, EOQ(B) = 3,162.28, EOQ(C) = 3.16, EOQ(D) = 7.07; d) Total costs for EOQ: A = $21.41, B = $51.62, C = $83.33, D = $161.42.

14.1   ΔNPV = $98,800 per year, relax credit standards.
14.2   ΔNPV = $58.1
14.3   ΔNPV(3) = $212.3, ΔNPV(4) = $69.21, ΔNPV(5) = $− 149.50.
14.4   ΔNPV = $68.75 per day.
14.5   ΔNPV = $285.4.

15.1   a) $r_e = 27.71\%$; b) $r_e = 15.89\%$; c) $r_e = 24.90\%$; d) $r_e = 27.86\%$; e) $r_e = 13.01\%$.
15.2   1. 15%; 2. 16.25%; 3. 14.86%.
15.3   a) Trade discount APR = 15.89%, Loan APR = 15.22%.
15.4   Field warehousing cost = $49,362; Line of credit cost = $59,727.
15.5   a) Borrow $136,986, Factor $103,986; b) Loan $r_c = 16.44\%$ per year, Factoring $r_c = 47.83\%$, Loan cost = $16,440 per year, factoring cost = $−100,950 per year.

15.6   a) Total cost (1) = \$3,416.67; (2) = \$4,000; (3) = \$2,300; (4) = \$3,500.

15.7   a) 57% of short-term financing, 34% of total debt, 29% of total financing.

15.8   a) \$258,621; b) \$ $-$ 7,656 = annual savings.

15.9   a) \$300,000.

15.10   a) \$320,000; b) 60 days; c) Net amount received $-$ Factoring = \$261,222, Receivables financing = \$249,600; e) APR factoring = 27.46%, Receivables financing = 16.40%.

15.11   b) Total dollar cost = \$252,360, Percentage cost = 26.37% (annual basis).

16.3 $\overline{R}_M = .088$; $\text{VAR}(R_M) = .0101$; $\sigma_M = .10$; $\overline{R}_F = .06$.

16.4 $\overline{R}_M = .16$; $\text{VAR}(R_M) = .0103$; $\sigma_M = .10$.

16.5   a) $\overline{R}_j = .17$; b) $\text{VAR}(R_j) = .0029$; c) $\sigma_j = .0539$.

16.6   a) $\overline{R}_j = .1625$; b) $\text{VAR}(R_j) = .01872$; c) $\sigma_j = .1368$; d) $\text{COV}(R_j, R_m) = .01244$; e) $\rho_{jM} = .9734$.

16.7   a) $\overline{R}_A = .17$, $\sigma_A = .11$, $\overline{R}_B = .116$, $\sigma_B = .07765$; b) $\rho_{AB} = .59474$; c) $\overline{R}_C = .1565$; d) $\sigma_C = .09538$.

16.8   a) $w_A = 1.00$, $R_p = .09$, $\sigma_p = .04$; $w_A = .75$, $R_p = .0925$, $\sigma_p = .0378$; $w_A = .50$, $R_p = .095$, $\sigma_p = .039$; $w_A = .25$, $R_p = .0975$, $\sigma_p = .0434$; $w_A = 0$, $R_p = .10$, $\sigma_p = .05$.

16.9   b) $w_i = .20$, $\sigma_p = 4.48$, $p = 18.41\%$.

16.10   a) $C = 150\%$, $\overline{R}_p = 12.15\%$, $\sigma_p = 15.82\%$; $C = 100\%$, $\overline{R}_p = 8\%$, $\sigma_p = 10.84\%$; $C = 50\%$, $\overline{R}_p = 3.85\%$, $\sigma_p = 6.06\%$; $C = 0\%$, $R_p = -.3\%$, $\sigma_p = 2.795\%$; $C = -50\%$, $\overline{R}_p = -4.45\%$, $\sigma_p = 5.55\%$; c) $w_C = .82$, $\sigma_p = 9.08\%$; d) $p = 27.76\%$.

16.11   a) .5; b) -50%, c) $\sigma^2(R_p) = .09$.

16.12   a) $b = .71129$; b) $\rho_{Mj} = .73976$; c) 54.68%.

17.3   a) A:E(CF) = \$4,500, B:E(CF) = \$5,100; b) $\text{NPV}_A = \$6,691.05$, $\text{NPV}_B = \$7,749.18$.

17.4 $R_A = 8\%$, $R_B = 10\%$, $R_C = 14\%$.

17.5   a) $R_j = 15\%$; b) NPV = \$211.32.

17.6   a) $\text{CV}:R_A = 14\%$, $R_B = 18\%$; $\text{SML}: R_A = 15\%$, $R_B = 12\%$.

17.7   a) $\lambda = 5$; b) $V_j = \$3,000$; c) $\overline{R}_j = 10\%$ (σ_M^2 rounded to .01).

17.8   a) $\overline{R}_M = .10$, $\text{VAR}(R_M) = .04$, $\sigma_M = .2$, $\overline{R}_1 = .20$, $\text{VAR}(R_1) = .18$, $\sigma_1 = .424$, $\overline{R}_2 = .10$, $\text{VAR}(R_2) = .122$, $\sigma_2 = .349$, $\text{COV}(R_1, R_M) = .08$, $\rho_{1M} = .943$, $\text{COV}(R_2, R_M) = .024$, $\rho_{2M} = .344$, $\text{COV}(R_1, R_2) = .004$, $\rho_{12} = .027$; b) $\overline{R}_p = .140$, $\text{VAR}(R_p) = .075$, $\sigma_p = .274$, d) $E(R_1) = .16$, $E(R_2) = .076$, $\text{NPV}_1 = \$34.48$, $\text{NPV}_2 = \$22.30$, choose No. 1.

17.9   a) $(\text{cef})^0 = 1$, $(\text{cef})^1 = .94643$, $(\text{cef})^5 = .75935$, $(\text{cef})^{10} = .57661$, $(\text{cef})^{20} = .33248$, $(\text{cef})^{30} = .19171$.

17.10   a) $\lambda = 5$, $V_j = \$2,000$; b) $\text{COV}(R_j, R_M) = 2\%$, $V_j = \$2,000$.

17.11 $E(R_P) = .172$, $E(R_Q) = .156$, choose Project Q.

17.12   a) .76; b) $\beta_s = 1.133$.

17.13 $\beta_j = .2355$.

17.14   a) $\beta_j = .131$; b) $k_e = 11.048\%$.

17.15   a) $k_1 = 14.8\%$, $k_2 = 21.4\%$, $k_3 = 12.1\%$; b) $\beta_f = 1.18614$; c) $\beta_s = 1.69449$; d) Keep Division 1; e) $\beta_1 = .97287$.

17B.3   b) $E(\text{NPV}) = \$-8,470$; c) $p(\$-60,900) = 2\%$; d) $p(\$21,700) = 12\%$; e) 41%.

18.3   Call price = \$4.18.

18.4 $C = \$7.02$.

18.5   128.06 calls.

18.6 $\sigma = .265$, $C = \$3.52$, $\sigma^2 = .07$.

18.7   a) $S = \$353,031$; b) $\$146,969$; c) $r = 24.23\%$.

18.8   a) $S = \$3,506,672$; b) $\$493,328$; c) $r = 12.85\%$.

18.9 $C = \$1.18$.

18.11 a) $B = \$20.77$; b) $k_e = 17\%$, $k_b = 11.5\%$.

18.12 a) $B = \$15.9591$; b) $S = \$117.897$; oppose the merger.

20.1   a) Bonner ROE $= 14.6\%$, Kirkeby ROE $= 16.8\%$; b) Bonner ROE $= 16.5\%$.

20.2   No leverage: $\overline{ROE} = .105$, CV $= .514$; 10% leverage: $\overline{ROE} = .112$, CV $= .518$; 50% leverage: $\overline{ROE} = .14$, CV $= .771$; 60% leverage: $\overline{ROE} = .131$, CV $= 1.046$.

20.3   b) $B/S = .4$, ROE $= 10.95\%$; $B/S = .8$, ROE $= 11.90\%$; $B/S = 1.0$, ROE $= 12.40\%$; $B/S = 1.2$, ROE $= 12.90\%$; $B/S = 1.6$, ROE $= 13.85\%$; c) $B/S = 1.46$; ROE $= 13.5\%$.

20.5   a) (1) DOL $= 1.5$; (2) DFL $= 1.45$; (3) DCL $= 2.18$; b) Bond financing EPS $= \$1.23$, DCL $= 3.90$; Stock financing EPS $= \$1.38$, DCL $= 2.91$.

20.6   a) $Q = 77,250$; b) DOL $= 1.193$, DFL $= 1.036$, DCL $= 1.236$; c) DCL $= 1.35$.

20.7

a) Sales:	$0	$700	$2,100	$3,500
Bond financing: EPS	$ − .71	$.29	$2.29	$4.29
Stock financing: EPS	$ − .11	$.60	$2.03	$3.46

c) Bond financing market value: *, $2.32, $10.32, $18.32, $26.32, $34.32, $42.32; Stock financing market value: *, $6.00, $13.10, $20.30, $27.40, $34.60, $41.70; f) Bond financing: $E(EPS) = \$2.29$, $E(p) = \$18.32$; Stock financing: $E(EPS) = \$2.03$, $E(p) = \$20.30$.

21.1   a) $V_U = \$12,000,000$, $V_L = \$16,000,000$.

21.2   a) (1) $k_U = 18\%$, (2) $k_s = 22.8\%$; b) (1) $k_U = 18\%$, $k = 14.4\%$.

21.3   a) (1) $.50$/share, (2) 10X, (3) 5/share, (4) $k = 10\%$; b) (5) $V_U = \$600$, $V_L = \$650$, (6) $.56$/share, (7) Market $= \$5.50$/share, Book $= \$5.00$/share, (8) 9.8214X, (9) $k_s = 10.18\%$, (10) $k = 9.23\%$, (11) 1.1X; c) (12) $V_U = V_L = \$600$, (13) $.50$/share, 120 million shares, (14) Market $=$ Book $= \$5$/share, (15) 1.0X, (16) $k_s = k_U = 10\%$; (17) $k = 10\% = k_U$, (18) 1.0X.

21.4 $k_r = 17\%$.

21.5   a) 18%; b) 13.2%.

21.6   6%.

21.7   a) After-tax cost $= 6.6\%$; b) 6.5%.

21.8 $k_{ps} = 11\%$.

21.10 a) 14%; b) 14%.

21.11 a) Equity financing $= \$25,000,000$; b) External financing $= \$15,000,000$; c) (1) $k_b = .066$, (2) $k_{ps} = .115$, (3) $k_r = .14$, (4) $k_e = .1467$; d) Equity cost $= .1440$; e) WACC $= 10.79\%$; f) WACC $= 10.99\%$; g) WACC $= 11.13\%$.

21.12 15.84%.

21.13 a) $g = 8\%$; b) Next year's EPS $= \$5.38$.

21.14 WACC (1) 12%, (2) 10.56%, (3) 11.40%, (4) 9.96%, (5) 13.33%, (6) 12.30%, (7) 16.53%, (8) 14.21%.

21B.1 b) $p_1 = .10$, $p_2 = .20$.

21B.2 b) $p_1 = .5305$, $p_2 = .4533$.

21B.3 Value $3,450 maximized with Debt $= \$3,000$.

21B.4 Plan X: $V(3,000) = 1,810$.

22.1   External equity $1,220,000.
22.2   Dividends $2,760,000.
22.3   Last year's dividend = $11.11.
22.5   a) Dividends = $1,237,500; b) Dividends = $2,025,000;
       c) Dividends = $3,250,000; d) Dividends = $2,250,000;
       e) Dividends = $4,750,000.
22.6   35%.
22.7   Capital stock = $1,000,000; Retained earnings = $1,500,000.
22.10 b) $12/share; c) $352/share.
22.11 a) S_A = $100, S_B = $100.
22.12 a) S_A = $6,480, S_B = $8,320.
23.1   a) P_A = $717.51, P_B = $626.56; b) P_A = $634.83, P_B = $536.42.
23.3   a) k_b = 10%; b) k_b = 8%; c) k_b = 6.67%.
23.4   a) (1) 14%, (2) 5%.
23.5   a) $1,125; b) $750; c) $1,000; d) (1) $1,096, (2) $779, (3) $1,000.
23.6 p_0 = $468.69.
23.7   a) V = $21.4286 million; b) V = $32.70; c) No growth: 7.1, Constant growth:
       10.9.
23.8   a) V = $58.4485; b) $114.6964.
23.10 a) EPS = $3.00, Average = $2.00, Dividends = $1.40, Average = $1.00, Book
       value = $24.00.
23.11 $42.42.
23.12 p_0 = $31.00.
23.13 a) V = $36.9 million; b) V = $52.32 million.

24.1   a) r = 14%; b) r = 12.98%.
24.2   13.6%.
24.3   a) Pure rights = 8%, stand-by = 5%, underwriting = 87%.
24.4   a) E(return) = $121,986.
24.5   a) Flotation = 5.02%, underwriting = 4.24%.

25.1 v_r = $3.
25.2   a) v_r = $2.50.
25.3   a) v_r = $2.50; b) Total assets: (1), (2), (3) = $19,150, (4) $17,925.
25.5   a) v_r = $2; b) v_r = 2.136.
25.6   c) 45,456 shares; d) 11.6%.
25.8   a) Current debt(%)/Long-term(%)/Equity(%): Present: 12%/44%/44%, Debt:
       10%/50%/40%, Equity: 10%/40%/50%; b) (1) $k_b/k_s/B$: Debt: 12%/16%/800, Equity:
       10%/12%/600, (2) Int. exp.: Debt, $86, Equity, $60, (3) Fixed charge coverage:
       Debt: 3.0X, Equity: 4.3X; c) Debt: $8.13/share, Equity: $10.23/share;
       e) Debt: k = 12.5%, Equity: k = 10.6%.

26.1   a) k = 13.2% annual ROR.
26.2   a) Fully amortized bond dur = −2.775; Balloon bond dur = −4.037, Discount
       dur = −5; b) Amortized PV = $829.62, dur = −2.641, Balloon PV = $760.77,
       dur = −3.887, Discount PV = $708.24, dur = −5.
26.3   a) k_s = 12%; b) V_L = $1,100; c) k = 11.34%; e) Debt k_s = .1225, Equity k_s = .1195;
       f) Debt S_1 = $1,042, p_1 = $10.42; Equity S_1 = $1,109, p_1 = $10.08;
       g) Debt V_L = $1,242, V_L equity = $1,209, h) Debt: k = 11.06% market,
       10.60% book; Equity: k = 11.36% market, 11.16% book.

26.5 a) Sales $0 $2,400 $3,000 $4,800
   Debt EPS $−.27 $.93 $1.23 $2.13
   Stock EPS $−.12 $.84 $1.08 $1.80
   b) Break even sales = $1,500;
   c)   Sales $600 $2,800 $3,600
   Market value Debt (P/E = 9) $ .27 $10.17 $13.77
        Stock (P/E = 10) $1.20 $10.00 $13.20
   d) Break even sales = $2,460; f) Bond CV = .5215, Stock CV = .4666.

26.7 NPV = $3,269,998.

27.1 a) L_t = $7,870; b) Buy = lease = $−19,890; c) L_t = $8,854, lease = $−22,378, buy = $−19,890.

27.2 a) NAL = $3,136.77.

27.3 NAL = $−28,286.10.

27.4 a) $2,521,600 net proceeds; b) Ratio 3:1 after; c) $−31,200.

28.1 a) $1,150.80; c) $50.80 loss per bond.

28.2 b) $2; c) $5; d) $10.

28.3 a) Fully diluted EPS = $2.88; b) v_r = $6; c) X = $19; d) $2.87.

28.5 a) Paid-in-capital = $138,000, Total claims = $500,000;
   b) Total claims = $687,500; c) (1) EPS = $2.90, Share price = $46.40; (2) EPS = $4.05, Share price = $64.86.

28.6 a) 13.22 shares; b) $37.82; c) 18% premium; d) 12.4%; e) 17.6%.

28.7 a) Total assets 1. = $625,000, 2. = $625,000, 3. = $975,000; b) Percent ownership 1. = 45%, 2. = 47%, 3. = 47%; c) EPS 1. = $.54, 2. = $.56, 3. = $.76; d) Debt ratio 1. = 22%, 2. = 22%, 3. = 50%.

28.8 a) B_0 = $726.11, B_6 = $766.37, B_{10} = $807.46; b) C_0 = $828, C_5 = $1,161, C_6 = $1,243, C_{10} = $1,629, C_{20} = $3,204; d) D_{c0} = $1,050, D_{c5} = $1,037.50, D_{c6} = $1,035, D_{c10} = $1,025; e) 6 years; h) ≈ 8%.

28.9 a) k_{ca} = 10.65%, k_{cb} = 11%; d) k_{ca} = 7.54%.

28.10 a) C_f = $20.91 million (straight debt); b) C_{fc} = $23.636 million (convertible debt).

29.1 Normal cost: Year 1 = $21,377, Year 2 = $24,596.

29.3 Dollar-weighted return: Year 1 = 7.8%, Year 2 = −12.4%, Year 3 = 17.6%, Year 4 = 2.0%, Year 5 = 14.7%, Year 6 = 3.4%; Time-weighted return: Year 1 = 7.8%, Year 2 = 0%, Year 3 = 5.3%, Year 4 = −7.3%, Year 5 = 20.6%, Year 6 = 3.4%.

29.4 β_B = 2.118, Predicted R_B = 2.57, Risk-adjusted abnormal return = 6.37%.

30.1 a) 12.5% decline; b) 16.7% increase.

30.2 a) $35.60 share price; b) 27% accretion; c) 68% dilution; d) Brunner = 9.2% decline, Powell = 81.6% increase; e) 19%; f) 12 years.

30.3 a) Dalton price = $10; Cory price = $30.00; b) Dalton = 1.6% decline; Cory = 195% accretion; c) $18.45.

30.4 a) (1) $76.80; (2) $69.96.

30.5 a) Total assets $4,500; b) Total assets $5,250.

30.6 a) NI/NW: 7.68%; b) Total assets $10 million; c) NI/NW = 12.21%; d) Fiscor NI/NW = 4.32%.

30.8　　a) Apex: $120 million, Allied: $180 million; b) Apex: $150 million, Allied: $150 million; d) 1. Apex: 1.33 shares Proxmore per Apex, Allied: 1.12 shares Proxmore per Allied, 2. With Apex $g = 6.6\%$, with Allied $g = 4.0\%$　3. With Apex EPS = $3.13, with Allied EPS = $3.59.

30.9　　g) Johnson-Koslow gain $144.49; Johnson-Landon gain $43.02.

30A.1　b) New EPS = $2.60, Vorno = $.40 dilution, Hondo = $1.60 accretion; c) New EPS = $3.20, Vorno = $.20 accretion, Hondo = $2.20 accretion.

31.1　　$2,300,000 available to general creditors.

31.2　　a) Total claims $373 million; b) Income available to common stock $3 million; c) $4.14 million increase; d) Required earnings are $6.9 million less.

31.3　　$600,000 liquidation value, $700,000 reorganization value.

31.4　　a) Cash from reorganization = $4,300,000.

31.5　　a) $Z = 1.772$.

32.1　　a) $X_1 = 211$ yen/$; b) $E_1 = \$.004739$ per yen; c) 7.78% devaluation; d) 8.42% revaluation.

32.2　　£ .125/fr 1.

32.3　　a) $R_{f0} = 15.9\%$; b) $R_{f0} = 33.8\%$; c) 2.1103 DM/$.

32.4　　a) $2,000 gain; b) $3,333 loss.

32.5　　a) $1,666,667 gain; b) $1,000,000 loss.

32.8　　a) 30.68%; b) $R_{f0} = 30.68\%$.

32.9　　a) 28.72%; b) $R_{f0} = 28.72\%$.

32.10　a) Net proceeds $1,040,000; b) Net proceeds $1,068,511; c) Net proceeds $990,000.

32.12　a) Net cost $96,000; b) Net cost = $90,533.60; c) Net cost = $103,500.

32.14　a) 2.86 DM/$; b) 14.4% Nominal U.S. rate; c) $X_f = 2.8636$.

Index